Welcome

It is our great pleasure to welcome you to the *2013 International Conference on In* *Interfaces (IUI'13)*. This year marks the eighteenth meeting of this conference, continuing its tradition of being the principal international forum for reporting outstanding research at the intersection of Human-Computer Interaction (HCI) and Artificial Intelligence (AI). The work that appears at IUI bridges these two fields and also delves into related fields, such as psychology, cognitive science, computer graphics, the arts, and many others. Members of the IUI community are interested in improving the symbiosis between humans and computers, increasing the intelligence of both in the process.

The call for papers attracted 195 submissions from Asia, Canada, Europe, Africa, and the United States. The program committee accepted 43 papers covering a diverse set of topics, including brain-computer interaction, social media analysis, automated design, and crowdsourcing. The program opens with a keynote by Professor Luis von Ahn on "Duolingo: Learn a Language for Free while Helping to Translate the Web," and closes with a keynote by Professor Monica S. Lam on "How Mobile Disrupts Social As We Know it." We also have an excellent poster and demonstration program consisting of 14 demos and 22 posters selected from a pool of 64 total submissions. In addition, the conference provides two exciting tutorials and four interesting workshops. The tutorials feature an introduction to Human Computation by Edith Law and an introduction to knowledge acquisition from the web and social media by Zornitsa Kozareva. The workshops cover topics ranging from interactive machine learning to IUI for developing worlds.

No conference of this size could be organized without the help of a large number of individuals who volunteer an enormous amount of their own time. Their names can be found in the following pages and each and every one of these extraordinary volunteers deserve our thanks. We want to especially recognize all of the members of the organizing committee, who put in countless hours over nearly a year to make the conference happen. If you see one of them in the hotel bar at the conference, please buy them a beverage of their choice. We must also thank our senior program committee for coordinating the review process and all 654 members of the program committee for providing high quality reviews that exceeded even our lofty expectations. Last, but certainly not least, we must thank the authors for providing the content for the program that is the foundation of any successful conference. We look forward to your presentations!

Finally, we must thank our sponsors, ACM, SIGCHI and SIGART, and our generous corporate supporters, Samsung, LG Electronics, FX Palo Alto Laboratory, Inc., RedWhale Software, IBM, Microsoft Research, and USC Information Sciences Institute.

We hope that you will find this year's program interesting and thought-provoking. We also hope the conference will provide you with a valuable opportunity to share ideas with other researchers and practitioners from institutions around the world, and that those shared ideas will manifest themselves in exciting papers at next year's conference. If you have any suggestions for how to improve the conference either this year or in the future, please do not hesitate to let us know.

Jihie Kim
IUI'13 General Chair
USC Information Sciences Institute, USA

Jeffrey Nichols
IUI'13 Program Co-Chair
IBM Research, USA

Pedro Szekely
IUI'13 Program Co-Chair
USC Information Sciences Institute, USA

March 19–22, 2013
Santa Monica, CA, USA

Association for
Computing Machinery

Advancing Computing as a Science & Profession

IUI'13

Proceedings of the 18th International Conference on
Intelligent User Interfaces

Sponsored by:
ACM SIGART and SIGCHI

Supported by:
Samsung, LG Electronics, FX Palo Alto Laboratory, Inc., RedWhale Software, IBM, & Microsoft Research

Association for
Computing Machinery

Advancing Computing as a Science & Profession

The Association for Computing Machinery
2 Penn Plaza, Suite 701
New York, New York 10121-0701

Notice to Past Authors of ACM-Published Articles
ACM intends to create a complete electronic archive of all articles and/or other material previously published by ACM. If you have written a work that has been previously published by ACM in any journal or conference proceedings prior to 1978, or any SIG Newsletter at any time, and you do NOT want this work to appear in the ACM Digital Library, please inform permissions@acm.org, stating the title of the work, the author(s), and where and when published.

ISBN: 978-1-4503-1965-2 (Digital)

ISBN: 978-1-4503-2093-1 (Print)

Additional copies may be ordered prepaid from:

ACM Order Department
PO Box 30777
New York, NY 10087-0777, USA

Phone: 1-800-342-6626 (USA and Canada)
+1-212-626-0500 (Global)
Fax: +1-212-944-1318
E-mail: acmhelp@acm.org
Hours of Operation: 8:30 am – 4:30 pm ET

Printed in the USA

Table of Contents

Session 5: Novel Input

Session 6: Common-Sense and Agents

Session 7: Emotion and User Modeling

Session 8: Mobile Applications

Session 9: Keynote Address

Session Chair: Pedro Szekely *(University of Southern California)*

Session 10: Visualization

Session 11: User Studies

Session 12: Tactile and Touch

IUI 2013 Conference Organization

General Chair:	Jihie Kim *(University of Southern California, USA)*
Program Chairs:	Jeffrey Nichols *(IBM Research – Almaden, USA)* Pedro Szekely *(University of Southern California, USA)*
Posters & Demo Chairs:	Oliver Brdiczka *(Palo Alto Research Center, USA)* Jalal Mahmud *(IBM Research – Almaden, USA)*
Workshops & Tutorials Chair:	Daniel Sonntag *(DFKI, Germany)*
Student Consortium Chairs:	Henry Lieberman *(Massachusetts Institute of Technology, USA)* Jane Hsu *(National Taiwan University, Taiwan)*
Treasurer:	Melinda Gervasio *(SRI International, USA)*
Sponsorship Chair:	Doug Riecken *(Columbia University, USA)*
Publicity Chair:	Gary Lee *(Pohang University of Science and Technology, South Korea)*
Social Media Chair:	Angel Puerta *(RedWhale Software, USA)*
Materials Chair:	Teresa Romão *(FCT/UNL, Portugal)*
Local Arrangements Chairs:	Kary Lau *(University of Southern California, USA)* Ricky Sethi *(University of Southern California, USA)*
Webmaster:	Calvin Hsu *(RedWhale Software, USA)*
Senior Program Committee:	Saleema Amershi *(University of Washington, USA)* Liliana Ardissono *(University of Torino, Italy)* Sumit Basu *(Microsoft Research, USA)* Mark Billinghurst *(HIT Lab NZ, New Zealand)* Larry Birnbaum *(Northwestern University, USA)* Marco Blumendorf *(TU Berlin, Germany)* Paul Buitelaar *(DERI, Ireland)* Andrea Bunt *(University of Manitoba, Canada)* Gaëlle Calvary *(University of Grenoble, France)* Fang Chen *(NICTA, Australia)* Wai-Tat Fu *(University of Illinois Urbana-Champaign, USA)* Paul Groth *(Vrije Universiteit Amsterdam, Netherlands)* Tracy Hammond *(Texas A&M University, USA)* Tim Hussein *(University of Duisburg-Essen, Germany)* Anthony Jameson *(DFKI, Germany)* Per Ola Kristensson *(University of St Andrews, UK)*

Senior Program Committee (continued):

Henry Lieberman *(Massachusetts Institute of Technology, USA)*
Kris Luyten *(Hasselt University, Belgium)*
Jalal Mahmud *(IBM Research – Almaden, USA)*
Louis Philippe Morency *(University of Southern California, USA)*
Tom Ouyang *(Google, USA)*
Tim Paek *(Microsoft Research, USA)*
Cecile Paris *(CSIRO, Australia)*
Fabio Paternò *(CNR-ISTI, Italy)*
Beryl Plimmer *(University of Auckland, New Zealand)*
Doug Riecken *(Columbia University, USA)*
Frank Shipman *(Texas A&M University, USA)*
Robert St. Amant *(North Carolina State University, USA)*
Qiang Yang *(Hong Kong SAR, China)*
Michelle Zhou *(IBM Research – Almaden, USA)*

Posters & Demonstrations Senior Review Committee:

Bo Begole *(Samsung, USA)*
Pradipta Biswas *(University of Cambridge, UK)*
Jilin Chen *(IBM Research – Almaden, USA)*
David Gotz *(IBM Research – Watson, USA)*
Eduardo Graells *(Universitat Pompeu Fabra, Spain)*
Tracy Hammond *(Texas A&M University, USA)*
Melanie Hartmann *(Technische Universität Darmstadt, Germany)*
Jochen Huber *(Technische Universität Darmstadt, Germany)*
Sanjay Kairam *(Stanford University, USA)*
Taemie Kim *(Accenture Technology Labs, USA)*
Per Ola Kristensson *(University of St Andrews, UK)*
Anuj Kumar *(Carnegie Mellon University, USA)*
Ranjitha Kumar *(Stanford University, USA)*
Aditi Muralidharan *(University of California, Berkeley, USA)*
John O'Donovan *(University of California, Santa Barbara, USA)*
Tim Paek *(Microsoft Research, USA)*
Aditya Pal *(IBM Research – Almaden, USA)*
Patrick Reignier *(INRIA Rhône-Alpes, France)*
Jianqiang Shen *(Palo Alto Research Center, USA)*
Daniel Sonntag *(DFKI, Germany)*
Awalin Sopan *(University of Maryland, USA)*
Jürgen Steimle *(MIT Media Lab, USA)*
Bongwon Suh *(Adobe Systems, USA)*
Naushad Uzzaman *(Nuance Communications, USA)*
Jesse Vig *(Palo Alto Research Center, USA)*

IUI 2013 Program Committee

Aaron Adler
Ana Afonso
Sebastian Ahrndt
Jumana Al Issawi
Dzmitry Aliakseyeu
Meryl Alper
Reza Amini
Robert Amor
Rangachari Anand
Margarita Anastassova
Elisabeth Andre
Adrienne Andrew
Lisa Anthony
Mark Antoniades
Ahmed Arif
Kenneth Arnold
Ron Artstein
Ilhan Aslan
Daniel Avrahami
Adnan Aziz
Sina Bahram
Ryan Baker
Saeideh Bakhshi
Matthias Baldauf
Tadas Baltrusaitis
Daniela Barbosa
Catalin Barbu
Barbara Rita Barricelli
Barbara Barry
Christian Bastien
Thomas Basuki
Jared Bauer
Joerg Baus
Amy Baylor
Russell Beale
Christoph Beckmann
Roman Bednarik
Bo Begole
Victoria Bellotti
Shlomo Berkovsky
Michael Bernstein
Sourav Bhattacharya
Nadia Bianchi-Berthouze
Timothy Bickmore
Jeffrey Bigham
Fernando Birra
Gilles Bisson
Sanat Bista
Pradipta Biswas
Rachel Blagojevic
Renaud Blanch
Matthias Böhmer
Sebastian Boring
Yevgen Borodin
Gianni Bosio
Jared Bott
Judy Bowen
Chris Bowers
Erin Brady
Kai Breiner
Joost Broekens
Jed Brubaker
Gerd Bruder
Paolo Buono
Eva Burneleit
Margaret Burnett
Marc Busch
Sven Buschbeck
Rafael Calvo
Jose Campos
Pedro Campos
Giuseppe Carenini
Luis Carriço
Scott Carter
Stefania Castellani
Marc Cavazza
James Caverlee
Federica Cena
Eva Cerezo
Matthew Chalmers
Remco Chang
Angela Chang
Kuen Chang
Duen Horng (Polo) Chau
Ciprian Chelba
Jilin Chen
Zebin Chen
Li Chen
Shiwei Cheng
Ed Chi
Lydia Chilton
Luca Chittaro
Eric Choi
Konstantinos Chorianopoulos
Jennifer Chu-Carroll
Jason Chuang
Karen Church
Cagla Cig
Jesse Cirimele
Alexis Clay
J. Edward Colgate
Nathalie Colineau
Cristina Conati
Karin Coninx
Natalie Connors
Colleen Cool
Andrew Correa
Dan Cosley
Enrico Costanza
Joelle Coutaz
Céline Coutrix
Nadine Couture
Benjamin Cowan
David Coyle
Henriette Cramer
Andrew Crossan
Danielle Cummings
Allen Cypher
Andreas Dünser
Maciej Dabrowski
Aba-Sah Dadzie
Florian Daiber
Massimiliano Dal Mas
Sashikanth Damaraju
Ionut Damian
José Danado
Chi Tai Dang
Andreea Danielescu
Waltenegus Dargie
Scott Davidoff
Jennifer Davidson
Randall Davis
Richard Davis
Nadja De Carolis
Alexander De Luca
Rogerio de Paula
Marco de Sá
Thierry Declerck
Alexandre Demeure
David DeVault
Anind Dey
Debayan Dhar
Jonathan Diehl
Stefan Diewald
Anke Dittmar
Wei Dong
Mark Dredze
Carlos Duarte
Emmanuel Dubois
Vijay Duddu
Susan Dumais
Bruno Dumas
Mark Dunlop
Sophie Dupuy-Chessa
Erik Duval
Achim Ebert
Patrick Ehlen
Jihad El-Sana
David England
Julien Epps
Parisa Eslambolchilar
Johannes Fähndrich
Christan Federmann
Jean-Daniel Fekete
Alexander Felfernig
Martin Field
Danyel Fisher
Daniel Fitton
Elizabeth FitzGerald
David Flatla
James Fogarty
Valérie Fointiat
Eelke Folmer
Manuel Fonseca
Peter Forbrig
Jill Freyne
Enrique Frias-Martinez

Christopher Fry
Maria Fugini
Roberto Furnari
Hayrettin Gürkök
Krzysztof Gajos
Dennis Galletta
Lisa Gandy
Feng Gao
Glenn Geers
Sven Gehring
Cristina Gena
Melinda Gervasio
Werner Geyer
Giuseppe Ghiani
Jeremy Gilbert Gilbert
Stephen Gilroy
Audrey Girouard
Alyssa Glass
Roland Goecke
Daniel Goldberg
Susan Goldman
Gene Golovchinsky
Antonio Gomes
Louis Gomez
Tiago Gonçalves
Dorian Gorgan
David Gotz
Anna Goy
Nicholas Graham
Wayne Gray
Stephen Green
Donatien Grolaux
Tobias Grosse-Puppendahl
Tudor Groza
Jens Grubert
João Guerreiro
Tiago Guerreiro
Mona Leigh Guha
Eija Haapalainen
Ferreira
Eben Haber
Mieke Haesen
Martin Halvey
William Hamilton
Alina Hang
John Hannon
Lynda Hardman
Chandra Harrison
Mountaz Hascoet
Kirstie Hawkey
Eiji Hayashi
Christopher Healey
Marti Hearst
Brent Hecht
Nathalie Henry Riche
Niels Henze
Eelco Herder
Nicolas Hernandez
Steffen Hess
Anne Hess
Wilko Heuten
Stacie Hibino
Michiel Hildebrand
Sherri Hiller
Ronald Hiller
Serena Hillman
Lauren Hinkle
Stacy Hobson
Christina Hochleitner
DJ Hoets
Paul Holleis
Jonathan Hook
M. Ehsan Hoque
Eric Horvitz
Gahangir Hossain
Hao-Wei Hsieh
Shih-Wen Huang
Weidong Huang
Cheng-Zhi Anna Huang
Jeff Huang
Hung-Hsuan Huang
Jochen Huber
Bowen Hui
Sazzad Hussain
David Huynh
Sungjae Hwang
Aulikki Hyrskykari
Francisco Iacobelli
Netta Iivari
José Macías Iglesias
Poika Isokoski
Jason Jacques
Christophe Jacquet
Jacek Jankowski
Bonnie John
Kristiina Jokinen
Anirudha Joshi
Christophe Jouffrais
Kshitij Judah
Jessica Jung
Marko Jurmu
Antti Jylhä
Chen Kai
Sanjay Kairam
Santosh Kalwar
Ece Kamar
Slim Kammoun
Shaun Kane
Ashish Kapoor
Evangelos Kapros
Sarvnaz Karimi
Judy Kay
Konstantinos Kazakos
Aisling Kelliher
Maximilian Kern
Cem Keskin
Mohammadreza Khalilbeigi
M. Asif Khawaja
Peter Khooshabeh
Hong-Hoe Kim
David Kim
Kenrick Kin
Felix Kistler
Aniket Kittur
Styliani Kleanthous
Isaac Knowles
Andrew Ko
Jeffrey Tzu Kwan
Valino Koh
Andrea Kohlhase
Farshad Kooti
Vassilis Kostakos
Ilkka Kosunen
Matthias Kranz
Onur Kucuktunc
Tsvi Kuflik
Katie Kuksenok
Todd Kulesza
Alexander Kulik
Ranjitha Kumar
Rohit Kumar
Shankar Kumar
Andrew Kun
Yen-Ling Kuo
Bum chul Kwon
Hao Lü
Shyong Lam
Edward Lank
Rosa Lanzilotti
Walter Lasecki
Joseph LaViola
Matthew Lee
Sang-su Lee
Chia-Hsun Lee
Gun Lee
Charlotte Lee
Bongshin Lee
Grzegorz Lehmann
Luis Leiva
Raimondas Lencevicius
Barbara Leporini
Cane Wing-Ki Leung
Yang Li
Wei Li
Anita Lillie
Brian Lim
Timm Linder
Christine Lisetti
Shixia Liu
W. Liu
Zhicheng Liu
Jiahui Liu
Xuan Liu
Li Liu
Benjamin Lok
Arminda Lopes
Vanessa Lopez
Joern Loviscach
Pengfei Lu
Jie Lu
George Lucchese
Maurizio Lucenteforte
Jake Luo
Michael Lyons
Allan MacLean
Rui Madeira

Paul Maglio
Archisman Majumdar
Apostolos Malatras
Maurizio Mancini
Cathy Marshall
Catherine Marshall
Stefan Marti
Jesús Ibáñez Martínez
Cindy Mason
Michael Massimi
Agnes Lisowska
Masson
Judith Masthoff
Justin Matejka
Diana Maynard
Davide Mazza
Kevin McGee
Patrick Mcnally
Amir Meghdadi
Gerrit Meixner
Sarah Mennicken
Greg Merkle
Marie-Jean Meurs
Daniel Michelis
David Milne
Tom Mitchell
Antonija Mitrovic
Takashi Miyaki
Andreas Möller
Khaireel Mohamed
Toni-Jan Keith
Monserrat
Stuart Moran
Tony Morelli
Alistair Morrison
Florian Mueller
Eric Mueller
Christian Mueller-
Tomfelde
Kasia Muldner
Cosmin Munteanu
Aditi Muralidharan
Dianne Murray
Mirco Musolesi
Moyen Mustaquim
Yukiko Nakano
David Navarre
Michael Nebeling
Luciana Nedel
Matei Negulescu
Nathan Nichols
Gabriel Nicolae
Hugo Nicolau
Laurence Nigay
Sylvie Noël
Shawn O'Banion
John O'Donovan
Ian Oakley
Zeljko Obrenovic
Amy Ogan
Patrick Oladimeji
Samuel Ollo
Alex Olwal
Constantin Orasan
Tihomir Orehovacki
Daniel Ortiz-Martínez
Sebastian Osswald
Derya Ozkan
Tyler Pace
Aditya Pal
Philippe Palanque
Shimei Pan
Jose Ignacio Panach
Adam Pantel
Nadia Pantidi
Young-Woo Park
Sun Young Park
Celeste Paul
Sharoda Paul
Heiko Paulheim
Brandon Paulson
Jose Manuel Sanchez
Pena
Lucas Pereira
Manuel Perez-Quinones
Simon Perrault
Annie Peshkam
Giovanna Petrone
Steve Pettifier
Mark Pfaff
Claudia Picardi
Martin Pielot
Jeffrey Pierce
Thomas Pietrzak
Luca Piovano
Peter Pirolli
Tim Plattner
Timothy Plattner
Till Plumbaum
Manoj Pooleery
Ana-maria Popescu
Benjamin Poppinga
Payam Aghaei Pour
Manoj Prasad
Pearl Pu
Angel Puerta
Shaolin Qu
Daniele Quercia
Aaron Quigley
Nitendra Rajput
Daniel Ramage
Sarvapali Ramchurn
Huaming Rao
Janet C. Read
Madhu Reddy
Steve Reeves
Tim Regan
Patrick Reignier
Katharina Reinecke
Gerhard Reitmayr
Christian Remy
Steve Renals
Franklin Reynolds
Sandra Richter
Andreas Riener
Chris Riesbeck
Mikko Rissanen
Alan Ritter
Brian Roark
Tyson Roberts
Simon Robinson
Ma. Mercedes Rodrigo
Ido Roll
Teresa Romão
Mario Romero
José Rouillard
Jonathan Rowe
Matthew Rowe
Tom Rowlands
Murat Russell
Heiki Ruuska
Rafal Rzepka
Amir Sadeghipour
Alireza Sahami
Alan Said
Krystian Samp
Ruth Sancho Huerga
Daniel Sandler
Vagner Santana
Carmen Santoro
Giuseppe Santucci
T. Scott Saponas
Sayan Sarcar
Dominique Scapin
Johannes Schöning
Florian Schaub
Chris Schmandt
Dominik Schmidt
Albrecht Schmidt
Paul Schmieder
Jodi Schneider
Bjoern Schuller
Stefan Schulz
Stephanie Schwartz
Amy Schwartz
Veit Schwartze
Jeremy Scott
Ahmed Seffah
Marino Segnan
Doree Seligmann
Ted Selker
Marcos Serrano
Ricky Sethi
Metin Sezgin
Izhak Shafran
David Shamma
Nikhil Sharma
Haifeng Shen
Jianqiang Shen
S. Sheppard
Sajad Shirali-Shahreza
Judith Siegel
Gabriel Skantze
J. David Smith
David Smith
Greg Smith
Yale Song
Yangqiu Song

Daniel Sonntag
Jean-Sébastien Sottet
Lucio Davide Spano
Adam Sporka
Richard Sproat
Milan Stankovic
Ben Steichen
Frank Steinicke
Oliviero Stock
Carlo Strapparava
Giota Stratou
Simone Stumpf
Bongwon Suh
David Sun
Kåre Synnes
Dalila Szostak
Aurélien Tabard
Paul Taele
Ronnie Taib
Federico Tajariol
John Tang
Jaime Teevan
Daniel Thalmann
Bruce Thomas
Amit Tiroshi
Cagdas "Chad" Toprak
Frank Trollmann
Raphael Troncy
Simon Tucker
Satish Ukkusuri
Amy Ulinski
Heather Underwood
Christina Unger
William Uther
Naushad Uzzaman
Kaisa Väänänen-Vainio-Mattila
Jan Van den Bergh
Benjamin Van durme
Marieke van Erp
Jeroen van Grondelle
Max Van Kleek
Andrew Vande Moere
Keith Vander Linden
Jean Vanderdonckt
Radu-Daniel Vatavu
Eduardo Veas
Jo Vermeulen
Fabiana Vernero
Keith Vertanen
Jesse Vig
Markel Vigo
Jean-Luc Vinot
Dong-Bach Vo
Juergen Vogel
Gualtiero Volpe
Emanuel von Zezschwitz
Earl Wagner
James Wallace
Hanna Wallach
Travis Waller
Hongan Wang
Yang Wang
Jieyu Wang
Xiaoyu Wang
Peter Wardrip
Catherine Watson
Jun Wei
Wei Wei
Nadir Weibel
Stephan Weibelzahl
Justin Weisz
Zhen Wen
Mark Whiting
Lynn Wilcox
Mathias Wilhelm
Jason D. Williams
John Williamson
Max Wilson
Raphael Wimmer
Christian Winkler
Maria Wolters
Pak Chung Wong
Min Wu
Mike Wu
Lexing Xie
Huahai Yang
Svetlana Yarosh
Ugan Yasavur
Tom Yeh
Lars Yencken
Ying Yin
Chuang-wen You
Jim Young
Gabriel Zachmann
Jakub Zavrel
Mi Zhang
Yanxia Zhang
Cheng Zhang
Yu Zheng
Erheng Zhong
Xiaomu Zhou
Jianlong Zhou
Kening Zhu
Yin Zhu
Juergen Ziegler

Posters & Demonstrations Reviewers

Sriram Karthik Badam
Sandra Baldassarri
Sumit Basu
Ajay Bhushan
Marc Busch
Amira Chalbi
Angela Chang
Alex Qiang Chen
Xiang 'Anthony' Chen
Ming Ki Chong
Massimiliano Dal Mas
Sashikanth Damaraju
Stefan Diewald
Honglu Du
Ruofei Du
Carlos Duarte
Varun Dutt
Ribel Fares
Robert Farrell
Feng Gao
Masitah Ghazali
Giuseppe Ghiani
Tiago Gonçalves
Alice Good
Visda Goudarzi
Mayank Grover
Serena Hillman
Christina Hochleitner
Gahangir Hossain
Pourang Irani
Teruaki Ito
Jacek Jankowski
Hyunggu Jung
Santosh Kalwar
Byungkyu Kang
Mohammadreza Khalilbeigi
Hong-Hoe Kim
Matthias Kranz
Sitwat Langrial
Walter Lasecki
Yann Laurillau
Luis Leiva
Li Liu
Can Liu
George Lucchese
Cristina Manresa Yee
Sampada Marathe
Tatu Marttila
Gregor Mehlmann
Emilie Mollenbach
Michael Nebeling
Sabrina Panëels
Lucas Pereira
Simon Perrault
Tamara Peyton
Bastian Pfleging
Martin Pielot
Manoj Prasad
Shaolin Qu
Janet C. Read
Mario Romero
Alan Said
Guarionex Salivia
Sayan Sarcar
Yann Savoye
James Schaffer
Florian Schaub
Lou Schwartz
Sajad Shirali-Shahreza
Lucio Davide Spano
Paul Taele
Nick Tanton
Minh-Triet TRAN
Philippe Truillet
Heli Väätäjä
Stephanie Valentine
Martin Voigt
Hana Vrzakova
Romain Vuillemot
Dhaval Vyas
Mark Whiting
Maria Wolters
Yanxia Zhang
Arkaitz Zubiaga

IUI 2013 Sponsors & Supporters

Sponsors: SIGART SIGCHI

Supporters: Samsung, LG Electronics, FX Palo Alto Laboratory (FXPAL), RedWhale Software, IBM, Microsoft Research

Duolingo: Learn a Language for Free while Helping to Translate the Web

Luis von Ahn
Carnegie Mellon University
5000 Forbes Avenue
Pittsburgh, PA 15213, USA
biglou@cs.cmu.edu

ABSTRACT

I want to translate the Web into every major language: every webpage, every video, and, yes, even Justin Bieber's tweets.

With its content split up into hundreds of languages — and with over 50% of it in English — most of the Web is inaccessible to most people in the world. This problem is pressing, now more than ever, with millions of people from China, Russia, Latin America and other quickly developing regions entering the Web. In this talk, I introduce my new project, called Duolingo, which aims at breaking this language barrier, and thus making the Web truly "world wide."

We have all seen how systems such as Google Translate are improving every day at translating the gist of things written in other languages. Unfortunately, they are not yet accurate enough for my purpose: Even when what they spit out is intelligible, it's so badly written that I can't read more than a few lines before getting a headache.

With Duolingo, our goal is to encourage people, like you and me, to translate the Web into their native languages.

Author Keywords

Crowdsourcing; human computation; education technology; natural language processing

ACM Classification Keywords

H.5.2 [Information Interfaces and Presentation]: User Interfaces - Interaction styles.

BIO

Luis von Ahn is the A. Nico Habermann Associate Professor of Computer Science at Carnegie Mellon University. He is working to develop a new area of computer science that he calls Human Computation, which aims to build systems that combine the intelligence of humans and computers to solve large-scale problems that neither can solve alone.

An example of his work is reCAPTCHA, in which over one billion people — 15% of humanity — have helped digitize books and newspapers.

Among his many honors are a MacArthur Fellowship, a Packard Fellowship, a Sloan Research Fellowship, a Microsoft New Faculty Fellowship, the ACM Grace Hopper Award, and CMU's Herbert A. Simon Award for Teaching Excellence and Alan J. Perlis Teaching Award. He has been named one of the "50 Best Brains in Science" by Discover Magazine, one of the 50 most influential people in technology by silicon.com, and one of the "Brilliant 10 Scientists" by Popular Science Magazine.

IUI'13, March 19–22, 2013, Santa Monica, CA, USA.
ACM 978-1-4503-1965-2/13/03.

Leveraging the Crowd to Improve Feature-Sentiment Analysis of User Reviews

Shih-Wen Huang[1], **Pei-Fen Tu**[1], **Wai-Tat Fu**[1], **Mohammad Amanzadeh**[2]
Department of Computer Science[1], Industrial & Enterprise System Engineering[2]
University of Illinois at Urbana-Champaign
{shuang51, ptu3, wfu, amanzad2}@illinois.edu

ABSTRACT
Crowdsourcing and machine learning are both useful techniques for solving difficult problems (e.g., computer vision and natural language processing). In this paper, we propose a novel method that harnesses and combines the strength of these two techniques to better analyze the features and the sentiments toward them in user reviews. To strike a good balance between reducing information overload and providing the original context expressed by review writers, the proposed system (1) allows users to interactively rank the entities based on feature-rating, (2) automatically highlights sentences that are related to relevant features, and (3) utilizes implicit crowdsourcing by encouraging users to provide correct labels of their own reviews to improve the feature-sentiment classifier. The proposed system not only helps users to save time and effort to digest the often massive amount of user reviews, but also provides real-time suggestions on relevant features and ratings as users generate their own reviews. Results from a simulation experiment show that leveraging on the crowd can significantly improve the feature-sentiment analysis of user reviews. Furthermore, results from a user study show that the proposed interface was preferred by more participants than interfaces that use traditional noun-adjective pair summarization, as the current interface allows users to view feature-related information in the original context.

Author Keywords
Human computation; crowdsourcing; interactive machine learning; sentiment analysis; user generated content

ACM Classification Keywords
H.5.2 [Information interfaces and presentation]: User Interfaces.

INTRODUCTION
With the rapid success of Web 2.0 technologies, user-generated content has become a major source of online information. One of the most notable examples is online reviews. Millions of people now write reviews on websites like Yelp or Amazon to express their opinions regarding different restaurants or products. These user-generated reviews can be very helpful for others to make wiser decisions.

However, extensive amounts of user-generated reviews are difficult for people to digest, creating a typical problem of information overload. There are two potentially conflicting goals when designing systems that leverage on user-generated reviews. First, the system should mitigate information overload by summarizing important information for the users; second, the system should allow users to express their experiences in their own words while at the same time allowing others to read their reviews in context. With the proposed system, we aim to provide a balance between the two.

Summarizing the information in user reviews based on related features and sentiment has proven to be an effective way to help users to digest the massive amount of information more efficiently. For example, Review Spotlight [33] performs feature-sentiment analysis and presents the results using noun-adjective pairs. Yatani *et al.* [33] showed that this interface can help users make decisions significantly faster, which demonstrates that feature-sentiment information can help users digest user-generated reviews more efficiently.

The feature-sentiment analysis in existing intelligent interfaces [13, 18, 33] typically incorporates two steps. First, it finds the features by identifying nouns with high frequency counts in the text. Second, after determining the features, it uses the adjective near each feature and a predefined glossary (e.g., SentiWordNet [9]) to determine the feature's orientation. However, researchers have pointed out that this unsupervised learning approach has two major disadvantages, which we will summarize below.

First, as mentioned in [12], this kind of analysis typically can discover only features that are explicitly discussed in the content. For example, consider the following sentence:

"While light, it will not easily fit in pockets."

This sentence is related to size of a product; however, it is very difficult for this unsupervised learning approach to discover the feature because the word "size" does not appear in the sentence [12]. This greatly undermines the utility of the algorithm since many opinions expressed in user-generated reviews are implicit, and they tend to elude discovery by unsupervised learning methods.

The second disadvantage is that this approach often makes mistakes in selecting useful features and deciding the sentiment orientation of the features. For instance, as mentioned in [33], "impeccable", which should be a positive word, has a very high negative score in their system. Illustrating similar mistakes made by the system, some of the system's users noted that the features they presented did not make much sense (as described in the paper [33]). These errors may lower the motivation to use a system as users perceive it to be unreliable.

One way to address these problems is to use labeled data and supervised learning to find the hidden features in the reviews. Supervised learning has demonstrated better performance than unsupervised methods in general [3]. Moreover, this approach can identify sentences related to a feature even if the feature itself is not in the sentence because it uses more than a single term in the sentences to classify. However, supervised methods are difficult, if not impossible, to implement in existing interfaces because it is difficult to motivate users to create a label for each sentence they write. Therefore, one big challenge for this approach is collecting labeled data. Finding a way to motivate users to provide labels is key to the success of this supervised approach.

To address the questions discussed above, *we propose a novel intelligent interface that collects training data directly from users as they generate reviews – a concept often called implicit crowdsourcing.* The system we built can perform feature-sentiment analysis in nearly real-time. As a result, it can provide predictions while a user is writing the review. If the user sees the prediction is wrong, the user can simply click the icons on the interface to correct the erroneous prediction. Therefore, instead of providing labels for every sentence in the review, users need only to correct some mistakes made by the system, which greatly reduces the effort necessary to provide feature-sentiment information. In addition, users are more motivated to provide labels because these labels are related to the accuracy of their own reviews. The collected data can be used as new training instances for the classifier. Moreover, increasing the number of training instances raises the coverage of the supervised learning algorithms [14]. Therefore, leveraging the crowd to collect user-generated labels allows the classifiers to provide more accurate predictions as the number of users in the system grows. To preview our result, the experiment shows that our supervised classifiers can achieve much higher F_1 scores than baseline models that discover feature-sentiment information using unsupervised methods.

Another drawback of many existing intelligent interfaces is that the feature-related information is summarized in a very compressed form (e.g., noun-adjective pairs). Although this has the advantage of allowing users to retrieve the feature-related information in the reviews more quickly, it also destroys the original context of the reviews, which often contain more than pure information, such as social cues, personal expression, etc. In contrast, the proposed system provides a highlighting function that highlights the feature-related information in its original context. This function integrates into the traditional review reading experience and creates a good balance between focusing on feature-related information and understanding the full reviews. In this study, we compared the two designs (i.e., noun-adjective pair summarization and highlighting) to observe what users liked or disliked about these two types of systems. To preview our results, we did find that most users preferred to see the original context rather than the purely summarized features, thus providing support to the design.

Overview of the paper

In the rest of the paper, we first will review related work on how crowdsourcing can be used to assist supervised learning and feature-sentiment analysis of user reviews. We will then describe the current system and how it differs from previous ones. Then we will perform two sets of evaluation. First, we will present results from a simulation experiment to demonstrate how the system can outperform previous systems that utilize unsupervised learning, and how the system can improve over time as more user-generated labels are collected to improve the classifier in the current system. Second, we will present results from a user study that tested whether review readers and writers would like the features of the current system. Specifically, we tested the extent to which review readers would like to see the context of user reviews instead of merely summarized reviews, and we tested whether the real-time feedback would encourage review writers to provide labels for their own reviews. Finally, we will discuss the implication of our results for the design of systems that rely on user-generated content in general, as well as the future direction of the current research.

RELATED WORK

Enhancing machine learning algorithms by collecting labeled data from crowdsourcing

Crowdsourcing has been proven as an effective way to solve various kinds of problems [11]. Individuals can easily recruit online workers from crowdsourcing platforms like Amazon Mechanical Turk (AMT)[1] to solve problems that are difficult for digital computers (e.g., text editing [1] and answering visual query [2]) at a very low cost. These examples have merely begun to demonstrate the potential of crowdsourcing as a social computing technique that can be applied in a wide range of situations.

One of the most notable application for crowdsourcing is collecting labeled data to improve the performance of machine learning algorithms. Von Ahn and Dabbish [29] pioneered the field by developing the ESP game, which recruits people to generate image labels while playing an online game. By 2008, this game had recruited 200,000 players and collected more than 50 million labels [30]. The collected labels then were used to improve Google image search. Other games [10, 31] and methods [22, 25, 26] also have been proposed to collect high-quality image labels to train computer vision algorithms.

[1]https://www.mturk.com

Figure 1. When reading reviews, users can highlight sentences that are related to the aspect which interests them by a single click.

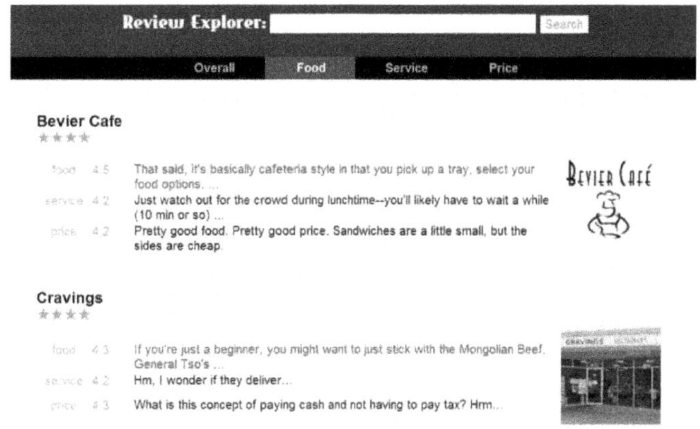

Figure 2. When browsing entities, the system allows users to sort them (e.g. restaurants) using their ratings of different features.

In addition to image labels, crowdsourcing also has been used to collect training data for natural language processing. Snow *et al.* [24] studied how the labeled data generated by the non-experts from AMT can be more cost-effective than those generated by experts. They also showed that the labels collected from crowdsourcing could successfully improve machine learning algorithms. There are also various workshops in NAACL [4], SIGIR [17], and WSDM [16] that aim at utilizing crowdsourcing to generate labeled data that are useful to data mining and information retrieval.

Instead of explicitly recruiting crowd workers to generate labeled data to enhance machine learning, Nichols *et al.* [19] proposed *implicit crowdsourcing*, a method that directly collects data generate by the users, which is different from traditional crowdsourcing that pays money to recruit workers from AMT to create labeled data. This allows the system to collect more data as the number of users increases. For example, they [19] found that by collecting status updates posted to Twitter, the system can successfully generate meaningful summaries of sporting events. This design is especially useful for supervised learning because the size of training data is essential to the performance of the algorithms [14]. Besides summarizing the data that have been already posted, the intelligent interface we built can generate the predictions in real time and involve users to correct the errors made by the system. As a result, our interface further uses artificial intelligence to assist users to generate labeled data more easily. To the best of our knowledge, this is a novel concept that has not yet been explored.

Intelligent interfaces for user reviews

Since user reviews contain much valuable information, many researches have proposed different methods to analyze the features and sentiments expressed in user reviews [20]. Hu and Liu [12] used the minimum support of association rule to identify frequent terms and phrases in user reviews as features. Many researchers [7, 21, 28, 32] also studied how to use machine learning algorithms to classify the sentiments expressed in user-generated reviews.

Recently, many intelligent interfaces have been developed to help users to understand feature-sentiment information in a huge amount of user reviews. Liu *et al.* [18] implemented Opinion Observer, an interface that uses bar charts to present the positive and negative sentiments of each feature. Carenini *et al.* [5] constructed a treemaps interface for users to interactively explore the information that interests them. In addition, they also designed a novel visualization for users to compare the feature-sentiment information between different entities [6]. Yatani *et al.* [33] developed Review Spotlight to present feature-sentiment information in user reviews using noun-adjective pairs in a tag cloud. Huang *et al.* [13] further group the similar features together to display feature-sentiment information in a more concise format. The biggest difference between the intelligent interface of our system and the existing ones is that: instead of summarizing the information using noun-adjective pairs, our system presents the information by highlighting the feature-related sentences in their original context. This allows the users to focus on feature-related information while still have the opportunity to explore other information in the reviews.

Moreover, intelligent interfaces also have been used to assist review writing. Dong *et al.* [8] developed Reviewer's Assistant, a browser plug-in that identifies the sentences written by previous users which might also be used by the current user and recommend them to the user. Their study showed that the system could suggest sentences that were actually written by the users. The current system also has an intelligent interface for review writing. Nevertheless, we aim at collecting feature-sentiment information that can be helpful to the readers instead of assisting reviewers to generate user reviews.

SYSTEM DESIGN AND IMPLEMENTATION

The proposed system incorporates two functions that help readers digest user reviews: first, it allows its users to highlight sentences based on the features they are interested in by a single click; this greatly reduces the amount of information that a user must read. (Figure 1) Second, users of the system can rank the entities based on their feature ratings, which are inferred directly from the contents. (Figure 2)

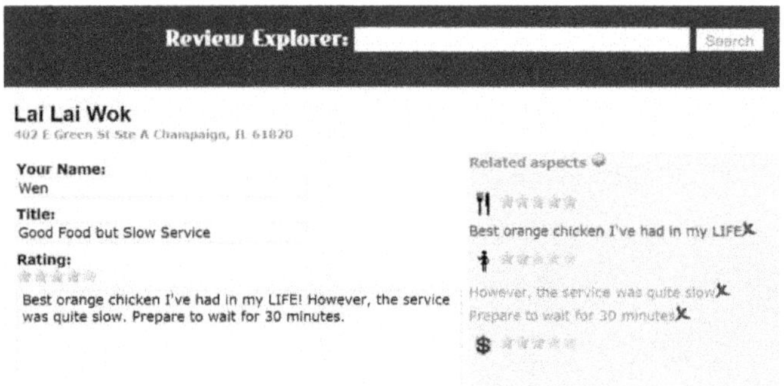

Figure 3. Users can click the icons on the interface to correct the erroneous predictions made by the system while composing reviews. For example, the cross sign near the sentences allow users to cancel the predictions made by the system. In addition, users also can click the stars to change feature-ratings.

To collect the information needed to perform the two functions mentioned above, the system also has a novel intelligent interface that conducts feature-sentiment analysis in real time. When a user is writing a review using the system, whenever the user finishes a sentence, the system would provide the user real-time predictions about the feature(s) that are related to it and the star ratings of the features. If the user feels that the predictions made by the system are wrong, they can simply click the icons on the interface to correct the errors. (Figure 3) A graphical representation of the design of our system is shown in Figure 4.

Data and features of the current system

The data used in the current system was retrieved from Yelp's Academic Dataset[2], which consists of 87,173 reviews of restaurants near 30 schools. In this study, we used three pre-defined features: food, service, and price. However, one should notice that the data and features of the system easily can be altered or expanded and are not limited to the current settings.

Supervised two-layer feature-sentiment analysis

To discover the related features of each sentence and the inferred ratings of the features, a supervised two-layer feature-sentiment analysis was conducted on each review in the corpus. A graphical representation of the flow of the two-layer analysis is shown in Figure 5.

The first layer of the analysis is the *sentence feature classification*. In this layer, the system decides if one sentence is related to a target feature or not. To initiate the classifiers of the system, we collected 5,000 labeled sentences by recruiting 194 workers from Amazon Mechanical Turk at a cost of $9.70 (from 4/11/2012 to 4/21/2012). The workers were asked to label whether a sentence was related to any of the three predefined features or to none of them (A sentence can be related to more than one feature). This is used to simulate the data generated by the initial users of our system. We preprocessed the text by stemming and removing stop words, and we converted these labeled sentences into unigram feature vectors.

[2]http://www.yelp.com/academic_dataset

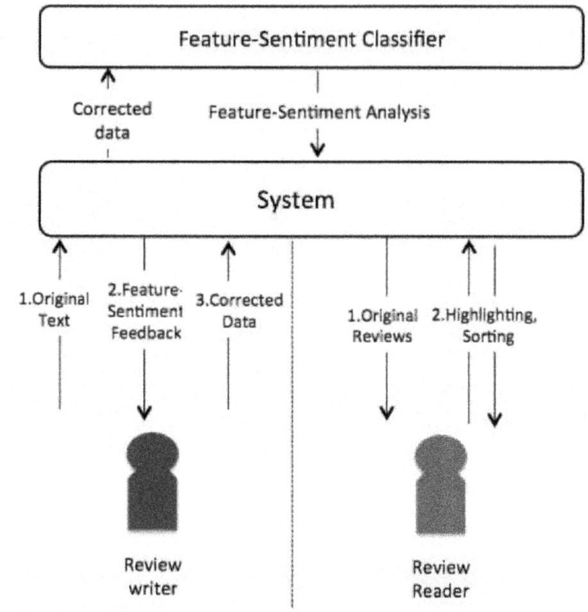

Figure 4. When user is writing a review using our novel intelligent interface, the system performs a real-time feature-sentiment analysis. The user can easily correct the erroneous predictions made by the system. The corrected data then is used to improve the classifiers to provide useful information for other users to digest the reviews.

Then, we used the SVM^{light} package[3] to train the classifiers on these feature vectors. If a sentence was related to a certain feature, its associated feature vector would be treated as a positive training instance for the classifier of that feature. In contrast, if the sentence is not related to that feature, its feature vector was used as a negative training instance. Finally, sentences that did not have labels in the corpus were converted into unigram feature vectors, and the system used the classifiers trained on the labeled sentences to classify the features related to the unlabeled sentences.

The second layer of the analysis is the *feature-rating prediction*, which predicts the star ratings of different features in each review. To construct the classifiers, we utilized the reviews and their associated star ratings in Yelp's academic dataset. First, the reviews with 4 or more stars were used as positive training instances and reviews with less than 4 stars were used as negative training instances. These reviews were converted to feature vectors and were used to train a positive-negative classifier using SVM^{light}. By a similar procedure, we built a 4-5-star classifier and a 2-3-star classifier[4]. These classifiers allowed us to predict the overall ratings of each review. For example, if a review was predicted as positive (more than 3 stars) by the positive-negative classifier, the system then would run the 4-5-star classifier to see if it should be classified as a 4-star review or a 5-star review.

Equipped with the rating classifiers, the system then predicts

[3]http://svmlight.joachims.org/

[4]We grouped 1-star reviews to the 2-star reviews category because there is only a very small portion of the reviews are 1-star

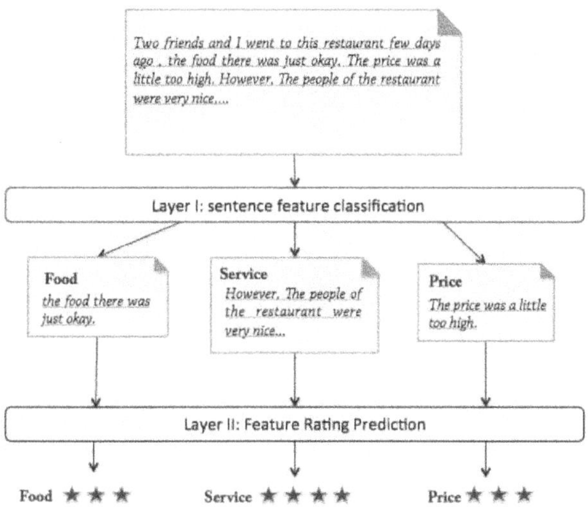

Figure 5. The flow of the two-layer feature-sentiment analysis. The system first classify the sentences with their related features. The sentences that are related to the same feature then are grouped together and are used to predict the rating of the feature.

the feature ratings of each review by classifying the star rating using only the contents that are related to a feature (based on the first layer analysis). For instance, when predicting the service rating of a review, the system would first find out which sentences related to service using the service-feature classifier. Then, these sentences would be grouped together and classified by the star-rating classifiers. Finally, the output of the classifier would be the service rating of the review.

Collecting corrected feature-sentiment information from users

To ensure the accuracy of the analysis made by the system and collect more training data to improve the performance of the classifier, the system provides an interface that can perform real-time feature-sentiment analysis while a user composes a review. Whenever the user finishes a sentence, the web-based system sends it to the server using AJAX. When the server receives the sentence, a Python script performs the text preprocessing and converts the sentence into a unigram feature vector that can be processed by the classifiers. Then the system conducts the two-layer feature-sentiment analysis using the SVM^{light} package. Finally, the result of the analysis is sent back to the interface on the client side. The whole analysis can be performed within one second, including the latency of the Internet, so for the user, the analysis seems to occur in real time.

If the predictions are wrong, the user can simply click the icons next to the predictions on the interface to correct them. For example, if a sentence is mistakenly classified as a sentence that is related to price but the user judges that it is not, the user can click the cross sign near the sentence to cancel this prediction and assign the sentence to other categories, or not to any existing category. If, for example, the sentence is judged to be related to food, the user can click the icon that represents food near the sentence to label it. Furthermore, if the star-rating predictions are wrong, the user can click the stars on the interface to change the ratings.

EXPERIMENTS

To evaluate whether our proposed method really improves feature-sentiment analysis, we manually labeled the related features (i.e., food, service, and price) of 1,000 sentences in the dataset and used these as gold standard test dataset. The system's ability to discover the related features of our proposed design and the baseline models was evaluated on this dataset.[5] In this study, we focused only on the ability to classify feature-related sentences of the proposed method and left evaluation of the ability to generate accurate feature-rating for future work. Specifically, we wanted to test two hypotheses:

H1: The supervised classifier in our design can achieve higher performance than a traditional unsupervised approach can.

H2: More training data improves the performance of the classifier.

Two experiments were performed to test the hypotheses. The details of these experiments are described below.

Experiment I: Comparisons between supervised and unsupervised methods

In this experiment, we compared the proposed supervised method to a baseline model with unsupervised learning to test if **H1** is true.

Method

Three sentence-feature classifiers (food, service, and price) were trained on 5,000 sentences labeled by AMT workers. We performed text preprocessing which includes stemming and removing the stop words of the sentences. The sentences then were converted to the feature vectors using a unigram model. Finally, we used SVM^{light} to train the classifiers on these feature vectors.

In addition, we built a baseline model similar to the ones in [13, 18, 33]. This unsupervised model used 434,664 sentences in the full data set. The data size is much larger than the 5,000 labeled sentences used in the supervised method. To identify the frequent features in the sentences, we first used the part-of-speech tagging function in NLTK[6] to find all the nouns and adjectives in the sentences. Then, we performed the same text preprocessing as in the supervised method. After that, the nouns (after stemming) that appeared in more than 1% of the total sentences were selected as the features. This threshold is the same as the minimum support used in [18]. We tried to vary the threshold to 0.1%, 0.5%, and 2%, but there were no significant differences in the results of the various thresholds. Therefore, only the results of the 1% threshold were reported. After the features were selected, the closest adjective to each feature was considered as the one

[5]We did not use the labels retrieved from AMT to evaluate the classifiers because we found that it contains many low-quality labels.
[6]http://nltk.org/

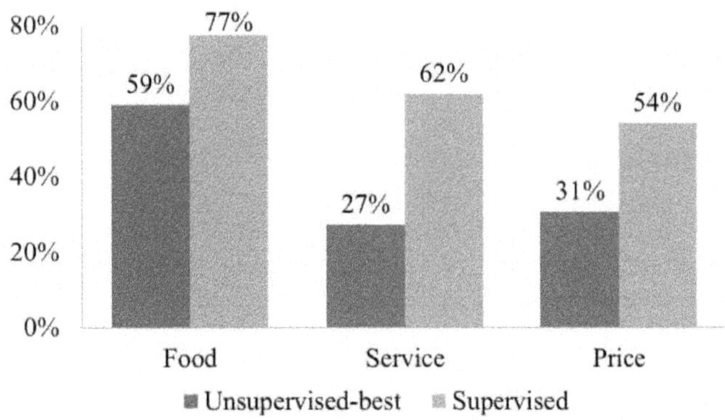

Figure 6. The comparisons between the F_1 scores of the supervised method and the best performance of the unsupervised methods. The results show that the supervised method can achieve much better F_1 scores than the unsupervised methods in all three features tested.

that described the feature. We then grouped the features using the Kullback-Leibler divergence [15] between the adjectives that described the features, which is the feature grouping method used in [13]. Finally, the top (5, 10, 20, 30) closest features to food, service, and price were assigned to them as sub-features. If one of the sub-features occurred in a target sentence, the sentence was classified as related to the main feature (food, service, or price).

Evaluation

We evaluated the systems on a 1000-sentence test data manually labeled by the authors. The precision, recall, and F_1 score were calculated using the formulas below:

$$\text{precision} = \frac{\text{\# feature-related sentences classfied correctly}}{\text{\# sentences classified as related to the feature}}$$

$$\text{recall} = \frac{\text{\# feature-related sentences classfied correctly}}{\text{\# feature-related sentences}}$$

$$F_1 = 2 \cdot \frac{\text{precision} \cdot \text{recall}}{\text{precision} + \text{recall}}$$

We used the F_1 scores to evaluate the performance of the classifiers because it is a weighted average of precision and recall. Since there is a trade-off between precision and recall, F_1 scores can evaluate the results more fairly [23]. The precision, recall, and F_1 scores of the supervised method and the unsupervised methods with various number of sub-features are summarized in the table 1, 2, and 3.

The results show that the proposed supervised method achieved much higher F_1 scores in classifying feature-related sentences. (Figure 6) When looking more carefully into the precision and recall of each classifier, we see that the supervised method can achieve much higher precision than the unsupervised methods can. In addition, although increasing features to the unsupervised methods allows them to outperform the supervised method in recall of two of the three features,

	5 feat.	10 feat.	20 feat.	30 feat.	supervised
Food	47.67%	51.69%	53.78%	51.99%	85.75%
Service	18.47%	18.39%	16.59%	17.09%	90.00%
Price	24.55%	16.29%	13.83%	11.91%	80.95%

Table 1. Precision of supervised method and unsupervised methods with different number of sub-features

	5 feat.	10 feat.	20 feat.	30 feat.	supervised
Food	30.09%	41.63%	61.09%	68.10%	70.50%
Service	34.33%	41.04%	50.75%	65.67%	47.01%
Price	31.68%	35.64%	49.50%	63.28%	40.50%

Table 2. Recall of supervised method and unsupervised methods with different number of sub-features

	5 feat.	10 feat.	20 feat.	30 feat.	supervised
food	36.89%	46.12%	57.20%	58.96%	77.38%
Service	24.02%	25.40%	25.01%	27.12%	61.76%
Price	30.60%	24.51%	22.22%	20.00%	53.99%

Table 3. F_1 scores of supervised method and unsupervised methods with different number of sub-features

the precision becomes unacceptably low (around 15%). The reason is that unsupervised methods would include many general terms as sub-features, which are not very helpful to the classification task. In contrast, the supervised method uses the unigram feature vector to determine whether one sentence is related to a feature. Therefore, the classification result is not dominated by any single term. In addition, the supervised method can discover some hidden patterns in sentences. For instance, consider the following:

"The food is superb and it comes out pretty fast."

This sentence is related to both food and service. By using an unsupervised method, the only feature that can be discovered is food because it is mentioned explicitly in the sentence. On the other hand, the supervised method used in our system can successfully capture both features because "fast" and "come" both carry meanings that are related to service, which is the hidden feature of this sentence. The supervised method can learn these implicit concepts (e.g., fast and come) to discover the hidden feature if it is trained on a massive amount of labeled data. As a result, the supervised method can achieve higher F_1 scores. The results therefore provide support to **H1** – using supervised learning to train the classifier can result in better performance than that achieved by traditional unsupervised methods. In particular, the current method can significantly improve precision because of the fact that many hidden variables that define the categories in user reviews cannot be easily identified by unsupervised methods.

Experiment II: Comparisons between the supervised methods with various training data size

In this second experiment, we varied the size of data that is used to train the supervised classifiers to see if **H2** is supported.

Method

We trained the classifiers on 0.5K, 1K, 2K, 3K, 4K, and 5K labeled sentences. These subsets of labeled sentences were selected randomly from the 5,000 labeled sentences collected from AMT as described in experiment I.

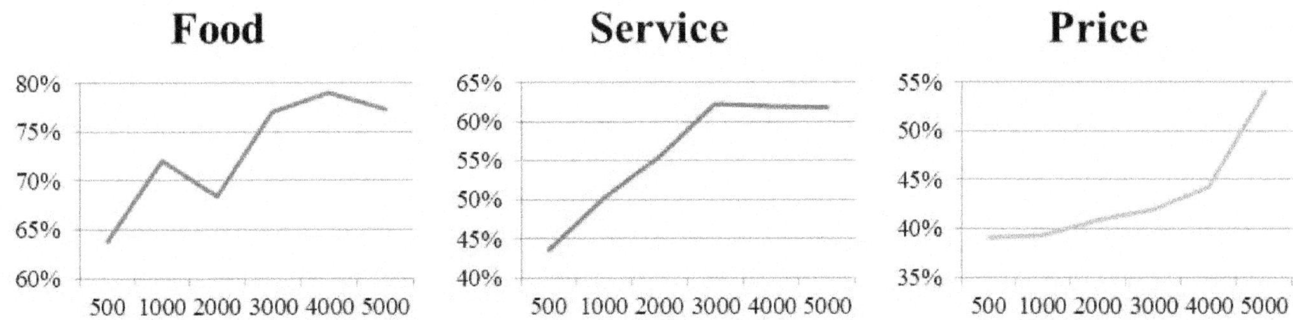

Figure 7. The F_1 scores of the feature-classifiers trained on various size of data. The results show that there was a very high positive correlation between the size of training data and the performance of the classifiers.

Evaluation

The precision, recall and F_1 scores of the feature-classifiers trained on various sizes of labeled sentences are summarized in the table 4, 5, and 6.

	500	1000	2000	3000	4000	5000
food	85.02%	82.13%	81.37%	82.90%	84.58%	85.75%
Service	95.00%	68.83%	70.93%	86.67%	85.53%	90.00%
Price	92.59%	96.15%	87.10%	78.38%	79.49%	80.95%

Table 4. Precision of supervised method on various size of training data

	500	1000	2000	3000	4000	5000
food	51.13%	64.19%	59.01%	72.07%	74.10%	70.50%
Service	28.36%	39.55%	45.52%	48.51%	48.51%	47.01%
Price	24.75%	24.75%	26.73%	28.71%	30.69%	40.50%

Table 5. Recall of supervised method on various size of training data

	500	1000	2000	3000	4000	5000
food	63.86%	72.06%	68.41%	77.11%	78.99%	77.38%
Service	43.68%	50.23%	55.45%	62.20%	61.91%	61.76%
Price	39.06%	39.37%	40.91%	42.03%	44.28%	53.99%

Table 6. F_1 score of supervised method on various size of training data

The results show that the performances of the classifiers clearly are positively correlated to the size of training data. The Pearson correlations between the size of training data and the F_1 scores of the feature classifiers for food, service, and price are 85%, 90%, and 89%, respectively. We also found that the improvements of the classifiers are mostly from recall. The Pearson correlations between the size of training data and the recall of the feature classifiers for food, service, and price are 81%, 79%, and 91% respectively. This shows that more training data can help the classifiers discover more hidden patterns in the data, which supports **H2**, that more training instances can enhance the performance of the feature classifiers. This also implies that when more users use the system, the classifiers behind the system can generate more accurate predictions because more training data can be collected from users.

Summary

To summarize, our experiments show that the proposed supervised method can be a better mechanism in classifying sentences by their related features than traditional unsupervised method. Moreover, increasing the training data can further improve the performance of the supervised classifiers, which means that collecting labeled data from users effectively enhances the feature-sentiment analysis of the system.

USER STUDY

We conducted a user study to gain more insight into how our interface impacts users and to answer the following three questions that are important to our theses:

1. Does the feature-sentiment analysis and highlighting function of our system help users digest the information in user reviews?
2. Is the highlighting function better than existing intelligent interfaces that summarize feature-sentiment by noun-adjective pairs?
3. Will users correct the erroneous predictions made by the system?

The first two questions show how our proposed interface helps readers digest user reviews and the last question lets us know if the system really can collect more corrected feature-sentiment information when the system is deployed in the wild.

Procedure

At the beginning of the study, the participants were asked to fill out a questionnaire collecting demographic information and asking how often they read and write user reviews. Then, we introduced our interface and its functions to the participant. After that, the participants were asked to read reviews about a restaurant using both our interface and Yelp's website[7]. When they finished reading, they were asked if the highlighting function of our interface helped them get useful information about the restaurant from the reviews.

Then, we introduced RevMiner[8] [13], an interface that uses noun-adjective pairs to summarize feature-sentiment information in the reviews to its users. (Figure 8) After the participants became familiar with the interfaces, we let them compare the noun-adjective pair summarization with our highlighting function. We chose to use the RevMiner interface

[7]http://www.yelp.com/

[8]http://revminer.com/

Food

food	amazing (13), delicious (27), great (32), hot (11), good (54)
thai food	amazing (5), best (50), great (5), authentic (9), good (9)
tofu	delicious (2), crispy (2), deep-fried (2), deep (5), fried (26)
thai	favorite (2), best (19), little, good (4), phad (2)
noodles	delicious (3), wide (4), thinner (2), flat (2), burnt (4)
menu	coolest (2), great (2), wooden (7), small (2), limited (2)
pad thai	amazing (3), delicious (3), great (4), tasty (2), good (4)
portions	great, huge, large (3), small (2), big (3)
peanut sauce	amazing (3), perfect (2), best (2), delicious (3), good (3)
phad thai	best (5), crisp, different, good (2), runny

Figure 8. Noun-adjective pairs visualization in RevMiner. We used RevMiner as an example to represent the interfaces that summarize feature-sentiment information using noun-adjective pairs.

because it was one of the most recently developed at the time this article was written, and because it was publicly available on the Web. We should point out that our intention was *not* to directly compare our interface to this particular interface. Instead, we are interested in comparing the general design between summarization using noun-adjective pairs (which are used primarily in RevMiner) and highlighting (which is used in our system).

Finally, we demonstrated the review-writing interface of our system, and asked the participants to write a review about a restaurant they recently visited using the interface. After they completed their reviews, we asked the participants whether they would use the interface to correct the feature-sentiment predictions when they were wrong.[9]

Participants

Thirteen college and graduate students (7 males and 6 females between the ages of 22 and 34) participated in this study. All of the participants read user reviews online at least once a month, and 8 of the 13 participants (62%) have experience in writing user reviews online. The study lasted approximately 30 minutes.

USER STUDY RESULTS

Highlighting helped participants digest user reviews

When comparing our interface with traditional review websites, 11 of the 13 participants (85%) suggested that the highlighting function helped them to understand more quickly the information contained in a massive amount of online reviews. One participant mentioned:

> *The highlighting function really helps me focus on the information I am interested in. I can get the information without spending time on the murmur of the reviewers.*

Although two participants thought this function didn't make significant differences, this result demonstrated that the feature-sentiment analysis and highlighting function were perceived as helpful for the majority of the participants in digesting the large number of user reviews.

[9]The exact wordings of our questions are listed in the appendix at the end of the paper.

More participants preferred highlighting over noun-adjective pair summarization

When participants were asked to compare our interface (highlighting) to RevMiner (noun-adjective pair), 6 of the 13 participants (46%) thought our interface was better, 3 of them (23%) thought RevMiner was better, and 4 of them (31%) thought it was a tie. The result suggests that about twice as many participants preferred the highlighting function, compared to those who preferred noun-adjective pair summarization. The reason was that the highlighting function allowed people to focus on the feature-sentiment information in its original context, which creates a good balance between focusing on some feature-sentiment information and the whole review. In contrast, the noun-adjective pair summarization allowed the participants to see only the compressed and fractured information, which was not easy for them to interpret. One of our participants noted:

> *I really like the first one (our interface) because it let me focus on some parts that I am interested in and I can also see its context. However, when reading reviews using the second one (RevMiner), I only see some short phrases. I have to first put them together to guess the meanings, so it takes more time and is hard to get the original context. This doesn't help me learn the experience of the previous users.*

The participants who favored noun-adjective pair summarization preferred it mainly because it offered more features than the three pre-defined features in our interface. However, this issue can be addressed by including more features in our system since the cost of adding new features is low.

Participants were motivated to correct erroneous predictions made by the system

After having the experience using our review-writing interface with real-time feature-sentiment analysis, 9 of the 13 participants (69%) expressed that they would correct errors made by the system. One of the participants mentioned,

> *When I write a review, I want to let others get my comments as clear as possible, so I care about the correctness of the information in the review and will correct the mistakes made by the system.*

Another participant said,

> *Because I read reviews using this system before, I know that my effort can help others understand my review, so I will provide the information even if it causes some extra work for me.*

This promising result demonstrates that the real-time feature-sentiment analysis does motivate users to correct the erroneous predictions of their own reviews. This is important as the system can collect more corrected labels to improve the classifier over time. We believe that the user's ability to see immediately how their reviews will be classified is an important feature that motivates users to provide a low-cost (one click) easy correction of the automatic classification.

Of course, the current study cannot directly prove that most users really would correct the mistakes made by the system. Nevertheless, when the number of users increases, even if only a small portion of them provide feedback, the system still can benefit from the feedback and enhance classification accuracy.

Summary

To summarize, our user study answered the three questions related to our theses. First, the highlighting function provided by the proposed system can improve the user's reading experience. Second, highlighting is at least as good as, if not better than, noun-adjective pair summarization because it preserves the original context of the feature-sentiment information as expressed by the review writers. Finally, the interface with real-time feature-sentiment analysis can successfully motivate users to correct errors made by the system, so the classifiers behind the system can be improved as the number of users increases.

DISCUSSION

Reducing effort in order to motivate users to correct erroneous predictions

Our interface reduces the effort needed to provide feature-sentiment information by performing real-time analysis, which requires only that users correct some mistakes made by the system instead of segmenting, labeling, and rating their reviews themselves. As a result, our user study shows that around 70% of the participants expressed that they would provide corrected feature-sentiment information. However, about 30% of the participants did say that they would not correct the erroneous predictions made by the system. When asked, they said the effort required needed to be further reduced. As one of the participants explained:

> *I know that correcting the errors can be helpful to my readers, but I think it's just too much work for me. I need to click many icons there to make them right. That's why I choose to just ignore the errors.*

Therefore, it is important for us to design interfaces that allow users to correct the errors more easily. In future, we would like to experiment with different interface designs to determine how to motivate more users to provide the corrected data. One possible way is to design an interface that allows users to drag the icons and sentences directly. On the other hand, given that most users said they would provide the label and the classifier could benefit from the input, fewer and fewer corrections would be needed for future users as the classifier became more accurate.

Including more features in the proposed design

Our user study shows that about 23% of the participants preferred the intelligent interface that used noun-adjective pair summarization (RevMiner). As suggested by the participants, the biggest advantage of the interface is that it has more features that interest them. In contrast, our system has only three pre-defined features. This problem can be solved easily by including more features, so it is not an inherent limitation of the system. Since the efficiency of the classifiers is pretty high, adding more features will not cause any technical problems when more features are added. However, additional features may introduce a different problem. As mentioned earlier, maintaining a low level of effort required is important for motivating users to provide the correct labels. However, adding more features may increase the effort, as users need to remember what the possible categories are. This also may make the interface more complex. Therefore, there is clearly a tradeoff between providing more detailed categories and information and maximizing usability.

Real-time feature-sentiment analysis can encourage users to generate more structured reviews

Although our system was not intended to help users write reviews with higher quality, we did see that the real-time feature-sentiment analysis affected the reviews generated by the users. As one of the participants mentioned after she wrote a review using our interface:

> *The results of the (feature-sentiment) analysis let me know which part I haven't mentioned in my review, so I will try to write some words that are related to that part.*

In our user study, we also found that participants would try to write something related to the three pre-defined features before they finished. This shows that the real-time analysis can encourage users to generate reviews that cover more features, which can improve the quality of reviews collected by the system. A controlled experiment that shows how the real-time analysis affects review quality can be done in the future.

The upper bounds of classification accuracy

In our experiment, the food-classifier reached the highest F_1 score at 4000 training instances, and the service-classifier reached the highest at 3000 training instances; however, the F_1 score of the price-classifier continued to grow even after 5000 training instances. The intuitive explanation for this is that there were more positive training instances for food and service in our randomly chosen training dataset, so the classifiers learned faster initially.

In the future, it would be valuable to perform a study to determine the upper bounds of classification accuracy. Once a classifier reaches its upper bound, the system could stop asking users to provide feedback for that classifier. This can reduce the workload of the users of the system.

CONCLUSIONS AND FUTURE WORKS

In this paper, we presented a novel intelligent system that performs a two-layer feature-sentiment analysis in real time. The system can provide real-time predictions to users who are writing user reviews, which makes it very easy for them to provide feature-sentiment information by simply correcting the erroneous predictions. Our user study shows that about 70% of the participants were willing to correct the mistakes made by the system, which means that the proposed interface can successfully utilize the power of the crowd to collect a massive amount of labeled data that can be used to train the supervised classifiers. Moreover, our experiment shows that the size of training data is positively correlated to the performance of the feature-sentiment analysis. As a result, we can expect that the analysis performed by the system can become more and more accurate as the number of system users increases.

In addition, we compared our system to existing intelligent interfaces with similar purposes. The results of our experiment show that the supervised method of our system can achieve much higher F_1 scores than traditional unsupervised methods can achieve. Moreover, our user study also shows that 46% of the participants preferred the highlighting function of our interface over the noun-adjective pair summarization, while only 23% of them preferred the summarization. This indicates that our system can provide more accurate feature-sentiment information and help users understand the information better than traditional interfaces with similar goals can.

The results of our experiment show that implicit crowdsourcing can be useful to improve supervised learning algorithm's ability to collect a huge amount of training data at no cost. The mechanism used in the proposed design also can be applied to other domains, like status updates in social media or contents in Q&A forums and is not limited to user reviews. However, there are still some limitations to the current design. One of the most essential issues is to find ways to further reduce the effort necessary for users to provide useful information. Moreover, it is also important to find a good way to include more features or even to let users input unspecified features themselves. We believe the work presented in this paper offers a good first step for more future studies that combine the strengths of intelligent interface and implicit crowdsourcing.

In the future, we would like to deploy our system in the wild to see if it really can help users and study how users interact with the system on a large scale. Furthermore, since the system involves its users to provide training data interactively, it is possible for us to include active learning [27] in our system design to further improve the performance of the supervised learning classifiers.

ACKNOWLEDGEMENTS

Many thanks to the anonymous reviewers for their valuable comments for us to improve the earlier draft of this work. We also would like to thank Siddharth Gupta for helping us implementing part of the system used in this study.

REFERENCES

1. Bernstein, M. S., Little, G., Miller, R. C., Hartmann, B., Ackerman, M. S., Karger, D. R., Crowell, D., and Panovich, K. Soylent: a word processor with a crowd inside. In *Proceedings of the 23nd annual ACM symposium on User interface software and technology*, UIST '10, ACM (New York, NY, USA, 2010), 313–322.
2. Bigham, J. P., Jayant, C., Ji, H., Little, G., Miller, A., Miller, R. C., Miller, R., Tatarowicz, A., White, B., White, S., and Yeh, T. Vizwiz: nearly real-time answers to visual questions. In *Proceedings of the 23nd annual ACM symposium on User interface software and technology*, UIST '10, ACM (New York, NY, USA, 2010), 333–342.
3. Blei, D., and McAuliffe, J. Supervised topic models. In *Advances in Neural Information Processing Systems 20*, J. Platt, D. Koller, Y. Singer, and S. Roweis, Eds. MIT Press, Cambridge, MA, 2008, 121–128.
4. Callison-Burch, C., and Dredze, M. Creating speech and language data with amazon's mechanical turk. In *Proceedings of the NAACL HLT 2010 Workshop on Creating Speech and Language Data with Amazon's Mechanical Turk*, CSLDAMT '10, Association for Computational Linguistics (Stroudsburg, PA, USA, 2010), 1–12.
5. Carenini, G., Ng, R. T., and Pauls, A. Interactive multimedia summaries of evaluative text. In *Proceedings of the 11th international conference on Intelligent user interfaces*, IUI '06, ACM (New York, NY, USA, 2006), 124–131.
6. Carenini, G., and Rizoli, L. A multimedia interface for facilitating comparisons of opinions. In *Proceedings of the 14th international conference on Intelligent user interfaces*, IUI '09, ACM (New York, NY, USA, 2009), 325–334.
7. Dave, K., Lawrence, S., and Pennock, D. M. Mining the peanut gallery: opinion extraction and semantic classification of product reviews. In *Proceedings of the 12th international conference on World Wide Web*, WWW '03, ACM (New York, NY, USA, 2003), 519–528.
8. Dong, R., McCarthy, K., O'Mahony, M., Schaal, M., and Smyth, B. Towards an intelligent reviewer's assistant: recommending topics to help users to write better product reviews. In *Proceedings of the 2012 ACM international conference on Intelligent User Interfaces*, IUI '12, ACM (New York, NY, USA, 2012), 159–168.
9. Esuli, A., and Sebastiani, F. Sentiwordnet: A publicly available lexical resource for opinion mining. In *In Proceedings of the 5th Conference on Language Resources and Evaluation (LREC06* (2006), 417–422.
10. Ho, C.-J., Chang, T.-H., Lee, J.-C., Hsu, J. Y.-j., and Chen, K.-T. Kisskissban: a competitive human computation game for image annotation. *SIGKDD Explor. Newsl. 12*, 1 (Nov. 2010), 21–24.
11. Howe, J. The rise of crowdsourcing. *Wired Magazine* (06 2006).
12. Hu, M., and Liu, B. Mining and summarizing customer reviews. In *Proceedings of the tenth ACM SIGKDD international conference on Knowledge discovery and data mining*, KDD '04, ACM (New York, NY, USA, 2004), 168–177.

13. Huang, J., Etzioni, O., Zettlemoyer, L., Clark, K., and Lee, C. Revminer: an extractive interface for navigating reviews on a smartphone. In *Proceedings of the 25th annual ACM symposium on User interface software and technology*, UIST '12 (2012), 3–12.
14. Kearns, M. J., and Vazirani, U. V. *An introduction to computational learning theory*. MIT Press, Cambridge, MA, USA, 1994.
15. Kullback, S., and Leibler, R. On information and sufficiency. *The Annals of Mathematical Statistics 22*, 1 (1951), 79–86.
16. Lease, M., Carvalho, V., and Yilmaz, E., Eds. *Proceedings of the Workshop on Crowdsourcing for Search and Data Mining (CSDM) at the Fourth ACM International Conference on Web Search and Data Mining (WSDM).*
17. Lease, M., Carvalho, V., and Yilmaz, E., Eds. *Proceedings of the ACM SIGIR 2010 Workshop on Crowdsourcing for Search Evaluation (CSE 2010).* Geneva, Switzerland, July 2010.
18. Liu, B., Hu, M., and Cheng, J. Opinion observer: analyzing and comparing opinions on the web. In *Proceedings of the 14th international conference on World Wide Web*, WWW '05 (2005), 342–351.
19. Nichols, J., Mahmud, J., and Drews, C. Summarizing sporting events using twitter. In *Proceedings of the 2012 ACM international conference on Intelligent User Interfaces*, IUI '12, ACM (New York, NY, USA, 2012), 189–198.
20. Pang, B., and Lee, L. Opinion mining and sentiment analysis. *Foundations and Trends in Information Retrieval 2*, 1–2 (2008), 1–135.
21. Pang, B., Lee, L., and Vaithyanathan, S. Thumbs up?: sentiment classification using machine learning techniques. In *Proceedings of the ACL-02 conference on Empirical methods in natural language processing - Volume 10*, EMNLP '02, Association for Computational Linguistics (Stroudsburg, PA, USA, 2002), 79–86.
22. Rashtchian, C., Young, P., Hodosh, M., and Hockenmaier, J. Collecting image annotations using amazon's mechanical turk. In *Proceedings of the NAACL HLT 2010 Workshop on Creating Speech and Language Data with Amazon's Mechanical Turk*, CSLDAMT '10, Association for Computational Linguistics (Stroudsburg, PA, USA, 2010), 139–147.
23. Rijsbergen, C. J. V. *Information Retrieval*, 2nd ed. Butterworth-Heinemann, Newton, MA, USA, 1979.
24. Snow, R., O'Connor, B., Jurafsky, D., and Ng, A. Y. Cheap and fast—but is it good?: evaluating non-expert annotations for natural language tasks. In *Proceedings of the Conference on Empirical Methods in Natural Language Processing*, EMNLP '08, Association for Computational Linguistics (Stroudsburg, PA, USA, 2008), 254–263.
25. Sorokin, A., and Forsyth, D. Utility data annotation with amazon mechanical turk. In *Computer Vision and Pattern Recognition Workshops, 2008. CVPRW '08. IEEE Computer Society Conference on* (june 2008), 1 –8.
26. Su, H., Deng, J., and Fei-Fei, L. Crowdsourcing annotations for visual object detection. In *Workshops at the Twenty-Sixth AAAI Conference on Artificial Intelligence* (2012).
27. Tong, S., and Koller, D. Support vector machine active learning with applications to text classification. *J. Mach. Learn. Res. 2* (Mar. 2002), 45–66.
28. Turney, P. D. Thumbs up or thumbs down?: semantic orientation applied to unsupervised classification of reviews. In *Proceedings of the 40th Annual Meeting on Association for Computational Linguistics*, ACL '02, Association for Computational Linguistics (Stroudsburg, PA, USA, 2002), 417–424.
29. von Ahn, L., and Dabbish, L. Labeling images with a computer game. In *Proceedings of the SIGCHI conference on Human factors in computing systems*, CHI '04, ACM (New York, NY, USA, 2004), 319–326.
30. von Ahn, L., and Dabbish, L. Designing games with a purpose. *Commun. ACM 51* (Aug. 2008), 58–67.
31. von Ahn, L., Liu, R., and Blum, M. Peekaboom: a game for locating objects in images. In *Proceedings of the SIGCHI Conference on Human Factors in Computing Systems*, CHI '06, ACM (New York, NY, USA, 2006), 55–64.
32. Wang, H., Lu, Y., and Zhai, C. Latent aspect rating analysis on review text data: a rating regression approach. In *Proceedings of the 16th ACM SIGKDD international conference on Knowledge discovery and data mining*, KDD '10, ACM (New York, NY, USA, 2010), 783–792.
33. Yatani, K., Novati, M., Trusty, A., and Truong, K. N. Review spotlight: a user interface for summarizing user-generated reviews using adjective-noun word pairs. In *Proceedings of the SIGCHI Conference on Human Factors in Computing Systems*, CHI '11, ACM (New York, NY, USA, 2011), 1541–1550.

APPENDIX: QUESTIONNAIRE

Q1: When reading user reviews, do you prefer the first interface or the second interface? Why?

Q2: When reading user reviews, do you prefer the highlighting function of the second interface or the noun-adjective pair representation of the last interface? Why?

Q3: When writing user reviews on the review writing interface you just used, would you correct the erroneous predictions made by the system? Why or why not?

Tailoring Recommendations to Groups of Users: A Graph Walk-based Approach

Heung-Nam Kim
University of Ottawa
800 King Edward, Ottawa, ON
K1N 6N5, Canada
hnkim@mcrlab.uottawa.ca

Majdi Rawashdeh
University of Ottawa
800 King Edward, Ottawa, ON
K1N 6N5, Canada
majdi@mcrlab.uottawa.ca

Abdulmotaleb El Saddik
University of Ottawa
800 King Edward, Ottawa, ON
K1N 6N5, Canada
elsaddik@uottawa.ca

ABSTRACT
With the rapid popularity of smart devices, users are easily and conveniently accessing rich multimedia content. Consequentially, the increasing need for recommender services, from both individual users and groups of users, has arisen. In this paper, we present a graph-based approach to a recommender system that can make recommendations most notably to groups of users. From rating information, we first model a signed graph that contains both positive and negative links between users and items. On this graph we examine two distinct random walks to separately quantify the degree to which a group of users would like or dislike items. We then employ a differential ranking approach for tailoring recommendations to the group. Our empirical evaluations on the MovieLens dataset demonstrate that the proposed group recommendation method performs better than existing alternatives. We also demonstrate the feasibility of Folkommender for smartphones.

Author Keywords
Social Recommender system; Group recommendation; Random walk with restarts

ACM Classification Keywords
H.5.3 **[Information interfaces and presentation]**: Group and Organization Interfaces

INTRODUCTION
With the current popularity of smart devices, such as smartphones and Smart TVs, users are experiencing a new convenient way of accessing rich multimedia content. For instance, Smart TVs, which offers more advanced capabilities in connectivity and experience through an Internet connection, enable users to view a limitless variety of content on their TV screen in addition to digital broadcast content. Consequentially, recommender techniques are becoming increasingly important, because users are also experiencing increasing difficulty with determining the most desirable content. While recommender systems have proliferated over the years, the large majority of the systems have been designed to recommend items (e.g., movies, videos, music, or TV programs) to individual users, depending on their personal interests [1]. It is, however, frequently the case that a group of people, such as friends, families, and colleagues, see multimedia content together [16]. Therefore, it would be a natural direction to develop recommender systems that make recommendations to groups of users; this is often referred to as group recommender systems [10]. More specifically, a recommender system may need to recommend different video and TV content to a viewer depending on whether they plan to view the content with their boyfriend/girlfriend or with their parents.

As a matter of fact, more and more research effort has been dedicated to group recommender systems, aiming at identifying items that satisfy individual preferences of all group members as much as possible. However, most existing studies have concentrated primarily on two aggregation approaches: (i) aggregating individual preferences to create a single group profile and then generating a recommendation list for this single group profile (referred to as the profile aggregation approach) [12, 14, 15, 21], and (ii) generating individual recommendation lists independently and then aggregating those lists to produce a single group recommendation list (referred to as the ranking aggregation approach) [2, 3, 8, 16]. Regardless of which approach is employed, both approaches have relied much on typical individual recommender techniques, such as collaborative and content-based filtering [1], in order to complete the entire group recommendation process. In addition, group recommendation paradigms that are based merely on aggregating either individual profiles or individual recommendations may often result in unsatisfactory recommendations to some of group members despite its simplicity. Therefore, the transition from individual recommendations to group recommendations still requires much more research effort, as the need for smart recommender services, from both individual users and groups of users, is expected to increase exponentially.

In this paper, we introduce Folkommender (Folk + Recommender)—a new recommender system based on a graph-based ranking method—that is designed to recommend multimedia content most notably to groups of

IUI'13, March 19–22, 2013, Santa Monica, CA, USA.

people, rather than to individual users; we henceforth use the term items to refer to multimedia content. Folkommender explores not only a positive aspect but also a negative aspect in a way that can achieve a general consensus among individual members about recommended items. From a graph viewpoint, the fundamental premises underlying our recommendation strategy are that (i) compelling items potentially suited to a certain group would be in close proximity to their past preferred items and (ii) inappropriate items for a certain group would be more closer to the items that its members have disliked in the past. To discover these two separate sets of items, we build two types of weighted user-item graphs derived from users' past preferences. We also incorporate social aspects of collaborative filtering in the graphs by assuming that (i) each member in a group is likely to prefer/hate an item that other similar users have previously liked/disliked and (ii) each member is likely to like/dislike an item similar to the items that they have previously liked/disliked. Using these graphs, we analyze two distinct random walks expected to visit particular items more frequently than other items: (i) a positive random walk that speculates about how much a group of users would like items and (ii) a negative random walk that speculates about how much a group of users would dislike items. Finally, we employ a differential approach, which considers both positive and negative rankings, for tailoring recommendations to a specific group.

RELATED WORK

We begin with the review of prior work on group recommender systems in this section. Since TV content is commonly enjoyed by groups of people, a growing number of studies have focused on the field of TV content/program recommendations for multiple viewers. In this domain, the profile aggregation approach has widely been used. Masthoff [14] studied a variety of aggregation strategies, including the Average model (that maximizes average satisfaction of individual members), the Least-Misery model (that maximizes satisfaction of misery), and the Most-Pleasure model (that takes the maximum of individual members), for building a group model derived from individual preferences. The author empirically assessed the effectiveness of different aggregation strategies for modeling a group of viewers watching TV together. In another study, Senot et al. [18] also investigated different group profiles obtained via various aggregation strategies for building accurate profiles according to groups' characteristics. Through experiments with a real dataset of TV viewings, the authors found that the Average model facilitated more accurate profiles for groups. Zhiwen et al. [21] proposed a TV program recommender system for multiple viewers, called TV4M. In the TV4M, each user profile was represented as a vector consisting of feature-weight pairs. For a group of users, the TV4M created a common group profile, also representable by a vector, by merging all members' profiles based on the total distance minimization. By using the merged profile, content-based filtering was exploited to recommend TV programs to the group of people. Sotelo et al. [19] presented a similar service, proposing an extension of AVATAR to establish a group recommender system in TV applications. This system adopted two different recommendation strategies depending on homogeneous groups and heterogeneous groups. For the homogeneous groups, it utilized the profile aggregation approach, whereas the ranking aggregation approach was employed for the heterogeneous groups.

Group recommender systems have also been studied in other application domains. McCarthy and Anagnost [15] developed a group preference arbitration system, called MusicFX, that determines music suited to a group of people working out together in a fitness center. O'Connor et al. [16] proposed PolyLens to recommend movies to small groups of users and discussed several design issues for group recommender systems. The PolyLens first predicted individuals' preference ratings for items by using user-based collaborative filtering and thus merged individual recommended lists based on the Least-Misery model. Berkovsky and Freyne [5] studied food recipe recommendations based on collaborative filtering. These authors evaluated the profile aggregation approach in comparison with the ranking aggregation approach, and identified that the former was superior to the latter in recipe recommendations. When aggregating individual preferences, this study considered several weighted models by assuming that some members of a group would have more influence than others. Amer-Yahia el al. [2] presented a consensus model aiming at maximizing group relevance, as well as minimizing group disagreement. For capturing disagreements between members of a group, the authors suggested two models, Average Pair-wise disagreements and Disagreement Variance, whereas the group relevance was computed by using the Average model or the Least-Misery model. This study demonstrated that incorporating disagreements between group members into a consensus function impacted positively on group recommendation. In another study, Gartrell et al. [8] proposed a new consensus function that considered three factors: a social factor, an expertise factor, and a dissimilarity factor. Based on the quantified social factor, different functions were flexibly used for aggregating individual recommendations. Baltrunas et al. [3] analyzed the effectiveness of group recommendations achieved by different rank aggregation techniques. Their experimental results demonstrated that the recommendation quality for homogenous groups did not tend to be affected by the group size. The authors also observed that the more similar users in a group, the more satisfied they are with recommendations. More recently, Kim et al. [12] introduced Commenders designed to recommend books for online communities. The Commenders exploited two filtering phases to improve both the recommendation effectiveness and the satisfaction of individual members. In the first phase, for a given group, the Commenders aggregated features of individual members' profiles, and then generated candidate books that other similar groups frequently purchased. During the second phase, these candidate books were further filtered out by measuring how each candidate book was relevant to each individual member.

Although the above-mentioned studies may present promising possibilities for group recommendations, those studies show several main differences with our study. Compared with prior work that used the ranking aggregation method, our work does not require computing individual members' ranking scores separately and, thus, does not require merging them for items. Instead, the proposed approach can estimate unified ranking scores of group members on items at the same time, by analyzing link-structures that represent users' past rating behaviors. On the other hand, the principal difference compared to the profile aggregation approach is that our approach does not create a single merged profile for a group. Rather, our ranking method speculates as to how close items are to every individual member and their rated items. More importantly, in our study we distinguish a group's positive preferences from its negative preferences in ways that may facilitate a better grasp of group preferences and thus minimize every individual user's dissatisfaction with recommended items.

DEFINITIONS AND NOTATIONS

For better understanding, we introduce the basic notations used in this paper and formalize the group recommendation problem. Throughout this paper, we use boldface, upper-case letters, such as **R**, to denote matrices; the corresponding italicized, upper-case letters with two subscript indices represent entries in the matrices, such as R_{ui}. We always use boldface lower-case letters, such as **r**, to denote vectors; **r**(i) refers to the ith element (or entry) of the vector **r**. Moreover, we use the notations m and n to denote the total number of unique users and items in a system, respectively.

The users' preference indicator exploited in this study is either a *5-point Likert scale* or *a binary scale* (e.g., like/dislike, thumbs up/down). For a set of m users $U = \{u_1, u_2,\ldots,u_m\}$ and a set of n items $I = \{i_1, i_2,\ldots, i_n\}$, we represent explicit past opinions (ratings) of whether or not the users have preferred the items by an $m \times n$ user-item matrix **R**; an entry R_{ui} is r such that $r \in \{1,\ldots, 5\}$ or $r \in \{1, -1\}$ if the uth user has rated the ith item, and is unknown otherwise. We denote by $\varnothing$ the unknown opinion. The group recommendation problem of our study is formally defined as follows: Given a user-item matrix **R** and a group of users $X \subseteq U$, the group recommendation is to identify an ordered set I_X of items that will be of interest to every individual member of group X such that $|I_X| \le K, \forall u \in X, i \in I_X$: $R_{ui} = \varnothing$.

A GRAPH WALK-BASED APPROACH TO GROUP RECOMMENDATIONS

In this section, we present a graph-based approach to ranking and recommending items that are tailored to a specific group. In our work, each user and item is represented as a node in a graph. From users' ratings, we derive two distinct link structures between users and items: a positive link structure and a negative link structure. To take advantage of collaborative social wisdom, we also incorporate neighborhood-based links into each link structure. On such link structures (graphs), we perform two separate random walks that periodically restart from specific nodes associated with a given group of users. On the basis of the random walks, we finally identify a set of ranked items that the group would like the most. In the remainder of this section, we elaborate how to model graphs from users' ratings, how to analyze two distinct random walks in regard to a given group, and how to rank (recommend) items for the group.

Building Relationship Graphs

Although the rating scale is fixed in the Likert-scale model, different users would have different rating behaviors for items. In our study, if a user's rating for a certain item is greater than that user's average rating $\breve{R}_u$, we call this rating a positive opinion for that item, and a negative opinion otherwise. In this context, we further split the user-item matrix **R** into two matrices: a positive matrix and a negative matrix:

- User-item positive matrix $\mathbf{R}^+$ whose entry represents the degree to which the corresponding row user has *liked* the corresponding column item, defined as follows:

$$R^+_{ui} = \begin{cases} R_{ui} - \breve{R}_u, & \text{if } R_{ui} > \breve{R}_u \\ 0, & \text{otherwise.} \end{cases} \quad (1)$$

- User-item negative matrix $\mathbf{R}^-$ whose entry represents the degree to which the corresponding row user has *disliked* the corresponding column item, defined as follows:

$$R^-_{ui} = \begin{cases} \breve{R}_u - R_{ui}, & \text{if } R_{ui} < \breve{R}_u \\ 0, & \text{otherwise.} \end{cases} \quad (2)$$

Note that we remove the rows consisting entirely of zeros from $\mathbf{R}^+$ and $\mathbf{R}^-$, implying that the corresponding users have no positive (or negative) opinions for any items. Analogously, we discard the columns of $\mathbf{R}^+$ and $\mathbf{R}^-$ consisting entirely of zeros, implying that the corresponding items have previously not received any positive (or negative) opinions. Accordingly, the dimensions of the rows and columns of both matrices are equal to or less than m and n, respectively.

Alternatively, in a situation where the binary rating scale (i.e., like/dislike) is employed for the preference indicator, $\mathbf{R}^+$ and $\mathbf{R}^-$ can be easily defined as follows:

- User-item positive matrix $\mathbf{R}^+$, defined as follows:

$$R^{+}_{ui} = \begin{cases} 1, & \text{if } R_{ui} = 1 \\ 0, & \text{otherwise.} \end{cases} \quad (3)$$

- User-item negative matrix $\mathbf{R}^{-}$, defined as follows:

$$R^{-}_{ui} = \begin{cases} 1, & \text{if } R_{ui} = -1 \\ 0, & \text{otherwise.} \end{cases} \quad (4)$$

Using $\mathbf{R}^{+}$ and $\mathbf{R}^{-}$, we build a bipartite signed, undirected graph $G_{BI} = (U \cup I, E^{+} \cup E^{-})$, whose nodes can be partitioned into two disjoint sets U and I such that each edge in E^{+} and E^{-} connects a node in U and a node in I. Weights on edges correspond to nonzero entries of $\mathbf{R}^{+}$ and $\mathbf{R}^{-}$.

Since, by definition, no two nodes within the same set are adjacent in the bipartite graph G_{BI}, there are no explicit links between pairs of two users or pairs of two items. In the following subsections, we additionally define two neighborhood graphs in which edges connects pairs of two nodes within the same set.

User-user neighborhood graph

In our study, for a given user, the user neighborhood is defined as the set of users who have exhibited preferred items similar to those of that user; this set is often called *k nearest neighbors* [6]. To identify such a neighborhood set, we employ the cosine similarity measure. For computing the similarity between two users, each user is treated as a *row* vector in the n dimensional item-space of the user-item matrix $\mathbf{R}$. Formally, the similarity between two users u and v is computed as

$$W_{uv} = \frac{\sum_{a \in I} R_{ua} \times R_{va}}{\sqrt{\sum_{a \in I} R^{2}_{ua}} \sqrt{\sum_{a \in I} R^{2}_{va}}} \quad (5)$$

Finally, for m users, the similarity of users can be represented as an $m \times m$ user-user similarity matrix $\mathbf{W}$. Since we consider the k nearest neighbors of each user, we set W_{uv} to the similarity value between a pair of two users u and v if the corresponding similarity value is greater than the k highest similarity value in the vth column of $\mathbf{W}$, and 0 otherwise. In other words, each column in the matrix $\mathbf{W}$ contains at most k nonzero values indicating the similarity values between the corresponding column user and the k most similar users. Note that all entries on the main diagonal in the matrix equal 0. We denote this resultant matrix as $\mathbf{W}_{k}$ where k is the number of similar users. By utilizing the matrix $\mathbf{W}_{k}^{\mathrm{T}}$ as an adjacency matrix, we define a user neighborhood graph $G_{U} = (U, E_{U})$ where E_{U} contains a directed edge $e(u,v)$ iff user v is user u's neighborhood such that $W_{vu} > 0$.

Item-item neighborhood graph

For a given item, the item neighborhood is defined as the set of items to which users have assigned ratings similar to what they do for that item; this set is often called *k most similar items* [7]. In the case of item-item similarities, each item is regarded as a *column* vector in the m dimensional user-space of $\mathbf{R}$. Therefore, for two vectors corresponding to the ith and jth columns of $\mathbf{R}$, the similarity between two items i and j is given by

$$V_{ij} = \frac{\sum_{a \in U} R_{ai} \times R_{aj}}{\sqrt{\sum_{a \in U} R^{2}_{ai}} \sqrt{\sum_{a \in U} R^{2}_{aj}}} \quad (6)$$

For n items, the similarity between every pair of two items can be represented as an $n \times n$ item-item similarity matrix $\mathbf{V}$. We also discard any unnecessary values for each item in a manner similar to the user-user matrix $\mathbf{W}_{k}$. We denote the resultant matrix by $\mathbf{V}_{k}$, where each column stores k most similar items to the column's corresponding item; in the matrix $\mathbf{V}_{k}$, V_{ij} is set to the similarity value between two items i and j, if the corresponding similarity value is greater than the k highest similarity value in the jth column of $\mathbf{V}_{k}$ and 0 otherwise. Additionally, all entries on the main diagonal in the matrix also equal to 0. In an item viewpoint, a directed neighborhood graph is defined as $G_{I} = (I, E_{I})$ where E_{I} contains a directed edge $e(i, j)$ iff item j is k most similar items to item i such that $V_{ji} > 0$.

Analyzing Random Graph Walks

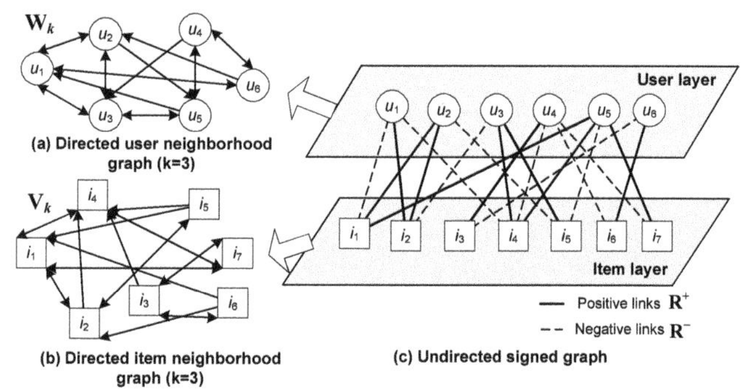

Figure 1. Two-layer signed graph model.

Figure 1 illustrates a two-layer signed graph. The basic intuition behind our group recommendation approach from a random walk viewpoint is that an item that is likely to be suitable for a particular group of users would tend to be highly reachable not only from the users of that group, but also from items that they have previously liked via paths of (strong) positive links. On the other hand, if a certain item tends to be highly visited by a random walk via paths of the group's negative links, the group of users would dislike such an item. With this aspect in mind, on our signed graph we perform two distinct random walks expected to visit particular items more frequently than other items: a *positive random walk* and a *negative random walk*. The former can only cross from one layer to another layer through positive links, whereas the latter can do so through negative links. Additionally, both walks can move to another node within the same layer via available (user or item) neighborhood links of a current node.

For the two random walks, we distinguish between positive and negative links, and separately construct two graphs: one graph only contains positive links between two different layers and another contains negative ones between them. The adjacency matrices **P′** and **N′** respectively corresponding to these graphs are represented by

$$\mathbf{P}'=\begin{pmatrix} \mathbf{W}_k & \mathbf{R}^+ \\ (\mathbf{R}^+)^{\mathrm{T}} & \mathbf{V}_k \end{pmatrix} \quad \mathbf{N}'=\begin{pmatrix} \mathbf{W}_k & \mathbf{R}^- \\ (\mathbf{R}^-)^{\mathrm{T}} & \mathbf{V}_k \end{pmatrix} \tag{7}$$

in which each entry's value (weigh) can be viewed as the link strength between a pair of nodes. We then normalize matrices **P′** and **N′** in order to obtain column-stochastic matrices **P** and **N** which are transition matrices of two Markov chains corresponding to two distinct random walks, respectively. Since transition probabilities are proportional to link-strengths, a random walker is more likely to traverse links of high strength.

Our study also incorporates the restart probability $d \in (0, 1)$ as in (Personalized) PageRank. That is, with probability d, a random walker jumps back (teleports) to a random node among a set of specific nodes (e.g., favorite items) and thus restarts from those nodes at each step [10]; a generally-accepted value for d is 0.15. For a given group, we compute two stationary distribution vectors that result from the positive and negative random walks using our transition matrices. Formally, the stationary distribution vectors of those random walks with restarts are defined as the solutions of the following equations:

$$\mathbf{r}^+ = (1-d)\mathbf{P}\mathbf{r}^+ + d\mathbf{v}^+ \tag{8}$$

$$\mathbf{r}^- = (1-d)\mathbf{N}\mathbf{r}^- + d\mathbf{v}^- \tag{9}$$

such that $\|\mathbf{r}^+\|_1 = 1$ and $\|\mathbf{r}^-\|_1 = 1$. $\mathbf{v}^+$ and $\mathbf{v}^-$ are probability vectors that allow non-uniform probabilities for teleporting to particular nodes.

In our study, different teleportation vectors $\mathbf{v}^+$ and $\mathbf{v}^-$ are built depending on a given group. Let $X = \{u_1, u_2,\ldots,u_{|X|}\}$ denote a group of users for recommendations. For group X, we denote by $I^+(X)$ and $I^-(X)$ the set of items *positively* and *negatively* rated by at least one of group X's members, respectively. Then, the non-normalized teleportation vectors, with regard to the ath entry, are respectively defined as:

$$\overline{\mathbf{v}}^+(a) = \begin{cases} 1 & \text{if} \quad a \in X, \\ U^+(a) & \text{if} \ a \in I^+(X), \\ 0 & \text{otherwise.} \end{cases} \tag{10}$$

$$\overline{\mathbf{v}}^-(a) = \begin{cases} 1 & \text{if} \quad a \in X, \\ U^-(a) & \text{if} \ a \in I^-(X), \\ 0 & \text{otherwise.} \end{cases} \tag{11}$$

where $U^+(a)$ is the number of group X's members who have *positively* rated item a in common and $U^-(a)$ is that of common members who have *negatively* rated item a; we normalize the teleportation vectors so that all entries sum to 1, i.e., $\|\mathbf{v}^+\|_1 = 1$ and $\|\mathbf{v}^-\|_1 = 1$. The salient concept behind the positive teleportation vector, which corresponds to attaching different importance to nodes, is that at every step, with some probability, a random walker teleports to members of the current group or items that the members have previously liked. In the case of a negative teleportation vector, a random walker teleports to items that group members have disliked in the past. Since $\mathbf{v}^+$ and $\mathbf{v}^-$ are non-uniform distribution vectors, a probability of a node to which a random walker teleports could differ from that of another node. The more the users liked an item, the higher the probability of teleporting to the item. Alternatively, we may be able to employ values in user-item positive and negative matrices $\mathbf{R}^+$ and $\mathbf{R}^-$ for setting items' entries of $\mathbf{v}^+$ and $\mathbf{v}^-$, respectively. We however give group members the same weights (i.e., ones) so that the random walks are not biased towards a specific member.

The resultant distributions contained in vector $\mathbf{r}^+$ correspond to the long-term probabilities of the positive random walk expected to visit specific nodes when the random walker periodically restarts from one of the nodes in X and $I^+(X)$, i.e., non-zero entries in $\mathbf{v}^+$, where the particular restart node is chosen non-uniformly at random. Accordingly, this vector $\mathbf{r}^+$ can be used for ranking nodes (particularly items) in regard to a given group X from a positive perspective, reflecting the degree to which items are in close proximity to the group. We regard items having high reachable probabilities as desirable items for group X. We name this resultant vector $\mathbf{r}^+$ a *positive ranking vector*. As opposed to the positive random walk, the negative random walk traverses negative links between users and items and thus is much more likely to visit items that a group of users would dislike. Therefore, the higher the probability an item has, the less its importance (ranking) for the group. We refer to this resultant vector $\mathbf{r}^-$ as a *negative ranking vector*.

Group Recommendations

Since individual members of a certain group may have different preferences of the same items, an effective method for capturing a consensus among members about items is critically impo

rtant to group recommender systems. When generating a recommendation list tailored to a group of people, we should take some questions into consideration [13]: Is it better to recommend items with which one person is as satisfied as possible? Or to recommend items with which no one is too dissatisfied? To minimize each individual member's dissatisfaction with recommended items, we employ a *differential* ranking approach that subtracts negative ranking scores from positive ranking scores. In other words, we consider not only how group users are likely to like an item, but also how they are likely to dislike that item when deciding on a final recommendation list. In this regard, we further compute the final ranking vector **r** as follows:

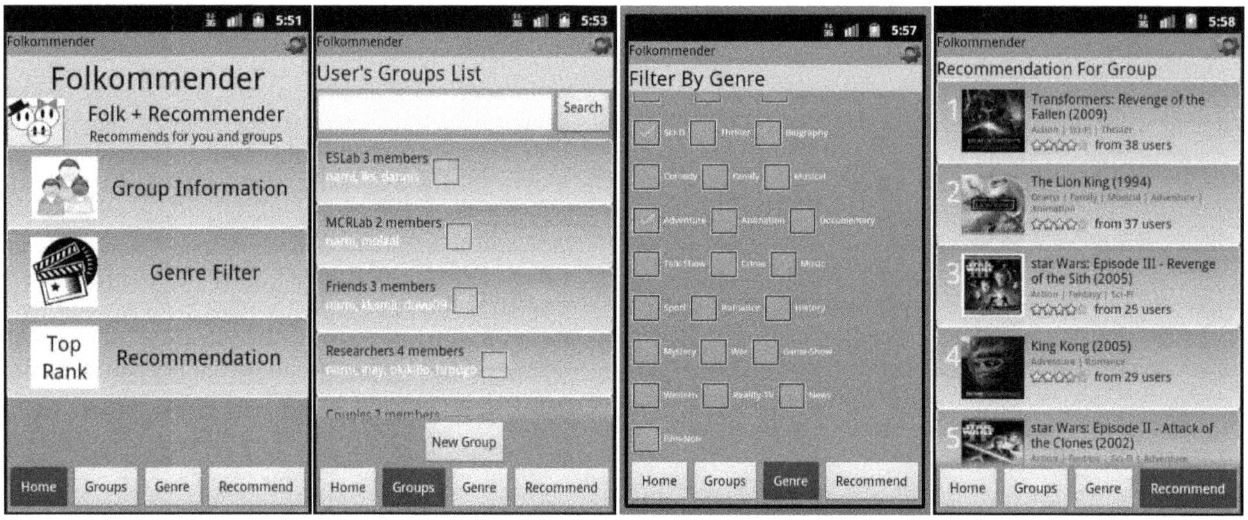

Figure 2. The Folkommender App screenshots, showing a main page, a group selection, genre filtering, and a top-ranked recommendation list.

$$\mathbf{r} = \alpha\mathbf{r}^{+} - (1-\alpha)\mathbf{r}^{-} \quad (12)$$

where $\alpha \in (0, 1)$ is a non-negative constant for adjusting the relative weighting between the positive ranking and the negative ranking. Note that for any given group X, the resultant ranking vector $\mathbf{r}$ contains a group view of preferences not only for users, but also for items. Since we aim to recommend items for a group of users, we ignore entries related to users. We call a value of an entry $i \in I$ in $\mathbf{r}$, $\mathbf{r}(i)$, a *group ranking score* of item i. The higher the ranking score of a particular item, the more desirable that item is for recommendations. Once $\mathbf{r}$ is estimated with respect to group X, we identify a set of K ordered items having the highest ranking scores and subsequently recommend those items to the group. It should be emphasized that our approach can be also employed for individual recommendations by assuming that a certain group consists only of a single user, i.e., $|X| = 1$. In this context, $\mathbf{r}$ will contain ranking scores solely for that user, resulting in "personalized recommendations" instead of group recommendations.

SMARTPHONE APPLICATION

Using our graph-based recommendation model, we have implemented a web-based Folkommender prototype that supports movie recommendations not only to groups, but also to individuals. Folkommender also has been designed to be served with smartphones. Figure 2 shows snapshots of a Folkommender application (App) working on an Android smartphone. The Folkommender App mainly consists of three steps to generate recommendations. The first step is to form a group to which Folkommender makes recommendations. Folkommender allows users to form groups in two ways: selecting their existing group list or creating a new group comprised of people on Folkommender. Individual users are also able to create themselves as a group in order to receive recommendations based exclusively on their personal interests. As one of the optional functions, users can choose genres to filter out movies according to the desired genres. If the genres are not selected, all genres are considered. In the final step, Folkommender displays the recommended movies according to their ranking scores for the selected group.

Beyond this smartphone App, Folkommender can be extended to a smart TV App—a web-based software program that works on a digital TV connected to the Internet—so that it can be directly accessible through TV screens. Since our App is currently running on an Android platform, it can be easily extensible to Android-based smart TVs, such as Google TV. As part of our future work, we plan to expand the Folkommender App to be optimized for smart TVs.

DATASET AND EVALUATION METHODOLOGY

Evaluating group recommender systems is generally harder than evaluating personalized recommender systems due to the absence of publicly available datasets containing both individual preferences and group preferences for items (e.g., numerical ratings, like/dislike). For the offline experiment, we used the MovieLens 100k dataset, consisting of 100,000 ratings (a 1-to-5 rating scale) from 943 users on 1682 movies. Since this dataset does not have group information, we artificially formed a number of groups for evaluation purposes.

Group Formation

When generating groups, we took account of two factors, group *size* and group *cohesiveness*, as per the suggestion in [2, 3]. We first selected items rated by at least 50 users. Subsequently, for each of those items, we identified users who have given the item a perfect rating of 5 in common and generated three different types of groups—that is, a *homogeneous* (similar) group, a *heterogeneous* (dissimilar) group, and a *random* group—from those users, with a predefined group size. Given an item i, for example, if six users, u_1, … u_6, have rated it in common with 5 points, we generated three groups, e.g., $X_1 = \{u_1, u_2\}$, $X_2 = \{u_3, u_4\}$, and $X_3 = \{u_5, u_6\}$, depending on the constraints of similarities among inner members of the groups. To define the degree of how similar/dissimilar group members are, we examined the distribution of cosine similarities between every pair of users in the MovieLens dataset. As a result, the average similarity was 0.178, with a standard deviation of 0.111. Accordingly, we formed a homogeneous group that was comprised of users who have similarities (between them) higher than 0.3, whereas a heterogeneous group consisted of users having similarities less than 0.17. For a random group, we randomly generated its members without any restriction on their similarities. Moreover, when forming groups, we considered four group sizes: 2, 3, 4, and 8. Table 1 displays the overall characteristics of the generated groups for our experiments.

Group type:	Similar	Dissimilar	Random
# groups	588	489	588
# unique users	578	565	644
Average per group			
Size	4.02	2.96	4.07
Similarity	0.423	0.143	0.305
Shared items	97.9	14.4	58.3

Table 1. Group characteristics used in our experiments.

Evaluation Protocol

To evaluate the performance of group recommendations, for each formed group, we withheld members' ratings on an item that all members have rated with 5 points and used this item as the test data for the group (i.e., one relevant item per group). The remaining rating data was employed as the training set for making group recommendations. Since every member in a group has greatly liked a test item in common, this item should appear earlier than other items (that every member has not yet rated) in a ranked list made by a group recommendation algorithm. Therefore, the goal of this test is to identify the relative place of the hidden relevant item within the total order of available items sorted by their ranking scores. To measure the recommendation quality with this dataset, we employed the Hit Rate (HR) at top-K [7], which judges how often a list of recommendations for a given group contains a test item that all members of the group have actually liked. Since recommender algorithms focus mainly on recommending high-quality items with higher ranks, we set the number of recommended items to 10 (i.e., top-10 recommendation).

Comparison algorithms

For comparison purposes, we experimented with the *Average* ranking aggregation model, which maximizes average satisfaction of individual members. Given a group X, the Average model computes a group score of a given item i as follows [2]:

$$\texttt{avg}_X(i) = \frac{1}{|X|}\sum_{u\in X}\texttt{score}(u,i) \qquad (13)$$

in which score(u, i) is a predicted preference score of user u for item i. For predicting individual scores, we exploited two straightforward Collaborative Filtering (CF) algorithms, a user-based CF [6] and an item-based CF [17], which have been widely adopted in group recommender algorithms [2, 3, 16, 19]. In addition to CF approaches, we also tested a variant of PageRank for a recommender system, called *ItemRank* [9]. In the experiment section, we denoted by AUCF, AICF, and AIRank the Average model with UCF, ICF, and ItemRank, respectively.

EXPERIMENTS AND RESULTS

This section compares the performance of our recommender method against that of the baseline methods. As noted in a number of previous studies, the size of the neighborhood k could influence the recommendation quality of neighborhood-based algorithms. Therefore, we carried out experiments by varying k from 10 to 30 with an increment of 10, and chose the value of k that yielded a higher rank for each group on each method. One point that is worth noting is that, in the MovieLens evaluation dataset, any further increases, beyond $k = 30$, either barely improved the performance or rather affected the degradation of the performance with regard to HR. For the differential ranking approach of Folkommender, defined in Equation (12), we also varied parameter α from 0.5 to 0.9 for adjusting the relative weighting between the positive and negative ranking vectors. As a result, we observed that higher values of α ($0.7 \leq \alpha \leq 0.9$) tended to lead to higher recommendation ranks. As a consequence, we reported the results obtained using two versions of Folkommender, one as the non-differential approach of Folkommender in which α was set to 1 (denoted as PosFolkR) and the other as the differential approach of Folkommender in which α was set to 0.8 (denoted as DifferFolkR).

AUCF	AICF	AIRank	PosFolkR	DifferFolkR
16.2%	15.9%	20.4%	22.1%	23.5%

Table 2. Hit-rate within the top-10 recommendations for all test groups.

We first measured HR values obtained using the previously mentioned five methods for all test groups (1665 groups in total) without considering their cohesiveness and size. Since users practically consider only the top part of a recommended list, this measure is useful to glance briefly the algorithms which on average tend to put hidden items in the very top positions. A summary of the principal results is shown in Table 2. As our study focuses on group recommendations, we intuitively expected that two main factors—group size and group cohesiveness—would affect the overall performance of each method. We therefore pay full attention to the influence of these two factors in more detail throughout the subsequent sections.

Evaluation of group cohesiveness

This section investigates the impact of group cohesiveness on the recommendation performance. In service of this objective, we calculated HR values depending respectively on homogeneous, heterogeneous, and random groups without consideration of group size.

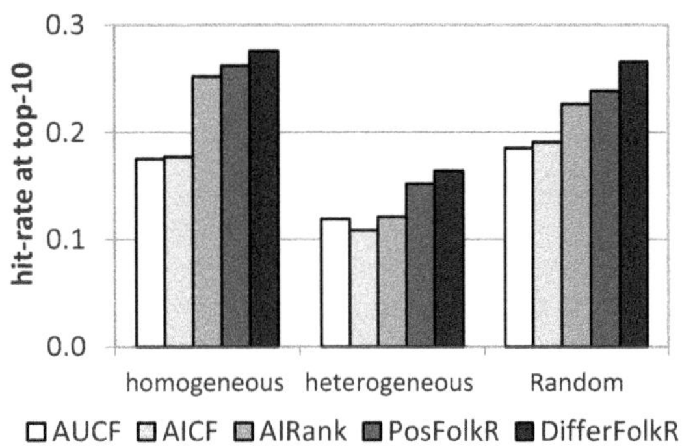

Figure 3. Hit-rate at top-10 recommendations with respect to different types of groups.

Figure 3 depicts the results for the three types of groups. As shown in the graph, it is clear that our Folkommender approaches, PosFolkR and DifferFolkR, performed significantly better than the baseline approaches on all occasions. For instance, for the homogeneous groups, the differential Folkommender strategy improved HR by 10% over AUCF, by 9.9% over AICF, and by 2.4% over AIRank, respectively. The results of the random groups did not qualitatively differ from those of the homogenous groups. Shifting attention to the results of the heterogeneous groups, we can also clearly see the superiority of the Folkommender methods. We also found that the recommendation performance trended downward as the overall similarity of group members decreased; that is, a significant HR disparity was clearly apparent between the homogeneous (or random) groups and the heterogeneous groups. This might be partially because the heterogeneous groups on our evaluation dataset were composed of a relatively small number of users compared with the homogeneous and random groups. This would be true in a real-world situation, as largely heterogeneous groups would be formed only rarely in practice. This aspect will be explored in more detail in the next section.

As mentioned earlier, a homogeneous group is comprised of users who have "similar" tastes, whereas a heterogeneous group is comprised of "dissimilar" users. To gain deeper insight into the impact of this cohesiveness on group recommendations, we further selected two different classes of groups according to the constraint of group members' similarity: (i) the average similarity of members is less than or equal to 0.1 (81 groups in total) and (ii) that of members is greater than or equal to 0.5 (141 groups in total). We then examined the HR values only for those groups. As shown in Table 3, the Folkommender approaches continued to surpass the baselines for both highly inner similar and dissimilar groups. A more interesting situation that we focus on is the highly heterogeneous groups; in this situation, DifferFolkR outputted the best results, implying that combining positive ranking scores with negative ones did help to improve the recommendation rankings. PosFolkR, however, achieved comparable results for the highly homogeneous groups.

To sum up, the performance of group recommendations depended somewhat on a state of cohesion inherent in groups. The more similar users in a group, the more accurately the algorithms identified suitable items for the group. Compared to the typical average methods, the differential Folkommender ranking strategy performs well in general. Incorporating negative ranking scores in creating a final ranking list proves to be effective for random or heterogeneous groups, but is not quite useful for the highly inner similar groups compared with the non-differential strategy.

	Group members' similarity	
	≤ 0.1	≥ 0.5
AUCF	13.4 %	14.2 %
AICF	4.9 %	21.3 %
AIRank	14.6 %	43.3 %
PosFolkR	17.1 %	47.5 %
DifferFolkR	22.0 %	48.9 %

Table 3. Hit-rate at top-10 with respect to highly heterogeneous groups and highly homogeneous groups.

Evaluation of group size

In this experiment, we investigated how sensitive each of the algorithms was regarding the number of users contained in groups. In addition to group cohesiveness, group size would constitute another significant factor that could affect the recommendation performance. To explore this impact, we measured HR values associated with different group size within homogeneous, heterogeneous, and random groups, respectively. Figure 4 depicts the results, showing how each method was affected by the size of groups. The number of groups per size is also plotted in the top of each bar chart. As shown, our Folkommender offers more benefits to small groups rather than to large groups. The results demonstrated that the Folkommender approaches were considerably superior to the CF approaches in the cases when group sizes were relatively small (i.e., group size ≤ 4). When the group size was 8 (i.e., large groups), AICF performed best particularly for homogeneous and random groups, but our differential approach still performed best for heterogeneous groups. Interestingly, AICF yielded uneven performance and seemed highly sensitive to the group size; in the large group case, AICF outputted the best results for homogeneous and random

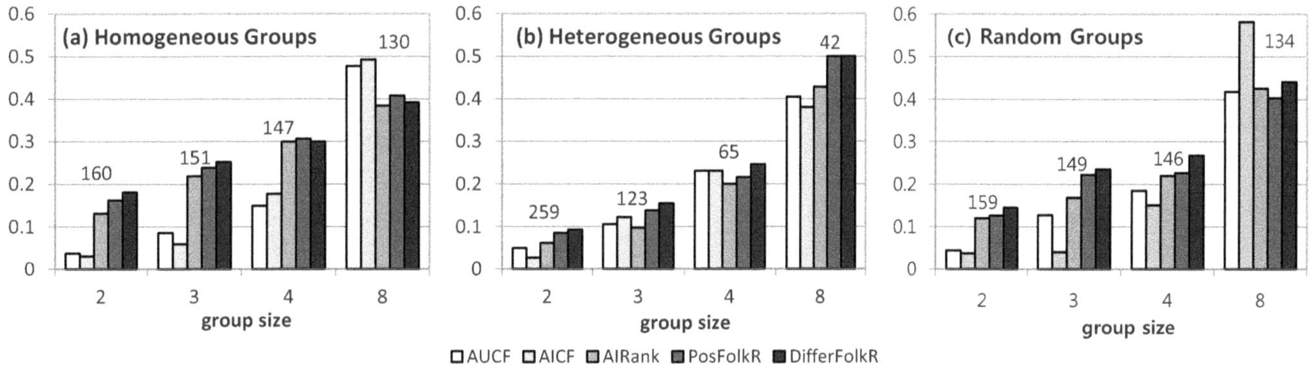

Figure 4. Comparisons of the hit-rate at top-10 according to different group size.

groups, but in the small group cases it outputted the worst results.

Our results also showed that the performance of all the methods in terms of HR appeared profoundly group size-dependent, regardless of whether or not group members were similar to one another. Surprisingly, it was determined that the HR values did tend to improve as the group size increased. For example, in the case of the homogenous groups consisting of two members, AUCF, AICF, AIRank, PosFolkR, and DifferFolkR demonstrated HR values of 0.038, 0.031, 0.131, 0.163, and 0.181, respectively; those values remarkably increased up to 0.477, 0.495, 0.384, 0.408 and 0.392, respectively, when the group size was 8. A similar upward trend was observed in the heterogeneous and random groups as well. These results might be caused by the fact that we judged how well each algorithm positioned a test item—that every member has previously rated with 5 points—at a higher rank for a given group. In this scenario, we found that numerous members contributed more to hitting the test item within their recommended list.

DISCUSSIONS AND OPEN ISSUES

There are several open issues and interesting tasks which could be performed so as to extend our work.

Since our graph-based recommendation method does not require any additional information about users or items aside from users' rating information, it could be potentially applicable to various recommendation contexts—for example, TV programs, social media, movies, music, and travel packages. Nevertheless, similar to most collaborative filtering-based methods, our method could suffer from rating sparsity-related problems. One problem that Folkommender could encounter is "cold start" cases wherein little or no information is known about users or items [1]. For example, an item newly added to the system cannot be recommended until sufficient users give the item their ratings. Analogously, cold start items that only a few users have rated would be positioned very rarely in the top part of a recommended list. Furthermore, when calculating group ranking scores, our method could be biased somewhat toward active members having a large number of ratings compared to other members. Consequently, the recommendation result could neglect opinions of cold start members who have previously rated very few items. These limitations raise some future theoretical and empirical research for more advanced recommender methods.

As shown by our experimental results, our method seemed not to be effective for large, homogeneous groups, particularly compared with AICF. In this work, we assumed that members in the same group have equal weight as we aimed to identify items that could satisfy all members as much as possible. In some cases, however, certain members would have more influence than others and thus be good leaders in their group recommendations. Since members in a homogeneous group have similar tastes in viewing multimedia content, influential members, particularly within "large" groups, may lead to good recommendations for their members. In teleportation vectors $\mathbf{v}^+$ and $\mathbf{v}^-$, we assigned the same values to entries of all members belonging to a specific group. However, it is possible to assign different values depending on the influence/importance particular users have in a group. We intend to investigate this impact on our recommendation performance in the future.

In our experiments, we tested the recommendation performance in a situation where groups are somewhat stable. However, we also need to concentrate on the dynamic nature of groups, which can turn into a flux over time. It is often the case that groups are temporally formed by people who have a common aim at a particular moment. Simply, we can compute the positive and negative ranking vectors, $\mathbf{r}^+$ and $\mathbf{r}^-$, using the power iteration method. In practice, however, it would not be possible to compute these ranking vectors naively with fixed iterations online in response to a temporal group's request, as those tasks are time-consuming processes. Thus, as with most recommender systems, we need pre-computation steps which can be accomplished offline. Fortunately, remarkable efforts have been made to facilitate the computation of PageRank-like algorithms [4, 20]. In particular, Jeh and Widom [11] proved a linear relationship between teleportation vectors and their corresponding personalized PageRank vectors. This linear relationship allows (personalized) PageRank scores to be obtained using a linear combination of *basis vectors* that are practically computed offline. Inspired by this study, at recommendation time, our positive and negative ranking vectors can be obtained from pre-computed basis vectors associated with a specific group; this computation approach could support fast recommendations online.

Our experiments showed that our group recommendation approach is fruitful in ranking hidden items. In the MovieLens dataset, however, the number of relevant items to a group in the test set may be a small fraction of the number of entire relevant items that are actually of interest to that group. This is because it is impossible that we collect the entire ground truth data about which items are of interest to each group. Accordingly, in our test scenario, we were not able to evaluate the appropriateness of many of the recommended items for a group as there is no preference information of that group for those items in the dataset. Accordingly, more in-depth studies with users are required to further validate the effectiveness of our method.

CONCLUSIONS

An effective service providing group recommendation is of undisputed value to users. In this paper, we developed a recommender system, which we call Folkommender, for recommending items to groups of users. Specifically, we model a two-layer signed graph that reflects both users' positive and negative opinions on items. We then exploit this graph for developing a graph-based differential ranking approach on group recommendation. This ranking approach examines random walks with restarts on two different link-structures derived from users' ratings in order to consider group ranking scores not only from a positive perspective but also from a negative perspective. Our experiments on the MovieLens dataset show that Folkommender performs better than existing alternatives most notably for small groups regardless of whether or not members are similar to each other. Additionally, our differential ranking strategy can be successfully leveraged to improve recommendation performance especially for heterogeneous/random groups.

REFERENCES

1. Adomavicius, G., Tuzhilin, A. Toward the next generation of recommender systems: a survey of the state-of-the-art and possible extensions. *IEEE Trans. Knowl. and Data Eng. 17*, 6 (2005), 734–749.
2. Amer-Yahia, S., Roy, S.B., Chawlat, A., Das, G., Yu, C. Group recommendation: semantics and efficiency. *Proc. VLDB Endow. 2,* 1 (2009) 754–765.
3. Baltrunas, L., Makcinskas, T., Ricci, F. Group recommendations with rank aggregation and collaborative filtering. *Proc. RecSys 2010*, ACM Press (2010), 119–126.
4. Berkhin, P. A survey on PageRank computing. *Internet Mathematics 2*, 1 (2005), 73–120
5. Berkovsky, S., Freyne, J. Group-based recipe recommendations: analysis of data aggregation strategies. *Proc. RecSys 2010*, ACM Press (2010), 111–118.
6. Breese, J.S., Heckerman, D., Kadie, C. Empirical analysis of predictive algorithms for collaborative filtering, *Proc. UAI-98*, Morgan Kaufmann (1998), 43–52.
7. Deshpande, M., Karypis, G. Item-based top-n recommendation algorithms. *ACM Trans. Information Systems 22*, 1 (2004), 143–177.
8. Gartrell, M., Xing, X., Lv, Q., Beach, A., Han, R., Mishra, S., Seada, K. Enhancing group recommendation by incorporating social relationship interactions. *Proc. GROUP 2010*, ACM Press (2010), 97–106.
9. Gori, M., Pucci, A. ItemRank: a random-walk based scoring algorithm for recommender engines. *Proc. IJCAI 2007*, AAAI Press (2007), 2766–2771.
10. Jameson, A., Smyth, B. Recommendation to groups. In The Adaptive Web, Lecture Notes in Computer Science 4321, Springer (2007), 596–627.
11. Jeh, G., Widom, J. Scaling personalized Web search. *Proc. WWW 2003*, ACM Press (2003), 271–279
12. Kim, H.K., Oh, H.Y., Gu, J.C., Kim, J.K.: Commenders: a recommendation procedure for online book communities. *Electronic Commerce Research and Applications 10*, 5 (2011), 501–509.
13. Konstan J. A., Riedl, J.: Recommender systems: from algorithms to user experience, *User Modeling and User-Adapted Interaction 22*, 1-2 (2012), 101–123.
14. Masthoff, J. Group modeling: selecting a sequence of television items to suit a group of viewers. *User Modeling and User-Adapted Interaction 14*, 1 (2004), 37–85.
15. McCarthy, J.F., Anagnost, T.D. MUSICFX: an arbiter of group preferences for computer supported collaborative workouts. *Proc. CSCW 1998*, ACM Press (1998), pp. 363–372.
16. O'Connor, M., Cosley, D., Konstan, J.A., Riedl, J. PolyLens: a recommender system for groups of users. *Proc. ECSCW 2001*, (2001), 199–218.
17. Sarwar, B., Karypis, G., Konstan, J., Riedl, J. Item-based collaborative filtering recommendation algorithms. *Proc. WWW 2001*, ACM Press (2001), 285-295.
18. Senot, C., Kostadinov, D., Bouzid, M., Picault, J., Aghasaryan, A., Bernier, C.: Analysis of strategies for building group profiles. *Proc. UMAP 2010*, Springer (2010), 40–51.
19. Sotelo, R., Blanco-Fernandez, Y., Lopez-Nores, M., Gil-Solla, A., Pazos-arias, J. TV program recommendation for groups based on multidimensional TV-Anytime classifications. *IEEE Trans. Consumer Electronics 55*, 1 (2009), 248–256.
20. Tong, T., Faloutsos, C., Pan, J.-Y. Fast random walk with restart and its applications. *Proc. ICDM 2006*, IEEE Computer Society (2006), 613 – 622.
21. Yu, Z., Zhou, X., Hao, Y., Gu, J. TV program recommendation for multiple viewers based on user profile merging. *User Modeling and User-Adapted Interaction 16*, 1 (2006), 63–82.

CatStream: Categorising Tweets for User Profiling and Stream Filtering

Sandra Garcia Esparza, Michael P. O'Mahony, Barry Smyth
CLARITY: Centre for Sensor Web Technologies,
School of Computer Science and Informatics,
University College Dublin (UCD), Belfield, Dublin 4, Ireland.
{sandra.garcia-esparza, michael.omahony, barry.smyth}@ucd.ie

ABSTRACT

Real-time information streams such as Twitter have become a common way for users to discover new information. For most users this means curating a set of other users to follow. However, at the moment the *following* granularity of Twitter is restricted to the level of individual users. Our research has highlighted that many following relationships are motivated by a subset of interests that are shared by the users in question. For example, user *A* might follow user *B* because of their technology related tweets, but shares little or no interest in their other tweets. As a result, this *all-or-nothing* following relationship can quickly overwhelm users' timelines with extraneous information. To improve this situation we propose a user profiling approach based on the topical categorisation of users' posted URLs. These topics can then be used to filter information streams so that they focus on more relevant information from the people they follow, based on their core interests. In particular, we present a system called *CatStream* that provides for a more fine-grained way to follow users on specific topics and filter our timelines accordingly. We present the results of a live-user study that shows how filtered timelines offer a better way to organise and filter their information streams. Most importantly users are generally satisfied with the categories predicted for their profiles and tweets.

Author Keywords

Real-time Web, User Profiling, Information Filtering, Classification

ACM Classification Keywords

H.3.3 Information Search and Retrieval: Information filtering; H.5.2 User Interfaces: Evaluation/methodology

INTRODUCTION

Twitter has had an incredible impact on the world's information flow and communication landscape. Today Twitter's 140m users generate about 340 million tweets a day[1], 25% of which contain URLs [2]. However, notwithstanding its success to date, we believe that there are a number of key challenges that quickly become apparent to new users, and that ultimately may limit the long-term efficacy of Twitter as an information sharing and discovery platform.

Twitter allows users to consume a stream of information generated by other users they have opted to follow. Such streams consist of short text messages (tweets) which can contain raw text, tags (hashtags) and URLs. Following a user in Twitter is an *all-or-nothing* affair, in the sense that all of their friends' tweets are shown in the user's information stream (i.e. their timeline). If the user has been judicious about the people and topics that they follow then the hope is that this stream of information will contain relevant content. This hope is often far from the reality however, because as Twitter users accumulate more and more friends, their streams quickly become polluted by a variety of content not all of which is relevant to their core interests. We note that this all-or-nothing following relationship is not just present in Twitter, but in many other information streaming services such as Tumblr or Pinterest.

To highlight this problem, in this paper we performed a live user study where we asked 45 participants to specify what categories they followed their friends on (we selected 10 friends at random) out of a set of 18 broad categories. After analysing their friends' tweets for those categories we found that on average only 53% of their friends' tweets (with URLs) were actually about the categories they were interested in. In other words, when users follow other users on Twitter, nearly half of their tweets are on topics that are not of interest to them.

This result shows a clear need for a system that facilitates the following of users only in relation to certain topics or categories. This is the challenge we wish to address and which contains two key elements. First, we need a way to automatically profile the topics of interests for Twitter users so that users can follow other users based on a subset of these interests. Second, we need a way to classify new tweets and filter those that are off topic. In this way, for example, we can recognize that user @Dogbert's interests include *technology*,

[1] `http://blog.twitter.com/2012/03/twitter-turns-six.html`
[2] `http://techcrunch.com/2010/09/14/twitter-seeing-90-million-tweets-per-day/`

research, and *music* and when user @Alice considers following @Dogbert she can do so with respect to *technology* only. Thus @Alice's timeline integrity will be preserved by filtering out @Dogbert's non-technology related tweets.

In this paper we have implemented a system called *CatStream* that incorporates these profiling and filtering capabilites in order to form a more topic-centric Twitter client that can deliver more relevant streams of information to end-users. CatStream's core component is a multi-category URL classifier that enables the system to categorise users and their tweets based on the URLs contained in them. Focusing on URLs is important because it provides a richer source of content for the purpose of topic classification.

In order to evaluate CatStream we have performed an online study with 45 participants. The result of this evaluation shows that most users would prefer to use a system that allowed to categorise and filter their streams in comparison to a standard Twitter client. Further, users are generally satisfied with the categories predicted for their profiles and tweets.

This paper is organised as follows. In the next section we describe related work that has been performed in the area of user profiling and information stream filtering. A description of the system, including the system architecture and the user interface is then presented. The process of selecting the URL classifier is explained and finally, a live user study to evaluate CatStream is described and results are presented.

RELATED WORK

Existing research has investigated different ways of profiling Twitter users. Some of the work has focused on using the content of tweets to represent the interests of users [5, 15, 23], while other researchers have also looked at hashtag information [1, 7].

However, analyzing tweets poses some significant challenges due to their short length, their noisy nature (i.e. spelling and grammatical errors, use of abbreviation, etc.) and the heterogeneous nature of their content. To deal with these challenges, researchers have also used external sources of information to enrich and disambiguate tweet content. For instance, richer user profiles can be built by extracting entity information (i.e. persons, events or products) using tools like OpenCalais [2, 17]. Further, in [14] the authors use Wikipedia to disambiguate tweets and extract categories of interest, while in [3] search engines are used as an external knowledge source to expand the content of tweets.

In this work we analyze the content of URLs, which are present in about 25% of tweets. While many tweets might not reveal much about a user's topical interests due to a lack of useful information (e.g. a large percentage of tweets consist of daily chatter), posted URLs provide a much richer source of information in terms of identifying the preferences of users for particular kinds of content (i.e. topics). In particular, our solution to user profiling consists on extracting categories of interest (i.e. high level topics such as *movies*, *sports*, *politics*, etc.) by using a multi-label text classifier to categorise URLs. One of the typical approaches to text categorisation uses machine learning techniques [10, 18, 24]. For example, naïve Bayes methods are commonly used in web page classification due to their high accuracy and simplicity [13, 22]. Support Vector Machines (SVMs) have also been used to classify web pages and in some work they report higher accuracy than naïve Bayes classifiers [8, 20].

Currently, some information stream services also perform user categorisation where a user is assigned a single category they are considered to be influential on. This is the case with Twitter and Pinterest, where such categorisation is used to suggest people to follow in these services. This approach works well for famous personalities (i.e. *@BarackObama* mostly tweets about politics) and other specialised users (*@BBCSport* just tweets about sports). However, for most users, this single-category assignation is rather limited since users tend to be have more diverse interests and post about many different topics. Thus, our approach offers a richer representation of users' interests which allows users to follow other users by a subset of topics they post about.

Filtering real-time streams has also been explored recently due to the increasing amount of information in those services. One of the solutions proposed to filtering information streams is recommender systems. For instance, the authors in [7] build user profiles using hashtags contained in the users' tweets and then use those profiles to recommend tweets. Similarly, user profiles have also been used to recommend news URLs to users [2, 5]. Recommending credible information in Twitter has also been investigated by [11], where a credibility score can be computed for a tweet about a particular topic using topic-specific credibility models.

Our solution to filtering information streams is treated as a categorisation problem rather than as recommendation problem. In this sense, categorisation techniques can be used to determine the category of each URL contained in a tweet and then by using category-based profiles we can select the tweets that are interesting to the user. Categorisation for filtering tweets has also been applied in [19] to classify Twitter messages into five categories (*news, events, opinions, deals* and *private messages*). Here, we also wish to filter micro-blogs but we apply filtering based on the category of the message rather than on the particular communication intention of the author.

This work focuses on the evaluation of CatStream, which incorporates the user profiling and filtering capabilities mentioned above. Our solution to both profiling and filtering is based on a multi-label URL classifier. For this reason in order to evaluate the quality of the user profiles and of the filtering of tweets we must first evaluate the performance of the categoriser on its own, which is described in section *Choosing the Classifier*. Further we also performed a live user study to evaluate CatStream which is explained in section *Online User Study*.

SYSTEM OVERVIEW

CatStream[3] is a system which categorises and filters information streams (currently on Twitter) based on category-based

[3]The system is currently live at `http://catstream.org`

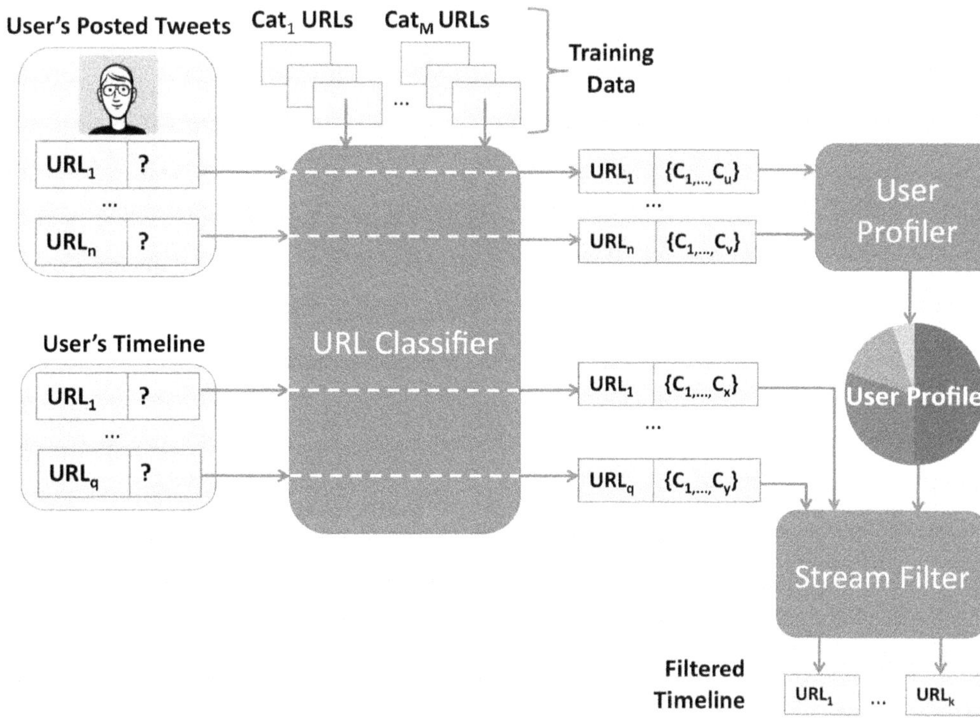

Figure 1. CatStream's System Architecture.

user profiles. Its main goal is to help users to better organise their Twitter streams in order to facilitate a more effective discovery platform. Currently CatStream focuses on tweets which contain URLs, since we believe they tend to contain more relevant content, and ignores those which are considered *daily chatter*. In fact, during our user study we asked users for what reasons they used Twitter and the most popular answer was to find news (82% of users). This establishes that Twitter is more of an information discovery network than a social network, as some might view it.

System Architecture

The architecture of CatStream (Figure 1), consists of three main components:

1. **URL Classifier.** The core of CatStream is a URL classifier which automatically assigns one or more categories to a tweet based on its URL content. This classification is performed in real-time using a naïve Bayes Multinomial classifier [12]. Currently, our classifier works with a set of 18 categories which correspond to topics such as *music*, *sports* or *health*.

2. **User Profiler.** The profiling component is responsible for constructing a category-based profile of a Twitter user. It does this by categorising the user's posted tweets (and retweets and replies) using the URL classifier, producing a weighted set of profile categories that reflect the topics that the user tends to post about. The purpose of the profile is two-fold. On the one hand a target user's profile is used as the basis for filtering the user's timeline, prioritising those tweets that conform to the users own interests. In addition, it is also used to provide the ability to follow users on certain topics; so for example a target user U_t might follow user U_i on topic T_j by selecting this topic from U_i's profile during the following process.

3. **Stream Filter.** The stream filter is responsible for filtering a target user's timeline. As mentioned above, CatStream uniquely provides Twitter users with the ability to *partially* follow other users, by indicating topics of interest during the following process. This means that instead of presenting the target user with a complete timeline of all of the tweets from the people they follow, CatStream filters these tweets based on the user's chosen topics as the basis for following.

Classifying Tweets

CatStream's profiling and filtering approach is fundamentally based on the ability to classify tweets containing URLs; that is, the ability to associate tweets with one or more topical categories based on an analysis of URL content. This classifier component, as shown in Figure 1, is implemented using a conventional machine learning approach, by training for a set of M categories using a set of labeled tweets to produce a classifier that is able to associate a new tweet Tw with a set of one or more category labels C_i as seen in Equation 1.

$$Classify(Tw) = \{c_1, ..., c_m\} \quad (1)$$

In this work, categories correspond to broad topics such as *music*, *sports* or *health*. For the purpose of obtaining labeled training data we source URLs from Twitter (using their Streaming API) that have been annotated with corresponding category hashtags (e.g. *#music*, *#sports*, *#health*). Thus, each training instance is a tweet containing a URL and an associated class label. For the purpose of training, the text of the URL provides the basic training data. In our work we have experimented with single-label and multi-label classifiers [18]. The former assigns a single major label to a tweet, while the latter has the option of assigning multiple labels. We will discuss the utility of both approaches in a later section.

From Tweets to Profiles

Given a classifier that can associate a tweet with one or more categories we can now adopt a straightforward approach to profile a given user. In CatStream, each user U_i is associated with a set of URLs (see Equation 2), which are the URLs that they have shared on Twitter (given the constraints of the Twitter API, for the purpose of our work we select URLs contained in the user's 200 most recent tweets).

$$U_i = \{URL_1 ... URL_n\} \tag{2}$$

Each of these URLs is then associated with one or more categories (using the classifier) and a count is maintained of the number of times that a particular category has been assigned to URLs for the target user. In this way, each user is associated with a weighted set of categories with a higher weight indicating that the user has posted more tweets on the corresponding topic (see Equation 3).

$$Profile(U_i) = \{(c_1, w_1), ..., (c_k, w_k)\} \tag{3}$$

For multi-label classifiers, where each tweet can be associated with a ranking list of categories, we using a straightforward positional weighting scheme so that primary categories count for more than secondary or tertiary categories. For example, if a tweet is associated with a ranked list of $C = \{c_1, ..., c_m\}$ categories then the weight w_r assigned to a category at rank r is calculated as per Equation 4.

$$w_r = 1 - \frac{r-1}{|C|}, where\ r = 1, .., |C| \tag{4}$$

From Profiles to Timelines

As mentioned above, a key purpose of the user profile is to provide other users with a perspective on a particular user, with respect to their main topics of interest. This then means that the *all-or-nothing* model of Twitter can be improved to allow for following relationships that are based on a combination of users and topics. Moreover, as a target user (U_t) follows other users based on subsets of their topics, CatStream can then filter U_t's timeline by eliminating posts from these users that are off-topic.

This can be achieved in a straightforward manner. Each target user, followed user (U_f) combination is associated with a set of topical categories based on the topics chosen by U_t when they chose to follow U_f; see Equation 5. To compute U_t's timeline (that is, the tweets they should see) CatStream requests the current tweets for U_t from Twitter; these are all of the tweets from the users that U_t follows since Twitter knows nothing of CatStream's categories or profiles.

$$FollowTopics(U_t, U_f) = \{c_1, ..., c_s\} \tag{5}$$

Each of these timeline tweets is classified in real-time by CatStream and filtered out unless its assigned categories support some minimal overlap with the categories chosen by U_t for the originator of the tweet. In other words, for U_t CatStream will only *keep* (that is, display) a tweet Tw from user U_f if and only if there is some overlap between the tweets categories and $FollowTopics(U_t, U_f)$; see Equation 6.

$$\begin{aligned} Keep(U_t, U_f, Tw) = \{FollowTopics(U_t, U_f) \cap \\ Classify(Tw)\} \neq \varnothing \end{aligned} \tag{6}$$

Obviously this approach to filtering has been chosen because of its simplicity. The choice of overlap threshold will be further explored as part of our future work. For example, an obvious extension of the above is to utlilise category weights during filtering more directly by, for example, calculating a cosine similarity between the *FollowTopics* and tweet categories so as to better reflect the relative priority of overlapping categories.

The User Interface

The CatStream system has been designed to emulate a conventional Twitter client and provides all the functionality one might expect in terms of allowing users to tweet, view/manage their profiles, view and follow other users, access timelines, tag tweets etc. Obviously, CatStream also introduces additional features based around its topic-based profiling and filtering components. We will briefly introduce these novel interface elements in what follows.

To begin with, Figure 2 shows a target user's profile. In this case user @Alice is looking at her own profile page which contains a range of categories that have been chosen based on an analysis of her tweets. By default these categories are *active* but a user can choose to *deactivate* a category if they wish. For example, we can see that @Alice has active categories such as *art & photography* and *travel & leisure* but has deactivated categories such as *health* and *music*. These may be temporary deactivations (for example, @Alice may only want to read about *sports* the day after her football team has played) or they may be more long-term, perhaps indicating that @Alice is generally not interested in that particular category.

Currently in CatStream a user's *active* categories are used to over-ride the filtering functionality in the sense that only tweets that match on active categories are considered by the

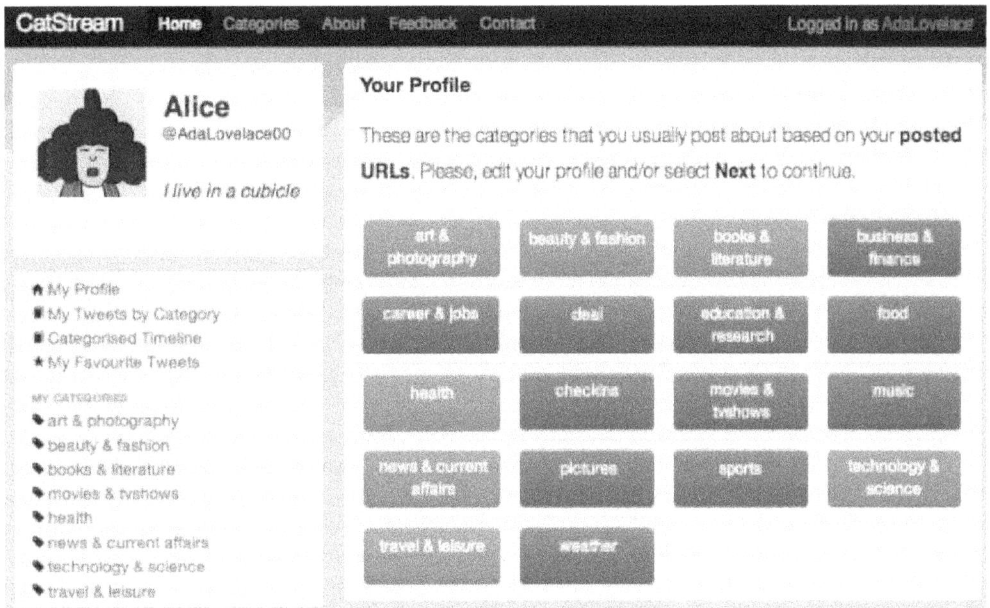

Figure 2. A typical CatStream profile.

filtering component. Thus, if @Alice follows another user @Dogbert on the topic of *music* then normally she will see all of @Dogbert's music tweets. However, if @Alice subsequently deactivates *music* in her profile the she will no longer see @Dogbert's music tweets.

Moving on, in Figure 3 we see @Alice's view of @Dogbert's profile page. In this case @Alice is already following @Dogbert and has chosen to do so based on topics such as *books & literature* and *music*. @Alice can choose to modify this relationship by deleting existing topics or adding new ones as appropriate. Again, the purpose of this is to support a more fine-grained following relationship between @Alice and @Dogbert, thereby ensuring that @Alice's timeline stays relevant with respect to the types of topics that matter to her and from the people she trusts with respect to these topics. Currently, the main filtering is performed using the topics from the user's profile page. Thus, by default, a user follows their friends on the set of topics that are active on her profile page, so that she is not obliged to select topics on an individual friend-by-friend basis. This filtering criteria also means that when a user activates a new topic of interest from her profile page for the first time, she will see the tweets on this topic from all her friends.

Finally, in Figure 4 we see CatStream's filtered timeline for user @Alice. Filtering can be switched on or off by the user, as shown. In this case, filtering is on and so @Alice sees the tweets in her timeline that are filtered based on her active categories and the categories by which she has chosen to follow users. Each tweet is shown in the normal way but augmented with real-time category information. A number of feedback options are provided so that users can delete/add categories, for example, which in the future can be used as part of an active learning approach to improving the core classifier.

CHOOSING THE CLASSIFIER

At this point we have motivated and described a novel approach to profiling and following users and filtering their stream content. The classifier approach at the core of CatStream has not yet been discussed in detail however. Before we discuss this element of CatStream it is worth highlighting that our main focus, at least at this stage of our work, is not to optimise the classifier to deliver a significant leap forward in content/text classification. Rather, our core objective is to explore this idea of a more personalised, topic-centric Twitter client by using a reasonably effective classifier. For this reason our approach to classification has largely been about harnessing existing classification technologies.

Single-label Classifier

Our starting point was to use a naïve Bayes multinomial classifier, which has been found to work well in the past for related classification problems [9, 12, 13]. By default this approach returns only a single class/category per classified tweet/URL. We used a bag-of-words approach to represent each URL, where the attributes of the classifier correspond to the terms appearing in the page pointed to by the URL, weighted according to the standard TF-IDF weighting function [21]. We also performed some basic preprocessing on the text, such as removing stop-words, special symbols and digits.

To evaluate this classifier we collected and downloaded the content of URLs for 18 different categories for tweets posted between September 2011 and January 2012. We removed duplicate URLs and selected 100 URLs at random for each category, producing a total of 1800 URLs. To begin with we performed a standard 10-fold cross-validation evaluation over this labeled data. Across the 18 categories, the average accuracy achieved by the classifier was 83.6% (σ = 6.3%).

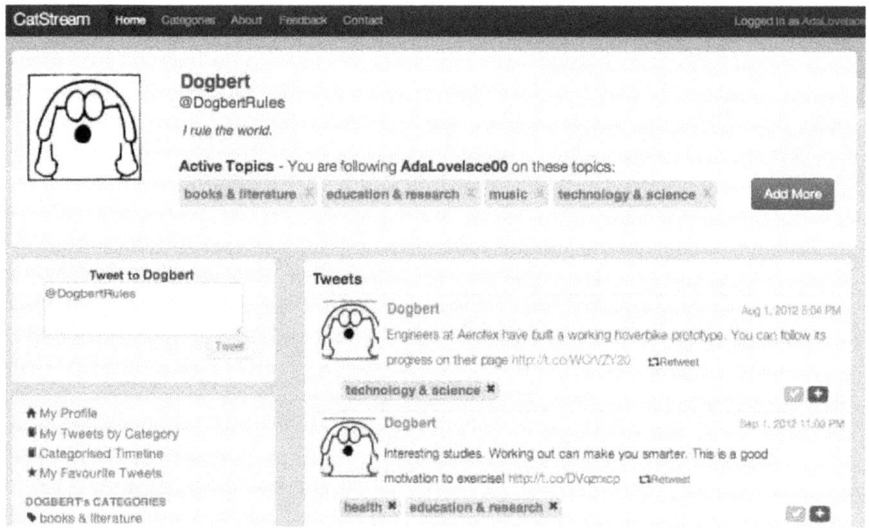

Figure 3. Following friends based on a subset of their profile topics.

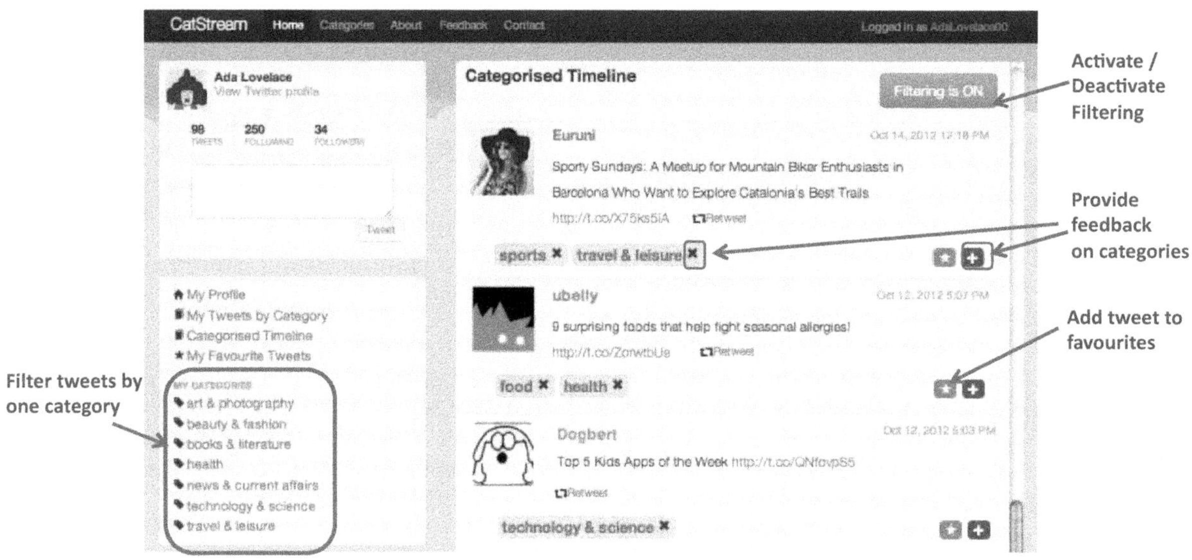

Figure 4. CatStream's categorised timeline.

We also performed a small online evaluation in an effort to benchmark the above offline results. We asked a group of 7 users to provide positive/negative feedback on the categories predicted for 50 random tweets; users were also invited to assign other categories to tweets as appropriate. The average prediction accuracy for these tweets was found to be 78.29% (σ = 7%), which although lower than the equivalent cross-validation accuracy is nevertheless in broad agreement.

Multi-label Classifiers

During the above experiment it became clear that one of the obvious shortcomings of our single-label approach was that tweeted URLs were more naturally associated with multiple categories, particularly given the set of categories that we use in CatStream. For this reason we chose to explore a multi-label classification approach.

To transform our single-label naïve Bayes classifier into a multi-label classifier version, we use the posterior probabilities assigned to each label (i.e. category) and which are returned by the naïve Bayes single-label classifier. We produce a label ranking by ordering the labels by their probabilities and pick the top L labels (typically L=2 or 3). We also implemented a variety of other standard classifiers (J48 [16], JRip [6], SVM [10] and Random Forest (RF)[4] with 500 trees) and re-evaluated their prediction accuracy across the 387 manually labeled tweets arising out of the small user study described above.

The accuracy results of this multi-label classifier evaluation are presented in Figure 5 as a graph of the percentage of tweets that were correctly labeled for each of the different classifiers at $L = 3$. We only show the performance for 16 categories as users did not provide feedback on tweets from the

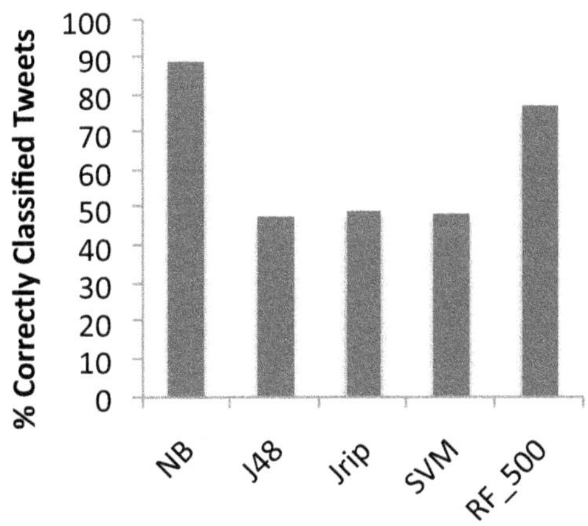

Figure 5. Comparison of Multi-label Classifiers (L = 3).

remaining 2 (*pictures* and *checkins*). The multi-label naïve Bayes classifier delivered superior overall accuracy. It also significantly outperformed the second place Random Forest on classification time; an important consideration given our need to perform real-time classification over a user's timeline of tens of tweets. Figure 6 also shows a more detailed analysis of the naïve Bayes approach on a category-by-category basis and highlighting the change in accuracy for $L = 1, 2, 3$. For the majority of categories classification accuracy is well in excess of 80%.

In the next section we perform a live-user study of CatStream with a naïve Bayes multi-label classifier as the core of the classification engine.The classifier was trained on the 1800 tweet/URL dataset described above.

ONLINE USER STUDY

To test CatStream in context we created a web application that allowed users to connect via their Twitter user credentials and evaluated it with 45 users who varied in ages from 18 to 55. All of the participants were active Twitter users to varying degrees; 77% used Twitter at least once per week while 14% used it on a monthly basis and 9% rarely used it. 62% of participants described themselves mainly as *consumers* of Twitter content, while 38% described themselves as both *producers* and *consumers*. The purpose of this study was to better understand how effective CatStream's classifier was performing by getting user feedback on the accuracy of their profile categories and the relevance of their filtered timelines. In addition the study also provided an opportunity to garner more general feedback on the perceived usefulness of the approach and the system as a whole.

Part 1 - Profile Accuracy

During the first part of this study users were presented with their profile page, complete with categories assigned to them based on their 200 most recent tweets that contained a minimum of 10 URLs. Unfortunately not all of the participants had sufficient tweets with URLs to use as a the basis for their profile and so the following results are based on a subset of 32 of the 45 users.

For the 32 users who did have sufficient tweets with URLs, their tweets contained a mean of 90 ($\sigma = 61$) URLs and CatStream predicted a mean of 4.35 ($\sigma = 2.09$) categories per user. Participants were asked to delete categories that did not apply to them and to add categories that they felt were missing. On average users deleted only 0.6 ($\sigma = 0.74$) categories and added 2.65 ($\sigma = 2.93$).

We can use this information to calculate versions of precision and recall for the predicted categories by treating deletions as irrelevant categories and additions as missing relevant categories. For example, the precision of a set of predicted profile categories is the number of predicted categories minus deletions divided by the number of predicted categories. And recall is the number of predicted categories minus deletions divided by the number of predicted categories minus deletions plus additions. This corresponds to a profile precision score of 0.9 ($\sigma = 0.14$) and a recall score of 0.68 ($\sigma = 0.27$). The mean of F1 was 0.73 ($\sigma = 0.21$). In other words, CatStream was performing very well when it came to predicting the primary categories that applied to users, rarely making incorrect category suggestions that were deleted by users. At the same time it was sometimes missing categories that users felt should be applied to their interests.

These results are very encouraging, especially in relation to the precision of the predictions. As to the missing categories, one explanation is that users were interested in categories that they would not usually post about. Another explanation is of course that CatStream only has access to each user's most recent tweets, which must represent an incomplete picture of their interests, and so it is entirely likely that the very categories that users tended to add as missing were not reflected in the subset of tweets that CatStream used for profiling. In a more open deployment setting it is likely that CatStream would be able to build a more complete picture of a user's interests.

Separately, it is worth highlighting that when users were asked to rate the overall accuracy of their profile pages on a 5-point scale from 1 (poor) to 5 (very good) the median rating was 4, again providing some additional encouragement that CatStream's profiling component is operating effectively.

Part 2- Tweet Classification for Timeline Filtering

For the second part of the study participants were asked to provide feedback on the accuracy of the categories assigned to their tweets in their timeline view (i.e. tweets which contain URLs from the people they follow). Figure 7 shows an example of the timeline view that was used for the purpose of this part of the study. It shows a fairly traditional Twitter timeline of tweets but, as previously discussed, each of the tweets is labeled with a set of predicted categories (computed in real-time by CatStream). Each tweet also has a pair of feedback icons. The 'tick' icon allows the user to confirm that they are happy with the categories assigned to the tweet as they are. The 'plus' icon allows them to add additional categories (either by choosing from one of the default categories or by providing a free-form category of their own).

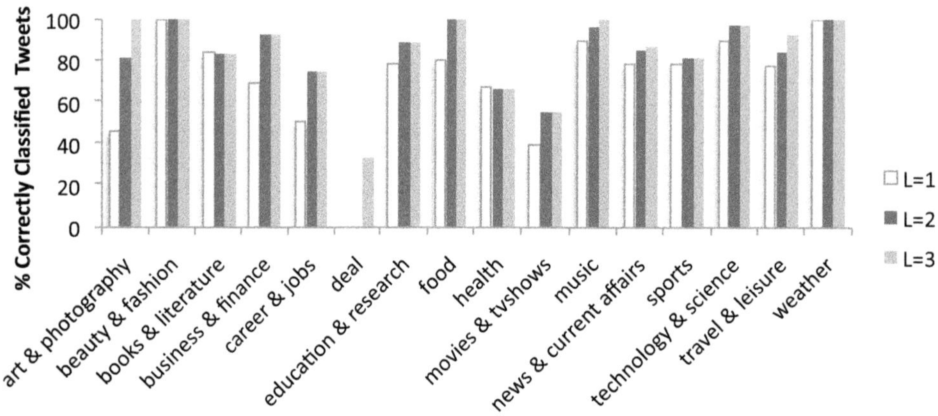

Figure 6. Percentage of correctly classified tweets per category for the top L labels achieved by the classifier.

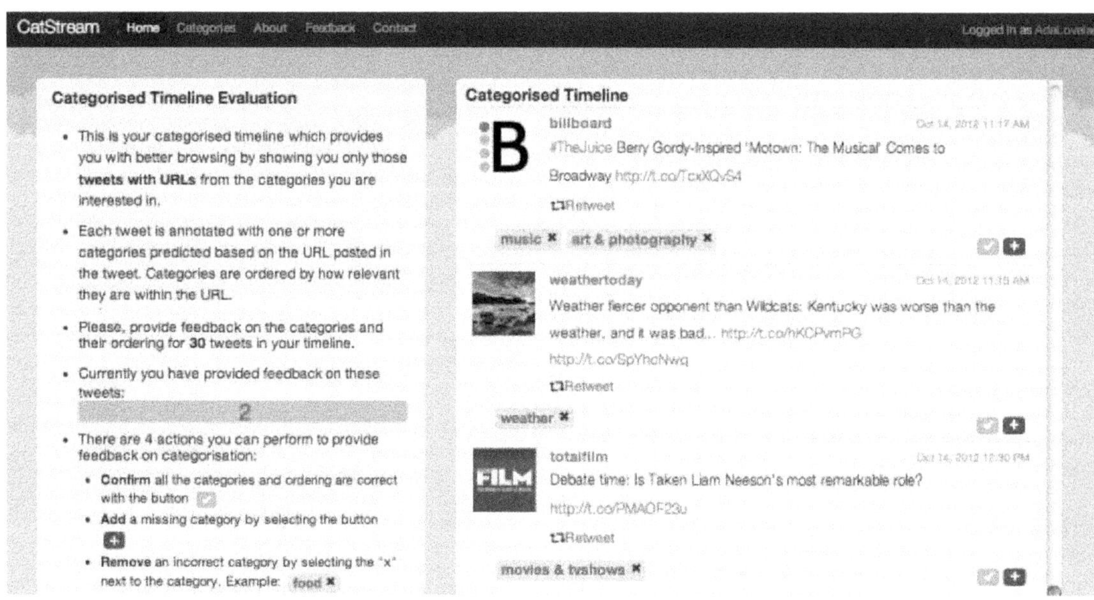

Figure 7. Timeline view showing tweets and annotated categories.

Each user was asked to provide feedback on a minimum of 30 URLs posted in tweets from their followers in their timeline; all 45 participants provided this feedback. In addition the more active users (those who had at least 30 of their own tweets with URLs) were encouraged to provide similar feedback but for their own posted tweets; only 25 participants were able to provide this feedback. In total users provided feedback for 2650 categorised tweets.

Participants confirmed that the predicted categories were correct (without change) for 64% of the tweets. They removed a category for only 8% of the tweets, added additional categories for 17% of the tweets and both removed and added categories for 11% of tweets. This demonstrates a similar feedback pattern as was found for profile pages in part 1 of this user study. Most of the time participants seemed happy with the categories assigned to tweets and tended to add categories more often than they deleted predicted categories.

For a given tweet we can predict the precision and recall scores for its predicted categories in a manner similar to that used in part 1 of the study. When we do this we obtain a mean precision and recall of 0.86 ($\sigma = 0.31$) and 0.81 ($\sigma = 0.33$) respectively. Mean F1 was 0.82 ($\sigma = 0.31$). Interestingly when we compare the accuracy of the predictions for a user's own tweets to the accuracy of their friends' (timeline) tweets we notice a mean F1 score for the former of 0.76 ($\sigma = 0.34\%$) versus 0.84 ($\sigma = 0.28\%$) for the latter. It is a matter for future work to determine whether this difference is due to actual poorer classification performance over each user's own tweets or whether it is based on user's having a higher degree of familiarity with the tweets they posted versus those their friends posted.

Interestingly, when participants were asked (as in part 1) to rate the accuracy of the classifier over their own tweets and the tweets of their friends on a 5-point scale from 1 (very inaccurate) to 5 (very accurate), the difference in the users' perceived quality was not so evident. In particular, the median

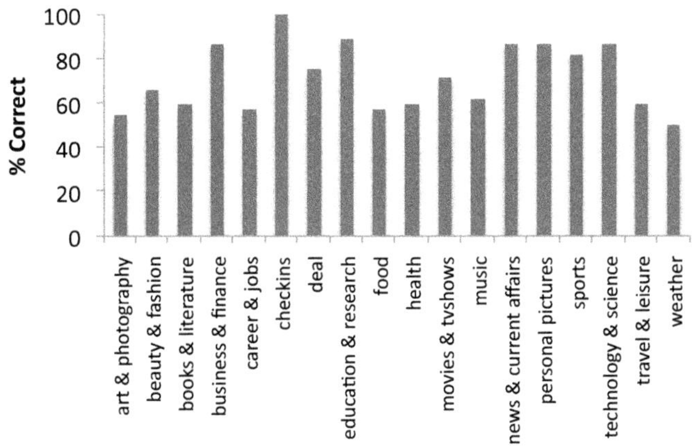

Figure 8. Percentage of times a category was correctly predicted.

ratings were 4 out of 5 for both the classification of friends and the user's own tweets.

Finally, in this part of the evaluation we also analysed the accuracy of the classifier across the 18 different categories by noting the percentage of times that a given category was accepted (that is, not deleted) for a URL posted in a tweet by participants. The results are presented in Figure 8 and show some variation in the performance of the classifier across the categories. Categories such as *news & current affairs, personal pictures, sports, technology & science* achieved accuracy levels in excess of 80%. In contrast categories like *art & photography, books & literature, career & jobs* did less well with accuracies in the range of 50%-60%. Once again this is a matter for future work. It is not clear whether this difference in accuracy is a result of some inherent difference in category complexity, or whether some categories are less controversial to the participants, or whether there is an issue with the training data. Certainly some of the less well-performing categories seem to correspond to classes of content that are perhaps less popular among Twitter users.

Part 3 - User Survey

CatStream offers a very different approach to providing users with access to their Twitter streams. Unlike conventional clients it adopts a more personalised approach, based on a finer-grained model of user following, that facilitates the active filtering of their timelines. The results above suggest that the mechanics of CatStream are working effectively, in the sense that the core classifier provides relatively good performance when it comes to predicting categories for unseen URLs posted in tweets. This in turn indicates that user profiles are a reasonably accurate reflection of user interests and their filtered timelines are more relevant. It does not however imply that users will be happy to engage with information streams in this fashion.

To better understand user engagement, participants completed the study by answering a simple questionnaire that focused on how useful participants found the approach, whether they would prefer it to a standard client, and whether they felt it helped them to find interesting content. The results are presented in Figure 9 and provides very strong evidence in favour of CatStream. For example, 91% of participants either agreed or strongly agreed that CatStream provided a useful service. 89% of people agreed or strongly agreed that they would prefer to use a client that incorporated CatStream-like profiling and filtering functionality. And more than 70% of people agreed or strongly agreed that it helped them find content that they were interested in. We believe these results are a strong indication that work in this line of research should be continued.

CONCLUSIONS

Twitter has proven to be an indispensable way for millions of users to keep up to date with the latest breaking news and updates from their friends. Many of us take the time to curate collections of influential Twitter users to follow so that we can benefit from a rich stream of information on topics that matter to us. Unfortunately Twitter's 'follower' model is very coarse grained, and it is increasingly responsible for polluting our timelines with irrelevant content. The core of this problem is that following a user is an all-or-nothing affair in Twitter, meaning that if a user follows another, all of the followed-user's tweets are presented even if, for example, the original user is only interested in technology related tweets.

In this paper we have described a novel system called CatStream that uses conventional classification techniques to profile Twitter users, based on the URLs they post in tweets, and filter their timelines based on the topics that matter to them. It is possible to partially follow users by following them with respect to certain topics and CatStream automatically filters out less relevant content from followed users.

We have described the results of a live-user trial which shows that CatStream is capable of effectively profiling users and that it provides a good performance when classifying tweets for the purpose of filtering our timelines. Feedback from live users has been extremely positive, with a majority indicating that they find the approach useful and preferable to conventional Twitter clients.

While in this work we focused on tweets with URLs, in the future we will expand our system so that tweets without URLs can also be classified using in-tweet content. In future work we will also complement the current set of broad categories with lower level topics in order to provide more detail into users' tweets and interests and thus better filtering techniques.

CatStream's current filters are manually selected by users of the system; however, in future work we will study approaches to automatically predict the topics that a user is interested in following for a given friend. For instance, replies and retweets can provide information about the topics users follow their friends for. Similar work was performed by [25] where topics were extracted from discussions between users in a social network.

Further, we plan to explore reinforcement learning and active learning techniques by mining feedback from users to further improve classification and filtering accuracy .

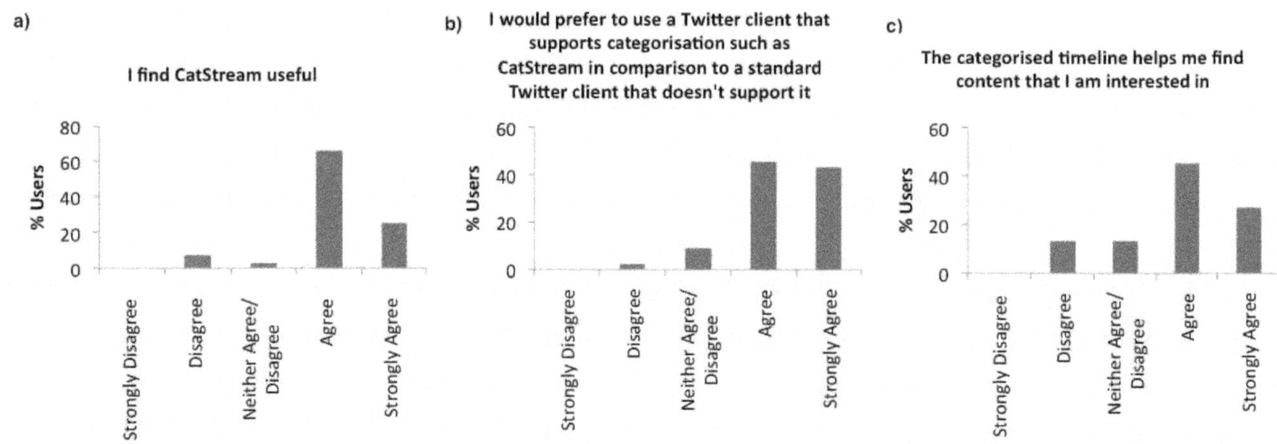

Figure 9. Survey answers.

REFERENCES

1. F. Abel, S. Araújo, Q. Gao, and G.-J. Houben. Analyzing cross-system user modeling on the social web. In *Proceedings of the 11th international conference on Web engineering*, ICWE'11, pages 28–43, Berlin, Heidelberg, 2011. Springer-Verlag.
2. F. Abel, Q. Gao, G.-J. Houben, and K. Tao. Analyzing user modeling on twitter for personalized news recommendations. In *Proceedings of the 19th international conference on User modeling, adaption, and personalization*, UMAP'11, pages 1–12, Berlin, Heidelberg, 2011.
3. M. S. Bernstein, B. Suh, L. Hong, J. Chen, S. Kairam, and E. H. Chi. Eddi: interactive topic-based browsing of social status streams. In *Proceedings of the 23nd annual ACM symposium on User interface software and technology*, UIST '10, pages 303–312, New York, NY, USA, 2010. ACM.
4. L. Breiman. Random forests. *Machine Learning*, 45(1):5–32, Oct. 2001.
5. J. Chen, R. Nairn, L. Nelson, M. Bernstein, and E. Chi. Short and tweet: Experiments on recommending content from information streams. In *Proceedings of the 28th international conference on Human factors in computing systems*, CHI '10, pages 1185–1194, New York, NY, USA, 2010.
6. W. W. Cohen. Fast effective rule induction. In *Proceedings of the Twelfth International Conference on Machine Learning*, pages 115–123. Morgan Kaufmann, 1995.
7. E. Diaz-Aviles, L. Drumond, L. Schmidt-Thieme, and W. Nejdl. Real-time top-n recommendation in social streams. In *Proceedings of the sixth ACM conference on Recommender systems*, RecSys '12, pages 59–66, New York, NY, USA, 2012. ACM.
8. S. Dumais and H. Chen. Hierarchical classification of web content. In *Proceedings of the 23rd annual international ACM SIGIR conference on Research and development in information retrieval*, SIGIR '00, pages 256–263, New York, NY, USA, 2000. ACM.
9. S. Garcia Esparza, M. O'Mahony, and B. Smyth. Further experiments in micro-blog categorization. In *Proceedings of the 22nd Irish Conference on Artificial Intelligence and Cognitive Science*, AICS '12, pages 156–165. Intelligent Systems Research Centre, 2011.
10. T. Joachims. Text categorization with support vector machines: learning with many relevant features. In *ECML '98: European Conference on Machine Learning*, pages 137–142, London, UK, 1998. Springer-Verlag.
11. B. Kang, J. O'Donovan, and T. Höllerer. Modeling topic specific credibility on twitter. In *Proceedings of the 2012 ACM international conference on Intelligent User Interfaces*, IUI '12, pages 179–188, New York, NY, USA, 2012. ACM.
12. A. M. Kibriya, E. Frank, B. Pfahringer, and G. Holmes. Multinomial naive bayes for text categorization revisited. In *Proceedings of the 17th Australian joint conference on Advances in Artificial Intelligence*, AI'04, pages 488–499, Berlin, Heidelberg, 2004. Springer-Verlag.
13. S.-B. Kim, H.-C. Rim, D. Yook, and H. Lim. Effective methods for improving naive bayes text classifiers. In *Proceedings of the 7th Pacific Rim International Conference on Artificial Intelligence: Trends in Artificial Intelligence*, PRICAI '02, London, UK, UK, 2002. Springer-Verlag.
14. M. Michelson and S. A. Macskassy. Discovering users' topics of interest on twitter: a first look. In *Proceedings of the fourth workshop on Analytics for noisy unstructured text data*, AND '10, pages 73–80, New York, NY, USA, 2010.
15. O. Phelan, K. McCarthy, and B. Smyth. Using twitter to recommend real-time topical news. In *Proceedings of*

the third ACM conference on Recommender systems, RecSys '09, pages 385–388, New York, NY, USA, 2009.

16. X. Qi and B. D. Davison. Web page classification: Features and algorithms. *ACM Computer Surveys*, 41(2):1–31, 2009.
17. D. Quercia, H. Askham, and J. Crowcroft. Tweetlda: supervised topic classification and link prediction in twitter. In *Proceedings of the 3rd Annual ACM Web Science Conference*, WebSci '12, pages 247–250, New York, NY, USA, 2012. ACM.
18. F. Sebastiani. Machine learning in automated text categorization. *ACM Computing Surveys*, 34(1):1–47, 2002.
19. B. Sriram, D. Fuhry, E. Demir, H. Ferhatosmanoglu, and M. Demirbas. Short text classification in twitter to improve information filtering. In *Proceedings of the 33rd international ACM SIGIR conference on Research and development in information retrieval*, SIGIR '10, pages 841–842, New York, NY, USA, 2010.
20. A. Sun, E.-P. Lim, and W.-K. Ng. Web classification using support vector machine. In *Proceedings of the 4th international workshop on Web information and data management*, WIDM '02, pages 96–99, New York, NY, USA, 2002. ACM.
21. C. J. van Rijsbergen. *Information Retrieval*. Butterworth-Heinemann, Newton, MA, USA, 1979.
22. Y. Wang, J. Hodges, and B. Tang. Classification of web documents using a naive bayes method. In *Proceedings of the 15th IEEE International Conference on Tools with Artificial Intelligence*, ICTAI '03, pages 560–564, Washington, DC, USA, 2003. IEEE Computer Society.
23. J. Weng, E.-P. Lim, J. Jiang, and Q. He. Twitterrank: finding topic-sensitive influential twitterers. In *Proceedings of the third ACM international conference on Web search and data mining*, WSDM '10, pages 261–270, New York, NY, USA, 2010.
24. Y. Yang and X. Liu. A re-examination of text categorization methods. In *SIGIR '99: Proceedings of the 22nd annual international ACM SIGIR conference on Research and development in information retrieval*, pages 42–49, New York, NY, USA, 1999. ACM.
25. M. Zhou, W. Zhang, B. Smith, E. Varga, M. Farias, and H. Badenes. Finding someone in my social directory whom i do not fully remember or barely know. In *Proceedings of the 2012 ACM international conference on Intelligent User Interfaces*, IUI '12, pages 203–206, New York, NY, USA, 2012. ACM.

Recommending Targeted Strangers from Whom to Solicit Information on Social Media

Jalal Mahmud Michelle X. Zhou Nimrod Megiddo Jeffrey Nichols Clemens Drews
IBM Research – Almaden
650 Harry Rd, San Jose, CA 95120
{jumahmud, mzhou, megiddo, jwnichols, cdrews}@us.ibm.com

ABSTRACT
We present an intelligent, crowd-powered information collection system that automatically identifies and asks targeted strangers on Twitter for desired information (e.g., current wait time at a nightclub). Our work includes three parts. First, we identify a set of features that characterize one's willingness and readiness to respond based on their exhibited social behavior, including the content of their tweets and social interaction patterns. Second, we use the identified features to build a statistical model that predicts one's likelihood to respond to information solicitations. Third, we develop a recommendation algorithm that selects a set of targeted strangers using the probabilities computed by our statistical model with the goal to maximize the overall response rate. Our experiments, including several in the real world, demonstrate the effectiveness of our work.

Author Keywords
Response Rate, Social Media, Willingness, Personality

ACM Classification Keywords
H.5.2. [Information Interfaces and Presentation]: User Interfaces

INTRODUCTION
Hundreds of millions of social media posts (e.g., tweets) are generated daily. Not only does the buzz of the crowd provide a great deal of information [12, 28, 36], but also creates a unique opportunity for building a new type of crowd-powered information collection systems. Such systems will *actively* identify and engage the right people at the right time on social media to elicit desired information. Assume that one wants to know the current wait time at a local popular restaurant. The system would then send such a request to those who are *able* (i.e., people tweeted being near the restaurant), *willing*, and *ready* to provide the wait time information. These systems have several advantages over other crowd-powered systems, such as Social Q&A [17].

First, it can collect information from people beyond one's own social network, especially when no one in their network may possess the desired information (e.g., no friends happen to know the wait time at a specific restaurant). Second, it can collect timely and potentially more accurate information from a crowd at an opportune time (e.g., people at an event) instead of passively waiting for opted-in information [3, 4, 5]. Third, it can collect balanced information from a diverse population by explicitly distributing questions across people with different perspectives, such as liberals and conservatives.

Although the systems described above have great potential and a recent study also demonstrates the feasibility of manually soliciting information from strangers on social media [27], there is so far little research in this space. To capitalize on the potential value of this approach, we are building an intelligent, crowd-powered information collection system, called qCrowd. Given a user's information request, qCrowd aids the user in collecting the desired information in four steps. First, it monitors a social media stream (e.g., twitter stream) to identify relevant posts (e.g., tweets generated from foursquare.com indicating people at specific locations). Second, it evaluates the authors of identified posts and recommends a sub-set of people to engage (Figure 1a). Third, it generates questions and then sends them to each selected person (Figure 1b). Fourth, it analyzes received responses and synthesizes the answers together.

In this paper, our focus is on the second step, the process of *automatically* determining the targeted strangers to engage on social media for an information collection task. This process is non-trivial for several reasons. First, the system must determine a person's qualification for the task—

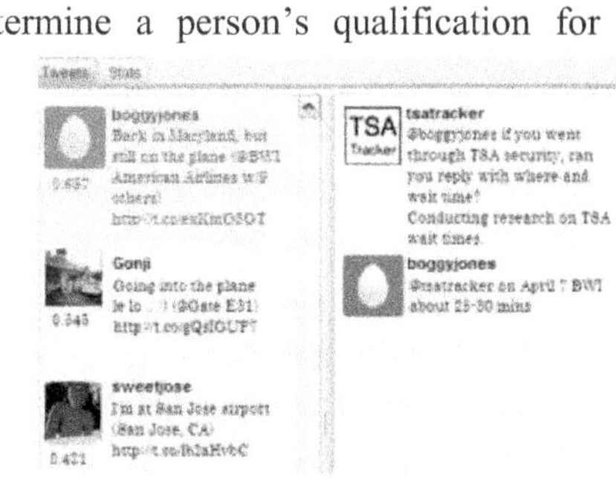

Figure 1. A screenshot of qCrowd. (a) left panel: system-recommended three people, and (b) right panel: the question sent and response received.

whether a person has the *ability* to provide the requested information, such as being at a specific location or having knowledge of a particular product. This requires analyzing the content of one's social media posts, which is often a difficult natural language processing task. Second, the system must determine how *willing* a qualified person is to provide the requested information. We hypothesize that one's willingness to respond to strangers may be related to one's personality traits [30], such as friendliness. However, it is unknown what and how exactly various personal traits influence one's willingness. In addition, accurately predicting one's willingness to respond is critical to the success of qCrowd, since a previous study shows that unwilling people not only would not respond, but are also likely to mark the information request as a spam if they do not understand the value of the request, which may result in suspended operations [27]. Third, qCrowd must determine how *ready* a person is to respond at the time of request. As seen later, one's readiness may depend on a number of factors, including the temporal characteristics of one's behavior and their most recent activity on social media. Again, there is little investigation in computationally measuring what and how various factors impact one's readiness to respond.

To address the challenges mentioned above, we build computational models to measure a person's *willingness*, *ability*, and *readiness* to respond based on one's behavior on social media. Since measuring one's ability is often domain or context dependent, currently we use a set of domain-specific rules to identify the targeted strangers who might possess the requested information. In the rest of the paper, we focus on the willingness and readiness models, which we believe are mostly domain agnostic.

Our work includes three parts. First, based on our real-world experiments and crowd-sourced surveys, we identify and compute a set of features that are likely to impact one's willingness and readiness to respond. These features capture various traits of a person, including one's personality and social interaction pattern. They are computed from several sources, including one's social media posts, social profile, and social media activities. Second, we train a statistical model to infer the contribution (weight) of each feature to one's willingness and readiness, which are then used to predict one's overall *likelihood to respond*. Third, we develop a recommendation algorithm that selects a subset of people based on the output of the statistical model. As explained later, our algorithm is designed to maximize the overall response rate of a request. Special care is thus needed to overcome the inherent imperfections (prediction errors) in any statistical models. To demonstrate the effectiveness of our approach, we have conducted extensive experiments including real-world, live experiments. Currently, we have implemented our models based on Twitter, which should be easily adapted to other social media platforms. As a result, our work offers three unique contributions.

- We build an extensible, feature-based model of predicting one's *likelihood to respond* to an information request on social media. Specifically, we identify a set of key features and their contributions (weights) to model a person's *willingness* and *readiness* to respond.
- We develop a recommendation algorithm that automatically selects a set of targeted strangers to maximize the overall response rate of an information request.
- We have applied qCrowd to real world scenarios. The results including demonstrated effectiveness provide validity and insights for building this new class of crowd-powered, intelligent information collection systems.

RELATED WORK

Our work is most closely related to a recent effort in studying the feasibility of directly asking targeted strangers on social media (Twitter) for information [27]. This work studies people's response patterns to questions in two domains and finds that it is feasible to obtain useful information from targeted strangers on social media with an average response rate of 42%. While their findings motivate our work, we advance their manual selection of targeted strangers by *automating* the selection process.

Our work is also related to a large number of efforts in online social Q&A services (e.g., [1, 2, 17]). Most of these services rely on volunteers to answer posted questions. To help get better answers faster, there are a number of efforts on automatically identifying suitable answerers for a given question [10, 20, 23, 24, 31, 40, 41]. Most of them however model the *ability* of potential answerers instead of their *willingness* or *readiness* to answer questions as we do.

Since we model a person's traits based on one's social media behavior, our work is related to a rich body of work on modeling people traits from social media, including location [13], demographics [33, 35], gender [35], personality [19], and political orientation [33, 35]. Like these works, we use one's social media posts and social networking activities (e.g., responding to other posts) to model personal traits, including personality and response behavior. Unlike these works, which model general traits of people, ours focuses on modeling the traits related to one's willingness and readiness to respond to a stranger's information requests on social media.

There is also work on studying and modeling people's responsiveness and availability in various situations (e.g., [8, 9, 26, 32, 38]). Closest to ours is studying response behavior in online social networks, such as Twitter [26, 32, 38]. While these studies focus on the behavior occurred *within* one's own social network [32, 38], ours examines how people would respond to *strangers* on an open social network. There is also work on modeling one's responsiveness to incoming instant messages [8] and availability [9] based on one's desktop computer activities. While we model similar traits of people (e.g., responsiveness and availability), our work differs in its use of one's social behavior, such as the content of their posts and social networking activities, which poses different technical challenges.

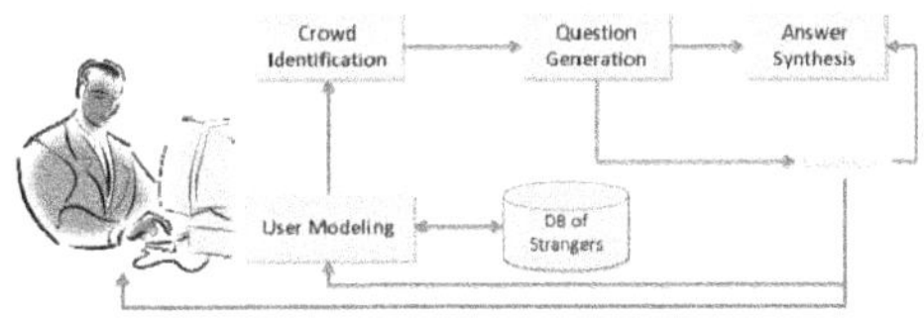

Figure 2. qCrowd overview.

OUR SYSTEM

We provide an overview of qCrowd and its applications.

Overview

As shown in Figure 2, qCrowd has four key components. The *user modeling* component creates a feature-based profile for each potential target on Twitter based on his/her tweeting activities, including the tweets posted. Each profile contains a set of computed features for modeling one's willingness, ability, and readiness to respond to a request. Such computed profiles are stored in a database. This component also updates the profile of a user who is already in the database. Based on a user's profile, the *crowd identification* component dynamically selects suitable targets to engage with. After a targeted person is identified, the *question generation* component generates a question suitable to the context (e.g., with a proper greeting) and then sends the question to the target via Twitter. The *answer synthesis* component parses and collates the received responses.

Unlike a traditional intelligent user interface that focuses on aiding human-computer interaction, qCrowd presents an intelligent user interface that facilitates human-computer-human interaction. In particular, it helps an information requester (e.g., a police officer) to better engage with a crowd (e.g., people happened to be near a crime scene) on social media to accomplish information solicitation tasks. The user interface of qCrowd is thus designed to facilitate such computer-mediated, human-human interaction. It allows a user to interact with qCrowd in one of three modes: (1) manual, (2) auto, and (3) mixed.

In the manual mode, a user (e.g., a marketer who wants to engage customers of a brand) watches a Twitter stream and manually selects individuals to send questions, composes the question, and synthesizes the answers received (Figure 3). In the auto mode, qCrowd performs these functions automatically but presents the results to the user (e.g., Figure 1). It can also run in a mixed mode, where one component (e.g., crowd selection) runs in the auto mode while another (e.g., question generation) runs manually. It always shows the user system-computed results (e.g., selected crowd) while allowing the user to interactively control the engagement process (e.g., editing and sending a question).

Our approach is easily applicable to different social platforms, as long as qCrowd has access to the needed information, such as one's social media posts and social interaction activities. It can then compute needed features and infer one's likelihood to respond to an information request. For example, in addition to our Twitter-based implementation, qCrowd technologies are also applied to enterprise social platforms, which support multiple types of social media activities, including online communities and forums.

Current Applications

Since many people disclose location-based information (e.g., where they are) or their opinions/experiences about a product or event on social media, we have built two applications focusing on collecting two types of information on Twitter: location-based information (e.g., airport security check wait time) and people's opinions about a product or service (e.g., cameras, tablets, and food trucks). While each is general enough to represent a class of applications, the two are also distinct enough from each other, which allow us to test the generality of our approach.

Our work should also be easily extended to support other types of information collections. For example, we are applying qCrowd to information solicitations in crisis and emergency situations, since its true potential is to collect time-sensitive information from a diverse population. However, there may be new challenges that we have not encountered in our current applications. For example, we may need to consider privacy concerns if soliciting potentially sensitive information about people.

DATA COLLECTION

To build a model for predicting one's likelihood to respond, we ran qCrowd in the manual mode to collect three data sets for both training and testing purposes. Our first two data sets were obtained in the process of collecting location-based information—airport security check wait time—via Twitter. Specifically, a human operator used qCrowd to manually identify people at an airport in the United States based on their tweets and then ask them for the airport security check wait time. Here is an example:

@bbx *If you went through security at JFK, can you reply with your wait time? Info will be used to help other travelers.*

Initially, one human operator asked 589 users and obtained 245 responses (42% response rate), which became our first data set *TSA-Tracker*-1. To collect more data in this domain, a different human operator then asked additional 409

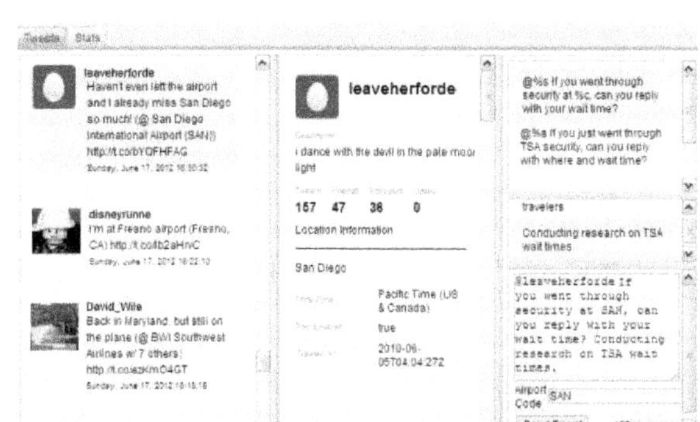

Figure 3. qCrowd user interface in the manual mode. The left panel shows a set of filtered (by rules) tweets of those at an airport. The human operator examines the profile of a user and decides whom to engage (middle panel). The right panel allows the operator to compose questions to send.

users and received 134 responses (33% response rate), which became our second data set, *TSA-Tracker-2*. Our third data set was obtained using the same method but by asking people on Twitter to describe their product/service experience. We asked people's opinions about three types of products: digital cameras, tablet computers, and food trucks. Here are two examples:

@johnny Trying to learn about tablets...sounds like you have Galaxy Tab 10.1. How fast is it?

@bobby Interested in Endless Summer. Sounds like you have eaten there. Is the menu large or small (for a food truck)?

A human operator asked 1540 users, and 474 responses were received (31% response rate). We refer to this data set *Product*. In each data set, we also collected the most recent tweets (up to 200 tweets) of each person engaged.

BASELINES

The human operators managed to achieve an average response rate of 31-42% in a manual process. The process however was found quite difficult as it required the human operators to read the relevant tweets and identify the right people to engage in real time. We thus created two baselines to assess the difficulty of the process and potential value of our automated approach. Our first baseline is to engage random people on social media without any filtering. Our second baseline is to let end users (crowd) identify and select targeted strangers to engage on social media.

Asking Random Strangers

To create a true baseline, we sent questions to random people on Twitter without considering their willingness, ability, or readiness to respond to these questions. Specifically, qCrowd *automatically* sent a question to a random person on Twitter at a fixed time interval (every 5 minutes). We created three different Twitter accounts and experimented with questions on three general topics: weather, public safety, and education. Here is an example question:

@needy Doing a research about your local public safety. Would you be willing to answer a related question?

Our aim was to send 250 questions on each topic. However, all three accounts were temporarily suspended by Twitter after sending a certain number of questions. On the weather topic, our system was able to send 187 questions and received only 7 responses. On public safety, 178 questions were sent and only 6 responses received. On education, only 3 responses were received after sending 101 questions. The response rates on all three topics were very low (well below 5% on each topic). This implies that it is ineffective to ask random strangers on social media without considering their willingness, ability, or readiness to answer questions. Moreover, the account suspension suggests that many people who received our questions may have flagged our account as a spamming account [27]. Thus, identifying the right people to engage is critical to the success of qCrowd.

Crowd as Human Operator

Our second baseline was created by crowdsourcing a human operator's task to test a crowd's ability to identify the right targets to engage. We were also curious about the criteria that a crowd would use to identify targeted strangers.

To do so, we conducted two surveys on CrowdFlower, a crowd-sourcing platform [7]. The first survey asked each participant to predict if a displayed Twitter user would be *willing* to respond to a given question, assuming that the user has the ability to answer. The second survey asked each participant to predict *how soon* the person would respond assuming that s/he is willing to respond. The participant was also required to provide an explanation of their prediction. We deliberately designed two separate surveys to understand a participant's criteria for judging one's willingness and readiness, respectively and to avoid potential interferences.

Willingness Survey

The first survey had two settings depending on what information of a Twitter user was displayed to the participant. In the first setting, only the user's tweets were displayed. In the second setting, the user's twitter screen name, twitter profile URL, and tweets were all displayed. For each setting, we randomly picked 200 Twitter users, 100 each from the *TSA-tracker-1* and *Product* dataset. In each setting, we recruited 100 participants on CrowdFlower, each of which was given 2 randomly selected users for prediction. We measured the crowd's prediction accuracy by comparing their predictions with the ground truth—whether the users responded to our requests in our data collection process.

In the first setting (displaying tweets only), our participants were 29% correct in their prediction. In the second setting, they were 38% correct. Since everything was the same in both settings except the amount of information disclosed about a potential target, the additional information displayed in the second setting helped the prediction. These results suggest that it is also difficult for the crowd to identify targeted strangers to engage. By the comments of the participants who made correct predictions, several types of information were used in their prediction.

Most (56.7%) mentioned that they made their predictions by observing people' past interaction behavior: *"Talks to others and responds", and "The user seems extremely social, both asking questions and replying to others".*

Some participants (10.45%) used one's activeness on Twitter as a predictor: *"This user tweets a lot, seems very chatty"*. Some participants (10.45%) used one's profile information: *"The user's job is Social Media representative..., his job involves answering questions"*; and *"being a social media guy and his tagline saying..."*

Several (6%) used one's re-tweeting behavior to predict: *"No (the person would not respond). Most of the tweets are retweets instead of anything personal"*. It is interesting to note that some were able to use one's personality (7.4%) for

Responsiveness Features	Computation
Mean Response Time, Median Response Time Mode Response Time, Max Response Time, Min Response Time	Avg(T), Med (T), Mod(T), Max(T), Min(T) T denote previous response times computed from users' past responses to questions asked in Twitter
Past Response Rate	N_R/N_D, N_R is the number of the user's previous responses and N_D is the number of direct questions the user was asked in Twitter.
Proactiveness	N_R/N_I, N_R is the number of user's responses and N_I is the number of indirect questions the user was asked in Twitter, where an indirect question does not contain mentions of the user's name

Table 1. Responsiveness features and their computation.

prediction: *"I think he won't respond. Doesn't seem to be very friendly"*.

We also examined how often the above types of information were used by participants whose predictions were *incorrect*. We obtained similar results: users' past responsiveness (identified by 41% of such participants), one's activeness (7%), profile information (6%), re-tweeting behavior (4%), and personality (3%), respectively. Since the participants used a similar set of factors regardless their prediction results, this suggests that none of the factors alone is perfect for identifying a potential responder.

Readiness Survey

Our second survey asked each participant to judge how *soon* a person would respond to an information request, assuming that the person would respond. We used a multiple choice question with varied time windows as choices (e.g., within an hour and within a day). In this survey, we randomly chose 100 people from our collected data sets (50 from *TSA-Tracker-1* and 50 from *Product*). We recruited 50 participants on CrowdFlower, each of which was given two randomly chosen people and their twitter handlers. We computed prediction correctness by comparing participants' predictions with the ground truth. For example, if a participant predicted that person *X* will respond within an hour, however, the response was not received in time, the prediction is then incorrect. Our participants were 58% correct. Through their comments, the participants identified several factors that helped them in their predictions: 25% thought that one's activeness (frequent users) and steadiness (consistent usage patterns) on Twitter were good indicators; 30% of them considered the promptness of a person's response on Twitter a good predictor.

Overall, our crowd-sourcing experiments were very valuable. We learned that it is difficult for an end user to identify the right targets to engage, which justifies our effort to automate the process by recommending suitable targets. Moreover, our participants used several criteria, including one's personality and responsiveness, to identify the right targets. These criteria provided us with an empirical base (feature categories) to build our computational model.

FEATURE EXTRACTION

To model one's willingness and readiness to respond to information solicitations on Twitter, we have identified five categories of features: *Responsiveness, Profile*, *Personality*, *Activity*, and *Readiness*. These features are mainly derived from one's tweet content, twitter profile, and social activities on Twitter. The first four categories, modeling a user's willingness to respond, were mainly identified by the participants in our first survey. The last category, modeling one's readiness to respond, was based on our second survey results but augmented to include additional features.

Responsiveness

According to our survey participants, one's response behavior on Twitter was the top factor for predicting one's likelihood to respond. We have thus identified two key features to measure one's overall responsiveness based on his/her tweeting behavior. One is *response time*, measuring how *quickly* a person normally responds to a post directed to him/her on Twitter. Our hypothesis is that the faster the person responds, the more likely the person is willing to do so. The other feature is *proactiveness*, measuring how active usually a person is to respond to any posts on Twitter including the ones not directed to him/her. The more proactive a person is, the more likely the person is willing to answer a request. Table 1 shows the two features and their variants. To compute the value of these features, qCrowd collects each person's interaction history, including one's responses to other individuals on Twitter.

Profile

Based on one's profile, our survey participants assessed the *socialness* of a person and used it as a predictor. We thus compute *CountSocialWords*, the frequency of social words appearing in a profile, including "*talking*" and "*communication*", adopted from the LIWC social process category [37]. We also added a set of words related to modern social activities, such as "*tweeting*" and "social network".

Personality

Some of our survey participants mentioned personality being one of the factors for predicting one's likelihood to respond. We hypothesize that one's personality traits, such as friendliness and extraversion, may be related to one's willingness to respond to strangers. Since it is impractical to ask a stranger on social media to take a personality test, we need to derive one's personality from his/her social media behavior. Several researchers have found that word usage in one's writings, such as blogs and essays, can be used to infer one's personality [16, 18, 19, 21, 25, 37]. Inspired by the existing work, we used the LIWC dictionary to compute one's personality traits [34, 37]. LIWC defines 68 different categories, each of which contains several dozens to hundreds of words [34]. For each person, we compute a LIWC-based personality as follows.

Readiness Features	Computation
Tweeting Likelihood of the Day	T_D/N, where T_D is the number of tweets sent by the user on day D and N is the total number of tweets.
Tweeting Likelihood of the Hour	T_H/N, where T_H is the number of tweets sent by the user on hour H and N is the total number of tweets.
Tweeting Steadiness	$1/\sigma$, where σ is the standard deviation of the elapsed time between consecutive tweets of users, computed from users' most recent K tweets (where K is set, for example, to 20).
Tweeting Inactivity	$T_Q - T_L$, where T_Q is the time the question was sent and T_L is the time the user last tweeted.

Table 2. Readiness features and their computation.

Let g be a LIWC category, N_g denotes the number of occurrences of words in that category in one's tweets and N denotes the total number of words in his/her tweets. A score for category g is then: N_g/N.

We exclude one's re-tweets when computing LIWC-based personality, since re-tweets are the content generated by others. Besides LIWC categories, psychologists have developed several personality models. One of the most well-studied is the Big5 personality model [15, 29]. It characterizes a person's traits from five aspects (also known as OCEAN): *openness*, *conscientiousness*, *extraversion*, *agreeableness*, and *neuroticism*.

Previous work [16, 18, 19, 21] has revealed correlations between Big5 personality [15] and LIWC-based features. More recently, Yarkoni [39] shows that correlations also exist between LIWC features and lower-level facets of Big5 [15]. Motivated by these findings and based on the word use in one's tweets, we compute one's additional personality features: Big5 traits and their lower-level facets.

To derive personality scores for each of the Big5 dimensions and their lower-level facets, we use the coefficients of correlation between them and LIWC categories [39]. We use a linear combination of LIWC categories (for which correlation was found statistically significant by Yarkoni [39]), where correlation coefficients are used as weights.

We extract a total of 103 personality features: 68 LIWC features, 5 Big5 traits, and 30 Big5 lower-level facets.

Activity

As indicated by our survey participants, one's demonstrated activity pattern on Twitter could signal one's willingness to respond. Intuitively, the more active a user is, the more likely the person will respond to a request. To capture this intuition, we compute two features: the total number of posts made overall (*MsgCount*) and daily (*DailyMsgCount*). These features were also used in prior works [14, 22] and help distinguish "sporadic" vs. "steady" activeness. We hypothesize that more "steady" users are more dependable and are more likely to respond when asked.

Several of our participants also noted re-tweeting as a factor to determine one's likelihood to respond. We thus incorporate one's retweeing behavior by two features: retweeting ratio (*RetweetRatio*), the ratio between the total number of retweets, and the total number of tweets sent, and daily retweeting ratio (*DailyRetweetRatio*), the ratio between the total number of retweets and the total number of tweets sent daily. These features help us distinguish users who create their own content vs. those who mostly retweet others' [11, 14]. We hypothesize that users who create their own content more often may be more willing to respond to a question, since responding involves content creation.

Readiness

Even if a person is willing to respond to a request, s/he may not be ready to respond at the time of request due to various reasons. For example, the person is in the middle of something and unable to respond immediately; or the person is experiencing a device malfunction (e.g., a dying battery) and unable to respond. The ability to predict one's readiness becomes more important when it requires time-sensitive responses, e.g., an information request in a crisis situation. However, one's readiness is highly context dependent and often difficult to capture as shown in our survey.

We thus use several features to approximate one's readiness based on the factors identified by our survey participants. Table 2 lists all the readiness features and their computation. Our rationale of choosing this set of features is two-fold. First, these features are good indicators of one's readiness from a particular aspect. For example, *Tweeting Inactivity* implies one's unavailability. A larger value suggests either that the person is busy and hence uninterruptible, or that s/he is out of reach. Second, these features are easy and fast to compute as only one's tweeting activity is used.

Feature Analysis

In total, we identify 119 features to model one's willingness and readiness to respond to a request on social media. Since we do not expect all features to contribute to the models equally, we performed a series of Chi-square tests with Bonferroni correction to identify statistically significant features that distinguish people who responded from those who did not. Using our *TSA-Tracker*-1 data set, we found 45 significant features (False Discovery Rate was 2.8%). In *TSA-Tracker*-2, we found 13 significant features (False Discovery Rate was 11.2%). For the *Product* data set, 33 features were identified as significant (False Discovery Rate was 4.2%). Table 3 shows a common set of five significant features belonging to four feature categories across all three data sets. We have also run extensive experiments with various feature combinations to hope to find a combination that has significantly discriminative power. We discovered a combination of four top features: *communication* (a LIWC feature), *past response rate*, *tweeting inactivity*, and *tweeting likelihood of the day*. As shown later, this combination produces very impressive prediction results.

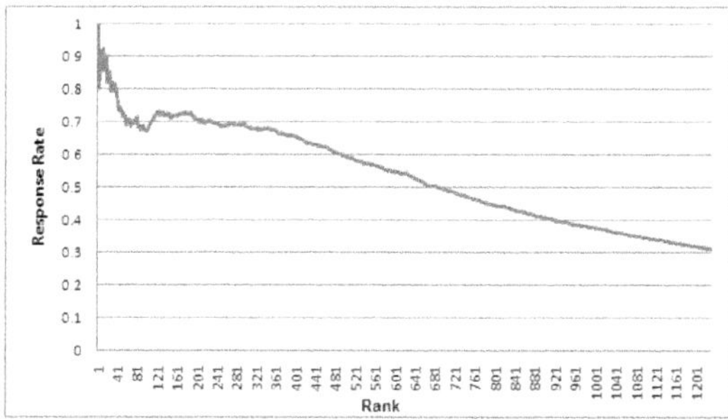

Figure 4. Response rate in the training set with rank of individuals. A response rate R_i is obtained when top i individuals are asked from the training set.

Figure 5. Response rate in the test set with rank of individuals. A response rate R_i is obtained when top i individuals are asked from the test set.

STATISTICAL MODELS

Using the features identified above, we build statistical models that predict a person's likelihood to respond. To do so, we partition each of our data sets randomly into *K* parts for *K*-fold cross validation. For each person in a training set, we compute all his/her features. The features and the person's response information (responded or not-responded) are then used to train a statistical model. Given a person in a test set and his/her computed features, the trained model outputs a probabilistic score that estimates the likelihood for the person to respond.

Formally, let $\boldsymbol{x}_i$ be the feature vector of the *i*th person in a data set, and y_i be the response label, such that if the person responded, $y_i = 1$; otherwise $y_i = 0$. In a simplified model, we assume that there is a unit benefit *B* of receiving a response and a unit cost *C* of sending a question. However, in reality, this assumption may not suffice. For example, the benefit of receiving additional answers to the same question may diminish as the number of answers grows. To build an accurate prediction model, we want to minimize prediction errors. Depending on the application, one type of error may be more costly than the other. For example, in one of our applications, the cost of sending a question may be much smaller than the benefit of receiving an answer. In this case, false negatives (e.g., missed people who would have responded) are more costly than false positives (e.g., selected people who do not respond).

However, most of the models typically do not differentiate two kinds of misclassification errors: false positive and false negative. By default, the classifier-building algorithm assumes that the designer wishes to minimize the overall misclassification rate. Similarly, a standard regression model does not distinguish between overestimating and underestimating probabilities, which in turn results in different types of misclassification errors.

Given the above considerations, we handle the difference in cost by properly weighing the training samples, assuming the unit cost and unit benefit. We weigh our training examples as follows. Positive examples (i.e., people who responded) are weighted by $B - C$, whereas negative ones (i.e., those who did not respond) are weighted by *C*. In other words, a false negative error, which is a misclassification of a positive example, incurs a missed-opportunity cost of $B - C$, where a false positive, which is a misclassification of a negative example, incurs a cost *C*.

We have used two popular statistical models in WEKA [6]: Support Vector Machines (SVM) and Logistic Regression, to predict the probability for a person to respond.

Past Response Rate (Responsiveness), ***Tweet Inactivity*** (Readiness), ***Excitement-Seeking*** (Personality), ***Cautiousness*** (Personality), ***DailyMsgCount*** (Activity)

Table 3. Statistically significant features and their category common to all three data sets.

RECOMMENDATION ALGORITHM

Our trained statistical model can be used in various ways to recommend a set of people to engage. The simplest is to use it as a binary classifier, which just predicts a person as a *responder* or *non-responder*. qCrowd can then engage those who are classified as responders. Alternatively, qCrowd can rank the people by the probability scores produced by the statistical models and then select the top-*K* to engage. However, due to inherent imperfections (prediction errors) in any prediction models, in reality, the predicted top-*K* people may not necessarily be the best choices who will maximize the overall response rate. To maximize the overall response rate for a given set of candidates, we thus have developed the following algorithm.

For each candidate *i*, our models compute a probability p_i. We then sort all candidates by the corresponding probabilities in a decreasing order: $\{\boldsymbol{p}_1,\ldots,\boldsymbol{p}_n\}$. We focus on intervals in this linear order rather than looking at all possible subsets of candidates. The justification for this restriction is that the linear orders generated by the models exhibit a good correlation with response rates. Figure 4 shows that in general the higher rank of an individual is, the higher the average response rate is (response rate achieved by asking all individuals with a higher rank). Here one's rank is determined by his/her computed probability. A person ranked first means his likelihood to respond is greater than or equal to that of rest. Figure 5 shows a similar curve when the model generated from a training set is applied to a test set. While both show that the probability to respond helps predict response rates, they also show that the top segment containing the highest ranked candidates may *not* produce the overall maximal response rate.

	TSA-tracker-1		TSA-tracker-2		Product	
	SVM	Logistic	SVM	Logistic	SVM	Logistic
Precision	0.62	0.60	0.52	0.51	0.67	0.654
Recall	0.63	0.61	0.53	0.55	0.71	0.62
F1	0.625	0.606	0.525	0.53	0.689	0.625
AUC	0.657	0.599	0.592	0.514	0.716	0.55

Table 4. Performance of prediction models.

Thus, our approach involves selecting an interval $[i, ,j]$ ($1\leq i < j \leq n$) from the training set, where the corresponding interval subset $\{p_i,\ldots,p_j\}$ produces an overall maximal response rate among all interval subsets. In our selection, we ignore short intervals at the top of the ranking. The rationale is that the variance in these small sets is large. A short interval that appears to produce a high response rate in the training set does not imply that the corresponding interval in the test set also has a high response rate. We also experimented with a restricted choice of intervals: choosing only those that extend to the top $[i, n]$. We have observed that restricting to intervals $[i, n]$ rather than $[i, j]$ produces sub-optimal results. The best subinterval $[i_r, j_r]$ in the training defines a corresponding sub-interval $[i_s, j_s]$ in the test set, based on percentiles. That is, if m is the cardinality of the test set, then $i_s = [(i_r{\cdot}m)/n]$ and $j_s = [(j_r{\cdot}m)/n]$.

We can also incorporate additional constraints in our interval selection. For example, if a minimum size of the interval is specified, our method will ignore intervals that are smaller than the specified minimum.

EVALUATION

To test the performance of our predictive models and recommendation algorithm, we have conducted an extensive set of experiments.

Evaluating Prediction Model

One key goal is to predict the *likelihood* for a stranger on social media to respond to our information requests. To evaluate the performance of our prediction models, we adopted a set of standard performance metrics including precision, recall, F1, and AUC (Area under ROC curve). For each data set, we performed 5-fold cross validation experiments with uniform weights, where $B - C = C = 1$.

Table 4 shows the results for different data sets using SVM and Logistic Regression. Overall, the SVM-based model

	TSA-tracker-1	TSA-tracker-2	Product
Baseline	42%	33%	31%
Binary classification	62%	52%	67%
Top-K selection	61%	54%	67%
Our algorithm	67%	56%	69%

Table 5. Comparison of average response rates for different recommendation approaches.

Interval Size	Optimal Interval	Response Rate	Recommendation Recall
25%	[67%, 92%]	76%	37%
50%	[46%, 96%]	68%	64%
75%	[19%, 94%]	53%	82%
100%	[0%, 100%]	31%	100%

Table 6. Response rate and recall by our recommendation algorithm with fixed size interval (Product Data, all features, SVM Model).

outperformed logistic regression. The SVM-based model for the *Product* data set also achieved the highest AUC value (0.716). Since the SVM-based model performed better in our experiments, we report various results obtained using this model in the rest of the paper.

Evaluating Recommendation Algorithm

As described earlier, our algorithm aims at selecting a targeted population to maximize the overall response rate. We thus compared the overall response rate achieved by qCrowd against our baseline. Our baseline is the response rates achieved by a human operator during our data collection process. For testing purpose, we used "*asking at least K% of people from the original set*" as a constraint to search for the interval that maximizes the response rate. We computed the response rates on all three data sets with varied K (e.g., K=5%, …, 90%) to find the respective optimal intervals. For comparison purpose, we also computed the response rates achieved using a simple binary classification (response rate is the precision of the predictive model) and simply selecting the top-K (e.g., K=5%, …, 90%.) people by their computed probabilities.

Table 5 shows the results achieved by different approaches. Our algorithm outperformed others in all three data sets.

Evaluating Recall of Recommendation

Although our goal is to maximize the overall response rate, we are also interested in finding out what percentage of actual responders that qCrowd can identify. This essentially measures the "recall" of our algorithm. When using a top-K selection, on average, the recall was 57%, 45%, and 63% for the three data sets, respectively. Using our recommendation algorithm, on average over varied K (the minimal percentage of people to ask), the recall was 57%, 46%, and 65%. Since the recall is affected by the number of people are actually engaged, we performed a set of experiments with varied, fixed interval sizes. As shown in Table 6, as the fixed interval size (in percentiles) increases, the response rate decreases and the recall improves. In practice, we want to find an "optimal" interval size that achieves a balanced high response rate (among the recommended most people would respond) and high recall (most of those who are likely to respond were recommended).

Evaluating the Use of Different Feature Sets

We also wanted to see the effect of different feature uses on response rates. Table 7 shows various response rates using

Feature Set	Response Rate		
	TSA-tracker-1	TSA-tracker-2	Product
All	0.79	0.72	0.78
Significant	0.83	0.75	0.82
Top-10 Significant	0.83	0.74	0.81
Top-4 features	0.82	0.73	0.83
Common significant features	0.81	0.72	0.82

Table 7. Response rates using our algorithm for different feature uses, minimum interval was 5%, SVM Model.

our algorithm with different feature sets when the minimum percentage to ask was set at 5%. The set of statistically significant features performed the best. It is notable that the top-4 features that we discovered (*communication*, *past response rate*, *tweeting inactivity*, and *tweeting likelihood of the day*) produced the best response rate for the *Product* data set and also performed well across all the data sets. Commonly significant features across all 3 data sets (listed in Table 3) also performed reasonably well. This implies that our features are fairly domain agnostic.

When we tested on varied K values (e.g., K=5%, …, 90%. etc.), we found that use of statistically significant features yields average response rates of 69%, 66%, and 72% for *TSA-tracker-1*, *TSA-tracker-2*, and *Product* data sets, respectively. These results show a significant improvement over our two baselines: (1) the response rate (<< 5%) achieved by randomly sending questions to strangers, and (2) the response rate (31-42%) achieved by a human operator during the data collection process.

Domain Sensitivity

We randomly selected 500 users from *TSA-tracker-1*, built a SVM-based model using commonly significant features, and then applied it to the *Product* data set and vice versa. The average response rates (with minimum interval size 5%) were 70% for *TSA-Tracker-1* and 64% for *Product*. This shows that our models are fairly domain independent.

Varied Cost and Benefit

So far we presented results with statistical models trained with equally weighed positive (responded) and negative (not-responded) examples, where B – C = C = 1. To test how our models perform with varied benefit and cost, we repeated our experiments with different benefit (B) to cost (C) ratio with C = 1. We observed varied response rates using our SVM-based model (Table 8). We noticed the slight improvement of response rates with the increased benefit (B) to cost (C) ratio. This validates our hypothesis that in a system like ours minimizing misclassifications of false negative errors improves prediction.

Live Experiments

In addition to evaluating the effectiveness of our work on previously collected data sets, we also conducted live experiments. qCrowd was set on the auto mode and dynamically selected strangers on Twitter to send them questions to collect security check wait time at different airports and product experience. In the first case, qCrowd used Twitter's Search API and a set of rules to first identify 500 users who tweeted about being at any US airport. From this set, it randomly asked 100 users for the security wait time. From the remaining 400 users, qCrowd used the recommendation algorithm to identify 100 users for questioning. It used the SVM-based model with the identified significant features of *TSA-tracker-1*. We waited 48 hours for the responses. 29 of the 100 users from the first set responded (29% response rate) and 66 out of the 100 users from the second set responded (66% response rate). The same process was repeated for sending product-related questions. The only difference was that the initial set of 500 users was identified using Twitter's Search API and a set of rules to detect users who had tweeted about digital cameras, tablet computers, or food-trucks. Response rate by random questioning was 26% and our algorithm achieved 60%. Thus, our live experiments also demonstrated the effectiveness of our work in a real world setting.

DISCUSSIONS

Compared to traditional social Q&A systems, our work offers two unique advantages: *activeness* and *timeliness* in collecting desired information. qCrowd *actively* seeks out and solicits information from the right people at the *right time* on social media. It is particularly suitable for collecting *accurate* and *up-to-date* information about specific situations (e.g., crowd movement at an airport) from the people who are or were just in the situation. However, the dynamic and complex nature of social media also poses unique challenges for us. Below we discuss several limitations of our current work and corresponding design implications for building this new class of systems.

Skew in the User Base

Our current model favors active users on social media. These users are associated with a higher level of willingness to be engaged and hence are more likely to be targeted by our system. As a result, the selected targets may be skewed. On the other hand, it is difficult to create a model that "promotes" inactive users due to a lack of information on these users. If not careful, engaging inactive, unknown users could jeopardize the success of the whole operation as demonstrated by our experiments. Therefore, our ongoing work is to develop methods that can identify "inactive" users, e.g., those similar to active ones in comparable aspects like personality instead of their activity patterns.

Benefit to Cost Ratio	*TSA-Tracker-1*	*TSA-Tracker-2*	*Product*
2	0.83	0.75	0.82
5	0.85	0.79	0.84
10	0.87	0.81	0.87
100	0.88	0.82	0.87

Table 8. Response rates achieved w/ different benefit to cost ratio, minimum interval 5%, SVM with significant features.

Modeling the Fitness of a Stranger to Engage

Currently, we focus on modeling one's likelihood to respond, based on this person's ability, willingness, and readiness to respond to a request on social media. However, our current model does not consider one's traits that may impact the overall *quality* of received responses or cause unexpected viral effects. For example, a more dutiful and trustworthy person may provide a higher quality response, while one's hatefulness might prompt malicious behavior on social media. Moreover, information exchange in qCrowd occurs mainly between the asker (the system) and answerer (a stranger), without any moderation by a larger group. This removes the potential reputation and filtering benefits of typical Social Q&A sites, like Quora, to govern the quality of crowd-sourced information. To ensure the quality of responses and prevent potential mischief, we thus must assess the overall *fitness* of a stranger to engage on social media. Beyond modeling one's likelihood to respond, a fitness model should include people traits that impact various aspects of an information collection process on social media, such as the quality of responses received and potential influence of various response behaviors.

Handling Complex Situations

Our current goal is to recommend the right set of strangers to achieve a particular response rate. While this can handle many real-world applications, it does not cover complex information collection situations. Suppose that our goal is to collect at least K data points (e.g., wait times) each hour at an airport. In practice, for a given hour, there may be not enough candidates—people who were at the airport and tweeted about their location. To handle such situations, we must model and estimate the size of the overall candidate pool in various situations. This may involve estimating the probability of people appearing at the desired location or the probability of publicizing their location on social media. In addition, different applications may have different cost and benefit measures of sending a request and getting a response, respectively. Such benefit or cost may also change as the responses are received. Assume that the goal is to obtain opinions from multiple people. The benefit of getting additional answers diminishes as the received answers start to converge. To systematically handle various constraints, an optimization-based model is then needed to incorporate all the constraints (including benefit and cost) into one objective function, which computes the net benefit. The goal of our recommendation is then to find a targeted population such that the net benefit is maximized.

Handling Unexpected Answers

Our goal is to ask a targeted population on social media to respond to our requests. Due to the public nature of social media, people who are *not* asked can still see our posted questions and may volunteer to provide us with an answer. For example, when collecting our *Product* data set, an owner of a food truck unexpectedly responded to one of our questions. Our current approach has not taken such situations into account. It would certainly be interesting to incorporate such situations into our methodology. This may also become a way to "grow" potential targets.

Protecting Privacy

Although people volunteer information about themselves on social media, they may not be fully aware how the disclosed information can be used or have complete control over the shared information. We have not conducted in-depth studies on how the people who were selected feel about the process and what their concerns might be. With such information, we can better tune our selection algorithms to exclude people who wish not to be engaged.

CONCLUSIONS

As hundreds of millions of people reveal themselves daily on social media like Twitter, our current research is on how to engage the right people at the right time on social media to crowd-source desired information. To achieve this goal, we are building qCrowd, an intelligent, crowd-powered information collection system. In this paper, we focus on qCrowd's ability to automatically identify and select the right strangers to engage on Twitter. Specifically, we have presented how we model and compute a stranger's likelihood to respond to an information request on social media.

Our current model measures one's willingness and readiness to respond based on a set of features derived from his/her social behavior on Twitter. Using this model, not only can we predict one's probability to respond to a question, but we have also identified a sub-set of features that have significant prediction power. Moreover, we have presented a recommendation algorithm that can automatically select a set of targeted strangers to engage based on their likelihood to respond with the goal of maximizing the overall response rate of the selected population. To validate our work, we have conducted an extensive set of experiments including live ones in a real-world setting. Our experiments demonstrate the effectiveness of both our prediction model and recommendation algorithm. In particular, our results show that qCrowd can achieve an average response rate over 65% in our two application domains, a significant improvement over the response rates achieved by a human operator in the range of 31-42%.

ACKNOWLEDGEMENTS

Research was sponsored by the U.S. Defense Advanced Research Projects Agency (DARPA) under the Social Media in Strategic Communication (SMISC) program, Agreement Number W911NF-12-C-0028. The views and conclusions contained in this document are those of the author(s) and should not be interpreted as representing the official policies, either expressed or implied, of the U.S. Defense Advanced Research Projects Agency or the U.S. Government. The U.S. Government is authorized to reproduce and distribute reprints for Government purposes notwithstanding any copyright notation hereon.

REFERENCES

1. WarriorForum – Internet Marketing Forums, http://www.warriorforum.com/

2. Slickdeals, http://slickdeals.net/forums/forumdisplay.php?f=19
3. Quora, http://www.quora.com/
4. Yahoo Answers, http://www.answers.yahoo.com
5. Facebook Questions, http://www.facebook.com
6. WEKA. http://www.cs.waikato.ac.nz/ml/weka/
7. Crowdflower. http://crowdflower.com/
8. Avrahami, D. and Hudson, Scott E. 2006. Responsiveness in Instant Messaging: Predictive Models Supporting Inter- Personal Communication, In *Proc. CHI 2006*.
9. Begole, J., Tang, J.C., Smith, R.E., and Yankelovich,N. 2002. Work rhythms: Analyzing visualizations of awareness histories of distributed groups. In *Proc. CSCW'02*.
10. Bouguessa, M. Dumoulin, B., and Wang, S. 2008. Identifying authoritative actions in question-answering forums: the case of Yahoo! answers: In *Proc. KDD 2008*.
11. Boyd, D. Golder, S., Lotan, G. 2010. Tweet, Tweet, Retweet: Conversational Aspects of Retweeting on Twitter. In *Proc.HICSS 2010*.
12. Chakrabarti, D., Punera, K.2011., Event Summarization using Tweets, In *Proc. ICWSM 2011*.
13. Cheng, Z., Caverlee, J., and Lee, K.2010. You Are Where You Tweet: A Content-Based Approach to Geo-locating Twitter Users. In *Proc. CIKM 2010*.
14. Castillo, C., Mendoza, M., and Poblete, B. 2011, Information Credibility on Twitter. In *Proc. WWW 2011*.
15. Costa, P.T.,Jr. & McCrae, R.R. 1992. Revised NEO Personality Inventory (NEO-PI-R) and NEO Five-Factor Inventory (NEO-FFI) manual. Odessa, FL: Psychological Assessment Resources.
16. Fast, Lisa A.; Funder, David C. 2008., Personality as manifest in word use: Correlations with self-report, acquaintance report, and behavior. Journal of Personality and Social Psychology, *Vol 94(2), 2008*.
17. Gazan, R (2011). Social Q&A. J. of the Amer. Soc. for Info Science & Technology, 62(12), 2301-2312.
18. Gill, A.J., Nowson, S., Oberlander, J. 2009. What Are They Blogging About? Personality, Topic and Motivation in Blogs, In *Proc. ICWSM 2009*.
19. Golbeck, J. Robles, C., Edmondson, M., Turner, K. 2011. Predicting Personality from Twitter. In *Proc. IEEE SocialCom*.
20. Guo, J., Xu, S., Bao, S., and Yu, Y. 2008. Tapping on the potential of Q&A community by recommending answer providers. In *Proc. CIKM 2008*.
21. Hirsh, J.B. and Peterson, J.B., 2009, Personality and language use in self-narratives Journal of Research in Personality.
22. Lee, K., Eoff, B.D. and Caverlee, J.2011. Seven months with the devils: A long term study of content polluters on Twitter. In *Proc. ICWSM 2011*.
23. Liu, X., Croft, W. B., and Koll, M.2005. Finding experts in community-based question-answering services, In *Proc. CIKM'05*, 315-316.
24. Jurczyk, P., and Agichtein, E., 2007, Discovering authorities in question-answering communities by using link analysis. In *Proc.CIKM 2007*.
25. Mairesse, F., Walker, M. 2006. Words Mark the Nerds: Computational Models of Personality Recognition through Language, In *Proc. of CogSci 2006*.
26. Morris, M., Teevan, J., and Panovich, K. 2010. What Do People Ask Their Social Networks, and Why? A Survey Study of Status Message Q&A Behavior. In *Proc. CHI,2010*.
27. Nichols, Jeffrey, Kang, Jeon-Hyung, 2012, Asking Questions of Targeted Strangers on Social Networks, In *Proc. CSCW2012*.
28. Nichols, J., Mahmud, J., Drews, C., 2012, Summarizing Sporting Events from Twitter., In *Proc. IUI2012*.
29. Norman,W. T. 1963. Toward an adequate taxonomy of personality attributes: replicated factor structure in peer nomination personality rating. Journal of Abnormal and social Psychology, 66:574-583.
30. O'Brien, T. and DeLongis, A. The interactional context of problem-, emotion-, and relationship-focused coping: The role of the big five personality factors. Journal of personality, 64(4):775–813, 1996.
31. Pal, A., Farzan, R., Konstan, Joseph A. and Kraut, Robert E,2011, Early Detection of Potential Experts in Question Answering Communities, In *Proc. UMAP 2011*.
32. Paul, S.A., Hong, L., and Chi, E.H., 2011. "Is Twitter a Good Place for Asking Questions? A Characterization Study", In *Proc. ICWSM'11 Posters*.
33. Pennacchiotti, M., Popescu, A.M. 2011. A Machine Learning Approach to Twitter User Classification, In *Proc. ICWSM 2011*.
34. Pennebaker, J.W., Francis, M.E., Booth, R.J., 2001, Linguistic Inquiry and Word Count. Erlbaum Publishers, Mahwah, NJ.
35. Rao, D., Yarowsky, D., Shreevats, A., Gupta, M. 2010, Classifying Latent User Attributes in Twitter, In *Proc. of SMUC'10*.
36. Sakaki, T., Okazaki, M., Matsuo, Y. 2010, Earthquake shakes twitter users: real-time event detection by social sensors, In *Proc. of WWW 2010*.
37. Tausczik, Yla R. and Pennebaker, James W, 2010. The Psychological Meaning of Words: LIWC and Computerized Text Analysis Methods, In. Journal of Language and Social Psychology 29(1) 24–54
38. Teevan, J., Morris, M., and Panovich, K. 2011. Factors Affecting Response Quantity, Quality, and Speed for Questions Asked via Social Network Status Messages. In *Proc. ICWSM 2011*.
39. Yarkoni, Tal. 2010. Personality in 100,000 words: A large-scale analysis of personality and word usage among bloggers. Journal of Research in Personality.
40. Zhang, J., Ackerman, M. S., and Adamic, L. 2007. Expertise networks in online communities: structure and algorithms. In *Proc. WWW, 2007*.
41. Zhou, Y., Cong, Z., Cui, B., Jensen, C.S., and Yao, J. Routing Questions to the Right Users in Online Communities. In *Proc. ICDE 2009*.

An Approach to Controlling User Models and Personalization Effects in Recommender Systems

Fedor Bakalov[1], **Marie-Jean Meurs**[2,3], **Birgitta König-Ries**[1], **Bahar Sateli**[2], **René Witte**[2], **Greg Butler**[2,3], **and Adrian Tsang**[3,4]
[1]Institute for Computer Science, Friedrich Schiller University of Jena, Germany
[2]Department of Computer Science and Software Engineering, Concordia University, Montréal, QC, Canada
[3]Centre for Structural and Functional Genomics, Concordia University, Montréal, QC, Canada
[4]Department of Biology, Concordia University, Montréal, QC, Canada

ABSTRACT
Personalization nowadays is a commodity in a broad spectrum of computer systems. Examples range from online shops recommending products identified based on the user's previous purchases to web search engines sorting search hits based on the user's browsing history. The aim of such adaptive behavior is to help users to find relevant content easier and faster. However, there are a number of negative aspects of this behavior. Adaptive systems have been criticized for violating the usability principles of direct manipulation systems, namely controllability, predictability, transparency, and unobtrusiveness. In this paper, we propose an approach to controlling adaptive behavior in recommender systems. It allows users to get an overview of personalization effects, view the user profile that is used for personalization, and adjust the profile and personalization effects to their needs and preferences. We present this approach using an example of a personalized portal for biochemical literature, whose users are biochemists, biologists and genomicists. Also, we report on a user study evaluating the impact of controllable personalization on the usefulness, usability, user satisfaction, transparency, and trustworthiness of personalized systems.

ACM Classification Keywords
H.5.2 User Interfaces: Natural language, User-centered design; H.5.4 Hypertext/Hypermedia: Architectures, Navigation, User issues

Author Keywords
adaptive hypermedia, personalization, user modeling, usability

INTRODUCTION
Personalized information systems emerged as an answer to the problem of steadily growing amounts of information and constantly increasing complexity of navigation in the information space that overwhelms the user. These systems are able to learn about the needs of individual users and to tailor the content, appearance, and behavior to the user needs. Examples of personalization range from online shops recommending products identified based on the user's previous purchases to web search engines sorting search hits based on the user's browsing history. The aim of such adaptive behavior is to help users to find relevant content easier and faster. To achieve such behavior, the system needs a user model providing information about users, e.g., about their interests, expertise, background, or traits. It also needs metadata of information resources and some logic or rules that govern how the resources must be delivered to users given their user model.

In most personalized systems, the user model and the process of adaptation are hidden from users. Users see only the resulting personalization effects. But they do not have direct access to the information the system collects about them and do not have control over the personalization behavior. This results in a number of grave usability and privacy problems. It violates two of Nielson's ten usability principles [15]: hiding user models *occludes the system status* and *hinders control over the system*. Jameson in [8] identifies further problems of personalized systems. Preventing users from accessing their user models and controlling personalization has a negative impact on the predictability and transparency of the system. It may also limit the user experience, i.e., due to incompleteness of the user model, the system may filter out relevant and important information. Finally, hindering users from accessing the user model violates privacy legislation of many countries [11, 17]. For instance, according to the German Act on the Protection of Personal Data Used in Teleservices (Gesetz über den Datenschutz bei Telediensten),

> "§7 User's right to information
> The user shall be entitled at any time to inspect, free of charge, stored data concerning his person or his pseudonym at the provider's. The information shall be given electronically if so requested by the user." [1]

To mitigate the usability and privacy problems, personalized systems must provide users full control over the user model and the personalization. However, introducing controllability into a personalized system brings a number of challenges: (1)

Since controllability of personalization has not yet become an integral feature of all personalized systems, an average user might not have developed the mental model of how to control the user model and personalization effects [6]; (2) Controlling adaptation is certainly not the main task the user wants to accomplish in an adaptive system. Therefore, the user might not have sufficient motivation to do it, especially if it requires training or specific skills; (3) In the case of systems applying complex adaptation rules, it might be difficult for users to understand the adaptation process and adjust it to their personal needs.

In this paper, we propose an approach to controlling user models and personalization effects in recommender systems. This approach leverages IntrospectiveViews, a visualization of semantic user models proposed by Bakalov et al. in [4]. It uses the visualization as a means to explain the adaptive behavior to users and to allow them to adjust this behavior to their preferences in an efficient and easy-to-use way. The approach allows users to directly see how a change in the user model affects the personalization. It also includes a method allowing users to apply personalization effects they like or to deactivate them. We present this approach using an example of a portal for biochemical literature, which provides a personalized single point of access to bibliography harvested from multiple scientific databases. Furthermore, we evaluate the impact of our approach on the perception of personalized systems by users, namely on the usefulness, ease of use, ease of learning, satisfaction, and trustworthiness.

The main contributions of this paper are twofold. First, it presents a method that can be applied in various recommender systems for empowering users to adjust user models and personalization effects to their needs and preferences. Second, it provides insights into how users perceive this control.

This paper is organized as follows. Section provides a short overview of the previous research related to controllable personalization and scrutable user models. Section outlines the system components required for controllable personalization in a content aggregating portal. Section presents a graphical user interface and interaction patterns for viewing and editing user models and adjusting personalization effects. In Section , we report on a user study evaluating the impact of giving users control over personalization. Finally, Section summarizes the paper and outlines the directions for our future work.

RELATED WORK

The usability and privacy problems of personalized systems have received much attention in the research areas of adaptive hypermedia and user modeling. A number of approaches have been proposed for scrutable user modeling. For instance, the um_view interface [5] allows traversing through a user model by expanding the tree of leaves and viewing detailed information about the items in the model. VlUM [20] and its successor SIV [9] are capable of visualizing large user models and enable users to get an overview of the whole model, view a subset of related beliefs, filter items by relevance, and obtain detailed information about the displayed items. STyLE-OLM [7] and ViSMod [22] visualize learner models using concept graphs and Bayesian Networks, respectively. However, most approaches to scrutable user modeling are primarily focused on allowing users to view information stored in the model. Little research has been conducted with respect to providing users full control over the user model, including edit operations on the model.

Even less research has been conducted with respect to bridging the changes on the user model initiated by users and the end effects these changes have on the personalization. Czarkowski [6] proposes a system for scrutable adaptive hypertext, in which personalized fragments of web pages are supplemented with textual messages showing what information from the user model was used for personalization. It also allows users to change user models, and hence influence the personalization in the system. More visual approaches to explaining the implication of changes in the user model are proposed by Kliger [10] and Tsandilas and Schraefel [19]. Kliger's PeerGlass architecture, next to personalized content, displays 3D visualizations of the parts of the user model that were used for personalizing the content. Additionally, it allows users to open the user model directly from the personalized page, make necessary changes in it, and see the effect on personalization. Similarly, the system proposed by Tsandilas and Schraefel displays the user model next to the personalized text. A change in the model is projected on the personalized text, so that the user can see the direct link between the user model and the personalization.

The three aforementioned approaches for explaining personalization effects leverage simple and relatively small user models. In contrast, our approach is suitable for the visualization of very large ontology-based user models. It empowers users to obtain an overview of the entire model, filter items, and zoom in and out. It shows semantic relations between items and provides additional information about selected items. It also allows users to edit the status of items, add new items, and delete items from the model in an intuitive and easy-to-use way. In addition, our approach supports multiple personalization effects for a single resource. It allows users to select effects they like for each resource individually. Finally, it allows user to switch personalization on and off.

SYSTEM ARCHITECTURE

In this section, we present the system architecture of a web portal that enables users to view and edit their user models and fine tune personalization effects. We describe the proposed architecture using the example of a portal providing personalized access to bibliography harvested from multiple scientific databases, such as PubMed[1]. The ultimate goal of this portal is to assist scientists in keeping track of relevant literature. To accomplish this goal, users must be able to search publications using keywords and other metadata attributes, e.g., author, title, or publication date. However, the number of returned search hits can be extremely large, e.g., for the search query "bacterial cellulose", the PubMed database returns more than five thousand hits. Therefore, the portal must

[1] http://www.ncbi.nlm.nih.gov/pubmed

provide a method for helping users to identify the most relevant hits. This can be achieved in a number of ways. For instance, the entire set of search hits can be sorted according to the relevance of the interests of individual users. Alternatively, the portal can foreground the most relevant of the user hits. It can also highlight the parts of retrieved content that is likely to be interesting for the user.

Below we describe a system architecture that provides components required for such adaptive behavior. It consists of four units displayed in Figure 1.

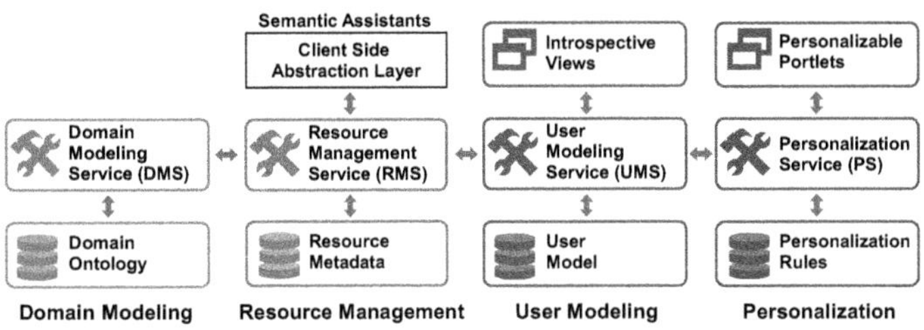

Figure 1. Portal system architecture

Domain Modeling Unit encapsulates the components responsible for storing, accessing, and managing the domain model representing the machine-processable description of the domain knowledge. The domain model is represented as an ontology, formalized in the Web Ontology Language (OWL)[2].

Resource Management Unit is responsible for harvesting and annotating literature from multiple scientific databases. For literature harvesting, we leverage the approach proposed by Schimratzki et al. in [16], whereas the semantic annotation of literature is achieved by processing the retrieved content with named entity extractors provided by the Semantic Assistants framework, an open source framework described in [21].

User Modeling Unit provides the models, mechanisms, and interfaces for managing information about users that are required for adaptation, namely, interests of individual scientists. It is designed as an overlay model: user interests are represented as an overlay of domain concepts defined in the domain ontology. For each concept, the user model stores information about the exact *degree* to which the user is interested in it. The user model is updated following a hybrid approach to user modeling proposed by Bakalov et al. in [3]. This approach supports automatic updates of the model based on a user's browsing history and the semantic structure of the domain knowledge model. Also, it enables users to update their profiles through the user model visualization presented in Section .

Personalization Unit stores personalization rules and provides mechanisms for performing personalization in the portal. As described in detail in Section , the portal content is delivered to users through personalizable portlets[3]. Users can view portlets in standard or personalized states. In a personalized state, users can choose between several personalization effects. For example, they can choose whether publications must be sorted by interest or chronologically. If a portlet is requested in a personalized view, the portlet invokes the personalization service. The service retrieves user personalization preferences to determine what personalization effects must be generated for the given portlet and user. It also retrieves metadata of the requested content and interests of the given user. Based on the metadata, user interests, and personalization preferences, it personalizes the content and passes it to the requesting portlet.

[2]http://www.w3.org/TR/owl-features/

[3]A portlet is a pluggable user interface component of web portals that provides a specific piece of content or an application

USER INTERFACE

The proposed framework was implemented and deployed on an IBM WebSphere Portal Server[4]. Figure 2 displays a personalized page that users see after they have logged in to the portal. This page consists of a number of portlets providing different types of content and functions. The *Query* portlet on the left displays a list of user search queries, which are used by the portal to retrieve publications from scientific databases. This portlet allows users to add, edit, and delete queries and organize them hierarchically. Upon a mouse click on a query, the portal will display a list of matching publications in the *Listing* portlet.

The *Listing* portlet allows users to request various types of semantic assistance on the content displayed. Users can view a list of named entities extracted from the publications or summaries of the publications. All types of assistance supported by the portlet can be seen in the *Semantic Assistants* menu, in which they can choose an assistant they want and set desired view options for the assistant results. Depending on the type of assistant, its results can be displayed in the source text, as an index, a map, or a text in a side portlet. For instance, Figure 2 displays results of the mycoMINE assistant [14], which extracts entities and facts related to fungal enzymes, such as enzymes, assays, genes, substrates and pH, temperature or activity assay conditions. The entities extracted by the assistant are underlined in the text of publications listed in the origin portlet. They are also displayed as an index in a side portlet. The index portlet lists all entities grouped by entity type. By hovering the mouse pointer over an entity in the index, all mentions of this entity will be highlighted in the text of publications. Users can also obtain some additional information about the extracted entities. By clicking an entity in the index, they can get all features of the entity, e.g., alias, abbreviations, and links to scientific databases.

Portal content and results of semantic assistants can be personalized by users. For most portlets, users can select whether they want to see the content in a personalized or a standard view. Users can switch between personalized and standard views using a personalization drop-down menu. This menu can be opened by clicking the heart icon on the portlet title bar. By selecting the *Turn personalization off* command, the portlet will be turned into standard view, i.e., no personalization will be applied on the content of the portlet. By selecting the *Turn personalization on*, the portlet will be displayed in a personalized view.

[4]`http://www.ibm.com/software/websphere/portal/`

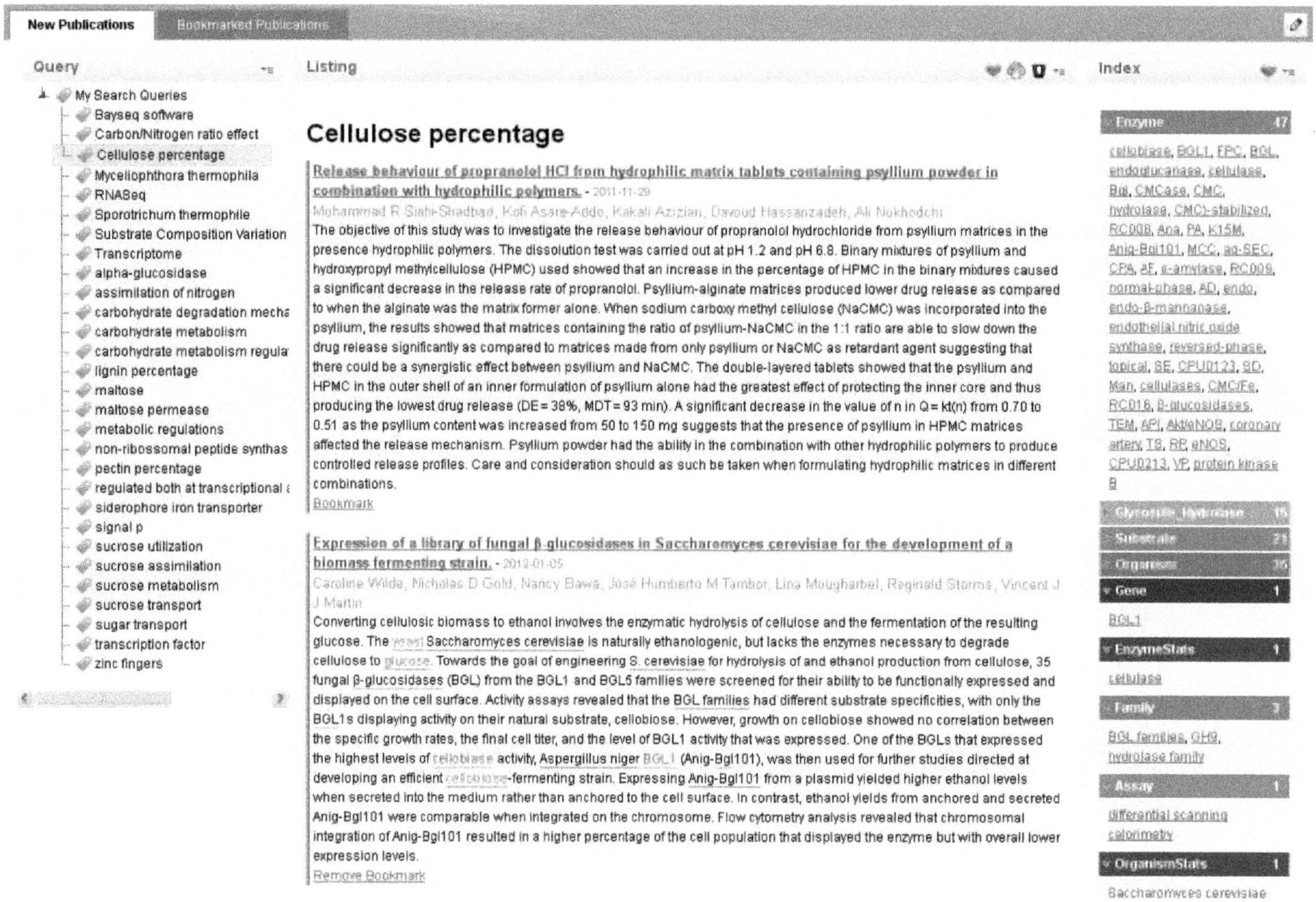

Figure 2. A portal page personalized to an individual user. The *Listing* portlet displays a list of publications sorted and color-coded according to interests of the user. The color codes match the color scheme of the user profile: red colored items represent interesting information. The *Index* portlet provides a personalized list of entities extracted from the publications. Likewise, the entities are sorted and highlighted using the user's interest profile.

In the personalized view, users can view and edit their interest profile, as well as define how the portlet content should be personalized. This can be done in a personalization options window, which can be opened by selecting the *Personalization options & interest profile* command from the portlet personalization menu. The personalization options window (Figure 3) is displayed as an overlay over the portlet. In the upper part, it displays the options for personalization supported by the portlet. The personalization options vary from portlet to portlet. For example, the *Listing* portlet, displaying a list of new publications, supports three personalization effects: (1) publications can be sorted according to the user interest profile; (2) the most interesting of the user publications can be highlighted by a color marker; (3) mentions of items from the user interest profile can be highlighted in the publications list. By selecting corresponding checkboxes, users can achieve the desired personalization effects in the portlet. User changes on the personalization options are immediately projected onto the portlet content.

For visualization of user profiles, we leverage the IntrospectiveViews interface proposed by Bakalov et al. in [4]. The interface (Figure 3) visualizes user interests using a metaphor of circular zones partitioned into slices, where each zone represents items of a certain interest degree and each slice represents items of a specific type, i.e., ontology class. The hot zone in the center displays items that users are strongly interested in. The cold zone at the circle edge displays items that users are not interested in. Items are grouped into circular sectors by type. The profile shown in Figure 3 displays items of such types as enzyme, gene, organism, strain, and some others. In addition to viewing, the visualization allows editing information in the model. It allows adding and deleting items, changing the interest degree, organizing items by type, defining user-specific types, and creating semantic relations among items.

Similarly to changes of personalization options, all changes in the interest profile made through the visualization are immediately projected onto the personalized content. For example, upon a change in the interest profile, the publications in the *Listing* portlet (Figure 2) will be resorted and the color markers of the most relevant publications will be updated. This helps users understand the connection between the user model and the end personalization effects. In turn, this should make the adaptive behavior more transparent and comprehen-

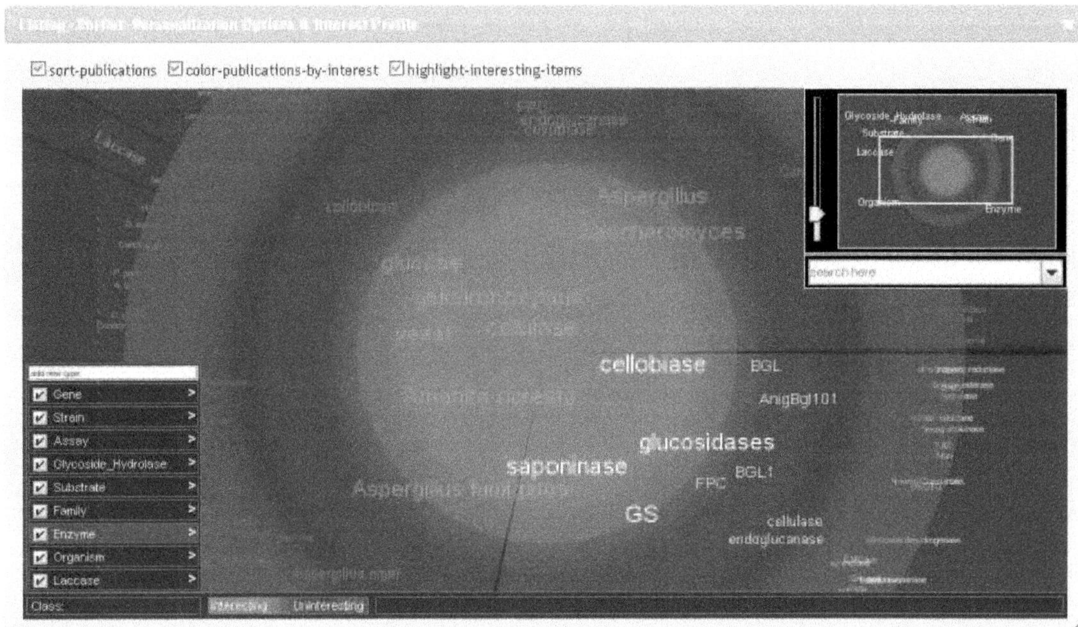

Figure 3. Personalization options and user interest profile

sible for users. This should also help users develop a mental model of affordance to control the adaptive behavior. In the next section, we evaluate whether these goals are achieved by our approach.

EVALUATION

We conducted a user study to evaluate the impact of our approach to controllable personalization on the subjective perception of a personalized system by users. More precisely, we aimed to assess how it affects the usefulness, usability, user satisfaction, and trustworthiness. Also, we aimed to collect user feedback with respect to possible improvements and enhancements of the approach.

The user study was conducted at the Concordia Centre for Structural and Functional Genomics (CSFG)[5]. The subjects of this study were seven employees of the center working in the Genozymes project[6], where the goal is to find novel ways of creating bioproducts and biofuels from green waste. Part of their work is the curation of characterized glycoside hydrolases[7] of fungal origin from the domain literature. The main background of the subjects is biology, chemistry, and genomics.

Study Design

For this user study, we used the personalized portal for biochemical literature presented in Section . The study was conducted in two phases. In the first phase, the subjects were provided with a version of the portal in which the control over personalization was blocked. The subjects knew that the portal collects information about their interests and personalizes its content. More precisely, publications in the portal were automatically sorted according to interests of individual users. Also, the text fragments of publications matching to items in the user model were highlighted by color. However, the subjects did not have access to the user model. They were also not able to switch personalization off or change personalization effects. The subjects were using this version of the portal for the entire duration of the first phase, which lasted two weeks.

At the end of the first phase, we asked the subjects to fill out a questionnaire. The questionnaire was designed based on the USE question set of Arnold Lund [13]. It includes questions regarding to the usefulness, ease of use, ease of learning, and satisfaction. Additionally, we added questions on the novelty and trust. In total, the questionnaire consists of 36 questions grouped into five categories. Figure 4 displays the complete lists of questions. For each question, the subjects were asked to cast a vote on a six-point Likert scale. The questionnaire was available online in the portal. The subjects were able to fill it out on their own computer at any convenient time. After all subjects had completed the questionnaire, we started the second phase of this study. In the second phase, the subjects were provided with a version of the portal that gives the user full control over personalization. In this version, they were able to access the user model, edit it and see the effects on personalization. They were also able to switch personalization on and off and fine tune personalization effects for individual portlets. The subjects were using this version for a period of two weeks. Table 1 provides the system usage statistics on selected interactions that subjects made during the study.

At the end of the second phase, they were asked again to respond to the same questionnaire that they filled out in the first phase. Additionally, we interviewed them. In the interview,

[5]`http://genomics.concordia.ca/`

[6]`http://fungalgenomics.ca`

[7]family of enzymes used to break down plant cell walls

Table 1. System usage statistics

Action	Total	⌀ User
Portlet content request	1369	195,57
Semantic assistant request	76	10,86
Personalization on/off	11	1,57
Personalization interface request	74	10,57
User model change	44	6,29
Personalization effects change	16	2,29

we requested subjects to speak out on the positive and negative aspects of the portal. We also asked them about additional functions and content they would like to have in the portal. The rest of this section presents the results of the two surveys and the interviews.

Results

The results of the two surveys are shown in Figure 4, with respect to individual questions of the survey questionnaire. As can be seen from the figure, providing users control over personalization has a considerable impact on the usefulness, usability, and user satisfaction of the personalized system. On average, the second version of the portal, in which users had control over personalization, received a 23% better rating than the version without the control. In the rest of this section, we discuss the results of the surveys and interviews with respect to the five categories of the questionnaire. We also present our findings with respect to the user modeling and user-driven changes on domain knowledge models of personalized systems.

Usefulness

The first version of the portal received relatively low rating in the *Usefulness* category. We attribute this to the prototypical state of the system and insufficient coverage of literature. In the interviews, most respondents said that they need the portal to be able to harvest publications from all the major scientific databases and to have at least two years of retrospective coverage. They also need a number of additional features, such as advanced search, functions for sharing publications, commenting, and rating.

However, the second version of the portal, which allows fine tuning of personalization, received a 24% better rating of the usefulness than the first version. Despite the prototypical state and low coverage of literature, the respondents rated the second version as a very useful tool that helps them to be more effective and productive. From the interviews, we found out that users like very much to be able to view and edit their interest profiles. They like the functions for applying different personalization effects to the portal content. Users especially like to be able to sort content according to the interest profile. The function for highlighting items from the user model in the text of portal pages was deemed useful as well. To avoid clutter on portal pages, users need to be able to select entity types they are mostly interested in. Only entities of the selected types must be highlighted in the portal.

Also, some respondents requested a function for rating portal content with respect to the relevance to their interest profile. Some said that they like to be able to flag uninteresting and

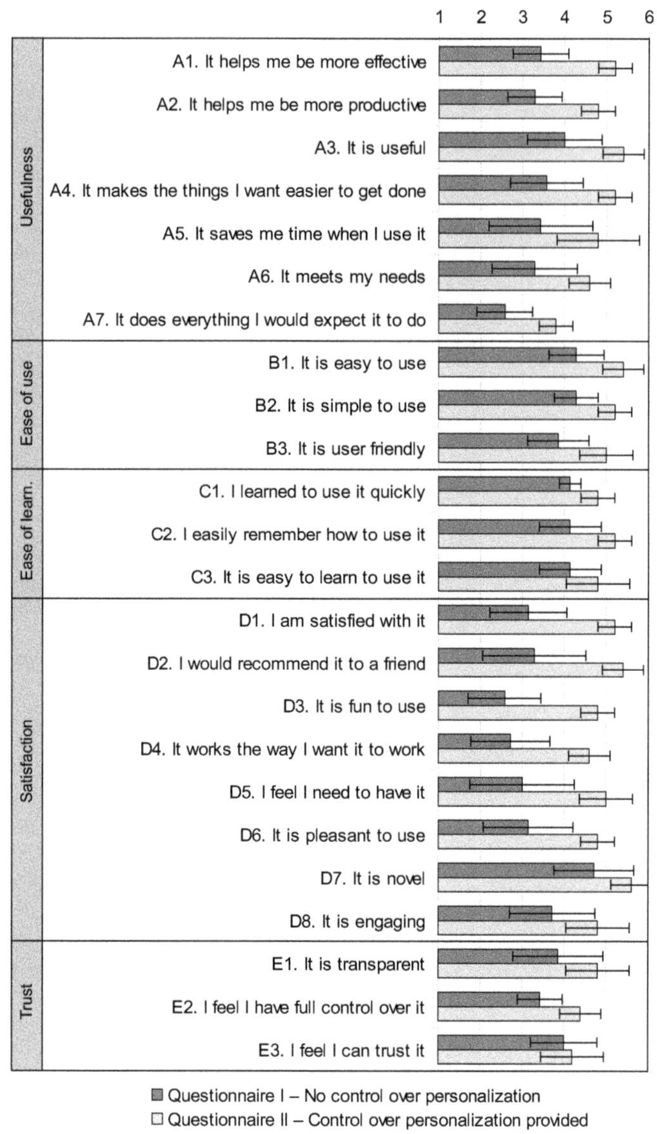

Figure 4. Questionnaire responses

irrelevant content and they want the portal to use this information for updating their interest profiles and improving the retrieval mechanisms. Additionally, we received a number interesting suggestions to further enhance the usefulness of controllable personalization in the portal. For example, several respondents said that they would like to have a function for setting alerts on certain parts of the user model in order to receive a notification when new relevant content becomes available.

Ease of Use and Learning

The version with controllable personalization received better ratings of the ease of use (18% increase) and the ease of learning (13% increase). The better rating in these categories is a surprising observation since the second version had a higher complexity than the first version, i.e., a higher number of control elements and functions. We attribute the improvement of the perceived usability of the second version to the gain of its outward attractiveness. A very strong correlation between the perceived ease of use and the subjective attractiveness of computer systems was first detected by Kurosu and Kashimura [12] and then confirmed in a number of replicated experiments by Tractinsky [18]. These studies reveal that users deem a visually attractive system more usable than its analog with a less attractive appearance.

In the case of the second version of the portal, the improvement of attractiveness is likely to be caused by the interactive visualization of user interests through IntrospectiveViews. The results of the previous study of the usability and hedonic aspects of this visualization [2] show that users deem the visualization visually attractive, engaging, pleasant, and fun to use. Hence, we argue that the integration of this visualization into a personalized system can improve not only its attractiveness, but also the perceived usability.

Satisfaction

In this category, we observed the highest increase of the rating in comparison with the other four categories. The respondents were 29% more satisfied with the portal in which they had control over personalization than with the portal where they did not have such control. All respondents were either satisfied or very satisfied with the second version.

We also observed a strong impact of the interface for controllable personalization on the emotional perception of the portal by users. The results show that the second version is deemed to be 37% more fun-to-use, 28% more pleasant, and 18% more engaging. Also, the willingness to recommend the system to a friend is 35% higher and the user's need to have the system is 33% stronger. This is an important observation because the emotional aspects influence the users' motivation to use their interest profiles for adjusting personalization. Hence, users are more likely to keep the information in the profile up-to-date and accurate. The accurate and complete information in user profiles, in turn, ensures the quality of personalization effects and the precision and recall of content recommendation.

Trust

We observed a 16% increase of the transparency of the second portal version in comparison to the first one. The user's feeling of having control over the system is increased too at the same rate as the transparency. During the interviews, all respondents said that they like to be able to know whether the content is personalized or not and what adaptations have been made. They also appreciated the access to their interest profiles and the ability to choose what personalization effects have to be applied to the content.

However, the results show only a marginal 3% increase of the trustworthiness. From the interviews, we found that some users do not care whether the portal collects information about their interests as long as it uses it for recommending relevant content, whereas others have significant concerns about their privacy. The difference of user attitude to the collection and usage of personal information can also be seen from a relatively high deviation in responses on questions E1 and E3. From these results we can conclude that different users have different concerns about privacy, hence they need different levels of control over their personal data. Those users who wish the highest degree of control should be able to delegate the management of their personal data to some trusted authority or to manage it locally on their desktops. They should be able to control what applications use their personal data and for what purpose.

User and Domain Modeling

The overall feedback with respect to user modeling is very positive. Users liked the function of using interest profiles for personalizing portal content. They liked that these profiles can be updated in both ways: unobtrusively based on the user interaction with the portal and explicitly by users. They also liked very much the visual interface for displaying and editing their profiles.

During the interviews, the subjects made a number of interesting suggestions with respect to a further enhancement of user modeling. Many subjects suggested allowing users to have multiple interest profiles. A user may work for several projects at one time. In different projects users may be responsible for different tasks. Therefore, the portal should allow users to create multiple profiles and to be able to select a profile for personalization effects in a given portal session. Also, respondents suggested having a group profile that reflects interests of a project team or a group of friends. Similar to personal profiles, the portal should allow users to select group profiles for generating personalization effects. In addition to that, some users are willing to share their interest profiles with their colleagues or friends. This function can be especially useful in corporate portals for senior staff and experts willing to share their knowledge with less experienced staff members, e.g., new employees or interns.

Also, one of the factors that had a negative impact on the user satisfaction with the portal is the incorrect classification of certain entities in the user profile. Users found it irritating. However, some of them said that they would be willing to correct the occasional misclassification by rearranging items in their interest profiles, i.e., by moving entities to the corresponding sectors on the interface for user model visualization. These corrections can be used by the portal to update the ontology representing machine-processable semantics of the domain knowledge. This information can be further used to improve the search and personalization in the portal.

It is important to mention the limitations of this study. Due to the small number of participants, it was not possible to conduct it with a control group. It also lacks counterbalancing of the system versions. Hence, we admit that the improved rating of the second version might be partially caused by the gain of the user experience with the system. Nevertheless, the study provides valuable insights into how users perceive the control over personalization. It also provides insights into how this control could be further enhanced.

CONCLUSIONS AND FUTURE WORK

In this paper, we have presented an approach to controlling user models and personalization effects in recommender systems. This approach enables users to access their user models that the system builds and uses for adaptation. It permits users to request a justification about the beliefs the system makes about their traits and override them if necessary. Also, it empowers users to get an explanation about personalization effects the system makes, based on the user profile. In addition, the approach allows users to set the desired degree of adaptivity: users can fine tune personalization effects or deactivate them at the level of individual content fragments.

We have reported the results of a user study, in which we evaluated the impact of our approach on the usefulness, usability, user satisfaction, transparency, and trustworthiness. The results show that the approach improves the usefulness of personalized systems. Users deem the mechanisms for controlling personalization provided by our approach easy, fun, and pleasant to use. This is an important result since the subjective attractiveness of these mechanisms is an essential requirement for motivating users to work with their user profiles and keep them up-to-date and accurate. This, in its turn, can improve the quality of personalization.

Also, the results of the user study show that our approach helps to solve the transparency and controllability problems that personalized systems have been criticized for. However, our findings with respect to the trustworthiness reveal that giving users full control over their user models alone is not enough to establish a sufficient level of trust between the user and a personalized system. Our results show that some users have significant concerns about their privacy, even though they have control over the user model and personalization effects.

The limitations of this user study are the small number of participants, the short duration of the study, and the lack of counterbalancing of the system versions. In our future work, we plan to evaluate the impact of this approach in a controlled experiment lasting a longer period of time and involving a larger number of subjects. Also, we plan to investigate methods for privacy management in order to improve the trustworthiness of personalized systems. In addition, we will further enhance our approach by incorporating the suggestions that we collected in this study.

Acknowledgements

We thank Justin Powlowski and all the participants of the user study for their time, patience, and valuable feedback. Funding for part of this work was provided by Genome Canada, Génome Québec and NSERC. Part of this research was sponsored by the IBM Ph.D. Fellowship Awards Program and the German Academic Exchange Service (DAAD).

REFERENCES

1. Act on the Protection of Personal Data Used in Teleservices (Gesetz über den Datenschutz bei Telediensten). Federal Law Gazette (Bundesgesetzblatt). Translation retrieved from http://www.iuscomp.org/gla/statutes/TDDSG.htm on April 12, 2012, 1997.
2. Bakalov, F., Knig-Ries, B., Hennig, T., and Schade, G. Usability Study of a Semantic User Model Visualization for Social Networks.
3. Bakalov, F., König-Ries, B., Nauerz, A., and Welsch, M. A Hybrid Approach to Identifying User Interests in Web Portals. In *Proc. of the 9th Int. Conf. on Innovative Internet Community Systems* (2009).
4. Bakalov, F., König-Ries, B., Nauerz, A., and Welsch, M. IntrospectiveViews: An Interface for Scrutinizing Semantic User Models. In *Proc. of the 18th Int. Conf. on User Modeling, Adaptation, and Personalization* (2010).
5. Cook, R., and Kay, J. The Justified User Model: A Viewable, Explained User Model. In *Proc. of the 4th Int. Conf. on User Modeling* (1994).
6. Czarkowski, M. *A scrutable adaptive hypertext*. PhD thesis, University of Sydney, 2006.
7. Dimitrova, V. STyLE-OLM: Interactive Open Learner Modelling. *International Journal of Artificial Intelligence in Education 17*, 2 (2003), 35–78.
8. Jameson, A. Adaptive interfaces and agents. In *The human-computer interaction handbook: Fundamentals, evolving technologies and emerging applications (2nd ed.)*. Erlbaum, 2003, 433–458.
9. Kay, J., and Lum, A. Building User Models from Observations of Users Accessing Multimedia Learning Objects. In *Adaptive Multimedia Retrieval*. Springer, 2004.
10. Kliger, J. Model Planes and Totem Poles: Methods for Visualizing User Models. Master's thesis, MIT Media Lab, 1995.
11. Kobsa, A. Personalized hypermedia and international privacy. *Commun. ACM 45*, 5 (2002), 64–67.
12. Kurosu, M., and Kashimura, K. Apparent usability vs. Inherent usability. In *Proc. of the ACM SIGCHI Conf. on Human Factors in Computing Systems (CHI'95)* (1995).
13. Lund, A. Measuring Usability with the USE Questionnaire. *Usability Interface 8*, 2 (2001).
14. Meurs, M.-J., Murphy, C., Morgenstern, I., Butler, G., Powlowski, J., Tsang, A., and Witte, R. Semantic text mining support for lignocellulose research. *BMC Medical Informatics and Decision Making 12*, Suppl 1 (April 2012), S5.
15. Nielsen, J. Enhancing the explanatory power of usability heuristics. In *Proc. of the SIGCHI Conf. on Human Factors in Computing Systems* (Boston, MA, 1994).
16. Schimratzki, O., Bakalov, F., Knoth, A., and König-Ries, B. Semantic Enrichment of Social Media Resources for Adaptation. In *Proc. of the Workshop on Adaptation in Social and Semantic Web held in conj. with the 18th Int. Conf. on User Modeling, Adaptation, and Personalization* (2010).
17. Schreck, J. *Security and Privacy in User Modeling*. PhD thesis, University of Essen, 2001.
18. Tractinsky, N. Aesthetics and apparent usability: empirically assessing cultural and methodological issues. In *Proc. of the ACM SIGCHI Conf. on Human Factors in Computing Systems (CHI'97)* (1997).
19. Tsandilas, T., and Schraefel, M. C. Usable Adaptive Hypermedia Systems. *New Review of Hypermedia and Multimedia 10*, 1 (2004), 5–29.
20. Uther, J., and Kay, J. VIUM, a Web-Based Visualisation of Large User Models. In *Proc. of the 9th Int. Conf. on User Modeling* (2003).
21. Witte, R., and Gitzinger, T. Semantic Assistants – User-Centric Natural Language Processing Services for Desktop Clients. In *3rd Asian Semantic Web Conference (ASWC 2008)*, vol. 5367 of *LNCS*, Springer (Bangkok, Thailand, 2008), 360–374.
22. Zapata-Rivera, J., and Greer, J. Externalising Learner Modelling Representations. In *Proc. of the Workshop on External Representations held in conj. with Int. Conf. on Artificial Intelligence in Education* (2001).

Automatic and Continuous User Task Analysis via Eye Activity

Siyuan Chen[1,2] **Julien Epps**[1,2]
[1] Electrical Engineering and Telecommunications
The University of New South Wales
Kensington, NSW, Australia
siyuan.chen@student.unsw.edu.au, j.epps@unsw.edu.au

Fang Chen[2]
[2]NICTA
Level 5, 13 Garden street,
Eveleigh, NSW, Australia
fang.chen@nicta.com.au

ABSTRACT

A day in the life of a user can be segmented into a series of tasks: a user begins a task, becomes loaded perceptually and cognitively to some extent by the objects and mental challenge that comprise that task, then at some point switches or is distracted to a new task, and so on. Understanding the contextual task characteristics and user behavior in interaction can benefit the development of intelligent systems to aid user task management. Applications that aid the user in one way or another have proliferated as computing devices become more and more of a constant companion. However, direct and continuous observations of individual tasks in a naturalistic context and subsequent task analysis, for example the diary method, have traditionally been a manual process. We propose a method for automatic task analysis system, which monitors the user's current task and analyzes it in terms of the task transition, and perceptual and cognitive load imposed by the task. An experiment was conducted in which participants were required to work continuously on groups of three sequential tasks of different types. Three classes of eye activity, namely pupillary response, blink and eye movement, were analyzed to detect the task transition and non-transition states, and to estimate three levels of perceptual load and three levels of cognitive load every second to infer task characteristics. This paper reports statistically significant classification accuracies in all cases and demonstrates the feasibility of this approach for task monitoring and analysis.

Author Keywords

Blink; pupil; fixation; saccade; cognitive load; perceptual load; task transition, task monitoring; task analysis.

ACM Classification Keywords

H.5.2 [Information Interfaces and Presentation]: User Interfaces.

General Terms

Human Factors; Measurement.

INTRODUCTION

The exploration of the structure of tasks and user behaviour in interaction is of great interest for developing intelligent systems in aiding user tasks [1,2]. However, unless interruption during tasks can be avoided, the role of such systems can be disruptive, as users now often multi-task, sometimes offloading control and responsibility to computers [2]. To design a truly supportive system, we must understand the contextual task characteristics and user behaviour during the interaction.

One way to understand how concurrent tasks are managed, what causes switches between them, and the nature of interruption, is through direct observation and subsequent analysis. In some studies [1,3,4], researchers spent hundreds of hours manually recording every event to identify and trace individual tasks. They reported the typical time involved in a task before switching, the levels of activity, the cause of the fragmentation and task timestamp, to name a few. Since the costs for direct observations are often high and the note taking speed can be limited, developing an automatic system, which can monitor user tasks and analyse their characteristics aforementioned, can have substantial benefit for an understanding of task patterns.

Current existing systems to monitor user tasks are mainly for interruption management. These systems rely on task models, which are expressed and represented by description languages, and tools to create task specifications. During task monitoring, events from instrumented application are compared to the task model for instructions and then decisions are made to manage task events [5], for example, a monitoring tool called DART [37]. A disadvantage of this kind of approach is that it assumes that the user's primary task is focused on the computing device, whereas increasingly this is not the case (e.g. GPS navigation in vehicles). Therefore, the motivation of this work is to detect task switching and some task characteristics without requiring any trace of task events (e.g. click to browse or open a file) that we can log and analyze. We used cues from user behaviours to infer and monitor tasks, instead of using task events. Such cues can preferably be obtained from user psychophysiological and behavioural signals since this approach does not interrupt the user performing the task.

Using eye activity for task monitoring has advantages over other psychophysiological and behavioural signals. Firstly, Eye activity contains three classes of information in the pupillary response, blink and eye movement (saccade and fixation). The correlations between the three classes of eye activity are low [6], and as a measure, eye activity is non-intrusive, objective and can be applied in broad scenarios. Furthermore, monitoring eye activity through cameras has been facilitated by recent eye tracking technology [34], making it more convenient and less intrusive.

In this study, we investigate the approach of estimating task transition, perceptual load and cognitive load imposed by tasks with the most sensitive eye features, towards real time, automatic task analysis in a multi-task switching situation. Our contributions are as follows: (1) We characterize task transition, perceptual load and cognitive load as task characteristics, and continuously detect task transition and estimate three levels of perceptual load and cognitive load every second to identify the time of switching, and the type and level of load caused by the task; (2) We employ three different classes of eye activity features to estimate task characteristics in a task switching environment, going beyond single and discrete task analysis; (3) We reveal the attributes of eye features for task transition detection, perceptual load and cognitive load estimation.

BACKGROUND AND RELATED WORK

With the increasing applications of mobile and ubiquitous computing, the interaction between user and computers has been extended to the interaction between user and computing systems in the user's surrounding context [35]. Unlike traditional interaction, where the primary tasks are often known, such as a control center [36], in this context, changes are often unforeseen and primary tasks are often unknown. However, to allow a system to usefully aid a user, information from both the context and user current states should be known [35]. Concerned with this, the three task characteristics provide informative details in terms of frequency, difficulty and sequence.

The first task characteristic of interest is task switching, which often occurs for a priority change and external interruptions [1]. It is an inevitable phenomenon that people cannot carry out multiple activities simultaneously because of their finite ability [1]. Intensive research related to task switching has often focused on the impact of interruption on users [2,7,9], and examined the more opportune moments for interruption [8,10]. In their studies, interruption tasks were designed and the task switching time was often known. The TaskPredictor2 system used a machine learning approach to detect undeclared switches between activities to support negotiated interruption. In order to do so, users have to explicitly declare a set of ongoing activities [38]. Few studies have attempted to automatically detect the moment when task switching occurs without logging task events like a mouse click. Studies in [1,3,4] are examples of such cases, where researchers manually recorded every event occurring in users' daily work in order to trace the patterns of the activities and tasks. The state of task transition, that is, the exact moment at which the task is switched, is critical to segment the time course in order to understand what prompted the switch.

In addition to task transition, we examine perceptual load and cognitive load, in an attempt to understand some of the generic attributes of the task. Perceptual load occurs when we are required to perceive many different items, or the same items with more demands on individual identification (e.g. identify an item colour and position at the same time), particularly in a short period of time [11]. It is a rather passive process, and some items cannot be perceived when perceptual load is high [11]. As high perceptual load can exhaust the available capacity for information processing, it is known for example that task display formats need to be carefully designed to reduce perceptual load [12,13]. Although perceptual load can be estimated by counting the number of items in a controlled environment (e.g. when the user is staring straight at a known application), it is not easy to estimate it when the items perceived are uncertain (e.g. when the user is mobile or focused on some other task). Current methods to indicate perceptual load include evaluating the task performance, training effectiveness [13], and fixation time on task displays [12].

Another factor that influences user behavior in interaction, which can be used to infer task characteristics, is cognitive load. In contrast with perceptual load, cognitive load is associated with working memory and increases with more demands on it [14]. It is a more active process than perceptual load [11]. There have been many research efforts to find sensitive psychophysiological and behavioral signals that are strongly correlated with cognitive load, in order to measure it. For example, the average accuracy of electroencephalogram (EEG) signals for classifying three load levels has been reported to be 43-90% with an increasing window size from 2-120 s in an n-back memory task [15]. With Functional near-infrared spectroscopy, the reported average accuracies for two levels of cognitive load ranged from 76%-94% in three single tasks [16]. An average accuracy of 81% for low and high cognitive load was reported using a combination of heat flux and electrocardiographic (ECG), where load levels were classified separately in each of the three task types [17]. Around 82% accuracy was achieved using a combination of EEG, ECG, electrooculographic (EOG) and respiration for two levels of cognitive load, where the levels were manipulated by the number of events [18]. The highest average accuracies for three levels of cognitive load were reported using speech, namely 72.6% and 88.5% in two different controlled datasets [19].

Although fair classification accuracies have been achieved for two or three levels of cognitive load measurement, most work used either one single task or a few discrete tasks without considering the continuity and task switching between different types and difficulties. Meanwhile, most studies typically reported averaged classification accuracies but not moment-to-moment results. More importantly, these psychophysiological and behavioral signals showed good correlation with cognitive load but not with perceptual load and task transition to date.

The viability of using eye features to distinguish task transition, perceptual load and cognitive load have been suggested in the literature [e.g. 20-22,24,39]; nevertheless, few studies used eye activity alone to distinguish the three task characteristics in real time for task monitoring and analysis. For example, studies reported the blink burst at the beginning and end of cognitive processes [20]. Meanwhile, blink is inhibited in more difficult tracking tasks [21] and increases in conversations and arithmetic tasks [20,22]. As another class of eye activity, pupillary response is sensitive to cognitive load. It is reported that pupil size increases in more difficult tasks and subsides at the boundaries of subtasks [10]. Fixation and saccade are another class of eye activity. Fixation is often used as a metric to indicate the difficulty of information extraction and the degree of importance of the element, while saccade often implies the difficulty of locating precise target positions [24,39].

METHODS

Data collection

To collect eye activity data in an intensive multi-tasking situation, we conducted an experiment in which three types of task, each involving a different level of perceptual load, and five levels of task difficulty (cognitive load) in each type of task, were deployed, as shown in Figure 1. These tasks were continuously performed, and switching between different types and levels of load was induced.

Perceptual load was controlled by the number of stimuli required to be perceived in each task type. The low perceptual load task was a mental arithmetic task, where four numbers were sequentially displayed in a 3-s interval, then participants used a mouse to select the correct answer from 10 displayed choices. The medium perceptual load task was a spatial task, where all task stimuli were displayed simultaneously, including the direction labels of two compasses, 12 radio buttons (displayed in a circle) indicating 12 directions, and a pointer to one of the 12 directions of the inner compass (inside the circle). Participants were required to identify the extent of the two misaligned compasses and click the corresponding direction of the pointer in the outer compass (outside the circle). The high perceptual load task was a search task, where 28 stimuli were not only simultaneously displayed in 28 boxes, which were evenly distributed in two rows and two columns, but also moved by one box every 3 s in one of the line directions: right, left, up and down. The target number was displayed for 2 s at the beginning of the task, and participants were required to click as many targets as possible, although there were only four targets in each task.

Cognitive load was induced by increasing the memory set, or the degree of the interactivity of task stimuli. In the arithmetic task, task difficulty levels were regulated by the number of digits for addition (up to 3 digits) and carries produced by addition. In the spatial task, the difficulty level was increased when the spatial compatibility between the two compasses was reduced by removing more direction labels. In the search task, the difficulty from level 1 to 5 was increased by increasing the number of the target digits from 1 to 5. Each digit was selected from {1,2,...,9} with minimum repetition. Distractors were selected to have similar digits as much as possible but in a different sequence, to prevent participants from only memorizing a few digits.

Tasks were continuously switched from one to another until a message displayed on the screen to indicate an end, for a

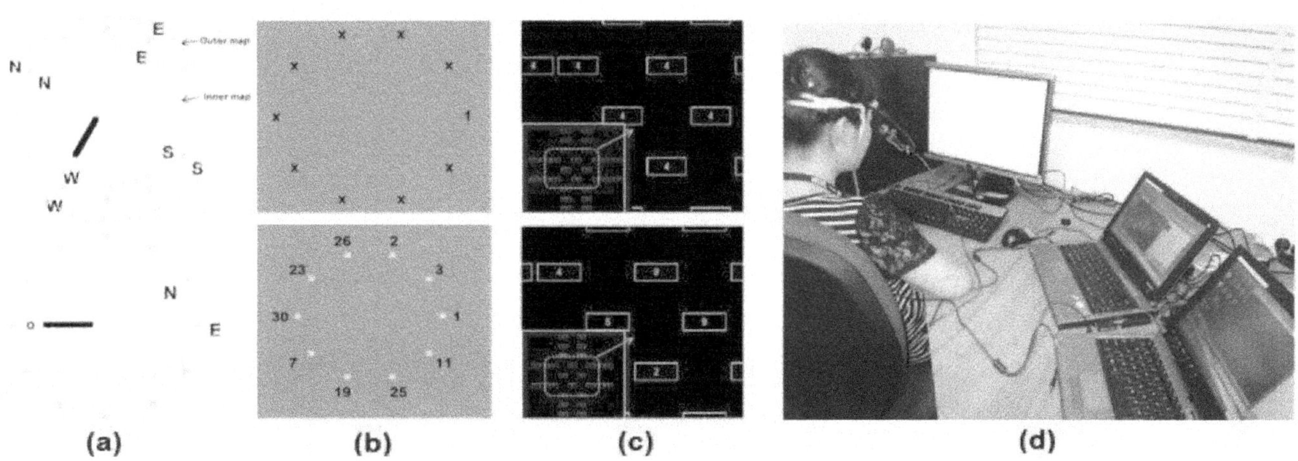

Figure 1. Screen shots of the spatial (a) (medium perceptual load (PL)), arithmetic (b) (low PL), search (c) (high PL) tasks and a participant at the end of the experiment (d). (a) The pointer always points to the inner map direction, and the N E S W labels always have clockwise ordering. The upper and lower images are examples of low and high cognitive load levels respectively. (b) One of the four addends replaces one of the ten placeholders (X) sequentially every 3 s (upper image) then multiple choices for the addition answer are shown (lower image). (c) A target number is initially displayed on every box for 2 s (upper image) then four different paths of numbers replace the target s (lower image) and move every 3 s. The lower left corner is the entire screen view of the task.

break. The arithmetic and spatial tasks were internally switched to the next task by a click to submit the answers, and the search task was externally switched, by ending automatically after 12 s. The executed task sequence was always one group of the three task types, followed immediately by another group of them. The sequence of the group was randomized permutations of cognitive load levels, 1 to 5, in groups of three task types, with repetition, therefore 125 ($5 \times 5 \times 5$) groups of three were generated in total. The randomized groups were then separated into six parts. The six parts were evenly allocated into two days. Before the three parts each day, there was a rating part where participants rated the task difficulty at the end of each task. Half of the participants began with the rating plus first three parts in the first day and half of them began with the rating plus other three parts. To make it more realistic in terms of luminance variation, we set the three types of task in different background colors, namely, white, gray and black for the spatial, arithmetic and search tasks respectively, since task switching is often associated with background change in real-world tasks.

Twenty-two participants completed all tasks in two different days after a short training period before the experiment. Each part had a duration of less than 25 minutes, and there was a 10-minute break between each part. Participants were required to wear a pair of safety glasses frames during tasks with two lightweight infrared web cameras mounted on it, pointing to each eye. Each web camera was connected to a laptop with USB 2.0 and the videos of eye activity were recorded in AVI format at 30 frames per second. The videos and the task presentation were synchronized at the beginning of each part by a button click and a long blink. The timestamp of each task was automatically recorded by the program. At the end of the experiment, each participant's eye length was measured in millimeters for later use.

Preprocessing

Video processing was carried out in order to identify the three classes of eye activity. Ellipse fitting was employed to estimate the pupil shape. The major axis length in pixels was measured as pupil size. Meanwhile, the minor axis length was recorded for the calculation of eccentricity with the major axis length, and the orientation of the ellipse was also recorded as a feature. The ellipse center position was logged as eye position for later fixation and saccade separation. Blinks were recorded when the pupil size was occluded by at least half.

The fitted ellipse was superimposed onto each video for visual inspection to ensure the true eye activity was correctly represented. False blinks, accounting for 1.2% of total blinks, were manually corrected. The axis lengths, orientation and eye position were linearly interpolated during blinks, and then passed through a median filter with length three frames to remove the noise caused by rapid eye movements. Pupil size was then converted to millimeters by the ratio of the true eye length and the eye length in the video. Fixation and saccade were separated by dispersion-based algorithms [25] using one degree of visual angle for at least 200 ms. As we did not detect the head motion, the fixation and saccade used in this paper were the relative fixation and saccade to the head position.

We defined the time span of 0.5 s before the end of the previous task to 0.5 s after the beginning of the current task as a task transition. This is based on an assumption of 0.5 s as the maximum latency of an eye activity response, from a stimulus to brain and brain to eye activity, as indicated by neuroimaging studies [26]. Therefore, a 1-s time window with 50% overlap was used in task transition detection. From the recorded task timeline, we labeled all time windows that crossed the instant of task beginning or end as task transitions in the ground truth.

Measured features

From the three classes of eye activity, we calculated a total of 29 features, including conventional statistics, from the time domain signals, frequency domain and entropy. All features were calculated from a time window of 1 s (1-s time window), and from a time window of 2 s (2-s time window), with 50% overlap along the two-hour task execution.

From the pupil data, we calculated the average pupil size (PDmean), pupil size range (PDrang), pupil size standard deviation (PDstd), average pupil orientation (POmean), pupil orientation range (POrang), pupil orientation standard deviation (POstd), average pupil eccentricity (PDeccMean), pupil eccentricity range (PDeccRange), and pupil eccentricity standard deviation (PDeccStd), over the time window. For perceptual load and cognitive load estimation, the above features were calculated after pupil baseline subtraction to reduce the light reflex effect. The baselines were the average pupil size during the 0.5 s at the end of each task transition. For this we assumed that each task transition had been perfectly detected.

Power spectral density from pupil time series was also considered, which indicates the average power in frequency domain. Due to the short length of time window, we used a parametric method for power spectrum estimation, which avoids spectral leakage and provides a better frequency resolution than FFT-based nonparametric methods (e.g. [23]). The Burg method for the autoregressive (AR) model was used and the AR model order was set to the length of time window divided by three [27] (this method can be implemented in Matlab). Eight average spectral power (Ave_psd) features were then computed on eight frequency bands, spanning 0.1 to 4 Hz (the first band is 0.1 to 0.5 Hz and the second band is 0.5-1.0 and so on).

Four blink features were of general interest. Blink number (blkNum) was calculated during the time window. Inter-blink interval (blkInterval) was the number of non-blink frames during the time window. Blink duration per blink number (blkDurPerNum) was the number of blink frames divided by the total number of blink. Blink product (blkProduct) was the multiplication of blink number per second and blink duration per second.

Fixation and saccade features were also investigated. From the time series, we calculated the number of fixations (fixNum) during the time window, the fixation duration per fixation (fixDur), the standard deviation of the fixation duration (fixDurStd), and the first difference of fixation duration (fixDurDiff). We also tried an entropy-based feature on fixation (fixEntropy), where an empirical probability mass function was generated by normalizing a sequence of fixation durations (in frames) by the total number of frames in the time window, and from this the Shannon entropy was calculated. For the saccade features, we computed the average amplitude of saccade (sacAmp), the standard deviation of saccade amplitude (sacAmpStd) and the first difference of saccade amplitude (sacAmpDiff).

Task transition detection

All features were computed from a 1-s time window, overlapped by 0.5 s, for task transition detection. Sensitive features were initially selected using a pilot test, in which the data from the first two parts of each day was taken as the pilot training set (half of them were randomly selected as validation set) and the data from the third part of each day as the pilot test set. Kappa scores were obtained from the classification decisions and the annotated ground truth. Data from the fourth part of each day was reserved for later use (testing data). The top 12 features ranked by the Kappa scores were collected as a full set of sensitive features.

Then the best features, from the full set of sensitive features, and classifier parameters were selected from training data to form the input of a classification system.

As task transition often consisted of three frames (i.e. the label for a time window) in series, a median filter of three frames was applied to the classifier output to remove rapid fluctuations due to noise.

Although we annotated task transitions based on timestamps, participants were at liberty to start or end the task at their own pace. Therefore it was difficult to find the exact time when participants began to engage in tasks with less than 0.5 s of error. Meanwhile, a shift in the task transition by one time window will cause an error of two incorrect time window labels in classification performance. Therefore, we reported the classification results for two schemes to get a sense of how close the detected task transitions were to the annotations.

Moment-by-moment Scheme: Task transition was detected every 0.5 s, and the classification performance was obtained by comparing the classification decision with the annotated ground truth frame by frame.

State-by-state Scheme: From the detected task transitions above, any transition with frames overlapping with the annotation was recognized as task transition, and declared as a task transition for classification performance calculation.

Perceptual load estimation

The perceptual load (low/medium/high) was estimated every 1 s independently of cognitive load, using the eye features derived from a 2-s time window, not including task transitions. Since blink and fixation features extracted over 1 s were not able to produce measurable magnitudes for perceptual load, as observed from the data, time windows of more than 2 s long should be considered in practice. The subsequent procedures were similar to those for task transition detection, but without median filtering.

Although we annotated the perceptual load of tasks based on the items required to be perceived, it is possible that participants perceived the items only when needed. Therefore, we reported the moment-by-moment classification results. However, to compare with the per-task ground truth annotation, we segmented the signals into task windows according to the annotated task transition, and aggregated the classifier outputs using majority vote during the task window [28]. The purpose of examining the moment-by-moment scheme and task-by-task scheme was to investigate the amount of fluctuation within tasks, and the influence of moment-by-moment load on the classification performance.

Moment-by-moment Scheme: Three perceptual load levels were estimated every 1 s. The classification performance was obtained by comparing the classification decision with the annotated ground truth frame by frame.

Task-by-task Scheme: From the estimated perceptual load levels above, we used the label that won the majority vote from a task window to represent the task.

Cognitive load estimation

Similarly to perceptual load estimation, features derived from a 2-s time window were selected for cognitive load estimation, without the influence of task transition. However, cognitive load is difficult to compare between tasks of different kinds [17]. Although we can annotate the five levels of difficulty as ground truth within each task, it does not necessarily mean that each level represents the same cognitive load across the different tasks. Meanwhile, in a realistic case, it is not feasible to train a model for each task, especially when the task is unknown. Therefore, we annotated three levels of cognitive load according to the average task performance scores across 22 participants, namely, low: 80-100%, medium: 60-79%, high: below 60%. The performance scores in the arithmetic task from level 1 to 5 are as follows: 99.1%, 97.3%, 88.1%, 56.7%, 31.3%; these in the spatial task from level 1 to 5 are as follows: 99.8%, 86.0%, 84.7%, 76.1%, 78.7%. Thus, level 1, 2, 3 in the arithmetic task and in the spatial task were annotated as 'low'; levels 4 and 5 in the spatial task were annotated as 'medium'; and levels 4 and 5 in the arithmetic task were annotated as 'high'.

Another important factor that can influence cognitive load measurement is the level of perceptual load of the task. According to the load theory of attention, cognitive control typically occurs in situations of low perceptual load [11], which implies that cognitive load levels during high perceptual load tasks may not be distinguishable. Therefore, high perceptual load tasks were excluded during model training. The classification decision for cognitive load was available only when the perceptual load was not high. Here we assume that perceptual load has been perfectly detected.

The other procedures and the schemes for classification decision were similar to that for perceptual load estimation.

Moment-by-moment Scheme: Three cognitive load levels were estimated every 1 s when the perceptual load was not high. The classification performance was obtained by comparing the classification decision with the annotated ground truth frame by frame.

Task-by-task Scheme: From the estimated cognitive load levels above, we used the label that won the majority vote.

Feature selection and classification

To lower the computational costs and shorten the runtime, we manually pruned the sensitive feature set to a number of subsets for further feature selection. The principle of the pruning is to contain two or three subsets where features are from each class of eye activity and the subsets where features are from different classes of eye activity. This is to minimize the negative influence on classification performance due to individual difference on sensitive features. For example, some participants have very low blink rate, which may result in blink features losing effect.

For classification, we selected logistic regression, for simplicity and to avoid overfitting, and employed a participant-dependent scheme. Considering the real time application, we did not use k-fold cross validation. The data partitions are as follows: data from the first three parts of each day formed the training data. Among the training data, 50% were randomly selected as a validation data to tune not only the regularization parameter but also the best subset of the features. Data from the fourth part of each day were used as the testing data.

Concerning the distribution of training data in each class, we needed to cope with a class imbalance problem. As easy tasks usually took less time than difficult tasks, this led to more training samples in difficult tasks when we used a time window with fixed length. This problem was more severe for task transition detection since the number of transitions was significantly less than that of non-transitions. To deal with this, we employed both downsampling and ensemble

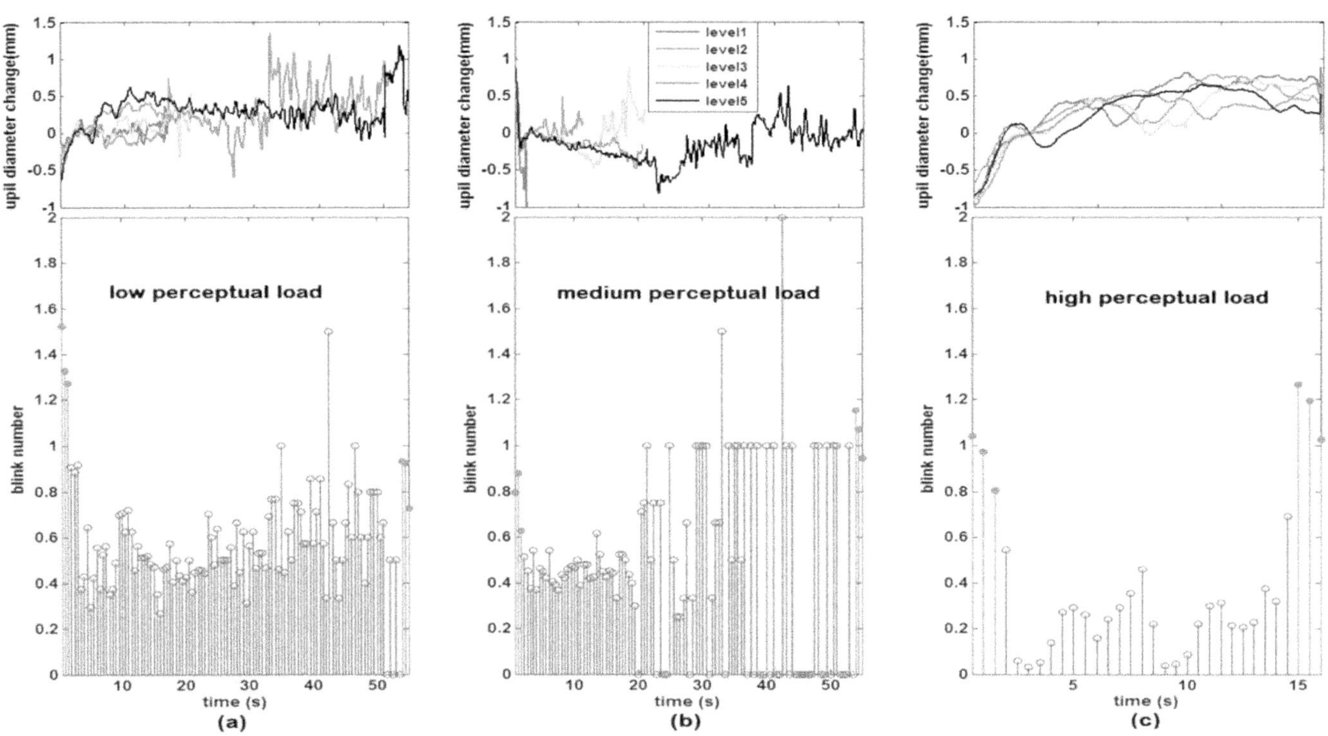

Figure 2. Examples of average pupillary response across five levels of cognitive load and average blink number in 1 s, from a participant in (a) the arithmetic task (low perceptual load), (b) the spatial task (medium perceptual load), (c) the search task (high perceptual load). Blink number shown in red with solid head denotes blink features occurring during task transition, and in blue with hollow head denotes occurring during non-transition states across all perceptual loads. This figure demonstrates that blink number in 1 s is sensitive to perceptual load and task transition. Pupillary response is sensitive to cognitive load in the low and medium perceptual load situations as generally pupil size was larger in high cognitive load (e.g. level 4 and 5) than low cognitive load (e.g. level 1 and 2) but this is not the case when perceptual load is high.

classifier schemes, where the number of classifier was the class imbalance ratio (integer). Each classifier was trained by the entire minority class and an equally sized, random subset of the majority class. The final predicted probability distribution was the averaged predicted probability from all the classifiers [29]. A test sample was then assigned the label corresponding to the maximum predicted probability.

We employed three metrics to describe the classification performance. Each of them was the averaged value across 22 participants. Correlation coefficient (*R*) measures the strength and direction of the relationship between the ground truth and the estimated labels. The absolute value of *R* in the ranges of 0-0.3, 0.3-0.7 and 0.7-1.0 can be considered to indicate weak, moderate and strong linear relationships respectively. Cohen's Kappa was also used, which measures the magnitude of classification agreement and takes into account chance agreement. Generally speaking, a Kappa score between 0.01 – 0.20 can be interpreted as having slight agreement, 0.21-0.40, fair agreement (above 0.20 is often interpreted as statistical significance), 0.41-0.60, moderate agreement and 0.61-0.80, substantial agreement. As the test samples are not balanced data for each class, we also reported the precision and recall for comparisons.

RESULTS

Task transition detection

Table 1 shows the top 12 most sensitive features for task transition. We can see that the average power in the frequency band of 0.5-1.0 Hz is the most sensitive feature. Meanwhile, all the sensitive features are from two classes of eye activity, that is, pupillary response (blue in Table 1) and blink (red in Table 1). Features from eye movements have little contribution to task transition. An example of a blink feature for task transition was depicted in the bottom figure of Figure 2, where the number of blinks was higher during task transition than during non-transition (notably the start of each new task) in each task.

Table 1. 12 eye features with Kappa score above 0.11 were selected as a full feature set for task transition detection.

Eye Feature	Kappa	Eye Feature	Kappa
Ave_psd_0.5-1.0	0.27	Ave_psd_2.0-2.5	0.15
Ave_psd_0.1-0.5	0.24	blkNum	0.11
PDrange	0.24	blkDurPerNum	0.11
PDstd	0.23	blkProduct	0.11
Ave_psd_1.0-1.5	0.22	blkInterval	0.11
Ave_psd_1.5-2.0	0.18	Ave_psd_2.5-3.0	0.11

Table 2 presents the classification performance in task transition detection. As expected, the results of the state-by-state scheme were far better than that of moment-by-moment scheme. As the precision and recall show, around one third of the task transition errors were due to transition shifts. Meanwhile, the value of *R* and Kappa score suggest a moderate linear relationship between the estimated and annotated task transitions, and a fair agreement in terms of classification.

Table 2. Classification results of task transition detection.

	R	Kappa	Precision	Recall
Moment-by-moment	0.35	0.33	38.7%	51.1%
State-by-state	0.61	0.59	60.7%	76.7%

Perceptual load estimation

Regarding the sensitive features for perceptual load, as Table 3 shows, blink features (in red) were the most sensitive features, followed by fixation and saccade (in green). The bottom panel of Figure 2 demonstrates that the average blink number in low and medium perceptual load tasks was higher than that in high perceptual load task. Pupillary response seems less influenced by perceptual load, since pupil size varied in a similar range in each perceptual load task, as the top panel of Figure 2 depicts.

Table 3. 12 eye features with Kappa score above 0.20 were selected as a full feature set for perceptual load estimation.

Eye Feature	Kappa	Eye Feature	Kappa
blkNum	0.30	fixDurStd	0.23
blkDurPerNum	0.29	fixNum	0.23
blkInterval	0.29	fixDur	0.23
sacAmp	0.27	fixEntropy	0.23
blkProduct	0.27	PDeccRange	0.21
fixDurDiff	0.24	PDeccStd	0.20

Table 4. Classification results of three levels of perceptual load estimation.

	R	Kappa	Precision	Recall
Moment-by-moment	0.45	0.42	60.5%	61.8%
Task-by-task	0.73	0.67	78.3%	78.6%

The classification performance for three levels of perceptual load estimation is presented in Table 4. The perceptual load fluctuations during tasks resulted in a 17% drop in precision and recall relative to the moment-by-moment scheme. Meanwhile, the linear relationship between the estimated and annotated perceptual load was moderate to strong and the agreement of classification was moderate to substantial, as indicated by the value of *R* and Kappa score.

Cognitive load estimation

As Table 5 shows, without the impact of high perceptual load, the average pupil size was the most sensitive feature for cognitive load. From the top panel in Figure 2, a distinct pattern of pupillary response to task difficulty levels can be observed in the low and medium perceptual load tasks, but not in the high perceptual load task. Meanwhile, the top 12 sensitive features were mainly from the classes of pupillary response (blue in Table 5) and eye movement (green in Table 5).

Table 5. 12 eye features with Kappa score above 0.08 were selected as a feature set for cognitive load estimation.

Eye Feature	Kappa	Eye Feature	Kappa
PDmean	0.25	POstd	0.09
sacAmp	0.15	fixDurStd	0.09
PDstd	0.13	Ave_psd_0.1-0.5	0.08
PDrange	0.12	sacAmpDiff	0.08
sacAmpStd	0.10	fixDur	0.08
PDeccRange	0.10	blkNum	0.08

Table 6. Classification results of three levels of cognitive estimation when the perceptual load was not high.

	R	Kappa	Precision	Recall
Moment-by-moment	0.29	0.26	50.4%	53.9%
Task-by-task	0.46	0.41	60.0%	64.9%

A 10% drop in precision and recall from the task-by-task scheme to moment-by-moment due to cognitive load fluctuations suggests that cognitive load has fewer fluctuations than perceptual load. Furthermore, the correlation between the estimated and annotated cognitive load in the two schemes was from weak to moderate. Correspondingly, the classification agreement was from fair to moderate, both of which were statistically significant.

DISCUSSION

Eye activity measures obtained in the present experiment achieved reasonably good classification performance in task transition detection, perceptual load estimation and cognitive load estimation. As shown in Table 2, 4 and 6, moderate and strong linear relationships between the estimated labels and ground truth were obtained in the state-by-state and task-by-task schemes. The values of R ranged from 0.46 to 0.73, implying that around 21% to 53% variations of task characteristics have been explained. Meanwhile, moderate and substantial classification agreements were achieved through all cases, suggesting that identifying the three task characteristics is far more than would be expected by chance. Furthermore, precision and recall was above 60% in the two-class transition detection, and above 77% in the three-class perceptual load estimation, and above 60% in the three-class cognitive load measurement. This supports the view that eye activity alone may be able to determine the task switching time, the type and level of load. Therefore, the proposed system can continuously perform task analysis in the task switching situation.

With regard to the real time implementation, the classification performance in our work was at 1 s resolution. However, the moment-by-moment classification did not provide high performance. One credible reason for this is that we lack the granularity in the ground truth, which only exists at task level. The influence of shifted task transitions on classification performance is illustrated in Table 2. Precision and recall increased from 38.7% and 51.1% to 60.7% and 76.7% if we tolerate task transition timing errors of up to 1 s. Furthermore, the performance of precision was higher than that of recall, suggesting that the number of detected task transitions was more than the annotated task transitions. When closely examining the results, we found that many detected false transitions were often close to the annotated task transitions. This may imply that participants did not engage in tasks immediately after each task switching, or disengage from tasks immediately before submitting answers. Meanwhile there were more detected false transitions in the arithmetic task than other tasks. This may suggest an occurrence of subtask switching, for example, when the 10 multiple choices were presented after the four addends displayed sequentially in the arithmetic task.

It is also possible that the classification performance of task transition and cognitive load were affected by task switching. As switching between different types and levels of load may result in different user behavior during task transitions and the subsequent tasks [30], our results represent the performance obtained in a task-switching situation, and might not be the optimum performance derived from a single task.

Except for the task switching impact, cognitive load measured across two types of task may also render its degradation in classification performance. Differently to previously reported work where a specific model for each task was trained, we experimented with a classification system that can accommodate tasks with low and medium perceptual load. The difficulty lies in that feature distributions across 1 to 5 levels of cognitive loads are different due to different perceptual loads, or the levels actually induced that are arbitrarily numbered 1 to 5 as an ordinal indicator of load level. Hence, a more objective approach to cognitive load measurement needs to be explored.

Although using performance score to annotate the ground truth may not be as desirable as using task design and/or subjective rating as a ground truth [22,33], this approach is promising, as indicated by the statistically significant classification performance, with a view to using cognitive load as a generic task characteristic for different tasks. It is important to note, however, that performance is not a measure of spare mental capacity [31,32], so this approach may be more reasonable for some situations than others.

To improve the classification performance of cognitive load, there may be a trade-off between the resolution (number of load levels), time window and accuracy for cognitive load estimation. In this study, 2 s may be too short for strong measurable changes in features, but some task durations were as short as 2 s in the easiest tasks. In practice, these are the parameters to be considered, and the values should be decided based on the application.

It is interesting to find that the sensitive feature sets for classifying task transition, perceptual load and cognitive load respectively comprised different classes of eye activity (as indicated by different colors in Table 1, 3 and 5). For task transition, the effective features are mainly from pupil power spectrum density, and blink. This is not surprising, because pupil size often drops rapidly at the end of one task and increases again when a new task begins [10]. This suggests that pupil size did not change frequently during a 1-s time window during task execution. Features for perceptual load are mainly from blink, fixation and saccade. This also agrees with previous studies in that blink, fixation and saccade are correlated with the number of items to be perceived [6,21], and confirms the efficacy of using fixation duration to indicated perceptual load [12]. For cognitive load, the major features were from pupil and eye movement, similarly to [22,24].

One implication from this study is that eye activity on its own may be sufficient to analyze the task characteristics described by task transition, perceptual load and cognitive load. Also, at least two classes of eye activity are capable to distinguish one of the task characteristics, which provide sufficient features for selection to overcome individual differences on feature preference. For example, the blink rate of three participants was too low to be used in this study; however, by selecting features from another class of eye activity, their classification performance achieved was fair. Furthermore, a task monitoring system can analyze tasks using a 1-s window, which may be suitable for many real time applications. Therefore, the implication for user interface design is that this system can play an important role in supporting user activity, like the TaskTracer project to recognize task switching [38] and the interruption manager to detect workload [10].

While this paper focused on general system configuration and data processing, we made efforts to design the experiment to be similar to a real world situation. For example, we used different types of task, different difficulties in each task, different background luminance in each task, different task switching sequences and different days for participants to perform the tasks.

We also processed the data in a way that is suitable for real time implementation. For example, the classifier was trained by the data from the first three parts of each day, where the optimum features and model parameters were tuned, and then the held-out data from the last part of each day was tested, and finally the results were reported every second. However, an assumption for perceptual load classification was that the current task transition had been correctly detected. The assumption for cognitive load classification was that both the current task transition and perceptual load were perfectly detected.

CONCLUSION

In this paper, we proposed a novel user task monitoring and analysis system that can automatically analyze the characteristics of the user's task in terms of task transition, perceptual load and cognitive load every second. Three classes of eye activity, spanning pupillary response, blink and eye movement (fixation and saccade), were collected from an experiment in which participants sequentially but continuously performed multiple tasks. Sensitive eye features were analyzed and selected for each task characteristics for classification. The experimental results demonstrate that using eye activity alone can produce good classification performance for each task characteristics in real time.

This work shows a promising system for directly and continuously observing user task patterns. Our work is the first to describe and apply a general-purpose approach for automatic task analysis to address the emerging problem of tracking task characteristics. The work also opens up a range of related problems for future work, including improving the accuracy of individual detection/estimation components, and investigating the generality of the approach with more types of task and interaction modalities.

ACKNOWLEDGMENTS

We thank all the volunteers for their time and effort. This research was supported by the Asian Office of Aerospace Research & Development, through Grant No. FA2386-12-1-4049."

REFERENCES

1. Smith, W., The Complex Structure of Office Works: Tasks, Activities and Modes, *OZCHI 2004*.
2. Bailey, B. P., Konstan, J. A., Carlis J. V., Measuring the Effects of Interruptions on Task Performance in the User Interface, In *2000 IEEE International Conference on Systems, Man, and Cybernetics*, 757-762.
3. Czerwinski, M., Horvitz, E. & Wilhite, S., A Diary of Task Switching and Interruptions, *CHI 2004*, Vienna.
4. Gonzalez, V.M. & Mark, G., Constant, Constant, Multi-tasking Craziness: Managing Multiple Working Spaces, *CHI 2004*, Vienna.

5. Bailey, B. P., Adamzyk, P. D., et al., A Framework for Specifying and Monitoring User Tasks, *Computers in Human Behavior*, 22 (2006), 709-732.
6. Chen, S., Epps, J., Ruiz, N., Chen, F., Eye Activity as a Measure of Human Mental Effort in HCI, *IUI 2011*.
7. Altmann, E. M., Timecourse of Recovery from Task Interruption: Data and a Model, *Psychonomic Bulletin & Review*, 14, 6 (2007), 1079-1084.
8. Adamczyk, P. D., Bailey, B. P., If Not Now, When: The Effects of Interruption at Different Moments Within Task Execution, *CHI2004*, Vienna.
9. Basoglu, K. A., Fuller, M., A., Sweeney, J. T., Investigating the Effects of Computer Mediated Interruption: An analysis of Task Characteristics and Interruption Frequency on Financial Performance, *Int. J. Accounting Information Systems*, 10 (2009), 177-189.
10. Iqbal, S. T., Adamczyk, P. D., et.al. Towards and Index of Opportunity: Understanding Changes in Mental Workload during Task Execution, *CHI 2005*, Portland.
11. Lavie, N., Hirst, A., de Fockert, J. W., Load Theory of Selective Attention and Cognitive Control, *Journal of Experimental Psychology*, 133 (2004), 339-354.
12. Lee, J., Forlizzi, J., Hudson, S. E., Iterative Design of MOVE: A Situationally Appropriate Vehicle Navigation System, *Int. J. Human-Computer Studies*, 66 (2008), 198-215.
13. Stedmon, A. W., Kalawsky, R. S., Hill, K., Cook, C. A., Old Theories, New Technologies: Cumulative Clutter Effects Using Augmented Reality, In *Proc. IEEE Int. Conf. on Information Visualization*, 1999, 132-137.
14. Paas, F., Tuovinen, J. E., Tabbers, H., Van Gerven, P. W. M. Cognitive Load Measurement as a Means to Advance Cognitive Load Theory. *Educational Psychologist* 38, 1 (2003), 63 - 71.
15. Grimes, D., Tan, D. S., Hudson, et,al. Feasibility and Pragmatics of Classifying Working Memory Load with an Electroencephalograph. *CHI'2008*.
16. Hirshfield, L. M., Gulotta, R., et. al. This is Your Brain on Interfaces: Enhancing Usability Testing with Functional Near-Infrared Spectroscopy, *CHI 2011*.
17. Haapalainen, E., Kim, S., Forlizzi, J. F., and Dey, A. K. Psycho-physiological Measures for Assessing Cognitive Load, *UbiComp 2010*, 301-310.
18. Wilson, G. F., Russell, C. A. Real-Time Assessment for Mental Workload Using Psychophysiological Measures and Artificial Neural Networks, *Human Factors*, 45, 4 (2003), 635-643.
19. Le, P., Ambikairajah, E., Epps, J., Sethu, V., Choi, E.H.C., Investigation of Spectral Centroid Features for Cognitive Load Classification, *Speech Communication*, 53, 4 (2011), 540-551.
20. Stern, J. A., Walrath, C., Goldstein, R., The Endogenous Eyeblink, *psychophysiology*, 21 (1984), 22-33.
21. Van Orden, K. F., Limbert, W., Makeig, S., Jung, T., Activity Correlates of Workload during a Visuospatial Memory Task, *The Journal of the Human Factors and Ergonomics Society*, 43 (2001), 111-121.
22. Chen, S., Epps, J., Chen, F., A Comparison of Four Methods for Cognitive Load Measurement, *OzCHI2011*.
23. Nakayama, M., Shimizu, Y., Frequency Analysis of Task Evoked Pupillary Response and Eye-movement, In *Proc. ETRA 2004*, 71-76.
24. Jacob, R. J. K., Karn, K. S., Eye Tracking in Human-computer Interaction and Usability Research: Ready to Deliver the Promises, *Mind*, 2003, 573-603.
25. Salvucci, D. D., Goldberg J. H., Identifying Fixations and Saccades in Eye-tracking Protocols, In *Proc. ETRA 2000*, New York, 71-78.
26. Laeng B., Sirois S. and Gredeback G., Pupillometry: A Window to The Preconscious? *Perspectives on psychological science*, 7(1), 2012, 18-27.
27. Proakis, J. G., Manolakis, D. G., *Digital Signal Processing*, Upper Saddle River, 2007, 986-1009.
28. Bulling, A., Ward, J. A., Gellersen, H., Troster, G., Eye Movement Analysis for Activity Recognition Using Electrooculography, *IEEE PAMI*, 33, 4 (2011), 741-753.
29. Klement, W., Wilk, S., Michalowski, W., Matwin, S., Classifying Severely Imbalanced Data, In *Proc. of the 24th Canadian conference on Advances in artificial intelligence*, 2011, 258-264.
30. Monsell, S., Task Switching, *Trends in Cognitive Science*, 7, 3 (2003), 134-140.
31. Yeh, Y. Y., and Wickens, C. D., Dissociation of Performance and Subjective Measures of Workload, *Human Factors*, 30 (1988), 111–120.
32. Parasuraman, R., Sheridan, T., B., & Wickens, C., D. Situation Awareness, Mental Workload, and Trust in Automation: Viable, Empirically Supported Cognitive Engineering Constructs, *Journal of Cognitive engineering and Decision Making*, 2, 2 (2008), 140-160.
33. Vidulich, M. A., Wickens, C. D., Causes of Dissociation between Subjective Workload Measures and Performance: Caveats for the Use of Subjective Assessments, *Applied Ergonomics*, 17, 4 (1986), 291-296.
34. Li, D., Babcock, J., Parkhurst, D. J., OpenEyes: a Low-cost Head-mounted Eye-tracking Solution, In *Proc. ETRA 2006*, 95-100.
35. Jameson, A., Modeling Both the Context and the User, *Personal Technologies*, 5, 1(2001).
36. Grootjen, M., Neerincx M. A., Veltman, J. A. Cognitive Task Load in a Naval Ship Control Centre: From Identification to Prediction, *Ergonomics*, 49, 12-13, (2006), 1238-1264.
37. Iqbal, S., Horvitz, E., Disruption and Recovery of Computing Tasks: Field Study, Analysis, and Directions, *CHI 2007*, San Jose.
38. Shen, J., Irvine, J., Bao, X., Goodman M., et al., Detecting and Correcting User Activity Switches: Algorithms and Interfaces, *IUI 2009*, Sanibel Island.
39. Chen, S., Epps, J., Automatic Classification of Eye Activity for Cognitive Load Measurement with Emotion Interference, *Computer Methods and Programs in Biomedicine*, 2012, DOI: 10.1016/j.cmpb.2012.10.021.

Agent Metaphor for Machine Translation Mediated Communication

Chunqi Shi
Kyoto University
Yoshida-Honmachi,
Sakyo-Ku, Kyoto
shi@ai.soc.i.kyoto-u.ac.jp

Donghui Lin
Kyoto University
Yoshida-Honmachi,
Sakyo-Ku, Kyoto
lindh@i.kyoto-u.ac.jp

Toru Ishida
Kyoto University
Yoshida-Honmachi,
Sakyo-Ku, Kyoto
ishida@i.kyoto-u.ac.jp

ABSTRACT
Machine translation is increasingly used to support multilingual communication. Because of unavoidable translation errors, multilingual communication cannot accurately transfer information. We propose to shift from the transparent-channel metaphor to the human-interpreter (agent) metaphor. Instead of viewing machine translation mediated communication as a transparent channel, the interpreter (agent) encourages the dialog participants to collaborate, as their interactivity will be helpful in reducing the number of translation errors, the noise of the channel. We examine the translation issues raised by multilingual communication, and analyze the impact of interactivity on the elimination of translation errors. We propose an implementation of the agent metaphor, which promotes interactivity between dialog participants and the machine translator. We design the architecture of our agent, analyze the interaction process, describe decision support and autonomous behavior, and provide an example of repair strategy preparation. We conduct an English-Chinese communication task experiment on tangram arrangement. The experiment shows that, compared to the transparent-channel metaphor, our agent metaphor reduced human communication effort by 21.6%.

Author Keywords
Machine translation mediated communication; interactivity; repair strategy; agent;

ACM Classification Keywords
H.5.m. Information Interfaces and Presentation: Miscellaneous - *Computer-mediated communication*

INTRODUCTION
Multilingual communication connects people from different nations, encourages business, and brings transnational cooperation. Given the success of famous companies, such as Facebook and Amazon, the need for multilingual communication is obvious. Thus, efficient support tools continue to receive more attention [9]. Machine translation always plays an important role in the implementation of such tools. For example, machine translation has been integrated in a communication support agent developed for multilingual participatory gaming [25]. However, machine translation has limits in terms of translation quality [26]. The translation errors continue to be the barrier for machine-translation-mediated (MT-mediated) communication. When MT-mediated communication is used for a cooperation task, it is necessary to translate the task-oriented dialog accurately. Generally speaking, a communication dialog can be tagged as task-oriented, emotion-oriented, or both [17]. According to social information process theory, emotion-oriented dialog involves not only the cognitive process but also the emotion transfer process. Task-oriented dialog mainly focuses on the acquisition of information in the task domain [3]. In machine translation of task-oriented dialogs, the accurate translation of concepts is the basis of successful information transfer [27]. Considering the limits of translation quality, it is hard to deal with machine translation errors in MT-mediated communication, even without considering the complex individual emotion-related factors, such as cultural background [15].

In view of the fact that machine translation errors cannot be ignored, we propose to shift from the transparent-channel metaphor to the human-interpreter (agent) metaphor. The agent metaphor was originally introduced by [10], in which *interactivity* is suggested as a new goal of the machine translator. Interactivity is the machine initiated interaction among the communication participants; it represents the ability to take positive actions to improve grounding and to negotiate meaning [10, 11]. Different from the traditional metaphor of machine translation as a transparent channel, interactivity makes it clear that translation errors are to be treated as channel noise. This noise can be suppressed through the efforts of the dialog participants.

In this paper we propose an implementation of the agent metaphor to enable interactivity. Interactivity is influenced strongly by the translation environment. Most translation environments involve the translation function and the user [5]. First, we have to mention the two characteristics of complex machine translation. One is the variable quality of machine translator output. The other is that, two messages expressing the same information can have widely different translation quality by the same machine translator. Second, in the transparent channel metaphor, the *activeness* of the user is ignored. Activeness plays an important role in interactivity. For example, certain people get better translation results than others because they can craft expressions that suit the characteristic of that machine translator. Thus, we need careful designs to promote interactivity.

We start by examining the machine translation of task-oriented dialogs. We list the typical translation errors leading to miscommunication. By analyzing the interactivity that can eliminate those errors, we formalize the requirements of an agent for encouraging interactivity. On one hand, the agent needs to know the translation quality. On the other, the agent needs to help the dialog participants adapt to the machine translator. Furthermore, we provide details of the design of the agent metaphor, including its architecture, interaction, and functions. In order to evaluate our prototype, we conduct an experiment on the multilingual tangram arrangement task. Next, we summarize what has been learned before discussing the limitations and implications of the current design.

MACHINE TRANSLATION MEDIATED COMMUNICATION

Machine Translation Mediated Communication Task

As an example, we established several sessions of a concrete English-Chinese communication task. The goal was the *tangram arrangement* task in which an English participant instructs a Chinese participant to construct a tangram object from seven shapes. Because of the geometric shapes, the words and phrases mainly fall into the geometry domain. Google Translate[1], one of the most popular online machine translation services, was used as the machine translator.

Communication Break Because of Translation Errors

Based on the observations made during these sessions, we analyzed the communication breaks occasioned by translation errors. In one observation, due to phrase concept mistranslation, the word "square" in the geometry domain was translated into "plaza" of another domain, because the word "square" is polysemous. The machine translator just provides the everyday meaning of the word, but its true meaning depends on the task domain. In the next observation, the mistranslated sentence is an imperative sentence that requests the receiver to conduct an act ("put something someplace"). The dialog participants often describe actions in imperative sentences, such as requests and commands. Machine translators often fail to translate imperative sentences as well as declarative sentences. Another observation is the mistranslation of inconsistent phrases (see Figure 1); the abbreviated reference ("the light one") is not translated accurately, and it is unnatural to stick to exactly the same expression globally. Such inconsistency easily leads to translation errors.

Analyzing miscommunication at the phrase, sentence, and dialog level is popular in machine-mediated communication research [14, 27]. These three observations of machine translation errors are picked up according to these levels: *phrase-level*, *sentence-level*, and *dialog-level*. Table 1 shows several existing works on examining mistranslation problems, providing suggestions and strategies for improving accuracy at each level. We summarize the mistranslation found in existing works. It shows that mistranslation often happens and can lead to communication breaks.

[1]http://translate.google.com/

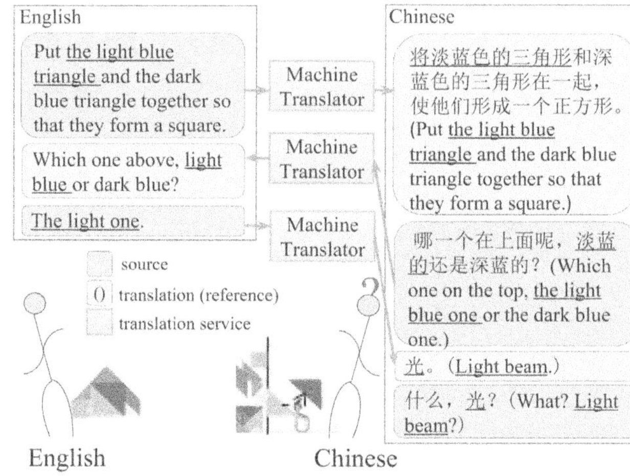

Figure 1: In English-Chinese tangram arrangement communication, the Chinese receives an inconsistent translated phrase and the communication breaks. (In this figure or following figures, the parentheses indicate references of Chinese-to-English translation.)

Level	Existing Works	Mistranslation
Phrase level	Extract and highlight inaccurate words [19], picture icons as precise translation of basic concepts [23].	Inadequate
Sentence level	Examine back-translation for sentence level accuracy check [18], Round-trip monolingual collaborative translation of sentence [7, 20].	Influent and inadequate
Dialog level	Examine asymmetries in machine translations [28], Predict misconception due to unrecognized translation errors [27].	Inconsistent

Table 1: Existing works on three levels and their corresponding mistranslation problems.

INTERACTIVITY AND AGENT METAPHOR

From Accuracy to Interactivity

When translation errors cannot be ignored in MT-mediated communication, the dialog participants can do nothing according to the transparent channel metaphor of machine translation (see Figure 1). The responses open to the machine translator fail to guarantee accuracy. If the dialog participants are encouraged to collaborate to eliminate such translation errors, the goal of the machine translator becomes to encourage interactivity. We studied what forms of interactivity could eliminate the translation errors expected. We replace the transparent channel model by introducing three interactions to eliminate translation errors (see Figures 2, 3, 4).

When translation failure is detected, the interaction process (see Figure 5) consists of: *(1)* Agent's effort to determine the *feature* of current dialog, *(2)* Agent's effort to *suggest*

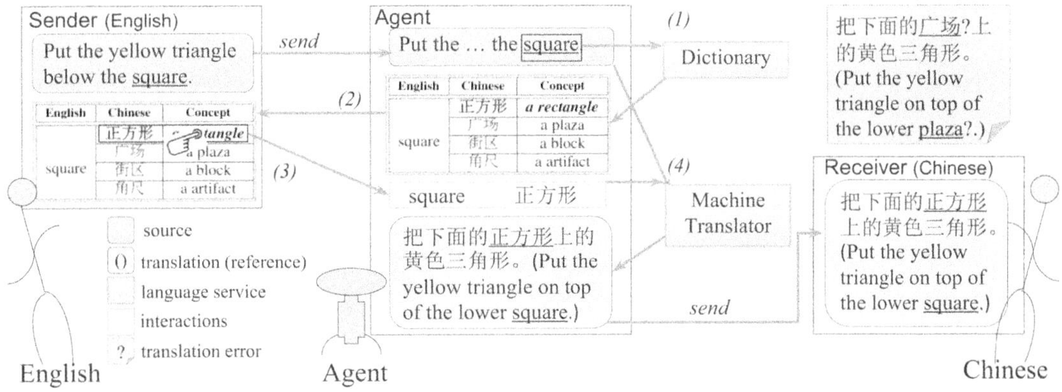

Figure 2: Interaction to handle inadequately translated phrase: *(1)* check the feature that the word, "square", has one-to-many dictionary results. *(2)* suggest the sender select the correct concept. *(3)* the sender chooses the target concept. *(4)* translate by the dictionary translator composite machine translator.

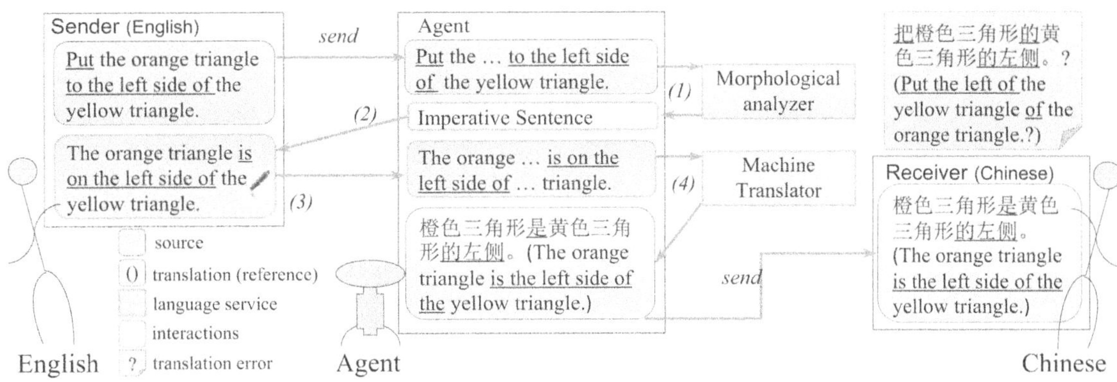

Figure 3: Interaction to handle mistranslated sentence. *(1)* check the feature that it is an imperative sentence starting with a verb. *(2)* suggest the sender rewrite the sentence into declarative version. *(3)* rewrite the sentence. *(4)* translate by the machine translator.

repair tips to the sender. Here, the human effort is referred to as "repair" as per machine translation mediated communication [11, 19]. *(3)* Sender's effort to repair the failure. *(4)* Agent's effort to translate the repaired message, and output an acceptable translation result. Given that there are multiple repair strategies, the agent has to decide the cause of the failure, send the appropriate repair suggestion to the sender. Other types of repair strategies, such as selecting phrases based on the prediction of available information [5], rephrasing based on back-translation results and sentence rewriting [19], can also be used.

Obviously, if the agent can initiate a proper interactivity with dialog participants, most translation errors can be eliminated. Still, we have to mention that the sensibility of dialog participants does not necessarily lead to the elimination of translation errors, because of the unpredictability of the machine translation function, and the uncertainty of the human repair action. Thus, the interactivity between the agent and dialog participants must be carefully designed to motivate participants by making their actions easy, even for monolingual neophytes.

Agent Metaphor for Interactivity

Our case study showed that interactivity can eliminate most translation errors. Here, we discuss why the agent metaphor is needed to establish such interactivity. Basically, there are two reasons for applying the agent metaphor: agent sophistication, and the role of the agent [13]. In this study, the agent metaphor offers *flexible autonomous behavior* and a *decision support function*.

Flexible Autonomous Behavior: Because MT-mediated communication requires online translation and interactivity, a proactive agent has the ability to avoid unnecessary operations. For example, process protocol based collaborative translation [8, 20] will go through the complete preset process flow, which is potentially inefficient. An agent enables flexible autonomous behavior, which is much more efficient.

Decision Support Functionality: Interaction will be triggered when translation errors are detected. After that, many decisions, such as translation error candidates, repair suggestions or extra translation improvement actions, need decision support functionality. A simple premise of this decision can be drawn from current translation quality. Through further design enhancement, the agent metaphor will gather additional

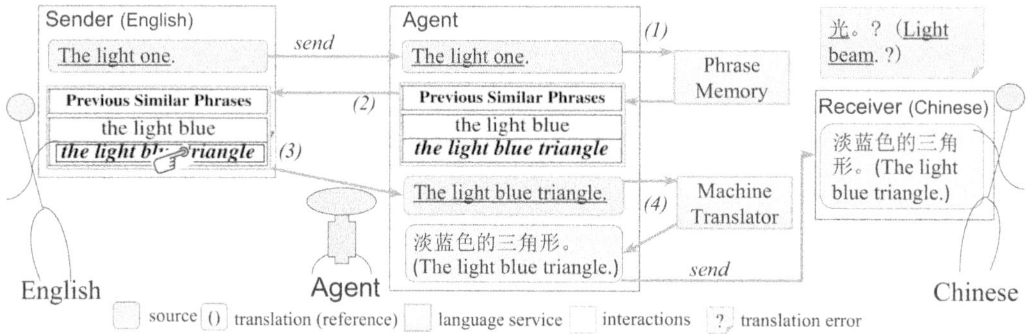

Figure 4: Interaction to handle inconsistently translated phrase. *(1)* check the feature of similar phrases existing in previous dialog. *(2)* suggest selection of appropriate previous phrase. *(3)* choose a replacement of the previous phrase. *(4)* translate by the machine translator.

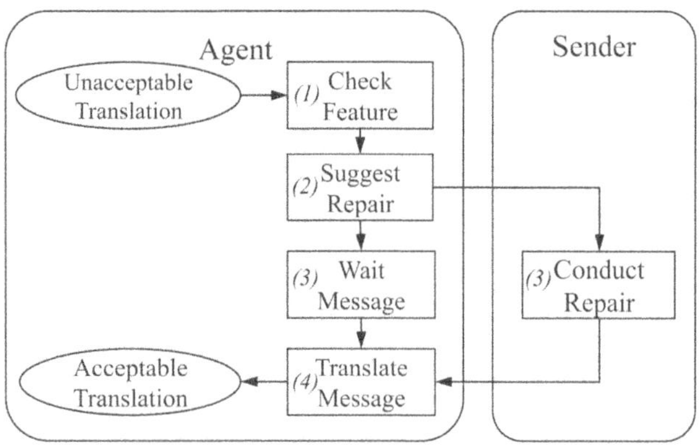

Figure 5: Four steps of the interaction process for one repair strategy: *(1)* Check Feature, *(2)* Suggest Repair, *(3)* Wait Message (Agent), Conduct Repair (Sender), and *(4)* Translate Message.

quality estimates or information from the participants. Thus, the agent metaphor has to sense the quality of current translations, build common consensus among dialog participants, and pass proper repair suggestions to participants.

DESIGN OF AGENT

Architecture

Our translation agent is designed around three agent phases: observation, decision, and action (see Figure 6).

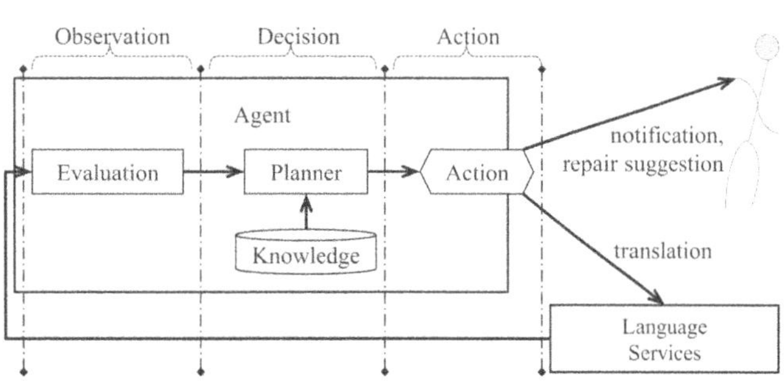

Figure 6: Architecture design of translation agent.

Observation Phase

The goal is to discern the translation quality of each message. An *evaluation* module will fill this role. Popular evaluation methods such as BLEU [21], METEOR [2], compare the lexical similarity between the translation result and a standard reference to calculate an evaluation score. Other quality estimation approaches, such as the set of quality features [24] can be considered. Previous studies use back-translation to predict potential translation errors [8, 18, 19, 20]. In this paper, back-translation and the BLEU method (maximum 3-gram, smoothed) are used as a simple way to trigger interaction.

Decision Phase

This phrase decides the actions to be taken. Here, a real time *planner* is necessary, and a knowledge base is needed to keep experience and/or policy. The planner is critical to establishing autonomous behavior and decision support. Two important facts should be mentioned here. One is that the agent needs the ability to process the dialog in real time. The other is that the activities of the dialog participants will provide uncertain results. This is because the participants might have limited ability to generate correct repair actions or the machine translation quality of each message is unpredictable. Accordingly, the planner should provide online planning and decision support to counter this uncertainty. The knowledge base will save and allow access to experience and policy.

Action Phase

Three types of actions are needed. First, to help the dialog participants get an idea of current quality, a *notification* action is needed. Second, the detection of an unacceptable translation triggers the *repair suggestion* action. The repair suggestion is the key to interactivity. Last, translation actions are needed to implement the different repair strategies.

For the actions of notification and repair suggestion, the demand is that the agent and dialog participants talk. We use a simple meta-dialog for this purpose. For the translation actions, the repair strategies in the observations of the last section require the dictionary service result, and the dictionary translator composition service (see Figure 2). These services will be provided through the Language Grid, a service-oriented platform [12]. Through Language Grid, several categories of atomic language services are available, including dictionary, parallel text, morphological analyzer, dependency parser, machine translators, etc. Meanwhile, several composite services are available, including dictionary-translator composite translation, multi-hop machine translation, and back-translation. Language Grid also provides a client that supports the invocation of both atomic and composite language services. People can develop their own version of services based on this client using Java programs. Language Grid platform support allows translation actions to be realized and invoked flexibly.

Autonomous Behavior and Decision Support

Sharing the status of translation quality between participants, and helping participants adapt to machine translation, are two goals of interactivity. Each communication dialog consists of many rounds of message transfer from one participant to the other. Through this transfer, the agent triggers interactivity. There are two message transfer states: *Acceptable* accuracy, and *Unacceptable* accuracy. If the former, after the message is translated into the other language, and the accuracy is accepted, the translated message is sent to the receiver. If the latter, the agent will notify the participants and pass repair tips to the sender who then repairs the message. The message will be sent to the agent again, and the message transfer process repeats.

Second, two interactivity goals should be met. Satisfying the first goal, sharing the status of translation quality between participants, is obvious. In the above Unacceptable accuracy situation, an informational meta-dialog will be triggered and a notification meta-dialog message will be sent to the sender. A decision on whether it is acceptable or unacceptable is needed. For the second goal, helping participants adapt to machine translation, achieving the goal is essential. Based on the previous case study of interactivity, we learned three points. The first point is that there is more than one repair strategy. This means that the agent has to decide which strategy should be taken. The second point is that repair is a four-step process {*feature, suggest, wait, translate*}. The third point is that the effect of any repair action is uncertain. The decision, deciding which repair strategy is to be selected under uncertainty, is especially important.

The agent has to decide whether to pass the message to the receiver, and if not, which repair strategy is to be taken. When the message is received, translated, and evaluated, the evaluation score is calculated via back-translation. The evaluation score determines whether the message is passed on or a repair strategy is needed. About the next decision, which repair strategy to adopt, the features of multiple repair strategies are checked and one is selected. These decision requirements can be met through a utility decision model [4]. The agent's autonomous behavior and decision support allow it to issue the appropriate repair strategy even under uncertainty.

Repair Strategy Example

An example of issuing the repair strategy "split", is explained. Here, we picked one rule from the AECMA Simplified English Standard [1], which is for technical manual preparation, and tried using it as the basis of a repair strategy, because simplified writing is effective in enhancing machine translation quality according to Pym's study [22].

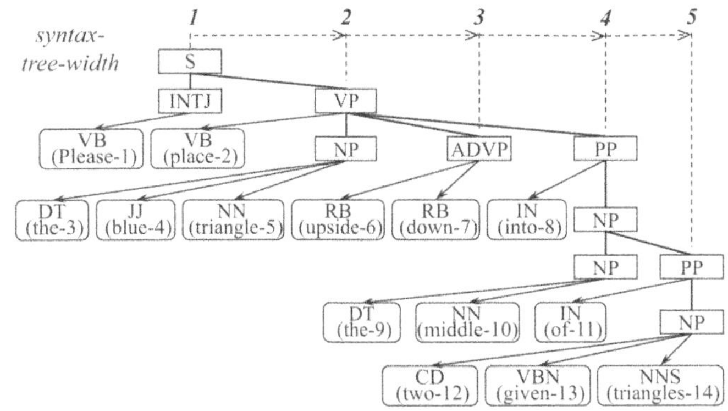

Figure 7: The *syntax-tree-width* feature of the repair strategy *split*: a width of non-leaf part of its constituency structure tree.

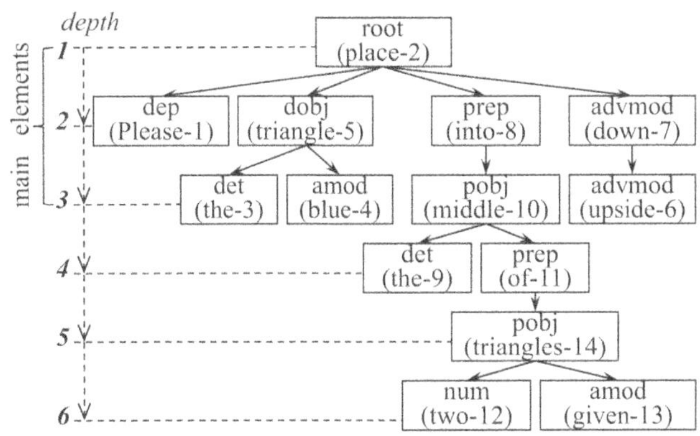

Figure 8: The *tips* for the repair strategy *split*: the core of the message, which is the main elements of the sentence with low depth (less than 4) in the dependency structure tree.

Simplified Writing Rule: use short sentences. Restrict sentence length to no more than 20 words (procedural sentences) or 25 words (descriptive sentences). Inspired by this rule, we developed the repair strategy "split". *Repair Strategy Split*: when an unacceptable translation is detected, if the message is a long and complex sentence, the repair tip is to split the source sentence into two sentences. *Feature of Split Strategy*: the literal length of the sentence is not directly used here. Instead, we choose the syntax-tree-width of its non-leaf syntax tree (see Figure 7). For example, the English message from the tangram arrange task, "Please place the blue triangle upside down into the middle of two given triangles.", is parsed into a constituency structure tree. The non-leaf part nodes form a non-leaf syntax, and its width is 5. Compared to the literal message length, this syntax-tree-width better represents the complexity of sentence structure.

Repair Suggestion: the tips are provided to help the sender undertake the repair. In this repair strategy, the core of the message, which is the main elements of the sentence with low

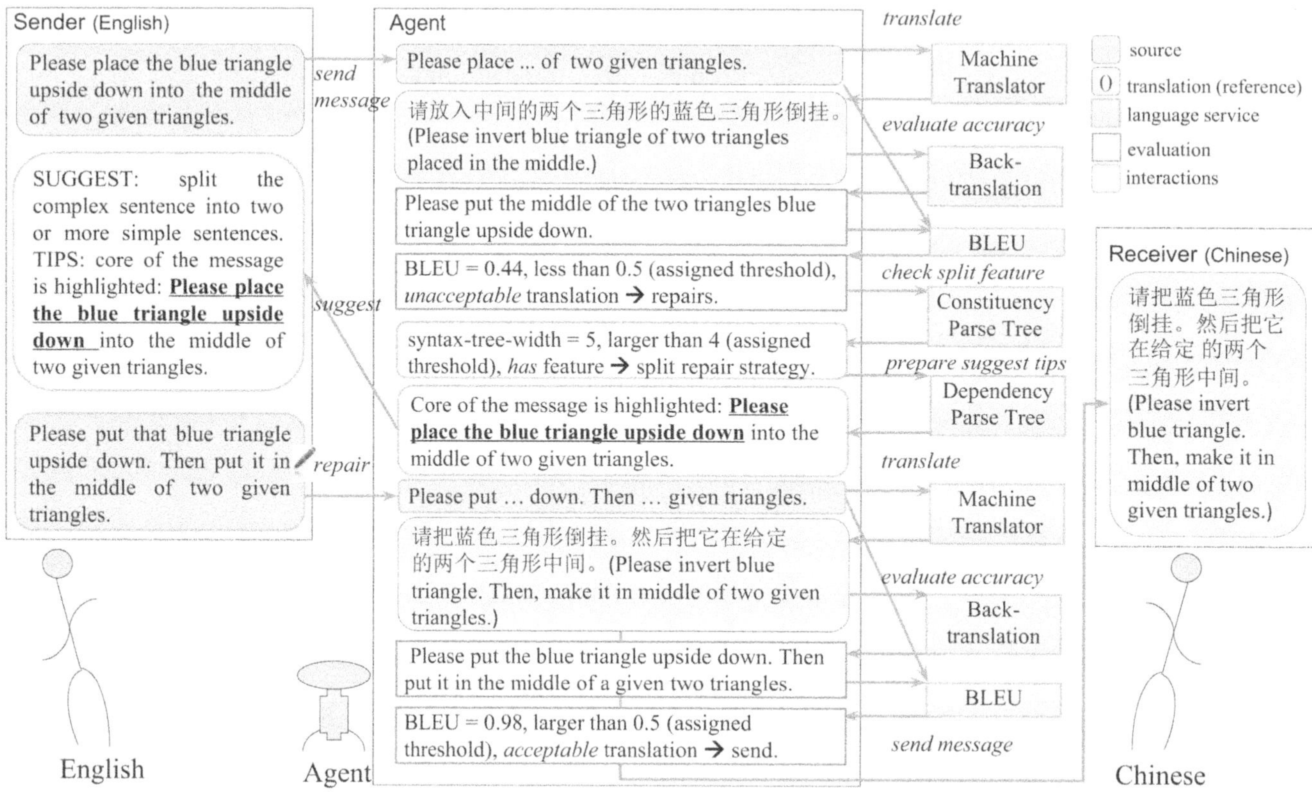

Figure 9: Example of agent's split strategy. Agent will follow the decision of sending message to receiver or starting repair strategy. Back-translation and BLEU evaluate translation quality (*accuracy*). The process steps of the repair strategy (see Figure 5) are given: check split feature, *the syntax-tree-width* (see Figure 7); suggest split with tips, *the core of the message* (see Figure 8); human repair; and translate the repaired message. Then, the evaluation shows that it becomes accepted.

depth (less than 3) in the dependency structure tree, is picked out for the sender (see Figure 8). This meta-dialog shows that, if the repair strategy is "split", then the suggestion and repair tips are passed to the sender (see Figure 9). The priority value is 0.5. It means that this will be the first message shown to the sender, if there is no higher priority meta-dialog defined for the IF premise. Both the constituency parse tree and dependency parse tree are from Stanford Parser [16], which is an open source Java implementation of natural language parsers. It provides a consistent interface for dependent parsers for English, Chinese, Arab, and German.

Here we describe the process of preparing our split repair strategy. According to our observation of the English-Chinese tangram arrangement sessions, we found instances in which this repair strategy was needed (see Figure 9). Obviously, the translated message is initially evaluated as unacceptable. We use the back-translation, the BLEU score, and the threshold for a simple decision. The usage of back-translation has been discussed a lot [8, 18, 19, 20]. The interaction process of split strategy is given and its result is shown (see Figure 9). The agent checks the feature of split strategy, prepares the suggestion tips, and feeds back the split suggestion. After the sender splits the message following the tips, the translation is evaluated again and it becomes accepted.

EVALUATION

Evaluation Methods

In order to evaluate the impact of the agent on interactivity, we conducted a controlled experiment, which compared the machine translator mediated transparent channel approach to the proposed agent mediated interactivity approach.

The Number of Human Messages per Turn Unit

We considered how the elimination of translation errors raised the efficiency of communication. Higher efficiency means that the information is transferred with fewer messages. According to conversation analysis [6], the *turn* is the basic unit interaction in the communication. Here, the tangram arrangement task can be divided into seven subtasks; there are seven pieces to be arranged. For each arrangement, the information transferred per turn unit, includes piece, rotation type, and position. The *number of human messages per turn unit* is defined as the number of messages sent by the human participants during one turn unit of the multilingual communication. It reflects the participants' effort to transfer the task information. For better data collection, after one message is sent, the participants were asked to wait for feedback before issuing the next message.

Normally, a turn unit consists of 2 messages: 1 information message from the sender and 1 feedback message from the receiver. Here, to transfer the square's position information, 4 messages are needed (the number of human messages is 4) because the translation error misleads the message receiver, and the receiver has a query. It should be noted that, in the agent metaphor, the repaired message from the sender is counted, for example, the number of human messages in the turn unit is 2 (two messages from the English sender) in the split strategy example (see Figure 9).

Experiment Preparation

An English-Chinese tangram arrangement communication task was conducted: an English user instructs a Chinese user how to arrange a tangram (see Figure 10). When the tangram is complex, this task is generally difficult to finish through text based messages, even for two native speakers. We set two limitations to make this task easier to finish. *Only use convex figures*[2]: there are only 13 convex figures. It is much easier to construct a convex figure. *Share initial state of tangram pieces*: both participants start with the same piece arrangement. With these two limitations, tangram arrangement focuses on communication.

Participants

For each tangram, we conducted the task using a single machine translator, a translation agent prototype, and bilingual translators. We randomly selected 5 tangram figures from the 13 convex figures. Two English and 2 Chinese participants, and 1 English-Chinese bilingual joined this experiment.

Repair Strategies for Agent Prototype

In this experiment the agent prototype knew three repair strategies; the *split* strategy of the last section, and the two repair strategies of Figure 2 and Figure 3: *phrase* and *rewrite*.

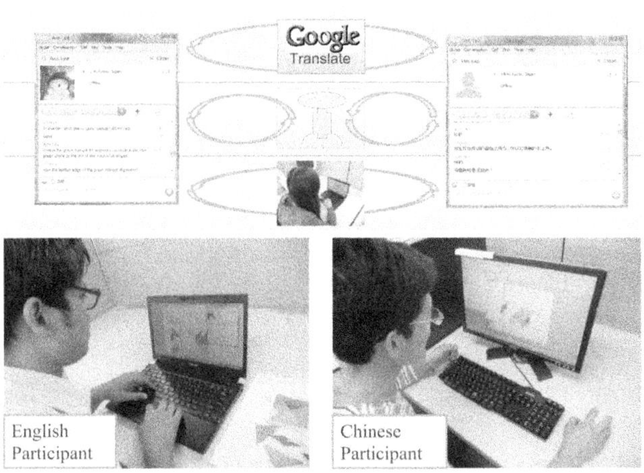

Figure 10: Experiment of English-Chinese (E-and-C) tangram arrangement through machine translator (MT), agent prototype using the wizard of OZ (Agent), and human bilingual (Human). There are two groups participants, E_1-and-C_1 and E_2-and-C_2 for this tangram arrangement experiment.

Result and Analysis

Each group was asked to finish 5 figures. The number of human messages and the average number of human messages in each turn were collected (see Table 2). The average number of human messages in each turn in human-mediated communication is 2.2. This shows that human-mediated communication is pretty efficient. The average number of human messages in each turn in machine translator mediated communication was 3.7. This shows that using machine translation almost doubles the participants' effort. Our prototype agent held the average number of human messages in each turn to 2.9, a **21.6%** improvement in communication efficiency.

Next, the total number of repair strategies in the English-Chinese dialogs was determined (see Table 3). First, the two different message senders had different repair strategies. Sender E_2's messages triggered more repair suggestions. The phrase and split strategies were used to almost the same extent. Second, different repair strategies took different amounts of time to complete. Here, the phrase strategy and split strategy were not activated as frequently as rewrite. This might be because there were few polysemous words, and the sentence structures were not too complex. We note that the senders used many imperative messages in the first instance.

Medium	Average Number of Human Messages		Average Number of Human Messages / Turn
	E_1-and-C_1	E_2-and-C_2	
MT	26.0	25.2	3.7
Agent	20.2	19.8	2.9
Human	15.6	14.8	2.2

Table 2: The average number of human messages and the average number of human messages in each turn unit for the 5 English-Chinese communication tasks.

Sender	Total Times of the Repair Strategies		
	Phrase	Rewrite	Split
E_1	6	21	9
E_2	5	17	10

Table 3: The total times of the repair strategies.

CONCLUSION

Implementing the agent metaphor proposed herein represents a paradigm shift to using interactivity to eliminate translation errors in machine-translation-mediated communication. We examined the translation errors found in the dialogs of multilingual communication, and showed that interactivity could support the dialog participants in eliminating translation errors efficiently. Thus, our goals were to create a consensus as to the current translation state and provide repair suggestions to the sender. Both are realized by our agent metaphor. Evaluation of translation accuracy is critical for the agent to determine the current translation state. Back-translation and automatic evaluation methods, such as BLEU, are used to evaluate accuracy. To realize the autonomous agent mechanism, the process of repair suggestion was analyzed, the situations of message transfer were described, and decision dependency was analyzed for autonomous behavior and decision support. Our agent uses decision-theoretic planning to make online decisions under uncertainty. Finally, we described our experiments on a tangram arrangement task with English-Chinese

[2]http://en.wikipedia.org/wiki/Tangram

task-oriented communication. The results showed that our agent prototype improved communication efficiency in the face of translation errors. The agent does help dialog participants raise the accuracy of translated messages.

ACKNOWLEDGMENTS

This research was partially supported by Service Science, Solutions and Foundation Integrated Research Program from JST RISTEX, and a Grant-in-Aid for Scientific Research (S) (24220002) from Japan Society for the Promotion of Science.

REFERENCES

1. AECMA. *A Guide for the Preparation of Aircraft Maintenance Documentation in the Aerospace Maintenance Language. AECMA Simplified English.* Brussels, 1995.
2. Banerjee, S., and Lavie, A. Meteor: An automatic metric for mt evaluation with improved correlation with human judgments. In *Proceedings of ACL2005* (2005), 65–72.
3. Bangalore, S., Di Fabbrizio, G., and Stent, A. Learning the structure of task-driven human-human dialogs. In *Proceedings of ACL2006* (2006), 201–208.
4. Bohnenberger, T., and Jameson, A. When policies are better than plans: decision-theoretic planning of recommendation sequences. In *Proceedings of IUI2001*, ACM (2001), 21–24.
5. Carl, M., Way, A., and Schäler, R. Toward a hybrid integrated translation environment. In *Machine Translation: From Research to Real Users*, vol. 2499 of *Lecture Notes in Computer Science*. Springer Berlin / Heidelberg, 2002, 11–20.
6. Goodwin, C., and Heritage, J. Conversation analysis. *Annual Review of Anthropology 19* (1990), pp. 283–307.
7. Hu, C. Collaborative translation by monolingual users. In *Proceedings of the EA2009*, ACM (2009), 3105–3108.
8. Hu, C., Bederson, B. B., Resnik, P., and Kronrod, Y. Monotrans2: a new human computation system to support monolingual translation. In *Proceedings of CHI2011*, ACM (2011), 1133–1136.
9. Inaba, R. Usability of multilingual communication tools. In *Usability and Internationalization. Global and Local User Interfaces*, vol. 4560 of *Lecture Notes in Computer Science*. Springer Berlin / Heidelberg, 2007, 91–97.
10. Ishida, T. Communicating culture. *IEEE Intelligent Systems 21* (2006), 62–63.
11. Ishida, T. Intercultural collaboration using machine translation. *IEEE Internet Computing* (2010), 26–28.
12. Ishida, T. *The Language Grid: Service-Oriented Collective Intelligence for Language Resource Interoperability*. Springer, 2011.
13. Jennings, N. R., and Wooldridge, M. Agent technology. Springer-Verlag New York, Inc., 1998, ch. Applications of intelligent agents, 3–28.
14. Kiesler, S., Zubrow, D., Moses, A. M., and Geller, V. Affect in computer-mediated communication: an experiment in synchronous terminal-to-terminal discussion. *Hum.-Comput. Interact. 1*, 1 (Mar. 1985), 77–104.
15. Kim, K.-J. Cross-cultural comparisons of online collaboration. *Journal of Computer-Mediated Communication 8* (2002).
16. Klein, D., and Manning, C. D. Fast exact inference with a factored model for natural language parsing. In *In Advances in Neural Information Processing Systems 15 (NIPS*, MIT Press (2003), 3–10.
17. Lemerise, E. A., and Arsenio, W. F. An integrated model of emotion processes and cognition in social information processing. *Child Development 71*, 1 (2000), 107–118.
18. Miyabe, M., and Yoshino, T. Accuracy evaluation of sentences translated to intermediate language in back translation. In *Proceedings of IUCS2009*, ACM (2009), 30–35.
19. Miyabe, M., Yoshino, T., and Shigenobu, T. Effects of repair support agent for accurate multilingual communication. In *PRICAI 2008: Trends in Artificial Intelligence*, vol. 5351 of *Lecture Notes in Computer Science*. Springer Berlin / Heidelberg, 2008, 1022–1027.
20. Morita, D., and Ishida, T. Collaborative translation by monolinguals with machine translators. In *Proceedings of the 14th IUI2009*, ACM (2009), 361–366.
21. Papineni, K., Roukos, S., Ward, T., and Zhu, W.-J. Bleu:a method for automatic evaluation of machine translations. In *Proceedings of the ACL2002* (2002), 311–318.
22. Pym, P. J. Pre-editing and the use of simplified writing for mt: an engineer's experience of operating an mt system. In *Translating and the computer* (London, 1990), 80–96.
23. Song, W., Finch, A. M., Tanaka-Ishii, K., and Sumita, E. picotrans: an icon-driven user interface for machine translation on mobile devices. In *Proceedings of the 16th IUI2011*, ACM (2011), 23–32.
24. Specia, L., Raj, D., and Turchi, M. Machine translation evaluation versus quality estimation. *Machine Translation 24* (2010), 39–50.
25. Tsunoda, K., and Hishiyama, R. Design of multilingual participatory gaming simulations with a communication support agent. In *Proceedings of the 28th SIGDOC2010*, ACM (2010), 17–25.
26. Wilks, Y. *Machine Translation: Its Scope and Limits*. Springer, 2009.
27. Yamashita, N., and Ishida, T. Automatic prediction of misconceptions in multilingual computer-mediated communication. In *IUI06* (2006).
28. Yamashita, N., and Ishida, T. Effects of machine translation on collaborative work. In *Proceedings of the 20th CSCW2006*, ACM (2006), 515–524.

Modeling Discussion Topics in Interactions with a Tablet Reading Primer

Adrian Boteanu
Worcester Polytechnic Institute
100 Institute Road Worcester, MA 01609
aboteanu@wpi.edu

Sonia Chernova
Worcester Polytechnic Institute
100 Institute Road Worcester, MA 01609
soniac@wpi.edu

ABSTRACT
CloudPrimer is a tablet-based interactive reading primer that aims to foster early literacy skills and shared parent-child reading through user-targeted discussion topic suggestions. The tablet application records discussions between parents and children as they read a story and leverages this information, in combination with a common sense knowledge base, to develop discussion topic models. The long-term goal of the project is to use such models to provide context-sensitive discussion topic suggestions to parents during the shared reading activity in order to enhance the interactive experience and foster parental engagement in literacy education. In this paper, we present a novel approach for using commonsense reasoning to effectively model topics of discussion in unstructured dialog. We introduce a metric for localizing concepts that the users are interested in at a given moment in the dialog and extract a time sequence of words of interest. We then present algorithms for topic modeling and refinement that leverage semantic knowledge acquired from ConceptNet, a commonsense knowledge base. We evaluate the performance of our algorithms using transcriptions of audio recordings of parent-child pairs interacting with a tablet application, and compare the output of our algorithms to human-generated topics. Our results show that words of interest and discussion topics selected by our algorithm closely match those identified by human readers.

Author Keywords
Context-Aware Computing, User and Cognitive Models, Dialog Analysis

ACM Classification Keywords
H.5.2. Information Interfaces and Presentation (e.g. HCI): User-centered design

General Terms
Design, Human Factors

INTRODUCTION
Currently there is significant interest in applications which track user interest and preferences while adapting to better suit individual needs. Such systems are found in numerous fields, ranging from commercial applications such as online shopping to research in adaptive tutoring ([5], [21]). CloudPrimer is a tablet-based interactive media and reading primer that seeks to foster early literacy skills by enhancing shared parent-child reading. The application is designed to provide an interactive reading experience and to guide readers through various game-like tasks, such as mixing colors and counting. The target age of the children is 3 to 5 years old. Children in this age group go through a rapid learning period during which it is particularly important for them to have interactions with adults, especially their parents, from which they can learn. We have developed an Android-based reading primer that audio records the conversation that takes place between the parent and child as they read an interactive story book. The long-term goal of our work is to facilitate greater parent-child engagement by learning discussion patterns from numerous interactions and to use these patterns during a live reading for suggesting new topics of conversation to broaden the parent-child interaction.

Modeling dialog topics in informal discussion presents a particular set of challenges. In free form discussions, the goals are not agreed upon in advance. Since the participants do not announce detailed intentions on how they expect the interaction to evolve, abrupt changes of subject are frequent. In this relaxed form, expanding the discussion in a direction from which all participants can benefit from the most takes precedence over debating a well defined topic. The main drivers of the conversation are the participants' interests, their relationship and any external inputs, such as a book or movie that they might be discussing.

The context and development of such interactions contrast with formal settings, such as written articles and news broadcasts. The latter have a distinct, professional, approach in handling a subject and describing it. Speakers in this context try to meet the expectations of a large public who does not offer real time feedback, so stating opinions and facts accurately is important. This is accomplished through a crisp discourse which uses names and jargon to anchor the readers' or viewers' focus of attention. In contrast, a casual conversation uses improvised references that are mostly relevant only for the other participants [11].

We designed a system for segmenting, annotating and analyzing spoken dialog data in order to model discussion topics that occur naturally in informal conversation. Taking into account the particular characteristics of such conversations, we incorporate common sense reasoning in evaluating the discussions.

Our system is divided into three major processing components: 1) gathering and annotating the dialog data, 2) modeling the discussion topic, and 3) making real time discussion topic suggestions to enhance the interactions. Our dialog corpus consists of parent-child reading discussions recorded at a local preschool, which have been transcribed to text using Amazon's Mechanical Turk [14]. This paper focuses on the second processing component, modeling the topic of discussion, which will form the basis for the topic suggestion system in our future work. The purpose of the topic modeling component is to summarize the discussion by tracking the readers' interests and produce topics that would seem reasonable to the average person if he/she were be listening to the conversation.

The main contributions of this paper are:

1. a method of assessing users' interest and focus as it changes over the course of the dialog
2. a two-phase topic modeling system that leverages commonsense reasoning

Both contributions are context independent and do not rely on background information about the dialog.

EDUCATIONAL CONTEXT

Early literacy is a term used to describe the stage of literacy development that occurs before children are able to read and write. During this stage, important abilities include cognitive skills, vocabulary development, phonemic awareness and letter knowledge. The development of early literacy skills through early experiences with books and stories has been critically linked to a childs reading and academic success. Repeated studies have shown that reading aloud to children and providing opportunities for them to discuss the stories that they hear is of utmost importance [2].

In recent years, electronic books have been introduced, aiming to promote early literacy and increase child engagement by including animation and sound effects in the stories. Scientific evaluations of these technologies have found that, although engaging, such devices do not effectively achieve educational goals when used alone [8]. Instead, recent studies highlight the importance of joint parent-child reading, showing that learning gains are achieved by combining the use of digital media with adult interaction [18].

Our system aims to foster early literacy skills through the development of an interactive tablet-based reading primer that promotes parental engagement in reading through the use of a targeted discussion topic suggestion system. The primer supports parents in their role as storytellers and teachers by providing suggestions for open ended discussion; Figure 1 presents a possible example.

Figure 1. Simulated in-story discussion suggestion via a dialog box.

Generating diverse and relevant discussion topics is critical to the success of this approach. As a result, instead of precoding a set of fixed topics, our work seeks to leverage a community of readers to crowdsource discussion topic suggestions using recorded interactions to suggest topics for new readers. Specifically, the Cloud Primer application 1) records discussions of parent-child pairs engaged in a reading activity, 2) identifies topics of discussion, 3) builds statistical models of discussion topic transitions, and 4) provides appropriately timed suggestions of discussion topics based on data gathered from across the community of readers. This paper focuses on the second challenge of identifying topics of discussion in transcribed speech.

Modeling topics requires understanding the particular interests of the readers as individuals and as a group. Compared to more traditional printed forms, interactive stories are rich in visual media and contain few words, both printed and spoken. Thus gathering enough personalized context information requires transcriptions of the verbal parent-child interactions. Otherwise the potential discussion topic suggestions would be limited by the relatively rigid and simple story structure.

Performing topic suggestions in real time poses many challenges. Speech recognition is highly unreliable for small children, thus our project relies on crowdsourcing through Amazon Mechanical Turk for speech transcription. Recent work [10] shows that audio transcription by non-experts on Mechanical Turk can be achieved with latency as low as 4 seconds with accuracy over 90%, which is sufficiently close to real time for our application. We anticipate that topic suggestions will lag approximately 10 seconds behind the discussion in the final application due to processing delays. Effective interface design, timing of suggestions and wording of suggestions pose additional future challenges for this work.

RELATED WORK

Several intelligent systems which learn from users have been designed in numerous areas. Such solutions include automated office managers [13], personified assistants [17] and smart house applications [1]. These systems either interact directly with the user, through messages or an avatar, or can change their behavior without explicitly notifying the user. The common approach between all these numerous applications is to create a personalized model by observing an individual user. Our work focuses on extracting relevant patterns from a large population. This will allow our system to have a more general and robust representation of what is relevant for a new reader.

Significant work has been done in tracking topics in news, scientific literature and meetings by using data mining methods and machine learning [9, 4]. However, in that context, topics have a different meaning, focusing on particular events or well defined problems. Common methods used for analysis include finding frequent words of interest and using data mining methods to predict their field. Unlike the casual and ambiguous discussions that we analyze in this project, these methods rely on precise definitions of keywords and historic events. One key difference in our work is that words with multiple meanings can be part of multiple topics, and the tracking process follows each particular meaning separately.

In this paper we introduce a metric for identifying and tracking words that that are relevant to the topic of the conversation. Existing metrics for finding relevant words, such as TF-IDF [16], rely on finding words that have a high frequency in a small subset of documents, differentiating them from other documents. Our project's final goal is to find both common discussion topics and their variations and make suggestions of how to enhance a given interaction based on previous experience.

The bag of words model is a common approach for simplifying text [20]. While the interest metric presented in this paper also reduces the transcriptions to significant sets of words, the key difference is that our approach produces a localized time sequence, as opposed to a single set of words that summarizes the entire text. Furthermore, the topic tracking component of our system takes into account the order in which words occur. Our algorithm for grouping words into topics also has some similarity with K-Means approaches for clustering words [19]. Both our raw topic formation and topic refinement techniques can be viewed as two clustering steps in a nonlinear space, using two different metrics (SVD distance and path length). However, the key differences are the absence of a cluster center and having the same word belong to multiple clusters. Because of these factors, our approach of topic formation is not affected by the initial starting words.

In order to understand how different topics relate to each other, it is important to understand the meaning or concept behind each word. ConceptNet is a freely available commonsense knowledge base and natural-language-processing toolkit which supports many practical textual-reasoning tasks over real-world documents, including topic-gisting, analogy-making, and other context oriented inferences [7]. ConceptNet forms a large graph of concepts connected through relations. From the ConceptNet project, we use the Divisi2 toolkit, which is a sparse singular value decomposition matrix of the graph relations, to measure the pairwise similarity distance between words; we also use the graph data directly.

Finally, in selecting the significant words, for this project we use a method loosely inspired on human short term memory for identifying words of interest that will be grouped into topics. Since the crowdsourced transcriptions already contain significant noise, with the prospect of speech recognition introducing even more noise if used, implementing a complex cognitive system such as ACT-R [3] would be ineffective. Thus, our method implements a simpler function that does not attempt to mimic human cognition.

OVERVIEW OF SYSTEM ARCHITECTURE

In this section, we present a high level description of our system; Sections Identifying Readers' Interest, Raw Topic Formation and Topic Refinement present the core contributions of this work in greater detail. Figure 2 presents the sequence of modules and the data flow. In Table 1 we present a running example that illustrates how the data is processed by each component.

- Dialog Data Collection: represents the crowdsourcing system used for data collection and annotation. Its output is a line by line transcription of the dialogue. This transcription may contain noise, such as misheard words or typos. A short example of this transcription is presented on the first row of Table 1.
- Preprocessing: prepares the transcriptions to be evaluated by the interest metric module. We preprocess the text by removing all stop words and other very common English words. Then we use the Snowball stemming engine [15] on all words. After this stage, the normalized text mostly consists of nouns, verbs and adjectives, all in stem form. Row two of Table 1 contains the result of preprocessing the dialog sample.
- Interest Metric Function: reads the preprocessed text in sequence, one word at a time, and outputs a set of words that, according to our algorithm, the readers are interested in. We consider each word from the preprocessed text a different time step. At each new time step, all words of interest are output as set. An example of how the output set changes through four consecutive moments in time is shown on row three of Table 1. Through this set of words we represent the current concepts that the speakers are interested in as they are talking.
- Topic Vocabulary Creation: creates a set of all words of interest selected across the entire interaction based on the output of the interest metric module above. We convert the word stems to lemmas using the vocabulary built at Stage 2 and build a vocabulary of lemmas, which can be searched in ConceptNet.
- Raw Topic Formation: constructs the raw topics based on the vocabulary of lemmas and the Divisi2 module of ConceptNet. The output of this module presents a starting point for refining topics.
- Topic Refinement: refines topics by exploring ConceptNet's graph structure. Unlike to the previous step, this process involves directly traveling across edges to identify the connected sub-graphs.

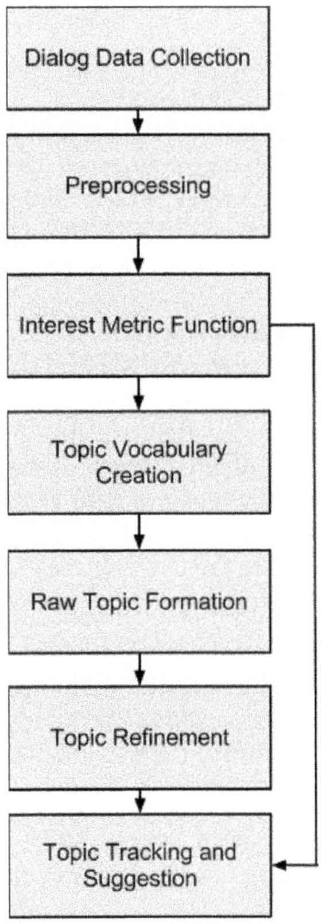

Figure 2. System block diagram.

- Topic tracking and suggestion: This module is a work in progress and is not described in detail in this paper. Using the above generated topics, we construct a Dynamic Bayesian Network in which each word from the vocabulary of lemmas built at Stage 4 is represented as a sensor node. The sensor nodes are connected to latent nodes, each representing a topics, according to the topics produced by Stage 6. We then apply EM on this network using the metric files resulted from Stage 3 to learn the network's parameters. Then, using the generated network, we plan to track topics across other discussions and make recommendations based on the inferred current topic.

IDENTIFYING READERS' INTEREST

The first step in grouping words by topic is to identify which words are the most relevant to the discussion topic. Written text and speech are very different in terms of phrasing, word selection and connectors. In particular, parents talking with their children have other goals beside transmitting a message, such as teaching new words [6]. We observed that parents often have to restate the goals and important concepts to keep their children on track. Another characteristic of dialog is that the density of topic-relevant words, such as nouns, verbs and adjectives, is low compared to a written document. The sequence in which the words are spoken is important for our purposes, since the system must both track topics and make suggestions for developing the discussion as it progresses during the interaction. Finally, crowdsourcing the audio data annotation with Amazon Mechanical Turk introduces noise due to misheard words, worker fatigue or laziness, providing an additional challenge.

Algorithm Stage	Data
1. Dialog Data Collection	Here you go, you have a purple duck. What's your favorite color? Um, purple. So baby duck is hungry, eat two beetles. The beetles? Yeah, that's the beetles. More, more. Those are ladybugs.
2. Preprocessing	purpl duck favorit color um purpl babi duck hungri eat beetl beetl yeah beetl ladybug want beetl need beetl need beetl want feed
3. Interest Metric Function)	Time step 0: {purple tap duck} Time step 1: {purple tap duck beetle} Time step 2: {purple beetle tap duck yeah} Time step 3: {purple beetle tap duck}
4. Topic Vocabulary Creation	{purple tap duck beetle yeah}
5. Raw Topic Formation	{blue purple green yellow different} {ant firefly cricket ladybug beetle} {owl bird duck} {need let want}
6. Topic Refinement	{blue purple green yellow} {different} {ant firefly cricket ladybug beetle} {owl bird duck} {need want} {let}

Table 1. Example of the results after each processing stage.

In this section, we introduce a metric for measuring how interested the user is in words occurring in dialog. Our scope is different from document categorization techniques that process a vast collection of documents searching for words that are both relevant and suitable for discerning among the collection. Instead, we track common words based on how significant they might be to the particular users when reading the story. One premise of the metric is that more frequent words, that have a higher local density, have greater importance. Particular for our scenario, parents often repeat words more than it would be necessary in an adult discussion, so that their children learn or focus on them [6]. Our second assumption is that if a word was spoken frequently during the interaction, it will regain a similar level importance in the conversation if it is mentioned again after a longer period of time. This assumption is inspired from the concept of short term memory, although our system does not attempt to replicate the cognitive process.

Interest Metric Function

We use a set structure to capture all unique word stems and associate each with two values, the interest metric value, m, and the word's relative frequency between its first and last occurrence, f. The system works in steps, one new word representing a new step, analyzing the words in the order in which they were spoken. At each step, the system updates the interest metric value for all words in the set, either increasing the interest metric value if the word occurred at the present step or decreasing it otherwise (Figure 3); new words are added to the set with a default initial metric value. The frequency of a word, f, is calculated in *updateFrequency*, as the number of the word occurrences divided by the total number of words in the interval between the first and the most recent occurrence of the word.

The interest metric value is updated by iterating through all the words in the set and calling the update function (Figure 4)

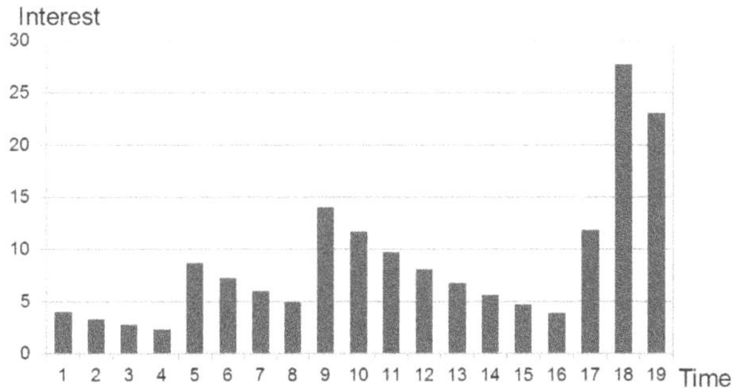

Figure 3. Example on how the interest metric value changes for a word as it is encountered at steps 1, 5, 9, 17 and 18. Note that for steps 17 and 18 the metric value is compensated for very frequent past occurrences.

on each word. If the current word does not match the word in the set, the interest metric value is lowered. If a match is found, the first step is to check (by comparing with the two thresholds on line 2) if the word was frequently spoken before but the current metric value is low. The value of f at this point reflects the previously calculated local frequency of the word. If these conditions are met, the interest metric value is compensated to take into account the readers talking about a word, although the word has not been spoken recently. Requiring both the metric value to be low and the previous local frequency to be high prevents the compensation being applied to common words that have a relatively high frequency but an uniform distribution.

On line 4 the metric function is then increased to mark the word's occurrence. This increase is applied to any word, if it occurs at the present time step. We then compute the new relative frequency over the entire span, from the first occurrence. This limits the number of times a word's interest metric is compensated because, as the discussion progresses, the frequency will gradually approach the average frequency of the word in the text. This enables elements that are present throughout the story, such as the protagonist, to be gradually replaced by newer and more local concepts, making it possible to offer the readers more varied suggestions that follow the story better. For the same purpose, we limit the maximum interest metric value a word can have.

1. $if\ w\ occurred:$
2. $\quad if\ (m < lowMetricThr)\ and\ (f > highFreqThr):$
3. $\quad\quad m \leftarrow m * \frac{a}{1-f}$
4. $\quad m \leftarrow b * (m + c)$
5. $\quad f \leftarrow updateFrequency(w)$
6. $else:$
7. $\quad m = \frac{m}{d} - e$

Figure 4. The algorithm for calculating the interest metric value. Lines 2 and 3 simulate the recent memories that the speakers would have about past discussions. For all the results presented here we used $a = 2, b = 2, c = 2, d = 1.1$ and $e = 0$, after taking into account the average number of words per sentence after preprocessing.

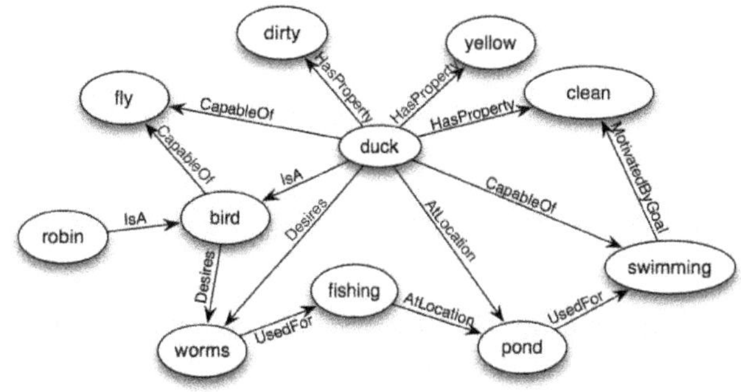

Figure 5. A small example of nodes and relations in ConceptNet

Topic Vocabulary Creation

After reading a new word and updating the interest metric values of the entire set, the module outputs the set of words that have the interest metric value higher than a given threshold. We consider these words to be relevant, or interesting, to the reader at that particular moment. The result is a sequence of sets of words, one per time step (example in row 3 of Table 1). At a given step, the output set can be void if no word has a high enough metric value.

In the final processing stage, words are converted from stem form to lemmas using the spell checking vocabulary with the NLTK library [12]. We also construct the vocabulary of words of interest using the entire metric file. This vocabulary forms the starting point for creating topics, which we present in sections Raw Topic Formation and Topic Refinement.

RAW TOPIC FORMATION

In this section, we describe the first stage of grouping the vocabulary of interest into discussion topics. This step produces rougher topics that are later refined. An example of a set of raw topics is given in Table 1.

The main source of knowledge for our topic creation algorithm is ConceptNet. In its latest version, the ConceptNet project scans online documents such as Wikipedia and compiles a common sense network that links concepts with oriented relations. For example, in the small concept network shown in Figure 5, the concepts 'Duck' and 'Bird' are in the relation 'IsA'. In order to use the stemmed words produced by the interest metric with ConceptNet, first we use the Natural Language Toolkit [12] to convert the word stems into lemmas. The reference vocabulary for retrieving the lemmas is created from the original transcriptions. The subsystem that groups words by topic uses the vocabulary formed by the words of interest; we merge all vocabularies from all discussions, resulting in a general topic model for the story as it was discussed by all readers. This model can be then applied to particular discussions for tracking topics. It is important to note that this general vocabulary of interesting words is much smaller than the vocabulary of the transcriptions, allowing us to use Bayesian networks, since the number of nodes is relatively small (20-30). We define a *topic* as a set of words relating to a common theme, without any particular order. Topics do not have names themselves and are defined only by the words that belong to them. This allows us to model each topic through the common sense relations between its constituent words. One key characteristic is that a word can belong to multiple topics at once. We allow this since words usually have multiple meanings.

The algorithm that constructs topics starts by removing a word from the vocabulary of interest and creating a new topic containing only that word. For all the remaining words in the set, we remove each word one at a time and, using ConceptNet, calculate the similarity distance between that word and all current topics. More specifically, using the sparse matrix Divisi2 toolkit from ConceptNet we compute the distance between the current word and each word in the topic using the singular value decomposition matrix [7]. If the value is above a threshold (i.e. the distance is small enough), the result counts as a positive vote that the word should belong to the topic. If a high enough percentage of words already in the topic give a positive vote, the new word is included in the topic. The process repeats itself until there are no more words in the vocabulary of interest.

We can control the specificity of each topic by adjusting both the minimum similarity threshold as well as the minimum percentage of votes. Figure 6 shows the base algorithm. Divisi2 returns a similarity value between two concepts, in the interval between -1 (completely opposite) and 1(identical). For example, by using a high minimum similarity (0.5) but a

```
topics = ϕ //the set of topics to be created
v = readVocabulary() //the vocabulary of interesting words
for each w in v :
  for each t in topics : //t is a topic:
    similar = 0 //number of votes from words from t
    //tw is a word belonging to the topic t
    for tw in t :
      if (similarity(w,tw) > similarityThreshold) :
        similar = similar + 1
    if similar > size(t) * minSimilarityVote :
      t = t ∪ w
  if w was not added to any existing topic :
    topics = topics ∪ w //create a new topic from w
```

Figure 6. Pseudocode for raw topic creation.

low voting percentage (50%) loose topics are generated, such as the following.

- ant owl bird ladybug duck
- noise tap
- color blue purple green yellow
- need say let want
- ladybug bird beetle
- happen let pass
- cricket bird
- purple different green
- yummy hungry
- firefly ladybug
- push angry

Using a lower similarity threshold (0.3) but a higher minimum voting percentage (85%) produces tighter topics, mostly because a newly introduced word has to have some association with most other words present in the topics, such as the following example:

- owl bird duck
- push tap
- blue purple different green yellow
- ant firefly cricket ladybug beetle
- push say let pass
- need let want
- push happen let pass
- yummy hungry

TOPIC REFINEMENT

The method we introduce in the previous section produces imprecise results. However, it has the advantage of speed over directly exploring the highly connected ConceptNet graph, segmenting the initially very large search space into smaller regions. In this section we introduce a method of refining those results by directly following the graph structure of ConceptNet, which traverses relation edges between concept nodes. ConceptNet contains two types of relations:

- Set relations – some examples are shown in Figure 5: 'IsA', 'AtLocation', etc.
- Concept relations, which have any form – for example, concepts 'Bread' and 'Sandwich' are linked by relation 'be in'.

As with any exploration of very large search spaces, the computational complexity increases dramatically with the depth of the search. From our experience, nodes with a degree of 30 or higher are common. The key idea of refining topics is to find connected components of the subgraph represented by the raw topic in ConceptNet.

We consider two concepts to belong to the same topic after refinement if there is a path between the two respective connected components of at most the length of the search depth. For example, if concepts 'Blue' and 'Red' are both connected by the 'Is A' relation to the concept 'Color', a search with the depth of 2 will consider them belonging to the same topic. Figure 7 shows in pseudocode the algorithm we propose for directly exploring the ConceptNet graph for refining topics.

The advantage of this approach is that it can eliminate any spurious associations introduced by approximating relations with Divisi2, without the high cost of searching in the initial large vocabulary. In our evaluation we found that the most practical search depth is 2. Table 2 shows how the search

```
p = φ
for w in t :
  candidates←the set of all nodes connected to w
             by a path of length d or less
  split ← True
  for q in p: //q is a refined topic:
    if q ∩ candidates = φ :
      q ← q ∪ {w}
      split ← False
  ifsplit = True :
    p = p ∪ {w}
```

Figure 7. Pseudocode for refining topics. t is the topic that is being refined, p is the resulting set of topics after separating the words from t and d is the search depth.

Raw topic	**{deer wing frog duck}**	**{owl bird duck}**	**{push happen let pass}**
Depth = 1	{deer}{wing} {frog}{duck}	{owl}{bird} {duck}	{push}{pass} {happen}{let}
Depth = 2	{deer}{wing} {frog duck}	{owl}{bird duck}	{push}{pass} {happen}{let}
Depth = 3	{deer}{wing} {frog duck}	{owl}{bird duck}	{push}{pass} {happen let}
Depth = 4	{deer} {wing duck} {frog duck}	{owl bird duck}	{push} {happen let pass}

Table 2. Topic refinement results for increasing search depths.

depth affects refining a small topic. In all these examples all types of relations are taken into account.

We found that restricting the search to only some relation types (for example traversing only relation edges 'IsA', 'CapableOf' and 'UsedFor') does not produce better results. Doing so leads to unpredictable output for a given depth because of missing or noisy links. In particular, concept relations, since they do not form a closed set, are difficult to account for in advance through preset filters. For example, one might expect concepts 'Owl' and 'Duck' to be both linked to 'Bird' by the 'Is A' relation, but as Table 2 shows, it takes more than 2 steps to associate them.

RESULTS EVALUATION

To evaluate the performance of our algorithms, we compared the results from three surveys conducted with human participants. In each of the surveys, the participants were presented with either a transcription or a set of words and were asked to answer questions regarding the topic of conversation or word grouping.

Interest metric

To evaluate the performance of our interest metric function, we compared its ability to pick out relevant words in a transcribed conversation to that of human readers. Participants were given short transcriptions of a conversation and were instructed to list five to ten words that captured the main topics of discussion. No information about the broader story plot was provided. In Table 3 we compare the output vocabulary of the interest metric function both with the union and the intersection of the survey responses; 14 participants provided responses to the first transcription, and 10 for the second.

Row 1 from Table 1 presents a short excerpt from one of the transcriptions used. The second column of Table 3 (Interest metric function) shows the vocabulary of important words produced by the interest metric algorithm when applied to the entire transcription. The third column contains the union of all words used by participants. Words that appear in both columns two and three are marked in bold. The fourth column presents the percentage of words from the metric function results that are in bold. Last two columns of the table show the words that were common between all survey respondents and the match percentage with our results.

Comparing our results with the union of all words used by the respondents shows the agreement between our results and the survey responses. The reduced size of the intersection of all survey vocabularies is an indicator of the overall disagreement between respondents. Since there is little agreement between the respondents and the word set is too small to reflect story details, there is no single commonly accepted answer to which we can compare our algorithm's results. However, trying to fully match the vocabulary union of all answers would lead to the inclusion of irrelevant words. Thus, we consider that our results provide a good compromise of general and specific words.

As shown in the 'Match union' column, a significant percentage of words identified by our interest metric function were also present in the survey answers. We found that part of the discrepancy between the columns can be attributed to the fact that (despite specific instructions not to do so) some survey participant answers included words that were not in the text, such as 'number', 'animal' and 'teach'. While these words accurately summarize parts of the discussion, they do not appear in the transcription (e.g., the parent is teaching the child counting and colors, but the word "teach" does not occur in the conversation). Unlike the human participants, our algorithm can only select words of interest from the transcribed words, which is why the density of bold words is higher in the second column compared to the third.

A second observation that we can make is that, while our interest metric module does not discriminate between nouns, verbs and adjectives, human respondents preferred nouns and adjectives to verbs and names. 57% of the words selected by the interest metric that were not matched by participant responses were verbs and names. Among words matched by participants, only 17% were verbs or names. This trend may suggest that humans focus on nouns the most when trying to get the gist of a conversation, though for our particular educational purpose we believe it is important to track all spoken words.

Overall, our interest metric output successfully matches a significant proportion from the words identified by human readers, while avoiding unrepresentative words.

#	Interest metric function	Survey answers vocabulary union	Match union	Survey answers intersection	Match intersection
1	**duck tap color beetle yellow walk ant** say want pass need happen **blue** different **yummy** anymore **purple angry** hurray **bird firefly ladybug cricket** let **baby eat play hungry green push grass**	**angry** animal **ant baby** back **beetle bird blue** butterfly centipede child **color cricket** day done dripping **duck eat** egg finger **firefly** fly frog game go good **grass green** have here help **hungry ladybug** learn **let** lullaby mouth music night open owl page parenthood past **play purple push** read red screen software **tap** teach touch **walk** words **yellow yummy**	70%	**bird tap duck purple**	100%
2	help **brown color** fox **puddle deer** slap **four baby rim** eat **cookie duck** run **arm** even use **feed** let buddy buggy floor six please three next rub **splash** call lot wet white tell **swim blue play good** hit may dive plug little gonna rain job **eight yellow** chris **tub** hold **day care count** kind name **bug many** work **hungry** know **page** turn nine fun five **want wing** talk jack	**feed swim color puddle duck deer** bath **four good** number learn children **day want** toys **count blue hungry arm baby bug splash** teach **white care** teen **brown play** ball giver book story parent you water **cookie tub** red **yellow rim wing** sound animals **eat many** dog **eight** tudy teach learn children school care **page** clap	42%	**duck cookie color**	100%

Table 3. Comparison between keywords identified by our approach, on the left, and keywords identified by human respondents, when given the same text to analyze.

Topic Refinement

We developed two surveys to evaluate the results of our topic refinement algorithm.

The first survey required participants to look through a list of words and select a subset of words that forms a common topic. For example, when presented with the set of words {*brown old long hello thing green yellow okay yes whole white red* } a possible response would be {*brown green yellow white red*}. In total 12 such topics were evaluated through surveys and the results were compared with the topic refinement algorithm output for search depths of 2 and 3. There were 12 participants in this survey, each evaluating only two topics from the 12 possible, amounting to 24 evaluations in total. Having a few evaluations per participant reduced the bias that a particular participant might introduce in the results. The answers for a question were considered to be in agreement only if they were identical.

The average agreement between the survey participants was 66%, which indicates a high probability of respondents disagreeing on selecting words to refine a topic. Table 4 shows, on average, how the survey results compare to our system's output. The table reports the percentage of participants for whom the topic was a *subset* of, exactly the *same* as, a *superset* of, or mostly *different* from the algorithm output. Table 5 shows sample results results of our system's output after topic refinement to participant responses and the classification result used in computing Table 4; for a given topic, the outputs for both search depths are included. These results show that a search dept of 3 produces topics with low cohesion since 58% of the survey results are subsets of the refined topic.

Search Depth	Subset	Same	Superset	Different
2	8.34%	41.66%	25%	25%
3	58.3%	0%	16.7%	25%

Table 4. Average topic refinement results compared survey responses.

The second survey consisted of a set of "odd word out" problems in which respondents were given a short list of words and instructed to select the one that did not fit with the others. The option 'None' was also available in the case that the participants considered that all words were similar. In total there were 26 topics. On average, each topic received 12 different evaluations from participants.

The average agreement between participants was 73.5%. The survey answers can be divided into two groups by agreement, high and low. For the nine topics which contained mostly verbs, the agreement ranged between 30% to 60% with an average of 45.4%. For the rest of the 17 topics, mostly formed by nouns, the agreement ranged between 75% and 100%, with a mean of 88.4%. This high agreement group of topics contains words that are interpreted similarly by the reviewers. In contrast, topics with low agreement contain words with multiple meanings, thus subjective to evaluate. Using a search depth of 2, the topic refinement algorithm matched the dominant decision of the survey answers for 47% of the topics – it either eliminated the same word or kept the topic unchanged. For a search depth of 3, the percentage is 29%. Table 6 presents a few examples of the survey questions, show-

Raw Topic	Survey Response	Depth 2 Result	Depth 2 Class	Search Depth 3 Result	Depth 3 Class
brown old long hello thing green yellow okay yes whole white red	brown green yellow white red	brown green yellow white red	same	brown hello thing green yellow okay yes whole white red	subset
chew tuck stop put let lay touch follow hello	chew tuck lay touch	(no topic)	different	chew lay follow hello	different
seven ten six three next four thing cant nine five eight hello	seven ten six three four nine five eight	three four nine five eight	superset	three next four nine five eight hello	subset

Table 5. Sample results between our approach for refining raw topics (second column) with survey responses.

Raw Topic	Outliers - Topic Refinement	Outliers - Survey Responses
Blue Purple Different Green Yellow	Depth 2, 3: Different	**Different (13/15)** Purple(1/15) None(1/15)
Ant Firefly Cricket Ladybug Beetle	Depth 2: Cricket Depth 3: None	Ant(2/15) Firefly(1/15) Cricket(2/15) Beetle(1/15) **None (9/15)**
Push Say Let Pass	Depth 2, 3: Push Say Let Pass (No common topic found)	Push(1/15) **Say(8/15)** Let(1/15) None(2/15)
Need Want Let	Depth 2, 3: Let	Need(1/15) Let(7/15) None(7/15)
Deer Wing Frog Duck	Depth 2, 3: Deer, Duck	**Wing(12/13)** Duck(1/13)

Table 6. Comparison between our approach and survey responses for refining raw topics. For the survey responses, the number of agreeing responses is shown as a fraction of the total responses for that particular question. If there is one, the predominant decision is in bold.

ing the raw topics, the words selected as outliers by the topic refinement algorithm, and words selected as outliers by the survey participants. Based on these results, we can conclude that our system best matches human respondents when analyzing topics composed of nouns. An exception to this is the example in the last row of Table 6, in which the algorithm was unable to differentiate animals (deer, frog, duck) from a limb (wing). We attribute such errors to currently missing edges in the constantly expanding commonsense knowledge network.

The most significant disagreement, both between our system and the respondents, and between the respondents themselves, occurs on topics consisting of verbs, such as in lines 3 and 4 of Table 6. These collections are more difficult to interpret, and refining the topic would imply adopting a specific angle. For example, on line 3 of the table, the consensus in selecting 'Say' might be that it is the only action that produces speech, but similar classifications can be found to eliminate other words.

This evaluation shows that, for the situations in which human respondents reach consensus on the constituency of a topic, our approach successfully matches that consensus.

CONCLUSIONS AND FUTURE WORK

The system described and demonstrated in this paper allows us to track readers' interest across a conversation and to build dialog topic models. It is a core component of a larger system designed to enhance conversations through real time topic suggestions. This will supplement the current touch input tablet application with the capability to offer intelligent feedback to it's users, making the learning experience more effective while retaining it's the game-like approach.

The methods we introduce are independent of the content of the discussion. When compared to human respondents' replies to the same task, our system's output is similar for both important word selection and topic generation. Because the survey respondents mostly agree with our system's output, we believe that the later stages of the project will provide meaningful hints for parents to develop conversations with their children.

We present an approach to track individual sessions of interaction with the tablet primer. By unifying all vocabularies of interest for all interactions of a parent with their child, we can build a general topic model for that family. We currently have work in progress to merge topics across families and create a generalized topic model for a story. This topic model, which will reflect meaningful trends of what families find interesting to talk about while reading the story, will be used to track topics and make suggestions in the deployment phase of the project.

Acknowledgments

We thank Cynthia Breazeal, David Nunez and Angela Chang for providing the interactive reading primer. This work was supported by the National Science Foundation award number 1117584.

REFERENCES

1. Bouchard, B., Bouzouane, A., and Giroux, S. A smart home agent for plan recognition. In *Proceedings of the fifth international joint conference on Autonomous agents and multiagent systems*, AAMAS '06, ACM (New York, NY, USA, 2006), 320–322.
2. Burns, M., Griffin, P., and Snows, C. Starting out right. a guide promoting children's reading success. wdc, 1999.
3. Douglass, S., and Ball, J. *Large Declarative Memories in ACT-R*. 2009, 222–227.
4. Eisenstein, J., and Barzilay, R. Bayesian unsupervised topic segmentation, 2008.
5. Feng, M., Heffernan, N., and Koedinger, K. Addressing the testing challenge with a web-based e-assessment system that tutors as it assesses. In *WWW '06 Proceedings of the 15th international conference on World Wide Web* (2006), 307–316.
6. Hausendorf, H., and Quasthoff, U. Patterns of adult-child interaction as a machanism of discourse acquisition. *Journal of Pragmatics 17* (1992), 241–259.
7. Havasi, C., Speer, R., and Alonso, J. *ConceptNet: A lexical resource for common sense knowledge*, vol. 5. John Benjamins Publishing Company, 2009.
8. Korat, O., and Shamir, A. The educational electronic book as a tool for supporting children?s emergent literacy in low versus middle ses groups. *Computers & Education 50*, 1 (2008), 110–124.
9. Krause, A., and Guestrin, C. Data association for topic intensity tracking. Tech. rep., In International Conference on Machine Learning (ICML, 2006.
10. Lasecki, W., Song, Y., Kautz, H., and Bigham, J. Real-time crowd labeling for deployable activity recognition, 2012.
11. Linell, P. *Approaching Dialogue*, vol. 1. John Benjamins Publishing Company, Philadelphia, PA, 1998.
12. Loper, E., and Bird, S. Nltk : The natural language toolkit. *Processing 1*, July (2002), 1–4.
13. Modi, J., Veloso, M., Smith, F. S., and Oh, J. Cmradar: A personal assistant agent for calendar management, 2005.
14. Paolacci, G., Chandler, J., and Ipeirotis, P. Running experiments on amazon mechanical turk, 2010.
15. Porter, M. Snowball: A language for stemming algorithms.
16. Ramos, J. Using tf-idf to determine word relevance in document queries, 2003.
17. Rich, C., and Sidner, C. L. Collagen: A collaboration manager for software interface agents. *User Modeling and User-Adapted Interaction 8* (1998), 315–350. 10.1023/A:1008204020038.
18. Segal-Drori, O., Korat, O., Shamir, A., and Klein, P. Reading electronic and printed books with and without adult instruction: effects on emergent reading. *Reading and Writing 23*, 8 (2010), 913–930.
19. Steinbach, M., Karypis, G., and Kumar, V. A comparison of document clustering techniques. In *In KDD Workshop on Text Mining* (2000).
20. Wallach, H. M. Topic modeling: beyond bag-of-words. In *Proceedings of the 23rd international conference on Machine learning*, ICML '06, ACM (New York, NY, USA, 2006), 977–984.
21. Weld, D., Adar, E., Chilton, L., Hoffmann, R., Horvitz, E., Koch, M., Landay, J., Lin, C., and Mausam, M. Personalized online education a crowdsourcing challenge. In *Workshops at the Twenty-Sixth AAAI Conference on Artificial Intelligence* (2012).

Semi-automatic Generation of Recommendation Processes and their GUIs

Hermann Kaindl[†], **Elmar P. Wach**[‡], **Ada Okoli**[◇], **Roman Popp**[†], **Ralph Hoch**[§], **Werner Gaulke**[$], **Tim Hussein**[$]
[†]Vienna University of Technology, Austria, kaindl@ict.tuwien.ac.at, roman.popp@tuwien.ac.at
[‡]STI Innsbruck, Austria, elmar.wach@sti2.at
[◇]Smart Information Systems, Austria, a.okoli@smart-infosys.at
[§]Dornbirn, Austria, hoch.ralph@gmail.com*
[$]University of Duisburg-Essen, Germany, werner.gaulke@uni-due.de, tim.hussein@uni-due.de

ABSTRACT
Creating and optimizing content- and dialogue-based recommendation processes and their GUIs (graphical user interfaces) manually is expensive and slow. Changes in the environment may also be found too late or even be overlooked by humans. We show how to generate such processes and their GUIs semi-automatically by using knowledge derived from unstructured data such as customer feedback on products on the Web. Our approach covers the whole lifecycle from knowledge discovery through text mining techniques to the use of this knowledge for semi-automatic generation of recommendation processes and their user interfaces as well as their comparison in real-world use within the e-commerce domain through A/B-variant tests. These tests indicate that our approach can lead to competitive results in terms of click-out rate, while requiring much less manual effort.

ACM Classification Keywords
H.5.2 User Interfaces: Graphical user interfaces (GUI)

General Terms
Design

Author Keywords
E-commerce; recommender systems; dialogue-based recommenders; model-based UI generation; ontologies.

INTRODUCTION
Dialogue-based recommendation processes have proven to be helpful tools in the area of e-commerce. Like content-based recommenders, they are based on explicit information about the items. According to [14], dialogue-based recommenders are especially helpful when users are looking for complex items that they do not buy very frequently (cars or computers, for instance). Manually creating and continuously optimizing such processes and their GUIs (graphical user interfaces), however, is laborious and error-prone.

*Ralph Hoch did this work while being with the Institute of Computer Technology (ICT) of the Vienna University of Technology.

In order to reduce the costs of creating a content- and dialogue-based recommendation process and its GUI for real-world use, we strived for automation. The recommender lifecycle proposed in this article makes use of knowledge sources on related products on the Web in order to generate recommendation processes semi-automatically.

To illustrate the approach, we use a running example based on a given product domain ontology (PDO). We use ontologies, since such formal representations can be more easily processed automatically than conventional, usually less structured product descriptions. The given PDO for mobile phones contains 74 properties representing various mobile phone features such as "face detection" or "operating system". These properties are referenced in the recommender dialogue to ask the end-users about their preferences (for instance, "Which operating system do you prefer?").

Within the automated recommender lifecycle, customer feedback on the products that are supposed to be recommended can be found as unstructured text on the Web. We use text mining techniques in order to adapt the PDO, including its annotations like recommendation priorities. Subsequently, the adapted PDO is used to generate a high-level abstraction of a recommendation process. Using domain-specific heuristics, this process is operationalized in all its details, including a GUI for its actual use by customers. We consider this an intelligent user interface supporting the customer in the course of browsing and potentially buying products. For instance, this approach ranked features higher that were related to the mobile phone display and the operating systems, while they were neglected or ranked differently in a human-generated version.

We deployed such a semi-automatically generated process in a real-world setting and compared its results to a process that was previously created manually. We use A/B-variant tests for this comparison. Data from real-world deployment of this new and automated approach provide empirical evidence of its usefulness. Deployed at a large e-commerce platform and tested with about 1,500 different customers, this approach increased the rate of customers who followed the recommendations by 14%. In addition to that, it reduced the manual adaptation work to very roughly half as much time. We regard the proposed recommender lifecycle as the major contribution of this paper, combining several mechanisms into an integrated approach that has proven to increase the quality of the recommendations while reducing manual effort.

The remainder of this paper is organized in the following manner. After discussing the state of the art, we introduce the recommender lifecycle, describing its components in detail. After that, we present an evaluation of this approach based on data obtained from real-world deployment. We conclude this paper by discussing the approach in a broader context.

STATE OF THE ART

To the best of our knowledge, no previous approach can directly be compared to the recommendation lifecycle proposed in this paper. However, several solutions for certain aspects of it have been proposed in the past. Dialogue- or critique-based recommenders have been in the focus of research for more than a decade [3, 18, 27]. In e-commerce, they have proven to be a good choice for guiding users through a variety of alternatives. While the user has a rather passive role in frequently used algorithms such as collaborative filtering [11], dialogue-based recommenders offer (and require) a higher degree of interaction between user and system. As a result, users tend to trust dialogue-driven recommendations more compared to recommendations generated by the system without interaction [30]. However, it is not trivial to select and order the questions that are supposed to be used in such a dialogue [5].

Explicit customer feedback to recommendations is rather scarce [15], so sources such as customer reviews or blog entries should be taken into consideration for revising the dialogue models according to recent trends or customer opinions. Data mining techniques have been proven to work well in the field of recommender systems [2]. They have, for instance, been used to identify the most salient features of products [12], to approximate user ratings [4], and to use this information directly during the recommendation generation process [16, 24, 32]. Mining and sentiment analysis techniques can be especially helpful, if collaborative filtering techniques do not yield meaningful recommendations due to sparsity problems [31].

In our case, ontologies build the foundation for the recommendations. Middleton et al. have introduced systems that use ontologies as a representation of user interests [19]. Ontological user profiling in recommender systems is also used by Sieg et al. [28]. Systems that use semantic product data [10] have been proposed as well. Hussein and Ziegler use product ontologies in combination with context ontologies for generating context-aware recommendations [13].

Mahmood and Ricci describe a conversational recommendation process as a sequential decision problem and model it as a Markov Decision Process [17]. A model of the user behavior is learned and used to acquire the adaptive strategy through Reinforcement Learning techniques. In this context, the system learns an optimal strategy by observing the effects of its actions on the final outcome of the recommendation sessions. Like in our approach, Aciar et al. use text mining techniques to analyze customer feedback [1]. However, their solution is not intended to be used in combination with conversational recommenders and does not provide a lifecycle like ours.

Website morphing as proposed by Hauser et al. [9] uses Bayesian Inference and Dynamic Programming to adapt layout and presentation of a Website to the user's preferred way of processing information. It focuses on how content is presented, while our approach creates a process and its content. In principle, these two approaches are complementary and could be combined.

THE PROPOSED RECOMMENDER LIFECYCLE

Figure 1 provides an overview of the proposed recommender lifecycle, illustrating the flow between the different steps. Initially, feedback is crawled and analyzed from customer reviews. Based on the results, the Product Domain Ontology (PDO) is updated, for instance by adding properties reflecting certain features that recently emerged for a type of product. The PDO then builds the foundation for discourse-based models, which in turn are used to generate concrete recommendation processes. Finally, the performance results of new recommendation processes are compared to those of existing ones using A/B tests. The dotted arrow indicates that the test results could be used to automatically adjust the PDOs again. This feature, however, is outside the scope of this paper.

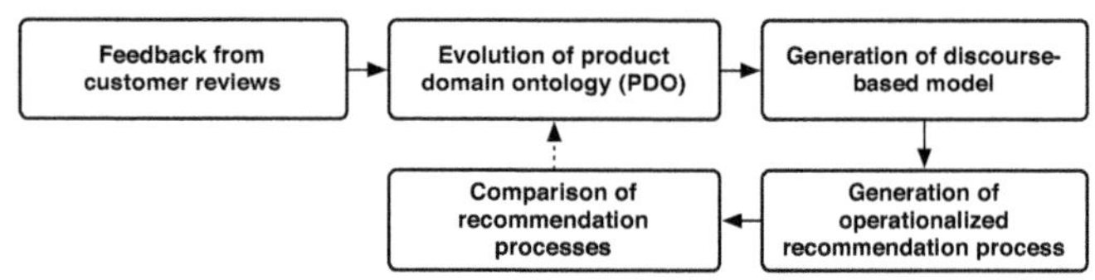

Figure 1. Overview of the recommender lifecycle.

Customer feedback on products

Discussing and reviewing products has become common in the modern Web. Users can express their opinion about a product on various sites. For example, many retailers such as amazon.com offer rating and feedback mechanisms for products offered. The approach presented in this paper analyzes customer feedback on products of a given product domain to identify the importance of certain features.

The underlying assumption for our approach is, that important features are discussed more often than unimportant ones. Hence, we count the number of appearances of features in the reviews. We do not take into account whether the feature is mentioned in a positive or negative way. We assume that the opinion about a feature is tied to the specific product and cannot be applied to the whole domain but the fact that the feature itself was mentioned makes it important.

Analysis of customer reviews is a major goal in the research of text- and opinion mining and several approaches are investigated [20]. Figure 2 illustrates the most important steps for processing customer feedback. The architecture is based on the approach for review analysis proposed by Hu and Liu [12] and was extended to support multiple feature detection techniques.

First, reviews are crawled from previously specified online sources. They are stored along with meta-data such as the respective publication date. Then, text mining algorithms are used to identify features mentioned in the reviews. We call these features *candidates*. These candidates are compared to

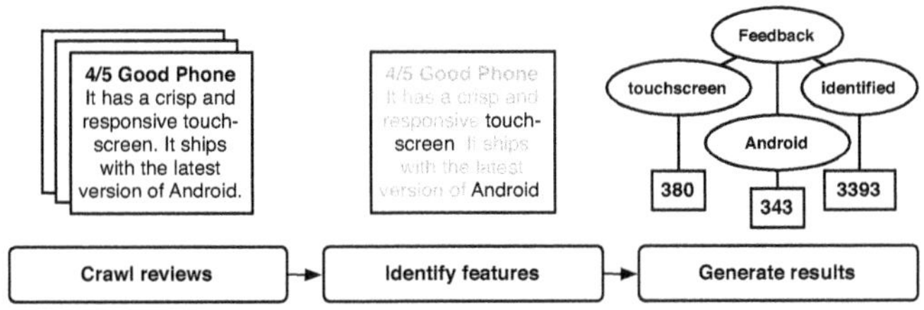

Figure 2. Steps necessary for feedback processing.

the features currently included in the PDO. Both candidates and existing features are counted and stored in a semantic representation for processing them later in the lifecycle.

The current implementation integrates supervised, unsupervised and probability-based algorithms for feature detection. Multiple Feature mining algorithms are used to even out shortcomings of the respective approaches. For example, the supervised associate rule mining algorithm proposed by Popescu and Etzioni [22] is used to detect features mentioned explicitly or implicitly. For each product domain, training data is, however, necessary. The unsupervised approach based on the ideas of Hu and Liu [12] does not need training data but is limited to features mentioned explicitly. It relies on the assumption that most of the features appear as nouns or in noun phrases. The probability-based word frequency algorithm proposed by Scaffidi et al. [26] uses a statistical approach to calculate probabilities for each mentioned noun in order to identify uncommon phrases as feature candidates.

After that, the feature lists obtained from these algorithms are compared to the features currently specified in the PDO, using the Levenshtein Distance algorithm for matching purposes. Candidates that could not be matched to features in the PDO are stored in order to be reviewed manually.

These steps are processed asynchronously. A scheduler crawls and analyzes new reviews on a regular basis.

Product domain ontology (PDO)

A PDO is the formal, explicit specification of a shared conceptualization of products and is specified in OWL DL[1]. In our case, the PDO includes both classes (concepts) and individuals as well as annotations (for example on priorities for the respective recommendation processes). The PDO should always contain the most important features for a certain product type. Thus, the PDO is adjusted regularly to reflect the results of the mining and analysis step.

Generally, ontologies may need to change if (i) there is an error in a prior version, (ii) a new way of modeling the domain is preferred, or (iii) a new terminology has been created[2]. In this research, customer feedback leads to reason (ii). The main research question is: How can feedback be utilized to facilitate PDO evolution with little or no human effort?

To answer the question, our recommender has been specified according to the adaptation strategy proposed in [29], and a feedback cycle has been established in which the feature relevance is fed back. This feedback metric is transformed into the Success Trend *ST*. The PDO is modeled according to GoodRelations[3] and evolved within that upper ontology. An excerpt of the PDO for mobile phones and related GoodRelations entities is depicted in Figure 3.

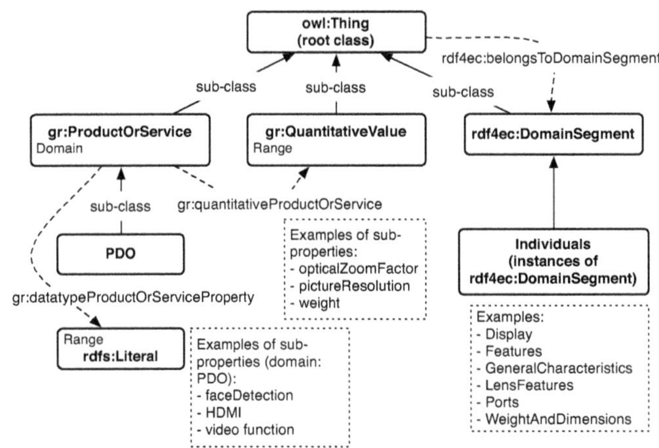

Figure 3. PDO 'MobilePhone' and related GoodRelations entities (excerpt). Solid lines indicate class relations, while dashed lines represent property relations.

The root class is `owl:Thing`, which has several sub-classes. Among them are GoodRelations classes[4] such as `gr:ProductOrService` or `gr:QuantitativeValue`. Instances of the class `rdf4ec:DomainSegment`[5] represent groups of properties used in the respective product domain such as *WeightAndDimensions*. The PDO for the running example has 11 DomainSegments and is modeled as a sub-class of the class `gr:ProductOrService`.

The features of a product are modeled as properties (for instance, the weight of a mobile phone). In OWL, a property maps elements of a certain *domain* onto elements of a certain *range*. *Object properties* map objects or classes onto other objects or classes, whereas the range for *datatype properties* are literals such as Boolean or integer values, for instance.

In our PDO, the class `gr:ProductOrService` is the domain for all properties. In case the feature is modeled as an object property (`gr:quantitativeProductOrServiceProperty`), the range is the class `gr:QuantitativeValue`. Examples of object properties are depth, height, and weight which are sub-properties of `gr:quantitativeProductOrServiceProperty`. In case the feature is modeled as a datatype property (`gr:datatypeProductOrServiceProperty`), the range is a literal (`rdfs:Literal`). Examples of datatype properties are android, keyboard, and touchscreen which are sub-properties of the property `gr:datatypeProductOrServiceProperty` and have as domain the class MobilePhone, which is the sub-class of the class `gr:ProductOrService`. Each property is correlated with one individual via the annotation property `rdf4ec:belongsToDomainSegment`.

[1]OWL DL provides sufficient expressivity and is still decidable
[2]www.w3.org/TR/webont-req/#goal-evolution
[3]www.purl.org/goodrelations
[4]Those entities start with the namespace `gr:`
[5]`rdf4ec` is a custom namespace.

Additionally, the property `rdf4ec:priority` represents annotations on the relevance of product features for the related recommendation processes. The domain of this annotation property is the class `owl:Thing` and the range is specified through the datatype `integer` with values [0...+100]. It indicates the importance of a property and is used for processing the explicit customer feedback. A higher value of `rdf4ec:priority` means that the question about this feature is more important and, hence, be asked earlier in the dialogue.

The explicit customer feedback gathers information about products based on PDO extractions and is thus PDO- and property-based. The corresponding metric is "Feature relevance", whose RDF includes the property (i.e., feature name) and its relevance based on the count of appearances on the Web over a period of time. It is defined as $Feat(t)$ with the range $[0 \ldots [$. $Feat(t)$ is converted into ST, which has the range $[0 \ldots +100]$, by calculating the new relevance of each property with the relative frequencies of the properties contained in the customer feedback. First, the maximum and minimum values of the properties as well as the sum of the values of all properties are determined and the interval for 100 classes is calculated. Second, the relative frequencies of the properties are calculated. Third, after having determined the classes and their bounds, the corresponding properties (i.e., the relative frequency of the property is within the bounds of the respective class) as well as the respective relevance are assigned to the classes. The new relevance is represented as given above (i.e., as annotation property `rdf4ec:priority`).

The feature relevance of the initial PDO was manually set to the same value for each property (i.e., all 74 properties had a priority of 30 as a heuristic guess, since only properties with high property values were used to generate the dialogues). Also, the triggering result of the A/B-variant test was manually designed. Subsequently, the customer feedback from the explicit customer feedback channel was retrieved, and $Feat(t)$ values for twenty properties were delivered (e.g., the property "android" describing the operating system appeared 343 times in the reviews). "keyboard" had the maximum $Feat(t)$, with a value of 500; "integratedRadio", however, was named only once. In total, all identified properties were discussed 3,393 times. The processing of the explicit feedback followed the three steps described above and finally led to the new priorities. Table 1 lists the development of `rdf4ec:priority` of the product features.

Table 1. Relevance changes of selected properties.

Property	$ST(t_0)$ (rdf4ec:priority)	$Feat(t_1)$	$ST(t_1)$ (rdf4ec:priority)
keyboard	30	500	100
touchscreen	30	380	77
android	30	343	69
flash	30	248	50
displaySizeInch	30	160	33
resolutionText	30	99	21
symbian	30	33	7
operatingSystem	30	23	6
integratedRadio	30	1	1

For properties that do not appear in the customer feedback, a specific function, the *Decay Function*, has been developed, calculating the priority for each of those product features. This function proposes a slight decrease of the relevance of a product feature (i.e., priority) in the first time period and a quicker decay later. This is due to the fact that the PDO already contains the priorities of product features derived from customer feedback earlier. Missing explicit customer feedback on a product feature should neither lead to its abolition nor to a strong decrease of its priority in a short time period. The Decay Function further proposes that the priority of a product feature will drop to zero (i.e., decay) after a certain period of time (e.g., in case a product feature has not been discussed for one year), which can be manually specified. It is a function: $Prio(t_0) \in \mathbb{N} \rightarrow Prio(t) \in \mathbb{N}$ where *Prio* is the priority of a product feature, t_0 is the point of time of the precedent customer feedback processing, and *t* is the point of time of the current customer feedback processing.

$$Prio(t) = Prio(t_0) + 1 - Rep * e^{\frac{t * \ln \frac{Prio(t_0)+1}{Rep}}{Decay}} \in \mathbb{N}$$

where *Prio(t)* is the priority of a product feature at time *t* (with 0.5 being rounded up), which is the point of time of the current customer feedback processing, *t* is the number of days from an initial date, *Prio(t_0)* is the priority of a product feature at time t_0, which is the point of time of the precedent customer feedback processing[6], *Rep* is the representativeness of not discussing a product feature, which reduces the priority of a product feature the more reliable the absence of a discussion is (the default value is +1), *Decay* is the number of days to a priority of zero (the default value is 365 days).

For the running example, the customer feedback processing was on October 28, 2011. The initial date is defined to be September 1, 2011 (i.e., the deployment of the prototype). Hence, *t* is 57 (i.e., 57 full days after September 1). With the default values for *Rep* and *Decay*, the new priorities are calculated to be 29.29, thus the initial priorities are decreased from 30 to 29.[7] Examples of properties that got this priority are bluetooth, GPS, integratedCamera, mp3Player, videoFunction, and WLAN.

After the feedback processing, a new PDO version is created. With the process described, the PDO adapts to the feedback automatically without any explicit, direct intervention from a human.

Recommendation processes as discourse-based models

From such an annotated PDO, we automatically generate a recommendation process on a conceptual level first. It is represented as a discourse-based model (for the background and a definition of such models see, for instance, [6, 23]). The Discourse Model, as its major part, essentially consists of questions and answers about those items annotated as important in the PDO, and their sequence.

Figure 4 shows an excerpt of such a Discourse Model. The related questions and answers are modeled as so-called *Adjacency Pairs* (shown as diamonds), with opening and closing Communicative Acts (shown as rounded rectangles). These

[6] A property that has never received customer feedback gets the value it had on the initial date

[7] 29.29 is rounded off to the next integer, which is 29

Adjacency Pairs are related to so-called *Discourse Relations*. In a model of such a recommendation process, only three types of Discourse Relations are used. The first one, `Sequence`, is shown as hexagon (since it is more specifically a Procedural Construct), the second, `Joint`, and the third one, `Background`, are shown as rectangles (since they are Rhetorical Relations). Because such a model can have many `Joint` relations and many Question-Answer Pairs, only one such element is shown each in order to visualize the pattern, which is repeated.

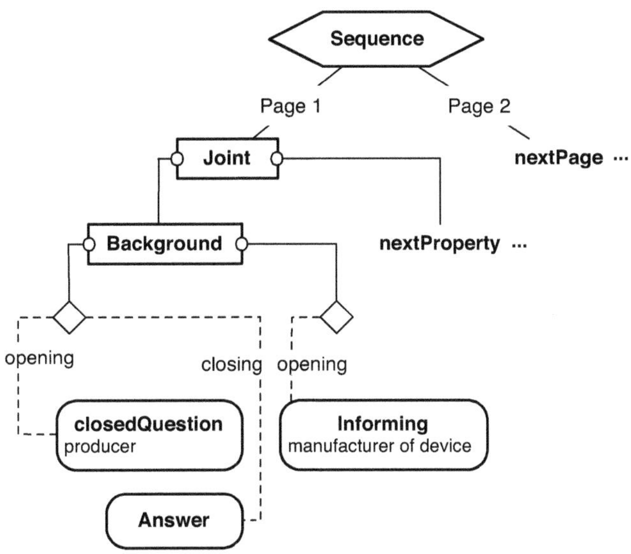

Figure 4. Excerpt of Discourse Model of recommendation process.

The automatic generation of such a model comprises two steps. First, our model-transformation approach transforms the instances of the PDO classes and their concrete datatypes and object property values into a model of the *content* of the communication (the Domain-of-Discourse model). Second, a set of model-transformation rules matches parts of the PDO (including its individuals) and transforms them automatically into corresponding parts of a Discourse Model. This step also defines the content of the Communicative Acts, so that the Discourse Model refers to the Domain-of-Discourse Model.

In the first step, all properties of the PDO are analyzed. Each property is stored as a datatype in the Domain-of-Discourse Model. For most of the datatypes, the values used by the individuals are added to the datatype. In case of numeric properties, only the minimum and maximum values are stored in the Domain-of-Discourse Model. All properties that are set on a minimum of 70% of the individuals are taken into account for further calculations in the second step, since it was observed in real-world practice over time that users trust the results more, if an answer leads to a sufficient number of products. The other properties are not used, since they do not seem to be relevant for a sufficient number of individuals.

In the second step, a Discourse Model is created. For each used property a question-answer pair is created according to a predefined template. Such a template consists of a *Question* and a corresponding *Answer* Communicative Act. These two Communicative Acts are connected with an *Adjacency Pair*. The description property of the transformed property is added to the defined Discourse-Model part with a *Background* relation connecting the Question-Answer Adjacency Pair with an *Informing* Communicative Act, containing the description. It is also possible that some properties of a domain segment are combined into a single question. This combination is applied, if there is more than one property of type Boolean. In our running example, the properties of the domain segment *Operating Systems* are combined. Several properties like *android*, *symbian*, *windowsMobile* have been combined to form a single question.

The generated parts of the Discourse Model are then sorted according to previously specified heuristics. An example of such a heuristic is, that the question for the producer property always has to be the first one. Another heuristic is, that questions for properties with a high priority are asked before properties with a lower priority. This sorted list is then divided into more logical units (eventually becoming pages in the resulting user interface). Each of these logical units has a configurable value of questions. In the Discourse Model, each of these logic units is represented with a *Joint* Relation, connecting the respective parts. The generated Joint Relations are connected then with a *Sequence* Relation specifying their order.

Operationalized recommendation process and its UI

Finally, the discourse-based models can be used to generate so-called *concrete user interfaces (CUI)* as depicted in Figure 5 as well as the actual recommendation processes that are eventually used on the Website. The CUI comprises both the structure of the process and the course of events, which defines how end-users navigate through the process.

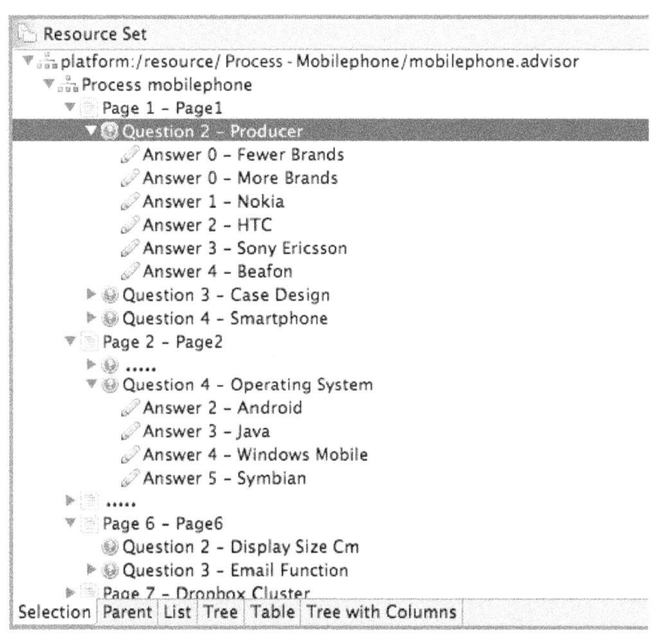

Figure 5. Advisor Model example at the CUI level.

Several heuristics are used for refining the discourse-based models and for transforming elements into concrete representations. The following list illustrates selected specifications of the question element:

- *String questions* have several predefined answer sets that are defined in the Domain-of-Discourse Model and refer to a specific property. The "Producer" property in Figure 5 represents such a question, as each answer (a brand in this case) is only related to one property.
- *Numeric questions* referring to specific properties enable to define a value range such as "Display Size Cm". Boundary values and step-width are defined in the Domain-of-Discourse Model.

Furthermore, a specific representation of each question type is defined. A numeric question, for example, can be represented by a single (minimum or maximum value) or double slider (range of values). In Figure 5 for instance, "Display Size Cm" represents a numeric question. Slider values, such as start and end value, are based on the actual values of the products and the specific representation is predefined in the Domain-Of-Discourse Model. Similar representations apply to the other question types. In addition to that, several other heuristics support the model transformation, covering for instance:

- text-patterns for questions,
- definition of background information,
- restricted answers per question,
- restricted answer selection per question, etc.

The resulting model comprises the logical layers used during a recommendation process. This means that a root element "process" serves as a starting point, containing an ordered set of pages. These pages are used as containers for question-answer pairs, where each question can have multiple related answers. Answers themselves can be restricted and special answer elements can be used to show/hide additional answers ("more"/"less" switch). Moreover, questions are based on product properties and have varying characteristics, which are rendered differently in the final user interface. Figure 6 illustrates an example with two different question types and their respective representations.

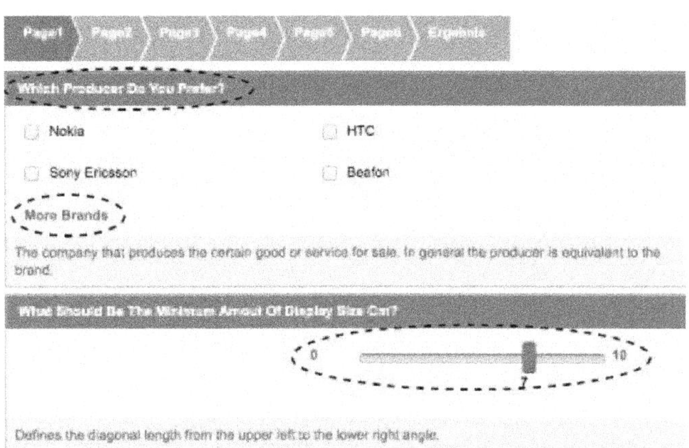

Figure 6. Example of a generated user interface.

Enabling the user to easily navigate through the process and to identify the important parts is mandatory. Thus, heuristics have been put in place to support this task. We demonstrate this behavior using the "Producer" property. Text-patterns are used to automatically generate meaningful questions that can easily be processed by end-users. Different approaches are used for different question types. In case of a string question, the text-pattern uses the property name to create a comprehensive question. Furthermore, the number of answers is limited and only a fragment is shown, so that customers are not overwhelmed by options. A special switch can be used to show/hide additional answers ("more"/"less" switch).[8]

A CUI model can be seen as a 1:1 mapping for the final user interface but still is independent from concrete implementations. One of the benefits of this method is that it facilitates manual adjustment of the process, if necessary, without changes at the implementation level. Adjustments can involve, for example, adding/deleting elements (pages, questions and answers) as well as changing question types. In addition to that, it facilitates the use of different implementations or layouts for the final user interface.

Figure 5 shows how a generated recommendation process model on the CUI-Level looks like. Technically, it is transformed into an RDF representation and stored in a database, serving as input for an already existing GUI-building component of the participating company. From this information on structure and content of the recommendation process, this component generates HTML-based GUIs as the one depicted in Figure 6. In essence, it queries the database with the RDF representation to automatically populate flexible HTML-based templates with the actual content such as questions, answers, and texts, and configures the layout according to the recommendation process model at hand. This does not require any modifications of source code.

The combination of actual instance data (e.g., products of a specific Web-shop) is done at runtime by an external engine, enabling a more flexible UI behavior than the runtime engine that some of the authors presented in previous publications [7, 23]. The engine used for recommendation generation allows the user to redefine his or her criteria and also to go back in the process.

EVALUATION

In order to measure the effectiveness of our approach, we compared the semi-automatically generated recommendation processes to manually created ones in a real-world retail setting.

General design

The study was designed and executed together with an Austrian company that offers recommendation process dialogues as a service for retailers. A large German online retailer (client of the Austrian company) was involved as well. The experiment ran for 14 consecutive days and involved 2,168 uninformed online customers, who accessed the recommendation processes to find suitable mobile phones.

[8] For the sake of simplicity, this is a simplified description of the CUI-Model. It is possible to parameterize the model transformation, and various heuristics are in place for different requirements.

Usually, the recommendation processes are designed manually by the company's project managers, who have the necessary domain knowledge and are skilled in designing successful recommendation processes for different online shops. The designed recommendation processes meet high quality standards and thus, can serve as a baseline for the evaluation. In addition to the effectiveness of the semi-automatically created recommenders, we also wanted to know if our approach can help reduce the manual effort required for the setup of recommender processes. Although we did not execute a specific study dedicated to this question, the evaluation process yielded some information regarding this aspect as well.

Study 1: Mobile phones

We used A/B-variant tests to measure the effectiveness of the semi-automatically generated recommendation processes for mobile phones. The manually created recommendation process (A) and the semi-automatically created recommendation process (B) were each displayed to approximately 50% of all customers who visited the retailer's Website within the test period. From July 7 to October 28, 2011, we crawled and analyzed a total of 4,044 reviews from amazon.com for the domain of mobile phones. Based on these reviews, 3,393 features were identified and compared to those in the existing PDO for mobile phones. For example, the feature "touchscreen" was mentioned 380 times, whereas "weight" was only mentioned 165 times.

Both the semi-automatically generated and the manually created recommendation processes order product features according to their relevance for users. This procedure is based on the underlying assumption that the effectiveness of a dialogue-based recommender systems increased, if the selectable product features were arranged by relevance. While human domain experts applied their domain knowledge to identify the relevance of product features, the semi-automatically generated recommendation processes exploited information from user reviews and the corresponding ranking of the product features within the PDO, which is explained above. At the time of the test, the manually created variants were about 7 months old.

For the evaluation, we applied the frequently used "click-out rate"[9] in order to measure the effectiveness of the process. In our case, it denotes the fraction of successful recommendations compared to the total amount of generated recommendations. A recommendation is regarded as successful, if the user requests details about the particular product or puts it in his or her electronic shopping cart.

Results of Study 1

Comparing the mobile phone recommendation process (Table 2), we found that the semi-automatically generated variant of the mobile phone recommendation process placed features such as *display* or *operating systems* on higher positions, while these were ranked differently or neglected by humans.

Moreover, product features that were related to Multimedia (Camera, Video, MP3) and Connectivity (WLAN, GPS, Bluetooth) were listed on lower positions within the semi-automatically generated variant. This suggests that these features have lost relevance over time, unrecognized by the domain experts. These results reflect the relevance of properties as given in Table 1. Here, the product features *touchscreen*, *displaySizeInch* and *resolutionText (Display)* and *android (Operating system)* received higher priorities than *videoFunction* and *mp3Player (Multimedia)* or *WLAN, GPS and Bluetooth (Connectivity)*.

Table 2. Comparison of ranking of properties in mobile phone recommendation processes. Left: Manually created process. Right: Semi-automatically generated process.

Left:

- Brand
- Price
- Multimedia
  - Camera
  - Video
  - MP3
- Connectivity
  - WLAN
  - GPS
  - Bluetooth
- Operating System
  - Android
  - Symbian

Right:

- Brand
- Price
- **Display**
  - Touch Display
  - Color Display
  - Display size
- **Operating System**
  - Android
  - Symbian
- Camera
- Connectivity
  - WLAN
  - GPS
  - Bluetooth

Table 3 shows the results of the A/B-variant test in which the semi-automatically generated mobile phone recommendation variant (B) was tested against a manually created variant (A).

Table 3. Results of A/B test with instances of the recommendation process generated (A) manually and (B) semi-automatically. UC: unique clients, CO: click-outs, COR: click-out rate.

Variant	UC	CO	COR
(A) Manual	1,068	421	0.394
(B) Generated	1,100	496	0.451

The method for comparing two proportions from univariate inferential statistics was used to calculate the results. The null hypothesis, which states that the two samples show no significant differences ($H_0 : variantA = variantB$), was tested. Additionally, the confidence interval was calculated in order to determine a lower and upper bound of the absolute difference between the two proportions.

A total of 1,068 unique clients used the manually created variant, which had 421 click-outs. The semi-automatic variant had 1,100 unique clients and 496 click-outs. The comparison of the two mobile phone variants shows, that the null hypothesis (H_0) should be rejected and a significant difference between the two variants exists ($z = -2.67, \alpha = 0.05$). With a confidence of 95%, the semi-automatic variant performed between 2% and 10% better in terms of absolute proportions than the manual variant ($\alpha = 0.05$).

Study 2: Other product categories

As a follow-up study, we carried out another one that included a total of seven product categories: Blu-ray player, camcorder, printer, receiver, video projector, DVD player and TFT screen. This study was set up analogously to the mobile phone study.

[9]Sometimes referred to as "click-through rate."

Results of Study 2

Table 4 sums up the results of the second study. For each domain the proportion was compared and tested, whether a significant difference between the two cases exists and H_0 should be rejected for $\alpha = 0.05$. Additionally, the range of the difference between the semi-automatic version and the manually created version is given with a confidence of 95%.

Table 4. Results and comparison of A/B-variant tests of recommendation process instances in 7 product categories — manually vs. semi-automatically generated process instance. $C_{A/B}$: unique clients for cases A (manual) and B (semi-automatic), $COR_{A/B}$: click-out-rates for cases A and B, $D(b,a)$: Difference from b to a with 95% confidence, z: computed z-value for the two proportions. Significant values are printed in bold. The null hypothesis is rejected for $\alpha = 0.05$.

Domain	C_A	C_B	COR_A	COR_B	$D(b,a)$	z
Blu-ray pl.	806	825	0.458	0.509	0..10%	**-2.071**
Camcorder	205	233	0.444	0.485	-5..13%	-0.860
DVD player	217	239	0.415	0.213	-28..-12%	**4.646**
Printer	382	364	0.683	0.547	-21..-7%	**3.834**
Receiver	677	686	0.316	0.319	-5..5%	-0.120
TFT screen	525	494	0.455	0.348	-17..-5%	**3.481**
Video proj.	156	173	0.429	0.462	-7..14%	-0.600

The semi-automatic advisor for Blu-ray player showed a significant difference over the manually created variant ($z = -2.071, \alpha = 0.05$) and performed between 0% and 10% better in terms of absolute proportions ($\alpha = 0.05$).

The comparison in the domains DVD player ($z = 4.646, \alpha = 0.05$), printer ($z = 4.646, \alpha = 3.834$) and TFT screens ($z = 4.646, \alpha = 3.481$) showed significant differences between the two proportions. In all three cases the semi-automatic version performed worse than the corresponding manually created one. The semi-automatic versions performed 12% to 28% (DVD player), 7% to 21% (printer) and 5% to 17% (TFT screen) worse in terms of absolute proportions than the manually created versions ($\alpha = 0.05$).

The domains of camcorder ($z = -0.860, \alpha = 0.05$), receiver ($z = -0.120, \alpha = 0.05$) and video projector ($z = -0.600, \alpha = 0.05$) showed no significant differences between the two variants and, therefore, H_0 cannot be rejected. The performance of the semi-automatic versions varied from -5% to 13% for camcorder, -5% to 5% for receiver and -7% to 14% for video projector ($\alpha = 0.05$).

Efficiency of the proposed approach

We interviewed several project managers of the Austrian company mentioned earlier who are usually involved in the (manual) setup of process recommendation systems. Depending on the complexity of the product domain, setting up or optimizing new advisors usually takes 1–2 days of work. This includes analyzing product reviews and pertinent Websites to identify the relevance that certain product features have to customers.

This task is followed by a reassessment of current recommendation processes and updating their contents according to the findings (restructuring questions and answers, adjusting the underlying product data structure, refining wordings and display).

With the support of the presented lifecycle to generate recommendation systems automatically, the domain experts were relieved of the manual research tasks and manual restructuring of the recommendation systems, which reduced the overall time required to several (6–8) hours. Thus, the automated process proposed in this paper led to a considerable reduction of manual effort.

DISCUSSION

The results of the studies suggest that the proposed lifecycle is capable of generating well-performing recommendation processes for real-life use.

However, analyzing the individual structures of the generated processes and their performance, led to the assumption that the automated approach works well for basic recommendation process structures. The three recommendation processes with significant negative performance (Printer, DVD Player, TFT screen) had more complex structures, in which the questions where interrelated (e.g., selecting a question triggered the display of an additional question), while this was not the case for the generated recommendation processes with significant positive performance (mobile phone, Blu-ray player). This preliminary assumption will be evaluated in future tests.

Measuring and comparing the efforts for the manual set up of recommendation processes to using the semi-automatic lifecycle showed that applying the latter led to a reduction of the manual work required by roughly half as much time.

Since our approach to generating recommender processes is semi-automatic, the question may arise what has to be done manually. First, the PDO was given and not automatically created. And of course, the whole machinery such as repositories, queries, transformation rules, etc. was manually devised. Once it had been set-up, however, it created the recommender processes fully automatically. Still, the selection of a new (generated) recommender process for deployment is done manually. This may be automated as well, however, once our closed optimization cycle will be available.

While our approach works and even results in recommendation processes applicable in practice, a few related questions should be discussed. In particular, is it necessary or, at least useful to generate a high-level model of such a process first? Although it seems possible to generate an operationalized process in one shot, we argue that a two-step approach is useful by analogy to compiler construction. Typically, intermediate languages are used on the way from a high-level programming language to machine code. These provide useful levels of abstraction for the compiler developers, and so does our high-level model of recommendation processes.

Still, the question remains, whether other kinds of languages or models could serve the same purpose, and possibly even better. This question cannot be answered with certainty as it stands, since our approach seems to be the very first along these lines.

As our discourse-based models are primarily used for specifying models on a high abstraction level for automated generation of user interfaces, how about the most often used approach for this purpose? Instead of discourse-based models, task-based *ConcurTaskTrees* [21] may be used for bridging the semantic gap between ontologies and user interfaces. ConcurTaskTrees facilitate modeling *tasks* and their causal and temporal relations. Such models are also being transformed into a user interface semi-automatically. However, we are not aware of any approach for generating ConcurTaskTrees out of ontologies.

UsiXML [8] is an XML-based specification language for user interface design. It allows specifying a user interface at different levels of abstraction, from high-level task models (like ConcurTaskTrees) to the concrete code of a user interface. Also for UsiXML, we are not aware of any approach for generating UsiXML models out of ontologies.

Since a recommendation process of the kind generated here primarily consists of pairs of questions and related answers, Communicative Acts as used in the discourse-based approach are an excellent fit for modeling them. In contrast, tasks would have to model questions and answers in the sense of corresponding interactions with a specific kind of user interface. So, while this would certainly be feasible, it appears to be less appealing than our approach.

From discourse-based Communication Models, it is possible to generate general-purpose graphical user interfaces according to [7] and even optimized ones for devices with small screens according to [25]. Contrasting them with the user interfaces generated for recommendation processes as explained above, it is clear that the latter are preferable in terms of usability.

As a matter of fact, they have been successfully used for real-world application of these recommendation processes. They are special-purpose, however, and their overall appearance was predefined, while only the content has been generated automatically for the given structure and with many given heuristics.

CONCLUSION

In this paper, we present a novel approach for semi-automatically generating dialogue-driven recommendation processes based on product ontologies. By analyzing product reviews, we were able to identify trends for product types automatically and to adapt these product ontologies accordingly. In rapidly evolving domains like mobile phones, the automated generation led to improved recommendation dialogues (in terms of click-outs).

The evaluation showed that our approach can reduce the effort for creating and adjusting the recommendation processes significantly. In addition, data from real-world deployment of this new and automated approach provide empirical evidence of its usefulness.

We are currently working on implementation and test of including automated feedback for the evolution of the PDO also from comparing recommendation processes during their deployment. It will close the loop for an optimization cycle, and this will hopefully improve the results further.

ACKNOWLEDGMENTS

This research has been carried out in the SOFAR project (No. 825061), partially funded by the Austrian FIT-IT Program of the FFG.

REFERENCES

1. S. Aciar, D. Zhang, S. Simoff, and J. Debenham. Recommender system based on consumer product reviews. In *WI '06: Proceedings of the 2006 IEEE/WIC/ACM International Conference on Web Intelligence*, pages 719–723. IEEE Computer Society, 2006.
2. X. Amatriain, J. M. Pujol, N. Tintarev, and N. Oliver. Rate it again: Increasing recommendation accuracy by user re-rating. In *RecSys '09: Proceedings of the 3rd ACM Conference on Recommender Systems*, pages 173–180. ACM, 2009.
3. R. Burke, K. Hammond, and B. C. Young. The FindMe approach to assisted browsing. *IEEE Expert*, 12(4):32–40, 1997.
4. J. Carrillo de Albornoz, L. Plaza, and P. G. A. Díaz. A joint model of feature mining and sentiment analysis for product review rating. In P. Clough, C. Foley, C. Gurrin, G. J. F. Jones, W. Kraaij, H. Lee, and V. Mudoch, editors, *Advances in Information Retrieval*, volume 6611 of *Lecture Notes in Computer Science*, pages 55–66. Springer, 2011.
5. M. Doyle and P. Cunningham. A dynamic approach to reducing dialog in on-line decision guides. In *EWCBR '00: Proceedings of the 5th European Workshop on Advances in Case-Based Reasoning*, pages 49–60. Springer, 2000.
6. J. Falb, H. Kaindl, H. Horacek, C. Bogdan, R. Popp, and E. Arnautovic. A discourse model for interaction design based on theories of human communication. In *Extended Abstracts on Human Factors in Computing Systems (CHI '06)*, pages 754–759. ACM, 2006.
7. J. Falb, S. Kavaldjian, R. Popp, D. Raneburger, E. Arnautovic, and H. Kaindl. Fully automatic user interface generation from discourse models. In *IUI '09: Proceedings of the 13th International Conference on Intelligent User Interfaces*, pages 475–476. ACM, 2009.
8. D. Faure and J. Vanderdonckt. User interface extensible markup language. In *EICS '10: Proceedings of the 2nd ACM SIGCHI Symposium on Engineering Interactive Computing Systems*, pages 361–362. ACM, 2010.
9. J. R. Hauser, G. L. Urban, G. Liberali, and M. Braun. Website morphing. *Marketing Science*, 28(2):202–223, 2009.
10. M. Hepp. Products and services ontologies: A methodology for deriving owl ontologies from industrial categorization standards. *International Journal on Semantic Web & Information Systems*, 2(1):72–99, 2006.

11. J. L. Herlocker, J. A. Konstan, L. G. Terveen, and J. Riedl. Evaluating collaborative filtering recommender systems. *ACM Transactions on Information Systems*, 22(1):5–53, 2004.
12. M. Hu and B. Liu. Mining opinion features in customer reviews. In *AAAI'04: Proceedings of the 19th National Conference on Artificial Intelligence*, pages 755–760. AAAI Press, 2004.
13. T. Hussein and J. Ziegler. Adapting web sites by spreading activation in ontologies. In *ReColl '08: Proceedings of the International Workshop on Recommendation and Collaboration*. ACM, 2008.
14. D. Jannach, M. Zanker, A. Felfernig, and G. Friedrich. *Recommender Systems: An Introduction*. Cambridge University Press, 2010.
15. G. Jawaheer, M. Szomszor, and P. Kostkova. Characterisation of explicit feedback in an online music recommendation service. In *RecSys '10: Proceedings of the 4th ACM Conference on Recommender Systems*, pages 317–320. ACM, 2010.
16. A. Levi, O. Mokryn, C. Diot, and N. Taft. Finding a needle in a haystack of reviews: Cold start context-based hotel recommender system. In *RecSys '12: Proceedings of the 6th ACM Conference on Recommender Systems*, pages 115–122. ACM, 2012.
17. T. Mahmood and F. Ricci. Learning and adaptivity in interactive recommender systems. In *ICEC '07: Proceedings of the 9th international Conference on Electronic Commerce*, pages 75–84. ACM, 2007.
18. L. McGinty and J. Reilly. On the evolution of critiquing recommenders. In F. Ricci, L. Rokach, B. Shapira, and P. B. Kantor, editors, *Recommender Systems Handbook*, pages 419–453. Springer, 2010.
19. S. E. Middleton, N. R. Shadbolt, and D. C. de Roure. Ontological user profiling in recommender systems. *ACM Transactions on Information Systems*, 22(1):54–88, 2004.
20. B. Pang and L. Lee. Opinion mining and sentiment analysis. *Foundations and Trends in Information Retrieval*, 2(1-2):1–135, 2008.
21. F. Paternò, C. Mancini, and S. Meniconi. ConcurTaskTrees: A diagrammatic notation for specifying task models. In *Interact '97: Proceedings of the IFIP TC13 6th International Conference on Human-Computer Interaction*, pages 362–369, 1997.
22. A.-M. Popescu and O. Etzioni. Extracting product features and opinions from reviews. In *HLT '05: Proceedings of the conference on Human Language Technology and Empirical Methods in Natural Language Processing*, pages 339–346. ACL, 2005.
23. R. Popp and D. Raneburger. A high-level agent interaction protocol based on a communication ontology. In C. Huemer, T. Setzer, W. Aalst, J. Mylopoulos, N. M. Sadeh, M. J. Shaw, and C. Szyperski, editors, *E-Commerce and Web Technologies*, volume 85 of *Lecture Notes in Business Information Processing*, pages 233–245. Springer, 2011.
24. S. Raghavan, S. Gunasekar, and J. Ghosh. Review quality aware collaborative filtering. In *RecSys '12: Proceedings of the 6th ACM Conference on Recommender Systems*, pages 123–130. ACM, 2012.
25. D. Raneburger, R. Popp, S. Kavaldjian, H. Kaindl, and J. Falb. Optimized GUI generation for small screens. In H. Hussmann, G. Meixner, and D. Zuehlke, editors, *Model-Driven Development of Advanced User Interfaces*, volume 340 of *Studies in Computational Intelligence*, pages 107–122. Springer, 2011.
26. C. Scaffidi, K. Bierhoff, E. Chang, M. Felker, H. Ng, and C. Jin. Red opal: product-feature scoring from reviews. In *EC '07: Proceedings of the 8th ACM Conference on Electronic Commerce*, pages 182–191. ACM, 2007.
27. S. Schmitt. simvar: A similarity-influenced question selection criterion for e-sales dialogs. *Artificial Intelligence Review*, 18(3-4):195–221, 2002.
28. A. Sieg, B. Mobasher, and R. Burke. Improving the effectiveness of collaborative recommendation with ontology-based user profiles. In *HetRec '10: Proceedings of the 1st International Workshop on Information Heterogeneity and Fusion in Recommender Systems*, pages 39–46. ACM, 2010.
29. E. P. Wach. Automated ontology evolution for an e-commerce recommender. In W. Abramowicz, L. Maciaszek, K. Wecel, W. Aalst, J. Mylopoulos, M. Rosemann, M. J. Shaw, and C. Szyperski, editors, *Business Information Systems Workshops*, volume 97 of *Lecture Notes in Business Information Processing*, pages 166–177. Springer, 2011.
30. B. Xiao and I. Benbasat. E-commerce product recommendation agents: Use, characteristics, and impact. *MIS Quarterly*, 31(1):137–209, 2007.
31. W. Zhang, G. Ding, C. L. Li Chen, and C. Zhang. Generating virtual ratings from chinese reviews to augment online recommendations. *ACM Transactions on Intelligent Systems and Technology*, 4(1), 2013.
32. C.-N. Ziegler, S. McNee, J. A. Konstan, and G. Lausen. Improving recommendation lists through topic diversification. In *WWW '05: Proceedings of the 14th International World Wide Web Conference*, pages 22–32. ACM, 2005.

Recommendation System for Automatic Design of Magazine Covers

Ali Jahanian[1], Jerry Liu[2], Qian Lin[2], Daniel R. Tretter[2], Eamonn O'Brien-Strain[2], Seungyon Lee[2], Nic Lyons[2], Jan P. Allebach[1]

[1]School of Electrical and Computer Engineering
Purdue University
West Lafayette, IN 47907, U.S.A
{ajahania, allebach}@purdue.edu

[2]HP Labs, Palo Alto, CA 94304, U.S.A
{jerry.liu, qian.lin, dan.tretter, eamonn.obrien-strain, claire.sylee, nic.lyons}@hp.com

ABSTRACT
In this paper, we present a recommendation system for the automatic design of magazine covers. Our users are non-designer designers: individuals or small and medium businesses who want to design without hiring a professional designer while still wanting to create aesthetically compelling designs. Because a design should have a purpose, we suggest a number of semantic features to the user, e.g., "clean and clear," "dynamic and active," or "formal," to describe the color mood for the purpose of his/her design. Based on these high level features and a number of low level features, such as the complexity of the visual balance in a photo, our system selects the best photos from the user's album for his/her design. Our system then generates several alternative designs that can be rated by the user. Consequently, our system generates future designs based on the user's style. In this fashion, our system personalizes the designs of a user based on his/her preferences.

Author Keywords
Visual design principles; aesthetics; layout; visual balance; color design; autonomous; recommendation; personalization

ACM Classification Keywords
H.5.2 Information Interfaces and Presentation: User Interfaces

H.1.2 Models and Principles User/Machine Systems - human factors, software psychology

General Terms
Human Factors; Design; Theory.

INTRODUCTION
In the information era, the representation of information via visual media is a desire for both personal and business means, though these consumers may prefer not to hire a professional to create designs for them. Personal communication through internet web services is becoming an essential part of contemporary life. New generations of communication devices also contribute to a need for the design of personal communication media. Hence, there is a great need and an increasing request for software applications that provide users with easy-to-follow steps for creating visual media, such as magazines, blogs, and other forms of self-publishing media. This need, in turn, inspires science and engineering to tackle the idea of visual media's automatic design.

An automatic design system, however, needs to take into account the key concepts of design and address the challenges that designers encounter when creating a design. The key concepts include: elements of design, principles in design, and aesthetics of design. By elements of design, we mean layout and visual balance considerations, typography, design of color, style, and context. Principles in design, however, refer to a number of rules that a designer may apply to accomplish the task of design. Aesthetics of design deals with the beauty of designs and how good a design is, considering both the form and function of a design. In fact, an automatic design system has to quantify these subjective concepts. Moreover, such a system has to perform the task of design automatically and autonomously. From a broader perspective, this system should be able to recommend to the user a number of designs and to customize the future designs for a user based on his/her personal preferences. Therefore, designing effective sets of interactions for user participation in the process of automatic design of visual media based on his/her preferences is required.

In this paper, we introduce a recommendation system for automatic design of magazine covers. Professional designers start a design by developing a concept to convey the message or purpose of the design. Similarly, our system guides the user to understand the purpose of his/her design. The purpose of a magazine cover design relates to the context of its cover image [11]. The context of the cover image has several aspects, including the color mood and the objects. At this stage, we focus on the color mood: we recommend a set of semantic descriptors to the user to understand his/her preferred color mood in his/her design. The system then selects a number of photos from the user's album based on his/her preferences and generates alternative designs.

We focus on magazine covers as an application of the idea of automatic design, especially because of the need for self-publishing designs in recent years. This need has also been addressed in prior work, such as [6] and [25]. There are now several tools and services for design of magazine covers. As an example, HP MagCloud websites [4] provide individuals as well as businesses the ability to design and upload magazine covers to share with others. Moreover, there are several on-line tools and apps for magazine cover design for amateurs, which is in contrast with tools that facilitate professionals for the design of magazine covers. Consequently, some well-known magazines such as Wired and Cosmopolitan have started offering design of personalized magazine cover as promotions to customers. As an example of other applications of our work, consider the case for providing non-designer designers with the opportunity to design magazine-like documents to communicate with specific target audiences. For instance, Greig et al. [14] suggests a system which creates a travel brochure, but it has to be enhanced by adding features that recognize how to design an effective cover. Other potential users include small non-profit organizations that need to design magazine covers and other magazine-like documents to generate excitement and credibility about their work, without hiring professional designers [6]. Furthermore, as we suggest in the discussion section, our work could be considered as a starting point to contribute to the idea of creativity support tools for both non-designer and designer users.

Our recommendation system is an extension of the automatic design system ADoMC, or Automatic Design of Magazine Covers, by Jahanian et al. [21]. Hence, we call our recommendation system R-ADoMC. Although we dedicate one section to ADoMC, we describe each part of R-ADoMC, including: Input User Interface, which suggests different purposes of a design to the user; Evaluation of Input Photos, which deals with the user's inputs; Designs User Interface, which provides a rating mechanism of the generated designs for the user; and Personalization of Designs, which recommends more designs based on the preferences of the user. We finally discuss the current limitations, challenges, and the future work. In the next section, we illustrate a common scenario that typically occurs with our users.

SCENARIO

Our users are non-designer designers, individuals and businesses who want to design without hiring a professional designer, while still wanting to create aesthetically compelling designs. Consider the following scenario: John has a pile of photos, and he wants to make a magazine cover with the best photo from the group. John also has a number of stories as his cover lines that he wants to place on the cover. He has thought about the priorities of his stories in terms of their importance. He knows what he would like to call his magazine title, but he may or may not have a predesigned masthead for his magazine title. John wants to make an attractive design, but he has no idea about the principles of design. The only thing that he knows is that he wants a "sporty and dynamic" design. Designers believe that if someone does not know how to design, he/she can easily make non-pleasing designs [20]. They also believe that any changes made in a design would lead to a different design, and the designer would have to start a new design from scratch. From the above input, R-ADoMC is implemented to create a design from start to finish. It does not allow any modifications on the user's part. Instead, it provides a number of designs to the user and lets him/her choose one. It also recommends a design based on the preference of the user. In John's case, R-ADoMC takes his photos and stories (i.e. cover lines), and then it suggests a number of adjectives to him that describe some possible kinds of design, e.g., "clean and clear", "dynamic and active", "elegant", "formal", etc. In the next sections, we discuss these adjectives, their origins, and the way that we deploy them to create a design.

RELATED WORK

We believe the work of visual media's automatic design, magazine covers in particular, is a multidisciplinary task that spans several different topics, including automated layout, color design, typography, computational aesthetics, and recommendation with personalization. The following subsections review the related work in each area and how we apply or extend the prior work.

Automated Layout

Automated layout – how to position the textual and graphical elements in the format of documents including newspapers and magazines – has been an active area of research activity. Lok et al. [28] and Hurst et al. [18] provide surveys of automated document layout techniques. Most of the related work is based on the concept of grids in design. We also use the idea of making and breaking grids, comprehensively discussed in [33]. The idea of automated layout has recently been used in design of photo-books [42], web-based magazines [17], and semi-automated magazine layout [25]. The main difference between the prior work and our work is perhaps the fact that we apply the layout onto a bitmap, or an image, as the background, or the canvas, rather than a white space. This requires dealing with the composition and complexity of the images, as well. In fact, our definition of white space is different, since we consider the non-salient part of an image as the white space. In this paper, we will describe how we find the salient and non-salient parts of an image, and how we use them to convey visual balance in a layout.

Color Design

Color design is a broad concept in design that ties with several well-known color models proposed by color theorists. In computer science and engineering, researchers have deployed some of these color theories, such as color harmony and complementary colors. [41] uses Matsuda's harmonious hue and tone templates as well as Kobayashi's color image scale to support users for the selection of colors for product design. [9] also uses Matsuda's harmonious templates for color harmonization in images. [31] studies color preferences provided from two color design websites Adobe Kuler [1] and COLOURLovers [3]. In our work, however, we use the well-known color theories of Itten [19], Matsuda [41], and

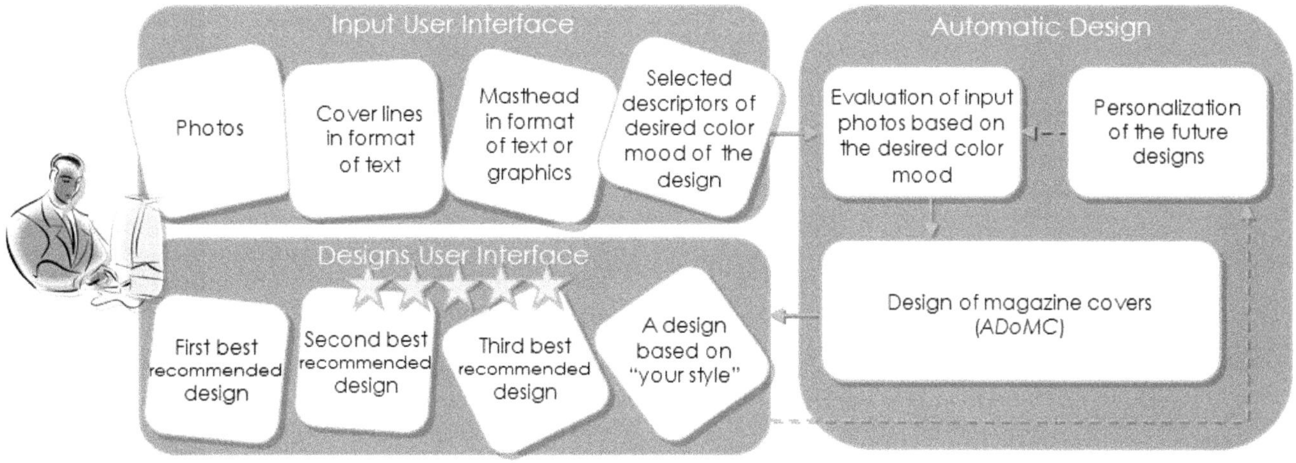

Figure 1: A schematic view of R-ADoMC. The user uploads his/her photos, cover lines, and masthead. Then, he/she chooses some recommended descriptors to indicate the desired color mood of his/her design. R-ADoMC evaluates the user's photos and chooses the best. It then sends the selected photos to the design engine. The generated designs will be shown to the user, who can rate the generated designs. The ratings will be considered for the user's future designs to recommend him/her one more design based on his/her style.

Kobayashi [32] to evaluate input cover images and to automatically choose colors for the cover lines of a magazine cover.

Typography

Typography in automatic layout is often considered as an optimization problem [18]. Knuth's work [23] is perhaps the most effective solution for typography. Recently, [27] suggests an algorithm based on Knuth's work for text fitting in arbitrary geometrical regions for digital publishing. The automatic text insertion in our typography is inspired by both [23] and [27], while dealing with text fitting in geometrical regions. Typography in design also deals with the aesthetics of typefaces and which typeface to choose for the purpose of a design [34]. Although we alternate the typeface of the textual elements in design of a magazine cover, choosing a good typeface for the purpose of a design is mentioned in the Discussion section as our future work.

Computational Aesthetics

Quantifying aesthetics of images is another trend of research. Birkhoff's [8] model is perhaps the first mathematical expression for aesthetics. [30] deploys Birkhoff's model for measuring aesthetics of layout of user interfaces on the screen. From another perspective, [13] develops a genetic algorithm for computing aesthetics of photo-albums. Datta et al. [10] applies a number of machine learning techniques in computational aesthetics of photos. However, machine learning techniques require defining effective features to quantify aesthetics and should be considered based on both function and form. That is why in our work aesthetics considerations are part of each module of design, e.g., aesthetics of color design or visual balance as well as the final design. Moreover, unlike other methods, we consider high level or semantic features (e.g. "clean and clear" colors) rather than just low level features (e.g. lightness of color). From a psychological viewpoint, [26] suggests an exploratory factor analysis for this purpose and lists a number of semantic terms in aesthetics of design. However, to the best of our knowledge, deployment of high level features in automatic design has not been considered in previous work. This is, in fact, part of this paper's contribution.

Recommendation Systems

Recommending a generated design from scratch for the user is another contribution of this paper. [16] discusses how designers can benefit from examples recommended by a recommending system to support their creativity in new designs. The main difference, however, is that in our work we create designs and recommend them to non-designer users. In recommendation systems, typically, prediction of a user's preferences is based on a rating data set, accumulated from the same user and similar users [5]. In our work, we personalize the future designs for a user by predicting his/her personal preferences in design and by inferring a style for him/her based on his/her ratings.

SOFTWARE FRAMEWORK

This section describes how we think about the problem of automatic design from the viewpoint of software engineering and computer science. We endeavor to quantify the elements and concepts in design and bring these subjective topics to the realm of objection. Our approach includes close collaboration with professional designers, magazine art directors and editorial boards, and journalists. The current software framework is the projection of a number of rules, mathematical expressions, and algorithms delineated and devised from the lessons we have learned so far. The following sub-sections describe each part of the system in more detail. We first start by looking at a schematic view of the framework and the relation of each part with others.

Schematic View

As Figure 1 illustrates, the system is comprised of three major parts: Input User Interface, Automatic Design Engine, and

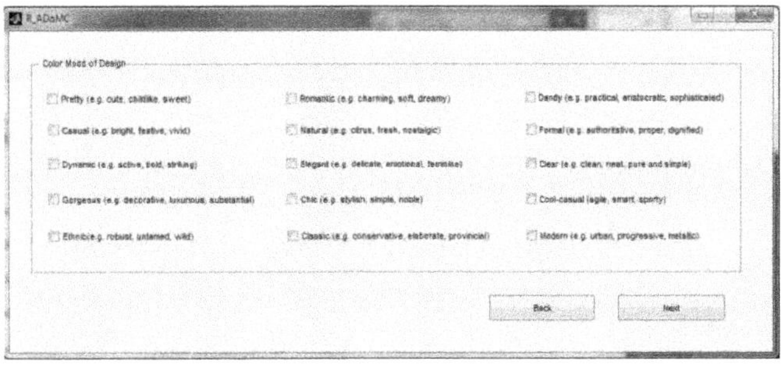

Figure 2: Descriptors for color mood of design. The user can tell R-ADoMC which color mood he/she wishes to convey in his/her design. These descriptors are suggested by [32] to relate the world of colors to the world of styles and human preferences.

Designs User Interface. The system first takes the user's inputs, which includes a collection of his/her photos, a number of text strings as his/her magazine cover stories (e.g. headline and byline), a masthead for the title in the format of a text string or a predefined logo, and a number of predefined adjectives describing the desired color mood of his/her design. The system then evaluates the user's photos based on his/her chosen adjectives. In this way, the system can order the input photos based on their aesthetics, including both form and functional aspects. The best photos are then sent to the design engine. This engine is called ADoMC and is based on work by Jahanian et al. [21]. The designs generated by ADoMC, which in turn pass a visual composition criterion, are presented as the final designs to the user by listing them in order of best design. The user can rate the generated designs using a five-star rating scale. The system incorporates the user's ratings in the personalization part to customize his/her future designs. In this fashion, the system will suggest to the user one more design among the other designs that he/she may like by indicating that it is based on "your style."

Input User Interface

A magazine cover has a main photo called a cover image, a title called a masthead, and a number of stories, including headline, byline, and other cover lines [11]. The user can upload his/her cover image, masthead, and cover lines to R-ADoMC. Users generally have a number of photos and may wonder which photo could be a good candidate for a magazine cover. On the other hand, since the context of the cover image influences the purpose of a magazine cover design, we recommend a list of adjectives to the user to describe several color moods in the context of a magazine cover. Although the context of a photo includes aspects other than color, at this stage of our work, we address only the color aspect. After the user chooses a set of adjectives, or color mood descriptors, R-ADoMC can evaluate the user's photos, rate them, and generate alternative designs. Figure 2 illustrates the menu of the color mood descriptors in R-ADoMC.

Evaluation of Input Photos

Computational aesthetics of photos is one of the recent interests in computer science and engineering. However, most of the related work is focused on a number of low level features in a photo, such as color distribution, texture, and objects [22]. These features are part of the aesthetics of photos, but they are context-free. Since a design has a mission and conveys a purpose to the audience, we also need a set of high level features to be able to describe a design and its color mood. Our solution to this challenge is inspired by the work on the Color Image Scale by Kobayashi [32]. Kobayashi has proposed a semantic view to the aesthetics of colors to relate the world of colors to the world of objects, life styles, and human preferences. Therefore, we use his work to quantify the mood of our designs from a semantic viewpoint. Kobayashi's Color Image Scale is an attempt to investigate the meanings that people may perceive from the colors and color combinations, from a number of psychological, systematic, and pragmatic approaches. This viewpoint comes from the idea of associating the physical attributes of the colors – hue, value, and chroma — to a higher level of abstract attributes of colors – warm-cool and soft-hard. Kobayashi and his institute, Nippon Color and Design Research, have conducted more than a decade of psychophysical experiments on colors. They asked individuals and groups of people to match a color and a combination of three colors with an adjective. Through factor analysis, a semantic differential method, and cluster analysis, Kobayashi came up with a list of adjectives as color descriptors or "color-images." Kobayashi then applied his scale to different color designs, for example, clothes, food, and several other industrial design applications [24]. Kobayashi later published his Color Image Scale in a book with the same name [32]. Today a Japanese website uses his work in a search engine for images [2]. Recently [37] has deployed Kobayashi's scale for image retrieval. We deploy the mathematical framework that [37] develops to implement Kobayashi's color scale for the purpose of image retrieval; hence, we use almost the same notation. We, however, use this framework to measure and evaluate the input photos for the purpose of a design. Kobayashi first defines 130 Basic Colors. He then defines 1170 3-Color Combinations and associates them with 180 adjectives (called color-images) or Labels. Each 3-Color Combination is also associated with a five-star rating that indicates the frequency of its usage. The Labels are later classified into 15 Patterns. The Patterns represent a number of selected terms in fashion and lifestyle. Kobayashi positions his 3-Color Combinations on a scale of warm-cool and soft-hard, and based on this arrangement, defines the boundaries of each Pattern. Figure 3 illustrates Kobayashi's Color Image Scale with the 15 Patterns and some of his 3-Color Combinations.

Our problem is how to locate a given image on Kobayashi's Color Image Scale. First we need to find a way to represent an image in sRGB color space in terms of Kobayashi's 130 Basic Colors. One way is to represent the image by its histogram. In other words, the problem is: how to convert the sRGB histogram of an image to its corresponding histogram in Kobayashi's 130 Basic Colors. To do so, we quantize the sRGB color space to a smaller space with 8 levels of R, 8 levels of G, and 8 levels of B. This leads to 512 sRGB colors, or bins. We obtain the Kobayashi's histogram of an image, denoted by h_K from the sRGB histogram of the image, denoted

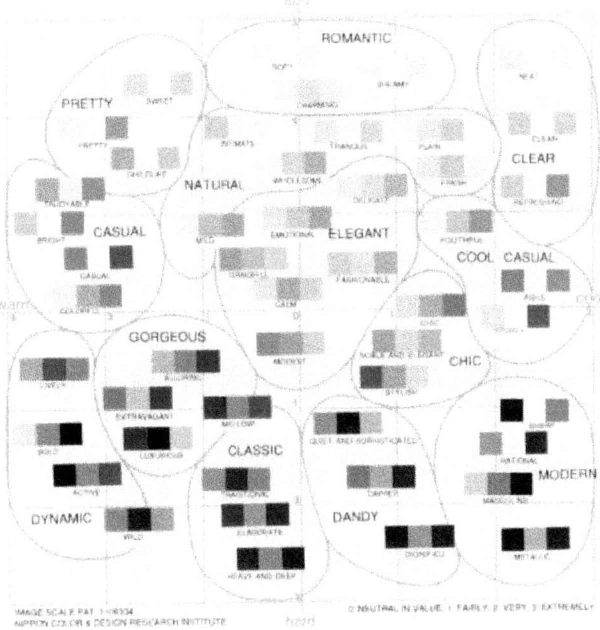

Figure 3: Kobayashi's Color Image Scale. Image taken from [32]. The contours show 15 patterns, labeled by all-capital letters. We use these patterns to describe the desired color mood of the design.

by h_{RGB}, according to the following Equation:

$$h_K = h_{RGB} \cdot T \tag{1}$$

Here T is the transformation matrix. We construct T by first converting both the quantized sRGB space and the 130 Basic Colors to CIELab color space. This space is perceptually uniform, and so we measure the distance between each pair of colors converted from these two color spaces in terms of their Euclidean distance in CIELab, denoted by $\triangle E_r$. We can then define the elements of the transformation matrix T:

$$t_{rl} = \begin{cases} 1 - \frac{\triangle E_r}{10} + 0.1 & \text{if } \triangle E_r \leq 10 \\ 0 & \text{otherwise} \end{cases} \tag{2}$$

where $r = 1, ..., 512$, and $l = 1, ..., 130$.

Hence, we obtain Kobayashi's histogram h_K of an image. The next step is computation of the distribution of any 3-Color Combination in the given image from its corresponding h_K. To do so, we first define the following notation to refer to a 3-Color Combination:

$$c_n^{(3)} = \{b_n^1, b_n^2, b_n^3\} \tag{3}$$

where $0 \leq b_n^i \leq 130$ denotes the index of a Basic Color.

Now we define h_σ as the distribution of the all 3-Color Combinations in a given image by:

$$h_\sigma = [\sigma_1, ..., \sigma_{1170}]^T \tag{4}$$

where

$$\sigma = \min(h_K(b_n^1), h_K(b_n^2), h_K(b_n^3)) \tag{5}$$

for $n = 1, ..., 1170$.

Next, we define matrix L as an index matrix to associate the 180 Labels to the 1170 3-Color Combinations:

$$L = \left[\vec{l_1} \ldots \vec{l_{180}}\right] \tag{6}$$

where L is a 1170×180 matrix and

$$l_{ij} = \begin{cases} 1 & \text{if label } j \text{ is associated to Color Combination } i \\ 0 & \text{otherwise} \end{cases} \tag{7}$$

Also, we define the diagonal matrix R, which contains the ratings of each 3-Color Combination. Hence, we obtain the distribution of each Label in an image by h_L as:

$$h_L = h_\sigma \cdot R \cdot L \tag{8}$$

Similar to Equations 6 and 7, we can define the matrix U as an index matrix to associate the 15 Patterns to the 180 Labels. Hence, we obtain the distribution of each Pattern in an image as follows:

$$P = h_L \cdot U \tag{9}$$

Finally, given the location of all the 180 Labels on the scale from the matrix E, we can obtain s, the location of the given image on the scale from:

$$s = h_L \cdot E^T \tag{10}$$

As an example, Figure 4 illustrates the location of an image on the Color Image Scale. In fact, we can find which of the Patterns, or in our word, color moods an image holds. The normalized values of matrix P give us a measure of closeness or similarity of an image to each Pattern. We use this measure to rate the user's photos and compute the best matches to Patterns. As we mentioned, this method deals with the high level features of an image's aesthetics. However, we also consider a low level feature in images, which is the layout composition of the image. We suggest this feature because the composition of the cover image heavily influences the visual balance and layout of the design of a magazine cover. Therefore, if an image maintains a busy composition, it will not be included among the final designs. At this stage, we equate the layout composition of an image with its visual saliency and compute it with the Graph-Based Visual Saliency algorithm [15].

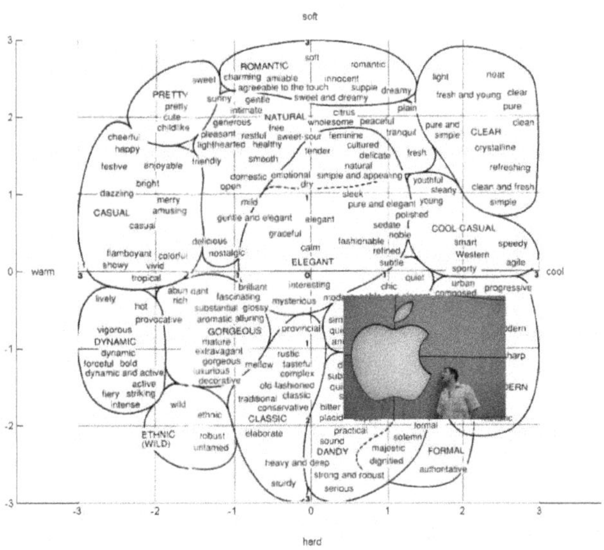

Figure 4: The location of an image on Kobayashi's Color Image Scale. This image is considered to be CHIC and MODERN according to this scale. The scale is taken from [32].

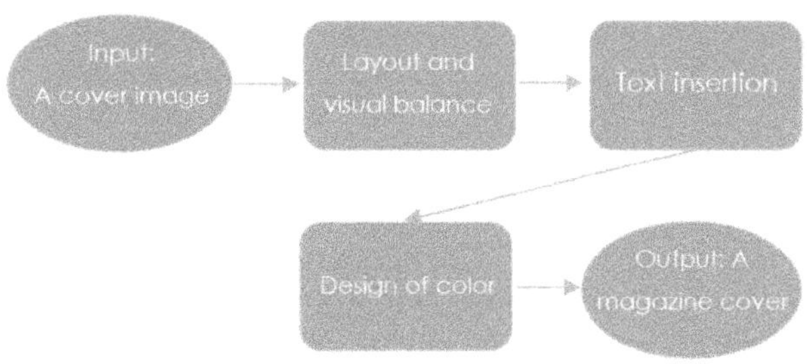

Figure 5: A schematic view of ADoMC. Image reproduced from [21].

Design Engine

After having a cover image selected by our evaluation mechanism, the next action is to design a magazine cover with it. This section is an overview to the automatic design of magazine covers (ADoMC) system [21]. A design process typically includes three modules: layout, typography, and design of color. Similarly, ADoMC quantifies and implements these modules. Figure 5 illustrates a schematic view of ADoMC.

Layout

As noted in [28], layout can be considered as a process that tries to solve the problem of positioning the visual elements while considering or determining their sizes. However, creating aesthetically pleasing layouts ties with visual balance considerations in design. Visual balance for designers means holding the property of "looking right" in a layout and can be considered as "visual weight" [29]. This term, the work of [30] in measuring aesthetics of layout, and the grid-based approach in layout [33], form the quantification approach of the visual balance of magazine cover layout in ADoMC, illustrated in Figure 6. In design, the form of the layout should follow the functionality of the design. For instance, the layout

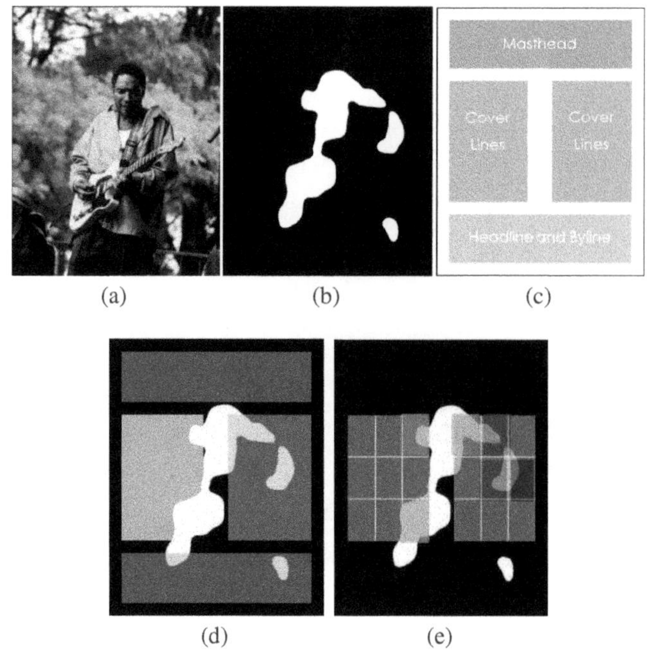

Figure 6: Layout decisions and visual balance considerations. a) An image. b) GBVS [15] binary mask. c) a general template for magazine covers. d) Fusion of general cover template (Figure 6.c) and GBVS binary mask (Figure 6.d). ADoMC [21] keeps the green region and discards the brown region, since the green region looks empty and is a good candidate to hold the cover lines. This decision is made by computing the visual balance as shown in part e (Figure 6.e). e) Computation of visual balance: different weights are assigned to the cells of the yellow grids on the left and right sides of the cover image: the darker the cells, the heavier the weights. Summing the product of each cell's weight and the number of salient pixels (white, here) gives us the weights of the left and right grids. The side with a lighter weight will be considered as an empty space to hold more elements, such as the texts of the cover lines. Images reproduced from [21].

of the magazine cover should be in a form that directs the eyes of the audience through the design [11]. Based on the advice of designers, ADoMC applies a general template for magazine cover layout (illustrated in Figure 6.c). This template, however, can be reformed based on the visual balance of the cover image. For visual balance considerations, ADoMC first finds the white spaces of the cover image. Here, white space on the background image means the regions of the image which are less busy relative to the other regions of the image. That is, ADoMC finds the non-salient segments of the image by deployment of the Graph-Based Visual Saliency algorithm (GBVS) [15]. ADoMC then fuses the binary GBVS mask with the general magazine cover template. The result yields the candidate regions for holding the textual elements on the cover. Finally, ADoMC applies grids on the image and assigns different weights to different cells of the grids to compute which candidate region should hold the textual elements. In this fashion, ADoMC conveys the visual balance in the layout of magazine covers.

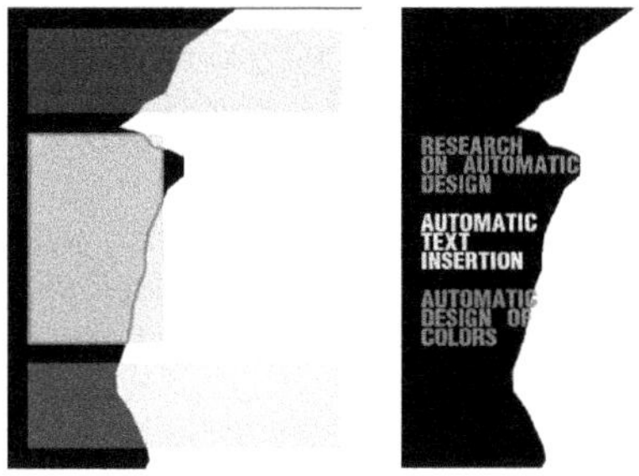

(a) (b)

Figure 7: Typography of cover lines for a magazine cover. a) Given the green region computed from Figure 6 as a candidate to hold cover lines, ADoMC [21] fits the text of the cover lines in it. It applies a form of text indentation to follow the boundaries of the green region. However, this process is performed in a way such that the size of the text is as large as possible for the purpose of legibility. b) Result of the automatic text fitting in the green region in (a). Images reproduced from [21].

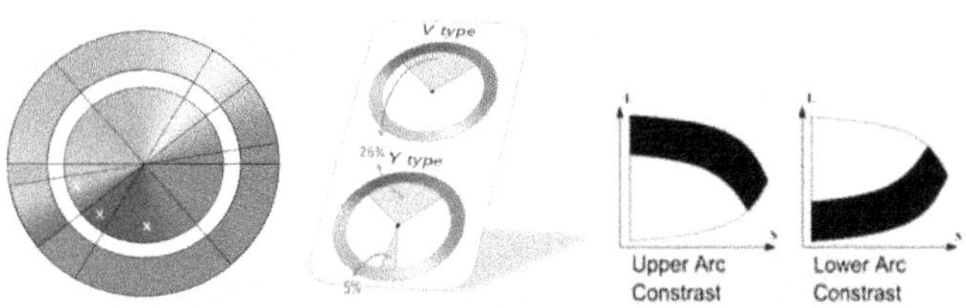

(a) (b) (c)

Figure 8: Color Design for masthead and cover lines. a) ADoMC [21] incorporates this complementary color wheel based on a continuous version of Itten's hue wheel. The crossed region inside the inner disc is discarded and replaced with the corresponding sectors in the outer ring. b) ADoMC uses these two templates of Matsuda's hue templates. The colors in the shaded sectors are considered to be in harmony. c) ADoMC uses these two templates of Matsuda's tone templates. The colors in the black arcs are considered to be in harmony. Images of (b) and (c) are reproduced from [9].

Typography

Where and how to put text, including the masthead, headline, byline, and other cover lines, is an important decision in design of magazine covers [11]. In our problem scope, by typography we mean the decisions that a designer makes about using different typefaces for different design purposes, the text size of the cover lines, priorities of the cover lines, and the problem of legibility of the text. According to professionals, the family of *Helvetica* is a good choice for a typical magazine cover. Better choices, however, relate to the class of magazine and will be considered in our future work. Similar to the preceding discussion for layout, we need to convey the priority and the hierarchy of the cover lines on the cover. Therefore, ADoMC assigns different sizes to the cover lines and lays them out based on their priority (specified by the user) starting from the top of the cover. Given a candidate region from the layout process, ADoMC inserts the text by applying a special form of indentation. This indentation is a pattern derived from well-known magazine designs. That is, designers usually give an indentation to the texts to align them with the boundaries of the salient segments of the cover image. This technique can be formulated as how to insert or fit a text in a geometrical region such that its indentation is most faithful to the shape of the region. ADoMC solves this problem as an optimization problem in which the maximum fidelity to the shape of the geometrical region and the maximum size of the text is desirable. Figure 7 illustrates the results of this solution for different numbers of cover lines with different words.

Color

Design of color for textual and graphical elements on a magazine cover is another challenge for magazine art directors [11]. In the automatic process of color design, one needs to address both aesthetics and legibility of the color text. In order to tackle the aesthetics of colors, ADoMC draws upon the well-known theories of color harmony. One of the most significant works in the area of quantifying aesthetics of colors is Itten's color harmony concept [19]. Itten defines seven kinds of color contrast: contrast of hue, light-dark contrast, cold-warm contrast, complementary contrast, simultaneous contrast, contrast of saturation, and contrast of extension. Among these contrasts, ADoMC applies the concept of complementary contrast to choose the color of the masthead. For the color of cover lines, ADoMC then uses Matsuda's hue templates [41] and [9], which are perhaps an extension of Itten's color harmony. The problem of illegible text may occur when the hue or the tone of the text in the foreground competes with the hue or the tone of its local background. Hence, for legibility of the text, Matsuda's tone templates are deployed as well as the hue templates. Figure 8.a illustrates how ADoMC customizes a continuous version of Itten's hue wheel. Figures 8.b and 8.c also illustrate the four (among eighteen) of Matsuda's hue and tone templates that are used. The reason for this choice is that these templates are more likely to occur in the contemporary context of well-known magazine cover designs, as analyzed and suggested by professional designers [20].

Designs User Interface

Getting the user to effectively visualize the results is a challenge when designing a user interface for recommendation systems. This, in turn, influences the personalization of the user's results. In our problem, we aim to present more than one design to the user in order to understand his/her design's purpose and to customize his/her future designs. We believe this is an added value for non-designers because it provides them designs that are aligned with their personal preferences and styles. In this fashion, we devise an interactive process between the automatic system and the user while creating a design, which also happens in practice between a professional designer and his/her client. Figure 9 illustrates R-ADoMC's user interface. R-ADoMC displays the first choice design in the main GUI and arranges two more design choices, along with a design based on the user's accumulated ratings in a separate panel. It also provides a five-star rating scale option by the user for these designs [38] provides a number of guidelines for choosing a rating scale, the options being unary ("like it"), binary (thumbs up/thumbs down), five-star, or a

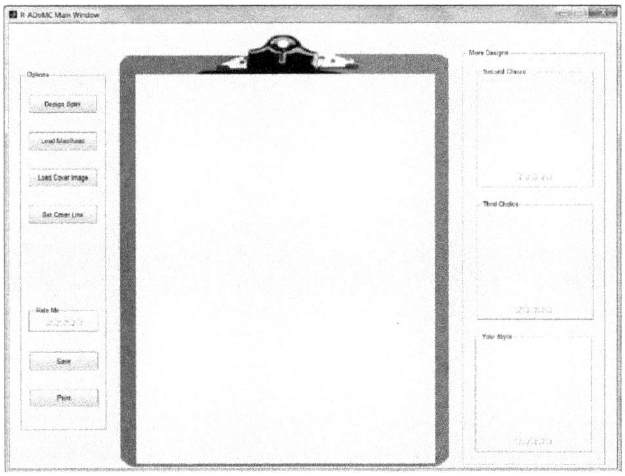

Figure 9: Designs UI for visualization of the designs generated in R-ADoMC. A rating option is available for each design, and the ratings will be considered in the user's future designs. The "your style" design is a representation of the idea of personalized designs for the user. The more that the user works with the system, the more that the system is able to personalize the future designs.

100-point slider. The degree of accuracy and user friendliness of the five-star method is a good choice for our work. In this way, we accumulate a better understanding of what kind of design the user likes, and consequently, we can customize his/her future designs.

Personalization of Designs

Is it legitimate to personalize designs? Although form follows function – or the context of a design should be aligned with the mission of the design – it can also be personalized. In fact, one way of thinking about personalization of a design is to think about the design's style, which comes from the preferences of a designer. There is a consensus between artists that each professional has his/her own style or signature, making some of the designers identifiable based on their designs even without their explicit identification. On the other hand, there might be alternative good designs for a specific purpose, and choosing one from several, ties with the personal preferences of the user. Hence, providing alternative designs and allowing a user to choose one design based on his/her personal preferences is an added value to the function of automatic design systems. Accordingly, R-ADoMC implements the idea of design personalization to support the user. As the user works more with R-ADoMC and rates the generated designs, the rating data is accumulated for future designs.

There are three different approaches for recommending an item in current recommendation systems, content-based, collaborative filtering, and a combination of both these known as hybrid [5]. At this stage, our system does not consider any collaborative filtering because its personalization procedure is single-user based rather than multiple-user based. As Figure 9 illustrates, the system suggests the personalized design as an extra design, labeled as "your style." To anticipate this personalized design from the previous ratings of the user, we define the prediction of the ratings of the generated designs as a linear regression problem. To solve this problem, we use the LASSO algorithm [40] with L_1 regularization.

EXPERIMENTAL RESULTS

Figure 10 illustrates several ordered results. Generally speaking, the results generated by ADoMC are acceptable to our professional designers. However, a set of psychophysical experiments to evaluate the results by users is part of our future work. The system is implemented in Matlab and takes a few minutes to present the results (for a photo album of about 100 images), on a 64-bit PC machine with a 2-core 3GHz Intel processor and 4GB of RAM.

DISCUSSION

R-ADoMC is a recommendation system for the automatic design of magazine covers, and the purpose of this system is to aid the non-designer designer in creating aesthetically compelling designs. After a user uploads his/her photos, the system first suggests a number of semantic features, e.g., "elegant," "dynamic and active," or "sporty," to describe the color mood for the purpose of his/her design. Based on these high level features and a number of low level features, such as the complexity of a photo's visual balance, our system then selects the most suitable photos from the user's album for his/her design. Following this, R-ADoMC generates several alternative designs that can be rated by the user. Consequently, the system generates future designs grounded in the user's style, thus personalizing the designs based on his/her preferences.

The feedback that we have received from professional designers suggests that our automatic designs are aligned with their intuition. However, there is a need to devise a solid framework to evaluate R-ADoMC's generated results. This problem is highly correlated with aesthetics measurements. Quantifying aesthetics is still a challenge in computer science and engineering. In our case, while seeking a good solution by discussing this problem with our partners in the School of Visual and Performing Arts at Purdue University, we found that there might be several alternative good designs. So, we might be able to restrict the problem to what is a bad design. That inspired us to follow the principles of design. We believe that our work, among other previous work, emphasizes the need of devising and designing a set of measures and user experiments to evaluate aesthetics of the visual design. It is also worthwhile to mention that one dimension of aesthetics is beauty, which might be perceived through personal interest and experience, as suggested by Frohlich in "Beauty as a Design Prize" [12] and also by Barthes [7]. This viewpoint supports the notion of personalized design, or "Your Style," which, as suggested in this paper, may leverage the transcendental experience of beauty. Moreover, as Frohlich suggests, the perception of beauty can be stimulated by the inclusion of a more subjective experience in design. This is another support for the idea of recommendation for automatic design, as it considers the user's preferences. In fact, in interaction design, engaging the non-designer designer in the process of a design's creation by having a personal experience can arouse the experience of beauty, and hence, aesthetics.

Figure 10: Generated designs by R-ADoMC. The results are ranked from the first to third choice of design, from the left column to the right. First row shows a "Pretty", "Romantic", and "Elegant" color mood. Second row shows a "Classic", "Natural" and "Cool-Casual" color mood. Third row shows a "Dynamic", and "Modern" color mood. Photos courtesy of Andrew Hancock (a, e, g, h), Sean Molin (c, d, f, i), and Martin O'Connell (b).

Although our framework provides personalized designs, we endeavor to develop a framework which generates designs that are effective in both the function and form of aesthetics. Keeping this in mind, there are a number of limitations in R-ADoMC that must be addressed. One limitation is that we reduce the dimensionality of a design's purpose to the color mood dimension, as well as visual complexity of the cover image. Although these two dimensions are important and influence the aesthetics of a design heavily, there exist other dimensions such as the objects in the cover image. This correlates with the context evaluations of the photos, and so these contextual factors need to be further investigated. Another limitation includes the hypothetical case that a user has an album of similar photos, e.g., all the photos are classified as modern in his/her album. While our system would provide several designs, we still require another feature or set of features to identify the ranking of these designs based on what the user needs. An additional limitation is that we do not consider specific typefaces for our typography, and this problem ties with the class of magazine, which contributes to defining a magazine's style. We aim to address design based on the class of magazines within our future work.

Our current system, R-ADoMC, is a software framework meant to emulate the process that a professional designer attends to when creating a design. In fact, one of the key components of this framework is developing an interactive process between the software and the user to understand what kind of design the user needs or wants. As also indicated by Swearingen et al. [39], understanding the user's needs is important in designing the interactions of recommendation systems. On the other hand, designing interactions for recommendation systems can also be expanded to contribute to the idea of creativity support tools. Creativity support tools facilitate users to "explore, discover, imagine, innovate, compose, and collaborate" [35]. However, as indicated by Shneiderman [36], creative work often begins by viewing previous projects and similar samples. Since R-ADoMC recommends alternative designs to the user based on his/her preferences, it can be an underlying framework for a creativity support system in visual design. If the user is unaware of key concepts in design or principles of design, it is an added value to recommend these semantic descriptors that make sense to him/her and help to describe a design. It is, however, more ambitious to escalate the creativity of our non-designer user in the design of visual media. This desire requires a series of effective interactions between the user and the system to include the user in the creative process of his/her design. Hence, we endeavor to evolve R-ADoMC's framework into a creativity support tool for the process of visual design and concept design for media.

ACKNOWLEDGEMENT

We gratefully thank David Sigman, Head of The Patti and Rusty Rueff School of Visual and Performing Arts at Purdue University, Hector Sanchez, Design Director of Indianapolis Monthly Magazine, Ryan Kough Gibboney, Art Director of Purdue Alumnus Magazine, and Petronio A. Bendito, Assistant Professor of Visual Communication Design, The Patti and Rusty Rueff School of Visual and Performing Arts at Purdue University, for their input on our automatic designs. We also gratefully thank Elana Cutter, from the Department of English at Purdue University, for her editorial reviews and creative words, which we used in the automatic design samples. This work is supported by HP Labs, Palo Alto.

REFERENCES

1. Adobe Kuler. `http://kuler.adobe.com/`.
2. amanaimages EVE. `http://amanaimages.com/eve/`.
3. COLOURlovers. `http://www.colourlovers.com/`.
4. HP MagCloud. `http://www.magcloud.com/`.
5. Adomavicius, G., and Tuzhilin, A. Toward the next generation of recommender systems: A survey of the state-of-the-art and possible extensions. *Knowledge and Data Engineering, IEEE Transactions on 17*, 6 (2005), 734–749.
6. Allebach, J., Segovia, M., Atkins, C., O'Brien-Strain, E., Damera-Venkata, N., Bhatti, N., Liu, J., and Lin, Q. An investigation of document aesthetics for web-to-print repurposing of small-medium business marketing collateral. In *Society of Photo-Optical Instrumentation Engineers (SPIE) Conference Series*, vol. 7540 (2010), 13.
7. Barthes, R. *Camera lucida: Reflections on photography*. Hill and Wang, 1982.
8. Birkhoff, G. D. *Aesthetics Measure*. Harvard University Press, 1933.
9. Cohen-Or, D., Sorkine, O., Gal, R., Leyvand, T., and Xu, Y. Color harmonization. In *ACM Transactions on Graphics (TOG)*, vol. 25, ACM (2006), 624–630.
10. Datta, R., Joshi, D., Li, J., and Wang, J. Studying aesthetics in photographic images using a computational approach. *Computer Vision–ECCV 2006* (2006), 288–301.
11. Foges, C. *Magazine Design*. RotoVision Press, Switzerland, 1999.
12. Frohlich, D. Beauty as a design prize. *Human–Computer Interaction 19*, 4 (2004), 359–366.
13. Geigel, J., and Loui, A. Automatic page layout using genetic algorithms for electronic albuming. In *Photonics West 2001-Electronic Imaging*, International Society for Optics and Photonics (2000), 79–90.
14. Greig, D., Hunter, A., and Slatter, D. Layout hierarchies for interactive design reuse. In *Society of Photo-Optical Instrumentation Engineers (SPIE) Conference Series*, vol. 8302 (2012), 12.
15. Harel, J., Koch, C., and Perona, P. Graph-based visual saliency. In *Advances in Neural Information Processing Systems 19*, MIT Press (2007), 545–552.
16. Herring, S., Chang, C., Krantzler, J., and Bailey, B. Getting inspired!: understanding how and why examples are used in creative design practice. In *Proceedings of the 27th International Conference on Human factors in Computing Systems*, ACM (2009), 87–96.
17. Hunter, A., Slatter, D., and Greig, D. Web-based magazine design for self publishers. In *IS&T/SPIE Electronic Imaging*, International Society for Optics and Photonics (2011), 787902–787902–6.
18. Hurst, N., Li, W., and Marriott, K. Review of automatic document formatting. In *Proceedings of the 9th ACM Symposium on Document Engineering (DocEng'09)* (2009), 99–108.
19. Itten, J. *The Art of Color*. Wiley, 1974.
20. Jahanian, A. Automatic magazine cover design. Master's thesis, Purdue University, 2011.
21. Jahanian, A., Liu, J., Tretter, D., Lin, Q., Damera-Venkata, N., O'Brien-Strain, E., Lee, S., Fan, J., and Allebach, J. Automatic design of magazine covers. In *IS&T/SPIE Electronic Imaging*, International Society for Optics and Photonics (2012), 83020N–83020N–8.

22. Joshi, D., Datta, R., Fedorovskaya, E., Luong, Q., Wang, J., Li, J., and Luo, J. Aesthetics and emotions in images. *Signal Processing Magazine, IEEE 28*, 5 (2011), 94–115.

23. Knuth, D., and Plass, M. Breaking paragraphs into lines. *Software: Practice and Experience 11*, 11 (1981), 1119–1184.

24. Kobayashi, S. The aim and method of the color image scale. *Color Research & Application 6*, 2 (1981), 93–107.

25. Kuhna, M., Kivelä, I.-M., and Oittinen, P. Semi-automated magazine layout using content-based image features. In *Proceedings of the 20th ACM international conference on Multimedia*, MM '12, ACM (2012), 379–388.

26. Lavie, T., and Tractinsky, N. Assessing dimensions of perceived visual aesthetics of web sites. *International Journal of Human-Computer Studies 60*, 3 (2004), 269–298.

27. Lin, X. Intelligent content fitting for digital publishing. In *Electronic Imaging 2006*, International Society for Optics and Photonics (2006), 60760J–60760J.

28. Lok, S., and Feiner, S. A survey of automated layout techniques for information presentations. In *Proceedings of Smart Graphics*, vol. 2001 (2001), 61–68.

29. Lok, S., Feiner, S., and Ngai, G. Evaluation of visual balance for automated layout. In *Proceedings of the 9th International Conference on Intelligent User Interfaces*, ACM (2004), 101–108.

30. Ngo, D., Samsudin, A., and Abdullah, R. Aesthetic measures for assessing graphic screens. *Journal of Information Science and Engineering 16*, 1 (2000), 97–116.

31. O'Donovan, P., Agarwala, A., and Hertzmann, A. Color compatibility from large datasets. *ACM Transactions on Graphics (TOG) 30*, 4 (2011), 63.

32. S., K. *Color Image Scale*. Kodansha Intern, 1991.

33. Samara, T. *Making and breaking the grid: a graphic design layout workshop*. Rockport Publishers, 2005.

34. Samara, T. *Typography workbook: A real-world guide to using type in graphic design*. Rockport Publishers, 2006.

35. Shneiderman, B. *Leonardo's laptop: human needs and the new computing technologies*. MIT Press, 2003.

36. Shneiderman, B. Creativity support tools: A grand challenge for hci researchers. *Engineering the User Interface* (2009), 1–9.

37. Solli, M., and Lenz, R. Color semantics for image indexing. In *CGIV 2010: 5th European Conference on Colour in Graphics, Imaging, and Vision*, IS&T (2010), 353–358.

38. Sparling, E., and Sen, S. Rating: how difficult is it? In *Proceedings of the Fifth ACM Conference on Recommender Systems*, ACM (2011), 149–156.

39. Swearingen, K., and Sinha, R. Interaction design for recommender systems. In *Designing Interactive Systems*, vol. 6, ACM Press (2002), 312–334.

40. Tibshirani, R. Regression shrinkage and selection via the lasso. *Journal of the Royal Statistical Society. Series B (Methodological)* (1996), 267–288.

41. Tokumaru, M., Muranaka, N., and Imanishi, S. Color design support system considering color harmony. In *Fuzzy Systems, 2002. FUZZ-IEEE'02. Proceedings of the 2002 IEEE International Conference on*, vol. 1, IEEE (2002), 378–383.

42. Zhang, X., Gao, Y., Atkins, C. B., Cheatle, P., Xiao, J., Chao, H., Wu, P., Tretter, D., Slatter, D., Carter, A., Penny, R., and Willis, C. Autophotobook: using technology to streamline photobook creation. In *Proceedings of the SPIE*, vol. 7540 of *Society of Photo-Optical Instrumentation Engineers (SPIE) Conference Series* (2010), 75400L–75400L–15.

LinkedVis: Exploring Social and Semantic Career Recommendations

Svetlin Alex Bostandjiev, John O'Donovan, Tobias Höllerer
Department of Computer Science
University of California, Santa Barbara
{alex, jod, holl}@cs.ucsb.edu

ABSTRACT
This paper presents LinkedVis, an interactive visual recommender system that combines social and semantic knowledge to produce career recommendations based on the LinkedIn API. A collaborative (social) approach is employed to identify professionals with similar career paths and produce personalized recommendations of both companies and roles. To unify semantically identical but lexically distinct entities and arrive at better user models, we employ lightweight natural language processing and entity resolution using semantic information from a variety of end-points on the web. Elements from the underlying recommendation algorithm are exposed through an interactive interface that allows users to manipulate different aspects of the algorithm and the data it operates on, allowing users to explore a variety of "what-if" scenarios around their current profile. We evaluate LinkedVis through leave-one-out accuracy and diversity experiments on a data corpus collected from 47 users and their LinkedIn connections, as well as through a supervised study of 27 users exploring their own profile and recommendations interactively. Results show that our approach outperforms a benchmark recommendation algorithm without semantic resolution in terms of accuracy and diversity, and that the ability to tweak recommendations interactively by adjusting profile item and social connection weights further improves predictive accuracy. Questionnaires on the user experience with the explanatory and interactive aspects of the application reveal very high user acceptance and satisfaction.

Author Keywords
User Interfaces; Visual Knowledge Representation; Hybrid Recommender Systems; Data Integration; Social Web

ACM Classification Keywords
H.5.2 Information Interfaces and Presentation: User Interfaces–*graphical user interfaces (GUI), user-centered design*

INTRODUCTION
Many of today's job search websites recommend jobs by simple matching of text descriptions to the job seeker's professional profile. The higher the correlation between the job description requirements and the job seeker's qualifications the more likely it is for a job to get recommended. This content-based matching method works to some degree, but it is narrow and ignores a wealth of social connections and other metadata that can potentially yield more interesting and diverse recommendations. For example, by looking at the jobs followed by other professionals with similar qualifications to some target user. We argue that it is valuable to take this so-called "social" information into account. We propose that a typical collaborative filtering approach can be used to identify professionals with similar backgrounds and reveal personalized job opportunities that are otherwise hidden. However, we find that in many cases there is insufficient overlap to generate useful predictions, so we look to the semantic web to bootstrap and augment the traditional approach. For example, a person graduating college might have a skill set very similar to someone who already has years of working experience after school, but these skill sets may be represented very differently in the two user-defined profiles. The jobs that the professional has held are of potential interest to the new graduate, and better techniques are needed to align these profiles as potential recommendation partners. Using these techniques, the *LinkedVis* interface helps users discover professionals with similar backgrounds who can in turn highlight potentially interesting companies and specific roles. For a job-seeker exploring possible career paths, it is typically useful to explore what-if scenarios. For example, one might want to answer questions such as: "What new jobs could I apply for if I became proficient in C++ programming?". LinkedVis enables users to answer such questions by leveraging underlying social and semantic information in a transparent manner via an interactive user interface. A video demo of the user interface can be viewed at [1]. To assess the performance of *LinkedVis*, a supervised laboratory study was performed using participants' real LinkedIn profiles and network connections. The study focused on aspects of recommendation accuracy, diversity and user satisfaction in three different interaction and control conditions within the *LinkedVis* system.

Contributions
The list below highlights the three core contributions in this paper. For each contribution, a discussion on design, implementation, evaluation and results are provided later.

[1] `http://www.youtube.com/watch?v=w7Q4JoYyEF4&hd=1`

Figure 1. Screenshot of the LinkedVis Recommender System.

- *A novel approach that uses NLP and entity resolution steps to improve traditional collaborative filtering for job recommendations.* An evaluation of our hybrid system is performed against purely social approaches in terms of recommendation accuracy, diversity, and computational costs. Offline experiments and a user study show that the hybrid approaches produce recommendations with higher accuracy and greater diversity at a higher computational cost that, for the purpose of our real-time user evaluations were absorbed in a one-time pre-processing step per user.

- *Real-time visualizations of the relationships between profile items, social connections, and the resulting recommendations, supporting explanation of the recommendation process.* A supervised user study of LinkedVis shows that recommending career opportunities through a user interface increases user satisfaction and provides explanation and transparency in the recommendation process.

- *An interactive control mechanism for the recommendation process at the data level and the algorithmic level.* An interaction method was designed to provide control over system settings that are generally not modifiable in modern career search websites. Users were able to modify the weights of their professional qualifications and connections. The interface was also designed to support what-if scenarios and let users see how adding new qualifications to their profile affects their suitability for certain companies and roles – this feature received the highest user satisfaction in the post-study questionnaire. Overall, our evaluation shows that interaction with the system in real time can improve recommendation accuracy and user experience.

RELATED WORK

This section provides a discussion of related research in the following two areas. 1) Recommender system algorithms and their hybrids, and 2) the role of interaction and visualization for recommendation systems.

Recommender Systems

Much research has focused on ways to automatically filter and personalize content for web users [24]. So called recommender systems aim to tailor a user's information by predicting the right item at the right time. There are a wide variety of approaches to recommendation, such as those algorithms we use through Amazon, YouTube, Netflix, Pandora and many other popular online applications that personalize content for users. Core techniques include content-based recommendation [16] [9] which is a rudimentary approach that simply matches text-based descriptions of a candidate item to those in a target users profile. These methods tend to suffer from problems such as narrowness, since they recommend items that are textually similar to those already in a user's profile. Content-based approaches also fall short on non-machine analyzable data such as music for example, where detailed text descriptions of content are generally not available. Collaborative filtering (CF) approaches [7][14][19][20][22], attempt to model the normal social process of asking a friend for a recommendation. In brief, CF algorithms generate recommendations based on the opinions of a neighborhood of users who have rated similarly in the past. CF methods perform well in rich data environments where there is plenty of overlap in user preference. They are capable of making good predictions on non-machine analyzable data such as music, since they rely on human evaluation of the candidate items. For the same reason, these methods tend to be less narrow than content-based approaches, and can produce serendipitous recommendations [20]. Another relevant class of recommender system algorithms use knowledge from domain specialists to produce recommendations. These are commonly known as knowledge-based or "expert" recommender systems [21].

Hybrid Approaches

Traditional recommender system techniques such as collaborative, content-based, and knowledge-based filtering, each have unique sets of strengths and limitations. For example, CF suffers from sparsity and early rater problems [20], while content-based approaches suffer from narrowness and require text descriptions. However, a hybrid approach can use one approach to make predictions where the other fails, resulting in a more robust recommender system [16]. Researchers have attempted to augment the traditional process of collaborative filtering with additional information such as trust models [18] to improve accuracy and robustness of the recommendations, while more recent work in [13, 17] refine the trust models used in [18]. Burke [6] proposes a taxonomy of different classes of hybrid systems and hybridization designs. For example recommendation algorithms can work in parallel before combining their results, may be pipelined such that the output of one algorithm is the input of the next, or may be combined into one monolithic algorithm. *LinkedVis* falls into the parallelized design class, since our approach firstly generates predictions from social sources, followed by semantic sources, and then applies a hybridization strategy afterwards.

Interfaces for Recommender Systems

Recommendations are now being delivered on a variety of devices and platforms, from small hand-held devices to 60 inch TV screens showing Netflix predictions on Roku or AppleTV devices for example. Accordingly. researchers have begun to place more focus on the role of the user interface interface in the recommendation process. Furthermore, evaluation mechanisms for recommender systems no longer focus solely on improving recommendation accuracy, but consider effects of interface elements in the overall evaluation process. For example, allowing for inspectability and control [26, 15] through interface elements improves overall acceptance of a recommendation [15, 4, 25]. However, there is some disagreement in the community as to what the appropriate levels of inspectability and control should be. [8] promotes the simpler UI, as do Netflix, while others [4, 15] argue the benefits of having greater transparency and control. The authors believe that it is important to have control available, and that the simple knowledge that control is available can have a bearing on a user's satisfaction with a recommender system. In the context of our LinkedVis system (Fig. 1), the interface can potentially be refined to just the predictions shown in the right column, with the remaining inspecability and control elements only shown on-demand, for those who wish to explore the system in more detail.

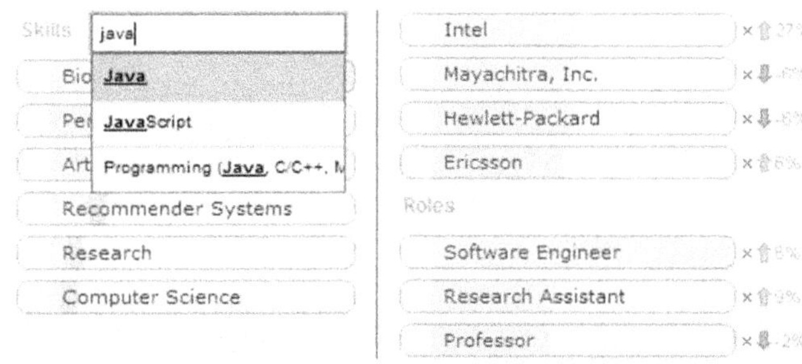

Figure 2. Illustration of the "what-if" scenario feature of *LinkedVis*. Users are able to add new hypothetical entities to their profile (left) and see how that affects the recommendations (right), i.e. whether the new entity brings them closer to their dream jobs.

DESIGN

The *LinkedVis* user interface provides a simple explanation of our collaborative filtering approach for discovering relevant entities: personal qualifications, connected professionals, companies, and roles (Figure 1).

Visualization

The interface is split into three distinct columns:

- *Profile*: The left column presents a semantically classified summary of the user's profile, such as educational background, previous and current jobs, and professional skills.
- *Connections*: The middle column consists of a list of connected professionals that have similar backgrounds to the user.
- *Recommendations*: The right column reveals grouped recommendations the user might be interested in, such as companies and roles.

An additional panel (right of the Recommendations column) provides detailed information about the last clicked entity.

Interaction

Each entity is weighted by our algorithms on a scale from 0 to 1 and is visually represented by a draggable slider. Via these sliders users are able to change the input weight of entities in their profile suggesting that for example their Ph.D. is more important than a part-time job they held at the dining commons. Weights of connected people can be changed to express how similar the user perceives those professionals to be. As the user drags a slider in his profile the weights of connected people change in real-time, and when weights of connected professionals are changed that also affects the recommendations in real-time. Users are able to explore what-if scenarios by adding qualifications to their profile and seeing how that affects their connections and recommendations. This is done via the "+" icon next to each profile group. Figure 2 illustrates this feature.

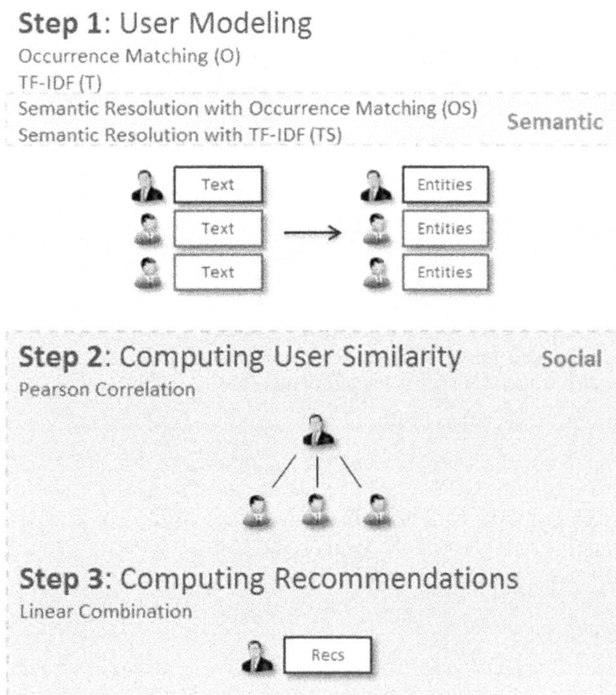

Figure 3. Three-step approach of *LinkedVis*.

APPROACH

As in most collaborative filtering methods, we need to model user profiles, design a metric for user similarity, and compute recommendations (Figure 3). These three steps are described in the following subsections.

User Modeling

`LinkedIn.com` is currently the dominant professional social network with more than 150 million users registered in more than 200 countries and territories[2]. We use the LinkedIn API to identify user's first connections. We then crawl the LinkedIn HTML pages related to the user and their connections. We parse the text out of each HTML file so that each user/connection is associated with a flat text file. These text files serve as the input for the algorithms described below. We treat each user/connection as a bag of weighted entities that describe it. For example, user X can be described by "MIT" and "software engineering" with respective weights of 0.8 and 0.6. We have designed four different approaches to model users and come up with these entities and their weights based on the user-associated text files:

- *Occurrence Matching (O)* : This simple model assigns a weight of 1 to each term (word) related to each user.

- *TF-IDF (T)* : This model uses "Term Frequency - Inverse Document Frequency" (TF-IDF)[3] to assign weights to each term. The input for the traditional TF-IDF approach is the corpus of text files describing the user and his connections.

- *Semantic Resolution with Occurrence Matching (OS)* : This model and the next involve alignment of semantic metadata, more specifically"semantic entity resolution". The idea is that we want to extract semantically meaningful entities for each user as opposed to just words. For example, the entity "Doctor of Philosophy" is more meaningful and descriptive than the terms "Doctor", "of", and "Philosophy". Our approach involves using the concept of "noun phrases" which are good topic markers in paragraph-long text descriptions [1, 12]. For each user, we identify noun phrases using a maximum entropy part-of speech tagger[4]. Then we resolve the noun phrases to real life semantic entities. Wikipedia presents the most evolved semantic graph in terms of completeness and non-redundancy [10], and therefore it is a good resource for entity-resolution. In order to map noun phrases to Wikipedia articles we rely on external callouts to a search engine. Previous work has been successful in turning search engines into knowledge bases [2, 3]. We identify the first article within the English Wikipedia that the search engine returns. This resolution approach helps us map phrases to semantically meaningful entities, i.e. "PhD", "Ph.D.", and "Doctor of Philosophy" will all map to the Wiki article `http://en.wikipedia.org/wiki/Doctor_of_Philosophy`. After we model each user in terms of semantic entities we assign a weight of 1 to each entity similarly to the *Occurrence Matching (O)* model.

- *Semantic Resolution with TF-IDF (TS)* : This model first uses the semantic entity resolution described in the previous model and then TF-IDF to assign weights to the semantic entities.

Computing User Similarity

After we model the user and his connections we want to rank the connection by how similar they are to the user in terms of their professional background. In order to compute user similarity we use a social collaborative filtering approach generally used in the field of recommender systems. We have adapted Pearson's correlation coefficient formula to account for the fact that entities in users' profiles are binary and do not contain scaled ratings. The similarity of each LinkedIn connection to the active user is given by:

$$W_{con_i} = \frac{TWCE_{user,con_i}}{\sqrt{TWE^2_{user} \cdot TWE^2_{con_i}}} \tag{1}$$

where $TWCE_{x,y}$ is the total weight of the entities x and y have common, and TWE_x is the total weight of user x's entities.

Computing Recommendations

The last step is to compute what companies and roles can be recommended based on the user similarities computed above. We compute the weight of each recommendation as the sum of the weights of all connections that contain the recommendation, i.e. the weighted sum.

[2]`http://en.wikipedia.org/wiki/LinkedIn`
[3]`http://en.wikipedia.org/wiki/Tf*idf`
[4]`http://www-nlp.stanford.edu/software`

EVALUATION

We carried out an evaluation of the system and its user interface via offline experiments and a user study. The evaluation focused on whether the system provides the contributions described in the beginning of this paper. We were interested in finding whether applying semantic entity resolution prior to performing social collaborative filtering improves the quality of the resulting recommended entities. We also measured the effectiveness of the visualization and interaction techniques provided by the user interface.

All evaluation was conducted on a Windows 7 64-bit computer (Intel Core i7-2670QM CPU at 2.2Ghz with 12GB of RAM) and the supervised user study used a 24-inch display with 1920x1080 pixel resolution. The web application and database were hosted locally.

EVALUATION VIA OFFLINE EXPERIMENTS

First, a set of offline experiments was performed over LinkedIn data collected for 47 users (27 male and 20 female, ages between 20 and 38) and their connections. 25 users were students and the rest were employed in industry. Users had 114.3 connections on average (SD=97.33). LinkedIn user connections data is not public and is only available through the LinkedIn API. In order to get a user's connections data the user had to approve a LinkedIn application that we created.

Leave-One-Out

We performed a leave-one-out cross-validation to compare the accuracy of the user models listed above. For each user in the collected data we extracted the companies and roles they have held. The 47 users had each worked for 3.82 companies on average, and served 3.86 different roles. We ran a leave-one-out analysis on that data using each user model. We measured how often the left-out entity appeared in the top N recommended entities, for N equals 1, 3, 5, 10, and 20. The analysis on companies and roles was done separately. The medians are presented in Figure 4.

In order to evaluate whether the semantic augmentation contributed to more accurate recommendations we performed paired tests. The leave-one-out accuracy data was not normally distributed so we chose a non-parametric counterpart of to the paired-samples t-test, the Wilcoxon Signed-Rank test. The analysis summarized in Table 1 was performed for the top 20 recommendations.

The Wilcoxon Signed-Rank tests revealed significant improvement in accuracy both on companies and roles. In terms of companies, for the *O* (Mdn=0.125) and *OS* (Mdn=0.25) models: Z=-2.973, p=0.001, and for the *T* (Mdn=0.33) and *TS* (Mdn=0.365) models: Z=-2.712, p=0.003. Moreover, in terms of roles, for the *O* (Mdn=0) and *OS* (Mdn=0.14) models: Z=-2.662, p=0.003, and for the *T* (Mdn=0.33) and *TS* (Mdn=0.33) models: Z=-2.122, p=0.014. Values ranged from 0 to 1 for all models.

The results from the analysis for the top 1, 3, 5, and 10 companies are summarized in Table 2. The semantic augmentation contributed to more accurate recommendations ($p<0.05$) in all cases except two: Z=-1.104, p=0.180 for top 10 companies and Z=-1.610, p=0.094 for top 1 roles for O-OS.

	Companies	Roles
Model	Mdn	Mdn
O	0.125	0
T	0.33	0.33
OS	0.25	0.14
TS	0.365	0.33

		Companies		Roles	
Model 1	Model 2	Z	P Val	Z	P Val
O	OS	-2.973	0.001	-2.662	0.003
T	TS	-2.712	0.003	-2.122	0.014

Table 1. Results from Wilcoxon Signed-Rank tests comparing the accuracy between the *O* and *OS* models and between the *T* and *TS* models over top 20 recommendations (df=46). Medians for the four models are presented in the top table and statistical significance values are described in the bottom table.

			Companies		Roles	
Model 1	Model 2	Top N	Z	P Val	Z	P Val
O	OS	20	-2.973	0.001	-2.662	0.003
		10	-1.104	0.180	-2.733	0.002
		5	-2.805	0.002	-2.733	0.002
		3	-2.088	0.022	-2.763	0.002
		1	-2.177	0.011	-1.610	0.094
T	TS	20	-2.712	0.003	-2.122	0.014
		10	-2.244	0.016	-3.131	<0.001
		5	-2.270	0.013	-3.237	<0.001
		3	-2.343	0.009	-4.077	<0.001
		1	-2.095	0.021	-3.114	0.001

Table 2. Results from Wilcoxon Signed-Rank tests comparing the accuracy between the *O* and *OS* models and between the *T* and *TS* models over top 1, 3, 5, 10, and 20 recommendations (df=46).

Diversity

As discussed in recommender system literature [11], predictive accuracy is not a sufficient measure of the performance of a recommender system. The "popular item" effect is a common problem in recommender systems, where predictions tend to include many popular items and not enough esoteric items. However, it is the correct prediction of these esoteric items that can have the biggest positive influence on user satisfaction. For example, it is not desirable for our system to recommend only big established companies but also startups.

We performed a diversity analysis on the different user models. For each company and role entity in the entire corpus of data we assigned a "popularity" score, i.e. a frequency score based on the number of the times the entity occurs in the whole corpus of data (Figure 5 left). The corpus contained 47 main users plus their connections, which accumulated to 5372 LinkedIn users total. The most popular roles were "Intern" and "Software Engineer" occurring 455 and 337 times respectively, and the most popular company was 'UC Santa Barbara" with 372 occurrences, which reflects the fact that the greater portion of our users were UC Santa Barbara students.

After we calculated frequencies for all companies and roles in the corpus, for each user we measured the total frequency of the top 20 recommended entities produced by each user model. The averages are presented in Figure 5 (right).

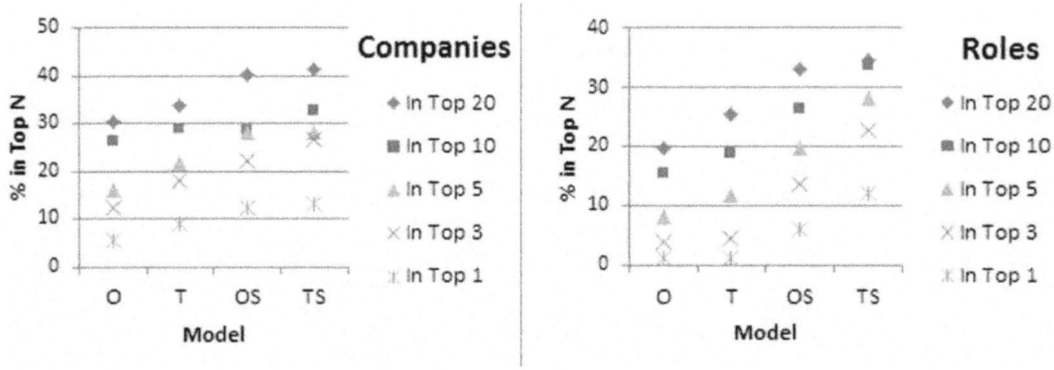

Figure 4. Leave-One-Out analysis results showing medians of how often the left-out entity appeared in the top N recommendations.

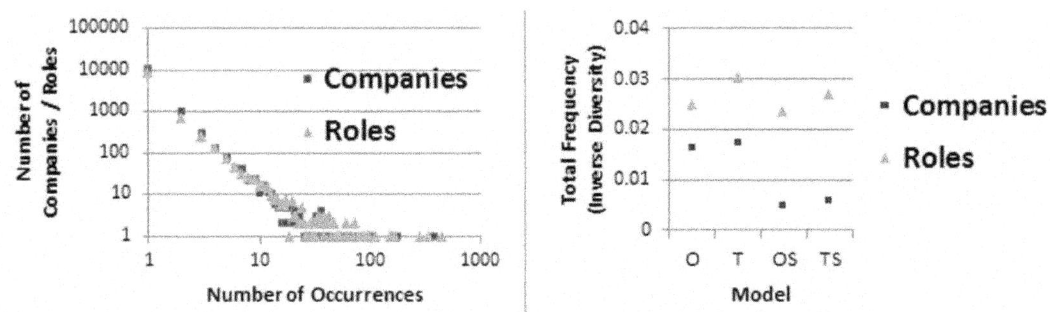

Figure 5. Results from the Diversity analysis. On the left, we show a histogram of the number of occurrences of companies and roles in the whole corpus of data (5372 LinkedIn users). The majority of the companies and roles, 85.8% and 85.3% respectively, occurred only once (10665 out of 12425 companies total and 8582 out of 10066 roles total). On the right, for each model we calculated the average frequency per user of his top 20 recommended companies / roles.

	Companies		Roles	
Model	Mean	StDev	Mean	StDev
O	0.016	0.010	0.025	0.012
T	0.017	0.010	0.030	0.013
OS	0.005	0.004	0.024	0.011
TS	0.006	0.004	0.027	0.010

		Companies		Roles	
Model 1	Model 2	t	P Val	t	P Val
O	OS	10.662	<0.001	1.744	0.044
T	TS	11.249	<0.001	3.771	<0.001

Table 3. Results from paired-samples t-tests comparing the frequency (inverse diversity) between the *O* and *OS* models and between the *T* and *TS* models (df=46).

Paired-samples t-tests were conducted to compare frequency (inverse diversity) between the *T* and *TS*, and between *O* and *OS* for both companies and roles. The results are summarized in Table 3.

The t-tests revealed significant differences in diversity both on companies and roles. In terms of companies, for the *O* (M=0.016, SD=0.010) and *OS* (M=0.005, SD=0.004) models: $t(46)=10.662$, $p<0.001$, and for the *T* (M=0.017, SD=0.10) and *TS* (M=0.006, SD=0.004) models: $t(46)=11.249$, $p<0.001$. Moreover, in terms of roles, for the *O* (M=0.025, SD=0.012) and *OS* (M=0.024, SD=0.011) models: $t(46)=1.744$, $p=0.044$, and for the *T* (M=0.030, SD=0.013) and *TS* (M=0.027, SD=0.010) models: $t(46)=3.771$, $p<0.001$.

These results suggest that the semantic augmentation produced more diverse recommendations.

EVALUATION VIA A USER STUDY

We conducted a supervised user study to obtain more insights on our main contributions in recommendation accuracy, explanation, and interaction. We gathered data implicitly and explicitly via pre- and post-study questionnaire. In the post-study questionnaire we asked questions to judge the perceived transparency and explanation of the system, and the quality of interaction.

Another goal of the study was to compare how different user models perform relative to one another in terms of recommendation accuracy. We compared all methods described in Section , plus an interactive method that let users change entity weights and improve the data. We looked for statistical significance of whether semantic computing can add value to standard user models, and whether the interaction method outperforms the best hybrid. As a base for the interaction method we chose the best performer out of the four non-interactive methods. In a pilot study involving six users we determined that *Semantic Resolution with TF-IDF (TS)* produces the best recommendations, and hence we named our interactive method *Interaction after Semantic Resolution with TF-IDF (ITS)*.

Setup

Each of the five methods produced a ranked list of recommended entities (companies and roles). We asked users to evaluate the relevance of these entities on a Likert scale (1 to 5 stars), which produces a "rating" for each entity. Users rated the top 10 results for each of the five methods, compiled into one randomized list, at the end of the study. We measured the "utility" of each ranked list of entities using Breeze's *R-Score* "utility" metric [5, 23] to determine a utility score for the list. The metric assumes that the value of recommendations decline exponentially based on position in the recommended list. The utility of a given recommendation list for user u is given by:

$$R_u = \sum_j \frac{max(r_{ui_j} - d, 0)}{2^{\frac{j-1}{\alpha-1}}} \qquad (2)$$

where i_j is the item in the jth position, r_{ui} is user u's rating of item i, (i.e. 1 to 5 stars), d is Breese's "don't care" threshold (experimentally chosen as 2 stars in our setting), and α is the half-life parameter, which we set to 1.5, controlling the exponential decline of the value of positions in the ranked list.

We performed one-way repeated measures ANOVA analyses for both companies and roles, with the independent variable being the user model and the dependent variable being the utility of the produced list of entities.

Note that users might have been biased to inflate relevance ratings of entities with higher value, for example giving a higher rating to "Google" than "LocalSoft" even though the user is better suited for the latter. This is due to the fact that bigger companies might be more desirable to work for. Our diversity analysis described in Section measures the level of entity popularity produced by each model. The analysis shows that the semantic models produce more diverse recommendations.

Participants

A total of 27 users participated in the user study, which lasted 41 minutes on average. The analyses used data from 20 participants as data for 7 participants was not logged correctly. We used the SONA[5] human subjects pool provided by the Department of Psychology at University of California, Santa Barbara to recruit participants. Out of the 20 participants 9 were male and 11 were female. Also, 15 were students: 5 pursuing a bachelors degree, 3 masters, and 7 doctorate, spanning 9 different majors. The other 5 participants were employed and working in the fields of the arts, sciences, and finance. The reported usage of LinkedIn was: 2 daily, 10 weekly, and 8 monthly. The way participants discover new career opportunities was mainly through personal connections, mailing lists, online job websites, and search.

Procedure

The study had four parts: a pre-computational step, a pre-study questionnaire, tasks, and a post-study questionnaire. It was required for each participant to have a LinkedIn account with at least 30 connections. Each participant was asked to approve a LinkedIn application through which we gathered their profile and connections data. Once the data was available we pre-computed all data necessary for the visualization. This step took no more than an hour for each user. The pre-study questionnaire was split into demographics and assessment of users' familiarity with and level of activity on LinkedIn and recommender systems. The following tasks were performed between the pre- and post-study questionnaires:

- *Preliminary Task*: In this task we explained what the system is about and asked users to familiarize themselves with the interface by clicking on a few entities and exploring how entities are connected.
- *Refinement Task*: Here we asked users to refine the visualization by changing some of the pre-computed weights for their profile items and connections. Users were able to see how the changes affected the weights of other entities in real-time.
- *What-if Scenario Task*: This task was designed for users to explore what-if scenarios. We asked users to add qualifications to their profiles that could potentially get them better jobs, such as new skills (i.e. Excel) and educational degrees (i.e. PhD), etc.
- *Rating Task*: Lastly, users were asked to rate the top 10 recommendations produced by each of the five approaches on a 1-to-5-star rating given in random order.

In the post-study questionnaire we asked questions related to transparency and explanation, and also interaction with the system.

		Companies				Roles			
Model 1	Model 2	Diff	Lower	Upper	P Val	Diff	Lower	Upper	P Val
OS	O	0.765	0.066	1.465	0.024	0.922	0.246	1.597	0.002
TS	T	0.774	0.075	1.474	0.022	0.772	0.097	1.448	0.016
ITS	TS	1.100	0.401	1.799	<0.001	1.306	0.631	1.981	<0.001

Table 4. Results from a Tukey post-hoc analysis of the user models: multiple comparisons of means with 95% family-wise confidence level

Recommendation Accuracy

We performed one-way repeated measures ANOVA analyses for both companies and roles, in which the independent variable was the user model and the dependent variable was the utility of the produced list of entities. Figure 6 shows the means of the five models over utility with 95% confidence intervals for companies and roles separately. The *Interaction after Semantic Resolution with TF-IDF (ITS)* model achieved the highest utility for both companies and roles, whereas, the simple *Occurrence Matching (O)* model reported the lowest utility. Mauchly's test did not show violation of sphericity against Model for companies (W(4)=0.39, p=0.06), and for roles (W(4)=0.43, p=0.10). The ANOVAs revealed a significant effect of the model variable on utility for both companies ($F(4, 76)=205.59$, $p<0.001$) and roles ($F(4, 76)=215.08$, $p<0.001$). To assess the statistical significance of pair-wise differences within our models, a Tukey post-hoc analysis was performed and the more interesting results were recorded in Table 4.

[5] `http://ucsb.sona-systems.com`

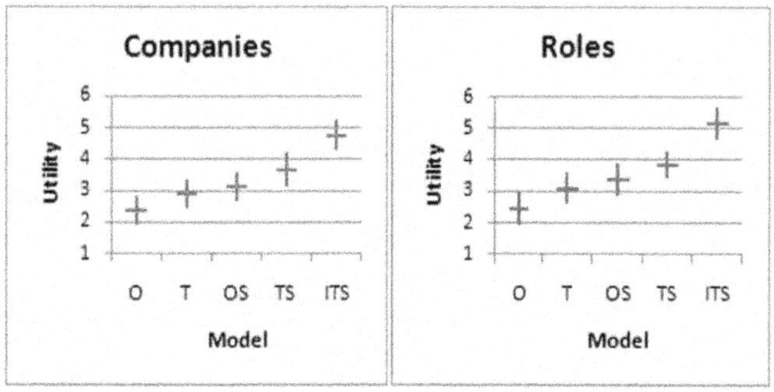

Figure 6. Plot of means of user models over utility with 95% confidence intervals.

Semantic vs. Non-semantic Results

In this section, we focus on the analysis whether our semantic models (*Semantic Resolution with Occurrence Matching (OS)* and *Semantic Resolution with TF-IDF (TS)*) perform better than the non-semantic models (*Occurrence Matching (O)* and *TF-IDF (T)*). The Tukey pair-wise test (Table 4) revealed that when both the *O* and *T* models were augmented with semantic computing, i.e. models *OS* and *TS*, there was an improvement in perceived recommendation accuracy for both companies and roles (($p=0.024$, $p=0.022$) and ($p=0.002$, $p=0.016$) respectively). This result indicates that semantic computing can be successfully used to improve the results of a purely social computing approach. We did not find significant difference between the two non-semantic models, *O* and *T*, and between the two semantic models, *OS* and *TS*.

Interaction Results

In terms of interaction, the Tukey pair-wise test showed that the interactive model, *Interaction after Semantic Resolution with TF-IDF (ITS)*, performed better than the *TS* model itself ($p<0.001$ for companies and roles). We tested interaction only over our best performing model in order to simplify the study. Testing over all models would require a between-subjects study with a significantly larger participant pool. The result indicates that interaction with the visualization helps users get better recommendation. This is a somewhat intuitive result because users can see the recommended entities.

User Experience

Figure 7 presents the results from the post-study questionnaire. The goal of the post-study was to examine the perceived quality of explanation within the system and the level to which users believed interaction was useful. All positively-phrased questions received scores higher than 4 on a 1-5 scale. The highest score of 4.6 was received for the more general questions "Was the system easy to use?" and "Was the system fun to use?".

In terms of explanation and transparency, users perceived that the system helped them understand the basis for their recommendations (4.3) and they felt like they found connections with similar backgrounds to their own (4.3).

The interaction features of *LinkedVis* were also positively perceived in the study. The highest score (4.6) was achieved by

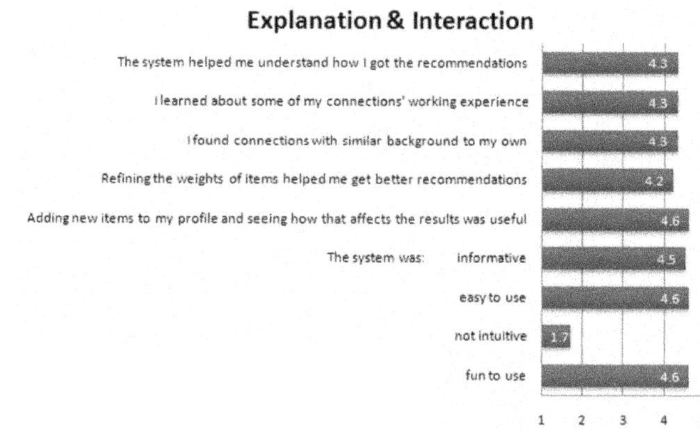

Figure 7. Post-study questionnaire results.

the what-if scenario feature of the user interface, i.e. the option to hypothetically add new entities to your profile and see how that affects the recommendations (Figure 2).

CONCLUSIONS AND FUTURE WORK

In this paper, we presented *LinkedVis*, a user interface for discovery of new career opportunities based on your professional social network. *LinkedVis* employs a collaborative filtering approach for finding similar connections in a target user's network, which is then augmented via semantic knowledge for user modeling and entity resolution. The interactive visual interface serves as an explanatory mechanism, and further, as an input modality for refining a user's profile and social connections and to exploring what-if scenarios in the career world.

We furthermore explored potential synergies that exist between social connections and associated semantic concept resolution for collaborative recommendation of jobs via the LinkedIn API.

A series of offline experiments and a user study were performed to evaluate the system in terms of integrating social network connections, semantic metadata, explanation and interaction into the recommendation process. The study results indicate that:

- Semantic entity resolution significantly increases user-rated recommendation accuracy and recommendation diversity in the job domain.
- Indication recommendation provenance and providing real-time illustration of the recommendation algorithm within a hybrid recommender system through a visual user interface resulted in high user satisfaction.
- Interaction with the social and semantic data relationships within a hybrid recommender system (allowing the adjustment of weightings for profile items and social connections, as well as enabling what-if analyses) can significantly improve recommendation accuracy and user experience.

The benefits of providing better explanation and control in recommender systems come at a cost. Every user interface has a learning curve as users need to spend time to understand the system and be willing to tweak it in the first place. The learning curve can be alleviated through better user interface designs that appeal to large audiences. In this regard, the qualitative findings from our post-study user questionnaire are highly encouraging, in that they indicated high levels of user enthusiasm and engagement with the system.

However, no matter how intuitive a system's user interface is, many users will often be satisfied with being given just a final recommendation. To accommodate groups of users with and without an interest in parameter control, we are interested in user interfaces that scale fluidly between basic and advanced user modes. Future work in this area may focus on how control and explanation can be provided by minimal intrusion on the user, evaluated by large-scale user studies on variants of popular recommender systems augmented with advanced views that provide different degrees explanation and interaction on demand.

ACKNOWLEDGEMENTS

The authors would like to thank Cha Lee and Sibel Adali for their input on analysis methods and credibility indicators for microblogs, respectively. This work was partially supported by the U.S. Army Research Laboratory under Cooperative Agreement No. W911NF-09-2-0053; by NSF grant IIS-1058132; by the Intelligence Advanced Research Projects Activity (IARPA) via Air Force Research Laboratory contract number FA8650-10-C-7060; and by the U.S. Army Research Laboratory under MURI grant No. W911NF-09-1-0553; The views and conclusions contained in this document are those of the authors and should not be interpreted as representing the official policies, either expressed or implied, of ARL, AFRL, IARPA, NSF, or the U.S. Government. The U.S. Government is authorized to reproduce and distribute reprints for Government purposes notwithstanding any copyright notation here on.

REFERENCES

1. Bendersky, M., and Croft, W. B. Discovering key concepts in verbose queries. In *SIGIR*, S.-H. Myaeng, D. W. Oard, F. Sebastiani, T.-S. Chua, and M.-K. Leong, Eds., ACM (2008), 491–498.
2. Bernstein, M. S., Suh, B., Hong, L., Chen, J., Kairam, S., and Chi, E. H. Eddi: interactive topic-based browsing of social status streams. In *Proceedings of the 23nd annual ACM symposium on User interface software and technology*, UIST '10, ACM (New York, NY, USA, 2010), 303–312.
3. Bostandjiev, S., O'Donovan, J., Hall, C., Gretarsson, B., and Höllerer, T. Wigipedia: A tool for improving structured data in wikipedia. In *Proceedings of the 2011 IEEE Fifth International Conference on Semantic Computing*, ICSC '11, IEEE Computer Society (Washington, DC, USA, 2011), 328–335.
4. Bostandjiev, S., O'Donovan, J., and Höllerer, T. Tasteweights: A visual interactive hybrid recommender. In *Proceedings of ACM RecSys '12 Conference on Recommender Systems* (Dublin, Ireland, 2012).
5. Breese, J. S., Heckerman, D., and Kadie, C. Empirical analysis of predictive algorithms for collaborative filtering. Morgan Kaufmann (1998), 43–52.
6. Burke, R. Hybrid recommender systems: Survey and experiments. *User Modeling and User-Adapted Interaction 12*, 4 (2002), 331–370.
7. Burke, R., Mobasher, B., Zabicki, R., and Bhaumik, R. Identifying attack models for secure recommendation. In *Beyond Personalisation Workshop at the International Conferece on Intelligent User Interfaces*, ACM Press (San Deigo, USA., 2005), 347–361.
8. Cremonesi, P., Garzotto, F., Negro, S., Papadopoulos, A., and Turrin, R. Comparative evaluation of recommender system quality. In *CHI '11 Extended Abstracts on Human Factors in Computing Systems*, CHI EA '11, ACM (New York, NY, USA, 2011), 1927–1932.
9. Goldberg, K., Roeder, T., Gupta, D., and Perkins, C. Eigentaste: A constant time collaborative filtering algorithm. *Information Retrieval 4*, 2 (2001), 133–151.
10. Halavais, A., and Lackaff, D. An analysis of topical coverage of wikipedia. *Journal of Computer-Mediated Communication 13*, 2 (2008), 429–440.
11. Herlocker, J. L., Konstan, J. A., Terveen, L. G., John, and Riedl, T. Evaluating collaborative filtering recommender systems. *ACM Transactions on Information Systems 22* (2004), 5–53.
12. Hulth, A. Improved automatic keyword extraction given more linguistic knowledge. *Proceedings of the Conference on Empirical Methods in Natural Language Processing (EMNLP 03)* (2003), 216–223.
13. Kang, B., O'Donovan, J., and Höllerer, T. Modeling topic specific credibility on twitter. In *IUI* (2012), 179–188.
14. Karypis, G. Evaluation of item-based top-n recommendation algorithms. In *Proceedings of the 2001 ACM CIKM International Conference on Information and Knowledge Management, Atlanta, Georgia, USA* (2001), 247–254.
15. Knijenburg, B., Bostandjiev, S., O'Donovan, J., and Kobsa, A. Inspectability and control in social recommenders. In *Proceedings of ACM RecSys '12 Conference on Recommender Systems* (Dublin, Ireland, 2012).
16. Melville, P., Mooney, R. J., and Nagarajan, R. Content-boosted collaborative filtering for improved recommendations. In *Eighteenth national conference on Artificial intelligence*, American Association for Artificial Intelligence (Menlo Park, CA, USA, 2002), 187–192.
17. O'Donovan, J., Kang, B., Meyer, G., Hllerer, T., and Adali, S. Credibility in context: An analysis of feature distributions in twitter. In *In proceedings at the 2012 ASE/IEEE International Conference on Social Computing, SocialCom, Amsterdam, The Netherlands.*, IEEE (2012), 167–174.
18. O'Donovan, J., and Smyth, B. Trust in recommender systems. In *Proceedings of the 10th international conference on Intelligent user interfaces*, ACM (2005), 167–174.
19. O'Sullivan, D., Wilson, D. C., and Smyth, B. Improving case-based recommendation: A collaborative filtering approach. In *Proceedings of the Sixth European Conference on Case Based Reasoning.* (2002), LNAI 2416, p. 278 ff.
20. Resnick, P., Iacovou, N., Suchak, M., Bergstrom, P., and Riedl, J. Grouplens: An open architecture for collaborative filtering of netnews. In *Proceedings of ACM CSCW'94 Conference on Computer-Supported Cooperative Work* (1994), 175–186.
21. Ricci, F., Rokach, L., Shapira, B., and Kantor, P. B., Eds. *Recommender Systems Handbook*. Springer, 2011.
22. Sarwar, B. M., Karypis, G., Konstan, J. A., and Reidl, J. Item-based collaborative filtering recommendation algorithms. In *World Wide Web* (2001), 285–295.
23. Shani, G., and Gunawardana, A. Evaluating recommendation systems. In *Recommender Systems Handbook*, F. Ricci, L. Rokach, B. Shapira, and P. B. Kantor, Eds. Springer, 2011, 257–297.
24. Shardanand, U., and Maes, P. Social information filtering: Algorithms for automating "word of mouth". In *Proceedings of ACM CHI'95 Conference on Human Factors in Computing Systems*, vol. 1 of *Papers: Using the Information of Others* (1995), 210–217.
25. Tintarev, N., and Masthoff, J. Effective explanations of recommendations: user-centered design. In *Proceedings of the 2007 ACM conference on Recommender systems*, RecSys '07, ACM (New York, NY, USA, 2007), 153–156.
26. Tintarev, N., and Masthoff, J. Designing and evaluating explanations for recommender systems. *Recommender Systems Handbook* (2011), 479–510.

Directing Exploratory Search: Reinforcement Learning from User Interactions with Keywords

Dorota Głowacka
Helsinki Institute for Information Technology HIIT
Dep. of Computer Science
University of Helsinki
glowacka@cs.helsinki.fi

Tuukka Ruotsalo
Helsinki Institute for Information Technology HIIT
Aalto University
tuukka.ruotsalo@aalto.fi

Ksenia Konyushkova
Helsinki Institute for Information Technology HIIT
Dep. of Computer Science
University of Helsinki
ksenia.konyushkova@helsinki.fi

Kumaripaba Athukorala
Helsinki Institute for Information Technology HIIT
Dep. of Computer Science
University of Helsinki
kumaripaba.athukorala@hiit.fi

Samuel Kaski
Helsinki Institute for Information Technology HIIT
Aalto University
samuel.kaski@aalto.fi

Giulio Jacucci
Helsinki Institute for Information Technology HIIT
Dep. of Computer Science
University of Helsinki
giulio.jacucci@helsinki.fi

ABSTRACT
Techniques for both exploratory and known item search tend to direct only to more specific subtopics or individual documents, as opposed to allowing directing the exploration of the information space. We present an interactive information retrieval system that combines Reinforcement Learning techniques along with a novel user interface design to allow active engagement of users in directing the search. Users can directly manipulate document features (keywords) to indicate their interests and Reinforcement Learning is used to model the user by allowing the system to trade off between exploration and exploitation. This gives users the opportunity to more effectively direct their search nearer, further and following a direction. A task-based user study conducted with 20 participants comparing our system to a traditional query-based baseline indicates that our system significantly improves the effectiveness of information retrieval by providing access to more relevant and novel information without having to spend more time acquiring the information.

Author Keywords
Adaptive Interfaces; Data Mining; Machine Learning; Recommender Systems; Information Filtering

ACM Classification Keywords
H.5.2. User Interfaces: User-centered design

General Terms
Information Retrieval

INTRODUCTION
In a typical interaction with an information retrieval system, the user expresses a specific information need, entered as a query, investigates the results returned by the search engine, and alters the query to direct the search to a chosen direction: a more specific subtopic or an alternative direction. As a result, users frequently have to carefully investigate the results to be able to reformulate their query. This behavior may have a confounding effect: result lists may be long and tedious to investigate, and relevant information may be widely scattered, and therefore hard for the user to extract [28].

Disadvantages of Query–Based Search Techniques
Searching for electronic information can be a multistage process. The information need evolves throughout the course of the search and even when the searched item is known, instead of jumping directly to the target, users typically navigate with small, local steps using their contextual knowledge as a guide. A recent survey found that users use long highly specific queries in less than a half of their searches, despite almost always knowing their information need upfront [26]. This allows users to specify less of their information need at once and provide a context in which to understand the intermediate results, but also lessens the users' cognitive burden by saving them from having to articulate exactly what they are looking for and allowing them to rely on established habits to get within the vicinity of their information need. Even in cases where users know what they are searching, it has been suggested that users try to avoid the cognitive overhead imposed by the difficulty of expressing their information needs exactly, by using simple and short queries and learning how to alter the query to achieve their goal. The effect of this finding becomes even more prominent in the case of exploratory information seeking, where users' needs are uncertain and underspecified in the first place, and to reduce the uncertainty users direct their search by exploring the information space step-by-step [25].

Relevance Feedback and IR Systems

While development usually aims at an optimal search engine that is able to return the best matching information based on a well-defined information need, the exploratory nature of the human information retrieval behavior has been addressed, e.g. by providing interactivity and control to users for better orientation and engagement [18, 26]. The first approach developed by the information retrieval community was the relevance feedback mechanism: users mark documents as relevant or non-relevant and the query model is updated based on the features present in the documents. Empirical studies have shown that experimental interactive IR systems benefit from term relevance feedback features [14]. However, evidence from user studies indicates that relevance feedback features are not used, or if they are, they are unlikely to result in retrieval improvements. Two main reasons for this were found [14]: (1) the relevance feedback often leads to a context trap, i.e. after a few iterations of feedback users have specified their context so strictly that the system is not able to propose anything new and users are trapped within the present set of results; (2) the cognitive load caused by the requirement to select relevant and non-relevant documents is high compared to typing in a new query and prevents users from actively engaging with the relevance feedback mechanisms.

Interface Design and User Feedback

The reason for the lack of use of relevance feedback has often been attributed to the specific intelligent user interface designs that do not allow users to conveniently provide feedback at a suitable level of granularity. Research has targeted to support users in giving feedback through a variety of techniques involving computational methods, to predict user needs based on the query history [1], rich user interface support with learning algorithms to assist users to comprehend the results and the existing information space [5, 8], and visualizing and summarizing the resulting information to enable faster relevance judgement of the quality of the information returned by the search engine [10, 13, 15, 19, 27].

Faceted Search and Search Context

The problem of getting trapped by context has been approached by using global features instead of contextual features or exploration techniques. One of the most successful ways to use global document set features in directing search is faceted search, also called faceted navigation or faceted browsing [30]. It is a technique for accessing information organized according to a faceted classification system, allowing users to explore a collection of information by applying multiple filters. A faceted classification system classifies each information element along multiple explicit global dimensions, enabling the classifications to be accessed and ordered in multiple ways rather than being based on contextually selected options. The problem with this approach is that the number of global features can be very large and users may have to be forced to select from a huge amount of options, making the user interface inconvenient and cognitively demanding [30].

Reinforcement Learning and Information Retrieval

Recent studies have shown that by modeling the search context, a system can provide much richer information about the search intention, limit the number of alternatives users need to select from to direct their search, and automate the tedious query reformulation process [29]. Reinforcement learning is a promising approach that can allow the system to utilize the search context in relevance feedback and, at the same time, to avoid the context trap. Reinforcement learning allows the system to trade between exploitation (moving towards more specific subtopics) and exploration (going towards alternative topics), and has been shown to be helpful in information retrieval [12, 23, 33]. Most of the existing work concentrates on using reinforcement learning for search personalization [23, 33]. Long-term implicit data acquisition is used to build user models that are then used as the basis for filtering content. In [22] a setting was introduced where the system learns the user preferences in an online manner without a labeled dataset, while taking into account similarities between documents and feedback from the users. Exploration–exploitation techniques are often used in tasks involving information retrieval or recommender systems, such as filtering [4], recommendation [12, 31, 34], ads placement [7, 17, 20] or image retrieval [3]. However, most of the information retrieval/recommender systems that employ reinforcement learning techniques rely on collecting information on users' habits and interests over a prolonged period of time, while in a typical search scenario users are more interested in the overall improvement of the search results within a given search session rather than hypothetical future search sessions.

Problem Solution

We propose that better support for exploration can be provided through learning from feedback on higher level representations of the data sets, such as topics or keywords, that are extracted from document features. This feedback provides enables applying machine learning techniques such as reinforcement learning to improve relevance, novelty and diversity of results. This allows users to direct their search using the offered keyword cues at any point of time without getting trapped in a context, or having to provide tedious document–level relevance feedback, or relying on implicit feedback mechanisms that may take long to converge. Users are experiencing diverse ways to interact with information, e.g. in smartphones and tablets, where multitouch revives the concept of direct manipulation as users expect visual representation of the option space, and rapid and incremental actions (and not only typing) [11]. Time is ripe fo the learning mechanism to predict the keywords based on the search session context and allow users to direct the search rather than merely re-ranking as in traditional personalization.

The resulting information access system couples advanced machine learning techniques with information visualization and interaction to boost exploratory search. The users can actively engage in an exploratory search loop where they manipulate article features such as keywords and ranking, and the underlying machine learning system offers them navigation options (keywords, articles) using an exploration–exploitation paradigm. We expect the search to become signicantly faster by allowing exploration and easier query manipulation. We have found a suitable abstract level on which it is convenient for the users to direct their search (in our case, the document keywords are the navigation options users can use to direct their search), and use observed interaction together with binary feedback to feed reinforcement learning–based optimization of further navigation options. We maintain that interactive choice of navigation options, such as topics and keywords, can facilitate exploration. We propose that this can support users in better directing the exploratory search nearer or further from the current context and following a direction.

System Assessment
We present results from a series of studies that demonstrate the benefits brought by the system. Computer simulations are first used to verify that it is beneficial to apply the reinforcement learning to user feedback on both the document features and the documents. A pre-experiment study is then carried out, aimed at evaluating the subjective experience and usability of the system. Finally, a task–based experiment with 20 subjects compares our system to a traditional query-based baseline. The performance is evaluated on three redefined measures based on the well known precision, recall and F-measures. They are redefined for the case of iterative queries, separately taking into account not only relevance but also obviousness and novelty. We also report the extent to which the suggested keywords are manipulated by users, as an indication of how much the system is used in directing the search.

SYSTEM OVERVIEW

The primary goal of the system is to assist scientists in finding and exploring the relevant literature on a given research topic quickly and effectively; although it can additionally be easily adapted to other domains. Reinforcement learning (RL) methods as well as visualization allow the user to assign relevance scores to the displayed keywords by moving them within the exploratory view provided by the system (keyword manipulation). Through keyword manipulation, the user can direct the search according to her interest, while the inbuilt RL mechanism helps the system to form a model of user's interests and suggest appropriate keywords in the next search iteration. The user modeling process is restarted once the user types in a new query and we build a new user model for each session to avoid the issue of "over-personalization". In this section, we describe the system design, its interface and the algorithms incorporated into the system.

Interface Design

The main idea behind the interactive interface is that instead of typing queries at each iteration, the user navigates through the contents by manipulating the keywords on the display, which results in new keywords appearing on the screen as well as a new set of documents being presented to the user. The user interface is presented in Figure 2 and an example search session in Figure 1.

The search starts with the user typing in a query, which results in a set of keywords being displayed in the circle on the left hand-side of the screen (exploratory view) and a set of articles being displayed on the right hand-side of the screen (Figure 2). The user can manipulate the keywords in the exploratory view to indicate their relevance: the closer to the center a given keyword is, the more relevant it is. The user can manipulate as many keywords as she likes in the exploratory view as well as drag keywords from underneath the displayed articles into the exploratory view to indicate their relevance to the search. After each iteration, new keywords and new articles are displayed. The search continues until the user is satisfied with the results.

We illustrate the interface and interaction design through a walkthrough that exemplifies a real information seeking task. In our example, a student writing an essay about "hand gestures" begins the seeking process by typing "hand gestures" as the query. The system retrieves a set of documents and adapts the content to match the user's feedback (Figure 1). On the first iteration, the documents and keywords are retrieved based on pseudo-feedback acquired from the top-ranked documents and visualized for the user. At this point, the students interest in "hand gesture recognition" increases (Iteration 1 in Figure 1) and she realizes that the keywords "language" and "communication" are not related to her information need. She provides feedback to the system by moving them outside of the exploratory view and by moving the keyword "recognition" to the center. The user then submits the feedback by clicking the center of the exploratory view. The system learns a more specific representation of the users information needs from the feedback, expresses it in terms of keywords, and retrieves and predicts a new set of documents and keywords (Iteration 2 in Figure 1). At the end of Iteration 2, the user decides to look at documents about "hidden Markov model". The document list now consists of documents related to "hand gesture recognition with hidden Markov models", but because of the novelty and diversity featured in the adaptation methods, the system also gives alternative keywords for the user to select. By moving them towards the center, the student could continue the seeking process.

System Design

The data flow from the system's perspective is illustrated in Figure 3. The three main blocks of the system are responsible for the initial retrieval and ranking of documents, and exploration in the keyword and the document spaces using RL.

The initial set of documents and their rankings are obtained through the Information Retrieval and Ranking module. Having received feedback on keywords, the system enters the exploratory loop. The explicit user feedback is sent to the Keywords Exploration and the Document Diversification modules. The Keywords Exploration module implements user model estimation using RL techniques (described below). The user model is a representation of the system's belief about the user's informational need at the current iteration of retrieval. The component receives feedback from the user and produces a list of keywords with weights which are passed on to the Information Retrieval and Ranking module, which predicts a new set of documents for the new search iteration based on the predicted user model. Thus, the dataset in the system is not static and it changes at every iteration based on the present, best estimation of the user model.

The Document Diversification module is responsible for determining the set and order of documents that are passed on to the Interface. The module uses exploration–exploitation

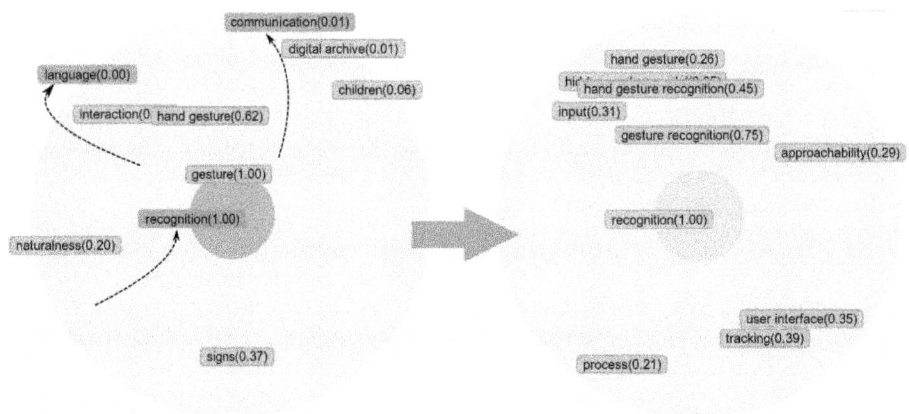

Figure 1. Feature manipulations. After receiving the initial set of keywords in the first iteration (left), the user indicates an increased importance of the keyword "recognition" by moving it towards the center of the exploratory view and indicates a reduced importance of the keywords "language" and "communication" by moving them outside the exploratory view. The keywords explicitly manipulated by the user are colored in orange. In the second iteration (right), new keywords have been predicted by the system on the basis of their estimated relevance and are positioned in the exploratory view. The new keywords can be distinguished by their orange borders.

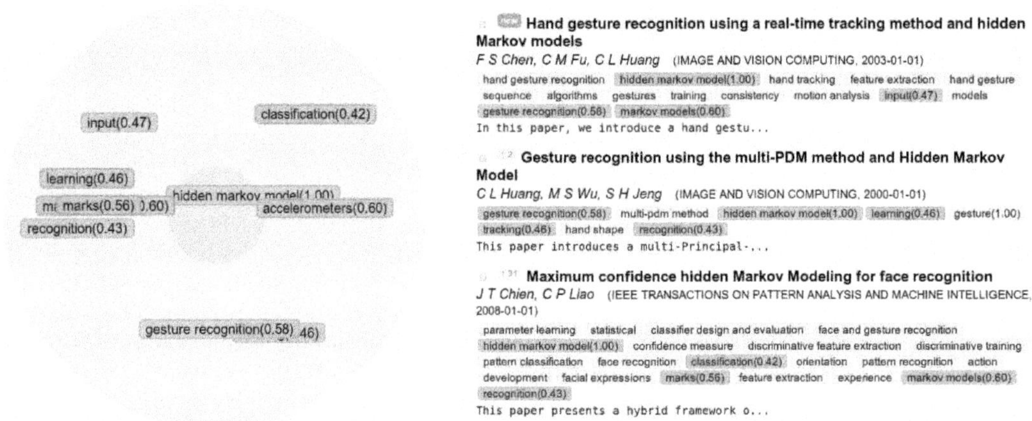

Figure 2. The document list after Iteration 2 has both new documents (labeled new) and documents whose rank increased from the previous round. The user has now obtained documents matching the information need. The exploratory view (left) also offers options for continuing the exploration in other potentially relevant directions, such as "accelerometers", "learning" or "classification".

techniques to sample a set of documents to display to the user, while keeping the ranking obtained from the Information Retrieval and Ranking module. The new set of documents is used in Keywords Exploration module to capture dependencies between keywords.

The user model is visualized in the exploratory view, which allows the user to give feedback to the system through keyword manipulation. A list of articles is also presented to the user. The system gets new feedback from the user and continues in the iterative feedback loop.

Retrieving and Ranking Documents

The system includes a separate retrieval model whose input is the user model and which produces a ranking for the documents and keywords attached to each of the ranked documents. The keywords are used to build a new estimate of the user model and the documents are shown for the user in the ranked order after diversification. The retrieval model allows a fast ranking of the top-n documents. This is motivated by a learning-to-rank approach where only the top-ranked documents and document features are used as the context for more

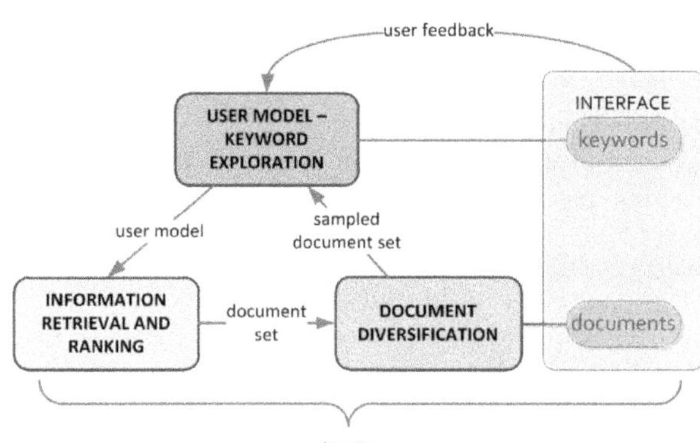

Figure 3. Overview of data flow in the exploratory search system

complex learning processes. In this way, we can reduce the number of documents and features that the RL methods have to deal with.

In order to estimate the relevance of each document d_j, we employ a standard language modeling approach of information retrieval. We estimate the initial ranking of documents d given a user model represented as the weighted keyword vector k consisting a weight $\hat{w}_i$ for each keyword. The ranking is computed according to the probability of documents given the user model. We use a probabilistic multinomial unigram language model. Documents are ranked by the probability that a query would be observed as a random sample from the respective document model. The probability of a document producing the user model is given by the language model M_{d_j} for document d_j by using maximum likelihood estimation (MLE):

$$\hat{P}(k|M_{d_j}) = \prod_{k_i \in k}^{i} \hat{w}_i \hat{P}_{mle}(k_i|M_{d_j}),$$

where M_{d_j} is the language model of document d_j and $\hat{w}_i$ is the estimation for the weight of a keyword k_i given by the present user model. Now the maximum likelihood of a keyword k_i is:

$$\hat{P}_{mle}(k_i|M_{d_j}) = \prod_{k_i \in k}^{i} P_\mu(k_i|d_j).$$

We avoid zero probabilities and improve the estimation by using the Bayesian Dirichlet smoothing [32]. The smoothed model is given by:

$$P_\mu(k|d_j) = \frac{c(k;d_j) + \mu p(k|C)}{\sum_k c(k;d_j) + \mu},$$

where the probability of a document generating a keyword is smoothed using the collection statistics $p(k|C)$, which is the estimate for a keyword k based on the whole collection C as opposite to only a relative count $c(k;d_j)$ in a single document d_j. The parameter μ is set to 2000 as suggested in the literature [32].

To keep the maximum likelihood estimation for the whole set of keywords occurring in the user model fast, we restrict the i being evaluated to the top ten keywords receiving the most of the weight mass at each iteration. The same set of keywords is also visualized for the user in the exploratory view.

User Model Estimation

We assume that the user is looking for a set of keywords related to her interest. The user feedback is given by a relevance score $r \in [0,1]$, where 1 indicates that the keyword is of high relevance. The user provides feedback by moving a keyword closer to or further from the center of the exploratory view: keywords in the center have relevance score 1 with the value getting smaller the further away from the center a keyword is moved (see Figure 1). Keywords placed on the edge of the exploratory view or beyond have relevance score 0. Keywords with relevance score 0 are excluded from appearing again in the exploratory view for the remainder of a given search session. The formal iteration protocol of is as follows:

- In each iteration, the system selects j keywords and presents them to the user.
- The user provides relevance scores $r_i \in [0,1], i = 1,\dots,j$ for the displayed keywords.

We assume that the relevance score r_i of a keyword k_i is a random variable with expected value $\mathbb{E}[r_i] = k_i \cdot w$, such that the expected relevance score is a linear function of the keywords. The unknown weight vector w is essentially the representation of the user's query and determines the relevance of keywords, i.e. the weight vector is the user model that describes user's interests and predicted directions based on the search history in the present session.

In order to preserve the dependency between the keywords and the documents, initially we represent each keyword k as a binary vector of length n, where n is the number of documents under consideration. The vector indicates the presence or absence of a keyword in a given document. In order to boost the significance of documents with rare keywords and to lower the significance of those with frequent keywords, we convert the binary vector representation of keywords into the *tf-idf* representation [24].

In order to help the user to explore the keyword space, we use LinRel [2], an algorithm that has already been proven to work well in other interactive retrieval systems [3]. At each iteration, LinRel suggests new keywords to be presented based on the feedback from the user obtained in previous iterations. The algorithm maintains a representation of the estimate $\hat{w}$ of the unknown weight vector w which maps keyword features to relevance scores. When selecting the next set of keywords to display, the system might simply select the keywords with the highest estimated relevance score. But since the estimate $\hat{w}$ may be inaccurate, this exploitative choice might be suboptimal. Alternatively, the system might exploratively select a keyword for which the user feedback improves the accuracy of the estimate $\hat{w}$, enabling better keyword selections in subsequent iterations.

In each iteration, LinRel obtains an estimate $\hat{w}$ by solving a linear regression problem. Suppose we have a matrix K, where each row k_i is a feature vector of keywords presented so far. Let $r = (r_1, r_2 \dots r_p)^\top$ be the column vector of relevance scores received so far from the user, where p is a number of iterations. Thus, LinRel tries to estimate $\hat{w}$ by solving the linear regression problem $r = K \cdot w$. Based on $\hat{w}$, LinRel calculates an estimated relevance score $\hat{r}_i = k_i \cdot \hat{w}$ for each keyword k_i. In order to deal with the exploration-exploitation trade-off, we present keywords not with the highest score, but with the largest upper confidence bound for the relevance score. Thus, if σ_i is an upper bound on standard deviation of relevance estimate $\hat{r}_i$, the upper confidence bound of keyword i is calculated as $r_i + \gamma\sigma_i$, where $\gamma > 0$ is a constant used to adjust the confidence level of the upper confidence bound. In each iteration, LinRel calculates:

$$s_i = x_i \cdot (X^\top \cdot X + \lambda I)^{-1} X^\top.$$

and the keywords that maximize $s_i \cdot r + \frac{\alpha}{2}||m_i||$ are selected for presentation.

Document Set Diversification

After each iteration, the search engine returns a list of ranked documents to display. In order to diversify the set of the displayed documents and expose the user to more novel documents, we sample l of documents from the ranked list provided by the search engine and display them to the user. In order to obtain this, we use the *Dirichlet Sampling Algorithm* [9]. The algorithm maintains weights α_i for all the documents in the set returned by the search engine, and we sample l documents from this list by sampling the Dirichlet distribution. A fast method to sample a random vector f from a n-dimensional Dirichlet distribution with parameters $\alpha = \{\alpha_1, \ldots, \alpha_n\}$ is to draw n independent random samples from the Gamma distribution

$$f \sim Gamma(\alpha, 1) = \frac{f^{\alpha-1}e^{-f_i}}{\Gamma(\alpha)}$$

and normalise the resulting vector f. In our case, the input is a vector α representing the weights or probabilities of each document, while the vector f represents a random number associated with each document. We display to the user the top l documents with the highest values of f_i. Thus, the higher the value of α, the more likely it is that the corresponding document will be selected.

After each search iteration, we updated the weights α of the entire document set. However, the users do not provide explicit feedback on all the documents, so we need to update the document weights based on the keywords selected by the users. Thus, the documents are partitioned into two sets. One set consists of documents containing in their feature representation a keyword that received positive feedback from the user, while the other set contains all the remaining documents. The documents that received implicitly positive feedback have their weights α_i increased by 1. After the weight updates, the vector α is normalized so that in future iterations we have a better estimation as to which documents might be more relevant to the user's interests.

EVALUATION METHODS

We conducted a set of studies to evaluate our system. We first performed a simulation study to automatically evaluate the role of exploration in different parts of the system. Based on the results of this study we chose the final setup of the system that was evaluated in a comparative user study. The comparative study included two conditions: our system that is from now onwards referred as RLR (Reinforcement Learning Retrieval) system, and a baseline system. Before the user study, we conducted a pre-experiment study to ensure the usability of the RLR system. Then, we ran the actual user study in order to evaluate the retrieval performance of the RLR system compared to the baseline system.

Data

We used a dataset including over 50 million scientific documents from the following data sources: the Web of Science prepared by THOMSON REUTERS, Inc., the Digital Library of the Association of Computing Machinery (ACM), the Digital Library of Institute of Electrical and Electronics Engineers (IEEE), and the Digital Library of Springer. The information about each document consists of: title, abstract, author names, publication year and publication forum. Both the baseline and RLR systems used the same document set.

Simulations

The RL techniques are incorporated into two modules of the RLR system: the Keyword Exploration module and the Document Diversification module. Thus, there were three possible configurations of the system: (1) RL in both the keywords and the articles space; (2) RL only in the keyword space; (3) RL only in article space. The fourth possibility, i.e. RL in neither of the components is equivalent to using traditional query-based informational retrieval systems and we tested this setting in the user studies. However, running user studies involving all four settings would have required a very large number of participants with similar research backgrounds, and so in order to assess the effectiveness of the RL methods, we first ran a set of simulations to define the system configurations to be used in the user studies. The purpose of the simulations was to identify which of the three settings would provide the user with the most diverse search results.

First, in a modelled situation of algorithm usage we estimated the optimal values of parameters of the algorithms. Next, we collected 10 examples of user's actions, i.e. keyword manipulations over ten iterations, while performing different searches. Each of the three system settings was run ten times using the collected user actions, i.e. for each setting we collected ten hypothetical searches with ten iterations each. We calculated the fraction of new articles appearing at each iteration in the studied systems. The setting with exploration in both keywords and documents gave us at least 20% more articles on average than other settings and this is the setting we applied in the users studies.

Pre-Experiment Study

The target of the Pre-Experiment study was to measure the general usability of the RLR system and the subjective usability of the search directing support of the RLR system. We used a task-based information retrieval evaluation method [16]: The participants performed search tasks with the system. In each task, the participant was asked to imagine that she is writing an essay on a given topic, and her task was to search and collect documents that she finds useful for the topic specified in the task description. Two tasks were defined and their topics were "semantic search" and "reinforcement learning". In order to preserve the exploratory nature of the task, we only recruited participants who have little knowledge in the topics of the tasks. We recruited ten participants who each performed one of the tasks using the RLR system. Once the participants completed the tasks, they filled two questionnaires to provide their subjective usability assessment on the system. As usability assessment questionnaires we used the standard System Usability Scale (SUS) [6] and a questionnaire based on user-centric evaluation framework named ResQue designed for the evaluation of recommender systems [21]. We used SUS because it is the most used, technology

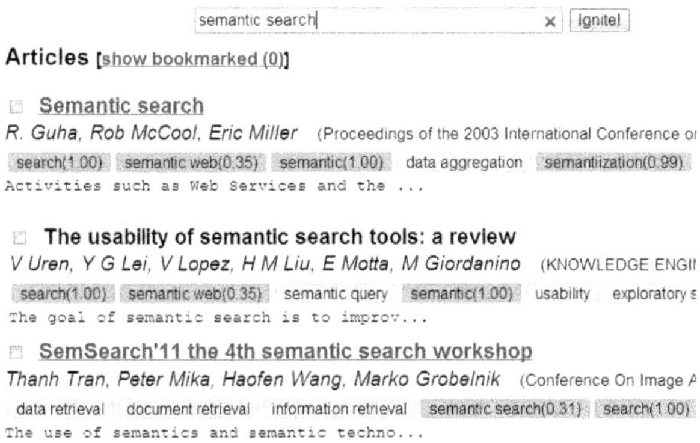

Figure 4. Screen shot of baseline system

independent questionnaire for measuring perceptions of usability. ResQue was chosen because it specifically measures the interaction adequacy and preference expression capabilities offered by a system. Participants used a five-point Likert scale to provide their answers for the ResQue questionnaire. In addition to the questionnaires we also conducted post task interviews with these participants to assess their subjective feedback on the characteristic features of the RLR system.

Baseline System

We used as the baseline a traditional query–based alternative, where neither user modeling, exploratory view nor diversification was used. The document retrieval algorithm was the same in both systems. In the baseline, users can express their information need only through typing queries and the results are presented as a list of documents followed by keywords in each document. Unlike in the RLR system, in the baseline system users cannot interact with the keywords visualized underneath each document to provide feedback; these keywords can only be used as clues for formulating queries. Figure 4 shows a screen shot of the baseline search user interface.

User Experiment

We conducted user experiments to compare the baseline and the RLR system. The aim of the experiments was (1) to evaluate the ability of the RLR system to support users in directing their search in an exploratory search setting, and (2) to measure the retrieval performance of the compared systems. We used a task-based information retrieval evaluation, where participants were situated in a scientific writing scenario. The participants were asked to imagine that they are writing an essay on a given topic and to answer a set of questions related to the topic. The participants used a given system to seek the information. The study used a between–subjects design in which half of the participants performed the task using RLR and the other half using the baseline system. We also counterbalanced between the tasks.

Tasks

We recruited two post-doctoral researchers as experts from the domains of information retrieval and machine learning to define the tasks. The task fields chosen by the experts were "semantic search" and "robotics". The experts wrote task descriptions using the following template: "imagine that you are writing a scientific essay on the topic of semantic search/robotics. Search scientific documents that you find useful for this essay". In order to provide clear goals for exploration, the experts provided the following guidelines on what content should be included in the essays:

- Robotics - This essay should include sub-fields, application areas and algorithms commonly used in the field of "robotics".
- Semantic search - This essay should include techniques used to acquire semantics, methods used in practical implementation and organization of results in semantic search.

Participants and Procedure

We recruited 20 researchers from our university to participate in this study. All the participants were either research staff or students (11 PhD researchers and 9 Masters students), and all had backgrounds in computer science or related fields. We particularly selected researchers as participants because our current database only consists of scientific documents. Therefore we needed participants who have experience in scientific document search. Prior to the experiment, we conducted a background survey of the participants to ensure that they have conducted literature search before and they are not expert researchers in the topics of the search tasks so that their prior knowledge will not influence the exploratory nature of the tasks. Prior to the study we provided training for each participant with the system that they are going to use in the experiment. We limited the time available to complete the task to 30 minutes to make sure that the participants were actively searching for the information during the experiment and had equal time to complete the task.

Data Logging

When the participants were performing tasks, we logged all their interactions with the system and all the articles and keywords presented by the systems in response to these interactions. Data logged from the interactions with the RLR system included details of the articles displayed, keywords predicted by the system, manipulated keywords, queries typed by the participants and times at which each interaction occurred. Similarly, from the baseline system we logged the queries typed, articles displayed, articles bookmarked by the participants and the times at which participants entered queries.

Ground Truth and Relevance Assessments

We pooled all the documents displayed to the participants in either condition, i.e. based on the logs we extracted all documents that were found by any user using either the baseline or the RLR system. Next, we asked the domain experts who defined the tasks to provide relevance assessments on these documents. In order to avoid any biasing of the expert assessments, the assessment process was double-blinded, meaning that the experts did not know from which of the two conditions the document originated nor for which of the participants the document was viewed. The experts provided relevance assessments on three levels: (1) relevance - whether this article was relevant to the search topic; (2) obviousness - whether this article is well known in a given research area; and (3) novelty - whether a given article was uncommon, yet showing a new aspect of the topic. Experts reviewed every article under each category and rated them as 1 if they belong to the category and 0 otherwise. This provided the ground truth that was used to evaluate the retrieval performance of the systems. To measure the quality of the relevance assessments, part of the assessments were conducted by two experts. We run the Cohen Kappa test to measure the inter-annotator agreement between the experts. Kappa indicated a substantial agreement (Kappa = 0.71, $p < 0.001$).

Retrieval Performance Measures

We defined three measures based on precision, recall and F measures of information retrieval to measure the performance of the two systems. We could not use these measures directly because in our setting users are shown a limited set of documents, i.e. top 50, on each iteration instead of the total ordering and the users perform several, but varying number of queries and interactions over time during a search session. The measures capture the performance of the system as a function of time when used to seek answers for the task. For example, if a user finds relevant documents on the first iteration, just ten seconds after starting to use the system, but the system does not assist the user to direct the search, then the performance may not be much better when investigated after 120 seconds of use. On the other hand, if the system assists the user to gain more relevant documents, the recall after 120 seconds may have been increased because the user could easily interact with the system to gain more relevant results.

We generalized the precision, recall and F measures to take into account the temporal dimension, where users cumulatively gain new information while searching. We start with a definition of cumulative document sets:

$$\cup_t = \bigcup_0^t documents,$$

which represents the cumulative set of documents being presented for the user, i.e. the union of documents from the start time 0 until time t. The rationale is that if the same documents are presented for the user in different moments of time, they are only added once in the $\cup_t$. We define temporal precision as:

$$P_t = \frac{\cup_t(relevant)}{\cup_t(retrieved)}.$$

It measures the proportion of relevant documents cumulatively shown to the user, compared to all documents cumulatively shown to the user until time point t. Similarly, the the temporal recall is defined as:

$$R_t = \frac{\cup_t(relevant)}{all\ relevant},$$

which measures the proportion of relevant documents cumulatively shown for the user compared to all relevant documents in the system.

The temporal recall is expected to grow over time as users are interacting with the system and viewing more documents, and the temporal precision is expected to stay the same or increase when users direct their search to more specific or more general, yet relevant documents. The best way to evaluate a system is to combine these measures to investigate how well the system is able to balance between precision and recall. The temporal F-measure is defined as:

$$F_t = \frac{2P_tR_t}{P_t + R_t},$$

which is the harmonic mean of R_t and P_t up to the time point t. These measures allow us to investigate how the precision–recall tradeoff develops over time and compare systems in task settings where users may use different queries at different points of time to find broad sets of articles. For example, by setting $t = 60$ seconds, we could investigate how many relevant articles a user was able to collect during the first minute of use by measuring R_t and what proportion of the collected articles were relevant by measuring P_t.

Aspect	Question	Mean (m) and Standard deviation(std)
Preference Elicitation	Provides adequate way to express preferences	m=3.93 std=0.583
Preference Revision	Provides adequate support to revise preferences	m=3.70 std=0.952
Interface Adequacy	layout of the system is clear	m=4.48 std=0.750
Interaction Adequacy	Offered me useful interaction options to express my information need	m=3.73 std=0.828
Ease of Decision making	I quickly became productive by using the system	m=3.60 std=0.894

Table 1. Summary of Results from the questionnaire based on ResQue framework

EXPERIMENTAL RESULTS

In order to measure the usability of the RLR system, we evaluated the feedback provided by the participants of the Pre-Experiment study. The RLR system received an average score of 79.5 out of 100 (standard deviation = 15.36) in the SUS questionnaire which shows that RLR is favored by the participants. Another questionnaire, based on the ResQue framework, consisted of questions addressing five different aspects of recommender systems. Table 1 presents a summary of the results, which show that the interface of the RLR system provides adequate support for the users to express and revise their preferences. Users also perceived the layout and the new interaction options of the RLR system to be clear. Finally, the users also indicated that with this system they performed more productively than before.

The post-task interviews with the participants also provided favorable results for the RLR system. The feature that received positive feedback from the majority of subjects was interactive keyword visualization, both in the exploratory view and underneath each article. Some comments from the participants were: "suggesting keywords make the system very easy to use and identify related keywords that I didn't know", "visual search is awesome, seeing the centrality of the keywords for the search from the circle", "I like the option of seeing keywords and both (de-)selecting and weighting them", "the rich keyword selection option provides new cues, even for the well known topics", "keyword visualization is very intuitive". Some of the participants commented that even though they like to see new keywords appearing after each interaction they prefer to have a back button to return back to the previously displayed keywords because sometimes keywords change too fast: "I would like to have a back button to go to previous results, so that I can try with new keywords and need not to worry about missing previous research results", "keyword view is changing too fast". Some of the participants liked the idea of performing fewer query alterations and providing more visual feedback using the mouse: "The fact that I could use the system only by using the mouse made it easy. So there was no need to constantly re-type the query". However, some of the participants found it difficult to judge documents without the citation count: "I am more used to judge articles based on citation data".

User Experiments Results

Table 2 shows the general system performance results from the user studies. In all the assessed categories, i.e. relevance, novelty and obviousness, the RLR system outperforms the baseline in terms of temporal F-measure, i.e. the measure of the quality of documents obtained throughout a search session. Temporal recall in the RLR system outperforms the baseline for all categories, while temporal precision in the RLR setting is greater only for novelty and non-obviousness. For temporal precision, the difference between the RLR system and the baseline was only 3% (69% against 72%). The RLR system beats the baseline in temporal F-measure due to the fact that it provides much better temporal recall while not sacrificing temporal precision.

The last row in Table 2 shows the numbers of relevant, novel, and obvious documents, as judged by the experts. These counts are derived from all the articles retrieved during all search sessions. Despite each experiments lasting the same amount of time, the RLR system provided the users with access to a much larger set of documents as users performed significantly more actions compared with the baseline system. With respect to *obviousness*, the number of articles displayed by both systems is not significantly different. Thus, the study indicates that both systems provide users with access to the most common, i.e. obvious, documents in a given research field, however, the RLR system exposes users to a higher number of relevant and novel articles that could not be easily found with a simple query-based search.

	Relevance		Novelty		Obviousness	
System	RLR	BL	RLR	BL	RLR	BL
F-measure	0.25	0.15	0.18	0.09	0.22	0.20
Precision	0.69	0.72	0.40	0.33	0.26	0.34
Recall	0.15	0.09	0.12	0.05	0.20	0.17
♯ of Articles	882	522	570	228	253	223

Table 2. Comparison of the performance of the RLR system and the baseline system (BL).

Search Performance

Figure 5 presents all the measures with respect to *relevance*. Figure 5a shows how temporal precision measure evolves as the search progresses. The RLR system is mildly outperformed by the baseline with the gap between systems shrinking over time. At the same time, the RLR system's temporal recall increases much faster than the baseline after 200 seconds and at the end of the search session reaches a much higher value (Figure 5b). The temporal F-measure shows how good the system is in balancing between these measures by taking their harmonic mean. The RLR's impressive temporal recall and similar performance with respect to temporal precision explains why the system outperforms the baseline in temporal F-measure after 200 seconds. We would like to stress the fact that within the first 200 seconds, the users on average preformed only one search iteration using the RLR system and spent a lot of time looking at the presented documents and keywords. Thus, the users do not need to wait for over 3 minutes for the RL techniques to take effect since the user model is instantiated right after the first search iteration.

An interesting finding is that in the first few minutes, the baseline performs slightly better than the RLR system. The same effect can be seen in Figures 6a and 6b with temporal F-measure with respect to *novelty* and *obviousness*. The baseline initially outperforming the RLR system with respect to *obviousness* is illustrated in Figure 6b. As the search begins, the baseline outperforms the RLR system, however, after a few minutes the average temporal F-measure of the baseline drops below that of the RLR system. A possible explanation is that at the beginning of the search, the users working with the baseline can easily create queries resulting in a large number of frequent or obvious documents. As the search progresses and the users need to think of more specific queries, temporal recall of relevant or obvious documents drops. However, when reinforcement learning is employed to build a user model, the user is able to direct the search more efficiently while at the same time preserving the search context. This helps users to preserve the precision of documents, but at the same time gain relevant documents faster than the baseline. We attribute this to the combination of user modeling and document diversification that allows users to better interact with the system and obtain a wider set of documents.

User Interaction

Users of the RLR system performed significantly more iterations (on average 14.7) than users of the baseline (on average 8) within the same time restrictions, which indicates that the RLR system allows the user to direct the search more easily through the displayed keywords, resulting in a high rate of interactions as the search progresses. As Figure 6c shows, at each iteration the system recommends new keywords to the user, which the user manipulates. The graph indicates that the keywords displayed and manipulated over time in the RLR system indeed support the users in directing their search and the users do take advantage of this opportunity.

SUMMARY AND CONCLUSIONS

To support users in directing the exploration of the information space during search, we developed an interactive infor-

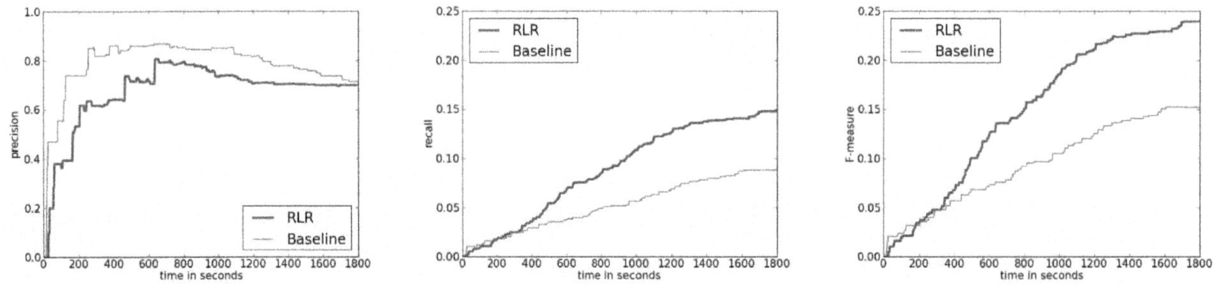

Figure 5. Average measures of relevance: temporal precision, recall and F-measure of the baseline and the RLR systems over a search session. The RLR system sacrifices little precision to get significantly higher recall, and outperforms the baseline in temporal F-measure after 200 seconds.

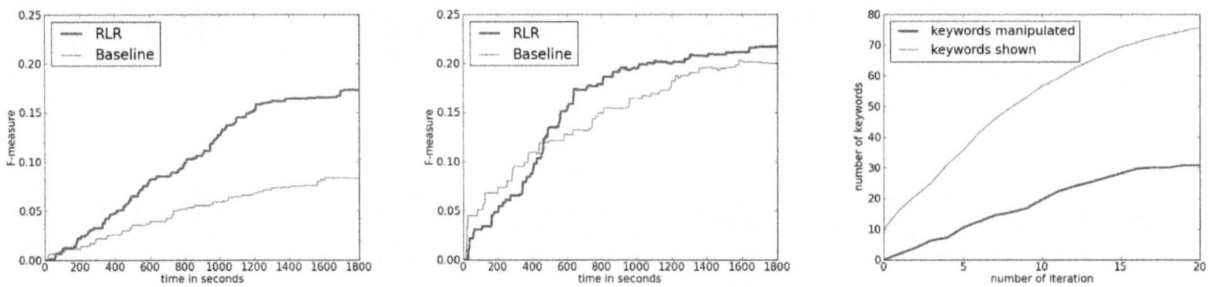

Figure 6. Average F-measure of the RLR system and the baseline system over the search session with respect to (a) novelty and (b) obviousness; (c) average cumulative number of keywords displayed and manipulated with the RLR system over the search session.

mation retrieval system that applies RL to user feedback on keywords. Besides writing queries, users can explore the information space by manipulating keywords on a display scoring them for interest. Such interactions result in predictions of new keywords and documents matching the user interest at the current iteration of retrieval. To achieve this, we developed three components: (1) Information Retrieval and Ranking, (2) Keywords Exploration, and (3) Document Diversification. The Information Retrieval and Ranking component allows fast ranking given the user model where only the top-ranked documents and document features are used as the context for the more advanced learning. The explicit user feedback is sent to Keywords Exploration that produces a list of keywords with weights which are passed on to the Information Retrieval and Ranking module as a user model estimation. The Document Diversification module is responsible for determining the set and order of documents that are passed on to the document list shown to the user. Our interactive information retrieval system is novel in the way that RL is applied not to feedback on documents but on higher-level features such as keywords. We carried out simulations to verify that RL should be applied to both Keywords Exploration and Document Diversification. A pre-experiment study confirmed that the system was functional and that users found it usable for exploration during search. Finally, we designed and carried out a task-based experiment comparing our system with a baseline query based system that did not offer user modeling, exploratory view or diversification. To be able to compare the performance of the two systems, we re-defined precision, recall and F-measures to take into account the fact that users perform several, and varying amount of different queries and interactions over time during a search session.

In all the categories assessed during the study, i.e. relevance, novelty and obviousness, our system outperforms the baseline in terms of the temporal F-measure, that is a measure of the quality of documents obtained through the search session. Analyzing differences in recall and precision in different categories, the results show that the RLR system provides much better temporal recall while not sacrificing the temporal precision, keeping it approximately the same or a bit better. The RLR system exposes users to a higher number of relevant and novel articles that could not be easily found with a simple query-based search system, but still gives access to the common ones. We further analyzed the temporal performance and user interaction finding evidence of how RLR supports users in directing search. When analyzing the performance over time, the F-measure for obviousness is better at the beginning for the baseline system while it becomes better for RLR only when RL is used to build a user model and the user is able to direct the search more efficiently. More importantly, the ability of users to direct search is emerging from the fact that users do score positively keywords recommended by RLR.

ACKNOWLEDGMENTS

The data used in the experiments is derived from the Web of Science prepared by THOMSON REUTERS, Inc.; the Digital Library of the Association of Computing Machinery (ACM); the Digital Library of Institute of Electrical and Electronics Engineers (IEEE), and the Digital Library of Springer. D. Głowacka and S. Kaski acknowledge the support of The Academy of Finland (Finnish Centre of Excellence in Computational Inference Research COIN, 251170).

REFERENCES

1. Alonso, O., Baeza-Yates, R., and Gertz, M. Exploratory search using timelines. In *SIGCHI 2007 Workshop on Exploratory Search and HCI Workshop*, no. 1 (2007).
2. Auer, P. Using confidence bounds for exploitation-exploration trade-offs. *Journal of Machine Learning Research 3* (2002), 397 – 422.
3. Auer, P., Hussain, Z., Kaski, S., A.Klami, J.Kujala, Laaksonen, J., Leung, A., Pasupa, K., and Shawe-Taylor, J. Pinview: Implicit feedback in content-based image retrieval. In *JMLR Workshop and Conference Proceedings: Workshop on Application of Pattern Analysis*, vol. 11 (2010), 51–57.
4. Balabanović, M. Exploring versus exploiting when learning user models for text recommendation. *User Modeling and User-Adapted Interaction 8* (1998), 71–102.
5. Baldonado, M., and Winograd, T. Sensemaker: an information-exploration interface supporting the contextual evolution of a user's interests. In *Proc. of SIGCHI* (1997), 11–18.
6. Brooke, J. Sus-a quick and dirty usability scale. *Usability Evaluation in Industry 189* (1996), 194.
7. Chapelle, O., and Li, L. An empirical evaluation of thompson sampling. In *Proc. of NIPS*, vol. 25 (2011).
8. Chau, D., Kittur, A., Hong, J., and Faloutsos, C. Apolo: making sense of large network data by combining rich user interaction and machine learning. In *Proc. of SIGCHI* (2011), 167–176.
9. Głowacka, D., and Shawe-Taylor, J. Content-based image retrieval with multinomial relevance feedback. In *JMLR Workshop and Conference Proceedings: 2nd Asian Conference on Machine Learning*, vol. 13 (2010), 111–125.
10. Havre, S., Hetzler, E., Perrine, K., Jurrus, E., and Miller, N. Interactive visualization of multiple query results. In *Proceedings of the IEEE Symposium on Information Visualization* (2001), 105.
11. Hutchins, E. L., Hollan, J. D., and Norman, D. A. Direct manipulation interfaces. *Hum.-Comput. Interact. 1*, 4 (Dec. 1985), 311–338.
12. Joachims, T., Freitag, D., and Mitchell, T. Webwatcher: A tour guide for the world wide web. In *Proc. of IJCAI* (1997).
13. Käki, M. Findex: search result categories help users when document ranking fails. In *Proc. of SIGCHI* (2005), 131–140.
14. Kelly, D., and Fu, X. Elicitation of term relevance feedback: an investigation of term source and context. In *Proc. of SIGIR* (2006), 453–460.
15. Kules, B., Wilson, M., Schraefel, M., and Shneiderman, B. From keyword search to exploration: How result visualization aids discovery on the web. *Human-Computer Interaction Lab Technical Report HCIL-2008-06, University of Maryland* (2008).
16. Leide, J., Cole, C., Beheshti, J., Large, A., and Lin, Y. Task-based information retrieval: Structuring undergraduate history essays for better course evaluation using essay-type visualizations. *Journal of the American Society for Information Science and Technology 58*, 9 (2007), 1227–1241.
17. Li, L., Chu, W., Langford, J., and Schapire, R. A contextual-bandit approach to personalized news article recommendation. In *Proc. of WWW* (2010).
18. Marchionini, G. Exploratory search: from finding to understanding. *Commun. ACM 49*, 4 (Apr. 2006), 41–46.
19. Matejka, J., Grossman, T., and Fitzmaurice, G. Citeology: visualizing paper genealogy. In *Proceedings of Human Factors in Computing Systems Extended Abstracts* (2012), 181–190.
20. Pandey, S., Agarwal, D., Chakrabarti, D., and Josifovski, V. Bandits for taxonomies: A modelbased approach. In *Proc. of ICDM* (2007).
21. Pu, P., Chen, L., and Hu, R. A user-centric evaluation framework for recommender systems. In *Proc. of RecSys* (2011), 157–164.
22. Radlinski, F., Kleinberg, R., and Joachims, T. Learning diverse rankings with multi-armed bandits. In *Proc. of ICML* (2008), 784–791.
23. Seo, Y., and Zhang, B. A reinforcement learning agent for personalized information filtering. In *Proc. of IUI* (2000), 248–251.
24. Spärck-Jones, K. A statistical interpretation of term specificity and its application in retrieval. *Journal of Documentation 28*, 1 (1972), 11–21.
25. Spink, A., Wolfram, D., Jansen, M. B. J., and Saracevic, T. Searching the web: The public and their queries. *Journal of the American Society for Information Science and Technology 52* (2001), 226–234.
26. Teevan, J., Alvarado, C., Ackerman, M. S., and Karger, D. R. The perfect search engine is not enough: a study of orienteering behavior in directed search. In *Proc. of SIGCHI* (2004), 415–422.
27. Terveen, L., Hill, W., and Amento, B. Constructing, organizing, and visualizing collections of topically related web resources. *ACM Transactions on Computer-Human Interaction (TOCHI) 6*, 1 (1999), 67–94.
28. Tombros, A., and Sanderson, M. Advantages of query biased summaries in information retrieval. In *Proc. of SIGIR* (1998), 2–10.
29. White, R. W., Bennett, P. N., and Dumais, S. T. Predicting short-term interests using activity-based search context. In *Proc. of CIKM* (2010).
30. Yee, K.-P., Swearingen, K., Li, K., and Hearst, M. Faceted metadata for image search and browsing. In *Proc. of SIGCHI* (2003), 401–408.
31. Yue, Y., and Joachims, T. Interactively optimizing information retrieval systems as a dueling bandits problem. In *Proc. of ICML* (2009).
32. Zhai, C., and Lafferty, J. A study of smoothing methods for language models applied to information retrieval. *ACM Trans. Inf. Syst. 22*, 2 (Apr. 2004), 179–214.
33. Zhang, B., and Seo, Y. Personalized web-document filtering using reinforcement learning. *Applied Artificial Intelligence 15* (2001), 665–685.
34. Zhang, Y., Xu, W., and Callan, J. Exploration and exploitation in adaptive filtering based on bayesian active learning. In *Proc. of ICML* (2003), 896–903.

Locating User Attention using Eye Tracking and EEG for Spatio-Temporal Event Selection

Felix Putze[1], Jutta Hild[3], Rainer Kärgel[1], Christian Herff[1], Alexander Redmann[3], Jürgen Beyerer[2,3], Tanja Schultz[1]

[1]Cognitive Systems Lab
Karlsruhe Institute of Technology
{felix.putze, christian.herff, tanja.schultz}@kit.edu

[2]Vision and Fusion Laboratory
Karlsruhe Institute of Technology

[3]Fraunhofer IOSB
{jutta.hild, alexander.redmann, juergen.beyerer}@iosb.fraunhofer.de

ABSTRACT
In expert video analysis, the selection of certain events in a continuous video stream is a frequently occurring operation, e.g., in surveillance applications. Due to the dynamic and rich visual input, the constantly high attention and the required hand-eye coordination for mouse interaction, this is a very demanding and exhausting task. Hence, relevant events might be missed. We propose to use eye tracking and electroencephalography (EEG) as additional input modalities for event selection. From eye tracking, we derive the spatial location of a perceived event and from patterns in the EEG signal we derive its temporal location within the video stream. This reduces the amount of the required active user input in the selection process, and thus has the potential to reduce the user's workload. In this paper, we describe the employed methods for the localization processes and introduce the developed scenario in which we investigate the feasibility of this approach. Finally, we present and discuss results on the accuracy and the speed of the method and investigate how the modalities interact.

Author Keywords
expert video analysis; event detection; eye tracking; EEG

ACM Classification Keywords
H.5.2 Information interfaces and presentation (e.g., HCI): User Interfaces: Input devices and strategies.

INTRODUCTION
In order to maintain a high level of security, video surveillance systems are used today in both civil and military environments. Video analysis is useful to detect conspicuous events – objects or situations – and to report time and place of their occurrence, i.e., to determine their temporal and spatial location. Despite progress in the development of automatic video analysis and tracking methods, the human video analyst still plays the central role in the event detection and dissemination process. In short, the task of expert video analysts can be described as a real-time visual search for events in imagery. To perform this demanding task successfully, the video analysts have to keep their focus of visual attention constantly on the dynamic video stream. To report the detected events, they additionally have to interact with the surveillance system, e.g., by marking the relevant item in the video image with a computer mouse. In this case, temporal and spatial event location is determined by the time the mouse button is clicked and the position of the mouse pointer at this juncture. However, due to ego motion or sensor motion, objects displayed in videos usually move, often even unpredictably. Furthermore, in contrast to static elements on graphical user interfaces events move into and out of the scene, being visible only for a limited time. Hence, mouse interaction is getting time-consuming and exhausting if repeated mouse pointer readjustments are necessary for successful event selection. Mouse interaction can even result in missed events when mouse click and pointer position do not coincide with time and place of the event. In security applications, this may lead to serious effects, hence, requiring a more efficient interaction technique.

A promising alternative is gaze-based interaction, which uses the user's gaze position on the screen – provided by an eye tracker – for pointing. As the pointing "device" is now always located at the video analyst's visual focus of interest, they do not have to divide their visual attention between event and pointing device any more. Though being inherently less accurate than mouse pointing [20], gaze pointing benefits by providing spatial event location with less mental and manual stress. A common method for temporal event location is the dwell time technique, i.e., the user consciously fixates the target object for a certain period of time [22] to actuate its selection. However, as the dwell time technique leads to unnatural eye movement behavior resulting in higher cognitive workload it is not suitable in expert video analysis. The other common method for temporal event location is to perform a button press [21,19]. However, it also requires a conscious action, inducing additional working memory load and adding additional latency to the reaction time. Video analysts may miss relevant events for a number of reasons, physical overload caused by multiple fast objects, distraction or fatigue caused by mental overload, or hesitation in unclear

IUI'13, March 19–22, 2013, Santa Monica, CA, USA.

situations. They might scan the scene as usual but fail to detect an event consciously and in consequence do not select and frame it. In this scenario, the gaze position might still lie near the event, thus indicating the spatial event location at least approximately (which may be enough as the material is often preprocessed using automatic object tracking techniques); but the temporal event location fails. It is well known [1] that humans react unconsciously to suspicious or in any case relevant events before reacting consciously or even if not reacting at all. This unconscious and very fast reaction can be measured by tracking brain activity related to perception and attention using EEG sensors. Thus, EEG measurement could be used for temporal event location, even when no explicit selection is performed. Also in combination with traditional selection mechanisms, EEG-based event detection can be used to detect false alarms caused by non-task fixation of an element, for example when the user is inattentive. In combination, eye tracking and EEG signal could provide a new method for determining both the spatial and the temporal conditions of an event.

EEG-based Brain Computer Interfaces (BCIs) have a long history of detecting events which catch their users' attention. The P300 speller paradigm [4] is one of the classic BCIs tracking the user's attention for letter spelling, designed for users who are incapable of any motor functions for communication. This paradigm relies on consecutive visual highlighting of all the letters (usually arranged in a matrix), which triggers a characteristic Event Related Potential (ERP), the P300 at about 300ms after the highlighting of the target letter. This ERP can be automatically detected from the EEG signal to derive the intended letter.

[6] and [7] propose a framework for human-aided computing for analysis of images. Instead of having human operators manually annotate a large number of images, they are presented a fast continuous stream of images they do not manually respond to. Instead, EEG is recorded during presentation and then automatically analyzed for the occurrence of neural markers related to certain images. While [6] relies on the user to mentally perform an active image classification, [7] solely exploits on the unconscious response of the user to the image to discriminate target from non-target images.

Also the combination of eye tracking and EEG is not completely new. [8] describes a hybrid point-and-click interface which allows self-paced operation of a BCI speller for text entry at arbitrary locations which are determined from eye gaze. [9] combines eye tracking and EEG to implement a visual-neural item selection process without manual intervention. Eye tracking is used to locate the user's attention in the spatial domain. The EEG signal is used to replace the traditional dwell time based selection of items. The approach is evaluated for a search-and-select task on a simple graphical user interface. In contrast to our proposed approach, their paradigm relies on actively issuing a mental command to trigger selection. The authors argue that this results in higher accuracy compared to implicit item selection. While their results support this finding, they also notice significantly higher reaction times for the active BCI compared to implicit methods.

In this contribution, a first step is made to examine the feasibility of robust spatio-temporal event detection without manual intervention by combining EEG and eye tracking data. We describe the experiment designed to investigate this question, the simple scenario which replicates certain typical tasks of video analysis in an abstracted and controllable fashion, and the collected data corpus. We analyze how accurate we can detect events from eye tracking and EEG recordings and how both modalities interact.

EXPERIMENTAL DESIGN

As our main objective is to provide a new technique for (nearly effortless) event detection to enhance gaze-based interaction, we decided to use a circle selection paradigm which is established in eye gaze interaction evaluation [18,19].

Experimental Paradigm

The experiment used three test paradigms. The initial paradigm 1 was an event counting task. A light-grey square with a size of 100 pixels is presented in the center of a grey background. To denote an event, the color of the square changed to red for 2s after a randomly chosen time span (>1.5s). The participants were told to continuously fixate the crosshair in the middle of the center square, and to count the number of events taking place. This setup is a very abstract model of observing a stationary object (e.g., a building) to detect relevant changes (e.g., someone entering).

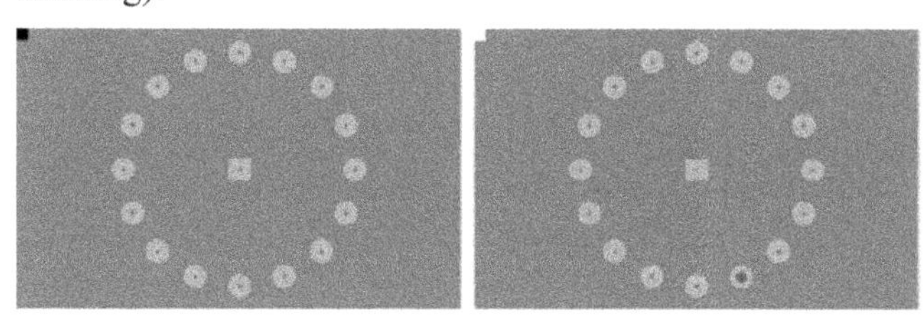

Figure 1: Visual stimulus for experimental paradigm 2.

Paradigms 2 and 3 were event selection tasks. Figure 1 shows the visual stimulus for paradigm 2. It comprises 16 circles with a diameter of 100 pixels, arranged in a circle around a center square with a size of 100 pixels. Circle size was chosen to match the accuracy of the eye tracker as reported by the manufacturer. The distance between the midpoint of the square and the midpoints of the circles was 500 pixels. Again, events occurred after randomly chosen time spans (>1.5s), and the red highlighting lasted always for 2s. This paradigm was designed according to suggestions made by ISO 9241-9, the standard for evaluating non-keyboard input devices, including the variant used by [19] to ensure a previously not known selection order. The participants had to perform event selection and were instructed to continuously focus the crosshair in the middle of the center square, and in case of an event (red highlighting), to change their focus onto the crosshair of the highlighted circle as fast as possible, keep focus there only until they were sure to have perceived the crosshair as a symbol and then to quickly move their focus back onto the center square.

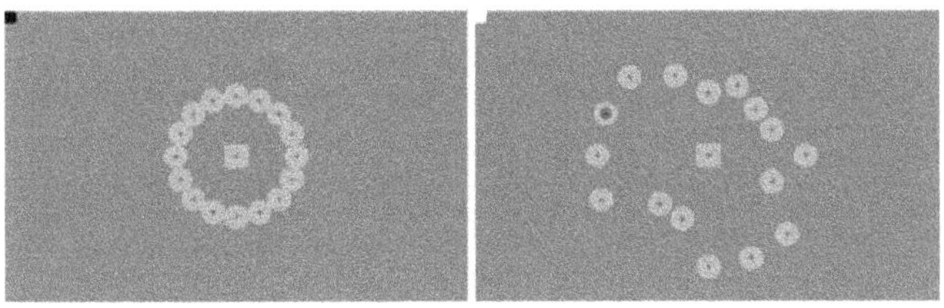

Figure 2: Starting configuration for paradigm 3 (left), visual stimulus during circle movement (right).

The visual stimulus of paradigm 3 is shown in Figure 2: Starting configuration for paradigm 3 (left), visual stimulus during circle movement (right). The design extends the stimulus of paradigm 2 into a moving object selection task. Now, circles moved radially with two different speeds which could change at random at the inner and outer reversal points for each point. Events were chosen to occur either at the reversal points (distance of 250 and 500 pixels, respectively), or in the middle between them. The instruction the participants got of how to perform the event selection was the same as for experimental paradigm 2. The benefits of this simple scenario are the ability to control distance to target for each trial and thus the variance in reaction time and it also avoids other confounding variables like overlapping events, different scanning strategies etc. The clear and abstract design also reflects the ability of well-trained and specialized expert video analysts to extract relevant information from a noisy video stream.

Every participant performed five experimental tasks. All participants started with an experimental task using paradigm 1. The number of events to count was ten. Then, each participant performed four tasks, switching between paradigm 2 and 3, starting with the static variant. The number of events was 32 for each task. Each of the 16 circles was highlighted twice. The highlighting order was randomized, and the highlighting orders for paradigms 2 and 3 were different. Overall, every participant had to perform 128 event selection trials for both paradigms combined. Prior to performing the tasks, every participant performed a training session, using the same order of experimental tasks, but with a reduce number of events (7 for paradigm 1; 8 for paradigms 2 and 3).

Data Collection

11 participants (9 male, 2 female) volunteered in our experiment. All of them were students or colleagues. Their ages ranged from 26 to 33 years (average = 28.6 years). All participants had normal or corrected to normal vision. Two were experienced eye tracker users, the others never used an eye tracker before.

For eye gaze measurement, a Tobii X60 remote eye tracker was used. It was placed beneath a 24''monitor (1920x1200 pixel) using a Tobii Monitor Mount. The eye tracker provides gaze data at a sampling rate of 60 Hz. According to the manufacturer, the eye tracker features an accuracy of 0.5°. As the participants viewing distance was about 65cm from the monitor, this corresponded to a "region of uncertainty" of about 1.13 cm or 43 pixels. As the Tobii X60 allows a freedom of head movement of 44x22x30 cm (W x H x D), we decided not to use a chin rest, as this would not be acceptable for expert video analysts, either. Eye tracker calibration was performed once, immediately before the participants started their first training task.

EEG was recorded using a BrainProducts actiCHamp recorder with 28 active electrodes arranged according to the international 10-10 system referenced at Pz and three monopolar Electrooculography (EOG) electrodes placed around the eyes according to [3]. See Figure 3 for the exact locations of the electrodes. Impedance was kept below 16kOhm for all electrodes. The EEG data was synchronized with the task and the eye tracking data using a photo diode attached to the screen above a marker box which switched color during events. This guarantees synchrony of data streams at a frame level.

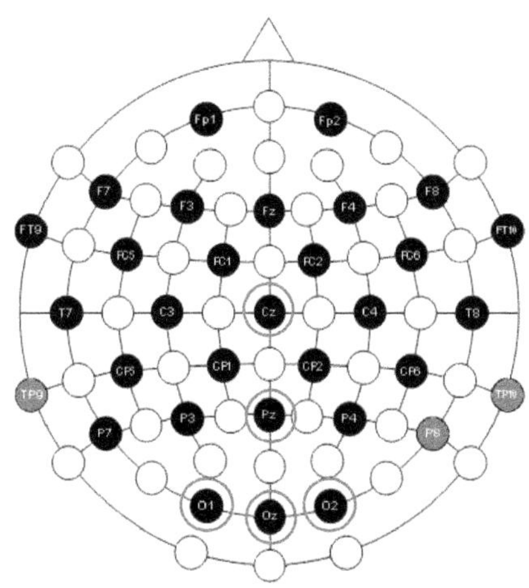

Figure 3: Electrode positions for EEG (grey locations are removed to serve as EOG electrodes). Electrodes marked in red are part of the *Reduced* electrode set.

METHODS FOR EVENT LOCALIZATION

Localizing events in time

For localization of the target events in time, we mainly make use of the recorded EEG data. We design a system which can detect the occurrence and perception of highlighting events depending on short segments of EEG data. We treat this task as a two-class classification problem of recognizing a presented segment of the EEG data stream as *trial* or *non-trial*. A trial is a segment which immediately follows the highlighting of an item on the screen while a non-trial is any other segment from the data with no or only small overlap with a trial. To approach this classification task, we cut out windows of 200, 300, 400, and 500ms duration after each highlighting event as trials and windows of the same length before each event as non-trials as we assume that this part of the data is closest to an idle condition. This selection of window sizes is within the physiologically plausible borders of a neural reaction and allows a trade-off between recognition accuracy and recognition latency. A shorter window results in a faster reaction time of the system to potentially time-critical events but also results in less data for accurate classification. Each extracted segment was normalized by subtracting means for each channel on a window of 150ms before the segment and filtered with a 1-10 Hz band pass filter to retain the coarse structure of the data.

Furthermore, we also differentiate two recognition modes: The *person-dependent* mode (PD) trains a classification model for each individual subject and is only tested on data of this person while the *person-independent* mode (PI) trains a classification model on the data of multiple subjects which do not include the test subject. A PI system is more convenient for the user as it does not require the collection of training data prior to a session. However, given the large individual differences expected in EEG data, we assume a PD system to perform better in terms of accuracy.

For feature extraction, we employ simple local temporal features by calculating and concatenating the signal mean across a fixed number of equidistant consecutive windows across the segment. This process is performed for each electrode and results are stacked. All feature vectors for one person are z-normalized to make them commensurable for the PI mode. Compared to more specialized feature sets as for example proposed in [11], this feature definition can be easily transferred to online recognition where a stimulus lock is not available. For PD mode, we select a smaller number of such windows to account for the smaller number of available training samples. It is also possible to work only on a limited set of electrodes. We define the electrode set *Full* which contains all 28 electrodes on the skull, and the electrode set *Reduced* which only contains the electrodes Cz, Pz, Oz, O1 the and O2. Those electrodes are associated with visual perception and event detection and are not located frontally, i.e. are less exposed to eye movement artifacts. Finally, the electrode set *EOG* contains the three EOG electrodes.

As a classification model, we employ a Support Vector Machine with Radial Basis Function kernels. For PD mode, the parameters C and γ were optimized for each subject on the respective training data following the suggestions of [4]. For the PI mode, we used the standard parameters of the LibSVM implementation [13] as we strive for a common parameter set independent of the training data.

Every EEG recording under non-clinical conditions is polluted with eye movement artifacts. This is especially true in this scenario where eye movement is enforced by the task and also triggered by and related to the expected brain activity. For many BCI applications, it is common practice to try to remove those using regression methods using EOG electrodes as predictor variables [3] or by removing certain components from a signal decomposition using Independent Component Analysis (ICA) [11]. However, as for example [10] discovers, eye gaze and EEG are intertwined at very subtle levels and it seems extremely challenging to reliably remove this effect for data collected in a non-clinical context. Even a segment which appears to be cleaned to an expert may still contain remains of artifacts or even artificial patterns introduced by the artifact removal procedure which may be invisible to the human eye but still exploitable by statistical machine learning. This may also happen to electrodes which would normally be largely clean of artifacts. We therefore refrain from any artifact correction beyond simple filtering. We will see that the EEG actually contains exploitable information on brain activity different from eye movement artifacts.

Localizing Events in Space

To localize an event in space, we can simply resort to the eye tracking output which after calibration yields absolute coordinates of the computer screen. We output the position of the first fixation after a saccade as target location.

In [2], it was shown that it is possible to predict gaze positions by EEG and EOG data due to the eye being a natural dipole that influences the electric potential of the surrounding tissue. This is still measurable at parts of the scalp farer from the eyes and leads to an offset in EEG/EOG data proportional to the degree by which the eye was moved. By placing multiple EOG electrodes at different locations near the eye, we can capture both horizontal and vertical eye movements. If the devices for EEG recording are already present for localizing events in time, this method could be used to replace the eye tracking system to go without an additional expensive device.

As the amplitude measured at the EOG electrodes is approximately proportional to the rotation of the eyeball, we can simply train two linear regression models for horizontal and vertical gaze positions, with the values of the EEG/EOG channels being the predictor variables and the predicted gaze positions being the dependent variables. To not over-represent eye gazes to the center, we only used 2s of data after each event for training. As preprocessing, the data is freed from linear trends and normalized piecewise to counter the effects of slow drifts in the data.

EVALUATION

Localizing Events in Time

For the evaluation of the systems, we work on three different data sets: Data recorded using paradigm 2 is collected in the *Static* data set, data recorded using paradigm 3 in the *Dynamic* data set. Each set contains 64 trials and 64 non-trials of 11 subjects. We also regard the data set *Fixed*, in which every event was presented at the location of the fixation crosshair.

We start the classification analysis with a person dependent evaluation. For each subject, we perform a 10-fold cross-validation on each of the data sets defined above and experiment with different window sizes and electrode subsets. As each data set is balanced for trials and non-trials, we can simply report recognition accuracy as quality metric. Table 1 summarizes recognition accuracy for all subjects for the data sets *Static* and *Dynamic*.

Size [ms]	Full	Reduced	EOG
200	0.93 / 0.93	0.91 / 0.91	0.66 / 0.67
300	0.94 / 0.94	0.91 / 0.91	0.89 / 0.89
400	0.95 / 0.95	0.90 / 0.91	0.94 / 0.95
500	0.97 / 0.96	0.91 / 0.91	0.95 / 0.96

Table 1: Average PD recognition rates for different electrode sets and different window sizes (in ms). Values for the static and the dynamic data set are given separately.

We notice that reliable PD event detection is possible for both data sets. We also see that already short windows of 200ms are sufficient for reliable event detection. This can be exploited to guarantee a high reaction time for a future online system. While the electrode sets *Full* and *EOG* yield slightly higher overall performance, we suspect this to be caused by task-dependent eye movement artifacts as by the experimental design, each saccade is a reaction to a perceived event. This conclusion is supported by the fact that *Full* exhibits a similar pattern of improvements for longer windows (which contain larger amounts of eye movements compared to short windows) like *EOG*, while *Reduced* does not react to those artifacts. For short windows, the EEG-based recognition outperforms the EOG-based system, profiting from its shorter latency in reaction to events.

In the next step, we study person-independent recognition which poses the additional challenge of handling individual differences but with the potential strength of exploiting more training material to estimate more reliable model. We evaluate the system in a leave-one-subject-out cross-validation. The average classification accuracy for different conditions is given in Table 2. Those results indicate that PI event detection is possible in a reliable way when enough training material is available to counter inter-personal differences. The advantage of the PD system compared to the corresponding PI system is always below 7% absolute and always below 2% absolute for both EEG-based electrode sets. This indicates that our system is able to identify universal patterns of event perception to compensate for individual differences.

Size [ms]	Full	Reduced	EOG
200	0.92 / 0.92	0.92 / 0.90	0.70 / 0.64
300	0.93 / 0.93	0.91 / 0.90	0.90 / 0.82
400	0.94 / 0.94	0.91 / 0.91	0.94 / 0.90
500	0.96 / 0.96	0.91 / 0.91	0.95 / 0.91

Table 2: Average PI recognition rates for different electrode sets and different window sizes (in ms). Values for the static and the dynamic data set are given separately.

We see that in general, the *Full* electrode set yields the best recognition performance but moving to the *Reduced* set only marginally effects accuracy as absolute performance drop is below 5% in all cases. We also note that already the EOG is able to predict the presence of an event. This is no surprise as in the given experiment a significant task-related deviation from the fixation point was strongly correlated with the occurrence of such an event. Still, we see that for short time frames of 200ms and 300ms, the EEG based recognition is much more accurate than the system using the EOG electrode set, even given the fact that the peak of average absolute EOG amplitude is already at 240ms. This means that even if the EOG reacts very fast to an event, it cannot reliably discriminate between task-related and non-task-related activity, especially in the dynamic condition were more visual distraction takes place. This fact also shows that we are able to detect the relevant EEG patterns despite the presence of EOG artifacts.

The advantage of EEG-based features for event detection becomes even clearer in cases where no task-related eye movement is present at all. This relates to situations in the application were an analyst is observing an object over a longer period of time, e.g., to count people moving into a house. To demonstrate that the system does not only learn leaked EOG artifacts and eye movement related EEG patterns, we repeat the PI analysis on the *Fixed* data set, in which no eye movement was necessary. Using the same recognition setup as for the other tasks, we see that the *Reduced* electrode set now is at least 23% absolute more accurate than the EOG-based system. Additionally, the previously observed advantage of the *Full* electrode set disappears, supporting the initial claim that the additional electrodes contain more task-dependent eye movement artifacts.

Size [ms]	Full	Reduced	EOG
200	0.85	0.77	0.55
300	0.86	0.87	0.59
400	0.87	0.89	0.66
500	0.88	0.89	0.66

Table 3: Average PI recognition rates for different electrode sets and different window sizes (in ms) for the *fixed* data set.

Localizing Events in Space

To get the eye gaze tracking performance results, for every trial (fixation on center square – saccade to highlighted object – fixation of highlighted object), saccadic reaction time (SRT), onset time of the first fixation on the highlighted object (FOT), and object hit or miss were determined. As a basis for the measurements, the collected gaze points were classified into either fixation points or saccade points, using the I-VT-algorithm [17]. Minimum fixation duration was set to 100ms. As no chin-rest was used, and as participants were allowed to move their head slightly in a natural way, the gaze data was expected to be noisy. Accordingly, a rather high velocity threshold of 50°/s proved to provide the best hit rates.

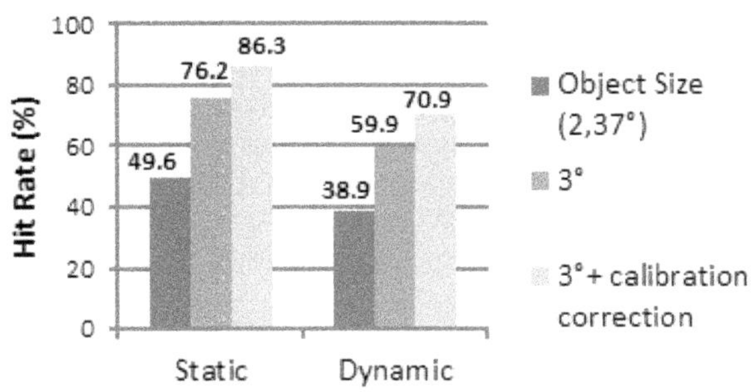

Figure 4: Hit rate for spatial event localization.

SRT was calculated as the difference between saccade onset time (= end time of last fixation on center square) and an object's highlighting time. As minimum human SRT, 150ms was chosen, a value in the middle of the range specified as "fast regular" saccades by [15]; trials with lower SRT were counted as an object miss. Saccade duration (SD) was calculated as the difference between the onset time of the first fixation on the object and the saccade onset time. As SD can be calculated by SD=2.2*amplitude (in visual angle, °)+21 [16], it was determined for every trial, and trials with a lower SD were counted as miss.

As the eye gaze data were rather noisy, the object hit rates (see Figure 4) were rather low if only based on a hit or miss of the real object size of 100 pixel (corresponding to 2,37° of visual angle), being 49.6% for static objects, and only 38,9% for moving objects. Using a virtual enlargement of the objects to a size corresponding to 3° of visual angle (126 pixel), the hit rates increase to at least 76.2% for static objects and 66.0% for moving objects. This enlargement can be made as the objects remain unambiguously selectable. Only objects in paradigm 3 can overlap when located at the inner reversal point. In this case, objects may overlap each of their two neighbors by up to 12.3% of their size. In our case, 12 of the 32 instances overlapped with one neighbor, 2 overlapped with both neighbors. To account for this, we conservatively adjust the hit rate of 66% by deducing 12.3%*(12/32) + 24.6%*(2/32) = 6.1%, resulting in a realistic hit rate of 59.9%. If in addition a simple calibration correction is used, which we derived from the average distance between gaze point and center of the square in paradigm 1, hit rates of 86.3% for static objects and of 70.9% for moving objects are obtained.

	SRT [ms]	FOT [ms]
Static	251 (62)	375 (86)
Dynamic	285 (90)	436 (133)

Table 4: Mean (and Std. Dev.) of SRT and FOT

Table 4 shows the SRT and the FOT achieved by analysis of the gaze data. For static object selection, both are shorter than for moving object selection, suggesting moving object selection to be the more difficult task which also makes it harder to automatically identify saccades and fixations.

For the evaluation of the EOG-based prediction of eye gaze, we used the output of the eye tracker as ground truth as a frame-based labeling was not available. The method was evaluated using cross-validation for each subject, training on three runs from the combined *static* and *dynamic* data sets and testing on the remaining one. We evaluated three different electrode sets: *Full*, *EOG* (as above), and *Full + EOG* (combining all 31 EEG and EOG electrodes). Averaged Pearson correlation is presented in Table 5. We see that we can achieve a correlation of up to 0.82 using all electrodes. While, as expected, the *EOG* electrode set beats the *Full* set, the EEG electrodes still add some information as the combined electrode set performs best. We also see that correlation of the horizontal axis is much more accurate than in vertical axis. This is a common effect caused by the vertical channel being more susceptible to drifts, artifacts and interference [14].

	Full	EOG	Full + EOG
R_X	0.69	0.80	0.82
R_Y	0.28	0.52	0.58

Table 5: Averaged correlation coefficients between predicted gaze position and ground truth.

DISCUSSION

In this paper, we performed first steps to implement and evaluate a system for nearly effortless spatio-temporal localization of events for expert video analysis. Our results show that we can perform person-independent localization in both time and space in a robust fashion. EEG-based event detection in time works with a very low latency and independent and despite of accompanying eye movements. Furthermore, we saw that we can locate events in space both using eye tracking and EEG/EOG data. We achieve a temporal accuracy of 91% and a spatial accuracy of 86.3% for the static paradigm 2 and of 70.9% for the dynamic paradigm 3. Assuming independence, we can expect to perform successful combined spatio-temporal localization for 78.5% (91% * 86.3%) resp. 64.5% (91% * 70.9%) of all cases. Temporal localization using EEG yields reliable results with a latency of 200-300ms, while a key-press or dwell time based technique would have an additional latency after FOT for selection.

The presented paradigm already represents a number of relevant situations in a video analysis scenario. Next steps will continue the analysis with the design of an ecologically more valid paradigm, including targets and non-target events.

REFERENCES

1. Bechara, A., Damasio, H., and Damasio, A.R. Emotion, Decision Making and the Orbitofrontal Cortex. In *Cerebral Cortex* 10, no. 3 (March 1, 2000): 295–307.
2. Hakenberg, J.P. Estimation of Gaze from EEG for Cursor Control. http://hakenberg.de, 2011
3. Schlögl, A., Keinrath, C., Zimmermann, D., Scherer, R., Leeb, R., and Pfurtscheller, G. A Fully Automated Correction Method of EOG Artifacts in EEG Recordings. In *Clinical Neurophysiology* 118, no. 1 (January 2007): 98–104.
4. Krusienski, D.J., Sellers, E.W., McFarland, D.J., Vaughan, T.M., and Wolpaw, J.R. Toward Enhanced P300 Speller Performance. In: *Journal of Neuroscience Methods* 167, no. 1 (January 15, 2008): 15–21.
5. Hsu, C.W., Chang, C.C., and Lin, C.J. A Practical Guide to Support Vector Classification, 2003.
6. Shenoy, P. and Desney S.T. Human-aided Computing: Utilizing Implicit Human Processing to Classify Images. In *Proceedings of the Twenty-sixth Annual SIGCHI Conference on Human Factors in Computing Systems*, 845–854. CHI '08. New York, NY, USA.
7. Gerson, A.D., Parra, L.C., and Sajda, P. Cortically Coupled Computer Vision for Rapid Image Search. In *IEEE Transactions on Neural Systems and Rehabilitation Engineering* 14, no. 2 (June 2006): 174 –179.
8. Yong, X., Fatourechi, M., Ward, R.K., and Birch, G.E. The Design of a Point-and-Click System by Integrating a Self-Paced Brain Computer Interface With an Eye-Tracker. In *IEEE Journal on Emerging and Selected Topics in Circuits and Systems* 1, no. 4 (December 2011): 590 –602.
9. Zander, T.O., Gaertner, M., Kothe, C., and Vilimek, R. Combining Eye Gaze Input with a Brain-Computer Interface for Touchless Human-Computer Interaction. In *International Journal of Human-Computer Interaction* 27, no. 1 (2010): 38–51.
10. Brunner, P., Joshi, S., Briskin, S., Wolpaw, J.R., Bischof, H., and Schalk, G. Does the 'P300' Speller Depend on Eye Gaze? In *Journal of Neural Engineering* 7, no. 5 (October 1, 2010): 056013.
11. Jung, T.-P., Makeig, S., Humphries, C., Lee, T.-W., McKeown, M.J., Iragui, V., and Sejnowski, T.J. Removing Electroencephalographic Artifacts by Blind Source Separation. In *Psychophysiology* 37, no. 2 (2000): 163–178.
12. Blankertz, B., Lemm, S., Treder, M., Haufe, S., and Müller, K.-R. Single-trial Analysis and Classification of ERP Components — A Tutorial. In *NeuroImage* 56, no. 2 (May 15, 2011): 814–825.
13. Chang, C., and Lin, C. LIBSVM: A Library for Support Vector Machines. In *ACM Trans. Intell. Syst. Technol.* 2, no. 3 (May 2011): 27:1–27:27.
14. Venkataramanan, S., Prabhat, P., Choudhury, S.R., Nemade, H.B., and Sahambi, J.S. Biomedical Instrumentation based on Electrooculogram (EOG) Signal Processing and Application to a Hospital Alarm System. In *Proc. ICISIP 2005*, IEEE Computer Society Washington, D.C., USA (2005), 535-540.
15. Gezeck, S., Fischer, B., and Timmer, J. Saccadic reaction times: a statistical analysis of multimodal distributions. *Vision research 37,* 15 (1997), 2119-2131.
16. Holmqvist, K., Nyström, M., Andersson, R., Dewhurst, R., Jarodzka, H., and Van de Weijer, J. *Eye tracking: A comprehensive guide to methods and measures.* OUP Oxford, 2011.
17. Salvucci, D.D. and Goldberg, J.H. Identifying fixations and saccades in eye-tracking protocols. In *Proc. ETRA 2000,* ACM Press (2000), 71-78.
18. Sibert, L.E. and Jacob, R.J.K. Evaluation of eye gaze interaction. In *Proc. Of the SIGCHI conference on Human factors in computing systems.* ACM Press (2000), 281-288.
19. Zhang, X. and MacKenzie, I.S. Evaluating eye tracking with ISO 9241 - Part 9. *Human-Computer Interaction. HCI Intelligent Multimodal Interaction Environments.* Springer, 2007, 779-788.
20. MacKenzie, I.S. An eye on user input: research challenges in using the eye for computer input control. In *Proc. ETRA 2010,* ACM Press, 2010, 11-12.
21. Ware, C. and Mikaelian, H.H. An evaluation of an eye tracker as a device for computer input. *ACM SIGCHI Bulletin 18,* 4 (1987), 183-188.
22. Jacob, R.J.K. The use of eye movements in human-computer interaction techniques: what you look at is what you get. *ACM Transactions on Information Systems (TOIS) 9,* 2 (1991), 152-169.

Subtle Gaze-Dependent Techniques for Visualising Display Changes in Multi-Display Environments

Jakub Dostal
School of Computer Science
University of St Andrews, UK
jd67@st-andrews.ac.uk

Per Ola Kristensson
School of Computer Science
University of St Andrews, UK
pok@st-andrews.ac.uk

Aaron Quigley
School of Computer Science
University of St Andrews, UK
aquigley@st-andrews.ac.uk

ABSTRACT
This paper explores techniques for visualising display changes in multi-display environments. We present four subtle gaze-dependent techniques for visualising change on unattended displays called FreezeFrame, PixMap, WindowMap and Aura. To enable the techniques to be directly deployed to workstations, we also present a system that automatically identifies the user's eyes using computer vision and a set of web cameras mounted on the displays. An evaluation confirms this system can detect which display the user is attending to with high accuracy. We studied the efficacy of the visualisation techniques in a five-day case study with a working professional. This individual used our system eight hours per day for five consecutive days. The results of the study show that the participant found the system and the techniques useful, subtle, calm and non-intrusive. We conclude by discussing the challenges in evaluating intelligent subtle interaction techniques using traditional experimental paradigms.

Author Keywords
multi-display environments; computer vision; subtle interaction; attentive user interfaces; notifications

ACM Classification Keywords
H.5.2 Information Interfaces and Presentation: User Interfaces—Windowing systems

INTRODUCTION
Modern computer workstation setups regularly include multiple displays in various configurations. With such multi-monitor or multi-display setups we have reached a stage where we have more display real-estate available than we are able to comfortably attend to. While the benefits of large or multi-display setups have been demonstrated in several studies (e.g. [2, 4, 7, 18]), it has also been suggested that this increase in display space will lead to usability problems [7], window management difficulties [4] and issues related to information overload [13].

Figure 1. A photograph of the display setup used in our study. The two 27-inch displays are bezel to bezel, which translates to approximately 45° angular difference at 76.5 cm distance from the user.

Another potential issue is change blindness: users' inability to detect significant visual display changes when there is a disruption in continuity such as a brief flicker or a shift in visual focus. However, the effects of change blindness in multi-display environments have not been extensively studied in the literature. In one study, DiVita and colleagues [8] report that change blindness was a significant factor for operators managing critical events using multi-display command and control systems with unattended displays.

In general, the increased display real-estate afforded by multi-display setups means that users are unable to attend to all of it at once. In particular, this point is reached when the total display area is so large that it does not fit within the user's field of vision. In this case, the user has to substantially turn their head to see different parts of the display environment. This situation eventually arises when the number of displays, or the distance between the displays, increases. For example, it is likely to occur when users are working with three displays aligned bezel to bezel (e.g. Figure 1). When the user is only able to observe part of the multi-display environment, changes occurring on the unattended displays are difficult to track.

Attentive user interfaces [20, 21] and distraction reduction techniques [17] have been extensively studied previously using a variety of context-sensitive eye- and gaze-tracking technologies. In contrast, *inattention*, and specifically technologies that track visual change on unattended displays, has received considerably less attention [21].

One example in the literature is Ashdown and Sato's [1] multi-display system, which uses head tracking to reposition the mouse pointer to the display the user attends to. Another example is the work by Kern et al. [14] on Gazemarks: a visual placeholder that indicates the user's last fixation on a display. Kern et al. [14] reported that the Gazemarks technique resulted in faster completion times in a map navigation task in a vehicle driving scenario. Finally, Bi and Balakrishnan [4] suggest further investigation of awareness of peripheral applications with large, single and dual desktop setups as a fruitful avenue for future research. However, research on change blindness in multi-display environments has shown that making users aware of changes in unattended displays is a significant challenge [8].

In the remainder of this paper we first contribute four visualisation techniques for assisting users in perceiving and tracking display changes in multi-display environments. Second, we present an accurate markerless system that is able to track the attended display using off-the-shelf web cameras and an evaluation of its performance and accuracy. Third, we present the results of a longitudinal case study in which a working professional used our system for 39.25 hours as part of his regular work activities. Finally, we discuss the challenges in evaluating subtle intelligent visualisation techniques.

APPROACH

We have designed four subtle gaze-dependent techniques for visualising display changes that we call FreezeFrame, PixMap, WindowMap and Aura. One can view our contribution within the attentive user interface framework proposed by Vertegaal et. al [21]. With respect to that framework, we are attempting to sense and communicate changes due to *inattention*.

Our techniques are designed to be used within an existing work context of the user. As a consequence, it is important that the techniques do not distract the user from their primary task. Therefore, our techniques are designed as *calm technologies*, as proposed by Weiser and Brown [23]. A calm technology *"moves easily from the periphery of our attention, to the center, and back"* where *"the periphery is informing without overburdening"* [23].

To be able to implement and deploy the non-intrusive visualisation techniques in an actual work environment, we have developed a system that is able to track the display the user is attending to and, by extension, the displays that are unattended. Importantly, our system is markerless and only relies on off-the-shelf web cameras for detecting users' gaze. This allows the system to be readily deployed in existing workstation setups. Our experimental results demonstrate that our system can accurately detect which display the user is attending.

As a subtle interface, our system does not naturally lend itself to a traditional evaluation approach, such as a short controlled experiment. Therefore, we instead carried out a qualitative longitudinal study to better understand the finer points and nuances of using visualisations as part of an ordinary multi-display environment. We recruited a working professional

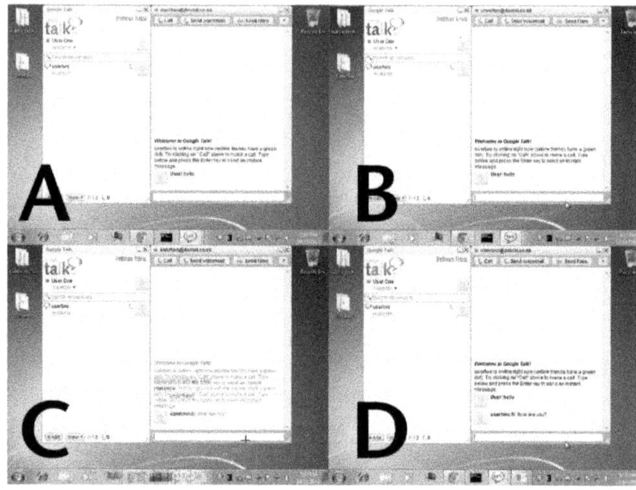

Figure 2. FreezeFrame reduces distractions by hiding visual change until the user shifts their visual focus back to the display. *A* shows the last frame before the user shifts visual focus away from this display. *B* shows a static frame of the unattended display before and during any visual change. *C* illustrates the dissolving of the old frame into the current display state. *D* shows the current display state.

who used our system during an entire workweek as part of his regular work activities. We recorded 39.25 hours of data in total. Our study shows that three out of four techniques highlighted visual changes in a subtle and non-intrusive manner. Additionally, the techniques reduced distractions and the participant found them useful when working in his regular multi-display setup.

In our study, distraction reduction was one of the main aims and benefits of using the techniques. In fact, the participant reported that before taking part in the study, he was unaware of how often he was distracted until he started using our techniques. This finding complements research into change blindness that suggests that people are not fully aware of their inability to perceive visual changes [3, 8]. Based on our study, we conjecture people may be unaware of the extent to which they get distracted by visual display changes in their environment. However, more work is required to firmly establish whether this hypothesis holds for other scenarios.

SUBTLE VISUALISATION TECHNIQUES

To assist users in noticing changes in multi-display environments, we have implemented four different subtle visualisation techniques for tracking visual changes on unattended displays. Each technique visualises display changes in a different manner. The term *visual focus* refers to an approximate direction of gaze (defined as the foveal field of vision). As gaze is a good approximation of the direction of attention [21], we use visual focus to approximate the direction of gaze. We will use the term *frame* to refer to a screenshot of the contents on a display at a specific point in time. All figures demonstrating the techniques use an instant message chat (specifically Google Talk) as an example scenario. The change that occurs while the user's visual focus is elsewhere is in all cases a new instant message appearing in the chat window.

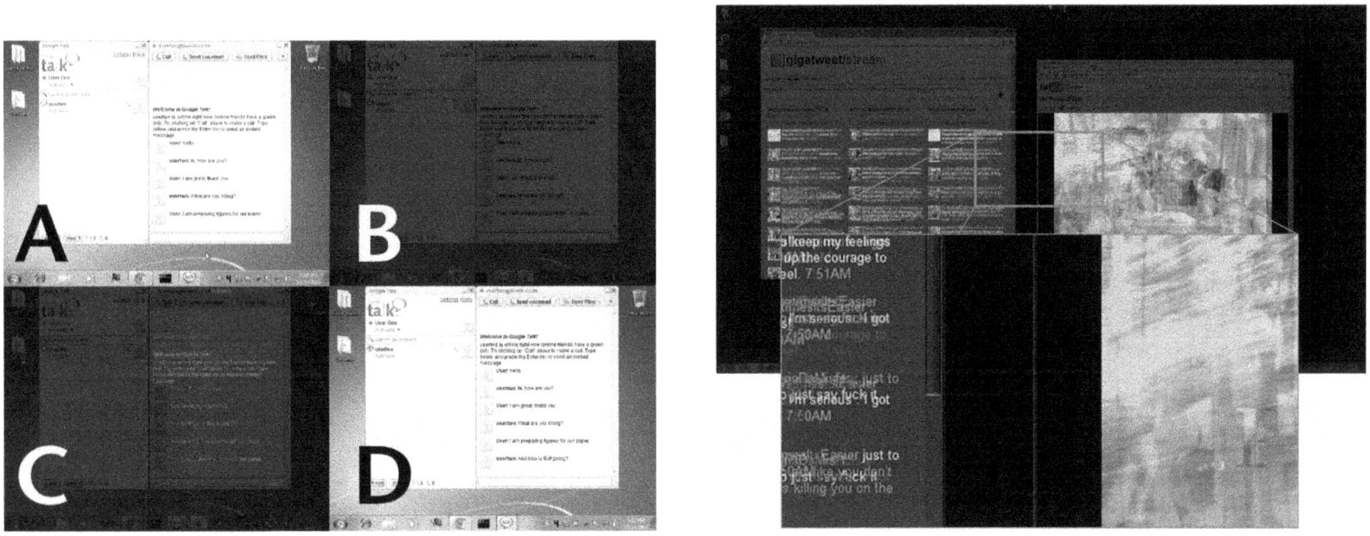

(a) (b)

Figure 3. An illustration of PixMap. Pixmap highlights visual changes over time on a pixel level. *A* shows the last frame before the user switches visual focus away from this display. *B* shows a frame of the unattended display before any visual change takes place. *C* illustrates how the technique visualises the change (a new instant message in the chat window) when it happens by brightening the pixels that changed in the chat window. *D* shows the current display state after the technique has been dissolved. Figure 3b shows a detailed example of change visualised as bright pixels.

FreezeFrame

FreezeFrame is the simplest technique, which hides visual changes on an unattended display until the user's visual focus shifts towards it again. FreezeFrame works as follows. Consider a user working with two displays (ONE and TWO). The user starts by attending display ONE. When the user switches visual focus from display ONE to display TWO, our gaze-detection system notices this focus shift. FreezeFrame then captures a frame of display ONE at the time the user shifted their visual focus to display TWO. This frame is then displayed on display ONE as a black and white static image. No visual change is then shown on display ONE until the user switches their visual focus from display TWO back to display ONE. When the user attends to display ONE again, the frozen black and white frame on display ONE dissolves, blending smoothly into the current state of display ONE over the next 1–2 seconds. Figure 2 and Video Figure 1.1 illustrate FreezeFrame.

PixMap

The PixMap technique is a temporal heatmap visualisation that shows the user the changes that occurred while the display was unattended. Following the scenario we previously described for FreezeFrame, when the user shifts their visual focus from display ONE to display TWO, display ONE is darkened to reduce distractions. While the user's visual focus is directed elsewhere, a frame (a screenshot of the contents of display ONE) is captured at regular intervals, approximately six times per second. A difference in pixel values between the two most recently captured frames is computed for the entire display and the change is visualised on display ONE. This continues until the user's visual focus returns to display ONE, at which point the visualisation is dissolved into the current desktop state of display ONE over the next 1–2 seconds. Figure 3 and Video Figure 1.2 illustrate PixMap.

We use the following formula to compute the value of pixels:

$$V_{new} = (V_{previous} \times Decay) + (V_{diff} \times Intensity)$$

where V_{new} is the new pixel value, $V_{previous}$ is the pixel value of the corresponding pixel in the previous iteration of the heat map. V_{diff} is the intensity of change between the last frame and the current frame measured as the difference in RGB values for the corresponding pixels. $Decay$ is a fraction denoting how quickly the current value should fade over time, and $Intensity$ defines how much of the intensity of V_{diff} will be added to the heat map.

The decay and intensity are empirically determined parameters. We set them as follows after testing the visual effect of different values:

$Decay = 0.01$, $Intensity = 0.5$.

WindowMap

WindowMap is a variation of the PixMap technique. Similar to PixMap, WindowMap also visualises changes that have occurred on an unattended display. However, instead of visualisation changes at the pixel level, WindowMap shows changes at the application-window level. WindowMap works identically to PixMap except that the amount of change in the unattended display is computed for application-window areas on the display instead for individual pixels. Figure 4 and Video Figure 1.3 illustrate WindowMap.

Again, the decay and intensity are empirically determined parameters. We set them, after testing, as follows:

$Decay = 0.02$, $Intensity = 0.75$.

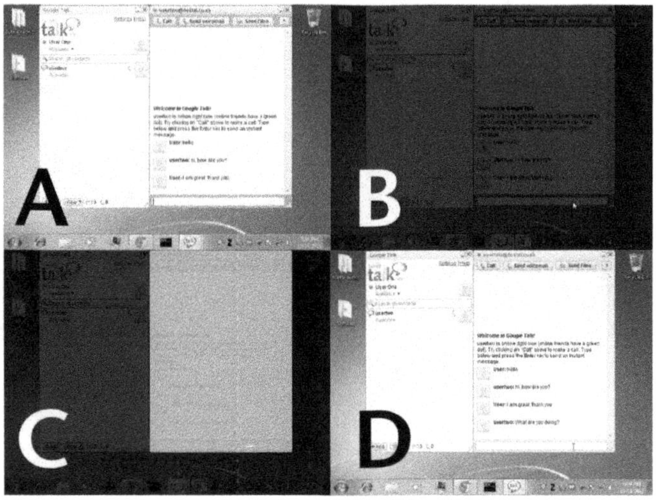

(a)

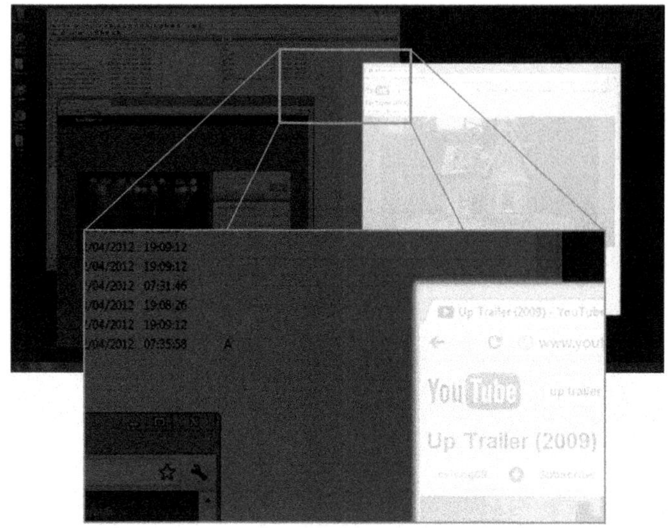

(b)

Figure 4. An illustration of WindowMap. It highlights visual change over time for individual application-windows. *A* shows the last frame before the user shifts visual focus away from this display. *B* shows a frame of the unattended display before any visual change. *C* illustrates how the technique visualises change (a new instant message in the chat window) as it happens by brightening the chat window. *D* shows the current display state after the technique dissolves. Figure 4b shows a detailed example of change visualised by brightening the application window, where the change occurred.

Aura

Aura visualises short-term display changes on an unattended display. Consider a user shifting their visual focus away from display ONE to Display TWO. Aura then first darkens display ONE to reduce distractions. Then Aura continually captures the last twenty frames of the unattended display at approximately one-second intervals. The change for a particular frame is then visualised as a thin rectangle around each window visible on the unattended display ONE. The brightness of the rectangle for each application window is proportional to how much the window in the frame changed in relation to the previous frame. Since Aura is tracking the changes for the last twenty frames, the visualisation ends up with twenty evenly spaced thin rectangles around each window. The closer a rectangle is to its window, the more recent the visualised change. Figure 5 and Video Figure 1.4 illustrate Aura. As the video figure illustrates, a window with many changes (such as a video player) results in cycles of bright rectangles, while a window with few changes (such as an instant messaging window) results in occasional bright rectangles.

DISPLAY-LEVEL VISUAL FOCUS DETECTOR

To enable the subtle visualisation techniques to be deployed to workstations, we developed a display-level visual focus detector using commodity hardware. Our system tracks users' gaze using web cameras mounted on the displays. The algorithm is an enhanced version of an algorithm described in our previous work [9]. It uses a display-level gaze direction detector based on the Viola-Jones feature detection algorithm [22], a computer vision algorithm that is readily available in the open source OpenCV library. Our system uses three specific classifiers. These classifiers have been shown to achieve high accuracy [5]. The first classifier (EP1) detects an eye-pair. The other two classifiers (LE and RE) detect the left and right eye respectively.

Using these classifiers we have designed a real-time algorithm that can detect eye-pairs with high accuracy and supports graceful degradation in situations when it is difficult to detect the user's eye-pair. When the system cannot reliably identify the user's left and right eyes, it attempts to infer an estimate based on an identified eye-pair area of interest. Algorithm 1 describes our gaze detection algorithm for a given image.

Evaluation

To ensure the visual focus detector was sufficiently accurate and robust to be deployed we carried out an evaluation with seven participants.

Method

The system was deployed to three dual-core iMac computers with 20-inch displays (1680×1050 pixel resolution). A Logitech C910 web camera was attached to each display. All computers were running the Windows 7 operating system. Each display was positioned at 76.5 cm from the user's default sitting position. This distance was based on the results of a study of comfortable viewing distances for computer displays, which reported this distance as the most comfortable viewing distance on average [10].

We tested six angular differences (15°, 30°, 45°, 60°, 75° and 90°). Figure 6a illustrates how angular difference was defined in the evaluation. The six different angles were chosen to sample the whole visual field of the participants. We recruited seven university students as participants (6 male). Their ages ranged between 19 and 26. Their skin colour and hairstyle varied but none of them wore reading aids.

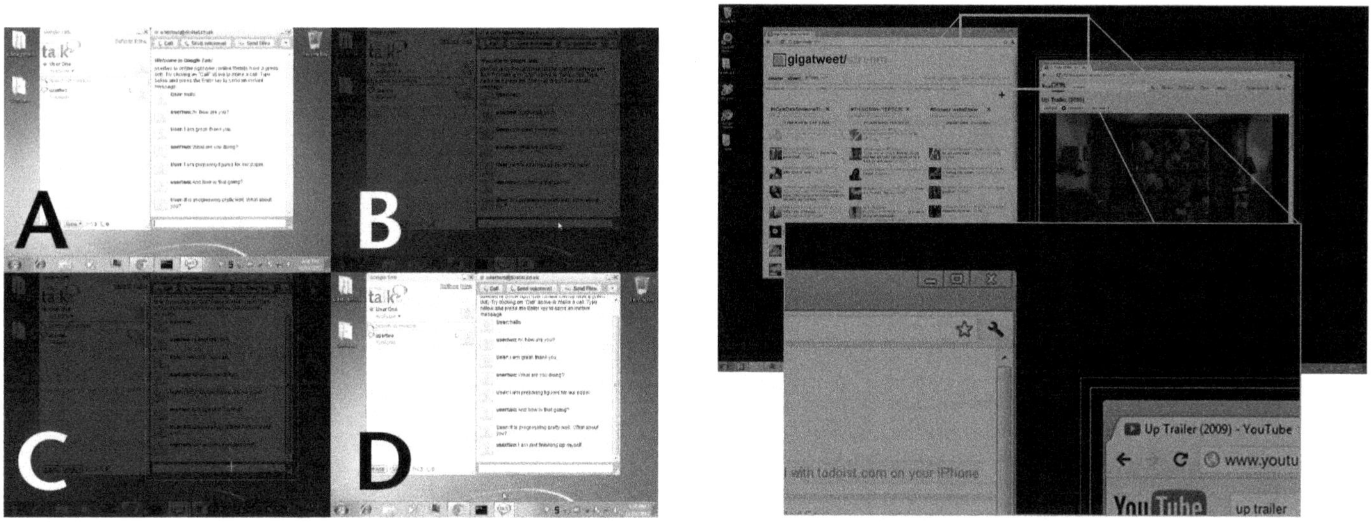

(a) (b)

Figure 5. An illustration of Aura. It highlights short-term visual changes by projecting a rectangular aura around each window. *A* shows the last frame before the user shifts visual focus away from this display. *B* shows a frame of the unattended display before any visual change. *C* illustrates how the technique visualises the change (a new instant message in the chat window) as it happens as a rectangle around the chat window. *D* shows the current display state after the technique dissolves. Figure 5b shows a detailed example of change visualised as rectangles of varying brightness projected around the application window where the change occurred.

Algorithm 1 Algorithm used by the Visual Focus Detector

find all possible eye-pairs in a given camera image using the EP1 classifier
for all detected eye-pairs **do**
  partition the rectangle containing the eye-pair horizontally into two parts (left, right) and add 20% horizontal and 60% vertical padding to each of the two parts;
  scan the left and right sub-area of interest for potential rectangles containing the left eye (using the LE classfier) and the right eye (using the RE classifier), respectively, and select the largest one in each case;
  if both sub-areas contain a detected eye **then**
    compute the pupil position for each of the eyes, store their location and the containing rectangles for the eyes;
  end if
end for
for all eye-pairs **do**
  if eye-pair has both eyes detected and the sizes of the rectangles containing each eye match each other more closely than current candidate **then**
    store this eye-pair as the best candidate;
  end if
end for
if there is a best candidate eye-pair **then**
  report a full detection, including the distance between the pupils within the area of interest in pixels;
else[no best candidate is found]
  report a partial detection with the largest eye-pair found as the most likely eye-pair;
end if

Each participant was asked to follow a sequence of spoken instructions directing them to look at a centre target (centre of a display) and side targets (centres of other displays) in turn. The participants were also instructed to keep their body facing the centre target and to only move their head and/or their eyes. As body position is not important during the actual detection, we wanted the participants to only move their head to exaggerate any possible effect imposed by the eye and head movement. They were asked to remain at the specified distance from the displays to maintain consistent viewing angles. For each examined angle, each participant spent approximately 25 seconds looking at the centre target and 20 seconds looking at each side target. This generated approximately seven minutes of video data per participant. Our algorithm then detected the participant's eyes for each video frame. Thereafter, the accuracy of our algorithm was assessed by visually comparing the algorithm's detection results against the ground truth in each image.

Results

Figure 6b shows the percentage of video frames with successful detections with our detection algorithm. The blue bars (first column) show the number of detections when the user is looking the centre of the display (true positives). The red bars (middle column) show the detections while the user is looking away from the display at a specific angle (false positives). The green bars (third column) show the overall accuracy of the algorithm.

For angular differences up to 45°, even though the algorithm performs perfectly in terms of true positives, the overall accuracy is significantly lowered due to the high number of false positives when the user is looking away. However, the amount of false positives steadily decreases as the angular dif-

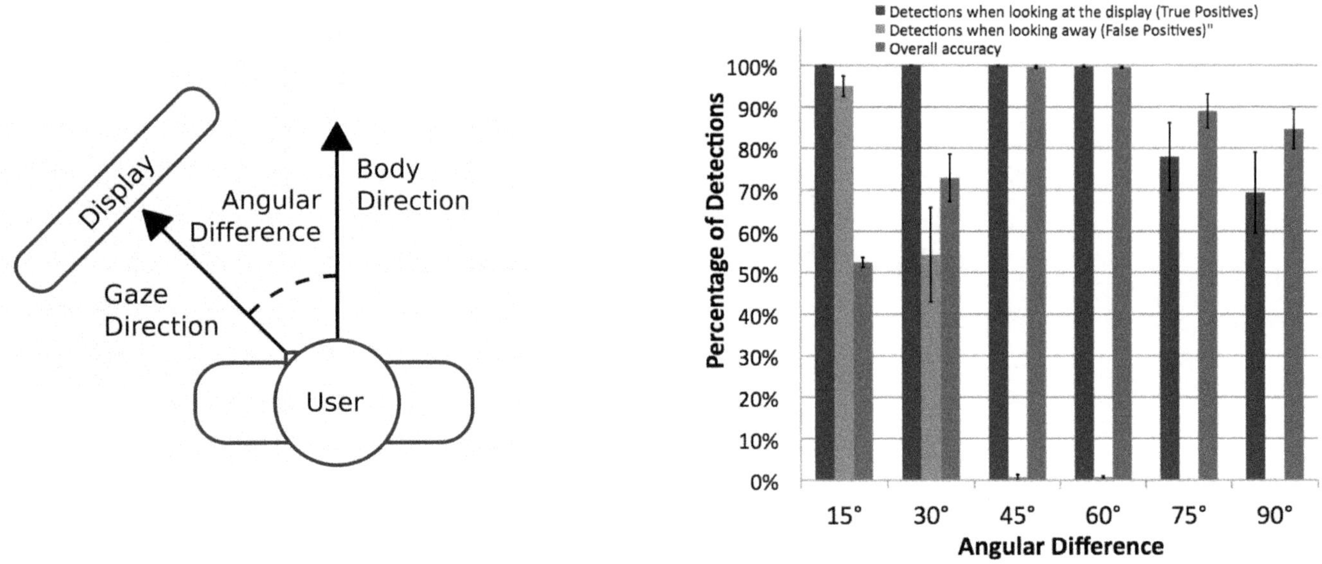

(a) A diagram illustrating how angular difference was measured in the evaluation of the visual focus detector.

(b) The results of our study of horizontal detection angles. The error bars show standard error.

Figure 6. The experimental setup (a) and the results (b) for our visual focus detector.

ference increases, and at a 45° angular difference the overall accuracy is higher than 98%.

For extreme angles greater than 60°, detection accuracy decreases substantially. In these cases, the participants tended to not move their head much, but instead move their pupils all the way towards the corner of their eyes to see the display. This was expected as we specifically instructed participants to not move their body, which is what would naturally occur. This meant that for much of the time the participants' eyes appeared very different from how they typically appear when they look straight at a display.

While we used 20-inch displays in this evaluation, the results are display size independent as the targets were positioned in the centre of the displays. A 45° angular difference provided the highest performance. As a calibration point, two 27-inch displays, positioned at a comfortable viewing distance 76.5 cm away from the user bezel-to-bezel, have an angular difference close to 45° (see Figure 1). We used two 27-inch displays in our setup for the longitudinal study, which we describe next.

LONGITUDINAL CASE STUDY

It is difficult to evaluate the effects of our subtle visualisation techniques as their behavioural influences require long-term use in realistic contexts. As has been observed in the literature, controlled experiments are poor constructs for evaluating such techniques, and a naïve application of a quantitative usability study risks generating misleading results [11, 16].

Therefore, we instead conducted a formative five-day qualitative case study with a working professional. We recruited a single participant with no prior knowledge of the system or the techniques. This participant was 24 years old, familiar with software development and a regular user of multi-display environments. The participant wore thin-rimmed glasses. Glasses do not have an effect on the display detector at short to medium distances. This effect only becomes noticeable at long distances when the eye-pair only occupies a small number of pixels in the camera image. Additionally, prior to the study, we extensively tested our display-level visual focus detector to ensure it would be able to accurately detect which display the participant attends to in his multi-display working environment.

The system was evaluated using a workstation configuration consisting of three computers, each with a high-resolution display. We used two 2010 iMac computers with 27-inch 2560×1440 pixel displays and a generic 2010 PC with a 24-inch 1920×1080 display. A Logitech C910 camera was attached to each display. Each camera provided a constant image stream of 1024×576 pixel images, which our system processed at 12 frames per second. All computers were running the Windows 7 operating system. Each display was positioned at 76.5 cm from the participant's preferred sitting position. However, the participant was instructed to sit comfortably and there was no restriction on their movement.

In this study, due to the size of the displays, the angular difference between the centres of the 27-inch displays was approximately 45° as measured from the 76.5 cm seating distance of the participant. This difference was maintained with the smaller 24-inch display for consistency. This setup represents a prototypical multi-display configuration, as a previous study has found that 45° angle between displays is a preferred setup among users [19].

Method

The participant was asked to use our multi-display setup for five days while performing his usual everyday work tasks.

The first day the participant was not exposed to a subtle visualisation technique. This approach was taken in order to obtain a baseline calibration point to compare the subtle visualisation techniques against. For the remaining four days, the four subtle visualisation techniques were deployed in the following order: WindowMap, FreezeFrame, PixMap and Aura. The participant was informed that some variant of an interaction technique that involves multiple displays would be used everyday but we did not inform the participant in advance of the particular technique that was used for a particular day. Further, the techniques were not demonstrated to the participant prior to the study.

Our system automatically logged the usage of specific displays, the time spent looking at each display, information about gaze switches between displays, the start and stop times for the techniques, and the method by which the technique was terminated (fade or user input).

The participant was also instructed to fill out two questionnaires each day. The first questionnaire was filled out immediately after the participant finished their work for the day and the second one the morning after. This meant we could ask the participant about both his immediate impression of a technique, and his impression of the technique the day after.

To complement the above methodology, we also used the Experience Sampling Method (ESM), which has been proposed as a methodology for evaluating pervasive and ubiquitous computing interfaces [6]. ESM enabled us to collect data of a higher granularity by presenting the participant with very brief questionnaires at approximately 30 minute intervals throughout the work day. The questionnaires asked about the participant's current task, his perceived frequency of display switching, and his familiarity with the technique. Finally, it included a comment area where the user could provide additional feedback. We collected between 9 and 15 samples per day, depending on the participant's physical presence and schedule. Additionally, one of the authors was present in the room for the entire duration of the experiment to administer the ESM questionnaires and to make visual observations.

Results

In total, we collected 39.25 hours of logged usage data (with a one second sampling rate), 9 questionnaires, and 61 ESM samples from our participant.

Display Utilisation

The participant spent a total of 31.66% of his time not attending to any of the displays due to various reasons such as meetings or paper-based work. Figure 7 shows the participant's display utilisation during the study as recorded in the system logs, adjusted to active-use time. Figure 7 makes it clear that the participant primarily attended to the centre display. This data suggests that the additional screens are mostly used for secondary or peripheral tasks. This is in line with previous research on the utilisation of multiple monitors [12]. In addition, based on our ESM samples and our visual observations, peripheral display tasks appear to be mostly related to social networking (Facebook, Twitter), instant messaging (MSN) or media streaming (Spotify). The peripheral displays were also commonly used as a point of reference for information such as documentation, server logs or an application programming interface (API). The participant also referred to the displays on either side, as well as activities performed on them, as peripheral.

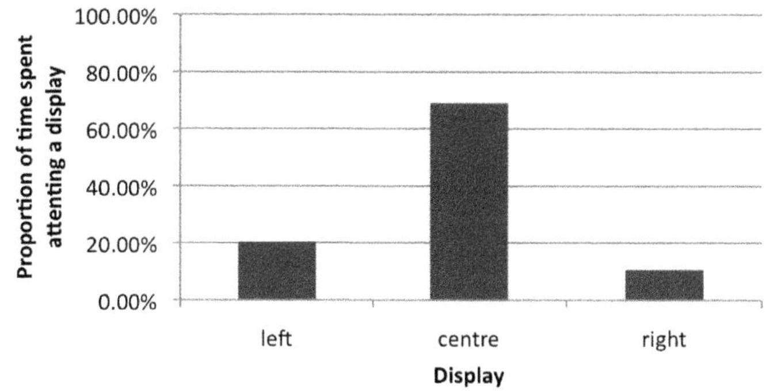

Figure 7. The distribution of display usage adjusted to active-use time.

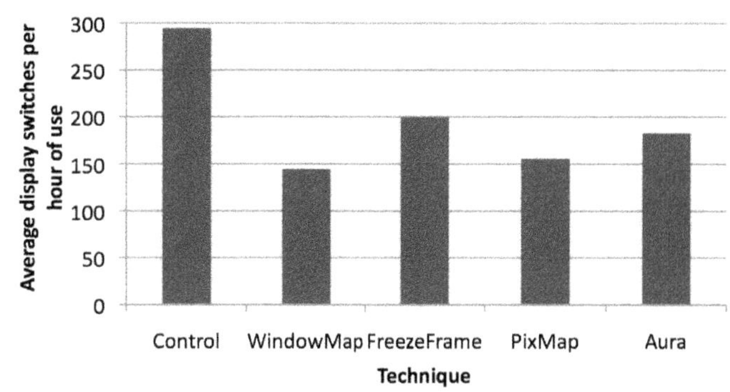

Figure 8. The average number of display switches per hour of use for each of the techniques.

Display Switching

Figure 8 plots the mean number of switches per hour of use for each technique. All four subtle visualisation techniques reduced the frequency of display switching by approximately a third or more compared to the baseline (which used no technique). FreezeFrame reduced the frequency of display switching by the smallest amount, only 32.5%. We conjecture this may be due to FreezeFrame's inability to dynamically visualise display change. This means that the only way for a user to check if there has been a change on the display is to switch visual focus to that display. Aura reduced the rate of display switching by 37.9%. We conjecture this may be due to the rectangular "aura" around the windows being too dim for the participant's peripheral vision to efficiently perceive it. Both PixMap and WindowMap reduced the rate of switching the most (47.2% and 51%, respectively). The similarity between the results of these techniques was expected due to their similar nature. We conjecture PixMap and WindowMap visualised change in such a way that the participant could use his peripheral vision to only react to changes that warranted his attention.

Our analysis of the subjective data suggests the participant had difficulty estimating his frequency of display switching.

According to the end-of-day questionnaires, the participant believed he was intensely switching displays during the day. His median rating on a seven-point Likert-type scale ("How often did you switch displays today? 1 = not at all, 7 = very often") was 7, and his minimum rating was 5. However, the ESM samples overall median rating for the study was 4 on the same seven point scale. While this still indicates that the participant felt he switched displays at least moderately frequently, the ESM rating is markedly lower. The participant perceived the display switches that happened during the work day as being more frequent at the end of the work day compared to the ESM samples taken throughout the day. Further, while the participant reported a high rate of display switching at the end of each day, based on the ESM samples he was subjectively display switching less often when the subtle visualisation techniques were deployed.

The high number of display switches shown in Figure 8 might be related to distractions caused by applications on the peripheral displays. The participant repeatedly noted that he was often distracted by pop-up notifications and other animated content on the first day of the study (the day none of the subtle visualisation techniques were used). On the other hand, the participant did praise every tested technique for their distraction-reducing qualities, be it through desaturation, decrease in contrast/dimming, or by only highlighting areas of the screen where a change was happening. This subjective data corroborates the measured frequency of display switching collected from our system logs (Figure 8).

Tasks and Display Switching

As part of our ESM sampling, we collected information about the primary task the user was performing at the time the sample was taken. This gave us coarse-grained information about the temporal distribution of the tasks during the study. Each task (or application use) specified by the participant was classified into a broader task category (see Table 1 for a list of task categories). Most of the task categories are self-explanatory. *Academic Reading* encompasses reading academic papers in PDF format and searching for papers online. *Internet Browsing* includes all other activities that use the browser, most often reading blogs and using social media.

Since the ESM samples were administered at approximately 30 minute intervals, the system logs with display switching data were divided into 15 minute segments. The timestamp of each ESM sample was used as a centre of the period during which the specified task was performed. This allowed us to estimate the time spent on each of the specified primary tasks and relate it to the number of display switches. Aside from the coarse estimation, a further limitation of this data is that we have little information about the secondary tasks performed. From the ESM samples and the observations of the study administrator, we are aware that the secondary tasks most often included a combination of internet browsing and social media use, instant messaging, media playback and server management through a terminal application.

Due to the unrestricted use of the computers, not all tasks were performed every day. We have therefore aggregated the data for all techniques together. While this does not allow for fine grained comparisons between techniques, it does allow us to see if there is a general trend towards distraction reduction for specific tasks (as all the subtle techniques should reduce distractions to some extent) and to compare different tasks with regards to the amount of display switching.

Task	Switches		Time [mins]	
	total	per min	active	total
Academic Reading	1035	2.43	425.42	540
Technical Reading	94	2.35	40.05	45
Graphical Editing	1207	3.33	362.72	450
Text Editing	583	2.45	237.52	315
Internet Browsing	200	3.07	65.08	105
Instant Messaging	308	5.13	60.08	105
Email	52	4.08	12.73	30
Other	133	3.19	41.72	45

Table 1. Display switches for specific tasks while the subtle visualisation techniques were running.

Table 1 shows the frequency of display switching for all the primary tasks performed during the four days the subtle techniques were used (as that is the larger, more diverse dataset). Apart from the total number of switches for a particular task, the table also shows the mean number of switches per minute of active computer use. In addition, the table shows the estimated total duration of each task over the four days, as well as the active computer usage time. The tasks with the highest mean number of switches per minute are the tasks which either tend to be multi-display (e.g. *Graphical Editing* with source information on one display and generated graphics on another) or tend to be of low importance, or glance-able (e.g. *Instant Messaging* and *Internet Browsing*). The high mean number of switches for email may be due to the short overall amount of time spent on the task and thus the result may not be very representative.

Task	Switches [per min]		Change
	Control	Techniques	
Graphical Editing	4.30	3.33	-22.62%
Text Editing	5.65	2.45	-56.56%
Instant Messaging	5.31	5.13	-3.40%

Table 2. The effect of subtle visualisation techniques on specific tasks.

Table 2 shows a comparison of three tasks that were performed both during the control day and the four days with subtle techniques. The table reveals the mean number of switches per minute for the two datasets. The subtle techniques decreased the number of display switches in all cases. In the case of *Instant Messaging* the change was small (3.4% decrease), which is likely due to the glance-able nature of instant messaging. However, for both of the editing tasks, the decrease is much more pronounced. The decrease for *Graphical Editing* is lower (22.62%) than for *Text Editing* (56.56%). This is probably because *Graphical Editing* is more expensive in terms of display space and thus is more likely to be used as a multi-display task, therefore requiring more frequent switches between displays. In either case, we can conclude that, especially for editing tasks, the subtle techniques successfully reduced the frequency of display switching.

Qualitative Analysis

In addition to investigating display utilisation and display switching, we interviewed the participant about the perceived usefulness of the techniques.

The first technique the participant used was WindowMap. Our observations indicate that the technique helped reduce distractions and allowed the participant to better focus on his primary task. For example, the participant stated that *"Dimming peripheral screens makes it easier to focus on [the main screen]."*

However, the timing design of WindowMap confused the participant. WindowMap was set up so the visualised changes would decay after approximately 20 to 30 seconds if no other changes occurred. This seems to have led to a situation, where the participant was noticing a change but was unsure about the timing of when the change occurred and whether or not it was continuous. However, we noticed a possible reduction in cognitive load when the participant processed events from the peripheral displays. For example, the participant stated that *"while waiting for a window to finish processing something, I was able to note the state change in my peripheral vision, which was more useful than randomly glancing over to check if it was done."* The participant ranked this subtle visualisation technique third in terms of perceived usefulness.

The second technique the participant used was FreezeFrame. FreezeFrame is a technique for re-establishing prior context before and after a display switch. FreezeFrame requires full visual focus and does not rely on users being able to notice changes in their peripheral vision. Our qualitative data indicates that this behavioural design of FreezeFrame helped the participant monitor longer-term changes more effectively: *"I find it very useful for more passive applications such as twitter. When glancing over, I have an immediate sense of what tweets are new, without being constantly distracted."* However, the fact that it required the participant's full visual focus meant that checking peripheral, yet time-sensitive applications, such as an instant messaging conversations created more of a distraction: *"I've found it useful to be able to glance at contact lists to see who's come online recently, because the change in the list is so easy to perceive, without distracting me while working."* Finally, while the participant felt the time-to-fade was too long, it was still considered the second most useful technique.

The third technique the participant used was PixMap. As previously noted, PixMap is similar to WindowMap in that it visualises changes over time. However, while WindowMap visualises display changes over time on the application-window level, PixMap visualises display changes over time on the pixel level. The participant perceived PixMap as more useful than WindowMap because it provided him with more fine-grained information, while also being more subtle. The participant reported that PixMap was particularly useful for applications that only resulted in smaller display changes, such as list updates: *"The 'trail' effect is particularly useful for gauging how lists have changed, such as on twitter - giving a glanceable way of telling how many new tweets there are."*

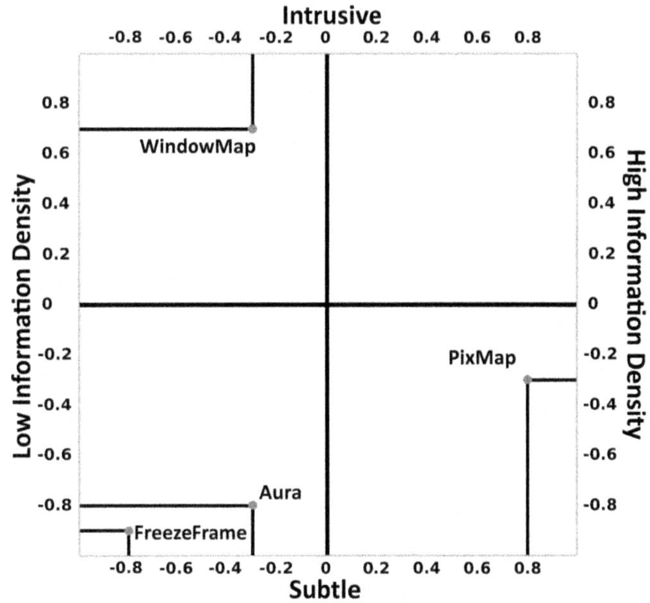

Figure 9. Mapping of all the techniques based on their perceived subtlety/intrusiveness (y-axis) and information density (x-axis).

The participant ranked PixMap as the most useful of all the subtle visualisation techniques.

The last subtle visualisation technique the participant tested was Aura. The participant felt it was useful for reducing distractions: *"Not distracting - keeps me focused!"*. Aura was perceived as very subtle, sometimes too subtle. In part this was because the visibility of the visual "pulses" that visualised the amount of change in the window at each of the past time steps depended on the background colour of the application. Since high activity was visualised as a white colour, this meant that when the background was white, it became difficult to perceive the change: *"I'm aware of change in some apps more than others. For example, one screen has two apps with dark colour schemes so the 'pulse' effect is more pronounced, whereas with apps with white backgrounds, I often miss any subtle change."* The participant ranked Aura as the least useful subtle visualisation technique.

Subtlety and Information Density

Figure 9 shows the participant's subjective mapping of the techniques in terms of their subtlety or intrusiveness and information density. Information density is a measure of the compactness of a particular technique in terms of the amount of useful information the technique displays. We noted that the ordering on the subtlety axis closely corresponds to the ranking of perceived subtlety reported by the participant in the daily questionnaires.

There was a separate question in the questionnaires about perceived contribution to increased productivity. Its ranking was exactly the same as for perceived usefulness. Since periphery-enhancing information is seen as one of the indicators of calm technologies [23], we expected the perceived usefulness of a technique to correspond with its perceived information density. However, this was not the case as the ranking of perceived usefulness was No Technique < Aura < WindowMap < FreezeFrame < PixMap, while for information density it was No Technique < FreezeFrame < Aura = WindowMap < PixMap. This means that while FreezeFrame was ranked low on information density, it was perceived as very useful.

LIMITATIONS AND FUTURE WORK

One limitation with our work is the way the system detects users' visual focus on a particular display. Our computer vision methods are dependent on inter-device angular difference. Since our system relies on a minimum angular difference between displays for accurate visual focus detection, users' multi-display environments may need to be modified to accommodate this. This can be done by either changing the size of displays, or their distance from the user.

Another limitation is that we rely on a five-day case study when we evaluate the implications and limitations of the four subtle visualisation techniques. Our choice to rely on a qualitative in-depth case study involving a single participant is unusual, and perhaps somewhat controversial. Studying a single participant limits our ability to make statistical inferences about the performance of subtle visualisation techniques for the general user population. However, in terms of the amount of data we collected, our 39.25 hours of data is approximately 2–3 times as much as what we would have collected if we carried out a traditional one-hour within-subjects controlled experiment with 16 participants. More importantly, it is very difficult to design a meaningful controlled experiment to evaluate the efficacy of subtle visualisation techniques. Unlike many other intelligent user interfaces, such as adaptive user interfaces and pointing amplification techniques, subtle visualisation techniques lack meaningful measures that can be collected within a relatively short amount of time. Further, lab-based studies de-contextualise the interaction techniques. For many intelligent interaction interfaces, this may not be a major issue. However, our subtle visualisation techniques are designed to be non-intrusive in users' regular working environments. There is therefore a substantial risk that de-contextualising the working environment in a laboratory study would have provided us with misleading results. In contrast, ESM enabled us to get a nuanced understanding of how our working professional perceived subtle visualisation techniques in a multi-display environment while carrying out his regular work.

Our work suggests that while our evaluation method works, it is also expensive. Therefore, a fruitful avenue for future work would be to develop alternative, more cost-effective, ways of evaluating subtle visualisation and interaction techniques. One possible direction is the design and evaluation model suggested by McCrickard et al. [15]. Although this model concentrates on notification systems, it could perhaps be broadened and adapted for use as a benchmark for evaluating subtle interaction techniques.

CONCLUSIONS

This paper explored subtle gaze-dependent techniques for visualising display changes in multi-display environments. We presented four subtle gaze-dependent techniques for visualising changes in unattended displays: FreezeFrame, PixMap, WindowMap and Aura.

To enable the visualisation techniques to be directly deployed to workstations, we also presented a system that automatically identifies the user's eyes using computer vision and a set of web cameras mounted on the displays. Our evaluation confirmed this system can accurately detect which display the user is attending to.

We studied the efficacy of the visualisation techniques in a longitudinal case study with a working professional. This participant used our system eight hours per day for five consecutive days. The results of the study showed that the techniques were successful in highlighting visual change, and in reducing distractions and the frequency of display switches for the participant. Further, three of the four techniques did so in a non-intrusive and subtle manner.

We also noted some challenges when evaluating subtle intelligent interaction techniques that require deployment in actual working contexts in order to generate meaningful data. In our study we used a combination of questionnaires, ESM sampling, observations and automatic logging. Our methodology proved successful for our case study, but it is also prohibitively expensive for a large-scale study. Our work points to potential avenues for overcoming these limitations through the use of an alternative evaluation methodology.

Our case study suggests that subtle visualisation techniques can indeed positively change the display attendance behaviour of a working professional who used these techniques as part of his regular work activities. However, many opportunities still exist for taking the technology further, both in terms of further refining the techniques, and in terms of identifying cost-effective means of evaluating the efficacy of such techniques. The subtle display of visual change information from unattended displays can alter our interactions and expectations of interfaces. Out of sight no longer means out of mind, when inattention is no longer an inherent cost but a new research and development opportunity.

ACKNOWLEDGEMENTS

This work was supported by the Engineering and Physical Sciences Research Council (grant number EP/H027408/1) and the Scottish Informatics and Computer Science Alliance.

REFERENCES

1. Ashdown, M., and Sato, Y. Attentive Interfaces for Multiple Monitors. In *CHI 2005 Workshop on Distributed Display Environments*, 4–5.

2. Baudisch, P., Good, N., Bellotti, V., and Schraedley, P. Keeping Things in Context: A Comparative Evaluation of Focus Plus Context Screens, Overviews, and Zooming. In *Proc. CHI 2002*, 259–266.

3. Beck, M. R., Levin, D. T., and Angelone, B. Change Blindness Blindness: Beliefs about the Roles of Intention and Scene Complexity in Change Detection. *Consciousness and cognition 16*, 1 (2007), 31–51.

4. Bi, X., and Balakrishnan, R. Comparing Usage of a Large High-Resolution Display to Single or Dual Desktop Displays for Daily Work. In *Proc. CHI 2009*, 1005–1014.
5. Castrillón-Santana, M., Déniz-Suárez, O., Antón-Canalís, L., and Navarro-Lorenzo, J. Face and Facial Feature Detection Evaluation: Performance Evaluation of Public Domain Haar Detectors for Face and Facial Feature Detection. In *Proc. VISAPP 2008*, 167–172.
6. Consolvo, S., and Walker, M. Using the Experience Sampling Method to Evaluate Ubicomp Applications. *IEEE Pervasive Computing 2*, 2 (2003), 24–31.
7. Czerwinski, M., Smith, G., Regan, T., Meyers, B., and Starkweather, G. Toward Characterizing the Productivity Benefits of Very Large Displays. In *Proc. INTERACT 2003*, 9–16.
8. DiVita, J., Obermayer, R., Nugent, W., and Linville, J. M. Verification of the Change Blindness Phenomenon While Managing Critical Events on a Combat Information Display. *Human Factors 46*, 2 (2004), 205–218.
9. Dostal, J., Kristensson, P. O., and Quigley, A. Estimating and Using Absolute and Relative Viewing Distance in Interactive Systems. *Pervasive and Mobile Computing* (2012). doi:10.1016/j.pmcj.2012.06.009
10. Grandjean, E., Hünting, W., and Nishiyama, K. Preferred VDT Workstation Settings, Body Posture and Physical Impairments. *Journal of Human Ergology 15*, 2 (1984), 99–104.
11. Greenberg, S., and Buxton, B. Usability Evaluation Considered Harmful (Some of the Time). In *Proc. CHI 2008*, 111–120.
12. Grudin, J. Partitioning Digital Worlds: Focal and Peripheral Awareness in Multiple Monitor Use. In *Proc. CHI 2001*, 458–465.
13. Intille, S. S. Change Blind Information Display for Ubiquitous Computing Environments. In *Proc. UbiComp 2002*, 1–16.
14. Kern, D., Keynes, M., and Schmidt, A. Gazemarks - Gaze-Based Visual Placeholders to Ease Attention Switching. In *Proc. CHI 2010*, 2093–2102.
15. McCrickard, D. S., Chewar, C. M., Somervell, J. P., and Ndiwalana, A. A Model for Notification Systems Evaluation - Assessing User Goals for Multitasking Activity. *ACM Transactions on Computer-Human Interaction 10*, 4 (2003), 312–338.
16. Olsen, D. R. J. Evaluating User Interface Systems Research. In *Proc. UIST 2007*, 251–258.
17. Shneiderman, B., and Benderson, B. B. Maintaining Concentration to Achieve Task Completion. In *Proc. DUX 2005*, 2–7.
18. Simmons, T. What's the Optimum Computer Display Size? *Ergonomics in Design 9*, 4 (2001), 19–25.
19. Su, R. E., and Bailey, B. P. Put Them Where? Towards Guidelines for Positioning Large Displays in Interactive Workspaces. In *Proc. INTERACT 2005*, 337–349.
20. Vertegaal, R., Dickie, C., Sohn, C., and Flickner, M. Designing Attentive Cell Phones Using Wearable EyeContact Sensors. In *CHI Extended Abstracts 2002*, 646–647.
21. Vertegaal, R., Shell, J. S., Chen, D., and Mamuji, A. Designing for Augmented Attention: Towards a Framework for Attentive User Interfaces. *Computers in Human Behavior 22*, 4 (2006), 771–789.
22. Viola, P., and Jones, M. J. Robust Real-Time Face Detection. *International Journal of Computer Vision 57*, 2 (2004), 137–154.
23. Weiser, M., and Brown, J. S. Designing Calm Technology. *World Wide Web Internet And Web Information Systems 1*, 1 (1995), 1–5.

Towards Cooperative Brain-Computer Interfaces for Space Navigation

Riccardo Poli
School of Computer Science and Electronic Engineering, University of Essex, UK
rpoli@essex.ac.uk

Caterina Cinel
School of Computer Science and Electronic Engineering, University of Essex, UK
ccinel@essex.ac.uk

Ana Matran-Fernandez
School of Computer Science and Electronic Engineering, University of Essex, UK
amatra@essex.ac.uk

Francisco Sepulveda
School of Computer Science and Electronic Engineering, University of Essex, UK
fsepulv@essex.ac.uk

Adrian Stoica
NASA Jet Propulsion Laboratory
California Institute of Technology
Adrian.Stoicajpl.nasa.gov

ABSTRACT

We explored the possibility of controlling a spacecraft simulator using an analogue Brain-Computer Interface (BCI) for 2-D pointer control. This is a difficult task, for which no previous attempt has been reported in the literature. Our system relies on an active display which produces event-related potentials (ERPs) in the user's brain. These are analysed in real-time to produce control vectors for the user interface. In tests, users of the simulator were told to pass as close as possible to the Sun. Performance was very promising, on average users managing to satisfy the simulation success criterion in 67.5% of the runs. Furthermore, to study the potential of a collaborative approach to spacecraft navigation, we developed BCIs where the system is controlled via the integration of the ERPs of two users. Performance analysis indicates that collaborative BCIs produce trajectories that are statistically significantly superior to those obtained by single users.

Author Keywords

Brain-Computer Interfaces; Space Applications; Cooperative Control; Pointer Control

ACM Classification Keywords

H.5.m. Information Interfaces and Presentation (e.g. HCI): Miscellaneous

INTRODUCTION

The work presented in this paper is the result of integrating recent techniques from single-user brain-computer interfaces as well as novel cooperative forms of these and applying them to a spacecraft navigation control task. We will review key literature in these domains in the following subsections.

Brain-Computer Interfaces

Brain-Computer Interfaces (BCIs) convert signals generated from the brain into control commands for various applications in different areas, like virtual reality and hands-free control of augmentative communication technologies [40, 1, 29]. BCI studies have shown that non-muscular communication and device control are possible and might serve useful purposes for people who cannot use conventional technologies, for example, because they are "locked-in" or lack sufficiently useful muscle control [5, 32]. Naturally, BCI systems can also be used by able-bodied users although, at the moment, they are not fast and reliable enough to replace other forms of control.

The signals used in BCI studies to date include P300 waves [13] and other ERPs [42], evoked potentials (EPs) [24], event-related desynchronization/synchronization (ERD/ERS) [25], activation patterns induced by mental task strategies [10], slow cortical potentials [4] recorded from the scalp, cortical neuron activity recorded by implanted electrodes (see [31] for a review), neuromagnetic signals recorded through megnetoencelography (MEG) [16], BOLD responses recorded through functional magnetic resonance imaging (fMRI) [38], activity-related, and localised brain oxygenation recorded through near infrared systems (NIRS) [9].

BCI for Pointer and Robot Control

Most of the approaches listed above concentrate on building BCI spellers. However, over the years, researchers have also targeted another area of BCI, often called Brain Machine Interfaces (BMIs) (see [19] for a review of BMI), which focuses on the *control* of physical systems, such as prosthetic devices, small wheeled robots [23] and autonomous wheelchairs [15]. Attempts have also been made at controlling humanoid robots, in which hybrid architectures integrate human-brain commands with elements of autonomous behaviour pre-implemented in the robot [2, 14]. However, those attempts have met limited success due to the intrinsic difficulty and unreliability of the classification process that transforms the brain signals into symbolic commands for a robot, a vehicle or a prosthesis.

There have also been attempts to develop BCI systems for the control of 2-D mouse pointers. Until recently, the most successful systems for this purpose had been those based on the detection of μ or β rhythms [41], those using invasive cortical interfaces (e.g., [11]) and those based on steady-state visually evoked potentials (SSVEP) [35, 39]. However, BCIs using basic rhythms require lengthy training periods before users can control them; invasive BCIs are not very practical, requiring surgery, presenting risks of infections, etc.; and SSVEP-based BCIs require gaze control.

To overcome some of the above limitations, BCIs for pointer control have been developed based on ERPs. ERPs are relatively well defined shape-wise variations of the ongoing EEG which are elicited by a stimulus and are temporally linked to it [20]. ERPs are rather appealing since, at least in principle, they offer a relatively high bit-rate, require no user training and can be recorded non-invasively. Focus has mainly been on the P300. This is a late appearing positive ERP with a latency of about 300 ms which is elicited by rare and/or significant stimuli. This makes it possible to use it in BCI systems to determine user intentions and commands.

Early work based on the P300 ERP include the system in [3], where rather long inter-stimulus intervals led to the pointer moving at the rate of one movement every 10 seconds, and the system in [28], where a speed of one cursor movement every 4 seconds was achieved but accuracy in detecting P300s was only about 50%. Recently, however, performance of P300-based BCIs for pointer control has started improving. We presented a more responsive P300-based mouse in [7]. However, while offline results were reasonably good, preliminary online tests and further offline analysis showed that the mouse pointer was hard to control. We later improved this system in [30], where a significantly more responsive and robust controller was obtained thanks to a change in the stimuli used to generate P300s. These two systems present one unique feature: they completely dispense with the problem of detecting P300s (a notoriously difficult task) by logically behaving as an analogue device (as opposed to a binary classifier). Also, they use a single trial approach where the mouse performs an action after every trial (once per second in [7] and once every 100 ms in [30]).

BCIs in the Space Domain

Over the last few years there has been some interest in understanding the possibilities offered by BCI technology in space applications. BCI robotic devices, surface rovers and semi-automatic manipulators are certainly the most relevant fields of application [6, 21, 22]. No such system has actually been built, but several researchers and both NASA and the European Space Agency have considered the potential advantages and limitations of BCIs in space. The results of the analyses have been mixed.

The potential advantages of BCIs for space applications include sending commands with minimum delays and high accuracy, astronauts collaborating in the control of machines such as robots and rovers [22], gaining machine control in conditions of restricted mobility and hands-free direct control of cabin instrumentation and equipment. However, as recently pointed out in [8], there are also factors that could limit the efficacy of EEG-based BCIs in a space environment. These include sensory and motor adaptation, microgravity, psychological stress, poor sleep and vestibular disturbances. Also, current information transfer rates and accuracy of BCIs are still too low for BCIs to be of real benefit for space applications.

While we do agree that the many potential benefits of BCI technologies are currently limited by the low communication bandwidth, recent advances in neuroscience and collaborative BCIs show that BCIs can be improved to an extent that they might become suitable for applications in the space domain.

Collaborative BCI

Recent studies on collaborative BCI seem to suggest that combining brain activity of several users involved in the same decision-making activity might give an advantage compared to decisions made with individual BCIs. In particular, Wang and collaborators [37] have compared the performance of single-user and collaborative (offline) BCIs in a task of movement planning. They proposed a system in which individual BCI subsystems solve the classification task independently and then a classifier integrates individual results. In experiments, through directly extracting information from the posterior parietal cortex and bypassing the motor related procedures, the BCI system could accelerate the motor response (via an artificial limb). The results show that there can be an advantage on the overall performance, compared to single user performance, when the brain activity of a group of individuals is integrated, the larger the group the better the overall performance (groups of up to 20 people were tested). Similarly [43] has proposed an online collaborative BCI that, using visual evoked potentials (VEP), can accelerate human response to visual stimuli.

We explored a collaborative form of BCI in [26] in an experiment where observers performed a simple visual matching task involving the rapid sequential presentation of pairs of visual patterns and had to decide whether the two patterns in a pair were the same. Visual stimuli were presented for insufficient time for the observers to be certain as to the decision. A composite feature was then developed, which optimally combined behavioural and neural measures in order to predict incorrect decisions. For group decisions, the use of a majority rule and three further decision rules were tested, which weigh the decisions of each observer based on their reaction times and the neural features. Results indicated that the integration of behavioural responses and neural features can significantly improve accuracy when compared with individual performances. Also, within groups of a particular size, the use of decision rules based on such features outperformed the majority rule.

Overall, studies of cognitive neurophysiology and collaborative BCI, such as those described above, seem to suggest that collaborative BCI can potentially provide significant improvements both in accuracy and speed with respect to conventional BCI systems. This seems also due to the fact that information on one's decision can be detected from the neural activity before a conscious decision is made and an overt response is given by an individual (see for example [36, 33]). Collaborative decisions based on neural activities seem to benefit particularly from this, as shown for example in [12], where sensory-related neural activity could predict collective decisions on a discrimination task as early as 200 ms after stimulus presentation and before an overt response was given, and in [37], as described above.

Multi-brain signal aggregation not only can facilitate rapid analysis of the environment and decision making, but can also assess characteristics such as group emotions, as shown in [34] where an experiment was described in which a group's emotional index was obtained by aggregating EEG and electromyographic signals from two individuals who were observing emotion-triggering images.

Contributions of this Article

In this paper we report on the application of a version of the analogue BCI system for 2–D pointer control we developed in [30] to a simulated spacecraft control task and we study the potential benefits of its extension to a collaborative multi-user BCI system.

In particular, we have coupled our pointer-control system [30] with a customised version of the Space Commander spacecraft simulator [18], where we modified both its galaxy and its controls to make it possible to control the simulator via pointer movements and to present less cluttered and simpler test conditions.

Although the *potential* applications of BCI to the space domain have previously been discussed in the literature (for example [8, 22]), at present there are no published reports of *actual* BCI applications in this domain. Our system, therefore, represents the first attempt at using a BCI to control a spacecraft simulator (although, admittedly in a highly simplified environment and with short simulations).

In the present study, we also investigated the possibility of two users jointly controlling the spacecraft via a collaborative BCI as a means of making the task less tiring and of increasing the speed and accuracy of the control. As indicated above, this is largely uncharted territory as only very recently the first ideas on cooperative BCIs have appeared in the literature [43, 37, 12, 26].

METHODS

Our BCI for the control of a space navigation simulator comprises two systems: the simulator itself (suitably adapted to satisfy the requirements of a BCI) and a BCI that converts brain activity into 2–D mouse-pointer movements, which are used for navigation control. Before the simulator could be used, the BCI had to be trained to recognise the ERPs of each user (as is normally required in BCI). Experimental sessions, therefore, consisted of a first part where suitable training (and test) data were collected and used to train the BCI, followed by a second part where the trained BCI was used to control the space simulator itself.

The following sections provide details of the BCI used, the collection of training and test data, the adaptations we made to the Space Commander simulator, and the methods we used to combine the ERPs from two users for joint pointer control.

BCI Pointer Movement

The BCI mouse we developed in [30] and have adopted here has a large pointer made up of eight circles arranged around an imaginary circle as shown in Figure 1(a). The circles are normally grey, but they flash in a periodic clockwise order, a flash of a circle consisting of a momentary change in colour, to either green or red (randomly selected). Each of the eight circles represents a direction. Flashes lasts for 100 ms with no delay in between flashes so that a full revolution is completed in 800 ms. When users want to move the pointer towards a specific direction, they focus their attention on the circle representing that direction (we call this a *target*) and try to mentally identify the colour of that circle every time it flashes, while attempting to ignore the other circles (*non-targets*). As a consequence of focusing attention on a target and identifying its colour, a P300 will be elicited in the user's brain when the target flashes, but not when non-targets flash (some non-targets might elicit a P300, but of a smaller amplitude than targets). It is precisely this effect that allows the BCI to control the mouse pointer.

In the system, ERPs are represented by a segment of 800 ms of EEG data called an *epoch*. Epochs start when each circle is flashed. Epochs of consecutive flashes, therefore, overlap.[1] Each epoch is passed to an ensemble of two hard-margin linear support vector machines (SVMs). These must be trained for each specific subject (as is traditional in BCI) to guarantee satisfactory performance. However, gathering a training set and training the SVMs takes only a few minutes. The training set is formed by epoch/desired-output pairs. Desired outputs are $+1$ for the epochs starting on the flash of a target (i.e., a circle pointing in the prescribed direction of movement), and -1 for the non-targets.

As in [30], after training, the SVMs' raw output was used as a score for ERPs: the higher the output, the more likely an ERP was generated by a target stimulus. The SVMs' score for each ERP was then turned into a vector pointing in the direction of the stimulus and with a length proportional to the score. To produce smoother trajectories, these micro-movements were integrated together using the following analogue integration strategy:

$$\Delta x = \sum_{\phi} (\text{most recent score in direction } \phi) \times \sin\phi$$

$$\Delta y = \sum_{\phi} (\text{most recent score in direction } \phi) \times \cos\phi$$

where $\phi \in \{0, \frac{\pi}{4}, \frac{\pi}{2}, \frac{3}{4}\pi, \pi, \frac{5}{4}\pi, \frac{3}{2}\pi, \frac{7}{4}\pi\}$.

Furthermore, to counteract the issues associated with eye-blinks and other muscular artifacts (which can generate sudden large movements of the pointer that users are then forced

[1] Naturally, this makes recognising P300s in the noisy EEG data much harder, but, overall, the resulting fast pace of stimulation allows higher information transfer rates.

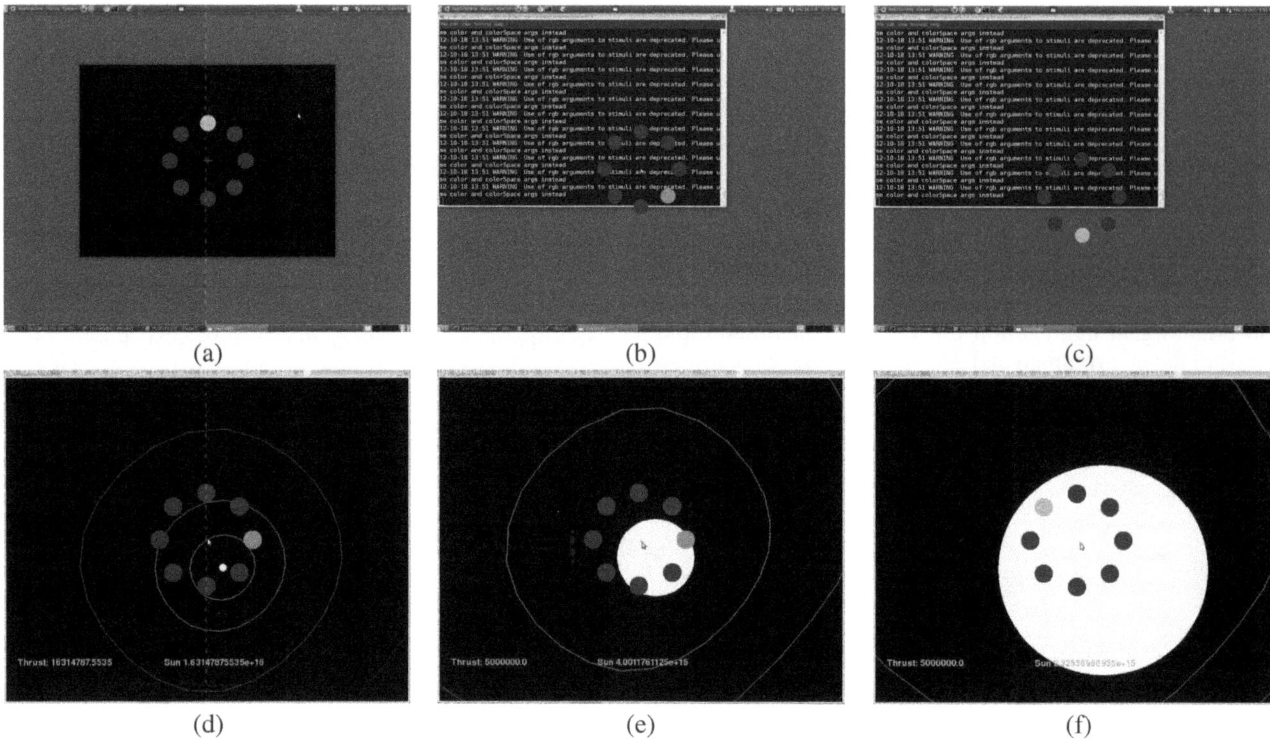

Figure 1. Different modes of operation of the system: (a) offline collection of training data with a static pointer on a black background, (b)–(c) two snapshots of the online collection of training data (and also of an independent test set) where the pointer moves and the background is the standard desktop of the Ubuntu operating system, and (d)–(e) three snapshots of the modified Space Commander simulator being controlled by our BCI.

to laboriously correct) we also implemented the additional post-processing strategy we evolved in [27].

Training and Test Sets

We gathered data from 3 participants. Participants were seated comfortably at approximately 80 cm from an LCD screen. Data were collected from 64 electrode sites using a BioSemi ActiveTwo EEG system. The EEG channels were referenced to the mean of the electrodes placed on either ear-lobe. The data were initially sampled at 2048 samples per second. We then band-pass filtered the data between 0.15 Hz and 30 Hz, and sub-sampled it to 32 samples per second. As indicated above, following each flash, an 800 ms epoch of the signal in each channel was extracted. At a 32 Hz sampling frequency, epochs contained 26 data points per channel. Thus, each epoch was described by a feature vector of $26 \times 64 = 1,664$ elements.

The training phase of each experiment was divided into three phases, Phase 1, 2 and 3, each including 8 short sessions with each session lasting approximately 25 seconds. All of the data acquired in one session were associated with the same target direction. Each participant carried out a total of 24 sessions, resulting in each of the 8 possible directions being the target direction for three sessions.

In Phase 1, comprising the first 8 sessions of the experiment, each session started with a blank screen and after 2 seconds the eight circles appeared near the centre of the screen. A red arrow then appeared for 1 second pointing to the target (representing the direction for that epoch). As previously indicated, subjects were instructed to mentally name the colour of the flashes for that target. After 2 seconds the flashing of the stimuli started. This stopped after a random number of trials, from 20 to 24, with a trial consisting of the sequential activation of each of the 8 circles. In other words, each session involved between $20 \times 8 = 160$ and $24 \times 8 = 192$ flashes. During Phase 1, the background remained black (as illustrated in Figure 1(a)), and the circular pointer remained static. The purpose of this first phase was the initial acquisition of a minimalist training set that we could then use to train a first ensemble of SVMs. This would then control the movement of the cursor in Phases 2 and 3, so as to make the conditions in these phases as close as possible to the conditions required in the real-time spacecraft navigation task.

After training the BCI with the approximately 1,400 training examples collected in Phase 1, in Phase 2 subjects performed a second set of 8 sessions. The BCI's active stimuli had the same duration and features as in the previous phase, but the background was not black and the mouse pointer was not static. Instead, as illustrated in Figures 1(b)–(c), we used a real desktop environment (as provided by the Ubuntu Linux operating system) and the pointer movement was controlled in real-time by the SVMs trained with the data collected in Phase 1. All filtering, classification and post-processing operations had to be performed within 100 ms.

In Phase 3 we acquired further data via a third set of 8 sessions. These were in exactly the same conditions as in Phase 2. However, we distinguish this phase from the previous one, because its data have been used for two different purposes in this study.

Firstly, the data were pooled with the data acquired in Phase 2 and used to retrain the BCI's SVMs on a larger and more realistic dataset before the system was used for the online spacecraft navigation task. We discarded the data from Phase 1 since these data had been acquired in slightly different conditions than those adopted in the real use of the system.

Secondly, the data from Phase 3 were also used as an independent test set for the analysis of the performance of both the single-user and the cooperative BCI. In this case we had to use the data from both Phase 1 and Phase 2 as a training set as we could not discard Phase 1 without incurring significant over-fitting.[2]

Modified Space Commander

After Phase 3, the subjects had a few minutes of rest and we then started their online sessions with our space simulator. We asked subjects to do up to 21 simulator runs. However, since each of these runs lasted 2 to 7 times longer than the sessions in Phases 1–3, we instructed subjects to feel free to stop the experiment when they felt too tired to continue. On average subjects did 17 such runs.

As indicated above, as a space simulator we created and used a customised version of the Space Commander spacecraft simulator (written in Python) [18]. Below we describe the modifications we made to this software for the purpose of our tests.

Firstly, we created a galaxy which only included the Sun. The users' aim was to pass within 0.26 light years from the Sun starting from 10 light-years away from it. So, we modified the code so that it automatically logged trajectories and stopped the simulator as soon as the space craft got within this distance from the Sun. If users failed to hit on the first pass, they had a chance to try to approach it again within a 3-minute simulation limit.

In terms of changes to the default user interface of Space Commander, we disabled all its mouse-button and keyboard controls, disallowed the spacecraft from rolling and directly connected the mouse pointer position to the control of the yaw and pitch of the spacecraft. Furthermore, we made the simulator's screen go black intermittently, to minimise interference with the active stimuli used in the BCI pointer (which remained visible at all times). The duty cycle was such that the galaxy was visible for 800 ms within each 5.6 s period. We also artificially expanded the diameter of the Sun by 5 times and added orbits around it (See Figures 1(d)–(e)) to help users find their way towards the Sun (even if it happened to go off the screen).

In addition, the simulation's initial velocity was randomly selected in such a way that, in the absence of suitable control, the spacecraft would almost always miss the Sun. More specifically, the direction of the initial velocity vectors was in the general direction of the Sun but it was off-course in the vertical and horizontal directions by angular displacements randomly selected in the range $[-5^\circ, +5^\circ]$. The magnitude of the initial velocity vector was 0.634 light-years/second. This very high velocity was needed to keep the simulation time reasonably short. However, in preliminary tests we found that approaching the Sun at such velocity was almost a shock for the subjects, so we introduced a velocity reduction mechanism which progressively slowed the approach speed down. The minimum this was allowed to drop was 0.032 light-years/second (corresponding to the artificial thrust of 5,000,000 units shown in Figures 1(e) and (f)). As a result of this, simulations lasted anywhere between 50 seconds (when the Sun was "hit" at the first pass) and 3 minutes (when time ran out).

[2]We discuss the implications of this in the "Results" section.

Cooperative BCI

In order to test the potential benefits and drawbacks of a cooperative BCI approach to the problem of space navigation, we created two methods for combining the ERPs of pairs of users. Our objective was to understand which method provided better performance and to see whether any of these would be superior to single-subject pointer control.

Both methods use exactly the same filtering and signal manipulation techniques of the BCI for 2–D pointer control for single users described previously. Also, both of them rely on the subjects having been exposed to exactly the same stimuli in exactly the same order in all the sessions of the three phases of collection of training and test data, which we ensure in our experiments. Timing information was also recorded in our EEG data files so that the ERPs from two subjects could be synchronised with sub-millisecond accuracy. In this way we were in a position to simulate exactly the conditions of two subjects performing our experiments together.

The first method combines the *input signals* to the BCI by averaging the ERPs from each subject before they are passed to a single ensemble of SVMs. This method presents the advantage of reducing the stochastic noise which always hampers the trial-by-trial recognition of target ERPs in EEG data by a factor $\frac{1}{\sqrt{2}}$ (i.e., by approximately 30%). However, there is always a significant variability in the shape and delay of ERPs in different subjects and averaging their ERPs may introduce significant distortions, which may in turn make their classification harder.

The second method combines the *outputs* of the single-user version of the BCI for the two subjects and averages the pointer movement vectors before they are executed. An advantage of this method is that the ERPs from each subject are processed by a ensemble of SVMs which was specifically trained on the data from that subject. This normally results in better classification accuracy (and this is why per-subject training is ubiquitous in BCI). Also, since the output vectors are noisy (due to the noise and variability in ERPs), averaging the vectors produced by two subjects produces a noise reduction (of the same magnitude as that of the first method), that is likely to result in better trajectories. However, we do not benefit from any reduction of the noise in input to the BCI, while the first method does.

RESULTS

Single-User Control of Pointer Movement

Let us start with the analysis of the performance of the BCI for pointer movement (on its own) when a single user controls it (we will test it in the Space Commander control task in the following section). This is important as in our previous work [30] all tests were performed with offline data and static displays (such as the one in Figure 1(a)), while here we are attempting to achieve online control (as in Figures 1(b)–(f)).

As we explained above, in these tests we used the data from Phase 1 and 2 as a training set and the data from Phase 3 as an independent test set. The data from Phase 1 were acquired in slightly different conditions than the other data (static vs dynamic pointer and black vs ordinary-desktop background). However, as we mentioned before, we had to use the data from both Phase 1 and Phase 2 as a training set as we could not discard the data from Phase 1 without incurring significant over-fitting.[3] Because of this misalignment between training and test set, the test-set results reported in this subsection and in the last subsection of this section are actually *lower bounds* on performance.

There are a number of ways of evaluating performance of the BCI controller of pointer movements. We adopted three: *AUCs*, *normalised path lengths* and *absolute angle deviations*. These are described in the remainder of this section.

We used the *Area Under the Curve* (AUC) of the Receiver Operating Characteristic (ROC) to assess the performance of the machine learning component of the system — an ensemble of two SVMs. The AUC is a well known summary for ROC curves that has been used widely in machine learning. It essentially characterises the behaviour of a classifier from the point of view of the trade off between producing false alarms and missing targets. A perfect classifier is one that never produces false alarms and never misses any targets. Such a classifier would have an AUC score of 1. A (useless) random classifier, on the other hand, would have an AUC of 0.5. So, the closer the AUC to 1, the better a classifier. In our work, AUCs were calculated using the efficient method proposed in [17].

The normalised path lengths and absolute angle deviations were introduced to evaluate the performance of the whole system. This requires an analysis of the trajectories produced by adding together the displacement vectors produced by system after the integration and post-processing phases. The *normalised path length* indicates how straight a trajectory is. This can be assessed by looking at how different a trajectory is from the line segment connecting its extremes. As indicated in Figure 2, this difference can be measured by simply comparing the path length of the trajectory (denoted as l in the figure) with the segment's length (d in the figure). The normalised path length is defined as the ratio between the two. The closer the normalised path length to 1 the better.

[3]We did considered the option of asking our subjects to acquire more training data, but we eventually discarded it to avoid their under-performing in the Space Commander task due to tiredness. When subjects start becoming tired, their attention levels drop and, as a consequence, their brain signals start changing. These changes include much reduced or even absent P300s where one would normally have robust ones. Also, as subjects become tired they tend to produce more muscular artifacts. So, after about one hour of experimentation (excluding subject preparation, which takes approximately 30 minutes) subjects wear out.

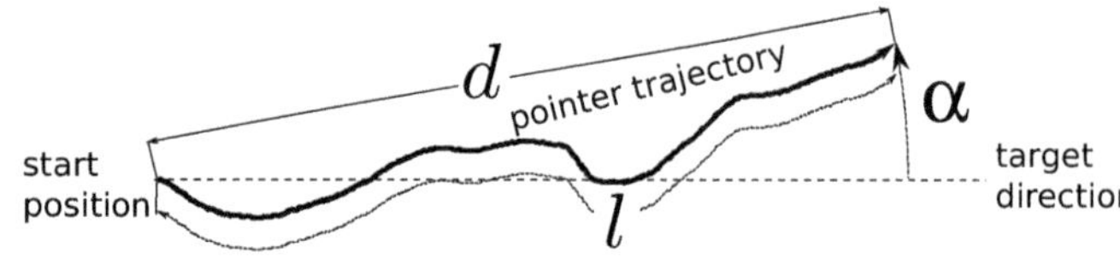

Figure 2. The overall performance of the BCI for pointer movement is evaluated based on the extent to which the pointer trajectory produced (thick line) is straight (the normalised path length, which, in the figure, is equivalent to $\frac{l}{d}$, where l is the length of the trajectory measured by "walking" along it) and by how much it deviates from the ideal direction (the absolute angle deviation, represented by the angle α in the figure).

Table 1. Single subject test-set performance at controlling pointer movement (see text for explanation of the three measures of performance).

Subject	*Absolute angle deviation*	*Normalised path length*	*AUC*
1	3.505	1.249	0.948941
2	6.727	1.275	0.879715
3	4.650	1.388	0.931228

The *absolute angle deviation*, instead, indicates how well a trajectory points towards the target direction. This can be assessed by measuring the angle between the line segment that we used to evaluate the straightness of the trajectory and the axis denoting the target direction (α in the Figure 2). Since it is not important whether the angle is positive or negative, we take its absolute value to represent performance, resulting in an absolute angle deviation. We measure this in degrees.

Table 1 reports the values of AUC score, normalised path length and absolute angle deviation on a subject by subject basis for the test data gathered in Phase 3. Normalised path lengths and absolute angle deviations were evaluated on the full trajectory produced by concatenating (after appropriate rotations) all of the outputs produced by the system for the sessions acquired in Phase 3 (approximately 1,400 movements). The full trajectories are shown in Figure 3.

It is clear from these results that all three subjects were able to control the mouse to a significant degree. Absolute angle deviations were small in all cases, normalised path lengths were reasonably close to 1, and AUC scores were on average above the 90% mark, which indicates very good performance (for BCI standards).[4]

Space Commander Runs

In the tests with Space Commander, we measured the success rate of our subjects (the fraction of runs where they were able to pass near the Sun) and we also studied their passage distances from the Sun.

We compared the results obtained by our subjects when using the system against two alternatives: (a) a static controller

[4]We will perform a deeper statistical analysis of single-user trajectories when we compare them to those obtained with cooperative control in a later section.

Table 2. Comparison of the success rates and mean passage distances from the Sun (in light-years) of the static controller (210 runs), the random-drifter (210 runs) and the controller based on our BCI mouse (51 runs).

Controller type	*Success Rate*	*Passage Distance*
Static	9.5%	0.671549
Random-drifted	6.2%	0.758904
BCI	66.7%	0.387318

that does not steer the spacecraft at all thereby always producing a rectilinear trajectory, and (b) a random-drifter which behaves as if the mouse pointer drifted randomly by a tiny random displacement at every simulation cycle (i.e., every $\frac{1}{60}$ of a second). This displacement was a zero-mean stochastic vector uniformly distributed in $[-1, +1] \times [-1, +1]$ (i.e., typically a sub-pixel amount).

Table 2 shows a comparison of the success rates and mean passage distances from the Sun of the static controller, the random-drifter and the controller based on our BCI mouse. It is clear that in the absence of intelligent control only between about 1 in 16 (for the random-drifter) and 1 in 10 (for the static controller) trajectories actually pass sufficiently near the Sun to trigger the system's stopping criterion. On the contrary on average our subjects were able to satisfy the criterion in 2 out of 3 runs. Mean passage distances confirm this observation with the mean distance for the BCI controlled runs being approximately 51% and 58% less than in the absence of control. Also, when we applied the one-tailed Kolmogorov-Smirnov test for two distributions to the passage distance data, we found that the BCI controlled runs resulted in passage distances which are highly statistically significantly superior to those obtained with both the random-drifter and the static controller (both p values being $< 10^{-17}$).

Cooperative Control of Pointer Movement

Let us now turn our attention to the analysis of the performance of the BCI for pointer movement when two users jointly control it. Cooperative control in such a complex task has never been attempted with a BCI.

As for the single-user analysis, also in these tests we used the data from Phase 1 and 2 as a training set and the data from Phase 3 as an independent test set. Also, as before, the misalignment between training and test set implies that the results reported here are actually *lower bounds* on performance.

We start from reporting our three performance indicators — AUC, normalised path length and absolute angle deviation — for each possible pair of subjects and for the two methods of achieving joint control: averaging the ERPs of the two subjects and passing them to a single ensemble of SVMs, or processing the ERPs of the two subjects independently through two separate ensembles of SVMs and then averaging the output vectors produced by the system.

Tables 3 and 4 show the results of these tests. Again, normalised path lengths and an absolute angle deviations were evaluated on the full trajectory produced by concatenating the outputs produced by the systems for the trials in Phase 3. The

Table 3. Cooperative BCI test-set performance at controlling pointer movement when using the average of ERPs and one ensemble of SVMs.

Subject	*Absolute angle deviation*	*Normalised path length*	*AUC*
1 & 2	4.075	1.264	0.920215
1 & 3	5.853	1.276	0.966195
2 & 3	3.322	1.322	0.938081

Table 4. Cooperative BCI test-set performance at controlling pointer movement when using two separate ensembles of SVMs

Subject	*Absolute angle deviation*	*Normalised path length*	*AUC*
1 & 2	2.376	1.127	0.911615
1 & 3	4.070	1.165	0.940064
2 & 3	1.965	1.146	0.902924

full trajectories for the two approaches to cooperative BCI control are shown in Figure 4.

It is clear from these results that, for all pairs of subjects, cooperative control of the BCI was either on par (for the ERP-averaging method) or very advantageous (for the separate SVM ensembles) over the single-subject tests. In particular, absolute angle deviations and normalised path lengths appear to be significantly better for the second form of cooperative control than for single subjects. This can also be seen by visually comparing Figures 3 and 4(b). Also, AUC scores on average are comparable but have significantly smaller variance in the cooperative BCIs, implying greater consistency in performance.

To verify whether the differences observed in the cumulative performance indicators reported above are statistically significant, we segmented the trajectories produced by the single-user method and our best cooperative method (based on independent SVMs) into their component trials (remember each trial represents a complete revolution of the flashing stimuli which correspond to 800 ms of data: 8 mouse movements, one every 100 ms). This gave us 176 trajectory segments. We then measured the absolute angle deviation and the normalised path length for each segment. Since the segments are paired across subjects and pairs of subjects (during training all subjects were presented with exactly the same sequence of stimuli), so are the values of these performance measures. Therefore, we could compare the distributions of performance for the segments with the one-tailed Wilcoxon signed rank test (which is a non-parametric test for paired data) to establish if the distribution of trial-by-trial trajectories was better for cooperative control or for single-user control.[5]

Table 5 shows the p values returned by the test when comparing the normalised path length and the absolute angle deviation of pairs and single subjects. All comparisons show that pairs produced statistically significantly better trajectories under both performance criteria than single subjects.

[5]Naturally, since we performed multiple pairwise tests, we applied the Bonferroni correction to the standard 5% significance level.

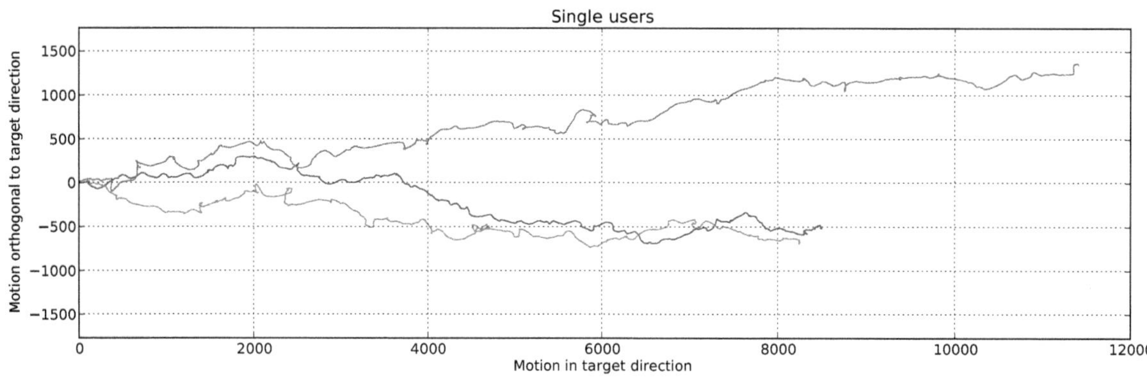

Figure 3. Trajectories produced by the BCI pointer control system for each of the three users when using the test data acquired in Phase 3.

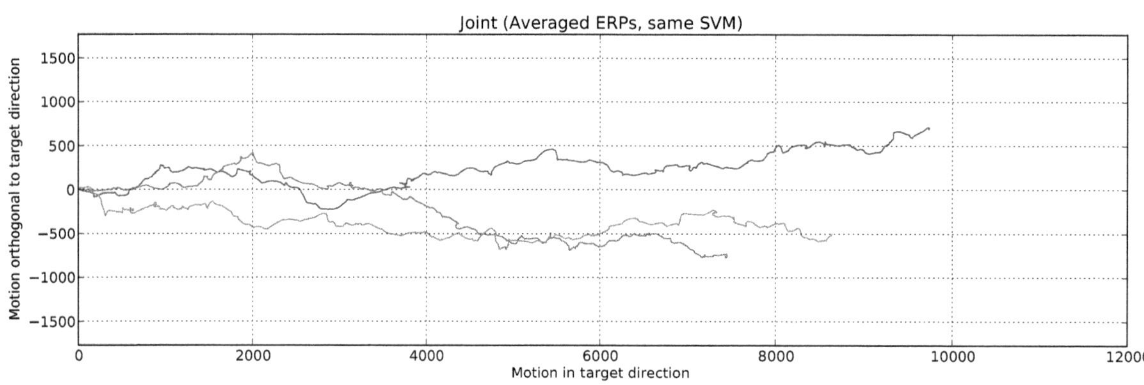

(a)

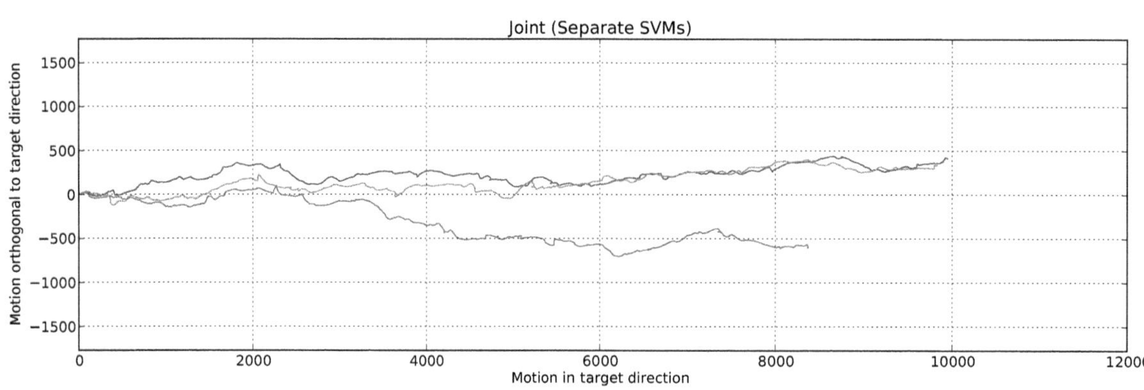

(b)

Figure 4. Trajectories produced by the system in the two cooperative-control configurations: (a) joint control obtained by averaging the ERPs of the two subjects and feeding them into a single (common) ensemble of SVMs, and (b) joint control obtained by sending the ERPs of the two subjects through two separate ensembles of SVMs and averaging the output displacement vectors produced by the system.

Table 5. Wilcoxon test p values for comparisons based on normalised path length (top) and on absolute deviation (bottom). Values in bold face are statistically significantly superior at the 5% confidence level (after Bonferroni correction). Values in italics are significant at a 10% confidence level (again after Bonferroni correction).

		...better than these?		
Performance measure	**Are these ...**	Subject 1	Subject 2	Subject 3
Normalised path length	Joint 1 & 2	$\mathbf{6.37502 \times 10^{-8}}$	$\mathbf{1.31414 \times 10^{-7}}$	$\mathbf{9.36245 \times 10^{-5}}$
	Joint 1 & 3	$\mathbf{2.7696 \times 10^{-8}}$	*0.00879649*	$\mathbf{8.39675 \times 10^{-6}}$
	Joint 2 & 3	**0.000142919**	**0.000502456**	**0.000232074**
Absolute angle deviation	Joint 1 & 2	$\mathbf{1.76193 \times 10^{-7}}$	$\mathbf{4.04779 \times 10^{-11}}$	$\mathbf{8.16628 \times 10^{-11}}$
	Joint 1 & 3	**0.000185374**	**0.00270251**	$\mathbf{1.10938 \times 10^{-10}}$
	Joint 2 & 3	**0.00254564**	$\mathbf{1.75272 \times 10^{-5}}$	$\mathbf{1.05116 \times 10^{-10}}$

DISCUSSION AND CONCLUSIONS

In this paper, we have studied the possibility of navigating a spacecraft via a BCI as well as the potential benefits of a collaborative BCI over a single-user one in relation to this task.

Although there have been previous reports analysing the potential benefits and drawbacks of BCI technology in the space domain [8, 22, 6], this is the first paper that describes an implementation and its actual testing in this domain. We would also like to note that only very recently the first explorations of cooperative BCIs have appeared in the literature [43, 37, 12, 26] and none of these have attempted to achieve anything as difficult as finely controlling a 2–D pointer on a screen in real-time as we have done in this article.

In tests of the single-user spacecraft navigation system, we have found that users managed to satisfy the success criterion for the simulation in more than $2/3$ of the runs. While this performance level is clearly inferior to what can be achieved using an ordinary mouse to control the spacecraft (where users would "hit" the Sun in 100% of the runs), it is actually a very good result considering the bandwidth and accuracy limits typical of brain-computer interfaces. This indicates that while BCI technology is still not quite ready for immediate deployment in space, it is inching its way towards becoming competitive and there is certainly ground for optimism for future space applications.

This study also provides an important contribution to collaborative BCI. Previous studies with cooperative BCIs have shown that collaborative systems can outperform single-user BCIs. However, in those studies this was achieved only when combining at least three users [37, 43, 26]. On the contrary, in this study we have found that combining the brain activity of two users already provides considerably improved performance over single-user BCI. This has important implications for cooperative BCI from a practical point of view, since wiring up more than two users may be impractical and expensive and may require difficult setups (in terms of space, screen technology, networking, etc.). Also, previous attempts used much simpler tasks and users were not actively and directly controlling a user interface (as we did).

There are several potential benefits of having multiple people control a BCI. One general advantage of cooperative control is noise reduction. Because the noise on the control signals from each user is typically uncorrelated, the noise on the resultant (cooperative) control signal is reduced. (With Gaussian noise, it would drop by a factor $1/\sqrt{2}$). However, there are additional advantages with our analogue approach the cooperation. For instance, with our interface the person which is more focused on the task will produce bigger ERPs and will thus (correctly) exert more control over the spacecraft motion. So, our cooperative control may suffer less from lapses of concentration (with rare uncorrelated lapses, some degree of control is almost always maintained over the spacecraft). Also, while with a single user the pointer can only move in 8 different directions (0, 45, 90, ... degrees), with two, many more directions can be achieved (e.g., if a user focused on a 0 degree direction, the other on a 45 degree one and they produced equal ERPs, the joint motion would be at a 22.5 degrees angle).

Our evaluation shows that there is promise for cooperative BCI in space applications, although, of course we are a long way away from seeing the first collaborative BCI in space.

We are aware that the simplicity of the simulation we have chosen can just barely qualify our system as an application in the space domain. We selected the spacecraft simulation to be particularly simple because we wanted to isolate the problem of real-time control from the problem of cross-talk deriving from having multiple potential obstacles, targets and controls of a more realistic environment. All of these would drive attention away from the main navigation task and would make it difficult to decide what to change to improve the interaction. By keeping the simulation and the interface to their bare bones, we were able to progressively modify them and obtain good real-time control. In the future we will implement and test a cooperative form of BCI for real-time spacecraft navigation to learn more about advantages, disadvantages and future prospects of cooperative technology and we will also look at progressively more complex scenarios to test the limits of our analogue BCI approach to user-interface control.

Of course, these approaches are not just limited to space applications. The key issues we had to solve was real-time control of a system which can accept analogue commands and the integration of such commands across users. In the future we also hope to extend the approach to other domains, including the control of robots and motorised vehicles.

Acknowledgements

The authors would like to thank the UK's Engineering and Physical Sciences Research Council (EPSRC) for financial support (grant EP/K004638/1, entitled "Gobal engagement with NASA JPL and ESA in Robotics, Brain Computer Interfaces, and Secure Adaptive Systems for Space Applications").

REFERENCES

1. Allison, B. Z., Wolpaw, E. W., and Wolpaw, J. R. Brain-computer interface systems: progress and prospects. *Expert Review of Medical Devices 4*, 4 (Jul 2007), 463–474.
2. Bell, C. J., Shenoy, P., Chalodhorn, R., and Rao, R. P. N. Control of a humanoid robot by a noninvasive braincomputer interface in humans. *Journal of Neural Engineering 5*, 2 (2008), 214.
3. Beverina, F., Palmas, G., Silvoni, S., Piccione, F., and Giove, S. User adaptive BCIs: SSVEP and P300 based interfaces. *PsychNology Journal 1*, 4 (2003), 331–354.
4. Birbaumer, N., Ghanayim, N., Hinterberger, T., Iversen, I., Kotchoubey, B., Kübler, A., Perelmouter, J., Taub, E., and Flor, H. A spelling device for the paralysed. *Nature 398*, 6725 (Mar 1999), 297–298.
5. Birbaumer, N., Hinterberger, T., Kübler, A., and Neumann, N. The thought-translation device (TTD): neurobehavioral mechanisms and clinical outcome. *IEEE Transactions on Neural System and Rehabilitation Engineering 11*, 2 (Jun 2003), 120–123.
6. Broschart, M., de Negueruela, C., Millán, J. d. R., and Menon, C. Augmenting astronaut's capabilities through brain-machine interfaces. In *Proceedings of the 20th International Joint Conference on Artificial Intelligence, Workshop on Artificial Intelligence for Space Applications* (1 2007).
7. Citi, L., Poli, R., Cinel, C., and Sepulveda, F. P300-based BCI mouse with genetically-optimized analogue control. *IEEE Transactions on Neural Systems and Rehabilitation Engineering 16*, 1 (Feb. 2008), 51–61.
8. Coffey, E. B., Brouwer, A.-M., Wilschut, E. S., and van Erp, J. B. Brainmachine interfaces in space: Using spontaneous rather than intentionally generated brain signals. *Acta Astronautica 67*, 1-2 (2010), 1–11.
9. Coyle, S. M., Ward, T. E., and Markham, C. M. Brain-computer interface using a simplified functional near-infrared spectroscopy system. *Journal of Neural Engineering 4*, 3 (Sep 2007), 219–226.
10. Curran, E. A., and Stokes, M. J. Learning to control brain activity: a review of the production and control of EEG components for driving brain-computer interface (BCI) systems. *Brain Cognition 51*, 3 (Apr 2003), 326–336.
11. Donoghue, J. Connecting cortex to machines: recent advances in brain interfaces. *Nature Neuroscience 5* (2002), 1085–1088.
12. Eckstein, M. P., Das, K., Pham, B. T., Peterson, M. F., Abbey, C. K., Sy, J. L., and Giesbrecht, B. Neural decoding of collective wisdom with multi-brain computing. *NeuroImage 59*, 1 (2012), 94–108.
13. Farwell, L. A., and Donchin, E. Talking off the top of your head: toward a mental prosthesis utilizing event-related brain potentials. *Electroencephalography and Clinical Neurophysiology 70*, 6 (Dec 1988), 510–523.
14. Finke, A., Knoblauch, A., Koesling, H., and Ritter, H. J. A hybrid brain interface for a humanoid robot assistant. In *33rd Annual International Conference of the IEEE Engineering in Medicine and Biology Society (EMBC2011)*, IEEE, IEEE (Boston, MA, USA, 30.08.2011 2011).
15. Galán, F., Nuttin, M., Lew, E., Ferrez, P., Vanacker, G., Philips, J., and Millán, J. A brain-actuated wheelchair: Asynchronous and non-invasive brain-computer interfaces for continuous control of robots. *Clinical Neurophysiololy* (2008).
16. Georgopoulos, A., Langheim, F., Leuthold, A., and Merkle, A. Magnetoencephalographic signals predict movement trajectory in space. *Experimental Brain Research* (Jul 2005), 1–4.
17. Hand, D. J., and Till, R. J. A simple generalisation of the area under the ROC curve for multiple class classification problems. *Machine Learning 45* (2001), 171–186.
18. Hilton, B. D. Space commander (version 0.4). `http://spacecommander.sourceforge.net/`, 2006.
19. Lebedev, M., and Nicolelis, M. Brain-machine interfaces: past, present and future. *Trends in Neurosciences 29*, 9 (September 2006), 536–546.
20. Luck, S. J. *An introduction to the event-related potential technique*. MIT Press, Cambridge, Massachusetts, 2005.
21. Menon, C., de Negueruela, C., del Millán, J., Tonet, O., Carpi, F., Broschart, M., Ferrez, P., Buttfield, A., Dario, P., Citi, L., Laschi, C., Tombini, M., Sepulveda, F., Poli, R., Palaniappan, R., Tecchio, F., Rossini, P. M., and Rossi, D. D. Prospective on brain-machine interfaces for space system control. In *57th Astronautical Congress* (Spain, 2–6 Oct 2006). paper IAC-06-D1.1.05.
22. Menon, C., de Negueruela, C., del Millán, J., Tonet, O., Carpi, F., Broschart, M., Ferrez, P., Buttfield, A., Tecchio, F., Sepulveda, F., Citi, L., Laschi, C., Tombini, M., Dario, P., Rossini, M., and Rossi, D. D. Prospects of brain-machine interfaces for space system control. *Acta Astronautica 64*, 4 (2009), 448–456.
23. Millan, J. D. R., Renkens, F., Mourino, J., and Gerstner, W. Noninvasive brain-actuated control of a mobile robot by human EEG. *IEEE Transactions on Biomedical Engineering 51* (2004), 1026–1033.

24. Müller, G. R., Scherer, R., Neuper, C., and Pfurtscheller, G. Steady-state somatosensori evoked potentials: Suitable brain signals for brain-computer interfaces? *IEEE Transactions on Neural Systems and Rehabilitation Engineering 14*, 1 (2006), 30–37.
25. Pfurtscheller, G., Flotzinger, D., and Kalcher, J. Brain-computer interface: a new communication device for handicapped persons. *Journal of Microcomputer Applications 16*, 3 (1993), 293–299.
26. Poli, R., Cinel, C., Sepulveda, F., and Stoica, A. Improving decision-making based on visual perception via a collaborative brain-computer interface. In *IEEE International Multi-Disciplinary Conference on Cognitive Methods in Situation Awareness and Decision Support (CogSIMA)*, IEEE (San Diego (CA), February 2013). (to appear).
27. Poli, R., Salvaris, M., and Cinel, C. Evolutionary synthesis of a trajectory integrator for an analogue brain-computer interface mouse. In *Applications of Evolutionary Computing, EvoApplications 2011*, C. Di Chio, S. Cagnoni, C. Cotta, M. Ebner, A. Ekart, A. I. Esparcia-Alcazar, J. J. Merelo, F. Neri, M. Preuss, H. Richter, J. Togelius, and G. N. Yannakakis, Eds., vol. 6624 of *LNCS*, Springer Verlag (Turin, Italy, 27-29 Apr. 2011), 214–223.
28. Polikoff, J. B., Bunnell, H. T., and Borkowski Jr, W. J. Toward a P300-based computer interface. In *Rehabilitation Engineering and Assistive Technology Society of North America (RESNA'95)*, Resna Press (Arlington, Va, 1995), 178–180.
29. Reza, F.-R., Z, A. B., Christoph, G., W, S. E., C, K. S., and Andrea, K. P300 brain computer interface: current challenges and emerging trends. *Frontiers in Neuroengineering 5*, 14 (2012).
30. Salvaris, M., Cinel, C., Citi, L., and Poli, R. Novel protocols for P300-based brain-computer interfaces. *IEEE Transactions on Neural Systems and Rehabilitation Engineering*, 1 (2012), 8–17.
31. Schwartz, A. B. Cortical neural prosthetics. *Annual Review of Neuroscience 27* (2004), 487–507.
32. Sellers, E. W., and Donchin, E. A P300-based brain-computer interface: Initial tests by ALS patients. *Clinical Neurophysiology 117*, 3 (Mar 2006), 538–548.
33. Soon, C. S., Brass, M., Heinze, H.-J., and Haynes, J.-D. Unconscious determinants of free decisions in the human brain. *Nature Neuroscience 11*, 5 (April 2008), 543–545.
34. Stoica, A. Multimind: Multi-brain signal fusion to exceed the power of a single brain. In *EST*, A. Stoica, D. Zarzhitsky, G. Howells, C. D. Frowd, K. D. McDonald-Maier, A. T. Erdogan, and T. Arslan, Eds., IEEE Computer Society (2012), 94–98.
35. Trejo, L. J., Rosipal, R., and Matthews, B. Brain-computer interfaces for 1-D and 2-D cursor control: Designs using volitional control of the EEG spectrum or steady-state visual evoked potentials. *IEEE Transactions on Neural Systems and Rehabilitation Engineering 14*, 2 (June 2006), 225–229.
36. Tzovara, A., Murray, M. M., Bourdaud, N., Chavarriaga, R., del R. Millán, J., Lucia, M. D., and Lucia, M. D. The timing of exploratory decision-making revealed by single-trial topographic EEG analyses. *NeuroImage* (2012), 1959–1969.
37. Wang, Y., and Jung, T.-P. A Collaborative Brain-Computer Interface for Improving Human Performance. *PLoS ONE 6*, 5 (May 2011), e20422+.
38. Weiskopf, N., Mathiak, K., Bock, S. W., Scharnowski, F., Veit, R., Grodd, W., Goebel, R., and Birbaumer, N. Principles of a brain-computer interface (BCI) based on real-time functional magnetic resonance imaging (fMRI). *IEEE Transactions on Biomedical Engineering 51*, 6 (Jun 2004), 966–970.
39. Wilson, J. J., and Palaniappan, R. Analogue mouse pointer control via an online steady state visual evoked potential (SSVEP) brain-computer interface. *Journal of Neural Engineering 8* (October 2011).
40. Wolpaw, J. R., Birbaumer, N., McFarland, D. J., Pfurtscheller, G., and Vaughan, T. M. Brain-computer interfaces for communication and control. *Clinical Neurophysiology 113*, 6 (June 2002), 767–91.
41. Wolpaw, J. R., and McFarland, D. J. Control of a two-dimensional movement signal by a noninvasive brain-computer interface in humans. *Proceedings of the National Academy of Sciences 101*, 51 (2004), 17849–17854.
42. Wolpaw, J. R., McFarland, D. J., Neat, G. W., and Forneris, C. A. An EEG-based brain-computer interface for cursor control. *Electroencephalography and Clinical Neurophysiology 78*, 3 (Mar 1991), 252–259.
43. Yuan, P., Wang, Y., Wu, W., Xu, H., Gao, X., and Gao, S. Study on an online collaborative BCI to accelerate response to visual targets. In *Proceedings of 34nd IEEE EMBS Conference* (2012).

Real-time Gait Classification for Persuasive Smartphone Apps: Structuring the Literature and Pushing the Limits

Oliver S. Schneider[1] oschneid@cs.ubc.ca
Karon E. MacLean[1] maclean@cs.ubc.ca
Kerem Altun[2] kerem.altun@kemerburgaz.edu.tr
Idin Karuei[1] idin@cs.ubc.ca
Michael M.A. Wu[1] mike.wu@alumni.ubc.ca

[1]Department of Computer Science
University of British Columbia
Vancouver, Canada

[2]Department of Mechanical Engineering
Istanbul Kemerburgaz University
Istanbul, Turkey

ABSTRACT

Persuasive technology is now mobile and context-aware. Intelligent analysis of accelerometer signals in smartphones and other specialized devices has recently been used to classify activity (*e.g.*, distinguishing walking from cycling) to encourage physical activity, sustainable transport, and other social goals. Unfortunately, results vary drastically due to differences in methodology and problem domain. The present report begins by structuring a survey of current work within a new framework, which highlights comparable characteristics between studies; this provided a tool by which we and others can understand the current state-of-the art and guide research towards existing gaps. We then present a new user study, positioned in an identified gap, that pushes limits of current success with a challenging problem: the real-time classification of 15 similar and novel gaits suitable for several persuasive application areas, focused on the growing phenomenon of exercise games. We achieve a mean correct classification rate of 78.1% of all 15 gaits with a minimal amount of personalized training of the classifier for each participant when carried in any of 6 different carrying locations (not known *a priori*). When narrowed to a subset of four gaits and one location that is known, this improves to means of 92.2% with and 87.2% without personalization. Finally, we group our findings into design guidelines and quantify variation in accuracy when an algorithm is trained for a known location and participant.

Author Keywords

Gait classification; activity detection; survey; mobile; persuasive computing; exercise games

ACM Classification Keywords

H.5.m. Information Interfaces and Presentation (e.g. HCI): Miscellaneous

General Terms

Human Factors; Design; Measurement; Performance

INTRODUCTION

As smartphones become more powerful and pervasive, developers and designers are using them to effect social or personal change — encouraging sustainable transport [9], facilitating free living for the elderly [35], and supporting individuals in being physically active [7]. The last has led to an abundance of smartphone-based exercise applications and games targeting the global concern of obesity: 10% of adults worldwide are classified as overweight or obese, a risk factor for many diseases [32]. In 2008, 31% of adults worldwide aged 15 and over were insufficiently active [33].

Modern smartphones have a wealth of sensing capabilities, such as accelerometers, gyroscopes, and Global Positioning System (GPS) units. These sensors allow for novel mobile applications to assess the user's context automatically, and permit implicit control of a system rather than requiring explicit control of an application (such as an intelligent music player that automatically pauses when a user stops running). This can support physical activity in a natural way, such as matching a song's beat to a user's running cadence (*i.e.*, step rate) to provide motivation [26], or the ambient display of physical activity, which has helped people maintain their exercise or weight management goals [6]. In particular, automatically sensing different gaits to help infer higher-level context lends itself well to applications involving physical activity. Applications can encourage activity in everyday choices, such as taking the stairs to the office rather than the elevator. Mobile exercise games can also benefit from sensing novel gaits as an input modality: accurate recognition of exercise is important for motivation [6], and many only use location-based sensing or approximations of overall physical activity [2, 11, 12, 17, 20, 30]. Different gaits are also valuable for other persuasive applications, fitting naturally with sustainable transport and unintrusive monitoring of the elderly to encourage positive life choices.

However, results for gait-related activity classification vary drastically in the related literature, obscuring the current state-of-the-art. Meanwhile, variation in methodology and problem characterization complicate finding the best match of algorithm to novel applications. To remedy this, we have identified key classification study dimensions, then organized them into a framework that makes explicit the algorithm's and/or its evaluation's intended target application, implementation details, and validation methodology. We use this framework to map closely-related work for mobile gait classification that is robust to different locations. Our map is intended as a tool for readers and researchers — a guide for different works and their key differences, a quick reference for study details, and a way to view the current state-of-the-art while placing results in the context of their methodology.

Related work posed within this framework revealed that our target of mobile exercise applications required sensing that is more robust to carrying location, and differentiates more gaits, than past work; this led to the creation of our own new algorithm. We classified 15 walking-category gaits suitable for a range of persuasive smartphone applications, especially exercise and games, and in describing this algorithm's analysis, we articulate our own study parameters within the proposed framework. Finally, we frame our results in design guidelines for using gait classification for mobile exercise applications.

RELATED WORK

Our related work is divided into two parts. In this section, we cover both the potential of gait classification for persuasive mobile applications and the current state of gait or gait-like activity classification using a triaxial accelerometer in a context analogous to a smartphone's.

Gait as Input for Mobile Exercise Applications

Using on-person sensors to support exercise is not new. Examples range from self-reported logging of exercise and nutrition to smartphone-based pedometers and GPS-based location sensing for running or cycling [10, 24, 26, 31]. More elaborate sensing solutions (in particular entailing a feedback and/or social networking element) have also been developed, such as Nike+, whose sensors can communicate with third party exercise equipment [25].

Recent studies have shown that physical activity monitoring can influence physical activity levels when coupled with an ambient display. Pedometers have been used to encourage participants to increase their daily step count via graphical fish avatars [23]. Findings from the "Houston" system, a mobile fitness journal application, suggest that though pedometers are motivating, non-walking activities must be supported. When Houston failed to report non-walking activities (such as climbing) correctly both to users themselves and via social network sharing, users were frustrated [6]. Better reporting was included with the followup system, UbiFit, which provides an ambient display of a garden growing when the user is active or achieves fitness goals [7]. UbiFit allowed automatic recording of some activities and manual entry of any activity, and this was better received by participants: the frustration encountered with Houston was not observed with UbiFit. Over 60 activities were reported, suggesting that automated systems will have to support a large number of activities.

Houston and UbiFit required external sensors, which users felt were large and unsightly — unsuitable for a pervasive application used in day-to-day life. Today's powerful smartphones have potential to reduce reliance on external sensors, but their on-board sensors require more elaborate processing. Exercise games have used accelerometers to infer overall activity level. NEAT-O-Games (Non-Exercise Activity Thermogenesis) are simple games that used hip-mounted external accelerometers to infer an overall physical activity level. Their goal is to increase "energy expenditure of all physical activities other than volitional sporting-like exercise," such as moving around to do chores [11, 12, 20]. Other common types of input for mobile exercise games include heart-rate monitors [5, 8] and location through GPS or wireless connection points [2, 17, 30].

However, at the time of this writing there are no exercise games that use gait as an input modality; that is, no exercise games directly take into account *how* the user is moving. Previous work on types of exercise game input has focused on situated rather than mobile contexts (*e.g.*, a stationary bike or vision-based system): a set of *abstract inputs* for existing exergames (or "active games"), later developed into a toolkit, has included gesture, stance, point, power, continuous control, and tap [3, 29]. Although some aspects of gait can be fit into these abstract specifications, emphasis was on non-mobile input techniques. There is a clear need to investigate how this new interaction modality could be used to support persuasive applications.

Accelerometer-based Gait Classification

Activity detection has been accomplished with great accuracy using an array of inertial measurement units (IMUs) attached at multiple points to the body (*e.g.*, [1]), but this approach is far too intrusive for pervasive persuasive applications. Recent results using smartphone sensors (or loose accelerometers approaching the context of a smartphone) cite a variety of success rates, up to 100% [19]. A closer look reveals that results vary depending on methodology, such as the number and type of classes (attributes to be classified; in this case, gaits or activities), the constraints placed on a phone's carrying method, or the number of participants. It is thus difficult to get an overall sense of mobile classification work, and how much progress we have made at solving various aspects of this problem. As such, we do not simply report on each study, but provide a structured survey of closely-related work.

In the next section, we present a framework for organizing mobile context-aware classification work, drawing upon specific studies for examples. An explanatory diagram of this framework can be found in Figure 1.

We then present a table of the most closely related studies organized by our framework in Table 1. Please note that we only report upon gait or gait-like classification with loosely carried smartphones. This excludes work in detecting the device's carrying location [22] or the use of gait as a biometric feature for identifying the user's identity [13, 28]. We expect that our framework will be applicable to mobile classification work in general, but charting that terrain is left to future work.

STRUCTURING MOBILE CLASSIFICATION

Our framework consists of three spaces: an *application space* that describes the overall goal and major problem description, an *implementation space* of classification approaches and

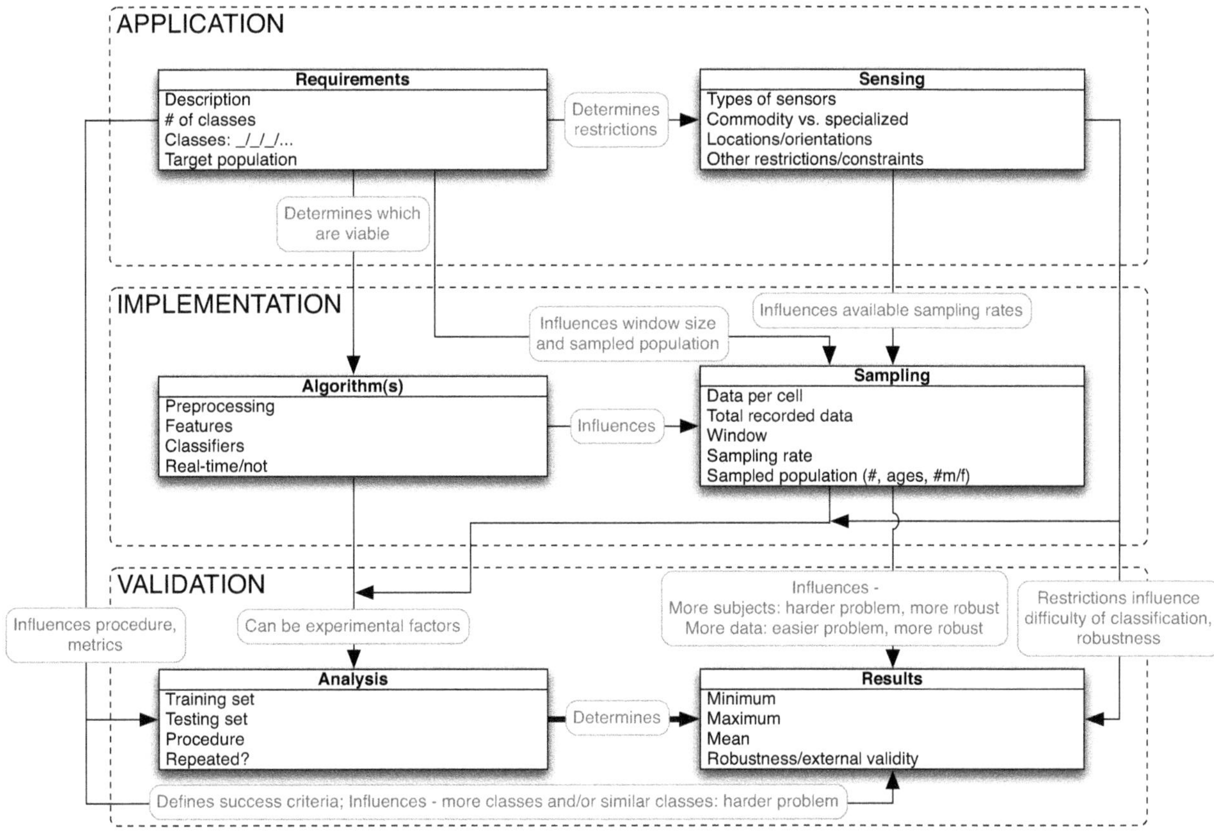

Figure 1: Framework for mobile context-aware classification work.

data collected, and a *validation space* of evaluation methodologies and results. We now describe the three spaces and six dimensions in more detail.

Figure 1 shows an explanatory diagram of this framework and the relationships between its entities. Each space is represented as a dashed box. Dimensions within each space are solid boxes (the term "dimension" is loosely defined; each is actually a collection of closely-related dimensions, but it is more useful to work with a lower-dimensional space).

Relationships between dimensions are represented with directional arrows, describing the influence of one dimension upon another. For example, when developing an interactive exercise game (described below under the Requirements dimension), this limits possible algorithms to those that can perform in real-time (influencing the Algorithm(s) dimension), which in turn restricts the available sample rate and window size, as real-time applications might require that the system reacts within a specified time period (influencing the Sampling dimension). As such, the framework can also be used as a flow chart to develop a study design – start by describing the requirements and follow the arrows.

Application Space

Classification research generally operates within a certain context to achieve a specific goal, *e.g.*, discriminating different gaits to track activity. This context can impose constraints that make classification more or less feasible. Two dimensions compose this space: Requirements and Sensing.

Requirements – The application space describes the task at hand. Is it to classify gaits, recognize a user, or detect a mode of travel? This dimension includes the number of classes and what they are. For example, Zhang et al.'s study classifies user gait and posture, recognizing 6 gaits: *walking*, *posture-transition*, *gentlemotion*, *standing*, *sitting*, and *lying* [35]. As well, the target user population are an important designation of the requirements. An exercise game designed for children will have different needs than an ambulatory monitoring system for physiotherapy in the elderly.

Sensing – What sensors are available to detect gaits, and what restrictions can we impose upon our users to facilitate sensing? Many studies seeking to use smartphones to infer context would like their system to work however the device is carried, but this is not always practical. This dimension makes chosen locations and other constraints explicit; this includes where the device is being carried or held, whether it is loose or fixed, and whether specialized equipment or commercially-available commodity hardware is required. For example, Huynh et al. use a sensor fixed to a backpack strap (a clear constraint) [15], but Kawahara, Kurasawa, & Morikawa allowed subjects carry commodity smartphones loosely in their pants pockets, chest pockets, and a personal bag [19].

	Schneider 2013	Khan 2010	Zhang 2010	Yang 2009	Kawahara 2007	Iso 2006	Huynh 2005
Requirements							
Task	Gait classification	Activity monitoring	Activity detection	Activity detection	Gait, device location classification	Activity detection	Activity detection
Target Population	Children, adults	Elderly	General	General	General	General	General
# of Classes	15	7	6	6	3-4	5	6
Classes	walk, fastwalk, jog, run, up/downstairs, walksideways/ backwards, narrow, penguin, twofoothop, toes, heels, knees, kickbum	walk, run, up/downstairs, cycle, vacuum, rest	walk, posture transition, gentle motion, stand, sit, lie	walk, run, drive, cycle, sit, stand	walk, run, sit, stand, *(sit & stand sometimes combined)*	walk, fastwalk, run, up/downstairs	walk, jog, skip, hop, ride bus, stand
Sensing							
Types of Sensors	Smartphone (Android)	Witilt 2.5 Sensor	Smartphone	Smartphone	Smartphone	Cellphone	Integrated sensor board
Specialized?	Commodity	Commodity	Commodity	Commodity	Commodity	Commodity	Specialized
Locations & Orientations	Front/back pockets, belt, arm, backpack, hand *(freely placed in each)*	Front left/front right/ rear trouser pockets, inner chest/jacket pockets	Belt *(horizontal orientation)*	Freely carried	Pants/chest pocket, bag	Breast/hip pocket	Affixed to backpack strap, consistent location
Algorithm(s)							
Preprocessing	*None*	Moving average	Kalman filter	Estimate gravity, split (x,y,z) into vertical and horizontal components	*None*	Pseudo-data created by rotating original signals	*None*
Features	Statistical features from time and frequency domains of X, Y, and Z axes	Spectral entropy, linear discriminant analysis of autoregressive coefficients, signal magnitude area	Accelerometer values	Several feature sets (factor in experiment); common statistical observations, cross correlation function	Average, variance, strongest frequency component, change in angle	Wavelet packet decomposition of periodogram, momentum from best basis	Statistical features on both time-domain and frequency-domain, light sensor, digital compass
Classifiers	Random forest with 500 trees	Hierarchical neural networks (resting, lower activity, upper activity; then activity)	Threshold rules to detect motion, SVMs for activity given motion/non-motion	Decision tree, naïve Bayes, kNN, SVM	Rule-based: detect orientation/location, then detect posture	Kohonen self-organizing map (KSOM)	K-means clustering for training, nearest cluster centroid for classification
Real-Time?	Yes	Yes	No	Yes	Yes	Yes	Yes
Sampling							
Total Recorded Data	9 hrs	24 hrs	2 hrs	192 min	~40 min	7.5 hrs	~200 min
Data Per Cell	28-42 seconds	2 to 8 minutes	*(not reported)*	10-30 minutes	~2.5 minutes	15 minutes	*(not reported)*
Window & Sampling Rate	2 seconds, ~26 Hz (variable sampling rate)	90 samples, 90 Hz	Segments of over 10s; sampling rate of 1 Hz	10 seconds, ~36 Hz	20 Hz, window varies with feature	3 seconds	0.25, 0.5, 1, 2, 4 seconds at 512 Hz
Sampled Population	12 subjects (6m/6f) Ages: 21-31 yrs Weights: 46-86 kg Heights: 155-183 cm	8 subjects (6m/2f) Age: mean 65, sd 3 yrs	10 subjects (7m/3f) Ages: 23-50	4 subjects	4 subjects	2 subjects	2 subjects
Analysis							
Training Set	For each participant, a randomly selected partition of 9 folds	60% of each subject (randomly selected)	One subject	3 subjects	3 subjects	*(not reported)*	800 cluster-means (4 of 5 folds of 1000 cluster-means)
Testing Set	For each participant, the remaining fold	40% of each subject (remaining)	All ten subjects (including training subject)	1 subject	4 subjects	*(not reported)*	remaining fold (200 cluster-means)
Procedure	10-fold cross validation	Train on several subject training sets, test on remaining subject testing sets	Train on one, test on all	10-fold cross-validation	Accuracy of gaits given device position	*(not reported)*	Cross validation
Repeated?	For each participant, 10 times (once per fold)	Until all subjects were a part of the testing set	No	For each feature set and classifier	No	*(not reported)*	5 times (one per fold)
Metric	Mean accuracy	Accuracy	Mean accuracy between motion and non-motion	Accuracy	Accuracy	Accuracy	Recall/(1-Precision) curves
Results							
Mean	78.1% - 92.2% (depending on gaitset and location)	94.4%	94.4%	Depends on classifier and feature set	N/A	~80%	N/A
Range/variation	68.1% - 100.0%	87% - 98%	87% - 98%	66.3% - 90.6%	96.7% - 100.0%	~73% - ~95%	N/A

Table 1: Map of related work, structured according to the framework presented in Figure 1. The new study reported in this paper is listed as 'Schneider 2013'.

Implementation Space

The Implementation Space describes the details of the solution, answering the question "How?" It has two dimensions: Algorithm(s) and Sampling.

Algorithm(s) – In this dimension, one describes both classification schemes as well as any preprocessing steps or unique notes about feature extraction. For example, Iso and Yamazaki generate pseudo-data by transforming their collected data rotationally [16]. This means that they may have some bias in their classifier (from similar patterns being artificially repeated), but they also making their classifier more robust to orientation, an important fact to consider when comparing different work. Because algorithms can become quite complex, we reserve this dimension to discuss high-level features, and direct readers to the papers themselves for details.

Sampling – The sampling dimension is the specific manifestation of a dataset for validation of the algorithm. As the amount of data collected has a large bearing on the results, it is important to describe both the overall amount of data collected and the amount per data cell – that is, how much data exists for each experimental factor (*e.g.*, gait/subject/location). If there is only a small amount of data in a data cell, then evaluation of the classifier may give lower results than if more data was collected. We also represent the relationship between time and number of observations in this dimension, by giving the sample rate and the window size (the amount of time or number of samples taken to constitute a sample used in classification. For example, Yang collects 10 to 30 minutes per data cell for a total of 192 minutes, and takes one observation from 10 seconds of data (with an accelerometer sampling rate of approximately 36 Hz) [34], while Khan et al. collect 2 to 8 minutes per data cell for a total of 24 hours of data, sampling at 90Hz with a window of 90 samples (1 second) [21]. Khan et al. clearly have more data, but are trying to classify observations with less data individually (1 second or 90 samples vs. 10 seconds or 36x10=360 samples), and less time spent with each gait or location. We include both sampling rate and window size to relate the number of observations to the amount of time.

Validation Space

Every technique must be evaluated. In this space, the dimensions of Analysis and Results have the most influence on the conclusions of a given study. As analysis necessarily varies with application area, generalization and comparison are difficult. However, this can be mitigated by clearly articulating both dimensions to provide context.

Analysis – The metrics that researchers use and the way that they compare results is extremely important. Most tend to use accuracy (the percent of correctly classified observations) as their metric, but classification techniques have several other ways to measure success, such as recall, precision, and F-measure. Some analyses might train on a single participant and test on several others (a difficult problem), while others might train on a subject and test on that same subject (which is expected to be easier).

Results – The actual metrics found during analysis. To facilitate comparison and access by algorithm consumers, we urge researchers to not just list an overall score (mean, etc.) but to also report the minimum, maximum, and mean. There is often a large variance of classification rates that is not captured in the mean alone.

Positioning Our Study

The goal of our user study is to explore previously unexamined areas with smartphone-based gait classification. Here, we demonstrate how the framework might be used by positioning our study within the established literature.

Looking at the Requirements dimension of Table 1, we see that previous studies have typically explored 5-7 gaits or activities, looking at common postures or modes of transport. We expand this to 15 gaits, looking at several atypical gaits suitable for exercise games. Along the Sensing dimension, we similarly examine more locations (6) than previously explored (5, [21]). With both of these dimensions, we explore a more challenging problem than does previous work.

In Algorithm(s) dimension, each study has its own algorithm, with some overlap (*e.g.*, SVM); ours introduces Random Forest. In this we are not necessarily introducing a challenge, but it illustrates how the framework can be used for a quick survey of past algorithm use and overlap between studies. In the Sampling dimension, a quick comparison establishes context for our study's results: the largest number of subjects and smallest reported length of data per data cell, a typical-to-large (but not largest) total amount of recorded data, and the use of a lower (but not lowest) sampling rate.

The Analysis dimension concisely describes how the final results were achieved, and highlights any difference from other studies. For example, in our evaluation, we both train and test our algorithm on each participant (effectively personalizing the algorithm, although we report non-personalized data) while other analyses might have other schemes, *e.g.*, training on one participant and testing on others. Finally, after examining this context, we use the Results dimension to compare how the different algorithms might perform given the analysis and dataset.

CLASSIFICATION STUDY

In order to inform gait as input for persuasive smartphone applications, in particular encouraging physical activity, we conducted a user study of novel gaits. In particular, we aim to explore rich and robust sensing by investigating more gaits and more carrying locations than in previous work. In essence, we pursued the most difficult manifestation of this classification problem to date, in order to identify baseline capabilities for mobile classification (which has been successful so far). We drew from 4 primary goals in this area: (a) to explore subtle differences for context-aware applications, investigating gaits that were similar (such as distinguishing jogging from rapid walking); (b) to explore novel gaits suitable for exercise applications, by involving different muscle groups; (c) to explore novel gaits that could be easily linked by metaphor to a child-friendly exercise game, such as marching like a soldier or walking on a tight rope; and (d) to connect

Category	Label	Verbal description
Pedestrian	walk	Walk normally
	fastwalk	Walk quickly
	jog	Jog, *if asked for clarification:* slow run
	run	Run, not necessarily a flat out sprint, but a run
	ascendstairs	Walk up the stairs as you normally would until you reach the top
	descendstairs	Walk down the stairs as you normally would until you reach the bottom
Exercise	toes	Walk on your toes
	heels	Walk on your heels
	liftknees	Walk while lifting your knees high in the air
	kickingbum	Walk while kicking your bum. You don't actually have to hit it, but do that motion
Game	twofoothop	Hop with two feet
	penguin	Walk like a penguin
	narrow	Walk as if on something narrow, like a tightrope
	walkbackwards	Walk backwards
	walksideways	Walk sideways

Table 2: Gaits and descriptions used in our data collection study.

modes of travel, such as cycling or driving. These four goals informed the generation of our gaits. As such, our target gaits were divided into *gaitsets*, sets of gaits grouped by their relationship to our four goals.

Gaits

With this in mind, we developed a set of gaits suitable for an exercise or context-aware game or application. After piloting, we retained 15 gaits organized into three gaitsets (Pedestrian, Exercise, and Game) corresponding to our first three goals; for scope and logistical reasons, our fourth goal of travel methods (the would-be Locomotion gaitset) is left to future work. We discovered during initial brainstorming that some gaits were consistently interpreted by participants (*e.g.*, walking on heels, walking like a penguin) but others were not (*e.g.*, skipping, walking like a zombie). To facilitate our user study and allow for a robust application, we decided to only use gaits that were consistently interpreted by a simple verbal or written description. To limit scope, all gaits had to involve directional movement and be bipedal - that is, we did not allow in-place activities like jumping jacks or walking on hands and knees. Our gaits are described in Table 2.

Gaits not involving stairs were performed outside in a random order. For logistical reasons, Ascend Stairs and Descend Stairs were performed either at the beginning or end of the trial; this was counterbalanced by participants, as was the order of Ascend Stairs and Descend Stairs.

Apparatus and Participants

Seven Samsung Galaxy Nexus smartphones running Android OS 4.0.1 (Ice Cream Sandwich) were used in the experiment, each loaded with a custom accelerometer logging application. Six were placed on the participant in the following locations: front pocket, back pocket, hip, hand, arm, and backpack. These six phones sampled the accelerometer at the highest rate allowed by the operating system (mean sampling period was 16.95 ms, standard deviation 28.75 ms, median 8.3 ms), and saved the sampled signals to a comma-separated value (CSV) file retrieved after the experiment. The final phone was held by the experimenter, and was used to record the start time and end time of each gait. The logging phones were synchronized with the experimenter's phone at the beginning of the experiment by having the experimenter simultaneously press buttons on the experimenter's phone and the logging phone. Analysis was conducted on a MacBook Pro laptop with a 2.7 GHz Intel i7 processor and 8 GB of RAM.

	Age (years)	Height (cm)	Weight (kg)
Minimum	21	155	46
Median	26	171.5	69.5
Mean	25.3	171.5	68
St. Dev.	2.96	9.71	14.14
Maximum	31	183	86

Table 3: Self-reported statistics from 12 participants.

12 participants (6 female, 1 left-handed) are hereafter referred to as P1 to P12. Table 3 reports summary statistics for self-reported age, weight, and height.

Algorithm

For our classification scheme, we use Random Forest, an algorithm that uses bagging with randomly selected subsets of features, constructing a decision tree for each bootstrap sample. Decisions are made by majority response of these trees. As the number of trees approaches infinity, the accuracy of a Random Forest classifier converges [4]; through piloting we found accuracy converged between 100 and 500 trees, and so use 500 trees. We used the implementation provided by Weka [14].

We used a 2-second window with 50% overlap to compensate for our small amount of data; this yielded a total of 35806 instances for our entire dataset. Our classification scheme and window were chosen as the best performing in a pilot study examining window sizes (2- and 4-second), classification schemes (SVM, Naïve Bayes, Multilayered Perceptron, and Random Forest), and axis-grouping (x/y/z, vertical/horizontal [34], and vector magnitude). We hereafter refer to our algorithm as "RF500".

Features are extracted using the Python programming language and Scipy software package [18]. Features were chosen to represent a large number of basic statistical observations of both time and frequency domain data: our gaits can have subtle differences. To address the variable sampling rate found in smartphones, we calculate the frequency spectrum of each window with the Fast Lombe-Scargle Periodogram (FASPER) algorithm [27].

For each axis (x, y, z), we take the following features: minimum, maximum, and mean values, variance, skewness, kurtosis, 25th percentile, median (50th percentile), 75th percentile, a ten-bin histogram (normalized to have the proportion of each value in each bin), the most powerful and least powerful spectral frequencies, a weighted average of spectral frequencies by spectral power, spectral variance, spectral entropy, and a ten-bin histogram of spectral powers (normalized to have the proportion of each value in each bin). In addition, we look at the Pearson correlation and corresponding p-value for each pairwise combination of the x, y, and z axes. Finally, we take the signal magnitude area (sum of the Euclidean or ℓ-2 norm of every x,y,z tuple).

A full analysis of feature quality is beyond our present scope. However, we observed no trends in feature contribution to results. We suspect that the Random Forest algorithm's performance might be influenced by an ability to examine subtle trends across all features.

We could not train the All Locations/All Gaits/All Participants data cell with RF500, as the 8GB of laptop memory was in sufficient for this dataset. This dataset is thus missing from our all-participants analysis. We use the equivalent algorithm with 100 trees ("RF100") for our confusion matrix involving all gaits (Figure 3); it is expected to perform similar to but slightly worse than RF500. These computational costs are only present when training the algorithm; once trained, RF500 can perform efficiently on mobile devices.

Results

We conducted our main algorithm analysis with location, gaitset, and participant as factors. That is, we examine the benefit of knowing them by training classifiers that assume specific levels (such as an algorithm that is trained only on Exercise gaits with Front Pocket as the location).

We conduct this analysis twice, once training and testing on all 12 participants ("All-Participant"), and once training and testing on each participant ("By-Participant"). For each location, gaitset, and (for by-participant analysis) participant, we conducted 10 iterations of a 10-fold cross-validation. Our results analyze the mean of each cross validation, giving 10 data points for each location/gaitset(/participant) combination. For both all-participant and by-participant analysis we planned an Analysis of Variance (ANOVA) to compare different factors. However, the Shapiro-Wilk test of normality

Gaitset	Location	Mean % correct
Exercise	Back Pocket	87.2
Exercise	Front Pocket	86.6
Exercise	Arm	85.3
Game	Front Pocket	85.0
Exercise	Belt	84.8
Exercise	Backpack	84.6
Game	Back Pocket	84.5
Pedestrian	Front Pocket	83.7
Exercise	Hand	83.4
Pedestrian	Back Pocket	82.6
Game	Arm	81.7
All Gaits	Front Pocket	80.1
Game	Backpack	79.9
All Gaits	Back Pocket	79.8
Game	Belt	79.6
Pedestrian	Belt	79.5
Game	Hand	78.9
Pedestrian	Backpack	78.9
Pedestrian	Arm	78.4
Pedestrian	Hand	77.2
All Gaits	Arm	74.5
All Gaits	Belt	74.4
All Gaits	Backpack	74.3
All Gaits	Hand	73.5

Table 4: All-participant means of gaitset/location accuracy. Chance ranges from $6.\overline{6}\%$ ("All Gaits") to 25% ("Exercise").

failed with a 5% level of significance on data cell residuals in both analyses (Exercise/Arm data cell in all-participant, W=0.83, p=0.037; 55 of 336 data sets in by-participant). We thus do not detect statistical effects for the three factors (location, gaitset, and participant), and could not conduct analysis through planned contrasts.

All-Participants

Confusion matrices have been produced with all locations across all-participants (*e.g.*, without personalization) for each gaitset in Figure 2, and for all gaits in Figure 3. Table 4 shows mean classification rates by gaitset and location.

By-Participant

Training the RF500 algorithm on each participant improves results with the short data collection time of 30s per gait and location, and reveals variability in individual differences; see Figure 4 for graphs of the effect of participants by gaitset and location. The top performing mean data classification rate was 100.0%, present in three data cells (involving two participants): Game/Front Pocket/P3, Game/Backpack/P9, and Exercise/Backpack/P3. The worst performing mean data classification rate was All Gaits/All Locations/P10 with a mean of 63.2% classification rate. Table 5 shows mean classification rates by gaitset and location. Due to space considerations, we only report the mean of each personalized Gaitset/Location result over all participants; as such, the extreme values of 63.2% and 100.0% do not appear in any tables.

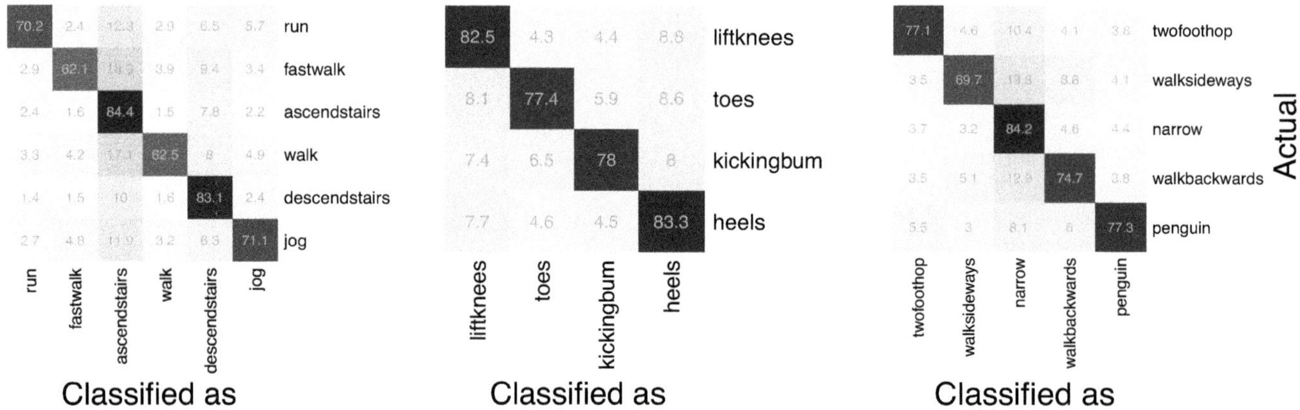

(a) Pedestrian (b) Exercise (c) Game

Figure 2: All-participant confusion matrices over all carrying locations for each gaitset (distinguishing only between gaits in the gaitset). Darker squares represent a higher classification rate. Numbers presented are percents of classification rates for each actual gait (rows sum to 100%).

Gaitset	Location	Mean % correct
Exercise	Belt	92.2
Exercise	Hand	91.0
Exercise	Arm	90.1
Exercise	Back Pocket	89.8
Exercise	Front Pocket	89.7
Exercise	Backpack	88.7
Game	Back Pocket	88.6
Game	Front Pocket	88.2
Pedestrian	Hand	87.9
Game	Hand	87.5
Game	Arm	87.4
Exercise	All Locations	87.3
Pedestrian	Front Pocket	87.0
Game	Belt	87.0
Pedestrian	Belt	86.7
Game	Backpack	86.3
Pedestrian	Back Pocket	86.0
Pedestrian	Arm	85.6
Pedestrian	Backpack	84.7
Game	All Locations	84.1
All	Front Pocket	83.0
Pedestrian	All Locations	82.7
All	Hand	82.3
All	Back Pocket	82.1
All	Belt	81.6
All	Arm	80.7
All	Backpack	80.1
All	All Locations	78.1

Table 5: By-participant means of gaitset/location accuracy rate. "All Gaits" results are highlighted in grey. Chance ranges from $6.6\bar{6}\%$ ("All Locations") to 25% ("Exercise").

DISCUSSION

Overall, the classification scheme performed with a varying range of success. In this section, we list our major conclusions to inform designers. We make an effort to compare our results with previous work whenever possible; please refer to our map (Table 1) for additional context.

Overall success

When trained and tested over all participants, accuracy ranged from 73.5% (All Gaits/Hand) to 87.2% (Exercise/Back Pocket), although we notably must exclude All Gaits/All Locations (due to limitations of computational resources), expected to be the worst performer. All are far larger than chance.

Overall, accuracy improved by about 5% when the algorithm was personalized (by-participant analysis). Although we cannot confirm statistical significance of this effect, it suggests that a short personalization session might improve classification rates. Even with personalization, though, there was a great deal of variation in accuracy: mean classification rates of each Gaitset/Location/Participant had extremes of 63.2% (minimum) to 100.0% (maximum). All classification rates are well above chance (the lowest classification rate, 63.2% compares to $6.6\bar{6}\%$ for all 15 gaits). For all locations and all gaits, after training on an individual for 30 seconds for each gait, the mean classification rate across all 12 participants was 78.1%.

For post-hoc analysis (analyzing a day's data for overall activity after-the-fact) we expect that both personalized and non-personalized algorithms (that is, trained on the user's data or not) could be sufficient for extremely high classification rates: Kunze et al. used a majority vote of several 1 second windows with 82% classification rate in 1 or more minute sequences to achieve 100% classification rate of walking vs not walking [22]. For real-time applications, a classification rate of 78.1% could be used with novel application design

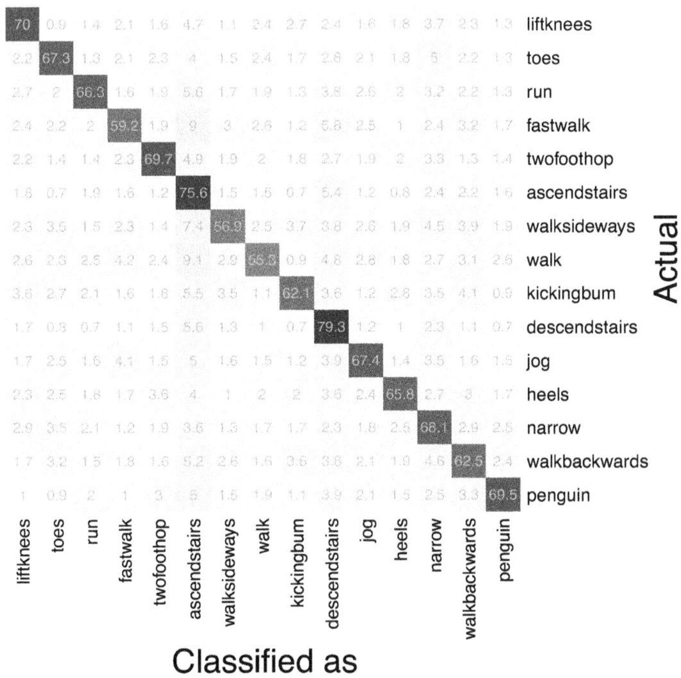

Figure 3: All-participants confusion matrix over all gaits and all carrying locations. Darker squares represent a higher classification rate. Numbers presented are percents of classification rates for each actual gait (rows sum to 100%).

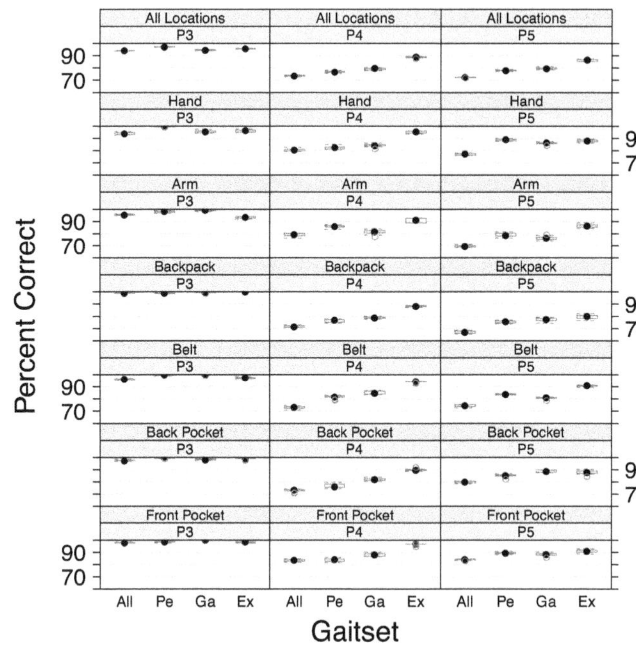

Figure 4: Bar-and-whiskers plot of gaitset performance for each of participants 3, 4, and 5 (chosen for illustrative purposes; P3's results are indicative of the high-performing participants P2, P3, and P9, while P4 and P5 are representative of the interactions present in the other 9 participants). Note the 3-way interactions between gaitset, location, and participant.

or game mechanics to improve perceived recognition rates. We also note that many of our gaits are very similar, and that careful pruning of the selection of gait could improve performance: our Exercise gaitset had a mean classification rate of 87.3% without knowledge of location when personalized, and achieved a mean classification rate of 92.2% when it was known to be mounted on the user's belt. Thus, our results are promising for robust classification of a wide variety of gaits.

Gait is a complex ecosystem of gaitset, location, and user

In Figure 4, we note interactions between location, gaitset, and participant. Different locations perform well with different gaitsets, and these vary depending on participant. With P3, we see a flat pattern across gaitsets and location — basically, the algorithm performed well for P3 regardless of location and gaitset. This pattern was observed for three participants: P2, P3, and P9; in fact, the 18 best performing data cells were from P3 and P9. No distinguishing demographic features stand out for these participants: both sexes are represented, heights and weights vary (155-183cm and 51-64kg respectively), and no notable behaviours were observed. This suggests that these gaits may work very effectively for certain individuals with minimal personalization (30 seconds per gait and location). If this is from gait interpretation, then it is possible that, if instruction is given to users, a wider variety of gaits could be effectively classified.

However, with other participants we see more variation (P4 and P5 are representative of the other 9 participants). Accuracy varies by participants and gaitsets when location is fixed. When the smartphone is carried in the hand, all gaitsets except for Exercise perform similarly for P4, but all gaitsets except for All Gaits perform similarly for P5. With different locations, more interactions appear; performance of all four gaitsets is similar for both P4 and P5 (but quite different from P3). We conclude that the performance of RF500 depends upon location, gaitset, and user, with intricate interactions.

In aggregate, Exercise does best and All Gaits worst

In general, the best performing gaitset tended to be Exercise, and the worst was the expected laggard, All Gaits. In the all-participant analysis, the top three performing data cells are Exercise data sets, and the worst four are from All Gaits (Table 4). In the by-participant analysis, the top 6 performing algorithms are Exercise sets, and the worst 6 performing algorithms are from All Gaits (Table 5). In both all-participant and by-participant analyses, the best performer for every location was Exercise, and the worst for every location was All Gaits. A close look at the by-participant results (Figure 4) shows that these results might change dramatically depending on the user even when the algorithm is personalized.

Gait similarity affects classification performance

Though there could be several reasons for the difference in performance of different gaitsets, such as the number of gaits within each gaitset, our findings suggest that the *types* of gaits chosen within each gaitset are an important factor. Major patterns in the all gaits confusion matrix follow, using "→" to indicate mis-classification. Mis-classification is not necessarily bidirectional.

As we can see in Figure 2, Exercise's gaits have fewer standout confusions with each other than the gaits in Pedestrian and Game, which is not surprising considering that Exercise is the best performing gaitset. Pedestrian has a number of confusions that suggest differences between these gaits are quite subtle, such as *walk → fastwalk* and *jog → fastwalk*. This is an expected result, and is consistent with the design of the Pedestrian gaitset to include very similar gaits. For the Pedestrian gaitset, then, we note that distinguishing between different categories of interpreted speeds of walking is challenging, and it may be best to only classify walking and jogging or running, or refer to cadence directly in applications.

In the Game gaitset we notice a dichotomy – two groups of gaits. Most gaits were mis-classified as *narrow*, especially *walksideways* and *walkbackwards*. The least confused gaits were *narrow → walksideways* and *penguin → walksideways*. We thus suggest that *narrow*, *walksideways*, and *walkbackwards* are similar, but different from *twofoothop* and *penguin* (which, unexpectedly, had a strong confusion with *penguin → twofoothop*). Ultimately, many of these gaits are similar to normal walking, and those that differ were more easily recognizable.

Pedestrian shows a number of confusions. As in the All Gaits confusion matrix (Figure 3), many were mis-classified as *ascendstairs*, and several were mis-classified as *jog*. Both *stairs* were often correctly distinguished from *jog* and *run*. Few gaits were confused with *run* and *walk*. Exercise demonstrates few standout confusions between its gaits. The most confused gait was *heels*, in that it has the darkest column excluding the diagonal element, followed by *liftknees*. The strongest individual confusion is *liftknees → heels*. *Toes* and *kickingbum* were confused with each other more than with the other two gaits.

Individual differences strongly influence gait recognition

Individual differences add an important dimension to the relationship between location and gaitset. This wide variation in individual differences for activity recognition is consistent with literature (Zhang et al. report 69% to 95.3% with their best classifier [35], Kunze et al. report 72% to 93% with a binary classifier [22]), but we are not aware of any previous work that has commented on or explored individual differences and their impact on gait. Furthermore, previous work has used a non-personalized algorithm for all participants; we demonstrate this effect *even when it is personalized via training on each participant, location, and gaitset*, suggesting that it is not merely error from the classifier, but could be an intrinsic component of each participant's gaits.

We thus suggest that future work attempting gait classification with gaits that might be susceptible to individual differences, such as the interpretation of unusual gaits or gaits with subtle differences, must accommodate these differences. We aim to pursue this in our future work.

CONCLUSION

In this work, we have given an argument for the role of gait classification in persuasive applications. We have identified a need for better comparison between different studies in this area, and provided a framework for comparison based differences in application area, implementation details, and validation methodology. We have used this framework to provide a map of relevant classification studies to help guide readers through the literature. Finally, we have provided our own contribution to real-time gait classification, looking at the difficult problem of classifying 15 novel, similar gaits considering 6 different carrying locations with only 30 seconds of data collected for each data cell.

There are limitations to our study that must be considered for interpretation and future work. As revealed by our framework, we have only a single algorithm, and a limited amount of data per data cell. More data could improve results, or make them more trustworthy. As well, there are two confounded variables in our study. First, our data was only collected once from each participant - individual differences could be a result of clothing or the phone orientation in addition to personal gait characteristics. Second, gaitsets do not have a consistent number of gaits: Pedestrian has 6 gaits, Game has 5, and Exercise has 4. We leave the investigation of these variables to future work. Finally, although we approach the problem of gait classification by exploring the limits of sensing, we suggest another angle for future work: examining how robust and accurate classification algorithms must be for use in persuasive mobile applications.

ACKNOWLEDGMENTS

We thank the reviewers for their insightful comments and our participants for their time and effort. This work was funded by the Natural Sciences and Engineering Research Council of Canada (NSERC) and received support from the Institute for Computing, Information and Cognitive Systems (ICICS) at UBC.

REFERENCES

1. Altun, K., Barshan, B., and Tunçel, O. Comparative study on classifying human activities with miniature inertial and magnetic sensors. *Pattern Recognition 43*, 10 (Oct. 2010), 3605–3620.
2. Bell, M., Chalmers, M., Barkhuus, L., Hall, M., Sherwood, S., Tennent, P., Brown, B., Rowland, D., Benford, S., Capra, M., and Hampshire, A. Interweaving mobile games with everyday life. In *Proceedings of the SIGCHI conference on Human Factors in computing systems*, no. April in CHI '06, ACM Press (2006), 417–426.
3. Brehmer, M., Graham, T. C. N., and Stach, T. Activate Your GAIM : A Toolkit for Input in Active Games. In *ACM FuturePlay 2010* (2010), 151–158.
4. Breiman, L. Random Forests. *Machine Learning 45* (2001), 5–32.

5. Buttussi, F., and Chittaro, L. Smarter Phones for Healthier Lifestyles: An Adaptive Fitness Game. *Pervasive Computing 9*, 4 (2010), 51–57.
6. Consolvo, S., Everitt, K., Smith, I., and Landay, J. A. Design requirements for technologies that encourage physical activity. In *Proceedings of the SIGCHI conference on Human Factors in computing systems - CHI '06*, ACM Press (New York, New York, USA, Apr. 2006), 457–466.
7. Consolvo, S., Klasnja, P., McDonald, D. W., Avrahami, D., Froehlich, J., LeGrand, L., Libby, R., Mosher, K., and Landay, J. A. Flowers or a Robot Army? Encouraging Awareness & Activity with Personal, Mobile Displays. In *Proceedings of the 10th international conference on Ubiquitous computing - UbiComp '08*, ACM Press (New York, New York, USA, Sept. 2008), 54–63.
8. Davis, S. B., Moar, M., Jacobs, R., Watkins, M., Riddoch, C., and Cooke, K. Ere Be Dragons : heartfelt gaming. *Digital Creativity 17*, 3 (Jan. 2006), 157–162.
9. Froehlich, J., Dillahunt, T., Klasnja, P., Mankoff, J., Consolvo, S., Harrison, B., and Landay, J. A. UbiGreen: investigating a mobile tool for tracking and supporting green transportation habits. In *Proceedings of the 27th international conference on Human factors in computing systems (CHI 2009)*, D. R. Olsen, Ed., vol. 09 of *CHI '09*, ACM SIGCHI, ACM (2009), 1043–1052.
10. Fujiki, Y. iPhone as a physical activity measurement platform. In *Proceedings of the 28th of the international conference extended abstracts on Human factors in computing systems - CHI EA '10*, ACM Press (New York, New York, USA, 2010), 4315–4320.
11. Fujiki, Y., Kazakos, K., Puri, C., Buddharaju, P., Pavlidis, I., and Levine, J. NEAT-o-Games: Blending Physical Activity and Fun in the Daily Routine. *Computers in Entertainment 6*, 2 (July 2008), Article 21.
12. Fujiki, Y., Kazakos, K., Puri, C., Pavlidis, I., Starren, J., and Levine, J. NEAT-o-Games: Ubiquitous Activity-based Gaming. In *CHI '07 extended abstracts on Human factors in computing systems - CHI '07*, ACM Press (New York, New York, USA, Apr. 2007), 2369–2374.
13. Gafurov, D., and Bours, P. Improved Hip-Based Individual Recognition Using Wearable Motion Recording Sensor. In *Security Technology, Disaster Recovery and Business Continuity*, T.-h. Kim, W.-c. Fang, M. K. Khan, K. P. Arnett, H.-j. Kang, and D. Ślzak, Eds., vol. 122 of *Communications in Computer and Information Science*. Springer Berlin Heidelberg, Berlin, Heidelberg, 2010, 179–186.
14. Hall, M., Frank, E., Holmes, G., Pfahringer, B., Reutemann, P., and Witten, I. H. The WEKA data mining software. *ACM SIGKDD Explorations Newsletter 11*, 1 (2009), 10–18.
15. Huynh, T., and Schiele, B. Analyzing features for activity recognition. In *Proceedings of the 2005 joint conference on Smart objects and ambient intelligence innovative context-aware services: usages and technologies - sOc-EUSAI '05*, ACM Press (New York, New York, USA, Oct. 2005), 159–164.
16. Iso, T., and Yamazaki, K. Gait analyzer based on a cell phone with a single three-axis accelerometer. In *Proceedings of the 8th conference on Human-computer interaction with mobile devices and services - MobileHCI '06*, ACM Press (New York, New York, USA, Sept. 2006), 141–144.
17. Jensen, K. L. v., Krishnasamy, R., and Selvadurai, V. Studying PH. A. N. T. O. M. in the wild. In *Proceedings of the 22nd Conference of the Computer-Human Interaction Special Interest Group of Australia on Computer-Human Interaction - OZCHI '10*, ACM Press (New York, New York, USA, Nov. 2010), 17–20.
18. Jones, E., Oliphant, T., Peterson, P., and Others. Scipy: Open source scientific tools for Python, 2012.
19. Kawahara, Y., Kurasawa, H., and Morikawa, H. Recognizing User Context Using Mobile Handsets with Acceleration Sensors. In *2007 IEEE International Conference on Portable Information Devices*, IEEE (May 2007), 1–5.
20. Kazakos, K., Fujiki, Y., Pavlidis, I., Bourlai, T., and Levine, J. NEAT-o-Games: Novel Mobile Gaming Versus Modern Sedentary Lifestyle. In *Proceedings of the 10th international conference on Human computer interaction with mobile devices and services - MobileHCI '08*, ACM Press (New York, New York, USA, Sept. 2008), 515–518.
21. Khan, A. M., Lee, Y.-K., Lee, S., and Kim, T.-S. Accelerometer's position independent physical activity recognition system for long-term activity monitoring in the elderly. *Medical & Biological Engineering & Computing 48*, 12 (Dec. 2010), 1271–1279.
22. Kunze, K., Lukowicz, P., Junker, H., and Tr, G. Where am I : Recognizing On-body Positions of Wearable Sensors. In *LOCA05: International Workshop on Location and Context-Awareness*, vol. 3479 (2005), 264–275.
23. Lin, J., Mamykina, L., Lindtner, S., Delajoux, G., Strub, H., Dourish, P., and Friday, A. FishnSteps: Encouraging Physical Activity with an Interactive Computer Game. In *8th International Conference on Ubiquitous Computing (Ubicomp 2006)*, P. Dourish and A. Friday, Eds., vol. 4206 of *Lecture Notes in Computer Science*, Springer Berlin Heidelberg (Berlin, Heidelberg, 2006), 261–278.
24. MapMyFitness Inc. MapMyRun, 2012.
25. Nike Inc. Nike+ Project, 2012.
26. Oliver, N., and Flores-Mangas, F. MPTrain: a mobile, music and physiology-based personal trainer. In *8th*

International Conference on Human Computer Interaction with Mobile Devices and Services (MobileHCI'06), M. Nieminen and M. Röykkee, Eds., ACM (2006), 21–28.

27. Press, W. H., Teukolsky, S. A., Vetterling, W. T., and Flannery, B. P. *Numerical recipes in C: The art of scientific computing: Second edition.* Cambridge University Press, 1992.
28. Sprager, S., and Zazula, D. A cumulant-based method for gait identification using accelerometer data with principal component analysis and support vector machine. *WSEAS Transactions on Signal Processing 5*, 11 (Nov. 2009), 369–378.
29. Stach, T., Graham, T. C. N., Brehmer, M., and Hollatz, A. Classifying Input for Active Games. In *Proceedings of the International Conference on Advances in Computer Enterntainment Technology - ACE '09*, ACM Press (New York, New York, USA, Oct. 2009), 379.
30. Stanley, K. G., Livingston, I., Bandurka, A., Kapiszka, R., and Mandryk, R. L. PiNiZoRo : A GPS-based Exercise Game for Families. In *Futureplay '10 Proceedings of the International Academic Conference on the Future of Game Design and Technology* (2010), 243–246.
31. Tudor-Locke, C. Taking Steps toward Increased Physical Activity: Using Pedometers To Measure and Motivate. *President's Council on Physical Fitness and Sports Research Digest 17*, 3 (2002), 3–10.
32. World Health Organization. WHO — Obesity and overweight, 2012.
33. World Health Organization. WHO — Physical Inactivity: A Global Public Health Problem, 2012.
34. Yang, J. Toward Physical Activity Diary: Motion Recognition Using Simple Acceleration Features with Mobile Phones. In *Proceedings of the 1st international workshop on Interactive multimedia for consumer electronics - IMCE '09*, ACM Press (New York, New York, USA, Oct. 2009), 1–10.
35. Zhang, S., Mccullagh, P., Nugent, C., and Zheng, H. Activity Monitoring Using a Smart Phones Accelerometer with Hierarchical Classification. In *6th International Conference on Intelligent Environments* (2010), 158–163.

Combining Acceleration and Gyroscope Data for Motion Gesture Recognition using Classifiers with Dimensionality Constraints

Sven Kratz
FX Palo Alto Laboratory
3174 Porter Drive, Palo Alto, CA, 94304, USA
kratz@fxpal.com

Michael Rohs
University of Hannover
Appelstraße 9A, 30167
Hannover, Germany
michael.rohs@hci.uni-hannover.de

Georg Essl
University of Michigan
Electrical Engineering and Computer Science
gessl@eecs.umich.edu

ABSTRACT
Motivated by the addition of gyroscopes to a large number of new smart phones, we study the effects of combining accelerometer and gyroscope data on the recognition rate of motion gesture recognizers with dimensionality constraints. Using a large data set of motion gestures we analyze results for the following algorithms: Protractor3D, Dynamic Time Warping (DTW) and Regularized Logistic Regression (LR). We chose to study these algorithms because they are relatively easy to implement, thus well suited for rapid prototyping or early deployment during prototyping stages. For use in our analysis, we contribute a method to extend Protractor3D to work with the 6D data obtained by combining accelerometer and gyroscope data. Our results show that combining accelerometer and gyroscope data is beneficial also for algorithms with dimensionality constraints and improves the gesture recognition rate on our data set by up to 4%.

Author Keywords
Motion Gestures; Mobile; Gesture Recognition; Accelerometer; Gyroscope; Sensor Fusion

ACM Classification Keywords
H.5.2

General Terms
Algorithms, Experimentation, Performance, Measurement, Human Factors

INTRODUCTION
A growing number of smart phones are being equipped with 3-axis gyroscopes in addition to 3-axis acceleration sensors. Combining the data from these two sensor types provides significantly more motion information compared to only using an accelerometer. On devices without a gyroscope, rotation can be approximated using accelerometers alone by using the direction of gravity as a reference for tilt. However, this approximation is not reliable in certain cases, i.e. when the device is rotated in the plane perpendicular to gravity, no tilt and thus rotation information can be obtained. The increase in motion information provided by gyroscopes can increase the recognition accuracy of motion gestures, which has been shown by previous work [4]. The higher recognition accuracy allows more complex gesture types to be used in mobile user interfaces, since the users can also add rotational components to their gesture inputs. Motion gestures can be used for a variety of applications on smart phones. These include gaming interfaces, where, for instance, the user interacts via a spell casting metaphor [1], entering special UI modes [11], UI navigation tasks [12] or user authentication [3].

It is desirable to have gesture recognizers for motion gestures on mobile devices that can be used early in the development of an application. This requires such algorithms be easy to implement and tune. Furthermore, for development on mobile devices in particular, it is beneficial for gesture recognition algorithms to be independent of specialized libraries or toolkits, in order to be able to deploy those algorithms on as many devices as possible.

Template-based techniques such as nearest-neighbor search are generally easy to implement and address most of the concerns mentioned previously. However, naïve template-based techniques will generally not compensate for variations in gesture execution time. A popular algorithm that does compensate for differences in time series is Dynamic Time Warping (DTW) [13]. Protractor3D [5] is a template-based technique developed for 3D acceleration data that compensates for rotational derivations between input sequences and templates by finding the optimal registration between input points and templates, in a way similar to Protractor [7], which only works with 2D data. A problem with Protractor3D is that this algorithm does not work with data dimensionalities greater than than 3.

In this paper we present a consensus-based approach using two instances of a template-based gesture recognizer (such as Protractor3D or DTW) to perform motion gesture recognition on the 6-D data obtained from an accelerometer-gyroscope pair. By analyzing a large corpus of motion gesture entries by users, we show that the combination of accelerometer and gyroscope data increases the gesture recognition rate by up to 4% on our data set. Our results indicate that combining acceleration data with rotation data from a 3-axis gyroscope will improve the gesture recognition rates for motion gestures entered on a mobile device. Reflecting on the results we obtained, we provide recommendations for the choice of a motion gesture recognizers for mobile applications.

RELATED WORK

DoubleFlip [11] addresses the problem of false positive gestures by employing a simple delimiter gesture (the "double flip" gesture) for entering gesture input mode. The criteria for choosing the "double flip" gesture were (1) the gesture being easy to perform and (2) the gesture being sufficiently distinct from everyday movement. To confirm the latter the authors investigated the false positive rate for a large corpus of everyday movement data.

Protractor [7] is a gesture recognition algorithm for touch screens. It is a template-based recognizer that resamples the gesture trace to get a vector with a fixed dimension, which is then translated to the origin and normalized. For each comparison with a template a rotation is performed that optimally aligns the input and template gestures. This is done in an efficient way using a closed-form analytic approach. *Protractor3D* [5] extends this idea to three dimensions. The approach is similar in principle to Protractor. However, finding a closed-form analytic solution in 3D is much more complicated. Compared to DTW, neither Protractor, nor Protracor3D do any kind of warping in the time domain.

Hoffman et al. [4] combined accelerometer and gyroscope data for gestural input. The addition of a gyrosope significantly increased their gesture recognition results. They used linear and AdaBoost [14] classifiers. Both of these methods can cope with high-dimensional feature vectors. In this paper we propose a method to leverage the additional motion data provided by a gyroscope with data-driven classifiers limited to three feature dimensions, such as Protractor3D.

EXTENDING PROTRACTOR3D WITH GYROSCOPE DATA

By design, Protractor3D cannot use data of a higher dimensionality than 3. This is inherent in the mathematics it uses to calculate the optimal registration between input points and templates. A simple extension to add support for gyroscope data in addition to accelerometer data is to run a second instance of Protractor3D in parallel on the gyroscope data. The remaining challenge is then to reconcile the two recognition results in order to determine which gesture has been recognized.

We propose a weighted approach that depends on the order of similarity of comparisons between input gestures and stored templates, i.e., templates that are less similar to the current input have a lower influence on the final recognition result. Our results indicate that the match with the lowest distance (or highest similarity) is most probably the gesture recognized. In other words, comparisons with a lower similarity are less likely to contribute to the decision on the recognition result.

Figure 1 shows pseudocode for the data combination algorithm (DCA) we devised. The algorithm returns the ID of

Inputs:
accResults: acceleration comparison results (list of gesture IDs sorted in descending order by similarity to the input)
gyrResults: acceleration comparison results (list of gesture IDs sorted in descending order by similarity to the input)
N: number of items in each of the comparison lists
bias: bias value determining influence of weaker comparisons
nGestureIDs: number of gesture classes (each class has a distinct ID)

```
counter = float[nGestureIDs]
for i=0 to N-1 do
    accRecogID = accRresults[i]
    gyrRecogID = gyrResults[i]
    counter[accRecogID] += 1.0/(bias*i +1.0)
    counter[gyrRecogID] += 1.0/(bias*i +1.0)
end for
bestGestureID = argmax(counter)
return bestGestureID
```

Figure 1. Data Combination Algorithm (DCA): pseudocode for a weighted approach to combine recognition results for accelerometer and gyroscope readings.

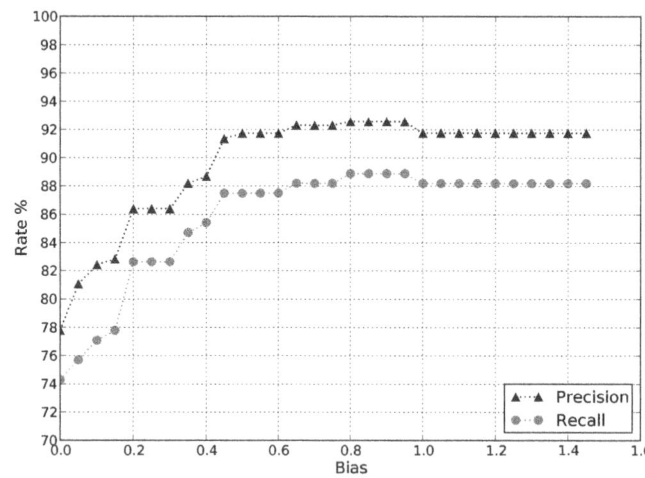

Figure 2. The influence of the bias variable in the weighted reconciliation algorithm. In this case $N = 5$. Choosing a $bias > 0.8$ does not further improve the gesture recognition rate, while giving each result an equal "vote" ($bias = 0$) generally results in a lower gesture recognition rate.

the best matching gesture. The *bias* variable determines the influence of comparison results according to their rank. Results with a low rank (i.e., lower distance to the input gesture) have a higher influence on the final matching result. The $argmax()$ function we used returns the index corresponding to the first occurrence if there are multiple occurrences of the same maximum value.

The DCA can be generalized easily to combine the results for more than two sensor data types. The only parameter of the algorithm that needs to be chosen specifically by the developer is *bias*. The optimal value for *bias* needs to be determined by analyzing existing user inputs. Figure 2 shows the influence of *bias* on *Precision* and *Recall*[1] results for our data set, where $0.8 \leq bias < 1.0$ provides the best result.

[1] for the definition of *Precision* and *Recall*, see Page 3, "Classifier Performance Metrics"

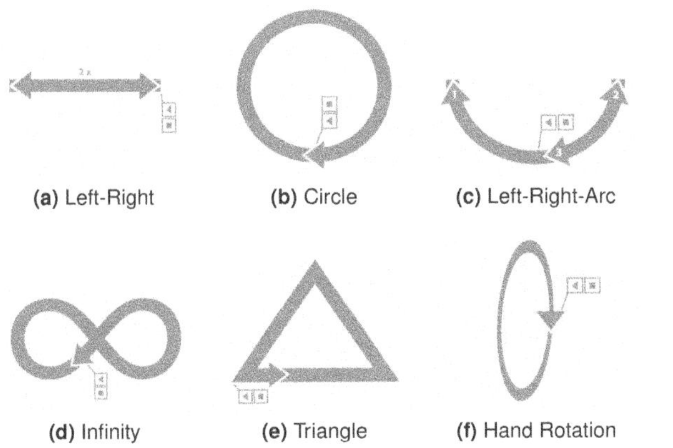

(a) Left-Right (b) Circle (c) Left-Right-Arc

(d) Infinity (e) Triangle (f) Hand Rotation

Figure 3. Visualization of the gesture classes we designed for input by the users.

COMBINING ACCELEROMETER AND GYROSCOPE DATA

To analyze the effects of combining 3-axis acceleration data with 3-axis rotation data for recognition by motion gesture recognizers, we present gesture recognition results for the following recognition algorithms: *Protractor3D*, *DTW* and *Regularized Logistic Regression (LR)* [6]. We chose DTW due to its popularity. We chose LR because it is, in contrast to DTW and Protractor3D, a feature-based machine learning algorithm that performs well with higher-dimensional data and it is still fairly easy to implement. LR is very efficient, since classification basically consists of multiplying a weight vector θ of a fixed length N (where N corresponds to the amount of features) with the features of the gesture input. Thus, compared with Protractor3D and DTW, the execution time of LR is independent of the number of training samples used.

Gesture Data Set

The gesture data for our analysis was gathered from 6 female and 9 male participants. All participants were right-handed, students and aged from 20 to 32 ($\mu = 24.3$, $\sigma = 2.9$). We compensated all participants with a small sum of money.

We designed six different gestures for the users to enter, as shown in Figure 3. Each participant provided a total of 15 samples for each gesture. Gestures were delimited using a *push-to-gesture* button. Recording of sensor data started when the button was pressed and ceased when the button was released. For all further analysis, we use the first 5 entries of each gesture by each user as (per-user) training templates and the corresponding last 10 entries for validation (also per-user). Our motivation for using the first 5 entries as training templates is because this reflects a realistic usage scenario for an mobile applications using personalized motion gestures. It is plausible to assume that new users would be required to train the system upon first use of the application.

In total, we recorded $15 \times 15 \times 6 = 1350$ gesture entries. 20 gesture entries had to be discarded, because they had too few samples due to erroneous entry. Our final data set size comprises 1330 gestures. Each gesture entry contains an average of 127 time-based data samples ($\sigma = 38.4$).

An iPhone 4 running a custom-built application, which provided logging and the push-to-gesture button interface, was used for recording gesture entries. We recorded the following data from the iPhone 4's accelerometer[2] and gyroscope[3] at a frequency of 80Hz: *acceleration*, *rotation rate* and *attitude*[4]. All acceleration values were measured in g, all rotation was measured in radians/second and attitude was given in Euler angles.

Recognition Results

We evaluated Protractor3D, DTW and LR for motion gesture recognition on the data set. As input to the algorithms, we used the following data and combinations thereof: *acc* (acceleration), *rot* (rotation), *att* (attitude), *acc-rot* (acceleration + rotation), *acc-att* (acceleration+attitude).

We configured Protractor3D to subsample and normalize the gesture entries to contain 64 samples. In order to keep the length of the feature representation for each gesture constant, we used the subsampled data generated by Protractor3D as input for LR. Each gesture was thus represented as a feature vector with a length of $64 \times 3 = 192$ for *acc, rot* and *att* and $64 \times 6 = 384$ for *acc-rot* and *acc-att*. For LR, we generated models for each gesture type for each user, and utilized per-user multi-class classification with a one-vs.-all strategy to classify the input gestures.

DTW used the unmodified sensor samples as input, as this algorithm is specifically designed to cope with length differences between inputs and templates. Our DTW implementation used the Euclidean (L^2) Norm as the distance function. We did not apply any step constraints for calculating the distance matrix.

Classifier Performance Metrics

As quantitative metrics for classifier performance, we use *Precision* (P), *Recall* (R) and F_1 score (F_1) [8, 9]. Given the amount of true positives tp, the amount of false positives fp and the amount of false negatives fn, Precision is defined as $P = tp/(tp + fp)$, i.e. the ratio of correct gesture recognitions out of all generated predictions. Recall is defined as $R = tp/(tp+fn)$, i.e. the ratio of correct gesture recognition out of all gestures in the data set. F_1 is defined as:

$$F_1 = 2\frac{PR}{P+R}$$

which represents a combined metric for the accuracy of a classifier and is based on the harmonic mean. The F_1 Score ranges from 0 to 1, where 1 is the best score obtainable.

Figure 4 shows the results for Precision (P), Recall (R) and F1-Score ($F1$) for the classifiers Protractor3D, DTW, and LR for each of the combinations of data types *acc* (acceleration), *rot* (rotation), *att* (attitude), *acc-rot* (acceleration + rotation), *acc-att* (acceleration+attitude). The combined data was evaluated using the DCA. In addition, we evaluated DTW and

[2]STMicroelectronics STM331DLH 3-axis MEMS accelerometer

[3]STMicroelectronics L3G4200D (equiv.) 3-axis MEMS gyroscope

[4]*attitude* represents the absolute change of rotation with respect to an initial reference frame, i.e. the device attitude at the beginning of a gesture recording.

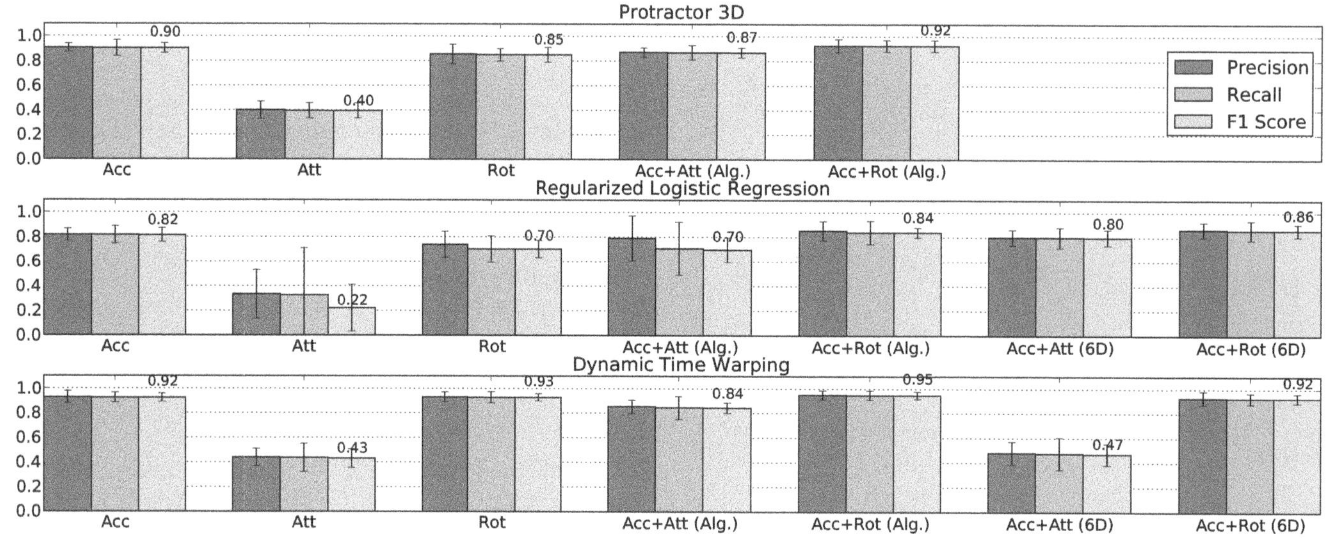

Figure 4. Mean recognition results for Protractor3D, Regularized Logistic Regression and DTW, for the data types accleration (*acc*), attitude (*att*), rotation (*rot*), acceleration+attitude *acc+att*), acceleration+rotation (*acc+rot*). "Alg." marks results the using the DCA. "6D" marks results using a 6D merged representation of accelerometer combined with gyroscope data. The error bars show the standard deviation. DTW with *acc+rot* using the combination algorithm achieved the best result with an F_1 Score of 0.95. The error bars show the standard deviation of the means.

LR without the DCA by using 6D feature vectors obtained by merging each 3D acceleration sample with its rotation counterpart. DTW with *acc-rot* and the DCA achieved the best result with an F_1 Score of 0.95, followed by Protractor3D using the same settings with an F_1 Score of 0.92. The best F_1 Score for LR was 0.86 using combined accelerometer and gyroscope data without the DCA. The lower score for LR suggests that a larger amount of training samples may be needed in order to obtain better results for this algorithm.

Statistical Analysis

We studied the effects of the *algorithm* (*P3D*, *DTW* and *LR*) and the *data type* (*acc*, *att*, *rot*, *acc+att* and *acc+rot*) on the mean F_1 score per gesture type. Not observing a normal distribution of the means, we ran Kruskal-Wallis tests for *algorithm* and *data type*, respectively. The results for *algorithm* ($H(2) = 9.46, p < 0.01$) and *data type* ($H(4) = 52.57, p < 0.001$) show significant effects. Non-parametric Dunn-Bonferroni [2] pairwise comparisons show a significant difference between *DTW* and *LR* ($Q = 20.45$, $p = 0.007$) for *algorithm*. Pairwise comparisons using the same method for *data type* unfortunately did not reveal significant effects between *acc* and *acc+rot* ($Q = -14.17$, $p = 0.1$), although we measured a 2%–4% increase in mean F_1 score depending on the algorithm used. The relatively low sample size $N = 18$ (mean values from 6 gestures $\times$ 3 algorithms) for each *data type* and the relatively small increase in F_1 score may not be sufficient to achieve $p < 0.05$ statistical significance in our case.

Algorithm Execution Times

For motion gesture recognizers, gesture recognition performance is not the only important criterion. The execution time is, arguably, equally important, especially on mobile platforms. The runtime of template-based approaches Protractor3D and DTW directly depends on the number of training templates, whereas this does not affect LR. To exemplify this for our data set, Protractor3D and DTW have to compare each of the 450 template gestures with 900 gesture entries, resulting in a total of 405,000 necessary comparisons for a single pass over the data set. For each comparison, DTW needs to construct a distance matrix with a size of $n \times m$, where n is the number of elements in the template and m of the sample, including evaluation of the distance function. A number of optimizations exist to improve the speed of DTW [10]. The results in this paper, however, reflect the performance of unoptimized DTW. Protractor3D does not have as much overhead as DTW, but still needs to complete the same number of comparison operations. By contrast, LR requires just 900 matrix multiplications to perform all predictions. Nevertheless, in comparison to DTW and Protractor3D, feature-based classifiers such as LR need a large number of training samples to work optimally, so developers face a trade-off between the time requested from users to enter training samples and the computational efficiency of the gesture recognizer.

Algorithm	Approx. Number of required comparisons	Profiled Cumulative Execution Time (s)	Average Processing Time per Gesture (s)
LR	900	0.4	0.004
Protractor3D	405,000	881	0.98
DTW	405,000	3966	4.4

Table 1. The approximate number of operations and the execution time (including data loading and pre-processing) required by the analyzed algorithms for a run on our data set. The average processing time per gesture was calculated by dividing the total execution time by the number of test samples in the training set. (Unoptimized) DTW is by far the slowest algorithm. LR has the lowest measured execution time as it performs only a single operation for each gesture in the validation set.

Table 1 shows the measured execution times for each algorithm when running on our data set. We implemented all gesture recognition algorithms in Python 2.7.1 using the *NumPy*, *SciPy* and *rpy2* libraries. All computation was performed on a Mac Pro with 2.66GHz Intel Core i7 processors. In order to measure the classifiers' execution time, we used Python's *cProfile* library. All classifiers were run exclusively as single-threaded applications and did not make use of parallel processing.

The comparison in Table 1 shows that the average per-gesture execution time of LR is two orders of magnitude lower than Protractor3D and three orders of magnitude lower than DTW. The runtime advantage of LR is thus very clear but the problem remains that this algorithm requires an optimization library in order to train models. Thus, the most beneficial use of LR would be in deployment-stage applications, with appropriate models for gesture recognition already trained, since the classification step does not require an optimization library. Protractor3D compares favorably with DTW, requiring about 4s less computation time. The measured processing time per gesture could be further improved by decreasing the subsampling size and switching from Python to a lower-level language such as C.

Summary and Discussion

Using a substantial data set, we analyzed the effect of adding the data of a gyroscope to accelerometer-based motion gesture recognition. In particular, we were interested in showing how adding additional gyroscope data affects dimensionally-constrained recognition algorithms, i.e. those that cannot process data of a dimensionality higher than 3. We devised a method to combine two or more dimensionally-constrained classifiers to perform motion gesture recognition for data dimensions greater than 3.

Confirming results obtained in previous work [4], our results indicate that combining accelerometer with gyroscope data leads to improvement in gesture recognition rates. Our key insight here is that also appears to work for simpler, template-based methods as well as dimensionally-constrained recognition algorithms, such as Protractor3D, using the data combination algorithm (DCA) we propose. Concretely, we observed 2%, 3%, and 4 % increases in F_1 score for Protractor3D, DTW and LR, respectively. Conversely, we observed that the proposed DCA does not improve the recognition rates of algorithms that can cope with higher-dimensional data, such as LR or DTW.

We recommend that developers choose their gesture recognition algorithm by (1) the number of training samples available (template-based approaches perform well, even with few training samples), (2) the performance constraints of their target devices (we obtained the highest F_1 score when using DTW, but it was also the algorithm with the highest execution time by far) and (3) the time available for coding during each iteration (template-based methods are easier to implement and deploy on different types of devices, since they do not require specialized libraries).

REFERENCES

1. Ballagas, R., Kratz, S.and Borchers, J., Yu, E., Walz, S., Fuhr, C., Hovestadt, L., and Tann, M. REXplorer: a mobile, pervasive spell-casting game for tourists. In *CHI'07 extended abstracts*, ACM (2007), 1929–1934.
2. Dunn, O. Multiple comparisons using rank sums. *Technometrics 6*, 3 (1964), 241–252.
3. Guse, D. Gesture-Based User Authentication on Mobile Devices using Accelerometer and Gyroscope (Master's Thesis). *Quality and Usability Group, Deutsche Telekom Laboratories, TU Berlin* (2011).
4. Hoffman, M., Varcholik, P., and LaViola, J. Breaking the status quo: Improving 3d gesture recognition with spatially convenient input devices. In *Virtual Reality Conference (VR), 2010 IEEE*, IEEE (2010), 59–66.
5. Kratz, S., and Rohs, M. Protractor3D : A Closed-Form Solution to Rotation-Invariant 3D Gestures. In *Proc. IUI 2011*, ACM (Palo Alto, CA, USA, 2011).
6. Lee, S., Lee, H., Abbeel, P., and Ng, A. Efficient L1 Regularized Logistic Regression. In *Proc. National Conference on Artificial Intelligence*, vol. 21, Menlo Park, CA; Cambridge, MA; London; AAAI Press; MIT Press; 1999 (2006), 401.
7. Li, Y. Protractor: a fast and accurate gesture recognizer. In *Proc. CHI 2010*, ACM (Atlanta, Georgia, USA, 2010), 2169–2172.
8. Makhoul, J., Kubala, F., Schwartz, R., Weischedel, R., et al. Performance measures for information extraction. In *Proceedings of DARPA Broadcast News Workshop* (1999), 249–252.
9. Powers, D. M. W. Evaluation: From precision, recall and f-measure to roc., informedness, markedness & correlation. *Journal of Machine Learning Technologies 2*, 1 (2011), 37–63.
10. Rakthanmanon, T., Campana, B., Mueen, A., Batista, G., Westover, B., Zhu, Q., Zakaria, J., and Keogh, E. Searching and mining trillions of time series subsequences under dynamic time warping. In *Proceedings of the 18th ACM SIGKDD international conference on Knowledge discovery and data mining*, ACM (2012), 262–270.
11. Ruiz, J., and Li, Y. DoubleFlip: a motion gesture delimiter for mobile interaction. In *Proc. CHI 2011*, ACM (2011), 2717–2720.
12. Ruiz, J., Li, Y., and Lank, E. User-defined motion gestures for mobile interaction. In *Proc. CHI 2011*, ACM (2011), 197–206.
13. Sakoe, H., and Chiba, S. Dynamic programming algorithm optimization for spoken word recognition. *IEEE Transactions on Acoustics, Speech and Signal Processing 26*, 1 (1978), 43–49.
14. Schapire, R. E. A brief introduction to boosting. In *Proceedings of the Sixteenth International Joint Conference on Artificial Intelligence*, IJCAI '99, Morgan Kaufmann Publishers Inc. (San Francisco, CA, USA, 1999), 1401–1406.

Mind the Gap: Collecting Commonsense Data about Simple Experiences

Jerry S. Weltman
Louisiana State University
Baton Rouge, Louisiana
jweltm2@tigers.lsu.edu

S. S. Iyengar
Florida International University
Miami, Florida
iyengar@cis.fiu.edu

Michael Hegarty
Louisiana State University
Baton Rouge, Louisiana
mhegar1@lsu.edu

ABSTRACT
In natural language, there are many gaps between what is stated and what is understood. Speakers and listeners fill in these gaps, presumably from some life experience, but no one knows how to get this experiential data into a computer. As a first step, we have created a methodology and software interface for collecting commonsense data about simple experiences. This work is intended to form the basis of a new resource for natural language processing.

We model experience as a sequence of comic frames, annotated with the changing intentional and physical states of the characters and objects. To create an annotated experience, our software interface guides non-experts in identifying facts about experiences that humans normally take for granted. As part of this process, the system asks questions using the Socratic Method to help users notice difficult-to-articulate commonsense data. A test on ten subjects indicates that non-experts are able to produce high quality experiential data.

Author Keywords
Knowledge Acquisition; Common Sense; Large-scale Collaboration

ACM Classification Keywords
H.5.2 **[Information Interfaces and Presentation]:** User Interfaces – Natural language; I.2.6 **[Artificial Intelligence]:** Learning – Knowledge acquisition; I.2.4 **[Artificial Intelligence]:** Knowledge Representation Formalisms and Methods.

General Terms
Human Factors; Design.

INTRODUCTION
In natural language, there are many gaps between what is stated and what is understood. Consider this simple story:

1) *Max was on the sofa, bored, all by himself. There was a pretty vase on a little side table. He went there and picked it up. He dropped it. Crash! This was fun!*

This simple narrative contains many unstated gaps that even the youngest reader could fill in, but a computer cannot:

- Max is probably a little boy
- Max is probably in a room
- At the start of the story, Max is probably in a sitting position
- Max sees the vase before going to it
- In order to pick up the vase, Max probably walks to the side table
- To walk to the vase, Max first stands up
- Etc.

Speakers and listeners fill in these gaps, presumably from some life experience. Even very young children have collected a wealth of life experiences needed to understand simple stories. As artificial intelligence (AI) critic and philosopher Hubert Dreyfus points out, regarding early attempts to program computers to understand language:

> The programs lacked the common sense of a four-year-old, and no one knew how to give them the background knowledge necessary for understanding even the simplest stories [2].

In the many years since Dreyfus's original 1972 publication, researchers still have not been able to devise a scheme for giving computer programs the background knowledge required for understanding simple stories.

Previous attempts to collect narrative data for automatic story understanding and general natural language processing (NLP) have failed to gain traction. AI workers initially experimented with canonical abstract life scripts such as going to a restaurant or children's party [15], but these scripts are difficult to build on a large scale because they require a great deal of expertise.

Some attempts to collect life experiences via volunteer crowdsourcing [17, 18, 20] also have faltered in part because it is quite difficult for non-experts to provide narratives at a granularity suitable for commonsense modeling. A more recent crowdsourcing experiment with collecting narratives [7] shows promise for inferring typical event ordering; however, the problem remains that people habitually omit what they consider to be obvious actions and states – information critical to commonsense modeling.

We propose a new methodology to help non-experts create experiential narratives. To address the natural tendency to omit details when describing an everyday experience, our methodology employs three novel techniques: 1) We model experience as a sequence of still frames, like the still images of an animation flip book. When animated, the frames expose gaps in actions; if the movement appears too abrupt, more frames need to be added. 2) We ask annotators to describe intention, emotion, location, and motion - information that is critical to a commonsense understanding of the situation. 3) We then ask annotators to explain the reason behind each description. Similar to the Socratic Method, we display the annotators' answers as a general rule, which exposes commonsense assumptions and encourages deeper explanations.

This methodology could be used as a basis for collecting detailed and coherent experiential data, which would be a fundamentally new type of resource for NLP as well as for general cognitive modeling. In the future, we envision a website that is a wiki-based collaboration, which means contributors view, discuss, and edit each other's work. The short scenes, or *experiences*, that contributors create would be open for discussion and would undergo many refinements as contributors hash out their meaning.

The overall project, called the Human eXperience Project (HXP), is a methodology and corresponding software framework that enables non-experts to create detailed narratives of simple everyday experiences. In line with the goals of McCarthy et al. outlined in [8], HXP focuses on *simple* experiences—activities and naïve mental states that one would expect to find in stories at the level of kindergarten or first grade. Concentrating on the knowledge found in children's stories helps make story understanding more tractable [8]. We know of no work that specifically focuses on collecting highly detailed child-centered experiences from non-experts. We believe that such a corpus would be a boon to statistically-oriented NLP. It would also help provide the raw data to develop new types of architectures for deep semantics and commonsense reasoning algorithms [1, 4, 10, 12, 16, 21].

We first describe the comic frames that form the basis of an experiential narrative. Then we show how users add the background, characters, and props. Next we discuss the annotation process: how the software guides the user to create statements and general rules of common sense to explain each statement. Then we describe a user test of the methodology, followed by related and future work.

COMIC FRAMES

To create an experience, a user first creates a series of comic strip frames, where each frame represents some

Figure 1: First six frames of "Max breaks the vase"

small slice in time (e.g. one second or less). Figure 1 shows the first six frames of an experience, entitled "Max breaks the vase," based on the events in (1). The frames depict a little boy named Max sitting in the living room with nothing to do. He notices a vase and picks it up. Later, he drops it on the floor with a crash (not shown here).

The format of the frames is not important at this point in the project; they can be drawings (either 2-D or 3-D), a series of photographs, or even a series of stills from a video. The only requirements are that there be multiple frames for each scene (we want a dynamic situation). For this example, we used Pixton, a free comic editing/sharing web site with reportedly hundreds of thousands of participants.[1]

When shown one after the other, the images give the illusion of animation. The goal is to make the animations appear fairly smooth. For example, an image of a boy on a sofa, followed by one of a boy next to a table, would be too abrupt; it would leave out the commonsense knowledge about how the boy gets to the table.

As an informal test, we asked two undergraduates to create some simple experiences along the style of Figure 1. After a few minutes of training, they were able to create a ten-frame narrative in about an hour.

For this paper, we will assume that the comic frames have already been created. We focus our attention on the most challenging aspect of the data collection: annotating each frame.

[1] http://pixton.com

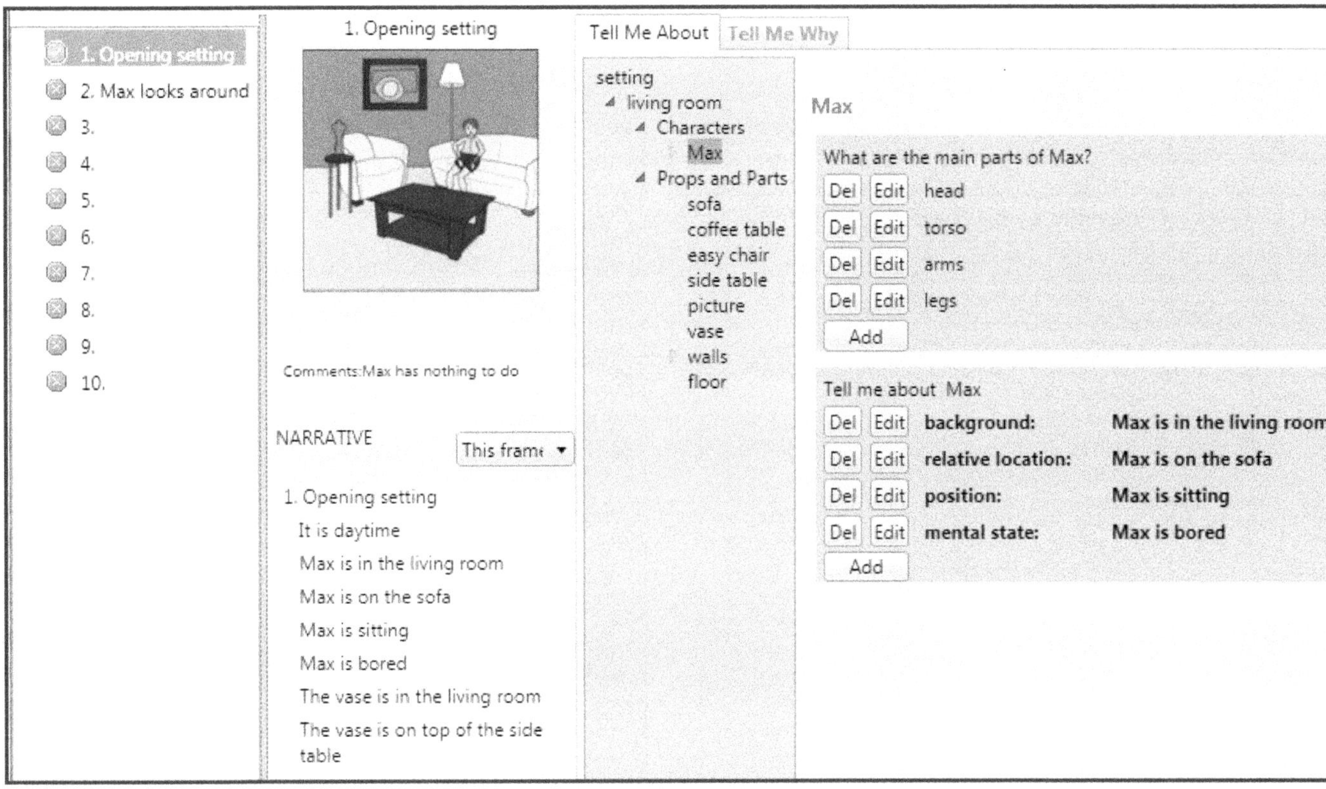

Figure 2: The opening setting after the user adds the background, character, and vase

BACKGROUND, CHARACTERS, AND PROPS

Similar to comics or movie editing software, the HXP software interface provides a set of stock background settings, characters, and props from which a contributor can populate a comic frame. Example backgrounds are a living room, kitchen, classroom, or park. Example props are a ball or vase, and example characters are a little boy and his mother.

There are currently a handful of stock backgrounds, characters, and props. The stock choices are pre-configured, but they can be edited by advanced users. (Capabilities of advanced users are currently not implemented.)

In our example experience, a user would select *living room* as the background setting. This setting comes pre-configured with many objects such as a floor, ceiling, four walls, and some furniture such as a coffee table. The user adds a vase to the frame by selecting from a list of stock props, then adds a boy from the stock characters, naming the boy *Max*. At this point, the user is prompted to input key commonsense information about Max: Max's room location, his body pose, and his mental state. Figure 2 shows the screen after the user has selected *on the sofa* for the location of Max, *sitting* for the body position, *bored* for his mental state, and *on top of the side table* for the room location of the vase.

THE ANNOTATION PROCESS

After selecting the background, character, and props, and providing key information about them, the software interface guides the user to add statements describing the characters and props. First we show an example of adding a statement using controlled natural language. Then we show how the Tell Me Why screen uses the Socratic Method to help users explain the reason for the statements.

Adding a Statement

When a user adds a statement, HXP does not parse free text, but rather structures the user input by using drop-downs and selections from controlled vocabularies. It provides feedback in natural language to show the meaning of the user's choices. This type of interface is called WYSIWYM for "What You See Is What You Mean" [14]. It controls the input so that all statements are unambiguous. All words in a statement are linked either to the WordNet [5] standard ontology or to the HXP database (for words and concepts not found in WordNet).

Figure 3 shows a screen to input "Max thinks the vase is pretty." Each of the six inputs is a drop-down choice based on the current state of the input.

In step 1, the user chooses from a list of mental states, including emotions such as *angry* and *glad* as well as complex states such as *belief* and *desire*. There are about 60 mental states currently in the system. Once the user has chosen *think,* the system displays "Max thinks some object has some state or action" and prompts the user to choose an object from this frame.

In step 2, the user chooses among all the objects that are in the frame, including all the props, parts of props, and characters. In this example, the user chooses *vase*, and the system displays "Max thinks the vase has some state or action."

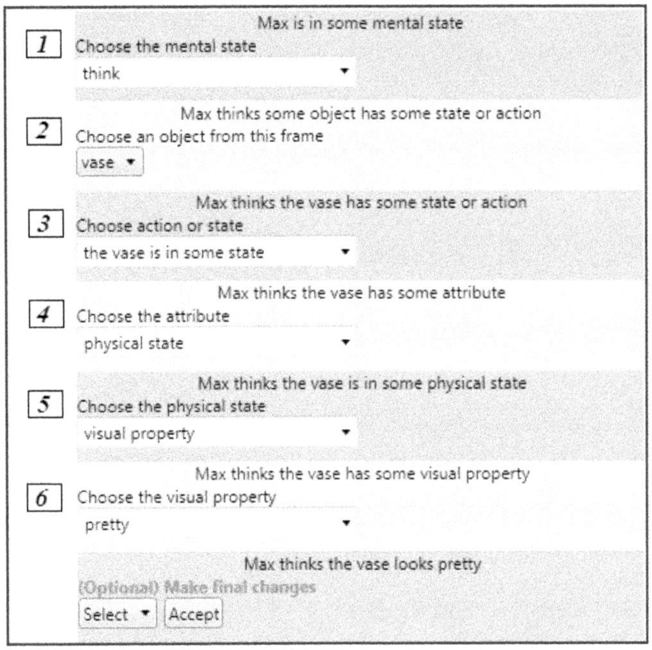

Figure 3: Input screens for the statement "Max thinks the vase looks pretty."

In step 3 the user is prompted to specify whether the vase is in some state or is doing some action. The user chooses *the vase is in some state* and continues on with the rest of the steps to drill down to *pretty*. Note, as a short cut, the user can simply type in *pretty* at any of the steps, starting at 3.

The underlying data structure representing each statement is a clause, containing a subject, predicate, optional arguments, and an optional subclause. In this example,

- Clause (subject="Max", predicate="think")
- Subclause(subject="vase", predicate="visual_attribute", argument="pretty")[2]

Different predicates require different input screens and argument structures. HXP has about a dozen general-purpose templates that control the structure of the predicate, and each predicate maps to a template. For example, there is a template for enumerated types like colors and shapes, and another template for relative location predicates like *next to*. In this example, *think* is mapped to a template that requires a subclause. Of course, there are many synonyms for *think*, such as *believe*, *imagine*, and *consider*. Users choose the most appropriate synonym, and different synonyms could map to different templates.

Tell Me Why

We have seen how a user creates statements that describe the objects in a frame. Now we will see how a user creates a generalized rule that explains each statement. Going back to Figure 2, we see that the user has created seven statements, starting at the top of the Narrative section with "It is daytime." The Tell Me Why tab at the top of the figure is red, indicating that the user has not explained the reason behind these statements. Figure 4 shows the corresponding Tell Me Why screen.

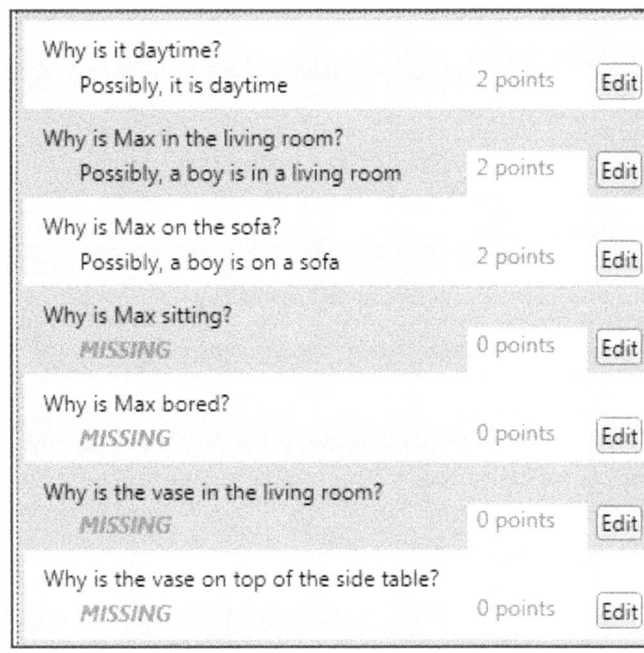

Figure 4: The Tell Me Why screen asks the user to explain each statement. The first three statements have been answered as simply "one of many possibilities." The other statements are unexplained.

As with any "Tell me why..." question, sometimes the answer is simply, "Just because I said so!" That is, the reason is too difficult to explain. In this example, there really is no good reason as to why daytime was chosen as the time of day. Therefore, the user chooses *This is just one of many possibilities* – the polite equivalent of "Just because!" Users always have the options of answering in this way, and this is perfectly fine, especially in the opening scene where the characters and setting are just being introduced.

However, even in the opening scene it is possible to provide a more informative answer to some questions. Let us look at the fourth question, "Why is Max sitting?" This

[2] For convenience of implementation, HXP considers predicate adjectives such as *pretty* to be binary relations.

statement can be explained in terms of the previous statement "Max is on the sofa."

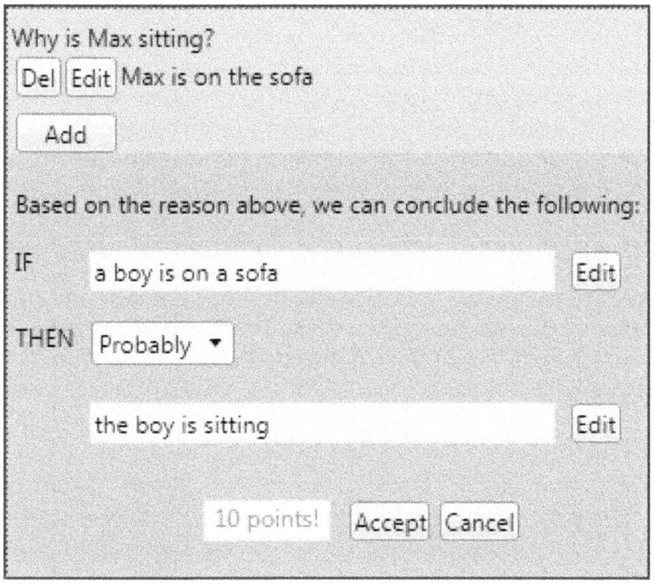

Figure 5: The user explains that we know that Max is sitting because Max is on the sofa. This explanation is then displayed as a general rule of common sense.

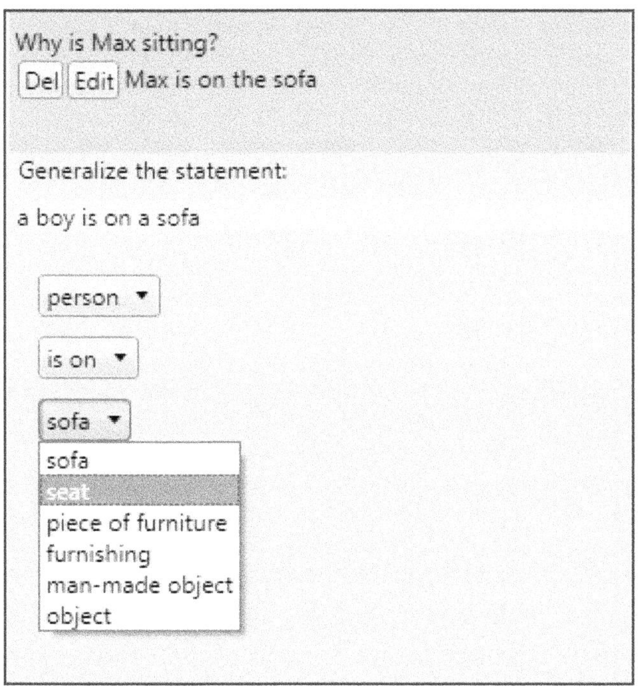

Figure 6: The user chooses hypernyms to generalize *a boy is on a sofa*. The user has already generalized *boy* to *person* and is now generalizing *sofa* to *seat*.

The relationship between being on a sofa and being in a sitting position is an unstated, but understood, rule of common sense. The HXP user interface guides the user through a series of screens to create this rule. First the user selects which of the previous statements somehow allow us to assume that Max is sitting. In this case, the user chooses the statement "Max is on the sofa." The system now restates this explanation as a general If-Then rule, as shown in Figure 5. The user has the option of editing the rule to make it more general. In this case, the user edits "a boy is on a sofa" and generalizes by choosing from the hypernyms for each noun. *Boy* has many hypernyms, including *male*, *child*, *person*, *living thing*, and *object*. Likewise, *sofa* has many hypernyms, including *seat*, *piece of furniture*, *furnishing*, *man-made object*, and *object*. The hypernyms are taken from WordNet, with a few modifications. In this example, the user's best generalization would be from *boy* to *person* and from *sofa* to *seat*.

Figure 6 shows the input screen for generalizing the statement. After generalization, the rule is:

2) IF a <u>person</u> is on a <u>seat</u>
THEN probably the <u>person</u> is sitting

To recap, a user first answered the question "Why is Max sitting?" by choosing a previous statement "Max is on the sofa." HXP then restated this explanation in terms of the general If-Then rule, shown in Figure 5. We have found that restating the explanation in this form exposes gaps in commonsense information and encourage users to add more detail.

Once satisfied that the rule seems to answer the question, the user proceeded to generalize it further, arriving at (2). At this point, not only has the user explained how we know that Max is sitting in this specific situation, but also the user has generated a useful rule for NLP, qualified by *probably*. In other words, given a situation where a person is on a seat, an NLP application could infer that the person is sitting, and the qualification of *probably* could be used to prioritize this rule over other possible rules.

The example illustrates the gap between what is stated and what is understood. In typical narratives, most people would assume that someone is in a state of sitting if the narrative says that the person is on a sofa.

It is instructive to look at another example to show the efficacy of this method. In Frame 2 of Figure 1, Max looks around for something to do. During the training portion of our user test, when asked why Max looks around, every one of the test subjects easily answered, "Max is bored," which is Max's mental state from Frame 1. This answer leads to rule (3), which seems correct.

3) IF a boy is bored
THEN probably the boy looks around

Moving on to Frame 3 of Figure 1, the question is much more difficult: Why does Max stand up? At first, each test subject tried to answer again that Max is bored, generating rule (4).[3]

4) *IF a boy is bored
THEN probably the boy stands up

The subjects were generally unhappy about this rule because the mere fact that a boy is bored does not generally lead to the boy standing up. In fact, we know that Max is getting up to go to the vase. To capture this intention, one subject added the statement to Frame 2: "Max is curious about the vase" and gave this new statement as the reason for why Max gets up, generating rule (5).

5) *IF a boy is curious about a vase
THEN probably the boy stands up

When the subject saw rule (5), the subject realized that curiosity was not enough to explain why Max stands up. Other subjects added statements about Max's intention, such as "Max desires to play with the vase" or "Max desires to examine the vase." But even these statements were judged to be insufficient as soon as they were presented as, shown in rule (6).

6) *IF a boy desires to examine a vase
THEN probably the boy stands up

In order for a rule to make sense, the subjects had to add statements indicating that the vase is not near Max, and that Max is sitting, generating rule (7).[4]

7) IF a boy is sitting
AND the boy desires to examine a vase
AND the boy is not near the vase
THEN probably the boy stands up

When the subjects viewed rule (7), it seemed right; it seemed to reasonably explain why Max stands up. Once the subjects felt that the rule reasonably explains why Max stands up, they generalized it to rule (8).

8) IF a <u>person</u> is sitting
AND the <u>person</u> desires to examine an <u>object</u>
AND the <u>person</u> is not near the <u>object</u>
THEN probably the <u>person</u> stands up

Generalized rules like (8) allow specific situations to be compared to a class of situations – very useful for commonsense modeling. But the process of creating the rules itself is also useful for commonsense modeling because it leads users to add more details. Of course, these additional details spawn even more statements. Why does Max desire to examine the vase? It is because Max sees the vase and perhaps Max thinks the vase is pretty. It is important to note, however, that the user can stop the Tell Me Why cycle at any time by choosing *This is just one of many possibilities*.

The confidences levels of *possibly*, *probably*, and *definitely* are deliberately non-precise. They represent what most people would assume if they were to fill in the gap between what is stated and what is understood in the context of a typical narrative.

To motivate users to add detail and general rules, we established a simple point system on each explanation. If a user takes the easy way out with the "Just because" answer, they receive the minimum points. But if they can explain a statement in terms of a previous statement, they receive more points. And if they can generalize the statement from, say, *boy* to *person*, they get even more points. Finally, the most points are obtained by increasing the confidence level from *possibly* to *probably* or to the highest level of *definitely*.

USER TEST

We conducted a test to assess the effectiveness of our methodology. There were ten subjects: five undergraduates (music, English lit., undecided, and two from biology), four professionals with at least a bachelor's degree (accounting, psychology, business computing, linguistics), and one high school student (ninth grade). Ages ranged from 15 to 54, with half below age 25. Half were male. The evaluation consisted of a one-on-one training session for about two hours, followed by a second session where we asked subjects to annotate a few frames until they had created enough statements and explanations to score 100 points (typically five statements). In the training session, we introduced the subjects to automated NLP and our goal of collecting simple life experiences. Then we went through the first three frames of "Max breaks the vase," creating statements and explaining them with general rules. In each case, the subjects breezed through the first two frames, but as soon as they encountered "Why does Max stand up?" in the third frame, they were stuck. We spent the majority of the training talking them through the process of filling in missing information and generating relevant rules. Consequently, all of the subjects were interactively guided to produce a rule similar to Rule (8) during the training.

In the second session, we asked subjects to drive the input, specifying the statements and rules. These sessions were always with individual subjects with no collaboration. Since this was an evaluation of the methodology, not the software per se, we handled the mouse and keyboard to relieve the subjects of worrying about screen navigation. However, one subject preferred to do the navigation.

[3] The (*) in rule (4) indicates the subjects found the rule unacceptable and subsequently changed it.

[4] One test subject added a separate mental state "Max desires to walk to the vase" with a similar explanation.

1. Opening setting
   It is daytime.
   Max is in the living room.
   Max is on the sofa.
   Max is sitting.
   Max is bored.
   The vase is in the living room.
   The vase is on the side table.
   Max is naughty.
   The side table is on the floor.

2. Max looks around the living room
   Max sees the vase.
   Max desires to be having fun.
   Max desires to break the vase.
   Max desires to drop the vase.
   Max desires to walk to the vase.

3. Max stands up
   Max is standing.
   Max is next to the sofa.

4. Max walks to the side table
   Max is near the side table.
   Max desires to pick up the vase.

5. Max grasps the vase
   Max is in contact with the vase.
   The arms are in contact with the vase.

6. Max picks up the vase
   The vase is not on the side table.
   The vase is over the side table.
   Max desires to turn with the vase.
   Max desires to turn from the side table.

Figure 7: User annotations from the first six frames. The numbered statements are frame captions, representing actions. The statements below each caption result from the action.

Two of the ten subjects were able to create statements, but were confused about how to create general rules and did not complete the test. The remaining eight created an average of 11.6 statements and explained them with general rules. It took about 1-1.5 hours to produce these statements, as subjects were still getting used to the methodology. Four of these eight found the process doable, but tedious and difficult. They were happy to do the minimum and finish, each creating about five statements. However, the other four subjects said that the program was cool and "nerdy fun." They produced an average of 20 statements, with the maximum of 25. All four voluntarily continued until all frames were annotated, adding about an additional half hour to the sessions. Two of them were motivated by the points awarded to each statement, and one in particular asked what others had done and made sure to double it.

Evaluating the data

Figure 7 shows the statements from the first six frames created by one of the more prolific subjects. The statements are rich in detail, capturing intention, emotion, location, and motion. Each of the numbered statements is a frame caption. Except for the Opening setting, the captions are actions and the statements below them are states that somehow result from those actions.

All of the captions and statements were created by the user. However, we directed the user in the first three frames as part of the training session. While space does not permit us to display all of the rules that were created for these frames, Figure 8, which shows the explanations for the statements in Frame 4, represents the type of rules collected.

The first line in Figure 8 begins an explanation of the caption of Frame 4: Why does Max walk to the side table? The explanation comprises three previous statements, which are generalized. That is, *object* stands for *vase*, *person* stands for *Max*, and *table* stands for *side table*.

Why does Max walk to the side table?
IF an object is on a table
AND a person desires to walk to the object
AND the person is standing
Probably, the person walks to the table

Why is Max near the side table?
IF a living thing goes to an object
Definitely, the living thing is near the object

Why does Max desire to pick up the vase?
IF a person is near a side table
AND a jar is on the side table
AND the person desires to drop the jar
Probably, the person desires to pick up the jar

Figure 8: Rules created to explain the statements in Frame 4.

The second block in Figure 8 begins the explanation of a state: Why is Max is near the side table? The explanation comprises just one previous statement, the caption itself, generalized so that *living thing* now stands for *Max*, *goes* stands for *walks*, and *object* stands for *side table*.

The third block in Figure 8 begins the explanation of the state: Why does Max desire to pick up the vase? The explanation comprises generalizations of three previous statements: Max is near the side table, the vase (generalized to *jar*) is on the side table, and Max desires to pick up the vase.

Each of the three rules in Figure 8 is excellent; they adequately explain the corresponding frame statement, and they are nicely generalized so that they may apply to many situations. The first and third rules are justified in having a confidence of *probably*, because they assert what usually one would expect given the statements in the antecedent. In contrast, the second rule has a confidence of *definitely*, which is appropriate because in the context of a typical narrative, if the text says that some living thing goes to some object, then an NLP application would almost always be correct in subsequently placing the living thing near that object.

It is interesting to note how each subject's interpretations are slightly different. In two of the interpretations, Max drops the vase because it is too heavy. In another, Max is a naughty boy and desires the break the vase from the onset. In another he is angry because he is being punished. There is no expected "true interpretation." We asked only that subjects come up with reasonable statements and explanations.

We instructed the test subjects to produce rules with a confidence of at least *probably* if they could come up with a justified explanation, and all the subjects tried hard to do so. We collected 95 rules with a confidence of either *probably* or *definitely*.

To rate each rule, we used a panel of three judges, consisting of the first author and two of the more enthusiastic test subjects. Each judge independently rated all the rules as either acceptable or unacceptable. An unacceptable rule had the confidence level too high or was missing at least one critical explanation. Rule (9) below is unacceptable because the object could be something that does not normally break when dropped. Rule (10) is unacceptable because, just because a person desires to do something, we cannot say that the person will definitely do it.[5]

9) IF a person picks up an object
   AND the object falls
   THEN probably the object breaks

10) IF a person desires to walk to an object
    AND the object is on top of a table
    THEN definitely the person walks to the table

The judges found 87% of the rules to be acceptable. The opinions were unanimous on 75% of the rules, and we took the majority opinion on the remaining 25%.

Discussion

In a ten-person user evaluation, eight people were able to contribute high quality, detailed data using this methodology. Of those eight, half found the process tedious and difficult, but half found it to be challenging and fun. We are encouraged by the results that 87% of the user-built rules were acceptable, particularly because we purposely did not choose computer science majors or AI fans. Crucially, subjects could easily understand the annotations of others and found it enjoyable to identify others' problems, as attested by the fact that two judges were test subjects themselves and had no previous experience with this process.

Clearly it is unrealistic to think that we can recruit armies of casual volunteers to use this framework for collecting experiential data. But with improvements in training and a wiki format where annotators view and discuss each other's work, we believe we may be able to tap into that small percentage of the vast web population who would enjoy collaborating on this difficult task.

RELATED WORK

There are a few closely related projects for collecting narrative data. Scheherazade [3] seeks to create a bank of annotated stories to advance text understanding and narratology. StoryNet [18] and ComicKit [20], both associated with MIT's Open Mind Common Sense (OMCS) project [19], attempted to collect stories specifically for commonsense reasoning. The next two subsections describe these projects and how they relate to HXP.

Scheherazade

The Scheherazade system (henceforth SCH) is a tool for annotating stories. It is intended to be used to create a corpus of annotated texts for automated narrative analysis. HXP shares many attributes of SCH. Both systems represent intentions and goals with causal links. Both systems specifically identify actors, locations, props, and narrative time slices (called "story points" in SCH). Finally, they both use a WYSIWYM user interface to guide the user input with minimum parsing. SCH allows non-experts to paraphrase general text, and it succeeds marvelously. Indeed, SCH is not merely a proof of concept; it is a mature, ready-to-use product. Nevertheless, SCH focuses on narratological issues of plot patterns and story structure rather than on collecting commonsense data. In contrast, HXP goes after difficult-to-articulate assumptions we make when we read a text.

OMCS Projects

There have been several attempts to use narrative structures for commonsense reasoning. Schank, Minsky, and colleagues introduced the concept of scripts and frames in the 1970s [15, 11]. Scripts are abstractions of event sequences based on many concrete experiences. Mueller created a database of scripts specifically for story understanding but noted the difficulty and tedium involved with trying to create them [13]. Creating a master script to generalize an activity is extremely difficult. Indeed, it

[5] We thank one of our test subjects for suggesting this guideline: an agent's intentions or desires are never enough to warrant a confidence level of *definitely*.

requires a great deal of expertise to find the quintessential sequence of events and roles that make up a generalized *type* of activity such as going to a restaurant.

On the other hand, almost anyone can describe what happens in a particular experience at a particular time and place. As Singh and colleagues point out in their motivation for OMCS's StoryNet, "it may be easier to tell and explain a specific story, which focuses the user on a specific set of characters, objects, and events, and their relationships, than to ask them to make a general rule-based theory in the abstract of some domain" [18]. One of the reported ideas to collect stories was to have people describe their own life stories. But this proved to be too unstructured. Another idea was to make use of the OMCS data to offer an easy-to-use interface for creating structured stories. Using a simple drag and drop interface, users were to take haphazard statements from the OMCS database and put them together into a more or less coherent narrative. The following story is a combination of seven statements:

> "I travel to an airport. I board a plane. I fly in an airplane. I put on safety equipment. I open a door. I see a cloud. I jump out of an airplane."

In exchange for the easy drag and drop input, the stories were not very engaging and therefore were probably less attractive for others to read.

Another OMCS-associated experimental project was called ComicKit. It offered a comic strip interface for telling stories. Figure 9 shows an excerpt from a ComicKit. It is a story about Alice, who wakes up depressed and decides to go on a walk.

Figure 9: ComicKit Story

The comic strip idea is a good way to engage users, as indicated by ComicKit's user test, where users reportedly reported a high degree of enjoyment. But ComicKit does not address one of the basic problems inherent with comic narratives: the stories require a lot of common sense to understand what happens in the space between the comic panels [9]. Although the comic strip format reportedly was fun for users, the lack of constraints on content and captions resulted in stories that were difficult for automated analysis.

Influenced by OMCS, Li and colleagues asked minimally paid workers on Amazon's Mechanical Turk to input natural language sentences describing typical life scenarios [7]. The project's workers were instructed to use fixed actor roles, with proper names, and simple one-verb sentences. The resulting narratives were amenable for parsing, and the results indicated that automatic analysis can produce graphs of ordered events. Unlike HXP however, Li et al.'s events are not constrained to small actions and are not causally explained. Therefore, the narratives tend to leave out a great deal of detail. The example narrative from this begins with two events: a) John drives to the restaurant and b) John stands in line. This level of granularity omits the detail of John's getting in the car, traveling along a road, parking the car, getting out, or going in the restaurant. It also leaves out commonsense information about why someone would go to a restaurant, use the car, stand in line, etc. In sum, Li's narrative data is valuable, but it does not attempt to represent the contextual details like HXP.

We agree with Singh and his colleagues that collecting specific experiences should be easier than formulating generalized scripts. The challenge is providing a framework to help non-experts contribute useful data. Our comic frames are limited in time and space to small actions appropriate for animation. The frames are richly populated with realistic background settings and props, which helps contributors show how objects change from one frame to the next. Although there is a lot of content freedom, the input methodology creates highly structured data.

For the initial stages of the project, we are focusing on child experiences, which narrows the narratives to concrete actions closely tied to basic needs and naïve desires. Although the HXP methodology is not specific to child-centered experiences, we find that non-experts have an easier time when they are instructed to annotate scenes at the level of a kindergarten or first-grade reader.

To our knowledge, there have been no successful attempts to use *non-experts* to capture the commonsense detail that HXP targets: narratives, richly described with mundane, commonsense detail that other projects normally omit, accompanied by general commonsense rules. Creating these narratives is time-consuming, but by making it possible for non-experts to do the work, the intellectually laborious task of articulating life experiences can be spread among many people.

FUTURE WORK

As a result of the user test, we identified several places where the software could be improved to encourage more detailed statements. The interface should explicitly prompt users to state the intentions/goals of the characters. Currently, it just prompts for the mental state. Also, the interface should remind users to check what states have changed from one frame to the next. Finally, we were hoping to get more statements about important sensory states, such as seeing the vase, touching the vase, and hearing the crash. We may have to add an explicit prompt for sensory states.

Our controlled natural language constructions are adequate for representing many simple experiences, but many more structures are needed. We need to add the capability of representing adverbs, comparisons, time durations, abstract concepts, group behavior, quantification, and simple dialog. Furthermore, to take the project from proof-of-concept to a fully functioning wiki collaboration, we need to implement the software as a thin client (i.e., access the program via Internet server) and add a host of features to make it more like a social networking site.

We are currently working to demonstrate the quality of the collected data by showing its inference potential. We will use forward chaining to predict what else might be true from a given statement. And we will use backward chaining to fill in the gap between what is stated and what might have been the reason behind the statement. While researchers have been demonstrating inference on manually prepared data since the early days of AI, in our case, we would be showing the efficacy of data manually prepared by non-experts aided by our software interface.

We should stress, however, that the goal here is *not* to build a rule-based NLP system; such a system would not scale up to handle a large database. Rather, the goal of HXP is strictly to collect highly structured, cohesive, generalizable data about the human experience, to be used for training scalable models or investigating new AI architectures.

Of course, a significant future challenge will be to motivate workers to participate in this project. In our small user test, some users were definitely motivated by the competition to get more points by adding more detail. They also had fun looking at other people's work and making comments and refinements. We believe other users would be motivated by a specific goal, say, creating experiences that correspond to a small corpus of children's stories similar to [8].

CONCLUSION

AI researchers have long recognized the importance of using narrative structures for natural language processing. However, attempts to narrow the problem to artificial worlds or specific domains do not scale up. Furthermore, attempts to use non-experts to provide simple stories from which commonsense can be extracted have also failed because it is so difficult for non-experts to articulate knowledge that seems so obvious.

To help non-experts create valuable narrative data, we have presented a novel methodology that focuses on simple experiences. We structure scenes into small time slices, guiding annotators to describe each frame, with particular focus on intent, emotion, location, and movement. Furthermore, we apply an automated Socratic Method to each user annotation to draw out hidden assumptions that humans make about common situations. The resulting narratives are in the form of highly structured and detailed time-ordered statements. As an added benefit, each statement is supported by a generalized rule that links *specific* situations to *classes* of situations. "Max is on a sofa" is specific situation. But rule (2) about a person on a seat is an abstraction that helps identify similarities between situations.

As [17] points out, commonsense knowledge in narrative form is contextualized; it relates situations, actions and effects. Our example narrative encodes many pieces of contextual knowledge – a person that is curious about an object might pick it up, which might mean that the person first moves to be near the object. A child that is bored in a living room might intentionally break a pretty vase. NLP applications could use this contextual knowledge to generate better translations, answer questions, and do other language understanding tasks.

HXP scenes consist of agents, actions, objects, mental states, and background setting – the same properties that cognitive scientists use to model cognition in the human brain [6]. In these models, the brain abstracts from concrete experiences as it performs essential cognitive tasks such as planning and interpreting the actions of others. If concrete experiences and abstractions of experiences are critical to cognitive processing, then we believe our methodology where users create specific experiences and explain them with generalized If-Then rules will be a fundamentally new type of resource, not just for NLP, but also for general models of human cognition.

ACKNOWLEDGEMENTS

We thank Stephen H. Elmer and Margit Link-Rodrigue for their valuable suggestions and help with this project.

REFERENCES

1. Aamodt, A. and Plaza, E. Case-Based Reasoning: Foundational Issues, Methodological Variations, and System Approaches. *AI Communications*, 7, 1 (1994), 39-59.
2. Dreyfus, H.L. *What Computers "Still" Can't Do: A Critique of Artificial Reason, Revised edition*. MIT Press, Cambridge, 1992.
3. Elson, D.K. and McKeown, K.R. Building a Bank of Semantically Encoded Narratives. In *Proc. LREC 2010*.
4. Fahlman, S.E. Using Scone's Multiple-Context Mechanism to Emulate Human-Like Reasoning. In

Proc. AAAI Fall Symposium on Advances in Cognitive Systems 2011.

5. Fellbaum, C. *WordNet: An Electronic Lexical Database*. MIT Press, Cambridge, MA., 1998.

6. Krueger, F., Barbey, A.K., and Grafman, J. The medial prefrontal cortex mediates social event knowledge. *Trends in Cognitive Sciences*, 13, 3 (March 2009), 103-109.

7. Boyang L., Appling, D.S., Lee-Urban, S., and Riedl, M.O. Learning Sociocultural Knowledge via Crowdsourced Examples. In *Proc. HCOMP 2012*.

8. McCarthy, J., Minsky, M., Sloman, A., Gong, L., Lau, T., Morgenstern, Mueller, E.T., L., Riecken, D., Singh, M., and Singh, P. An architecture of diversity for commonsense reasoning. *IBM Systems Journal*, 41, 3 (2002), 530-539.

9. McCloud, S. *Understanding Comics: The Invisible Art*. Harper Perennial, New York, 1994.

10. Minsky, M. *The Emotion Machine: Commonsense Thinking, Artificial Intelligence, and the Future of the Human Mind.* Simon & Schuster, New York, 2007.

11. Minsky, M. *A Framework for Representing Knowledge*. Technical Report. Massachusetts Institute of Technology, Cambridge, MA, 1974.

12. Mueller, E.T. Modelling Space and Time in Narratives about Restaurants. *Literary and Linguistic Computing*, 22, 1 (2006), 67-84.

13. Mueller, E.T. *Natural Language Processing with ThoughtTreasure*. Signiform, New York, 1998.

14. Power, R., Scott, D., and Evans, R. What You See Is What You Meant: direct knowledge editing with natural language feedback. In *Proc. ECAI 1998.*

15. Schank, R.C. and Abelson, R. P. *Scripts, Plans, Goals, and Understanding*. Lawrence Erlbaum, Hillsdale, NJ, 1977.

16. Schubert, L.K. Turing's Dream and the Knowledge Challenge. In *Proc. AAAI 2006*, AAAI Press (2006), 1534-8.

17. Singh, P. and Barry, B. Collecting Commonsense Experiences. In *Proc. K-CAP 2003*.

18. Singh, P., Barry, B., and Liu, H. Teaching machines about everyday life. *BT Technology Journal*, 22, 4 (October 2004), 227-240.

19. Singh, P., Lin, T., Mueller, E.T., Lim, G., Perkins, T., and Zhu, W.L. Open Mind Common Sense: Knowledge Acquisition from the General Public. In *Proc. ODBASE 2002.*

20. Williams, R., Barry, B., and Singh, P. ComicKit: Acquiring Story Scripts Using Common Sense Feedback. In *Proc. IUI 2005,* ACM Press (2005), 302-304.

21. Zarri, G.P. *Representation and Management of Narrative Information : Theoretical Principles and Implementation*. Springer-Verlag, London, 2010.

Learning Non-Myopically from Human-Generated Reward

W. Bradley Knox
Massachusetts Institute of Technology
Media Lab
Cambridge, Massachusetts
bradknox@mit.edu

Peter Stone
University of Texas at Austin
Department of Computer Science
Austin, Texas
pstone@cs.utexas.edu

ABSTRACT
Recent research has demonstrated that human-generated reward signals can be effectively used to train agents to perform a range of reinforcement learning tasks. Such tasks are either episodic—i.e., conducted in unconnected episodes of activity that often end in either goal or failure states—or continuing—i.e., indefinitely ongoing. Another point of difference is whether the learning agent highly discounts the value of future reward—a myopic agent—or conversely values future reward appreciably. In recent work, we found that previous approaches to learning from human reward all used myopic valuation [7]. This study additionally provided evidence for the desirability of myopic valuation in task domains that are both goal-based and episodic.

In this paper, we conduct three user studies that examine critical assumptions of our previous research: task episodicity, optimal behavior with respect to a Markov Decision Process, and lack of a failure state in the goal-based task. In the first experiment, we show that converting a simple episodic task to non-episodic (i.e., continuing) task resolves some theoretical issues present in episodic tasks with generally positive reward and—relatedly—enables highly successful learning with non-myopic valuation in multiple user studies. The primary learning algorithm in this paper, which we call "VI-TAMER", is *the first algorithm to successfully learn non-myopically from human-generated reward*; we also empirically show that such non-myopic valuation facilitates higher-level understanding of the task. Anticipating the complexity of real-world problems, we perform two subsequent user studies—one with a failure state added—that compare (1) learning when states are updated asynchronously with local bias—i.e., states quickly reachable from the agent's current state are updated more often than other states—to (2) learning with the fully synchronous sweeps across each state in the VI-TAMER algorithm. With these locally biased updates, we find that *the general positivity of human reward creates problems even for continuing tasks*, revealing a distinct research challenge for future work.

Author Keywords
reinforcement learning; modeling and prediction of user behavior; end-user programming; human-agent interaction; interactive machine learning; human teachers

ACM Classification Keywords
H.1.2 User/Machine Systems: Miscellaneous

INTRODUCTION
The constructs of reward and punishment form the foundation of psychological models that have provided powerful insights into the behavior of humans and other animals. Reward and punishment are frequently received in a social context, from another social agent. In recent years, this form of communication and its machine-learning analog—reinforcement learning—have been adapted to permit teaching of artificial agents by their human users [4, 14, 6, 13, 11, 10]. In this form of teaching—which we call interactive shaping—a user observes an agent's behavior while generating *human reward* instances through varying interfaces (e.g., keyboard, mouse, or verbal feedback); each instance is received by the learning agent as a time-stamped numeric value and used to inform future behavioral choices. Here the trainer considers his or her reward to encompass colloquial concepts like "reward" and "punishment", "approval" and "disapproval", or something similar.[1]

Interactive shaping enables people—without programming skills or complicated instruction—to specify desired behavior and to share task knowledge when correct behavior is already indirectly specified (e.g., by a pre-coded reward function). Further, in contrast to the complementary approach of learning from demonstration [1], learning from human reward employs a simple task-independent interface, exhibits learned behavior *during* teaching, and, we speculate, requires less task expertise and places less cognitive load on the trainer.

Concepts and definitions
Interactive shaping can be framed as having two different objectives. The *task objective* represents what the trainer is attempting to teach and determines an agent's *task performance*. For instance, when training an agent to play Tetris [6], the task objective might be maximizing the number of lines cleared per game or stacking as many blocks to the far right as

[1]The term "punishment" is used here only in psychological and colloquial contexts. In artificial intelligence, the term "reward" includes both positively and negatively valued feedback.

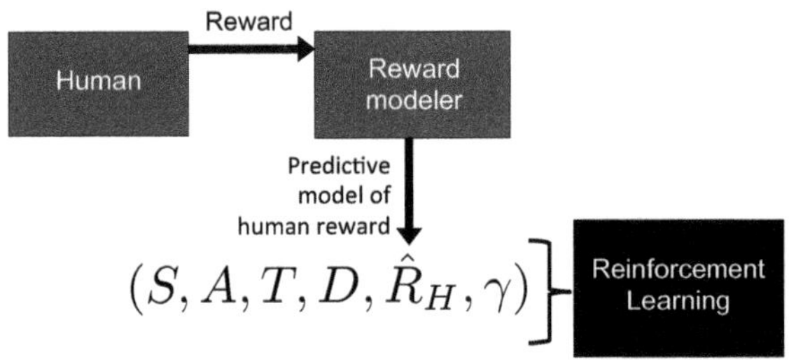

Figure 1. An illustration of the agent's learning algorithm, where inputs *to* the human are not represented. Human reward instances change the predictive reward model $\hat{R}_H$, which is used as the reward function in an MDP. A reinforcement learning agent learns from the most recent MDP.

possible; the trainer decides the task objective unless it is prespecified and communicated to the trainer, as we do for experimental purposes. The agent has no access to the trainer's task objective; setting aside the possibility of pre-programmed a priori knowledge (without loss of generality), we observe that the agent instead only experiences its own state-action history and the reward instances given by the trainer. Thus, the learning agent needs its own objective, which we define with respect to the human-generated reward it receives. Following this approach, any solution to the interactive shaping problem includes two parts: (1) a *reward-based objective* for the agent and (2) a learning algorithm that effectively improves on this objective with experience.

We focus on the space of reward-based objectives used in reinforcement learning (RL) for Markov Decision Processes (MDPs) [12]. MDPs are denoted as $\{S, A, T, R, \gamma, D\}$.[2] RL algorithms seek to learn policies ($\pi : S \rightarrow A$) for an MDP that improve its discounted sum long-term reward—i.e., its *return*—from each state, where return is expressed as $Q^\pi(s, \pi(s))$ and defined in terms of reward as $Q^\pi(s,a) = \sum_{t=0}^{\infty} E_\pi[\gamma^t R(s_t, a_t)]$ (with $0^0 = 1$). We refer to return-maximizing policies as *MDP-optimal*; on the other hand, policies that maximize the task objective are called *task optimal*.

For the experiments described in this paper, a Markovian model of human reward, $\hat{R}_H$, is learned from human reward instances. This model completes an MDP specification for the agent to learn in, $\{S, A, T, \hat{R}_H, \gamma, D\}$ (Figure 1). Thus, the output of $\hat{R}_H(s, a)$ for an agent's current state s and action a is the actual reward experienced by the learning agent. In this research, we seek to find reward-based objectives such that algorithms that perform well on the reward-based objective *with reward functions modeled on human trainers' reward* also perform well on the task objective. If we were concerned only with optimal behavior (we are not), this goal could be restated as finding reward-based objectives such that MDP-optimal behavior is also task optimal.

[2]Here, S and A are the sets of possible states and actions; T is a function describing the probability of transitioning from one state to another given a specific action, such that $T(s_t, a_t, s_{t+1}) = P(s_{t+1}|s_t, a_t)$; R is a reward function, $R : S \times A \rightarrow \Re$, with a state and an action as inputs; $\gamma \in [0, 1]$ is a discount factor, controlling how much expected future reward is valued; and D is the distribution of start states for each learning episode.

An important aspect of reward-based objectives is temporal discounting, which is controlled by the γ parameter of MDPs. As shown in the expression of return above, when $\gamma = 0$ the objective is fully myopic. A fully myopic agent only values the reward from its immediate state and action; expected future reward is not valued. At the other extreme, an agent with a $\gamma = 1$ objective values near-term reward equally to reward infinitely far in the future. When $\gamma \in (0, 1)$, future reward is discounted at an exponential rate, making near-term reward more valuable than long-term reward. Higher γ values result in a lower discount rate.

An additional dimension of MDPs is *episodicity*: whether the task is episodic or continuing. In an episodic task, the agent can reach one or more episode-terminating states, which are called *"absorbing states"* in the RL literature [12]. Upon reaching an absorbing state, the learning episode ends, a new episode starts with state chosen independently of the reached absorbing state, and the agent experiences reward that is not attributable to behavior during the previous episode. Absorbing states often either represent success or failure at the task, constituting *goal states* or *failure states*; we call tasks with goal states "goal-based". In contrast to an episodic task, a continuing task is ongoing, wherein all reward is attributable to all past behavior, if discounting permits.

As we describe more specifically later in this section, we explore the impact on task performance of the agent's reward-based objective along four dimensions: (1) the discount factor, (2) whether a task is episodic or continuing, (3) whether the agent acts approximately MDP-optimal or is less effective in maximizing its return, and (4) the effect of having a failure state as well as the goal state. In addition to understanding the effects of these four dimensions on the agent's task performance, this paper concerns two questions: How can an agent learn from human reward at low discount rates (i.e., non-myopically, with high discount factors)? What benefits are conferred by low discount rates?

Background

A critical precursor to this work is our investigation of the impact of discounting in goal-based, episodic tasks [7]. Investigating the six previous projects that we know to have involved learning from positively and negatively valued human-generated reward [4, 14, 13, 11, 9, 10] (including by email with corresponding authors), we identified a curious trend: all such projects have been much more myopic—i.e., using high discount rates—than is usual in RL. We hypothesized that a cause of this pattern is the general positivity of human reward. More specifically, if the previously observed positive bias in human reward creates at least one "positive circuit"—i.e., repeatable sequences of behavior that net positive total reward—then an MDP-optimal agent in an episodic, goal-based task *will avoid the goal* if acting without discounting, since the absorbing state of the goal prevents accrual of further reward. To investigate this hypothesis, we previously conducted a user study of agent training in a simple grid-world task (shown later in Figure 4), varying the experimental conditions only by the discount factor in the agent's reward-based objective. Experimental results showed (1) that higher

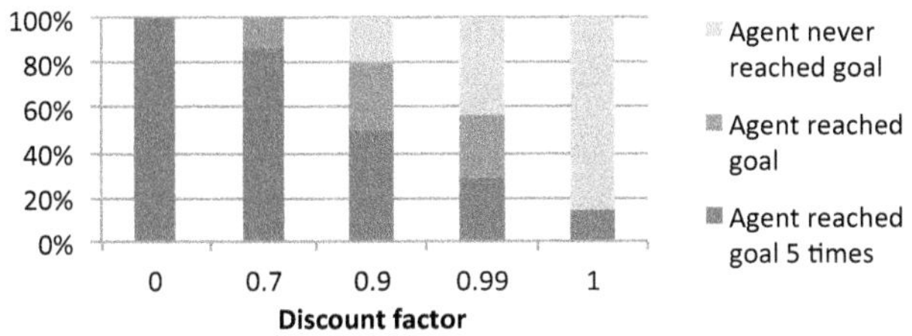

Figure 2. Success rates by discount factor for our prior experiment.

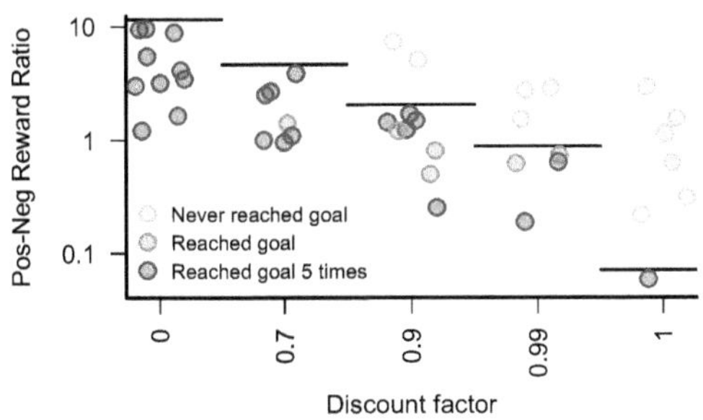

Figure 3. From our prior experiment, the ratio of cumulative positive reward to cumulative negative reward given by each trainer, separated by discount factor condition and task performance. X-axis jitter was added for readability. Within each condition, a horizontal line was placed above the mark for the highest ratio at which a subject trained the agent to reach the goal at least once.

discount rates (i.e., lower γs) led to better performance, (2) that lower discount rates result in more negative reward overall (fittingly, since increased negativity helps address the positive circuits problem), and (3) that successful trainers at lower discount rates give more negative reward than do unsuccessful ones. Additionally, 66.7% of trainers across all conditions created at least one positive circuit, meaning that those agents would never greedily reach the goal if discounting at $\gamma = 1$. The results of this experiment are reproduced in Figures 2 and 3.

Preview of experiments

Using adaptations of the same task, experimental design, and agent algorithm—which we dub VI-TAMER—this paper includes **three user studies** that examine three important assumptions of our prior work:

1. The task is episodic.
2. The agent can act approximately MDP-optimally with respect to the agent's current predictive model of human reward.
3. The task has a goal state but lacks failure states.

The task and agent algorithm are described in detail in the *Continuing-task experiment* section.

Repeating our prior experiment in a continuing version of the same task—in what we call the **continuing-task experiment**—we make the following four observations. First, we find for discount factors $\gamma < 1$ that task performance of MDP-optimal policies during training is generally high and independent of discounting; in contrast, such policies do not perform well at high γs when the task is episodic. Second, strong correlations observed in their episodic-task experiment disappear. Third, in this investigation, the $\gamma = 0.99$ condition with the VI-TAMER algorithm is the *first known instance of successful learning from human-generated reward at a low discount rate* (i.e., a high gamma with relatively long time steps). Fourth, in two additional tests using the training data from this continuing-task experiment, we find evidence for the theoretically based conjecture that low discount rates facilitate the communication of higher-level task information—e.g., the location of the goal rather than the exact sequence of steps to reach it. Such higher-level information enables learning that is more robust to environmental changes, better guides action in unexperienced states, and leads the agent to learn policies that surpass those known to the trainer.

In our second experiment—the **local-bias experiment**—we examine task performance under low discount rates *when the agent cannot generally act approximately MDP-optimally*. This experiment is motivated by an anticipation of converting VI-TAMER to more complex tasks, where MDP-optimal behavior is intractable. Specifically, we focus on an agent that updates the values of state-action pairs with a *local bias*, meaning that pairs reachable within a few steps of the agent's current state receive more updates than those further away. Such locally biased updates are a common characteristic among RL algorithms. With such local bias, we find that performance decreases, apparently because of further problems created by the positivity of human reward.

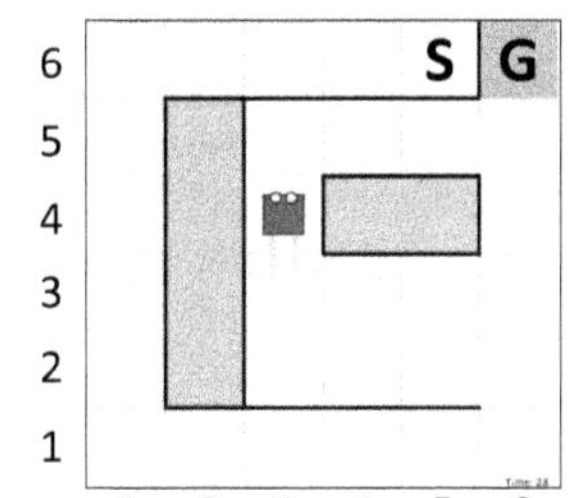

Figure 4. The baseline grid world task. To display the agent's actions and state transitions to the trainer, (1) wheel tracks are drawn from the agent's previously occupied cell, and (2) the simulated robot's eyes point in the direction of the last action. The start and goal cells are labeled 'S' and 'G' respectively.

Our third experiment—the **failure-state experiment**—boosts the generality of conclusions from the previous two experiments (and our prior experiments [7]) by adding a failure state to the goal-based task and then repeating the $\gamma = 0.99$ conditions from these previous experiments. The results from this failure-state experiment follow patterns observed in the previous experiments, though sometimes with less significance (likely because of smaller effect sizes).

In the following section, we describe baselines for the agent algorithm, the task, and the experimental design. In each of the subsequent three sections, one of the three experiments is described along with an analysis of its results. We then conclude the paper.

BASELINES FOR THE TASK, AGENT, AND EXPERIMENT

Here we describe baseline versions of the task, the agent, and the experiment, which are equivalent to those for the grid-world experiment from our prior work [7]. Unless otherwise specified, this baseline set is used in each of this paper's experiments. Given space requirements, we keep these descriptions at a high level. Full details can be found at `http://www.cs.utexas.edu/users/bradknox/papers/13iui/`.

The task

The task is a grid world with 30 states, shown in Figure 4. At each step, the agent acts once by moving up, down, left, or right, and attempted movement through a wall results in no movement during the step. Task performance metrics are based on the time steps taken to reach the goal. The agent always starts a learning episode in the state labeled "**S**" in Figure 4. The shortest path from the start state requires 19 actions. Each time step lasts approximately 800 ms.

In the episodic version of this task, the goal state is absorbing. In the continuing version, upon transitioning into the goal, the agent instead experiences a transition to the start state. Consequently, reward received in one "episode" can be attributed to state-action pairs in the previous "episode" (and farther in the past). Though reaching the goal in the continuing version does not mark the end of an episode, *we continue to use the word "episode" to refer to the periods of time that are divided by the attainment of the goal.* Another valid perspective for the reader is to assume the task is fundamentally episodic and that the continuing version is simply tricking the agent to make it experience the task as continuing.

The agent

In all experiments a model of human reward, $\hat{R}_H$, is learned through the TAMER framework [6], and the output of this model provides reward for the agent within an MDP specified as $\{S, A, T, \hat{R}_H, \gamma, D\}$. Figure 1 illustrates this scenario. During training, human reward signals form labels for learning samples that have state-action pairs as features; a regression algorithm continuously updates $\hat{R}_H$ with new features. For experiments in this paper, the TAMER module represents $\hat{R}_H$ as a linear model of Gaussian radial basis functions (RBFs) and updates the model by incremental gradient descent, as in our prior work [7]. One RBF is centered on each cell of the grid world, effectively creating a pseudo-tabular representation that generalizes slightly between nearby cells.

During training for all experiments, human reward was communicated via the '/' and 'z' keys on the keyboard, which respectively mapped to 1 and -1. This mapping to 1 and -1, though not infallible, is an intuitive choice that is similar to that of related works that explain their exact mappings [14, 13, 10, 11]. Additionally, this interface allows richer feedback than it superficially appears to for two reasons. First, reward signals are asynchronous to actions, so the rate of reward signaling determines intensity. Second, to account for delays in giving feedback, the causal attribution of each reward is distributed across multiple recent time steps by TAMER's credit assignment module [5], further adding variety to the label values of samples for training $\hat{R}_H$.

The agent seeks to improve its return—i.e., its reward-based objective—with respect to the current $\hat{R}_H$, $\sum_{t=0}^{\infty} E[\gamma^t \hat{R}_H(s_t, \pi(s_t))]$, but we empirically evaluate the agent by task performance metrics that are not reward-based (see the list of statistical tests in description of the baseline experiment below). The reinforcement learning algorithm used by the agent is value iteration [12] with greedy action selection. However, unlike traditional value iteration (in which the algorithm iterates until state values converge), here one update sweep occurs over all of the states every 20 ms, creating approximately 40 sweeps per step. The agent's value function is initialized to zero once, at the start of training only, for reasons discussed in the analysis of the second experiment. We call this value iteration algorithm with TAMER-based modeling of human reward "VI-TAMER".

Because the agent in this experiment learns from a frequently changing reward function, behaving optimally with respect to the current reward function is difficult. For the simple task we have chosen, value iteration creates approximately MDP-optimal behavior with small lag in responding to changes to the reward function, a lag of a few time steps or less. Thus, *we can be confident that observed differences between experimental conditions can be attributed to the reward-based objective, not deficiencies in maximizing that objective.*

The experiment

All experiments were conducted through subjects' web browsers via Amazon Mechanical Turk. Subjects were randomly assigned to an experimental condition. They were prepared with video instructions and a period of controlling the agent followed by a practice training session. During these instructions, subjects are told to give "reward and punishment" to the green "Kermitbot" to "teach the robot to find the water as fast as possible." Trainers were left to determine their own reward strategies, possibly including rewarding every time the agent acts as they would have acted or rewarding highly when the agent reaches the goal.

The actual training session stopped after the agent reached the goal 10 times (i.e., 10 episodes) or after 450 steps, whichever came first (unless otherwise specified). This stopping time is the only difference between these baseline components and our prior grid-world experiment, in which trainers were stopped after the first of 5 episodes or 300 time steps [7].

A training sample is removed from analysis if it fulfills any of the following conditions: the sample was created from the second or later time that a specific worker acted as a subject, the log file is incomplete, the user mistyped his or her condition-specifying user ID such that the condition was incorrectly specified, or the user gave less than 2 instances of feedback per 100 time steps, which we consider to be non-compliance with our experimental instructions.

Because we repeat many of the same statistical tests throughout this paper, we define and name our more common tests here:

- *Fisher Success* - a Fisher's Tests comparing outcomes of reaching the goal all N times or not by condition, where N is specified as a threshold
- *MWU Episodes Finished* - a Mann Whitney U test where the dependent variable is the number of episodes completed before training was stopped
- *MWU Time To Goal* - a Mann Whitney U test where the dependent variable is how many steps occurred before the agent reached the goal for *the first time*

- *Spearman Success* - a Spearman correlation test of the ratios of positive to negative reward and success within a specific condition

CONTINUING-TASK EXPERIMENT

In the experiment described in this section, we investigate the impact of the discount rate when a task is continuing. For episodic tasks, we previously argued that a positive reward bias among human trainers combined with high discount factors can lead to infinite behavioral circuits—created by what we call "positive circuits"—and consequently minimal task performance [7]. For episodic tasks, we found that myopic discounting (low γs) avoids this problem; the *Introduction* describes these prior results in more detail. However, positive circuits may only cause severe problems in episodic tasks, since an agent reaching an absorbing goal state is effectively penalized; it is exiting a world rich with positive reward. We examine another strategy to remove this penalty: formulate the task as continuing, making the goal a gateway to more opportunity to accrue reward. Unlike for episodic MDPs, the optimal policy of a continuing MDP is unaffected by adding a constant value to all reward; thus, the positivity of human reward should not present the same problem for MDP-optimal policies in continuing tasks.

Experiment and analysis of results

This experiment uses the baseline agent, experimental design, and continuing task, repeating our prior experiment almost exactly, only changing the task to be continuing as described in *The task*. For consistency with the previous experiment, we analyze data from the first 5 episodes that occur before the 301st time step and also retain the $\gamma = 1$ condition, even though such discounting is generally inappropriate for continuing tasks. 25 subjects were run per condition, and one subject in the $\gamma = 0.9$ condition was replaced by another subject for not following instructions (a practice followed only in this experiment). After filtering, for γs of 0, 0.7, 0.9, 0.99, and 1, there were respectively 20, 21, 20, 23, and 23 subjects. Figures 5 and 6 show results (presented analogously to Figures 2 and 3).

In comparison to our prior episodic-task experiment [7], the results in the continuing-task version are markedly different. As shown in Figure 5, the task success rate at $\gamma = 1$ is lower than at other conditions, which we expect given that this discounting is generally avoided for continuing tasks to make rewards in the finite future meaningful. The other discount factors create similar task performance, with $\gamma = 0.99$ achieving the highest mean rate of full success. Fisher-Success tests with a 5-episode threshold find a marginally significant difference between $\gamma = 0.99$ and $\gamma = 1$ conditions ($p = 0.0574$); no other pairwise comparisons between conditions are significantly different.[3]

[3]Note that episodicity cannot affect a $\gamma = 0$ agent, making this condition identical to the $\gamma = 0$ condition of our prior experiment. The difference in success rate at $\gamma = 0$ in the two grid world experiments is likely because of either randomness—their difference is insignificant by a Fisher-Success test with a 5-episode threshold ($p = 0.2890$)—or this experiment, run at a different time, sampled from a lower-performing population.

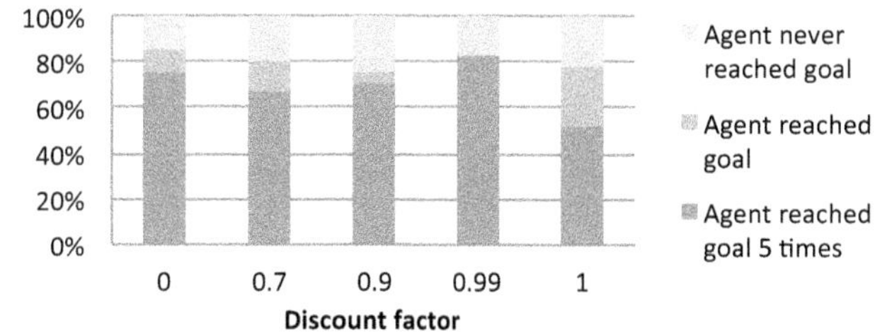

Figure 5. Success rates for the continuing-task experiment by discount factor.

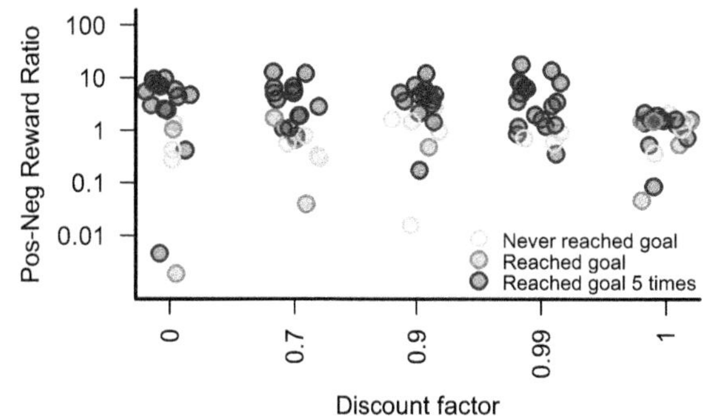

Figure 6. For the continuing-task experiment, ratio of cumulative positive reward to cumulative negative reward given by each trainer (with x-axis jitter).

Patterns exhibited by the ratios of cumulative positive reward to cumulative negative reward among trainers (as shown in Figure 6) also differ from the episodic experiment. Specifically, there is no significant correlation between the ratios of fully successful trainers and discount factor when $\gamma = 1$ is excluded (Spearman coefficient $\rho = -0.0564$, $p = 0.6628$), though the correlation is significant with $\gamma = 1$ included ($\rho = -0.3233$, $p = 0.0050$). Further, the relationship between reward positivity and task performance is closer to the intuitive expectation that high-performance agents receive more positively-biased reward: ratios and success categories (no, partial, and full success) are significantly correlated in the $\gamma \leq 0.9$ conditions (Spearman's coefficient $\rho > 0.595$, $p < 0.006$ for all $\gamma \leq 0.9$) and $\rho > 0$ as well for the other conditions, though the correlation is insignificant.

*For this task and this approximately MDP-optimal RL algorithm (*VI-TAMER*), converting the task to continuing does indeed appear to remove the adverse impact of reward positivity at high discount factors, overcoming the positive circuits problem.* However, based only on the roughly equivalent task performance for all $\gamma < 1$ conditions, the choice of which discounting to use is unclear. In the next subsection, we investigate whether higher-level task information was communicated by the trainer, making learning more robust to changes to the environment or more general at certain γ values.

Benefits of non-myopic learning

At non-myopic discount rates (i.e., γs near 1), reward can communicate a desired policy, the goals of the task, or a mix of the two. Using the full training data from this experiment (up to 10 episodes or 450 time steps), we now investigate whether the trained agents do learn more than a policy. Since $\gamma = 1$ is generally inappropriate for continuing tasks, we ex-

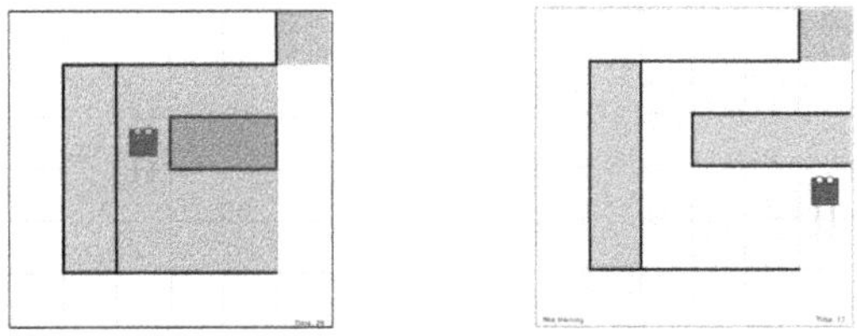

(a) (b)

Figure 7. Illustrations of the two tests of the benefits of non-myopic learning, testing agent performance after training. (a) Starting from (highlighted) states off the optimal path. (b) Blocking the optimal path.

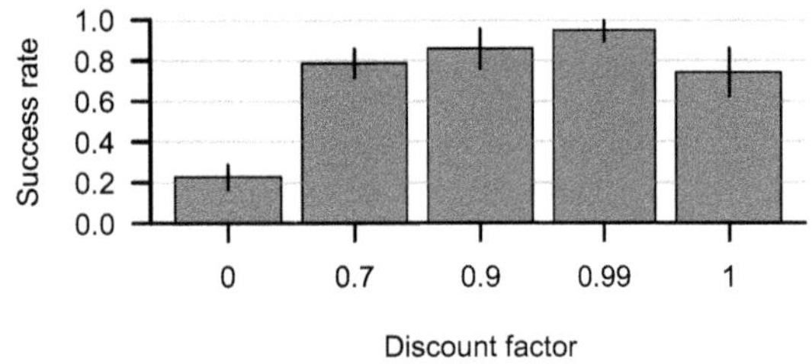

Figure 8. Mean rate of successfully trained agents reaching the goal in less than 100 time steps *from the 10 states off of the optimal path.* **Standard error bars are calculated using a single agent's success rate as one sample.**

pect $\gamma = 0.99$ to yield the best results. We restrict our analysis to those agents successfully trained to get to the goal 5 times in less than 300 steps. Thus, we effectively ask, *given that an agent learns a good (and usually optimal) policy from human reward, what else does the agent learn?*

We first test the learned policy from 10 states that are not along the optimal path from the start state, which are highlighted in Figure 7a. These states may have never been experienced by the agent during training, in which case $\hat{R}_H$ is built without any samples from the state. Simple policy generalization from nearby, optimal-path states would help in only some of these 10 states, so the ability of the agent to get to the goal reflects whether the agent has learned some information about the task goals. Agents that had learned their policies at higher γs were more often able to get to the goal in less than 100 time steps (Figure 8). 18 of 19 successfully trained agents in the $\gamma = 0.99$ condition reached the goal from every tested state. We note though that different discount factors might lead to different levels of experience in these tested states, providing a confounding factor.

In the second test, an obstacle is placed in the state two cells below the goal (Figure 7b), blocking the optimal path, and we then determine whether the agent can still reach the goal in less than 100 time steps. Thus, we test the effects of changing the task-optimal policy but keeping constant the task goal: get to the goal state as quickly as possible. For the two state-action pairs that previously transitioned into the newly blocked state, the agent's reward function is modified to output 0 to reflect the agent's lack of knowledge about how the trainer would reward these transitions. In the $\gamma = 0.99$ condition, 9 of 19 successfully trained agents reached the goal. One agent from each of the $\gamma = 0.9$ and $\gamma = 1$ conditions also reached the goal (of 14 and 12 total, respectively); no agents with $\gamma < 0.9$ did.

These analyses support the conjecture that agents taught with higher discount factors learn about the task goals themselves, making the agents generally more robust to changes in the environment and more able to act appropriately in previously unexperienced states. That agents may learn task goals raises the tantalizing prospect that, under the right circumstances, an agent receiving reward from a human trainer could learn a policy that is far superior to that envisioned by the trainer. These benefits of non-myopic learning underscore the importance of creating algorithms for complex, real-world tasks that can learn non-myopically. As the next two sections confirm, achieving this goal is non-trivial.

LOCAL-BIAS EXPERIMENT

In considerably more complex domains than the 30-state grid-world task used in our continuing-task experiment, agents will likely be unable to perform value iteration with iterating sweeps over the entire state; even ignoring the possibility of continuous states or actions, some tasks simply contain too many states to quickly and repeatedly perform temporal difference updates on all states. In anticipation of scaling the high-γ, continuing-task approach found successful in the previous experiment, we implemented a version of value iteration that learns asynchronously, which we call aVI-TAMER. Instead of updating each state once and then repeating as in VI-TAMER,[4] aVI-TAMER updates state-action pairs through the Monte Carlo tree search strategy Upper Confidence Trees (UCT). UCT-based search has been successful in tasks with especially large state spaces [8], originally in games like Go [2] but also in more general reinforcement learning tasks [3].

aVI-TAMER is mostly identical to VI-TAMER: the human reward model $\hat{R}_H$ is learned as before, using TAMER; a tabular action-value function is maintained; and the agent acts greedily with respect to that function. Unlike VI-TAMER, aVI-TAMER's "planning" consists of repeatedly considering different possible 40-step trajectories from its current state. Transitions from these trajectories provide updates for value iteration.[5] Planning trajectories are chosen by UCT [8], where the search tree is reset at the start of each time step to respect the corresponding change to the reward function $\hat{R}_H$ at that step, which generally makes past search results inaccurate. The confidence value for UCT is 1.

For this aVI-TAMER algorithm, the number of updates to each state's value differs considerably among states; in contrast, between sweep iterations in our value iteration implementation, all states have been updated an equal number of times. Instead of a balanced distribution of updates, state transitions that can quickly be reached from the current state receive many more temporal difference updates than transitions

[4] VI-TAMER is not synchronous in the strictest sense—where the entire sweep across state updates with the same value function—but we find this term "asynchronous" useful for distinguishing these two approaches.

[5] Using experienced transitions for action-value-updating value iteration is only valid for deterministic policies and transitions, as we have here. Also, note that the update mechanism is not itself Monte Carlo.

from less "local" states. For complex tasks in general, this bias towards local updating appears desirable, since an effective learning agent will likely visit regions of the state space that are worth understanding more often than areas that can be ignored during learning. Additionally, this local updating bias occurs in a large fraction of common RL algorithms (e.g., Sarsa(λ), Q-learning, and Monte Carlo tree search algorithms). We chose aVI-TAMER as a representative of this class of algorithms because it learns much more quickly than most other locally-biased algorithms. However, we recognize that there may be unforeseen benefits from the worse MDP-based performance of these other algorithms, similar to aVI-TAMER in the following section's failure-state experiment outperforming VI-TAMER in the episodic framing of the task.

This experiment departs from the baseline set of agent, task, and experiment specifications only by the inclusion of aVI-TAMER as the algorithm for two conditions. Since this investigation is focused on the effect of locally-biased updates on a high-γ algorithm, all three conditions calculate return with $\gamma = 0.99$. We are primarily interested in two conditions: VI-cont and aVI-cont, which respectively denote VI-TAMER and aVI-TAMER acting in a continuing version of the task. Note that this VI-cont condition is identical to the $\gamma = 0.99$ condition of the continuing-task experiment of the previous section; it is rerun here to account for the differing population that subjects will be drawn from. As a third condition called aVI-epis, we added aVI-TAMER in an episodic version to see what gains are retained by making the task continuing when updates are locally biased. The results of this experiment are shown in Figures 9 and 10. All results concern the full duration of training unless otherwise specified . 26 subjects were run per condition, resulting in the following number of samples by condition after filtering: VI-cont, 22; aVI-cont, 19; aVI-epis, 18.

We observe that the results for the VI-cont condition are similar to that of the equivalent $\gamma = 0.99$ condition in the continuing-task experiment (shown in Figures 5 and 9). The performance is insignificantly higher in this experiment by a Fisher-Success test with a 10-episode threshold ($p = 0.1085$). *This experiment further supports the assertion that the* VI-TAMER *algorithm successfully learns from human-generated reward at high discount factors in the continuing task.*

Effect of local bias in the continuing task

Comparing the two continuing conditions of this experiment—VI-cont and aVI-cont—*locally biased updates result in worse performance than* VI-TAMER*'s uniform updates* (Figure 9). This difference is highly significant by the 10-episode Fisher-Success test ($p = 0.0001$) and by a MWU-Episodes-Finished test ($p = 0.0016$). We also consider how many steps it took the agent to reach the goal *the first time*: a MWU-Time-To-Goal test is also highly significant ($mean_{VI-cont} = 93.45$; $mean_{aVI-cont} = 272.11$; $median_{VI-cont} = 70$; $median_{aVI-cont} = 250$; $p < 0.0001$), indicating that the change to locally biased updates slows early learning.

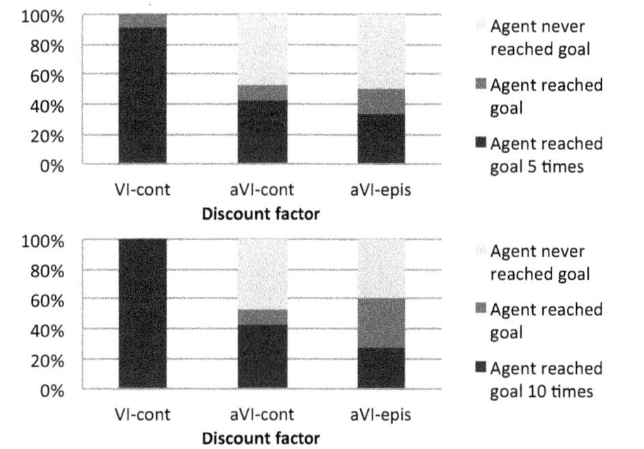

Figure 9. Success rates by condition for the local-bias experiment. Through their bias towards updating "local" states, the aVI-TAMER conditions create behavior that is farther from MDP-optimal for the current reward function than is behavior learned by VI-TAMER. The top plot shows success with the stopping points used for Figures 5 and 6, the first of 5 episodes or 300 time steps. The lower plot displays success with this experiment's stopping points, the first of 10 episodes or 450 time steps.

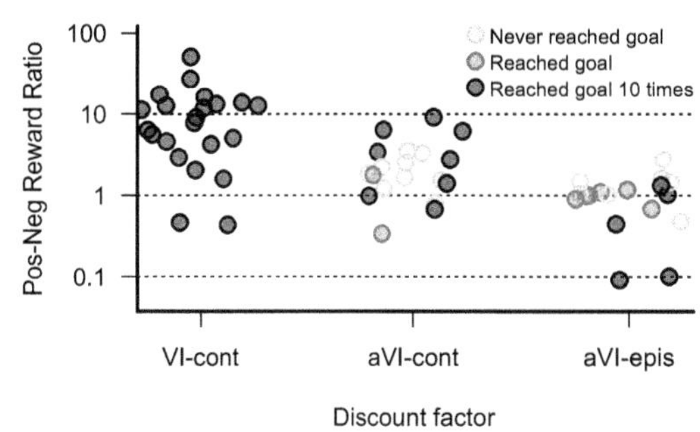

Figure 10. For the local-bias experiment, ratio of cumulative positive reward to cumulative negative reward given by each trainer (with x-axis jitter).

VI-TAMER effectively performs 4800 temporal difference updates per time step (40 sweeps $\times$ 30 states $\times$ 4 actions per state with deterministic transitions), compared to medians of 589 for the aVI-cont group and 1004 the aVI-epis group. Though aVI-TAMER's updates—dependent on the subject's computer—were less frequent, we doubt this difference is a meaningful factor in the results; a four-fold increase in aVI-TAMER's update speed would add less than one level of depth to its exhaustive search tree (which is extended by greedy roll-outs to reach the full trajectory depth of 40).

Other than the number of updates per step, the only difference between aVI-TAMER and VI-TAMER in the continuing conditions is which state-action values are updated. We suspect that the locally-biased character of aVI-TAMER's updates is interacting with the positivity of human reward to lower the aVI-TAMER's algorithm's performance. Specifically, local bias causes nearby states to receive more updates, and the positivity of reward—with an action-value function initialized to 0, as in all experiments of this paper—makes states that are updated more often appear more desirable, consequently strengthening the local bias even further. In early learning, the aVI-TAMER agent will not learn the true values of states along its MDP-optimal path if it does not get near

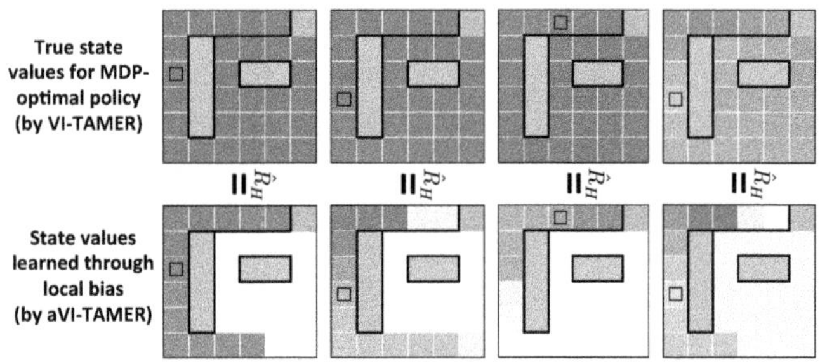

Figure 11. Heat maps showing value functions learned by VI-TAMER and aVI-TAMER, where both maps in a column was created through the same experience trajectory. Both learn from a training log from the VI-TAMER condition, containing a sequence of state-action pairs and time-stamped human reward signals. Training is stopped during the *first* step at which the reward function specifies the task-optimal path to the goal. 4 logs were chosen from the 22 of the VI-cont condition at varying time-to-first-goal values. The VI-TAMER algorithm used to create these heat maps performs 2000 update sweeps per step, increasing from the 40 per step in the experiment to approximate the MDP-optimal value function with further accuracy. The aVI-TAMER algorithm experiences the same trajectory, learning from 1000 planning trajectories per step. Each heat map shows state values after learning of $\hat{R}_H$ is stopped and the corresponding algorithm performs one step worth of updates. The deepest red corresponds to highest value of both value functions in the column, and white squares represent the lowest values, which is 0 or less in all four columns. The location of the agent at the trajectory's stopping point is shown by an agent-sized square.

those states, and policies that bring the agent back to previously experienced—and thus highly valued—states will be followed. The value-function heat maps in Figure 11 support this explanation of the performance differences; states that are far from experienced states often have not been updated even once and retain their original state values of 0.

One apparent solution to this problem of overly local exploration—optimistically initializing the action-value function—is not an option in complex domains for two reasons. First, optimism leads to thorough exploration of the state-action space. Such exhaustive exploration during training would frustrate, exhaust, and confuse the trainer, since such exploration would include much behavior that goes against the trainer's feedback, making the agent appear unresponsive and unable to learn for a considerable period. Thorough exploration would also sacrifice the fast learning that is one of the chief appeals of interactive shaping. Planning-only exploration from optimistic initialization, where the agent's actual actions are greedy, might be possible, but it would be greatly complicated by the following second reason that optimistic initialization is problematic: the reward function $\hat{R}_H$ is constantly changing during training. If the agent reinitializes its action-value function optimistically each time step, it forfeits all knowledge gained during previous time steps about action values under similar $\hat{R}_H$s, knowledge that should be critical to learning quickly to perform well with the new $\hat{R}_H$. On the other hand, if the agent only initializes at the beginning of training, then it will not explore with new $\hat{R}_H$s, largely removing the impact of optimistic initialization. Another option, optimistically initializing $\hat{R}_H$ directly, also generally creates exhaustive exploration.

Effect of episodicity for locally biased learning

Given that the locally biased updates of aVI-TAMER worsen performance compared to the approximately MDP-optimal performance of VI-TAMER, we now ask whether the choice of episodic or continuing formulations still has an appreciable effect in the context of aVI-TAMER's locally biased updates. Comparing these two conditions by the same three statistical tests applied above to compare the VI-cont and aVI-cont conditions, none are significant (*all* $p > 0.49$) and the corresponding means, medians, and proportions for the tests are quite similar across conditions.

The ratios of positive to negative reward in Figure 10 are negatively and significantly correlated with success for aVI-epis (Spearman-Success test, $p = 0.035$; $\rho = -0.50$) and uncorrelated for aVI-cont (Spearman-Success test, $p = 0.45$; $\rho = 0.19$), following the pattern observed from the continuing-task experiment for VI-TAMER. We also look at how often an agent *relapses* into sub-optimal task performance after an episode that is completed in minimal time. As mentioned previously, uniformly raising the value of all rewards by a constant value does not affect the MDP-optimal policy for a continuing task but often will for an episodic task. Consequently, we suspect that trainers will generally give more positive reward after their agent acts optimally (though their reward is not necessarily uniformly higher), which may cause more problems for the episodic aVI-TAMER condition. In the aVI-cont condition, of the 11 agents that finish an episode in minimal time during the first five episodes, 36.6% subsequently relapse into non-optimal behavior before reaching the 10-episode or 450-time-step endpoint. In the episodic condition, 77.7% of the 9 such agents do. This difference is marginally significant in a Fisher's test ($p = 0.0923$).

In overall performance, aVI-TAMER-guided updates do not clearly benefit from making the task continuing. However, we do observe that success in the continuing version still appears unrelated to reward positivity. Additionally, the relapse rate is lower in the continuing task. We suspect that these strengths of the continuing version are balanced against one advantage of the episodic version, that there is a simple but counterintuitive method for teaching the agent to act task-optimal: giving only negative reward. This hypothesis informs the following experiment.

FAILURE-STATE EXPERIMENT

In this experiment, the task is further manipulated to have a failure state that is closer to the start state than the goal state, as shown in Figure 12. In the episodic version of this task, both failure and goal states are absorbing state; in the continuing version, transitions to either create a transition to the start state. When this modified task is episodic, giving only negative reward will create MDP-optimal policies that fail by repeatedly looping through the failure state. In designing this task, we hope to represent the large class of tasks for which failure can be achieved more quickly than the goal (e.g., driving to a destination without crashing). In this task, we predicted that the continuing version would outperform the episodic version by a greater margin. This experiment tests both this prediction and the generality of the results from the other experiments, which thus far have been exclusively demonstrated in a goal-only task.

We use the same algorithms and discount rate ($\gamma = 0.99$) as in the previous experiment, adding as a fourth condition the VI-TAMER algorithm with the episodic version of the task, making this a full 2x2 experiment. We refer to the new condition as VI-epis. Except for an additional instruction to make the agent avoid the failure state—a "black pit that takes [the agent] back to the start"—the experiment was conducted identically as the baseline experiment until the agent reaches the goal a 10th time. If a trainer reaches that point, instead of stopping the experiment we allow the user to continue training until all 450 time steps have passed. We made this adjustment to add resolution among the most successful trainers (e.g., between trainers who would get the agent to the goal 11 times or 18 times). 20 subjects were run per condition; after filtering the data (see *The experiment* for details), the number of subjects were as follows: 15 for VI-cont, 16 for VI-epis, 14 for aVI-cont, and 14 for aVI-epis.

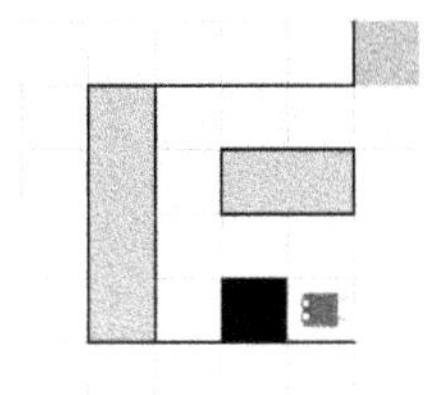

Figure 12. The task with a failure state added.

Results from this experiment are described by Figures 14 and 15 and the table of statistical test results in Figure 13. Generally speaking, we observe the same performance patterns as in the experiments with the goal-only task, though these patterns are less pronounced. VI-cont performs best in all comparisons, significantly so in 5 of 6. For both VI-TAMER and aVI-TAMER algorithms, performance is better for the continuing version of the task, except for aVI-TAMER's mean rank of time to goal from the MWU-Time-To-Goal test, where aVI-epis is insignificantly better than aVI-cont. Interestingly, the new comparison between VI-epis and aVI-epis reveals that the agent performs better in the algorithm with locally biased updates, aVI-epis. We suspect that this result arises because the sub-optimality of aVI-TAMER makes it less likely to find existing positive circuits, which could prevent the agent with a $\gamma = 0.99$ reward-based objective from going to the goal. In other words, failing to achieve an undesirable objective can be better than achieving it. This result raises the surprising prospect that the combination of an agent objective that poorly aligns MDP-optimal and task-optimal behavior combined with an agent that poorly maximizes that objective might produce better results than can be achieved by any considerably sub-optimal agent attempting to maximize a perfectly aligned objective.

We also examine reward positivity (Figure 15). For both VI-TAMER and aVI-TAMER, reward was more positive in the continuing version of the task, which fits observations from the two experiments on the goal-only task. In VI-epis, there is a marginally significant negative correlation between success and reward positivity by the Spearman-success test ($\rho = -0.4266$, $p = 0.0994$); this correlation is insignificant for the other 3 conditions. Overall, we see that episodicity has a smaller effect on reward positivity in this failure-state task than in the goal-only task. We suspect that this observation is connected to a previously described effect of adding the failure state: that the simple strategy of always giving negative reward, without regard for the state or action, no longer creates MDP-optimal behavior that is also task-optimal.

From analyzing these results, we believe that adding the failure state affected the ease of training in both positive and negative ways. As an alternate absorbing state to the goal, the failure state generally forces trainers to give more discriminating reward (e.g., the arbitrarily all-negative strategy for the episodic version becomes unsuccessful). In comparison to the goal-only task, on the other hand, the aVI-TAMER algorithm preformed better overall in both the continuing and episodic versions of the failure-task; this increase might be due in part to the failure state being used as an intermediate "goal" that the learner makes updates for, goes to, and then gets experience and reward for those states near it, which then help it go to the real goal. Because of these multiple factors that likely affect performance (as well as randomness and different subject populations at different experiment times), we hesitate to draw strong conclusions from comparisons *across* experiments. However, we can say that this experiment does not reveal an increased performance difference between the aVI-epis and aVI-cont conditions, as we had predicted.

Nonetheless, the results from this experiment give additional empirical support for the generality of the patterns that have been identified previously in this paper, showing that they appear when the task contains both desirable and undesirable absorbing state. Most important among these patterns are that (1) performance is better for a continuing formulation of the task—especially when the agent acts approximately MDP-optimally as with the VI-TAMER algorithm—and that (2) the choice of the best algorithm for complex tasks, where MDP-optimal behavior is generally intractable, is a challenging direction for future work.

CONCLUSION

Any solution to the problem of interactive shaping—i.e., learning sequential tasks from human-generated reward—requires the definition of a reward-based objective and an agent algorithm. Building on previous work [7], this paper examines the relationship between reward discounting rates, episodicity, reward positivity, acting approximately MDP-optimally or not, and task performance. These relationships are examined thoroughly in a goal-only task and are examined further for non-myopic discounting only in a task with both goal and failure states. The table in Figure 16 summarizes our findings.

We see four main contributions in this paper:

1. empirically finding that for approximately MDP-optimal agents, converting the otherwise episodic grid-world task to a continuing task (a) enables successful training at non-myopic discount rates, (b) removes negative correlations between reward positivity and discount factor values, and (c) removes negative correlations between reward positivity and task performance within non-myopic conditions;

	VI-epis			aVI-cont			aVI-epis		
Test	Fisher Success	MWU Eps. Finished	MWU Time to Goal	Fisher Success	MWU Eps. Finished	MWU Time to Goal	Fisher Success	MWU Eps. Finished	MWU Time to Goal
VI-cont	**p<0.0001, VI-cont**	**p=0.0022, VI-cont**	**p=0.0128, VI-cont**	p=0.2635, VI-cont	**p=0.0574, VI-cont**	**p=0.0257, VI-cont**			
VI-epis							**p=0.0365, aVI-epis**	**p=0.0615, aVI-epis**	p=0.5222, aVI-epis
aVI-cont							p=0.4401, aVI-cont	p=0.5823, aVI-cont	p=0.4593, aVI-epis

Figure 13. Statistical tests for comparisons of interest. Each cell contains the p-value for the corresponding test as well as the name of the condition that performed better on the metric, which could be highest proportion of success, highest mean ranking of episodes finished, or lowest mean ranking of time to first goal. (The Mann-Whitney U test converts samples to rankings.) Cells with p-values below 0.1 are emboldened.

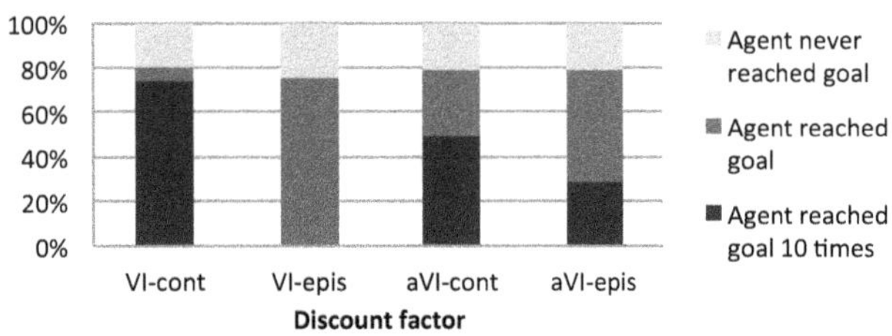

Figure 14. Success rates by condition for the failure-state experiment, which investigates the effects of locally-biased updates (the aVI-TAMER conditions) and episodicity when there is both a goal state and a failure state.

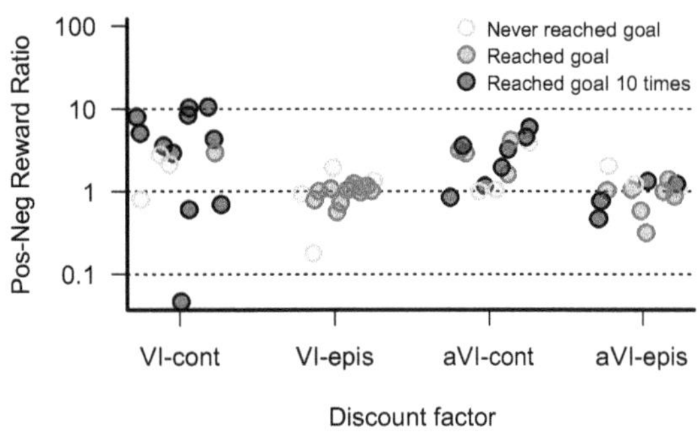

Figure 15. For the same experiment, the ratio of cumulative positive reward to cumulative negative reward given by each trainer (with x-axis jitter).

2. achieving the first known instance of consistently successful training of a non-myopic agent by live, human-generated reward signals;
3. demonstrating that successfully trained agents with non-myopic objectives learn higher-level task information, making them more robust to changes in their environments and better able to act from states in which they lack experience;
4. and showing that when the agent's MDP-based performance is worsened—as it must be for complex tasks—by the common practice of locally biased learning, task performance worsens significantly in continuing tasks.

This paper represents a step forward in the effort to create effective algorithms for learning from human reward. We note, however, that more analysis is required to establish the generality of our observations. Changing the reward-giving interface, the mapping of reward cues (e.g. keys) to scalar values, the instructions to trainers, our algorithmic choices, and the task to be learned—though all carefully chosen to avoid overt bias—might create qualitatively different results.

	Approximately MDP-optimal (VI-TAMER)	Locally biased learning (UCT-driven aVI-TAMER)
Episodic	• Effective with **few** trainers • Success **negatively correlated** with reward positivity in both tasks	• Effective with **some** trainers • Success **negatively correlated** with reward positivity in goal-only task
Continuing	• Effective with **almost all** trainers • Success **independent** of reward positivity in both tasks	• Effective with **some** trainers • Success **independent** of reward positivity in both tasks

Figure 16. Qualitative summary of this paper's experimental conclusions on non-myopic learning.

From this research, we believe that the greatest future contributions of learning from human reward will come from non-myopic objectives and will likely be in continuing tasks. However, we expect that naively designed agents with biases towards local updates—agents often well-suited for complex tasks—will ineffectively learn from human reward even in continuing tasks; the problems of reward positivity extend beyond episodic tasks. Identifying algorithms that learn non-myopically from human-generated reward in complex domains—where approximately MDP-optimal behavior will likely be impossible—remains a critical research question.

Acknowledgments

This work has taken place in the Personal Robots Group at the MIT Media Lab and in the Learning Agents Research Group (LARG) at UT Austin. LARG research is supported in part by NSF (IIS-0917122), ONR (N00014-09-1-0658), and the FHWA (DTFH61-07-H-00030). We thank George Konidaris and Rich Sutton for fruitful discussions on discounting human reward.

REFERENCES

1. Argall, B., Chernova, S., Veloso, M., and Browning, B. A survey of robot learning from demonstration. *Robotics and Autonomous Systems 57*, 5 (2009), 469–483.
2. Gelly, S., and Silver, D. Achieving master level play in 9× 9 computer go. In *Proceedings of AAAI* (2008), 1537–1540.
3. Hester, T., and Stone, P. Learning and using models. In *Reinforcement Learning: State of the Art*, M. Wiering and M. van Otterlo, Eds. Springer Verlag, Berlin, Germany, 2011.
4. Isbell, C., Kearns, M., Singh, S., Shelton, C., Stone, P., and Kormann, D. Cobot in LambdaMOO: An Adaptive Social Statistics Agent. *Proceedings of The 5th Annual International Conference on Autonomous Agents and Multiagent Systems (AAMAS)* (2006).
5. Knox, W. B. *Learning from Human-Generated Reward*. PhD thesis, Department of Computer Science, The University of Texas at Austin, August 2012.
6. Knox, W. B., and Stone, P. Interactively shaping agents via human reinforcement: The TAMER framework. In *The 5th International Conference on Knowledge Capture* (September 2009).
7. Knox, W. B., and Stone, P. Reinforcement learning from human reward: Discounting in episodic tasks. In *21st IEEE International Symposium on Robot and Human Interactive Communication (Ro-Man)* (September 2012).
8. Kocsis, L., and Szepesvári, C. Bandit based monte-carlo planning. *Machine Learning: ECML 2006* (2006), 282–293.
9. León, A., Morales, E., Altamirano, L., and Ruiz, J. Teaching a robot to perform task through imitation and on-line feedback. *Progress in Pattern Recognition, Image Analysis, Computer Vision, and Applications* (2011), 549–556.
10. Pilarski, P., Dawson, M., Degris, T., Fahimi, F., Carey, J., and Sutton, R. Online human training of a myoelectric prosthesis controller via actor-critic reinforcement learning. In *IEEE International Conference on Rehabilitation Robotics (ICORR)*, IEEE (2011), 1–7.
11. Suay, H., and Chernova, S. Effect of human guidance and state space size on interactive reinforcement learning. In *20th IEEE International Symposium on Robot and Human Interactive Communication (Ro-Man)* (2011), 1–6.
12. Sutton, R., and Barto, A. *Reinforcement Learning: An Introduction*. MIT Press, 1998.
13. Tenorio-Gonzalez, A., Morales, E., and Villaseñor-Pineda, L. Dynamic reward shaping: training a robot by voice. *Advances in Artificial Intelligence–IBERAMIA* (2010), 483–492.
14. Thomaz, A., and Breazeal, C. Teachable robots: Understanding human teaching behavior to build more effective robot learners. *Artificial Intelligence 172*, 6-7 (2008), 716–737.

Westland Row Why So Slow? Fusing Social Media and Linked Data Sources for Understanding Real-Time Traffic Conditions

Elizabeth M. Daly, Freddy Lecue, Veli Bicer
IBM Research
Dublin, Ireland
firstname.lastname@ie.ibm.com

ABSTRACT
The advent of real-time traffic streaming offers users the opportunity to visualise current traffic conditions and congestion information. However, real-time information highlighting the underlying reason for tail-backs remains largely unexplored. Broken traffic lights, an accident, a large concert, or road-works reveal important information for citizens and traffic operators alike. Providing such information in real-time requires intelligent mechanisms and user interfaces in order to (i) harness heterogeneous data sources (volume, velocity, variety, veracity) and (ii) make derived knowledge consumable so users can visualize traffic conditions and congestion information making better routing decisions while travelling. This work focuses on surfacing relevant information and explaining the underlying reasons behind traffic conditions. To this end, static data from event providers, planned road works together with dynamically emerging events such as a traffic accidents, localized weather conditions or unplanned obstructions are captured through social media to provide users real-time feedback to highlight the causes of traffic congestion.

Author Keywords
Intelligent user interfaces; text mining; social media; crowd-sourcing; semantic reasoning

ACM Classification Keywords
H.5.2. [Information Interfaces and Presentation]: User Interfaces; H.2.8. [Database Management]: Database applications - Data mining.

INTRODUCTION
Much research in smarter cities focuses on analyzing and understanding traditional information sources such as static census data, city wide information resources such as event databases and dynamic streaming data from real-time sensors. However, user generated content can provide information outside the scope of traditional data sources [10]. For example, traffic sensors such as GPS units and loop detectors may identify delays or emerging traffic jams, but are unable to capture the whole picture in order to differentiate between an unplanned protest, unexpected weather conditions or a broken down car. Social media streams, such as twitter, however have shown to be valuable information sources for such events [1, 10].

Traditional data sources have the advantage of reliability, governance, and the quality may be known a priori. Depending on these traditional data sources alone, however, does not come without its challenges. Managing and updating many different data sources that greatly vary according to volume, update rate and reliability means assuming freshness and completeness is impossible to guarantee. Information streams from social media and user generated content on the other hand can have low reliability, little governance and can vary significantly in terms of quality. However, user generated content can capture real-time information which can augment traditional data sources. These views of the city combined, can support a richer and more complete view by merging the reliability of traditional data sources with dynamic less reliable social media streams.

In the context of traffic, the availability of real-time road conditions has lead to the ability to visualize congested roads[1] and provide alternative routes, however, surfacing the reason for congestion to users remains unexplored. In this paper we present Dub-STAR (Dublin's Semantic Traffic Annotator and Reasoner) which merges city data sources and social media, and captures relevant insights in order to provide real-time explanations of abnormal traffic conditions, such as delays. The contributions of this paper are as following: (i) a social media extension for traffic diagnosis, (ii) an intelligent interface to easily capture real-time insight of dynamic traffic conditions, (iii) a geo-coder to parse user generated content, all evaluated in terms of accuracy and usability.

The remainder of this paper is organized as follows. In Section 2 we comment on related work. Section 3 presents the

[1] `https://maps.google.com/`

Dub-STAR system, our Semantic Traffic Annotator and Reasoner, designed to explain real-time traffic conditions in the city of Dublin. Section 4 reviews our semantic-based approach. Section 5 harnesses crowd-sourced traffic updates through a novel natural language processing algorithm which is presented. Section 6 reports some experimental results in terms of accuracy, performance and usability. Finally, Section 7 concludes our work.

RELATED WORK

Traffic control rooms have the ability to visualize current conditions through traditional sensors such as loop-detectors and traffic cameras, detecting traffic jams as they emerge using domain knowledge and expertise. However the automated and real-time explanation of traffic conditions through merging heterogeneous data sources including social media feeds has not been tackled.

In previous work the underlying cause for a traffic anomaly has been inferred (i.e., road congestion) by aggregating and interpreting external and heterogeneous data sources [4]. The work presented in this paper extends [4] by considering social media feeds to capture real-time updates of traffic conditions. We make use of semantic representations to classify types of anomalies in traffic situations (e.g., delay, incident), and semantic matching techniques to surface possible causes and related social media updates (e.g., AARoadWatch, Dublin LiveDrive, GardaTraffic) that can explain the current traffic conditions.

Valle et al. applied semantic web technologies and machine learning techniques for predicting road traffic conditions in the city of Milano [11]. Our work goes further as we aim to explain traffic conditions. To this end our approach merges Artificial Intelligence diagnosis techniques with social media analytics. Semantic representation is required for automatically interpreting diagnosis results in any open environment i.e., domains such as traffic where causes are not trivially linked to their effects.

Social media provides a valuable source of real-time information and insights into the physical world. Starbird et al. examined how twitter users disseminated information and coordinated during a flood [10]. Sakaki et al. use a domain specific classifier to detect earthquake events [9]. Becker et al. use discovered clusters of related words or tweets to detect events [1]. Popescu et al. detect events from twitter using knowledge of known entities [8]. Nicholas et al. use twitter to automatically generate summaries of sporting events where key moments are detected through a rapid increase in the number of messages [6].

Much of this work addresses the challenges associated with event detection in the diverse and noisy twitter stream. In this paper we aim to overcome these issues by harnessing domain specific, reputable and focused twitter sources, while still extracting useful information in order to detect traffic related events. Another key difference in this work is that we do not limit ourselves to geo-coded twitter feeds and consider the city to be known a priori. The added-value of our work relies also in the fusion of relevant data sources, from different channels, i.e., streams for social media, and static data from city event sources, using semantic and common representations for existing Linked Open Data vocabularies from DBPedia[2].

Previous work has focused on assigning locations to twitter users, however, the granularity is at the city-level. Cheng et al. propose a probabilistic approach based on the content of the tweet and reported user profile locations [2]. Eisenstein et al. introduced a method for modelling linguistic properties, identifying consistent regions to predict locations [3]. Mahmud et al. use a combination of classifiers to predict at city level the location of the user [5]. Our work departs from this direction by taking the question of identifying the city out of the equation and focuses on geo-coding at street level accuracy.

DUB-STAR

This section presents Dub-STAR, Dublin's Semantic Traffic Annotator and Reasoner, designed to explain traffic conditions in the city of Dublin. First of all, we review the system interface, then we present its architecture. We describe the approach for explaining abnormal traffic conditions using city event data. We then present a geocoding algorithm to harness non-geocoded traffic related social media feeds and how these inputs are utilized as valuable data sources into the Dub-STAR system.

System Interface and User Interaction

Dub-STAR combines city information sources and social media inputs in order to provide real-time traffic information helping highlight events and incidents that could be causing congestions in Dublin city. An example screen shot of the Dub-STAR web client is presented in Figure 1. It shows a zoomed in section of Dublin where the red lines show traffic congestion in real-time and the red bubbles show that a related alert has been identified by the Dub-STAR system. As can be seen, a traffic accident has occurred at this location which was identified through a traffic based twitter stream. At the same time on a connected street a protest is underway and has been highlighted as a related incident. The left hand panel shows a summary of the recent types of updates detected in the city in order to enable the user to filter on specific event types. The right hand panel shows the heterogeneous data sources being considered as inputs and annotation of traffic conditions.

The embedded map enables the end-user to zoom in and out filtering events based on alert type. The size of the bubbles is based on the number of updates for that area, highlighting hotspots of the city as they emerge. Users may zoom into specific locations, clicking on alerts associated with any part of Dublin city.

System Architecture

The overall system architecture is presented in Figure 2 and consists of the following core components:

1. *Historical Training.* Historical data regarding road conditions, congestion and events in the city are used to train the

[2]`http://dbpedia.org/`

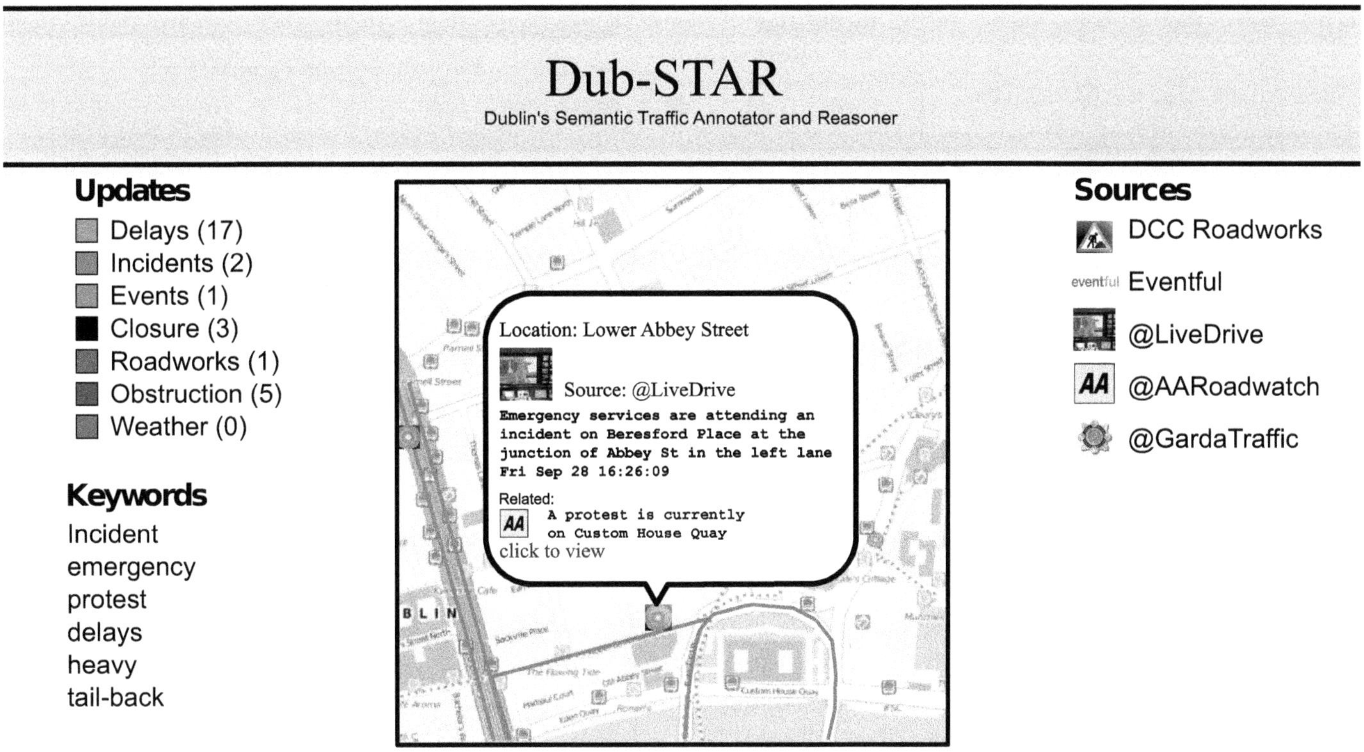

Figure 1: Dub-STAR Web Client: Alerts are shown on a map of the city which supports zoom-in/zoom-out navigation. The size of the alert symbols are based on the number of updates reflecting that location. The left hand panel shows a summary of the recent types of updates detected in the city in order to enable the user to filter on specific event types. The right hand panel shows the heterogeneous data sources being considered as inputs and annotation of traffic conditions.

diagnosis process. An off-line diagnoser is extracted using the methodology presented in [4] by contextualising historical congestion data into its spatial and temporal domain using the road network of the city. Details are provided in *Semantics-based Traffic Diagnosis* section.

2. *Semantic Matching.* Once the training phase is complete, links between events and congestion are inferred. Real-time events are evaluated as possible causes on the basis of: semantic similarity to previous congestion causing "semantically similar" events (i.e., events which are similar type, have similar tags etc.), the time window of the event, the road network and the connectivity between the potential source of congestion and the input request. Inputs from social media are also considered on the basis of the time window and the spatial relationship between the input request and the geo-coded social media input.

3. *Semantic Interpretation.* The candidate responses are ranked based on confidence and presented to the user. The confidence is evaluated based on a spatio-temporal relationship between abnormal conditions and its potential causes.

4. *Geo-Coding.* Inputs that originate from social media and SMS messages must first be geo-coded before being included into the semantic matching process. The geo-coder supports free text inputs, automatically extracting and mapping the input to a geographic coordinate which will be explained in greater detail in the following sections.

5. *Multi-Modal User Interface.* The ability to support free text location based requests enables the system to support three methods of request inputs to the Dub-STAR system. The geo-coder is used to pre-process requests from twitter and SMS messages. The web client supports requests based on a map location and therefore may bypass the geo-coder.

SEMANTIC-BASED TRAFFIC DIAGNOSIS

Diagnosis is a reasoning task which comprises of connecting causes of an anomaly to its effects. In a transportation and road traffic context, traffic diagnosis provides a means of explaining anomalies or abnormal conditions such as congestion in real-time based on previously observed conditions.

Approach

We use semantic web technologies in order to integrate heterogeneous data and enable semantic analytics. A road segment is defined as *congested* if we observe that the speed of at least two buses on the same segment is lower than 5km/h in a time window of 10 minutes, using Dublin City Bus SIRI data (described below). The potential causes for congestion takes

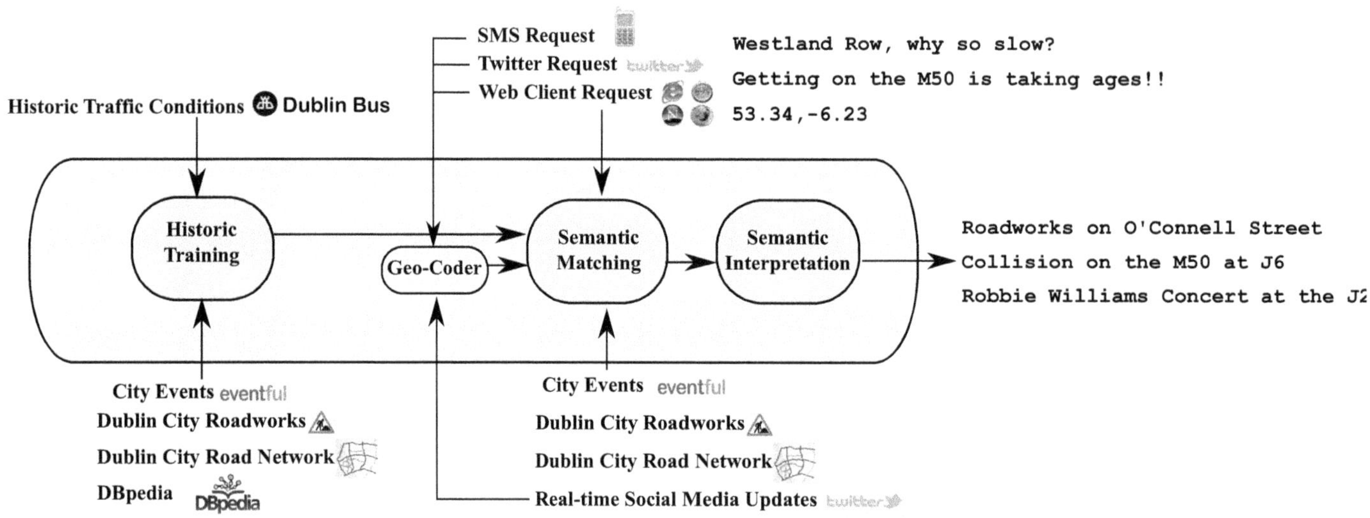

Figure 2: High level system overview of the Dub-STAR System.

into consideration background knowledge (i.e., semantic descriptions of events and road works) and dynamic knowledge (e.g., a music event is active in a given window time) using existing Linked Open Data vocabularies from DBPedia and the Dublin City Road Network.

Our approach, as part of the Dub-STAR system in Figure 2, implements an off-line diagnoser which aims to capture *historical observations of congestion* and their *causes* over a predetermined *time window*. For example, Canal street was congested on May 1st, 2012 from 6:00pm to 7:12pm due to a concert in the Aviva stadium and road works on Bath avenue. For the real-time diagnosis of new instances of congestion "*similar*" occurrences (e.g., similarly congested roads during the same time frame) and "*semantically similar*" causes (e.g., close to an event of type concert) are retrieved. The similarity estimation is computed with respect to semantic descriptions of congestion and its causes and the spatial connectivity of events with respect to the road network of the city, ensuring that the infrastructure of the city is considered.

Data Sources

The city data sources considered for computing the off-line diagnoser and the on-line experiments are as follows:

Dublin Bus SIRI: The XML SIRI[3] dataset consists of historical events where road segments have been classified as "congested" or "cleared" derived from GPS traces of 1000 buses in Dublin, updated every 20 seconds.

The resulting road status have then been represented along space (latitude, longitude and road segments) and time dimensions (i.e., start, end-time of congestion and clearance roads) and encoded in RDF (Resource Description Framework: W3C standard for metadata data model[4]) using respectively W3C standards `http://www.w3.org/2003/01/geo/wgs84_pos` and `http://www.w3.org/2002/12/cal/icaltzd`. The space and time-based descriptions of events and road works have been similarly encoded, mainly for linking data entities from heterogeneous sources along those two dimensions.

Eventful: Eventful[5] is a web service for sharing events which contains rich representations of both events, venues and organizers. All considered XML-based events have been encoded in RDF, where their categories and types have been enriched using concepts from the Linked Open Data cloud.

DBPedia: DBPedia provides a consistent structure of terms for the LOD and is used to classify the type and categories of events in the Eventful dataset, matching each event to DBPedia concepts. This pre-processing step enables similarity comparisons of events based on their semantic classification.

Dublin Road Works: Dublin City Council releases the planned roadworks for the year through the Dublinked Open Data portal[6]. Additionally, the scheduled disruptions for the week ahead are released through their website[7]. Along with the location and type of road works taking place the predicted severity and impact of the roadworks are included.

Dublin City Road Network: LinkedGeoData[8] provides an RDF representation of the road network and can be used to identify road segments linked throughout the city.

[3]SIRI (Service Interface for Real Time Information) is a standard for exchanging real-time services and vehicles - http://siri.org.uk

[4]`http://www.w3.org/RDF/`
[5]`http://api.eventful.com`
[6]`http://dublinked.ie/datastore/datasets/dataset-217.php/`
[7]`http://www.dublincity.ie/RoadsandTraffic/ScheduledDisruptions/Documents/Traffic_News.pdf`
[8]`http://linkedgeodata.org/About`

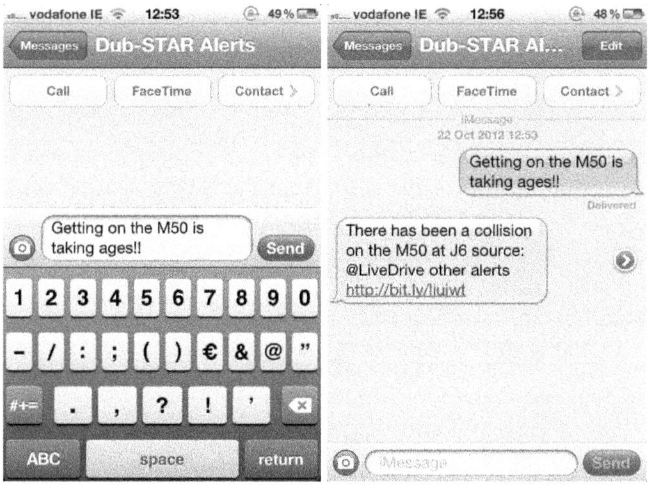

Figure 3: Dub-STAR SMS Client

All data sources have been encoded in RDF, using the metadata of its organizer, venue, type and associated tags for city events, and contractor area of work, traffic impact and asset type for road works. Besides handling seamless integration of data entities, RDF encoding of data has been shown to be very efficient for semantic reasoning on event types, allowing automatic classification of events through type specification.

CROWD-SOURCED TRAFFIC ALERTS

Information resources such as Eventful and scheduled roadworks provide a rich structured view of the city. Traffic, however, is a domain where crowd sourcing, in a low tech form, has been active for many years before the advent of twitter and smart phones. Radio stations have long used listeners to request traffic updates providing on the ground insights and updates of the state of the city. The information gained through such reporting has previously remained locked in radio station control rooms and broadcast to their listeners. Through the use of twitter this information can now be broadcast to a larger audience and harnessed as an information source in order to annotate and explain real-time traffic congestion. Alerts may come to the traffic authority in the form of SMS messages or tweets, however a challenge remains that many of these reports come in the form of free text and are not geo-coded. Even if the twitter messages were geo-coded, the location is potentially out of date by the time the message is sent. Additionally, if they originate from a traffic specific twitter feed relaying real-time traffic information, the geo-coded information reflects the location of the feed provider rather than the location the message is referring to.

As a result, the ability to assign accurate locations to free text messages creates the opportunity to harness otherwise unavailable real-time information in the city. Additionally it enables users to query the system in a free text manner using either twitter or traditional SMS messages.

Geo-coding User Generated Content

We present a natural language processing algorithm which extracts location based keywords in order to assign a geo-coded location to a free text input message.

Location Dictionary and Index: The OpenStreetMaps osm file is used as the foundation for the location based dictionary. Each node and waypoint with the `highway` tag is collected and the nodes connected to the way points are also used. The result is a collection of named locations, longitude, latitude and related terms associated with the location. For example, a waypoint may be called the South Eastern Motorway, on that waypoint is a node that connects two motorways the M50 leading to Dundrum on the R113. In this case all keywords associated with the location are used, i.e., South Eastern Motorway, M50, Dundrum and R113. These text and location pairs are then inserted into a Lucene[9] index which provides a dictionary of location terms and a collection of retrievable documents based on their keywords.

Geo-coding Algorithm The geo-coding algorithm processes the user generated text in a number of steps. The flow and an example are illustrated in Table 1 while the details of the approach are as follows:

- *Input:* The input message is fed into the geocoder. These messages can be in the form of an SMS message or collected through a twitter feed.
- *Cleanse:* The message is normalized by removing punctuation and lower cased. Keywords such as rd, ave, st are expanded to road, avenue and street respectively.
- *Extracting Location Text:* Each word is used to perform a dictionary lookup in order to assess whether this term exists in the index. Additional processing is done to merge patterns of a single letter beginning with R (route), N (national road), M (motorway) or J (junction) followed by a digit which is a typical pattern for road annotations, e.g., R66. If the word is not found in the index a spell checker is used to identify possible replacements that closely match. In the example shown in Table 1 the space between N and 11 is removed and the misspelling of Kilmacud has been corrected.
- *Generate N-Grams:* The location based terms are then used to generate n-grams of the possible word combinations.
- *Validate N-Grams:* A lookup on the index for each n-gram is performed. If no document exists with these possible location keywords appearing together, the n-gram is removed.
- *Filter N-Grams:* Not all n-grams that exist in the index are valid enough to warrant a separate clause in the search query. If an n-gram only contains keywords such as street, road, drive, place, etc. then it is removed.
- *Generate Search Query:* A lucene search query containing a clause for each n-gram is created. Each n-gram is boosted

[9] `http://lucene.apache.org/`

Step	Function	Input Message
1	Input	There has been a collision on the N 11 inbound just before Lower Kilmacuod Rd in the right lane
2	Clean	there has been a collision on the **n 11** inbound just before **lower kilmacud road** in the right lane
3	Extract Location Text	n11 lower kilmacud road lane
4	N-Grams	[kilmacud, kilmacud road, kilmacud road lane, lane, lower, lower kilmacud, lower kilmacud road, n11, n11 lower, n11 lower kilmacud, road, road lane]
5	Validate N-Gram	[kilmacud, kilmacud road, lane, lower, n11, road]
6	Filter N-Grams	[kilmacud, kilmacud road, lower, n11]
7	Generate Search Query	kilmacud OR "kilmacud road"$\hat{2}$ OR lower OR "n11"$\hat{5}$
8	Search Output	Kilmacud Road Lower = 53.28864,-6.1977253

Table 1: Example Dub-STAR Geocoding.

based on two factors: either the length of the n-gram taking into account that if a user has gone to the trouble of writing a longer string representing the location that it may be more significant than a shorter phrase [7], or whether the n-gram matches the pattern of a route, national road, motorway or junction. These n-grams are given a boosting factor of 5 representing their significance in the location based information despite being a single word.

- *Search Output:* The resulting lucene query is issued to the search index with a customized scorer that ignores the TF-IDF scores of the terms, scoring documents on the number of keywords overlapping in the search query with the index document. The highest ranking result document is used as the latitude and longitude and assigned to the input message.

Semantically Annotating

Another challenge of utilizing crowd-sourced data for traffic diagnosis is to understand the type of alerts received in free text form. An important task is to extract the nature of the update and to annotate them with the correct classes such as `delay`, `incident`, `roadwork`, or `concert`. For example, the first alert in Figure 3 *"Getting on the M50 is taking ages!!"* reports a `delay` on the M50, whereas the alert in Figure 1 indicates a `incident` on the road.

For this paper, we use a simple dictionary approach in order to assign tags to the input messages with example keywords shown in Table 3. The geo-coded, annotated messages are then fed into the semantic matching process as an additional data source providing real-time updates. Given historical training is not available for social media inputs, the semantic matching process utilizes the road network (i.e., road segments links and their nature e.g., bi-directional, one way) to identify spatially linked updates returned as possible explanations for current traffic conditions.

EXPERIMENTAL EVALUATION

Evaluation Data

The training and classification phase were performed using roadworks and Eventful data for the time period of 01/01/2011-31/12/2011 and the inferred congestion using SIRI data for the entire year of 2011.

Category	Sample keywords
delay	slow, tail-back, busy, back up, delay
incident	crash, accident, incident, danger
event	concert, gig, protest, parade, festival
closure	roadblock, closed, access, restrictions
roadworks	roadworks
obstruction	blockage, blocking, parked
weather	flood, rain, sun, fog, frost, snow

Table 2: Sample Classification Keywords.

In order to evaluate the Dub-STAR system, we collected a dataset of tweets from three reputable sources of traffic information in Dublin, Ireland; LiveDrive, AARoadwatch and GardaTraffic. The user feed was collected through the Twitter API for the months of August and September 2012, with the volume over these two months shown in Figure 4. During this period Dublin experienced a number of events that caused closures and additional traffic issues throughout the city. August 15th for example shows a large spike associated with the Olympic Homecoming ceremony which resulted in traffic restrictions in the city center. The Tall Ships festival took place on the weekend of August 23rd[10]. This peak is followed closely by another smaller peak on August 30th where an American football parade took place before a game between Notre Dame and Old Navy. The first of three peaks in September on the 14th was due to two concerts, Robbie Williams and Leonard Cohen, co-occurring on the same evening in city center venues. The data set contains events associated with traffic congestion ranging from a taxi strike and protests to fallen trees and flooding to a driver stopping to rescue two signets on the motorway.

The traffic twitter feed from these three sources were used to manually infer real world traffic events that occurred during the months of August and September in the city of Dublin. Each event was manually geo-coded and classified into the categories shown in Table 3.

The summary of events consisted of 719 representative events. Below shows a sample input entry from the @LiveDrive twitter stream. It is important to note that only

[10] `http://www.dublintallships.ie/`

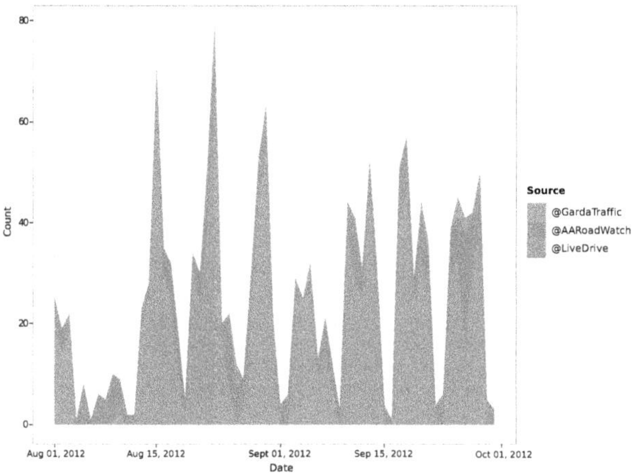

Figure 4: Twitter Traffic

Category	Number
delay	455
incident	179
event	34
closure	18
roadworks	16
obstruction	9
weather	8

Table 3: Breakdown of Input Events.

the date and the geo-location are used to simulate input requests to the Dub-STAR.

Input Entry:

```
@LiveDrive Just had a text from a listener
who has been queuing to get off at J7 Lucan
for an hour: they only started at J9 Red Cow
Date: 28/09/2012 17:45:30
Location:  53.32,-6.37
```

Example Output:

```
@GardaTraffic Gardai at scene of 4 car
collision on M50 northbound between jcn9
Naas rd and jcn7 Palmerstown - traffic
down to 2 lanes - expect delays
Date: 28/09/2012 17:40:06
Location: 53.31,-6.37
```

Geocoding Evaluation

In order to evaluate the geo-coding algorithm, the manually annotated and geolocated inputs are compared. The latitude and longitude of the annotated input is used as a lookup to the road network. Given a number of the locations include junctions and places where two roads meet, multiple street segments could be valid locations assigned to the message. As a result, we evaluate the accuracy according to two criteria: *exact match*, where both location and road names are the same; *connected match*, where the algorithmically geo-coded location is connected through the road network to the manually geo-coded road.

Figure 5 a) shows the accuracy of the geo-coder based on all inputs. As can be seen the accuracy is only 35% for the exact match criteria and 54% for the connected match. This is due to the fact that over 30% of the input events contained more than one location for example "Most of the city moving fine now. Some delays remaining on Malahide Rd: Swords Rd: Strand Rd and the N11 from Donnybrook Church to clear UCD". The manual annotation extracted delay reports for four distinct locations and the geo-coder currently uses the best first match. This highlights a limitation of the current algorithm. When examining the geo-coder accuracy on unique messages (i.e., messages with multiple locations are used as inputs once rather than repeated for each location) the exact match accuracy increases to 50% and the connected match accuracy increases to 80%.

The spatial accuracy of the geo-coder is also evaluated using the measure of distance between the manually geo-coded input and the geo-coding algorithm output, Figure 5 b). Similarly to the results based on the road network, the accuracy is reduced when considering all inputs. However, when matching unique messages nearly 50% are accurate with an error range of 500 meters and reaches nearly 100% within a threshold of 2km. Though 2km may appear to be poor accuracy, given a large portion of the roads are motorways or main roads that act as the arteries of the city and the radius of the city spans for nearly 30km this performance is promising. Additionally, when merged with traditional sensors such as loop detectors, where candidate locations may be polled for evidence of congestion in order to select the most probable match, we believe this accuracy may be improved greatly.

Explanations Precision and Recall

Figure 6 shows the coverage, precision and recall of the resulting explanations returned by Dub-STAR. The coverage shows the number of input queries, $i_{queries}$, where an output was returned. An output match, $O_{returned}$, is any entry that could be related to the input query, this could include reports of delays from connected locations, notification or roadworks or ongoing events. Without the input of social media events only 41% of the queries provided a result. This is to be expected given the high number of input queries where the underlying reason was due to collisions or weather conditions. With the inclusion of social media data sources coverage increases to 78%.

$$Coverage_{any} = \frac{O_{returned}}{I_{queries}} \quad (1)$$

A number of the entries returned from social media however may simply include related reports of delays and though potentially useful in order to see other locations that are experiencing congestion and how many users are also reporting delays. These entries do not provide an underlying reason for the observed delay. As a result, we evaluate the number of results that contain a valid explanation. We consider a valid explanation, $O_{explained}$, to be an entry tagged with one of the following: event, incident, disruption, roadworks, closure or weather. When excluding social media all of the returned

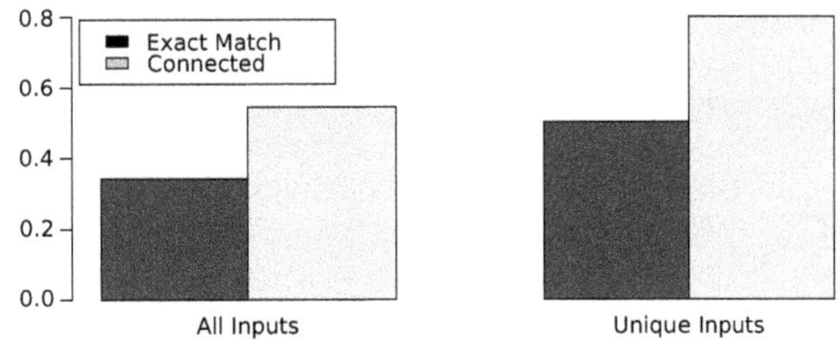

(a) Roads Network

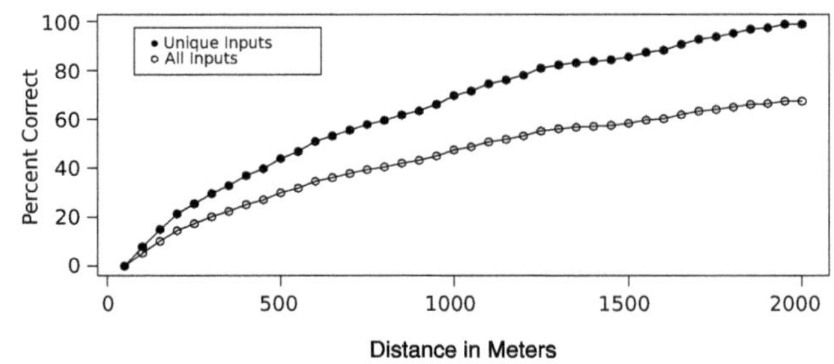

(b) Spatial Distance

Figure 5: Geo-coder Accuracy

entries contained a possible explanation. When considering social media sources nearly 70% of the entries returned did include a possible explanation.

$$Coverage_{explained} = \frac{O_{explain}}{I_{queries}} \qquad (2)$$

Only 35% of the manually annotated inputs contained an explanation E_{input}, the remainder were simply reporting delays. In order to evaluate the accuracy of explanations provided we evaluate whether the explanation returned by DubSTAR matched the reason provided in the input event. For example, if the input event states "Four parked buses on Charlotte's Way are causing delays on Camden St outbound and Richmond St inbound" which has been manually classified as `obstruction`, returns an explanation also classified as `obstruction`, then the explanation is determined to be correct, $E_{correct}$. We define $recall$ as the number of correct explanations, $E_{correct}$ normalized by the number of input explanations, E_{input}.

$$Recall = \frac{E_{correct}}{E_{input}} \qquad (3)$$

In the case where social media sources are excluded the recall is only 10% which is a facet of the number of input requests related to real-time information regarding obstructions, collisions and weather conditions. When including social media as an input the recall increases to 78%.

$$Precision = \frac{E_{correct}}{E_{returned}} \qquad (4)$$

More than one reason could be responsible for the observed congestion, for example a collision may have occurred on a street segment at the same time as a protest is currently under way. It is difficult to evaluate relevance of all the returned entries, however of those that could be classified as correct, $E_{correct}$, the precision of the algorithm is approximately 20%, as shown in figure 6 . Though precision can be improved through a combination of increasing the confidence threshold, reducing the time window and the boundary box of diagnosis, this does come at the expense of recall being reduced.

End-User-based Evaluation

Live Drive CityFM is a radio station run by Dublin County Council. The radio station broadcasts during the morning and evening peak traffic times. Listeners are incentivised to provide real-time updates to the station by offering free parking vouchers, requesting a song of their choice and the general understanding that if they contribute useful information that benefits others, they too benefit from the contributions of others. The team consists primarily of three members, the radio presenter who communicates the updates to the listeners, the producer who monitors incoming alerts and a camera controller who has access to a number of the traffic cameras in the city when trying to clarify reported issues. The authors conducted semi-structured interviews with this team on location at their office. The interviews were transcribed and a number of common themes emerged from these interviews, which we describe below.

Aggregating City Data: The producer must currently manually compile a list of events occurring in the city for the week ahead, taking into account roadworks, concerts and sporting events in order to give accurate updates and alerts to their listeners. When asked if returning events and roadworks as possible explanations related to user requests the team emphasized the utility of such a feature,

> "anything that saves us time and gives us a better picture of what is going on in the city would be really useful".

User contributed events: We asked the team whether they find the information they get from listeners useful in terms of identifying accidents given they have access to traffic cameras. It turns out the crowd-sourced alerts are their primary source of information for such incidents,

> "we find out about the majority of accidents from our listeners so their contributions are really important. Though we have access to traffic cameras we don't have coverage in many areas."

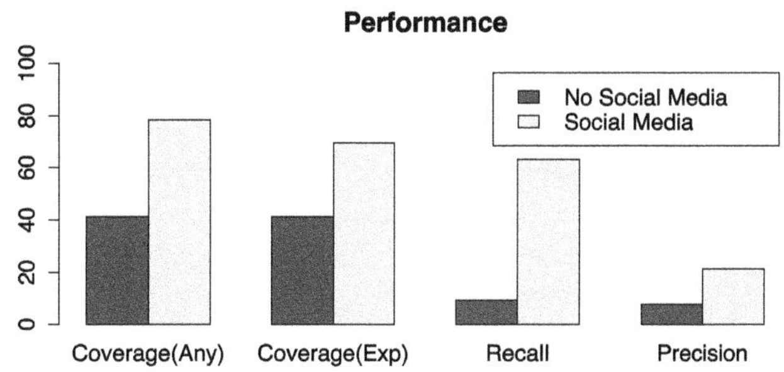

Figure 6: Performance Evaluation of Retrieval.

Use of Twitter vs SMS: The team highlighted that twitter is an increasing source of information where traditionally the majority of updates from listeners came in the form of SMS messages,

> "our following on twitter is growing by the day, we still get alot of SMS alerts but they are definitely increasingly coming from twitter. This could be because it's free and they don't have to pay for the text message."

Accuracy: Given the large amount of input the team receives from listeners we wanted to understand whether all information is relayed or whether they are cautious in the information they give out.

> "Accuracy is really important to use. If the listeners can't trust our updates then they will no longer participate so we really try to verify information, so showing supporting information such as how many people have also tweeted that something is occurring at the same location is really valuable."

Evidence: Not all events occurring in the city result in congestion, so before raising an alert to listeners the team highlighted the value of users validating that a problem is occurring.

> "Some roadworks might just be maintenance on the footpath so it is hard to tell which ones could cause a problem and which ones won't. If we advertise that there are roadworks on a particular route, we could even cause traffic congestion by scaring them away from a route when it wouldn't have caused a problem after all. So we would be cautious about advising users of roadworks unless we see they might be causing a problem".

Reputation: Understanding the source of updates can be a key indicator of the accuracy, as a result the reputation of the source and surfacing this to the user should be considered.

> "Sometimes people defined delays differently, we certainly have some users who might exaggerate a little and then we have others who are very loyal contributors and we really know we can trust their content. Having a way to see an indication of history of the person contributing the update would really make that easier."

User Interface: The team were shown the Dub-STAR system and updates from October 24th 2011, when extensive flooding occurred, were replayed to them in a simulation.

> "I really like the user interface, it is really clean and simple to use. I also particularly like that the size of the bubble is based on the number of updates referring to the same area. And being able to filter on specific types of events could be really useful."

On days such as that of October 24th, 2011 the ability of the team to keep up with the volume of inputs becomes very difficult. As a result, when it is busy they get less time to see the updates which is potentially when listeners need the updates the most.

Text mapping: The team explored the geo-coding of the message stream and highlighted a potential requirement of allowing user inputs to the location index.

> "We use a lot of way points like shopping centres and petrol stations when giving locations or use short names like the LMR for the Long Mile Road or SCR for the South Circular Road. It would be really great if we could add our own labels to locations."

CONCLUSIONS AND FUTURE WORK

The Dub-STAR system presents a novel mechanism of fusing traditional city data sources with real-time social media updates in order to surface and highlight the underlying causes of current traffic conditions. The contributions of the paper are as following: (i) a social media extension for traffic diagnosis, (ii) an intelligent interface for easily capture real-time insight on time changing traffic conditions, (iii) a geo-coding interpretation of user generated content. The accuracy of both the geo-coding algorithm and the explanations supports that this solution warrants further exploration. One limitation identified through the evaluation is that the current algorithm only supports matching a single location to a single message. However, as was seen, a large number of messages refer to more than one location. Through our interviews we identified a number of avenues to be considered including capturing the reputation of the contributing source and supporting user defined location terms.

The evaluation presented here focused on dedicated, reputable traffic based twitter sources. Our next step, is to conduct a large scale experiment capturing user inputs as they are directed at these twitter streams.

We believe this work provides a valuable contribution fusing static and dynamic data streams towards explaining why Westland Row is so slow.

REFERENCES

1. Becker, H., Naaman, M., and Gravano, L. Beyond Trending Topics: Real-World Event Identification on Twitter.
2. Cheng, Z., Caverlee, J., and Lee, K. You are where you tweet: a content-based approach to geo-locating twitter users. In *Proceedings of the 19th ACM international conference on Information and knowledge management*, CIKM '10, ACM (New York, NY, USA, 2010), 759–768.
3. Eisenstein, J., O'Connor, B., Smith, N. A., and Xing, E. P. A latent variable model for geographic lexical variation. In *Proceedings of the 2010 Conference on Empirical Methods in Natural Language Processing*, EMNLP '10, Association for Computational Linguistics (Stroudsburg, PA, USA, 2010), 1277–1287.
4. Lécué, F., Schumann, A., and Sbodio, M. L. Applying semantic web technologies for diagnosing road traffic congestions. In *Proceedings of the 11th International Semantic Web Conference (ISWC)* (2012).
5. Mahmud, J., Nichols, J., and Drews, C. Where Is This Tweet From? Inferring Home Locations of Twitter Users (2012).
6. Nichols, J., Mahmud, J., and Drews, C. Summarizing sporting events using twitter. In *Proceedings of the 2012 ACM international conference on Intelligent User Interfaces*, IUI '12, ACM (New York, NY, USA, 2012), 189–198.
7. Pfeifer, U., Poersch, T., and Fuhr, N. Retrieval effectiveness of proper name search methods. *Information Processing & Management 32*, 6 (Nov. 1996), 667–679.
8. Popescu, A. M., Pennacchiotti, M., and Paranjpe, D. Extracting events and event descriptions from Twitter. In *Proceedings of the 20th international conference companion on World wide web*, WWW '11, ACM (New York, NY, USA, 2011), 105–106.
9. Sakaki, T., Okazaki, M., and Matsuo, Y. Earthquake shakes Twitter users: real-time event detection by social sensors. In *Proceedings of the 19th international conference on World wide web*, WWW '10, ACM (New York, NY, USA, 2010), 851–860.
10. Starbird, K., Palen, L., Hughes, A. L., and Vieweg, S. Chatter on the red: what hazards threat reveals about the social life of microblogged information. In *Proceedings of the 2010 ACM conference on Computer supported cooperative work*, CSCW '10, ACM (New York, NY, USA, 2010), 241–250.
11. Valle, E. D., Celino, I., Dell'Aglio, D., Grothmann, R., Steinke, F., and Tresp, V. Semantic traffic-aware routing using the larkc platform. *IEEE Internet Computing 15*, 6 (2011), 15–23.

Curating and Contextualizing Twitter Stories to Assist with Social Newsgathering

Arkaitz Zubiaga
Computer Science Department
Queens College and Graduate Center
City University of New York
New York, NY, USA
arkaitz@zubiaga.org

Heng Ji
Computer Science Department
Queens College and Graduate Center
City University of New York
New York, NY, USA
hengjicuny@gmail.com

Kevin Knight
Computer Science Department
Information Sciences Institute
Univ. of Southern California
Marina del Rey, CA, USA
knight@isi.edu

ABSTRACT

While journalism is evolving toward a rather open-minded participatory paradigm, social media presents overwhelming streams of data that make it difficult to identify the information of a journalist's interest. Given the increasing interest of journalists in broadening and democratizing news by incorporating social media sources, we have developed TweetGathering, a prototype tool that provides curated and contextualized access to news stories on Twitter. This tool was built with the aim of assisting journalists both with gathering and with researching news stories as users comment on them. Five journalism professionals who tested the tool found helpful characteristics that could assist them with gathering additional facts on breaking news, as well as facilitating discovery of potential information sources such as witnesses in the geographical locations of news.

Author Keywords

newsgathering, user-interface, social media, trends, scoop

ACM Classification Keywords

H.5.m Information Systems: Information Interfaces and Presentation - Miscellaneous

INTRODUCTION

Social media is steadily growing as it gains importance as an information source to learn about current affairs. More specifically, the microblogging service Twitter, where users can post short messages known as tweets, is becoming the *par excellence* social media to catch up on recent news and events. The brevity of tweets and the increasing usage of mobile devices are facilitating to quickly share information from anywhere at anytime, and thus make Twitter the first venue where news break in many cases, anticipating news media [19]. This phenomenon is giving rise to an ever stronger citizen journalism, where millions of users share about, discuss, comment on and illustrate recent happenings on a daily basis. The participation of a large community of users enables access to an unprecedented volume of real-time information, constituting a gold mine for journalists to research the news and search for sources for ideal news reporting.

Journalists constantly track numerous sources with the aim of discovering and researching breaking news stories as soon as they happen. This process is known as *newsgathering*, by which they try to collect as much information and sources as they can for a subsequent well-researched news reporting step. While journalists have traditionally relied on authoritative information sources for newsgathering, the growth of social media is picking up steam as an additional participatory information source fed by citizens. In addition, collecting information by citizens in social media allows to approach to the readers by reporting news in a broader, more democratic, and culturally more relevant way [29]. Furthermore, taking advantage of information and media shared by citizens enables extensive coverage of news as never seen before due to limited reach of journalists themselves, both geographically and culturally. However, this open participation often produces an overwhelming amount of informal and noisy information, which makes it difficult to identify and grasp the main contents. Despite the potential existence of valuable and sometimes unique information in that mess, some journalists are still skeptical about using social media as a source, given the endeavor needed to curate its contents.

With the aim of making newsgathering from social media an easier experience, especially for journalists, we have developed TweetGathering, a tool for curated and contextualized access to Twitter stories early on as news break. Distilling Twitter, an open platform where users can share and comment on all kinds of matters, often riddled with pointless chatter, we provide enhanced access to trending stories that are likely to be newsworthy. The enhancements include curation of contents for faster access to salient information, addition of context for easier understanding of events that are not familiar to the reader, and improved access to contributors for the discovery of potential sources such as witnesses.

Five journalism professionals were invited to test the tool. By interviewing them and evaluating their user experience, we have found numerous features and visualizations that could be helpful to journalists in the social newsgathering process. TweetGathering is expected to assist collecting additional facts on breaking news, as well as facilitating discovery of potential information sources such as witnesses in the geographical locations of news.

TWITTER, NEWS, AND JOURNALISM

Twitter is a hodgepodge that, among many other kinds of contents, includes a bonanza of news [14]. It can be considered as an ambient media system where users get information from both established media and each other, but where not everything is an act of journalism [11]. It has shown the ability to quickly spread the stories of community's interest, which the site reflects as *trending topics*. These trending topics are often produced by breaking news [38], whereupon users can contribute, comment and spread. This often produces a great deal of citizen journalism contents that build on and enrich news. Popular examples of citizen journalism on Twitter include the Hudson River plane crash photo in 2009, or the witness photo in the 2012 Empire State shooting, among many others.

The emergence and success of the participation of users in news sharing through Twitter has strengthened citizen journalism. Journalism is evolving toward a participatory paradigm [35] as the participation of readers in the distribution of news and supply of information is becoming fundamental [27, 36]. News is becoming a participatory activity, as people contribute their own stories and experiences and post their reactions to events [31]. This quickly attracted journalists and news organizations to be part of the social media service, both for distributing breaking news quickly and concisely, and for soliciting story ideas, sources and facts to a community of users [12]. News organizations have stepped into social media to tell about breaking news and recent events, conceiving it as a new medium akin to traditional sources [29]. In fact, the recent trend of news organizations is to be anywhere, anytime, on any platform [30]. It enables to be closer to the community by engaging new readers, and to be on top of news and events as they occur.

Besides a powerful platform for the dissemination of breaking news, social media presents an unprecedented opportunity to catch the scoop from citizen's updates, to quickly learn more about recent news, and to find sources for further news research. In this work, we present our efforts toward developing a friendly interface for easier newsgathering from the social media jumble.

RELATED WORK

We discuss relevant research on the identification of news stories from social media, and visualizations that assist journalists with the optimal utilization of social media.

Sankaranarayanan et al. [32] presented one of the first approaches to identify whether or not a tweet is related to a news. They use a set of 2,000 handpicked Twitter users as a seed, and assume that they are always sharing news to identify tweets by other users. Unfortunately, their approach does not identify news stories initialized by unknown users, and do not consider that those users might be sharing tweets that are not related to news. Phelan et al. [28] focused on recommending news to Twitter users by assuming the news identification utilizing external sources such as RSS feeds from news media. Zubiaga et al. [38] presented a real-time approach to categorize emerging trending topics in a topology of four types of trend triggers: news, current events, memes, and commemoratives. They present a set of language-independent features that accurately identify the type of trigger each trending topic belongs to. In this work, we use the social features suggested by them as one of the inputs to our news ranking system. Similarly, Naaman et al. [25] introduced a taxonomy of trending topics, but they did not deal with its classification. Other studies have focused on analyzing the credibility of tweets [5], studying the evolution of trending topics [1, 6], performing behavioral studies of tweets [19], and studying the spread of news in social media [22, 26].

There have been some studies on the development of user interfaces to assist journalists with the use of social media. Marcus et al. [24] presented TwitInfo, a tool that identifies peaks in the tweeting activity as sub-events that occur in events, with the aim of assisting with the summarization of events. Diakopoulos and Shamma [9] developed a tool that visualizes temporal dynamics of sentiments in tweets during a political debate. More recently, Diakopoulos et al. [8] presented a tool to help journalists identify eyewitnesses in the context of an event. We believe that the present is the first research work on a user interface to assist journalists in curating and contextualizing social media stories for newsgathering.

There are online services that leave the description of a trending topic in hands of users. WhatTheTrend[1] stores Twitter's trending topics, and collects users' definitions. Being maintained by users, definitions often delay, and it does not provide an alternative to automatic identification of news. Alternatively, [34, 33] automate the summarization of topics in a single definition by looking at common phrases found in tweets, while [37] look at spikes in the tweeting activity to automatically create real-time summaries of events.

Despite the interest in mining conversations and trends from Twitter, and the increasing interest of journalists and news organizations in the power of social media as a news source, as far as we know no previous research dealt with the facilitation of an effective newsgathering from social media sources. This work attempts to fill this gap by studying the development of a social newsgathering tool.

SOCIAL MEDIA AS A SOURCE FOR NEWSGATHERING

On a recent study, Knight [17] analyzed the use of social media sources to research the news related to the Iran protests in 2009. He found that social media sources are sometimes hidden in news reporting, but social media, and especially Twitter, is often used and quoted. The meta-journalistic discussions about the use of Twitter imply that journalists are much more reliant on social media as a source than is apparent from an analysis of the articles. Social media is changing the way news are gathered and researched. Traditionally, the newsgathering has been known as a *gatekeeping* process [3], i.e., news organizations receive news stories while they choose which of them should be ultimately published. First with collaborative news websites like Digg, and now with other social media services like Twitter, it is becoming a *gatewatching* process [4], where news organizations have the chance to observe what the community is considering as newsworthy, and what they are contributing to the news. Twitter being a

[1] http://www.whatthetrend.com

rich source of breaking news, the need for *gatewatching* increases. However, social media poses new challenges, where a great many individuals post no end of updates, which aggregate to the mess. Successfully exploiting this information source provides an unprecedented way of covering news.

Figure 1. Interface of Twitter search.

Figure 1 shows the interface of Twitter's search. The interface is similar to a traditional web search engine, where a selected set of tweets are displayed, sorted by relevance. Although the sorting algorithm used by Twitter is not known, it appears to be limited to a combination of number of retweets and recency. Along with a set of tweets in the right column, the interface shows some media items on the left column: people, top videos, and top images. What Twitter labels as "people", for instance, is just a set of profile images of the top users for a story, that help neither find who these users are, nor what these users have posted about. To look for more details about any of these users, one has to click on them to open a new page, which leads to leaving the search page being browsed. In addition, the new page might not show the tweets in the conversation being analyzed, but the whole timeline of the user, which may contain irrelevant information.

Having analyzed Twitter's interface, and the needs to make it easier to understand trending stories, to grasp the story being discussed in a conversation, and to research it, we describe the two top shortcomings we detected: (i) the overwhelming amounts of content, and (ii) lack of context.

Shortcoming #1: Overwhelming Amounts of Content

On one hand, given the interest that a trending story arouses in the community of users, the number of tweets about the story increases, which in turn creates a big amount of tweets being shared about it. This produces overwhelming amounts of tweets about a story, often mixed with tweets that, instead of sharing or commenting on a news, are making fun of it or introducing spam. This makes it difficult to identify and understand the main information within the story, and to discover users who are involved as sources to be followed. Thus, we believe that curating these tweets would benefit the task of following the story and identifying the main contents.

Shortcoming #2: Lack of Context

On the other hand, a trending story presents several issues that are not easy to understand without further help. Breaking news being mentioned in a Twitter story may have occurred anywhere in the world, and have anyone involved in it. It is common to have news breaking in the country where it occurs, but later becoming international news as it spreads. Depending on the prior knowledge of the user analyzing the story, it becomes challenging to understand what is going on when the majority of the tweets are written in an unknown language, or the people and organizations involved are unknown. Geographical and cultural differences play an important role in understanding certain news. This suggests the necessity to translate tweets when needed, as well as to incorporate some context to help understand who or what are involved. Having tweets translated and contextualized would in turn make the user feel closer to the story and better understand it.

INTERFACE DESIGN

The user interface of TweetGathering aims to provide easy navigation through recent stories being discussed on Twitter. The tool is designed as a standalone web application that meets the standards to be rendered by all major browsers. It is also designed so that everything can be browsed within a single tab of the browser, so there is no need to open additional tabs or windows. Besides the contents collected from Twitter, and what the tool itself displays, it provides access to external URLs included in tweets. This is done by loading external URLs in a floating iframe on top of the tool, to avoid opening new windows or tabs. To facilitate access to and run-through of recent stories at all times, the prototype is composed of a navigational list of stories on the left, and a bigger panel on the right to explore the story of the user's choice.

Overall, the interface aims to be as easy to adapt as possible for a user who is familiar with Twitter. For this, tweets retain the original format, with the profile image on the left side, and the username, the text of the tweet, the timestamp, and the ability to perform a set of actions such as reply and retweet on the right. Figure 2 shows the interface of the TweetGathering prototype, with the main tab for a sample story loaded on the right panel.

The right panel includes all the information related to the selected story, with the main information on the initial tab, and having chance to access additional information and features from the other tabs. The initial tab is mainly composed of a box where tweets are loaded, and a set of features around to navigate through tweets. These features aim to help contextualize and characterize a story, which we describe with details in the next section. The tweet box is initially loaded with a set of representative tweets, with the aim of curating the contents and providing the most salient tweets. When clicking on the features surrounding the box, the tweets relevant to the selected feature will be visualized in the box.

TECHNICAL DEVELOPMENT

In this section, we describe the data gathering process we followed on Twitter to retrieve stories to conduct the user stud-

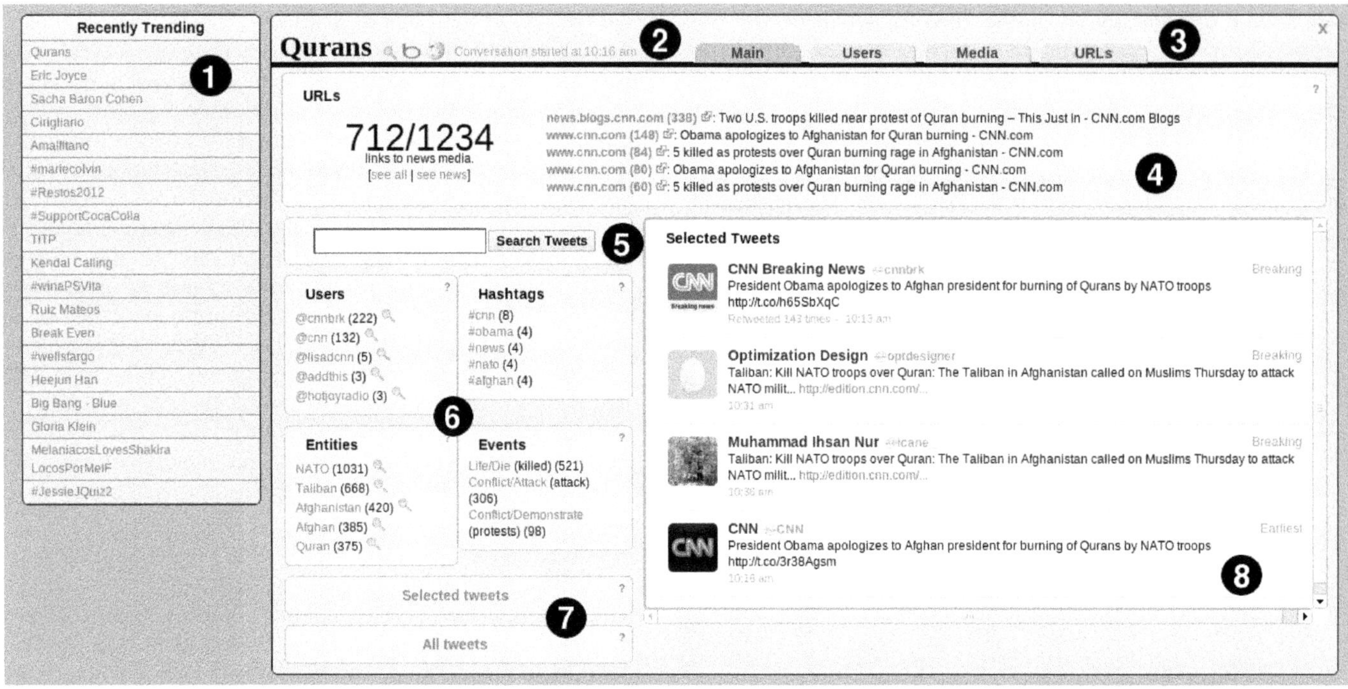

Figure 2. Interface of TweetGathering. 1) List of recently trending stories, sorted by newsworthiness, 2) Title, descriptions, and start time of the story being explored, 3) Tabs for additional navigation, 4) Summary of URLs, 5) Search engine, 6) Users, hashtags, named entities and events found in the story, 7) Access to selected tweets and all tweets, 8) Tweet box.

ies, and elaborate the processing we did on this data to provide the user with enhanced information on the user interface.

Dataset

In order to build and test the TweetGathering prototype, we relied on Twitter's worldwide trending topics as a source of potential breaking news. Twitter shows, at all times, a list of top 10 trending terms that are being mentioned outstandingly at the very moment. We tracked these trending topics from February 1 to 28, 2012, and randomly sampled a set of five topics per hour. For each of these trending topics that we collected, we also gathered up to 1,500 tweets[2] that contained the term, that is, the most recent tweets that gave rise to the trending topic. This gathering process resulted in a final set of 2,593 trending topics, and a total of 3,629,089 tweets associated with them. As we rely on worldwide trending topics, the stories are related to issues from several countries, which produces an ideal input for the purposes of this research of helping understand stories that not always are culturally or geographically close to the user. The collected data is also diverse in terms of languages used, where English amounts to a 57.8% of the tweets, but other languages contain large amounts of tweets: Spanish (14.9%), Portuguese (7.6%), Dutch (4.2%), Indonesian (3.1%), Italian (3.1%), etc.

For evaluation purposes, each of the trending topics was manually annotated as newsworthy or not by 3 annotators. Determining whether a story is newsworthy is not an easy task, since it can depend on many factors that are ultimately an editor's decision [10]. To make it easier to decide what is newsworthy, the annotators were instructed to annotate as newsworthy those trending topics whose underlying story was later covered by major news media. We asked the annotators to provide the URL of a news story, and the domain of the URL provided by them had to be listed on The Paper Boy[3], a comprehensive directory of online worldwide news media, to be considered as valid. A trending topic would not be deemed newsworthy if the URL provided as a proof did not match the requirements. The annotation resulted in a final set of 358 newsworthy trending topics, with a 92.3% inter-annotator agreement. We split the dataset into a development set, composed of the first three weeks –i.e., February 1 to 21–, and a test set with the last week –from February 22 to 28.

Since we collected tweets for stories that recently trended on Twitter, it is not always likely that newsworthy stories will contain links pointing to news media. By labeling as news media all the links with a domain listed on The Paper Boy, and otherwise not, we analyzed the characteristics of newsworthy and unnewsworthy stories. Figure 3 shows the ratio of links pointing to news media from tweets in newsworthy and unnewsworthy stories. In both cases, the number of links pointing to news media is usually low. Although the number of links to news media is more likely to be smaller for unnewsworthy stories, there is no clear difference. Note that for half of the newsworthy stories, less than 0.05 of the links point to news media. This reveals that the early discovery of news from Twitter is not as easy as following or tracking links

[2]Due to the limitation of Twitter's search API to the last 1,500 tweets for a given query.

[3]http://www.paperboy.com/

to news media, but also requires more complex searching and processing.

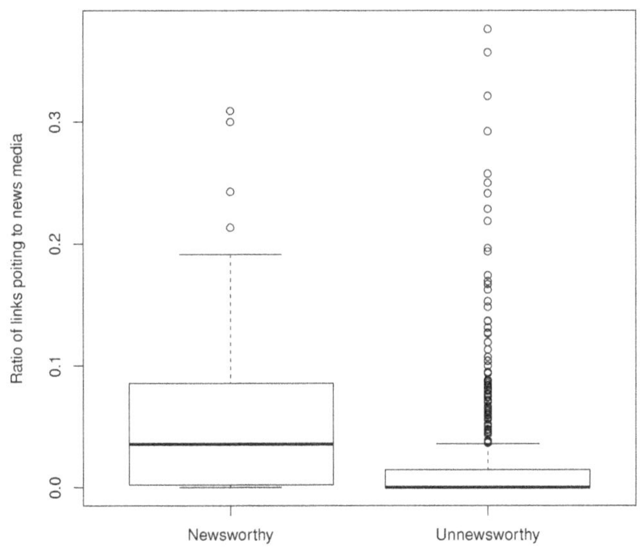

Figure 3. Ratio of links pointing to news media.

Feature Extraction

The newsgathering prototype includes a number of additional features to help with curation and contextualization of trending topics. Next, we enumerate and describe the technical details of these features:

Machine translation of tweets. We used automatic translation software to translate non-English tweets into English. After we translate these tweets, we can extract English-based features from them, and users can read them. Automatic translations were provided by SDL plc[4], whose statistical translation engines processed 98.1% of the non-English tweets in our collection. Of the top 20 non-English languages, SDL's engines covered 19 (the exception being Icelandic), while overall, tweets in 27 of the 46 represented languages were translated.

Ranking trending topics by newsworthiness. Having a large number of stories trending every day on Twitter, it is convenient to provide the chance to more easily identify top stories. With this purpose, we rank the trending stories as they come out, so that we can include a new story at its corresponding position in the ranking. We use Support Vector Machines (SVM [7]) to create the rankings, specifically *SVM-light* [16]. Although SVM is originally designed for text classification, the output provided in the form of margins that refer to confidence can be used as values to rank. We split the development set into groups of two weeks for training, and the remaining week for testing. We evaluate with three-fold cross-validation.

[4]http://www.sdl.com/

We use two different kinds of features for the ranking: (i) vectors of term frequencies (TF) from tweets translated into English, and (ii) social features, as suggested by Zubiaga et al. [38], including 15 features concerning diversity and sharing characteristics, which were demonstrated to accurately classify trending topics in a typology that includes news as one of the categories. Besides the comparison of these two kinds of features separately, we also combine them by using classifier committees [21]. Classifier committees add up the outputs of both classifiers, getting the most of them, and often improving the results of each of them.

Figure 4 shows the averaged results for top positions of ranking trending stories by newsworthiness. We use the Normalized Discounted Cumulative Gain (nDCG [13]) as a measure, which evaluates the effectiveness of a ranking considering that higher positions will have a higher influence on the measure. The results show that the TF approach on translated tweets does better than the social features for the top positions, but the social features improve in positions after 10. However, combining them solves this issue, outperforming both of the independent approaches, and high level performance is achieved, especially for the top positions. Thus, we rely on the combined approach, as inferred from the development set, when ranking new stories from the test set.

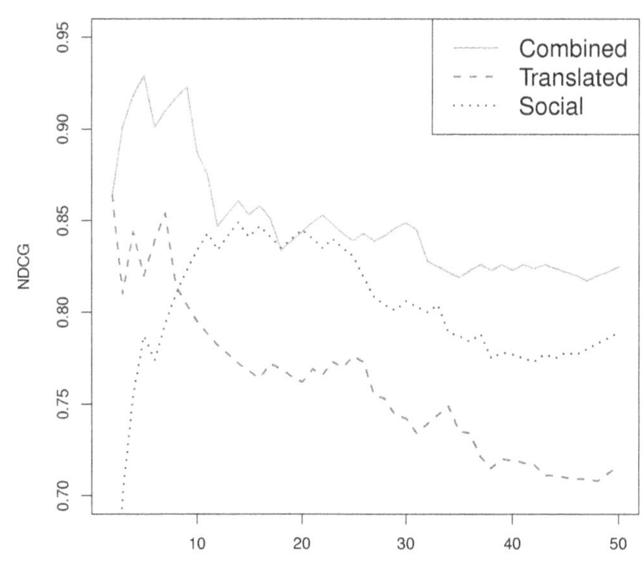

Figure 4. nDCG values for top 50 stories ranked by newsworthiness.

URL lengthening and statistics. When tweets contain links, they tend to be shortened to save characters. The short URLs hide the actual URL to the users, and so they need to click on it to check where it actually points to. Moreover, different short URLs often redirect to the same URL, so it is necessary to resolve the final URLs to get actual statistics of the use of URLs, and to find out the most popular URLs. Therefore, we resolved all the short URLs to their final URLs. With those, we can create a ranking of the most popular URLs, the top of which is shown on the interface. On the other hand, we categorize the final URLs as news or not. A URL was considered as news when its domain belongs to news media, i.e., when its domain is listed as a news media on The Paper Boy. The tool visualizes the number of URLs contained in the story as well as the fraction that belongs to news media, and the top five URLs categorized as news are shown. These top five URLs are accompanied by the title of the page as gathered from the HTML tag `<title>`, so it is easy to know what it is about without clicking on it. The user can click on any of the URLs to preview its contents, and can also switch to the "URLs" tab for the full list of URLs in the story. The number of news URLs does not mean to refer to the newsworthiness of the story, since newsworthy stories frequently lack news URLs early on when they break. Instead, it aims to estimate the extent to which the news has already been covered by news media, or it recently broke on Twitter with no media coverage yet.

Selection of Representative Tweets. We aim to provide the user with a set of representative tweets that outline the main contents of the story being analyzed. We extract the following four types of tweets as the most representative:

- *Most retweeted:* the most retweeted tweet is straightforward to get, as the one that has been re-shared most.
- *Most frequent:* we select the most frequent tweet as the one that best matches with the vocabulary used in the whole conversation. To find this tweet, we weigh each tweet in the story by adding up the frequency of each term in the whole story. The tweet with most common terms is assigned the highest weight.
- *Trendiest:* we call the trendiest tweet that making the biggest difference from the tweets seen on previous days. The idea of selecting this tweet is to get rid of those tweets that are frequent in many trending stories on Twitter, e.g., *Hey, let's make this trend, please RT!*. To do this, we rely on a language modeling approach using the Kullback-Leibler Divergence (KLD [18]). By computing the divergence of terms in the story being analyzed to the terms seen in previous stories (i.e., those in the development set), we can extract the tweet that is more diverse from usual tweets. This tweet will be the one that maximizes the sum of its terms' diversity values.
- *Earliest:* It is not easy to determine which is the earliest tweet that starts a story. In some cases, there might be mentions before the story broke, which are not actually related to the story. After performing a set of empirical experiments on the development set, we found that finding the earliest tweet with common vocabulary compared to later tweets does well. Thus, we select the tweet containing one of the top 3 terms in the story as the earliest tweet. Besides showing the earliest tweet as one of the selected representative tweets, this also allows us to show the start time of the story on Twitter, which is shown on the header, next to the title of the story.

On the interface, we group them into two types of tweets: (i) *breaking tweets*, which include the most retweeted, the most frequent, and the trendiest, and (ii) the *earliest tweet*. We group the first three tweets since the differences are mainly technical, but they have similar meanings in practice for the user.

Twitter features. There are a number of features that are inherent to Twitter, which we preprocess to facilitate navigation through the tool. We show lists that contain the top of these features, accompanied by the number of appearances in the story, while clicking on them shows the tweets that contain the selected feature:

- *Users.* We extract the top users who tweeted or are mentioned by others in a conversation. This enables us to generate the list of top users that are relevant in the story. The user information not only includes the username, but also additional information including the description and location of the user, when available.
- *Hashtags.* Hashtags are terms preceded by #, referring to an important concept within a tweet, usually meant to categorize the tweet in a conversation. We extract the top hashtags within a story, as a summary of representative concepts or categories that users chose for the story. Hashtags are often a combination of several words into a single string. For instance, users can utilize the hashtag `#unitedstates` to refer to the *United States* without explicit tokenization. Without prior normalization of these hashtags, it might be difficult to read, and especially to process and contextualize since it is unlikely that Wikipedia will have an entry with that name when looking up its meaning. To alleviate this, we analyze all the occurrences of the hashtag in the story. When the hashtag has been capitalized in some cases, we rely on the most frequent capitalization as the tokenization of the hashtag. Thus, if the most frequent capitalization is `#UnitedStates`, we tokenize it by starting a new word on each capital letter, for easier understanding.
- *Images and videos (Media).* On a separate tab, we show the thumbnails for top images and videos that appear in the conversation, sorted by the number of occurrences. Each media is accompanied by the tweet(s) that include it, as well as the top users associated with it. Different from Twitter's original interface, which is limited to thumbnails, the added context aims to describe the media, as well as to identify the top sources.

Named entities. Using information extraction techniques, we identify the named entities that are mentioned in the story. Types of named entities we identify include person, location, and organization names. We apply a high-performing name tagger [23] to extract these names. The tagger adopts the linear-chain CRFs [20] as the learning method, and incorporates multi-layer local features based on ngrams, case and shape, Part-of-Speech, chunking, gazetteers, Brown Cluster [2], as well as sentence-level and document-level features such as the position and the frequency of the name candidates. The interface shows a ranked list of top names mentioned in a story, as well as their number of occurrences, while clicking on them loads associated tweets in the tweet box.

Descriptions of names. In some cases, the user of the tool might be unfamiliar with the names, locations, or organizations involved in the story, especially when the story originates from a different country, language or culture. To provide background on the names extracted in the story, we gather their descriptions from the structural knowledge base DBpedia[5]. As a description, DBpedia provides the initial sentences of the corresponding article on Wikipedia. In case this information is not enough, additional alternatives are given to preview the whole Wikipedia article, as well as to look for the term on the Bing[6] search engine.

Events. Events play an important role in the context of news. With events, we aim to provide the user with the key happenings that are mentioned in a story, e.g., death, resignation, or attack. We apply a state-of-the-art English event extraction system [15] to extract events from tweets. The system combines pattern matching with a set of Maximum Entropy classifiers incorporating diverse lexical, syntactic, semantic and ontological knowledge. It takes raw documents as input and conducts some pre-processing steps. The texts are automatically annotated with part-of-speech tags, parsing structures, entities, time expressions, and relations. The annotated documents are then sent to the following classifiers: to distinguish events from non-events; to classify events by type and subtype; to distinguish arguments from non-arguments; to classify arguments by argument role; and given a trigger, an event type, and a set of arguments, to determine whether there is a reportable event mention. Each component can produce reliable confidence values. As for named entities, the top events are shown with their number of occurrences, and clicking on each of them loads associated tweets.

Locations of users. It is often difficult to identify the location of users, since many of them do not provide any details. In this work, we rely on the location of users as specified in their settings. However, the location field in the settings is a string that can be set to anything like "somewhere in the world" or "at home" instead of a location that can be mapped. 20.2% of users in the development set have this field empty, so we cannot easily guess where they are. Also, users specify locations with different levels of granularity, e.g., a few users give the specific coordinates, while some users say they are in *New York City*, and others only say they are in the *USA*.

Search engine. The interface incorporates a query-based search engine that allows the user to look for the terms of their interest, especially to explore subtopics in tweets. The search enables manually curate the contents by filtering with the term(s) of their choice. The search engine will return the tweets matching the input query as an AND search of the query terms, so that more restrictive searches can be done by using more terms. The match between query terms and tweets is not limited to full tokens, so that searching for a term also retrieves usernames and hashtags with that name.

[5]http://dbpedia.org/
[6]http://www.bing.com/

Access to all tweets. The interface also provides access to all the tweets in the story, so the user can explore the whole conversation when needed.

Some of the features described above rely on methods that might be inaccurate in some cases, such as NLP techniques. Tweets being short and often with an incomplete grammar present an extra difficulty to get accurate results when using NLP techniques. However, relying on stories of tweets rather than single tweets considerably alleviates this issue by putting together the outputs and relying on the top items of combined results. A quantitative evaluation of NLP outputs would be needed to precisily measure the accuracy of such techniques, which in this case has been qualitatively evaluated through journalists' undertanding during user studies.

EVALUATION

In this section, we describe the user studies we conducted to assess the TweetGathering prototype, and present comments and findings collected from these studies.

User Study

The evaluation of TweetGathering was carried out with five journalism professionals who fit the characteristics of actual users of a social newsgathering tool. All of them are native English speakers, have a Twitter account and are familiar with social media, and have long been following the microblogging system to catch the scoop and research news in numerous situations. The studies were conducted in a newsroom, one by one, where they had the chance to play around with the tool while they were thinking aloud about anything they did or found. The prototype was fed by the trending topics in the test set, and each of the interviewees used a specific snapshot of the prototype in different dates and times within the week of the test set. Therefore, each of them used the tool in a real scenario with the stories that trended recently in that specific moment, so they could analyze the utility of the tool to discover news, as well as the utility of curation and contextualization provided for a newsgathering process. We interviewed them about their prior experiences before they used the tool, and also afterward to learn about their feelings while using the tool. The stories shown to them in the user study were previously known to us, but not necessarily to journalists –they did remember a few of the news shown, but they were unaware of most of the news. While journalists were thinking aloud while using the tool and commenting on their findings, we verified that their understanding of the story was the correct one.

Even though two of the interviewees admitted that they never or rarely tweet, all of them follow a number of Twitter accounts on a near-daily basis. They do believe that Twitter opens up a tremendous oportunity to access information shared by users as well as to identify potential sources and witnesses to follow. However, they find that the number of tweets sent during breaking news is overwhelming, and it is difficult to identify the useful information and relevant users. Actually, one of them pointed out that *"I know journalists who are not willing to use Twitter, because they feel overwhelmed by all the information, and that requires a big effort to follow"* (P2). At this point, they feel the need of a curation tool to make easier the task of researching breaking news.

News Discovery
Given a real scenario of recently trending stories, the participants could explore them in search of breaking news that they would be interested in learning more. They followed different strategies to navigate through the trending stories provided in the left menu. While two of them looked at the top ranked stories, and clicked on the one of their top interest, the other three read through all the list of stories before clicking on one. One of them noted that *"the ranking is very helpful, since the stories in the bottom of the list are mostly memes and pointless conversations, so I can easily get rid of them"* (P1).

After clicking on and exploring some stories, we asked each of them about the main features they were relying on to check whether a story is likely to be about a newsworthy event. They were quite unanimous on this, commenting that they were mostly relying on the selected subset of tweets, as a good summary of the story. Three of them, however, added that they rather looked at the summary of URLs first. When the URLs point to news, only the titles of the URLs are self-explanatory but, otherwise, they looked at the selected tweets. One of them added that *"the navigation through the tool is really easy, as it conveniently enables you to catch the scoop as you click on a news story and find out whether the story is worth exploring in more detail for later news reporting"* (P5).

Curation of Stories
One of the main characteristics introduced in the prototype is the curation of contents, due to the overwhelming amounts of tweets shared in a story. The participants made exhaustive use of the selected tweets that appear initially in the tweet box, which is the main feature of the tool in terms of curation. *"I usually find that Twitter conversations are full of spam and people making fun instead of talking about the actual news, and I need to skip many of the tweets since they are off-topic to me. Having a few tweets selected really helps me discover salient tweets instead of doing it manually"* (P3). Overall, they did not find a great difference among the three tweets labeled as "breaking", but they believe they are similarly helpful and complementary in some cases. However, the "earliest tweet" arouses much more interest in them, since they believe that it might be the source, the tweet that broke the news, so it can be worth following what that user says next, or even contact the user to ask for additional information or an interview.

The search engine is another feature that enables curation, although this requires prior selection of the terms. They did not use the search engine very frequently, but they did find some possible utility in it: *"I would use it to look for users that are in a specific location, for instance. This is something that I miss on Twitter when exploring a story"* (P2).

Finally, the machine translation of tweets also contributes to curation of contents. One of them did not realize that the tweets were originally written in another language for a specific story, but she noticed it having seen the location of the story; *"it is very helpful to have the tweets translated into English, so I don't have to wait to later tweets written in English. This is certainly a story that will soon become internationally popular, and it is important to quickly catch the scoop"* (P4).

Contextualization of Stories
The other main characteristic introduced in the prototype is the contextualization of the story, which we accomplish by extracting a set of features from tweets, and describing some of them. The participants did not doubt that having context besides tweets is of utmost help.

The feature they liked most for contextualization is the summary of URLs in the story. Besides helping to consider the story as newsworthy or not, they also agree that it is helpful to find context. They find it really helpful to see the final URLs instead of the shortened ones, and to have the chance to open them in the tool without switching tabs. *"It all depends on whether the story contains links to news media. When it does, I can research the news written by others, while in the event that there are no links to news media, I can explore the links to check where they are pointing to and what they are about"* (P2).

The next features they used most are the lists of users, named entities, hashtags, and events. *"Those really help place the story into context and see who is involved. It's not easy to get all that information at first glance from tweets. And they have counts associated, which somewhat reflects the importance of each item. I was looking for the highest numbers, and found interesting things that you don't realize from reading through tweets."* (P2). They also found interesting utilities of these four features:

- Users: *"I'd say that the list of users is the most interesting of these four features. We often look into the contributing users to find sources, or even witnesses that might be reporting on the news. We rely on those as information sources, and sometimes contact them to learn more"* (P5).
- Named entities: *"The list of names reveals, in some cases, where is the story possibly happening, and so makes it easier to locate it. Likewise, being able to easily identify involved people and organizations, with the additional feature of describing them, rapidly places the news into context, especially when it is culturally new to me"* (P1).
- Hashtags: *"Although hashtags don't seem to be as useful as other features, it is sometimes worth exploring the ones that are co-occurring with the story. I was really wondering why #ows appears so frequently in a story about #wellsfargo, that's something I needed to look into more detail"* (P3).
- Events: *"Events can be good in some cases, to see what people are commenting on the story. It's not only about the story itself. I found in a story about a political announcement that a popular event being mentioned in the tweets was resignation, this must be a strong community that wants this politician to step down"* (P4).

Among the stories they had to analyze, there were stories from other countries. Besides being written in foreign language, some of the people and organizations involved were unknown to them. They had to use the external sources provided to describe them. *"I really had no idea who this guy was, so I was unable to say how newsworthy this story could become. Then I saw that he is a participant from reality show. I'm no longer interested in the story, that's not of interest to me"* (P5).

None of them really needed to go to the "all tweets" section, because they could find the essential information from the rest of the features. Two of them tried it out to see how it would look like without having all the enhanced information, and one of them said: *"this is what I usually see, and it is really overwhelming. It takes much longer to grasp the story and find the people, organizations, and locations involved in the story. I'd say it's fine to have it somewhere in the tool, as an alternative if it ever is needed, but it's secondary. I would rarely use it"* (P1).

Finally, the start time of the story helped find how old a story is. *"It's hard to know when a story started, that's not available anywhere. I'd rely on that time to have an idea"* (P3).

Overall Utility and Final Remarks

Overall, the participants liked the features provided to curate and contextualize the tweets of a story. *"I find it very easy to use. Everything is well organized on a single page, and I can explore all the features from here, without leaving the tool"* (P1). They would appreciate having the chance to customize the stories listed, for instance, by including the topics of their interest, the trending topics of specific areas, or stories from the users they follow, which altogether becomes overwhelming to follow on a daily basis. *"I need something like this for my work. With a few customizations to follow the information of my interest, and having it running in real-time, I would switch to this tool"* (P4).

The participants also mentioned some features that they would like to see on the tool:

- Two of them commented that they would like to know what is the location of a story. Currently, the name of the location might appear among the named entities listed by the tool. However, the use of more sophisticated techniques could help determine the location, mapping the stories for easier browsing.
- One of them suggested that, besides having a ranking of tweets, a categorization of the stories by topic would be interesting to follow specific topics.
- Other suggestions were related to customization and having an account to log in on the tool. These suggestions include being able to ban certain topics/users as spam they no longer want to hear from, or being able to bookmark a story to check it again later.

DISCUSSION

This paper explores the identification of news from stories that appear in Twitter's lists of trending topics. Trending topics are a convenient way of identifying recently emerging conversations on Twitter's stream. However, the exploration of stories does not need to be limited to trending topics as presented by Twitter. Alternatively, the identification of emerging conversations from Twitter streams would allow to customize desired stories to be presented, which is not within the scope of this work. Additionally, the system can straightforwardly be applied to specific events, so that it makes easier to find breaking news associated with those specific situations. For instance, the presented prototype could also be suitable for emergency journalism, curating and contextualizing events such as protests, hurricanes or quakes, where the user could input a query, getting the information for the associated story. Also, we believe that the ability to have an account and to log in on the tool would benefit the user experience, having access to stories of the user's interest in a customized way.

CONCLUSION

In this paper, we have introduced TweetGathering, a prototype tool that facilitates social newsgathering from Twitter for journalists. The presented tool aims to make it easier for journalists to find out and research breaking news, by curating and adding context to stories made up by short and often contextless tweets. We have conducted user studies with five journalism professionals to evaluate and get feedback on the prototype tool. These studies brought to light numerous features of the tool that may assist journalists with gathering additional facts on breaking news, alleviating the difficulty of understanding stories from other countries, cultures, and languages, and facilitating discovery of potential information sources.

The feedback received from journalists has also brought to light some future challenges for further improvements on the tool. First, it would benefit from incorporating customized contents, so that it provides personalized lists of stories to each user. Second, the limited features of Twitter in terms of geographical locations of users requires the analysis of sophisticated techniques to determine the locations of both stories and users. And third, we aim to roll out an updated version of the tool to journalists for its use in newsrooms in real-time. This will enable us to quantify the gains provided by the newsgathering tool as compared to using Twitter's original interface.

Acknowledgments

Thanks to Daniel Marcu of SDL for assistance with translations, and to Nicholas Diakopoulos for discussion and comments on an early version of the prototype. This work was supported by the U.S. Army Research Laboratory under Cooperative Agreement No. W911NF- 09-2-0053 (NS-CTA), the U.S. NSF CAREER Award under Grant IIS-0953149, the U.S. NSF EAGER Award under Grant No. IIS-1144111, the U.S. DARPA Deep Exploration and Filtering of Text program and CUNY Junior Faculty Award. The views and conclusions contained in this document are those of the authors and should not be interpreted as representing the official policies, either expressed or implied, of the U.S. Government. The U.S. Government is authorized to reproduce and distribute reprints for Government purposes notwithstanding any copyright notation here on.

REFERENCES

1. Asur, S., Huberman, B., Szabo, G., and Wang, C. Trends in social media: Persistence and decay. In *5th International AAAI Conference on Weblogs and Social Media* (2011).
2. Brown, P., Desouza, P., Mercer, R., Pietra, V., and Lai, J. Class-based n-gram models of natural language. *Computational linguistics 18*, 4 (1992), 467–479.
3. Bruns, A. Gatewatching, not gatekeeping: Collaborative online news. *Media International Australia Incorporating Culture and Policy: quarterly journal of media research and resources 107* (2003), 31–44.
4. Bruns, A. Gatekeeping, gatewatching, real-time feedback: new challenges for journalism. *Brazilian Journalism Research 7*, 2 (2011), 117–136.
5. Castillo, C., Mendoza, M., and Poblete, B. Information credibility on twitter. In *Proceedings of the 20th international conference on World wide web*, WWW '11, ACM (New York, NY, USA, 2011), 675–684.
6. Cheong, M., and Lee, V. Integrating web-based intelligence retrieval and decision-making from the twitter trends knowledge base. In *Proceedings of the 2nd ACM workshop on Social Web Search and Mining* (2009), 1–8.
7. Cortes, C., and Vapnik, V. Support-vector networks. *Machine learning 20*, 3 (1995), 273–297.
8. Diakopoulos, N., De Choudhury, M., and Naaman, M. Finding and assessing social media information sources in the context of journalism. In *Proceedings of the 2012 ACM annual conference on Human Factors in Computing Systems*, CHI '12, ACM (New York, NY, USA, 2012), 2451–2460.
9. Diakopoulos, N., and Shamma, D. Characterizing debate performance via aggregated twitter sentiment. In *Proceedings of the 28th international conference on Human factors in computing systems*, ACM (2010), 1195–1198.
10. Harcup, T., and O'neill, D. What is news? galtung and ruge revisited. *Journalism studies 2*, 2 (2001), 261–280.
11. Hermida, A. From tv to twitter: How ambient news became ambient journalism. *M/C Journal 13*, 2 (2010).
12. Hermida, A. Twittering the news. *Journalism Practice 4*, 3 (2010), 297–308.
13. Järvelin, K., and Kekäläinen, J. Cumulated gain-based evaluation of ir techniques. *ACM Transactions on Information Systems (TOIS) 20*, 4 (2002), 422–446.
14. Java, A., Song, X., Finin, T., and Tseng, B. Why we twitter: understanding microblogging usage and communities. In *Proceedings of the 9th WebKDD and 1st SNA-KDD 2007 workshop on Web mining and social network analysis*, ACM (2007), 56–65.
15. Ji, H., and Grishman, R. Refining event extraction through unsupervised cross-document inference. In *Proc. of ACL, the Annual Meeting of the Association of Computational Linguistics* (2012).
16. Joachims, T. Text categorization with support vector machines: Learning with many relevant features. *Machine learning: ECML-98* (1998), 137–142.
17. Knight, M. Journalism as usual: The use of social media as a newsgathering tool in the coverage of the iranian elections in 2009. *Journal of Media Practice 13*, 1 (2012), 61–74.
18. Kullback, S., and Leibler, R. On information and sufficiency. *The Annals of Mathematical Statistics 22*, 1 (1951), 79–86.
19. Kwak, H., Lee, C., Park, H., and Moon, S. What is twitter, a social network or a news media? In *Proceedings of the 19th international conference on World wide web*, WWW '10, ACM (New York, NY, USA, 2010), 591–600.
20. Lafferty, J. D., McCallum, A., and Pereira, F. C. N. Conditional random fields: Probabilistic models for segmenting and labeling sequence data. In *ICML* (2001), 282–289.
21. Larkey, L., and Croft, W. Combining classifiers in text categorization. In *SIGIR*, ACM (1996), 289–297.
22. Lerman, K., and Ghosh, R. Information contagion: An empirical study of the spread of news on digg and twitter social networks. In *ICWSM* (2010).
23. Li, Q., Li, H., Ji, H., Wang, W., Zheng, J., and Huang, F. Joint bilingual name tagging for parallel corpora. In *Proc. The 21st ACM International Conference on Information and Knowledge Management (CIKM 2012)* (2012).
24. Marcus, A., Bernstein, M., Badar, O., Karger, D., Madden, S., and Miller, R. Twitinfo: aggregating and visualizing microblogs for event exploration. In *Proceedings of the 2011 annual conference on Human factors in computing systems*, ACM (2011), 227–236.
25. Naaman, M., Becker, H., and Gravano, L. Hip and trendy: Characterizing emerging trends on twitter. *Journal of the American Society for Information Science and Technology 62*, 5 (2011), 902–918.
26. Naveed, N., Gottron, T., Kunegis, J., and Alhadi, A. C. Bad news travel fast: A content-based analysis of interestingness on twitter. In *WebSci '11: Proceedings of the 3rd International Conference on Web Science* (2011).
27. Paulussen, S., Heinonen, A., Domingo, D., and Quandt, T. Doing it together: Citizen participation in the professional news making process. *Observatorio (OBS*) 1*, 3 (2007).
28. Phelan, O., McCarthy, K., and Smyth, B. Using twitter to recommend real-time topical news. In *Proceedings of the third ACM conference on Recommender systems*,

RecSys '09, ACM (New York, NY, USA, 2009), 385–388.

29. Phillips, A., et al. Old sources: New bottles. *New media, old news: Journalism and democracy in the digital age* (2010), 87–101.

30. Picard, R. Blogs, tweets, social media, and the news business. *Nieman Reports 63*, 3 (2009), 10.

31. Purcell, K., Rainie, L., Mitchell, A., Rosenstiel, T., and Olmstead, K. Understanding the participatory news consumer. *Pew Internet and American Life Project 1* (2010).

32. Sankaranarayanan, J., Samet, H., Teitler, B., Lieberman, M., and Sperling, J. Twitterstand: news in tweets. In *Proceedings of the 17th ACM SIGSPATIAL International Conference on Advances in Geographic Information Systems*, ACM (2009), 42–51.

33. Sharifi, B., Hutton, M., and Kalita, J. Experiments in microblog summarization. In *Proc. of IEEE Second International Conference on Social Computing* (2010).

34. Sharifi, B., Hutton, M., and Kalita, J. Summarizing microblogs automatically. In *Proc. of NAACL* (2010).

35. Singer, J., Domingo, D., Heinonen, A., Hermida, A., Paulussen, S., Quandt, T., Reich, Z., and Vujnovic, M. *Participatory Journalism: Guarding Open Gates at Online Newspapers*. Wiley, 2011.

36. Stassen, W. Your news in 140 characters: exploring the role of social media in journalism. *Global Media Journal African Edition 4*, 1 (2011).

37. Zubiaga, A., Spina, D., Amigó, E., and Gonzalo, J. Towards real-time summarization of scheduled events from twitter streams. In *Proceedings of the 23rd ACM conference on Hypertext and social media*, ACM (2012), 319–320.

38. Zubiaga, A., Spina, D., Fresno, V., and Martínez, R. Classifying trending topics: a typology of conversation triggers on twitter. In *Proceedings of the 20th ACM international conference on Information and knowledge management*, CIKM '11, ACM (New York, NY, USA, 2011), 2461–2464.

Detecting Boredom and Engagement During Writing with Keystroke Analysis, Task Appraisals, and Stable Traits

Robert Bixler
University of Notre Dame
384 Fitzpatrick Hall
Notre Dame, IN 46556
rbixler@nd.edu

Sidney D'Mello
University of Notre Dame
384 Fitzpatrick Hall
Notre Dame, IN 46556
sdmello@nd.edu

ABSTRACT
It is hypothesized that the ability for a system to automatically detect and respond to users' affective states can greatly enhance the human-computer interaction experience. Although there are currently many options for affect detection, keystroke analysis offers several attractive advantages to traditional methods. In this paper, we consider the possibility of automatically discriminating between natural occurrences of boredom, engagement, and neutral by analyzing keystrokes, task appraisals, and stable traits of 44 individuals engaged in a writing task. The analyses explored several different arrangements of the data: using downsampled and/or standardized data; distinguishing between three different affect states or groups of two; and using keystroke/timing features in isolation or coupled with stable traits and/or task appraisals. The results indicated that the use of raw data and the feature set that combined keystroke/timing features with task appraisals and stable traits, yielded accuracies that were 11% to 38% above random guessing and generalized to new individuals. Applications of our affect detector for intelligent interfaces that provide engagement support during writing are discussed.

Author Keywords
Affect detection; keystroke dynamics; boredom; engagement; free text.

ACM Classification Keywords
Categories and subject descriptors: H.5.m [Information Interfaces and Presentation]: Miscellaneous

INTRODUCTION
One of the primary goals of the field of Affective Computing is to develop intelligent systems that can detect and respond to users' affective states [28, 29]. In general, affective systems can be subdivided into three categories: systems that detect affect, systems that express affect, and systems that experience affect (i.e., artificial emotions). Although each type of system has far-reaching applications in a myriad of research domains, detecting affect is an integral component in designing applications that intelligently communicate with users and assist them in performing their tasks.

The Affective Computing community has recognized the importance of detecting affect and a wide array of methods have been developed [see 3, 27, and 35 for reviews]. The preeminent modality associated with affect is that of the face, presumably due to the well-known links between affect and facial expressions [13, 26, 31]. A second modality that has received considerable attention is speech and it has been shown that paralinguistic features of speech can serve as an important index into affect [18, 21]. Text analysis is a third type of modality that has been heavily researched as evidenced by the nascent field of sentiment analysis [25]. The fourth modality includes physiological signals, such as the electrical conductivity of the skin, electrical activity of the heart, and activation of muscles in the face. These measures of peripheral physiology can be complemented by measures of central physiology such as fMRI and EEG [24]. Other measures that have received somewhat less attention include eye gaze, postures, and gestures [3].

There are some important factors that must be considered when evaluating the usefulness of any particular modality for affect detection. These are: 1) validity of the signal as being diagnostic of affect, 2) reliability of the signal in a real-world environment, 3) time resolution of the signal, and 4) cost of implementation and intrusiveness of the sensors. Although significant advances in the development of functional affect detection systems have been made over the last decade, most of the current systems fail to achieve one or more of these desirable features.

Taking a somewhat different approach from the common modalities discussed above, the present paper focuses on the use of *keystroke analysis* to develop fully automated affect detectors while individuals perform a writing task with a computer interface. The working hypothesis is that an analysis of users' keystrokes can yield information that signals their affective states. The focus is not on *what* specific content is generated, but on *how* the content is generated.

There are many attractive aspects of keystroke analysis for affect detection. Keystroke analysis requires no extra hardware beyond the already present computer and keyboard. All that is required is software to record and analyze the keystrokes, so the method is unobtrusive, cost effective, and scalable. Keystrokes are transferred directly from the keyboard to the data collection software, resulting in a reliable signal with negligible interference. Because each keystroke event occurs within a short time frame of the previous keystroke, enough data can be gathered to detect and respond to affect in a timely manner. The only unknown factor is how accurately keystroke analysis predicts affect, which is the focus of the present work. We begin by briefly reviewing some of the research on keystroke analysis as an affect detection channel followed by an overview of the present study.

Previous Work on Keystroke Analysis and Affect

Although not directly relevant to affect detection, the largest body on keystroke analysis is in research on authentication systems. These systems aim to identify individuals based on their unique typing patterns. The most distinctive variation of keystroke-based authentication systems is fixed text versus free text. Most attempts at keystroke authentication involve developing a profile while users type a pre-determined text [2, 17]. This profile is then compared to any subsequent attempts to log in as that user. Free text analysis consists of logging the keystrokes during the user's session without any constraints on what the user can type, and comparing similarities between the authentication profile and patterns observed during typing [16]. Considerably less research has been done in this area as fixed text analysis has a much lower error rate – a measurement that is paramount in authentication systems [5].

There have been a few studies that have used keystroke analysis for affect detection. Vizer et al. [32] explored the possibility of detecting users' stress by continuously monitoring keyboard interactions. Their features consisted of timing, keystroke, and linguistic information. They tested their models with both raw and standardized data in order to minimize subject variability. They reported that their classification rates using standardized data were consistent with those achieved by other researchers using different methods such as facial recognition, speech analysis, and a pressure-sensing mouse.

Khanna and Sasikumar used a suite of classifiers in WEKA to distinguish between positive, negative, and neutral affect based on fixed text [19]. Their data was collected while users re-typed text from chosen paragraphs. After copying the paragraphs, users were instructed to indicate their affective state during the typing task. The classifiers that performed best were BF Trees and J48, with correct classification rates of 89.0% and 84.1% for detecting negative affect from neutral affect and correct classification rates of 86.4% and 88.9% for detecting positive affect from neutral affect.

A most recent study by Epp et al. [14] collected both fixed and free text and analyzed models for six different affective states. During their experiment they collected 10 minutes of free text prior to a questionnaire that asked users which affect they were experiencing. Following the questionnaire was a passage from Alice in Wonderland which the user was instructed to type as a sample of fixed text. They then created models based on either the fixed or free text samples.. Their best performing models all used fixed text and achieved accuracies of 77.4%-87.8% with kappas ranging between .55 and .75.

Overview of Current Study

Keystrokes are never generated in a vacuum, but are always coupled to an underlying activity. The target activity in the present study was a writing activity that involved the composition of essays on a variety of different topics. Writing is an activity that lends itself to keystroke analysis, because the purpose of writing is to generate content, which involves keystrokes in most cases. There is also evidence which suggests that affective states might be tied to both the topics and processes of writing, so it is important to understand the affective states that arise during writing and how they influence writing outcomes [12, 22]. In line with this, the purpose of this paper is to develop automated methods to monitor the moment-to-moment affective states that individuals experience while writing about topics that vary in emotional intensity. The hope is that the automated methods can be integrated into intelligent interfaces that can help students develop writing proficiency by detecting and responding to their affective states (this is discussed in more detail in the General Discussion section).

Our proposed approach varies from the previous work on keystroke analysis reviewed above in several key ways. First, we attempt to detect affective states that naturally occur in the context of an ongoing activity, rather than inducing affect or tracking affect before or after writing. Second, we attempt to classify affect in 15 second intervals, which is a considerably shorter time frame compared to other free text methods. Third, the granularity of our affect classification is finer; instead of either distinguishing between positive and negative affect or detecting a particular affective state, we are distinguishing between either two or three non-basic affective states as discussed in the next section. Fourth, our models include features, such as number of pauses, which appear in very few studies on keystroke analysis. Fifth, in addition to the keystrokes themselves, our models also include information at two additional levels of granularity. These include the writer's appraisals or impressions of the writing task prior to writing (task appraisals) and relevant measures of writer's individual traits (stable traits). Finally, unlike the majority of research on keystroke analysis which uses fixed text entry methods, we pursue free text analysis because it offers a glimpse into the mechanics of writing, which we hypothesize conveys affect.

We begin by first describing the data set used to collect training data for the affect detection models. Next, the feature engineering, selection, and model building phases are discussed. This is followed by the results of a cross-validation analysis. Finally, an overview of our major findings, a discussion of limitations, possible resolutions, and potential applications are discussed.

DATA COLLECTION

Participants

The participants were 44 U.S. undergraduate students (68% female; mean age of 19.9 years; 45% Caucasians, 52% African Americans, and 3% "Other") who participated for course credit.

Essay Topics

The study involved relatively fine-grained tracking of affective states while participants wrote essays on three different topics: (a) academic topics which were obtained from the writing portion of the American College Testing (ACT) test, (b) socially charged issues like abortion and the death penalty, and (c) personal emotional experiences such as recent angry or happy experiences. These three topics were selected because they reflect a continuum with respect to their expected emotional impact, ranging from the affectively neutral academic topics to the affectively charged personal emotional experiences, with the socially charged topic lying in between these two extremes.

In order to increase interest in the writing activity, participants were allowed to choose one subtopic from a list of options under each topic. Academic topics were adapted from the writing portion of the ACT and subtopics included "time spent in high school", "the use of class discussion", and "social skills being taught in schools". Socially charged subtopics included "abortion", "gays in the military", and "the death penalty". Subtopics for the personal emotional experiences condition involved writing about one of six basic affective states (anger, disgust, fear, happiness, sadness, and surprise).

Stable Trait Measures (Individual Differences)

In order to account for within subject differences, we collected stable traits for each subject. The trait measures we used were *scholastic aptitude, writing apprehension, and exposure to print.* Participants' self-reported ACT scores were used as the measure of scholastic aptitude. Self-reported ACT scores have been found to correlate with actual test scores [4], so we have some confidence in this measure.

Writing apprehension was measured with the validated 26-item Writing Apprehension Test (WAT) [9]. The WAT is a self-report inventory where participants respond to a series of statements (e.g., "I avoid writing", "I'm nervous about writing") via a 5-point Likert scale. As recommended by Daly and Miller [9], the test was modified for use outside of the classroom by removing six items pertaining to classroom composition activities. Scores on the WAT can range from 20 to 100, with lower scores indicated more writing apprehension.

Exposure to print was measured with the Author Recognition Test [8]. Participants were presented with a list of names of 42 popular authors (e.g., J. R. R. Tolkien, Dean Koontz) and they had to place a check mark by each author they recognized. The version of the measure we implemented did not have any distracter items; hence, scores were computed as the proportion of authors that were correctly recognized.

Task Appraisal Measures

Participants completed a Task Appraisal Questionnaire prior to writing each essay. The questionnaire used a six-point scale to collect information on participants: (1) *interest* in the topic, (2) how often they *discussed* the topic, (3) how *comfortable* with the topic they were (important for socially charged issues), (4) how *confidant* they were in their ability to write a good essay (5), how much *effort* they would put into writing, (6) their *perceived enjoyment* while writing, and (7) how *personally connected* they were to the topic.

Procedure

Essay Writing

Participants were given 10 minutes to write an essay on each of the three topics. The order of topics was counterbalanced across participants with a 3 × 3 Latin Square. For each topic, they were asked to select one of the subtopics listed above. They typed their essays on a computer interface. Each keystroke was logged along with a timestamp from the beginning of both the session and essay and the number of milliseconds since the last keystroke. Videos of participants' faces and computer screens were also recorded.

Retrospective Affect Judgment

Participants provided self-judgments of their affective states immediately after the writing session. Similar to a cued-recall procedure [10, 30], the judgments for a participant's writing session began by playing a video of the face along with the screen capture video on a widescreen monitor. The screen capture included the writing prompt and dynamically presented the text as it was written, thereby providing the context of the writing session. Participants were instructed to make judgments on what affective states were present at any moment during the writing session by manually pausing the videos. They were also instructed to make judgments at each 15-second interval. The fifteen affective states available to select were: anger, contempt, disgust, fear, happiness, sadness, surprise, boredom, confusion, delight, engagement, frustration, anxiety, curious, and finally, neutral.

It is important to mention three points pertaining to the present affect judgment methodology. Offline judgments were used because they allow monitoring of participants' affective states at multiple points, with minimal task interference, and without participants knowing that these states were being monitored during completion of the learning task. Second, this retrospective affect-judgment method has been previously validated [30], and analyses comparing these offline affect judgments with online measures encompassing self-reports and observations by judges have produced similar distributions of emotions [6,7]. Third, the offline affect annotations obtained via this retrospective protocol correlate with online recordings of facial activity and gross body movements in expected directions [11]. Although no method is without its limitations, the present method appears to be a viable approach to track emotions at a relatively fine-grained temporal resolution.

Affect Distributions

The retrospective affect judgment protocol yielded 5,551 affect judgments across the 44 participants. The distribution of affective states supports two major conclusions. First, the fourteen affective states cumulatively accounted for 78.9% of the observations, while neutral was reported for the remaining 21.1% of the observations. Second, only six out of the 14 affective states (excluding neutral) occurred with some regularity. The most frequent affective state was engagement with an occurrence rate of 35.4% followed by boredom at 26.4%; these two states comprised approximately half of the observations (51.8%). We chose to focus on engagement, boredom, and neutral in this study because they comprised 72.9% of the observations and the remaining affective states were either observed at very low frequencies or inconsistently observed across participants.

MODEL BUILDING

Three types of features were used for the present analysis: keystroke/timing features, task appraisals, and stable traits. ACT scores, WAT scores, and exposure to print were used as stable traits among all subjects. The seven pre-essay questions were used as task appraisals for each essay. These two sets of features have been described in the previous section, so we focus on keystroke/timing features here.

Keystroke and Timing Features

The list of keystroke and timing features is presented in Table 1. These 12 features were reduced from a larger set of 19 based on tolerance analyses, which was used to identify multicollinearity among features.

Features were computed in 15 second intervals, with each interval culminating in an affect judgment (see above). The features can be subdivided into four types: relative timing features, keystroke content features, keystroke timing features, and pausing behaviors. *Relative timing features* consist of the time of an interval relative to the start of the session or essay. *Keystroke verbosity features* consist of features measuring the number of certain keystrokes such as backspaces or the overall number of keystrokes in an interval. *Keystroke timing features* consist of various descriptive statistics of the latency between keystrokes, such as the largest latency or the mean latency between keystrokes in an interval. Finally, *pausing behavior features* consist of the number of each type of pause within an interval.

Outliers were taken to be values greater than three standard deviations away from the mean and were not included in the data that we built our models with. This data set is referred to as the *raw* data set because no additional transformations were performed other than outlier treatment.

	Description
Relative Timing	
Session Time	Elapsed time from start of session
Essay Time	Elapsed time from start of essay
Keystroke Verbosity	
Verbosity	Number of keys within the interval
Backspace Use	Number of backspaces within the interval
Keystroke Timing	
Largest Latency	Largest time difference between keystrokes within interval
Smallest Latency	Smallest time difference between keystrokes within interval
Mean Latency	The mean of all the differences in time between keystrokes within the interval
Median Latency	The median of all the differences in time between keystrokes within the interval
Pausing Behaviors	
0.5 Second Pauses	The number of pauses above .5 seconds and below 1 second
1 Second Pauses	The number of pauses above 1 second and below 1.5 seconds
1.5 Second Pauses	The number of pauses above 1.5 second and below 2 seconds
2 Second Pauses	The number of pauses above 2 second and below 3 seconds

Table 1. Keystroke and Timing Features

Models

We created models with four different combinations of features: keystroke/timing features alone; keystroke/timing features with stable traits; keystroke/timing features with task appraisals; and all three types of features.

In addition to models on the raw features, we also created models with standardized features, models that were downsampled to the affect state with lowest frequency (boredom), and downsampled models with standardized features. Downsampling was used to eliminate imbalance arising from uneven class labels since models that are built on uneven data have a tendency to skew classification towards the majority class. Downsampling can improve classification rates in instances where there is an uneven distribution of class labels, as was the case for our data. Standardization (i.e., z-scores) was done by subject on only the keystroke/timing features, and was used to reduce between-subject variability. Standardization was performed after downsampling.

In addition to the boredom, engagement, neutral discrimination, we also created three two-affect models. This resulted in a model distinguishing boredom from engagement, one distinguishing engagement from neutral, and one distinguishing boredom from neutral.

We used WEKA implementations [34] of nine different classifiers for supervised classification: J48, NaïveBayes, BayesNet, SMO, DecisionTable, OneR, RandomForest, RandomTree, and REPTree. For models with downsampling, we ran the tests with ten different randomly downsampled datasets and took the average values over the ten runs.

We validated our results using the *leave several subjects out* method. Specifically, we split our data into two groups, with 66% of subjects in one group and the remaining 33% in the other. We then trained the models on the first 66% and tested on the other 33%. The leave-several-subjects out method ensures that the models generalize to new subjects because the same subject is either in the training or the testing group, but never both. By splitting our data by subject, we emulate the situation of encountering new subjects with a previously trained model, ensuring generalization. We did this a total of ten times, and took the average kappa values and accuracies for each classifier over those ten runs.

RESULTS

A total of 5,760 models (4 affect discriminations × 4 data sets × 4 features × 9 classifiers × 10 iterations per classifier)

Model	Best Classifier	Kappa
Boredom-Engagement-Neutral		
Keystroke/Timing	DecisionTable	0.036
Keystroke/Timing + Task Appraisals	BayesNet	0.100
Keystroke/Timing + Stable Traits	NaiveBayes	0.116
Keystroke/Timing + Task Appraisals + Stable Traits	**BayesNet**	**0.171**
Boredom - Engagement		
Keystroke/Timing	NaiveBayes	0.021
Keystroke/Timing + Task Appraisals	NaiveBayes	0.270
Keystroke/Timing + Stable Traits	RandomForest	0.357
Keystroke/Timing + Task Appraisals + Stable Traits	**REPTree**	**0.374**
Engagement - Neutral		
Keystroke/Timing	NaiveBayes	0.105
Keystroke/Timing + Task Appraisals	SMO	0.087
Keystroke/Timing + Stable Traits	SMO	0.127
Keystroke/Timing + Task Appraisals + Stable Traits	**NaiveBayes**	**0.156**
Boredom - Neutral		
Keystroke/Timing	BayesNet	0.102
Keystroke/Timing + Task Appraisals	**NaiveBayes**	**0.132**
Keystroke/Timing + Stable Traits	J48	0.121
Keystroke/Timing + Task Appraisals + Stable Traits	BayesNet	0.115

Table 2. Kappa and accuracy for each data and feature set

were estimated. The raw data performed better or almost as well as the standardized and downsampled data. As raw data is more ideal to use for real world purposes, we decided to focus on this data and the results for the models on standardized and downsampled data are not discussed further.

The results for the classifier that yielded the best average performance across trials for a given combination of affect discrimination and feature set are shown in Table 2. The kappa values of the best feature set within each classification task have been bolded. We use kappas instead of accuracy to interpret the results, because kappas correct for random guessing, which is of concern due to an uneven distribution of priors of the three affective states.

From the table it is easy to see that classification between boredom and engagement (kappa = .374; accuracy = 87.0%) was the easiest to perform. The best model for the three-way boredom- engagement-neutral discrimination yielded a kappa of 0.171 with an accuracy of 56.3%, which is approximately half of the kappa of the boredom-engagement discrimination. This is presumably due to difficulty associated with discriminating boredom and engagement from neutral (best kappas of 0.132 with an accuracy of 65.0% and 0.156 with an accuracy of 68.4%, respectively).

The effect of the different feature sets is apparent from the table, as well. With the exception of the boredom and neutral discrimination, in general using all three types of features resulted in the best kappa values. The average kappa value for the feature set with all three features across the four discriminations was 0.204. The next best feature set was the combination of keystroke/timing features and stable traits, which resulted in an average of 0.180. The third best feature set was the set with both task appraisals and keystroke/timing features, with an average of 0.147. The feature set with only keystroke/timing features resulted in the lowest kappas, with an average of 0.066.

The results highlight several key points. First, the best model for discriminating boredom, engagement, and neutral resulted in a kappa value of 0.171, or approximately 17% above chance. This suggests that it is possible to automatically discriminate between boredom, engagement, and neutral by coupling keystrokes and timing data with information on task appraisals and stable traits related to the writing task.

Second, the fact that the highest kappa was between boredom and engagement, while kappas for the other three-way discriminations were on par and lower, suggests that the classifiers experienced difficulty in separating boredom and engagement from neutral compared to discriminating boredom from engagement. This is what could be expected since boredom and engagement are on two opposite sides of a continuum with neutral in between.

Third, there was an interaction between feature set and affect discrimination. Specifically, the keystroke/timing level features alone yielded very low kappas for the three way-classification (kappa = .036, accuracy = 54.4%). This is because they were not very useful in discriminating boredom from engagement (kappa = .021, accuracy = 82.0%), although they could discriminate both boredom and engagement from neutral (kappas of .105 with an accuracy of 68.6% and .102 with an accuracy of 66.0%, respectively). A combination of task appraisals and stable traits along with keystroke/timing features was needed to discriminate between the three states.

Fourth, the feature set with the keystroke/timing features and stable traits generally performed better than either the keystroke/timing features alone or keystroke/timing features coupled with task appraisals. This indicates that the stable traits were more useful than the task appraisals for the discriminations.

GENERAL DISCUSSION

Scalable and accurate affect detection has and always will be one of the predominant goals of affective computing. As noted in the Introduction, some affect detection methods currently in use have limitations, such as obtrusiveness and cost, which keystroke analysis overcomes. Due to the prevalence of typed entry, we hypothesized that keystroke analysis is an attractive alternative to either replace or complement other affect detection methods. We tested this hypothesis by investigating how accurately we could discriminate among natural occurrences of boredom, engagement, and neutral during a writing task. By doing so, we have expanded upon a relatively small amount of previous research pertaining to affect detection using keystroke analysis by using keystroke/timing features in conjunction with stable traits and task appraisals to distinguish between boredom, engagement, and neutral. In this section, we take stock of our major findings, discuss applied implications, and discuss limitations and potential areas for future work.

Major Findings

Our results were illuminating in a number of ways. First, we have shown that it is possible to discriminate between boredom, engagement, and neutral using keystroke analysis and both task appraisals and stable traits relevant to writing. Our work differed from previous research on keystroke based affect detection (see Introduction) in terms of our focus on free text, tracking of non-basic emotions, finer-grained temporal resolution for affect detection, a feature set that couples keystrokes with task appraisals and stable traits, validation methods that generalize to new learners, and the fact that naturalistic experiences of affect were being tracked.

Second, standardizing and downsampling the data did not provide a significant increase in classification rate over raw data. This is a significant advantage for real-world implementation because raw keystroke data is immediately available as input to the classifiers. Third, classification was improved by combining keystroke analysis with both task appraisals and relevant stable traits. Although this requires additional data collection (see below), it may be worth the improvement in detection. Fourth, we found that distinguishing between boredom and engagement was easier than distinguishing either boredom or engagement from neutral.

Finally, it is important to note that the models were built using purely free text keystroke analysis. Free text keystroke analysis is a more accurate representation of real world situations than fixed text keystroke analysis, and as such is more appropriate for dynamic affect detection. Our results indicate that free text keystroke analysis may be a reasonable avenue for consideration in affect detection systems.

Application of Findings to Intelligent User Interfaces

The present findings are applicable to any user interface that utilizes keyboard for user input. The most immediate application are systems that monitor affect during writing. This is an important application area because writing is increasingly being considered to be a crucial 21st century skill since the ability to write proficiently is a critical component of success in many professional endeavors. The impetus on writing can also be witnessed in the formal education system. Standardized tests in the U.S., such as the ACT, SAT, and GRE, have recently added sections that evaluate an applicant's writing proficiency. Unfortunately, despite the increased focus on writing in the education system, there is evidence to suggest that the average student lacks the necessary skills to effectively communicate their ideas in written text. For example, according to a National Assessment of Educational Progress report, only 23% of 8th graders and 31% of 12th graders in the U.S. were considered to be "proficient" writers and there was no significant change since 2002 [23].

Considering the high stakes placed on writing competency several educational applications have been developed to automatically score written essays and provide formative feedback on writing quality. Some of these include the Intelligent Essay Assessor, E-Rater, Summary Street, and Writing Pal [1, 15, 20, 33]. Unfortunately, these systems have focused on the cognitive aspects of writing, while ignoring the affective ones. The present research can alleviate this problem by automatically detecting when engagement is waning and the student risks disengaging from the writing task due to boredom. This educational application can use this information to intervene accordingly, such as changing topics when the student is bored. The affect detectors developed in this study could also be instrumental in furthering understanding the role of affect in developing writing proficiency by affording automated measurement of engagement and boredom, which are presumably correlated with writing outcomes.

The present focus on keystroke and timing analysis makes it quite easy to incorporate our models into intelligent writing-support applications that detect and respond to affect. The analysis of keystroke, timing, stable traits, and task appraisal features can all be implemented easily through software. Data for keystroke and timing features can be collected unobtrusively while users type on the keyboard. Stable traits can be collected with short questionnaires; taking no longer than five minutes while a user creates their profile for the first time. Task appraisals can be collected with a brief series of questions before each writing task, which can also be done with minimal interruption. This data is collected before the task begins, so there is little infringement on the writing process. Since collecting data for task appraisals and stable traits is done quickly, it is not infeasible to incorporate these features into a real world situation.

Our research is focused on affect during writing, which extends farther than educational systems. Detecting affect might be beneficial in the workplace or on a personal computer as well. Continuous monitoring of affect through keystroke analysis could help create systems that can soothe a user becoming frustrated with an aspect of their work or re-focus a user that is becoming bored. A personal computer could detect when a user is becoming sad and might make an attempt to cheer them up. These situations are somewhat different than typing from an essay writing standpoint, but interaction with a keyboard invites the opportunity for unobtrusive affect detection regardless of the situation.

Limitations and Future Work

There are a few limitations of the methods we employed. First, the highest accuracy for the boredom, engagement, and neutral discrimination was 56.3%, which, although approximately 17% better than chance, is quite modest. That being said, we do have some confidence in the generalizability of our models, because these results were obtained for previously unseen subjects through the leave several subjects out cross-validation method. Second, we did not perform feature selection other than removing features that exhibited multicollinearity. Employing feature selection would reduce the number of features being used and may improve classification as well. Third, we only investigated affect in 15 second intervals because this is when humans provided affect judgments. Different interval lengths might be more or less appropriate for affect detection. Fourth, we investigated whether our models generalize to new learners through the leave several out method, but we did not assess the extent to which they generalize to new topics.

Future work could be focused in several areas. It would be useful to investigate if feature selection improves performance of the classifiers. Instead of looking at 15 second intervals, it might be possible to analyze a continuous stream of keystrokes. Our models were built from data within the subject but independent of the essay – it might be informative to study trends within each essay as well. Whether these and other advances result in notable improvements in accuracy awaits further research and empirical testing.

ACKNOWLEDGEMENTS

Special thanks to Caitlin Mills for leading the data collection and to Rebekah Combs, Rosaire Daigle, Nia Dowell, Ally Dobbins, Melissa Gross, Blair Lehman, and Amber Strain for help with data collection. This research was supported by the National Science Foundation (NSF) (ITR 0325428, HCC 0834847, and DRL 1235958). Any opinions, findings and conclusions, or recommendations expressed in this paper are those of the authors and do not necessarily reflect the views of the NSF.

REFERENCES

1. Attali, Y., & Burstein, J. (2006). Automated essay scoring with e-rater® V. 2. *The Journal of Technology, Learning and Assessment*, *4*(3).
2. Bleha, S., Slivinsky, C., & Hussien, B. (1990). Computer-access security systems using keystroke dynamics. *Pattern Analysis and Machine Intelligence, IEEE Transactions on*, *12*(12), 1217-1222.
3. Calvo, R. A., & D'Mello, S. K. (2010). Affect detection: An interdisciplinary review of models, methods, and their applications. *IEEE Transactions on Affective Computing, 1*(1), 18-37. doi: 10.1109/T-AFFC.2010.1
4. Cole, J. S., & Gonyea, R. M. (2010). Accuracy of self-reported SAT and ACT test scores: Implications for research. *Research in Higher Education, 51*(4), 305-319. doi: 10.1007/s11162-009-9160-9
5. Crawford, H. (2010). Keystroke dynamics: Characteristics and opportunities. In *Privacy Security and Trust (PST), 2010 Eighth Annual International Conference on* (pp. 205-212). IEEE.
6. Craig, S., D'Mello, S., Witherspoon, A., & Graesser, A. (2008). Emote aloud during learning with AutoTutor: Applying the facial action coding system to cognitive-affective states during learning. *Cognition & Emotion, 22(5),* 777-788.
7. Craig, S., Graesser, A., Sullins, J., & Gholson, J. (2004). Affect and learning: An exploratory look into the role of affect in learning. *Journal of Educational Media, 29*, 241-250.
8. Cunningham, A. E., & Stanovich, K. E. (1997). Early reading acquisition and its relation to reading experience and ability 10 years later. *Developmental Psychology, 33*(6), 934-945.
9. Daly, J., & Miller, M. (1975). The empirical development of an instrument to measure writing apprehension. *Research in the Teaching of English 9*(3), 242-249.
10. D'Mello, S., & Graesser, A. (2011). The half-life of cognitive-affective states during complex learning. *Cognition & Emotion, 25*(7), 1299-1308.
11. D'Mello, S., & Graesser, A. (2010). Multimodal semi-automated affect detection from conversational cues, gross body language, and facial features. *User Modeling and User-adapted Interaction, 20(2)*, 147-187.
12. D'Mello, S., & Mills, C. (in review). Emotions during emotional and non-emotional writing.
13. Ekman, P. (1992). An argument for basic emotions. *Cognition & Emotion*, *6*(3-4), 169-200.
14. Epp, C., Lippold, M., & Mandryk, R. L. (2011). Identifying emotional states using keystroke dynamics. In *Proceedings of the 2011 annual conference on Human factors in computing systems* (pp. 715-724). ACM.
15. Foltz, P. W., Laham, D., & Landauer, T. K. (1999). The intelligent essay assessor: Applications to educational technology. *Interactive Multimedia Electronic Journal of Computer-Enhanced Learning*, *1*(2).
16. Gunetti, D., & Picardi, C. (2005). Keystroke analysis of free text. *ACM Transactions on Information and System Security (TISSEC)*, *8*(3), 312-347.
17. Joyce, R., & Gupta, G. (1990). Identity authentication based on keystroke latencies. *Communications of the ACM*, *33*(2), 168-176.
18. K., & Litman, D. J. (2011). Benefits and challenges of real-time uncertainty detection and adaptation in a spoken dialogue computer tutor. *Speech Communication, 53*(9-10), 1115-1136. doi: 10.1016/j.specom.2011.02.006
19. Khanna, P., & Sasikumar, M. (2010). Recognising Emotions from Keyboard Stroke Pattern. *International Journal of Computer Applications IJCA*, *11*(9), 24-28.
20. McNamara, D. S., Raine, R., Roscoe, R., Crossley, S., Jackson, G. T., Dai, J., & Graesser, A. C. (2012). The Writing-Pal: Natural language algorithms to support intelligent tutoring on writing strategies. *Applied natural language processing and content analysis: Identification, investigation, and resolution. Hershey, PA: IGI Global.*
21. Metallinou, A., Wollmer, M., Katsamanis, A., Eyben, F., Schuller, B., & Narayanan, S. (in press). Context-Sensitive Learning for Enhanced Audiovisual Emotion Classification. *IEEE Transactions on Affective Computing*.
22. Mills, C., & D'Mello, S. K. (2012). Emotions during writing on topics that align or misalign with personal beliefs. In S. Cerri, W. Clancey, G. Papadourakis & K. Panourgia (Eds.), *Proceedings of the 11th International Conference on Intelligent Tutoring Systems* (pp. 638-639). Berlin Heidelberg: Springer-Verlag.

23. NAEP. (2007). The Nation's Report Card: Writing 2007.
24. Nijholt, Anton, & Desney S. Tan (2010). *Brain-Computer Interfaces: Applying our Minds to Human-Computer Interaction*. Springer.
25. Pang, B., & Lee, L. (2008). Opinion mining and sentiment analysis. *Foundations and Trends in Information Retrieval, 2*(1-2), 1-135
26. Pantic, M., & Patras, I. (2006). Dynamics of facial expression: Recognition of facial actions and their temporal segments from face profile image sequences. *IEEE Transactions on Systems, Man, and Cybernetics, Part B., 36*(2), 433-449. doi: 10.1109/tsmcb.2005.859075
27. Pantic, M., & Rothkrantz, L. (2003). Toward an affect-sensitive multimodal human-computer interaction. [Review]. *Proceedings of the IEEE, 91*(9), 1370-1390. doi: 10.1109/jproc.2003.817122
28. Picard, R. (1997). *Affective Computing*. Cambridge, Mass: MIT Press.
29. Picard, R. (2010). Affective Computing: From Laughter to IEEE. *IEEE Transactions on Affective Computing, 1*(1), 11-17.
30. Rosenberg, E., & Ekman, P. (1994). Coherence between expressive and experiential systems in emotion. *Cognition & Emotion, 8*(3), 201-229.
31. Valstar, M. F., Mehu, M., Jiang, B., Pantic, M., Scherer, K., Jiang, B., Valstar, M., Pantic, M., Valstar, M., & Jiang, B. (in press). Meta-Analysis of the First Facial Expression Recognition Challenge. *IEEE transactions on systems, man, and cybernetics. Part B, Cybernetics.*
32. Vizer, L. M., Zhou, L., & Sears, A. (2009). Automated stress detection using keystroke and linguistic features: An exploratory study. *International Journal of Human-Computer Studies, 67*(10), 870-886.
33. Wade-Stein, D., & Kintsch, E. (2004). Summary Street: Interactive computer support for writing. *Cognition and Instruction, 22*(3), 333-362.
34. Witten, I.H., Frank, E., Trigg, L., Hall, M., Holmes, G. & Cunningham, S.J. (1999). Weka: Practical machine learning tools and techniques with Java implementations. Hamilton, New Zealand: University of Waikato, Department of Computer Science.
35. Zeng, Z., Pantic, M., Roisman, G., & Huang, T. (2009). A survey of affect recognition methods: Audio, visual, and spontaneous expressions. *IEEE Transactions on Pattern Analysis and Machine Intelligence, 31*(1), 39-58.

Informing Intelligent User Interfaces by Inferring Affective States from Body Postures in Ubiquitous Computing Environments

Chiew Seng Sean Tan **Johannes Schöning** **Kris Luyten** **Karin Coninx**
Hasselt University
tUL – iMinds
Expertise Centre for Digital Media
3590 Diepenbeek, Belgium
firstname.lastname@uhasselt.be

ABSTRACT
Intelligent User Interfaces can benefit from having knowledge on the user's emotion. However, current implementations to detect affective states, are often constraining the user's freedom of movement by instrumenting her with sensors. This prevents affective computing from being deployed in naturalistic and ubiquitous computing contexts. In this paper, we present a novel system called mASqUE, which uses a set of association rules to infer someone's affective state from their body postures. This is done without any user instrumentation and using off-the-shelf and non-expensive commodity hardware: a depth camera tracks the body posture of the users and their postures are also used as an indicator of their openness. By combining the posture information with physiological sensors measurements we were able to mine a set of association rules relating postures to affective states. We demonstrate the possibility of inferring affective states from body postures in ubiquitous computing environments and our study also provides insights how this opens up new possibilities for IUI to access the affective states of users from body postures in a nonintrusive way.

Author Keywords
Affective Computing; Posture Tracking / Detection; Social Behavior; Emotion Recognition; Ubicomp; Intelligent User Interfaces.

ACM Classification Keywords
H5.2 [Information interfaces and presentation]: User Interfaces. – Interaction Styles.

General Terms
Performance; Experimentation; Design; Human Factor.

MOTIVATION
Weiser's vision of ubiquitous computing [35] is not longer a vision as pointed out by Abowd [1] and Rogers [28]. With the increase of computational power that is available in our environments and the quality of sensors, ubiquitous systems that are embedded in our environment can take better decisions on how to support our daily routines and activities. This is exactly the context-awareness that has been most prominently advocated by Dey et al. [12] to frame interaction within the situation of the user. Although the *context of use* in general has been widely explored to improve usability of Ubicomp systems, we argue further improvements can be accomplished by taking into account the *context of the user*, more specifically the *affective state* of a user. For interaction in an Ubicomp environment, a system, that detects the affective states of the users, should maintain the freedom of movement of the users by not instrumenting them with additional sensors.

Researchers have demonstrated the huge potential of including the affective states of users to inform UIs by approaches such as multimodal fusion [14] and data-centric modeling [21]. However, affective computing has not been deployed in ubiquitous computing environments yet. A leading question for this challenge is: How does one detect and represent the emotions that affective systems should implement in ubiquitous computing environments? This question in turn leads us to determine whether current sensors are able to deliver the advantages of affective computing in our research domain. Recently Aviezer et al. [36] highlighted the role of body postures in expressing and perceiving emotions. They showed in their Science article that body posture is as expressive as facial expression for distinguishing positive and negative emotions.

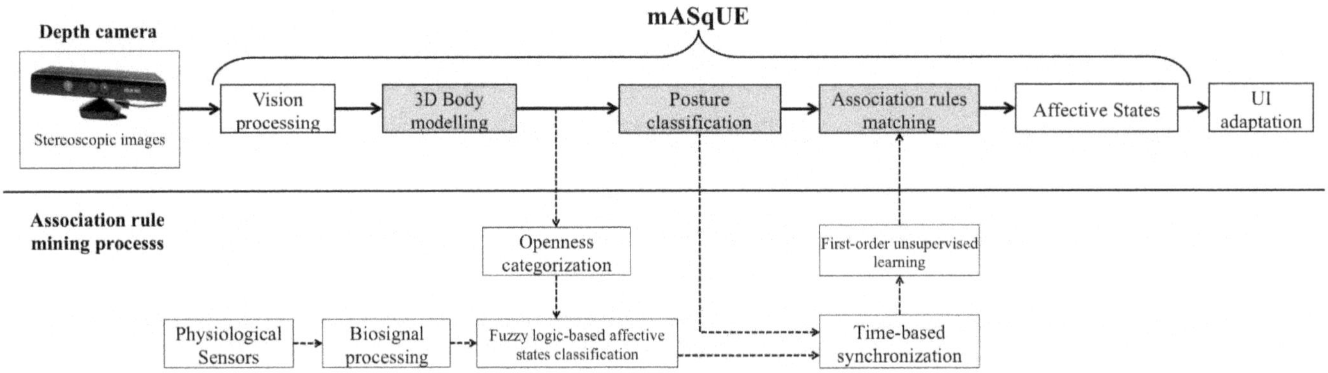

Figure 1: mASqUE affective state detection: By fusing the postural information with physiological sensors measurement (dotted lines) we are able to mine a set of association rules. The three main parts are highlighted with grey filled boxes. This set then can be used to detect affective states with posture detection only (solid lines) and inform UIs.

We identify three practical limitations emerging from current sensor implementations and use them to guide our system design mainly relying on body posture. (1) *Bound to the desktop*: the detection range of the aforementioned input modalities restricts users' mobility. As an example, systems that use facial expressions or voice intonation analysis compel users to situate themselves directly in front of a camera or microphone, usually mounted on top of a computer screen. For that reason, we decided to use cheap commodity hardware and designed our system to work in ubiquitous computing environments. (2) *Not always "on"*: certain emotional cues of the users are undetected due to the device's functionality. Similar to the above example, systems that detect and track lip movement or voice intonations depend on the users' speech formation. Body postures constantly cover many communicative functions. They may replace speech during dialogue, or when speech is not used at all. Similar to body postures, ubiquitous computing systems are also always available to provide their computation functionalities and are constantly engaging with their users. Hence, using ubiquitous computing systems to detect postures ensures the continuous access to user's emotions cues. (3) *Heavy user instrumentation*: users are also affected by a device's presence (e.g. wireless sensors) throughout their normal activities. Systems based on physiological information require users to wear specialized instruments such as sensors that can detect galvanic skin response or heart rate, which burden their natural behavioral and mental response. Automatic visual detection of body movements and postures does not distract users, as no wearable instruments are required and also does not require user to constantly focus on a computer screen.

INTRODUCTION

As outlined above, we present mASqUE (Affective State detection in Ubiquitous Computing Environments), which is aimed to overcome these problems. It is a novel system that addresses the key limitations imposed by typical Ubicomp environments. mASqUE merely examines users' body postures so that their dominant affective states can be inferred. We present a 3D body-modeling technique tailored for tracking even subtle body postures with an off-the-shelf depth camera. Our system is designed to passively and unobtrusively detect affective states when the whole body is detected and tracked, which usually means the user is standing. Although this can also be considered as a limitation of our system, there are other solutions that work for non-standing positions [18, 23]. mASqUE works on the principle of using a set of association rules that allow inference of someone's affective state from their body postures (as illustrated in Figure 1). We found several affective states that are expressed through body postures in a naturalistic manner.

We used a mining process involving a series of experiments to obtain the set of association rules. We first looked for clear associations to dominant affective states and postures people take. To find these, we compared posture information with physiological sensor data from the users, which were captured at the same time. In this stage, we used the traditional input data: the user's arousal and valence, as defined by [29], which have proven to be useful and reliable, together with the openness values. We then transformed this information to affective states and correlated them with the detected postures. Openness is derived from posture information as well. The characterization of openness levels enables us to gain insights of the attitude of the users. Attitudes commonly refer to the general evaluations people hold regarding various objects, issues, and people [25]. With that, we derive a set of association rules to cover ten affective states, consistent with the ones described by Breazeal and Scassellati [6]. The set of ten affective states comprises of five basic affective states: content, excitement, frustration, calm, and boredom, which are also described by Russell's Affect Grid [29]; and another five affective states (overjoy, accepting, stern, disgust, anger) as described by [6]. Our system, mASqUE, uses the association rules to decide what the most likely dominant affective state is, merely based on body postures. By including "openness" as an additional categorization of affective states, we are able to use a fine-grained definition of affective states. In contrast to physiological measurements, which are based on distinctive patterns of the autonomic nervous system inside the body, openness is observed through bodily movements, such as postures, to determine for the varying degrees of emotions. A low openness level can indicate an emotion that shows greater intensity of animosity. For example, frustration in a neutral openness level can be intensified to become anger. When the openness level drops, this indicates that the user is being aggressive, introvert or unapproachable.

With these components in place, we have a system that captures the context of the user and provides information on the dominant affective state of the user.

RELATED WORK

Affective systems, equipped with different sensory modalities, are able to detect and recognize emotions of the users. Their applications range from troubleshooting for interactive systems [4] to enhancing game experience with play technology [19]. Different modalities and affective models are being used, such as voice intonation analysis with a corresponding Pleasure-Arousal-Dominance model [14] or physiological instrumentation being used with arousal and valence in addition to a third affective dimension (engagement [23]). For a comprehensive overview on emotion recognition using different modalities and affective models, we refer readers to the survey of Gunes et al. [15].

Interactive systems with affective computing capabilities have been previously studied. Ball and Breese [4] developed an affective system, which utilize a four-dimensional affective model to develop a character-based interface for software troubleshooting. Their affective model includes dominance and friendliness alongside with arousal and valence to model the traits that appear to be most critical to interpersonal relationships. AffectAura, developed by McDuff et al. [23], utilizes a combination of video, speech, physiological, and activity information to provide visualization of the user's affective states in desktop work-related context. They used valence, arousal, and engagement to model user states, where engagement in this case refers to the user's level of work-related commitment. However, both systems are highly dependent on the speech characteristics (and also physiological instrumentation [23]) to determine the classification of emotionally communicative behaviors. This dependency creates practical limitations (mentioned in previous section) for the users in ubiquitous computing environments.

Gilroy et al. [14] used a multimodal fusion approach for video and speech to interpret the dimensional representations of emotion. Their work focuses on the EMG electrode placements to establish the pleasure dimension using Pleasure-Arousal-Dominance model during physiological measurement. Lance and Marsella [20] used motion capture to collect data of the head, eye, and body movement of actors performing emotionally different gaze shifts. They also used a Pleasure-Arousal-Dominance model. Their work involves gaze behaviors and emotional expressiveness in animation of virtual characters. Wagner et al. also explored fusion methods for multimodal emotion recognition with a special focus on missing data for real-time applications [34].

Bolls et al. [5] used facial electromyography (EMG) and physiological measurements to determine the valence of user and explore the effects of user's arousal on attention and memory. They used arousal, valence and dominance to measure and determine the relationship between valence from radio messages and cognitive functions. These studies, however, mainly focused on improving sensor measurements or performance accuracy and did not strive for incorporating their work in ubiquitous computing environments.

Probably the work most similar to ours is that by Kleinsmith et al. [19], who used posture information to determine a set of affective states in an interactive play context. However, they used potency and avoidance to indicate the level of control to influence emotionally significant people, events, or situations, which is grounded in the work of Mehrabian [24]. Our affective model, which differs from theirs, uses openness to indicate how approachable the users are by the expansiveness or contractiveness of their body postures. Our use of openness is inspired by Ekman and Davidson [11]. We describe openness as one's behavioral closeness to another person in interpersonal space. Furthermore, our approach does not rely on additional instrumentation – body markers in Kleinsmith's case – to acquire visual information. Markers can also be problematic outside of a laboratory context, which is not a problem for mASqUE. Additional benefit of our work is the use of affordable and highly accessible hardware (Microsoft Kinect).

SYSTEM OVERVIEW OF MASQUE

Our system, mASqUE, consists of three main parts as can be seen in Figure 1 (grey filled boxes). The first part of mASqUE is the **3-dimensional body model** (for kinematic analysis of the whole body using vision processing techniques) that also discriminate the openness level of the users. The second part is the **posture classifier** (for body posture classifications using 3-dimensional body modeling) that maps the kinematical and semantical features to an extended range of postures commonly observed in naturalistic, conversational settings. The third part is an **association rule matcher**, which is used to deduce the affective states from the detected postures. The association rules are derived from a mining process that we will describe later in this section.

mASqUE's approach for converting (sets of) postures into affective state is based on the stages in affective signal

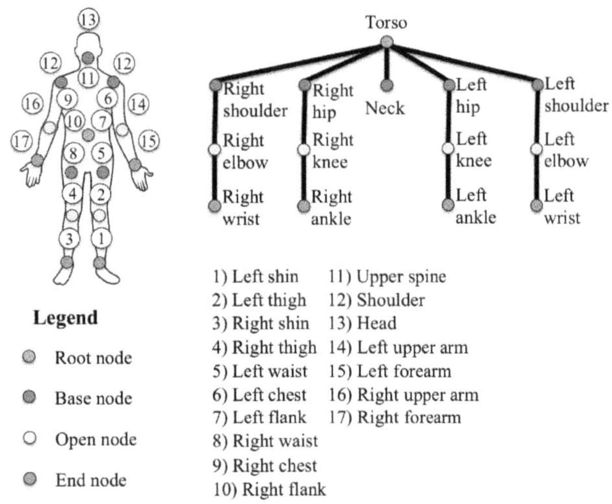

Figure 2. Link model with joints represented by hierarchical nodes. The 14 joints (shown as colored nodes) are connected to the 17 numerated body parts.

processing defined by Picard [26]. First, the low level information (postures) is captured by a sensing device (a MS Kinect). Next, we detect patterns in these postures that indicate a specific prominent affective state. The affective states we are able to classify are deduced from Russell's Affect Grid [29]. Finally, we convert these states into high-level representations of goals and preferences for emotion synthesis. This final stage gives us symbolic data that can be used by affective systems to reason about their situations. In the following we discuss the three main parts of the mASqUE system is detail.

Vision-based approach for 3D Body Modeling

We delineate a set of postures typically identified in psychology literature [30]. The postures can be described with a combination of primitives in the body lean, arms, head, and legs [3]. The eleven postures we use are Hand-on-chin, Hand-near-hip, Hand-behind-neck, Arm Crossed, Limbs Restrained, Limbs Relaxed, Legs Crossed, Foot Forward (Left), Foot Forward (Right), Lean Forward, and Lean Sideward. We developed a 3D body model for identifying body kinematics that can be used to correlate the abovementioned postures with different types of limbs.

The skeletonization method to detect the body structure from the human silhouette [13] is the basis for our approach. In contrast to Fujiyoshi and Lipton [13] we used a 17-links model compared to their simpler "star" skeleton to represent the human body. However, for capturing more subtle posture cues (e.g. to enable posture tracking during human conversations) we extract additional features related to the quality of body movement. Based on this information, we introduce a model-based kinematic framework that is able to characterize body language in a conversational setting. Our 3D body model is represented with a link model that is made from a set of limbs that are segments being connected together by means of joints. Our 17-links model comprises of fourteen body joints and seventeen limbs (as can be seen in Figure 2). We measure rotations and transitions of fourteen monitored body joints using the kinematic framework. Details on posture classification are provided in the next subsection, which is based on the measurements of body articulations (i.e. joint angle) and quality of body movement (i.e. Region of Interest movement).

Classification based on Postures

As an input for the posture classifier we use depth images from the Microsoft Kinect depth camera system. Basic skeletonization and tracking is provided by the OpenNI SDK from PrimeSense. The OpenNI SDK also allows us to detect significant body parts for our 3D body modeling including the head, tips of the feet, and tips of the hands, hips, knees, elbows, and the torso. We build a tracking algorithm on top of OpenNI that is tailored for detecting postures. The algorithm includes a combination of temporal scaling and spatial transformation parameters for tracking the significant body parts.

To increase the precision of our 3D body model, when subtle changes in postures occur, we implemented the 2D image tracking algorithms of Comaniciu [9] (i.e. kernel-based object tracking to monitor movement of the joints that are being tracked at per-pixel level) and color histogram model matching to measure the background noise caused by the transitioning of body postures. With our 3D body model, we can extract the angles of fourteen monitored body joints and track the following kinematic and semantical features: the body articulation measurement (i.e. flexion and pivot angles of each monitored body joint) and quality of body movement (i.e. quantification assessment of the tracked Region of Interest (ROI) that is superimposed on each joint).

Flexion refers to the rotation in the direction of the limb and pivot refers to the rotation laterally across the limb. The quantification assessment for quality of body movement uses a kernel-based object tracking to determine the number of Meanshift iterations for the ROI movement from the previous position at per-pixel level. Color histogram model matching is also included in the quantification assessment to measure the Mahalanobis distance, which is used to detect outliers (background noise) in data association of the color histogram patterns along image sequences. All of these features are combined to create a 44-element feature vector that is updated every 200 milliseconds. A feed-forward neural network with a backpropagation learning algorithm executes the posture recognition algorithms (one for each defined posture).

Association rule matching to infer affective state

Statistical analyses are used by the association rule matcher to make inferences about the affective state in real-time. We

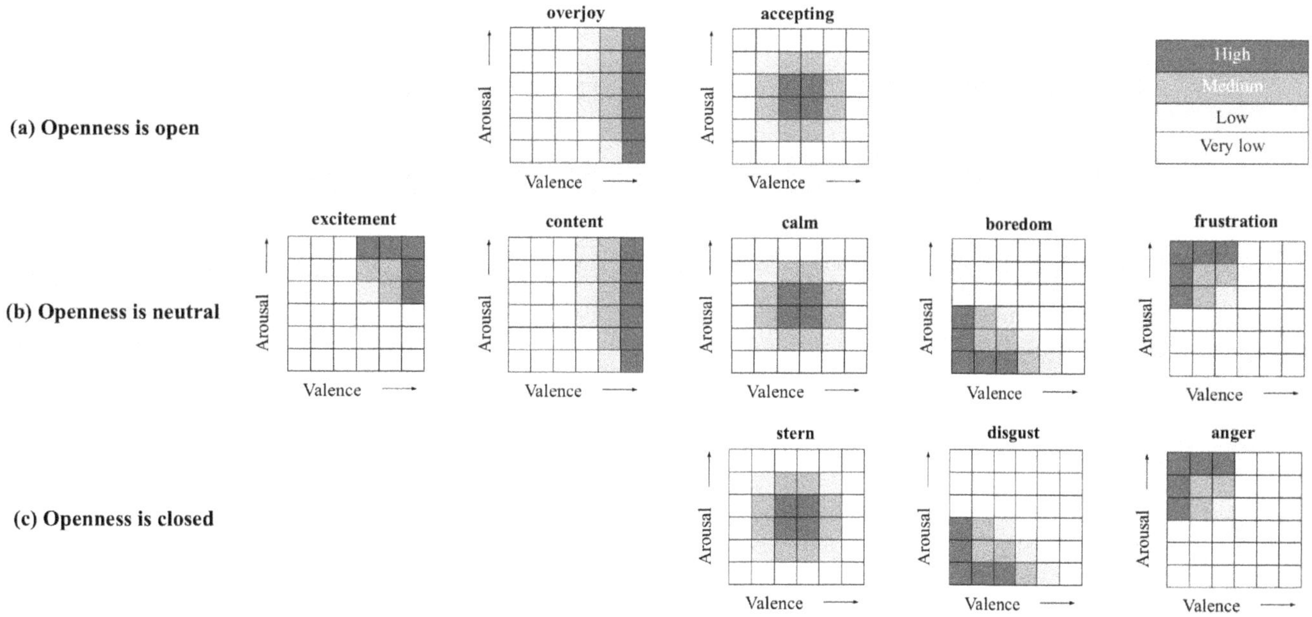

Figure 3: Representation of levels of emotions in arousal-valence space. (middle row) The results with openness being neutral are same as the results by Mandryk [19]. (top and bottom rows) Using the same set of representation of levels of emotions, we defined additional emotions with different openness levels (i.e. open and closed).

accumulate the posture information every 200 milliseconds over a moving window of 2 seconds and rank the postures according to their posterior probabilities. The three postures with highest posterior probability are then selected to determine a corresponding match with the association rules.

PROCESS FOR MINING ASSOCATION RULES

The association rules are derived by a mining process that took the results we obtained from a study on postures as input. This study was conducted primarily to observe the postures during different emotionally-led conversations.

We developed an affective state classifier, which uses fuzzy logic to combine posture information and physiological measurements to identify an extended range of affective states.

Classification for an extended range of Affective States

Our affective state classifier is based on the combination of two classification approaches: vision-based openness categorization and physiological-based arousal-valence classification. The affective state classification uses the continuous values of arousal, valence and openness to mathematically model a set of emotions (see Figure 1).

Openness categorization based on Postures

We use the posture information from our vision-based posture recognition approach to provide the openness categorization in the detected postures. The transformations from posture to openness value, which provide a symbolic representation of an individual's behavior, is derived from Burgoon [7] and Clore [8]. They have evaluated different body behaviors to identify those that can distinguish a positive attitude from a negative one. We then relate these body behaviors (such as expansive arm and body movement, postural relaxation, direct body orientation and forward lean of the upper body) to our posture descriptions. This openness categorization can also potentially be implemented in game systems to provide appropriate empathic feedback for the players to improve their game experience. For example, the game feedback can adapt to the openness level (such as players are showing negative signs of approachable attitude) and it provides the relevant support to the players with encouraging comments after a game when they are slouching their shoulders instead of making harsh cynical comments.

To confirm the level of openness conveyed by each of the postures suitable for naturalistic and ubiquitous computing contexts, we asked human observers to appraise their emotional content. We created hypothetical scenarios using guidelines from Scherer et al. [31] to capture non-acted postures from 10 pre-test participants. We then manually selected a total of 57 variations of the user postures and annotated them as test patterns. A total of 60 observers have been recruited from Amazons Mechanical Turk services to rate each test pattern on its level of openness from 1 (not approachable at all) to 7 (very approachable). The faces in the test patterns were pixelated to prevent observers from interpreting emotion from facial expression. The between-groups multivariate ANOVA results show that the postures can be grouped into three distinct levels. Postures with high levels of openness ($M = 4.43$, $SD = 1.54$) were indeed rated significantly higher than postures with mid level of openness ($M = 3.85$, $SD = 1.57$), $F(59) = 0.476$, $p < .001$; $r = 0.002$. Similarly, postures with low level of openness (M

= 3.36, SD = 1.49) were rated significantly lower than postures with mid level of openness, $F(59) = 0.467$, $p < .001$; $r = -0.113$. We then related the three levels of openness (high, mid, and low) to the respective labels: open, neutral, and closed.

Fuzzy logic implementation for Affective State Classifier

The affective state classifier uses a fuzzy logic implementation for determining the affective patterns that can be used to differentiate a set of emotions. Fuzzy logic provides the advantages of modeling uncertainty and also resembling the way humans think, reason and perceive about its situational information [2]. A typical fuzzy logic system uses a collection of fuzzy membership functions and rules to handle inexact, uncertain and vague concepts in an appropriate manner to reason about data.

Our classifier combines both physiological-based arousal-valence classification and vision-based openness categorization. This approach is similar to Mandryk's [22] which also utilized two fuzzy logic models for determining user emotions: the first model transforms physiological signals as a direct indication of user experience into arousal and valence, and the second model transforms the changes in arousal and valence according to the openness (category) level into a set of ten affective states.

To capture the physiological information, we used Thought Technology's ProComp Infiniti hardware and Biograph software. Arousal and valence values were then derived from these four physiological signals: Galvanic Skin Response (GSR), Heart Rate (HR), Electromyography of the corrugator supercilii muscle for frowning (EMG_{frown}), and Electromyography of the zygomaticus major muscle for smiling (EMG_{smile}). Similar to [22], we also faced the issue that there are no established guidelines for transforming arousal and valence according to the openness categorization into a set of emotions. We defined the membership functions and the rules to translate arousal, valence, and openness using the basis of the circumplex model of emotion [29], related works from Mandryk [22] and Breazeal [6]. For the transformation involving arousal-valence space at different levels of openness, fifteen trapezoidal membership functions that are evenly distributed are used for the inputs of arousal, valence and openness. Arousal and valence are each represented in six levels: veryLow, low, midLow, midHigh, high, and veryHigh. Openness is represented in three levels: closed, neutral, and open. For each of the three openness levels (see section above), the physiological information is mapped on the two-dimensional arousal-valence space, forming a set of 2D points that can be used as input to a fuzzy logic model.

There are 156 fuzzy logic rules to transform the input values from arousal, valence and openness into the ten affective states. The ten affective states comprise of five new affective states in addition to the set of basic affective states. The set of basic affective states can be derived from

Posture combination	Affective States
Foot Forward (Right) + Lean Sideward Lean Forward + Lean Sideward + Foot Forward (Right)	**Overjoy**
Hand-near-hip + Lean Sideward	**Excitement**
Foot Forward (Right) + Hand-on-chin Foot Forward (Right) + Hand-behind-neck + Hand-on-chin	**Content**
Foot Forward (Right) + Hand-near-hip + Legs Crossed	**Accepting**
Limbs Constrained + Legs Crossed Arms Crossed + Lean Sideward + Limbs Relaxed Lean Sideward + Legs Crossed + Hand-on-chin	**Calm**
Foot Forward (Left) + Limbs Constrained + Lean Sideward Arms Crossed + Hand-on-chin Arms Crossed + Hand-near-neck + Lean Sideward	**Stern**
Arms Crossed + Limbs Relaxed + Lean Sideward Arms Crossed + Limbs Constrained Limbs Constrained + Foot Forward (Right) Hand-on-chin + Hand-behind-neck	**Boredom**
Limbs Constrained + Hand-near-neck Hand-near-hip + Legs Crossed Legs Apart + Limbs Constrained + Legs Crossed	**Frustration**
Arms Crossed + Hand-on-chin Hand-near-neck + Limbs Constrained	**Disgust**
Hand-on-chin + Arms Crossed Limbs Constrained + Hand-on-chin + Foot Forward (Right) Arms Crossed + Hand-near-hip	**Anger**

Table 1. This table shows the association rules representative of correlation between postures and affective states. We assumed that the interaction partner is located at the direction where the foot forward is pointing to the right side i.e. Foot Forward (right).

the transformation of arousal and valence, when openness is neutral, based on a set of 71 fuzzy logic rules. We assumed the default for the openness level is neutral for these 71 fuzzy logic rules as they can be described and depicted on an arousal-valence plane. The fuzzy logic rules were generated to map the levels of arousal and valence to the five basic affective states: content, excitement, frustration, calm, and boredom. The details for this representation of the levels of emotion are shown in Figure 3 (middle row, b), which is based on our data and replicate the results of Mandryk. Note that we replace the emotional category of Challenge from [22] with Calm, as Challenge is derived from Csikszentmihalyi's [10] and Mandryk's [22] application domain of gaming whereas Calm is more suited for general contexts.

The details for the representation of levels of the new set of emotion are shown in Figure 3 (top and bottom rows, a and c). The five additional affective states are: overjoy, accepting, stern, disgust, and anger. As such, we reused the 71 fuzzy logic rules, which are described earlier for the set of five basic affective states. The additional 85 rules are derived from the first set of 71 fuzzy logic rules by

Fuzzy logic-based affective state classifier	Inferred from the mASqUE System									
	Overjoy	Excitement	Content	Accepting	Calm	Stern	Boredom	Frustration	Disgust	Anger
Overjoy	276	0	0	5	0	0	0	0	0	0
Excitement	9	445	0	0	14	2	0	0	0	0
Content	0	0	37	0	0	0	0	0	0	0
Accepting	0	0	0	393	0	1	0	0	0	0
Calm	0	0	0	0	304	0	0	0	0	0
Stern	0	1	1	0	5	488	0	0	0	1
Boredom	0	0	0	0	0	0	220	0	0	0
Frustration	0	0	0	1	4	0	0	507	1	1
Disgust	0	0	0	0	0	1	0	0	66	0
Anger	0	0	0	0	0	3	0	0	0	188

Table 2. The confusion matrix shows the performance of prediction of the affective states we derived from participants using postures only. The numbers indicate the frequency of the different detected affective states.

factoring two other openness levels (i.e. open and closed). For example, stern (when openness is closed) has the same representation of levels of emotion as calm (when openness is neutral).

Association rules mining in a naturalistic and ubiquitous computing context

The procedure of this study consisted of pairs of users engaging in a series of unrehearsed, minimally structured conversations that invoked emotions, both negative and positive. Eighteen participants were recruited within our research facility and subdivided in nine pairs. All participants participated out of free will, were in good health and were informed on the goals and procedure of the tests, as well as on the data being captured. The participants included 8 postgraduate students and 10 researchers, all of who had worked together in projects. Participants were paired in a fashion that maximized the frequency of daily interaction within each pair. In each pair, one participant was monitored (physiological measurement and posture tracking). Nine participants were monitored (six male and three female, ages ranged from 25 to 39). Before each trial, we explained to the participants that there would be two conversational sessions with a brief intermission. Both participants were encouraged to maneuver freely and express themselves physically with no restrictions on bodily movements or postures. Each conversational session took 15 minutes. The participants were debriefed at the end of the experiment and informed on the details of the experiment. We collected over 9 hours of video recordings for synchronizing the results from both the physiological measuring equipment and stereoscopic camera system. This resulted in over 3600 samples where postures were identified with the corresponding physiological measurements captured during that posture.

RESULTS AND ANALYSIS

From the association rules mining process, we extracted a set of association rules using rule-induction. The association rules mining process is illustrated by the dotted lines in Figure 1. The body postures were first synthesized with expressions of emotions in the time-based synchronization. Of the 3606 samples collected from our experiment, only 2974 instances were able to be validated for the completeness of data. The resulting affective states were then used to facilitate a response directly from the posture input. Next, we implemented a first-order unsupervised learning technique, which employs the Tertius and Predictive Apriori algorithms in the open source WEKA machine learning software package [16]. The result of the association rules is as shown in Table 1.

A standard 10-fold cross-validation approach was used for testing. We used the J48 implementation of the C4.5 decision tree [27] to construct a pruned decision tree based on the data from our experiment. Our pruned tree consists of 50 nodes and 45 leaves. The decision tree outputs a set of temporal decision rules, which we used to supplement our classification of affective states. We then generated a hierarchy of general to specific categories that is useful for inferring the affective states from postures. Table 2 presents the confusion matrix of the decision tree, which shows the results of the fuzzy logic-based affective state classification and the results inferred from the mASqUE system. The match instance rate is 98.32%. As can be seen in Table 2, mASqUE returns similar results as using the fuzzy logic-based affective state classifier. It is interesting to see, that e.g. for "excitement" similar affective states were inferred such as "calm" or "overjoy". Note that there is no generally accepted baseline for comparing system that detects affective states. We showed that our system can reproduce the same results as using physiological measurements for each openness levels.

MASQUE EVALUATION

We conducted a user evaluation to determine the performance of mASqUE, involving 10 participants (3 female, 7 male); aged are between 23 and 31. The participants are a mix of 5 undergraduate students, 2 graduate students, and 3 research staff members. The participants were asked to evaluate mASqUE for 30 minutes by acting out the postures in a simulated conversation with a research assistant. The purpose was for the participants to provide their postures as input to the mASqUE system and observe the inferred affective states. After the evaluation we conducted a semi-structured interview.

The quantitative responses of the users about their affective states from the semi-structured interviews were averaged. The means are presented in Figure 4 (bottom). We performed comparisons using ANOVA on the affective states inferred from mASqUE. Comparing the frequency of occurrence with the Likert scale ratings of the users (comparing top with bottom results in Figure 4), we found the results to be consistent for seven affective states (overjoy, excitement, content, boredom, frustration, disgust, anger); however, we found out that accepting, calm, and stern are being significantly different ($p < .05$) from the seven affective states mentioned above, $F(1,20) = 6.163$, $p = .006$.

The consolidated qualitative responses from the interviews show that the appropriate mapping of postures to the intended affective states can be clearly inferred based on the association rules (which in our case map the affective states from a limited combination of postures as shown in Table 1). Our result is very much in line with the notion that emotion spaces are multi-dimensional and can reliably distinguish basic emotions. Although the emotions that we have represented in Figure 3 occupy distinct points in the arousal-valence emotion space, this is still not an exhaustive description. For a more definitive model for mapping postures to affective states, we posit that a comprehensive study on body postures in different social domains will be needed to obtain a set of more generalized, reliable association rules. Regarding the performance of mASqUE, three participants were skeptical and considered the selection of the ten emotions in Table 1 as still too narrow. The other seven participants expressed general satisfaction with the degree of correctness for characterizing the multi-facet emotions in their overall user experience. One of these seven participants made the following comments "Personally, I do not have a (mental) set of postures for specific emotion. Knowing the affective states that I am having, will allow me to discriminate my self-expression." Another participant stated: "The extensive range of emotions allows me to try out different possibilities of body movement and understanding their impact on my perceived emotion".

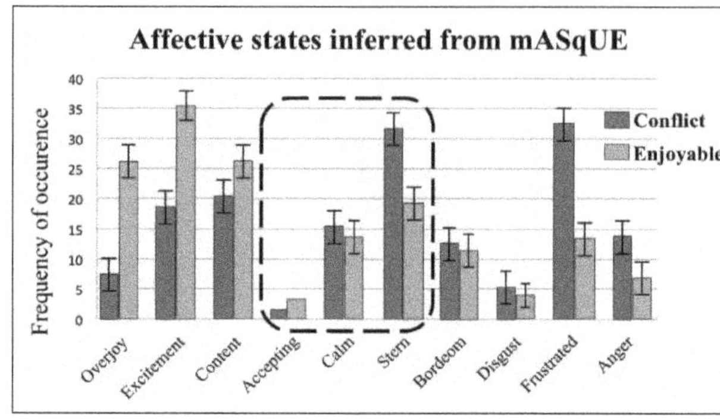

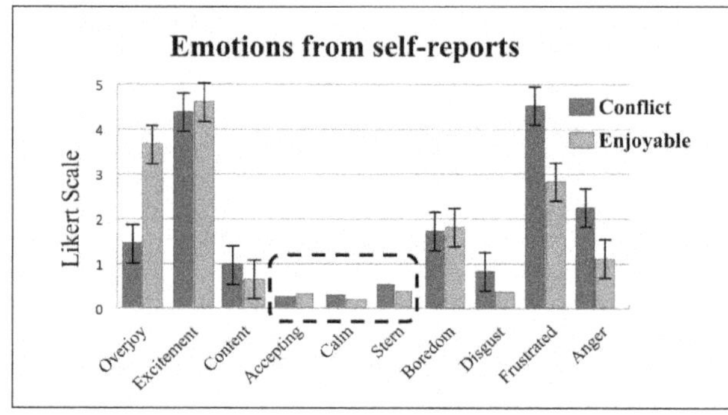

Figure 4. Mean values of affective states inferred from mASqUE (top) and emotions from self-reporting (bottom). The error bar show one standard deviation across the 9 monitored participants. (Bottom) Error bar for Accepting, Calm and Stern are not displayed. Their error rates are 0.03, 0.03, 0.01 and 0.15, 0.03, 0.01 respectively for conflict- and enjoyable oriented conversations. Notice that the mean values are only significantly different for Accepting, Calm, and Stern comparing the mASqUE system to the self-reports as indicated with the dotted box.

DISCUSSION

An analysis of the user evaluation showed that mASqUE is suitable for deployment in ubiquitous computing environments as its rich, extensive range of emotion representations (i.e. affective states) is able to inform intelligent user interfaces about the user's emotion. This is especially important for evaluating user experience in ubiquitous computing environments because the spontaneous affective response of the user can be determined during the process of interaction in real-time, not the outcome of verbal conversation. We have shown that our system can reproduce the same results as using physiological measurements for each openness level.

Besides that, the following two subsections also discuss the potential impacts of affective states detection in ubiquitous computing environments within the area of IUI.

Benefits of extending the emotion space

By adding the openness categorization to complement the arousal-valence emotion space, we are able to extend the arousal-valence emotion space from five basic affective states to ten affective states. We notice in our study that the complexity in making choices increases when allowing participants to choose from the ten emotional categories for qualitative evaluation in their self-report. We can refer to [33] for the explanation that people tend to simplify their decision-making processes using some form of heuristics, which in turn introduces judgmental errors and makes the assessment of own behaviors erroneous. This underlies an important role that body posture has for informing the IUI with five more affective states using the openness categorization.

Our system takes a global approach for emotion scaling, so a user's affective state is given as a percentage of the maximum value (i.e. Excitement). As seen in Figure 4, frustration and anger are significantly lower as measured by the frequency count for affective states compared to overjoy and excitement, which are only moderately lower. Although self-reporting from post evaluation interview had deviated from our mASqUE system, we can use the subjective self-reports to provide an explanation for our observation. Subjects taking part in the experiments were feeling excited in general with our expectation of certain exotic and novel experiences during the experiment. Although a user may be angry, and may rate anger as fairly high on a 5-point scale, this rating will be relatively low compared to the feeling of overjoy throughout the experiment.

Enriching the affective evaluation

In addition, mASqUE is able to characterize valuable information about affective states that cannot be extracted from the subjective self-reporting approach. In other words, mASqUE is able to detect affective states that are negligibly rated by the self-report. As shown in Figure 4, mASqUE shows a significantly higher distribution of accepting, calm and stern, whereas in self-reporting these emotions are negligibly rated.

From a biological perspective, these three emotions (accepting, calm and stern), which we describe with calm descriptions in the emotion representation (Figure 3), result in a delay of emotional response as they take a longer time to process cognitively. These emotions could be overtaken by other emotions with shorter response time (e.g. anger, frustration, excitement, and overjoy), which are linked to the biological emotion stimuli. However, it is important to detect these calm-related emotions as they have a positive and beneficial effect on a variety of decision-making processes [17].

Future research is necessary to be carried out in order to define how powerful the influence of a posture in the recognition of an emotion actually is in ubiquitous computing environments. An application of mASqUE, is Bro-Cam [32]. With Bro-Cam we explored the possibility to provide empathic feedback for videogame players. The body posture of a player at the end of a game round was mapped (this mapping was simply done using a MT survey) to humoristic statement to improve the players game experience. Results from a user study [32] also validate the positive effects that this empathic feedback (with a very simple mapping) had on the player's game experience. To underline the potential of mASqUE we describe two scenarios where our system can exploit its full potential in the area of IUI in the following section.

INTERACTION SCENARIOS

With this work we provide additional information to the users that need to communicate with each other. Especially when users collaborate over a distance, the information we get from each other's body language can get lost. For tasks that require a tight collaboration between users, being aware of each other's affective state can make a huge difference. Even when co-located, users might not be familiar with each other and thus have difficulties in recognizing each other's affective states. In this section we illustrate how our approach can improve collaborations by means of two example scenarios that apply mASqUE for improving collaboration. The first example covers the support for information-sensitive conversations, while the second provides an example for intense remote collaboration.

1) During information-sensitive conversations, such as during doctor-patient conversations, ensuring sufficient empathy makes a huge difference. Trained professionals can do this during co-located conversations, but when doing them remotely using e.g. video conferencing, this is often problematic. mASqUE provides clues on the affective states and openness of conversation partners thus are able to guide a doctor when and how to reveal sensitive information and follow-up on the effects of her message. mASqUE tells us, besides the basic affective states, when someone is open for new information and ideas. During a video conferencing session, mASqUE presents to the doctor its readings using a straight-forward interface: it tells the doctor what the most dominant emotion is being deduced and what the level of openness is presented as a number ranging from 1 (not approachable) to 7 (very approachable). The doctor can subsequently steer a conversation in such a way the patient will be most comfortable in receiving new information.

2) Similar to the previous example, when people collaborate during intense tasks, mASqUE helps to make this collaboration more efficient and reliable. When a lab technician has to perform a critical task for example in a nuclear lab and is being guided by an expert remotely (since experts are sparse in this area), providing the most complete

view of the lab technician will make guidance fit better to the personal needs and individual state of mind. In this case mASqUE will notify the expert when the lab technician will be insecure or anxious when performing a certain activity. This will ensure that the expert pays extra attention at those stages since these require more help. In the opposite case, mASqUE can reveal when the lab technician becomes too relaxed and can intervene (anticipate) on activities that require the full attention of the lab technician.

These two short examples described above present possible application domains with the field of IUI for which we envision mASqUE to play a crucial role. The subtle information emitted by our body language can be used by mASqUE to determine affective states in various Ubicomp environments.

CONCLUSION

With mASqUE we demonstrated a new way to infer affective states from body postures in a ubiquitous computing environment. Using an unobtrusive technique, such as posture tracking with a depth camera, mASqUE opens up a huge design space for further IUI applications. By freeing the users from the desktop, having the system "always on" and with no user instrumentation we overcome the main limitations as described in the introduction. As also described later, one can imagine various scenarios, such as remote lab training, human-to-human conversations, point-of-sales interactions, or games, where this system is applicable. By adding vision-based posture recognition, we enable a new affective categorization (i.e. openness) to determine the degree of user's behavioral closeness to another person or object in the interpersonal space. Our fuzzy logic-based affective state classifier for combining both physiological-based arousal-valence and vision-based openness values is able to scale beyond the limited range of basic emotions. The analysis also shows mASqUE is able to detect affective states (accepting, calm, and stern) – with positive and beneficial effect on decision-making processes – that are negligibly rated in the subjective self-reports. mASqUE opens up new possibilities for informing IUI about the affective states of users from their body postures in a nonintrusive way.

ACKNOWLEDGMENTS

We would like to thank Mieke Haesen for her valuable feedback and comments on this paper.

REFERENCES

1. Abowd, G.D. What next, ubicomp? celebrating an intellectual disappearing act. In *Proc. Ubicomp 2012*, ACM Press (2012), 31-40.
2. Abraham, A. Rule Based Expert Systems. In *Handbook for Measurement Systems Design*, Sydenham, P. and Thorn, R. (Eds.), John Wiley and Sons, London, UK, 2005, 920-931.
3. Argyle, M. *Bodily Communication*, Taylor and Francis, Abington, UK, 1988.
4. Ball, G. and Breese, J. Relating Personality and Behavior: Posture and Gestures, *Affective Interactions*, Paiva A.M (Ed.), LNAI 1814 (2000), 196-204.
5. Bolls, P.D., Lang, A. and Potter, R.F. The Effects of Message Valence and Listener Arousal on Attention, Memory, and Facial Muscular Responses to Radio Advertisements. *Communication Research* 28, 5 (2001), 627-651.
6. Breazeal, C. and Scassellati, B. A Context-Dependent Attention System for a Social Robot. In *Proc. IJCAI 1999*, Morgan Kaufmann Publishers (1999), 1146-1153.
7. Burgoon, J.K., Buller, D.B., Hale, J.L. and de Turck, M.A. Relational messages associated with nonverbal behaviors. *Human Communication Research* 10, 3 (1984), 351-378.
8. Clore, G.L., Wiggins, N.H. and Itkin, S. Gain and loss in attraction: Attributions from nonverbal behavior. *Journal of Personality and Social Psychology* 31, 4 (1975), 706-713.
9. Comaniciu, D., Ramesh, V. and Meer, P. Kernel-Based Object Tracking. *IEEE Trans. Pattern Anal. Mach. Intell.* 25, 5 (2003), 564-575.
10. Csikszentmihalyi, M. *Flow: The Psychology of Optimal Experience*, Harper Perennial, New York, USA, 1991.
11. Davidson, J. and Ekman, P. *The Nature of Emotion: Fundamental Questions*, Oxford University Press, New York, USA, 1994.
12. Dey, A.K. Understanding and Using Context. *Personal Ubiquitous Comput.* 5, 1 (2001), 4-7.
13. Fujiyoshi, H. and Lipton, A.J. Real-time Human Motion Analysis by Image Skeletonization, In *Proc. WACV'98*, IEEE Computer Society (1998), 15-21.
14. Gilroy, S.W., Cavazza, M.O. and Vervondel, V. Evaluating multimodal affective fusion using physiological signals. In *Proc. IUI 2011*, ACM Press (2011), 53-62.
15. Gunes, H., Schuller, B., Pantic, M. and Cowie, R., Emotion Representation, Analysis and Synthesis in Continuous Space: A Survey. In Proc. FG'11, Workshop on EmoSPACE 2011, 827-834.
16. Hall, M., Frank, E., Holmes, G., Pfahringer, B., Reutemann, P. and Witten, I.H. The WEKA data mining software: an update. *SIGKDD Explor. Newsl.* 11, 1 (2009), 10-18.
17. Isen, A.M. Positive Affect and Decision Making. Lewis, M. and Haviland-Jones, J.M. (Eds.) *Handbook of Emotions*, New York, USA, 2000.
18. Kapoor, A., Burleson, W. and Picard, R.W. Automatic prediction of frustration. *Int. J. Hum.-Comput. Stud.* 65, 8 (2008), 724-736.

19. Kleinsmith, A. and Bianchi-Berthouze, N. Recognizing Affective Dimensions from Body Posture. In *Proc. ACII 2007*, Springer-Verlag (2007), 48-58.
20. Lance, B. and Marsella, S.C. Emotionally Expressive Head and Body Movement During Gaze Shifts. In *Proc. IVA 2007*, Springer-Verlag (2007), 72-85.
21. Legaspi, R., Fukui, K., Moriyama, K., Kurihara, S., Numao, M. and Suarez, M. Addressing the problems of data-centric physiology-affect relations modeling. In *Proc. IUI 2010*, ACM Press (2010), 21-30.
22. Mandryk, R.L. and Atkins, S. A fuzzy physiological approach for continuously modeling emotion during interaction with play technologies. *Int. J. Hum.-Comput. Stud.* 65, 4 (2007), 329-347.
23. McDuff, D., Karlson, A., Kapoor, A., Roseway, A. and Czerwinski, M. AffectAura: an intelligent system for emotional memory. In Proc. CHI 2012, ACM Press (2012), 849-858.
24. Mehrabian, A. Pleasure-arousal-dominance: A general framework for describing and measuring individual differences in Temperament. *Current Psychology* 14, 4 (1996), 261-292.
25. Petty, R.E. and Cacioppo, J.T. *Attitudes and persuasion: Classic and contemporary approaches*, Westview Press, Colorado, USA, 1996.
26. Picard, R.W. *Affective Computing*. The MIT Press, Cambridge, Massachusetts, 1997, Ch. 5,6,and 7.
27. Quinlan, J.R. *C4.5: programs for machine learning*. Morgan Kaufmann Publishers Inc., California, USA, 1993.
28. Rogers, Y. The Changing Face of Human-Computer Interaction in the Age of Ubiquitous Computing. *Usability for e-Inclusion*, LNCS 5889 (2009), 1-19.
29. Russell, J.A., Weiss, A. and Mendelsohn, G.A. Affect Grid: A single-item scale of pleasure and arousal. *Journal of Personality and Social Psychology* 57, 3 (1989), 493-502.
30. Scheflen, A.E. and Scheflen, A. *Body Language and the Social Order: Communication As Behavioral Control*. Prentice-Hall, New Jersey, USA, 1972.
31. Scherer, K.R., Wallbott, H.G. and Summerfield, A.B. *Experiencing Emotion: A Cross-Cultural Study*, Cambridge University Press, New York, USA, 1986.
32. Tan, S., Schöning, J., Schneider Barnes, J., Luyten K. and Coninx, K. *Bro-cam: Improving game experience with empathic feedback using posture tracking.* In Proc. of the 8th International Conference on Persuasive Technology, (2013)
33. Timmermans, D. The impact of task complexity on information use in multi-attribute decision making. *Journ. Behavioral Decision Making* 6, 2 (1993), 95-111.
34. Wagner, J., Andre, E., Lingenfelser, F. and Kim, J. Exploring Fusion Methods for Multimodal Emotion Recognition with Missing Data. *IEEE Trans. Affect. Comput.* 2, 4 (2011), 206-218.
35. Weiser, M. The computer for the 21st century. *Scientific American*, 1991, 94-104.
36. Aviezer, H., Trope, Y., and Todorov, A. Body cues, not facial expressions, discriminate between intense positive and negative emotions. Science 338, 6111 (2012), 1225–1229.

Indexing Cognitive Workload Based on Pupillary Response under Luminance and Emotional Changes

Weihong Wang*
National ICT Australia
University of New South Wales
weihong.wang@nicta.com.au

Zhidong Li*
National ICT Australia
University of New South Wales
zhidong.li@nicta.com.au

Yang Wang
National ICT Australia
University of New South Wales
yang.wang@nicta.com.au

Fang Chen
National ICT Australia
University of New South Wales
fang.chen@nicta.com.au

ABSTRACT
Pupillary response is a popular physiological index of cognitive workload that can be used for design and evaluation of adaptive interface in various areas of human-computer interaction (HCI) research. However, in practice various confounding factors unrelated to workload, including changes of luminance condition and emotional arousal might degrade pupillary response based workload measures such as commonly used mean pupil diameter. This work investigates pupillary response as a cognitive workload measure under the influence of such confounding factors. Video-based eye tracker is used to record pupillary response during arithmetic tasks under luminance and emotional changes. Machine learning based feature selection and classification techniques are proposed to robustly index cognitive workload based on pupillary response even with the influence of noisy factors unrelated to workload.

Author Keywords
Cognitive workload; feature extraction; machine learning; pupillary response

ACM Classification Keywords
H.5.2 Information Interfaces and Presentation: User interfaces - Evaluation/methodology

General Terms
Human Factors; algorithms; experimentation

*First authors

INTRODUCTION
In recent years, cognitive workload evaluation has become an important topic in various areas of human-computer interaction (HCI) research, such as adaptive automation and training, air traffic control, gaming, and in-car safety [3]. Traditionally computer systems are built with an assumption that users can adapt to the human computer interfaces. As a result, users need instruction, training, and practice to develop skills to interact with the interfaces, which sometimes can be very inefficient. Cognitive workload evaluation provides a promising and enduring approach to build adaptive interaction systems, which is able to adapt to users' behavior and their ability to attend, learn, and perform different tasks. Specifically, with the assistance of cognitive workload evaluation, such adaptive interface is able to be aware of users' current mental status and change its manner of presentation and interaction with the users, so that the user experience can be improved substantially. Cognitive workload measures can also be used to evaluate the efficacy of HCI systems.

Cognitive workload can be estimated through subjective rating, task performance, and physiological response. Especially, physiological response based measure is a viable and attractive approach to assess cognitive workload for HCI research. The extensive range of physiological measures, which are involuntary and sensitive to workload variations, includes brain wave, eye activity, heart rate, respiration, skin conductance etc. Among these techniques, eye activity are relatively suitable for HCI research, as it provide physiological indexes of cognitive state in a convenient and real-time manner.

Pupillary response is one type of eye activity based workload measure and it has attracted increasing attention with the appearance of video-based eye tracker in recent years [27]. There are abundant literatures on the correlation between pupillary response and cognitive workload in the last two decades. Pupillary response has been widely applied as an effective indicator of cognitive workload in various cognitive tasks including arithemtic task, driving task, memory task, visual search task, etc. In recent studies [11, 19, 4], pupillary response was measured through video-based eye tracking and different pupillometric measures (features) were extracted and analysed. Although there is little doubt that pupillary response is a useful measure of variations in mental workload, pupillary response is also found to be sensitive to confounding (or noisy) factors unrelated to cognitive tasks, such as changes of illumination and emotional states [15, 26, 29]. Thus in practice comprehensive treatments need to be taken to deal with such factors when using pupillary response as a workload index.

To help understand and evaluate the effectiveness of pupillary response based workload measures, Galvanic skin conductance (GSR) is also employed under the noisy factors in the second experiment of this study. GSR is another type of physiological measure involving workload effects. The GSR data reflects the activities of sweat glands, which can be used to identify the cognitive workload during various tasks [16, 17]. Like pupillary response, GSR data can also be continuously recorded at high frequency rate [18], so that subtle changes can be easily captured during tasks. In recent years, GSR has also been investigated for the measurement of mental status involving cognitive workload or other factors such as stress. [25] evaluated the correlation between GSR data and cognitive workload in multimodal user interface. In addition, GSR based morphological features including amplitude, recovery time and latency have been employed for stress measurement during cognitive processes [24, 14]. It was reported that GSR could be affected by emotion arousal as well. In Bradley et al.'s experiment, comparing to when participants viewed neutral pictures, skin conductance became larger when they viewed unpleasant or pleasant pictures [2].

This study takes an initial step to analyse the problem of robustly evaluating cognitive workload based on physiological response data under complex environments (e.g. changes of luminance condition and emotional arousal). Our contributions are three-fold: 1) Study pupillary response as a cognitive workload measure under luminance and emotional changes. 2) Propose an adaptive workload measure (based on Haar-like feature) to effectively describe the dynamic characteristics of physiological response even under the effect of noisy factors. 3) Apply machine learning algorithm (Boosting algorithm) to automatically classify cognitive workload. We also comparatively study the effectiveness of workload classification using pupillary response or GSR data individually, as well as the fusion of both physiological data.

In the following sections, Section 2 introduces the related work of cognitive workload measurement based on pupillary response. Section 3 analyses pupillary response data from an experiment of arithmetic tasks with luminance changes. Section 4 analyses pupillary response from another experiment of arithmetic tasks with changes of both luminance condition and emotional arousal. Section 5 presents the machine learning algorithm used for feature selection and workload classification. The proposed techniques are concluded in Section 6.

RELATED WORK

Previous studies have shown that pupillary response provides a sensitive and reliable measure for cognitive workload under constrained luminance condition. To study task-evoked pupillary responses, [1, 10] conducted experiments consisting of various tasks such as language processing, reasoning, searching, and perception. Pupil dilation was found to be a reliable indicator of processing load during the tasks. It has been demonstrated in [9] that a whole task can be divided into different types of subtasks and the workload changes during task execution. [11] found subtle changes of pupil size induced by cognitive workload variations could be detected by remote video eye tracker. In their experiment, the eye tracker provided effective pupillometric measurement of cognitive workload.

Pupil size could also be affected by changes of luminance condition in the visual field during cognitive tasks [12, 6]. Empirical studies showed that luminance condition has greater influence on pupil dilation comparing with cognitive workload. [12] reported that larger changes in the pupil diameter occur in response to illumination changes than those to information processing. [21] investigated the effects and the interaction of cognitive workload and luminance changes in a gaze-controlled human-computer interaction task. There were three difficulty levels and two levels of background brightness (black and white) in the task. The experimental result showed that pupil size was significantly influenced by the factor of task difficulty and the factor of background brightness and there was no interaction between the two factors.

[15] proposed the index of cognitive activity (ICA) method to detect cognitive workload under different luminance (dark and bright) conditions. The pupillary response was decomposed by wavelet transformation into detailed signals and de-noised signals. Then the high oscillation part in the de-noised signal was used to determine the existence of workloads. Experimental results demonstrated that ICA was effective to detect cognitive workload. It is worth noting that in their work a single noisy factor (luminance changes) is considered when evaluating cognitive workload, while this study is trying to classify cognitive workload under the influence of multiple factors (luminance and emotional changes).

[28] proposed a fine-grained feature extraction method for cognitive workload measurement to deal with luminance changes in pupillary response data. In their work, the whole task period was divided into several intervals corresponding to different stages of the cognitive task. For each interval, normalized average pupil diameter was employed for workload measurement. It has been noted that the feature extraction strategy depends on the setting of the specific task, so it can be difficult to apply the technique to other applications involving dissimilar task types.

Another common element influencing the pupillary response is emotional arousal. Stanners et al. examined two psychological interpretation of pupillary response, namely emotional arousal and cognitive workload and found that cognitive workload took priority over emotional factor in affecting pupillary response [26]. [2] conducted a picture viewing experiment which utilized a set of selected pictures from the International Affective Picture System (IAPS) [13]. They found that under controlled luminance condition, pupillary changes became larger when participants viewed emotionally arous-

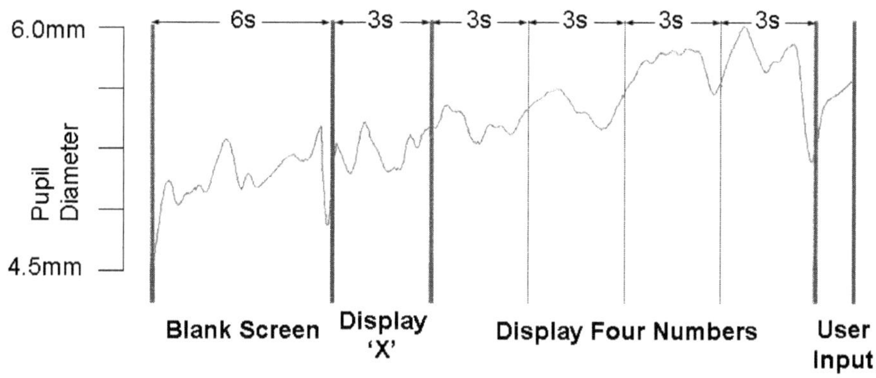

Figure 1. Time setting of an arithmetic task.

ing pictures, regardless of whether these pictures were pleasant or unpleasant. [20] examined pupil size variation during and after auditory emotional stimulation. The experimental results showed that compared with the process with neutral stimuli, the pupil size was significantly larger in the process with emotionally positive or negative stimuli.

EXPERIMENT 1

Participants and Apparatus

Thirteen 24-to-46-year-old male subjects are invited to participate the experiment. Subjects all have normal or corrected-to-normal vision. Each subject is rewarded with a small-value gift for his participation.

We use a remote eye tracker (faceLAB 4.5 of Seeing Machines Ltd) to record the pupillary response data of each subject. The remote eye tracker continuously measures the subjects' pupil diameters at a sampling rate of $50Hz$. Visual tasks are displayed on a 21-inch monitor with a screen resolution of 1024 by 768 pixels.

Experiment Design

Each subject is seated in office environment and performs arithmetic tasks under different luminance conditions on the monitor screen. The arithmetic tasks are designed to have four difficulty levels, and there are four levels of background brightness, resulting in 16 different task types in total.

In each arithmetic task, four different numbers are displayed sequentially on the center of the screen and each number is displayed for three seconds. Each subject is asked to sum up the numbers and then choose the correct answer on the screen through mouse click. There is no time limit for the subject to choose an answer. The difficulty level of the task is determined by the range of the numbers. In the first (lowest) difficulty level, numbers range from 0 to 1 (binary number); in the second difficulty level, numbers range from 1 to 9 (1-digit number); in the third difficulty level, numbers range from 10 to 99 (2-digit number); in the fourth (highest) difficulty level, numbers range from 100 to 999 (3-digit number). At the beginning of each task, a blank screen with the same brightness level as the rest of the task is shown for 6 seconds. Then before the first number appears, different number of letter "X" are displayed at the center of the screen for 3 seconds. The number of "X" indicates the number of digits in the arithmetic task. Figure 1 depicts the setting for each arithmetic task.

In order to produce noisy luminance change signals in the pupillary response data, different levels of background luminance is shown on the screen. This is done by setting grayscale values for the four levels of background brightness (L1, L2, L3, and L4) as 32, 96, 160 and 224, respectively. Before each arithmetic task, a blank background is displayed for 6 seconds.

Procedure

Each subject has a practice before the experiment (data of the practice is not recorded). The experiment starts with one-minute's rest period with black background displayed on the screen. There are two tasks for each trial type, so each subject performs 32 arithmetic tasks in total. The tasks are randomly presented during the experiment. The experiment lasts about 22 minutes for each subject.

Subjective Rating and Response Time

To validate the overall effectiveness of cognitive workload experiment design, an ANOVA test is applied on the subjective rating scores and response time for the four levels of task difficulty. The subjective rating scores are obtained from the subjects after the experiment. The scores range from 1 to 9 (1 is the easiest and 9 is the hardest). Figure 2 shows the average subjective rating scores from all the subjects. It can

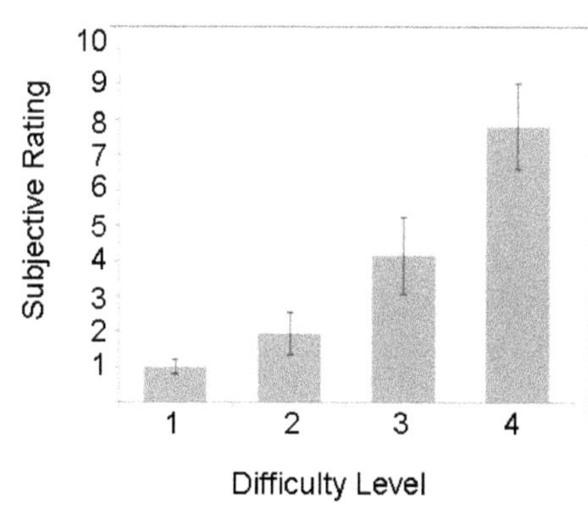

Figure 2. Subjective rating of task difficulty.

be seen that there exists significant difference among the subjective rating of different task difficulty levels ($F = 108.63$, $p < 0.05$ in ANOVA test). Response time (user input) of subjects in arithmetic tasks are also extracted and analysed. Figure 3 shows the average response time of different task difficulty levels. It is clear that higher difficulty level corresponds to larger response time ($F = 62.59$, $p < 0.05$ in ANOVA test). The analysis on subject rating and response time indicates the effectiveness of task difficulty setting.

Workload Measurement

In this section we study pupillary response based workload measurement under changes of luminance condition.

Pupillary response during eye blinks is ignored in the data preprocessing. Firstly, a coarse-grained analysis is performed to examine how background brightness and cognitive workload affect the pupillary response. The average pupil diameter is used to describe the pupillary response during the tasks. Figure 4 demonstrates the average pupil diameters under different task difficulty levels and background brightness conditions. Under the same difficulty level, we can see that the pupil diameter decrease with the increase of the brightness level, and under the same brightness level, the pupil diameter has an upward trend with the rise of the difficulty level. Such observation indicates that pupil diameter is influenced by both background brightness and cognitive workload. However the figure also reveals that luminance condition is a superior factor over cognitive demand in pupil diameter changes, as the pupil diameter corresponding to the highest task difficulty under the highest background brightness is smaller than that corresponding to the lowest task difficulty under the lowest background brightness. ANOVA tests applied on the average pupil diameters under background brightness conditions and difficulty levels agree with the above observations. Statistical significance is obtained in the ANOVA tests for the four background brightness conditions ($F = 7.19$, $p < 0.05$), while statistical significance is not found in the ANOVA test for the four task difficulty levels ($F = 1.3, p = 0.2839$). The above analysis indicates that the average pupil diameter is too coarse a measure to effectively assess cognitive workload with the influence of noisy factors such as luminance change. To solve this problem, we require a workload measure to both characterize cognitive workload and adapt to changes caused by the

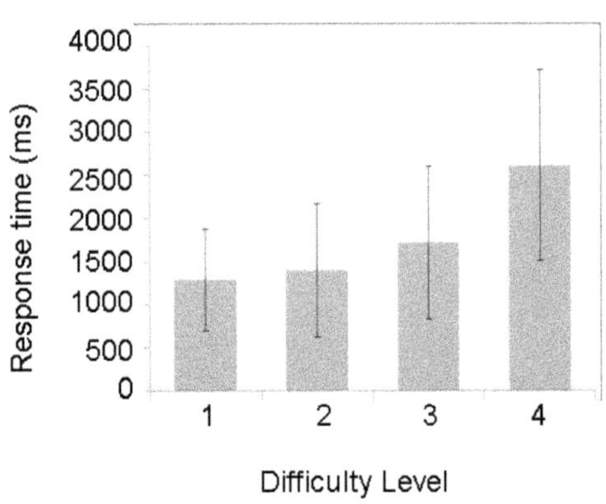

Figure 3. Response time.

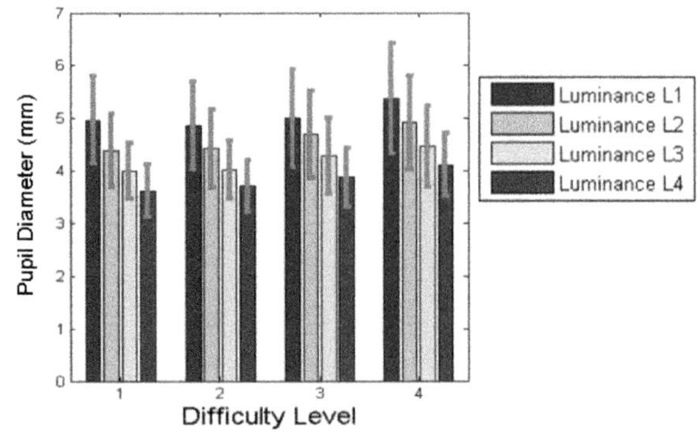

Figure 4. Pupil diameter under different task difficulty levels and background brightness conditions.

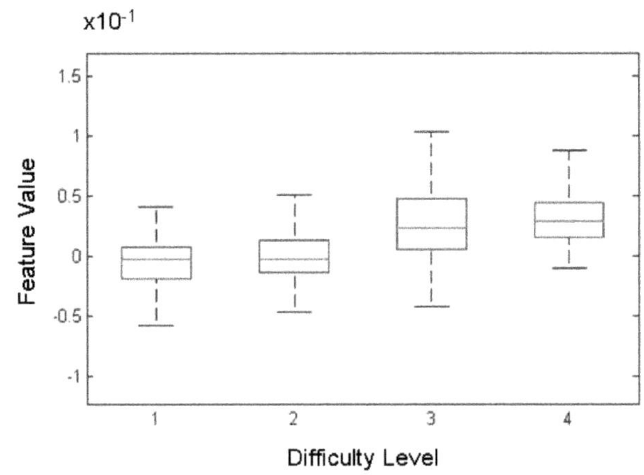

Figure 5. Box plot of pupillary response based feature values (sample minimum, lower quartile, median, upper quartile, and maximum) corresponding to different task difficulty levels.

confounding factors. As discussed in previous work [9], a task can be divided into subtasks and workload changes during task execution, hence workload/pupillary response during a task could be viewed as a dynamic process. In this work we empirically propose a mean-difference feature, which divides each task period into two half intervals, to capture the dynamic change between the first half and the second half. The value of the mean-difference feature is computed as the difference between the average pupil diameter in the first half interval and that in the second half interval. To test its feasibility, distribution of the feature values extracted from different difficulty levels is shown in Figure 5. It can be clearly seen that even with the interference of background luminance changes,

Table 1. ANOVA tests for each pair of task difficulties based on pupillary response data.

Difficulty level	2	3	4
1	$F = 2.45$, $p = 0.13$	$F = 23.17$, $p < 0.05$	$F = 39.19$, $p < 0.05$
2		$F = 12.52$, $p < 0.05$	$F = 22.05$, $p < 0.05$
3			$F = 0.43$, $p = 0.52$

Figure 6. Experiment setup.

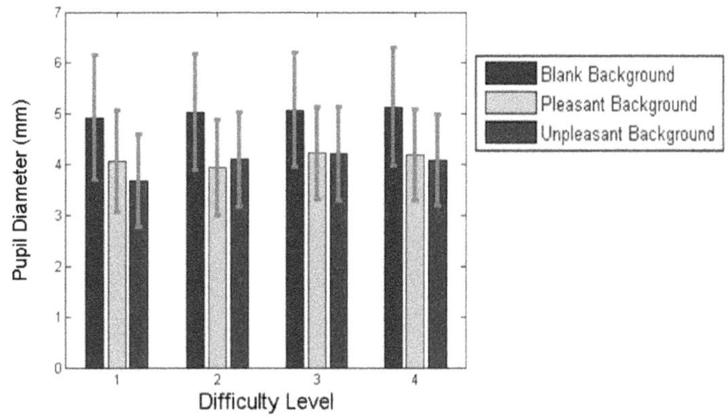

Figure 7. Pupil diameter under different task difficulty levels and background conditions.

the pupillary response based feature value rises as the task difficulty level goes up. In the corresponding ANOVA test, statistical significance ($F = 15.43$, $p < 0.05$) is obtained for the four task difficulty levels. ANOVA tests for each pair of difficulties are also performed and the results are in Table 1. In the corresponding two-way ANOVA test, statistical significance is obtained for the task difficulty levels ($F = 30.85$, $p < 0.05$) but not for the background brightness conditions ($F = 1.2$, $p = 0.3084$).

In conclusion, the proposed mean difference feature provides an effective measure for cognitive workload assessment even under the changes of luminance condition. Cognitive workload assessment under emotional arousal is investigated in the next experiment.

EXPERIMENT 2

Participants and Apparatus

In this experiment, twelve 24-to-35-year-old male participants perform arithmetic tasks under the changes of luminance condition and emotional arousal.

We use the same remote eye tracker as in experiment 1 to record pupillary response data and use a GSR sensor (ProComp Infiniti of Thought Technology Ltd) to record skin conductance data. The experiment setup is demonstrated in Figure 6.

Experiment Design

The experiment is composed of three parts. In the first part, the arithmetic task is undergoing with blank background (black screen). In the second and third parts, the arithmetic task is undergoing with pleasant and unpleasant background images shown on the screen.

The design of each arithmetic task is similar to that in experiment 1. During each task, the subjects are asked to sum up 4 different numbers and then choose the correct answer through mouse click. At the beginning of a task, the same "X" displaying period appears for 3 seconds before the first number is displayed. The arithmetic tasks have the same four task difficulty levels as those in experiment 1. The difference between experiment 1 and experiment 2 comes from the setting of background condition. In the first part of experiment 2, blank background is displayed on the screen. In the second and the third parts, pleasant and unpleasant background images are displayed during the tasks. Eight pleasant images ($mean\ valence = 7.1, mean\ arousal = 5.7$) and eight unpleasant images ($mean\ valence = 2.8, mean\ arousal = 4.8$) are selected from the IAPS database. The average luminance (Y value) of the pleasant images is 57.7, and 57.8 for the unpleasant images.

Procedure

At the beginning and the end of the whole experiment, each subject has a one-minute rest with black screen. Eight arithmetic tasks are randomly given in each experiment part (two for each difficulty level). The experiment lasts about 15 minutes for each subject.

Workload Measurement

In this section we study pupillary response and GSR based workload measurement under changes of both luminance condition and emotion arousal.

The average pupil diameters under different task difficulty levels and background conditions are presented in Figure 7. It is shown that with the blank background, the pupil diameter increases when the task difficulty level rises. But this trend is not observed for the pupil diameters with the pleasant and unpleasant background images, as the pupillary response could be affected by the changes of both luminance condition and emotional arousal. It can be seen in the figure that the pupil diameter under the highest task difficulty with emotional background images is smaller than that under the lowest task difficulty with the blank background. The phenomenon is consistent with the observation of previous empirical research that luminance conditions prioritize over cognitive demands and emotional arousal in pupil diameter changes. Statistical significance is not obtained in the ANOVA test on the average pupil diameters for the pleasant and unpleasant background images ($F = 0.0002$, $p = 0.99$), nor for the four task difficulty levels ($F = 0.17$, $p = 0.91$).

The same mean-difference feature as that in experiment 1 is used to measure cognitive workload based on the pupillary

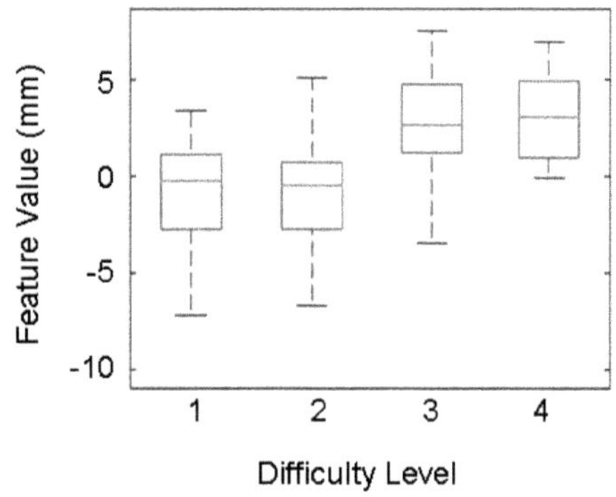

Figure 8. Box plot of pupillary response based feature values corresponding to different task difficulty levels.

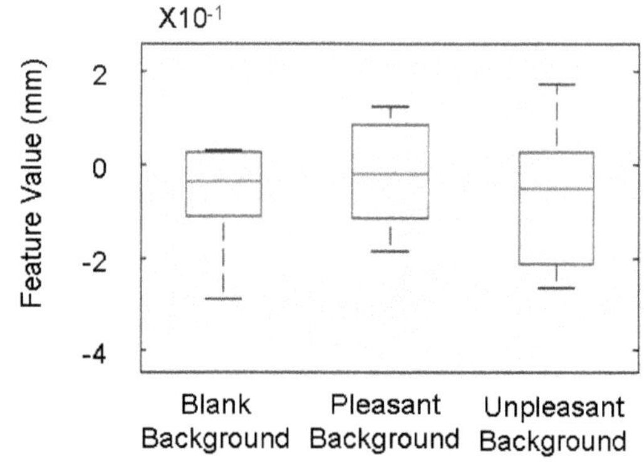

Figure 9. Box plot of pupillary response based feature values corresponding to different background conditions.

response data. The distribution of the feature values corresponding to different task difficulty levels is shown in Figure 8. It is shown that even with the change of background luminance and emotion arousal, the pupillary response based feature value increases as the task difficulty level increases, and statistical significance ($F = 3.59$, $p < 0.05$) is found in the corresponding ANOVA test. ANOVA tests for each pair of task difficulties are also performed and the results are in Table 2.

Figure 9 also shows the distribution of mean-difference feature values under different background conditions (blank, pleasant and unpleasant background images). The mean-difference feature does not exhibit significant difference under different conditions of emotional arousal ($F = 1.09$, $p = 0.35$ in the corresponding ANOVA test). In the corresponding two-way ANOVA test, statistical significance is obtained for the levels of task difficulty ($F = 6.1$, $p < 0.05$) but not for the conditions of emotional arousal ($F = 0.35$, $p = 0.7062$). The statistical results indicate that comparing with cognitive workload, the pupillary response based feature is less sensitive to emotional arousal in our experiment.

The skin response of each subject is also recorded during the experiment and the GSR based measurement of cognitive workload is investigated. The distribution of average GSR value during the task period under different task difficulty levels and background conditions is computed and it is found that the average GSR value cannot effectively distinguish different task difficulty levels ($F = 0.01$, $p = 0.99$ in corresponding ANOVA test). Similarly we use the mean-difference feature to characterize cognitive workload based

Table 2. ANOVA tests for each pair of task difficulties based on pupillary response data.

Difficulty level	2	3	4
1	$F = 5.45$, $p < 0.05$	$F = 0.45$, $p = 0.5$	$F = 16.3$, $p < 0.05$
2		$F = 10.36$, $p < 0.05$	$F = 16.56$, $p < 0.05$
3			$F = 0.87$, $p = 0.35$

on GSR data. The mean-difference feature does not exhibit statistical significance for the different task difficulty levels ($F = 1.83$, $p = 0.16$ in the corresponding ANOVA test;). Meanwhile the mean-difference feature demonstrates significant difference for the different conditions of emotional arousal ($F = 3.78$, $p < 0.05$ in the corresponding ANOVA test). In the two-way ANOVA test, the mean-difference feature exhibits statistical significance for the task difficulty levels ($F = 3.12$, $p < 0.05$), but not for emotional arousal conditions ($F = 2.58$, $p = 0.078$).

In conclusion, the proposed mean-difference feature, especially for pupillary response, provides an effective indicator for cognitive workload assessment even under the influence of emotional arousal. It is worth noting that the above ANOVA analysis is conducted at the group level. For fine-grained analysis at individual level, machine learning based techniques are proposed for workload classification in the next section.

WORKLOAD CLASSIFICATION

This section studies workload classification based on pupillary response and GSR data. The mean-difference feature used in previous sections is empirically derived through manual inspection of the experimental data. Such manual feature selection heavily relies on individual experience, so it cannot guarantee optimal features to be selected, which may impair the performance of cognitive workload classification. Manual feature selection is also ineffective when the number of available features becomes large.

In order to avoid such disadvantage, machine learning based feature selection and classification could be used to index cognitive workload. In this work, feature space is enriched by generating a large number of dynamic features which are denoted as Haar-like features [5]. Boosting algorithm [22, 7] is applied to automatically mine the most discriminative Haar-like features for cognitive workload classification. The proposed machine learning approach does not depend on specific task design and does not require baseline calibration, which is generally applicable to various cognitive processes. The detailed explanation of the solution is as follow.

Feature Selection and Workload Classification

Haar-like feature is related to Haar wavelet [5]. Haar wavelet is a step function taking values 1 and -1 on $[0, 0.5)$ and $[0.5, 1)$ respectively. The name "Haar-like feature" is from its intuitive similarity with Haar wavelets. The time period of a Haar-like feature is divided into halves and the value of the Haar-like feature is the difference of the average value of the first half against that of the second half. The application of Haar-like feature is inspired by the mean-difference feature described in previous sections. The mean-difference feature has been demonstrated as an effective measure for cognitive workload. For physiological signal over certain time period, the corresponding Haar-like feature could be viewed as a dynamic version of mean-difference feature. This motivates us to extend mean difference feature and propose Haar-like features to describe workload changes in different stages of the whole task. As a task can be divided into several subtasks/stages, each subtask/stage could be characterized by a Haar-like feature. A Haar-like feature is identified by its temporal size (the size of each half) and its centre location. We denote the temporal size as r, the centre location as t. By varying the temporal size and the centre location, a large number of Haar-like features can be generated, which represent dynamic characteristics of physiological signals in different scales over time. Figure 10 shows examples of Haar-like features obtained from pupillary response data.

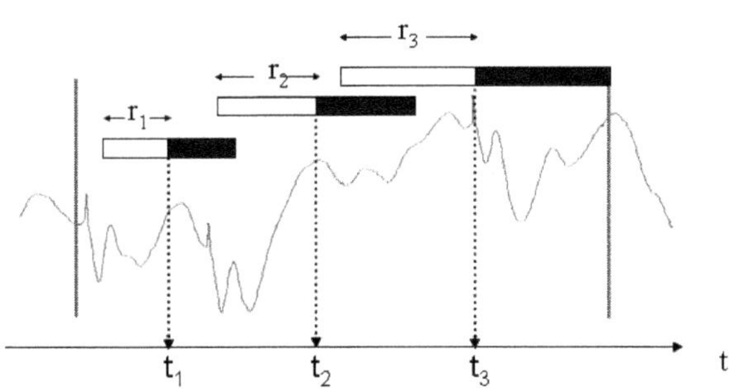

Figure 10. Examples of Haar-like features. r represents temporal size and t represent the centre location of a feature. Feature value is computed as the difference of average value of the white part and that of the dark part.

The large number of Haar-like features (more than $3,600$ features in this work) may contain a certain amount of redundancy and some features are sensitive to noisy factors such as luminance variation and emotion arousal. To simultaneously maximize the accuracy of workload classification and minimize the impact of noisy factors, machine learning technique is used for automatic feature selection and workload classification. The feature selection process is critical to obtain the subset of most useful features discriminating different workload levels and suppress non-relevant features. At the same time, the selected features are optimally combined to maximize the performance of workload classification. Boosting is one widely used machine learning algorithm suitable in this work. The detailed explanation of Boosting algorithm is in Appendix.

For our implementation, in the feature generation process, Haar-like features are generated from the pupillary response data and GSR data. The temporal size of features ranges from 0.1 second to 6 seconds and the centre location of features shifts over a task period with step size 0.1 second. With all the combination of different temporal sizes and centre locations, we generate about $3,600$ Haar-like features. Each Haar-like feature is combined with a weak classifier, so we have $3,600$ weak classifiers. Then the Boosting algorithm takes the training samples and the weak classifiers as input and selects the best weak classifiers (features) and constructs a final strong classifier. It is worth noting that the whole process of feature selection requires no human input or intervention. The trained strong classifier is then used on new subject data for cognitive workload classification. We use leave-one-out cross-validation (LOOCV) to estimate the classification accuracies. Specifically, we run the classifier training and testing the same number of times as the number of subjects. In each time, data of one subject is reserved for classifier testing and the data of the rest of subjects are used in the training. We obtain a testing accuracy each time. The final accuracy is the average accuracy of all the testing accuracies.

Experiments are conducted on pupillary response data to evaluate the performance of the Boosting algorithm with the proposed Haar-like feature. The experiment data is the same as in experiment 1 and experiment 2. We have performed both two-class classification (task difficulty level 1 and 2 versus task difficulty level 3 and 4) and four-class classification.

Results on Pupillary Response

ANOVA tests are performed on the selected features for Boosting based workload classification in experiment 1 and experiment 2 data respectively. Statistical significances ($F = 69, p < 0.05$ for experiment 1 data and $F = 12.68, p < 0.05$ for experiment 2 data) are obtained. Moreover, effect size for ANOVA computed on the selected features for two-class classification is 0.58, and 0.35 for four-class classification, which indicates the effectiveness of Haar-like feature based Boosting.

Table 3 is the accuracies (percentage of correct classification) of two-class and four-class classification based on pupillary response data from experiment 1 and experiment 2 respectively. Boosting can achieve about 80 per cent testing accuracy for two-class classification and about 45 per cent for four-class classification.

Table 3. Workload classification accuracies based on pupillary response data for experiment 1 and experiment 2.

	Two-class	Four-class
Experiment 1	79.3%	45.0%
Experiment 2	79.2%	43.2%

Figure 11 and Figure 12 demonstrate the distributions of selected Haar-like features in terms of feature temporal size r and centre location t respectively for four-class classification. We can see that the Boosting algorithm tend to select features with large temporal size and features located in the middle of task period, which indicates that those features are relatively discriminative for workload classification.

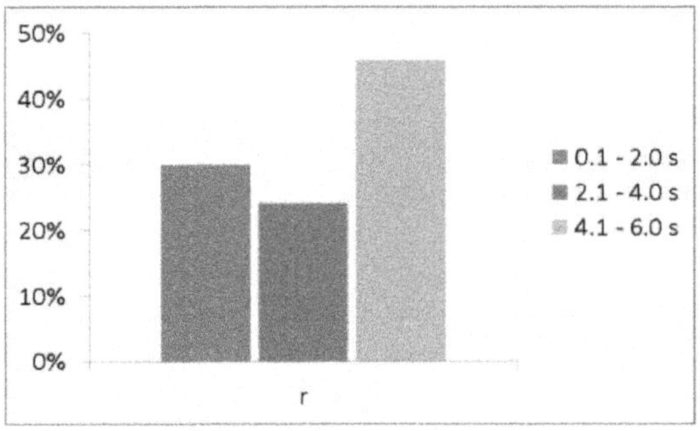

Figure 11. Distribution of feature size for Haar-like features used in workload classification based on pupillary response for four-class classification.

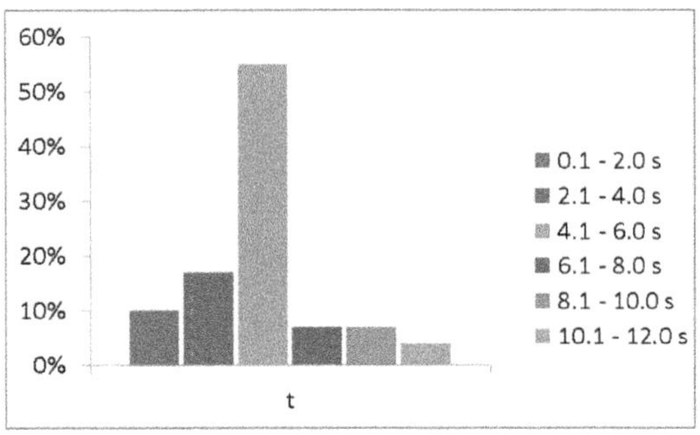

Figure 12. Distribution of feature centre for Haar-like features used in workload classification based on pupillary response for four-class classification.

Results on the Fusion of Pupillary Response and GSR Data

GSR data from experiment 2 is also tested by the Boosting algorithm with Haar-like features. The two-class and four-class classification accuracies are 67.3% and 36.9% respectively. We can see that neither two-class nor four-class classification accuracy is as good as those based on pupillary response, which indicates that pupillary response is more effective than GSR for workload classification. This observation is consistent with later experimental results based on the fusion of pupillary response and GSR data.

Table 4 shows accuracy of two-class and four-class classification for fusion of pupillary response data and GSR data from experiment 2. Data fusion could be naturally achieved by the Boosting algorithm. Haar-like features extracted from both pupillary response data and GSR data are put together for feature selection and workload classification during the classifier training process. The classification performance based on the fused data is slightly better than that based on the pupillary response data alone and much better than that based on the GSR data alone, as data fusion can provide richer feature space for classifier construction.

Table 4. Workload classification accuracy based on the fusion of pupillary response and GSR data for experiment 2.

	Two-class	Four-class
Accuracy	82.1%	45.8%

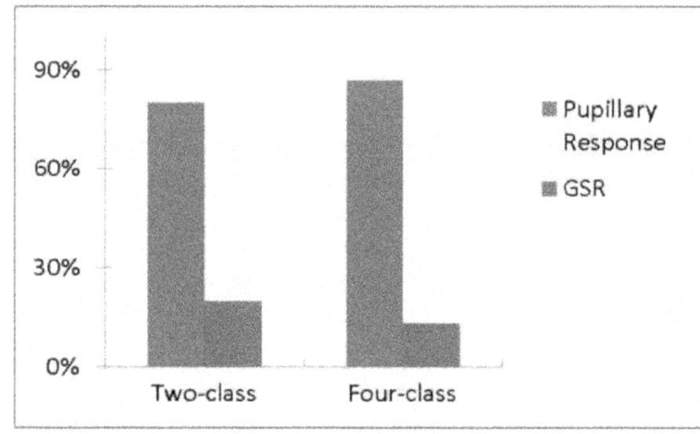

Figure 13. Proportions of pupillary response based features and GSR based features selected for workload classification.

In Figure 13, we also compare the proportion of pupillary response based features against that of GSR based features used by the two-class and four-class workload classifiers. We find that the features extracted from pupillary response data are dominant. This indicates again that pupillary response is more useful than GSR for cognitive workload classification in our experiment.

CONCLUSION

This work investigates cognitive workload indexing based on pupillary response under the influence of confounding factors such as luminance condition and emotional arousal. The proposed mean-difference feature and its extension (Haar-like features) have been demonstrated to effectively characterize physiological responses of cognitive workload under luminance and emotional changes. Boosting based feature selection and classification has been employed to robustly classify workload even under the influence of those noisy factors. The proposed technique could be applied to various applications involving cognitive workload evaluation under complex environments. In our future work, more complex tasks such as driving task and visual search task will be investigated to evaluate the proposed techniques.

APPENDIX

Boosting [22, 7] is a classification technique which performs feature selection and classifier construction simultaneously. It is a general ensemble learning algorithm, which creates an accurate strong classifier H by iteratively combines a number of moderately inaccurate weak classifiers h. The definition of strong classifier is a classifier that has high classification accuracy on the data set, while a weak classifier is a classifier with accuracy just larger than a random guess. The final strong classifier can be defined as:

$$H(x) = \begin{cases} 1 & \text{if } \sum_{i=1}^{T} \alpha_i h_i(x) \geq 0; \\ -1 & \text{otherwise,} \end{cases} \quad (1)$$

where α_i is a weight coefficient; $h_i(\cdot)$ is a weak classifier and T is the number of weak classifiers. Each weak classifier is normally attached with a feature, so the process of combining weak classifiers in Boosting is equivalent to feature selection process.

Algorithm 1 AdaBoost algorithm

Input: n training samples (x_1, y_1), ... , (x_n, y_n) where $y_i = -1, 1$ for negative samples and positive samples respectively

Output: a Boosting classifier $H(x)$

Initialize sample weights: $w_{1,i} = \frac{1}{n}, i = 1...n$.

for $t = 1 \to T$ **do**

  Normalize the weights: $w_{t,i} \leftarrow \frac{w_{t,i}}{\sum_{j=1}^{n} w_{t,j}}$.

  Find the classifier h_t:$X \to \{-1, +1\}$ that minimizes the error with respect to sample weights w_t: $h_t = \arg\min_h \varepsilon$, where $\varepsilon = \sum_{i=1}^{n} \frac{1}{2} w_i |h(x_i) - y_i|$.

  The corresponding error of h_t: $\varepsilon_t = \sum_{i=1}^{n} \frac{1}{2} w_i |h_t(x_i) - y_i|$.

  Calculate $\alpha_t = \frac{1}{2} \ln \frac{1-\varepsilon_t}{\varepsilon_t}$.

  Update sample weights: $w_{t+1,i} = w_{t,i} \exp(-\alpha_t y_i h_t(x_i))$.

end for

The final strong classifier is

$$H(x) = \begin{cases} 1 & \text{if } \sum_{i=1}^{T} \alpha_i h_i(x) \geq 0; \\ -1 & \text{otherwise,} \end{cases}$$

AdaBoost [8, 23], an Adaptive version of Boosting, is employed in this work. During the process of constructing a strong classifier, AdaBoost maintains weights over the training samples; the sample weights are the reflection of the importance of training samples. Initially, sample weights are all equal. In order to select those features that are most discriminative of a given problem, in each iteration of the training process, AdaBoost selects a new weak classifier with the minimal weighted classification error with respect to the training sample weight distribution, which means the newly selected weak classifier can guarantee the more important samples (samples with higher weights) are classified correctly. Then the weights of incorrectly classified samples are increased, so in the next iteration, AdaBoost can focus on these incorrectly classified samples. The process of AdaBoost algorithm is shown in Algorithm 1.

ACKNOWLEDGEMENT

Authors would like to express gratitude to Kun Yu for his helpful discussion on this work. National ICT Australia (NICTA) is funded by the Australian Government as represented by the Department of Broadband, Communications and the Digital Economy and the Australian Research council through the ICT Centre of Excellence program. This work is funded by AOARD grant FA2386-12-1-4049 "Robust Multimodal Cognitive Load Measurement".

REFERENCES

1. Beatty, J. Task-evoked pupillary responses, processing load, and the structure of processing resources. *Psychological bulletin 91*, 2 (1982), 276.
2. Bradley, M., Miccoli, L., Escrig, M., and Lang, P. The pupil as a measure of emotional arousal and autonomic activation. *Psychophysiology 45*, 4 (2008), 602–607.
3. Cain, B. A review of the mental workload literature. Tech. rep., Defence Research and Development, Canada Toronto, 2007.
4. Chen, S., Epps, J., Ruiz, N., and Chen, F. Eye activity as a measure of human mental effort in hci. In *Proceedings of the 16th international conference on Intelligent user interfaces*, ACM (2011), 315–318.
5. Chui, C. *An introduction to wavelets*, vol. 1. Academic Pr, 1992.
6. Farmer E, B. A. Review of workload measurement, analysis and interpretation methods. Tech. rep., European Organisation for the Safety of Air Navigation, 2003.
7. Freund, Y. Boosting a weak learning algorithm by majority. *Information and computation 121*, 2 (1995), 256–285.
8. Freund, Y., and Schapire, R. A desicion-theoretic generalization of on-line learning and an application to boosting. In *Computational learning theory* (1995), 23–37.
9. Iqbal, S., Adamczyk, P., Zheng, X., and Bailey, B. Towards an index of opportunity: understanding changes in mental workload during task execution. In *Conference on Human Factors in Computing Systems: Proceedings of the SIGCHI conference on Human factors in computing systems*, vol. 2, Citeseer (2005), 311–320.
10. Iqbal, S., Zheng, X., and Bailey, B. Task-evoked pupillary response to mental workload in human-computer interaction. In *CHI'04 extended abstracts on Human factors in computing systems*, ACM (2004), 1477–1480.
11. Klingner, J., Kumar, R., and Hanrahan, P. Measuring the task-evoked pupillary response with a remote eye tracker. In *Proceedings of ETRA* (2008), 69–72.
12. Kramer, A. Physiological metrics of mental workload: A review of recent progress. *Multiple-task performance* (1991), 279–328.
13. Lang, P., Bradley, M., and Cuthbert, B. International affective picture system: Affective ratings of pictures and instruction manual. Tech. rep., University of Florida, 2005.
14. LimaU, C., Rennieb, C., Barryc, R., Bahramalib, H., Lazzarob, I., Manorb, B., and Gordonb, E. Decomposing skin conductance into tonic and phasic components. *International Journal of Psychophysiology 25* (1997), 97–109.
15. Marshall, S. The index of cognitive activity: Measuring cognitive workload. In *Human factors and power plants, 2002. proceedings of the 2002 IEEE 7th conference on*, IEEE (2002), 7–5.
16. McEwen, B., and Sapolsky, R. Stress and cognitive function. *Current opinion in neurobiology 5*, 2 (1995), 205–216.

17. Miller, L., and Shmavonian, B. Replicability of two gsr indices as a function of stress and cognitive activity. *Journal of personality and social psychology 2*, 5 (1965), 753.

18. Paas, F., Tuovinen, J., Tabbers, H., and Van Gerven, P. Cognitive load measurement as a means to advance cognitive load theory. *Educational psychologist 38*, 1 (2003), 63–71.

19. Palinko, O., Kun, A., Shyrokov, A., and Heeman, P. Estimating cognitive load using remote eye tracking in a driving simulator. In *Proceedings of the 2010 Symposium on Eye-Tracking Research & Applications*, ACM (2010), 141–144.

20. Partala, T., and Surakka, V. Pupil size variation as an indication of affective processing. *International Journal of Human-Computer Studies 59*, 1 (2003), 185–198.

21. Pomplun, M., and Sunkara, S. Pupil dilation as an indicator of cognitive workload in human-computer interaction. In *Proceedings of the International Conference on HCI* (2003).

22. Schapire, R. The strength of weak learnability. *Machine learning 5*, 2 (1990), 197–227.

23. Schapire, R., Freund, Y., Bartlett, P., and Lee, W. Boosting the margin: A new explanation for the effectiveness of voting methods. *The annals of statistics 26*, 5 (1998), 1651–1686.

24. Setz, C., Arnrich, B., Schumm, J., La Marca, R., Troster, G., and Ehlert, U. Discriminating stress from cognitive load using a wearable eda device. *Information Technology in Biomedicine, IEEE Transactions on 14*, 2 (2010), 410–417.

25. Shi, Y., Ruiz, N., Taib, R., Choi, E., and Chen, F. Galvanic skin response (gsr) as an index of cognitive load. In *CHI'07 extended abstracts on Human factors in computing systems*, ACM (2007), 2651–2656.

26. Stanners, R., Coulter, M., Sweet, A., and Murphy, P. The pupillary response as an indicator of arousal and cognition. *Motivation and Emotion 3*, 4 (1979), 319–340.

27. Wilson, G. F. Operator functional state assessment. Tech. rep., Research and Technology Organisation, North Atlantic Treaty Organisation, 2004.

28. Xu, J., Wang, Y., Chen, F., and Choi, E. Pupillary response based cognitive workload measurement under luminance changes. *Human-Computer Interaction–INTERACT 2011* (2011), 178–185.

29. Xu, J., Wang, Y., Chen, F., Choi, H., Li, G., Chen, S., and Hussain, S. Pupillary response based cognitive workload index under luminance and emotional changes. In *Proceedings of the 2011 annual conference extended abstracts on Human factors in computing systems*, ACM (2011), 1627–1632.

Exploring 3D Gesture Metaphors for Interaction with Unmanned Aerial Vehicles

Kevin P. Pfeil
University of Central Florida
Orlando, FL
kevin.pfeil@knights.ucf.edu

Seng Lee Koh
University of Central Florida
Orlando, FL
ksenglee@knights.ucf.edu

Joseph J. LaViola Jr.
University of Central Florida
Orlando, FL
jjl@eecs.ucf.edu

ABSTRACT
We present a study exploring upper body 3D spatial interaction metaphors for control and communication with Unmanned Aerial Vehicles (UAV) such as the Parrot AR Drone. We discuss the design and implementation of five interaction techniques using the Microsoft Kinect, based on metaphors inspired by UAVs, to support a variety of flying operations a UAV can perform. Techniques include a first-person interaction metaphor where a user takes a pose like a winged aircraft, a game controller metaphor, where a user's hands mimic the control movements of console joysticks, "proxy" manipulation, where the user imagines manipulating the UAV as if it were in their grasp, and a pointing metaphor in which the user assumes the identity of a monarch and commands the UAV as such. We examine qualitative metrics such as perceived intuition, usability and satisfaction, among others. Our results indicate that novice users appreciate certain 3D spatial techniques over the smartphone application bundled with the AR Drone. We also discuss the trade-offs in the technique design metrics based on results from our study.

Author Keywords
3D Interaction; User Studies; Robots

ACM Classification Keywords
I.2.9 Robotics: Operator Interfaces; H.5.2 User Interfaces: Interaction Styles

General Terms
Design, Experimentation

INTRODUCTION
Human Robot interface design is becoming an increasingly important topic as the robot industry matures. One approach to these interfaces is through the use of upper body 3D interaction techniques. There is opportunity for a more natural and intuitive user interface involving such techniques, or as part of an overall multi-modal interface. An interaction technique based on 3D gestures or poses, especially techniques that do not require touch or wearable devices, is more desirable due to its ease of reconfigurability and programmability [6].

IUI'13, March 19–22, 2013, Santa Monica, CA, USA.

Figure 1. Giving a 3D interaction command to the UAV

One approach in 3D interaction design that facilitates understanding of the techniques is the use of metaphors, which are prevalent in many commercial games using motion control, such as WarioWare: Smooth Moves[1] and Dance Central 2[2]. These metaphors could be used outside of entertainment, such as in Human Robot Interaction (HRI). However, we have not found much work that addresses the qualitative and quantitative attributes of 3D interaction, specifically 3D gestures, within HRI. A compelling reason for this lack of work could be that incorporating metaphors into 3D interaction design, or the design process itself, is usually technology-driven as opposed to user-driven. Most of the user studies we found were also conducted in software-based simulations, such as video games, despite markedly dissimilar user experiences between live, virtual and constructive test-beds [1]. With the arrival of low-cost robotics such as the Parrot AR Drone and Roomba, we attempt not only to address usability with 3D gesture interfaces, but also explore the configuration and performance of what we perceive to be commonly understood metaphors applied to body gestures that can be implemented for both remote and proximate interaction with robots.

The type of 3D interaction on which we focus upon in this paper is direct and explicit teleoperations of robots with ap-

[1] http://www.nintendo.com/sites/software_warioware.jsp
[2] http://www.dancecentral.com/

plications to assistive robotics, or in military domains such as reconnaissance or search and rescue. We chose UAVs, given their extensive use in the aforementioned application domains, and their availability for domestic purposes mostly as entertainment apparatus. Taking inspiration from common gestures and physical control devices, we implemented a set of five upper-body gesture techniques to fly the UAV in all degrees of freedom using the Microsoft Kinect. With the release of the Microsoft Kinect 1.5 SDK onwards, both standing and seated skeletal tracking are supported even at Near Depth Range; this feature allows us to explore metaphors for gesture sets that perform similar tasks for a wider context of user profiles.

RELATED WORK

There has been a significant amount of literature reported on the successful extraction of gestures and poses or their subsets, such as hand/finger gestures, to communicate and perform Human Robot Interaction (HRI) tasks via 3D interaction techniques [2] [3] [11].

Guo et. al. explored interaction with robots using different tangible devices such as the multiple Wii-motes and the keyboard [4]. Although they did use motion control versus traditional input devices, they still relied on usage of additional hand-held technology to assign commands to their robot. We explore interaction with robots without any grasping or wearing any tracking devices.

Lichtenstern et. al. [7] explored commanding multiple robots using 3D selection techniques that do not require tangible devices. However, they did not explore different methods of 3D spatial interaction and solely reported their facilitation for selection and coordination of movements of multiple-robot teams.

Sugiura et. al. [10] implemented a multitouch interface with a mobile device, such as a smartphone, to operate a bipedal robot via finger swipes and taps. Finger contact on the display is performed with natural finger expressions or gestures that mimic the robot's bipedal actions such as walking, turning, kicking, and jumping. Our work focuses upon teleoperation of UAVs without physical contact with any tracking devices, and we also explore and analyse metaphors that may not be as straightforward as simple mimicry of the robot's locomotion via finger walking.

Ng et al. [8] explored a falconeering metaphor for interacting with an AR drone. However, they used a Wizard-of-Oz experiment set-up and with emphasis on studying human-robot social interaction inside collocated spaces. Our work is a full technical implementation using the Microsoft Kinect SDK and we do not differentiate interaction techniques for either collocated or remote teleoperations, with the gesture sets pertaining to each metaphor applicable to both sets of scenarios.

There have been many retrospective works reported on using body gestures to control robots, but they emphasize more on technical implementations for prototyping purposes [9] [10] [11]. Instead, we report the results of qualitative and quantitative metrics in a user study for the teleoperation of UAVs.

3D INTERACTION TECHNIQUES

Design Process

We aim at developing multiple 3D gestural interfaces based on metaphors that we regard as natural when applied to UAVs. By observing the physical nature and movement of the UAV, we were inspired to develop interaction techniques. We ultimately developed five interaction techniques to study. We regard these developed techniques as natural and hoped the participants also found these as natural.

Keeping in mind that users would be holding poses, we attempted to factor in parameters that would affect the overall usability of the technique. For instance, we believe that the neutral position, or the "do nothing" command, should be the least strenuous activity for the user. In other words, if a pose must be met by the user for the UAV to keep its course, the user should feel as comfortable as possible. Further, issuing commands to the UAV should not be difficult to do or require much energy; they should be easy for the user to perform and simple enough so that they become second nature. We wanted the reaction time of the UAV to be as fast as possible, so we did not use gesture recognition algorithms or complex gestures. Rather, we use specific heuristic values to allow for faster results.

After deciding on the interaction techniques based on the chosen metaphors, we developed the gestural commands to operate the UAV. The next sections describe the metaphors and the physical interactions that were used to control the UAV.

Selected Metaphors

Five techniques in all were created and assigned a moniker to assist the user in remembering the underlying motions to control the Drone:

- First Person
- Game Controller
- The Throne
- Proxy Manipulation
- Seated Proxy

We consider these five techniques to be built on easy metaphors to understand, and we attempt to generate command lists that follow the theme of the metaphor and are easy to use. See Figure 2 for examples of each technique.

First Person

This technique is based on the metaphor of the user assuming the pretense role of an aircraft. Children at play can sometimes be found mimicking an airplane, with their arms out to the side, "flying" around a playground. The technique was built to mirror this seemingly natural pose, where the user keeps the arms out to the side as if they were aircraft wings. To move the UAV to either side, the user would lean in the corresponding direction; to turn the Drone, the user would simply rotate the torso to the appropriate direction. To have the UAV climb or fall, the arms would respectively go up above the head or down below the waist. When the user leans forward or backward, the UAV would move in that direction.

We observe that it is possible for the user to give complex commands to the UAV using this method with low rates of accidental input. Due to this seemingly natural metaphor we expected performance to be positive. We also expect this technique to be favourable due to its simplicity.

Game Controller

This technique was developed using the metaphor where the user's arms assume the role of a typical set of control sticks found on a game controller. In many first person shooter games available for consoles, the left joystick traditionally controls translation of a character while the right joystick commands rotation. In this interface, the user's forearms operate in a similar fashion. When designing the interface, we originally intended for the hands to be in the air, where the elbows are bent at 90 degree angles. We quickly realized the amount of strain required to keep the arms in the air, so we ultimately rotated the entire interaction to counter this. As a result, the neutral position for the user is to hold the arms as if they were resting on a chair, but in a way that the shoulders are relaxed. When the left arm is angled right or left, the UAV would move in the corresponding direction. The right arm, when moved in the same way, would command the UAV to change its heading, respectively. To allow for vertical climb and fall, the right arm is raised or lowered, respectively, and to allow forward and backward translation, the left arm is moved in the same fashion.

Although this technique seems to involve a weaker metaphor, we wanted to explore this type of interaction where minimal movements of the user can still issue commands to the UAV. With these gestures, the user has more opportunity to assign complex commands to the UAV because both hands are independent of each other. Our expectation is that due to the minimal movement required to issue commands and the ease of combining commands, this technique would be favourable.

The Throne

We formed this interaction technique on the metaphor of the user assuming the role of a king or queen. The typical depiction of a monarch giving commands to a subject is always through the use of one hand, using minimal amounts of energy. For this technique, the user is seated in an armchair. The arm rests are used for the neutral position, meaning no command is given. Using one hand only, the Drone can be navigated up, down, left, right, and forward by simply pointing in the respective direction. The command to move back is to bring the hand towards the shoulder, as if to beckon the Drone backwards. Rotation for the Drone can be achieved by rotating the opposite hand to the left and right.

For this technique, the hand movements seem very simple. We expected this technique to be not only the most comfortable technique, due to the lack of strain on the user's legs, but the easiest one to use, because one hand can control the UAV almost entirely.

Proxy Manipulation

This technique was built on a metaphor that allows the user to visualize moving the Drone as though it was grasped in the user's hands. The hands are placed in a comfortable area directly in front of the user this is the neutral position. In order to manipulate the Drone, the user would move the hands forward, indicating the intent to push it in that direction; to bring it backward, the user would make a pulling gesture by bringing the hands near the shoulders. Turning the UAV in a direction involved moving one hand forward and the other hand backward, as though it was being steered. The user would lift the hands to raise the UAV, and conversely lower them to let the UAV descend. In order to strafe left or right, the user would position the hands one over the other, as if the UAV was being tilted in the corresponding way.

The concept of holding an imaginary UAV seems to be a very easy metaphor for a user to understand, and we expect highly favourable results from this technique. Because all commands are given in tandem using both hands, misplacing one hand typically renders no action by the UAV; we find this favourable because it helps to prevent accidental commands being given through errant gestures.

Seated Proxy Manipulation

This final technique was generated as an alternative for the original Proxy Manipulation method. The user takes a seated position, and most commands match the original s However, the left and right strafing is conducted in an different fashion. Opposed to applying imaginary tilt through the use of one hand over the other, the strafing is conducted by using both hands to pull the Drone to either side. This way, all commands are given to the drone by keeping the hands level on one plane.

We expected this technique to allow for a similar experience as the Proxy Manipulation, with the only exception in the comfort factor; it seems obvious that seated gestures would be preferred due to the lack of strain on the user's legs.

Parrot AR Drone Smartphone App

In addition to our interaction techniques, the user could also interact with the UAV using the native smartphone app developed by Parrot. We use an Android device containing an accelerometer for our study. To have the UAV rotate, the right thumb swipes on the screen and holds until the desired angle is achieved. Height can be adjusted by swiping up or down. To translate the UAV, the left thumb is held on the screen and the smartphone is physically rotated in the desired direction, affecting the accelerometer component that is used to generate commands.

USER STUDY

The goal of our study is to measure performance of the interaction techniques we developed, and evaluate parameters that may be important to the user when interacting with UAVs. The techniques are intended for rotorcraft, but similar variants can apply to fixed-wing UAVs. We aim to begin to answer the following questions:

- Are there specific interaction techniques that are more effective than others?
- How are specific interaction techniques more ergonomically appreciated?

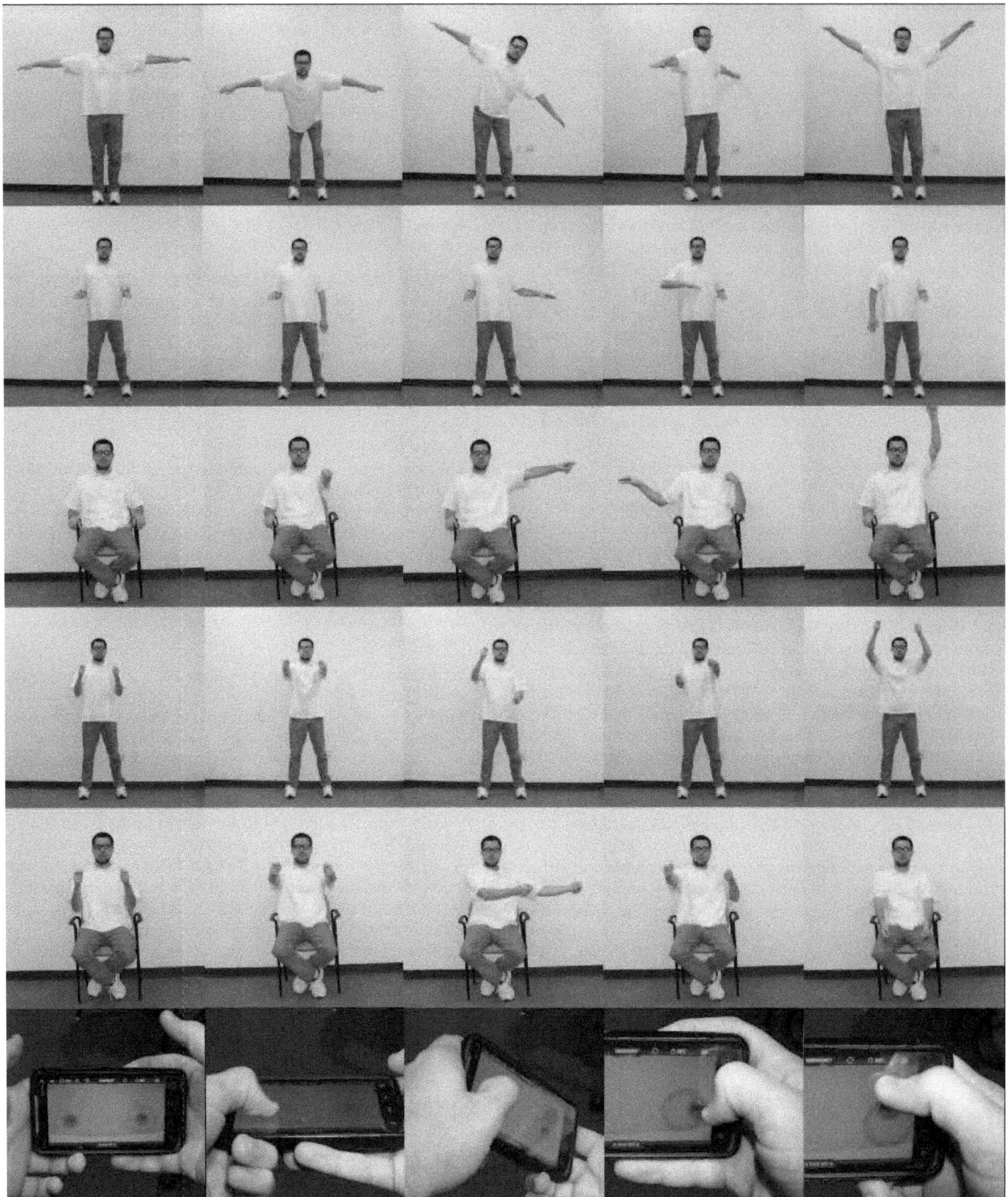

Figure 2. Examples of the various poses for each of the interaction techniques. From Top to Bottom: First Person, Game Controller, The Throne, Standing Proxy Manipulation, Seated Proxy Manipulation, Smart-phone App. Commands shown are examples of neutral positions, forward/backwards, strafe left/right, turn left/right, and up/down, in order per technique.

- Can 3D interaction outperform traditional control devices to control UAVs?
- Do more elaborate metaphors allow for easier understanding of the interaction?

We expect to find at least one technique that is not only more effective than others, but also more natural, among other factors. We also expect to find at least one technique that outperforms the default input method that acts as the control variable, in this case a smartphone application.

Subjects

14 students (10 male and 4 female) from the University of Central Florida were recruited to participate in the study. 11 are graduate students. The ages ranged from 20 to 37 and the median age is 28. Only 2 have ever interacted with the AR Drone prior to the user study, but half reported prior experience using remote controlled vehicles. 10 of the participants have used a Microsoft Kinect before.

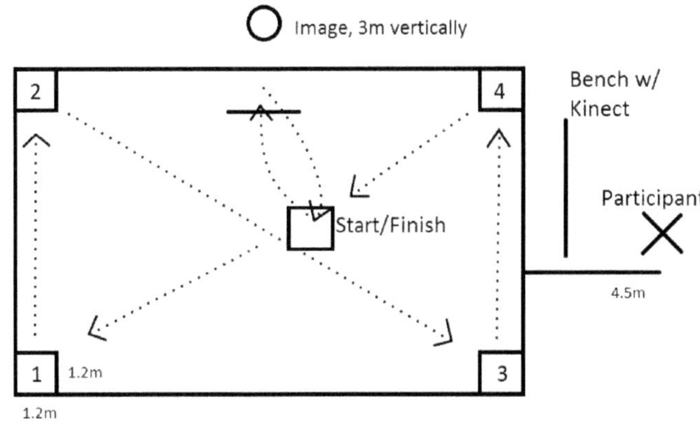

Figure 3. Layout of the test space for the user study. The user was placed away from the area for a full view of the environment. The UAV was to navigate from the start to the numbered way points in order. The UAV was required to turn towards the user before moving from point 2 to point 3. After the Drone arrived back at the start, it was to look at the image outside of the test area before landing at the finish.

Devices and Software

We selected the Parrot AR Drone 2.0 to serve as our test UAV. The AR Drone is a quadrotor vehicle equipped with two cameras: one facing forward and one facing downwards. It is bundled with a smartphone app that allows joystick-like control; our hand-held device was a HTC Evo 4G that has an accelerometer required to work the application. We used skeletal data extracted with Microsoft Kinect SDK to develop our interaction techniques. In order to push the commands to the AR Drone through the Kinect, we made use of an open source C-sharp project developed by Endres, Hobley, and Vinel[3], which allows PC communication with the Drone, and developed our interfaces in it. We ran this application on a computer running the 64-bit Windows 7 Operating System, with 8 GB RAM, a 2.3GHz Intel I7 processor, a 1920 x 1080 resolution on a 17" screen, with a 2GB NVIDIA GeForce GTX 660M graphics card. Because the software application did not display the camera feed for the AR Drone 2.0 at the time of the conducted study, we used FFPlay[4] to rapidly decode the image stream and display it on the laptop.

Test Space

To conduct our study, we arranged for a space of approximately 15m long, and 6m wide. No obstacles were within this safe area, but there were walls and objects outside of the border. The user was located approximately 4.5m from the shorter side, with the Kinect stationed in front of the user. Although this can create parallax error due to the length, we decided that it was beneficial for the user to see the entire space directly in front, requiring a smaller field of view. In each corner of the test space, way points were placed with a 1.2m by 1.2m area. The Drone's beginning and ending location was another way point located in the middle of the two long sides, but closer to the user, for an easier view of the Drone's take-off and land. Near the middle of the long side of the space, a visual target was placed outside of the boundaries, approximately 3m in height. This was used as part of the experimental tasks, which required the camera of the Drone to view the image.

Trial Design

Participants used all techniques in a random, unique order. Before performing a run, the user was given ample time to become familiar with the interaction technique. Up to 5 minutes of free usage was allowed before starting the timed trial, but the user could opt to begin before 5 minutes elapsed. During our initial pilot studies, expert users were able to complete the course with any technique in just over one minute. We feel that the 5 minutes of training time, as well as a 5 minute maximum to complete the course, is ample time for a successful run. During familiarization, all commands were tested by the user and inverted flying was suggested.

In order to evaluate user ability to navigate the AR Drone with each described technique, we involved the way points of the test area and required the user to fly through them at any height. Because parallax error affects the user's ability to perceive the Drone's location at further distance, we used a human line judge to inform the user of successful way point achievement. The order of the way points was constant between users. Starting with the landing pad and working forward to the left, the Drone would fly in a "figure 8" with no navigational restrictions, with the exception of one key constraint. Upon reaching the second way point and needing to fly towards the other side of the area, the Drone was required to turn so that it faced the user; this forced an understanding of the inverted commands, as left/right and forward/backward were now switched, from the user's point of view. To assist with this task, the camera was available at all times on the laptop screen or on the smartphone. Once the figure 8 was completed, the Drone flew towards an image set-up beyond the boundaries of the test area. It did not need to cross the borders of the space; rather, it needed only to look directly at the image. The line judge would assure proper positioning of the Drone, or the camera feed was checked to ensure the im-

[3]https://github.com/shtejv/ARDrone-Control-.NET
[4]http://ffmpeg.org/index.html

In-Between Questionnaire
The interface to fly the Drone was comfortable to use.
The interface to fly the Drone was confusing to me.
I liked using the interface.
The gestures to fly the Drone felt natural to me.
It was fun to use the interface.
I felt frustrated using the interface.
It was easy to use the interface.
The Drone always moved in an expected way.

Table 1. Questions asked to the user for Rate and Rank.

age was being viewed. After completing all tasks, the Drone would proceed to land on the point where it began, with some buffer due to drift while landing. It was possible to fly the Drone too far out of bounds, but the user had a chance to recover without penalty. If a crash occurred due to losing control of the Drone or errantly clipping an object, the Drone was reset to the landing pad.

Quantitative Metrics

On successful runs, the total time from rotor start-up to rotor shut-down was recorded. Up to 3 attempts per interaction technique were allowed for a user. If the Drone crashed at any point, the Drone and timer were reset, and a new try was conducted. After any third failed run, the maximum time allowed, five minutes, was recorded for that run.

Qualitative Metrics

After using every interface, the participant was given a questionnaire to rate key qualities about the interface, according to their experience. Using a 7-point Likert scale, where 1 means strongly disagree and 7 means strongly agree, participants were asked the following questions listed in Table 1.

Each participant was also asked to fill a post-questionnaire at the end of the entire experiment. We asked the user to rank each technique based on the same criteria in Table 1 plus one additional question that asks the participants to rank their overall experience. This ranking ensures that there can be no ties in any category.

RESULTS AND DISCUSSION

Analysis of Trial Completion Times

Figure 4 illustrates the mean completion time of trials with each 3D interaction technique and the smartphone app. If a participant could not complete the course within 3 tries, we gave the cap of 5 minutes as a penalty for that technique, and all participants who finished the course did so under the 5 minute cap. Only 1 participant could not complete the course with any technique. Except for the Throne, each technique had either one or no participants who failed the course.

We used a 6-way repeated measures ANOVA analysis to test for significant differences in the mean completion times between all interaction techniques and smartphone app in our study. If there were any significant differences found between the groups, we use matched-pair t-tests to look for interesting differences between any 2 sets of interaction techniques in our post-hoc analysis. For instance when using the smartphone app as the control, we perform a t-test comparison with each of the other techniques at α=.05, resulting in a total of five comparisons. Type I errors inside the t-tests are controlled by using Holm's Sequential Bonferroni adjustment [5].

Positive Feedback
I was impressed by how cool and novel it is.
The metaphor of holding the drone is easy to understand.
Fun and intuitive.
The controls were efficient.
Better control of the Drone.

Table 2. Positive comments captured by users for Standing Proxy.

Significant differences were found between the interaction techniques and smartphone app in their trial completion times ($F_{5,13} = 4.201, p < 0.002$). However, using pairwise t-tests with the smartphone app as the control, we found no significant differences with the interaction techniques. Completion times from 'The Throne' technique was the cause of the significant differences between the groups, due to less than half of the participants not being able to complete the trial. We proceeded to do pairwise t-tests with the 'The Throne' technique as the control instead. Significant differences between The Throne and the other interaction techniques were found, except for the smartphone app (Seated Proxy t=3.164, $p < 0.007$; Standing Proxy t=3.037, $p < 0.01$; First Person t=2.796, $p < 0.015$; Game Controller t=2.607, $p < 0.022$). Figure 4 implies that the mean completion time for the smartphone app is comparable with The Throne technique.

Although users had ample time to become familiar with The Throne, we believe the gestural commands were not well-tuned. Additionally, we perceive difficulty when users attempt to recover from unexpected UAV behaviour. Confusion paired with very simplistic gestural commands yielded poor performance.

ANALYSIS OF QUALITATIVE DATA

We used a non-parametric Friedman test on our post questionnaire qualitative metrics to check for any significant differences in their medians. If any significant differences were found between the groups, we use Wilcoxon signed rank tests to look for differences between the interaction techniques with the smartphone. Type I errors are controlled by using Holm's Sequential Bonferroni adjustment [5]. Quite similar to the quantitative time completion analysis, we found no significant differences in any the qualitative metrics, except for "Fun" ($\chi^2 = 14.776, p < 0.01$) and "Likeability" ($\chi^2 = 12.342, p < 0.03$). The interaction technique that was significantly different than the others was the Standing Proxy, which benefited from a greater appreciation from the participants. Table 2 contains comments collected from the users after their experience.

Overall, user feedback indicates the Proxy techniques to be the best out of the 5 developed 3D interactions. The smartphone application was regarded as the best interface by 4 of 14 participants, whereas the Standing Proxy was ranked the highest by 6 of 14. The Throne technique was regarded as

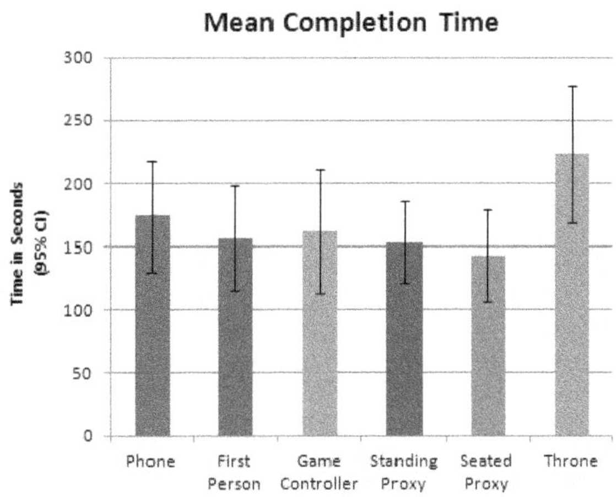

Figure 4. Mean completion time for each interaction technique. There were subtle differences in performance of all techniques, except for The Throne, which did not perform well.

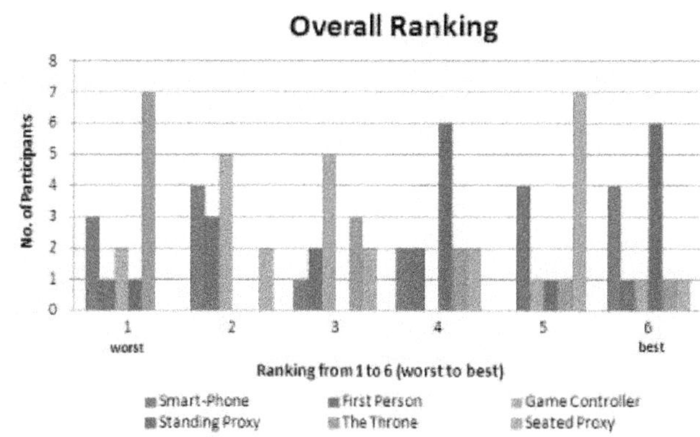

Figure 5. Histogram of user rankings for the interfaces overall. Users indicate that the Standing and Seated Proxy techniques are better to use than the others.

the worst technique by half of the participants. Figure 5 illustrates the rankings for each interaction technique.

The First Person technique felt the most natural, according to user feedback. According to some participants, because the underlying metaphor is very easy to understand, most of the commands did not need to be explained. Users also commented that they did not even think about what gesture to perform when they needed it; they felt it was second nature, as we expected. Figure 6 depicts the user rankings of perceived naturalness of each technique.

The Throne and the Game Controller techniques were both very confusing to the users as shown in Figure 7. As previously discussed, The Throne was the worst in terms of trial completion time, and it was also ranked very poorly overall by the users. That is due to the confusion the users perceived when attempting to recover from the UAV's incorrect movements. The Game Controller was also perceived as confusing, most likely due to the weaker metaphor that the technique was built on. If the neutral position was intended for the hands to be constantly in the air as originally designed, there may be opportunity for improved perception. However, the tradeoff for this switch in stance would be any comfort currently achieved. Like The Throne, it is easy to give inadvertent commands due to the minimal hand movements needed to pilot the UAV.

The smartphone app was ranked the most comfortable more times than our 3D techniques due to the absolutely minimal movements needed to command the UAV. However, the Standing and Seated Proxy techniques were also regarded as comfortable, with the Standing Proxy being the better of the two; this is due to fewer movements needed to perform a strafe. We expected the Seated Proxy to be more comfortable due to less strain on the legs, but since interaction only occurred for up to 5 minutes, user fatigue may not have had time to reach a level that would have caused annoyance. The First Person technique was regarded as very uncomfortable, which is understandable, as the user needs to not only keep the arms spread at all times, but also lean in different directions to command the UAV. Figure 8 depicts user rankings of perceived comfort levels of each technique.

Figure 9 details the overall rankings of the participant's disposition towards the factor of "Likeability." All but one of the users ranked the Standing Proxy technique positively. This user's comments include "turning was frustrating" but we observed the user performing the turning interaction task incorrectly. The other users had no problem with any of the commands and liked the interface overall. 9 of the 14 participants also ranked the Seated Proxy technique highly, as we expected due to the Standing and Seated versions being very similar. Comments from the participants indicate that they preferred the hand-over-hand method to strafe the UAV opposed to the horizontal movement for both hands. As illustrated in Figure 2, the strafing is conducted in a rather extreme manner. Transitioning between strafes left and right involves the user to move the arms from one side to the complete opposite side, whereas the Standing Proxy strafing only involves easier movements for the arms. This is an interesting find, as this helps show that even though the metaphor is easy to understand, the design of the actual commands still need to be considered.

Figure 10 depicts user frustration when using each interaction method. There was no clear advantage by any the methods that reduced frustration levels. Looking to user ratings for this metric, it seems that the median level of frustration, on the 7-Point Likert scale, is 2, with the exception of the Throne. This suggests that although there may have been some discomfort or confusion when using a technique, it was not enough to ultimately frustrate the user.

Half of the participants ranked the Standing Proxy technique as the most fun, as shown in Figure 11. Interestingly, the smartphone app was regarded as one of the least fun interaction techniques. We attribute this finding to the idea that exaggerated gestures may be regarded as more fun for a user, whereas a more simple mode of input does not necessarily bring enjoyment. We originally believed that the most fun interface would be that which yielded the best performance in task time, but does not seem to be the case. In general, it seems that the use of motion control is more fun for a user than standard methods of input.

Figure 12 depicts ranking of user perception of the ease of use for each interaction technique. The Proxy techniques were generally regarded positively in this regard, with 9 of 14 users reporting the Seated Proxy positively, and 11 of 14 regarding the Standing Proxy technique positively. The smartphone app was also very easy to use, but some users did have trouble using it. We observed some users rotating the smartphone too far when trying to translate the UAV; in this way, the UAV would either not move in the desired direction, or it wouldn't move at all. User feedback indicates that the Proxy techniques were easy to understand and also easy to perform.

Figure 13 measures the ranking of the UAV's movements in an expected fashion while navigating it with each technique. Half of the users found the UAV moving expectedly when using the smartphone app. The Proxy techniques were again regarded positively, indicating that user gestures agreed with how the UAV was expected to move when navigating the course. The Throne technique did not allow for expected movements by many of 11 of 14 participants.

LESSONS LEARNED

Although we cannot directly generalize our results to other forms of robots, we expect that our methodology for developing the 3D interaction techniques used in this study can be applied to creation of future user interfaces. Metaphors are efficient facilitators for design teams to brainstorm potentially efficient techniques in 3D gestural user interfaces, as it helps both designers and users to form a natural cognitive mapping between perception of a system and its actual machine operations. By introducing metaphors to the designed gestural command sets, we can estimate the benefits and drawbacks for a technique in a known usage context. For instance, we did expect the First Person technique to perform well as it used a very simple metaphor to comprehend, but we also expected strain on the user's body. Our questionnaires confirmed our suspicion. Analysing the qualitative results of each technique, our initial suspicions for each technique have been confirmed or denied.

First Person

We originally believed the First Person technique to be very favourable as an interface to command the UAV, but this was only true to an extent. Users did find this method to be natural, fun, and not confusing, but was ultimately regarded as a mediocre interface due to the amount of discomfort brought on by the excessive movements needed to give commands. We would not recommend this type of interface for prolonged usage, but perhaps for entertainment purposes. Paired with the AR Drone's front-facing camera, this would be a ideal interface to use when exploring an open world with a UAV.

Game Controller

Our initial reaction to the Game Controller technique was that it would allow an easier time to interface with the UAV in a more complex way. Since both arms can be used independent of each other and are used to give separate commands, more complex commands can be used to fly the UAV (such as turning while flying forward and climbing higher). By allowing the users to navigate the UAV in this way, we expected performance to increase. However, the participant feedback indicates that the interface is not as natural as the others, and it is also very confusing. Due to both arms being independent from each other, the user was able to give inadvertent commands in more than one way at a time. We observed users accidentally flying the UAV to the ground while attempting to fly in a straight line, which was caused by the user forgetting to maintain the neutral position. In prior pilot studies, experts were able to use this technique effectively, however; we would suggest that this technique be used only after ample training.

The Throne

From our results, we found the Throne technique to perform the worst; half of the users could not complete the course, and we attribute this poor result to the technique's requirement of very minimal movements from the user in order to operate the UAV. The Throne technique is essentially a pointing gesture,

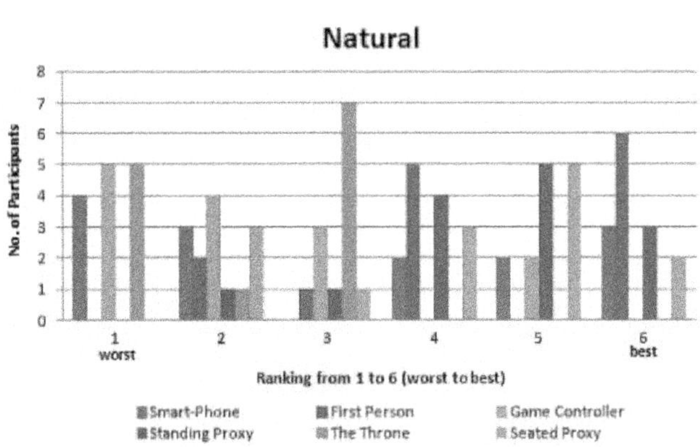

Figure 6. Histogram of user rankings of Naturalness. The First Person technique was perceived as the most natural to use by 6 of 14 participants.

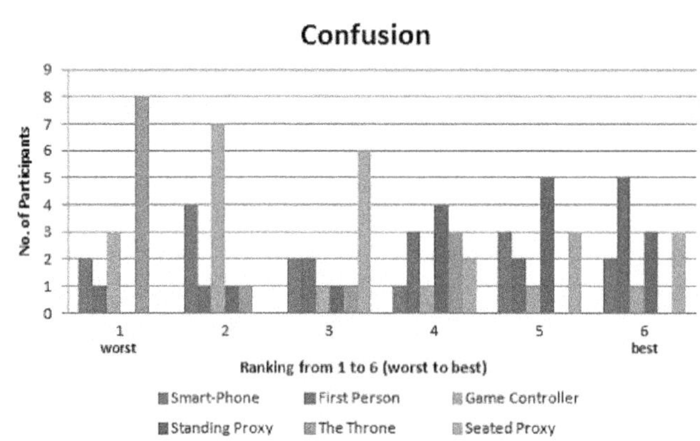

Figure 7. Histogram of user rankings of Confusion. The Throne was the most confusing for nearly all participants, and the First Person technique was regarded as least confusing.

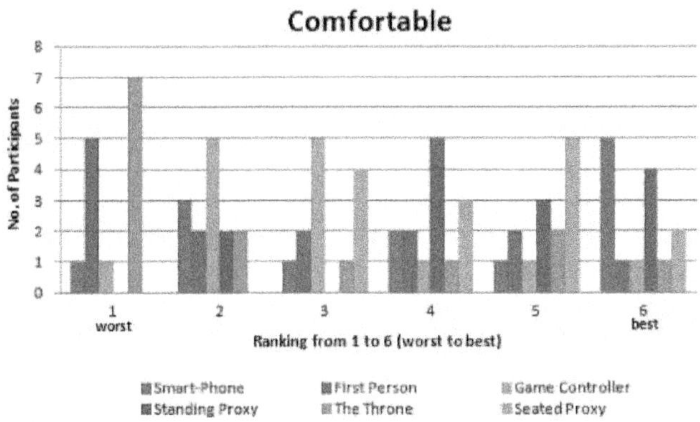

Figure 8. Histogram of user rankings of Comfort. The First Person technique was perceived as the most natural to use by 6 of 14 participants.

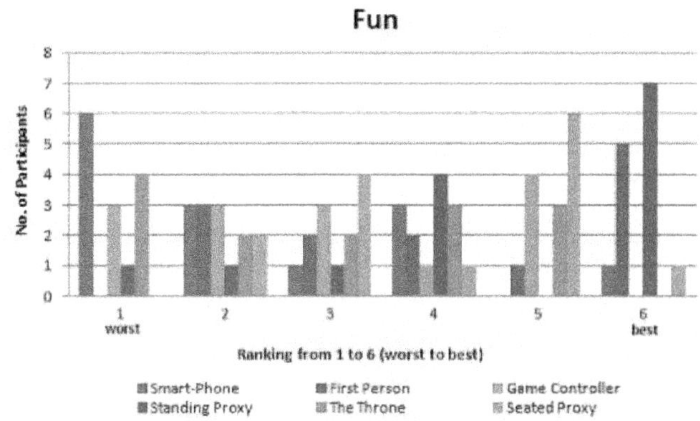

Figure 11. Histogram of user rankings of Fun. 7 of 14 participants indicate the Standing Proxy technique was the most fun, and 6 indicate the Smart-Phone App was the least fun.

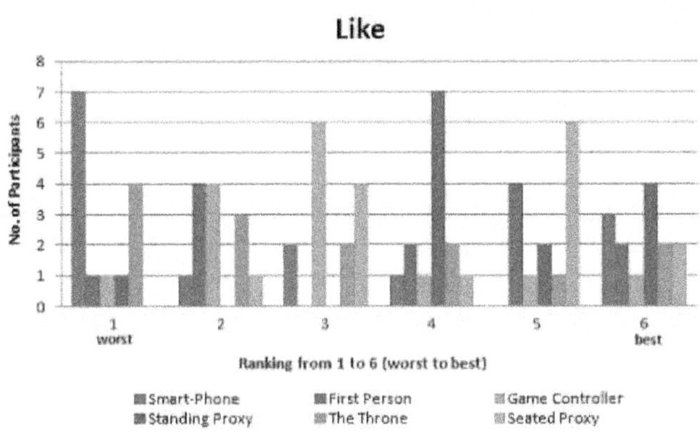

Figure 9. Histogram of user rankings of Likeability. All but one user ranked the Standing Proxy positively.

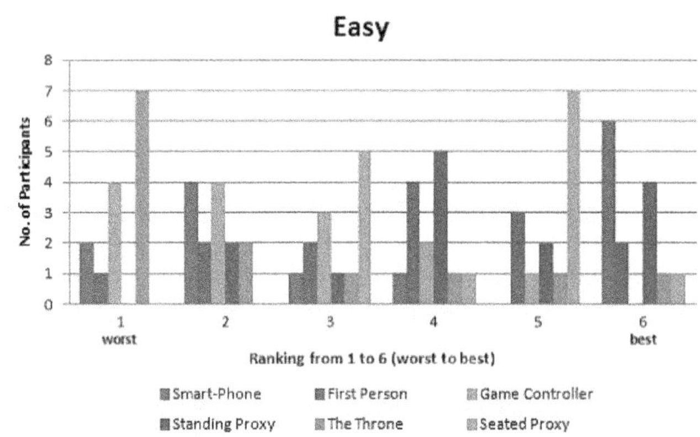

Figure 12. Histogram of user rankings of Easiness. The smartphone app was regarded as the easiest, and among the 3D interaction techniques, the Proxy techniques were regarded favourably.

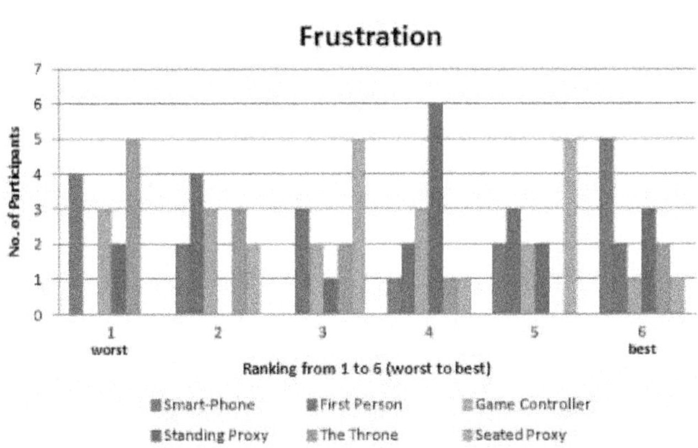

Figure 10. Histogram of user rankings of Frustration. The Seated Proxy technique was well regarded as a non-frustrating technique, and The Throne was generally most frustrating.

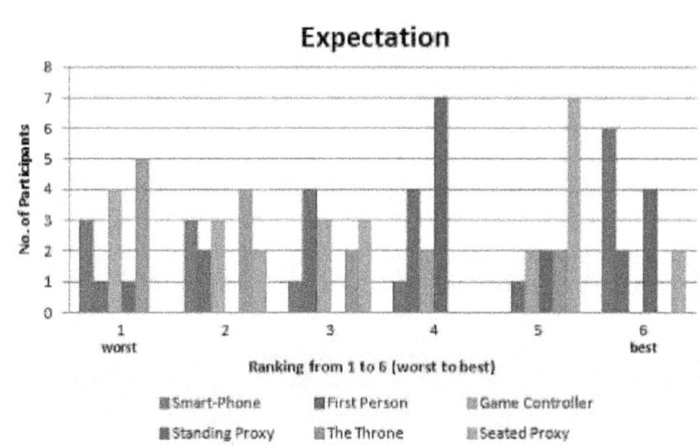

Figure 13. Histogram of user rankings of Expectation. The smartphone app was mixed with both positive and negative feedback; the proxy techniques were generally regarded as positive.

with some modification, and when a user becomes confused or the UAV moves towards an obstacle, incorrect commands can be very easily dictated. Similarly, inadvertent commands can be given by accidentally moving the hand in any direction. We do not expect this kind of technique to be useful in many domains due to the difficult nature of its use, and therefore would not recommend its use.

Standing and Seated Proxy

In contrast to The Throne and Game Controller, the Proxy techniques require both arms in tandem to perform any command. Although this somewhat requires more user effort, we find that accuracy is greatly improved, as inadvertent commands are less likely to occur. Incorrect commands are also reduced because the user is required to move the body more purposefully to the correct gesture for the desired command. Users regarded these techniques highly among all of the recorded factors, indicating that this style of interaction may be the best out of the ones we developed. We would therefore recommend use of these techniques over the others to navigate a UAV.

FUTURE WORK

We plan on further evaluating user preference over other techniques not reported here, and we also plan on attempting to find a technique that can potentially combine all of the positive attributes reported here by the test subjects. Although this study did compare 3D interaction to a control device, we plan on further comparing differences between 3D interaction techniques to other traditional input devices, such as the keyboard, joystick, and typical R/C controllers. Further, we want to explore the development of 3D interaction techniques for different robot platforms, including ground vehicles and humanoid robots, and attempt to find natural techniques to improve current HRI interaction standards. Lastly, we plan on applying our findings to multiple in-tandem robot teams instead of just one standalone agent.

CONCLUSIONS

We developed 3D interaction techniques using the Microsoft Kinect SDK to control the AR Drone 2.0. A user study was performed that evaluated the participants' disposition towards each interface on multiple levels. We find that users appreciate the designed techniques that are built on easy and understandable metaphors, which ultimately serves for better interaction. Our test subjects preferred our Proxy Manipulation techniques, regardless of the posture, over others that were still regarded as fun or perceived as natural. Due to varying results in the factors of comfort, likeability, naturalness, and overall perception, we conclude that there may be a correct usage for each of these techniques when applied in a proper domain; for instance, the Proxy techniques may be best suitable for non-recreational use, whereas the First Person technique may be more suited for entertainment purposes. Of course, it remains to be seen if other techniques that we did not explore in this study can provide better results and be regarded highly among users. However, from our initial exploration on techniques to control UAVs such as the AR Drone, we find that those which provide the best user experience also leverage metaphors that closely associate with the UAV's nature.

ACKNOWLEDGEMENTS

This work is supported in part by NSF CAREER award IIS-0845921 and NSF awards IIS-0856045 and CCF-1012056. We would also like to thank the members of the ISUE lab for their support, and the anonymous reviewers for their useful comments and feedback.

REFERENCES

1. Dean, F. S., Garrity, P., and Stapleton, C. B. Mixed Reality: A Tool for Integrating Live, Virtual & Constructive Domains to Support Training Transformation. In *The Interservice/Industry Training, Simulation & Education Conference (I/ITSEC)*, vol. 2004, NTSA (2004).
2. Fikkert, W., van der, P. V., and Nijholt, A. Gestures in an intelligent user interface. In *Multimedia Interaction and Intelligent User Interfaces: Principles, Methods and Applications*, L. Shao, C. Shan, J. Luo, and M. Etoh, Eds., no. Multim in Advances in Pattern Recognition. Springer Verlag, London, September 2010, 215–242.
3. Gadea, C., Ionescu, B., Ionescu, D., Islam, S., and Solomon, B. Finger-based gesture control of a collaborative online workspace. In *Applied Computational Intelligence and Informatics (SACI), 2012 7th IEEE International Symposium on* (may 2012), 41 –46.
4. Guo, C., and Sharlin, E. Exploring the use of tangible user interfaces for human-robot interaction: a comparative study. In *Proceedings of the SIGCHI Conference on Human Factors in Computing Systems*, CHI '08, ACM (New York, NY, USA, 2008), 121–130.
5. Holm, S. A simple sequentially rejective multiple test procedure. *Scandinavian Journal of Statistics 6* (1979), 65–70.
6. Lambrecht, J., Kleinsorge, M., and Kruger, J. Markerless gesture-based motion control and programming of industrial robots. In *Emerging Technologies Factory Automation (ETFA), 2011 IEEE 16th Conference on* (sept. 2011), 1 –4.
7. Lichtenstern, M., Frassl, M., Perun, B., and Angermann, M. A prototyping environment for interaction between a human and a robotic multi-agent system. In *Human-Robot Interaction (HRI), 2012 7th ACM/IEEE International Conference on* (march 2012), 185 –186.
8. Ng, W. S., and Sharlin, E. Collocated interaction with flying robots. In *RO-MAN, 2011 IEEE* (31 2011-aug. 3 2011), 143 –149.
9. Nguyen, T. T. M., Pham, N. H., Dong, V. T., Nguyen, V. S., and Tran, T. T. H. A fully automatic hand gesture recognition system for human-robot interaction. In *Proceedings of the Second Symposium on Information and Communication Technology*, SoICT '11, ACM (New York, NY, USA, 2011), 112–119.
10. Sugiura, Y., Kakehi, G., Withana, A., Fernando, C., Sakamoto, D., Inami, M., and Igarashi, T. Walky: An operating method for a bipedal walking robot for entertainment. In *ACM SIGGRAPH ASIA 2009 Art Gallery & Emerging Technologies: Adaptation*, SIGGRAPH ASIA '09, ACM (New York, NY, USA, 2009), 79–79.
11. Urban, M., and Bajcsy, P. Fusion of voice, gesture, and human-computer interface controls for remotely operated robot. In *Information Fusion, 2005 8th International Conference on*, vol. 2 (july 2005), 8 pp.

AppFunnel: A Framework for Usage-centric Evaluation of Recommender Systems that Suggest Mobile Applications

Matthias Böhmer
DFKI GmbH
Saarbrücken, Germany
matthias.boehmer@dfki.de

Lyubomir Ganev
Saarland University
Saarbrücken, Germany
luboganev@gmail.com

Antonio Krüger
DFKI GmbH
Saarbrücken, Germany
antonio.krueger@dfki.de

ABSTRACT
Mobile phones have evolved from communication to multi-purpose devices that assist people with applications in various contexts and tasks. The size of the mobile ecosystem is steadily growing and new applications become available every day. This increasing number of applications makes it difficult for end-users to find good applications. Recommender systems suggesting mobile applications are being built to help people to find valuable applications. Since the nature of mobile applications differs from classical items to be recommended (e.g. books, movies, other goods), not only can new approaches for recommendation be developed, but also new paradigms for evaluating performance of recommender systems are advisable. During the lifecycle of mobile applications, different events can be observed that provide insights into users' engagement with particular applications. This gives rise to new approaches for evaluation of recommender systems. In this paper, we present *AppFunnel*: a framework that allows for usage-centric evaluation considering different stages of application engagement. We present a case study and discuss capabilities for evaluating recommender engines by applying metrics to the *AppFunnel*.

ACM Classification Keywords
H.3.3 Information Search and Retrieval: Relevance feedback

Author Keywords
Recommendation; mobile apps; usage-centric evaluation.

INTRODUCTION
In recent years mobile phones have evolved from single-purpose to multi-purpose devices. In particular, this was facilitated by improved hardware and more effective programming capabilities. While earlier mobile phones provided only fixed and limited functionality, i.e. phone calls and short messaging services, current smartphones can be customized by their owners to extend functionality with new applications, also called *apps*. The advent of mobile app stores eased the process of distributing and installing mobile apps. This resulted in apps of various types and quality being made available for end-users. The number of app downloads is anticipated to surpass 81.4 billion in 2013.[1] In January 2013, there are more than 700,000 apps available for both Apple's iPhone and for the Android platform.[2] The number of available apps is steadily increasing. This results in end-users being overwhelmed by quantity, and finding good apps can become a difficult task.

Given this problem and the fast growth of the mobile ecosystem, recommendation of mobile apps became a research topic of increasing interest. Current approaches mainly focus on social aspects (e.g. [9, 1]), context awareness (e.g. [26, 21, 13, 8]) and characteristics of app markets (e.g. [20]). Exploiting context seems especially promising since smartphone usage is subject to perpetually changing contexts [12, 6, 24]. As such, the set of required apps also varies according to the user's changing tasks, e.g. from picture taking, to navigating, to looking for a restaurant. Mobile apps are a special type of items to be recommended: their usage is not only conditioned by users' contexts, but also the usage of a mobile app itself can be tracked alongside the user's interaction with the app — due to an app being a software process that can be observed [6]. Most importantly smartphone use can be characterized by "dead" apps: fewer than half of installed apps are actually being used [22]. Therefore, choosing installations as the evaluation metric might result in even more apps residing unused on a user's device. Consequently, new approaches for evaluating app recommender systems are required: They need to go beyond ratings, click-through-rates or download statistics. Hence, this paper gives rise to new paradigms for evaluating mobile app recommender systems.

Our two key contributions are: (1) We introduce a usage-centric approach for observing people's engagement with mobile apps on different stages along apps' lifecycles beyond installations. Therefore, we adopt the concept of conversion funnels to the mobile ecosystem and present *AppFunnel*. Based on that, we can track the performance of different recommender engines according to this funnel. (2) We present results of a case study of *AppFunnel*.

[1] http://www.gartner.com/it/page.jsp?id=2153215
[2] List of digital distribution platforms http://is.gd/pzjWb6

This shows capabilities for ascertaining the performance of different recommender engines by applying metrics to the *AppFunnel*. Further, we discuss preliminary findings showing that a context-aware recommender engine performs better when aimed on short-term usage at the time of the recommendation request, and a non-context-aware engine performs better when addressing long-term usage of apps.

RELATED WORK

Work that relates to ours covers mobile app recommendation, conversion funnels and user-centric evaluation.

Recommendation of Mobile Apps

Woerndl et al. [25] present the first recommender system suggesting mobile applications. It exploits context features and is based on capturing the installations of applications related to the context (basically location). The recommender engine is based on a hybrid engine following a multi-dimensional approach. Jannach and Hegelich [11] evaluate recommender engines suggesting game applications on a mobile internet platform. They found that the personalization of recommendations results in an increased number of views and sales. Yan and Chen [26] present the *AppJoy* system: a recommender system that suggests mobile applications on the *Google Play Market*. It is based on application usage data that is modeled according to the recency, frequency and duration of the application usage. Yan and Chen show that their recommendation approach based on implicit usage data performs well without explicit user input; they evaluated their system by comparing usage times of recommended and not-recommended apps. Davidsson and Moritz [8] present the *Applause* system, which is a recommender system that exploits users' locations to recommend apps. In particular *Applause* tends to exploit context to be able to recommend applications instantly without collecting any additional user data. Girardello et al. [9] present *AppAware*: an app suggesting recommender system that is based on people's application installations, uninstallations and updates. The system recommends applications based on their popularity, i.e. how many times an app was installed without removal. Böhmer et al. [5] present the prototype of a recommender system for mobile applications called *appazaar*[3]. We used this system as a testbed for the research presented in this paper. In [6] Böhmer et al. present a large-scale study on mobile application usage. Therefore they define an app's lifecycle to consist of installation, open, close, update, and removal events. Their findings can be exploited for context-aware recommendation of apps, e.g. news apps are more popular in the morning, and games at night.

Context-aware models for recommendation of mobile applications have recently been presented by Karatzoglou et al. [13] and Shi et al. [21]. Both papers present tensor-factorization based models that perform better than state of the art context-aware approaches and non-context-aware approaches when using app usage as implicit feedback. Also, Shi and Ali [20] present a recommender engine that addresses characteristics of mobile app markets. Their model is based on app usage as implicit feedback and specially tailored towards mobile app markets that have heavier heads and longer tails in their distributions.

However, none of the related works on mobile app recommendation uses a usage-centric model based on how engaged a user is with an application for evaluation. This is what this paper aims to do.

Conversion Funnels

A *conversion funnel* describes an action sequence, e.g. from showing an ad to a user, to the user clicking on the ad, to the user eventually purchasing the advertised product. The paradigm of *conversion funnels* is mostly used in the domains of marketing and advertising. Bagherjeiran et al. [2] present a ranking method for scheduling ads that is optimized for different stages of the conversion funnel. Their model enables a more efficient targeting of ads towards conversions. For online advertising, Becker et al. [4] provide insight into the relationship between landing page types, query classes, and conversion. They conclude that the majority of ad landing pages fall into three distinct classes: home pages, sub pages, and search result pages. Furthermore, the authors correlate these classes with conversion data provided by advertisers to show that the *conversion rate* (i.e., the proportion of certain users who take a predefined, desirable action, such as a purchase, registration, download, etc., as compared to simply page browsing) varies considerably according to these classes. Rosales et al. [18] provide a detailed analysis of conversion rates in the context of non-guaranteed delivery for display advertising. They formalize the problem of predicting the post-click conversion, i.e. conversions after a user clicks on a referring ad. The authors further provide fundamental properties of the post-click conversion process based on contextual information including a comparison between click-through rate and conversion rate.

In this paper, we apply the concept of conversion funnels to the domain of mobile application recommendation. The nature of mobile apps — being pieces of software that can be observed during an app's lifecycle [6] — allows us to define an action sequence that relates to engagement with an application.

Usage-centric Evaluation

Hayes et al. [10] propose an online evaluation framework for recommender systems that tackles issues related to the dynamically changing conditions in the wild. Instead of measuring absolute engine performance, it performs a comparative measure of how one recommendation strategy performs against another as part of a real world online system used by a community of users. The authors argue that the relative comparison provides both recommender engines with the same resources

[3]`http://appazaar.net`

and that they suffer from the same negative impact of data changes, thus providing fair evaluation in an online scenario. Swearing and Sinha [23] argue that the effectiveness of recommender engines is not solely determined by the quality of the algorithm. Instead they suggest that trust, explanations, serendipity, and user-customizable filters are important factors for effective recommendation. Also, McNee et al. [16] argue that accuracy metrics alone cannot be used to judge usefulness of recommendations and therefore propose new user-centric directions for evaluating recommender systems. They define three aspects of the recommendation process that accuracy metrics cannot measure: similarity of recommendation lists, serendipity, and importance of user needs and expectations. Pu et al. [17] examine combined criteria for usability and satisfaction and conceptualize a unifying recommender systems evaluation framework, called *ResQue*. It consists of thirty-two questions and fifteen constructs aiming at measuring qualities of recommended items, systems' usability, usefulness, interface and interaction qualities, users' satisfaction with the systems, and influence of these qualities on users' behavioral intentions. In the same line of thinking, Knijnenburg et al. [14] present a framework for user-centric evaluation of recommender systems linking system aspects to user behavior aspects to explain why and how a recommender's user experience evolves. Finally, Konstan and Riedl [15] argue that we need a more diverse set of measures to evaluate the user experience of recommender systems.

In our work, we present a usage-centric perspective and its capabilities for the evaluation of recommender engines that suggest mobile apps.

CONCEPT OF APPFUNNEL

Stages of App Engagement

To ascertain an app's usefulness for a user, we adopted the concept of conversion funnels [2]. The final conversion represents the conversion of a recommended application to one that is used in the long-term. In order to reach this conversion, users go through several stages that represent different events resulting from their interactions with recommended apps. As depicted in Figure 1, we can distinguish four different stages in a user's action sequence for determining a conversion funnel for a mobile application after it was recommended.

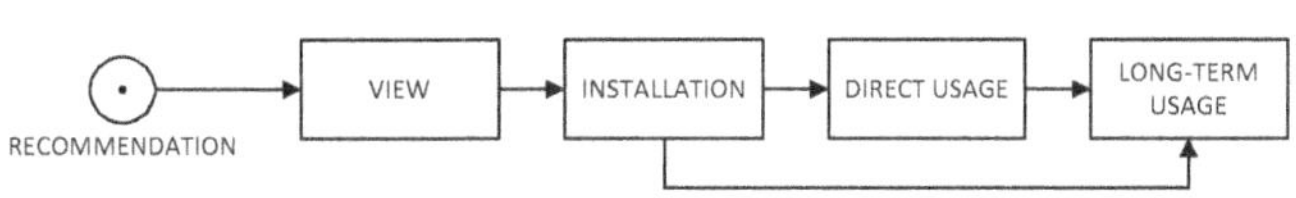

Figure 1. The *AppFunnels*'s stages along a user's app interaction sequence.

After the recommendation of a list of applications to the user, the first stage that an app can reach is the *view stage*. It happens when a user clicks on a particular app from the list of recommended apps. This stage reflects the lowest level of interest that a user might have in an recommended application; it can be elicited by the name, the icon, other users' ratings, or the category of the application. By retrieving application details, he can view additional information like a description, screenshots, or other users' comments.

The *installation stage* appears when the user downloads and installs an application. This stage reflects an even stronger interest in the application. Furthermore, an installation of an app signals that the user actually finds that application interesting enough to try it based on its description and other users' feedback. For some apps, this also means that the user is willing to pay for the application.

Directly after installation, an app might reach the *direct usage stage*. This reveals that a user launches the application shortly after it has been installed, which reflects the next interest level, i.e. he is interested enough to directly try it. Another reason might be that he needs the recommended app in his current context and expects it to be useful. As such, this event is optional and might not appear for applications that are not launched right away. Instead, the user might leave the application and try it later.

Finally, an application might reach the final stage of *long-term usage*. This stage represents the final conversion which reflects the strongest possible level of interest in a recommended app: it reveals that a recommended app turned out to be useful and engaging. In comparison to the previous stages, this one can only be determined from post-processing historical app-usage data, and not from observing a single event resulting from a user's app interaction. As we show in the next section, an app's relative usage time can be used to determine a threshold for considering app usage to be long-term usage.

The four stages in this funnel can only be reached sequentially following the arrows shown in Figure 1. Every stage can be traversed several times, always starting from the *view stage*, if a user has uninstalled an application and retrieves a recommendation again.

Determining Long-term Usage

For determining the long-term usage of an app, we calculate its relative usage $r = u/t \in [0, 1]$, with u denoting the number of days during which the application was used and t denoting the total number of days that the application was installed. The granularity of days is reasonable, since the quotient r for relative usage should address long-term usage and the question is whether a user keeps using an app at all. Aggregating based on days additionally compensates for the effect that app usage varies during the course of a day [6].

The relative usage is influenced by an app's type, meaning that some applications naturally have a higher and others a lower relative usage; e.g. communication apps are used more often than applications providing functionality that is solely useful in particular situations like shopping on the weekend [6]. Based on the data provided through *appazaar* [6], this can be illustrated with the two

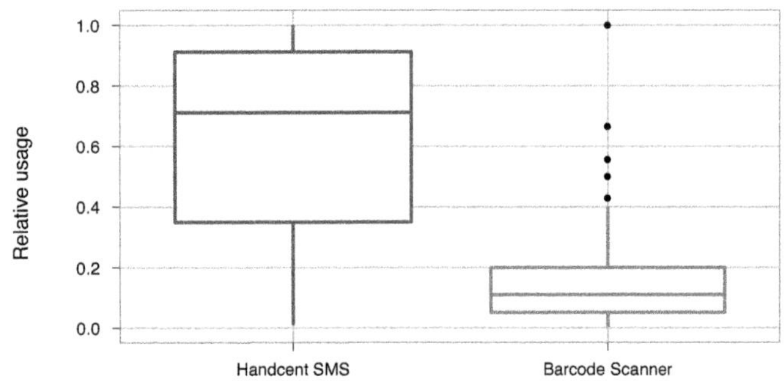

Figure 2. Relative usage of two apps (paired data of 197 users).

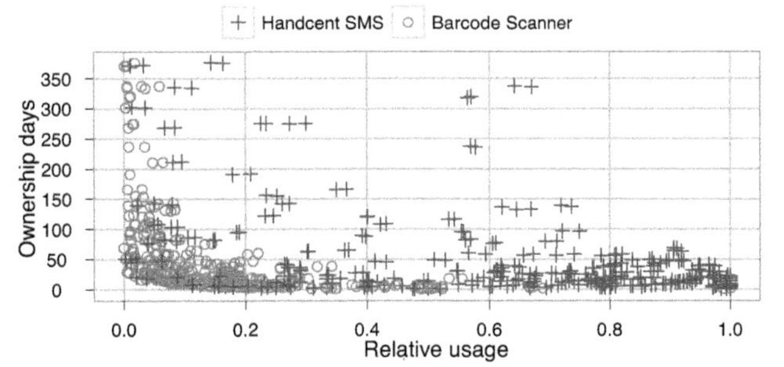

Figure 3. Relative usage versus number of ownership days of two apps (paired data of 197 users).

applications *Handcent SMS* (a popular free messaging application for smartphones) and *Barcode Scanner* (provides users with the ability to scan barcodes containing various types of information such as website links or contact information). Figure 2 depicts the relative usage of these two applications across 197 users. The lower and higher borders of the boxes depict the lower and higher quartile, respectively; we considered only paired cases. The plot shows a significant difference (*Wilcoxon signed-rank test,* $W{=}16510$, $Z{=}11.77$, $p{<}.001$, $r = 0.59$) in the relative usage of these two apps, with a high relative usage for *Handcent SMS* and a low relative usage for *Barcode Scanner*. The median relative usage for *Handcent SMS* is about 71%, denoting that people use this app nearly 5 days per week; median relative usage for *Barcode Scanner* is 11%, meaning that people use it on less than one day per week.

A user removing an application does not necessarily mean that it has not provided any benefit to the user, especially if the user owned the application for a long period of time. Therefore, such cases require additional analysis of the amount of time that the application was owned by the user and further comparison with other users. For example, if a user uninstalls an application after a period of time that is longer than the median ownership time of all other users, then his relative usage reflects a potential long-term engagement despite the fact that he uninstalled the app. In addition, this approach can also detect events when a user initially does not like an application and uninstalls it after a short ownership time. For example, if an application is installed, used and uninstalled on the same day, it would have a high relative usage of 1.0. For our example, such relative usages are shown in the bottom right corner of Figure 3 for people who used *Handcent SMS* for only a short time. If one particular application is kept by the majority of users for a long time, it can be assumed that the users who have installed the application for only a short time have just tried the application and directly rejected it, thus in this case the high value of the relative usage does not reflect a genuine long-term engagement and should be ignored.

CASE STUDY OF APPFUNNEL

We conducted a case study to examine the validity of our approach and explore possible conclusions that can be drawn based on data collected from the *AppFunnel* framework. Thus, we implemented the proposed framework within a deployed app recommender system and put it to the test in the wild.

Testbed

We used the *appazaar* recommender system provided by Böhmer et al. [5] as our testbed. The system has already been installed by 6,680 users[4]. We do not know any demographic information about our users, but since our testbed *appazaar* is deployed on the *Google Play Market*, we may assume that those people who have installed the *appazaar* application are a good representation of those people who can be expected to use a mobile app recommender system.

In our testbed we had to add a *view market stage* between the *view stage* and the *installation stage*. This is specific to *appazaar* since it builds upon, but is not integrated into, *Google Play Market* itself. The only way to recommend apps for installation on Android devices is to forward the user to the *Google Play Market* (where he has to grant the app's permission request). Figure 4 sketches the screens a user traverses from the view stage to long-term usage. The *view market stage* is reached when a user decides to review details about an app. The user reaches a screen where he can read other users' feedback about the app and install it. Since the user has to perform an additional click this event reflects a stronger "want-to-try level" of interest towards the application.

Applying Metrics to the AppFunnel

We extended the testbed to collect data about the given recommendations and the corresponding action sequences taken by users as determined by our conversion funnel. As such, for all given app recommendations, we kept track of which stages the recommended apps reached (view / view market / installation / direct usage / long-term usage).

In analogy to well-known and widely-used metrics like click-through-rates or pay-per-click we can define metrics for recommended applications reaching the different stages and conversions between those stages. In our case study we have chosen metrics for the different stages in the form of counters for how many apps have reached

[4]According to Google Play's Android Developer Console.

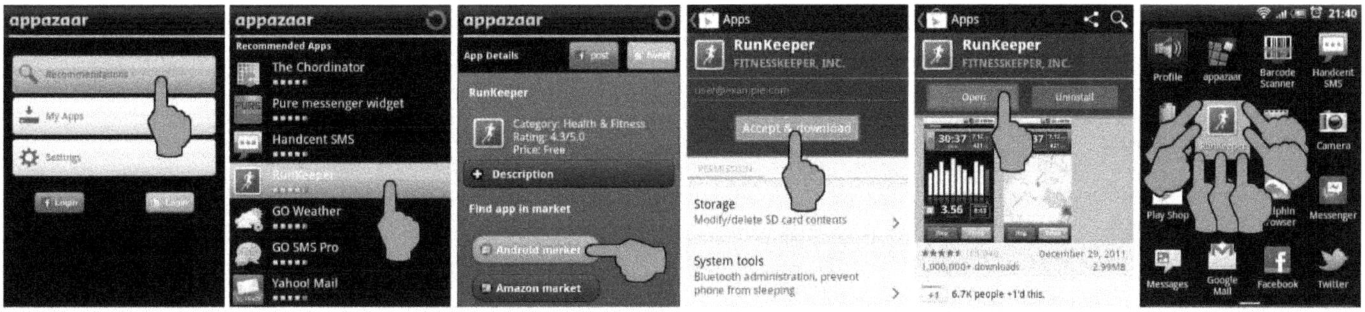

(a) recommendation (b) view (c) view market (d) installation (e) direct usage (f) long-term usage

Figure 4. Examples of screens a user sees when traversing the stages of our testbed's conversion funnel. This usage-centric action sequence can be captured for evaluation of the different recommender engines.

a certain stage, e.g. the long-term usage metric is the number of apps that have been used in the long-term. Conversion rates are the quotients of two counters of stage events, e.g. the ratio of the number of people who viewed a recommended app to the number of people who used it in the long term.

Recommender Engines under Test

The focus of this paper is on the *AppFunnel* as an evaluation framework and not on investigating new engines themselves. Therefore we have used the recommender engines that already have been developed and deployed within *appazaar* for testing our framework. As shown in Table 1, the engines under test can be classified according to the two dimensions of personalization and context awareness. The personalized engines take information about specific users into account, i.e. their app usage histories. The context-aware recommender engines generate recommendations based on users' current context, e.g. time, location, and previously used apps.

	Non-personalized	*Personalized*
Context-less	– App popularity	– Usage-based CF
Context-aware	– App-aware filtering	– Location-aware CF – Time-aware CF

Table 1. Design space of tested recommender engines.

Within *appazaar*, users' requests for app recommendations have been scheduled to the different recommender engines randomly. This allows for counter-balanced within-subject testing of the engines. All engines that are utilizing collaborative filtering are implemented based on the *Apache Mahout* framework.[5]

It is worth mentioning that not every recommender engine was able to produce results for every request. The system suffers from the cold-start problem [19], in particular for the context-aware engines. When no recommendation could be presented to the user respectively, no user interaction with the recommendation list was possible, and as a result no *AppFunnel*-related data was collected. However, to present apps to the user regardless, the fallback strategy for all engines is to return a random set of applications. Since the interaction with such random data does not contribute to the evaluation of the engines themselves, we do not take into account this data for the presented evaluation framework.

App Popularity

The first recommender engine implemented in *appazaar* is based on apps' popularities measured by their usage. Since installations alone do not reveal much about the quality of an application[6], this engine ranks applications according to their popularity based on their global usage in terms of total number of launches. This engine is neither personalized nor context-aware. Therefore, this engine was able to return results for all issued requests for recommendations, since it did not require any specific additional data.

Usage-based collaborative filtering

The second engine implements collaborative filtering. It utilizes users' app usage data as implicit feedback encoded as binary values for user/item pairs: 1 meaning a user has used an app and 0 meaning a user has never used the app. This engine is personalized, but not context-aware. The core of this engine was implemented using a user-based collaborative filtering algorithm. Therefore, it suffers from the cold-start problem and cannot recommend any applications to users that are new to the system, or to those who did not upload app usage data.[7]

App-aware filtering

This recommender engine is based on the idea that people's usage sessions between screen-on and screen-off have a specific contextual scope. For instance, there is an increased likelihood that people stay with games once they have used a game, or with social apps once they have used a social app [6]. Also, for app usage prediction the preceding app is a strong predictor [22]. Therefore, this app-aware engine recommends applications that are similar to those that have been used recently within the same session. The app-aware filtering is a context-aware but non-personalized approach. Since this engine is based on the apps recently used by the user, this engine has failed whenever the user asked for recommendations without having used an app other than *appazaar* previously in the same session.

[5] `http://mahout.apache.org/`

[6] Jakob Nielsen, `http://goo.gl/KR09G`

[7] Users could opt out from uploading data for privacy reasons.

Time-aware collaborative filtering

The type of apps people use changes during the course of the day, e.g., news applications are more likely to be launched in the morning, and multimedia apps are more likely to be launched in the evening [6]. To exploit this phenomenon, we implemented a recommender engine that incorporates the hour of the day as an additional piece of context information. We extended the previously described collaborative filtering engine following a context-splitting approach [3] and multiplex a user's identity by the 24 hours of the day. As a result, the user-at-time/item pairs denote whether a user has used an application at a specific time of the day or not. This engine suffers from the cold-start problem similarly to the other two engines based on the collaborative filtering algorithm. Its range of possible contextual values is, however, limited to a set of discrete values denoting the hour of the day.

Location-aware collaborative filtering

Location has a high impact on mobile information needs [12], and app usage patterns [24]. Therefore — analogously to the time-aware engine — we also tested an engine that exploits the location of mobile device usage. This engine is also based on the context-splitting approach, modeling pairs of user-at-location/item denoting whether a user has used a specific app at a certain location or not. This engine is personalized and context-aware. This recommender engine suffers from the same problem as the *usage-based collaborative filtering*, because it also uses the collaborative filtering algorithm. Its success rate is further decreased by its location awareness, since there are simply too many different locations defined by geographic coordinates. Locations have been discretized into cells of approx. 30m x 30m (to match e.g. sizes of peoples' homes, offices, or stores). As a result, only a limited number of popular locations include enough usage data that can be used by the collaborative filtering algorithm to produce a successful recommendation; otherwise it just fails.

For the location-aware engine, the data is split to a higher degree than for the time-aware engine. Having only 24 hours in a day allows more application usage data to be used by the collaborative filtering algorithm for a particular hour than for a particular location.

Results

The main purpose of our case study was to examine the capability of the *AppFunnel* framework to evaluate different recommender engines by applying metrics. The following analysis does not aim to find the best performing recommender engine, but to illustrate various observations that can be made by investigating the experimental data that can be collected by means of the *AppFunnel*-based framework.

The data was collected from December 5, 2011, to March 5, 2012, i.e., over a period of three months. In total it contains 287 *AppFunnel* events (204 views, 50 market views, 20 installations, 8 direct usages, 5 long-term usages) contributed by 45 users. The events are distributed across the tested recommender engines as follows: 137 for *app-popularity filtering*, 47 for *usage-based collaborative filtering*, 35 for *app-aware filtering*, 48 for *time-aware collaborative filtering*, and 20 for *location-aware collaborative filtering*.

Within our testbed, the determination of direct usage is performed directly on the users' smartphones. If a user launches a recommended application within five minutes after its installation, this usage is considered to be a direct usage. In order to determine long-term usage of a recommended application, we perform several steps offline. Firstly, we calculate all applications' relative usage across all users who have used it. For each particular application we then pick the lower quartile of users' relative usage values as a threshold. If a particular user's relative usage is higher than this threshold, we consider his usage of this particular app as a long-term usage. Thereby we filter out those app users who had the app installed but did not use it long enough for the application to be considered as engaging long-term usage. Secondly, we calculate the median ownership time for the application across all users who have used it. If a particular user's ownership time is less than the median ownership time, this ownership is filtered out from long-term usage. Thereby we exclude those cases where people have a high relative usage but only had the app installed for a very short time, as discussed earlier.

For a comparison of the recommender engines' performances, the data collected from the *AppFunnel* cannot be applied directly, because of the varying number of successful recommendation lists that each engine has produced. Therefore, we normalized the number of counted *AppFunnel* stages by the number of successful recommendation lists returned per engine. The resulting data represents the average number of events related to recommended applications per successful recommendation list. Since every resulting recommendation list can contain more than one application which people might interact with (see Figure 4, left), the relative number of action sequences per stage can be more than one. This normalization counteracts the fact that not every recommender engine was able to produce a result set for every request. The data is shown in Figure 5.

Conversion Stages

The conversion stage metric depicts how many applications have reached a certain stage in the *AppFunnel*. It appears that the *app-popularity based engine* resulted in the most views of recommended applications. Having a relative number bigger than 1 means that on average people have viewed more than one app from a list of apps recommended by this engine. As for all tested recommender engines, there is a steep drop-off in numbers for the following stages, as Figure 5 shows.

The *usage-based collaborative filtering engine* resulted in the second most views of recommended applications.

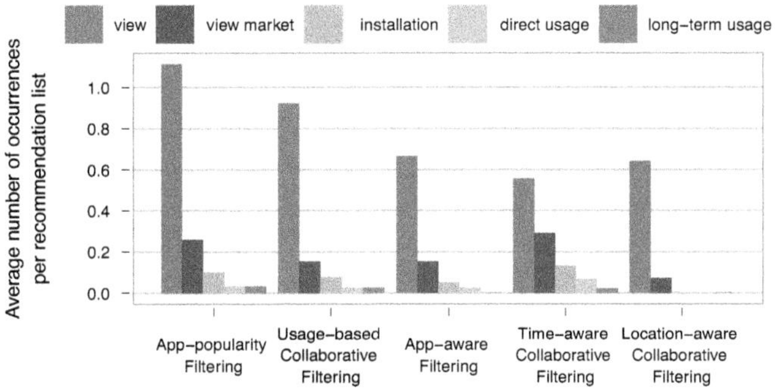

Figure 5. Average number of events counted per recommender engine and *AppFunnel*'s stages.

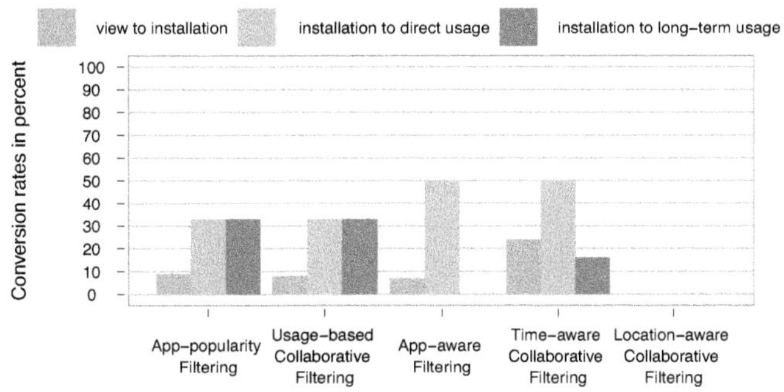

Figure 6. Conversion rates of engines under test. The location-aware CF did not result in any of these conversions (see Figure 5).

However, this engine also shows a steep drop-off after the view event. This engine successfully generated a great initial impression with applications that look interesting enough for the users initially, but are discarded after they are reviewed in detail.

In contrast to the previous two engines, the *app-aware engine* has a lower number of views of recommended apps. In addition, this engine has produced only direct usage and no long-term usage interests, which can also be a result of users just installing similar applications driven by curiosity. Users tried the installed apps immediately, but did not use them regularly in the long term.

The *time-aware collaborative filtering engine* has resulted in the least view events. However, out of all engines, this one has the highest number of action sequences that have reached the three stages of view market, installation and direct usage. Although this engine has recommended applications that resulted in long-term usage, these are fewer than the number of apps that were directly used after they were installed.

The *location-aware collaborative filtering engine* not only has the lowest success rate of all the engines, but it is also the only engine that has not resulted in any installed or used applications. This is interesting, since it even has a slightly higher number of view counts than the time-aware engine. Although the number of views was not less than for the other context-aware engines, there is already a larger gap between the view and the market stage. This engine had no installations, and therefore also had no direct or long-term usage.

Conversion Rates

The conversion rate metric denotes the relative number of action sequences that users follow from one stage to the next. As it can already be seen in Figure 5, the higher the stage within an action sequence, the fewer events occur. Therefore, for all transitions a conversion rate naturally is between 0 and 1 (including endpoints). Although it is possible to calculate conversion rates between all successive stages of a conversion funnel, the most interesting ones related to mobile application usage are: *view to installation*, *installation to direct usage*, and *installation to long-term usage*. These conversion rates are shown in Figure 6. They are based on the absolute and normalized numbers that also have been taken into account for Figure 5.

From the view stage to installations, the engine based on *app-popularity* has a conversion rate of 9%. Overall, for all engines only a few people installed applications that they viewed. In general, the conversion rates from installations to usages — either direct or in the long term — are higher. For the app-popularity engine, both conversion rates (*installation to direct usage* and *installation to long-term usage*) are higher than 30%.

The *usage-based collaborative filtering* engine has a conversion rate of 8% from views to installations. The conversion rates from *installation to direct usage* and *installation to long-term usage* are both higher than 30% — same as the app-popularity based engine. This shows that for these two engines, many users who found apps interesting enough to install them actually also tried them immediately and kept them in the long term.

The *app-aware filtering* engine has a 7% *view to installation* conversion rate which is almost equal to the *app-popularity* and *usage-based collaborative filtering* engines. This engine has not resulted in any *long-term usage* stages; therefore its *installation to long-term usage* conversion rate is 0%. In contrast, the *installation to direct usage* is 50%. It can be inferred that applications recommended by this engine provide a specific functionality, which is useful at the current moment but is not needed on regular basis.

The *time-aware usage collaborative filtering* engine has the highest *view to installation* conversion rate: 24%. Further, its *installation to long-term usage* conversion rate is 16%. Similarly to the *app-aware filtering* engine, it has a high *installation to direct usage* conversion rate of 50%. Since this engine recommends apps that are typically used at the same time of the day in which the recommendation request is sent, it can be expected to have a high *installation to direct usage* conversion rate.

Since there have been no installations for apps that were recommended by the *location-aware recommender engine* (see Figure 5), there are no conversion rates for this engine.

At the bottom line it can be seen that the two contextless recommendation engines resulted in more views of recommended applications than the others. However, the preliminary results of our case study suggest that the two context-aware engines resulted in the highest conversion rates from installation to direct usage, while the two context-less engines resulted in highest conversion from installation to long-term usage.

DISCUSSION

Recommender Engines under Test

It is not surprising that the recommender engine based on apps' popularities resulted in the most views. It is known that naive non-personalized approaches can compete with well-elaborated algorithms [7]. While naive approaches are much easier to design and implement, the more elaborate recommender engines used in this paper require more testing and fine-tuning.

The high number of views of the app-aware filtering engine might be a result of their similarity with some applications that the users have just used in the same session. This engine recommends similar applications, which very often contain similar keywords in their names or have similar icon symbols. Thus, the users might be driven by curiosity to find out more about these new apps.

The bad performance of the location-aware engine might be a result of the same factor that causes the low success rate of this engine: locations defined by geographical coordinates might result in too fragmented usage data that is too sparse and therefore not suitable for a valuable collaborative filtering, which follows from the splitting approach. Optimization of this particular engine is the subject to future work. However, the *AppFunnel* framework allowed us to trace down this issue in the first place. If we had taken a conventional evaluation approach, e.g. solely based on click-through-rates, the location-aware engine would have been ascertained to have a better performance than the time-aware engine. Only the usage-centric *AppFunnel*-based approach enabled us to investigate this issue by keeping track of user actions following on the view of a suggested app. And only this approach enabled us to find that while the location-aware engine resulted in clicks, it did not result in user value in terms of direct or long-term usage.

Since the time-aware engine recommends such applications as are typically used at the same time of day as the recommendations are requested, it was expected to have a high relative number of direct usage.

Two additional events that can be tracked along a mobile app's lifecycle are updates and uninstalls of an application [6]. However, the update does not tell much about a user's engagement with the application, since frequency of updates is specific for each particular app and its developer, and updates can be done automatically without any user intervention. Additionally, we do not consider the removal of an application as feedback. This can also be exploited, but requires further refinements and post-processing, since the removal cannot be taken as an additional stage in the *AppFunnel* as such. Firstly, the removal is more of a negative sort of feedback, and the *AppFunnel* currently is based on positively growing engagement from stage to stage. Secondly, not every user necessarily removes an application he does not need anymore (e.g. he can also remove only the icon of the app from his home screen). Contrary to this, the *AppFunnel*'s stages compulsorily follow from the user's intent.

Application of AppFunnel

It was interesting to see that — irrespective of the location-aware engine — the two context-aware engines caused different user actions than the two context-less engines. The results of our case study suggest that the performance of the different paradigms of recommender approaches are more diverse in terms of stages reached after a recommended item was clicked on, i.e. *installations* and *direct usages* or *long-term usages* are more diverse than *views*, especially in terms or conversion rates. This suggests that the usage-centric evaluation approach — as introduced by *AppFunnel* — enables a more elaborate evaluation of recommender engines that suggest mobile applications and their design goals, e.g. fostering download and installation counts, or providing instant support in the form of apps that can be used directly, or pursuing user benefit in terms of long-term application engagement.

Choosing from AppFunnel's Metrics

Recommender systems are commonly implemented into e-commerce websites for the sake of increasing turnover and revenue. We argue in the line of Konstan and Riedl [15] that incorporating user experience into algorithms will affect the user's benefit from a recommender, and that a more comprehensive set of measures than currently used are required. For the recommendation of mobile applications, the *AppFunnel* goes beyond measuring the quality of a recommender engine in terms of installations. In the case of paid apps, an increase in revenue is already realized as soon as the customer installs a recommended app. This, however, is only an intermediate stage that an app can reach in the *AppFunnel*. Especially when considering that a large portion of installed apps are lying idle [22], it is reasonable to conclude that recommending for installations alone is myopic and should not be the top-priority goal.

Based on *AppFunnel*, we can reason on the quality of a recommender engine beyond commonly applied metrics, like *click-through-rate* and *pay-per-click events*. However, we suggest considering the metrics we introduced as additional metrics for evaluation of recommender engines rather than as a replacement. Our metrics aim to extend evaluation from a vendor's view to a usage-centric view of recommender system performance — i.e., which app was of actual use in the current context or in the long term.

As we have seen in the case study, one metric might conflict with others. One engine might not perform best in all metrics. How to choose and ascertain the metrics has to be decided according to a recommender engine's design goal. As seen in our case study, a context-aware engine might achieve good results when observing direct usage, but have bad results when taking into account long-term usage. This is sufficient for a context-aware recommender engine, since its goal is to address actual user needs, while a recommender engine generally modeling user taste should aim for good performance according to long-term usage.

We did not take into account applications prices. The price might impact whether an app will be installed or not, but this rather is an attribute of the app instead of being inherent to the app usage. Applying the AppFunnel approach one might find a recommender engine recommending expensive apps to a user who only installs free apps with bad view-to-installations conversion rate.

Our case study shows that by applying the *AppFunnel* and incorporating the metrics we introduced, one can investigate the performance of recommender engines for different goals. In our case, we realized that an engine with average performance in terms of clicks performed poorly in terms of usage.

CONCLUSION

In this paper, we presented *AppFunnel*: a usage-centric evaluation-framework for the evaluation of recommender systems that suggest mobile applications. The main part of this framework is the usage-centric concept of a conversion funnel for tracking mobile application engagement: from viewing a recommended application, to installing it, to over using it directly, to using it in the long term. The *AppFunnel* allows for evaluating recommender engines beyond click-through-rates and download statistics. We have implemented and tested our framework based on a system deployed in the wild, and presented results of applying metrics to the *AppFunnel*. Though the testbed's recommender engines are simplistic, we were able to find that the ones addressing the current context of the user show a higher performance in direct usage, while non-contextualized recommender engines result in a higher long-term usage of installed applications.

REFERENCES

1. Z. Ahmet and K. V. V. Mattila. Mobile service distribution from the end-user perspective: the survey study on recommendation practices. In *Proc. of CHI EA '12*, 2012.
2. A. Bagherjeiran, A. O. Hatch, and A. Ratnaparkhi. Ranking for the conversion funnel. In *Proc. SIGIR 2010*.
3. L. Baltrunas and F. Ricci. Context-based splitting of item ratings in collaborative filtering. In *Proc. of RecSys '09*, pages 245–248, 2009.
4. H. Becker, A. Broder, E. Gabrilovich, V. Josifovski, and B. Pang. What happens after an ad click?: quantifying the impact of landing pages in web advertising. In *Proc. of CIKM '09*, pages 57–66, 2009.
5. M. Böhmer, G. Bauer, and A. Krüger. Exploring the Design Space of Recommender Systems that Suggest Mobile Apps. In *Proc. Workshop CARS*, 2010.
6. M. Böhmer, B. Hecht, J. Schöning, A. Krüger, and G. Bauer. Falling asleep with angry birds, facebook and kindle - a large scale study on mobile application usage. In *Proc. MobileHCI*, 2011.
7. P. Cremonesi, Y. Koren, and R. Turrin. Performance of recommender algorithms on top-n recommendation tasks. In *Proc. of RecSys '10*, 2010.
8. C. Davidsson and S. Moritz. Utilizing implicit feedback and context to recommend mobile applications from first use. In *Proc. of CaRR '11*, pages 19–22, 2011.
9. A. Girardello and F. Michahelles. Appaware: which mobile applications are hot? In *Proc. MobileHCI*, 2010.
10. C. Hayes, P. Massa, P. Cunningham, P. Avesani, and P. Cunningham. An on-line evaluation framework for recommender systems. In *Workshop on Personalization and Recommendation in E-Commerce*, 2002.
11. D. Jannach and K. Hegelich. A case study on the effectiveness of recommendations in the mobile internet. In *Proc. of RecSys '09*, pages 205–208, 2009.
12. E. Kaasinen. User needs for location-aware mobile services. *Pers. and Ubi. Comp.*, 7(1):70–79, 2003.
13. A. Karatzoglou, L. Baltrunas, K. Church, and M. Böhmer. Climbing the app wall: Enabling mobile app discovery through context-aware recommendations. *Proc. of CIKM'12*, 2012.
14. B. P. Knijnenburg, M. C. Willemsen, Z. Gantner, H. Soncu, and C. Newell. Explaining the user experience of recommender systems. *User Modeling and User-Adapted Interaction*, pages 1–64, Mar. 2012.
15. J. A. Konstan and J. Riedl. Recommender systems: from algorithms to user experience. *User Modeling and User-Adapted Interaction*, 22(1):101–123, Apr. 2012.
16. S. M. McNee, J. Riedl, and J. A. Konstan. Being accurate is not enough: how accuracy metrics have hurt recommender systems. In *Proc. of CHI EA 2006*.
17. P. Pu, L. Chen, and R. Hu. A user-centric evaluation framework for recommender systems. In *Proc. RecSys 2011*.
18. R. Rosales, H. Cheng, and E. Manavoglu. Post-click conversion modeling and analysis for non-guaranteed delivery display advertising. In *Proc. of WSDM 2012*.
19. A. I. Schein, A. Popescul, L. H. Ungar, and D. M. Pennock. Methods and metrics for cold-start recommendations. In *Proc. of SIGIR 2002*.
20. K. Shi and K. Ali. GetJar mobile application recommendations with very sparse datasets. In *Proc. of KDD '12*, KDD '12, 2012.
21. Y. Shi, A. Karatzoglou, L. Baltrunas, M. Larson, A. Hanjalic, and N. Oliver. TFMAP: optimizing MAP for top-n context-aware recommendation. In *Proc. of SIGIR '12*, 2012.
22. C. Shin, J.-H. Hong, and A. K. Dey. Understanding and prediction of mobile application usage for smart phones. In *Proc. UbiComp*, 2012.
23. K. Swearingen and R. Sinha. Beyond algorithms: An HCI perspective on recommender systems. *ACM SIGIR 2001 Workshop on Recommender Systems*, 2001.
24. H. Verkasalo. Contextual patterns in mobile service usage. *Pers. and Ubiq. Computing*, 13(5), 2009.
25. W. Woerndl, C. Schueller, and R. Wojtech. A hybrid recommender system for context-aware recommendations of mobile applications. In *Proc. of ICDEW '07*, 2007.
26. B. Yan and G. Chen. AppJoy: personalized mobile application discovery. In *Proc. of MobiSys '11*, 2011.

Making Graphic-Based Authentication Secure against Smudge Attacks

Emanuel von Zezschwitz, Anton Koslow, Alexander De Luca, Heinrich Hussmann
Media Informatics Group, University of Munich (LMU), Amalienstr. 17, 80333 Munich, Germany
{emanuel.von.zezschwitz, alexander.de.luca, hussmann}@ifi.lmu.de, koslow@cip.ifi.lmu.de

ABSTRACT
Most of today's smartphones and tablet computers feature touchscreens as the main way of interaction. By using these touchscreens, oily residues of the users' fingers, smudge, remain on the device's display. As this smudge can be used to deduce formerly entered data, authentication tokens are jeopardized. Most notably, grid-based authentication methods, like the Android pattern scheme are prone to such attacks.

Based on a thorough development process using low fidelity and high fidelity prototyping, we designed three graphic-based authentication methods in a way to leave smudge traces, which are not easy to interpret. We present one grid-based and two randomized graphical approaches and report on two user studies that we performed to prove the feasibility of these concepts. The authentication schemes were compared to the widely used Android pattern authentication and analyzed in terms of performance, usability and security. The results indicate that our concepts are significantly more secure against smudge attacks while keeping high input speed.

Author Keywords
Mobile; Security; Authentication; Smudge; Attacks.

ACM Classification Keywords
H.5.m. Information Interfaces and Presentation (e.g. HCI): Miscellaneous

General Terms
Human Factors; Security; Design.

INTRODUCTION
The smartphone became a ubiquitous device of the users' daily life. In connection with mobile internet, it empowers its owner to check emails, surf the web or perform financial transactions in almost every situation. As a consequence, various sensitive data is either stored on the device or can be accessed with it [11]. Thus, the access to the mobile device has to be secured and user authentication nowadays is an indispensable part of mobile interaction. Most deployed authentication methods are based on challenge and response, where a secret token (e.g. PIN) has to be entered to authenticate. As mobile devices are often used in public settings, the input can easily be observed by an attacker and the user's password is exposed. Such direct observational attacks are called shoulder surfing. They have been an object of research for many years (e.g. [5, 4, 9, 14]).

IUI'13, March 19–22, 2013, Santa Monica, CA, USA.

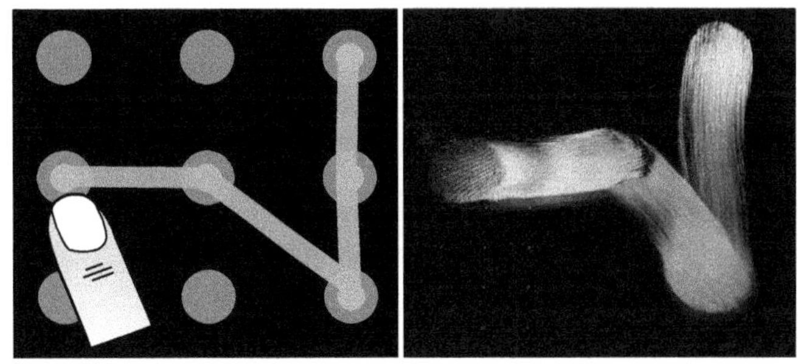

Figure 1. The Android pattern "3 6 9 5 4" (left) and the corresponding smudge (right). The oily residues expose not only the performed pattern, but also the direction in which it was drawn.

In addition to these well-known direct observational attacks, a new security threat was recently discovered [3], which is based on the fact that most smartphones and tablet computers use touchscreens as the main way of user interaction. Every time the user touches the screen, oily residues remain on the device's display. Figure 1 gives an example. When in possession of the device, an attacker can use these residues, called smudge, to deduce the owner's password, even if the input task was not directly observed. This approach is called a "smudge attack".

Graphical authentication methods like Android patterns, which were introduced by Google in 2010[1], seem to be prone to such attacks. At the same time, graphical authentication has advantages compared to alphanumeric methods (e.g. passwords cannot be based on user data) and some approaches exploit the human motor memory [15] or the pictorial superiority effect [12, 16]. In addition, using graphical approaches seems to be more joyful for some users.

The goal of this work was to find usable graphic-based methods, which are particularly secure against smudge attacks. In this paper, we present the design process of such systems and report on two user studies that we performed to prove the feasibility of our concepts.

[1] Android 2.2 platform highlights: `http://developer.android.com/about/versions/android-2.2-highlights.html`, last accessed: 01/07/2013

RELATED WORK

In general, graphical authentication can be categorized into searchmetric, locimetric and drawmetric systems [13].

Searchmetric systems (e.g. [6, 7]) require the user to identify predefined items from a set of randomly chosen images. While there are concepts, which are secure against shoulder surfing (e.g. [19]), such systems were not yet analyzed in terms of smudge attack vulnerability. However, as most concepts present their challenging sets in a randomized order, we assume that this approach is fairly secure.

Locimetric systems like Passpoints [18] require the user to select specific predefined positions within a picture. When used on touchscreens, these systems seem to be very prone to smudge attacks as oily residues do directly correspond to the selected regions of the image. In addition, it is difficult to select specific regions on a small mobile display and thus this approach seems to be inappropriate for mobile authentication.

Drawmetric systems like Draw-a-Secret [10] and Passdoodles [17] require the user to draw a specific shape, which was defined during enrollment. As Google's pattern concept fits in this category, drawmetric methods seem to be most relevant for graphical authentication on mobile devices. We argue that Android patterns are a restricted and thus usability-optimized version of the Draw-a-Secret authentication. Instead of relying on freely drawn shapes, Android patterns are drawn along a maximum of nine possible dots, which are arranged in a $3*3$ matrix. Aviv et al. [3] analyzed Android patterns in terms of smudge attack vulnerability and revealed that passwords are very often exposed by such an attack. With camera based smudge attacks, 68% of the patterns could be identified under perfect conditions and even after a simulated usage most of the passwords were exposed.

One possible solution to the problem of smudge attacks is the introduction of an additional security layer. De Luca et al. [8] add an implicit authentication layer to an Android like pattern authentication. As a consequence, access is only granted, when the right pattern is entered and the way the authentication is performed matches the stored attributes of the user (e.g. same speed, pressure, etcetera). Thus, such an approach can prevent successful smudge attacks as the right pattern does not necessarily give access to the device. Other approaches add an additional task to the basic authentication. For example, WhisperCore [2] requires the user to wipe the screen after the pattern was entered. By wiping the screen additional smudge is added and the residues of the pattern cannot easily be identified anymore. The drawback of this approach is based on the fact that authentication is never the user's primary goal [1]. Thus adding an additional task to the already cumbersome authentication might lead to frustrated users.

In this paper, we propose three novel input mechanisms, which were developed based on a thorough design process. One system belongs to the drawmetric category and is based on Google's pattern scheme. Instead of adding an additional minimal task or implementing an additional security layer, we add randomization to defend smudge attacks. The other two systems are searchmetric-like systems, but are token-based instead of relying on images. The concepts were evaluated in two user studies using low fidelity and high fidelity prototypes. Using the Android pattern authentication as baseline, we gathered comparable data in terms of security, performance and usability. The security analysis was based on the approach of Aviv et al. [3] and confirmed that Android patterns are very prone to smudge attacks. At the same time, the results indicate that our concepts are significantly more secure against smudge attacks than Android patterns and that authentication speed and error rates are kept in a good range.

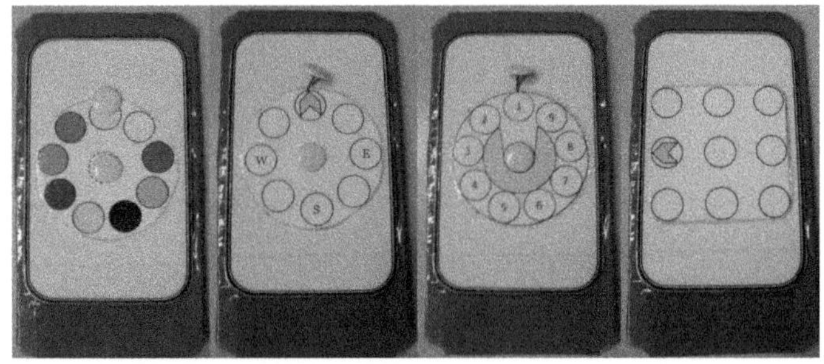

Figure 2. The paper prototypes of the four candidate concepts: *marbles*, *compass*, *dial* and *pattern rotation* (from left to right). Interactivity was achieved using movable elements.

THREAT MODEL

During everyday usage, interaction with mobile devices is far beyond authentication. As authentication takes place multiple times a day and the phone is primarily used for other tasks, there are several residues on the display distracting the deduction of the password. In addition, smudge attacks are hard to accomplish without being in possession of the device and without specific lighting conditions [3].

In this work, we intend to evaluate the security of our approaches in a worst case scenario. Therefore, we assume that *a*) the attacker is in possession of the device and *b*) does have perfect lighting condition as well as a camera to perform the attack. In addition, we assume that *c*) the touchscreen was cleaned before the authentication took place and *d*) the user authenticates only once, before the smudge attack is performed. Thus, there is no smudge on the display apart from the user password. We argue that this is the perfect condition to perform a smudge attack and therefore, the worst case in terms of security.

PAPER PROTOTYPING PRE-STUDY

Based on two brainstorming sessions and the analysis of existing systems, four candidate concepts were designed. We firstly realized them as low-fidelity paper prototypes (see figure 2) and evaluated them in a first user study.

Candidate Concepts

The proposed input mechanisms were explicitly designed in a way to leave smudge traces, which are not easy to interpret. This was achieved due to *a*) randomized distribution of the security tokens, *b*) consecutive blurring of the residues within one authentication or *c*) rotating the view port and thus hamper the deduction of the underlying values.

Marbles

This concept (figure 2, left) is based on the randomized distribution of nine colored "*marbles*". A password consists of up to nine different colors, multiple usage of the same color within one password is allowed. To authenticate, the user is required to drag the colored marbles in the right order into the center of the screen. Each input consists of one distinct dragging operation. The marbles are randomly arranged each time the user authenticates.

Compass

Compass is a drawmetric concept (figure 2, second from left). Instead of a $3 * 3$ matrix known from Android patterns, the dots are arranged in circular order. This order is the same for every authentication. Smudge attack resistance is achieved by randomly rotating the circle of dots. The current orientation is indicated by an arrow and the initials of three cardinal points. A password consists of up to eight connected dots, while each dot can be visited only once. To authenticate, a password is drawn by connecting the dots in the right order.

Dial

This concept (figure 2, second from right) is based on consecutive blurring of residues. A password consists of an arbitrary sequence of the digits one to nine. To authenticate, the user is required to drag the digits in the right order into the center of the screen. The approach uses the metaphor of a dial plate and thus, the numbers have to be dragged within the black margins. To reach the center of the screen, the white opening under the digit "one" has to be used. Thus, the same path is used multiple times within one authentication. While the numbers stay in constant order, the dial (view-port) is randomly rotated within a range of 45°.

Pattern Rotation

This concept (figure 2, right) is based on the Android pattern authentication. Thus, a pattern connects up to nine dots, which are arranged in a $3 * 3$ matrix. To authenticate, the user is required to redraw the pattern. The only modification compared to the original approach is that the matrix is randomly orientated on the screen and the current direction is indicated by an arrow. Two different versions were tested: a 90° version with four different directions and a 360° version allowing an arbitrary orientation on the screen.

Paper Prototype User Study

To gain insights into the feasibility of the concepts and to gather design implications for the final systems, a user study based on the paper prototypes was conducted.

User Study Design

We used a repeated measure within participants design. The independent variables were *authentication system* with five levels (*marbles, dial, compass, pattern 90, pattern 360*) and *password origin* with two levels (*given, self-selected*).

Authentication system was counterbalanced based on a Latin square design, *password origin* was alternated. Qualitative data was collected via a questionnaire and via video recording.

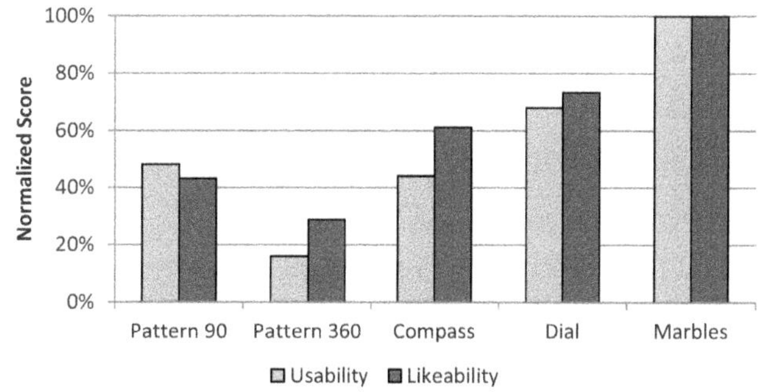

Figure 3. The normalized usability and likeability ranks. *Marbles* scores best in both categories, while *pattern 360* is rated worst.

Procedure

Each user had to use each prototype to create a password and to authenticate using a given password. Each test case started with a short training task and ended with a questionnaire about the usability, likeability and the perceived security of the tested approach. Interactivity of the paper prototypes (e.g. rotation) was simulated by the examiner. The sessions were filmed to get further insights into user behavior and interaction problems. At the end of the session a questionnaire was used to compare and rank the concepts.

Participants

The systems were tested by twelve experienced smartphone users, whose mean age was 22 (19-26) years. Seven participants were female, five male. Ten users stated to use lock screens on their phone, nine of them used Google's pattern authentication, one used PIN. Three (25%) participants stated to be familiar with smudge attacks.

Preliminary Results

The results are based on 6-point Likert scales and user rankings. The Likert scale based questions were answered after each concept was tested, while the ranking was performed after all concepts were used.

Likeability

The likeability ratings are shown in figure 3. The participants ranked the systems according to their willingness to use them on a daily base. The results were normalized for better comparison. Most users would use *marbles*, while both *pattern rotation* approaches scored worst.

In addition, we asked users after each test run if they would use the respective system. The results support the data of the likeability ranking as only three (25%) users would use *pattern 360* and four (33%) would use the *pattern 90* system. The *compass* would be used by eight (66%) participants, nine (75%) users stated, they would like to use the *dial* authentication and eleven (92%) users would like to use *marbles*.

Usability

Usability was subdivided into the two aspects "easy to use" and "easy to understand". Figures 4 and 5 present the respective results. Data was collected using Likert scales ranking from "very good" to "bad".

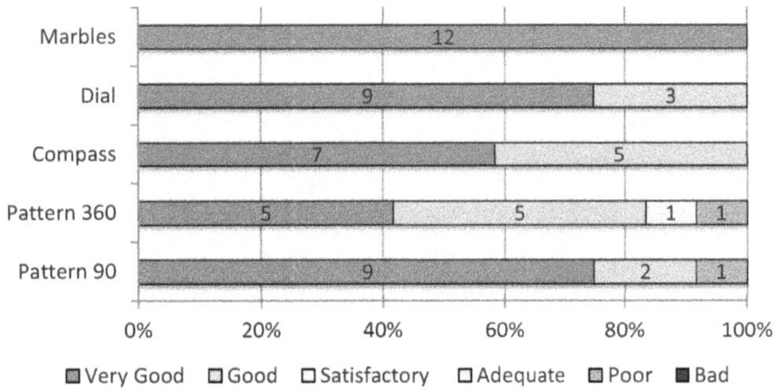

Figure 4. The comprehensibility ratings of the five concepts. *Marbles* is rated best as all participants attested very good understandability.

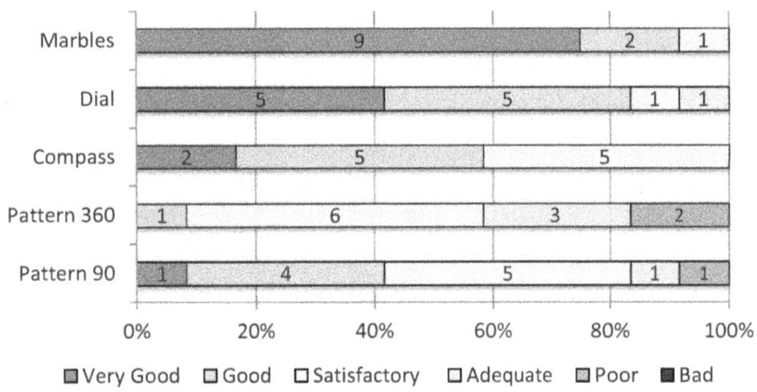

Figure 5. The usability ratings of the five concepts. *Marbles* scores best, while *pattern 360* led to most interaction problems.

Based on the median values, the understandability of all systems is rated "good" or "very good". However, the usability ratings are more diverse. Only *marbles* was attested "very good" usability. According to the participants, the *dial* and the *compass* system still provide "good" usability. Both *pattern rotation* approaches seem to be more difficult to use as usability was rated "satisfactory". Users reported that these systems demand elevated concentration. Similar statements were given according to the *compass* approach. In contrast to the in-between ratings, the *pattern 90* system was preferred to the *compass* approach in the final rankings (see figure 3).

FINAL CONCEPTS AND PROTOTYPES

Based on the results of the first user study, we decided to further analyze the feasibility of the *marbles* authentication approach. In addition, we chose the *pattern 90* approach to be further evaluated. Even if it scored worse than the *dial* system in terms of usability and likeability, we preferred this approach for two reasons: *1*) we were interested in, what impact view port rotation really has on the usability and security aspects, when compared to the Android approach. *2*) We wanted to provide a drawmetric based solution as this category is most widely used on mobile devices and thus, smudge attack protection is very relevant.

In addition to these two systems, a third system was developed during the second design phase. The *marble gap* (see figure 6, right), which is a modification of the *marbles* approach tested in the pre-study. The *marble gap* restricts reuse of identically colored marbles and has therefore the potential

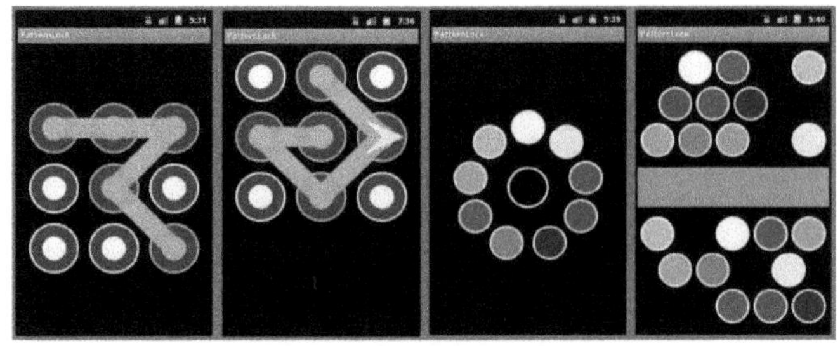

Figure 6. The four prototypes of the user study: *Android pattern* (baseline), *pattern 90*, *marbles* and *marble gap* (from left to right).

to positively influence the creation of more secure passwords. These three novel concepts and Google's pattern approach (baseline) were implemented in high fidelity prototypes using the Android SDK. In the following, the four concepts are presented in detail.

Android Pattern

The *Android pattern* approach was implemented according to the Google standards. A password is based on a pattern, which connects a maximum of nine dots. It is not allowed to visit the same dot multiple times. Due to Android specific restrictions, the theoretical password space of this approach is $389,112$ [3]. Figure 6 shows the used prototype on the most left picture.

Pattern 90

The *pattern 90* approach works analog to *Android patterns*. To prevent smudge attacks, the view port is randomly assigned and the position on the screen is alternated. The theoretical password space matches the one of *Android patterns*. The example of figure 6 shows a matrix, which was positioned on top of the screen and clockwise rotated by 90°. The underlying password of the example is "*4 2 6 8 5*".

Marbles

As no relevant shortcomings were detected, the marbles approach was implemented the same way it was tested in the pre-study. A password consists of an arbitrary sequence of marbles (colors). After a marble is dragged in the center, it immediately reappears on its prior position. The positions are kept during one authentication but rearranged at the beginning of each new attempt. The theoretical password space of this approach has no upper bound. The third image from the left of figure 6 shows the interface of the used prototype.

Marble Gap

The *marble gap* is a modification of the *marbles* approach. The most right image of figure 6 shows the interface of this concept. In contrast to the circular arrangement of the *marbles* approach, the user interface of *marble gap* is divided into three sections. The top and the bottom section present the marbles in a randomized order. The section in the center is called gap.

To authenticate, users have to drag the marbles in the right order anywhere into the gap. Marbles with the same colors do have the same values and thus it does not matter for the password, if the intended color is chosen from the top or from the bottom of the screen. After a marble was dragged into the gap, it disappears from the screen and cannot be used anymore. The prototype used in the user study featured ten different colors of which each was present two times. Thus, user passwords could comprise the same color two times maximum and the password length was restricted to 20 characters (theoretical password space $\approx 13.17 * 10^{12}$).

Another interesting aspect, which might lead to more secure passwords, is based on the fact that marbles of the same color are equally distributed over the top and the bottom section. When choosing the same color twice, one has to drag elements from the bottom and the top; in contrast, when choosing different colors one can drag marbles from one side only. This interplay of password complexity and input effort might lead to the selection of passwords, which are based on more different colors. As a consequence, high entropy in user chosen passwords is supported.

USABILITY AND SECURITY USER STUDY

The final concepts were evaluated in a user study to get insights into their usability, performance and security. In this section, we provide details on the design and the conduction of the study and report on the results.

User Study Design

The user study was based on a repeated measures factorial design. The independent variables were *authentication concept* with four levels (*Android pattern, pattern 90, marbles, marble gap*), *password origin* with two levels (*given, self-selected*) and *run* with three levels (*one, two, three*). The order of *authentication concept* was counterbalanced using a Latin square, *password origin* was alternated and *run* represented successful authentications.

Quantitative data was collected via logging mechanisms, qualitative data was collected with a questionnaire. For further analysis, the study was filmed and pictures of the device's touchscreen were taken after successful authentications. As an incentive, 10 Euro vouchers were handed out to the participants.

Experimental Setup

The prototypes were tested on an HTC Google Nexus One device. The smudge attack setup consisted of a camera (Canon EOS 1000D) and a strong light source (Arri 650W spot light) from above. The device was placed in front of the camera using a paperboard platform. The distance to the camera was approximately 20 cm, the angle between object lens and touchscreen was 60°. The setup can be seen in figure 7, it was not modified during the whole study. In addition to the smudge attack setup, the sessions were filmed using a Canon FS 306 camcorder, which was placed behind the participant and targeted on the touchscreen of the device. The web-based questionnaire was filled out using a laptop computer.

Passwords and Procedure

This section describes the guidelines of the passwords, which were used to test the described concepts. In addition, the procedure of the user study is explained in detail.

Figure 7. To perform smudge attacks, an HTC Nexus One was placed under an Arri 650W spot light and in front of a Canon EOS 1000D. Under such overexposed conditions, even minor residues become visible.

Passwords

The results of the pre-study revealed that the length of five was most often chosen for the approaches *pattern 90* and *marbles* and that theoretical security is comparable at this length. Therefore, we decided to restrict the password length for all tested systems to the length of five distinctive tokens. The given passwords of *marbles* and the *marble gap* approach were composed with a maximum of one repeated color. The passwords for the pattern approaches were composed with diverse, but counterbalanced input complexity. Half or the patterns were exclusively based on directly adjacent dots, while the other half comprised larger distances between dots. User generated passwords were also restricted to the length of five, but we did not restrict the repetition of same tokens to get insights into the password composition behavior with the respective system.

Based on five activated dots, the theoretical password space of the *Android pattern* and the *pattern 90* approach is 10,672. This is influenced by Android specific restrictions. For example, it is not possible to activate a dot, which is not a direct neighbor without activating the direct neighbor, if all three dots are in line. Given that repeated colors are allowed, the password space of *marbles* with five tokens is 59,049 (15,120 without repeated colors). As the *marble gab* allows each color to be chosen twice at maximum, the theoretical password space is 64,800 (30,240 without repeated colors).

Procedure

After an introduction to smudge attacks, the tasks of the user study were explained to the participant. To preserve privacy, each user was assigned an ID. Based on this ID, the order of *authentication concept* and *password origin* was defined. Each concept was tested twice (alternating *password origin*) using the following procedure: *1*) During a training phase, the user tried out the respective system until she stated to understand the approach. *2*) After the training, the touchscreen was cleaned using a microfiber cloth and the device was given back to the participant. *3*) The user entered the respective password. *4*) If the authentication was correct, a photo of the touchscreen was taken using the described setup. If the au-

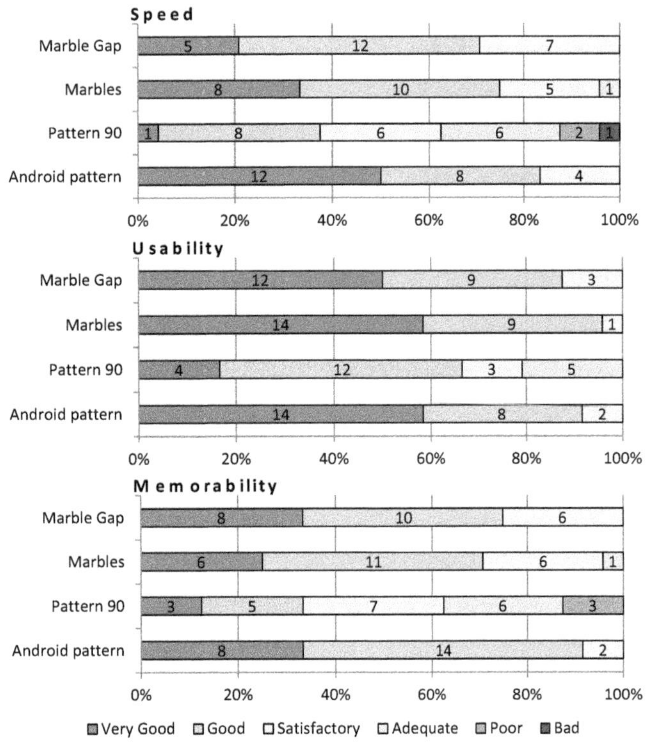

Figure 8. The qualitative results of the Likert scale analysis. While *pattern 90* is rated worst in terms of usability, authentication speed and memorability, both *marble* based approaches are rated comparable to the *Android pattern*.

thentication failed, the process started over with step 2. 5) After the picture was taken, the user had to successfully authenticate two more times. Failed authentications were repeated. While the user had the possibility to look up the password for the first and the second authentication, the third authentication had to be performed without such memory aid.

After all concepts were tested, the user filled out a questionnaire. The questionnaire collected data about the usability and performance of the concepts and demographical data of the user. In the end of the study, a 10 Euro voucher for an online shop was handed out to the participant.

Participants

24 participants took part in the user study. The mean age was 25 years (19-33). Eight users were female, 16 users were male. They were experienced touchscreen users as 23 (96%) used a smartphone on a daily base. However, only 13 (54%) users knew about smudge attacks. Seven users used patterns, six used PIN to protect their device. The rest of the group did not use secure lock screens.

USER STUDY RESULTS

In this section, we report on the results of the user study. The results are based on quantitative data of the log files and qualitative data of the questionnaire as well as photos and videos.

Authentication Speed

Authentication speed is distinguished in orientation time and input time. The orientation time is the time span between the

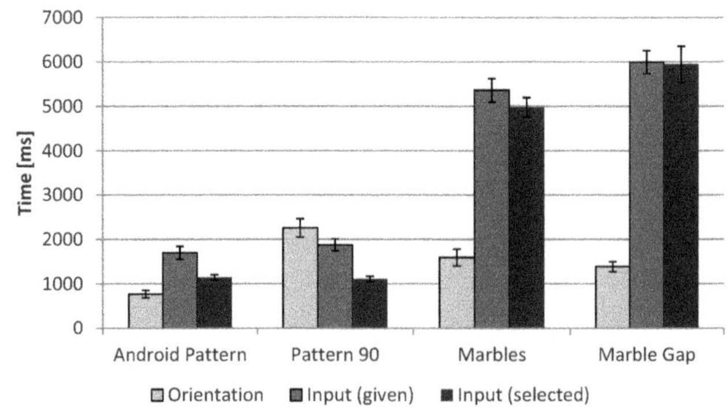

Figure 9. The average orientation time and the average input time of all systems. While input times of the *marble* approaches are significantly higher than the input times of the pattern systems, users of the *pattern 90* system need more time for orienting themselves, than for entering the password.

start of authentication and the user's first touch event. Thus, it represents the time a user needs to orient herself. With the first touch event, the input time starts. The input time ends when the password is confirmed or the authentication is cancelled. It is very important to analyze the orientation time as the data input only represents one aspect of the whole authentication process.

Data

Authentication time was analyzed based on successfully completed attempts. Input times are therefore based on 576 samples (*24 users* $*$ *2 password origins* $*$ *4 authentication concepts* $*$ *3 runs*). Due to an error in the log files, only the third authentication attempt (*run*) of each user could be used as a basis for the orientation time. Thus, the analysis of orientation time is based on a smaller set of 192 samples (*24 users* $*$ *2 password origins* $*$ *4 authentication concepts* $*$ *1 run*). However, the last run seems to be best suited for this analysis as users were already trained using the specific password two times. We excluded outliers in both data sets using the doubled standard deviation as an upper and lower boundary.

Results

We performed a repeated measures ANOVA of the orientation and input times to analyze the effects of *authentication concept*, *password origin* and *run*. The results are shown in figure 9. For better comparison, the input times of figure 9 were also based on the third run.

According to the orientation times, no significant main effects were found for *password origin* ($p > .05$). In contrast, there are highly significant main effects of *authentication concept* on the orientation time ($F_{2.1,48.4} = 16.64, p < .001$, Greenhouse-Geisser corrected: $\epsilon = .69$). Post-hoc tests reveal that users needed significantly ($p < .001$ for all contrasts) more time using the *pattern 90* ($Mn = 2254ms, SE = 206$), *marbles* ($Mn = 1592ms, SE = 188$) and *marble gab* ($Mn = 1383ms, SE = 113$) systems than using the *Android pattern* approach ($Mn = 768ms, SE = 84$). Furthermore, the *pattern 90* approach led to the highest orientation times and performed significantly worse than *marbles* and *marble gap* ($p < .05$).

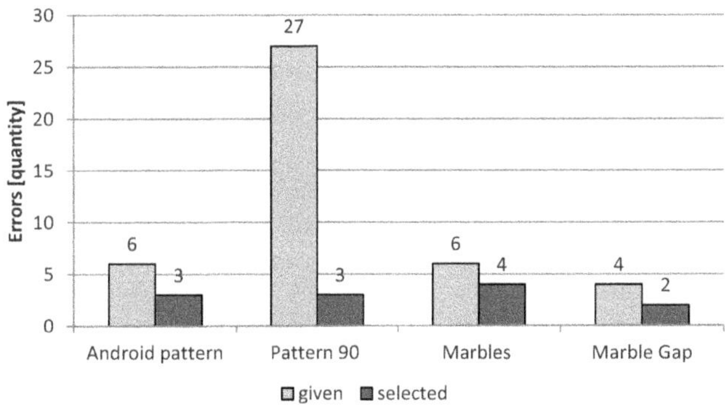

Figure 10. The amount of failed authentications. Given passwords led to significantly more errors than self-selected tokens. The *pattern 90* approach was most affected by errors.

In terms of the input time, highly significant main effects were found for *authentication concept* ($F_{2.1,41.6} = 315.32, p < .001$, Greenhouse-Geisser corrected: $\epsilon = .69$) and *password origin* ($F_{1.0,20.0} = 27.25, p < .001$). No significant main effects of *run* were found ($p > .05$). Post-hoc tests reveal that *marbles* ($Mn = 5233ms, SE = 199$) and *marble gap* ($Mn = 5982ms, SE = 261$) have significantly higher input times ($p < .001$) than *Android pattern* ($Mn = 1611ms, SE = 111$) and *pattern 90* ($Mn = 1664ms, SE = 97$). The *password origin* does not significantly influence these contrasts ($p > .05$). In addition, the input times of marble-based and pattern-based approaches are not significantly different, when compared to each other ($p > .05$). This is true for given and self-selected passwords.

However, the *password origin* has a highly significant effect on the input performance within both pattern-based concepts ($p < .001$). The participants entered passwords significantly faster, when they were self-selected. Both marble-based concepts were not affected by *password origin*.

Interestingly, the participants' perception differs from the results of the quantitative data. Based on the median values, users ranked the *Android pattern* system to be "very fast", both *marble* approaches "fast" and the *pattern 90* approach to be the slowest ("satisfactory") (see figure 8, speed). The same order was found in the final rankings, even though *pattern 90* actually performed second best in terms of authentication speed.

Error Rate and Usability

Failed authentications are distinguished in simple and critical errors. Simple errors are based on authentication sessions, which fail one or two times. Productive systems (e.g. ATM) most often allow a maximum of three attempts to authenticate, before user accounts are locked. Therefore, if an authentication fails three consecutive times, it is interpreted as a critical error.

Data

The data is based on 192 authentication sessions. Each session was finished after three successful attempts. In addition, qualitative data of the questionnaire is analyzed to get further insights into the usability and memorability of the systems.

Results

In summary, 55 authentication attempts failed, thus the error rate based on all authentications was 9.5%. Only one critical error was logged. This occurred in the third run of using the *pattern 90* system with a given password.

We performed a repeated measures ANOVA to analyze the influence of *authentication concept*, *password origin* and *run* on failed authentication attempts. Significant main effects were found for *authentication concept* ($F_{3.0,40.0} = 5.99, p < .05$, Greenhouse-Geisser corrected: $\epsilon = .58$) and for *password origin* ($F_{1.0,23.0} = 8.15, p < .05$). No significant main effect was found for *run* ($p > .05$). In addition, a significant interaction effect was found for *authentication concept* $*$ *password origin* $*$ *run*, ($F_{3.5,80.0} = 2.99, p < .05$, Greenhouse-Geisser corrected: $\epsilon = .58$). Figure 10 shows the amount of failed authentications based on *authentication concept* and *password origin*.

Post-hoc tests regarding the *authentication concept* reveal that significantly more errors were made using the *pattern 90* ($n = 30$) system than using any of the other system ($p < .05$ for all contrasts). Fewest authentications failed with the *marble gap* ($n = 6$). Using the *Android pattern*, nine authentications failed, using *marbles* ten errors were logged.

The contrast of self-selected and predetermined passwords reveals that significantly more errors were made, when the password was given ($p < .05$). 78% ($n = 43$) of all failed authentications were based on given passwords. This is mainly caused by the *pattern 90* approach, where 90% ($n = 27$) of all errors were based on given patterns.

The users' perception supports the quantitative data. Our users stated that the rotation of the *pattern 90* approach was "cumbersome" and "demanded high cognitive load". Our participants' comments reveal that most errors occurred, because the users were confused by the orientation and draw their patterns in the wrong direction. The median values of the usability ranking reflect these problems as *pattern 90* was rated "satisfactory", while all other systems were rated "good" (see figure 8). In addition, our users confirmed that self-selected passwords were easier to use on all systems. While *marble gap*, *marbles* and *Android patterns* were rated "very easy", when used with self-selected passwords, the rating dropped to "easy", when given passwords had to be used. According to the *pattern 90*, users rated the difficulty "satisfactory", when used with self-selected passwords and "poor", when used with given passwords. In the final ranking, *marble gap* was voted the easiest system; *Android pattern* was second, *marbles* third. *Pattern 90* was confirmed to be the most difficult approach.

As memorability is hard to measure in a lab experiment, we have to limit the analysis on the users' perception. In figure 8, the memorability ratings based on 6-point Likert scales are shown. The memorability of the *Android pattern* system was rated best. Based on the median, this aspect was rated "very good", when the password was self-selected and "good", when passwords were given. Both marble-based approaches were rated "good" independently from *password*

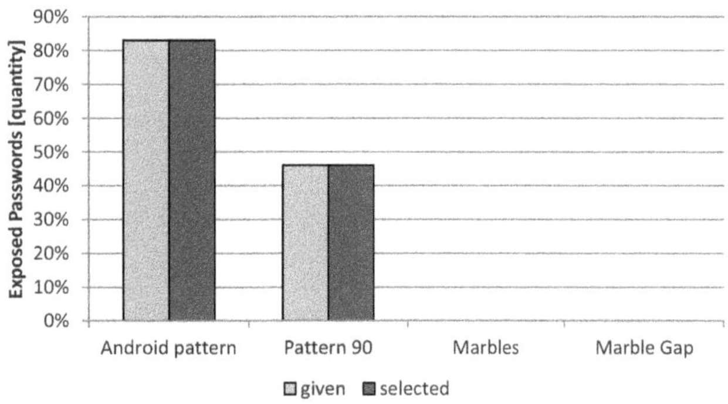

Figure 11. The percentage of exposed passwords. No passwords could be deduced from *marble*-based approaches. The *Android* approach is most prone to smudge attacks, but *pattern 90* is also vulnerable to smudge attacks, especially when the attacker has multiple guesses.

origin. However, memorability was rated slightly better, when self-selected passwords were used and the memorability of *marble gap* seems to be better, than the memorability of *marbles*. *Pattern 90* was rated worst according to this aspect. User stated that memorability was good with self-selected patterns and satisfactory with given patterns.

Security Evaluation

Since the focus of this work is smudge attack secure systems, the security evaluation is restricted to such an attack. We like to point out that there are other security threats like shoulder surfing, which are out of the scope of this work.

Data

Smudge attacks were performed based on the pictures taken during the user study. For each authentication system, one image of the self-selected password and one image of the given password were analyzed. Thus, the results are based on 192 samples. The pictures were not edited (e.g. adjusting contrast) to obtain the same conditions for each participant. Figure 12 shows one example of each concept. It has to be mentioned, that these images show optimal results and there have also been images, which had less oily residues on the screen.

The smudge attacks were performed by a security expert, who was highly familiar with the authentication systems, but had no knowledge about the used passwords. Before each attack, he was informed about the current system and the *password origin* (self-selected, given). Each attack consisted of a maximum of three guesses. The attacker was allowed to zoom and rotate the images, but no other transformations were used.

Results

Figure 11 presents the quantitative results of the security evaluation. The *Android pattern* approach is most vulnerable to smudge attacks. 20 (83%) self-selected and 20 (83%) given passwords were exposed. Eight smudge attacks failed, because none or too little smudge was visible on the display. As one can see in figure 12, left, the oily residues on the touchscreen are clearly exposing the set of activated dots *1 4 5 6 7*. In theory, there are two patterns matching this token set, but due to overlapping smudge, the right order *7 4 1 5 6* can be

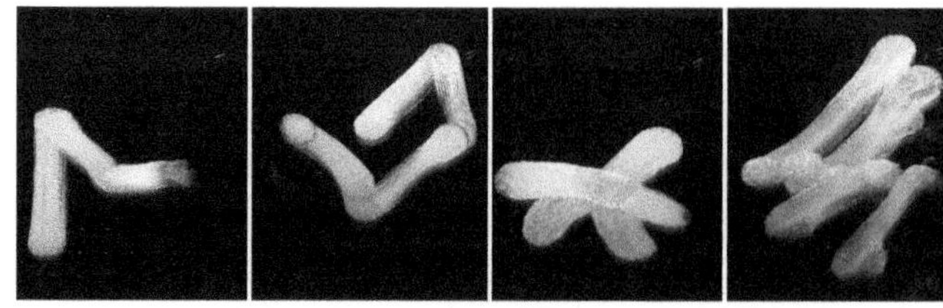

Figure 12. Examples of the pictures used for the smudge attacks. *Android pattern*, *pattern 90*, *marbles* and *marble gap* (from left to right). The images are not edited (except cropping).

deduced as well. In detail, 60% of these patterns were exposed during the first attack and the rest was found by a second guess. A third try did not improve the attacker's success rate. This indicates that, whenever enough smudge is visible on the screen and the attacker has multiple guesses, the right password can be deduced. Only two participants left almost no residues on the touchscreen and thus neither the self-selected nor the given pattern was exposed. With the *pattern 90* system, eleven (46%) self-selected and eleven (46%) given passwords could be derived. The smudge patterns of this approach (figure 12, second from the left) can be interpreted in four different directions. Since the attacker had three guesses per image, the chance to find the right pattern was 75%, whenever enough smudge was on the touchscreen. The analysis of single attempts supports this assumption as 36% of the exposed patterns were found in a first guess and another 32% were exposed during the second attack. In contrast to *Android patterns*, the third attempt further improved the success rate as 32% of the patterns were derived at this point. Another aspect, which makes *pattern 90* vulnerable, is due to the fact that in some cases additional smudge allows guessing how the device was grasped, which gives an additional cue, in what direction the pattern was entered.

Both marble-based approaches are very secure against smudge attacks. Based on the randomized order of the security tokens, the oily residues do not give enough information to deduce the password and thus no password was exposed. However, both approaches allow deriving some information about the composition of the password, which can restrict the password space for further attacks. Since the *marble gap* does not allow selecting marbles of one section multiple times, this information can be used whenever smudge is detected on only one of the two segments. The same is true for *marbles* providing that the attacker knows the length of the password and the amount of distinctive residues matches this value (vice versa repeated colors can be detected).

The analysis of the Likert scale based data reveals that the participants perceived the *Android pattern* as significantly less secure than the other three approaches. The security of the *Android patterns* system was rated "adequate", while the security of *pattern 90*, *marbles* and *marble gap* was rated "good". In the final rankings, *marble gap* was rated most secure, *marbles* was second, *pattern 90* was third and the *Android pattern* approach was ranked last place. This ranking matches the results of the quantitative analysis and indicates that users have a good understanding of security.

User Acceptance

To evaluate the user acceptance, users had to rank the systems according to likeability. In addition, we asked the participants if they would like to use the respective system on a daily base.

Android patterns were placed first according to likeability, the *marbles* approach was ranked second, *marble gap* was set on the third place. The *pattern 90* approach was the least favored concept. Correspondingly, most participants ($n = 22$, 92%) would use the Android approach on a daily base. The two participants, who refused using this concept, stated that it was not secure enough. Furthermore, 18 (75%) people would use *marbles* and 16 (67%) participants would use *marble gap* on a daily base. Criticism on these approaches was mostly related to the use of color coded tokens. People, who did not want to use these concepts, suggested the use of numbers or symbols instead. Only ten (42%) participants would use the *pattern 90* approach on a daily base. Most users, who did not want to use this approach, stated that entering the pattern needed too much spatial imagination and rotating the mobile device for each authentication was cumbersome.

DISCUSSION

The quantitative analysis of authentication speed reveals that *Android patterns* performed best in the study and thus, randomization does negatively influence the input time and the orientation time. However, marble-based approaches and the *pattern 90* system comprise different aspects of randomization and these aspects affected the authentication speed in different ways. The random orientation of the view-port mainly influences the time a user needs to orient herself, while the randomized arrangements of security tokens had more impact on the input time.

Connected to this, the conflict of the measured speed values and the users' perception is very interesting. While the *pattern 90* approach was actually the second fastest system, it was ranked to be the slowest. In contrast, both marble-based approaches, which actually performed significantly slower than the *pattern 90* approach, were rated faster. This result indicates that high orientation times were more annoying for users than high input times.

In addition, the *password origin* significantly influenced the input speed of both pattern-based approaches. When using these systems, users entered self-selected passwords significantly faster than given passwords. The input time of both marble-based approaches was not affected by this aspect. We assume that this is based on the fact that patterns provide a wider range of input complexity compared to marble-based passwords. When users had the chance to choose their passwords, they selected patterns, which were easier and thus faster to enter than given passwords.

The overall error rate was low, considering that users were not familiar with the systems and not used to the passwords. While both marble-based approaches performed well and error rates were comparable to the *Android patterns*, the *pattern 90* system led to significantly more failed authentications. 90% of these authentication errors using the *pattern 90* approach were based on given passwords. This supports the assumption that patterns cause more interaction problems, when input complexity is not controlled by the user and whenever it is possible, users tend to choose simple patterns. A complex system like *pattern 90* might reinforce this problem.

The security analysis reveals that *Android patterns* are highly vulnerable to smudge attacks and thus confirms the findings of Aviv et al. [3]. However, the risk of smudge attacks is individually diverse as some users did not leave enough residues on the display to be attacked. The *pattern 90* approach was significantly more secure against smudge attacks than *Android patterns*, but still exposed passwords. Thus, the additional benefits in terms of security seem not to justify the drawbacks in usability. The security of both marble-based approaches is excellent as not a single password could be deduced.

Taking all these aspects into account, the *pattern 90* approach seems not usable and not secure enough and thus has to be discarded. However, the analysis of this concept gave valuable insights into the interplay of authentication performance and user perception. In contrast, both marble-based approaches performed well in terms of usability and security. Therefore, we argue that these concepts are promising candidates for a smudge attack secure mobile authentication, which is usable and highly accepted by the users.

LIMITATIONS

Even if the study was carefully designed, there are some limitations concerning the experiment and the collected data, we would like to address.

Since we performed a short term lab study, we were not able to examine training effects and how our concepts affect memorability. All passwords were new to the users and therefore, we assume that performance would improve on all systems when they were used with well-known and memorized passwords. In addition, we assume that password composition was influenced by the fact that the participants did not have to protect real sensitive data. If the respective systems would be used in the wild, users would potentially create more secure passwords and the difference between given passwords and the user-selected ones would be smaller.

In terms of generalizability, we have to mention that the data is based on 24 users only and can therefore only give indications on the performance of the proposed systems. However, based on the thorough design of the study and since multiple samples were collected per user and per system, we argue that our data is valid.

CONCLUSION AND FUTURE WORK

In this paper, we analyzed the vulnerability of *Android patterns* to smudge attacks and proposed alternative more secure graphic-based authentication concepts. The concept development was based on a thorough design and evaluation process. In a first step, candidate concepts were found and paper prototypes were built and evaluated in a user study. In a second step, the results of the paper prototype analysis were used to develop the final concepts, which were implemented for Android smartphones and evaluated in terms of usability, performance and security. The results were set in relation to the *Android pattern* approach.

While one pattern-based concept (*pattern 90*) had to be discarded as the trade-off between usability and security was not sufficient, we found two promising token-based concepts. The systems are significantly more secure against smudge attacks than *Android patterns*. In addition, error rates were low and authentication speed was perceived comparably fast. The likeability scores of both systems support the assumption that our concepts are actual candidates for smudge attack secure and usable graphical authentication systems on mobile devices.

In addition, we presented general findings about user authentication. Firstly, the *marble gap* approach indicates the existence of an interplay of input complexity and password complexity. Based on this approach, the input complexity of stronger passwords seems lower than the input complexity of weak passwords. We argue that this aspect might be used to implicitly teach users to create stronger passwords. Secondly, the results of the distinct analysis of authentication speed indicate that high orientation times are more annoying than high input times.

In future work, we will evaluate the proposed concepts in a long-term field study to gather insights into training effects, password composition behavior and the memorability of such passwords. In addition, we plan to integrate shoulder surfing in our analysis and evaluate our concepts according to such attacks. Furthermore, we like to address the interplay of input complexity and password complexity in our upcoming research.

REFERENCES

1. Adams, A., and Sasse, M. Users are not the enemy. *Communications of the ACM 42*, 12 (1999), 40–46.
2. Airowaily, K., and Alrubaian, M. Oily residuals security threat on smart phones. In *Robot, Vision and Signal Processing (RVSP), 2011 First International Conference on*, IEEE (2011), 300–302.
3. Aviv, A., Gibson, K., Mossop, E., Blaze, M., and Smith, J. Smudge attacks on smartphone touch screens. In *Proceedings of the 4th USENIX conference on Offensive technologies*, USENIX Association (2010), 1–7.
4. Bianchi, A., Oakley, I., Kostakos, V., and Kwon, D. The phone lock: audio and haptic shoulder-surfing resistant pin entry methods for mobile devices. In *Proceedings of the fifth international conference on Tangible, embedded, and embodied interaction*, ACM (2011), 197–200.
5. Bianchi, A., Oakley, I., and Kwon, D. S. The secure haptic keypad: a tactile password system. In *Proceedings of the SIGCHI Conference on Human Factors in Computing Systems*, CHI '10, ACM (New York, NY, USA, 2010), 1089–1092.
6. Brostoff, S., and Sasse, M. Are passfaces more usable than passwords? a field trial investigation. *PEOPLE AND COMPUTERS* (2000), 405–424.
7. De Angeli, A., Coutts, M., Coventry, L., Johnson, G., Cameron, D., and Fischer, M. Vip: a visual approach to user authentication. In *Proceedings of the Working Conference on Advanced Visual Interfaces*, ACM (2002), 316–323.
8. De Luca, A., Hang, A., Brudy, F., Lindner, C., and Hussmann, H. Touch me once and i know it's you!: implicit authentication based on touch screen patterns. In *Proceedings of the 2012 ACM annual conference on Human Factors in Computing Systems*, ACM (2012), 987–996.
9. De Luca, A., Von Zezschwitz, E., and Hußmann, H. Vibrapass: secure authentication based on shared lies. In *Proceedings of the 27th international conference on Human factors in computing systems*, ACM (2009), 913–916.
10. Jermyn, I., Mayer, A., Monrose, F., Reiter, M., Rubin, A., et al. The design and analysis of graphical passwords. In *Proceedings of the 8th USENIX Security Symposium*, Washington DC (1999), 1–14.
11. Karlson, A., Brush, A., and Schechter, S. Can i borrow your phone?: understanding concerns when sharing mobile phones. In *Proceedings of the 27th international conference on Human factors in computing systems*, ACM (2009), 1647–1650.
12. Madigan, S. Picture memory. *Imagery, memory and cognition* (1983), 65–89.
13. Renaud, K., and De Angeli, A. Visual passwords: cure-all or snake-oil? *Commun. ACM 52*, 12 (Dec. 2009), 135–140.
14. Roth, V., Richter, K., and Freidinger, R. A pin-entry method resilient against shoulder surfing. In *Proceedings of the 11th ACM conference on Computer and communications security*, ACM (2004), 236–245.
15. Shadmehr, R., and Brashers-Krug, T. Functional stages in the formation of human long-term motor memory. *The Journal of Neuroscience 17*, 1 (1997), 409–419.
16. Standing, L. Learning 10000 pictures. *The Quarterly journal of experimental psychology 25*, 2 (1973), 207–222.
17. Varenhorst, C., et al. Passdoodles: A lightweight authentication method. *Research Science Institute* (2004).
18. Wiedenbeck, S., Waters, J., Birget, J., Brodskiy, A., and Memon, N. Passpoints: Design and longitudinal evaluation of a graphical password system. *International Journal of Human-Computer Studies 63*, 1 (2005), 102–127.
19. Wiedenbeck, S., Waters, J., Sobrado, L., and Birget, J. Design and evaluation of a shoulder-surfing resistant graphical password scheme. In *Proceedings of the working conference on Advanced visual interfaces*, ACM (2006), 177–184.

SmartDCap: Semi-Automatic Capture of Higher Quality Document Images from a Smartphone

Francine Chen Scott Carter Laurent Denoue
FX Palo Alto Laboratory
Palo Alto, CA USA
{chen, carter, denoue}@fxpal.com

Jayant Kumar
University of Maryland
College Park, MD USA
jayant@umiacs.umd.edu

ABSTRACT
People frequently capture photos with their smartphones, and some are starting to capture images of documents. However, the quality of captured document images is often lower than expected, even when an application that performs post-processing to improve the image is used. To improve the quality of captured images before post-processing, we developed the Smart Document Capture (SmartDCap) application that provides real-time feedback to users about the likely quality of a captured image. The quality measures capture the sharpness and framing of a page or regions on a page, such as a set of one or more columns, a part of a column, a figure, or a table. Using our approach, while users adjust the camera position, the application automatically determines when to take a picture of a document to produce a good quality result. We performed a subjective evaluation comparing SmartDCap and the Android Ice Cream Sandwich (ICS) camera application; we also used raters to evaluate the quality of the captured images. Our results indicate that users find SmartDCap to be as easy to use as the standard ICS camera application. Also, images captured using SmartDCap are sharper and better framed on average than images using the ICS camera application.

Author Keywords
Mobile computing; mobile capture; image analysis; documents

ACM Classification Keywords
H.5.2 User Interfaces; I.7.5 Document Capture: Document analysis, Scanning

INTRODUCTION
Mobile devices with cameras are rapidly proliferating and are being used to capture media at an ever-increasing rate. Furthermore, document scanning applications in particular generally rank among the most downloaded enterprise applications on the Android and iOS application stores, with several individual applications having more than a million downloads. Unfortunately, the quality of document photos, even using specialized applications, is often poor. Although cameras on mobile devices have increasingly higher resolutions, the small camera size, uneven lighting conditions, and other contextual issues often conspire to make using a camera phone to capture a high quality image of a document difficult. Even if a user tries to carefully position the document in the camera's preview screen, the quality of the final image may still not be as good as expected. Some possible causes for poor image quality include:

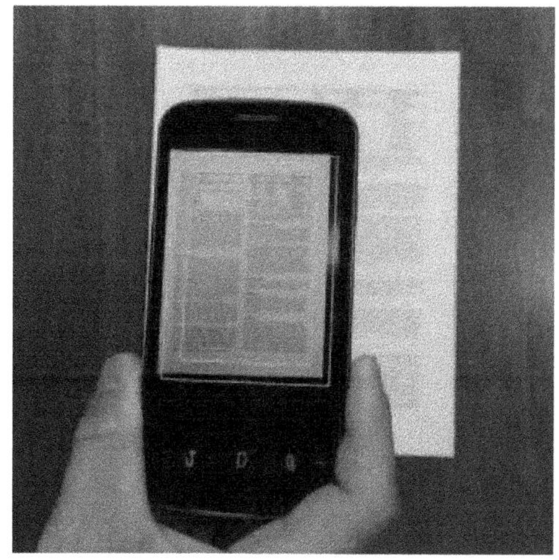

Figure 1. Using SmartDCap to take a high quality document image.

Focus: With small viewers, it may not be obvious when the focus is poor. At the close ranges used for capturing page images, small hand movements can cause blur, and autofocus does not always correctly determine focus. In addition, the camera may occasionally refocus without warning.

Framing: The captured photo may crop part of the desired content or include too much extraneous context (and therefore the resolution is lower than it could be) because it is hard to simultaneously check that multiple edges are correctly framed. A framing aid based on structured light was developed for capturing documents using a regular camera [14]. Although this approach improved framing, it is not currently feasible for use with smartphones.

Rotation: The frame of the camera image may be rotated relative to the page, resulting in lower resolution characters.

Shadows and poor lighting: Poor lighting results in lower image quality. A slower shutter speed is often used to com-

Figure 2. Sharpness can vary due to limited depth of field.

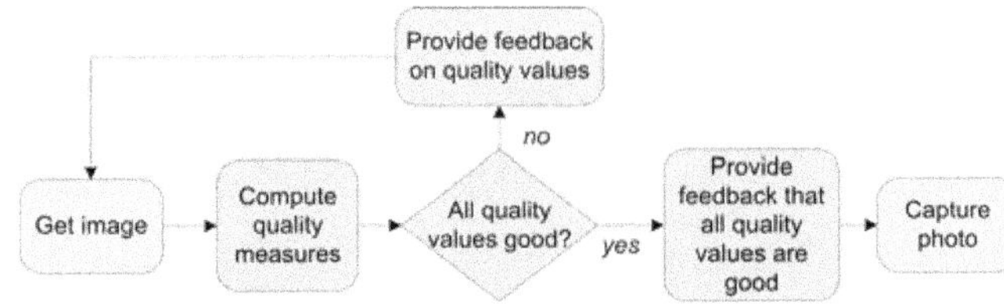

Figure 3. SmartDCap analyzes video preview frames in realtime, communicates their quality to the user, and automatically snaps a photo when the image quality is high.

pensate under low light conditions, with the consequence that small hand movements result in blur. The act of taking a picture may itself lower the quality of the image, especially if the user casts a shadow by leaning over the document. Sometimes the shadow is not apparent when looking at the paper, but appears exaggerated in the captured photo.

Depth variation: Due to limited depth of field in most smartphone cameras, a photo of a page or other items that fill the camera screen may have blurry regions if the camera plane is not relatively parallel to the plane of the page. For example, if the user holds their camera to one side, as someone sitting might do when photographing a page on their desk, the camera may not be able to uniformly bring into focus the different depths at close range. This is illustrated in Figure 2, where the text at the top of the page is blurrier than the text at the bottom.

Although post-image processing can address some of these issues, some information may be lost and artifacts can be introduced. The resulting quality is not as good as a photo of a flat page captured straight-on so that it is aligned with the plane of the camera sensor, closely framed for high resolution, and with good lighting.

In this paper we present our *Smart Document Capture* (SmartDCap) system for semi-automatic, higher quality capture of the content of a document page. SmartDCap provides realtime feedback to users about the likely quality of an image of a flat document page and automatically snaps a photo when the quality is acceptable, allowing the user to lean away from the document so as not to interfere with the captured image. We describe the two measures used to estimate image quality, sharpness and framing, and show that the sharpness measure correlates well with perceived sharpness of document and scene images. We also describe a subjective study evaluating the ease of using our SmartDCap application and the Android Ice Cream Sandwich (ICS) camera application. We also present an evaluation of the quality of captured images.

RELATED WORK

Many applications for the iPhone and Android perform post-processing to improve pictures people have taken of business cards and document pages. For example, Genius Scan[1], CamScanner+[2], TurboScan[3] and CamCard[4] offer features such as automatic and semi-automatic detection of the edges of a business card or page and perspective correction, color correction, exporting the document in formats including JPG and PDF, and supporting email and sharing of the document. ClearCam[5] merges several rapid-fire photos into a single higher-resolution image. With these document-capture applications, the offered features are applied to an image that has been captured in the usual way: look at the phone's screen, decide when a shot of a document page is good, and press a button. The applications do not help a user to capture a better image, but perform post-processing to try and improve whatever image was captured. However, there is a limit on how much the post-processing methods can improve a poorly captured image. For example, when post-processing to sharpen an image is applied to an image with varying sharpness, as in Figure 2, the blurrier regions will often still appear blurrier.

In contrast, our focus is on improving the quality of captured document images *at the time of capture*. With our method, the user need not try and determine when the capture conditions are good. Instead, the user only has to adjust the phone until SmartDCap detects the image quality is good. The resulting higher quality images captured using SmartDCap can then be improved even further using any of post-processing methods employed by other capture applications. Because SmartDCap provides higher quality images to begin with, the post-processed images should be of at least as high quality as the regularly captured images, if not higher. For example, SmartDCap encourages pages to be captured straight-on, so there is minimal blurriness from limited depth of field.

Many cameras now use face detection or smile detection to provide feedback when one or more people are visible in a camera viewer. Some Casio cameras have an Auto Shutter mode[6]. The Anti Blur Auto Shutter will automatically capture a photo when the camera is stationary. This is especially useful for capturing sharper images when subjects are moving. However, a stationary camera alone may not be adequate for capturing sharp document images; in the close range used to take photos of pages, the camera autofocus does not always work correctly. Thus, an image may be blurry even if the camera is stationary. Casio also offers Auto Shutter for Panning, Smile Detection, and Self Portrait modes. However, none of these are applicable to capturing document pages.

[1]https://play.google.com/store/apps/details?id=com.thegrizzlylabs.geniusscan

[2]http://itunes.apple.com/us/app/camscanner/id388624839

[3]http://itunes.apple.com/us/app/turboscan-quickly-scan-multipage/id342548956

[4]http://creativeoverflow.net/camcard-application-review/

[5]http://itunes.apple.com/us/app/clearcam/id364930963

[6]http://www.exilim.eu/euro/exilimcard/exs10/editing/#editing/autoshutter

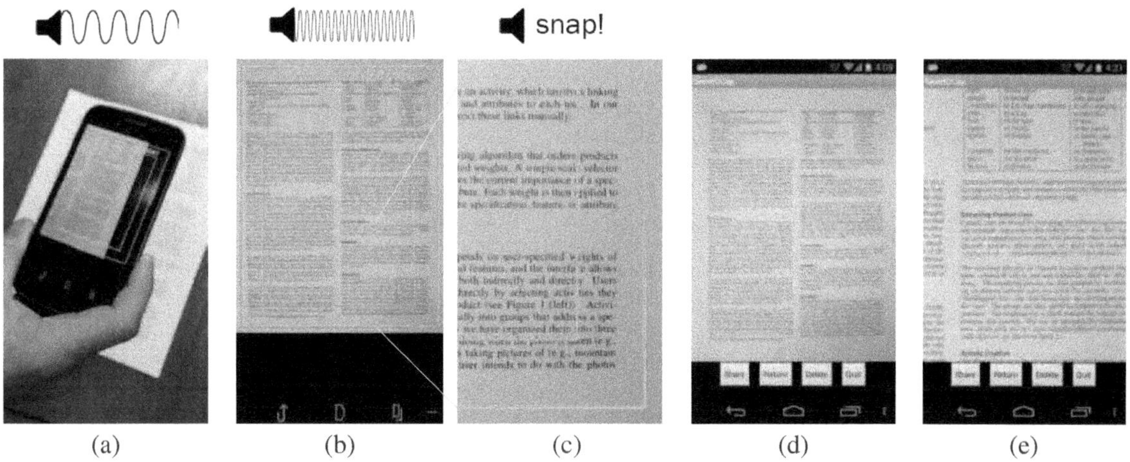

Figure 4. Capturing a photo with SmartDCap. (a) At first, as the user positions the device, the auditory feedback tone frequency and sharpness score are low. (b) As the document sharpness score increases, the feedback tone frequency increases. (c) Once the photo is sharp and the edges of the text or image regions to be captured are between the two green overlaid rectangles, the application snaps a photo. (d) The user can then review the shot before sharing it, deleting it, or taking another photo. (e) The user can also pan and zoom the captured image to verify its quality.

A few systems have been developed which provide feedback on framing an image. NudgeCam [2], which provides hints at point-of-capture to help users take a high quality video. [17] and EasySnap [19, 7] couple real-time image processing with audio feedback to help the visually impaired center a text region of interest for taking a photo. In [17], tones at different pitch and tempo "based on the distance on the screen from the current position to the target" were used as feedback, where the target is text in street scenes. EasySnap [19, 7] gives verbal feedback, such as "Go Left" and "Turn Right". The version in [19] has a "document" mode that provides audio feedback for centering and aligning text but does not handle pictures on a page. In contrast, the framing in SmartDCap is more precise and focused on how well text and/or pictures in a document fill the photo. Additionally, shots of any region sufficiently separate from the rest of the page content, such as one or more columns, a part of a column, a figure, or a table, can be taken. Another difference is that SmartDCap automatically determines when to take a photo.

Our contributions in this paper include a method for capturing higher quality images of documents *at the time of capture*, which enables even higher quality final images after post-processing, and a simple-to-use application, SmartDCap, that determines when to capture an image.

SMART DOCUMENT CAPTURE

The SmartDCap application helps a user to capture higher quality images of a document from a smartphone. The application can run on a phone with no external support – it only needs access to the phone's camera.

The application has three distinct stages: *analysis* of video preview frames; *capture* of a high resolution photo; and *user review* of the captured photo.

Analysis As the camera views the document, the system analyzes the preview frame using two distinct quality scores that characterize image sharpness and framing (Figure 3). The two scores are used to determine whether the image quality is high enough for capturing a good photo. The phone translates these scores into feedback to the user. Past work has found that real-time feedback can improve task performance in mobile-video applications [11], that such applications should support multiple different types of feedback to match the demands of different environments [6], and that non-speech, auditory feedback in particular can enhance visual interactions on a mobile device [20]. In SmartDCap, feedback is presented as a visual score displayed on the screen as well as audio trills and tones, where lower scores are mapped to low frequency tones and higher scores are mapped to high frequency tones (Figure 4a,b). In designing the auditory feedback, we employed a common method for auditory graphing: the data values, i.e., sharpness estimates, were mapped to the frequency of a short tone, so that increasing pitch corresponds to increasing sharpness [13, 18]. The sharpness values were clipped to a minimum and maximum value to limit the frequency range. The tones were relatively short to better accommodate quick changes in sharpness, but long enough to allow users to perceive pitch. Although sound frequency is a relative perception for most people, in SmartDCap the tones are played up to five times a second (after each sharpness computation a tone corresponding to the current sharpness value is played if a sound is not currently being played to allow for a short pause between tones) so that a user only need be concerned with whether the pitch is rising. Also during the analysis stage, the screen of the camera has overlaid two rectangles, which we refer to as *framing rectangles*, that indicate where the text or page content should extend as in Figure 4a-c. With the camera in autofocus mode, the user holds the phone approximately over the region of interest, and then waits until the feedback tones are high and constant in pitch to indicate that the image is sharp and in focus. As the user adjusts the position of the phone so that edges of the content of interest fall between the two rectangles, the camera continues to provide sharpness feedback.

Capture When both sharpness and framing quality are good, a short trill, an earcon [1], is played to alert the user that a photo is about to be automatically captured (Figure 4c). The user should try to hold the camera still while the picture is captured to minimize motion blur, especially in dim light. When both sharpness and framing quality are good in a second video frame, a second short trill at a higher pitch is played and the system automatically takes a photo of the document.

Review Since the application analyses video preview frames but snaps a high resolution photo, there can be a brief delay in the handoff between the video preview analysis and the photo capture. Though unlikely, it is possible that the device moves between the time the last video frame was analyzed and the time the phone snapped the high resolution image. For this reason, it is important to provide a pannable, zoomable view to allow the user to review the captured image (Figure 4d,e). From this view the user can share the photo with an external application, take a photo of a new page, or delete the current image and reshoot the current page.

We implemented our quality measures and the SmartDCap interface on the Android platform. We have tested the application on a variety of devices running Android 4.0.x (ICS) as well as Android 4.1.x (Jelly Bean). For the purposes of this paper and the evaluations described later, we deployed the application to a Galaxy Nexus running ICS. Computation of the sharpness estimates and the character-based framing measures in Android Java was too slow for real-time use. So to compute the quality measures quickly enough for real-time feedback, the measures were implemented in native C++ and called methods from the Android port of the OpenCV library[7]. We found that in the native implementation, the time to estimate framing quality was negligible compared to the time to estimate sharpness. For common technical articles, our native implementation processed approximately 2-5 frames/sec, depending in part on the complexity of the image. Note that this rate applies only to the framing and sharpness feedback – since processing was run on a thread separate from the camera the video content was shown to the user at the default frame rate. We next describe the computation of the image quality measures used by SmartDCap.

Quality Measures

Two different measures are used to estimate when the camera is in a good position for taking a photo: 1) image sharpness and 2) framing quality. We do not explicitly compute the orientation of text lines to estimate how well they are aligned with a camera edge. While this may improve results, this is computationally expensive, which we try to minimize for real-time mobile capture. Instead, as described below, the simple-to-compute image sharpness measure and framing quality measure indirectly give an indication of text line alignment.

Image Sharpness

We developed an efficient method for estimating the sharpness of the preview image that is computed on-the-fly on a smartphone. Several top-performing, perceptually-motivated, sharpness measures for scene images are based on the width of edges (sharper edges have smaller edge widths) measured in pixels e.g., [3, 12]. However these measures are slow to compute and do not perform well on text, which has sharp edges that often only three or fewer pixels wide. Instead of measuring edge width in pixels, a coarsely quantized value, we estimate the sharpness of an edge based on the "slope" of gray-scale intensities. We compute the slope by integrating the second derivative of gray-scale intensities over a small window around an edge. Since the second derivative will be close to zero away from an edge, summing outside the edge does not affect the computed slope. Thus our method is less sensitive to pixel width quantization than computing slope directly. Taking a digital derivative by computing differences, the second derivative at pixel $I_{k,j}$ is computed digitally as a difference of differences, $(I_{k+2j} - I_{k,j}) - (I_{k,j} - I_{k-2,j})$, assuming pixel width is a constant that can be ignored. The sharpness, $S_x(i,j)$, in the x-direction at median-filtered edge pixel $I_{i,j}$ located at (i,j) in an image, is computed as the digital integral (i.e., sum) of the magnitude of the second derivative of median-filtered pixel values, normalized by the magnitude of the change in contrast over a window:

$$S_x(i,j) = \frac{\sum_{i-w \le k \le i+w} |(I_{k+2,j} - I_{k,j}) - (I_{k,j} - I_{k-2,j})|}{\sum_{i-w \le k \le i+w} |g_{k,j} - g_{k-1,j}|}$$

where $g(k,j)$ is the grayscale intensity of a pixel at (k,j) in the image and w is a parameter defining window size. In practice, we set $w = 3$. Because we do not care whether slope is positive or negative, slope magnitudes are used. The denominator provides normalization for different contrast levels; it was noted in [3] that as contrast increases, the width of just noticeable blur decreases. The pixel at i,j is defined to be sharp in the horizontal direction if $S_x(i,j) > T$, where the threshold T is learned from a set of images labeled for sharpness.

Our measure for estimating the overall sharpness of an image, ΔDoM, combines the proportion of edge pixels that are sharp in the horizontal and vertical directions using the Frobenius norm:

$$\Delta DoM = \sqrt{\left(\frac{\#sharpPix_x}{\#edgePix_x}\right)^2 + \left(\frac{\#sharpPix_y}{\#edgePix_y}\right)^2}.$$

Dataset	*Method* JNB	CPBD	ΔDoM
Doc	0.43	0.31	0.63
LIVE	0.84	0.94	0.89
CSIQ	0.77	0.89	0.84

Table 1. Spearman rank correlation of perceived image sharpness with three sharpness estimation methods on a document image dataset and two scene image datasets.

Image Sharpness Evaluation We evaluated how well our ΔDoM sharpness measure corresponds with perceived sharpness on three datasets:

Doc 135 document page images contributed by 27 smartphone users. Each page was labeled for sharpness by 21-25

[7]http://opencv.willowgarage.com/wiki/

	Method		
Dataset	JNB	CPBD	ΔDoM
Doc	33.63	55.46	3.91
LIVE	2.25	1.05	0.27
CSIQ	1.71	0.68	0.26

Table 2. Computation time per image (in sec) for three sharpness estimation methods on a document image dataset and two scene image datasets.

(a) (b) (c)

Figure 5. Images that do not meet framing quality constraints: (a) page is rotated (b) text area is too small (c) all four margins are bad.

Mechanical Turk workers from a pool of 76 workers (the judgments of seven workers who had poor agreement with the other 76 workers were removed).

LIVE A freely available image sharpness dataset[8] [16]. We used the Gaussian-blurred subset composed of 174 images labeled for sharpness by 24 subjects.

CSIQ A freely available image sharpness datase[9] [8]. We used the Gaussian-blurred subset composed of 150 images labeled for sharpness by 35 subjects.

We compared how ΔDoM performs against two leading perceptually-based sharpness measures, JNB [3] and CPBD [12], for estimating the sharpness of photos of natural scenes. Table 1 shows the Spearman rank correlation between manually labeled sharpness and sharpness estimates by the JNB, CPBD and ΔDoM measures. We observed that on the Doc dataset, ΔDoM performed best among the measures. We observed that ΔDoM also performed competitively with JNB and CPBD for predicting the sharpness of the blurred scene images in the LIVE and CSIQ datasets.

We also compared the computational speed of the three methods by measuring the average time it took to process an image on each of the three datasets. A 64-bit 2.83 GHz Intel Core2 Quad Windows 7 machine with 4 GB of memory was used for all computations. A MatLab implementation of ΔDoM was used for comparison against the freely available MatLab implementations of JNB and CPBD. Each method and dataset combination was run three times and the median of the average times is shown in Table 2. Note that ΔDoM is significantly faster than JNB and CPBD. Unlike the JNB and CPBD methods, ΔDoM does not require computing multiple time-consuming exponentials, Canny edge-detection, or counting pixels for edge-width computation.

[8]http://live.ece.utexas.edu/research/quality/subjective.htm

[9]http://vision.okstate.edu/?loc=csiq

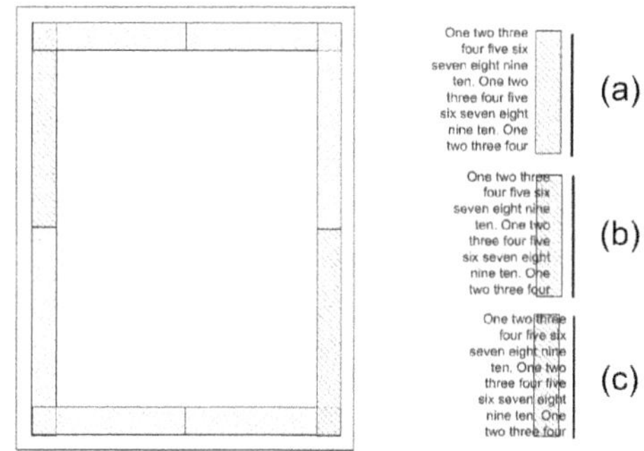

Figure 6. Quiet Margins in an image are required to extend from each edge to inside the nearest hashed/colored area. There are two zones along each edge in the left figure. The quiet margins meet framing quality constraints for a zone on the right side in (b) but not in (a) or (c).

Framing Quality

A document should be well aligned to the preview image. Unlike scanned images, capture conditions when using a mobile device are not controlled and the camera may be so close that no margins or full columns are in view, or so far that other irrelevant objects are in view. Three examples of poorly framed text are shown in Figure 5. When taking a photo of a document page, a user may wish to photograph the whole page or only part of the columns in a page. Identifying the edges of the page can be used to frame a whole page, but not text columns or regions such as a figure or table.

To identify whether the content is well-framed, we offer a simple method for estimating framing quality that can be computed in real-time on a smartphone. While many page segmentation techniques have been proposed, e.g. a comparison of six methods is given in [15], these techniques are not directly applicable to camera-captured images of document pages due to many factors [10], including lack of consideration for real-time computation on a mobile device and the assumptions of flatbed scanning without extraneous objects and of pages being printed on white paper. Rather than performing full page segmentation, we draw from a subset of page segmentation methods to identify "gutters" of white space between columns of content to estimate whether framing along an edge is good.

We focus on the width of the "gutter" between a text column and another column or edge of the page, which allows a user to frame regions of a page in addition to whole pages. We refer to these gutters as **Quiet Margins** and the width of a gutter as a 'quiet margin size'. The permissible quiet margin size is constrained between a minimum (0.02 * imageWidth) and maximum (0.08 * imageWidth), represented in Figure 4a-c by the outer and inner green framing rectangles, respectively. A minimum quiet margin size helps ensure that a column is not cropped; a maximum quiet margin size helps ensure that most of the image is filled with the region of interest. Although the background could be cropped as done by many applications such as those mentioned in Related Work, the resulting resolution of the text content decreases as the background area increases. To enforce rotation restrictions, two zones along each edge are checked for whether the quiet margin values are acceptable. The allowable range of the inside

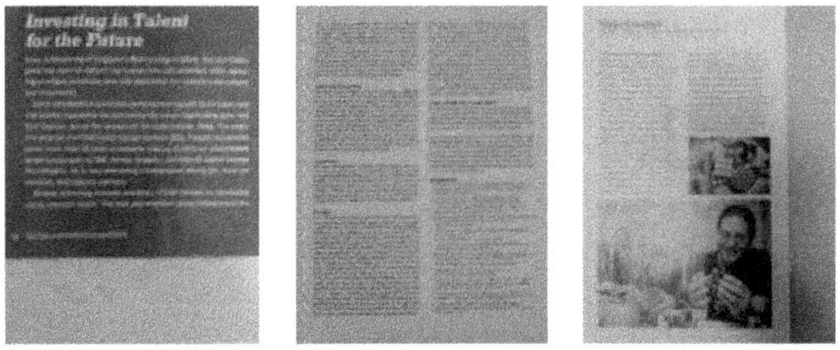

(a) (b) (c)

Figure 7. Captured images that meet framing quality constraints: (a,b) left, right and top margins meet constraints (c) top, bottom and left margins meet constraints.

edge of quiet margins with two zones per side is shown by the hashed, colored areas in Figure 6.

A number of features can be used to estimate quiet margin size, including pixel values, text character locations, and feature point locations. Independent pixel-based and connected component-based methods have been developed for page segmentation [15]. We chose to use a combination of these two complementary approaches: (1) pixel-based works well on uniform backgrounds and handles photos, and 2) character-based works well on text, handles non-uniform backgrounds better than pixel-based, but does not handle photos with gradual color changes well.

Pixel-based Our pixel-based method for estimating quiet margin size is similar to computing pixel-based projection profiles [9], but is computed over only part of a page for efficiency. Specifically, the image is first binarized, and then a row/column of pixels in a zone starting at the edge is processed. A row/column is classified as 'quiet' if it contains fewer than a small, pre-defined number of foreground pixels, thus allowing for some noise in a margin. To handle different colored backgrounds, the background color of a zone is identified as the predominant color of the row/column along the edge of that zone. A zone is labeled as 'good' if the first non-quiet row/column from the edge falls within the hashed areas in Figure 6.

Character-based To estimate quiet margin size based on character locations, our approach is similar in spirit to identifying gutters by computing a projection profile of all connected components, as in [5], but more efficient. To identify character-size components, contours of edges are identified by first converting the image to grayscale, applying Canny edge detection, and then applying connected component analysis. Next, connected components of a size and aspect ratio that are not in a range appropriate for text characters are filtered out. The location of the bounding box of each remaining connected component is computed and assigned for consideration in one or more zones. For example, the bottom zone along the right margin in Figure 6 (red) considers all bounding boxes which have a centroid in the bottom half of the image. Next, rather than creating a profile of connected component bounding boxes with values for each pixel along an edge, we examine only the locations of one side of the bounding boxes in the zone for efficiency. For example, again using the bottom zone in the right margin, only the locations of the right edge of bounding boxes are examined. To remove noisy characters from consideration while preserving characters at the right edge of a paragraph, a small number of the rightmost characters (up to 10) are ignored unless they are aligned with at least three other bounding boxes in a direction roughly parallel to the edge. The difference between the rightmost remaining value and the right edge of the image serves as an estimate of the right margin; the bottom right zone is 'good' if the margin falls in the (red) hashed area (see Figure 6b). To handle non-text regions, the number of characters is counted, and if there are too few, it is noted. The margin size is computed similarly for the other zones. A zone that was noted as having too few characters is labeled 'good' if the other zone associated with the same edge has been labeled 'good'.

An edge is labeled as a good quiet margin if each zone of an edge is determined to be good by either the pixel- or character-based methods. At least three good quiet margins are required in order for the framing of the page image to be considered acceptable, as illustrated by the examples in Figure 7. Note that quiet margins can handle different colored backgrounds and photos on a page, as well as text. Also note in (a) and (c) that by requiring only three, rather than four, edges to have good margins, we can capture parts of pages that do not completely fill the image and yet are well-framed.

Combined Quality Measures

The Image Sharpness and the Quiet Margins measures are used together by the SmartDCap system for providing feedback and determining when the image quality is high enough for taking a photo. Image Sharpness is used first to indicate the sharpness of the preview image. If the preview is sharp enough for capturing a photo, then the Quiet Margin measure is checked simultaneously. When both the framing is good and the preview image is in focus the camera can automatically capture a photo. When both measures jointly indicate good image quality, many of the issues outlined in the Introduction are ameliorated:

Focus: Image Sharpness indicates when the image is sharp.

Framing: Quiet Margins constrain the framing to be relatively straight.

Rotation: Quiet Margins constrain the amount of rotation allowed.

Shadows and poor lighting: When there are shadows over the image or poor lighting, the edges are not as sharp, and so the Image Sharpness measure will be lower.

Depth variation: When taking a photo from the side, both the Image Sharpness and the Framing Quality measures will be poor.

EVALUATION

We conducted a subjective evaluation to compare the *ease of using* SmartDCap versus a standard camera application. We also evaluated the *quality* of the captured photos.

In our evaluations, we compared SmartDCap and the Android ICS camera application (shown in Figure 9). We chose to

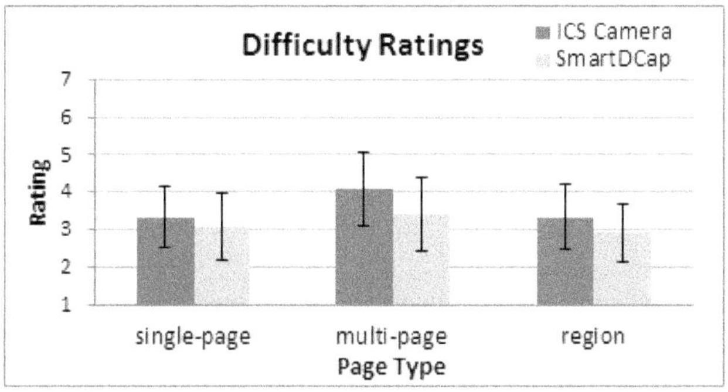

Figure 8. Mean difficulty ratings with 95% confidence intervals for images captured by the ICS camera application and SmartDCap by page type. Rating of 1 is easy, 7 is difficult.

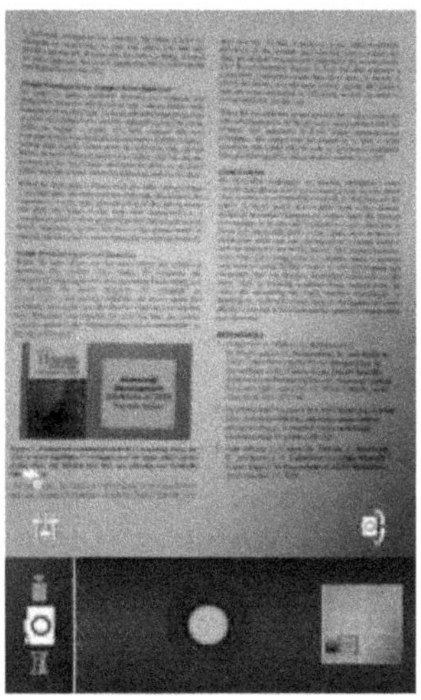

Figure 9. The default Android ICS camera application used in the evaluation. The application automatically focuses when taking a photo. Users could view the previously taken image by clicking on its thumbnail (lower right).

compare against the ICS camera application since it comes pre-installed on the device and is therefore the default camera application for most users. Although we could compare against other capture applications, the improvements that they offer are done *after* capture; those same post-processing improvements can also be applied to the images captured by SmartDCap. Comparing to the default application allows us to test whether SmartDCap improves the quality of photos captured *before* post-processing.

Subjective Evaluation

For our subjective experiment, we used a Galaxy Nexus with both the ICS camera application and SmartDCap installed. The SmartDCap display was as shown in Figure 1, except that the sharpness score was rotated 90 degrees clockwise and located inside the upper right corner of the inner framing rectangle. All of our 12 subjects used both SmartDCap and the ICS camera application; half the subjects used SmartDCap first. Before a subject used an application, instructions and a demo were given on its use. Both for SmartDCap and the ICS camera application, users were instructed to take photos in focus and to fill the camera view with the content of interest and parallel to the viewer edges. Users were also told

	Factor	*F-value*	*Significance*
sharpness	lighting	666.19	$p < 0.01$
	capture method	25.32	$p < 0.05$
framing	lighting	51.51	$p < 0.05$
	capture method	142.23	$p < 0.01$

Table 3. Significant factors for sharpness and framing

to minimize shadows as well as possible. For SmartDCap in particular, subjects were instructed to adjust the position of the camera to align the content to be captured so that at least three edges of the desired content were between the framing rectangles, and then to hold the position until the camera took a photo. For each application, the subjects first practiced using the application and then were asked to take good photos of three types of documents: a single brochure-type page, pages from a 4-page paper, and a close-up of a picture on part of a page. After a photo was taken using either application, the subjects could check the image quality by panning and zooming the captured image. For both applications, the subjects were allowed to take photos of a page until they were satisfied with the quality of the photo. We decided on this approach rather than asking subjects to take only one photo of a page since it better reflects observed practices.

After taking one or more photos of each of the three page types using one application, subjects were asked to rate on a scale of 1 (easy) to 7 (difficult) how hard it was to capture an acceptable image for each type of document. We also questioned participants about their experience with SmartDCap features, asking them to rate (using the same scale) the difficulty of aligning the document content boundary between the green framing rectangles, and, from 1 (agree) to 7 (disagree), whether the auditory feedback helped them understand when they needed to adjust the camera, whether they understood how to adjust the camera, and whether they preferred to have the application capture images automatically. We also asked participants to provide open-ended feedback about the strengths and weaknesses of each application.

Half the subjects were run in a poorly lit ("dim") room and half in a well-lit ("bright") room to examine how the capture applications perform under both conditions. Images may be less sharp under dimmer lighting due to a slower shutter speed combined with small hand movements. Because documents are photographed at close range, small hand movements are relatively noticeable.

Thus the factors that may affect the difficulty scores are application (ICS camera application vs. SmartDCap), task type, and lighting. We performed a 3-way ANOVA on these factors with difficulty score as the dependent variable; Figure 8 shows difficulty ratings by application type and task type. These results indicate that SmartDCap is not any harder to use than the ICS camera application. In addition, some users reported that SmartDCap makes photo review easier.

Feedback from the subjective questions specific to the SmartDCap application revealed that users were conflicted about aligning a document with the green rectangles. While users overall rated the task as moderately difficult, others found that

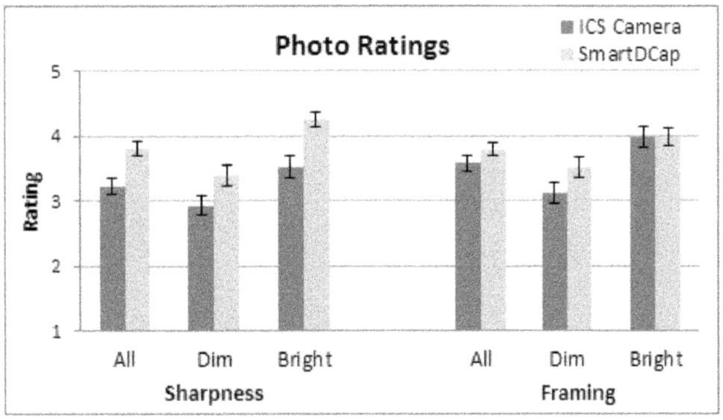

Figure 10. Mean ratings with 95% confidence intervals for sharpness and framing of captured images using the ICS camera application and SmartDCap under dim, bright, and combined (all) lighting conditions. Rating of 1 is poor, 5 is excellent.

the "green borders [helped] line up edges." They also relied more on the visual feedback than the audio feedback, and suggested that the application show a "visual indication of which edge is an issue" when framing a document. Users were particularly fond of the automated capture feature, which made it "much easier to concentrate on framing region of interest ...." They also appreciated not "having to press the button which messes up focus."

Image Quality Evaluation

To evaluate the quality of the captured photos, three people not in the subjective study were asked to rate the sharpness and framing of photos taken during the study on a scale of 1 (poor) to 5 (excellent). Since some of the subjective study participants experimented with the applications to try out different options, we presented (in random order) only the last photo of each page captured by each participant, for a total of 6 photos/(subject&app) * 12 subjects * 2 apps = 144 photos.

We ran a 2-way ANOVA with repeated measures on the factors of lighting (dim and bright) and capture method (SmartDCap or ICS camera application) with *sharpness* as the dependent variable. Both lighting and capture method were main effects, with lighting more significant. We also ran a 2-way ANOVA with repeated measures on the factors of lighting and capture method with *framing* as the dependent variable. Both lighting and capture method were again main effects, but with capture method more significant (Table 3). There were no significant interactions between factors.

More detailed results are shown in Figure 10. Note that both measures of image quality are better under bright light, as has been noted by others (e.g., JotNot[10], TurboScan). One-sided t-tests at the 0.05 level of significance indicate that SmartDCap captured sharper images than the ICS camera application under both dim ($p = 0.002$) and bright ($p = 1.588e^{-6}$) lighting conditions. And under dim lighting, framing using SmartDCap was significantly better ($p = 0.006$).

DISCUSSION AND PROPOSED REFINEMENTS

Our evaluations indicate that SmartDCap captures sharper, better-framed images semi-automatically and is as easy to use as the standard ICS camera application. SmartDCap's framing guides for closely-framed images result in higher resolution of the captured context while reducing the number of extraneous pixels. Although it is difficult for a user to simultaneously check that all four edges are well-framed when capturing closely-framed photos of document content, SmartDCap reduces the difficulty by offering guides for framing and automatically deciding when to capture, allowing users to focus on framing. The result is that the content is captured well-framed, at a higher image resolution, and sharper, both because the user does not press any buttons (which can cause camera movement) and because the application requires a minimum image sharpness before snapping a photo.

Photos captured by SmartDCap can be processed using the types of post-processing techniques that other capture applications offer, such as perspective and tone correction, to further improve the captured image. Because the SmartDCap images are of higher quality to begin with, the processed images should be of at least as high quality as those captured using other apps.

Capture applications that offer perspective correction may implicitly encourage a user to capture pages from one side, often resulting in some regions of the photo being blurrier, especially when capturing larger areas, such a page, than when capturing smaller areas such as business cards. Even with simple post-processing of the image offered by capture apps, parts of the photo will often still be blurrier. In contrast, SmartDCap checks sharpness over the entire image so that the whole page is more uniformly sharp.

Based on user comments, we propose several refinements to SmartDCap. Two areas that our study suggests changes would be beneficial are the framing rectangles and capture speed under dim lighting. We further propose an extension of SmartDCap usage.

In our experiments, the distance between the framing rectangles was set to be relatively small and to be close to the edge of the mobile display. This was to force a page to be captured straight on and to force the page content to fill a large proportion of the image for best quality. This could be relaxed a bit by decreasing the size of the inner rectangle so that images could be captured slightly off to the side, but the edges of the page would still be in focus. Another refinement to help a user during alignment is for the framing lines to change color or disappear to indicate which edges are well-aligned.

Another issue raised in our experiments is that capture is slower in a dimly lit room. Originally, a single sharpness threshold was hardwired in the program. However, attaining a sharp image is much easier in bright light, where the shutter speed is faster, than in dim light. At the possible expense of capturing somewhat blurrier images, a slider could be added to the interface to allow users to set the sharpness threshold. Alternatively, the system could automatically adjust the threshold based on the best recent sharpness values. A minimum allowed sharpness could be used to prevent blurry images from being considered when computing a threshold. An example of the computation of minimal required sharpness is

[10]http://itunes.apple.com/us/app/jotnot-scanner-pro/id307868751

to compute a running average of the most recent sharpness values greater than the minimum sharpness:

$$thresh_{sharpness} = \frac{1}{N} \sum_{t=i-N}^{i} s(t) - \alpha$$

where $s(t)$ is the sharpness value of the tth frame with a value greater than the minimum, N is the number of frames used in the estimate and set to a relatively small value, e.g., 3, and α lowers the $thresh_{sharpness}$ so that images can be captured more quickly, but may be blurrier.

We can also expand our work on automatic, high quality capture of the content of a document page to provide for efficient capture of multi-page documents. We note based on observation that as a user moves a camera and/or page into position while SmartDCap is working, the page content is not well framed and the image is not sharp enough for capture since movement results in blur and the varying distance between the camera and the page results in the image being mostly out of focus. We can extrapolate that similarly, as a page is being removed from view or turned over, the image will not be well-framed or sharp enough for capture. Based on this and evidence from our experiments that SmartDCap can take high quality shots automatically, we can optionally allow users to advance to the next page in the document immediately and wait to review all captured images as a group after scanning the whole document, which could increase scanning speed.

Finally, we may be able to improve the audio feedback in SmartDCap using earcons [1] or auditory icons [4] to communicate more specific directions to users during capture, such as "move left/right", "move closer", or "light too low".

CONCLUSIONS

People continue to take an increasing number of photos with mobile devices. Even so, capturing a sharp, well-framed page or region of a page is more challenging than capturing a scene. In this paper we presented the SmartDCap system for helping people capture better document images. SmartDCap provides real-time feedback on image quality and automatically captures an image when the quality measures are good. The measures are based on image sharpness and framing of document content, where the content can be either full pages or portions of page columns. SmartDCap makes it easier to capture good photos of document content by allowing a user to focus on framing while freeing them from having to simultaneously decide when sharpness and framing are good and then indicating that a photo should be captured. Our users rated SmartDCap at least as easy to use as the ICS camera application. Furthermore, rating of the captured images showed that the sharpness of the images captured by SmartDCap is significantly better under different lighting conditions and the framing is significantly better overall.

With SmartDCap, higher quality photos are captured *before* any post-processing is applied. Post-processing techniques that other capture applications offer, such as perspective and tone correction, can be applied to photos captured by SmartDCap to further improve the captured images. Results from our evaluations of SmartDCap led us to propose refinements to simplify its use and to propose how it can be used as the basis of a mobile document capture system that more efficiently captures multi-page documents.

REFERENCES

1. Brewster, S., Wright, P., and Edwards, A. An evaluation of earcons for use in auditory human-computer interfaces. In *Proc. of the INTERACT '93 and CHI '93 Conf. on Human Factors in Computing Systems*, ACM (1993), 222–227.
2. Carter, S., Adcock, J., Doherty, J., and Branham, S. Nudgecam: toward targeted, higher quality media capture. In *Proc. of the ACM Intl. Conf. on Multimedia* (2010), 615–618.
3. Ferzli, R., and Karam, L. A no-reference objective image sharpness metric based on the notion of just noticeable blur (JNB). *IEEE Transactions on Image Processing 18*, 4 (2009), 717–728.
4. Garzonis, S., Jones, S., Jay, T., and ONeill, E. Auditory icon and earcon mobile service notifications: intuitiveness, learnability, memorability and preference. In *Proc. of the SIGCHI Conf. on Human Factors in Computing Systems*, ACM (2009), 1513–1522.
5. Ha, J., Haralick, R., and Phillips, I. Recursive x–y cut using bounding boxes of connected components. In *Proc. of the Intl. Conf. on Document Analysis and Recognition*, vol. 2, IEEE (1995), 952–955.
6. Hoggan, E., Crossan, A., Brewster, S., and Kaaresoja, T. Audio or tactile feedback: which modality when? In *Proc. of the SIGCHI Conf. on Human Factors in Computing Systems*, ACM (2009), 2253–2256.
7. Jayant, C., Ji, H., White, S., and Bigham, J. P. Supporting blind photography. In *Proc. of the ACM SIGACCESS Conf. on Computers and Accessibility* (2011), 203–210.
8. Larson, E., and Chandler, D. Most apparent distortion: Full-reference image quality assessment and the role of strategy. *Journal of Electronic Imaging 19*, 1 (2012).
9. Lee, S., and Ryu, D. Parameter-free geometric document layout analysis. *IEEE Transactions on Pattern Analysis and Machine Intelligence 23*, 11 (2001), 1240–1256.
10. Liang, J., Doermann, D., and Li, H. Camera-based analysis of text and documents: a survey. *Intl. Journal on Document Analysis and Recognition 7*, 2 (2005), 84–104.
11. Liu, C., Huot, S., Diehl, J., Mackay, W., and Beaudouin-Lafon, M. Evaluating the benefits of real-time feedback in mobile augmented reality with hand-held devices. In *Proc. of the SIGCHI Conf. on Human Factors in Computing Systems*, ACM (2012), 2973–2976.
12. Narvekar, N., and Karam, L. A no-reference image blur metric based on the cumulative probability of blur detection (CPBD). *IEEE Transactions on Image Processing 20*, 9 (2011), 2678 –2683.

13. Nees, M., and Walker, B. Data density and trend reversals in auditory graphs: Effects on point-estimation and trend-identification tasks. *ACM Transactions on Applied Perception (TAP) 5*, 3 (2008), 13.

14. Pollard, S., and Pilu, M. Building cameras for capturing documents. *Intl. Journal on Document Analysis and Recognition 7*, 2 (2005), 123–137.

15. Shafait, F., Keysers, D., and Breuel, T. Performance evaluation and benchmarking of six-page segmentation algorithms. *IEEE Transactions on Pattern Analysis and Machine Intelligence 30*, 6 (2008), 941–954.

16. Sheikh, H., Sabir, M., and Bovik, A. A statistical evaluation of recent full reference image quality assessment algorithms. *IEEE Transactions on Image Processing 15*, 11 (Nov 2006), 3440–3451.

17. Vázquez, M., and Steinfeld, A. Facilitating photographic documentation of accessibility in street scenes. In *CHI Extended Abstracts on Human Factors in Computing Systems*, ACM (2011), 1711–1716.

18. Walker, B., and Kramer, G. Mappings and metaphors in auditory displays: An experimental assessment. *ACM Transactions on Applied Perception (TAP) 2*, 4 (2005), 407–412.

19. White, S., Ji, H., and Bigham, J. Easysnap: Real-time audio feedback for blind photography. In *Adj. Proc. of the ACM Symposium on User Interface Software and Technology* (2010), 409–410.

20. Yu, Y., and Liu, Z. A user study of visual versus sonically-enhanced interfaces for use while walking. In *Proc. of the ACM Intl. Conf. on Multimedia* (2010), 687–680.

Functionality-Based Clustering using Short Textual Description: Helping Users to Find Apps Installed on their Mobile Device

David Lavid Ben Lulu
The University of Haifa
Information Systems Department
Haifa 31905, Israel
dbenlu02@campus.haifa.ac.il

Tsvi Kuflik
The University of Haifa
Information Systems Department
Haifa 31905, Israel
tsvikak@is.haifa.ac.il

ABSTRACT
In recent years, we have witnessed the incredible popularity and widespread adoption of mobile devices. Millions of Apps are being developed and downloaded by users at an amazing rate. These are multi-feature Apps that address a broad range of needs and functions. Nowadays, every user has dozens of Apps on his mobile device. As time goes on, it becomes more and more difficult simply to find the desired App among those that are installed on the mobile device. In spite of several attempts to address the problem, no good solution for this increasing problem has yet been found. In this paper we suggest the use of unsupervised machine learning for clustering Apps based on their functionality, to allow users to access them easily. The functionality is elicited from their description as retrieved from various App stores and enriched by content from professional blogs. The Apps are clustered and grouped according to their functionality and presented hierarchically to the user in order to facilitate the search on the small screen of the mobile device.

Author Keywords
Data mining, Human–Computer Interaction, Clustering, Smartphone Apps, Mobile, Short and Sparse Text, Text Similarity, Visualization

ACM Classification Keywords
H.5.2 [Information Interfaces and Presentation]: User

Interfaces - Interaction,

H.3.3 [Information Search and Retrieval]: Text Mining,

H.3.1 [Information Storage and Retrieval]: Content Analysis and Indexing;

INTRODUCTION

Smart mobile era
Smartphones have changed and continue to change our lives beyond recognition, as they combine the capabilities of cellular phones with advanced computing technologies. These devices enable their users to download web content, take high resolution pictures, make high quality video calls, use location-based services, transfer data to other devices, make use of three dimensional graphics, and connect to external accessories. Mobile sensing [1] is a growing field that serves as a telecommunication platform, allowing its users to sense location and motion, and share audio and text as well as visual information. People use these devices in every situation; they are always available and enable their users to remain constantly connected, resulting in a true revolution in terms of how people connect and use the web.

According to global marketing research, in 2012 smart phones were in use by 50.4 percent of consumers in the USA[2]. Smartphone shipments will grow from the 494 million in 2011 to 1.16 billion in 2016 [3] and 10 billion in total will exist [4]. According to a UK telecommunications regulator (Ofcom) [5], research on smartphone usage revealed that users have a unique relationship with their mobile phones: 37% of adults and 60% of teenagers admit to being addicted to their smartphone. Smartphones are changing social behavior: over half of adults use their mobile phones while socializing and almost a quarter use them during mealtimes and even in the bathroom (22%). We are in an age in which, by using mobile Apps, people are able to do almost anything from any location without having to be physically at their personal computer.

Mobile App booms
In mid-2007, Apple released the first iPhone and about a year later, the App Store opened, allowing people to publish and sell their Apps as well as download Apps published by others. This was the point at which the snowball known as mobile Apps began to roll. Google, Nokia, and Microsoft quickly joined the battle and became competitors in this growing market by creating their own App stores. At the beginning of 2011, the American Dialect Society chose the word "App" as the word of the year for 2010 [6]. A mobile App is piece of computer software developed to be

executed on a specific mobile operating system and run on hardware such as smartphones, tablet computers, automobiles, gaming consoles, and other mobile devices. They are designed to help users perform specifics task with a specific purpose: reading and writing emails, calendar management, gaming, factory automation, banking, order-tracking, and many more [7]. The mobile ecosystem has evolved dramatically over the past few years. Apple recently published that their App store contains more than 550,000 Apps that were downloaded 25 billion times [8], at a rate of about 48.6 million Apps per day. This rate does not appear to be decreasing [9]. As time goes on, it becomes harder and harder simply to find a needed App among all the Apps that are installed on the device.

Based on the above, we can predict more and more situations where people search their cellular Apps for the right App for a specific task. Here is an example. In the morning the mother activates the shopping list App, and records all the products she needs, to be sent to the father's mobile device. Meanwhile the father scans the newspapers. The daughter, on the way to school, takes a few filtered photos and shares them on a social network. In the afternoon, after a quick arcade game, the son goes out for a run and listens to music while recording data from the run. The daughter takes her blood pressure using a dedicated App and immediately activates a video conversation and tells her father the recommendations she received. When the father finishes work, he drives to the supermarket with the shopping list, and on the way receives location-based traffic and weather updates. The mother edits documents with her business partner on the other side of the world and takes a break to purchase flights after she checks their financial situation. Most of the activities described above are done using about 15 different mobile Apps that the user has to search among the dozens of Apps installed on the mobile device.

Installed App discovery

According to the Flurry[1] Mobile Analytics Firm, the average user has 65 Apps installed on his or her mobile device and spends more time using them than surfing the internet: about 94 minutes per day [10]. The median for iPhone users is 108 Apps [11]. In TechCrunch [12], Sara Perez noted the difficulty of finding the desired installed App. Since the average user uses only 15 Apps per week, most of the Apps that are installed on the device are used much less frequently. Thus, if during a trip you run into a squirrel and you want to take a picture of it with your favorite filter App, by the time you find it, the squirrel has already disappeared. In many cases the name of the App bears no indication of its function and therefore association- or related word-based searches do not provide the desired results. Adam Pash [13] describes the problem as it applies to iPhone users. When they drag one App onto another in order to make a folder, iOS offers only vague categories such as "Tools", "Reference", or "Productivity". Organization of items using categories is fine for libraries, movies, and music, but not for Apps. Attempts to hunt down an App using this method can be exhausting and therefore folders must be made based on the main functions (Actions) of the Apps. This type of manual arrangement will increase the speed at which the desired App is found and launched.

Figure 1: self-organizer - from App mess to functional folders

RELATED WORK

The problem of App discovery in App Stores

There are more than a few Apps that try to address this problem, most of which require manual organization of Apps into folders or through label definition [14]. These Apps place an emphasis on a quality interface that makes Apps organization easy. There are a few Apps that automatically sort the installed Apps into a limited number of categories (internet, system, Apps, multimedia, etc.) based on the App features and not on the functional content [15]. These Apps do not provide a proper solution to the problem. This work suggests using unsupervised machine learning for clustering Apps based on the short description of their functionality, as retrieved from various App stores and professional blogs on the web. We define a unique representation for Apps, based on their functional characteristics as elicited from their textual descriptions, as illustrated in Figure 1. Using this representation, we cluster them for hierarchical presentation on the small screen of a mobile device. An additional problem that will be solved is the difficulty in classifying Apps as they are downloaded. Our application, at the time of the download, will find similarities between the App description and the existing clusters, allowing accurate cluster assignment. If the new

[1] http://www.flurry.com/

App cannot be assigned to any existing cluster, the application will be assigned to the closest cluster, or will perform re-clustering with the permission of the user.

The threshold of a million Apps in the various App stores has already been crossed, and finding a suitable App in the ocean of existing ones is not a simple task. The problem of App discovery in these stores is becoming more and more difficult over time [16] [17]. This is a serious problem that the store operators, as well as 3rd party developers, have been trying to solve for the past two years by adding sections and developing mechanisms to optimize searches with the help of quality matrices (downloads, recommendations, ratings). These attempts had not been successful [18]. There are applications that suggest relevant Apps in the store by analyzing actual usage of the Apps already installed on the user's device [19]. AppBrain offers an Android Apps search based on popularity rankings and rating in various time sections and categories [20]. Quixey allows one to search based on functionality that the system has learned using information gleaned from the network [21]. AppsFire suggests Apps based on trends in social networks and allows location-based searches [22]. Uquery also performs social searches based on selections made by the user's social network contacts [23]. Xyologic suggests potential Apps by analyzing the number of downloads and the quality of the advertisers across different countries and through the various operating systems [24]. Chomp allows App searches based on App activity [25] [26]. The race of these commercial companies to hunt down the right App that matches the user's search is still in progress.

App search

Recently, Shanahan [27] discussed the need for functional search in order to solve the big challenge of App search and how to match Apps with users' needs. He found that the majority of queries are functional in nature or task-centric. He concluded that App search is non-trivial like other search methods, such as multimedia or web search. The representation of Apps requires more research. Furthermore, existing methods and features are unlikely to be effective and require an essentially different approach. Rudolf [28] describes how a perfect App search engine should work according to three stages: (1) Classify all Apps into topics; (2) guess the intent of the user; (3) find the best App among the topics. An effective search engine should at least disambiguate the results and guide the user to a proper topic. It computes various popularity and quality signals from social interactions in the App store. Gabrilovich et al. [29] introduced the concept of a contextual App search that relies on action needs. Classical IR is centered on the concept of an information need, which can be satisfied by (reading) one or more documents. Yet, people rarely search merely to satisfy their curiosity; rather, they search the Web to get things done. They suggested search engines that, instead of offering a multitude of web pages, return Apps that directly help the users accomplish their tasks.

Computer Desktop Organization

Before we offer our solution to the installed App problem, we take a look at the long-standing problem of computer desktop organization, which is similar to our problem. Quite a few desktops are cluttered with icons and the users search for documents or folders among tens of icons. The user has difficulty finding a specific icon and he wants to manage his desktop icons quickly and maintain an attractive and ordered desktop. During the last two decades, many studies have focused on this subject. Barreau et al. [30] concluded from a user behavior study that users prefer a location-based search for finding files and to use three types of information: ephemeral, in process, and not important (archived). Bergman et al. [31] showed that changing the Windows default from Details to Icons would reduce retrieval time by 41%. Voida et al. [32] presented an activity-based desktop interface. The prototype uses action as the primary organizing principle. They developed a method for tagging activities and their constituent resources using semantically meaningful labels. Bruce et al. [33] suggested that Participants' Wishful Thinking is a nearly human automated solver that magically facilitates the management of personal information collections. There are several commercial tools addressing this problem: Fences arranges cluttered desktop icons into shaded areas, which become movable and sizable containers so that one can clean up the mess into useful groups of shortcuts, such as folders, files, websites, or optionally hide them altogether [34]. Launchy is a search utility. It indexes files in specific folders and shortcuts in the start menu to allow quicker access to programs and browsing to the relevant files, and can launch programs, documents, and bookmarks with just a few taps on the keyboard [35]. RocketDock is an application launcher. It provides a clean interface on which to drop shortcuts for easy access and organization, with each item completely customizable [36]. Rklauncher, Orbit and Standalonestack are a launcher's widgets that provide attractive, quick shortcuts of any folder on the desktop [37][38][39].

As can be seen, there are already quite a few solutions for logically organizing icons on the PC desktop. However, the fundamental difference between a desktop and a mobile is the ratio between the number of icons and the screen size. In the mobile device, the problem is significantly more severe. While on the desktop there is usually enough space and arrangements can be flat and one-dimensional, on the mobile better solutions are needed, which may be hierarchical or multi-dimensional. The solutions proposed above are based on the difference between the files, that is, the file extensions indicate the various file types. On the mobile, there is no such option, since all Apps are of the same type. It is necessary to understand what lies behind any App.

FUNCTIONALITY BASED APPS CLUSTERING

Prior studies, after mining the App price, reviews, ratings, and number of downloads from the Appstores, identified a correlation between the downloading rate and the price and rating of Apps [40]. Similarly, economists extract the length of the App description and assess the demand for it [41]. Researchers have identified App usage patterns from smartphone trace logs to predict App launches before they occur in order to solve the slow App launch problem [42] and to identify diverse usage behaviors [43]. Minelli et al. [44] performed mining on a number of open-source Android Apps. He discovered that App software characteristics differ from classical software systems in source code structure, APIs usage, and evolution process.

We suggest a new way to address the installed App search problem by clustering the Apps based on their functional similarity as represented by their descriptions. This will ease and expedite the process of finding them. To achieve this, we need to address the following challenges:

1. Searching for Apps descriptions;
2. Eliciting the functionality of Apps from their textual description;
3. Clustering Apps based on their functionality representation;
4. Presenting the results to the user in an attractive and interactive way;
5. Evaluating the effectiveness of the new approach.

We address the first three challenges in a three-stage process as illustrated by Figure 2: Web mining; Text Preprocessing; and Hierarchical Clustering.

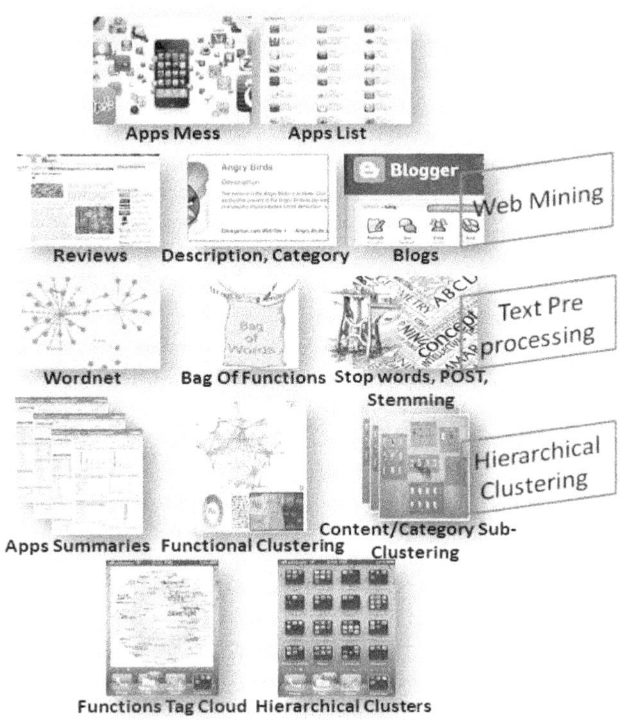

Figure 2: Process stages and components

Web Mining

Once Apocalypse is installed on a smartphone, it extracts the list of Apps installed on it. The process begins with the mining of the App description and category from the virtual store and from the home page of the App (when available). In addition, a web search is performed to extend the description with the content of reviews published in blogs and articles. The purpose of this action is to elicit sufficient content for the next stages (Figure 3 presents an example of an App enriched description).

The #1 Mobile Travel app includes flight and car search, hotel search and booking, Flight tracker and My Trips, so you have your itinerary at your fingertips.
And of course, KAYAK for Android is free.

****

Enriched by professional blogs http://intransit.blogs.nytimes.com

****

Kayak has upgraded its iPhone app, allowing users to book flights, hotel rooms and car rentals on their mobile phones.
Kayak's new app was partly inspired by travelers who used the mobile app to search for flights but found it so time-consuming to complete additional reservations...

Figure 3: App description example (kayak)

Text Preprocessing

The textual description undergoes classical information retrieval processing: stop words are removed; stemming and part of speech tagging are performed. To reduce the difference between the descriptions, the algorithm replaces synonyms and verbs, actions, and objects that express the same function under the function keyword with a canonical representation of the function. The set of function keywords, such as read, track, share, play, watch and more, will be created automatically using Verbnet [45] and synonyms will be abstracted using Wordnet [46] and Bing synonyms [47]. Words not included in the dictionaries as technological words or contemporary abbreviations will be combined into groups manually. (IMs/ mms/ sms/ message => Chat; Knowledge, education, test, quiz=> learn; song, sound, Mp3, radio => Listen; etc.). Because the order of words has no significance, the app algorithm uses the classic bag of words (BOW) model. Finally, a weighted vector of terms representation is constructed (using term and document frequencies, TF-IDF that reflects how important a word is in representing a document in a collection). Similarly, the algorithm performs bag of functional words (BOF).

Hierarchical Clustering

The representing vectors (illustrated in Figure 4) are used as input to the functionality-based clustering process. In this stage, the most similar Apps are clustered into groups based on their functional similarity. Clusters of Apps are obtained as a result (allowing an App to be duplicated into multiple clusters). For each cluster that passes the threshold number of Apps in a cluster (say 6), further clustering is performed (sub-clustering). This can be done according to several criteria. We chose to focus on two major criteria, grouping according to similarity in content or Appstore category.At the end of the hierarchical clustering stage, three levels of hierarchy are formed. Within the top layer there are functional clusters, while the layer below contains clusters based on Content or Category similarity. This layer is optional and exists only if in the top layer there are some large clusters. The lower level is the Apps themselves. In every level of hierarchy, objects are arranged by frequency of use.

Nu	App Name	App Category	Task 1	Task 2	Task 3
1	Learn English with babbel.com	Education	Spell	Learn	
2	Ant Smasher Free	Arcade & Action games	smash	crushe	
3	TED	Education	Watch	Listen	Learn
4	Period Calendar Tracker	Health & Fitness	Tracke	Back	Restore
5	Netflix	Entertainment	Watch	Browse	Rate
6	Calorie Counter - MyFitnessPal	Health & Fitness	Tracke	counte	
7	MP3 Music Download V6	Entertainment	manage	download	Listen
8	Mp3 Search and Download Pro	Music & Audio	Search	Download	
9	File Manager	Business	Manage	explore	browse
10	Domino's Pizza USA	Lifestyle	order	Find	remember
11	IQ Test	Health & Fitness	Test	finish	
12	My Days - Period & Ovulation	Lifestyle	track	Forecast/predict	Backup
13	Menstrual Calendar	Medical	Track	Forecast/predict	Back
14	Draw Something Free	Brain & Puzzle games	draw	guesse	
15	Scramble With Friends Free	Brain & Puzzle games	Spell	guesse	
16	Words With Friends Free	Brain & Puzzle games	Spell	guesse	
17	Speed Anatomy Quiz Free	Medical	test	Learn	play
18	Bible	Books & Reference	Read	leran	translate
19	Dictionary.com	Books & Reference	Spell	leran	Read
20	Ringdroid	Media & Video	edit	Listen	record
21	Ringtone Maker Pro Free	Media & Video	Make/create	Listen	
22	Talking Lily Panda Free	Libraries & Demo	Talk	listen	repeat

Figure 4: Functionality mining from apps descriptions (manual)

The final results are presented to the user: clusters are presented in functional folders, and Content or Category clusters appear as frames within each cluster, as illustrated in Figure 5. If there are too many folders (say, over 16), the user is presented only with function names as a polygon map or tag cloud. If the number of folders is particularly high (say, over 40), hierarchical agglomerative clustering will take place where similar folders will be clustered into fewer, more abstract folders. A rise of one level in the hierarchy allows grouping similar functions into a super-cluster, meaning that the number of folders will take one frame (outside the scope of this paper). The above algorithm is illustrated by the pseudo code of Figure 6.

INITIAL RESULTS

As a first step in the process, before defining and implementing the algorithm, we explored the possibility of using a short Apps description as an input to the text processing and clustering process. We wanted to ensure that it is possible to create meaningful clusters based on the short textual descriptions.

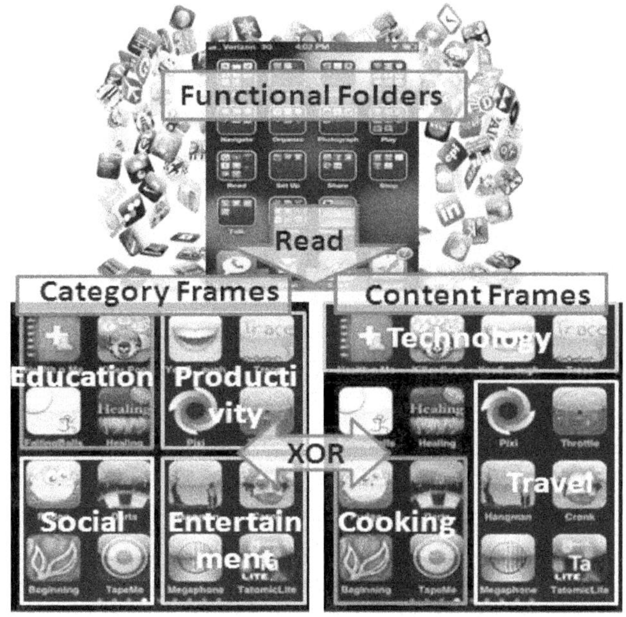

Figure 5: FBC Output- a. Functional folders b. "Read" folder Apps clustered by category and by content

We focused on Android Apps because the problem is more prominent on smartphones that support the Google operating system. On August 5th, 2012, the descriptions of 120 Apps were downloaded from the Google Play Appstore. These were the 120 Apps with the highest rating, the highest number of downloads, and an impressive growth rate. It is probable that a large portion of them will be on most of the mobile devices in the world. The rankings are based on two Apps-ranking websites from the list of the most popular Android Apps of all time. There are 30 categories in the store; a minimum of 3 Apps were taken from each category [48] [20]. The average number of words in an App description is 146. A significant portion of these descriptions contain information that is not related to the nature of the App.

Feasibility Study

We performed two experiments, the first for clustering Apps by the content of their descriptions, and the second for clustering Apps by category. We used carrot2 [49] clustering algorithms with Aduna [50] visualization. In every experiment, three algorithms were compared: Lingo [51], Suffix Tree Clustering (STC) [52], and Bisecting k-means [53]. The textual description underwent carrot2 default preprocessing. The linguistic preprocessing includes the following components:

1. Stemming: folding grammatical variations of words into their "base" forms.
2. Stop words: ignored terms that are meaningless in the language.
3. Stop labels: avoiding labels that should not be considered clusters.

```
Functionality Based Clustering Algorithm
1.   appsList = Extract apps names (Smartphone);
2.   appsInClusterThreshold = 6;
     Web mining:
3.   For each app in appsList :
 3.1.   appsCategoryList [app] = Get store Category ( app);
 3.2.   appsDescList [app] = Get store Description (app);
 3.3.   if ( appsDescList [app] <= shortDescription )
   3.3.1.   appsDescList [app] = Enriching Description (appsDescList [app] );
     Text Preprocessing:
4.   For each app in appsList
 4.1.   appsDescList [app] = StopWords Removal (appsDescList [app]);
 4.2.   appsDescList [app] = Stemming (appsDescList [app]);
 4.3.   appsDescList [app] =  POST (appsDescList [app]);
 4.4.   appsDescList [app] = Reducing the difference between
        words using Wordnet (appsDescList [app])
 4.5.   appWordVecList[app]= BOW (appsDescList [app]);
 4.6.   appsFuncVecList[app]= BOF (appsDescList [app] );
     Hierarchical Clustering:
5.   funcClusters = Functional clustering (appsFuncVecList) ;
6.   funcClusters = Clusters Arrangement (funcClusters) ;
7.   For each cluster in funcClusters
 7.1.   If ( number of apps  > = appsInClusterThreshold)
   7.1.1.   contentSubClusters = ContentClustering
            (appWordVecList[cluster]);
   7.1.2.   categorySubClusters =CategoryClustering (appsCategoryList
            [cluster]);
   7.1.3.   subClusters = contentSubClusters xor categorySubClusters;
   7.1.4.   subClusters = Sub-Clusters Arrangement (subClusters);
   7.1.5.   For each subCluster in subClusters
     7.1.5.1.   subCluster = Apps Arrangement (subCluster);
8.   Display the results to the user
```

Figure 6: FBC Algorithm Data Set

The algorithms have various quality and performance characteristics due to the difference in their main clustering principle. The Lingo algorithm has a key feature, reversing the traditional clustering pipeline. It starts from the identification of cluster labels and only subsequently forms final clusters by assigning Apps descriptions to the labels. In order to find the labels, for all input Apps descriptions, Lingo builds a term description matrix. For better matrix estimation, low dimensional space is obtained by creating base vectors from matrix separation. Each weighted vector of terms gives rise to one cluster label. Each label has the App description in which the label's words appear. This completes the Lingo clustering process. According to the STC, a Generalized Suffix Tree (GST) is built for all input App descriptions. To identify words and terms that appear more than once in the input, they are passed to the GST. Each word or term gives rise to one base cluster. Final clusters are generated by merging base clusters. The two algorithms presented above, have two characteristics in common. In both, the created clusters can overlap, meaning that one description can be assigned to more than one cluster. Moreover, a particular number of descriptions can remain unclustered. Another algorithm that can be used to perform this task is Bisecting k-means, a generic clustering algorithm. It creates non overlapping clusters and does not produce unlabeled groups, unlike Lingo and STC. Its current limitation is that it labels clusters using individual words; not all cluster's App descriptions may correspond to the words included in the cluster label [47].

The experimental results were examined using four parameters: Clusters overlap, Cluster diversity, Cluster labels, and Unlabeled Apps (as shown in Table 1).

Clustering by	Parameter / Algo	Clusters overlap	Cluster diversity	Cluster labels	Apps Unlabeled
Category	Lingo	Y	more balanced	Descriptive ,longer labels	9
	STC	Y	Few big clusters	Shorter labels	14
	K-Means	N	lack in balanced	Not describe all apps in the cluster	0
Content	Lingo	Y	A lot of small clusters	More precise	28
	STC	Y	Balanced	Appropriate	13

Table 1: Clustering algorithms comparison

The first experiment compared the algorithms in content-based clustering. K-means was eliminated for two reasons. The first is that the algorithm does not create overlapping clusters. The overlap is necessary because the App can belong to multiple clusters, and our objective is that once a user enters a cluster he will find what he needs. The second reason is that cluster labels may not always describe all the Apps in the cluster. Finding a solution for this issue is very problematic; because our objective is that the labeling will detect the commonality of all Apps within the cluster. We found that STC outperformed the Lingo algorithm. We focused on the aspects of cluster diversity and cluster labels. Unlabeled Apps will be a significant parameter only after customized Apps descriptions preprocessing. Regarding cluster diversity, we would like clusters to be balanced. STC performed this task better. In terms of meaningfulness, STC and Lingo gave a reasonable but not sufficient cluster labeling. Lingo cluster labels were a little more precise. After considering the results as they appear in Table 1, we conclude that STC is more suitable for content-based clustering. The second experiment was to find the appropriate algorithm for clustering by category according to the extended title of the App description. As shown in the table, Lingo achieved satisfactory results and was more balanced. After performing these experiments, we concluded that for more balanced clusters we should adjust the cluster number to the cluster Apps number. We strive to avoid a large number of unlabeled Apps, but we cannot prevent it using the selected algorithms. Furthermore, not all Apps clustered together correctly. Unlabeled Apps and cluster quality require further research. It is clear that we need to perform customized App description preprocessing in order to achieve better content-based representation. We should remove all words related to advertising or marketing information, directions for operation, technical problems and final updates ("Free," "service," "device," "Note," "best," "fastest," "versions," etc.).

CONCLUSIONS AND FUTURE WORK

The feasibility study showed that the short descriptions of Apps seem to be sufficient for clustering them. Following these encouraging results, we intend to implement and evaluate the suggested novel Apps representation based on their functionality, and use unsupervised machine learning for functionality-based Apps clustering, in order to allow users to access them easily. The main challenges we will address and resolve are:

1. How can we extract the functionality from the Apps description? This will involve using ontologies and semantic reasoning in order to extract the functionality of an App from its general description.
2. How do we cluster Apps based on their functionality representation? While the feasibility study showed the possibility of using short descriptions for clustering, the question is whether the even shorter functional description will be sufficient for meaningful clustering
3. How do we present the results in a user-friendly way? Given the small screen size of the mobile device, presenting the clustering results to the user while allowing easy search and browsing becomes a major challenge.

For evaluation purposes, we will build a dataset that will include Apps descriptions. The Apps will be manually clustered based on their functionality, and we will use this manually annotated dataset for evaluating the performance of the suggested approach, using several clustering methods (similarly to the feasibility study). We will evaluate the performance of the clustering using a classical clustering measure, such as Adjusted Rand Index. Finally, we will evaluate the perceived quality of the process in a user study comparing:

1. A default state: 120 Apps whose icons are presented on smartphone screens (current situation).
2. Existing methods: the same 120 Apps will be clustered by current applications that automatically organize Apps.
3. The same Apps clustered based on their functionality.

The participants will be asked to evaluate the clustering methods in terms of the ease and speed of finding apps.

REFERENCES

1. Lane, N.D., Miluzzo, E., Hong L., Peebles, D. Choudhury, T., Campbell, A. A survey of mobile phone sensing, Communications Magazine, IEEE , vol. 48, no. 9, pp. 140-150, Sept. 2010
2. America's new mobile majority: a look at smartphone owners in the U.S., Nielsen, Mar. 2012, http://blog.nielsen.com/nielsenwire/?p=31688, accessed Oct. 20th, 2012
3. Nearly 1 Billion Smart Connected Devices Shipped in 2011 with Shipments Expected to Double by 2016 , International Data Corporation (IDC), Mar. 2012 http://www.idc.com/getdoc.jsp?containerId=prUS23398412, accessed Oct. 20th, 2012
4. Cisco Visual Networking Index: Global Mobile Data Traffic Forecast Update, 2011–2016 , Cisco, pp.3; Feb. 2012,http://www.cisco.com/en/US/solutions/collateral/ns341/ns525/ns537/ns705/ns827/white_paper_c11-520862.pdf , accessed Oct. 20th, 2012
5. Communications Market Report: UK, Ofcom, pp.6, Aug. 2011, http://stakeholders.ofcom.org.uk/binaries/research/cmr/cmr11/UK_CMR_2011_FINAL.pdf, accessed Oct. 20th, 2012, accessed Oct. 20th, 2012
6. Zimmer B., Barrett G., Metcalf A. "App" 2010 Word of the Year, as voted by American Dialect Society , American Dialect Society, pp.1-2, Jan. 2011, http://www.americandialect.org/American-Dialect-Society-2010-Word-of-the-Year-PRESS-RELEASE.pdf, accessed Oct. 20th, 2012
7. Mobile app ,Wikipedia,2012, http://en.wikipedia.org/wiki/Mobile_app, accessed Oct. 20th, 2012,
8. Apple's App Store Downloads Top 25 Billion , Apple, Mar. 2012, http://www.apple.com/pr/library/2012/03/05Apples-App-Store-Downloads-Top-25-Billion.html, accessed Oct. 20th, 2012
9. Horace D. App developers receive $12 for each iOS device sold , Asymco, Feb. 2012 http://www.asymco.com/2012/02/19/app-developers-get-12-for-each-ios-device-sold/, accessed Oct. 20th, 2012
10. Newark-French C. Mobile App Usage Further Dominates Web, Spurred by Facebook , Flurry, Jan. 2012, http://blog.flurry.com/bid/80241/Mobile-App-Usage-Further-Dominates-Web-Spurred-by-Facebook, accessed Oct. 20th, 2012
11. Infographic: iOS Apps vs. Web Apps, Appsfire, Jan. 2011, http://blog.appsfire.com/infographic-ios-apps-vs-web-apps/, accessed Oct. 20th, 2012
12. Perez S. App-ocalypse , Techcrunch, Dec. 2011 http://techcrunch.com/2011/12/18/app-ocalypse/, accessed Oct. 20th, 2012
13. Pash A. Organize your Apps by action instead of category for a more intuitive find-and-launch system, Lifehacker, Feb. 2012 http://lifehacker.com/5882749/organize-your-apps-by-action-instead-of-category-for-a-more-intuitive-find+and+launch-system, accessed Oct. 20th, 2012
14. Apps Organizer, Fabio Collini,2012, https://play.google.com/store/apps/details?id=com.google.code.appsorganizer
15. Auto App Organizer, ZeroTouchSystems, 2012, https://play.google.com/store/apps/details?id=com.utility.autoapporganizer&feature=related_apps#?t=W251bGwsMSwxLDEwOSwiY29tLnV0aWxpdHkuYXV0b2FwcG9yZ2FuaXplciJd, accessed Oct. 20th, 2012
16. The problem of app discovery, Dimoso, May 2012. http://www.dimoso.com/2012/05/08/the-problem-of-app-discovery/#.UAko-GGFAht, accessed Oct. 20th, 2012

17. Kim, R. App discovery: the challenge that keeps beckoning, Gigacom, Mar. 2012, http://gigaom.com/2012/03/02/app-discovery-the-challenge-that-keeps-beckoning/, accessed Oct. 20th, 2012
18. Cheng J. App Store's new sections still don't solve discovery problems, Arstechnica, May 2012 http://arstechnica.com/apple/2012/05/app-stores-new-sections-still-dont-solve-discovery-problems/, accessed Oct. 20th, 2012
19. Yan and B., Chen G. AppJoy: Personalized mobile application discovery, In Proc. ACM MOBISYS, 2011. http://www.cs.uml.edu/~glchen/papers/appjoy-mobisys-2011.pdf, accessed Oct. 20th, 2012
20. Appbrain,2012, http://www.appbrain.com/, accessed Oct. 20th, 2012
21. Quixey,2012, https://www.quixey.com/, accessed Oct. 20th, 2012
22. Appsfire,2012, http://appsfire.com/, accessed Oct. 20th, 2012
23. Uquery,2012, http://www.uquery.com/, accessed Oct. 20th, 2012
24. Xyologic,2012, http://www.xyologic.com/, accessed Oct. 20th, 2012
25. Chomp,2012, http://chomp.com/, accessed jun. 20th, 2012
26. Siegler M. Apple Acquires Chomp; App Store Search and Discovery to Be Completely Revamped , Techcrunch, Feb. 2012 http://techcrunch.com/2012/02/23/apple-chomp/, accessed Oct. 20th, 2012
27. Shanahan J. G. , Glover E. J. Bridging the app gap: from web search to app search via functional search™ , Workshop on the Appification of the Web, April 2012
28. Rudolf M., In pursuit of a perfect App search engine, Workshop on the Appification of the Web, April 2012
29. Gabrilovich E., From information needs to action needs: towards contextual app search and recommendation, Workshop on the Appification of the Web, April 2012
30. Barreau, D. K. and Nardi, B. A. Finding and reminding: File organization from the desktop. SIGCHI Bulletin 27, 3 (1995), 39-43.
31. Bergman O., Whittaker S., Sanderson M., Nachmias R., Ramamoorthy A., How do we find personal files? The effect of OS, presentation & depth on file navigation, to appear in proceedings of the Conference on Human Factors in Computing Systems (CHI 2012)
32. Voida S., Mynatt E.D., Edwards W.K. Re-framing the desktop interface around the activities of knowledge work. Proc. UIST 2008, ACM Press (2008), 211-220.
33. Bruce H., Wenning A., Jones E., Vinson J., Jones W. Seeking an ideal solution to the management of personal information collections. Information Seeking in Context Conference - (ISIC) 2010, (2010).
34. Fences, Stardock, 2012, http://www.stardock.com/products/fences/, accessed Oct. 20th, 2012
35. Karlin J. Launchy ,2010,http://launchy.net/, accessed Oct. 20th, 2012
36. RocketDock, Punk Labs, 2008, http://rocketdock.com/, accessed Oct. 20th, 2012
37. RK Launcher, Cogeco, 2005, ,http://home.cogeco.ca/~rklauncher/, accessed Oct. 20th, 2012
38. Orbit, Ecocardio, http://www.ecocardio.com.br/orbit/, accessed Oct. 20th, 2012
39. Standalonestack , Chrisnsoft, http://www.chrisnsoft.com/standalonestack, accessed Oct. 20th, 2012
40. Harman M., Jia Y.; Zhang Y. App store mining and analysis: MSR for app stores, Mining Software Repositories (MSR), 2012 9th IEEE Working Conference on , pp. 108-111, 2-3 June 2012
41. Ghose A., Han S. Estimating demand for mobile applications, in preparation to submit to Management Science.
42. Yan T., Chu D., Ganesan D., Kansal A., Liu J. Fast app launching for mobile devices using predictive user context ; MobiSys '12 Proceedings of the 10th international conference on Mobile systems, applications, and services. pp. 113-126, 2012
43. Xu Q., Erman J., Gerber A., Mao Z., Pang J., Venkataraman S. Identifying diverse usage behaviors of smartphone apps. In IMC. ACM, 2011
44. Minelli R., Software Analytics for Mobile Applications, June 2012
45. Schuler, K. K. VerbNet: A broad-coverage, comprehensive verb lexicon. Univ. of Pennsylvania, 2005.
46. George A. Miller (1995). WordNet: A Lexical Database for English. Communications of the ACM Vol. 38, No. 11: 39-41.
47. Bing Synonyms API , http://datamarket.azure.com/dataset/bing/synonyms , accessed Dec. 21th, 2012
48. Androidrank,2012, http://www.androidrank.org, accessed Oct. 20th, 2012
49. Carrot2,2012, http://project.carrot2.org/, accessed Oct. 20th, 2012
50. Aduna ,2012,http://www.aduna-software.com/, accessed Oct. 20th, 2012

51. Osiński S., Stefanowski J., Weiss D. Lingo: Search results clustering algorithm based on singular value decomposition. Advances in Soft Computing, Intelligent Information Processing and Web Mining, Proceedings of the International IIS: IIPWM'04 Conference, Zakopane, Poland, 2004, pp. 359-368

52. Zamir O., Etzioni O. Web document clustering: a feasibility demonstration, in: Proc. of the 19th International ACM SIGIR Conference on Research and Development in Information Retrieval. pp. 46-54, 1998

53. Steinbach M., Karypis G., Kumar V. A comparison of document clustering techniques, Proc. Text Mining Workshop, 2000.

Real-time Hand Interaction for Augmented Reality on Mobile Phones

Wendy H. Chun
Unaffiliated*
Los Angeles, CA
wendyhchun@gmail.com

Tobias Höllerer
Department of Computer Science
University of California, Santa Barbara
holl@cs.ucsb.edu

ABSTRACT
Over the past few years, Augmented Reality has become widely popular in the form of smart phone applications, however most smart phone-based AR applications are limited in user interaction and do not support gesture-based direct manipulation of the augmented scene. In this paper, we introduce a new AR interaction methodology, employing users' hands and fingers to interact with the virtual (and possibly physical) objects that appear on the mobile phone screen. The goal of this project was to support different types of interaction (selection, transformation, and fine-grain control of an input value) while keeping the methodology for hand detection as simple as possible to maintain good performance on smart phones. We evaluated our methods in user studies, collecting task performance data and user impressions about this direct way of interacting with augmented scenes through mobile phones.

Author Keywords
Augmented Reality; Hand-based Interaction; Mobile Phone; Gesture Recognition

ACM Classification Keywords
H.5.2 Information Interfaces and Presentation: User Interfaces: Input devices and strategies.

INTRODUCTION
Mobile Augmented Reality (AR) applications have historically been deployed on experimental laboratory systems, using bulky setups of mini-computers, sensors, and large head-mounted displays. These instrumentation constraints posed major obstacles to widespread acceptance of AR technology. With the arrival of embedded AR devices in the form of smart phones, people can now experience AR applications more easily, without setup restrictions, anywhere, and at any time.

*major portions of this work were performed while this author completed her MS degree in Computer Science at UC Santa Barbara

Augmented Reality has been demonstrated widely on mobile phones, with many different applications such as games, navigation and references. In the beginning, many of these applications were less about interaction and focused more on information display on the top of our real world [1]. As AR applications became increasingly interactive, e.g. through gestures on a phone's touch screen, the possible scope of applications was extended. Our motivation stems from the successful demonstration of direct free-hand gestures in AR [2, 3, 8, 13, 19], and our aim is to enable such direct interaction in the "magic lens" of smart-phone based AR.

In this project, we implement hand-based Augmented Reality interaction in real-time on a mobile phone. We design several different interaction types, allowing a user to move and scale an AR object, as well as to control a continuous value (mapped for demonstration purposes to the transparency of a virtual object). We believe that the ensuing direct interaction is very applicable in many smart-phone based AR applications. We evaluate the accuracy and robustness we achieved with our methods through user evaluations. The results indicate that our prototype is functional and engaging. We use a very simple computer vision methodology in order to maximize responsiveness of the interface even on less powerful computational platforms.

We organize this paper into four parts: first, we put our work in perspective of related work, discussing how hand interaction in AR environments has previously been implemented, and comparing our approach. Next, we present the interaction techniques we designed, and explain the implementation of the system. Then we report on several user studies that we conducted, detailing procedure, results, and discussion. Finally, we conclude with an overall discussion and an outlook for future work.

RELATED WORK
Previous work [3, 13, 19] on hand-based interaction between a user and the augmented reality environment has been demonstrated using multiple fiducial markers on both moving and stationary objects. FingARTips by Buchmann et al. [3] implemented hand interaction employing multiple stationary markers on the ground, and others attached to the user's fingers. They utilized ARToolKit [10] to find the relationship between the ground and fingers to detect the gestures. The paper addressed potential occlusion problems by placing markers on three finger joints, resulting in a somewhat encumbered experience. Three gestures (grabbing, dragging, and releasing a virtual object) were distinguished by taking

into account pose estimation differences among fingertips as well as finger poses relative to the object and ground (stationary markers). While the method produced promising results in public demonstrations and informal user studies, high setup costs and user encumbrance restricted broad adoption.

Other works, such as [8, 17] partially addressed encumbrance issues due to multi-marker use by attaching color stickers on fingertips. Recently, Hürst et al. [8] implemented various interaction capabilities on mobile phones by employing the system's sensor data, and color markers on fingertips. They showcased single- and dual-finger interactions and conducted user studies to evaluate their techniques on the mobile phone. Finger-based 2D translation tasks were compared against gestures utilizing the phone's touch screen and orientation sensors, and the results showed that in terms of task time, touch-screen interaction outperformed the other approaches. Although the finger-based interaction scored the lowest performance, a high score of fun-engagement level indicated the potential for gaming applications. The authors adopted this feedback, prototyping dual-finger interaction on a virtual board game, including translation, scaling, rotation, and incorporating visualization. Gestures were recognized based on the location, distance, and center point between two fingers. The results showed that translation using two fingers performed comparably to single-finger interaction, but in a post-study survey users rated dual-finger interaction slightly higher. Even though the paper presented the potential of dual-finger interaction on the mobile phone, one shortcoming was the lack of full-fledged 3D interaction. The authors mentioned that full 3D localization was difficult and noisy due to unintended camera motion; thus, they restricted their practical evaluations to 2D interactions. They also applied color stickers that prepared only certain fingers for the interaction. Our work addresses the problem of unintended camera motion, and lets users express their gestures with unmarked fingers of their choice.

Many prototypes implemented on higher-performance systems [5, 15, 16] integrated sophisticated computer vision algorithms (e.g. [21]) to find the hand and detect gestures more robustly in less-restricted scenes, demonstrating that gesture recognition can be rather complex and computationally expensive, depending on the working environment. On the lower-performance hardware afforded by mobile phones, simpler approaches have to be devised to run at practical speed. Baldauf et al. [2] suggested the use of fixed skin-color segmentation and morphological filtering to find fingertips in the image plane. This work focused mainly on the tracking technique, and it has not been demonstrated and evaluated as part of a complete interaction solution featuring different types of interaction and comparative performance evaluations. Seo et al. [20] estimated the palm pose by filtering potential hand regions based on skin color and subsequently applying a distance transformation to find the biggest area. The virtual object appeared on top of this detected region and could move along with the palm. The work however did not address sequential gestures, such as flicking or scaling. Both of these last two projects also suffered from relying solely on skin color when segmenting the hand, because it would be difficult to continuously recognize the hand when the working environment included big portions of skin-color materials such as a wooden desk.

INTERACTION TECHNIQUES

We implemented three different user input gestures to be recognized by our system. We restricted our system to three gestures that are commonly used on touch screen: swiping, scaling, and value adjustment (as by a slider) to experiment with the possibilities of hand interaction techniques on mobile phones both quantitatively and qualitatively. To optimize learnability, we designed our gestures to be similar to existing touch screen gestures.

To demonstrate and test the gestures, we apply transformations to an AR object: a virtual object superimposed on top of an ARToolkitPlus [23] marker. While the world reference frame is defined by the marker, our gestures are all recognized using fast and simple markerless computer vision algorithms.

- Translate (move left, right, up, or down): When the hand moves from outside of the scene toward the marker, the virtual object moves based on the hand direction (pushing the object in a certain direction).

- Scale (increase and decrease size): Similar to a touch screen zoom gesture, when a user makes a pinch or unpinch (spread) motion, the virtual object scales down or up.

- Adjust value: A continuous value is controlled as the hand comes closer to or further away from the marker. We illustrate this by adjusting the transparency of a virtual object: more opaque as the hand comes closer to the marker, and more transparent when the hand gets retracted further. In order to lock in the desired transparency value, the user removes the hand quickly.

IMPLEMENTATION

Without loss of generality, we built our prototype system on top of ARToolKitPlus [23], ported to a Nokia N900 smart phone, running Maemo 5.

After marker detection, we detect and track the hand in the scene using color and motion cues. We assume that a user holds the phone in one hand and uses the other for interaction with the scene. The first approach we pursued aimed to identify frame-to-frame optical flow and classify it by velocities (to distinguish camera motion from motion of the hand in the scene). While Lucas-Kanade optical flow [14], which ranges among the faster computer vision techniques, has good applicability for hand-tracking on laptops or workstations, we soon experienced the computational constraints of our mobile phone platform. Calculating optical flow on each frame, or even just every 5-10 frames, slowed down the overall performance considerably. In our initial implementation, the frame-rate dropped to about 1-5 fps when utilizing this method. Instead, as a fast alternative, we first applied background subtraction and then used simple motion segmentation algorithms to detect the hand gestures.

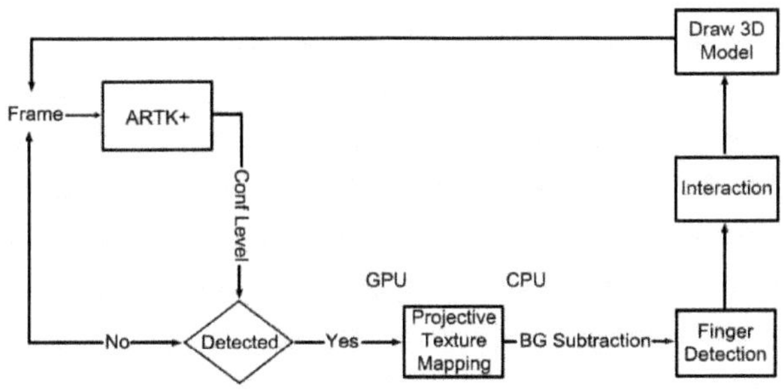

Figure 1. Flow diagram of our application

Background Subtraction

Background subtraction works well when the camera stays in a static position, but in our use case, in which a user holds the phone in one hand, we have to cope with intermittent camera motion. As shown in Figure 1, after the marker is detected, we employ a Projective Texture Mapping [6] step, projecting the reference camera image onto the scene geometry, which in our simple demo application is simply the plane defined by the recognized marker, and capturing a virtual image of that scene from the current camera position. Assuming a close-to-planar scene, we can thus remove the background even in presence of camera motion, and classify all remaining image differences as candidate interaction motion (a second classification step will filter out only skin-colored motion pixels). To improve performance, we compute this inside the GPU in parallel, modifying the framebuffer directly. This method works fast, causing little performance loss (we observed frame rates dropping from 30fps to 27 fps). Once the GPU returns the framebuffer that obtains the projected reference background frame from the current camera viewpoint, it is compared against the current camera frame via subtraction.

The question arises when to capture a new reference background frame. Simply re-capturing the background every n frames is not an option because when a hand is present in the scene, it would be taken as part of the background. Instead, we make use of the fact that this style of interaction (one hand performing a gesture while the other is framing the view) is usually performed while the camera stays close to stationary; We tend to move a camera around to see the virtual object from different angles when we do not interact with the scene. Based on this assumption, the background update will be made when $\Delta x \geq 20.0mm$ or $\Delta y \geq 20.0mm$ or $\Delta z \geq 20.0mm$ where Δx, Δy, and Δz are the absolute camera position differences since the last background frame was taken. Otherwise, when the background update is on hold, our finger detection algorithm is applied to recognize an interaction.

Interaction

After the background subtraction step, the hand can be detected much faster and more accurately than trying to detect it from a raw input frame. There are many algorithms to detect the hand in various environments, e.g. based on color [12, 22], motion flow [14], shape detection [18], and statistical information [9]. Combining multiple hand detection methods will improve the overall accuracy but it will also slow down the overall performance, especially in mobile phone applications. We take a very simple approach, applying color segmentation to detect the hand from the scene. Different color spaces have been suggested for the skin color range; to avoid the cost of color space conversion, RGB color was chosen for this project.

Normalizing RGB is crucial because it will remove any intensity changes and thus, it will address illumination problems and increase accuracy. After normalizing the RGB image, we performed a skin color filter to the region around the AR marker. To save a computational cost and since we are mostly interested in interaction in the region around the virtual object, we restricted the search window to three times the area of the marker (pose-estimation). We used an RGB skin color range as suggested by Kovac et al. [12].

We split the search window into a 4 by 4 grid (Figure 2 (d)). The size of this grid was determined experimentally as a good compromise between speed and necessary accuracy for the gestures we chose to implement and evaluate (see also Section on User Studies). For each grid cell, we compute the percentage of skin-color pixels, $P(skin_n)$, the number of skin-colored pixels divided by total number of pixels in $grid_n$. We implemented two different modes for the interaction: discrete event detection and continuous value adjustment. For the discrete mode, we manually set the threshold value for each cell, that is if $P(skin_n)$ is greater than the threshold value, $grid_n$ is hit. For the continuous value adjustment, we record how much the hand occludes that grid cell. In this case, each cell is not governed by a threshold, but the amount of hand occlusion in each cell, $P(skin_n)$, is used to change a value dynamically, for instance opacity. Figure 2 illustrates the three different interaction techniques: discrete (A and B), and continuous value adjustment (C) mode.

We use the discrete mode when we need to make a sequential gesture, such as for translation or scaling. For instance, scale-down or up uses a pinch motion and we split the detection into two parts: When $P(skin_{n1})$ is greater than the threshold value in a certain starting grid cell and next (within 10 frames from first detection) the corresponding neighbor grid cells obtain $P(skin_{n2})$ that is greater than the threshold value, then we trigger the interaction. On the other hand, we use the continuous mode for an interaction that continuously changes a value, similar to a slider. In our case, the virtual object remains transparent until the hand goes closer to the marker, which increases the opacity. The farther the user retracts the finger, the more transparent the object becomes. To lock in a certain degree of transparency, the user quickly removes the finger.

SPEED

Our application renders the augmented video stream at 640×480 resolution on the phone's display, but we internally use 320×240 resolution for all image processing steps to reduce computation time. Table 1 shows time measurements for each step, revealing that GPU to CPU read-back and image filtering took the most time. Even though the GPU processes

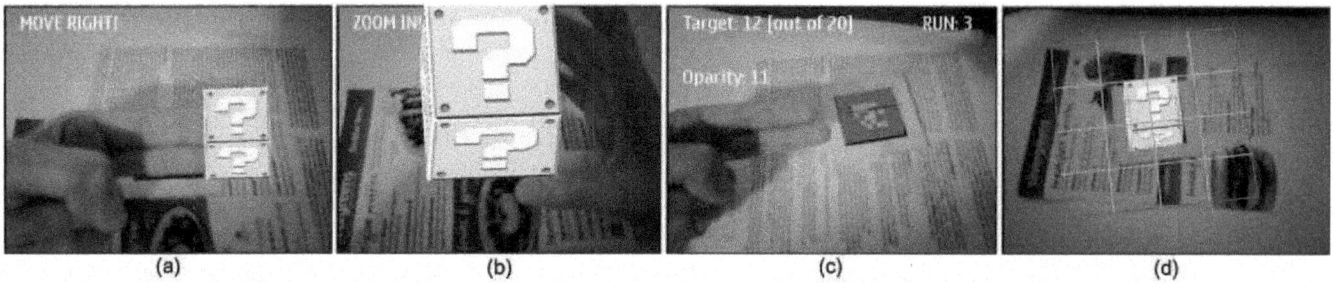

Figure 2. (a) and (b) show translation and scaling interaction. (c) shows continuous value adjustment, applied to box transparency. In this experiment, the user attempts to match a target opacity value. (d) shows (as debug information) the 4×4 grid board we use to track the hand.

Task	Processing Time (msec)
Marker Detection	8.72
Background Subtraction	9.27
Transfer GPU to CPU*	22.60
Image Filtering*	82.63
Skin Region Detection*	12.31
Interaction Detection	0.00

Table 1. Performance timings for each task (in ms)
* tasks are called every 5 frames; all others are called every frame

the projective texture mapping and background subtraction quickly, a challenge arises when we need to access this output from the CPU. We resolved this issue by only requiring a direct pixel access every 5 frames, which experimentation revealed to be sufficient for robust performance. Image filtering is applied after background subtraction, filling any holes that resulted, and smoothing out noise. After prolonged informal experimentation, we determined that applying the erosion and dilation steps three times would result in a sharp reliable segmentation, but this turned out to be a large workload. These expensive tasks (marked with * in Table 1) are thus called only every 5 frames whereas all others are called every frame. This all adds up to a total performance time of approximately 41.5 ms per frame. Since we initially started out with a rendering rate of 30 fps for simple AR marker detection, we now end up with an 18-20 fps overall frame rate, which is still a “reasonable” speed for interactive use.

USER STUDIES

We conducted two different studies to measure the accuracy and robustness of the application, and to observe if the hand interaction using the mobile phone is usable. We conducted both studies back-to-back, the two studies being independent of each other. The total length of the two studies was a maximum of 45 minutes. We recruited 30 participants, who were from different backgrounds, with a mean age of 24.6 years (23 females with a mean age of 24.1 years, and 7 males with mean age 26.4). The test environment was not constrained to a single place, but each test was conducted in a different place, using flat working surfaces which varied in color and texture. Before we started each trial, we determined how familiar a user was with smart phones and Augmented Reality, and established the participant's dominant hand. Participants received standardized instruction and training with our methods, all part of the 45 minutes. We asked users to hold the phone in their non-dominant hand and to use their dominant hand for the interaction.

Goals

The first study measured the time for continuous value control. We speculated that as the range from which to choose the target value becomes wider (e.g. from [1,10] to [1,30]), selecting the target value would become more difficult to control. We were interested in locating any range of drastic performance drop-off to determine the best suitability of our 4×4 grid-board method. A random number was chosen from three different ranges, [1,10], [1,20], or [1,30], and displayed on the screen (Figure 2 (c)). The users' task was to move their hands/fingers in or out the AR scene to control the value to match the displayed number. Every 10 seconds, if users could not finish the task, the system would time out, recorded 10 seconds as the maximum time, and move on to the next random number; otherwise, the completion time was recorded internally and the next trial started. We asked users to do this task 75 times, with 25 trials from [1,10], 25 from [1,20], and 25 from [1,30], in random order.

Our second study tested the performance of hand-held versus tripod setups (Figure 5 (b) depicts a typical tripod scene). One major point of interest with our proposed method was the intended system use which differed slightly from related work: users hold the phone in one hand and use the other for the interaction while enabling 6-degree-of-freedom interaction. We hypothesized that since our method addressed the issue of (slight) camera motion, we would get about the same results from non-stationary (hand-held) camera setups as with stationary (tripod) camera setups. We randomized the order of conditions. For hand-held setups, we asked users to hold the phone any which way they preferred and also let them switch hands if they deemed it more natural. We had four different gestures: Move a box left, right, up, and down in random order, 25 times for each direction. For each task, we displayed the requested direction on the screen and we asked users to complete the trial in 3 seconds. We simply recorded whether users completed the task within that time frame or not. We asked users to do 100 trials, 50 with the camera on a tripod and 50 with the camera in hand.

Results

Our pre-study survey showed that 83% of the participants own smart-phones, and that among these participants the predominant average usage of smart phone was between every

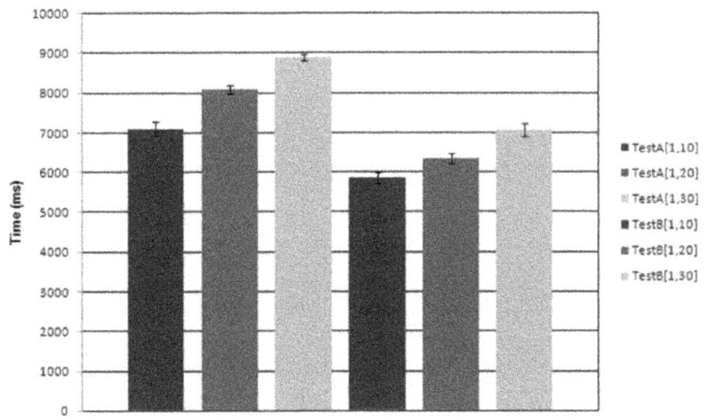

Figure 3. Results of Continuous Value Experiment based on *TestA:* whole data, and *TestB:* successfully completed trials only.

hour to every few hours. 27% of the participant knew or had heard of Augmented Reality before, generally from the web or through applications such as games, but they reported their familiarity level with AR as low (average of 1.3, with median of 1, on a 1-5 scale).

Task	Completed	Full data		Completed data	
		Mean	SD	Mean	SD
[1,10]	69.2%	7102.2	946.5	5866.8	718.6
[1,20]	53.6%	8076.7	590.0	6338.7	776.6
[1,30]	39.3%	8886.8	410.4	7068.9	837.9

Table 2. Results of continuous value adjustment

Table 2 reports the results of our first (continuous value adjustment) test, with the collected dataset sliced two ways: The full dataset represents all 2250 runs (25 runs × 3 ranges × 30 participants) we collected during the study. The completed dataset on the other hand represents only those tasks that participants were able to finish within 10 seconds. Table 2 lists the completion rate of each range (after removing three outlier participants, who did not follow instructions correctly, the probabilities improved to 75.3%, 57.1% and 42.4%).

For each dataset, we measured the average time (ms) to complete the number for each of the three different ranges. An ANOVA for the full dataset revealed significant differences ($F(2, 87) = 51.4$, and p = $1.8 \times 10^{-15} < 0.05$). Moreover, post-hoc analysis using Tukey's HSD test demonstrated that since all possible differences were greater than HSD, all groups are significantly different from each other. An ANOVA for the completed dataset also revealed significant differences ($F(2, 87) = 18.1$ and p = $2.63 \times 10^{-7} < 0.05$). Here, a post-hoc analysis using Tukey's HSD test showed that HSD = 479.4, with $|M_1 - M_2| = 471.9$, $|M_2 - M_3| = 730.2$, and $|M_3 - M_1| = 1202.1$, and thus no significant difference between the [1,10] and [1,20] groups, but differences among the other groups ([1,20], [1,30] and [1,10], [1,30]). Figure 3 illustrates these results.

We also tested the collected data for a learning effect, i.e. do later trials tend to exhibit increased performance? Over all participants, the average time in ms for the first 25 runs was 8008.9 (SD=676.3); for the next 25 runs, it was 8096.8 (SD=649.7); and for the last 25 runs, it was 7997.0 (SD=830.1). In this case, an ANOVA test revealed no significant differences ($F(2, 87) = 0.17$ and p = $0.84 > 0.05$). Similarly, a t-test between the first 25 runs and last 25 runs showed $t(29) = 0.081$ and p = $0.94 > 0.05$, implying that there was no significant difference. We did not observe a learning effect over time with this task.

Our results confirmed that the value adjustment task became more difficult with the interval to pick the target value from widening. We did not observe a drastic timing change between any two of the three different ranges. Instead, the difficulty level appears to rise nearly linearly from range [1,10] to range [1,30]. The average time for range [1,10] was 7102.2ms (5866.8ms for completed trials), which appears to be surprisingly long for the gesture, and the completion rate was 69.2%, which is fairly low. These quantitative results support that it is difficult to make fine-grin adjustments using our 4×4 grid approach, and this puts a limit on the range of hand gestures we can gainfully implement. As a result, we need to re-consider the use of the 4×4 region for gestures demanding high precision.

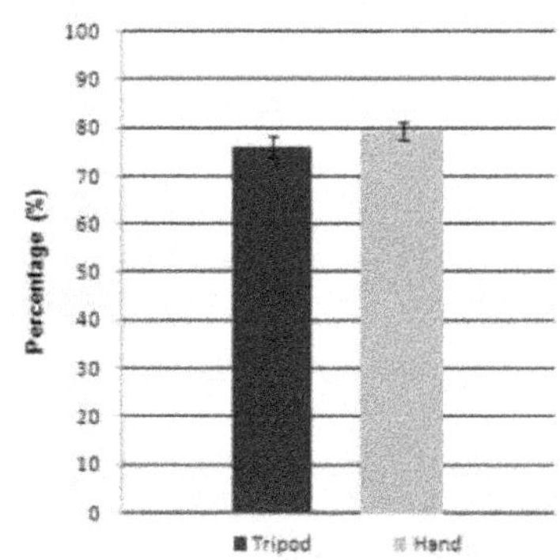

Figure 4. Completion rates for Experiment 2 (movement task) for camera on tripod (*left*) and camera in hand (*right*)

The second experiment measured the success rates of triggering discrete translation events for camera-in-hand versus camera-on-tripod setups (Figure 5). The results displayed in Figure 4 show that the average rate of completing the task within 3 seconds with the camera on a tripod was 0.76 (SD=0.13) and for camera-in-hand it was 0.79 (SD=0.10). A t-test ($t(29) = -2.08$ and p =$0.047 < 0.05$) revealed that there was a significant difference between the tripod and hand setups, with the camera-in-hand setup performing better. From the data, we also checked if there were any ordering effects, i.e. did it matter if a user first did the tripod-based test or the camera-in-hand test? T-tests revealed no significant difference from what modality was performed first.

Our analysis contradicted our initial hypothesis that the two setups would perform equally well. We obtained the unexpected result that our camera-in-hand setup performed slightly better than the tripod setup. It is difficult to find exact quantitative reasons of why the camera-in-hand mode might have outperformed the tripod mode. After all, the differences

	Experiment 1		Experiment 2		
	Fun to use	Easy to control	Easy to control	Move physically	Tripod-Hand
Strongly disagree (1)	0%	6.7%	0%	0%	16.7%
Disagree (2)	0%	26.7%	0%	0%	13.3%
Somewhat disagree (3)	0%	33.3%	6.7%	3.3%	6.7%
Neutral (4)	3.3%	23.3%	3.3%	10%	6.7%
Somewhat agree (5)	26.7%	10%	20%	26.7%	3.3%
Agree (6)	26.7%	0%	30%	13.3%	13.3%
Strongly agree (7)	43.3%	0%	40%	46.7%	40%
Mean (Likert scale)	6.1	3.0	5.9	5.9	4.6

Table 3. Post-study questionnaire results using a 7-point Likert scale; data from 30 participants. For the last column (Tripod-Hand), 1 indicated an absolute preference for the tripod setup and 7 for the camera-in-hand setup

were not huge. What can be concluded is that our method of dealing with slight camera movements was successful enough as not to lead to performance handicaps in this study. Post-study survey comments indicated an alignment of user performance with user preferences: Some users who preferred the tripod setup scored high on the tripod due to "easiness" because they liked having "both hands free" and thus, they did not have to "worry about switching hands for the interaction", such as between move gestures to the left and to the right. On the other hand, some users preferred the camera-in-hand, because for the tripod setup it was "harder" to see the virtual object "from a certain angle", and "tripod legs were an obstacle for the interaction".

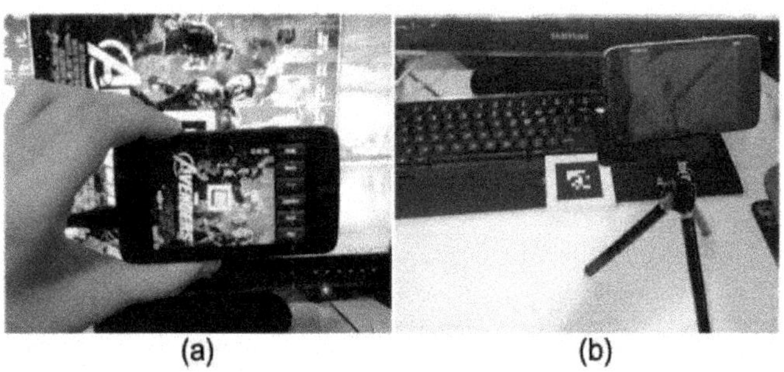

Figure 5. Two different setups: (a) camera-in-hand and (b) camera-on-tripod

Discussion

After the first test, we asked users about how fun the application was and on a scale from 1 (not fun) to 7 (very fun), our average score was 6.1 (median = 6). In exit interviews participants mentioned that it was "like a game application" and that they derived a "must-win" feeling during the study. We also think that the low familiarity level with AR (1.3 according to our pre-study survey) might have been a contributing factor, in that experiencing a method that users were not familiar with was "entertaining" to them. However, the score for the easiness of locking in the correct target number in experiment 1, from 1 (very hard) to 7 (very easy) scale, was only 3.0 (median = 3). As our results on completion rate also demonstrated (Table 2 shows 69.2%, 53.6%, and 39.3% for the different ranges), it was possible that frustration with fine-grain adjustments brought down this score. Table 3 shows more detail about two experiments' post-survey result.

On the second test, the average score on easiness of control in 1 (hard) to 7 (easy) scale was 5.9 (median 6). The discreteness of this task contributed to better completion rates. We also asked if users felt like they were moving the box physically, and on a scale from 1 (not really) to 7 (absolutely) scale, the result was 5.9 (median 6). This is a high value, considering that there was no force feedback. A shortcoming of the experience was that the box always moved with the same velocity in only four directions.

Despite many users' positive feedbacks about our proposed method, we also received some complaints, such as "tiring shoulder". Particularly, some critical comments came in response to the first test, when users had to hold the phone continuously for each task that took up to 10 seconds. This might mean that gestures that requires longer interaction times could face acceptance problems. For instance, one of the possible solutions that Hürst et al. [8] suggested was to focus on applications that requires gestures less frequently.

A question arises if direct hand interaction is a better solution compared with current state-of-the-art touch-screen gestures. As the results from our first experiment indicate, based on the completion rate, time, and post-survey feedback, controlling a small value using our proposed method was not easy. However, interacting with a 3D AR object and environment through gestures on a 2D screen observing the 3D scene also has its potential problems. The fixed and potentially very small size of a smart-phone display screen doesn't lend itself well to larger-motion gestures, especially when the distance between the camera and the AR object increases, making the interaction footprint on the display very small (through perspective projection). Further experiments are needed to make quantitative comparisons for various scenarios. Although touch screens offer a very reliable and thoroughly established mode of interaction, for controlling 3D AR scenes the jury is still out on what interface metaphor might work best.

Quantitative results from our second experiment revealed a success rate of 79% for users being able to complete a flicking/pushing task within 3 seconds. We conducted a brief analysis, applying keystroke-level model (KLM-GOMS) [4, 7, 11] theory to predict the time of a related swiping gestures on the touch screen, so that we can informally compare it against our method. We split our discrete method into two parts: the mental act, through which users cognitively prepare for the task that they need to achieve (flicking in a certain direction), and the pointing event, for which users move a finger around the touch screen to achieve the goal (just like moving a mouse cursor). We predict the time of using the discrete method on the touch screen to amount as approximately 2.3 seconds. This time can vary depending on the distance between the screen and finger and other factors. It is likely that touch-screen input will yield higher success rates and altogether faster response times than our through-the-camera-phone hand gestures. However, the benefits of direct-manipulation for AR object manipulation is a potential plus for the proposed method, as evidenced by the positive post-study survey feedback and specifically the question on the realism of interaction.

Conclusions

In this paper, we introduced a simple yet novel approach for interacting with virtual content in AR environments observed through camera smart phones, using our unencumbered hands for gestural input. Our results demonstrate that we can successfully address the problem of potential camera motion during gesture detection using projective texture mapping and background subtraction, obtaining acceptable correctness rates for simple scenes while maintaining good frame rates.

Our first evaluation experiment showed that this type of hand interaction might not (yet) be a good fit for subtle adjustment motions, as evidenced by users' difficulties in controlling small interval values; we think that button, keypad or other physical sources of input might still be a better fit in this case. Our second study demonstrated acceptable performance (correctness rate) of using a discrete sequential gesture detection for a translation event, at a reasonable speed. Our post-study survey comments highlight some potential promise of direct-manipulation gesture interaction with AR scenes (high engagement and physical realism). The hand-based interaction was perceived as "fun" and "easy to control" (for the discrete method). There is a distinct difference in features and affordances between a touch screen and our proposed method. A touch-screen interface is a common and accepted gesture tool in mobile phones, which users are thoroughly familiar with and which works robustly and, in conjunction with the right interface elements, very advantageously. We are not arguing or even targeting a complete replacement of this interaction modality. We do think, however, that our work, as well as other recent work in the area of hand gesture recognition highlights specific potential of 3D interaction using finger gestures to directly manipulate an AR scene. We have demonstrated the feasibility and potential uses of such technologies using camera smart phones. Based on reasonable accuracy, robustness, and positive feedbacks we received, we conclude that direct hand interaction in phone-based AR is a modality that should be considered to complement others.

We realize that improvements are desirable in terms of long-term-use ergonomics, robustness and reliability. We will consider the design of infrequent gestures as Hürst et al. suggested, and we also plan to collect more data on user behaviors to optimize gesture design. Our current 4×4 grid restricts possible gestures, as detailed adjustments are difficult to achieve. Future work will consist in tracking individual fingers more efficiently and robustly, for instance by applying multiple hand detection algorithms in parallel while keeping performance high. We would like to expand our method to more and more fine-grained gestures, such as freely rotating virtual objects or moving objects in any direction with different velocities. User studies will be required to investigate if 3D interaction 'in the air' has advantages over existing and more established display-based interaction methods, both qualitatively and quantitatively. Once we make progress towards these goals, one of the possible applications in which we can utilize and showcase our new direct manipulation gestures would be a virtual storybook, in which users can interact with characters and scenery through life-like 3D gestures, hopefully enhancing the Flow and Presence afforded by such an environment.

ACKNOWLEDGMENTS

We thank the anonymous reviewers for their helpful comments and suggestions. This work was partially supported by NSF CAREER grant IIS-0747520.

REFERENCES

1. Azuma, R., Baillot, Y., Behringer, R., Feiner, S., Julier, S., and MacIntyre, B. Recent Advances in Augmented Reality. *IEEE Computer Graphics and Applications 21*, 6 (Nov. 2001), 34–47.

2. Baldauf, M., Zambanini, S., Fröhlich, P., and Reichl, P. Markerless Visual Fingertip Detection for Natural Mobile Device Interaction. In *Proceedings of the 13th International Conference on Human Computer Interaction with Mobile Devices and Services*, MobileHCI '11, ACM (New York, NY, USA, 2011), 539–544.

3. Buchmann, V., Violich, S., Billinghurst, M., and Cockburn, A. FingARtips: Gesture Based Direct Manipulation in Augmented Reality. In *Proceedings of the 2nd International Conference on Computer Graphics and Interactive Techniques in Australasia and South East Asia*, GRAPHITE '04, ACM (New York, NY, USA, 2004), 212–221.

4. Card, S. K., Moran, T. P., and Newell, A. The Keystroke-Level Model for User Performance Time with Interactive Systems. *Communications of the ACM 23*, 7 (July 1980), 396–410.

5. Chan, L.-W., Kao, H.-S., Chen, M. Y., Lee, M.-S., Hsu, J., and Hung, Y.-P. Touching the Void: Direct-Touch Interaction for Intangible Displays. In *Proceedings of the SIGCHI Conference on Human Factors in Computing Systems*, CHI '10, ACM (New York, NY, USA, 2010), 2625–2634.

6. Everitt, C. Projective Texture Mapping. Tech. rep., NVDIA, 2000. `https://developer.nvidia.com/content/projective-texture-mapping`.

7. Holleis, P., Otto, F., Hussmann, H., and Schmidt, A. Keystroke-Level Model for Advanced Mobile Phone

Interaction. In *Proceedings of the SIGCHI Conference on Human Factors in Computing Systems*, CHI '07, ACM (New York, NY, USA, 2007), 1505–1514.

8. Hürst, W., and van Wezel, C. Gesture-based Interaction via Finger Tracking for Mobile Augmented Reality. *Multimedia Tools and Applications* (2012), 1–26. 10.1007/s11042-011-0983-y.
9. Jones, M. J., and Rehg, J. M. Statistical Color Models with Application to Skin Detection. *International Journal of Computer Vision 46*, 1 (Jan. 2002), 81–96.
10. Kato, H., and Billinghurst, M. ARToolKit, 2003. `http://www.hitl.washington.edu/artoolkit/`.
11. Kieras, D. Using the Keystroke-Level Model to Estimate Execution Times. Unpublished Report, `http://www.pitt.edu/~cmlewis/KSM.pdf`, 1993.
12. Kovac, J., Peer, P., and Solina, F. Human Skin Color Clustering for Face Detection. In *EUROCON 2003. Computer as a Tool. The IEEE Region 8*, vol. 2 (Sept. 2003), 144 – 148 vol.2.
13. Looser, J. *AR Magic Lenses: Addressing the Challenge of Focus and Context in Augmented Reality*. PhD thesis, University of Canterbury, New Zealand, 2007.
14. Lucas, B. D., and Kanade, T. An Iterative Image Registration Technique with an Application to Stereo Vision. In *Proceedings of the 7th international joint conference on Artificial intelligence - Volume 2*, IJCAI'81, Morgan Kaufmann Publishers Inc. (San Francisco, CA, USA, 1981), 674–679.
15. Malik, S., Ranjan, A., and Balakrishnan, R. Interacting with Large Displays from a Distance with Vision-Tracked Multi-finger Gestural Input. In *Proceedings of the 18th annual ACM symposium on User Interface Software and Technology*, UIST '05, ACM (New York, NY, USA, 2005), 43–52.
16. McDonald, C., Malik, S., and Roth, G. Hand-Based Interaction in Augmented Reality. In *Haptic Virtual Environments and Their Applications, IEEE International Workshop 2002 HAVE* (2002), 55–59.
17. Mistry, P., Maes, P., and Chang, L. WUW - Wear Ur World: A Wearable Gestural Interface. In *CHI '09 Extended Abstracts on Human Factors in Computing Systems*, CHI EA '09, ACM (New York, NY, USA, 2009), 4111–4116.
18. Potamias, M., and Athitsos, V. Nearest Neighbor Search Methods for Handshape Recognition. In *Proceedings of the 1st international conference on Pervasive Technologies Related to Assistive Environments*, PETRA '08, ACM (New York, NY, USA, 2008), 30:1–30:8.
19. Reitmayr, G., and Schmalstieg, D. Mobile Collaborative Augmented Reality. In *Proceedings of IEEE and ACM International Symposium on Augmented Reality*, IEEE Computer Society (2001), 114–123.
20. Seo, B.-K., Choi, J., Han, J.-H., Park, H., and Park, J.-I. One-Handed Interaction with Augmented Virtual Objects on Mobile Devices. In *Proceedings of The 7th ACM SIGGRAPH International Conference on Virtual-Reality Continuum and Its Applications in Industry*, VRCAI '08, ACM (New York, NY, USA, 2008), 8:1–8:6.
21. Vatavu, R. D., Pentiuc, Ş., Chaillou, C., Grisoni, L., and Degrande, S. Visual Recognition of Hand Postures for Interacting with Virtual Environments. *Advances in Electrical and Computer Engineering 6*, 13 (2006), 55–58.
22. Vezhnevets, V., Sazonov, V., and Andreeva, A. A survey on Pixel-Based Skin Color Detection Techniques. In *Proceedings of the 13th International Conference on the Computer Graphics and Vision* (Sept. 2003), 85–92.
23. Wagner, D., and Schmalstieg, D. ARToolKitPlus for Pose Tracking on Mobile Devices. In *Proceedings of the 12th Computer Vision Winter Workshop*, CVWW '07 (2007), 139–146.

How Mobile Disrupts Social as We Know It

Monica S. Lam
Computer Science Department
Stanford University
Gates Building, Room 307
353 Serra Mall
Stanford, CA 94305
lam@cs.stanford.edu

ABSTRACT

Every computer revolution changes our lives dramatically; so will mobile devices. Mobile devices enable billions of people to capture, share, interact, and consume real-time personal media in new and creative ways. In addition, being devices owned by individuals, they can form an autonomous computing fabric that frees us from the domination of existing centralized proprietary social networking services.

This talk presents a system architecture called Musubi (Mobile, Social, and UBIquitous) that combines a novel and natural mobile social experience with a clean architecture that lets users choose different cloud backup services. In addition, Musubi is an app platform that makes it easy to create privacy-honoring social apps. This can open up new markets for social and collaborative apps in fields like education, health and businesses, where centralized proprietary services are inappropriate. A fully working prototype of Musubi is available on both the Android and iPhone app store.

Author Keywords

Mobile computing; social computing; social networks; software architecture.

ACM Classification Keywords

C.2.1 [Network Architecture and Design]: Distributed networks; H.5.3 [Group and Organization Interfaces]: Collaborative computing

BIO

Monica S. Lam has been a Professor in the Computer Science Dept. at Stanford University since 1988, and the Faculty Director of the Stanford MobiSocial Computing Lab. She received her PhD in Computer Science from Carnegie Mellon University. Her current research interest is in creating open social computing platforms. She has worked in the areas of high-performance computing, computer architecture, compiler optimizations, security analysis, virtualization-based computer management, and mobile/social software architectures. She is a co-author of the "Dragon Book." Together with her students, she founded MokaFive Inc. in 2005 and MobiSocial Inc. in 2012. Monica is an ACM Fellow.

IUI'13, March 19–22, 2013, Santa Monica, CA, USA.
ACM 978-1-4503-1965-2/13/03.

User-Adaptive Information Visualization - Using Eye Gaze Data to Infer Visualization Tasks and User Cognitive Abilities

Ben Steichen, Giuseppe Carenini, Cristina Conati
Department of Computer Science,
University of British Columbia, Vancouver, Canada
{steichen, carenini, conati}@cs.ubc.ca

ABSTRACT
Information Visualization systems have traditionally followed a one-size-fits-all model, typically ignoring an individual user's needs, abilities and preferences. However, recent research has indicated that visualization performance could be improved by adapting aspects of the visualization to each individual user. To this end, this paper presents research aimed at supporting the design of novel user-adaptive visualization systems. In particular, we discuss results on using information on user eye gaze patterns while interacting with a given visualization to predict the user's visualization tasks, as well as user cognitive abilities including perceptual speed, visual working memory, and verbal working memory. We show that such predictions are significantly better than a baseline classifier even during the early stages of visualization usage. These findings are discussed in view of designing visualization systems that can adapt to each individual user in real-time.

Author Keywords
Adaptive Information Visualization; Eye-tracking; Adaptation; Machine Learning.

ACM Classification Keywords
H.5.m.

INTRODUCTION
Information Visualization is a thriving area of Human-Computer Interaction that aims to help users in managing and understanding increasing amounts of information. While visualization systems have gained in terms of general usage and usability, they have traditionally been designed using a one-size-fits-all approach, typically ignoring an individual user's needs, abilities and preferences. In order to better assist each individual user during visualization tasks, recent research has started to investigate novel *user-adaptive* visualizations that can dynamically infer relevant user characteristics and provide appropriate interventions tailored to these characteristics. Initial research of user-adaptive visualizations have already provided evidence for improved user performance (e.g. time on task, task accuracy), for instance by using click behavior to infer and adapt to suboptimal usage patterns [14], or by using a user's visualization selections to infer and adapt to a user's visualization expertise and preferences [15]. In terms of intervention mechanisms, these initial systems have typically investigated recommending visualizations that are most suitable for the current task and/or appropriate for a particular user's preference and expertise.

Our long-term goal is to extend such research on user-adaptive visualization in a number of aspects. First of all, we aim to expand the set of adaptation characteristics towards general (low-level) visualization task types, task complexity, as well as users' cognitive abilities (other than expertise) that have been shown to influence visualization performance. Secondly, while existing research has looked at improving visualization performance solely using information on a user's direct interaction (e.g. mouse clicks), we aim to provide assistance using additional (and potentially complementary) non-interactive data sources (e.g. eye tracking). Thirdly, while existing work has focused on interventions that recommend alternative visualizations, we envision to also deliver interventions that can dynamically help the user with the current visualization (e.g. through highlighting relevant visualization elements).

In this paper, we address the first two aspects by investigating to what extent a variety of visualization tasks and three different cognitive abilities (perceptual speed, visual working memory and verbal working memory) can be inferred from a user's eye gaze behavior. We focus on gaze behavior because visual scanning and processing are fundamental components of working with any visualization (and the only components for non-interactive visualizations). Specifically, we ask the following two research questions:

Q1. To what extent can a user's current task and/or long-term cognitive abilities be inferred from eye gaze data?

Q2. Which gaze features are the most informative?

The motivation of this particular work is two-fold. First of all, in order to provide appropriate adaptive support, an adaptive system needs to know about the user's *current task*. For example, if the system knows that the user is currently trying to "filter" based on a particular data series, the system could adaptively deemphasize non-relevant data to reduce the user's cognitive load. Similarly, if a system knew a user's *cognitive abilities*, appropriate interventions could be provided to better assist this user. For example, since low perceptual speed has already been shown to lead to lower performance (in terms of speed and accuracy) [3][31][29], such users would benefit most from adaptive interventions.

Secondly, by analyzing which features are most informative, we may get an initial insight into what type of interventions would be most suitable. For example, as will be shown in the paper, different Areas of Interest (AOI) of a visualization provide considerable information about different task/user characteristics. Such results suggest that adaptations that are particularly tailored towards these AOIs may be most effective in order to support different tasks and/or user characteristics.

The remainder of this paper is structured as follows. First, we provide an overview of related research in adaptive visualization, eye tracking, as well as the most recent findings on the impact of individual user differences in visualization. Next, we present the user study that provided the gaze data for our research. This is followed by a series of classification experiments that we ran on this gaze data to answer the research questions outlined above. Finally, we conclude with a discussion of the overall findings and outline several directions for future work.

RELATED WORK

Adaptation and personalization have long been established as effective techniques to support individual users in a variety of tasks and applications, including personalized search [27], adaptive hypermedia [27], desktop assistance [19], as well as e-learning [19]. By contrast, information visualization research has traditionally maintained a static, one-size-fits-all approach by ignoring an individual user's needs, abilities and preferences. In particular, early automatic visualization systems have focused only on adapting the visualization to task or data properties that are known *a priori* [2][22], rather than dynamically inferring individual properties *during* visualization usage. An exception to this non-adaptive paradigm is presented in [15], where users' visualization expertise and preferences are dynamically inferred through monitoring visualization selections (e.g. how long it takes a user to decide on which visualization to choose). Using this inferred level of user expertise and preferences, the system then attempts to recommend the most suitable visualizations for subsequent tasks. Results from the user studies in [15] show that the recommendations indeed lead to better user performance in terms of task effectiveness (i.e. accuracy), as well as user efficiency (i.e. time on task). However, this work does not actively monitor a user *during* a task, and thus cannot adapt in real-time to help the user with the current task. In contrast, the system developed by Gotz and Wen [14] actively monitors real-time user behavior during visualization usage in order to infer needs for intervention. In their work, interaction data (i.e. mouse clicks) are constantly tracked in order to detect suboptimal usage patterns, i.e. activities of users that are of a repetitive (hence inefficient) nature. Each of these sub-optimal patterns indicates that an alternative visualization may be more suitable to the current user activity. The patterns used in their paper include *scanning* (i.e. a user is iteratively inspecting over similar visual objects), *flipping* (iteratively changing filter constraints), *swapping* (repeatedly re-arranging the order of data dimensions) and *drilling* (repeatedly filtering down along orthogonal dimensions). Once these patterns are detected, the system triggers adaptation interventions similar to those in [15], namely they recommend alternative visualizations that may be more suitable for the current activity (for example, the location of a set of hotels may be best viewed using a map visualization, rather than a user having to repeatedly drill down to this information for each result). However, there are a number of shortcomings of this work. First of all, the usage patterns, as well as the respective visualization recommendations are determined by experts a priori, rather than being based on experimental findings. Secondly, their system is only able to provide adaptations for visualizations that allow users to interact directly with the visualizations, either through mouse clicks or other forms of direct user input. This approach therefore does not work if a user is simply "looking" at a visualization without manipulating its controls/data. Thirdly, the patterns do not try to infer general (low-level) visualization tasks (e.g. *filter*, *compute derived value*). Lastly, their approach does not attempt to adapt to any individual user characteristics.

As mentioned before, since visual scanning and processing are fundamental components of working with *any* visualization (they are in fact the only components for non-interactive visualizations), it is important to consider eye-tracking as a source of real-time information on user behavior. Although such technology is currently confined to research environments (mostly due to the high cost of eye tracking devices), the rapid development in affordable, mainstream eye tracking solutions (e.g. using standard webcams) will enable the widespread application of such techniques in the near future [25]. In the field of cognitive and perceptual psychology, the use of eye tracking has long been established as a suitable means for analyzing user attention patterns in information processing tasks [21]. Similarly, research in this field has investigated the impact of individual user differences on basic reading and search tasks [24]. More recently, the fields of human-computer interaction and information visualization have also started to use eye-tracking technology to investigate trends and differences in user attention patterns and cognitive/decision processing. Such research has typically focused on either identifying pattern differences for different visualizations

[13] or task types (e.g. reading vs. mathematical reasoning) [18], or on explaining differences in user accuracy between alternative interfaces [23]. However, such studies have generally only attempted to gain insights into differences in gaze behaviors for different tasks and/or interfaces, rather than providing a means for directly driving adaptive systems. In particular, such analyses have typically consisted of offline processes that require further human analysis (e.g. manually analyzing eye gaze coordinate plots [18]). In terms of actually using raw eye tracking data for real-time prediction, most research has so far focused on identifying cognitive processes while performing non-visualization activities, for example during exploratory e-learning [20][4], quizzes [5], simple puzzle games [7], or information search tasks (e.g. word search) [26]. By contrast, our gaze-based work focuses on information visualization, where a user's main activity is to perform simple visualization lookup and comparison tasks.

It is also important to note that none of the above approaches have attempted to adapt to user differences other than expertise. However, recent research has shown that other user traits can in fact significantly influence task performance, especially in the field of information visualization. For example, Ziemkiewicz et al. [32], as well as Green and Fisher [16] have looked at the influence of a user's personality traits, showing that locus of control (internal vs. external) can impact visualization performance. Similarly, cognitive measures such as perceptual speed and visual working memory have been shown to influence a user's ability to complete a task effectively [3][31]. For example, it has been shown that users with high perceptual speed had significantly faster completion times and accuracy on certain tasks. These results have been confirmed and extended in a recent study by Toker et al. [29], where perceptual speed, working memory, and user expertise were shown to influence not only a user's task performance, but also satisfaction regarding different visualization types. More specifically, they showed that depending on the respective cognitive abilities, users performed differently and preferred different visualizations. Most recently, it was also found that such individual user differences have an impact on different user eye gaze measures [28], which directly serves as the motivation for the work in this paper on using gaze data to dynamically identify and adapt to user cognitive abilities.

USER STUDY

To reiterate, this paper is part of our ongoing work on designing user-adaptive information visualizations. In particular, our research studies both the effect that different user characteristics have on visualization performance, as well as the real-time detection of task and user characteristics in order to be able provide appropriate interventions (note that this paper only focuses on the latter part). For these purposes, we designed and ran a user eye tracking study with two basic visualization techniques, namely bar graphs (Figure 1, top) and radar graphs (bottom). By choosing two different types of visualizations, we aimed to investigate the generalizability of our results.

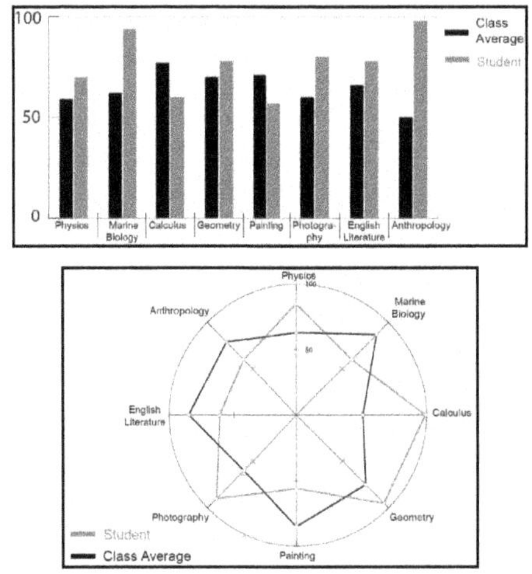

Figure 1. Sample bar (top) and radar graph (bottom)

Bar graphs were chosen because they are one of the most popular and effective visualization techniques. We chose radar graphs because, although they are often considered inferior to bar graphs on common information seeking tasks [10], they are widely used for multivariate data. Furthermore, there are indications that radar graphs may be just as effective as bar graphs for more complex tasks [29].

Study Tasks

As part of the study design, we developed a set of tasks that varied both in *task type* and *task complexity*. In terms of different *task types*, we based our questions on a set of general visualization tasks that had been identified by Amar et al. to be "representative of the kinds of specific questions that a person may ask when working with a data set" [1]. In particular, out of this taxonomy we chose the following five types: *retrieve value (RV), filter (FI), compute derived value (CDV), find extremum (FE),* and *sort (SO)*. Each of the tasks required users to evaluate student performance values in eight different academic courses (using an artificial data set). The tasks were chosen so that each of our two target visualizations would be suitable to support them. In order to vary the task complexity, we differentiated between *single* and *double* tasks. Single tasks required participants to compare one student's performance with the class average for 8 academic courses (e.g., "In how many courses is Maria below the class average?"), whereas double tasks required participants to compare the performance of two students with the class average (e.g., "Find the courses in which Andrea is below the class average and Diana is above it?"). In total, our study comprised 5 single tasks, one for each task type (i.e. RV1, FI1, CDV1, FE1, SO1), and 4 double tasks (RV2, CDV2, FI2a, FI2b), meaning that the most fine-grained task type/complexity classification could consist of 9 classes (see classification experiments).

Cognitive Abilities

The long-term user traits that we investigated in this study consisted of the following three cognitive abilities: *perceptual speed* (a measure of speed when performing simple perceptual tasks), *verbal working memory* (a measure of storage and manipulation capacity of verbal information), *and visual working memory* (a measure of storage and manipulation capacity of visual and spatial information). Perceptual speed and visual working memory were selected because they were among the perceptual abilities explored by Velez et al. [31], as well as among the set that Conati and Maclaren [3] found to impact user performance with radar graphs and a Multiscale Dimension Visualizer (MDV). We also chose verbal working memory because we hypothesized that it may affect a user's performance with a visualization in terms of how the user processes its textual components (e.g., legends).

Study Procedure

Thirty-five subjects (18 female) participated in the experiment, ranging in age from 19 to 35. Participants were recruited via advertising at our university, with the aim of collecting a heterogeneous pool with suitable variability in their cognitive abilities. Ten participants were CS students, while the rest came from a variety of backgrounds, including microbiology, economics, classical archaeology, and film production. The experiment was designed and pilot-tested to fit in a single session lasting at most one hour. Participants began by completing tests for three cognitive measures[1]: a computer-based OSPAN test for Verbal Working Memory [30] (lasting between 7 and 12 minutes), a computer-based test for Visual Working Memory [11] (10 minutes long), and a paper-based P-3 test for Perceptual Speed [8] (3 minutes long). The experiment was conducted on a Pentium 4, 3.2GHz, with 2GB of RAM and a Tobii T120 eye-tracker as the main display. Tobii T120 is a remote eye-tracker embedded in a 17" display, providing unobtrusive eye-tracking. After undergoing a calibration phase for the eye-tracker, participants performed 14 tasks per visualization (2x5 *single* and 1x4 *double*). The presentation order with respect to visualization type was fully counterbalanced across subjects. For each task, users were presented with a radar/bar graph displaying the relevant data, along with a textual question. Participants would then select their answer from a drop-down list and click OK to advance to the next task. The experimental software was fully automated and coded in Python.

Eye tracking measures & features

An eye-tracker captures gaze information through fixations (i.e., maintaining gaze at one point on the screen) and saccades (i.e., a quick movement of gaze from one fixation point to another), which can be analyzed to derive a viewer's attention patterns. For our experiments we generated a large set of eye-tracking features by calculating statistics upon basic eye-tracking measures (see Table 1).

Basic gaze measures	**Description**
Fixation rate	Rate of eye fixations per milliseconds
Number of Fixations	Number of eye fixations detected during an interval of interest
Fixation Duration	Time duration of an individual fixation
Saccade Length	Distance between the two fixations delimiting the saccade (d in Fig. 2)
Relative Saccade Angles	The angle between the two consecutive saccades (e.g., angle y in Fig. 2)
Absolute Saccade Angles	The angle between a saccade and the horizontal (e.g., angle x in Fig. 2)

Table 1. Description of basic eye tracking measures.

Of these basic measures, *Fixation rate*, *Number of Fixations* and *Fixation Duration* are widely used in eye tracking studies. In addition, we included *Saccade Length* (e.g., distance d in Fig. 2.), *Relative Saccades Angle* (e.g., angle y in Fig. 2) and *Absolute Saccade Angle* (e.g., angle x in Fig. 2.), as suggested in [12], because these measures are potentially useful for summarizing trends in user attention patterns within a specific interaction window, e.g., if the user's gaze follows a planned sequence (as opposed to being scattered).

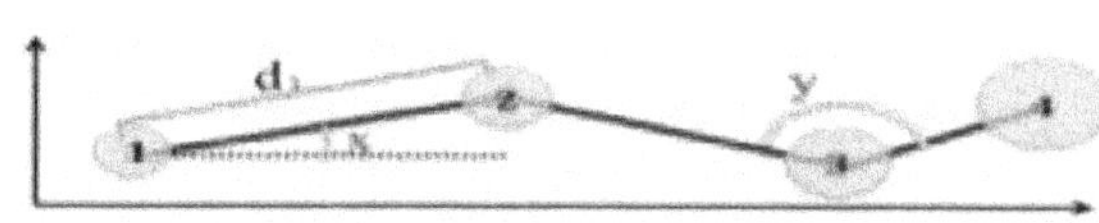

Fig. 2. Saccade based eye measures

In order to extract individual eye tracking features, the raw gaze data from the Tobii eye tracker was processed using customized scripts[2] written in the Python programming language. The scripts compute statistics such as sum, average and standard deviation over the eye tracking measures with respect to: (i) each overall task in the study, to get a sense of the complete interaction with the task (*task-level measures* from now on) and (ii) specific areas of interest (AOI), identifying parts of the interface relevant for understanding a user's attention processes during each task (*AOI-level measures* from now on). A total of five AOIs were defined for each of the two visualizations.

These regions were selected in order to capture the distinctive and typical components of the two visualizations used in the study. Figures 3 and 4 show how these AOI map onto bar and radar graph components respectively.

[1] Note that these tests measure long-term cognitive traits, as opposed to short-term cognitive load. Therefore these tests do not have to be run during/in between tasks.

[2] These scripts are currently being generalized and will soon be released as an open-source toolkit named EMDAT (Eye Movement Data Analysis Toolkit).

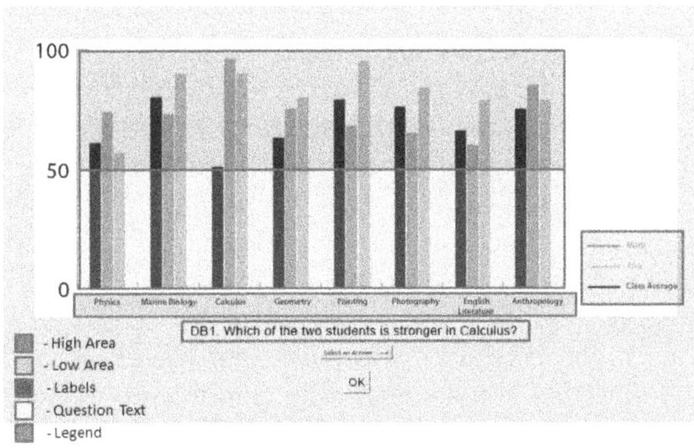

Figure 3: The five AOI regions defined over a bar graph

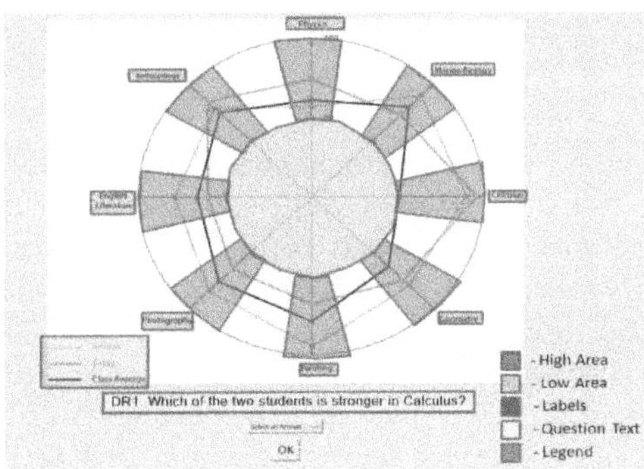

Figure 4: The five AOI regions defined over a radar graph

High Area: covers the upper half of the data elements of each visualization. This area is the graphical portion of an Infovis that contains the relevant data values. On the bar graph, it corresponds to a rectangle over the top half of the vertical bars (see Figure 3); for the radar graph, it corresponds to the combined area of the 8 trapezoidal regions covering the data points (see Figure 4).
Low Area: covers the lower half of the data elements for each visualization.
Labels: covers all the data labels in each graph.
Question Text: covers the text describing the task to be performed.
Legend: covers the legend showing the mapping between each student and the color of the visualization elements that represent her performance.

The selection of these five AOIs is the result of a trade-off between having detailed information on user attention over areas that are salient for task execution, and keeping the number of AOIs manageable for real-time computation. Overall, a total of 79 features were calculated from the gaze data (see Table 2). For experimental purposes, we differentiated between a feature set that contained all features, including task-level and AOI features (called the *Full* set from now on), and one that did not contain features relating to AOIs (called the *No AOI* set), i.e. only containing the task-level features. This differentiation was chosen in order to evaluate the relative information gain attained when AOI features are available to the system.

TASK-LEVEL FEATURES
Fixations: *Total Number of Fixations, Fixation rate*
Fixation Durations: *Sum, Mean, Std. deviation*
Saccade Length: *Sum, Mean, Std. deviation*
Relative Saccade Angles: *Sum, Mean, Std. deviation*
Absolute Saccade Angles: *Sum, Mean, Std. deviation*
AOI-LEVEL FEATURES (for each AOI)
Total number of fixations in AOI
Sum & Mean of fixation durations in AOI
Time to first fixation in AOI
Time to last fixation in AOI
Longest fixation in AOI
Proportion of Total Number of Fixations in AOI
Proportion of Total Fixation Durations in AOI
Prop. number of Transitions From this AOI to every other AOI (5 separate measures)

Table 2. Eye Tracking Features

CLASSIFICATION EXPERIMENTS

The classification experiments described in this section use the above-mentioned features to infer a number of task and user characteristics. In particular, we investigate the extent to which these characteristics can be inferred from gaze data (Q1), as well as what gaze features are most important for classification (Q2).

First, we provide a quick overview of the experimental process used for classification. This is followed by a detailed analysis of each of the classification results, which includes classification accuracy for *task type* (at different granularities) and *task complexity*, as well as accuracy on classifying the three user cognitive abilities of *perceptual speed*, *visual working memory* and *verbal working memory*. In addition, we ran a classification experiment for predicting the currently active *visualization type* (i.e. bar graph vs. radar graph), to evaluate the extent to which this information can be inferred when it is not available to the system (i.e., if the visualization system and the eye tracking component are independent). We conclude with a summary of the overall results, as well as a discussion regarding the extent to which these results could be used for providing adaptive visualizations.

Experimental process

Given the gaze features described in the previous section, we generated a number of datasets to simulate partial observation of gaze data during each task, e.g., only the first 10%, 20%, 30%, etc. These datasets were generated to simulate classification accuracies *while* a user is still interacting with (i.e., looking at) the visualization. The goal of this analysis is to investigate the feasibility of real-time interventions when integrating the classification component into a live user-adaptive visualization system.

We used the WEKA data mining toolkit [17] for model learning, as well as evaluation. For model learning, we tried a number of different classifier types (Decision Tree based, Support Vector Machine, Multilayer Perceptron, and Logistic Regression) with feature-selection and 10-fold cross-validation for model evaluation. In all our experiments, Logistic Regression (LR from now on) was the classifier with the highest accuracy. In the following sections, the performance of this classifier is evaluated on both the *Full* and *No AOI* data sets. As a baseline for comparison, we use a classifier that always selects the most likely class (thus failing in all cases of the other classes), e.g., for task complexity, the baseline classifier would always predict a task to be *single*, since there are more *single* tasks overall (thus failing in all cases of *double* tasks). Results are generated using the WEKA experiment API with the default 10(repetition) * 10(cross-validation) setting, and statistical significance is tested using t-tests with Bonferroni adjustment on pairwise comparisons between the different classifiers. All reported results are statistically significant (at $p<0.05$), unless mentioned otherwise. In cases of two-class classifications, we also present the strongest features generated by feature selection. For simplicity, in the case of multiclass classifications we do not present the results of feature selection in detail. Instead, we discuss the impact of features only with respect to the performance of the *Full* vs. *No AOI* datasets.

Classification results for task characteristics

As explained in the *study procedure* section, users performed tasks of varying *type* and *complexity*. In this section we present classification results when tasks are defined at different levels of granularity.

Task type – 9 tasks

The most fine-grained analysis splits tasks into 9 different classes, one for each separate question type-complexity combination used in the study, e.g. *single retrieve value (RV1), double retrieve value (RV2)*, etc. Because of the high number of classes, this case represents a difficult multiclass classification challenge, with a baseline classification accuracy of only 15.45%. Nonetheless, the LR classifier using the full feature data set (LR-Full from now on), reaches a classification accuracy of 56.60% after seeing all the available data (see Figure 5), and starts having significantly higher accuracy than the baseline after seeing only 10% of the data.

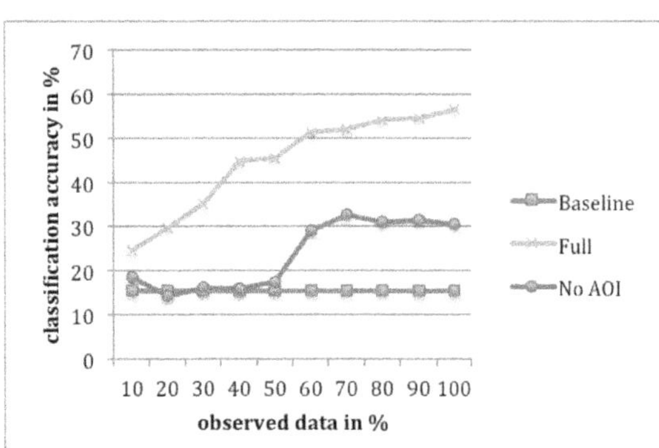

Figure 5. Task type – classification accuracy (9 different tasks)

Moreover, classification accuracy grows continuously as more gaze data becomes available, going over 50% after seeing 60% of the data (as shown in Figure 5). The average classification accuracy over time for LR-Full is 44.81%. Results are not as good for the LR classifier using the No-AOI dataset (LR-NoAOI from now on). The average accuracy over time for this classifier is 23.80% and its maximum accuracy after seeing all the data is 30.61%, both statistically significantly lower than the corresponding accuracies for LR-Full. Moreover, the accuracy of LR-NoAOI classifier is not statistically significantly better than the baseline until after seeing 60% of the data. These differences in performance for the *Full* vs. *No AOI* data sets indicate that AOI-related features have a strong impact on classification accuracy for task type at this granularity.

Task type- 5 tasks

In addition to the fine-grained task analysis involving 9 different tasks, we also investigated classifying task type from gaze data when type is defined at a coarser level of granularity that ignores the complexity difference between *single* and *double* tasks, e.g., ignoring the difference between *retrieve value* when one student is involved (RV1) as opposed to when two students are involved (RV2). Ignoring this difference leaves us with 5 different classes, corresponding to 5 different task types from Amar's taxonomy (i.e., *retrieve value (RV), filter (FI), compute derived value (CDV), find extremum (FE),* and *sort (SO)*). From the point of view of inferring task type with the goal of providing adaptive interventions specific to tasks types, this 5-class classification task is very meaningful, because the classes represent general tasks types recognized as being common in information visualization.

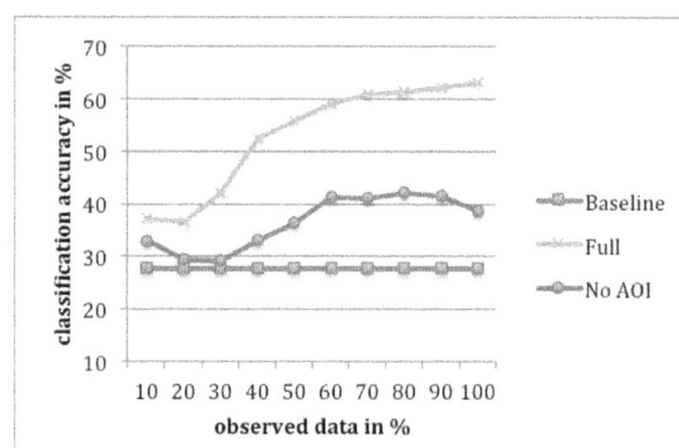

Figure 6. Task type – classification accuracy (5 tasks)

For this experiment, LR-Full reaches an average accuracy of 53.18% over time, an accuracy of 55.84% after seeing 50% of the data, and a maximum accuracy of 63.32% after seeing all the data. LR-Full statistically significantly outperforms the baseline's accuracy (27.863%) from the start. As was the case with 9 tasks, removing AOI-related features statistically significantly reduces accuracy, as shown by the performance of LR-NoAOI in Figure 6. This classifier reaches an average accuracy of 36.61% over time, an accuracy of 36.34% after seeing 50% of the data, and a maximum accuracy of 42.25% after seeing 80% of the data. Moreover, this classifier only starts to be statistically significantly better than baseline after seeing 40%.

When analyzing sources of errors in the confusion matrix, we found two pairs of tasks that are most often confused with each other. The first pair involves the tasks *compute derived value* (CDV) and *filter* (FI). For example, in 57% of the cases where CDV was misclassified, the predicted class was FI. This result is not surprising, since both of these tasks essentially involve applying a filter to all data values (e.g. finding values above a given threshold), with the difference being that CDV requires an additional computation (e.g. "in how many courses is student x above the class average"). Thus, FI can be regarded as a subtask of CDV for the questions used in our study. In fact, as noted by Amar et al., the *filter* task "... is used as a subtask in many other questions". Adaptations that particularly support this *filter* task may therefore also be of use to CDV tasks if they contain such a subcomponent. The second pair of tasks often confused with each other involves *find extremum* (FE) and *sort* (SO). For example, in 38% of the cases where FE was misclassified, the predicted class was SO. This result is again not surprising given the nature of these two tasks. *FE* involves going through all values to find the highest value(s) from a set of values, whereas SO involves sorting all values from highest to lowest. Thus, *FE* essentially involves a subpart of the steps necessary to perform an *SO* task. This finding confirms the observation in the Amar et al.'s taxonomy that *"sorting is generally a substrate for extreme value finding"* [1].

The aforementioned relations between the two pairs of frequently confused tasks suggest that combining each pair into one new task type, and building a classifier that can recognize this combined type is still valuable for adaptation, since adaptations could be provided to support the common subtask. Thus, in the next section we evaluate the accuracy of a classifier for task type that involves three classes: FI-CDV (combined), SO-FE (combined) and retrieve value (RV).

Task type - 3 tasks

When considering only 3 different task types, LR-Full reaches an average accuracy of 68.42% over time, an accuracy of 70.55% after seeing 50% of the data, and a maximum accuracy of 76.24% after seeing all the data. LR-Full statistically significantly outperforms the baseline's accuracy (48.14%) from the start.

As was the case with 9 and 5 tasks, removing AOI-related features statistically significantly reduces accuracy, as shown by the performance of LR-NoAOI in Figure 7. This classifier only reaches an average accuracy of 50.71% over time, an accuracy of 51.20% after seeing 50% of the data, and a maximum accuracy of 54.12 after seeing 70% of the data. Moreover, this classifier is only statistically significantly better than baseline between 50-70% of the data observations.

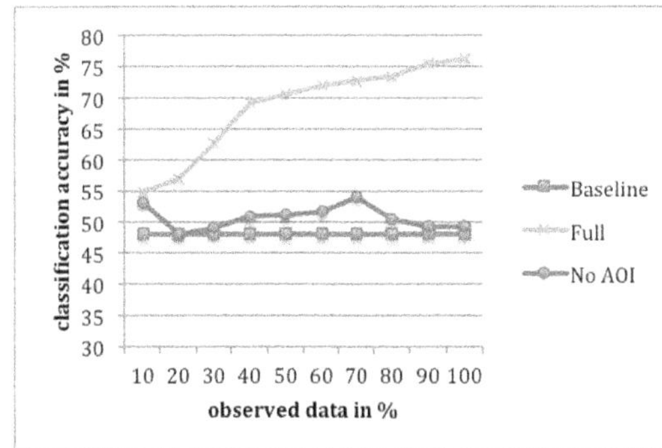

Figure 7. Task type – classification accuracy (3 tasks)

Task types – summary of results

In summary, we found that, across all task type granularities, LR with the full data set outperformed both the baseline and LR with the *No AOI* data set, showing the importance of having AOI-related features for task-type classification. Figure 8 summarizes the results in terms of average accuracy over time. As expected, accuracy for all the classifiers increases as task granularity gets coarser. Although only the classification of three tasks with the LR-Full classifier reaches accuracies that may be suitable for providing reliable task-based interventions, we see these results as being very important, for two reasons. First, as we argued earlier, suitable interventions can be provided even if task type is recognized at this coarser level. Second, our results have been obtained by using relatively simple eye-gaze features that do not capture gaze patterns beyond simple transitions between two AOIs. Using more complex gaze patterns or additional sources of information to guide classification (see discussion section), it is likely that we can increase accuracy on all our classification tasks.

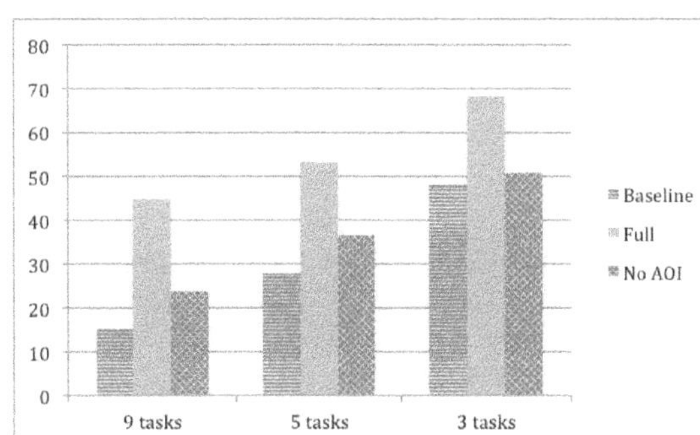

Figure 8. Task type – average classification accuracy over time for different task granularities

Task complexity

The classifier in this experiment predicts if the user is attending to a task of the *single* or *double* scenario. As discussed in the user study section, this distinction provides a measure for *task complexity*. LR-Full is still the most accurate classifier, with statistically significantly higher average accuracy (80.39%) over time than both the baseline classifier (72.69%) and LR-NoAOI (74.76%). It should be noted that, at 72.69%, the baseline accuracy is relatively high in this experiment, since users performed more than twice as many *single* tasks than *double* ones. Nevertheless, both LR classifiers performed higher, with accuracies reaching up to 84.45% for the full data set (see Figure 9). Accuracy again improved with more data being observed, and each of the feature sets outperformed the baseline after relatively low amounts of observed data (LR-Full is statistically significantly higher from the outset; LR-NoAOI after 40% of the data has been observed).

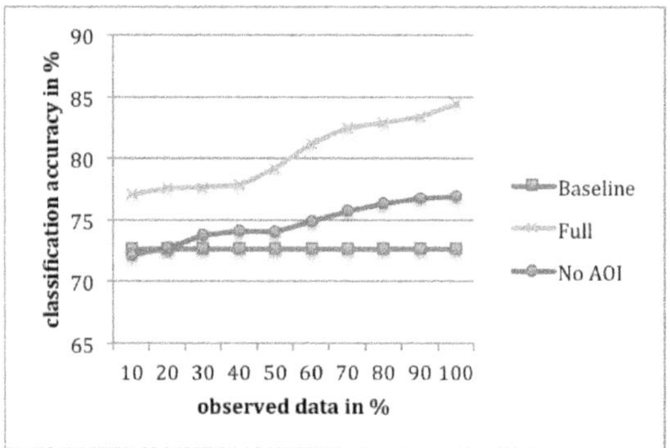

Figure 9. Task complexity – classification accuracy

Since task complexity consists of a simple two-class classification, it is also interesting to look into the more detailed feature selections and coefficients in order to analyze which exact features were contributing most to the classification (note that for multiclass logistic regression involving n classes, this analysis would involve analyzing n-1 feature selection results). Due to space limitations, we will only discuss the strongest features for LR-Full. With increased task complexity, we found that the use of the graph *legend* increased considerably, both in terms of proportionate amount of time spent (compared to all other AOIs), as well as in terms of transitions (i.e. there were more transitions to and from the legend). This result shows that an increase in data series has an effect on how much users may need to refer back to the legend during a visualization task, as to be expected. Nevertheless, it is an interesting finding that such an increase in complexity can be captured in real-time using simple eye gaze measures, which will in turn allow a user-adaptive system to provide adaptations for more complex tasks (e.g. provide support for better legend access and processing).

Classification results for Cognitive Abilities

In this section, we discuss classification results relating to inferring a user's level of visual working memory, verbal working memory, and perceptual speed. The specific task of each of the three classifiers is to infer if a user belongs to either the High or Low category for that measure (based on a median split). In addition to reporting the classification accuracy, we will also discuss the gaze features that have the highest impact on classification.

In general, we found similar results across the three classification experiments. First of all, we found that LR-Full statistically significantly outperformed both the baseline and LR-NoAOI, with average accuracies for LR-Full ranging between 56-60%. While these average accuracies were rather low, it has to be noted again that these experiments are solely based on simple eye tracking measures, which may be improved using additional sources of information (see overall result discussion).

Several interesting observations were made when analyzing the accuracies at different data cut-off points. In particular, for each of the experiments, the peak accuracy of LR-Full was actually found after 20-40% of the data had been observed, as opposed to after all the data had been observed (as found in previous experiments). This pattern suggests that a user's cognitive abilities most strongly affect a user's gaze patterns during the initial phase of a visualization task (clearly presented in Figures 10, 11, 12), and that these patterns are increasingly "diluted" by other factors (e.g. task type) as the task goes on.

For *visual working memory*, the peak accuracy of 58.92% occurred after 40% of the data had been observed (see Figure 10). When analyzing the features that received the highest coefficient during feature selection for LR-Full, we found that the time to first fixation for *text, label* and *high* AOIs played an important role in classifying users. We found that high visual working memory users had lower times to first fixation (indicated by a negative coefficient), meaning that they were very quick at scanning the various AOIs of the visualization.

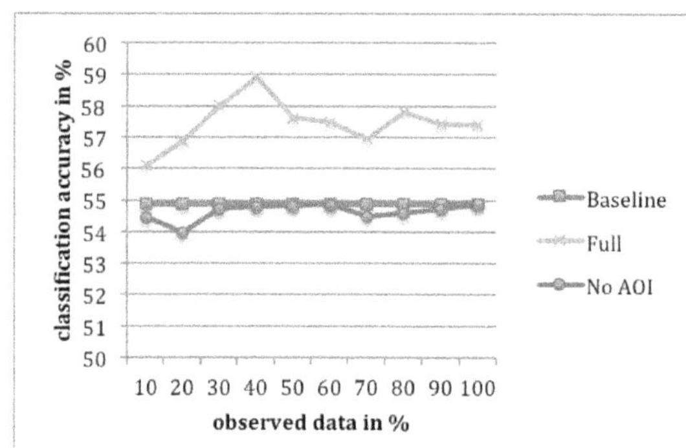

Figure 10. Visual Working Memory – classification accuracy

Similarly, for *verbal working memory*, the highest classification accuracy for both LR-Full (63.86%) and LR-NoAOI (61.09%) was found after observing only 20% of the data (see Figure 11). When analyzing the feature selection results for LR-Full, we found that features related to the *text* and *label* AOI most strongly contributed to the classification accuracy. In particular, high verbal working memory users spent less time in the text AOI, both overall and in proportion to other AOIs. Since users are most likely to read the question text at the beginning of each task, it therefore seems intuitive that the highest accuracies were found after only 20% of the data had been observed.

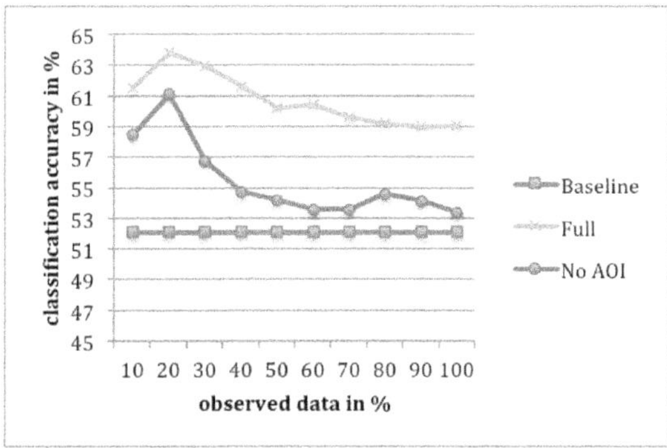

Figure 11. Verbal Working Memory – classification accuracy

A similar pattern was observed for the perceptual speed classification experiment, where the highest accuracy for LR-Full (59.84%) was found after only 20% of data had been observed (see Figure 12). When analyzing the feature selection results, we found that features related to the *label* and *legend* AOIs had the strongest coefficients. In particular, we found that high perceptual speed users had a lower number of fixations in the legend. This finding may indicate that low perceptual speed users would benefit from adaptations relating to this particular AOI (e.g. through highlighting, facilitating easier access, etc.). In addition, high perceptual speed users had a shorter *longest fixation* and a higher *fixation rate*.

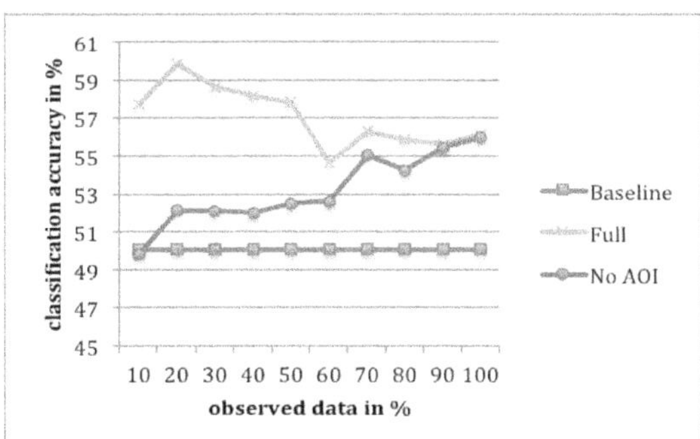

Figure 12. Perceptual Speed – classification accuracy

Visualization type

As shown in the classification results above, the inclusion of AOI-related features is critical towards generating predictions for both task types and cognitive measures. Having such AOI-related features requires knowing which visualization is currently active. While there are scenarios in which this information is indeed available to an adaptive component (i.e. if the adaptation component is part of the visualization system), this is not always the case. For example, if an adaptive component were to run as a standalone system in parallel to a separate visualization system (e.g., in the context of an information retrieval task when the user gets back a visualization, or in case the adaptive component acts as a complement to statistical analysis tools, etc.), it would be first necessary to infer the currently active visualization type in order to utilize the right AOIs for accurate task/user classifications. Thus, in this section we present results on whether visualization type can be inferred from gaze data. Since AOI information would not be available for this task, LR-Full is not applicable in a realistic scenario. For the LR-NoAOI classifier, the average accuracy is 64.56%, which is statistically significantly higher than the baseline (52.69%). As shown in Figure 13 (note that LR-Full is included for completeness), the accuracy of LR-NoAOI continuously grows as more gaze data is observed, reaching 66.34% after 50% of the data has been observed, and a maximum of 70.26% after all data has been observed. All accuracies are statistically significantly higher than baseline after only 20% of the data has been observed. While these results are encouraging, further research needs to be conducted in terms of improving accuracies in order to employ such techniques in a live system (see discussion).

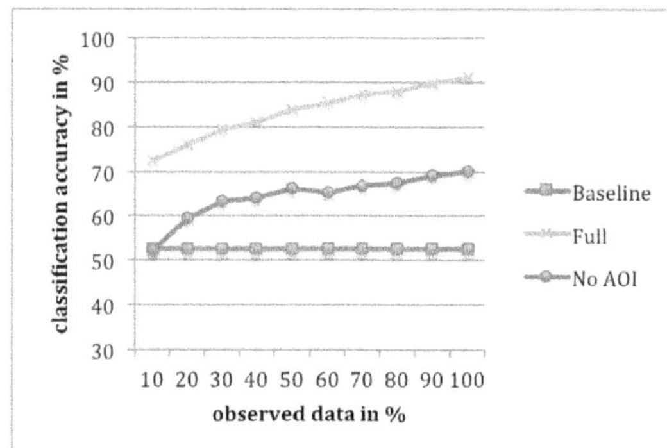

Figure 13. Visualization type – classification accuracy

Regarding the feature selection for this NoAOI classifier, we found that users have different viewing patterns in terms of *path angles*. Specifically, users have more horizontal viewing patterns in the bar graph (lower *mean absolute path angles*) and more "erratic" saccades (higher *standard deviation of absolute path angles*), whereas in the radar graph users follow a circular trajectory to view the various data points (indicated by a higher *mean of absolute path angles*), and have more uniform saccades due to the proximity of the labels to the respective data points (indicated by a lower *std. dev. of absolute path angles*).

Summary of Results & Discussion

As outlined in the introduction, the specific goals of our experiments were to investigate the extent to which a user's current visualization task and/or long-term cognitive abilities could be inferred solely based on eye gaze data (Q1), as well as which gaze features would be the most informative (Q2). By running a number of classification experiments and analyzing in detail the effects of different feature sets, we have found several interesting findings regarding these research questions.

We found that a user's eye gaze behavior provides evidence about each of the visualization tasks and cognitive abilities. In particular, we show that for each classification task, gaze-behavior-based predictions outperform a baseline classifier (Q1). Moreover, we show that for most of the predictions, the classification accuracy is statistically significantly higher even after only partial data observations. We have shown that for some experiments, accuracy is actually highest at the beginning of each task, indicating that a user's eye gaze at this time may contain the most relevant information regarding the target characteristics. These results provide very encouraging evidence that user eye gaze behavior could indeed be used for driving adaptive systems, particularly given that the experiments used a relatively simple set of features.

It may be argued that from a practical point of view, the accuracies are not yet high enough to be exploited in a live system. In particular, the accuracies relating to the cognitive abilities yielded results that were only in the 55-60% range. However, depending on the nature of the intervention/ guidance that is being provided, it can be envisioned that if the system is unsure about the user's classification, some minimal adjustments can be done, followed by continued tracking to see if performance improves. Nevertheless, further research should be conducted in order to improve the presented accuracies. On the one hand, we envision that the addition of sequence features (e.g. scan path patterns) could provide even more information about the various task and user characteristics. On the other hand, eye tracking data could be integrated with other sources, for example interaction data if such information is available. Similarly, there are further sources of information that could potentially be added to such a system, for example it may be possible to infer the user's task through automatic graph analysis (e.g. based on computer vision techniques [9]) or natural language processing (e.g. by processing a visualization's caption).

We obtained very interesting results regarding the more fine-grained details of each classification experiment. In particular, we found that depending on the goal of the classification, different features are most informative for different task/user characteristics (Q2). For example, we found that the label usage increases for more complex tasks, suggesting that users could benefit from interventions relating to this particular AOI. Similarly, we found that for low perceptual speed, users spend more time in the legend, suggesting such users may benefit from interventions that particularly relate to this AOI (e.g. giving such elements more emphasis or providing easier access). Such detailed analyses thereby not only provide evidence to what extent different characteristics can be inferred, but also how a system may adapt to individual differences.

In terms of general trends regarding the most informative features, we found that for each of the classification runs, AOI-related features were crucial towards more accurate predictions. It may therefore be argued that in order to build effective adaptive visualizations, a system needs to be aware of the currently active visualization. We therefore also showed that, even in the case of the system not knowing this information a priori (e.g. if the adaptive component is not directly attached to the visualization), it is possible to infer this visualization type solely based on a user's eye gaze with 70% accuracy. Again, this accuracy may potentially be improved with additional, more sophisticated features such as sequential scan paths.

While our experiments have only investigated two simple visualization techniques, there are many results that may be generalized to a wider array of visualization designs. In particular, we have shown that many of the important features are actually based on generic AOIs that are common to most types of visualizations, such as a graph's labels or legend. Similarly, while the study only focused on an artificial data set involving student grades, the actual tasks were derived from an established set of general, low-level analysis tasks for information visualization [1] and may therefore be generalized to other application domains.

Lastly, while our experiments have shown results regarding the classification of different task and user characteristics, i.e. *what* to adapt to, and to a certain extent *how* to adapt, more work needs to be carried out in terms of predicting *when* adaptive assistance is required. In particular, further research is necessary relating to the identification of potential user confusion or cognitive overload, which is related to the detection of "sub-optimal usage patterns" that was discussed in related work by Gotz and Wen [14]. Similarly, if a system were able to detect "how well" a user is currently doing (i.e. if the system could infer user performance), adaptive assistance could be provided in cases of "bad" eye gaze patterns.

CONCLUSIONS & FUTURE WORK

In conclusion, we have presented research results showing that a user's eye gaze is a valuable source to infer a number of task and user characteristics. In particular, we have shown encouraging results using simple machine learning techniques on simple eye tracking metrics, even after only partial data has been observed. The study has therefore provided a first step towards our long-term goal of designing user-adaptive information visualizations.

The next step of this research is to design user studies that focus on the effect of different adaptive interventions (e.g. highlighting, drawing reference lines, recommending alternative visualizations) on a user's performance, both in general, and in relation to different tasks and individual user differences. These studies will also need to focus on different degrees of intervention intrusiveness, for example comparing fully-adaptive vs. mixed-initiative approaches. Following this investigation, we hope to develop a fully integrated adaptive information visualization system, which is able to dynamically provide adaptive interventions that are informed by real-time user behavior data. Lastly, we will investigate the detection of user performance and/or confusion, and we will investigate the usage of more complex features such as sequential scan paths to improve on the results presented in this paper.

REFERENCES

1. Amar, R.A., Eagan J., & Stasko, J.T. Low-Level Components of Analytic Activity in Information Visualization. In 16th IEEE Visualization Conference, (2005), 15-21.
2. Casner, S. M. A task-analytic approach to the automated design of graphic presentations. ACM Trans. on Graph., 10(2), (1991), 111-115.
3. Conati, C., & Maclaren, H. Exploring the Role of Individual Differences in Information Visualization. In Proceedings of the working conference on Advanced visual interfaces (AVI '08). ACM, New York, NY, USA, (2008), 199-20.
4. Conati, C., & Merten, C. Eye-tracking for user modeling in exploratory learning environments: An empirical evaluation. Know.-Based Syst., 20(6), (2007), 557-574.
5. Courtemanche, F., Aïmeur, E., Dufresne, A., Najjar, M., & Eboa, F.H.M. Activity recognition using eye-gaze movements and traditional interactions. In Proceedings of In-teracting with Computers, (2011), 202-213.
6. Dillon, A., & Shaap, D. Expertise and the perception of structure in discourse. Journal of the American Society for Information Science, 47(10), (1996), 786-788.
7. Eivazi, S., Bednarik, R. Predicting Problem-Solving Behavior and Performance Levels from Visual Attention Data. In the proceedings of 2nd Workshop on Eye Gaze in Intelligent Human Machine Interaction at IUI 2011, (2011), 9-16.
8. Ekstrom, R., French, J., Harman, H. and Dermen, D, Manual from Kit of Factor-References Cognitive Tests. Educational Testing Service (1976), Princeton, NJ.
9. Elzer, S., Carberry, S., & Zukerman, I. The automated understanding of simple bar charts. Artif. Intell. 175(2), (2011), 526-555.
10. Few, S. Keep Radar Graphs Below the Radar - Far Below: Information Management Magazine, (2005).
11. Fukuda, K., & Vogel, E.K. Human variation in overriding attentional capture. Journal of Neuroscience, (2009), 8726-8733.
12. Goldberg, J.H. & Helfman, J.I. Comparing Information Graphics: A Critical Look at Eye Tracking, BELIV '10, (2010), 182-195.
13. Goldberg, J.H. & Helfman, J.I. Eye tracking for visualization evaluation: Reading values on linear versus radial graphs. Information visualization 10(3), (2011), 182-195.
14. Gotz D., & Wen, Z.. Behavior-Driven Visualization Recommendation. ACM Int. Conf. on Intelligent User Interfaces, (2009), 315-324.
15. Grawemeyer, B. Evaluation of ERST – an external representation selection tutor. In Proc. of the 4th int. conf. on Diagrammatic Representation and Inference (Diagrams'06), (2006), 154-167.
16. Green, T. M. & Fisher, B. Towards the personal equation of interaction: The impact of personality factors on visual analytics interface interaction. In IEEE Visual Analytics Science and Technology (VAST), (2010), 203-210.
17. Hall, M., Frank, E., Holmes, G., Pfahringer, B., Reutemann, P., & Witten, I.H. The WEKA Data Mining Software: An Update, SIGKDD Explor., 11 (1), (2009).
18. Iqbal, S.T., & Bailey, B.P. Using eye gaze patterns to identify user tasks. In: The Grace Hopper Celebration of Women in Computing, (2004).
19. Jameson, A. (2008). Adaptive Interfaces and Agents. The human-computer interaction handbook: Fundamentals, evolving technologies and emerging applications (2nd ed.), pp. 433–458.
20. Kardan, S., Conati, C.: Exploring Gaze Data for Determining User Learning with an Inter-active Simulation. Proc. 19th intl. conf. on user modeling, adaptation, and personalization, (2012), 126-138.
21. Keith, R. Eye movements and cognitive processes in reading, visual search, and scene perception. Eye Movement Research Mechanisms, Processes, and Applications. North-Holland Press, (1995).
22. Mackinlay, J. Automating the design of graphical presentations of relational information. ACM Trans. on Graph., 5(2), (1986), 110-141.
23. Plumlee, M.D., & Ware, C. Zooming versus multiple window interfaces: Cognitive costs of visual comparisons. ACM Trans. Comput.-Hum. Interact, 13, 2, (2006), 179-209.
24. Rayner, K. Eye movements in reading and information processing: 20 years of research. Psychological Bulletin 124, (1998), 372-422.
25. Sesma, L., Villanueva, A., & Cabeza, R. Evaluation of pupil center-eye corner vector for gaze estimation using a web cam. In Proceedings of the Symposium on Eye Tracking Research and Applications (ETRA '12), (2012), 217-220.
26. Simola, J., Salojarvi, J., & Kojo, I. Using hidden Markov model to uncover processing states from eye movements in information search tasks. Cognitive Systems Research. 9, (2008), 237-251.
27. Steichen, B., Ashman, H., & Wade, V. A comparative survey of Personalised Information Retrieval and Adaptive Hypermedia techniques. Information Processing & Management, 48 (4), (2012), 698–724.
28. Toker D., Conati C., Steichen B., & Carenini G. Individual User Characteristics and Information Visualization: Connecting the Dots through Eye Tracking. In Proc. of the ACM SIGCHI Conference on

Human Factors in Computing Systems, (CHI 2013), (2013), (to appear).

29. Toker, D., Conati, C., Carenini, G., & Haraty, M. Towards Adaptive Information Visualization: On the Influence of User Characteristics. In Proc. of the 19th international conference on user modeling, adaptation, and personalization, UMAP, (2012), 274-285.

30. Turner, M. L., & Engle, R.W. Is working memory capacity task dependent? Journal of Memory and Language, 28(2), (1989), 127-154.

31. Velez, M.C., Silver, D., & Tremaine, M. Understanding visualization through spatial ability differences. Proceedings of Visualization, (2005), 511-518.

32. Ziemkiewicz, C., et al. How Locus of Control Influences Compatibility with Visualization Style. Proc. IEEE VAST, (2011), 81-90.

glueTK: A Framework For Multi-Modal, Multi-Display Human-Machine-Interaction

Florian van de Camp
Fraunhofer IOSB
Karlsruhe, Germany
florian.vandecamp@iosb.fraunhofer.de

Rainer Stiefelhagen
Karlsruhe Institute of Technology
Karlsruhe, Germany
rainer.stiefelhagen@kit.edu

ABSTRACT
As new input modalities allow interaction not only in front of a single display, but enable interaction in the whole room, application developers face new challenges. They have to handle many new input modalities, each with its own interface and requirements for pre-processing, deal with multiple displays, and applications that are distributed across multiple machines. We present glueTK, a framework that abstracts from the complexities of these input modalities, allows the design of interfaces for a wide range of display sizes, and makes the distribution across multiple machines transparent to the developer as well as the user. With an example application we demonstrate the wide range of input modalities glueTK can support and the functionality this enables. GlueTK moves away from the focus on point and touch like input modalities, enabling the design of applications tailored towards interactive rooms instead of the traditional desktop environment.

Author Keywords
Application frameworks;multi-modal interfaces

ACM Classification Keywords
H.5.2 Information interfaces and presentation: User Interfaces. - Graphical user interfaces.

General Terms
Design, Human Factors

INTRODUCTION
A wide range of new input modalities are becoming mature enough to be used in real world applications. The introduction of the Kinect has shown, that there is much interest in new input technology. It has also shown, that the focus of interaction broadens from thinking just in terms of display coordinates, to the human in front of the display. Other computer vision technology offers an even wider spectrum of information about humans that can be used for interaction. For an application developer however, it is still hard to make use of all this information. Current frameworks are mostly WIMP based and therefore do not offer interfaces for modalities other than mouse and keyboard. In many cases this has led to using touch like input modalities to emulate mouse input, which severely limits the real potential of this new generation of input modalities that can provide richer and more natural ways of interaction. Post-WIMP frameworks have been proposed, but they take care of handling almost exclusively touch like input modalities.

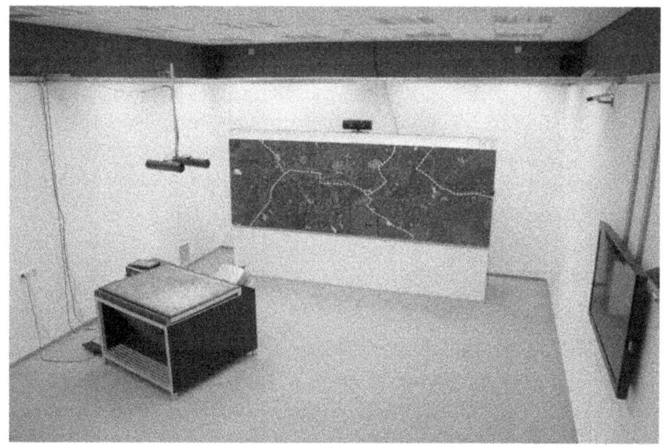

Figure 1. Room setup with back projection video wall and digital table

When Xerox created the Star with the mouse as an input modality, they completely rethought the user interface [15]. Unlike previous text based interfaces they tailored the interface towards making use of the potential of a computer mouse. This example shows, for all new input modalities, input (handling new input modalities) and output (display of content) can not be considered independent of each other.

GlueTK is a framework for handling both, input and output, which allows the output to be tailored towards the properties of the input modalities and the input modalities to be improved by utilizing knowledge about what is currently being displayed. In addition, glueTK abstracts away from the fact that applications are distributed across multiple machines and displays by introducing a network transparent signal and slot system.

The requirements for such a framework pose many challenges. A large variety of input modalities has to be handled, which are connected in completely different ways and provide not only touch like data but completely orthogonal input data as well. Since many input modalities are concerned with persons in the whole room rather than in front of a single display, multiple display devices with different aspect ratios, resolutions and sizes, ranging from smartphones to display walls of many meters in size have to be handled. And because multiple displays are involved, the framework has to abstract from the fact that multiple machines and applications are involved; neither the application developer nor the user wants to worry about this. The framework has to allow for transparent communication and data transfer across applications and machines. All components of the framework have to meet high performance requirements as the input needs to trigger instant visual feedback and allow for low latency interaction. The latency of the whole interaction chain from input handling to display update has to be minimal to allow for fluent, natural interaction.

The remainder of the paper is structured as follows: First we will discuss related work, followed by a description of glueTK's architecture and its components. Using an example application for crisis control rooms we give an insight to what kind of applications can be created using glueTK. A final conclusion will both summarize and give an outlook on the future plans for glueTK.

RELATED WORK

There have been several approaches to handle touch and touch-like input modalities. Especially for table top displays, multi touch has gained much popularity and several frameworks have been created with such a display in mind [7, 26, 11, 16, 24]. While these frameworks deal with the many different technologies enabling multi touch they are mostly limited to touch and multi touch like modalities. As the table top display is the focus for these frameworks, they do not support inter display and inter machine interaction.

Other projects move away from a single display to allow interaction in a room. The intelligent room project [5] is one, that aims at providing an intelligent room, without any displays, that users can interact with in a star-trek like fashion. The system integrates multiple input modalities by utilizing "agent-based layers" in which each agent offers an abstraction of the component it wraps, so the application developer doesn't have to deal with it in detail. One of the main goals of the interactive workspace project by Johanson et al. [14] is the design and use of rooms that contain one or more large displays. The use of these is not tailored towards the multiple modalities and display sizes for the most part, but towards using readily available technology such as websites and traditional WIMP applications. They implemented an "Event Heap" that is used as a central entity to distribute events between all machines and interfaces. A specific application of multiple input modalities for collaborative work on multiple devices has been presented by Bragdon et al. in [4]. Instead of presenting a generic approach to implementing such applications, they focus on the combination of touch and pointing as well as the social acceptability of gestures in an office setting.

Krumm et al. [17] present one of the few systems that go beyond touch-like modalities for interaction. In their system, they use a multi person tracker to control certain functionality of an intelligent room. However their focus is the tracking system itself that has to cope with the challenges faced in such an environment and not the use or integration of the tracking system for interaction. Fernandes et al. [8] describe a middleware framework that allows the use of multiple modalities that can easily be exchanged if they offer overlapping capabilities.

There has been a lot of work on fusing multiple input modalities [9, 23, 18]. There are frameworks to accomplish the fusion of multiple input modalities in a generic fashion such as MUDRA [13]. The focus is the fusion itself and therefore only touch-like modalities or naturally related modalities such as speech are considered in most cases. Most of the work on multi modal input ignores the question of the corresponding user interface. However as Oviatt [20] points out, output is part of a multi modal interaction. Melchior et al. [19] describe a toolkit that deals with many issues of multi display interaction, especially data and widget transfer between displays. While supporting multiple displays, devices and platforms, for input and output they rely on the traditional WIMP paradigm and also focus on working on a single device at a time. The ROSS API [28] is a toolkit that allows communication between multiple devices to exchange input and output data. The main focus is a nested structure to organize devices and modalities within a room. One of the few examples of frameworks that include dedicated output is PyMT [12]. They state that current GUI toolkits are WIMP based and therefore not built for the new range of input modalities. Rendering user interfaces tailored towards multi touch interaction is a part of PyMT. This allows them to build applications that take into account the features multi touch has to offer compared to a mouse, and also deal with its properties. PyMT is build for touch like input modalities and while the control of input and output would allow for it, they do not make use of the knowledge about what is displayed on the screen to improve the input modalities.

While most frameworks only focus on the input modalities, mostly ignoring the display of user interfaces and the actual interaction with displays, glueTK provides one coherent framework to handle input as well as create user interfaces and drive multiple display devices. GlueTK supports not only touch and pointing like modalities and speech, which are rather common, but also enables the use of information from systems like person tracking, head pose estimation and face identification for interaction.

GLUETK

In the following sections we will describe the glueTK architecture and how it deals with the challenges involved in creating multi-display applications utilizing a large variety of input modalities. One of the main challenges is making all different input modalities easily available, as they come with a wide variety of interfaces, data representations, and they require different kinds of pre-processing. Displays vary in physical size, aspect ratio, and resolution, this is both challenging from a performance perspective but also from a design perspective as user interface elements have to be tailored towards these different configurations. Since many new input modalities, like pointing gestures, are not necessarily bound to a single display, glueTK applications can span across multiple displays that are driven by different machines. Because of this necessary separation, glueTK has to deal with communication and data transfer across machines to make this distribution transparent to the application developer and the end user. GlueTK is implemented in C++ and uses the Clutter toolkit [1] for rendering. To seamlessly integrate the multi modal and multi display aspects of glueTK, Clutter is completely wrapped and invisible to the developer. For network communication we use a middleware based on the publish/subscribe communication paradigm, developed in our research group. GlueTK is split into two separate libraries: glueInput and glueOutput. GlueInput provides a clean interface to input modalities and takes care of all pre-processing and adaptation so the developer only has to deal with one coherent interface. GlueOutput offers an easy way to build efficient interfaces for a large variety of display types, from smartphones to high resolution video walls, connected to one or multiple machines in a network. In many cases, it is not an option to rewrite existing applications using glueTK. In these cases, glueInput can be used without glueOutput to integrate new input modalities into an existing application.

The contributions of this paper are:

- A network transparent signal and slot system
- A flexible and simple interface to modalities beyond mouselike input and context aware preprocessing
- A generic framework for creating cross machine and cross display user aware applications
- A way to enable the use of new modalities in existing applications without limitation of the modalities potentials

GLUETK ARCHITECTURE

As an introduction to the components that make up glueTK and how they work together, Figure 2 illustrates the architecture with some exemplary components. Along with the following description, this is intended to give an overview of the architecture before the components will be described in more detail.

The input modalities are displayed on the left. FaceID, a face recognition system, which outputs progress information about the identification process, Persontracker, a multi person tracking system which generates a list of coordinates of persons in a room, a pointing gesture recognition system, and a gyro mouse, which outputs relative display coordinates. While FaceID, Persontracker and pointing recognition send their information via a local network, the gyro mouse has a USB interface. For each of those input modalities there is a corresponding event handler on the right. The goal of the event handlers is to gather data from the input modalities, do pre-processing and add functionality. All event handlers push the final information as signals to the event manager. Besides managing all event handlers and being the central point of communication for all input data, the event manager also takes care of subscribing to network streams. This way, if multiple event handlers need the same data, there is no need to subscribe to them separately in each event handler. Context handlers subscribe to signals of other event handlers and generate additional information. The 3D pointing directions of the pointing system, for example, are mapped to displays in the room this way.

Because many displays can be used in a glueTK application that are driven by different machines, intra machine as well as inter machine communication and data transfer are important aspects of glueTK. To make the differentiation easier, a glueTK application consisting of several applications in the traditional sense is from here on called "glue application". All applications that make up such a glue application, communicate using a network transparent signal and slot system, which also takes care of the communication within each application. The proxy event handler takes care of distributing local signals via the network to all other applications and making the received signals available locally. This way, within a glue application there is no difference between a signal from within the same application and a signal from a different application running on a different machine.

To distribute these signals to the right slots of the right widgets, the signal manager keeps track of connected signals and slots using a mapping table. Every time a signal comes in, either from a local widget or from the event manager, the signal manager checks if any slots are connected to it and calls the corresponding slots if that is the case. If only glueInput is used, the signal manager constitutes the interface to any third party software. If both glueInput and glueOutput are used, a derived signal manager also initializes the display and manages the rendering of all widgets.

Widgets are interface elements created from basic building blocks provided by glueTK. A widget can offer slots that can be connected to any signal, be it for communication with other widgets, e.g. a button click triggering the display of an image, or for reacting to data from input modalities, e.g. moving the widget to the display position provided by the gyro mouse, to create a cursor.

GLUE INPUT

The input layer takes care of getting information from input modalities to the application developer. This way, instead of having to deal with a multitude of different interfaces to get the input data, all information is provided via one coherent interface.

Event manager

The event manager is the entity between the event handlers and the user interface. By having one central component for communication between input and output layer, many duplications can be avoided. It allows for a single, clean interface between the layers, which makes it easy to separate them. To provide input modalities with context information, glueTK applications always provide information about the state of the user interface elements (position, size, state etc.) to the event manager where event handlers can access this information.

If glueInput is used to connect modalities to an existing application, the application developer can provide context information at run time which is made available to the event handlers to exploit this information. For delivering input data from any modality to the user interface, glueTK allows for similar flexibility. All input data is provided as signals which can be mapped to functions as will be shown below. This way, the developer has a coherent way of accessing all data,

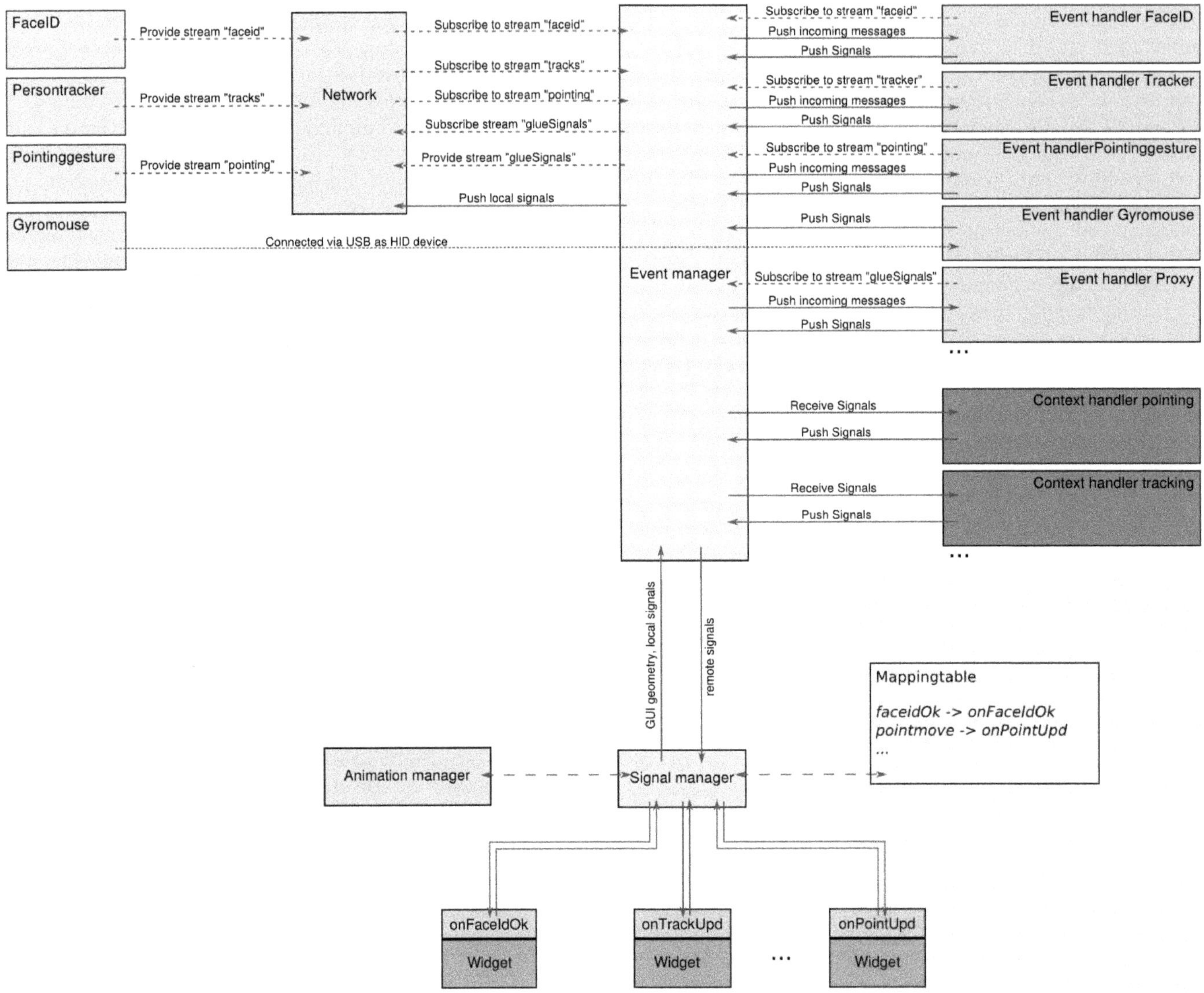

Figure 2. glueTK architecture overview with exemplary input modalities and corresponding event handlers

independent of the actual formatting, protocols or required pre-processing the modalities rely on.

Event handlers

Input modalities come with a wide variety of interfaces. This ranges from devices directly connected via USB, requiring special drivers or emulating a mouse, to systems running on different machines, communicating via a network. Because this variety of sources complicates the handling of multiple modalities, glueTK abstracts from them at the earliest possible point using event handlers. While many established input devices can simply be wrapped by an event handler, so their input data can be accessed in a generic fashion, there are many new modalities that can be greatly improved in the event handler. Two examples for improvement are data filtering and added functionality. Unlike the input device itself, the event handler has access to the current state and layout of the user interface. This allows for taking this context information into account when filtering data to, for example, make use of assisting technologies like force fields [3]. An example for added functionality is the click event we added to our pointing gesture recognition system. The pointing gesture recognition system only provides the pointing direction. To actually interact with an interface it lacks a way to trigger a click. An easy way to implement a click functionality is a dwell timer - keeping the pointing arm at the same position for a certain amount of time triggers a click. Instead of implementing this feature inside the pointing gesture recognition system it was implemented within the corresponding event handler. This way, the event handler will only start the dwell timer if the gesture points towards a click able object. Also, the event handler can easily pass information about the dwell progress to the application, which provides the user with immediate visual feedback as illustrated in Fig. 3. As the pointing gesture recognition is not as robust and accurate as a mouse, the amount of filtering applied to the pointing data can be increased when close to a click able object to assist the user in keeping the cursor still.

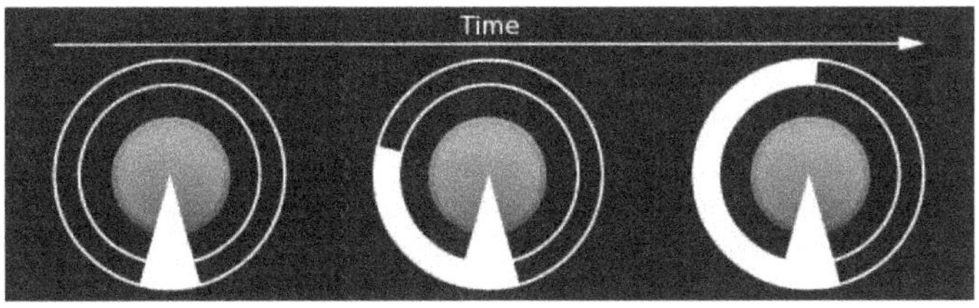

Figure 3. Visual feedback when clicking a button

Context handlers

While it is common to make raw input data like coordinates from a person tracker available, in many cases application developers do not want to deal with the details of this information as this would require additional logic in the interface. To abstract from this low level information, context handlers subscribe to the signals from one or more event handlers and provide higher level information, again as signals, to the application. In the case of a person tracker, the kind of high level information could be relations of persons to displays (eg. "person_x_left_display_y""). In case of pointing modalities that are detached from a specific display and simply provide pointing directions in the room coordinate system, the data has to be mapped to the displays in the room to provide display coordinates that can actually be used to interact with an interface on a screen. Context handlers are, however, not limited to abstracting from data from a single event handler. Fusion of both similar modalities and heterogeneous modalities can be done within a context handler. For example, using both person tracker and pointing system data, the detected pointing directions can be associated with the corresponding persons. This allows to differentiate between a multipoint gesture by a single person and two single point gestures by two different persons.

COMMUNICATION

GlueTK provides a communication mechanism based on the signal and slot concept [27]. It is used to provide the input data from the event handlers to all applications within the glue application. This makes input modalities usable in a whole room independent of the actual machine they are connected to. In addition, the same mechanism is used to allow widgets to communicate with each other, again independent of what machine they reside on, and to transfer widgets between displays and therefore machines.

Signals and slots

The idea of a signal and slot system is, that objects can send signals containing arbitrary information which - if connected - are received by other objects and will execute special functions, so called slots. This concept allows for very flexible, asynchronous communication. Unlike previous implementations, a distinctive feature of the signal and slot implementation in glueTK is that local signals are automatically distributed over the network and are available to all parts of the glue application. Therefore the way signals and slots are connected in most implementations:

```
connect(Object1, Signal1, Object2, Slot2)
```

Is extended to support the connection of signals and slots across several applications:

```
connect(App1, Object1, Signal1,
        App2, Object2, Slot2)
```

This allows to connect one specific signal to one specific slot. The identifiers in the connect command are just strings, so there is no need to have access to the objects in code, and signals and slots can be connected at any point, in any part of the glue application. In many cases it can be convenient to address all applications or all slots or all objects. To achieve this, any identifier in the connect command can be substituted by the wildcard character "*".

```
connect(App1, Object1, Signal1,
        *, *, hide())
```

Every interface element has default slots for common functionality, one of them is the "hide" slot, which hides the element when called. The above command connects a single signal to all "hide" slots of any object in any application and would hide all interface elements without addressing each individually. Independent of what machine an input modality is connected to, independent of where widgets reside, the communication is always based on this signal and slot system and that is all the developer has to deal with.

Widget transfer

As glue applications can spread across multiple screens, users should be able to move widgets across screens without worrying about the underlying technical details. This allows for example, to attach a personal menu widget to a person's position in the room and have the menu show up on the display closest to the person. Or to simply drag a widget from one display to another. Making this possible however, is not trivial, as screens can be connected to different machines. So moving a widget from one screen to another might actually require the widget to be transferred to a completely different machine. While the network transparent signal and slot system abstracts from the fact that a glue application runs across multiple machines to drive multiple displays with regard to the communication, signals are designed for low latency communication and are therefore not suitable for transferring large amounts of data. The transfer of a widget can be triggered explicitly or by setting its position relative to a different screen. It is then serialized as JSON data, attaching binary data as encoded strings. The data is transferred to the target machine via a network connection, where a new widget is then created by deserializing this data. To avoid delays in case of large attached binary data (large textures for example), widgets have a flag which, when set, causes them to be synchronized. This means that every machine keeps a continuously updated copy of the widget. This way, if the widget is transfered across displays, the data is already available on the target display. This allows to move widgets across displays, no matter if these displays are connected to the same machine, running a single application or if they are connected to different machines, running different applications.

Signal manager

The signal manager is the link between the input and output layer. All signals from input modalities or other applications, that come in via the event manager, are passed to the signal manager. Using a mapping table, it looks up which slots are connected to incoming signals and calls the corresponding functions. The signal manager also offers the bidirectional interface for developers, to integrate the input modality abstraction of glueTK into existing applications.

For a glue application, the signal manager is extended to also drive connected displays and manage the rendering of widgets. It passes any signals emitted by the widgets to the event manager, so they are available within the whole glue application. As the signal manager is highly multi threaded, there is no limit to the number of simultaneous signals that can be passed on and handled, which is important when dealing with not only multi touch, but multi person, multi touch on large display walls.

GLUE OUTPUT

GlueOutput is responsible for creating and rendering user interfaces on displays. Despite the fact that these displays vary greatly in size, resolution and aspect ratio, the goal is to offer the application developer an easy and flexible way to create user interfaces for an arbitrary range of displays. For this reason, glueTK offers elementary building blocks, that allow for easy assembly of custom, interactive widgets that can be connected to input modalities as well as communicate with each other. While this requires additional work, it allows to build widgets specifically tailored towards the properties of the available input modalities as well as screen sizes and resolutions.

Widgets

In existing GUI toolkits, widgets intend to solve one specific input task, usually obtaining one well defined type of value from the user. There are common sets of widgets that provide input elements for the most common types of values. This causes users to get used to certain ways information is asked from them and makes them feel comfortable even with unknown applications as many parts of that application are in fact, well known. This kind of reuse is possible if the input modalities as well as the range of display sizes and resolutions stays the same. Of course it is possible to simply scale such widgets to any screen size, but that would most definitely not result in an optimal interface. Also, given the wide range of modalities glueTK supports, not all input modalities would work with widgets tailored towards mouse use.

In most cases, this means that custom widgets, to allow user input, have to be created. This way, the best possible interface can be created given the target displays and input modalities. To assist users in the creation of such custom widgets, glueTK contains building blocks for images, videos, text, maps and web content that can be easily combined. Every building block has a set of default properties such as position, size, rotation, etc. so that placement and manipulation is the same for all types of building blocks. Each widget created from one or more of these building blocks, has the ability to offer slots to allow access to its functionality. These slots can be connected to signals from input modalities to, for example, set the widget's position to that of a person in front of the display to make the widget follow the person.

Animation manager

The animation manager allows to apply a predefined set of animations to any widget to provide visual feedback to the user. In addition, every property of a widget can be manipulated with custom animations to create more appealing interfaces. Animations are applied by calling a slot in the animation manager, which allows their use at any point in the glue application, even across displays and machines. When dealing with input modalities that are not universally known, providing this kind of feedback is important as users tend to need more guidance.

EVALUATION AND EXAMPLES

To demonstrate the functionality of glueTK, an application for a next generation control room has been implemented. In addition to this overview of functionality that glueTK enables, we evaluated the network transparent signal and slot system with regard to its performance, as it is an important aspect of the high flexibility described above. It is therefore important that its performance does not constitute a bottleneck for the framework. We did not evaluate the rendering performance since we rely on the external Clutter library [1]. As Clutter is OpenGL based, the performance is highly dependent on the utilized hardware and display resolutions. We do however drive displays up to 2160p with a single NVIDIA GTX480 and up to eight XGA displays using two low end NVIDIA GF9600GT without having any performance issues.

Performance evaluation

There are four ways signals are used within glueTK: from event handlers to widgets of the same application, from widgets to other widgets within the same application, from event handlers to remote applications and from widgets from one application to a remote application. There is, however, no difference internally between sending a signal from an event handler to a widget or from another widget. For evaluation we therefore differ between internal signals within the same application and remote signals, between separate applications that run on different machines. Most signals are lists of parameters which result in rather small amounts of data which have to be transferred. For evaluation, we chose a typical signal size of 342 characters ($\sim 0.33kbyte$) and for comparison a 76480 characters signal ($\sim 74kbyte$ or about twice the text of this paper). For remote signals we used two machines in a switched gigabit ethernet network. We transfered 100000 signals 10 times. The time from sending a signal to triggering the target slot was measured. The following table shows the averaged results as the number of signals per second.

type/size	342 characters	76480 characters
local	115500.11sps	111844.31sps
remote	6690.75sps	407.84sps

Considering that most input modalities, which usually produce higher traffic than inter widget communication, update with 50Hz or less, the performance of the network transparent signal and slot system leaves enough room to not cause any significant latency.

Control Room Application

While glueTK is a generic framework which has been used to build different applications, we present a control room application as a specific example. The task of a control room is the planning and dispatching of relief squads, to deal with disaster situations. Each user is typically assigned a role according to the continental staff system which assigns a certain set of tasks and responsibilities. Cohen at al. [6] have shown early on that technology can assist users in command and control environments. So unlike current, rather low tech rooms, the goal of the "smart" control room is to allow multi modal interaction with a multitude of displays and devices to make the use of technology more intuitive and efficient. In the following, an example scenario will be described that shows some aspects of the application and how glueTK manages a wide variety of input modalities ranging from person tracking to head pose estimation and display devices from a $9cm$ smartphone to a $427cm$ video wall. We will first describe the involved hardware and software components.[1].

The main display is a $4m \times 1.5m$ back projection video wall with a resolution of $4096px \times 1536px$ which serves as an overview of the whole geographic region of the area of authority. A $0.9m \times 1.2m$ digital back projection table with a resolution of $1400px \times 1050px$ serves as an interactive workstation for specific assignments. Tablet computers can be used on the table as high resolution digital magnifiers and annotation boards as described in [10]. On a total of 4 machines (Intel QuadCore 2.4Ghz) with 10 cameras (9 Axis 211a, 1 Logitech Quickcam Pro), we have six computer vision components running:

A commercial face recognition system [2] using a webcam attached to the right side of the video wall. Four cameras around the video wall are used to build a 3D reconstruction of the area in front of the video wall and derive pointing gestures from that information as described in [22]. A person tracking component utilizing a camera with a fish eye lens in the ceiling can track multiple persons throughout the whole room. At the digital table, a stereo camera set up allows the use of not only pointing gestures, but also the detection of more detailed hand gestures as described in [21]. A marker tracker can locate and identify tablet computers and smart phones on the digital table using a MCMXT-Marker [10] based tracker. Finally, a head pose estimation system [25] uses a camera that observes the person standing in front of the digital table and analyses the persons' focus of attention.

The task of the glueTK application is to make use of all the information these components provide and create user interfaces on the displays to assist users in assessing the situation and plan missions for the relief units, based on the information about incidents coming in. One example usage of the application will be described in the following, highlighting what happens behind the scene to make the interactions possible.

[1] A video of the smart control room application is available at: http://www.youtube.com/watch?v=cTDqDbBrysk

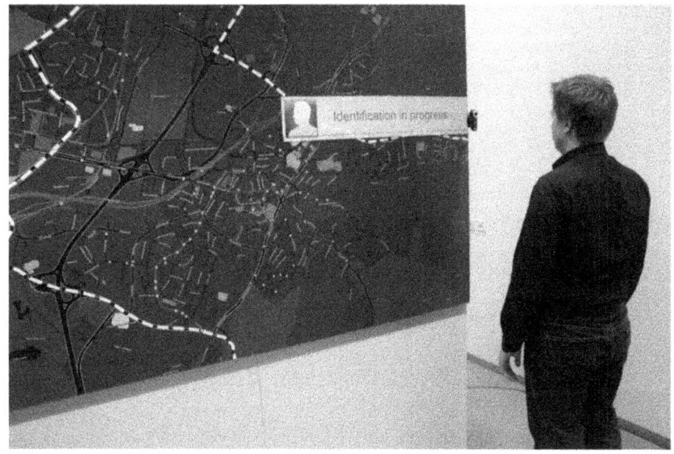

Figure 4. Visual feedback indicating the face identification in progress.

The video wall displays an overview map of a city while the digital situation table displays a small subsection of the map in greater detail. A person, S1, is standing at the digital situation table as another person, S2, comes in. S2 starts his shift, and needs to get an overview at the videowall of what is going on in the city. To be able to use the system, he has to identify himself by looking into the webcam attached to the side of the video wall. The face identification component sends out status information like *face_detected*, *identification_in_progress* and *successfulid_idX* or *unknown_person*. A face identification event handler receives these status messages via the network and makes them available as signals in the glueTK application. A face identification widget gives the user visual feedback about the ongoing identification progress by providing slots to display banners (see Figure 4) that are connected to these signals. A personal menu widget has a slot that is connected to the *successfulid_idX* signal, which causes the personal menu belonging to S2 to appear right in front of him after identification.

To make the personal menu appear right in front of S2 it needs information about the person's location as well. To provide this information as signals, so it is readily available to the widgets, there is a tracking event handler that receives updates about the locations of all persons in the room. At the video wall, since it is such a large display, the location information is not only used to make the menu appear at the person's location initially but it also follows the person as he walks along the video wall.

The map used on the video wall is rather minimal to avoid clutter on the overview. However, S2 can get more detailed information by selecting a map overlay tool from his personal menu. To do this, he simply points to the according icon in his personal menu (Figure 5).

A few things happen in the background at this point. First of all, there is an context handler for the pointing gesture component that detects dwell based clicks, while giving visual feedback as described above. As mentioned before, the personal menu follows the person along the video wall. This can be a problem if the person tries to select an item from the menu. To make this easier the pointing signal is not only con-

Figure 5. Pointing gesture to select items in the locked menu.

Figure 6. Map layer selection with pointing gesture on the digital table.

nected to the cursor but also to the personal menu, that will lock in place if it is pointed at. The map overlay that appears, displays a more detailed map in a rectangular region around the pointing direction and moves with the pointing gesture across the whole wall. With another click the overlay can be dismissed.

Now that S2 got an overview, he joins his colleague at the table and walks from the video wall to digital table. The personal workspace automatically follows S2 from the video wall to the table. A context handler uses the information about the person's position and the displays' positions, to generate signals like *at_wall* or *at_table* which are connected to corresponding slots of the personal menu widget and trigger a display transfer. Here, glueTK abstracts away from the fact that these are different displays driven by different applications running on different machines. The user has a coherent experience of interacting with one room-embracing glue application.

While S1 and S2 are at the table an alarm message about an explosion is displayed at the video wall. Both go up to the video wall and their respective personal workspaces appear in front of them. They can now collaborate at the wall by using additional tools from their workspaces to analyse the alarm with respect to the overall situation.

To actually plan the deployment of relief squads in detail, they move back to the table. To signal anyone looking at the overview wall that this alarm is taken care of, one of the operators loads the alarm message into his personal workspace using a pointing gesture. By doing so, the event is now assigned to him and as soon as he arrives at the digital table, it moves and zooms the map to the location of the explosion.

At the digital table, special hand gestures allow different map manipulations. With all five fingers stretched out the map can be moved, with two fingers stretched out the map can be zoomed with both hands, and a single stretched out finger triggers a click signal (see Figure 6).

Since glueTK gets information about the head pose orientation of the person in front of the digital table, it can keep track of what display the operator currently looks at. While both are focused on the table, planning the deployment of relief squads, another alarm comes in which is only displayed on the table. If the operator in front of the table looks up to the video wall, the alarm is displayed there as well with additional information to help him understand the global context. The operator can then point from the table to the alarm on the wall to acknowledge the message. Even so, this pointing gesture is detected by the cameras above the table, which are connected to the machine that drives the table display, glueTK makes this information available globally, so it can be used to interact with the video wall as well.

Another operator S3 comes in with a smart phone to transfer some images he took to the video wall. He can control a special cursor on the wall using the phone's gyroscope and transfer the pictures by clicking on them. Of course the transfer works both ways, so to get the deployment blueprint S1 and S2 created on the table, the smart phone can be placed on it, where it is located and identified using a marker on its back. The transfer is initiated by placing one finger on the table and another on the smart phone.

All of the described components and functionality is implemented and works in real time. The full glue application has been presented at CeBIT 2011 and proven to work within the challenging conditions of an exhibition booth.

CONCLUSION

In this paper, we presented a framework for creating multi modal applications that can span across multiple displays and machines. A generic approach is used to handle any input modalities, not limited to touch like modalities, they are made available through a single coherent interface. It allows for bidirectional communication to enable the use of context information. As many modalities targeted do not provide touch like data, this context information is important and input data can not simply be used to emulate a mouse as it is common practise in many frameworks with a focus on point and touch input. This abstraction layer can be used independently in existing applications without drawbacks, to integrate new input modalities. The presented framework assists in the creation of interfaces for a wide range of display sizes, aspect ratios, and resolutions. The distribution of user interfaces across displays and machines as well as all communication, is transparent to the application developer as well as the end user. In an example application for crisis response rooms, we demonstrated the integration and interaction of many input modalities like gestures, person tracking, face identification, headpose orientation, a gyroscope as well as the utilization of multiple displays in a room. While glueTK has already been used by other people than the original developers, in the future we would like to make glueTK available to a greater audience. As for extending glueTK, we will explore ways of providing more complex widgets, which are still usable independent of screen sizes and connected modalities, and further improve the use of context information as this becomes more important in such complex environments.

Acknowledgements

This work is supported by the Fraunhofer-Gesellschaft Internal Programs under Grant 692 026.

REFERENCES

1. Clutter toolkit. *http://www.clutter-project.org* (accessed October, 2012).
2. Videmo face sdk. *http://videmo.de/products* (accessed October, 2012).
3. Ahlström, D., Hitz, M., and Leitner, G. An evaluation of sticky and force enhanced targets in multi target situations. In *4th Nordic conference on Human-*, no. October (2006), 14–18.
4. Bragdon, A., Deline, R., Hinckley, K., and Morris, M. R. Code Space : Touch + Air Gesture Hybrid Interactions for Supporting Developer Meetings. In *ITS* (Kobe, Japan, 2010).
5. Brooks, R. A. The intelligent room project. In *Proceedings of the 2nd International Conference on Cognitive Technology*, CT '97 (Washington, DC, USA, 1997), 271–.
6. Cohen, P. R., Johnston, M., McGee, D., Oviatt, S., Pittman, J., Smith, I., Chen, L., and Clow, J. Quickset: multimodal interaction for simulation set-up and control. In *Proceedings of the fifth conference on Applied natural language processing*, ANLC '97, Association for Computational Linguistics (Stroudsburg, PA, USA, 1997), 20–24.
7. Echtler, F., and Klinker, G. A multitouch software architecture. In *Proceedings of the 5th Nordic conference on Human-computer interaction: building bridges*, NordiCHI '08, ACM (New York, NY, USA, 2008), 463–466.
8. Fernandes, V., Guerreiro, T., Araújo, B., Jorge, J., and Pereira, J. a. Extensible middleware framework for multimodal interfaces in distributed environments. In *Proceedings of the 9th international conference on Multimodal interfaces*, ICMI '07, ACM (New York, NY, USA, 2007), 216–219.
9. Flippo, F. A Framework for Rapid Development of Multimodal Interfaces. In *Design* (2003).
10. Geisler, J., Eck, R., Rehfeld, N., Peinsipp-Byma, E., Schutz, C., and Geggus, S. Fovea-tablett : A new paradigm for the interaction with large screens. In *Human Interface and the Management of Information.*, vol. 4557 of *Lecture Notes in Computer Science*. 2007, 278–287.
11. Gokcezade, A., Leitner, J., and Haller, M. Lighttracker: An open-source multitouch toolkit. *Comput. Entertain. 8*, 3 (Dec. 2010), 19:1–19:16.
12. Hansen, T., Hourcade, J., Virbel, M., Patali, S., and Serra, T. PyMT: a post-WIMP multi-touch user interface toolkit. In *Proceedings of the ACM International Conference on Interactive Tabletops and Surfaces*, ACM (2009), 17–24.
13. Hoste, L., Dumas, B., and Signer, B. Mudra: A Unified Multimodal Interaction Framework. In *Proceedings of ICMI 2011 13th International Conference on Multimodal Interaction* (2011), 97–104.
14. Johanson, B., Fox, A., and Winograd, T. The Interactive Workspaces project: experiences with ubiquitous computing rooms. *IEEE Pervasive Computing 1*, 2 (Apr. 2002), 67–74.
15. Johnson, J., Roberts, T. L., Verplank, W., Smith, D. C., Irby, C. H., Beard, M., and Mackey, K. The xerox star: A retrospective. *Computer 22*, 9 (Sept. 1989), 11–26, 28–29.
16. Kaltenbrunner, M., and Bencina, R. reactivision: a computer-vision framework for table-based tangible interaction. In *Proceedings of the 1st international conference on Tangible and embedded interaction*, TEI '07, ACM (New York, NY, USA, 2007), 69–74.
17. Krumm, J., Harris, S., Meyers, B., Brumitt, B., Hale, M., and Shafer, S. Multi-camera multi-person tracking for EasyLiving. *Proceedings of the third International Workshop on Visual Surveillance* (2000), 3–10.
18. Lalanne, D., Nigay, L., Palanque, P., Robinson, P., and Vanderdonckt, J. Fusion Engines for Multimodal Input : A Survey. *Interfaces* (2009), 153–160.
19. Melchior, J., Grolaux, D., Vanderdonckt, J., and Van Roy, P. A toolkit for peer-to-peer distributed user interfaces: concepts, implementation, and applications. In *Proceedings of the ACM SIGCHI symposium on Engineering interactive computing systems*, EICS '09 (New York, NY, USA, 2009), 69–78.
20. Oviatt, S., and Cohen, P. Perceptual user interfaces: multimodal interfaces that process what comes naturally. *Communications of ACM 43*, 3 (Mar. 2000), 45–53.
21. Peinsipp-Byma, E., Geisler, J., and Bader, T. Digital map and situation surface: a team-oriented multidisplay workspace for network enabled situation analysis. J. T. Thomas and D. D. Desjardins, Eds., vol. 7327, SPIE (2009), 732703.
22. Schick, A., Camp, F. v. d., Ijsselmuiden, J., and Stiefelhagen, R. Extending touch: towards interaction with large-scale surfaces. In *Proceedings of the ACM International Conference on Interactive Tabletops and Surfaces*, ACM (2009), 117–124.
23. Serrano, M., Nigay, L., Lawson, J.-y. L., Ramsay, A., Murray-smith, R., Denef, S., and Augustin, S. The OpenInterface Framework : A tool for multimodal interaction. In *Design* (2008), 3501–3506.
24. Shen, C., Vernier, F. D., Forlines, C., and Ringel, M. Diamondspin: an extensible toolkit for around-the-table interaction. In *Proceedings of the SIGCHI conference on Human factors in computing systems*, CHI '04, ACM (New York, NY, USA, 2004), 167–174.
25. Voit, M., Nickel, K., and Stiefelhagen, R. Neural network-based head pose estimation and multi-view fusion. vol. 4122, Springer (2007), 291–298.
26. Wang, X., Zhou, Q., and Xin, Y. The construction and application of multitouch interactive platform based on touchlib. In *Proceedings of the 2011 4th International Conference on Intelligent Networks and Intelligent Systems*, ICINIS '11, IEEE Computer Society (Washington, DC, USA, 2011), 153–156.
27. Weis, T., and Geihs, K. Components on the desktop. In *Proceedings of the Technology of Object-Oriented Languages and Systems*, TOOLS '00 (Washington, DC, USA, 2000).
28. Wu, A., Mendenhall, S., Jog, J., Hoag, L. S., and Mazalek, A. A nested api structure to simplify cross-device communication. In *Proceedings of the Sixth International Conference on Tangible, Embedded and Embodied Interaction*, TEI '12, ACM (New York, NY, USA, 2012), 225–232.

Optimizing Temporal Topic Segmentation for Intelligent Text Visualization

Shimei Pan[1] Michelle Zhou[2] Yangqiu Song[3] Weihong Qian[4] Fei Wang[1] Shixia Liu[5]

[1]IBM Research-T.J.Watson, USA
{shimei, fwang}@us.ibm.com

[2]IBM Research Almaden, USA
mzhou@us.ibm.com

[3]HKUST, Hong Kong
yqsong@gmail.com

[4]IBM Research China, China
qianwh@cn.ibm.com

[5]Microsoft Research Asia, China
shliu@microsoft.com

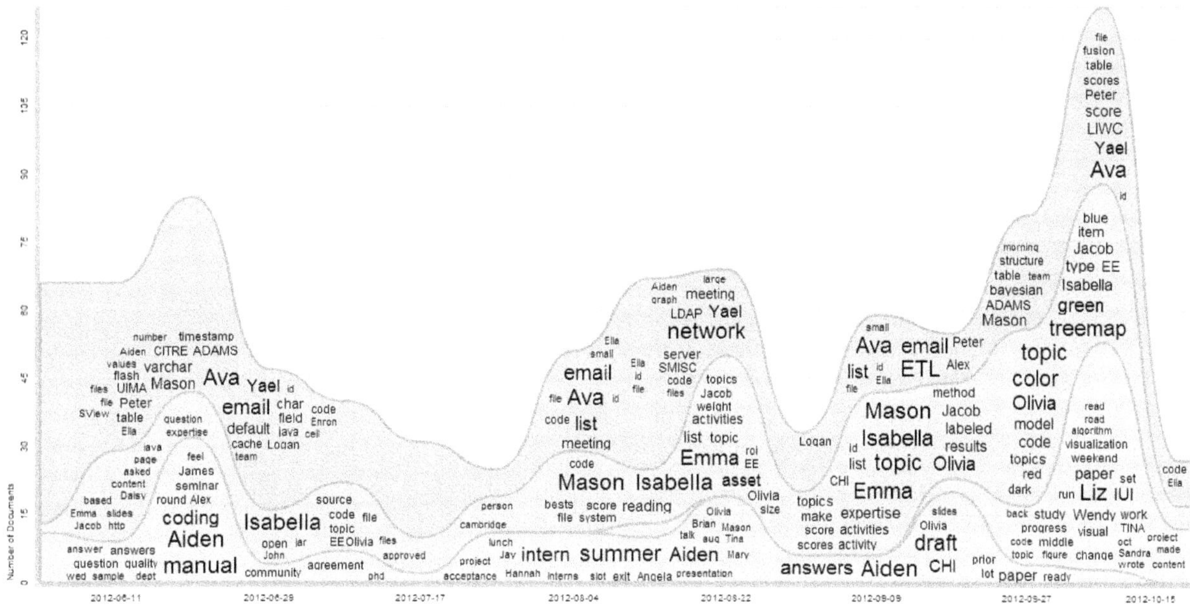

Figure 1. TIARA-generated visual text summary showing four topic layers.

ABSTRACT
We are building a topic-based, interactive visual analytic tool that aids users in analyzing large collections of text. To help users quickly discover content evolution and significant content transitions within a topic over time, here we present a novel, constraint-based approach to temporal topic segmentation. Our solution splits a discovered topic into multiple linear, non-overlapping sub-topics along a timeline by satisfying a diverse set of semantic, temporal, and visualization constraints simultaneously. For each derived sub-topic, our solution also automatically selects a set of representative keywords to summarize the main content of the sub-topic. Our extensive evaluation, including a crowd-sourced user study, demonstrates the effectiveness of our method over an existing baseline.

Author Keywords
Text visualization, topic-based, constrained clustering.

ACM Classification Keywords
H.5.m. Information interfaces and presentation (e.g., HCI): Miscellaneous. [**Artificial Intelligence**]: Natural language Processing – *text analysis.*

INTRODUCTION
To aid users in effectively gleaning insights and locating critical information from large collections of text documents, we have developed a topic-based, interactive visual analysis tool, TIARA [22]. TIARA provides two main functions. First, it *automatically* generates a time-based visual text summary that conveys key topics derived from a large collection of text. Second, it supports a rich set of interactions that allow users to further explore the created visual summary and examine the text collection from multiple aspects. Figure 1 is an output of TIARA, where each colored layer represents an automatically derived topic. Each layer is depicted by a sequence of word clouds, summarizing the topic content at each time interval. At each time

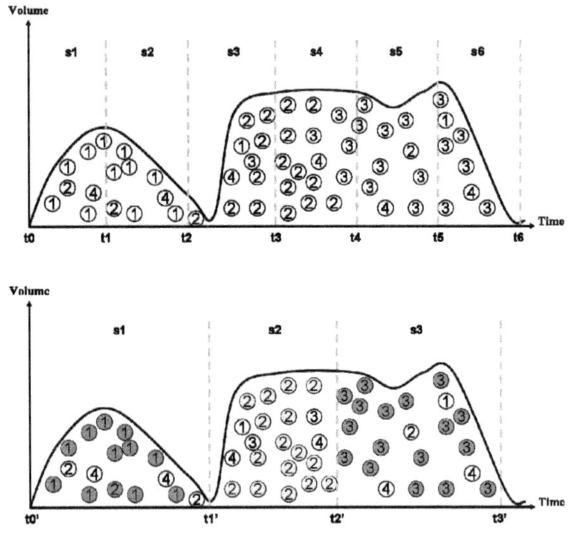

Figure 2. (a) Top: segmented (s1-s6) by fixed time intervals (t1-t6); and (b) Bottom: optimized segmentation (s1-s3). Each numbered circle denotes a document in a specific sub-topic.

point, the height of a layer encodes the "strength" of the topic—the number of documents covering the topic at that time. A user can also interact with this visualization, e.g., retrieving text snippets and a full document [22].

To automatically derive the topics shown above, TIARA performs two key tasks: topic extraction and temporal topic segmentation. *Topic extraction* is to automatically derive a set of topics (e.g., sports and politics) from a text collection (e.g., news articles). *Temporal topic segmentation* is to break an extracted topic into a set of sub-topics along the time line so that a user can easily track the temporal evolution of the topic. There are many research efforts on topic extraction, including clustering [16, 32] and probabilistic topic modeling [7, 17, 24]. Currently, TIARA uses the Latent Dirichlet Allocation (LDA) model [7] to automatically extract a set of topics. Although TIARA used simple heuristics to the second task, there is little in-depth research in this area. In this paper, we propose a systematic approach to temporal topic segmentation.

Temporal topic segmentation is to split a continuous topic into a sequence of sub-topics over time. It further consists of two steps. First, it must identify a set of meaningful, time-based, semantic transitions to split a topic into multiple, linear non-overlapping temporal segments. Second, it must extract a set of representative keywords to summarize the content of each segment. Both steps are non-trivial, since the system must satisfy a diverse set of constraints, including semantic, temporal, and visual constraints.

Constraint 1: *Capturing significant topic transitions.* One of our goals is to help users detect how a topic evolves over time, in particular, identify whether and how the content of a topic has shifted and when. Existing time-based visual text summaries split a topic into multiple temporal segments by a fixed time interval (e.g., monthly) [22]. In reality, however, semantic transitions of a topic may not occur in pre-determined, fixed time intervals (Figure 2a). In such cases, chopping up a topic "unnaturally" along fixed time points not only would miss the natural topic transitions, but may also result in visual redundancies. For example, segments S1 and S2 contain semantically similar content (Figure 2a). To capture natural topic transitions, a temporal segment boundary should be placed near where a significant topic shift occurs (e.g., t2 in Figure 2a)

Constraint 2: *Identifying sub-topics with temporal locality.* To effectively visualize topic transitions over time, we are interested in discovering sub-topics that exhibit temporal locality. *Temporal locality* of a topic is a time interval where the documents covering the topic appear most prominently. As shown in Figure 2(a), for example, sub-topic 4 does not have temporal locality, since the documents on this topic are distributed over the entire time span. In contrast, the temporal locality of sub-topic 1 is time interval t0–t2.

Constraint 3: *Respecting visual segment boundaries.* As shown in Figure 1, word clouds representing topic segments are placed in a topic layer. To best use the available space in each topic layer, a spatial layout algorithm is often used to place the keywords in the formed peaks and valleys [22]. However, the temporal localities of sub-topics may not be aligned with these visual peaks and valleys. For example, the preferred temporal boundary for sub-topic 1 is t0–t2 in Figure 2(a), which does not line up with the visual boundary t0'–t1' in (b). If we do not respect natural visual shapes, the space use may not be optimal (e.g., placing the keywords for sub-topic 1 in t0–t2 versus t0'–t1'). Moreover, placing a word cloud representing the same topic *across* visual boundaries will disrupt the visual flow. For example, sub-topic 2 spans t2–t4, across the natural visual boundary at t1'. Ideally, temporal and visual boundaries should be aligned to produce a semantically coherent *and* visually pleasing display. Using the above examples, segmenting the topic at t1' is much preferable than at t2.

To address the challenges described above, we develop an optimization-based approach to temporal topic segmentation, including the selection of representative keywords for summarizing each identified temporal segment. Our approach systematically incorporates a set of constraints, including semantic, temporal, and visual constraints. It then satisfies them simultaneously to optimize topic segmentation and keyword selection. To demonstrate the effectiveness of our work, we have conducted both algorithmic and end user evaluations. Our results show significant improvements over an established baseline. As a result, our work offers two unique contributions:

1. Our optimization-based approach to temporal topic segmentation is effective, as it satisfies a diverse set of semantic, temporal, and visualization constraints for creating a time-based, visual text summary.

2. Our constraint-based framework is extensible, since it can easily incorporate additional constraints when needed (e.g., geo-spatial constraints to group together segments originated from the same geo-location).

In the rest of the paper, we first summarize related work before giving an overview of our tool. We then explain our approach in detail on temporal topic segmentation, followed by the evaluations. We also discuss limitations of our work and potential improvements before concluding.

RELATED WORK

Similar to our work, document segmentation [5, 10, 19, 20, 23, 29] is to identify a set of topic transitions in a single or multiple document(s). There are a number of approaches to single document segmentation, such as detecting segmentation points by specific speech or lexical cues [29], identifying lexical or semantic changes between adjacent text blocks [19, 20], and probabilistic topic segmentation [10, 23]. On the other hand, multi-document segmentation takes multiple *similar* documents (e.g., multiple news articles from different sources reporting the same event) to find a set of sub-topics on the shared topic [21, 28]. Compared to the existing work on document segmentation, ours focuses on *temporal* segmentation of a set of heterogeneous documents, which has not been addressed before. Moreover, we must consider *visual* constraints during topic segmentation to ensure an effective temporal visualization of the derived-segments.

Similar to our goal of investigating topics along time, there is a rich body of work on temporal topic analysis [2, 8, 12, 30, 31, 33]. The main purpose of these works is to incorporate time as an *input* to improve topic discovery results. For example, one effort is to discover how the topics in one year evolve from those of the previous year [8]. In such a model, documents are first grouped by a *fixed* time frame (e.g., per year). A topic model is then used to derive multiple topics from the documents in each time frame. In contrast, our work is to identify and *output* proper time frames that best segment a topic by satisfying a set of semantic, temporal, and visualization constraints.

Our work is also related to existing efforts in creating topic-based, interactive visual text summarization systems [11, 15, 22]. These works focus on developing visual metaphors and interactions that allow users to understand and explore the derived topics. To generate a time-based, visual summary, these systems also need to segment topics along a timeline. However, existing approaches are often ad hoc. For example, in our earlier work on topic segmentation, the temporal segment boundaries are mainly determined by visual constraints, such as the peaks and valleys of a topic layer [22]. If a topic layer has too few natural visual segment boundaries (the shape of the topic layer is mostly flat), additional segment boundaries are then introduced using fixed time intervals. Nonetheless, such approaches cannot guarantee that the derived temporal segments capture the correct significant topic transitions. In contrast, here we present a systematic approach to temporal topic segmentation by balancing a diverse set of constraints.

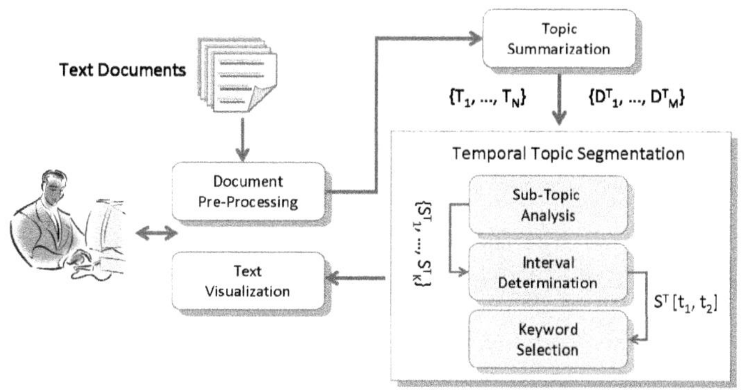

Figure 3. System overview.

SYSTEM OVERVIEW

Figure 3 provides an overview of TIARA. The input to TIARA is a collection of text documents. The *document pre-processing* component first extracts the title and the main body text (e.g., the body of a news story) and related meta data (e.g., the author and time information) from each document. The extracted information is then sent to the *topic summarization* component, which now uses an LDA-based approach to automatically extract a set of topics. Each derived topic is associated with a set of documents.

Given a derived topic (T) and a set of documents covering the topic $\{D^T_1, \ldots, D^T_M\}$, the *sub-topic analysis* component identifies a set of sub-topics $\{S^T_1, \ldots, S^T_K\}$ that satisfy a set of semantic, temporal, and visualization constraints. The *interval determination* component computes the temporal boundary for each sub-topic $S^T[t1, t2]$. Finally, the *keyword selection* component identifies a set of keywords to represent each derived sub-topic. Given the derived topics and sub-topics, the *text visualization* component generates a time-based, interactive visual text summary. Our focus below is on the three components highlighted in red.

OUR APPROACH

We describe our approach in two parts: (1) we describe a three-step process that uses constraint-based topic analysis to identify a set of sub-topics of a given topic in a linear, non-overlapping temporal sequence; and (2) we present a keyword selection method, which selects a set of representative keywords to summarize each derived sub-topic.

Temporal Segmentation

There are three main steps in temporal segmentation: (1) constraint generation, (2) topic analysis with the generated constraints, and (3) temporal segment boundary determination based on the topic analysis results.

Step 1: Generating Visual and Temporal Constraints

As mentioned earlier, our goal is to identify temporal sub-topics that satisfy a set of semantic, temporal, and visual constraints. Since typical topic analysis already incorporates latent semantic constraints [7, 27, 32], there is no need to encode semantic constraints explicitly. We thus need only encode temporal and visual constraints. To incorporate these constraints into a constraint-based topic modeling process, we represent them as must-links and cannot-links that enforce specific relationships between two documents [6, 27, 32]. More specifically, *must-link* ensures that related documents be in the same sub-topic (e.g., documents A and B should be in the same sub-topic), while *cannot-links* indicate that related documents should *not* be associated with the same sub-topic (e.g., documents C and D should be in different sub-topics).

Given a derived topic and a set of documents D relevant to the topic, we add a must-link or a cannot-link between each document pair d_i and d_j in D as follows:

(1) Adding a *cannot-link* constraint between d_i and d_j if they fall in different visual segments. Here visual segment boundaries are computed by our visualization component prior to topic segmentation. Since each document is associated with a time stamp, we use its time stamp to determine which visual segment the document falls in. Whenever possible, our goal is to place the keywords representing a sub-topic in a single visual segment instead of across the boundaries of two visual segments. To achieve this goal, the added cannot-links discourage documents falling in different visual segments to form a single sub-topic.

(2) If the temporal distance between the two documents is within a threshold ∂ (e.g., within a week), add a *must-link* between them. These must-links encourage documents that are temporally close to each other to be in the same sub-topic. As a result, these constraints help discover the temporal locality of sub-topics.

(3) Otherwise, if the temporal distance between the two documents is above a threshold Δ (e.g., above 6 months), add a *cannot-link* between them. These cannot-links will prevent temporally distant documents from being placed in the same sub-topic. In other words, these links discourage the formation of sub-topics that do not have temporal locality.

Here, thresholds ∂ and Δ are used to define the temporal proximity of two documents. Currently, both values are set empirically based on the properties of the target dataset (e.g., the time span and the distribution of documents).

Note that, multiple constraints may co-exist between a pair of documents. For example, two documents fall in two visual segments, so a cannot-link will be added in step (1). Since they are also temporally close enough, a must-link will also be added in step (2). In such cases, we must assign priority to different constraints. Currently, the priority is given to visual constraints. Our rationale is that the number of visual constraints is far fewer than the number of the temporal constraints. Our heuristic promotes more specific visual constraints and prevents them from being overpowered by more general temporal constraints.

After the must-links and cannot-links are generated, we employ constraint-based topic analysis to derive sub-topics that satisfy these constraints.

Step 2: Performing Constraint-based Topic Analysis

To incorporate the visual and temporal constraints specified above in a topic modeling process, we employ constraint-based topic analysis. There are two families of constraint-based topic analysis: (a) Constrained LDA [3, 4, 24] and (b) constrained clustering [6, 27, 32]. Since constrained LDA is a relatively new effort, without extensions, none of the existing methods can encode the temporal and visual constraints that must be satisfied in our application. We thus decide to use constrained clustering.

Constrained clustering is a class of semi-supervised clustering algorithms that allows a system to incorporate additional user or application constraints during clustering. Frequently, these constraints are soft constraints and not all of them will be satisfied in the final solution. In general, constrained clustering is formulated as constraint-based optimization where its objective function captures both cluster coherence and additional constraints. This property fits our goal quite well, since it ensures the semantic coherence of discovered sub-topics while satisfying additional temporal and visual constraints.

Among all the constrained clustering algorithms, we adopt *constrained co-clustering* for two reasons. First, it is flexible as it can cluster multiple variables simultaneously. Traditional constrained clustering methods that cluster one random variable at a time are special cases of constrained co-clustering methods. Second, it is more effective in text analysis than one dimensional clustering, since it can cluster documents and words jointly [16]. To leverage the state-of-the-art constrained co-clustering methods, we decide to experiment with two top-performed algorithms but with very different clustering frameworks: Constrained Information-Theoretic Co-Clustering (CITCC) [27] and Constrained Co-Clustering with Non-negative Matrix Tri-Factorization (CCCTriNMF) [32].

CITCC combines the benefits of information-theoretic co-clustering with constrained clustering for textual documents [27]. It utilizes a two-sided hidden Markov random field to model both the document and word constraints. In *CITCC*, the clustering process is formulated as constraint-based optimization with the following objective function:

$$\begin{aligned}&\arg\min D_{KL}(p(D,V,\hat{D},\hat{V} \| q(D,V,\hat{D},\hat{V})\\&+\sum_{d_{m_1}}^{M}\sum_{d_{m_2}\in M_{d_{m_1}}} E(d_{m_1},d_{m_2}\in M_{d_{m_1}})\\&+\sum_{d_{m_1}}^{M}\sum_{d_{m_2}\in C_{d_{m_1}}} E(d_{m_1},d_{m_2}\in C_{d_{m_1}})\\&+\sum_{v_{i_1}}^{V}\sum_{v_{i_2}\in M_{v_{i_1}}} E(v_{i_1},v_{i_2}\in M_{v_{i_1}})\\&+\sum_{v_{i_1}}^{V}\sum_{v_{i_2}\in C_{v_{i_1}}} E(v_{i_1},v_{i_2}\in C_{v_{i_1}})\end{aligned} \quad (1)$$

where $D=\{d_1,..,d_M\}$ and $V=\{v_1,..,v_V\}$ are document and word sets, $\hat{D}$ and $\hat{V}$ are the document and word clusters, M_{d_m} and C_{d_m} are the must-links and cannot-links on the latent document cluster label L_{d_m} for document d_m. Similarly, M_{v_i} and C_{v_i} are the must-links and cannot-links on the latent word cluster label L_{v_i} for word v_i; E is the energy function for must-links and cannot-links.

In contrast, *CCCTriNMF* [32] is matrix-factorization-based, constrained co-clustering. Similar to CITCC, the constraints are encoded as must-links and cannot-links. It finds a solution to optimize the following objective:

$$\min_{G_1\geq 0, G_2\geq 0}\left\|R_{12}-G_1SG_2^T\right\|^2+Tr(G_1^T\Theta_1G_1)+Tr(G_2^T\Theta_2G_2) \quad (2)$$

where R_{12} is a co-occurrence document and word matrix, G_1 and G_2 are the cluster indicator matrices for document and word. $Tr(G_1^T\Theta_1G_1)$ and $Tr(G_2^T\Theta_2G_2)$ are penalties for violating the must-link and cannot-link constraints of documents and words, and Θ_1 and Θ_2 are penalty matrices.

Step 3: Determining Temporal Boundaries

Although Step 2 derives a set of document clusters representing a set of sub-topics, the clusters have not yet been assigned temporal boundaries. In Step 3, we employ two methods to determine the temporal boundaries of derived sub-topics: (1) by cluster centers and radiuses, and (2) by smoothed labels.

Cluster Center and Radius-based (CR) Based on the constrained clustering results, we extract the *temporal center* and the *temporal radius* for each derived document cluster (sub-topic). The *temporal center* ***c*** of a document cluster is defined as the median time stamp after sorting all the documents in the cluster on the time line, half of them is before ***c*** and half is after ***c***. The *temporal radius* ***r*** of a cluster is used to define a range **[*c-r, c+r*]** so that *x%* of the documents in the cluster are within that range. Normally, *x* is set empirically based on the target data set. Figure 4 shows the cluster centers and radiuses of two document-clusters.

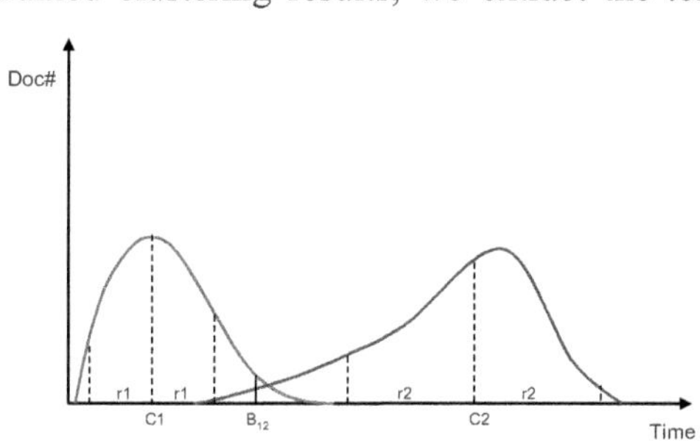

Figure 4. Cluster center and radius-based segmentation.

To associate the clusters with time, we sort all the clusters on the time line based on their temporal centers. The segment boundary between two adjacent clusters c_1 and c_2 is determined based on their cluster radiuses. Given distance d between the centers of two adjacent clusters, the segment boundary $b_{1,2}$ is decided by:

$$b_{1,2} = c_1 + \frac{r_1}{r_1+r_2}\times d \quad (3)$$

Since the size of the derived clusters can be imbalanced (e.g., some clusters are with thousands of documents, while others may only have a few), we performed smoothing to remove clusters that are "too small to visualize effectively". Here, we consider a cluster whose size is less than 10% of the average cluster size "too small to visualize".

Smoothed Label-based (SL). Our second approach is to use a sliding window to determine temporal boundaries of the derived clusters (sub-topics) [5, 13, 20]. We first directly sort all the documents on the timeline based on their time stamps. We then use a sliding window of size *N* to examine *N* documents at a time and identify those whose cluster labels do not conform to the main cluster where the majority lies. Such a document is then re-assigned to the main cluster within the window. Based on the smoothed document labels, a temporal boundary occurs whenever there is a change of cluster labels between two adjacent documents on the time line. In our experiments, *N* was set empirically based on the target dataset. In general, larger window size will result in smaller number of segments. Similar to the *CR*-based algorithm, "small clusters" may be removed during *SL* segmentation due to "smoothing".

Selection of Representative Segment Keywords

After Step 3, each document cluster (sub-topic) is now associated with a temporal boundary, which is called a *temporal segment*. For each temporal segment *S*, we select a set of topic keywords to best summarize the documents in the segment. The method for selecting topic keywords varies depending on which clustering algorithm is used.

For CITCC, the rank of a word v_i is computed using:

$$r_{v_i\in S} = \sum_{k_v} q(\hat{d}_{k_d}, \hat{v}_{k_v})q(v_i \mid \hat{v}_{k_v}) \quad (4)$$

For each word v_i in any of the documents in segment S, we compute the rank of the word r_{v_i} by formula (4) where $\hat{d}_{k_d}$ is the document cluster associated with segment S, $q(\hat{d}_{k_d}, \hat{v}_{k_v})$ is the probability of a word cluster $\hat{v}_{k_v}$, k_v =1, 2, 3. …, K, be associated with the document cluster $\hat{d}_{k_d}$, and $q(v_i \mid \hat{v}_{k_v})$ is the probability a word v_i is associated with the word cluster $\hat{v}_{k_v}$.

To improve efficiency, here we only focus on the *most relevant word clusters*. The relevant word clusters for a document cluster $\hat{d}_{k_d}$ are defined as those whose $q(\hat{d}_{k_d}, \hat{v}_{k_v})$ is above a certain threshold.

For CCCTriNMF, the rank of a word v_i is computed using:

$$r_{v_i} = [S.G_2^T]_{k,i} \quad (5)$$

where S is the cluster center matrix in equation (2), G_2^T is the transpose of the word cluster indicator matrix G_2, k is the document cluster label associated with the current segment, and i is the word index of v_i.

Based on the word ranks defined in equations (4) and (5), we retrieve the top-K keywords to represent each segment.

ALGORITHMIC EVALUATION

To test the performance of our approach, we first conducted a set of experiments to measure the performance of our algorithms in different settings.

Data Sets

We used two data sets in our experiments. The first data set is a collection of 7000+ emails over the course of two years. The second is a collection of 13,000+ New York Times articles, published during the time period of six months.

Settings and Baseline

TIARA first ran LDA topic modeling on each of our data set to derive N topics. For emails, N was set to 10. For news articles, N was set to 30.

For each of the N topics, we extracted all the documents relevant to the topic. A document k is considered relevant to a topic i if its LDA-derived document topic probability $\theta_{k,i}$ is above a threshold; or if $\theta_{k,i}$ is the highest among all the $\theta_{k,j\ (j \neq i)}$ if none is above the threshold. In our experiments, the threshold was set to 0.4 for emails and 0.3 for news articles. For each LDA-derived topic, we then ran our temporal segmentation algorithms. We repeated the same process 10 times, each with a different random seed for CITCC and CCCTriNMF. All the results presented here are the averages over 10 random runs across all the N topics.

For comparison, we used the previous version of TIARA as a baseline [22]. This is the first and only method known to us that performs temporal topic segmentation for text visualization. The temporal boundaries in the baseline were determined first by visual segment boundaries, augmented with additional segments based on fixed time intervals to make the total number of segments the same as the document cluster number used in CITCC and CCCTriNMF. To select segment keywords, the baseline computed the rank of a keyword in each temporal segment based on its segment-specific *tf*idf* scores. Here, *tf* is the accumulative frequency of a word in all the documents in a segment. *idf* is computed the same way as that in typical IR tasks. We used the top-K keywords for each segment.

Metrics

We used three objective metrics to evaluate our algorithms.

Topic Completeness measures how relevant the selected segment keywords are to the current topic. As shown in Figure 1, the semantics of a topic is defined by the keywords associated with all the segments in the topic. Thus, one critical role played by these keywords is to help users understand the semantics of a topic. A high score in topic completeness indicates that it is easy for a user to grasp the overall semantics of a derived topic through the keywords in all temporal segments. In contrast, a low score implies that the extracted segment keywords may not be a good representation of the topic.

Table 1. Experimental results on two data sets. Except for visual alignment, all the numbers in bold represent significant improvement over the baseline. The bold numbers with * in visual alignment represent significant difference between the two segmentation algorithms under the same clustering condition.

Method	Topic Completeness		Topic Distinctiveness		Visual Alignment	
	Email	NYT	Email	NYT	Email	NYT
Baseline	.260	.426	.103	.005	.000	.000
CITCC-CR	**.561**	**.575**	.079	**.111**	.082	.050
CITCC-SL	**.561**	**.573**	.077	**.118**	**.067***	**.043***
CCCTriNMF-CR	**.440**	**.494**	**.128**	**.147**	.097	.066
CCCTriNMF-SL	**.432**	**.479**	**.115**	**.156**	.095	.068

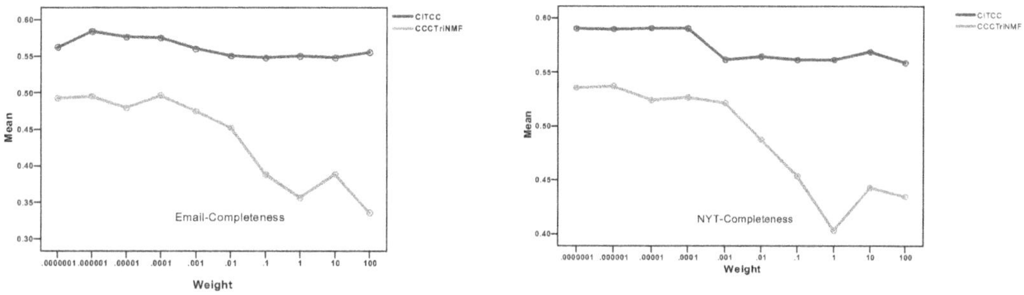

Figure 5. The impact of constraint weight on topic completeness.

To compute topic completeness, for each topic, we compare the union of all the keywords in all the derived segments (sub-topics) with the original top 50 keywords derived by LDA for that topic. Based on the number of overlapping keywords, we compute *precision* to measure among all the keywords in the segment keyword union, the percentage of which also belongs to the top 50 topic keywords derived by LDA. We also compute *recall* to measure among all the top 50 keywords from LDA, the percentage of which also appears in the union of all the segment keywords. Finally, we compute the *F-measure,* the harmonic mean of precision and recall, as the overall assessment for topic completeness. The completeness score in Table 1 is the average *F-measure* over all the topics over 10 random runs.

Topic Distinctiveness measures how one segment differs from another based on their associated keywords. It helps us evaluate how well the temporal segments produced by our algorithm capture significant topic transitions. Here, we use the average pair-wise Jensen-Shannon (JS) divergence to measure the distinctiveness of two sets of keywords. Suppose that a topic is segmented into L parts. Each segment l has a normalized keyword histogram h_l s.t. $\sum_m h_l(m) = 1$ where m is the word index in the vocabulary.

Given two normalized keyword histograms h_i and h_j, first we compute the Kullback-Leibler (*KL*) divergence:

$$D_{KL}(h_i \| h_j) = \sum_{k=1}^{V} h_i(k) \log \frac{h_i(k)}{h_j(k)} \quad (6)$$

Then we compute the Jensen-Shannon divergence:

$$D_{JS}(h_i \| h_j) = \frac{1}{2} D_{KL}(h_i \| \bar{h}) + \frac{1}{2} D_{KL}(h_j \| \bar{h}) \quad (7)$$

where $\bar{h} = 1/2(h_i + h_j)$. The final distinctiveness score of a topic is the average pair-wise JS score over all the segments in a topic. After deriving the topic distinctiveness score for each topic, we then compute the average over all the topics over 10 random runs.

Visual Segment Alignment measures how well the derived temporal segments align with visual segments. While our first two metrics evaluate the semantic coherence of derived temporal segments, this metric evaluates how well our algorithm satisfies the visualization constraints. Here the visual segment boundaries were pre-computed by our system based on the shape of each topic layer. We computed the average distance between each visual segment boundary and its nearest temporal segment boundary inferred by our algorithms. We normalized the distance so that it is in the range of [0, 1]. Here, the lower the score (distance) is, the better the alignment is. The scores shown in Table 1 are the averages over all the visual segment boundaries for all the topics over 10 random runs.

Results and Analysis

As shown in Figure 5 for *topic completeness*, all our algorithms outperformed the baseline on both data sets. The difference is statistically significant based on paired *t*-test ($p<0.001$). This result strongly suggests that by employing constrained clustering, our algorithm is much more capable of identifying topic-related keywords. Low topic completeness score often means it is hard for users to grasp the semantics of a topic based on the sum of the segment keywords. Moreover, between the two clustering algorithms, CITCC-based methods performed better than CCCTriNMF-based methods for topic completeness ($p<0.001$).

For *topic distinctiveness*, CCCTriNMF-based approaches performed the best on both data sets. They performed significantly better than the baseline ($p<0.001$). They also performed significantly better than the CITCC-based methods ($p<0.001$). Note that the topic distinctiveness scores for the baseline system in both data sets are quite low (**Error! Reference source not found.**). Since the baseline used only visual boundaries and fixed time intervals to do segmentation, this may cause redundancies by splitting similar content into multiple segments (e.g., S1 and S2 in Figure 2(a)).

For *visual segment alignment*, since by definition, the alignment score for the baseline is always 0, we did not compare our results with the baseline. Instead, we compared the performances between our two temporal alignment algorithms (i.e., *CR* versus *SL*) under the same clustering condition. Based on paired-t test, if used in combination with CITCC, the SL-based algorithm performed significantly better than the CR-based method on both datasets ($p<0.001$). There is no statistically significant difference

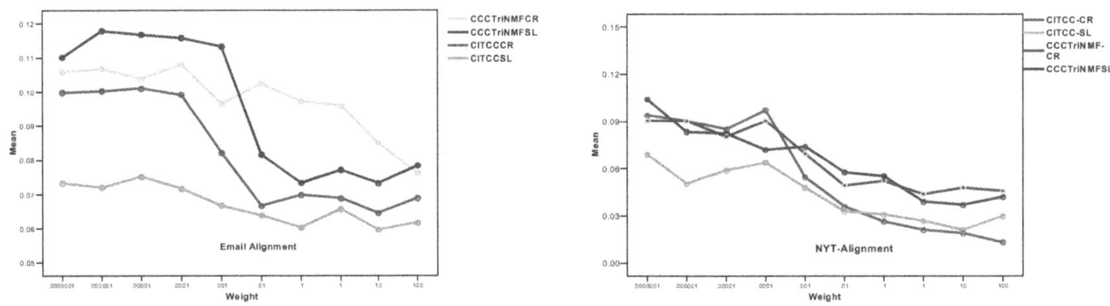

Figure 6: The impact of constraint weight on visual alignment.

between these two approaches, if they were used in combination with CCCTriNMF.

Since both CITCC and CCCTriNMF attempt to strike a balance between discovering coherent sub-topics and satisfying additional visual and temporal constraints, we also investigated how constraint weight affects the results. In this experiment, we varied the weights of must-links and cannot-links in CITCC and CCCTriNMF from 0.0000001, the lowest, to 100, the highest.

Figure 5 shows the impact of weight on topic completeness on both datasets. As shown in Figure 5, the topic completeness is mainly determined by the constrained clustering algorithms (i.e., CITCC or CCCTriNMF) and not sensitive to the two temporal segmenting algorithms (CR or SL). We thus show the average topic completeness for each clustering method, regardless of the segmentation algorithm used. As shown in Figure 5, when the weight of constraints increases, the topic completeness for CCCTriNMF deteriorates significantly. In contrast, CITCC holds its performance much better than CCCTriNMF.

Similarly in Figure 7, we show how constraint weight affects topic distinctiveness. Here, in CCCTriNMF (the green lines), when the constraint weight increases, the distinctiveness of the segments increases slightly. In contrast, for CITCC (the blue lines), increasing constraint weights seems having little impact on email data and negative impact on the news data on the topic distinctiveness.

Moreover, the impact of constraint weight can be clearly observed in Figure 6, which shows how visual alignment scores change with the constraint weights on two data sets. Each curve in these graphs represents a combination of clustering (CITCC and CCCTriNMF) and temporal segmentation algorithm (CR and SL). As shown in these graphics, when the weight increases, the alignment score decreases, indicating a better visual-temporal boundary alignment. This trend holds regardless of the data set, the clustering algorithm used, and the temporal alignment algorithm used. These results are significant and demonstrate the effectiveness of our work in satisfying visualization constraints. Moreover, among the four combinations that we have investigated, CITCC-based algorithms outperformed CCCTriNMF-based ones; and the combination of CITCC_SL performed the best in most situations.

USER STUDY

In addition to our algorithmic evaluation, we also designed and conducted a crowdsourced user study to evaluate the effect of our work on user task performance. Specifically, we evaluated how our method aided users in their text analytic tasks against the baseline.

Data and Method

In this study, we used the email data set, since we need to compare the user task performance against the ground truth that we have already known. Moreover, we focused on testing TIARA's capability in helping users perform practical text analysis tasks. For this purpose, TIARA created two visualizations (Figure 8). Figure 8(a) shows the temporal segmentation results of a topic produced by the baseline [22]. Figure 8(b) displays the results of our CITCC_SL

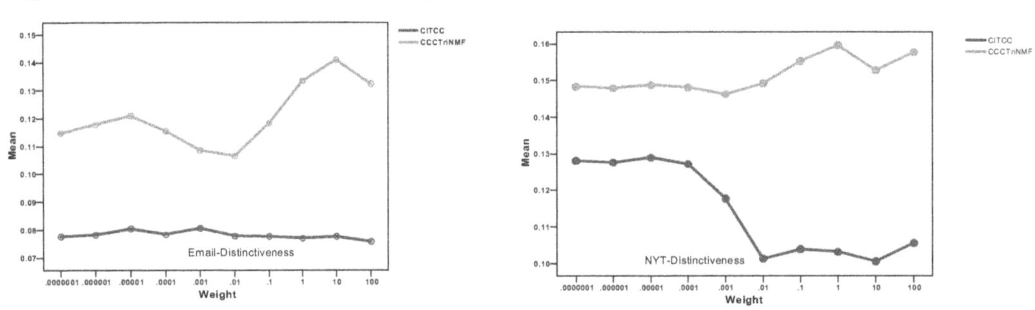

Figure 7. The impact of constraint weight on topic distinctiveness.

algorithm, since it outperformed others in most cases by our algorithmic evaluation. The displayed topic involved 155 emails, dated from 6/1/2012 to 10/10/1012. The two visualizations were the same (e.g., size, color, and shape) except the location and content of the keyword clouds.

We designed two surveys, one for each visualization. The surveys contained identical instructions and questions except the visualization. Each participant was first given a brief introduction to the task, including the data and the visualization. S/he was then instructed to view the visualization carefully to answer four multiple-choice questions, each of which is a text analytic task to gain an understanding of the selected topic. The first two questions (Q1 and Q2) were designed to test a user's overall understanding of the derived topic. The next two questions (Q3 and Q4) tested a user's understanding of specified sub-topic(s) and associated temporal information.

Q1: *Who is most involved in Project X in its entire course?*

Q2: *What are the main sub-topics discussed in this project?*

Q3: *When did event E occur?*

Q4: *Which event(s) occurred during the time frame X?*

We used a between-subject design and sent 50 assignments for each survey on CrowdFlower [1], a crowdsourcing platform. To ensure the quality, we recruited workers located in the U.S. only and also limited a worker to work on only one of the two surveys once. We collected 51 responses for the baseline and 54 responses for our method.

Study Results and Analysis

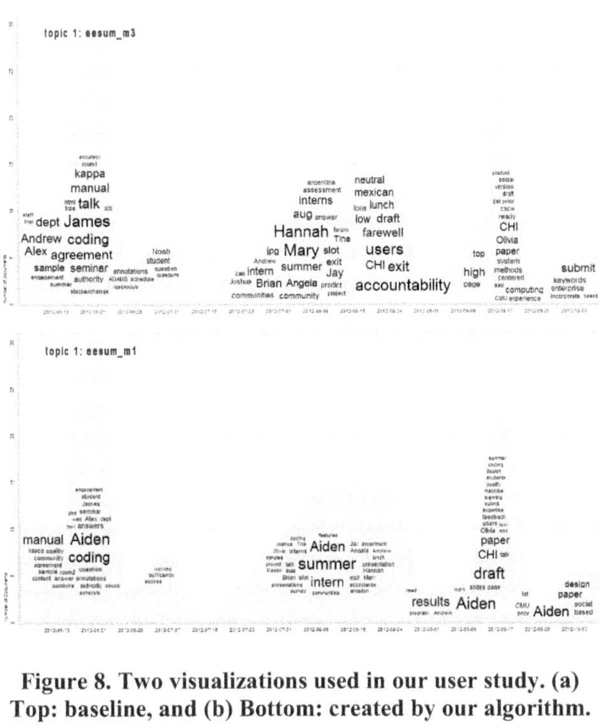

Figure 8. Two visualizations used in our user study. (a) Top: baseline, and (b) Bottom: created by our algorithm.

From the collected survey results, we examined two metrics. One is *task completion time*, which was computed using the job start and submission time automatically recorded by CrowdFlower. The other is *task success rate*, measuring the percentage of correct answers that a participant produced. Overall, the participants who used Figure 8(b) took longer (*mean* = 4.8 minutes) to complete their tasks than those with the baseline (*mean* = 4.2 minutes), although the difference was not significant ($p<0.08$ based on independent samples *t*-test). However, these participants achieved a much higher task success rate (*mean* = 81% for our method versus 18% for the baseline). The difference is statistically significant ($p<0.001$). This means that although those participants spent a bit more time, they were able to perform the analytic tasks much better using the visualization produced by our method.

We further examined the effect of different tasks on the task success rate since our survey included two types of analytic tasks: (1) achieving an overall understanding of a topic (Q1 and Q2), and (2) extracting specific aspects of a derived temporal sub-topic (Q3 and Q4). We found that the difference in task success rate was even greater in Type 1 task, 83% vs. 6%, while smaller, 79% vs. 30%, for Type 2 task.

We believe the difference is because our topic segmentation approach models latent semantics of sub-topics and ensures that extracted temporal segments are semantically coherent and distinctive (consistent with our *topic completeness* and *topic distinctiveness* evaluation). In contrast, the baseline relies on only a *tf*idf* based model, and important concepts (especially those appearing often in all the documents) might be discounted without showing up prominently in the display. Moreover, without a coherent topic model, the keywords selected by the baseline were disconnected. In contrast, our method selected keywords that are semantically and temporally meaningful.

As demonstrated by our study, the ability to capture semantic and temporal coherence of sub-topics and their representative keywords is critical to effective visual text analysis. Users often rely on the temporally distributed word clouds to interpret and differentiate sub-topics. In this study, however we did not separately test the effect of visual coherence (e.g., alignment with visual segment boundaries) on user task performance. Further studies are needed to verify the impact of visual coherence on user task performance.

DISCUSSION

One distinct advantage of our approach is its extensibility, as new constraints can be easily incorporated in a topic analysis process. Here we briefly discuss handling of new types of constraints and limitations in our current work.

Handling New Types of Constraints

It is quite straightforward for our model to support new types of constraints, such as geo-spatial constraints. Assume that we want to gauge the opinions posted on social media (e.g., Twitter) towards the 2012 US presidential candidates by geographical locations over time. In this case, we want to group the posts not only based on their semantic themes and temporal localities, but also by the authors' geolocations. To achieve this goal, we just need to incorporate must-links and cannot-links that indicate geographical relationships between two documents based on the locations of their authors. TIARA can then perform topic analysis while balancing *all* the constraints, including the geo-spatial constraints. In short, our approach is easily applicable to new situations where new types of constraints need to be incorporated in topic analysis.

Content-based Modeling of Document Time

To segment a topic temporally, we must obtain the temporal information of each document. Currently, we associate a document with a time stamp, which, in most cases, is the document creation time (e.g., when an email is sent or a news article is published). To capture content-based temporal information, we must then perform temporal information extraction for each document, e.g., inferring the temporal intervals of described events. Although there are multiple temporal reasoning models in natural language processing, finding a suitable tool that can handle a large collection of documents with high accuracy is non-trivial [25].

Setting Model Parameters

In our current framework, we need to set multiple model parameters, such as word and document cluster number, the size of the sliding window for SL-based segmentation, and weights of various constraints. Although we can use heuristics to estimate the parameters for a data set based on its characteristics (e.g., size of the data set), in reality, the parameters will still need to be tuned empirically for each new dataset. Optimizing such parameters for each dataset *automatically* is an active research topic in Machine Learning and beyond the scope of the paper.

Topic Analysis with Enriched Constraint Models

Currently, we allow the use of must-links and cannot-links between a pair of documents/words to specify additional constraints in a topic modeling process. In reality, constraints could be far more complex. For example, we may want to specify finer-grained temporal/visual constraints between two documents that a must-link or cannot-link cannot capture [26]. While there are many sophisticated constraint models and solvers that we could leverage, the key challenge is how to incorporate such models with topic analysis that handles complex latent semantic constraints. Even more challenging is how to satisfy all the constraints *efficiently* when millions of documents are involved.

CONCLUSION

To create an effective, time-based visual summary of text, in this paper, we present a constraint-based topic analysis approach to temporal topic segmentation. Given a topic derived from a set of text documents, our approach automatically splits it into a set of sub-topics (segments) spanning over multiple linear, non-overlapping temporal intervals. It does so by systematically incorporating and simultaneously satisfying a diverse set of constraints, including semantic, temporal, and visualization constraints. As a result, our approach produces semantically coherent temporal segments that capture significant topic transitions. Moreover, the identified temporal boundaries are aligned with the natural visual boundaries of a topic layer to optimize the use of space for displaying each word cloud, summarizing each sub-topic.

We have also conducted extensive experiments to measure the performance of our methods by three objective metrics: topic completeness, topic distinctiveness, and visual segment alignment. Our results have demonstrated the significant advantage of our method over an existing baseline. In particular, our Constrained Information-Theoretic Co-Clustering (CITCC) topic analysis with the Smoothing Label temporal alignment approach performs the best in most cases. Furthermore, our crowdsourced user study demonstrates the effectiveness of our work in aiding users completing practical text analysis tasks.

REFERENCES

1. http://www.crowdflower.com
2. Alonso, O., Gertz, M. and Baeza-Yates, R. 2009. Clustering and Exploring Search Results using Timeline Constructions. *CIKM'09*, 97-106.
3. Andrzejewski, D., Zhu, X., Craven, M., and Recht, B. 2011. A Framework for Incorporating General Domain Knowledge into Latent Dirichlet Allocation using First-Order Logic. *IJCAI'2011*, 1171-1177.
4. Andrzejewski, D., Zhu, X., and Craven, M. 2009. Incorporating Domain Knowledge into Topic Modeling via Dirichlet Forest Priors. *ICML*, 4.
5. Banerjee, S. and Rudnicky, A. 2006. A TextTiling Based Approach to Topic Boundary Detection in Meetings. In proceedings of *the Interspeech*. pp 57-60.
6. Basu, S., Bilenko, M. and Mooney, R. 2004. A Probabilistic Framework for Semi-Supervised Clustering. *SIGKDD'04*, 59-68.
7. Blei, D., Ng, A. and Jordan, M. 2003. Latent Dirichlet Allocation. *J. of Mach. Learn. Res.*, 3:993–1022.
8. Blei, D., Lafferty, J. 2006. Dynamic topic models. *ICML'06,* 113–120.
9. Basu, S., Banerjee, A., and Mooney, R. J. 2002. Semi-supervised clustering by seeding. *ICML'02*, 27-34.
10. Brants, T., Chen, F. and Tsochantaridis, I., 2002 Topic-based document segmentation with probabilistic latent semantic analysis, *CIKM' 02,* 211 – 218.
11. Carenini, G., Ng, R. Pauls, A.2008: Interactive multi-media summaries of evaluative text. *IUI'08*, 124-131.

12. Chi, Y., Song, X., Zhou, D., Hino, K. and Tseng, B. 2007. Evolutionary spectral clustering by incorporating temporal smoothness. *SIGKDD'07*, 153-162.
13. Chu, C.-S.J. 1995. Time Series Segmentation: A Sliding Window Approach. *Information Sciences*, 85 (1):147-173.
14. Chuang, J., Ramage, D., Manning, C., and Heer, J. 2012. Interpretation and trust: designing model-driven visualizations for text analysis. *CHI'12*, 443-452.
15. Cui, W., Liu, S., Tan, L., Shi, C., Song, Y., Gao, Z., Qu, H., and Tong, X. Textflow: Towards better understanding of evolving topics in text. *IEEE Trans. Vis. Comput. Graph*. 17, 12 (2011), 2412–2421.
16. Dhillon, I., Mallela, S. and Modha, D. 2003. *Information* Theoretic Co-Clustering. *SIGKDD'03*, 89–98.
17. Dredze, M., Wallach, H., Puller, D., and Pereira, F. 2008. Generating Summary Keywords for Emails Using Topics. *IUI'09*, 199-206.
18. Galley, M., McKeown, K., Fosler-Lussier, E. and Jing., H. 2003. Discourse Segmentation of Multi-party Conversation. *ACL'03*, 562–569.
19. Hearst, M. 1994. Multi-paragraph segmentation of expository text. *ACL'94*, 9-16.
20. Hearst, M. 1997. TextTiling: Segmenting text into multi-paragraph subtopic passages. *Computational Linguistics*, 23(1):33-64.
21. Jeong, M. and Titov, I. 2010 Multi-Document Topic Segmentation. *CIKM'2010*, 1119-1128.
22. Liu, S., Zhou, M., Pan, S., Qian, W., Cai, W., Lian, X. 2009. Interactive Topic-based Visual Text Summarization and Analysis, *CIKM'09*, 543-552.
23. Misra, H., Yvon, F., Jose, J. and Cappe, O. 2009. Text segmentation via topic modeling: an analytical study. *CIKM '09*, 1553-1556.
24. Ramage, D., Manning, C. and Dumais, S. 2011. Partially Labeled Topic Models for Interpretable Text Mining. *SIGKDD'11*, 457-465.
25. Sanampudi, S. and Kumari, G. Temporal reasoning in natural language processing: a survey. *Intl. J. of Comp. Apps*. 1(4): 53-57, 2010.
26. Schrier, E., Dontcheva, M., Jacobs, C., Wade, G. and Salesin D. *.IUI '08*, Adaptive layout for dynamically aggregated documents. 99-108.
27. Song, Y., Pan, S., Liu, S., Wei, F., Zhou, M. and Qian, W. 2010. Constrained co-clustering for textual documents. *AAAI'2010*, 581-586.
28. Sun, B., Mitra, P., Giles, C., Yen, J. and Zha, H., 2007. Topic segmentation with shared topic detection and alignment of multiple documents. *SIGIR'07*, 199-206.
29. Tür, G., Stolcke, A., Hakkani-Tür, D. and Shriberg, E. 2001. Integrating prosodic and lexical cues for automatic topic segmentation, *Computational Linguistics,* 27(1), 31-57.
30. Wang, F., Tong, H. and Lin, C. 2011. Towards Evolutionary Nonnegative Matrix Factorization. *AAAI'11, 501-566.*
31. Wang, C., Blei, D. and Heckerman, D. 2008. Continuous Time Dynamic Topic Models. *Proc. on Uncertainty in AI*, 579-586.
32. Wang, F., Li, T. and Zhang, C. 2008. Semi-Supervised Clustering via Matrix Factorization. *SIAM'08*, 1-12.
33. Wang, X. and McCallum, A. 2006. Topics over time: a Non-Markov Continuous-Time Model of Topical Trends. *SIGKDD'06*, 424-433.

Visualizing Recommendations to Support Exploration, Transparency and Controllability

Katrien Verbert[1,4], Denis Parra[2,3], Peter Brusilovsky[2], Erik Duval[4]
[1]Department of Computer Science, Eindhoven University of Technology, Eindhoven, The Netherlands
{k.verbert@tue.nl}
[2]School of Information Sciences, University of Pittsburgh, 135 North Bellefield Avenue, Pittsburgh, PA 15260, USA {dap89, peterb}@pitt.edu
[3]Department of Computer Science, PUC Chile, Santiago, Chile
[4]Departement Computerwetenschappen, KU Leuven, Celestijnenlaan 200A, B-3001 Leuven, Belgium
{erik.duval@cs.kuleuven.be}

ABSTRACT

Research on recommender systems has traditionally focused on the development of algorithms to improve accuracy of recommendations. So far, little research has been done to enable user interaction with such systems as a basis to support exploration and control by end users. In this paper, we present our research on the use of information visualization techniques to interact with recommender systems. We investigated how information visualization can improve user understanding of the typically black-box rationale behind recommendations in order to increase their perceived relevance and meaning and to support exploration and user involvement in the recommendation process. Our study has been performed using TalkExplorer, an interactive visualization tool developed for attendees of academic conferences. The results of user studies performed at two conferences allowed us to obtain interesting insights to enhance user interfaces that integrate recommendation technology. More specifically, effectiveness and probability of item selection both increase when users are able to explore and interrelate multiple entities – i.e. items bookmarked by users, recommendations and tags.

Author Keywords

User interfaces for recommender systems; information visualization; user studies.

ACM Classification Keywords

H.5.2. Information interfaces and presentation (e.g., HCI): User interfaces. H.5.m. Information interfaces and presentation (e.g., HCI): Miscellaneous.

General Terms

Human Factors; Design; Experimentation.

INTRODUCTION

Interactive information visualization and recommendation techniques have both been explored as ways to help people deal with abundance of information. The main advantage of interactive visualization is that a multi-dimensional representation allows the user to more easily see multiple aspects of data while being in control when exploring information. The main advantage of the traditional recommendation approach is that offering a clear list of items ranked by perceived interest reduces cognitive overload associated with exploring a rich set of items.

In this paper, we present our research on the combination of both approaches. We investigated how graphical representations and the ability to combine a personalized prospect offered by a recommender engine with other valuable prospects can improve user trust in the results offered by the black-box recommender engines and increase user ability to find interesting items.

Our work has been motivated by the presence of multiple *relevance prospects* in modern personalized social tagging systems. An important feature pioneered by social tagging systems and later used in other kinds of social systems is the ability to explore different *community relevance prospects* by examining items bookmarked by a specific user or items associated by various users with a specific tag. Items bookmarked by a specific user offer a *social* relevance prospect: if this user is known and trustable or appears to be like-minded (bookmarked a number of items known as interesting) a collection of his or her bookmarks is perceived as an interesting and relevant set that is worth to explore for more useful items. Similarly, items marked by a specific tag offer a *content* relevance prospect. Items related to a tag of interest or a tag that was used to mark many known interesting items are also perceived as potentially relevant and worth to explore. In this context, a ranked list of recommended items offered by a specific recommender engine can be considered as yet another *personalized* relevance prospect.

The problem that we address is that existing personalized social systems do not allow their users to explore and combine multiple relevance prospects. Only one prospect can be explored at any given time – a list of recommended items, a list of items bookmarked by a specific user or a list of items marked with a specific tag. We believe that exploring a single prospect is not sufficient since none of the prospects could be fully reliable and trustable by the users (that includes recommendations generated by black-box engines). In this context, the ability to combine prospects might offer a more reliable and attractive way to explore information. For example, knowing that a specific item has been not only recommended by a recommender engine, but also bookmarked by two trustable users can remarkably increase user trust in the quality of this item.

To solve the aforementioned problem and to offer users an approach to explore and combine multiple relevance prospects, we suggest a specific interactive visualization approach. This visualization embodies suggestions offered by various recommender systems *as recommender agents* that can be perceived as being analogous to human users and as a result, exportable in parallel with the relevance prospects offered by users and tags in social systems. We believe that using interactive visualization can increase the transparency of the recommendation process and allow the users to be in control of their exploration.

A special issue on interfaces for recommender systems [25] illustrates the interest and importance of intelligent interfaces for recommender systems. Such interfaces are investigated to provide new capabilities to the users of the recommender system to search, browse, and understand the results of the recommendations. In our work, we focus on the use of *information visualization techniques* to support such new capabilities. The research contribution of this work is threefold:

1) First, we present a novel and synergetic approach to combine multiple relevance prospects that include *personalized relevance* as offered by different recommenders and *social relevance* as offered in social bookmarking systems. In this approach, recommender systems are presented as agents and their interrelationship can be explored (i.e. a user can explore which items are suggested by multiple recommender agents). In parallel, real users and their bookmarks are shown and users can explore both interrelationships between users as well as interrelationships between agents and users. Third, a user can explore tags and interrelationships between tags, users and agents. To our knowledge, this combination has not yet been invetigated as a way to support exploration and controllability, and to increase trust and acceptance of recommendations.
2) Second, we present a user interface which serves to both explain the provenance of recommendations in a transparent way and to support exploration. Users can browse bookmarks of other users, tags and suggestions of recommender agents as a basis to find relevant items.
3) Third, we present the results of a study that evaluated the usefulness of this interactive interface with 21 users. In this study we attempted to assess how the ability to control and combine entities involved in the recommendation process can influence user performance and satisfaction.

This paper is organized as follows: first we present related work in the area of user interfaces for recommender systems. Then, we introduce TalkExplorer, an interactive visualization of users, tags, talks at a conference and recommendations for conference attendees. The evaluation of this visualization at conferences is presented next. Finally, we discuss the results of this case study, lessons learnt and future research opportunities.

BACKGROUND AND RELATED WORK

Recommender systems

Recommender algorithms can be broadly categorized in three areas:

1. *Collaborative filtering* (CF) recognizes commonalities between users or between items on the basis of explicit or implicit relevance indications [13] such as ratings [3] and tags [25]. Implicit data used by recommender systems include actions like reading [21] or watching TV series [14]. Starting from the active user, user-based CF first identifies a neighborhood of similar users to then recommend items based on the nearest neighbors' top preferences. On the other side, item-based CF identifies similarly rated items, and then uses these similar items to identify the recommendations. CF is the most widely implemented and most mature technology [6].
2. *Content-based filtering* matches descriptions of items to descriptions of users [26]. This approach bases predictions on information about individual users and items, and ignores contributions from other users.
3. *Hybrid recommender systems* combine recommendation techniques, to gain better performance with fewer drawbacks [6].

Although these algorithms have been implemented and validated on a large scale in several application areas [22], there are important challenges that need to be addressed before recommendation can realize its full potential.

1. Collaborative recommendation techniques often suffer from *cold start* issues, i.e. they cannot make effective recommendations for new users or for new items that have no explicit or implicit relevance indicators yet [7].
2. It is *difficult to explain* the rationale behind recommendations to end users [12]: the complexity of recommendation algorithms often prevents users from comprehending recommended results and can lead to *trust* issues when recommendations fail.

3. Allowing users to *control* the way they can sort lists of recommendations [17] or the neighbors' contribution in a social recommender [18] has shown a positive effect in user satisfaction. However, there are several ways that users can control elements in the interface: which are the most effective for the user experience?

The design and development of user interfaces for recommender systems has gained increased interest. Such interfaces are researched to provide new capabilities to search, browse, and understand the results of the recommendations [27]. Among others, explaining recommendations to provide transparency and to increase trust has been extensively investigated [28]. In most cases, such explanations are presented in plain text and indicate why a specific item is suggested to a user – such as *"Because you have selected or highly rated: Movie A"*.

In addition to supporting transparency, we are particularly interested to enable interaction with recommender systems as a basis to support exploration and controllability. In recent years, some research has been done to visualize recommendations to enable such new capabilities. We elaborate on existing work in this area in the next section.

Visualizing recommendations

Most existing work in the area of visualizing recommendations focuses on interaction with collaborative filtering recommender systems. PeerChooser [23] is a visual interactive recommender that uses a graph-based representation to show relations between users and recommended items of a collaborative filtering recommender system. Similarly, SmallWorlds [10] allows exploration of relationships between recommended items and similar friends, in multiple layers of similarity. These systems enable users to explore such relationships as a basis to provide transparency and to support the user to find new relevant items. Pharos [31] is a social map-based recommender system that visualizes a summary of social network activity of different communities. The system uses topic modeling [4] to provide new users with an overview of the site, alleviating the cold start problem.

Some systems focus specifically on tags that are used by social recommenders. SFViz (Social Friends Visualization) [11] visualizes social connections among users and user interests in order to increase awareness in a social network and to help people find potential friends with similar interests. This system uses a Radial Space-Filling (RSF) technique [9] to visualize a tag tree and a circle layout with edge bundling to show a social network.

FaceTag [29] is a tool that helps users see the relationship between user-generated tags and recommended facets in a classification scheme. Tagsplanations [30] presents both tag relevance (the degree to which a tag describes an item) and tag preference (the user's sentiment toward a tag) as a basis to explain recommendations. Kammerer et al. [15] designed a tag-based search browser to recommend relevant tags for further search. Research on this stream focuses on information and meta-information concerning items, and ignores the users who contributed such information and relationships among those users [11].

More recently, TasteWeights [5] has been introduced as a system that allows users to control the importance of friends and peers in social systems to obtain recommendations. Similar to our work, TasteWeights introduces the concept of an interface for hybrid recommender systems. The system elicits preference data and relevance feedback from users at run-time and uses these data to adapt recommendations to the current needs of the user. To our knowledge, this is one of the first systems that enables interaction with a hybrid recommender system and that can be adjusted by end users to control the output of the systems. In our work, we extend this concept of visualizing and combining the output of multiple recommenders as a basis to support exploration and controllability. While our work also enables end users to explore intersections of multiple recommenders (and hence in this respect we build on concepts that have been introduced by TasteWeights), the major difference and innovation of our work is that we allow end users to combine multiple *relevance prospects* in order to increase the perceived relevance and meaning of items. Our visualization embodies suggestions offered by various recommender systems *as recommender agents.* Items bookmarked by a specific user offer a *social relevance prospect:* if this user is known or appears to be like-minded a collection of her bookmarks is perceived as an interesting and relevant set that is worth to explore. Similarly, items marked by a specific tag offer a *content relevance prospect.* To our knowledge, this combination of multiple relevance prospects (agents, tags and real users) has not yet been explored as a way to support exploration and controllability, and to increase trust and acceptance of recommendations. Secondly, to our knowledge, our work is the first attempt to evaluate whether enabling end users to combine multiple relevance prospects increases the effectiveness and probability of item selection.

TALKEXPLORER

TalkExplorer is an interactive visualization tool that enables users to explore and bookmark research papers and talks at a conference using recommender agents and social data (tags, bookmarks, and connections to other users). The visualization was built as a component of the conference support system *Conference Navigator 3*. We first present Conference Navigator 3 (hereinafter CN3) and the recommendation functionalities that it provides. Then, we present the objectives of visualizing recommendations and details on the design and development of TalkExplorer. Evaluation results are presented in the next section.

Conference Navigator

Conference Navigator 3 is a social personalized system that supports attendees to academic conferences [24].

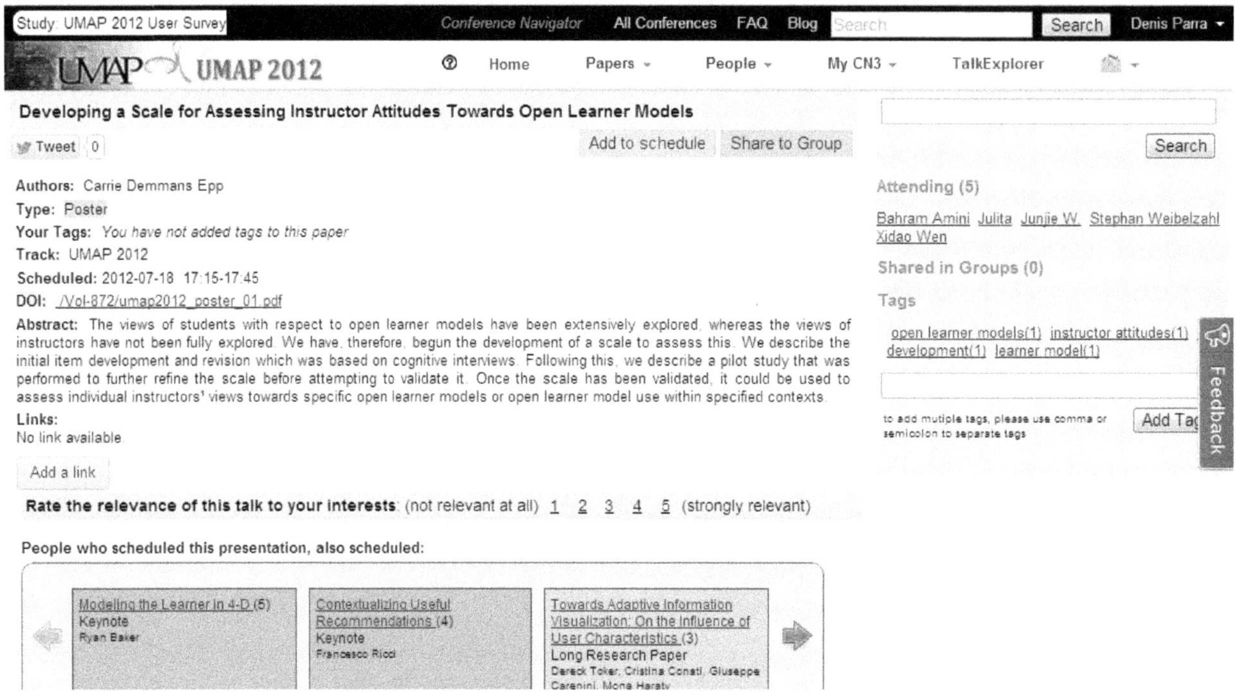

Figure 1: Talk details page in Conference Navigator 3 (CN3)

At the time of writing, 18 conferences have been supported by CN3. Among different features, Conference Navigator 3 provides a conference schedule, a list of the conference talks and details of each talk (Figure 1). It also provides information about people related to the conference, such as the list of attendees and the list of authors. Users can add papers to create a personal schedule, they can add tags to each talk, and they can also connect with other CN3 users by following them (unidirectional relationship) or connecting with them (bidirectional relationship). Social information collected by CN3 is extensively used to help users find interesting papers. For example, in the page called "Top Items", CN3 summarizes the most popular articles, the most active people, their institutions, and also the most popular tags associated to the papers.

When visiting talk information, as shown in Figure 1, users can also see who *scheduled* each talk during the conference and which tags were assigned to this talk. This social information is also used to provide links to similar papers ("People who scheduled this presentation, also scheduled:") mimicking the well-known Amazon.com's suggestions [19]. Similarly, when visiting a user page, other users can see which talks she is planning to attend (given that personal privacy settings provide access to this information). Finally, talks marked with a specific tag by the community of users can be explored.

In addition to social information access, CN3 offers personal recommendation of talks and papers. CN3 supports two kinds of recommendations: content-based and tag-based. The content-based engine constructs the user interest profile as a vector of terms with weights based on TF-IDF [1] using the content of the papers that the user has scheduled. Then, it recommends papers that match the profile of interests. The tag-based recommender engine makes use of the tags that users associate to conference talks. By matching user tags (tags applied by a target user) with item tags (tags assigned to different talks by the community of users) using the Okapi BM25 algorithm [20], the engine identifies relevant talks and suggests them to the active user.

Visualizing recommendations, tags and users

In the original CN3, ranked links produced by the content-based and tag-based recommenders are presented in separate pages and can be used by users to find new talks. In addition, users can explore bookmarks and tags of other users as a basis to explore new items. In this paper, we are particularly interested in assessing the potential influence of perceived relevancy and meaning of recommended items when we enable end users to explore and combine these multiple relevance prospects.

TalkExplorer is an interactive visualization developed on top of data collected by CN3.

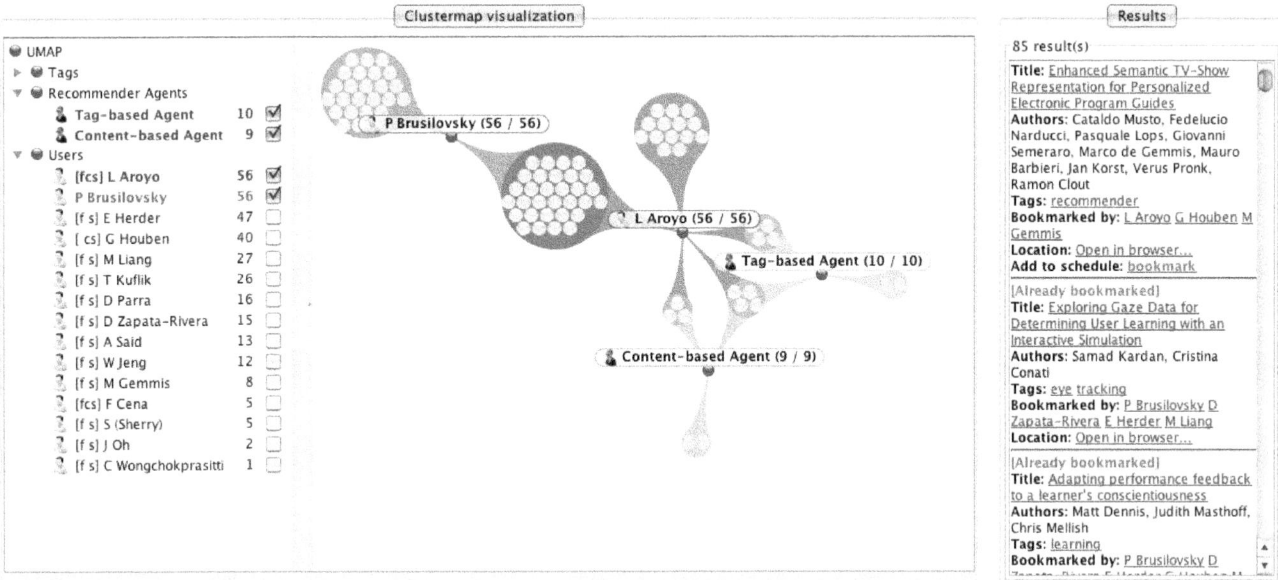

Figure 2: TalkExplorer

The interface serves to both explain the provenance of recommendations in a transparent way and to support exploration and control by end users. More specifically, users can browse and interrelate bookmarks of other users, tags and suggestions of recommender agents in order to find relevant items.

The visualization is implemented as a Java applet and uses the Aduna clustermap visualization library [1]. This software library visualizes sets of categorized objects and their interrelationships. The library has been used in related research to explore the interaction of users, resources and tags in social tagging systems [16]. In this past research, the library was deployed on top of delicious.com data to explore bookmarks of users and to support exploratory search. We adapted this initial version to visualize the interactions of users, tags, and *recommender agents* in terms of conference talks that they have in common – as illustrated in Figure 2. The objective was to explore new ways to enable end users to interact with recommender engines and items that are suggested to them.

Recommender systems are presented as talk-collecting agents so that interrelationship can be explored. In parallel, real users and their bookmarks are shown, and users can explore both interrelationships between users as well as interrelationships between agents and users (i.e. which other users have bookmarked talks that are recommended to them by one or more agents). In addition, relationships with tags can be explored to identify relevant items. We are hypothesizing that visualizing these relationships can help users to find relevant talks to attend at a conference, and that this visualization can provide transparency and increase trust.

As shown in Figure 2, fifteen users from the neighborhood of the active user are shown and users can explore items that these other users have bookmarked. The selection of the neighborhood users is based on two types of explicit CN3 links - i.e. users that the active user follows (user name preceded by [f] in Figure 2) and connections (user name preceded by [c]), respectively. In addition, users that have similar interests based on common bookmarks are shown in this neighborhood (preceded by [s]). The output of two CN3 recommendation algorithms is shown as items selected by the content-based and the tag-based recommender agents in parallel to bookmarks of real users and to bookmarks associated with specific tags.

TalkExplorer allows users to explore the three different relevance prospect mentioned above using a three-component interface shown in Figure 2. On the left side, the entity selection panel allows users to select tags, users and recommender agents to be added and displayed in the canvas area. This canvas area, at the center of the applet, shows a clustermap visualization - i.e., different clusters of talks linked by connected components. The labeled circles in this canvas area represent entities: users, recommender agents or tags. Yellow circles represent individual talks, and the bubbles that involve them represent clusters of talks.

In Figure 2, two users are shown (P Brusilovsky and L Aroyo), as well as suggestions of the tag-based and content-based recommender agents. The cluster map visualization enables users to explore relationships between items that are associated with different entities (i.e., recommended by an agent, bookmarked by a user, tagged with a tag). For instance, a user can see which users have bookmarked a talk that is suggested to them by a recommender agent by exploring the intersection of the agent and a specific user. Users can arrange the different entities displayed in the canvas by dragging them with the mouse.

Finally, the rightmost panel shows the detailed list of talks. This can be a list of all the talks presented in the canvas area, or a subset of them related to the selected entity. For example, if a user clicks on a specific user name in the canvas area, the papers that the selected user has bookmarked are presented in the list. If a user clicks on a cluster (for example, the cluster showing talks that were bookmarked by a user and a specific agent) the list of these talks is presented.

EVALUATION

We evaluated TalkExplorer at two conferences where CN3 was used as the main conference assistance system: ACM Hypertext 2012 conference in June 2012 (HT 2012) and User Modeling, Adaptation, and Personalization conference in July 2012 (UMAP 2012). Both evaluations were performed with attendees of respective conferences using real conference data (i.e., using actual talks and schedules and bookmarks, tags and ratings of the conference participants). Users were asked to explore conference talks using the visualization provided by TalkExplorer. As explained in the previous section, the visualization provided access to the content-based and tag-based recommender agents and allowed to explore talks bookmarked by users or tagged with community tags.

Participants

In the HT 2012 evaluation, fourteen users participated in a controlled experiment at the conference. We inquired about the number of Hypertext conferences participants have attended, as well as their knowledge of recommendation and visualization techniques, respectively. The latter were rated on a five point Likert scale. On average, participants attended 1.5 conferences in the past (std. deviation 0.732). Most of the participants have knowledge about or expertise with visualization techniques (average 4.285, std. deviation 0.7). In addition, familiarity with recommendation techniques is high – although less extensive than with visualization techniques (average 3.7, std. dev. 0.8).

Seven participants of the UMAP 2012 conference participated in the second study of our visualization. They had a high familiarity with visualization techniques (mean 4.2, std. deviation 0.76) and a relatively high familiarity with recommendation techniques (mean 3.7, std. deviation 0.95). On average, participants attended 2 UMAP conferences (std. deviation 1.5).

Tasks

We asked users to complete three tasks:

1. In the first task, they were asked to find a new relevant talk to attend by exploring talks that users in their neighborhood bookmarked (Task 1 – T1)
2. In the second task, subjects had to find a new relevant talk by exploring the content-based and tag-based recommender agents (Task 2 – T2).
3. In the third task, they were asked to find a new relevant talk by exploring the tags (Task 3 – T3).

Data collection

Data was collected in two ways. The think aloud protocol was used during the experiment to facilitate the collection of relevant feedback from participants. We recorded the screen and voice of participants using Camtasia Studio [8]. Afterwards, participants were asked to fill out a survey inquiring about their needs at a conference and the usefulness of the visualization to address these needs.

Results

To assess the value of interactive multi-prospect visualization offered by TalkExplorer, we have analyzed the way in which users *explore* and *use* the visualization. In the remainder of this section, we refer to selectable users, agents and tags as *entities* in the visualization. Papers or talks associated with these entities are referred to as *items.* We refer to *intersections* of entities when multiple entities were selected at the same time and their common items were explored.

We measured the *effectiveness* and *yield* of different combinations of entities to gain insight in the relative success rate of different combinations of entities to find relevant items.

Effectiveness measures how frequently a specific combination type produced a display that was used to bookmark at least one interesting item. It is calculated as the number of cases where the exploration of this combination type resulted in a bookmark, divided by the total number of times this combination type was explored. For instance, the set of items of a related user was explored 75 times by all participants. 23 of these sets were used to bookmark a new item. Thus, the effectiveness of exploring the set of items of a specific user is 23/75=31%. The number of item sets explored and the item sets used to bookmark a relevant talk, as well as the *effectiveness*, are presented in Figure 5.

In addition, we counted the number of items in the sets where the selection was made to check *yield* (productivity) of different kinds of sets. The yield of a specific combination type was measured by summing up the total number of selections made from each combination type, divided by the total number of items that were shown in the combinations where the selection was made. In other words, yield measures a chance of a random item shown in a specific combination type to be useful (i.e. bookmarked by the user). Yield results are presented in Figure 6.

Figure 3 presents an example where the active user, E Duval, used the intersection of two other users as a basis to find a relevant item. In this example, E Duval used the set of 8 items in the intersection of two other users (P Brusilovsky and D Parra) to find an item. The yield indicates the number of selections made from a specific set of entities divided by the sum of the number of items in this set (8 in the example presented in Figure 3).

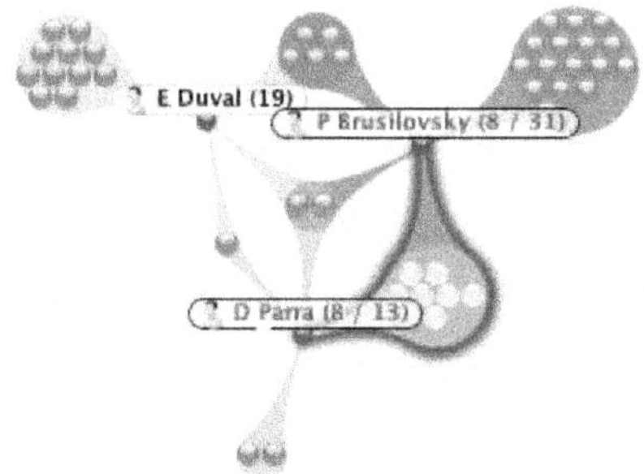

Figure 3: Exploring an intersection: items bookmarked by 2 users but not yet bookmarked by the active user

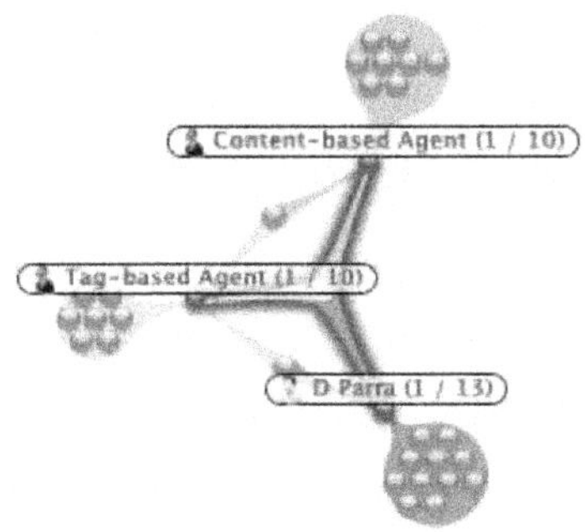

Figure 4: Talk in intersection of agents and another user

For the intersection of 2 users, twice an item was selected out of 2 items and twice an item was selected out of a set containing 1 item. We have yield or probability of selection of (1+1+1+1)/(2+2+1+1)=0.66.

Task 1

In the first task (T1), users were asked to find a relevant talk by exploring bookmarks of users in their neighborhood. Results are presented in Figure 5 and Figure 6. The set of items of one specific user with whom the active user is related was explored 75 times by all participants. 23 of these sets were used to bookmark a new item. The number of items in these 23 sets is 276. Thus, the effectiveness of 23/75 = 31% (first top bars in Figure 5) and the yield is 23/276 = 8% (first bar in Figure 6).

Fifteen users explored intersections of two related users focusing on talks that they have not yet bookmarked (as illustrated in Figure 3). This kind of set was used to bookmark a talk 4 times (effectiveness = 27%) and the sum of items in the used sets was 6 (yield = 66%).

Talks in the intersection of three or four other users were explored 12 and 6 times and used 5 and 3 times, respectively (effectiveness of 42% and 50%). The number of items in the selection set was 14 and 7, respectively (yield of 37% and 43%). As we can see from this data, the general trend is clear: the sets that allow users to explore the overlap of several prospects are both more effective and have higher yield. Moreover, there is a general tendency for effectiveness and yield to increase when more entities are used in the selection process. Small fluctuations within the general trend can be explained by the small sample.

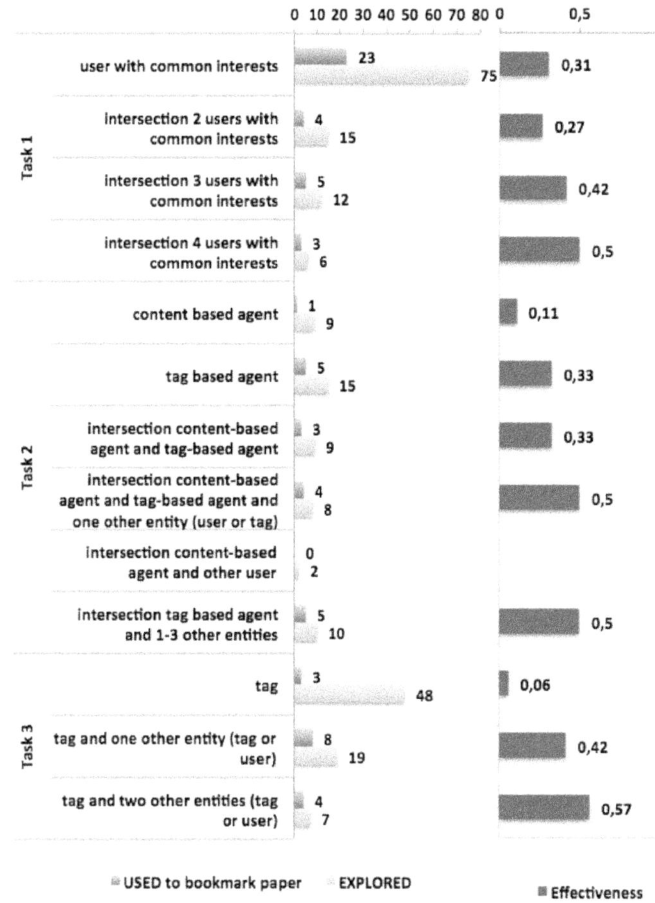

Figure 5: Summary of actions explored, used to bookmark a paper, and effectiveness of those actions.

Task 2

In the second task (T2), users were asked to find a relevant talk by exploring the output of recommender agents (a content-based and a tag-based agent). Results are presented in Figure 5 and 6, the middle set with 6 possible actions.

One out of nine users found a relevant talk by exploring suggestions by the content-based agent that were not related to any other entities on the screen (effectiveness=11%, yield=11%). Five out of 15 users found a relevant talk by exploring suggestions of the tag-based agent. Three out of nine users found relevant items by exploring the intersection of agents (i.e. talks that were suggested to them by both the content-based and the tag-based agent). Four out of eight users found relevant items by exploring the intersection of the agents with another entity. Figure 4 presents such an example.

The set of items of the content-based agent in combination with another user was explored twice, but not used to find a relevant item. The tag-based agent in combination with one or more entities was successful in 50% of the cases. The results presented in Figure 5 indicate the same trend: a higher number of entities (prospects) involved in the intersection increases the effectiveness and the yield of the resulting set.

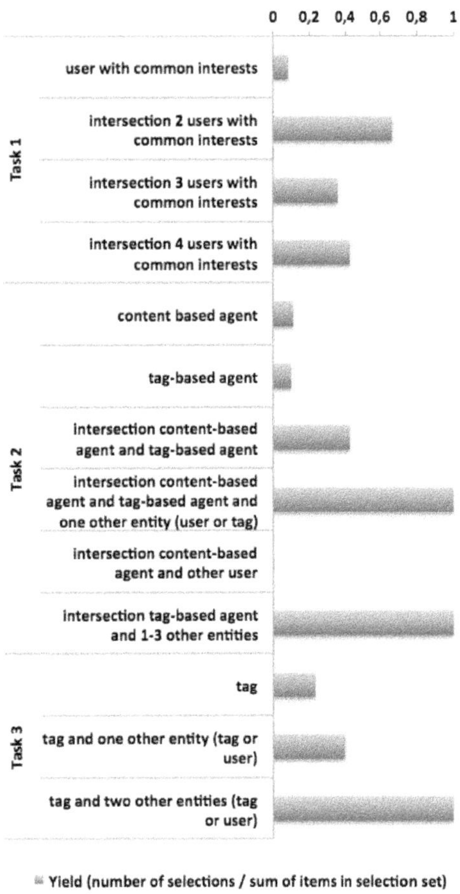

Figure 6: Summary of yield results

Task 3

In the third task (T3), we asked users to find interesting talks by exploring tags that were added by users to talks. Results are presented in the bottom set of 3 actions in Figure 5 and Figure 6.

As the data shows, using a single tag prospect (i.e., exploring items related to one selected tag) results in the lowest effectiveness registered in the study – as only three users were able to find a relevant item (effectiveness 6%). The sum of the number of items in the set when a selection was made was 13 (yield 3/13=23%).

Combining a tag prospect with one or more additional entities was more effective. 19 users explored the combination of a tag with another entity and 8 users used this intersection to bookmark an item (effectiveness=42%, yield=40%). A tag in relation to two other entities was effective in 57% of the explored cases. Some users indicated that they particularly liked this functionality – as this allows them to retrieve specifically items of their topic of interest from users they know or who have a high reputation in the field.

Summary of results

Effectiveness and yield results are summarized in Figure 7. Overall, these results indicate that effectiveness of an explored set increases once more entities are integrated. Similar trends are observed when we look at yield. These results indicate that the probability of selecting an item from a set increases if more entities are overlapped.

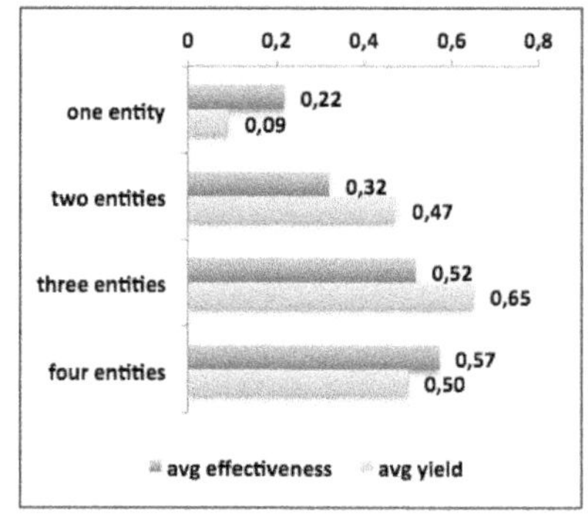

(a)

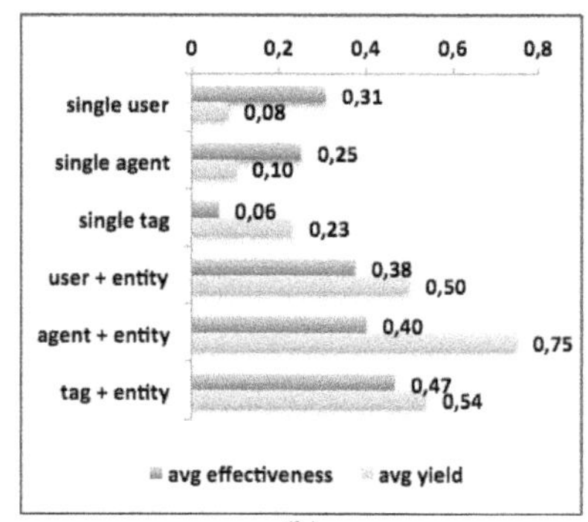

(b)

	Significance effectiveness	Significance yield
multiple vs. one entity	0.003469	0
user vs. (user + entity)	0.5934	0
agent vs. (agent + entity)	0.3417	0
tag v/s (tag + entity)	0	0.1

(c)

Figure 7: Summary of effectiveness and yield results

In Figure 7.a, we can see that the effectiveness and yield increases from 22% and 9% when a single entity is used to 57% and 50% when 4 entities are used. In Figure 7.b, we can see that yield increases from 8% when the set of items of one user is used, 10% when the set of items of one recommender agent is used and 23% when the set of items of one tag is used to 50% when the intersection of a user and another entity used, 75% when the intersection of an agent with another entity is used and 54% when a tag is used in combination with another entity. There is a significant difference in effectiveness when a tag is used in combination with another entity (see Figure 7.c). Effectiveness differences between users and agents in combinations with other entities are not significant. In general, effectiveness and probability of item selection is significantly higher when multiple entities are used (first row Figure 7.c). These results illustrate that enabling end users to explore interrelationships between prospects (sets of items in the overlap of entities) increases the probability of finding a relevant item.

The results also allow us to make several interesting observations. First, it is interesting to note that the least effective kind of set is the set of items related to exactly one tag (6% effectiveness). Incidentally, this is the only option to use tags for item exploration offered in many tag-based system. As shown by our data, the systems that do not allow exploring items related to combinations of several tags are not doing a good service to their users.

In contrast, exploring a prospect of a single related user in relation to the target user is a relatively effective approach – almost 1/3 of explored combinations produced bookmarks. It shows that the prospects of human users are more valuable (and trustable) than prospects offered by tags.

Overall, these results illustrate the added value of enabling users to combine social and personalization features of recommenders as a basis to increase the relevance and value of suggested items.

Questionnaire results

To collect user subjective feedback, we used a questionnaire. Its goal was to inquire about needs and issues that users have when attending a conference and the extent to which our visualization addresses those needs and issues. This questionnaire was used to collect some preliminary feedback and included only a few questions we considered important at this stage. We elaborate in the next section on the use of standardized questionnaires.

Figure 8 presents the results of our questionnaire on a five point Likert scale. The first column of bar charts presents answers to questions that inquire about the importance of issues and needs at a conference. The second column presents to which extent TalkExplorer addresses these needs and issues. The results indicate that conference attendees perceive 'finding relevant talks at a conference' as an important need (median 5) and that TalkExplorer addresses this need in a good way (median 4). 'Being aware which talks my friends are attending' is also perceived as important (first column) and most participants indicate that this need is addressed by TalkExplorer (second column). 'Being aware which talks people I follow are attending' is considered less important and is also not so well addressed by our tool (median 3). 'Finding other users who have similar interests' is important for many participants (median 4) and is addressed well by TalkExplorer (median 4). 'Gaining insight into why talks are recommended' is important for many, but not all, participants. This need is addressed well by TalkExplorer according to most, but again not all, participants (median 4).

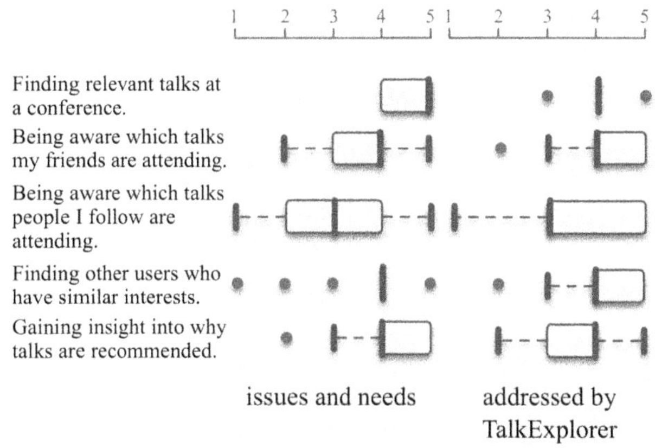

Figure 8: questionnaire issues and needs

In addition, we inquired about perceived usefulness of the visualization to support transparency and exploration. These results are presented in Figure 9 and indicate that participants perceive the visualization as useful because it gives more insight than a plain list of talks (median 4). In addition, most participants liked our idea of adding agents in parallel to real users as a means to find interesting talks (median 4) – among others to compare relevancy of recommendations (median 5).

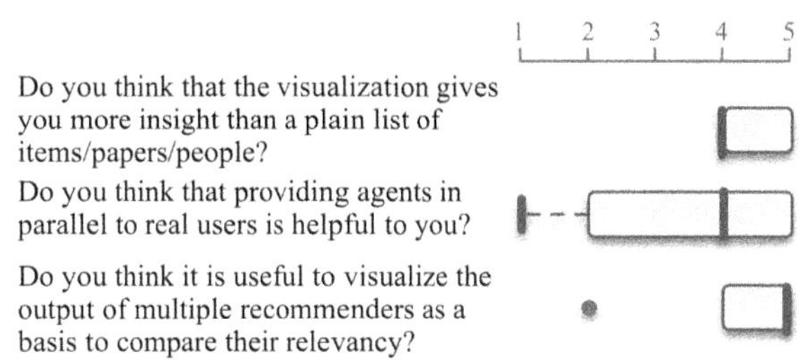

Figure 9: perceived usefulness

Think-aloud data analysis

An analysis of think-aloud data revealed some usability issues with the visualization and some additional insights into the usefulness of combining multiple relevance prospects. This data indicates that it was not clear why 15 users are shown in the neighborhood of a user. Participants asked why some users are shown by default and how these users are selected. Explaining the rationale of the selection of these users, such as the similarity match based on common bookmarks, can potentially resolve this issue. In addition, it would be interesting to explore how users can navigate through interest data of all users – while still distinguishing potentially more relevant bookmarks from users with common interests. People recommendation as opposed to recommendation of papers and talks was another suggestion from a participant.

Moreover, when users removed themselves from the visualization and explored bookmarks of other users only, it was not clear for them which of these items were already in their schedule. We resolved this issue for the UMAP evaluation by indicating in the right side panel whether a talk is already bookmarked (see Figure 2). Using different colors in the canvas could be a second solution.

Finally, participants remarked that they particularly liked combining tag prospects with agents or user prospects – as this functionality enables them to identify talks of a specific topic of interest from a set of recommended items or items from a user. These remarks illustrate the perceived usefulness of combining multiple prospects and are also reflected in the data presented in Figure 7. These data indicate that effectiveness of individual tags is significantly lower than a tag in combination with another entity.

DISCUSSION

Evaluation results presented in the previous section indicate that ability to combine visually multiple relevance prospects (i.e., bookmarks of users, suggestions of recommender agents and talks marked by specific tags) is perceived as useful to increase the relevance and value of recommendations. Results from our questionnaire are generally positive and indicate that participants value our visualization as a way to gain insight into why talks are recommended. In addition, they indicate that such a visualization gives more insight than a typical ranked list of recommendations.

Interaction patterns indicate that users often explore relationships between entities to find relevant items. Although items of one specific user were explored most often to find a relevant item (see Figure 5, first row), the effectiveness and probability of selecting an item is significantly lower than with intersections of multiple entities. Moreover, interrelating tags with other entities increase their effectiveness significantly (as summarized in Figure 7).

While these results illustrate the usefulness of visualizing and combining recommendations, tags and users, there are several limitations to this study that should be articulated and addressed in follow up studies. First, we asked users to explicitly explore users in their neighborhood, recommender agents and tags in three separate tasks. While results of these tasks give some interesting insights in the usefulness of these entities and the way users interacted with additional entities during these tasks, we cannot draw strong conclusions about the relative effectiveness of tags, users and agents in this way. The order of the tasks may have had an influence on the effectiveness of these entities. Moreover, we explicitly asked to explore these entities. In a follow up study, we are capturing interactions of users with the visualization in an open setting where users are free to explore various entities. Such a study and analysis of interaction patterns will yield more accurate data with respect to relative effectiveness of tags, users and agents. Second, participants at both UMAP 2012 and HT 2012 are highly knowledgeable on topics of recommendation and visualization and so they might not be representative of the general conference audience. Third, the questionnaire we used was a preliminary set of questions we assembled to gather initial feedback. In a follow up study, we plan to conduct more elaborate surveys based on standardized questionnaires to assess accuracy, diversity and novelty. Such studies are necessary to gain insight in other potential benefits that this interface can offer to end users.

CONCLUSION AND FUTURE WORK

In this paper we have presented and discussed the results of two studies involving conference attendees that select relevant talks by making use of the TalkExplorer visualization tool, embedded in CN3. TalkExplorer allows users to explore items (talks) by combining different entities (users, tags, recommender agents). After analyzing the users' behavior and their answers in a survey, we highlight three results.

First, to the best of our knowledge, the recommender systems literature offers neither studies that represent recommender algorithms as agents nor systems that let users interact with and combine the output of recommendation algorithms with social prospects. Our results indicate that this can be a significant contribution to the area of user interaction in recommender systems, and we plan to expand our research in this area to other domains beyond paper suggestions. We also plan to investigate different ways that users can apply to control and combine the output of several recommendation methods.

Second, results of our questionnaire indicate that end users perceive our interactive visualization. However, it is still an open question what is the impact of *personal characteristics* (such as expertise, and the users' visual processing fit) on the usefulness of our approach, and how different ways to manipulate the interface that the system offers its users might influence user performance and satisfaction.

Finally, users show a better performance finding relevant items – in terms of the number of actions needed to discover relevant items – by foraging for additional evidence. In TalkExplorer, users accomplish that by intersecting the preferred items of several users, items associated with tags, and agent recommendations. This opens research opportunities for studying further the benefits of interactive recommender interfaces in terms of user trust in the systems, transparency and satisfaction.

ACKNOWLEDGMENTS

The authors would like to thank Joris Klerkx for making available the source code of his framework code. In addition, we thank all the participants of the user studies for their participation and useful feedback. Research of Katrien Verbert was supported by postdoctoral fellowship grant of the Research Foundation – Flanders (FWO). The authors would like to thank the anonymous reviewers for their valuable feedback and suggestions.

REFERENCES

1. Aduna clustermap. http://www.aduna-software.com/technology/clustermap

2. Baeza-Yates, R.A. and Ribeiro-Neto, B. Modern Information Retrieval. Addison-Wesley Longman Publishing Co., Inc., Boston, MA, 1999
3. Bennett, J. and Lanning, S. The Netflix Prize. *Communications of the ACM*, 52, 10 (2007), 8 pages. Citeseer.
4. Blei, D.M., Ng, A.Y. and Jordan, M.I. Latent dirichlet allocation. *The Journal of Machine Learning Research*, 3, (2003), 993-1022
5. Bostandjiev, S., O'Donovan, J. and Höllerer, T. TasteWeights: a visual interactive hybrid recommender system. In *Proceedings of the sixth ACM conference on Recommender systems* (RecSys '12). ACM, New York, NY, USA (2012), 35-42.
6. Burke, R. Hybrid Recommender Systems: Survey and Experiments. *User Modeling and User Adapted Interaction*, 12, 4 (2002), 331–370.
7. Burke, R. Evaluating the dynamic properties of recommendation algorithms. In *Proceedings of RecSys10: fourth ACM conference on Recommender systems*, ACM Press New York, NY, USA (2010), 225–228.
8. Camtasia Studio: http://www.techsmith.com/camtasia.html
9. Chuah M. Dynamic aggregation with circular visual designs. In *Proceedings of the IEEE Symposium on Information Visualization* (1998), 35–43
10. Gretarsson, B., O'Donovan, J., Bostandjiev, S., Hall, C. and Höllerer, T. SmallWorlds: Visualizing Social Recommendations. *Comput. Graph. Forum*, 29, 3 (2010), 833-842.
11. Gou, L., You, F., Guo, J., Wu, L. and Zhang, X. SFViz: interest-based friends exploration and recommendation in social networks. In *Proceedings of the 2011 Visual Information Communication - International Symposium* (VINCI '11). ACM, New York, NY, USA (2011), 10 pages.
12. Herlocker, J.L., Konstan, J.A. and Riedl, J. Explaining collaborative filtering recommendations. In *Proceedings of CSCW00: ACM conference on Computer supported cooperative work*, ACM Press (2000), 241–250
13. Herlocker, J.L., Konstan, J.A., Terveen, L.G. and Riedl, J.T. Evaluating collaborative filtering recommender systems. *ACM Trans. Inf. Syst.*, 22, 1 (2004), 5–53.
14. Hu, Y., Koren, Y. and Volinsky, C. Collaborative filtering for implicit feedback datasets. In *Proceedings of the 2008 Eighth IEEE International Conference on Data Mining.* IEEE Computer Society, Washington, DC (2008), 263–272.
15. Kammerer, Y., Nairn, R., Pirolli, P. and Chi, E. H. (2009). Signpost from the masses: learning effects in an exploratory social tag search browser. In *Proceedings of the SIGCHI Conference on Human Factors in Computing Systems* (CHI '09). ACM, New York, NY, USA (2009) 625-634.
16. Klerkx, J. and Duval, E. Visualising social bookmarks. *Journal Of Digital Information*, 10, 2 (2009), 40 pages. Multimedia Research Group, U. of Southampton.
17. Knijnenburg, B.P., Reijmer, N.J.M. and Willemsen, M.C. Each to his own: how different users call for different interaction methods in recommender systems. In *Proceedings of the fifth ACM conference on Recommender systems* (RecSys '11). ACM (2011), 141-148.
18. Knijnenburg, B.P., Bostandjiev, S., O'Donovan, J. and Kobsa, A. Inspectability and control in social recommenders. In *Proceedings of the sixth ACM conference on Recommender systems* (RecSys '12). ACM, New York, NY, USA (2012), 43-50.
19. Linden, G., Smith, B. and York, J. Amazon.com recommendations: item-to-item collaborative filtering. *IEEE Internet Computing*, 7, 1 (Jan/Feb 2003), 76-80.
20. Manning, C.D., Raghavan, P. and Schtze, H. Introduction to Information Retrieval, Cambridge University Press, New York, NY, 2008
21. Morita, M. and Shinoda, Y. Information Filtering Based on User Behavior Analysis and Best Match Text Retrieval. In *SIGIR 1994: Proceedings of the 17th Annual International ACM SIGIR Conference.* Springer-Verlag New York, Inc., New York, NY, USA (1994), 272–281.
22. Nageswara, R.K. and Talwar, V.G. Application domain and functional classification of recommender systems a survey. *DESIDOC Journal of Library and Information Technology*, 28, 3 (2008), 17–35
23. O'Donovan, J., Smyth, B., Gretarsson, B., Bostandjiev, S., and Höllerer, T. PeerChooser: visual interactive recommendation. In *Proceedings of the twenty-sixth conference on Human factors in computing systems* (CHI '08). ACM, NY, USA, 2008, 1085-1088.
24. Parra, D., Jeng, W., Brusilovsky, P., Lopez, C. and Sahebi, S. Conference Navigator 3: An Online Social Conference Support System. Poster at UMAP 2012. Montreal, Canada.
25. Parra, D. and Brusilovsky, P. Collaborative filtering for social tagging systems: an experiment with CiteULike. In *Proceedings of the third ACM conference on Recommender systems* (RecSys '09). ACM, New York, NY, USA (2009), 237-240.
26. Pazzani, M.J. and Billsus, D. Content-Based Recommendation Systems. In P. Brusilovsky, A. Kobsa, and W. Nejdl, editors, *The Adaptive Web*, volume 4321 of LNCS (2007), 325–341. Springer-Verlag, Springer.
27. Riedl, J. and Dourish, P. Introduction to the special section on recommender systems. *ACM Trans. Comput.-Hum. Interact.* 12, 3 (Sept.2005), 371-373.

28. Tintarev, N. and Masthoff, J. Designing and Evaluating Explanations for Recommender Systems. *Recommender Systems Handbook*, (2011), 479-510

29. Tonkin, E., Corrado, E. M., Moulaison, H. L., Kipp, M. E. I., Resmini, A., Pfeiffer, H. D. and Zhang, Q. Collaborative and Social Tagging Networks. *Ariadne*, 54. (2008).

30. Vig, J., Sen, S. and Riedl, J. Tagsplanations: explaining recommendations using tags. In *Proceedings of the 14th international conference on Intelligent user interfaces* (IUI '09). ACM, New York, NY, USA (2009), 47-56.

31. Zhao, S., Zhou, M.X., Yuan, Q., Zhang, X., Zheng, W., and Fu, R. Who is talking about what: social map-based recommendation for content-centric social websites. In *Proceedings of the fourth ACM conference on Recommender systems* (RecSys '10). ACM, New York, NY, USA (2010), 143-150.

Dynamic Text Management for See-through Wearable and Heads-up Display Systems

Jason Orlosky
Osaka University
Osaka, Japan

Kiyoshi Kiyokawa
Osaka University
Osaka, Japan

Haruo Takemura
Osaka University
Osaka, Japan

{orlosky@lab., kiyo@, takemura@} ime.cmc.osaka-u.ac.jp

ABSTRACT

Reading text safely and easily while mobile has been an issue with see-through displays for many years. For example, in order to effectively use optical see through Head Mounted Displays (HMDs) or Heads Up Display (HUD) systems in constantly changing dynamic environments, variables like lighting conditions, human or vehicular obstructions in a user's path, and scene variation must be dealt with effectively.

This paper introduces a new intelligent text management system that actively manages movement of text in a user's field of view. Research to date lacks a method to migrate user-centric content such as e-mail or text messages throughout a user's environment while mobile. Unlike most current annotation and view management systems, we use camera tracking to find dark, uniform regions along the route on which a user is travelling in real time. We then implement methodology to move text from one viable location to the next to maximize readability. A pilot experiment with 19 participants shows that the text placement of our system is preferred to text in fixed location configurations.

Author Keywords

Scene analysis; wearable display; heads up display; content stabilization; text placement; view management

ACM Classification Keywords

H.5.2 User Interfaces: *Theory and methods*

INTRODUCTION

Wearable Computing and Text Overlay

In recent years, the world of mobile computing has seen a drastic increase in the development of wearable display systems. Google's Project Glass, Epson's Moverio, and the Silicon Micro Display are just a few examples of display systems that allow users to view content overlayed onto their immediate environment while mobile. This type of technology has various benefits, such as allowing virtual information to be displayed onto real world objects, giving a simultaneous view of digital content and real world environment, and faster access times to information. Although these devices can be incredibly useful and augment human ability, various studies on technologically induced intersensory conflict, readability, and fatigue show that it is still difficult for users to acclimate to content viewed through see through displays [7, 14, 15]. Secondly, since text is typically viewed in a fixed location on an HMD screen, people, vehicles, and noise in the background of a user's path can interfere with tasks, especially with reading text. Similarly, in vehicle HUD systems, displayed content such as speedometer reading, directions, and map information can interfere with visibility. For example, Figure 1 below shows the most common method for displaying text on an HMD, affixing it to the center of the viewing screen. Interferences such as reflected sunlight, non-uniformity, and color variation all interfere with reading text. This type of hindrance to reading speed has been shown on numerous occasions [5, 10]. In addition to interfering with tasks, digital content that occludes real world objects can pose a threat to a user's safety.

If a user could reach out, grab, and place overlayed text in a desired location, he or she might choose a dark or uniform surface where cars and pedestrians are unlikely to interfere. So, we sought to answer the question: How should content that is overlayed onto the real world be moved through one's environment? More specifically, how can text overlay and text movement be automated in real time? When choosing an appropriate region for text in the real world, a large number of factors play a part in that choice, affecting factors like readability, eye fatigue, and ease of use.

Figure 1. Example of an e-mail viewed through an HMD in a dense environment (simulated).

Video see-through displays can alleviate some of these problems by modulating real world images, but cannot solve all the problems completely, and are not ideal for all applications. On the other hand, optical see-through displays are often more suitable for vehicles or military applications for example, but have larger problems with readability due to luminance and inability to modulate or manipulate the background image. Because of these difficulties, the effects of background surface, lighting conditions, and other environmental interactions have been well studied [5, 10]. However, the continued moving of content, such as e-mail and messaging, through one's environment have been largely overlooked, especially when users are mobile. In order to provide a new foundation for managing dynamic content and improve the usability of optical see-through HMD and HUD systems, we implemented an intelligent text management system that allows user centric text to move along a user's path in real-time.

PREVIOUS WORK

Related research primarily focuses on two areas:
1) Studying and improving readability of text in AR and 2) view management and layout of annotations in both real-world augmented and virtually submersed environments.

Readability Studies

A variety of studies are available on text readability in mixed AR literature, many of which focus on the relationship between text color and background [5, 8, 10]. In order for text to be readable, the user should be able to clearly view text against various scenery and lighting conditions. In 2004, Leykin et. al. used a pattern recognition approach to detect readable surfaces on static images using training data [10]. They used mean intensities of the text compared to the surrounding region to determine whether an area is readable or unreadable as well as a rating scale for readability. Their method was assessed as suitable for video see-through displays and suggest that their technique is suitable for view management systems.

Gabbard et al. later conducted a study using an optical see-through display to determine optimal readability for various surfaces such as brick, foliage, and pavement [5]. Billboard configurations were also tested; for example, instead of using the environment as a background, a single color "billboard" was displayed through the HMD that functioned as a background, and text was displayed as if pasted onto the billboard. Participants sat still while gazing at a particular text style and background and times for reading text strings showed that green text and billboard drawing styles resulted in the fastest responses for readability. Therefore, we chose bright green text for use in our method and attempted to fit text to areas that effectively function as billboards, which will be described in more detail later. Many other studies focus on text readability, but only do so in submersive virtual environments such as games, video, and 3D simulations. Although they provide useful insights about how to manage text in a simulated environment, they are not as relevant to real-world and mixed-AR applications.

Annotation and View Management

This area of study focuses on how to display annotations, labels, and descriptive information in AR. Studies conducted in simulated 3D environments are more relevant in this case because management algorithms and strategies are less dependent on whether the environment is real or simulated.

The most recent and closest work to ours is likely the annotation placement method developed by Makita et. al. In 2009 [13]. Via camera, this method estimates where annotations should appear by detecting humans located in real-world indoor environments, and subsequently places an annotation such as a name or image over an individual's body. The algorithm is penalty based, giving stronger likelihood to higher body locations such as the head or torso. It is implemented in real time, but does not take into account scene background or complexity for readability.

Prior to Makita, a more comprehensive work on view management was conducted by Bell et. al. using a see-through optical display [2]. They developed an algorithm to manage large numbers of building descriptions, images, and other annotative information that would otherwise overlap or clutter the viewing screen. By taking into account temporal continuity, occlusion, and screen constraints, the method arranged annotations in real time to maximize visibility. Like many other annotation methods, the algorithm is considered to be "greedy," is non-optimal, and like Makita et. al., does not take into account scene background for text readability [1].

Other information management frameworks include more specific methods and classifiers for managing annotations in environments where space and screen limitations are present. Most of these methods are designed for gaming, advertising, labeling of individual parts of 3D objects, and other label placement [12, 13, 19, 20].

Environment Centric vs. User Centric Information

Before continuing, it is important to make the distinction between "environment centric" and "user centric" information presented to the user when using a see-through display. Similar classifiers exist that provide guidelines for annotation permanence [20] and whether head, body, or world are better locations for workspaces [3]. We present a new classification that is useful when determining whether content should be permanently fixed to an object in the environment or whether it should travel with the user. Though some types of information fall in both categories, the distinction is often easy to make.

Environment Centric

The primary feature of this type of information is that it has a strong relationship between content and environment location. Examples include building descriptions, landmark information, billboard advertisements, and a majority of object annotations. The nature of this type of information is local to the object in the environment. For example, when displaying the name of a building, the information is most useful if affixed to the building itself. There is little need to move the information from its static, world-relative location to a new point in the user's field of view. A majority of current text placement research focuses on annotative and environment centric content [2, 12, 18, 19].

User Centric

In this case, there is a much stronger relationship between content and user. In e-mail, for example, the purpose of interaction is communication, and content is location independent since an e-mail can be received and read from anywhere there is a wireless connection and access terminal. The location of text in the environment is irrelevant to the meaning of the conversation between users, so it makes little sense to establish a permanent location for the e-mail. Other examples of this type of information include social networking feeds, weather information, interactive maps, speedometer readings, and non-annotative text. To date, placement and movement of user-centric information in real world environments has not been well addressed.

Further Motivation

Several of the studies mentioned above suggest that the frameworks proposed could be used as part of an active management system [5, 10]. Some active management systems exist, but only make attempts at managing annotations and text affixed to certain objects in the world [12, 19]. The question of how to appropriately manage and move user-centric text still remains unanswered. Furthermore, algorithms for detecting readable areas exist, but are not always implemented in real time, do not find the best area for readability, and provide no methodology for moving text from one readable area to the next [2, 13, 19].

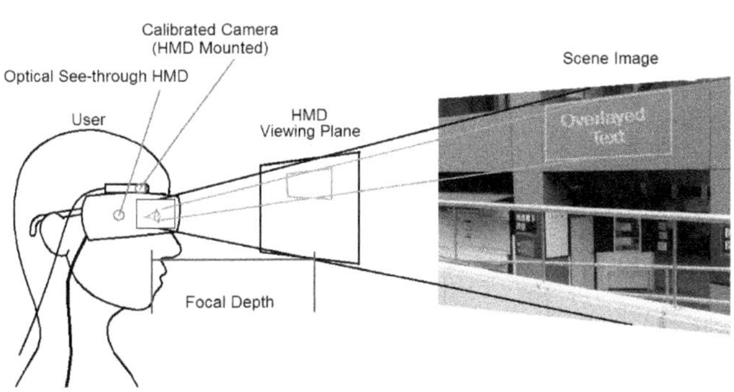

Figure 2. HMD, mounted camera, focal plane, and background image with overlayed text.

FRAMEWORK AND ALGORITHM FUNDAMENTALS

Overview

Keeping the previously mentioned challenges in mind, we designed our system to address them in several different phases. First, the system recognizes viable (dark, uniform) text locations in the real world using camera analysis. This analysis takes methods like Makita et. al.'s a step further since it can be used in any environment without prior knowledge of the scene [13]. It then affixes text to the most viable area, rotates the text to a stable orientation, and repeats this process from frame to frame. When a viable area becomes non-viable or leaves the user's field of view, the system moves text to a new area, maximizing the window of time in which the text is most viewable, and at the same time avoiding environmental interference. In each of the following subsections, we will describe the theory behind the framework as well as the details of how each component was implemented.

Selecting Viable Regions for Text

The first step in our framework is to find an appropriate location for text. Though many factors were taken into account, we primarily focused on detecting two scene features, darkness and uniformity, to find the best location.

As Gabbard et. al. and Leykin et. al. both showed, lighter text on a dark, uniform background is one of the more visible display styles [5, 10]. Out of light text colors, bright green (#00FF00) was chosen due to its contrast with colors of a majority of man-made structures, predominantly gray. Though placing dark text on a white background is also a highly readable display style, it is not currently feasible with see-through displays because of their inability to reproduce black due to transparency. White "billboards" also result in frequent occlusion of other scene objects and decreased visibility, so we opted for placing bright green text over dark backgrounds as shown in figure 2. Though bright green works in many environments, complement colors should also be considered, especially in environments with dense foliage or greenery. Because active modulation of text color is a relatively complex problem for dynamic environments, implementing a complement color based algorithm is not included in this paper, though we do plan to address it in later works. Lastly, based on a study conducted by Scharff et. al. in 1999, text size was not determine to have a significant effect on readability, so an appropriate text size should be selected based on viewing distance and the dimensions of the HMD or HUD screen [17].

In essence, our method finds dark, uniform rectangular regions that resemble black billboards and then applies a best fit algorithm based on the dimensions of displayed text or content, which are both parametrized. To display e-mails or short messaging content, 8-10 pixel wide characters are used, resulting in between 40 and 55 characters per line.

Figure 3. Heatmap showing viability in red where: redder = more viable and where the best point is colored bright green.

Required angular height and width of the dark areas in the camera image are calculated based on the focal distance of the HMD viewing plane shown in figure 2. Though selecting only dark regions or only uniform regions to display text is a valid method for finding readable areas, evenly weighting darkness and uniformity results in a larger number of unique regions in the scene to display text. A viability rating for darkness and uniformity is calculated at every point in the image, and a best *x,y* position is selected after rating all points in the image. We first calculate an average pixel intensity for the whole image, then, to rate a single point in the image, we use all pixels in the rectangle surrounding that pixel, sum grayscale intensities to calculate darkness, and take the standard deviation to determine uniformity. Rectangle size is determined by the dimensions of desired text. See figure 3 for the resulting heatmap showing good points in a sample image (black = less viable, redder = more viable) and the best point in the image (bright green square). Text is then redrawn on the HMD viewing plane in a position calculated from and centered around the previously selected best point in the real world. Because humans and automobiles are not typically dark, uniform surfaces, this method also functions similarly to an object avoidance algorithm in addition to maximizing readability.

Algorithm

```
WHILE camera is on
  CALCULATE average pixel intensity for current frame
  FOR each pixel in the current frame
    FOR all pixels in desired text display area (rectangular)
      CALCULATE relative darkness-to-intensity metric
      CALCULATE uniformity (standard deviation)
      IF darkness + uniformity > previous viability rating
        THEN current pixel is new best point ENDIF
    ENDFOR
  ENDFOR
  REDRAW text on new best point
ENDWHILE
```

Content Movement

Because ideal regions for text often change significantly from frame to frame due to changing lighting conditions, text would sporadically alternate locations in the user's field of view if moved to a better ideal region every time. This type of movement is difficult for the eye to follow, so to maximize readability, we developed and incorporated a decision making algorithm that determines when and how to migrate text to a new location.

We use two primary schemata: 1) Move text directly to the next ideal location if the change in ideal location is only due to camera movement, and 2) only move to new, distant locations in the environment if the current location has become much worse than the new one. The results of these schemata are that 1) text remains in the same region in the environment despite a user's normal head movement, and 2) text is migrated to new viable regions in the environment only when the current region has become non-viable when compared to the new region. The difference between head movement and changing of viable location is computed via a predetermined threshold value. One more attribute is a running average of the last n positions, resulting in a smoothing effect when migrating text to a new region.

Algorithm

```
CALCULATE expected maximum head movement
CALCULATE expected minimum distance for a change in
viable locations in the environment (non-head movement)
SET thresh to a pixel value between the above calculations
WHILE selecting a new point
  IF distance to new best point < thresh
  THEN Current best point is new best point ENDIF
  IF distance to new best point > thresh AND
    new viability rating of best point /
    scaled distance to new best point
    > viability rating of old best point
    THEN Current best point is new best point ENDIF
ENDWHILE
```

Text Orientation and Stability

Finally, in order to relieve technologically induced intersensory conflict, we built stabilization into our method. This means that we rotate text to an angle aligned with objects in the scene or to other features in the environment. This is most applicable to HMD screens since text is typically screen stabilized (fixed to the user's head position), which results in a disparity between real world and augmented information. Real world billboards or signs do not move synchronously with a user's head, so in order to counteract this disparity, we present two methods to align text with the environment and categorize situations in which each method is appropriate. Text is stabilized in 2D based on a study by Chen et. al. that shows text overlayed in 2D HUD configurations is more readable, especially in dense or crowded environments [4].

Gravity-stable

Gravity-stable means that text is always aligned perpendicular to earth's gravitational field and is also referred to as world-stable [3]. Since this method can be accomplished with accelerometers, it is appropriate for noisy environments where scene analysis may be difficult or when a user's or vehicle's movement in the vertical plane is smooth. If a user is walking quickly or is in an environment where sporadic movements are necessary, noisy acceleration readings can result in poor stabilization.

Region-stable

A new method for stabilization and one of the contributions of this paper is region-stable alignment, which means that text is aligned to the surface or surrounding surfaces on which text is overlayed. From a user's point of view, man made surfaces do not always appear to be aligned with gravity. In figure 1, for example, though the HMD screen is roughly aligned with gravity, buildings that are also aligned with gravity appear to be at an angle in the image. If text is aligned over the buildings, it should be aligned parallel to the structure's apparent orientation rather than to gravity. Aligning to a single surface does not necessarily result in the best stabilization since angles of 3D objects can vary greatly within a small area. Stabilizing to the surface of an object also requires prior knowledge of 3D scene geometry. With our method, we can calculate a metric for region-stability that does not require this prior knowledge.

To find alignment of the region in the user's field of view, we start by extracting all detectable lines in the current frame using Hough's pattern detection algorithm [6], weighting their respective angles according to line length, and calculating an average angle for the entire viewing region. The image in figure 4 shows detected lines and stabilized text. Because lines in man made structures (buildings, walls, street lines, windows, etc.) are often longer and straighter than natural lines (branches, clouds, body parts, etc.), weighting longer lines more heavily in the angle calculation results in better stabilization. Text is then rotated to the resulting angle for each frame.

Algorithm

STORE all detected lines from image in an array
FOR all lines in array
  CALCULATE line angle and length
  Compensate for the fact that detected horizontal lines are perpendicular to real world gravity
  UPDATE average weighted angle with current angle value with weight based on line length
ENDFOR
Rotate text to average weighted angle of all lines

Sparse sampling for efficiency

The device for which this algorithm is most useful is likely a head mounted display with a built-in camera. Since HMD input devices are typically small and constricted by low processing power, we also developed a way to use the above algorithms with sparse sampling. Instead of rating the region around every single pixel for darkness and uniformity, every n^{th} pixel can be sampled for similar results. For example, when a 250 x 200 pixel area for text is desired, sampling every 5th pixel for both x and y would still result in a sample size of 50 x 40 (2000 pixels per rectangle), more than enough to calculate ratings for both darkness and uniformity. This means that our method can easily be scaled for smaller devices with limited capability.

Figure 4. Lines detected by the Hough lines algorithm and resulting stabilized text.

EXPERIMENTAL EVALUATION

In order to provide an initial evaluation of our method, we sought to determine whether the system will pick similar regions to a human when choosing locations for text and to see if those locations are preferred to fixed location configurations. To test this, we set up a pilot experiment where participants picked a region of an image which they thought was most appropriate for text. From each participant's selections, we could then compare how close their selections were to the selections of our system. We would also be able to compare whether our system was better at selecting a location for text than if left at a fixed position on the image, centered for example. Although this type of experiment is not adequate to test system usability in general situations, it gives us a basic comparison of the algorithm's selections and human decisions.

Setup

The experiment included 19 participants, ranging from age 19 to 67, with an approximately even number of males and females. Participants were asked to view a set of 20 images with the same 25x25 matrix of bright green character strings (A1 to Y25) overlayed onto each image as shown in figure 5. All images were 1024x768 pixels in resolution and viewed on participants' personal computer monitors. Spacing was set at 30 and 37 pixels between vertical and horizontal character strings, respectively.

Figure 5. Segment of an image overlayed with green character strings.

Images were chosen prior to applying the algorithm to avoid bias, so we did not know what region the system would select or what region users would pick in advance. We sent a web based questionnaire to each participant that contained all 20 images. They were then asked to enter the character string corresponding to the most appropriate region for text in each image, and took as much time as they wished. Though conducting the experiment in various outdoor and indoor locations with both HMD and HUD systems would be more appropriate to evaluate usability, we first sought to conduct a simple comparison of human and system choices. Using images allowed us to test the algorithm independent of device and let us pick geographically dispersed locations as well as a large number of backgrounds. Though aspect ratios and color variations of monitors differ, the effects were considered negligible since all images viewed by the same user were viewed on the same monitor.

Results

To show whether our system selected similar text regions as the human participants, we first plotted both user selected and system selected points for each image as shown in figure 6.

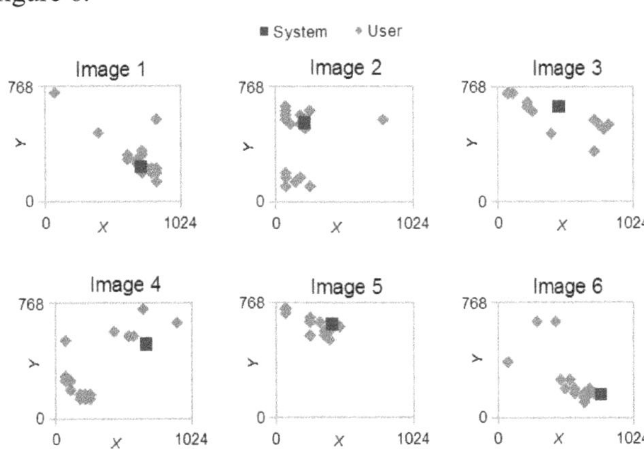

Figure 6: Plots of user selected points and system selected points for 6 of the 20 experiment images.

User selections are orange diamonds and system selections are blue squares. *X* and *Y* coordinates of each plot correspond to the *x* and *y* coordinates of each image in the experiment. Next, we calculated the euclidean distance between all 20 user selected points and each system selected point for each image. For example, in figure 6, image 1 has an average euclidean distance of 157 pixels, and image 4 has a distance of 498 pixels. Only the first 6 plots are shown in order to conserve space, but should provide a good visual comparison of user and system selected points. The average euclidean distances for each image are shown in table 1, and the average for all 20 images is 267 pixels.

Image # (bold columns) and average euclidean distance (non-bold columns).							
1	157	**6**	231	**11**	401	**16**	338
2	211	**7**	302	**12**	369	**17**	240
3	324	**8**	303	**13**	129	**18**	253
4	498	**9**	279	**14**	210	**19**	153
5	170	**10**	160	**15**	183	**20**	432

Table 1. Average euclidean distances between all 20 user selected and system selected points for each image.

With these results, we cannot state that our method completely resembles human behavior, however, through qualitative analysis we can make the claim that our system chooses similar regions to a human to a certain degree. For example, in the plot of image 1 in figure 6, it is clear that our system picked a point similar to a majority of user selections. 16 of 19 users chose to place text in the lower right corner of the screen, just like the system did. 10 of those 16 people chose a location within 100 pixels of the system selected location. 6 of those 16 people chose a location within 160 pixels of the system selected location. The remaining 3 people selected a point on a different section of the image that was over 300 pixels away from the system selected location. So, for all images, we show how many user selected points were within 50, 100, 150 and 200 pixel distances of the system selected points from all images, which are listed in table 2.

Euclidean distance to system selected points in pixels	Number of user selected points within that distance (out of 380 points total)
200 pixels	187 points (49.2%)
150 pixels	149 points (39.2%)
100 pixels	105 points (27.6%)
50 pixels	34 points (8.9%)

Table 2. Number and percentage of points selected by the user within various euclidean distances from system selected points.

Points within 50 pixels would be extremely close, whereas over 200 pixels would not be considered close or in the same area. For reference, on a standard 17 inch monitor, 50 diagonal pixels are equivalent to about 0.66 inches (1.5 centimeters).

We then compared our system selections to 5 different fixed view configurations, including upper left (UL), upper right (UR), lower right (LR), lower left (LL), and center (C). Center text was located at the very center of each image, *y* positions of upper and lower texts were at 330 pixels above and below center, and *x* positions of left and right texts were at 250 pixels left and right of center. As a quantitative comparison, we showed the average euclidean distance between all configurations and user selected points, and conducted a one way analysis of variance (ANOVA) for the system vs. each fixed view configuration as shown in table 3. Images were established as the control, and system, UL, UR, LR, LL, and C were independent variables, allowing for a pairwise comparison of our system to each fixed view configuration. The results of F show a strong effect between euclidean distances of system selected points and and all fixed configuration locations.

Average of euclidean distances between all user selected points in all 20 images and:		ANOVA for system vs. fixed configurations	
System Selected	267 pixels	$F_{1,18}$	P
LR Fixed	557 pixels	50.6	< .01
LL Fixed	477 pixels	23.5	< .01
UL Fixed	423 pixels	15.5	< .01
UR Fixed	511 pixels	55.1	< .01
C Fixed	342 pixels	12.4	< .01

Table 3. Table showing average euclidean distances between each configuration and participant selected points across all images (left) and pairwise ANOVA results between system and fixed configurations (right).

Since the averages of system selected locations were closer to any of the fixed selections and since an effect was shown for each pairwise comparison, we can conclude that locations selected by our system are preferred to locations permanently fixed to points on the presented images.

Other considerations

One important point to note is that several images had several good (though not ideal) points that were selected by users. For example, a majority of user selections in figure 6, image 2, are grouped in two areas, the upper left and lower left side of the image. Our algorithm picked the location nearest to the majority of user selections in the upper left corner, however, this is not reflected when taking the average euclidean distance between all 20 user points and the system selected point.

Secondly, though the experiment we conducted is adequate to show the basic effectiveness of our algorithm, an experiment using see-through optical HMD and or HUD systems would be necessary to fully measure usability. Experiments testing distraction, fatigue, and virtual simulation sickness also deserve further testing.

DISCUSSION

While our suggested methods provide a basic framework for moving and stabilizing an overlayed text throughout the real world, they are by no means comprehensive. However, we believe problems with more complex environments can be solved with feature tracking, object detection, or other context analysis algorithms. Especially when attempting to manage user-centric text, our methods provide a good foundation.

Interaction With Text and Content

Although our algorithm deals mostly with the viewing of text, users still need methods for interaction. At the very least, a user should be able to scroll through text and transition between windows or programs. Though camera tracking of finger and hand are possible for gesture recognition, a method that is likely more simple and intuitive is to give the user a wireless touch based surface to interact with. Using a touch-screen phone, belt-worn touch pad, or touch screen watch will allow click, scroll, and relative pointing and would not require constant visual contact.

In addition to scrolling through text or window management, there are also a variety of input methods that not only allow users to enter text while walking but do not require the user to maintain constant eye contact with the input device. Devices such as the AlphaGrip, Torso Keyboard, Gestyboard, Twiddler, and voice recognition do not need constant visual contact like a software keyboard would [9, 11, 16].

Dealing with scene complexity

As scene/lighting complexity increase, more specific methods for dealing with variation become necessary. In addition to the software solutions we mentioned before like feature tracking, there are several methods appropriate for dealing with some of these complexity challenges.

For example, in noisy images where there may be many small viable regions instead of several large ones, text can be scaled down in size or broken up into smaller bits. Twitter feeds or text messages could be placed throughout the environment in a logical manner much like signs are placed on either side of a street.

Lastly, for wide field of view applications, a fish-eye lens could be affixed to the camera to increase the area of analysis. In this case, instead of moving text to new regions on the HMD when previous regions leave the viewing screen, an indicator could be used to show the direction of off-screen text or other content, especially for mobile workspaces [3]. Messages, feeds, and miscellaneous smaller notifications would be ideal for this type of display.

FUTURE WORK

As future work, we plan to improve our system by developing a learning algorithm that adapts region selection methodology based on user selected areas. Much like using training data, a learning algorithm would not only make our method more effective, but allow for automated customization based on individual users.

We also plan to implement fast feature tracking in order to improve our stabilization method as well as expand methodology for moving text through the environment.

CONCLUSION

In this paper, we improve upon previous methods for displaying text in AR, combine those methods into a single framework, and implement a scalable system for managing text that can run in real time. The system allows text viewed through an HMD to move with the user as the user travels throughout various environments and maximizes times where text is viewable by finding dark, uniform regions. This method can serve as a foundation for managing user-centric text and provide useful insights for other content or view management research.

ACKNOWLEDGMENTS

Many thanks to family, friends, and mentors for their help and support. This research was funded in part by Grant-in-Aid for Scientific Research (B), #22300043 from Japan Society for the Promotion of Science (JSPS), Japan.

REFERENCES

1. Azuma, R., and Furmanski, C. Evaluating label placement for augmented reality view management. In *Proc. ISMAR 2003.* 66-75.
2. Bell, B., Feiner, S., and Höllerer., T., View Management for Virtual and Augmented Reality. *Proc. UIST 2001.* 101–110.
3. Billinghurst, M., Bowskill, J., Jessop, M., Morphett, J. A Wearable Spatial Conferencing Space. *Proc. ISWC 1998.* 76-93.
4. Chen, J. Testbed Evaluation of Navigation and Text Display Techniques in an Information-Rich Virtual Environment. *Proc. VR 2004.* 181-289.
5. Gabbard, JL., Swan II, Hix, D., Schulman, RS., Lucas, J., Gupta, D. "An Empirical User-Based Study of Text Drawing Style and Outdoor Background Textures for Augmented Reality", Technical Papers, *IEEE Virtual Reality 2005.* 11–18.
6. Hough, P.V.C. "Methods and means for recognizing complex patterns," U.S. Patent 3 069 654, 1962.
7. Huckauf, A., Urbina, M. H., Böckelmann, I., Schega, L., Mecke, R., Grubert, J., Doil, F., Tümler, J. Perceptual issues in optical-see-through displays. *Proc. APGV 2010*, 41-48.
8. Jankowski, J., Samp, K., Irzynska, I., Jozwowicz, M., Decker, S. Integrating Text with Video and 3D Graphics: The Effects of Text Drawing Styles on Text Readability. *Proc. CHI 2010,* 1321-1330.
9. Koskun, T., Artinger, E., Pirritano, L. Gestyboard: A 10-finger-system and gesture based text input system for multi-touchscreens with no need for tactile feedback. *Proc. APCHI 2012.*
10. Leykin, A., and Tuceryan, M. Automatic Determination of Text Readability over Textured Backgrounds for Augmented Reality Systems. *Proc. ISMAR 2004,* 224-230.
11. Lyons, K., Starner, T., Plaisted, D., Fusia, J., Lyons, A., Drew, A., and Looney, E. W. Twiddler typing: one handed chording text entry for mobile phones. *Proc. CHI 2004.* 671-678.
12. Maass, S., Döllner, J. Dynamic Annotation of Interactive Environments using Object-Integrated Billboards. *Proc. WSCG 2006.* 327-334.
13. Makita, K., Kanbara, M., and Yokaya, N., View Management of Annotations for Wearable Augmented Reality. *Proc. ICME 2009*, 982-985.
14. Mon-Williams, M., Wann, J.P., and Rushton, S. "Binocular Vision in a Virtual World: Visual Deficits Following the Wearing of a Head-Mounted Display," Ophthalmic and Physiological Optics, vol. 13, no. 4, 1993, 387-391.
15. Nelson, T.W., Roe, M., Bolia, R., Morley, R. Assessing Simulator Sickness in a See-through HMD. *Proc. Image 2000 Conference.* Scottsdale, Arizona 10-14 July 2000.
16. Orlosky, J. Katzakis, N. Kiyokawa, K. Takemura, H. Torso Keyboard: A Wearable Text Entry Device That Can Be Used While Sitting, Standing or Walking. *Proc. APCHI 2012*, 781-782.
17. Scharff, L. , Ahumada, A. J., and Hill, A. Discriminability Measures for Predicting Readability, Human Vision and Electronic Imaging IV, *Proc. SPIE 1999,* 270-277.
18. Tanaka, K., Kishino, Y., Miyamae, M. , Terada, T., and Nishio, S. An information layout method for an optical see-through head mounted display focusing on the viewability. *Proc. ISMAR 2008.* 139–142.
19. Thanedar, V., Hollerer, T. Semi-automated Placement of Annotations in Videos. Technical Report #2004-11, UC, Santa Barbara 2004.
20. Wither, J., DiVerdi, S., Hollerer, T. "Annotation in outdoor augmented reality." Computers & Graphics Volume 33, Number 6, December 2009. 679–689.

Team Reactions to Voiced Agent Instructions in a Pervasive Game

Stuart Moran, Nadia Pantidi, Khaled Bachour
Joel E. Fischer, Martin Flintham, Tom Rodden
Mixed Reality Lab
University of Nottingham, UK
{firstname.surname}@nottingham.ac.uk

Simon Evans and Simon Johnson
SlingShot
Bristol, UK
{firstname.surname}@slingshoteffect.co.uk

ABSTRACT
The assumed role of humans as controllers and instructors of machines is changing. As systems become more complex and incomprehensible to humans, it will be increasingly necessary for us to place confidence in intelligent interfaces and follow their instructions and recommendations. This type of relationship becomes particularly intricate when we consider significant numbers of humans and agents working together in collectives. While instruction-based interfaces and agents already exist, our understanding of them within the field of Human-Computer Interaction is still limited.

As such, we developed a large-scale pervasive game called 'Cargo', where a semi-autonomous ruled-based agent distributes a number of text-to-speech instructions to multiple teams of players via their mobile phone as an interface. We describe how people received, negotiated and acted upon the instructions in the game both individually and as a team and how players initial plans and expectations shaped their understanding of the instructions.

Author Keywords
Human-agent interaction; in situ; instructions; pervasive games

ACM Classification Keywords
H.5.2 [Information Interfaces and Presentation]: User Interfaces - Interaction styles.

INTRODUCTION
Intelligent interfaces continue to revolutionize the relationship between humans and computers. A product of this is that the default and comfortable position of users instructing and controlling computers is changing. As we continue to offload complex tasks and responsibility to machines, we will more frequently experience systems and interfaces that deliver instructions for *us* to follow. This role reversal becomes increasingly important in highly complex, dynamic and demanding time critical circumstances such as disaster response. Such complexity will require groups of humans and intelligent interfaces to *seamlessly* exchange instructions in order to effectively co-operate. While expert, diagnostic, support and recommender systems have been successfully deployed for some time, to date, exploring and understanding the instruction of users in HCI is still limited [26]. Without this understanding, agent based instruction systems may function inefficiently, or at worst, fail to achieve compliance from humans. This would be of particular consequence in safety/time critical systems.

In light of this, our goal in this paper is to probe a number of issues centered on how people respond to instructions from a semi-autonomous agent-based system. In particular, we are interested in investigating:

- How do people make sense of unstructured or ambiguous information from a software agent?
- How do groups of people work together while under agent instruction?
- What makes people trust instructions, and what might cause them to not comply?

To explore these issues, we have developed a large-scale, 'in the wild' pervasive game called Cargo. Within the game, a semi-autonomous rule-based agent distributes a number of voice instructions to multiple teams of players via their mobile phones as an interface. This approach allowed us to study the visceral reactions and interactions of a large number of human teams receiving instructions in situ, in real time and under pressure. The results highlight the process by which players interpret instructions, negotiate their meanings, as well as how these are intertwined with the relationship between the players and the agent. We conclude the paper with a number of emerging design recommendations to consider when creating agent systems which instruct teams of humans.

BACKGROUND
Within the field of Human-Computer Interaction, there is a wide range of literature on the interaction between humans and agents. However the tendency is to focus on a one-to-one relationship. The functionality and practical application of such collaboration is limited to specific types of problems and tasks. When we begin to consider increasingly large-scale complex environments and challenges, such relationships start to lose value. Hence, one growing field of research in human-agent interaction is

the exploration of significant numbers of individual agents and humans acting in human-agent collectives (HACs).

Human Agent Collectives

HACs will have the ability to help solve, support and/or manage extremely dynamic and time-constrained tasks and problems that humans cannot easily complete alone. One clear example of how such collectives might work is in disaster response [10], where agents could assist in data collection in inaccessible areas (e.g. scouting aerial drones), and decision-making (e.g. knowledge of the 'bigger' picture that may be incomprehensible to humans). The means by which the interaction takes place in HACs is a vital issue, and intelligent user interfaces are important in facilitating human-agent co-operation and teamwork [20,25]. In situations such as these, an inherent part of this teamwork is the exchange of instructions as part of an on-going communication [21].

Agents as Instructors

For successful co-operation with agents, humans need to be open to being directed [25], and able to engage with agents at a peer level [15]. As such, it is important to understand the different roles and relationships between humans and agents in HACs. Agents are capable of managing complex information that would overwhelm humans [1], and giving them the role of the instructor is ideal. This places the agent as an intelligent interface between the humans and the complex information they need to complete their task. For example, there is a large body of work on the ways agents have been used to support collaborative workplaces such as in the management of emergencies [23] and damage control [4]. Agents can also take on more formal advisory roles such as 'doctors', assisting patients and medical staff in diagnoses [5,8], or as a personal tutor [13].

While this prior work is interesting, it can be argued that instructing is not necessarily the primary function of many agents: they simply explain concepts, diagnose problems or provide recommendations. This raises the question, what would it mean for a human to receive direct and specific instructions from an agent, as opposed to passive recommendations? Moreover, how might this play-out in teams of humans, with different views and perceptions?

Instructing Teams

In human-agent teamwork, it is important that agents are viewed as proactive *'team players'* [6] [28] and not simply as 'puppets' [27]. In their role as an instructor, agents will need to make decisions and be capable of dealing with issues of authority, responsibility, coordinated actions and group decisions [27]. There are a variety of examples where software agents directly instruct teams, including control rooms [18], flight decks [12] and command-and-control situations [16]. While the interaction between human and agents in these systems is readily established, the ways humans *interpret* and *negotiate* instructions can affect the way they are carried out.

Interpreting Instructions

While efficiently communicating correct information can help reduce the cognitive burden of interpreting instructions [6], the source can influence the way it is interpreted and evaluated. For example, incomplete or ambiguous information received from an agent may be perceived as unreliable but as credible if from a human [7]. Humans will also react differently depending on the timing of the instruction in relation to the local situation [19]. Although, reactions to instructions are not based purely on the current experience and situation, but are also affected by interactions pre- and post-instructions [9,14].

While interpretations of instructions can differ in many ways, it is the consequences of these interpretations that are ultimately important – the way they are (or not) translated into practical activities [24]. However the post-instruction activities of humans may not always be predictable or expected. As such, an instructing agent needs to be able to adapt its recommendations to a situation as it unfolds. This means relying on a group wide shared understanding of the situation [14][6]. Unfortunately, this understanding might not be the same for all team members [14][28], so negotiation becomes important to the team dynamic.

Negotiating Instructions

Negotiation about the goals and actions of a human-agent team is a key aspect to collaboration, and is enabled by sharing a common frame of reference [27]. The purpose of negotiation is to reduce any discrepancies between the *shared* frame of reference, and the *actual* frame of reference [22], a common source of breakdowns in co-ordination [6]. That is, negotiation enables a team to resolve potential changes to their current state or agreed plan of action. There are different approaches that can be adopted when human-agent teams negotiate, including *debative* and *integrative* negotiation [22]. Debative negotiation initiates when new information is shared which highlights a discrepancy or interference with current activities. However, if this information were to coincide with current activities and was introduced by an individual, then integrative negotiation initiates.

When receiving instructions, teams of humans have been known to make *their own* negotiations. Such negotiations can take place silently where, for example, humans that are experienced at working together have been observed making group decisions without the need to communicate it to an agent [22]. This can be problematic for an agent, as missing information could render any further attempts at instruction or negotiation inappropriate [3]. This demonstrates that *observability*, in addition to *directability*, is essential to the success of co-operative systems [6].

Negotiation is unlikely to occur in safety critical systems, where an agent has a greater appreciation and understanding of the wider situation. Even so, there are examples of agents that will act if their instructions are ignored. For example, a collision agent instructing pilots on maneuvers will take action itself if sufficient time expires and the situation becomes critical [12]. This is often a necessity because the additional cognitive load of interacting with an agent can cause a breakdown in the co-operation under time critical situations [22]. There are also many examples of situations that are free from risk and consequence, which present humans with options for ignoring or misusing instructions. For example, drivers have been known to follow the directions offered by in-car satellite navigation, irrespective of external warnings, such as road signs or unexpected changes in the quality of road. As a result, some drivers have actually driven their cars off-road and directly into rivers as a consequence of their over reliance and confidence in the directions given [29].

The main limitations of studies on agents and instructions are that they are restricted to a small number of individuals and are generally conducted in laboratory conditions or simulations. Furthermore, the critical nature of their purpose adds (necessary) constraints to how freely teams interpret and negotiate the instructions. Hence, to explore systems instructing ***teams of humans*** on a ***larger scale***, ***in situ*** and with ***fewer constraints on actions***, a different approach is needed.

METHOD

Pervasive games are recreational experiences that make use of pervasive technologies such as smart phones, wireless technologies and sensors with the aim of extending the gaming experience into the real world [2]. They are frequently used as a research tool for exploring complex social and technological issues in an engaging way [e.g. disaster response [10]. The primary benefit of pervasive games is the fact that they can be situated, which can lead to improvements in the efficacy of the behavioral observations made [11]. Pervasive games have already been established as a tool for exploring instructions, although limited to a linear experience, and a small number of individuals receiving instructions from human performers [26]. This motivated the development of 'Cargo', and the use of a semi-autonomous rule-based software agent, which automatically sends hundreds of verbal instructions to significant numbers of individuals, distributed in teams.

CARGO

Cargo is a mixed reality street game with elements of treasure hunt and tag. The theme of the game is that a team of six to eight players is trying to help one member (called Cargo) escape the city before being caught by police. Players race against the clock in an attempt to gather enough credits to win the game. In order to collect enough credits, players must visit, or check in, at a number of these game stations scattered around the city. When a player checks in, the station either rewards them with credit or, if the station is "dead", wipes out their credit total. Players need to figure out which stations are dead and which ones are live. They are aided in that by a software agent we call the Instructor, who calls players on their phones with relevant in-game information. In the game rules, the only information given to players regarding the Instructor is the following:

> "You will get calls giving useful information. Using the information from these calls will be vital to your success or failure."

Figure 1. A game station (left) is a computer with an RFID reader and a target where players scan their RFID tags, and a player (right) swipes his ID on the box and awaits feedback.

Implementation

The system is implemented as a server-client architecture. Each game station is a PC running a simple python script that handles player check-ins. A Phidgets [30] RFID reader is attached to each station, as well as a loud speaker to provide direct feedback to the players. The hardware is packaged in a cardboard box with an area on the top marked with a target indicating where the RFID reader is placed. Players have RFID-tagged plastic cards associated with their player profile. Players can then swipe a card on the target area of the cardboard box (see Figure 1), and the station gives audio feedback on whether or not that check-in was successful. The game station sends all check-in data to the main game server where all the game logic is handled. The architecture is represented in Figure 2.

The game server is a Django web application that uses an SQLite engine to store the game state. It provides several views on the game state for online game management such as a player registration page and game-authoring tools for defining what messages players will receive. The web view also allows the remote configuration of game stations, as well as monitoring their status through periodic pings that the stations send back to the server. The game uses a commercial cloud API for making voice calls. The server communicates with the API through HTTP requests to trigger JavaScript code that makes a voice call and uses text-to-speech to read out a personalized message to the player in a continuous loop until the player hangs up.

The Instructor

The Instructor is a semi-autonomous rule-driven software agent that monitors the game state and player check-ins and sends out appropriate instructions. Every time a player checks in, the agent evaluates the game state against a sequence of conditions and takes the appropriate action if any. Figure 3 shows the rules the agent follows when calling players with information

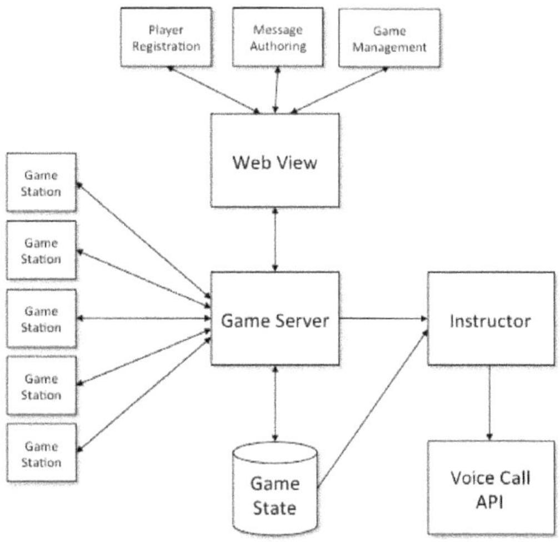

Figure 2. System architecture.

It is important to note that the information the agent provides to the players is always correct. For example, the Instructor never recommends that a player visit a dead game station that would cause them to lose their credits. The highlighted condition in the chart is the most commonly occurring and is one of primary interest to us. It triggers anytime a player checks in at a live station and thus gains credits. If that player had not been instructed to go to a particular station, or if they were checking in at the station she was instructed to go to, she would receive a new recommendation for the next station:

> *"Hi Sally Smith, I heard there are a lot of points to be had at Albion House on Broad Street. It is in your best interests to head there now."*

If however she checked in at a location different from one she was recommended, she would receive a call questioning her trust in the Instructor:

> *"Sally Smith looks like you did not follow my advice about going to The Big Chill on Small Street. Do you not trust me Sally Smith?"*

When multiple players in the same team check in to a location triggering this condition, several of them might receive a recommendation for the next station, and while all recommendations lead them to live stations, the actual stations may differ. Thus players on the same team often receive instructions from the Instructor telling them to go to different locations. The Instructor also tells players not to check in if they are Cargo, when they have enough credit to win the game, and when one player loses their credits. In addition to the automated messages, the game management interface allows Instructor calls to be manually triggered. These include Start and End Game messages.

Event and Deployment

Cargo was developed in collaboration with SlingShot [31] a street game developing company based in a British city to headline on the annual 'interesting games' festival (igFest

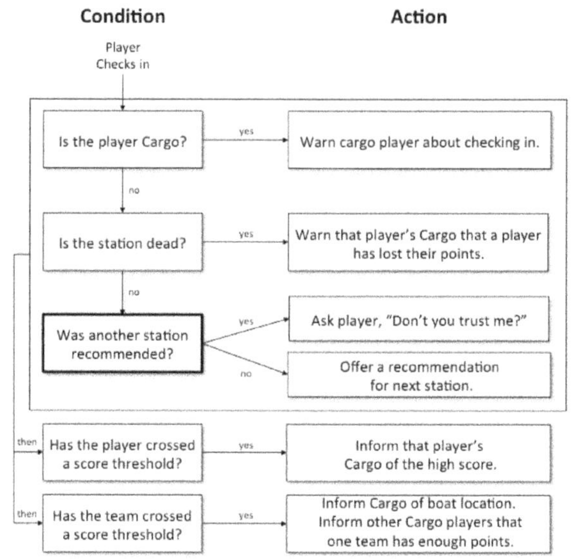

Figure 3. Rule Chart for Instructor.

[32]). A total of 112 players participated in the game (71 players in the first session and 41 in the second). Players purchased tickets priced at 15 British Pounds to participate in the game. For both game sessions, 14 game stations were setup around the city center area resulting in a game area approximately 600 meters long and 300 meters wide. The locations chosen for these stations were varied and included pubs, cafes, bookshops and art galleries.

Players arrived at the festival headquarters approximately half an hour prior to the start of each game and were registered into the system (including their phone numbers) and given game packs that included their RFID card, some game instructions and a map of the game area. They were then asked to go to the center of the game area and await further instructions. Once all teams were ready, a manually triggered call was initiated, and the Instructor simultaneously informed players the game had begun.

Each game lasted one hour, and a total of 1310 Instructor phone calls were made to the players. When a team had collected enough points to win the game, they were given one last call and told to get on a boat that will leave the city at a certain time from a given location. When the game time elapsed, the remaining players were given a similar call directing them to "the losers' boat." Two small ferries were awaiting the players at the end of the game.

During the course of the game, a researcher shadowed each of four teams (two in each session) and filmed their entire game experience. Short semi-structured interviews were conducted and recorded after the game with some players (not only ones that were shadowed). Our findings in the next section are predominately based on the analysis of these video recordings, supported by game logs collected on the server.

FINDINGS

This section describes how people *received, negotiated* and *acted upon the instructions* in the game both *individually* and *as a team*. These descriptions are presented in context i.e. taking into account there were different types of instructing messages; each team had different game play and group dynamics. More specifically, regarding the four teams observed, three of them had quite high cohesion, probably relating to the fact that a number of players knew each other beforehand. The fourth team had comparatively low cohesion and several conflicts emerged during the game. Further, the players' initial plans and expectations, their assumptions regarding the Instructor, as well as the timing and the location instructions were delivered were shown to have shaped the way instructions were understood, negotiated and followed, or not, by the players.

Relating to the Instructor

The way players interpreted and acted upon instructions throughout the game was shaped to a great extent by their perceptions and assumptions regarding the Instructor. How players talked to and about the Instructor; issues relating to its perceived authority and degrees of trust are presented.

Referring and talking to the Instructor

Initial impressions about the phone calls and the Instructor were positive; players were amused while receiving their first phone call; one player commented on the voice and the content: *"It was nice to hear your name recorded in a computerized voice".*

The players answered the phone calls by saying "hello" and answered "yes" when their name was mentioned similar to the way they might respond to an actual person on the other end of the line. However when referring to the Instructor, the players quite often used 'it' (*"see what **it** says..."*; *"wait **it** says I need a new identity"*) or 'they' (*"**they** tried to break us up"*) and less often 'he' (*"**he** knows I changed my identity"*). The use of 'they' was interchangeable as for some players it represented people such as the policemen that were after them and for others it referred to machines or computers. Sometimes when referred to as 'he' or 'they', the Instructor was ascribed human qualities and reactions: *"he is annoyed I didn't follow."*

Authority and Obedience

Throughout the game, the central role of the instructions meant that players assigned authority to the Instructor. Players not only debated or made assumptions about what the Instructor was capable of, mostly regarding penalizing for not following instructions, but also critical milestones of the game such as who the Cargo will be were attributed to the Instructor: *"So is it the Artificial Intelligence that is gonna decide whose name it is (the Cargo)?"*

The authority assigned to the Instructor often triggered dilemmas on obedience. Teams were undecided as to whether they should follow the instructions and how to do so *"let's go to where we were told"*, or whether this was a trick, as part of the game *"What if it is a trap?"* Likewise, players were sometimes torn between following what they were individually advised and what the rest of the team had or was about to decide to do: *"I think I should go to the one he told me."* Players also reported feelings of anxiety following non-compliance to the instructions:

> *"It was quite intimidating ... When we didn't follow its instructions, it rang me and told me off. Made me feel a bit worried."*

In the interviews following the game, one player even related the game with Milgram's well-known experiment on obedience [17]: *"I reckon it was like that voice, that experiment where you were told to shock someone and you listened to the authority."*

Trust

The Instructor's authority was recognized either implicitly or explicitly; however, authority did not coincide with trust. Building up from the first phone call and what followed in the next few stations, players created a *persona*, a stereotypical perception of whether the Instructor was on their side or trying to make them lose the game or just confuse them; and accordingly trust was built or not around the stereotype adopted by the team or individual players.

In the interviews after the game had ended, several players reported trusting the Instructor:

> *"... Because everywhere I went to a place it told me, there were points; I had no reason to not trust"*

However, during the game, when players had to continuously make sense of the information given and the situation, many of them expressed disbelief and mistrust to the Instructor:

> *"P1: Should we try and ignore all messages cause they probably just are trying to pull us apart? P3: Maybe, we don't know yet. P2: I think it is false information"*

> *"So basically the computers are lying to us, that's what's going on. The automated messages are lying."*

For some teams/players, this persona remained stable (usually as a negative one) despite opposing evidence such as being sent to locations with credits; yet for others it was renegotiated throughout the game:

> *"P3:I have never believed it; has anyone believed it here yet? P1:I believe it now. When we went to the rummer, we got points and I had been told from the start (to go there)."*

Receiving instructions

While the content of the phone calls involved both individual and team information, the calls were delivered individually. Upon ringing, players moved away from their team to pick up the call or stayed behind when walking/running. In the teams with high cohesion, players were observed to rejoin the team once the voice message started repeating. They walked towards where the majority of the team was gathered and shared the content of the message with their teammates. On some occasions information was shared with others with a delay. For the less cohesive teams, sharing did not occur, or did so rarely.

Sharing

Players shared the information they received on the phone calls by announcing it to the rest of the team or nearby players. "*I have just got a phone call saying I should go to the Albion Bar on Broad Street.*"

Sharing was manifested by body language during or after receiving the call. Players often drifted away or stayed behind when walking to listen to the phone call for the first time. They would then approach the rest of the team while the message was repeated and shared its content with the rest of the team.

In addition to verbal announcements, sharing instructions also took place by one player sharing the phone with another player or putting the phone on speaker (Figure 3).

Figure 3. Second player on the left is getting instructions on the phone and sharing with her team; at some point she cannot hear what it is said and asks another player to have a listen for her: *"P1:I cant make out…to Dal, to Dalgo Place… (passes the phone to P2 while the message repeats) P2: It says don't you trust him because you didn't go to Photographique (P2 gives the phone back to P1) P1:Oh! Is it Photographique, I cannot hear what they say!"*

Delaying

Sharing often happened in a delayed fashion, usually due to the timing of the instruction. Players received phone calls while already running towards a location or when their teammates were swiping at a station, which made it hard to stop and share the information. Yet in the high cohesion teams, players handled that delay in sharing by stopping at times to coordinate action (described in next section).

Apart from such coincidental delays in sharing, there were occasions that the delay was purposeful and planned. For example, in one team, the Cargo did not immediately openly reveal he was the Cargo. Instead he confided this information gradually and to only two teammates at a time. Between walking to stations, he approached pairs of teammates and in low voice told them he was the Cargo and that they had to be careful as the police were after him. This delay was intended and served the purpose of protecting the Cargo's identity not only from the policemen but also from other teams' players that were in vicinity.

Withholding

Not all players shared their information; withholding mostly occurred in the teams with low cohesion. This was also indicated strongly by body postures during or after the phone call; players turned their backs or moved much further away from the team and stayed there until the end of the phone call (Figure 4).

A few players did not reveal any of the information they received to others in the team even when specifically asked; although most players only partially withheld information. Withholding was more common among the Cargo players and for information that involved teammates potentially having an advantage or disadvantage against others e.g. 'one player in your team has enough points to finish the game on their own.'

Figure 4. Players drifting away and remaining separated from the team while receiving phone calls.

Negotiating instructions

Upon receiving instructions, players negotiated to decide on what to do next. Negotiation involved interpreting the value of the information in terms of its content and its implications for action, which mostly involved consideration of possible consequences from not following instructions. As part of the negotiation, players also developed tactics to deal with the different instructions; and debated to resolve or avoid conflicts when possible.

Interpreting

Players interpreted the instructions based on the content and the intentionality they assigned to the Instructor. In terms of the content, ambiguous information such as the instructions sending players to different locations engaged players into debates about whether instructions should be followed or not and, if so, in what way. Information that related to the credit state (and potential win) of other players or teams were also found to be ambiguous and occasionally led to mistrust between team members.

> *"P4:You know something don't you? C:I don't know anything(...)P4:I think we should ditch the Cargo (laugh)"*

However, most interpretations related to the Instructor and its intentions. As mentioned earlier, as the game unfolded, players developed a character for the Instructor and based on that inferred whether its messages were meant to help them or trick them.

> *"It is (the instructor) a bit too insistent and you are like 'hang on a minute!' are you shanking me?" "The machine is luring us to fake places"*

Mistrust towards the Instructor influenced and was influenced by the team's game play. For example, teams chose not to go to locations where it was guaranteed they would earn credits as a result of not trusting the Instructor. One team even considered not going to the end location after being informed the game was over and they had lost because they thought that was a trick. Equally when a team had decided upon a specific game play such as '*staying together*', all information against their gameplay was considered irrelevant and not trustworthy: "*You know we have all been given different information, so ignore it.*"

Debating over possible consequences

Further, players debated about possible consequences of not following instructions, in particular, during the first few check-ins of the game. After they received the message telling them they did not go to where was suggested and were asked whether they trusted the messages:

> "*I was told off.*" / "*What if there is some kind of penalty if we don't swipe in order?*"

They were concerned whether their disobedience meant they would not get any more calls and as a result; some players insisted strongly that the whole team should go where they were told. In response to such interpretations of consequences and value-based attributions to the messages, teams developed game tactics.

Tactics for dealing with instructions

Interpretation was followed or, more often, closely intertwined with planning and forming game tactics. Depending on what meanings were assigned to the messages, the Instructor and perceived consequences, teams and individuals formed different tactics to deal with the consequences of following instructions or not. For example, if instructions were perceived to be accurate and the Instructor trustworthy, the team dealt with the varying location messages by splitting into smaller groups to go check in at the instructed location and regroup at the next.

With regards to the potential consequences of disobeying the instructions, one team developed a tactic to test what happens to those that follow instructions or not. The tactic involved one player following to the letter what the messages were telling them and the others just checking in any station independently of the messages. Another tactic that was introduced by individual players was to follow the team to the location but do not check in if that was not the instructed location. In this way, players avoided being 'told off' to the next call and resolved the dilemma of whether they were meant to check in stations that they were not told to go: "*I am not going to cash in here because it told me to go somewhere else.*" A similar tactic used at one point but later dropped was to have the player who had received the instruction to the specific location to check in first at that location in the hope that they would earn extra points.

The episode that follows is an example of how one team went about interpreting the instructions, debating over consequences and formed tactics to deal with them:

(Players looking at maps) P1: I am just going to go to the church P2: Ok. P3: Mine is at St Nicholas Market P4: Where? P5: For the first three or four we should just go together P1: Should we go to mine?

P5: The Church, yeah, well just wait for us (some players enter another location) P5: I am not going to cash in here because...P1 they told you to go somewhere else. P5: Yes, right. P4: But I think you need more points (to win the game) P5: Right but it is this idea of following instructions

P4: Ok, ok. (his phone rings) Let see what it says now that I have followed it (moves further away to pick up the phone and soon after returns to the team) guys guys I have got St Stevens now too!

(They all head to St Stevens but the debate continues so they stop in front of the church) (...) P4: why did you get told off for? P1 and P5: For not going to where I was told. P4: You get told off but you still get the points. P5: Yeah but at some point should we not do it cause we are not doing what they are saying...

P4: What about, one person doesn't do what it says, the rest of us kind of do what it says and one person religiously does what they say to even it out? P5: I have done it P6: I haven't P4: so you keep doing it and see what happens.

Resolving conflicts

Conflicts occurred when players, receiving different instructions and with various interpretation of these instructions, needed to agree on their next action. Such conflicts were more common to teams with low cohesion as the players did not know each other and could not easily agree to a single course of action.

Most conflicts arose from the differing information with regards to where players were advised to go next and troubles reconciling individual obedience versus team play: "*We have been sent to different places, so do we go together or do we split up*?"

Several players felt strongly that they had to follow the instructions: *"I think I should go to the one he told me"; "Have to follow the instructions"* and this made it harder for conflicts to be resolved especially in the beginning of the game when the consequences of disobedience were unclear. Withholding information relating to the calls also resulted in conflicts, in particular when members of the team went missing/collecting points without notifying the rest of the team:

> *"P1: Why have you gone off and abandoned us? P2: What? I went off to get some more points. P3: Oh, that's dodgy!"*

When were instructions not followed

A thorough look to the game data reveals instances or circumstances that fostered the likelihood of players not following instructions. The priorities set by the team as part of their game play, the mistrust to the Instructor, group dynamics and cohesion and conditions such as the location and the timing of when the instruction was given all contributed less or more to the likelihood of disobeying instructions.

Gameplay priorities

The gameplay that a team had chosen for itself guided to a great extent how instructions were negotiated. Priorities were set implicitly or explicitly and sometimes this meant some instructions came second. For example, when players perceived '*staying as a team'* as the main goal of the game, this resulted in them ignoring instructions that were suggesting splitting up or individual action to be taken.

> *"P2: Why don't we try and ignore all the messages? They are probably trying to pull us all apart. P3: Maybe. P4: I think it is false information"*

> *"May I remind everyone that among our main priorities is to protect the Cargo?"*

Mistrust to the message and/or the Instructor

As described earlier players interpreted the content of each message and assigned intentionality to the Instructor that was delivering them. When previous instructions had not led to expected successful outcomes (earning credits), it was more likely that future instructions would not be followed. For instance, several teams went to a location they had been instructed expecting to earn more than 100 points which did not happen, so in the future, they ignored other instructions to locations: *"No I didn't trust it cause everything was 100 points"*

Proximity

In the case of instructions to specific locations, the distance between current location and instructed location was found to play a significant role as to whether instructions were followed or not. Specifically, when the instructions were about locations that were not in close proximity to the current location of the team, it was more likely that they were not followed.

> *"P1:The Lanes on Nelson Street . P2: The Lanes. P3: We have just been told to go to the Lanes. P4: I have just been told to go to John Street, but the Lanes are pretty close. P2: Let's go to the Lanes then. P1: The Lanes!"*

Team dynamics

The way the team was socially structured also related to whether instructions would be followed. The dynamics of the team as we described earlier shaped how instructions were negotiated and acted upon. Further, in some cases, one or two people acted as leaders within the team, which meant they decided on where the team went to next and what instructions were to be followed or not.

Mishearings and misunderstandings

Often instructions were not followed as a result of the information being misheard or not fully understood by the player who received them. The game being played in a noisy street environment and also the computerized voice of the Instructor led to messages being misheard by players.

Misheard information was then relayed to the team leading to confusion among the players, or equally to mistrust towards the Instructor, both of which resulted in instructions not being followed. One example of the latter was when right after a call, a player communicated to his team that the Instructor was lying. When asked why is that, he replied: "*Because we got a message saying that we all lost our points"*. Since that was not the case, the player assumed that the system was lying; however, such a message did not exist in the system, the player had just misheard the information.

Timing

The point in time that instructions were delivered was also found to be relevant to whether players would follow them or not. For example, if instructions were delivered while players were running, it was likely that they would not be followed and potentially not even received. Similarly, players' availability and receptivity to instructions was also restricted by the danger factor of the policemen. In the next episode, players are negotiating on the instructions while a policeman sneaks up on them. Players run away and none of the instructions are followed at this point.

"P5: I have been told to go the Bank but others have been told to go to the Lanes…P2: So why are we going…hey you guys, guys let's come together. We have been told different information.

P3: We got three different venues so let's have a look at the map (team comes together and open their maps (cop is right behind them). P1: (whispering) There is a man behind us that we need to avoid (starts walking away and two other players follow him.

P2: Hey guys, shouldn't we stick together as we need to catch the boat together?" (Rest of players realize there is a cop behind them)

(Everyone starts running away)

DISCUSSION

This work aimed to explore issues regarding an agent delivering instructions to teams of humans and did so in the context of a pervasive game played in the streets of a British city. Contrary to previous work, we were interested in how teams and not individuals received and negotiated instructions. A further contribution of this work relating to the field of human-agent interaction is the methodology itself. There is no precedent of a large-scale pervasive game to be used before to explore human-agent interaction. As shown, the benefits of such an 'in the wild' deployment compared to software simulations or purely lab-based experiments are significant: detailed descriptions of what took place can assist in unfolding the complexities in the interaction between humans and agents, including visceral or environmental aspects of decision-making (e.g. fatigue, fear); and provide pointers for further experimental investigation.

This work has uncovered the ways teams and individuals engaged with the agent and followed (or not) its instructions with an emphasis on how shared understanding and negotiation were realized. These two areas have been established in existing work [6][27] as vital to human-agent interaction and particularly challenging for human agent coordination. In this work, as part of sharing and negotiating, players had to make sense of ambiguous information and this was shown to be informed by assumptions about the character of the Instructor, leveraging the perceived goals of the game and other contextual information against the received information. Often negotiating meant that teams/players would not follow the instructions despite the fact that in the game pack it was stated that the information given through the Instructor is "*useful*" and "*vital*" for the game. The instructions were further always correct, in the sense that they did not send the players to any dead stations, and yet players ignored them with ease.

A main consideration from this is that any assumptions about obedience, trust – and equally intelligence – that might have been built in the design of the agent were challenged, and exposed the fragility of such systems. The assumptions relating to the Instructor and the persona developed around it, shaped notions of trust and mistrust that were paramount not only to the following of instructions but also to the intra team relations and communication. With this in mind, it is important to consider ways in which the interface can be more sensitive or contingent to the context at hand. Investing into building a relationship with the agent, potentially through interfaces of conversation - rather than discrete instruction messages - that take into account the on-going assumptions and allow for human-machine reconfigurations [22] is a more appropriate design approach. Likewise, a trustful agent will more easily inspire a change of priorities within the team if needed. In the next section, we provide recommendations for design that address the insights from this work.

Design Recommendations

We provide five recommendations that address the issues discussed above. While these recommendations have emerged from a context of an agent instructing teams, we believe they are relevant to human-agent interaction design in general and can be applied equally to cases of agents instructing individuals.

Reliability is subjective. Trust in the agent does not depend on the reliability of its instruction, but in the user's perception of this reliability. It is not sufficient for the agent to give useful and correct information to a user in order to establish trust. Agents that rely on user's trust for their instructions to be followed must thus provide correct information and at the same time ensure that the user perceives this information as correct. Otherwise it must provide a mechanism for correcting user's perception when they do not match what is desired.

Users are dynamic; agents should be too. The relationship between users and agents is not static. It evolves over the course of the interaction. One limitation of our agent is that while its relationship with the subjects changed over time, its own behaviour remained the same, leading to divergence between how some users interpreted its instructions and how it expected them to be interpreted. An agent instructing users needs to adapt when it becomes clear that the user is no longer interested in following their instructions. The agent should provide ongoing feedback as a part of the process of updating the shared model of the situation [21], and overcome the barriers associated with disinterested users.

Ignored instructions are not equivalent to non-compliance. Users are not always able to follow instructions for a variety of reasons. Users may not fully comprehend or appreciate the systems activities, or feel that the instructions conflict with their immediate goals [6]. This may be attributed to the relative 'invisibility' of the agent's intentions and activities, increasing the cognitive demands on users to interpret and evaluate the instructions given [28]. A consequence is, that rather than engaging with the agent, users revert to manual or direct control, often in an attempt to reclaim their own understanding or control of the situation [6]. An agent should not judge lack of compliance to its instructions as a sign that the user is purposefully not following instructions.

Agent instruction needs to take team cohesion into account. In unstructured teams, when an individual acts a single point of delivery of agent instructions, then the role and position of that individual within the team strongly impacts how those instructions are handled. When an agent becomes part of a team, this role becomes critical for the interaction between team and agent. Hence, the agent should make allowances for this in terms of the timing, format and content of any communications [28]. The agent's presence can also add additional co-ordination demands to specific members of the team [6]. An agent may need to send out the same instruction to multiple individuals or select an individual of higher standing within the team to send instructions to. This is part of a global strategy to ensure the agent's actions are synchronised and consistent with the team [6].

Manners matter. Simply delivering instructions to users is not sufficient. It is also important to consider the manner in which they are delivered. The fact that the Instructor called users on their phones and addressed them with their real names had a strong influence on the users' willingness to engage with it. The anthropomorphic nature of the agent's behaviour, especially when asking users, "Don't you trust me?" led to a significant change in how users decided to proceed in their engagement with the Instructor.

FUTURE WORK

The study presented in this paper was an initial exploration on the use pervasive games to study how teams of users respond to agent instructions. Its design was not meant to mimic real world scenarios, nor extract generalizable findings. It was rather focused on creating an engaging gaming experience for players. However, some of the core mechanics of the game share similarities with various real-world scenarios where agents will need to instruct teams of people under pressured conditions and issues such as trust and authority, timing and proximity that were found in our game will be of high importance. For instance, in the case of emergency evacuation/crowd control, an agent may collect information from a number of sources (drones, sensor infrastructure, local authorities) and instruct groups of people on available exit points; or in the case of urban search and rescue, where an agent may coordinate and instruct teams regarding worksites or potential hazards.

Our focus now moves towards establishing a more empirical approach that would produce more concrete a generalizable results. Of particular interest is studying more realistic models of human-agent interaction, for example by focusing on two-way interaction where human users would provide feedback to the agent instructor, rather than the simple one-way communication used in Cargo. In addition, more controlled experiments will be required to compare different configurations of instructing humans via agents: agents directly instructing humans, agents instructing humans through human intermediary, or humans instructing humans through agent intermediaries.

CONCLUSIONS

In this paper, we set about exploring how teams of humans respond to instructions from an intelligent agent. To explore these issues in situ and on a large scale, we developed a pervasive game called Cargo, which sees the Instructor, a semi-autonomous agent, use text-to-speech to direct teams of players (via their mobile phones) around a city in the UK. Our observations indicate that the teams' interpretation of, and compliance with, instructions were shaped predominately by their perceptions and assumptions of the agent. Many participants attributed an authoritative characteristic to the agent, and trust was built (or lost) as the relationship was developed over the period of the game. Upon receipt of instructions by individuals, information was shared with the team in different ways, and frequently led to team members negotiating their next actions. Based on the findings, we presented five design implications to consider when creating intelligent interface systems that instruct teams of humans.

ACKNOWLEDGMENTS

This work was supported by EPSRC Grant No. EP/I011587/1.

REFERENCES

1. Ball, M. and Callaghan, V. Introducing Intelligent Environments, Agents and Autonomy to Users. *Proceedings of the 7th International Conference on Intelligent Environments (IE '11)*, (2011), 382–385.
2. Benford, S., Magerkurth, C., and Ljungstrand, P. Bridging the physical and digital in pervasive gaming.

Communications of the ACM (CACM) 48, 3 (2005), 54–57.

3. Benotti, L. and Denis, A. Giving instructions in virtual environments by corpus based selection. *Proceedings of the 12th Annual Meeting of the Special Interest Group on Discourse and Dialogue (SIGDIAL '11).*, (2011), 68–77.

4. Bulitko, V.V. and Wilkins, D.C. Automated Instructor Assistant for Ship Damage Control. *Proceedings of the Sixteenth National Conference on Artificial Intelligence and the Eleventh Innovative Applications of Artificial Intelligence Conference Innovative Applications of Artificial Intelligence AAAI '99/IAAI '99*, (1999), 778 – 785.

5. Chan, V., Ray, P., and Parameswaran, N. Mobile e-Health monitoring: an agent-based approach. *IET Communications 2*, 2 (2008), 223–230.

6. Christoffersen, K. and Woods, D.D. How to make automated systems team players. *Advances in human performance and cognitive engineering research 2*, (2002), 1–12.

7. Cuevas, H.M., Fiore, S.M., Caldwell, B.S., and Strater, L. Augmenting Team Cognition in Human-Automation Teams Performing in Complex Operational Environments. *Aviation, Space, and Environmental Medicine 78*, 1 (2007), B63–B70(8).

8. Doswell, J. and Harmeyer, K. Extending the 'Serious Game' Boundary: Virtual Instructors in Mobile Mixed Reality Learning Games. *Proceedings of the Digital Games Research Association International Conference (DiGRA 2007)*, (2007), 524–529.

9. Fiore, S.M., Salas, E., Cuevas, H.M., and Bowers, C.A. Distributed coordination space: Toward a theory of distributed team process and performance. *Theoretical Issues in Ergonomics Science 4*, 3-4 (2003), 340–364.

10. Fischer, J., Jiang, W., and Moran, S. AtomicOrchid: A Mixed Reality Game to Investigate Coordination in Disaster Response. *In Mobile Gaming Workshop (MOGA) 2012 as a part of Proceedings of the 11th International Conference on Entertainment Computing (ICEC 2012)*, (2012), 572–577.

11. Fischer, J.E., Flintham, M., Price, D., Goulding, J., Pantidi, N., and Rodden, T. Serious Mixed Reality Games. *In Proceedings of Mixed-Reality Games Workshop as a part of the International Conference on Computer Supported Cooperative Work (CSCW'12)*, (2012).

12. Hexmoor, H. and Heng, T. Air Traffic Control Agents: Landing and Collision Avoidance. *Proceedings of International Conference in Artificial Intelligence, (IC-AI '00).*, (2000).

13. Heylen, D., Nijholt, A., op den Akker, R., and Vissers, M. Socially Intelligent Tutor Agents. *Proceedings of Intelligent Virtual Agents (IVA '03)*, Lecture Notes in Artificial Intelligence (2003), 341–347.

14. Koschmann, T., LeBaron, C., Goodwin, C., and Feltovich, P. The mystery of the missing referent: objects, procedures, and the problem of the instruction follower. *Proceedings of the 20th Anniversary Conference on Computer Supported Cooperative Work (CSCW '06)*, ACM New York, NY, USA (2006), 373–382.

15. Maes, P. Agents that reduce work and information overload. *Communications of the ACM 37*, 7 (2007), 30–40.

16. McGrath, S., Chacón, D., and Whitebread, K. Intelligent Mobile Agents in Military Command and Control. *Proceedings of the Autonomous Agents Workshop on Agents in Industry*, (2000).

17. Milgram, S. *Obedience to Authority: An Experimental View*. Harper Perennial Modern Classics, 2009.

18. Mittrup, I., Smarsly, K., Hartmann, D., and Bettzieche, V. An Agent-Based Approach to Dam Monitoring. *Proceedings of the 20th CIB W78 Conference on Information Technology in Construction.*, (2003), 239–246.

19. Murata, K., Enomoto, M., Arimoto, Y., and Nakano, Y. When Should Animated Agents Give Additional Instructions to Users? - Monitoring User's Understanding in Multimodal Dialogues. *International Conference on Control, Automation and Systems, ICCAS '07.*, (2007), 733 – 736.

20. Murthy, S., Akkiraju, R., Rachlin, J., and Wu, F. Agent-Based Cooperative Scheduling. *Proceedings of AAAI Workshop on Constraints and Agents*, AAAI Press (1997), 112–117.

21. Norman, D.A. The 'problem' with automation: inappropriate feedback and interaction, not'over-automation. *Philosophical Transactions of the Royal Society of London. B 327*, 1241 (1990), 585–593.

22. Pacaux-Lemoine, M.-P. and Debernard, S. Common work space for human–machine cooperation in air traffic control. *Control Engineering Practice 10*, 5 (2002), 571–576.

23. Schaafstal, A.M., Johnston, J.H., and Oser, R.L. Training teams for emergency management. *Computers in Human Behavior 17*, 5-6 (2001), 615–626.

24. Suchman, L.A. *Plans and Situated Actions: The Problem of Human-Machine Communication.* Cambridge University Press, 1999.

25. Sukthankar, G., Shumaker, R., and Lewis, M. Intelligent Agents as Teammates. In Eduardo Salas, S.M. Fiore and M.P. Letsky, eds., *Theories of Team Cognition: Cross-Disciplinary Perspectives*. 2012, 313 – 343.

26. Tolmie, P., Benford, S., Flintham, M., et al. "Act Natural": Instructions, Compliance and Accountability in Ambulatory Experiences. *CHI '12 Proceedings of the SIGCHI Conference on Human Factors in Computing Systems*, (2012), 1519–1528.

27. Traum, D., Rickel, J., Gratch, J., and Marsella, S. Negotiating over Tasks in Hybrid Human-Agent Teams for Simulation-Based Training. *Proceedings of the Second International Joint Conference on Autonomous Agents and Multiagent Systems (AAMAS '03)*, ACM New York, NY, USA (2003), 441–448.

28. Woods, D.D. Human-centered software agents: Lessons from clumsy automation. In S. J. Flanagan, T. Huang, P. Jones, & S. Kasif, ed., *Human centered systems: Information, interactivity, and in.* Washington, DC: National Science Foundation, 1997, 288–293.

29. http://cars.uk.msn.com/features/sat-nav-catastrophes Accessed on 09/01/2013.

30. http://www.phidgets.com Accessed on 09/01/2013.

31. http://slingshoteffect.co.uk/ Accessed on 09/01/2013.

32. http://igfest.org/ Accessed on 09/01/2013.

Recommending Energy Tariffs and Load Shifting Based on Smart Household Usage Profiling

Joel E. Fischer*, Sarvapali D. Ramchurn+, Michael A. Osborne~, Oliver Parson+, T. Dong Huynh+, Muddasser Alam+, Nadia Pantidi*, Stuart Moran*, Khaled Bachour*, Steven Reece~, Enrico Costanza+, Tom Rodden*, Nicholas R. Jennings+

*University of Nottingham
Nottingham, UK, NG8 1BB
joel.fischer@nottingham.ac.uk

+University of Southampton
{sdr,op106,tdh,moody,ec,nrj}@
ecs.soton.ac.uk

~University of Oxford
{mosb,reece}@
robots.ox.ac.uk

ABSTRACT
We present a system and study of personalized energy-related recommendation. AgentSwitch utilizes electricity usage data collected from users' households over a period of time to realize a range of smart energy-related recommendations on energy tariffs, load detection and usage shifting. The web service is driven by a third party real-time energy tariff API (uSwitch), an energy data store, a set of algorithms for usage prediction, and appliance-level load disaggregation. We present the system design and user evaluation consisting of interviews and interface walkthroughs. We recruited participants from a previous study during which three months of their household's energy use was recorded to evaluate personalized recommendations in AgentSwitch. Our contributions are a) a systems architecture for personalized energy services; and b) findings from the evaluation that reveal challenges in designing energy-related recommender systems. In response to the challenges we formulate design recommendations to mitigate barriers to switching tariffs, to incentivize load shifting, and to automate energy management.

Author Keywords
Energy tariffs; recommender systems; load shifting; personalization; smart grid; demand response.

ACM Classification Keywords
H.5.m. Information interfaces and presentation (e.g., HCI): Miscellaneous.

INTRODUCTION
In the face of dwindling fossil fuel resources, energy security and efficiency has emerged as one of the key global concerns of our time. Many countries have implemented political, societal and technological initiatives to respond to the challenges of how to become more energy efficient [8]. For example, initiatives in the UK include the roll out of *smart meters,* a key technology associated with the idea of the *smart grid* [9]. Essentially, the smart grid will serve as an "information technology backbone" [15]. Two-way information flow between suppliers and consumers is essential for smart grid technologies aimed at making the grid more energy efficient, such as *demand side management.* For example, 'dynamic' or 'time-of-use' pricing have been suggested as techniques to reduce peak demand by encouraging *load shifting* of demand through higher prices at peak times to off-peak periods [31]. These techniques raise major challenges for interactive and intelligent systems design to support the consumers' understanding and control of their energy usage in this complex environment. For example, recommender systems have been proposed [18] in order to empower users to play an active role in demand side management.

Research into demand side technologies has been embraced by HCI and adjacent computing disciplines, and domestic energy consumption has emerged as a key application domain. In particular, efforts have been focused on persuasive technologies that provide feedback on consumption to raise awareness or to promote conservation behavior [5,13,24]. However, research has also shown that despite raised awareness, comfort and everyday habits can prevent true change [30]. For most people in the 'developed world', the fact that energy (still) is a readily available 'commodity' often appears to fail to engage people sufficiently to care. In spite of predictions of annual energy bills exceeding £1,500 for the average UK household [12], a recent study has shown that people spend as little as two hours per year to shop for energy tariffs [32].

Against this background, we present a system and evaluation that takes on the challenges of people's limited interest in energy tariffs and explores reactions to load shifting advice. The premise behind AgentSwitch is that the future proliferation of monitoring devices such as smart meters connected to online data stores will lead to intelligent services that process, analyze and reason based on energy usage data. AgentSwitch presents a novel prototype of such a service, recommending energy tariffs and load shifting based on energy usage profiles (EUP). Our research interest focuses on how user interaction with such systems might best be supported. We evaluate the system through a user study consisting of task-based walkthroughs and interviews. Our findings highlight perceived barriers to switch to cheaper tariffs. In particular, for recommendations of shifting appliance usage to different times, it appears that more benefits than monetary savings are required to incentivize changing behavior in this way.

MANAGING ENERGY ON THE DEMAND SIDE

HCI systems to encourage conservation often provide multiple views of users' energy usage at various levels of temporal granularity, and may for example combine these with persuasive messages sent to the user's inbox [17]. Recently, this focus on *consumption feedback* has been critiqued for its 'one size fits all' approach that glosses over people's differences in motivations [14], and can reduce energy issues to an optimization problem [5]. An inherent rationalistic orientation that feedback leads to reduction does also not take into account that everyday practices are often driven by comfort and convenience rather than by rational calculations [30]. A recent review of the field has also called for more engagement with the opportunities smart grid systems hold to promote energy efficiency and reductions in costs for consumers, producers and the environment [24].

Smart grid and smart home energy management

A key question for our research is how can smart grid technologies support consumers in becoming more energy efficient without impeding too much on their comfort and convenience. As the US Department of Energy writes in their report introducing the smart grid:

"Consumers are not interested in sitting around for an hour a day to change how their house uses energy; what they will do is spend two hours per year to set their comfort, price and environmental preferences – enabling collaboration with the grid to occur automatically on their behalf and saving money each time." [13: 20].

More automated approaches to home energy management have been proposed that rely on machine learning and multi-agent systems [1], e.g., to enable automatic appliance control [26], home heating based on occupancy [29], or off-grid home energy management [2].

The work presented here engages with these proposals. Firstly, AgentSwitch is designed as a service that consumers could use only once or twice a year to optimize their energy use. Secondly, we are interested in users' reactions to personalized recommendations on how much they can save by shifting loads to off-peak times, under current tariffs and assuming no automation. Will the potential savings be perceived as sufficient to motivate behavior change? In this light, what are people's attitudes towards automation to support load shifting?

Recommender Systems and Energy

At the time of writing, the consumer in the UK can choose between 24 energy providers that offer plans with many different payment options, energy sources, fixed price and tiered tariff structures. Currently, 'Economy7' is the most common tiered tariff type that offers a cheaper rate for a seven-hour period during the night. Consumers also need a special meter installed in their homes to switch to this tariff. Conceivably, consumers may find choosing the right energy tariff a daunting task. Hence, a recommender systems approach proposed to cope with the problem of information overload [21] appears to be worth investigating.

Generally speaking, recommender systems can be distinguished by whether they employ a content-based or a collaborative strategy (or a mix of both) [21]. They have been applied to the energy domain, for example to support building automation [18]. Context-aware and model-based recommender systems have also taken into account behavior [19] and user state in time [16]; approaches that are more closely aligned with the energy usage profiling our work relies on. Price comparison websites also employ profiling to support selecting appropriate products such as insurances, mobile phone contracts and energy tariffs. Such services usually require the user to manually provide parameters of preference to narrow the choices. In contrast, our approach relies on the analysis of pre-recorded data to enable *personalized* price comparison based on energy usage. Potential privacy issues related to access to this kind of fine-grained data have been highlighted [28], and will also be explored in the evaluation.

We draw on a user-centric evaluation framework for recommender systems [25] to guide the evaluation of our system. In the context of giving energy advice, literature shows that prior domain knowledge and commitment to save energy are important factors that influence the intention to follow advice [7,22]. To evaluate our system, the intention to follow recommendations is an important indicator of usefulness, in addition to factors relating to the predicted information, such as confidence and intelligibility, as well as potential issues with privacy.

AGENTSWITCH SYSTEM ARCHITECTURE

AgentSwitch relies on energy data collected from household-level monitoring to compute personalized recommendations. The web service is implemented as a RESTful Django web application,[1] consisting of a number of core modules (see figure 1). The system setup is designed for a deregulated electricity market (e.g., the consumer can chose between various suppliers and tariffs) as found in a number of countries across the world. Its modular design should make it relatively straightforward to plug in other tariff data sources and metering equipment available than the ones used in our deployment.

Household monitoring

The evaluation presented in this paper is based on data collected during a three-month deployment in 18 households in the UK. The technical setup consisted of a commercially available current sensor (CT-clamp) wirelessly transmitting Watt readings to an off-the-shelf In-home display (IHD). A low-power (< 8W), small form-factor computer connected

[1] http://hac.ecs.soton.ac.uk/agentswitch

to the display aggregates the readings and pushes them to the data store via the home's broadband every 5 seconds.

Data store

AgentSwitch retrieves the user's personal energy data from the data store that exposes an API for authentication and data requests. The user logs in to authorize AgentSwitch to retrieve their data, which is explained in the UI. The data is only handled for the duration of the session; it is not stored persistently by AgentSwitch. The data store is part of a bigger vision in which a multitude of web and mobile applications provide personalized energy-specific services. The user authorizes the applications to use their energy data that is stored in a single secure online location.

Energy usage profiling

Once the actual energy data is retrieved from the data store, an EUP for the whole year is predicted based on the actual data. Annual consumption estimates are a required input parameter for the energy tariff API. We use a Gaussian process (GP) to model power consumption as a function of time, using scaled national average consumption to provide a mean function. The latter embeds seasonal variations within our model, meaning that we can provide accurate power consumption prediction on yearlong scales even with sparse data. We can then employ this GP model to estimate the integral of power consumption over a year, giving an estimate of a household's total annual energy consumption. This technique is known as Bayesian Quadrature (BQ), a model-based means of numerical integration [10]. In this work, we adapt the technique for quasi-periodic energy consumption signals emerging from the weekly cycles of typical domestic consumers.

Evaluating BQ

We evaluated the efficacy of this approach with the data collected during the deployment: we divided the data into a set of training data (one third of the collected data) and test data; the goal was to accurately predict the total energy usage given only training data. Results reported in more detail in [27] show that the approach generates more accurate predictions than simpler alternatives.

A key challenge for the prediction module is computation time: users are usually unwilling to wait more than a few seconds to receive recommendations. The Bayesian quadrature algorithm requires fitting a GP to the data, an expensive operation that scales as $O(N^3)$ in the length of the data, N. To tackle this problem, we aggregated our data, therefore reducing its size. Rather than using all minute-by-minute observations, we supplied to the model only observations of the total energy consumed in an hour. This was found to have negligible effect on predictive accuracy due to the redundancy in the finer-grained observations. Training the hyperparameters of the GP is a particularly computationally demanding process. We therefore trained most hyperparameters on a fixed set of training data off-line, reducing the required processing for the on-line module to

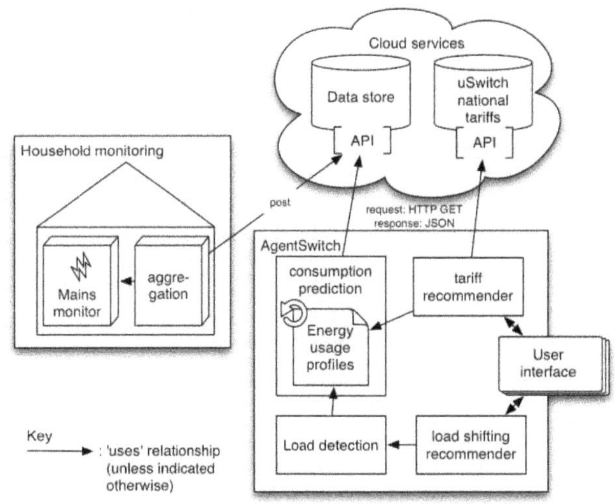

Figure 1. AgentSwitch system and infrastructure.

about 0.02 seconds for N=5 and 0.4 seconds for N=500, for example.

uSwitch API wrapper

AgentSwitch makes essential use of national tariff data provided by uSwitch.com, a price comparison website that provides its up-to-date energy tariff information through an API. In AgentSwitch the user selects their tariff details from a set of locally available tariffs retrieved from uSwitch (e.g., supplier and plan details). The recommender module then uses the details (e.g., unit rates, thresholds) to compute annual cost estimates based on personal usage profiles.

Load detection

Deferrable loads (non-overlapping uses of the washing machine, clothes dryer or dishwasher) are detected from the aggregate household-level data. Loads from these appliances share similar profiles, and therefore a template can be constructed to match the behavior of all of them. To detect deferrable loads disaggregation is performed using a variant of the hidden Markov model approach described by Parson et al. [23]. The disaggregation module takes a list of time-stamped energy readings and returns a list of deferrable loads. However, due to the lack of training data and low data granularity, it is very hard to determine which of the three appliances generated an individual load. Whether the accuracy of such appliance-level disaggregation is sufficient from the user's perspective is investigated in the evaluation.

User interface

The GUI (e.g., see figure 3, 4 and 5) has been iteratively developed from wireframe sketches through several rounds of expert walkthroughs. The following key considerations have driven the development.

Minimize manual user input

A key feature of AgentSwitch compared to existing commercial price comparison websites is that the user does not have to provide parameters detailing their energy consumption. Arguably, manual input is error prone, can be tedious, and important details like the proportion of daytime vs. nighttime consumption are difficult to estimate. In AgentSwitch, after the user logs on they only have to provide a postcode (to select the right set of locally available tariffs). Their usage profile is computed from their actual energy data fetched from the data store. Comparison of their current tariff to the list of available tariffs is optional, which requires the user to manually provide parameters detailing their current tariff to the system.

Explanation driven by data provenance
Throughout the AgentSwitch UI, care is taken not to overload views with information. Instead, more information is provided on demand through hover-overs and links. Availability of explanations of system actions was deemed important in concordance with findings in the literature on recommender systems [6]. In order to support understanding and confidence in the recommendations, explanations are constructed using the *provenance* of data used in computations. Provenance information is modeled using the W3C PROV Data Model [20], which captures the various relationships between (data) entities, activities (e.g. consumption prediction, load disaggregation), and agents (e.g. the user, uSwitch, the data store). For example, using such traces, users may be able to identify incorrect predictions of yearly consumption, or justify changes to daily routines to make significant savings.

In particular, due to its potential to raise concerns related to privacy and confidence in the accuracy of the presented information, the following explanations are provided on demand:

- Explanations justifying why personal data is required and how personal energy data is handled.
- Explanations describing how the presented information was computed, including its provenance (i.e., its origin).

Familiar concepts
Throughout the application, interface concepts were deployed that we hoped most people would be familiar with. In addition to visual layout inspired by existing price comparison websites, we adopted the concept of *authorizing an application to use your data*. Users should be familiar with this for example from logging on to OAuth-enabled social networking application clients. It is conceivable that future third party energy applications will be able to request usage of users' energy data stored in a private online repository in the same way, much like initiatives such as Green Button[2] already advocate.

EVALUATION

The key objective for AgentSwitch is to provide a useful and trustworthy personalized service that allows the user to make an informed decision on how to save by switching tariffs or shifting energy usage. As outlined in the previous section, this is realized through various modules that compute information surfaced by the UI. Drawing on [25], the focus of the evaluation is on how users with genuine personal energy data perceive AgentSwitch with regards to

Participant	Colleague	Home occupancy	Age, gender	Occupation
P1	Yes	2	29, m	PhD student
P2	No	1	32, f	Marketing manager
P3	No	4	48, m	University manager
P4	Yes	2	34, m	Researcher
P5	No	4	34, f	Artist
P6	No	2	35, f	Translator
P7	No	3	49, f	Housewife
P8	Yes	2	25, m	PhD student
P9	Yes	2	27, m	Researcher
P10	Yes	3	55, m	PhD student

Table 1. Participant details.

- **usefulness** and use cases of provided functionality,
- **provenance** (Where did this data/figure come from?),
- **comprehensiveness** (Is all the desired information present?),
- **confidence** (Do users trust that the information is accurate?),
- **intelligibility** (Is it possible to understand the information, and the way it was computed?),
- **actionability** (Will users do anything as a result of this information?) of the information, and
- **privacy** issues and emerging attitudes towards the use of personal energy data to drive the service.

We chose to employ a task-based interface walkthrough and also asked our participants to 'think aloud' while completing the tasks. After the walkthrough, a researcher conducted a semi-structured interview to investigate their experience of using AgentSwitch in more detail. We recorded video, audio and screencasts during the procedure. For qualitative analysis, the statements made during the walkthrough and the interview were coded and grouped according to emerging broader themes, of which the quotes present in this paper are representative [4]. Before we present the results from the study, we briefly describe participant recruitment, procedure, walkthrough tasks, and interview structure.

Participants

To evaluate AgentSwitch's core functionality, it is essential that there is a sufficient amount of energy data available for each user. Hence, we recruited 10 participants that took part in a study approximately one year earlier during which we recorded three months worth of their home's electricity usage data aggregated to 5min intervals (in Watt-hours). In the earlier study, participants had been exposed to real-time and historic electricity feedback delivered via various devices such as an In-home display (IHD), a web app, and text messages. Each participant was from a different household with varying occupancy (see table 1). Due to the

[2] www.greenbuttondata.org

sensitive nature of conducting a long-term study in their homes, participants had been recruited among colleagues that were not involved with the research (5) and friends of friends (5). The only requirement we had is that they frequently handled energy bill payment in their household.

Procedure

We invited our 10 participants to come to one of three sessions in a meeting space in the local University. We asked them to have their current energy tariff details to hand as they were required for the study. Two of the sessions had three participants; the other session had four.

Upon arrival we briefed participants on the study procedure and gained informed consent. We then demonstrated uSwitch to them, a commercial price comparison website. The site offers energy tariff comparison based on annual usage data users have to input manually. The purpose of the demo was to acknowledge an underlying service we built on, but also to give participants the opportunity to compare AgentSwitch to an existing solution.

One researcher accompanied one participant to a laptop set up in a separate and quiet part of the lab. The browser already displayed the landing page of AgentSwitch. Participants received printed task instructions for the walkthrough. The researcher then remained with the participant throughout the walkthrough, encouraged them to think aloud and clarified or helped where necessary. Finally, interviews were conducted. The entire procedure usually lasted about 45 minutes.

Walkthrough tasks

To evaluate AgentSwitch's core functionality in use, we designed a set of walkthrough tasks to be completed by each participant. Participants were tasked to answer a set of questions that required them to explore most of AgentSwitch's UI. We wanted to ensure participants engaged with most of the functionality in a systematic and comparable way, to enable later discussion about the actual figures AgentSwitch presented.

Tasks were ordered in increasing complexity and in keeping with the order of interface transitions. Participants had to find information by engaging with the following features:

- Estimation of annual cost for their current tariff (figure 3).
- Breakdown of annual cost into daytime and nighttime (if they had an Economy7 tariff) (see figure 3).
- Cheapest recommended standard and Economy7 tariff, and estimated cost and savings compared to their current tariff (see figure 4).
- Potential savings by shifting 20% of daytime usage to nighttime (based on their own Economy 7 tariff, or else based on the cheapest Economy7 tariff).
- Percentage of their overall use accounted for by detected deferrable loads (washing machine, dish washer, or tumble dryer) (see figure 5).

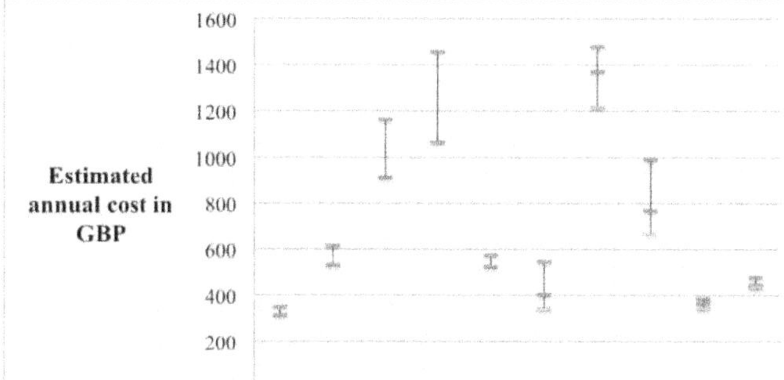

	P1	P2	P6	P7	P9	P3	P4	P5	P8	P10
current tariff	352	615	1164	1456	574	546	1479	989	368	482
cheapest available tariff	313	531	912	1065	525	406	1373	768	385	447
shifting 20% usage to nighttime						342	1218	669	342	437

Figure 2. Estimated annual cost for current tariff, cheapest available tariff, and when shifting 20% of usage from daytime to nighttime (for participants on Economy 7 tariffs).

- Potential savings by shifting all of the detected deferrable loads from daytime to nighttime (see figure 5).

Interviews

A researcher conducted a semi-structured interview per participant after the walkthrough. Aside from allowing for first impressions and overall comments or concerns, questions were designed for participants to elaborate on perceived usefulness and whether and for what reasons they would use AgentSwitch again in the future. Questions also probed their understanding of the provenance of the information, their confidence in the accuracy, and whether they would consider switching tariffs or shifting usage as a result of using the service. Lastly, questions probed potential privacy issues as well as attitudes towards more autonomous systems that perform actions like switching tariffs automatically on the user's behalf.

RESULTS

Participants found AgentSwitch relatively easy to use and easy to make sense of. The fact that all of the participants said they would use the site again speaks to its perceived usefulness. Confirming initial motivations, participants' comments suggest that the domain of energy tariffs only attracts usage once or twice per year, or less often.

We begin by giving an overview of the personalized figures AgentSwitch presented, and how they were typically made sense of and perceived by our participants. We then move on to present qualitative findings from a thematic analysis of statements participants made during the walkthrough and the interview.

Personalized recommendations

AgentSwitch found cheaper tariffs for 9 of our 10 participants, with estimated annual savings between £35 and £391 (M=£132) if they switched to the cheapest tariff. In addition, AgentSwitch calculated that participants with an Economy 7 tariff could save an additional £26-£110 if they shifted 20% of their overall usage to the cheaper night rate of the two-tiered tariff (see figure 2).

Figure 3. Screenshot of annual cost estimates (a) and breakdown (b) for P3's current tariff.

Making sense of the recommendations

The following transcript from the walkthrough illustrates how a participant is using and making sense of the presented information, discovering discrepancies in the predictions compared to his provider (see figure 3). This participant has brought paperwork detailing his power company's estimations of their annual cost.

[Reading the results page] *Estimated Annual cost. That must be using the data you hold. You reckon it'll cost us, electricity wise 540 pounds a year* - [looks down at paperwork] *which.... They* [the supplier] *think is a lot more. By 200 pounds worth. Because - they reckon I'm gonna use a lot. I'm thinking the majority is at 16p during the day. So... let's see how you break it down first of all.* [clicks on 'show cost breakdown' – reading breakdown] *Day rate* - [looks down] *yea. that's the difference. It's 200 pounds - it's virtually 170 pounds difference in the day rate. The night rate is virtually the same -so, it's in the day rate, that it's a big difference.* [P3]

Perceived accuracy of the predictions

AgentSwitch estimates annual consumption cost of the current tariff on the basis of a three-month data sample. For the purpose of this paper, more important than the accuracy of the predictions is how participants perceived the accuracy of the predicted figures. We anticipated that a certain level of perceived accuracy was important to further engage with and trust information provided by the system.

P1 and P7 perceived the estimate of the annual bill as about right, while P4, P5 and P6 felt that is was higher than expected; and P2, P8, P9 felt it was lower than expected (P10 does not comment). This discrepancy in the data does not necessarily lead to a distrust of the system, as P3 puts it,

*I mean, **the thing that struck me was the difference first of all between what you estimate my cost should be. And what they're*** **[the power company]** ***estimating it should be.** I mean, the interesting thing is why are they estimating an awful lot more than you are?* [P3]

This statement illustrates how confidence in the presented information extends beyond immediate system usage:

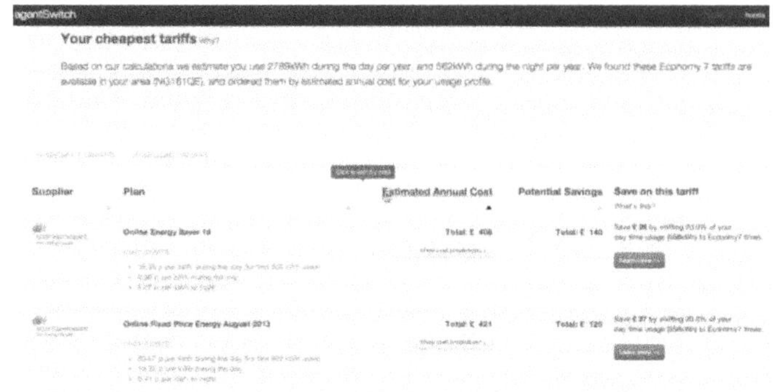

Figure 4. 2 of the recommended cheapest available tariffs for P3.

*I'd want to make sure that information is accurate. I don't know how I would... I mean I supposed I would have to look up my... go back through my bills to double check. I think I only feel that way because I know that this system is new. And I know also that the data that was collected was over a certain period of time. Whereas if let's say I was involved in a year-long, or even six months actually... **If I'd have been involved in a six month project, where over six months my data is collected, and I knew that this technology, the glitches and issues, were ironed out, then I would be quite happy to trust the information** I was being given and I would switch, definitely.* [P5]

Barriers to following advice on switching

Despite that cheaper tariffs than the one they were currently on were presented to 9 out of 10 participants, they presented many accounts of the barriers that made the prospect of switching tariffs less desirable.

Inconvenience

Despite efforts of consumer-oriented agencies, switching tariffs and particularly providers is perceived by all of our participants as an inconvenience.

*I get the impression that you could just keep moving. Your whole life, and **it's a bit of a pain every time**... you get the whole welcome pack and things. It's not something I want to do all the time.* [P1]

*One of the reasons why we haven't changed our energy provider was because I did uSwitch and I found it was such **a hassle to go through the process of changing**.* [P5]

Switching tariffs [...] *I mean, it's a **necessarily horrifying and complicated process** anyway, ahem, because there are so many different suppliers.* [P4]

(Not) knowing the provider

Another stated barrier for switching is unfamiliarity with the provider that offered the cheapest tariff. P3 states that they prefer to be with a supplier that actually owned the infrastructure as well and were not just providing a service. This could be described as a 'reputational effect'.

Disagreeing with the provider's policy

Prior experience and attitudes towards the recommended provider play a role in why switching is rejected. P7 says they would not switch to the provider who offered the cheapest tariff *...because* ***I object to their selling techniques, I object to them on a moral [basis]****...* [P7]

Environmental vs. monetary motivation

'Green' motives can outweigh monetary incentives to switch. P7 goes on to highlight that they are on their current tariff for environmental reasons.

The reason we're with the tariff is because, ***it's the green side of it****, I know we're using electricity, we all are but I kind of justify it by thinking well if that's being offset slightly by them* [current supplier] *investing in renewable energy, so I know its not the cheapest, but that's not why I use them.* [P7]

Satisfied with the current provider's service

There can be a myriad of other reasons why users might prefer to stay on their current tariff, or with their current supplier. For example P1 states,

[current supplier] ***has a really cool website*** *which lets me see what I'm using... I think if that need was filled by some kind of personal energy monitoring then... the appeal of* [current supplier] *might go away a little bit. And then maybe I'd think about changing then.* [P1]

Cost of switching

The current supplier can sometimes penalize switching providers before the end of a contract (for example on a fixed term tariff). In addition, the procedure of signing up with a new supplier can also be associated with costs, monetary or in terms of time spent.

... ***what kind of penalties there might be for changing****, if that information is available, I don't know; and perhaps in the new tariffs, what kind of procedure is expected to be followed, do I need to do anything with it (...) even if it does give you a nice button, sometimes you are not really sure where is that going to take you to; it requires a lot of information.* [P2]

Incompleteness of AgentSwitch

The prematurity of the prototype meant that energy tariffs could not be covered comprehensively. For example, combined gas and electricity tariffs ('dual fuel') were excluded from the system as AgentSwitch relied solely on electricity usage data.

...the only slight problem is that because I have a dual plan, I don't know if this... ***I don't think this takes it into account****. Because obviously you're not monitoring gas use. I suppose if the system existed that would allow me to do that I would* [consider switching]. [P4]

However, consulting other sources can probably mitigate problems with incompleteness:

I will probably go into for example the [supplier] *website and check the details again. I think this is very useful in terms of,* ***it gives you the idea*** *of what is the cheapest and what is the second cheapest,* ***so I will probably go into the cheapest and the second cheapest and check their websites and decide which one to go for****.* [P6]

Thresholds for switching

The perhaps most obvious reason not to switch is that savings are not perceived to be high enough to incentivize switching.

It's ***not actually as much savings as I thought****. There's a threshold... it's not worth changing supplier for 2 pounds a year. It might be worth it for 40 pounds a year... maybe... I'm more inclined now after having a look at this I'd say... to.. to think about changing. But I probably won't. I'm not on a tragic tariff.* [P1]

In fact, participants often talk about the threshold that potential savings have to exceed to motivate them to investigate switching further.

I did do a price comparison on a website once, I think it was after I had been in the flat for a year so I had an annual figure and I think it said ***the most I would be able to save was 60 pounds over a year so I decided it was not worth moving****. But with these kinds of savings I think it would be worthwhile* [P2]

We're still talking of ***2-300 pound difference, which - is... worth exploring****. So I'd be like... right OK, tell you what,* [clicks Economy 7 tariff tab, see figure 4] *give me a screen print of that and I'll take it home, start to have a look, dig into it.* [P3]

I think it was like 60 quid ***and for a saving of 60 pounds over a whole year it just felt like it was more hassle*** *to change [...]* ***whereas with this it's actually telling me that I could save almost 300 pounds*** *by a combination of changing my behavior and changing my tariff. So it's much more clear* [P6].

Interestingly, automation of switching could perhaps lower this threshold, as P6 elaborates.

If it's just 50 quid for a year's worth of energy, to me it's not worth the hassle cause I've had the experience before of switching providers. Whereas ***if there was a system that could do it for you****, if that system worked fairly effectively,* ***then the saving of 50 pounds or even 10 pounds is worth it****. Because there's little effort in doing that.* [P6]

Autonomous switching

Whether this is seen as a blessing or a curse seems to depend on the perceived accuracy of the system as experienced in the walkthrough

But ***it's discredited itself by giving me incorrect savings amounts****!* [P1]

as well as whether a host of conditions could be met by such an autonomous system:

Yes, I'd be quite happy to, ***as long as I had some notification and control over it*** *I'd be quite happy for an agent to change my tariff between energy companies. ... It*

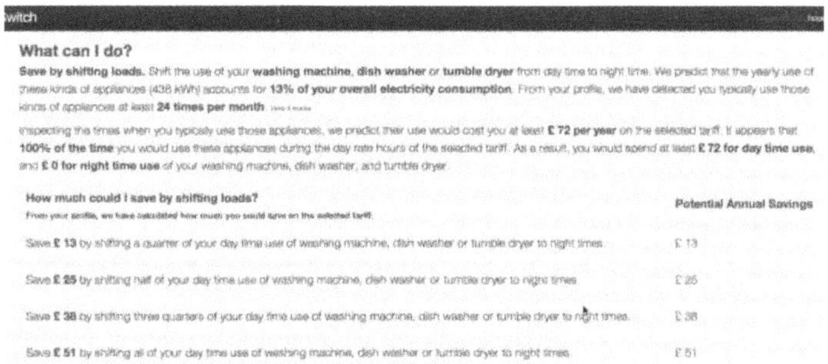

Figure 5. Participant P3's load shifting advice.

would have to be set up sufficiently cleverly that ***it would notify me when it was gonna do it and ask me whether I was willing to do it - for each time****. The reason why is that I'd want to know what's coming out of my bank account in any given month. So, as long as it has some* ***limiting factors****, like, I want to be on a* ***monthly direct debit and I don't want to spend more than X****, or something like that, then, I'd be quite happy for it to flick around.* [P4]

Load shifting

The load detection module made more specific recommendations possible, enabling detailed advice of how many loads users typically run, what their footprint is, how much they can save by shifting them and so on (see figure 5). People have their own ways of making sense of how the system is able to present this kind of information to them

You can tell the heavy loads they would have come on during - well all the time you're monitoring - say you've looked at where the heavy loads are and say - right ok, if they moved into the night time tariff then they would have done this, I can understand where the information could be gleaned from. Because of the information you collected. It's nice to see it all together. [P3]

Aside from praise, this participant also flags up the risk involved with running appliances during night time, which

... we are reluctant to do ... because of ***risk of them going up in flames*** *... as we know a couple of people that had those issues. So we tend not to ...* [P3]

Furthermore, the actual savings by shifting loads are perhaps not high enough to outweigh the cost of shifting.

The ***shifting the loads is not going to do us a great deal****. Behavior wise-we're* ***more comfortable with it being run during the day even if it costs us an extra 30 pounds a year****. That isn't a problem.* [P3]

In addition to noting that the potential for load shifting is limited to certain appliances, it was also noted that accommodating for shifting these loads comes with an extra cost.

That would probably mean ***buying a timer, or indeed a washing machine with a timer on it****. So washing I could do at night, and the dishwasher could go on at night... cooking as I say, I might struggle.... 'Wake up everybody, time for dinner'. I* ***mean paying off a timer switch, I've no idea what one costs, but say it's 20 pounds****, that's stupid... that's a complete waste of time, for the hassle factor.* [P7]

Understanding 'saving by shifting'

Whilst the concept of 'saving by switching' was familiar to all of our participants, the potential to save costs by shifting loads to different times of day with cheaper rates was novel to most of them. Hence, the information related to potential additional savings through shifting is sometimes misunderstood, and usually takes users more effort to make sense of.

I find it difficult to imagine an interface which is clearer... but ***it is a bit confusing at times****. You have to* ***stop and think about what you're looking at*** *and what the savings actually mean.* [P1]

People struggle perhaps especially because there are two kinds of recommendations related to savings (switching and shifting), which could be separated more clearly.

I mentioned before about the potential savings and then the savings on this tariff there isn't a clear indication of how those things are different and how they relate to one another. [P5]

However, once people make sense of the information, they appreciate its value.

I do think the breakdown of ***how much you can save by moving things - by moving energy usage to different times*** *is really interesting. Not so much, just saying, you know, you'll get some savings. But saying, you know,* ***here are actual, genuine numbers****, 'if you move THIS percentage of your usage.' Which - if you're talking about, erm, tumble dryers, dish washers, these are things than can easily be moved. You don't want to move your kettle, toaster, you know. It's really nice, it kinda just reminds you of the stuff. And that's a whole, kind of, area I hadn't thought about, since the last study... moving stuff to doing them at night, particularly.* [P4]

Provenance of information

When asked whether it was clear where the data came from and how the information was computed, none of our participants explicitly mention any of the features of the UI that support explanations. Instead, participants orient to the previous study in their responses.

I know they're based on real usage - ***because I watched it being recorded****, and I reviewed what it was saying* [P4]

Moreover, through this orientation participants may have gained a more favorable view of AgentSwitch.

Maybe because I went through the previous process and I was able to see my data and how the data was collected and so on, so it might be ***because I'm aware of how the data was collected that I feel that I can trust to a certain degree, I have a better understanding of what is actually there...if***

that wasn't the case and I wasn't aware perhaps I wouldn't be quite so quick to trust it. [P5]

Privacy

Records of energy data – especially if recorded continuously over a period of time – are sensitive pieces of information as people's behavior can be inferred from it to a certain degree. Two of our participants point out the ability to infer whether people are not at home from (near-) real-time energy consumption data. While these concern relate to energy data being publicly available, participants also voice concerns regarding sharing of energy data with energy suppliers.

If you're not in touch with any of the companies*, if the companies can't see it...****then that's not a problem****. I would only want my provider to know what tariff I'm on. I wouldn't want other people to say 'Ah, you're on this tariff, we can save you money', so that's none of their business.* [P2]

Other comments suggest that the personal benefit derived from recording and analyzing the information may mitigate concerns about sharing the data with the supplier.

The live information that's being produced by my activity and my family's activity, I'm not completely comfortable about organizations having access to that data and potentially selling that data to one another. Without it actually benefiting me. Whereas ***this I think can demonstrate that there is more benefit than what I've seen before****.* [P5]

A couple of participants also point out that the voluntary nature of use is essential, which implies consent to the data being used to provide a service.

Well ***you don't have to use it****, so I'm gonna guess that if you were concerned about privacy in that way, then you wouldn't be using it at all.* [P7]

This participant puts it in more technical terms, and raises an issue of control over data and autonomous systems.

But this is kind of interesting because ***it is a pull service rather than a push service****. So I'm asking it to use my data to tell me something interesting, rather than IT is using my data to tell me something interesting. That distinction is what's important to me in terms of privacy.* [P4]

DISCUSSION

The findings reveal a set of barriers to switching despite that 9 out of 10 of our participants could save by switching. With regards to shifting loads, aside from some difficulties understanding the concept due to novelty, participants furthermore largely struggled to see the benefits in shifting. We now discuss the findings and suggest ways to overcome the barriers, and relate our findings back to broader concerns in the literature.

Making advice easier to follow: barrier-free switching

The study has revealed people's manifold barriers to switching. What can be done to address these barriers? Fundamentally, energy policy and regulation needs to be implemented to enable interaction designers to build better systems. For example, to make switching more convenient (e.g., enabling one-click switching), to commit energy providers to be more transparent about the provenance of the energy sold to consumers (e.g., to enable choosing tariffs based on the proportions of the energy-mix), and so on.

Some barriers are also more directly attributable to the system design, which can be addressed through improvements. Trust is a core issue for recommender systems [21]. To be perceived as trustworthy by users is important for these kinds of intelligent and complex systems [6], especially when they involve personal data [28]. Therefore, we suggest the following design recommendations:

Have a complete product base

Focus on the determining factors that help people make a decision. In the case of energy tariffs, in addition to pricing structure we found information on the provider (e.g., their policies, practices, area of operation etc.), and contractual details (e.g., on payment, duration, and penalties for premature cancelation), potential additional services of the provider (e.g., web tools and apps), and gas and dual fuel tariffs to be decisive factors that were not covered sufficiently by the current prototype of AgentSwitch.

Know the product recommended to be replaced

To help users make an informed decision on whether to switch to another supplier, the system needs to take into account the details of the current tariff. Does the current contract allow switching, are there any penalties associated with leaving the provider, how do other aspects of the current provider compare to the one to switch to?

Support different levels of motivation

People have different attitudes, beliefs and values. In addition to rationalistic price comparisons, people may want to base their decisions on prior attitudes, for example on environmental impact, or emotional persuasion, for example through positive reinforcement [14]. In terms of AgentSwitch, information on the environmental impact of the tariff could have helped to make an informed decision in this vein (e.g., the actual provenance of the electricity distributed to the home).

Make following recommendations as convenient as possible

Even if regulation means 'one-click' switching is not possible, improvements to the system that makes switching more convenient might be as simple as populating an email template with the desired tariff details, or making the relevant provider's website available with one click.

Reveal provenance and certainty of predictions on demand

People did not explicitly mention that they used the explanations to support intelligibility of the system (echoing recent findings [6]), but their orientation towards the previous study in which their data was recorded suggests that an understanding of the provenance of the predictions was important overall. In real-life settings (e.g., without the presence of explaining researchers), availability of explanations how the predictions were arrived at in terms of provenance of the raw data used is likely more important to be perceived as trustworthy.

In addition, statistical methods of predictions yield probability values that indicate the level of certainty associated with the prediction. It may also be of value to take into account the level of certainty when presenting the predictions. Whether and how to present uncertainty in intelligent UIs is a key question for future work.

Incentivizing load shifting

The study revealed participants' manifold cost/benefit trade-offs with regards to incentivizing switching tariffs and shifting loads. The analysis highlights that these barriers differ contextually by person, activity, provider, perceived reward, and so on.

Particularly, the responses suggest that the monetary benefits of load shifting under current tariff structure (e.g., Economy7) did not sufficiently motivate our participants to change their behavior. Incentives to shift loads may be more attractive in the future with rising prices. However, even small savings may be important for some; fuel poverty is a core problem in low-income communities [11].

For load shifting in particular, the onus is on governmental policy and energy providers to create the infrastructure and services to incentivize load shifting. For example, the anticipated roll out of smart grid technologies may lead to the introduction of dynamically priced tariffs to incentivize load shifting. The price structure of these dynamic, multi-tier tariffs can be expected to provide a larger monetary incentive.

In addition, once the smart grid is in place, interactive systems can then be realized that aim to motivate load shifting in similar ways to current prevailing research and system design to motivate reductions in energy consumption [13,17]. One approach might be to convey to consumers the environmental benefits of load shifting (e.g., avoiding peak demand and thus reducing carbon emissions). New kinds of 'smart' persuasive technologies could draw on grid data to dissuade use in high-demand periods, and reward consent not just with money, but also with game-like rewards or environmental praise. In future work we will investigate providing such incentives in addition to monetary incentives especially where the latter are not sufficiently high.

Towards autonomous energy management

The study has also revealed people's attitude towards systems that automate switching and shifting. The anticipated increase in convenience seems to lower the (monetary) threshold in savings required to make switching worthwhile. The results support recent findings that people are not interested in spending a great deal of time optimizing their home energy management [32]. This finding supports the potential of investing in research towards (semi-) autonomous home energy management.

However, participants' comments suggest that accuracy of the predictions is essential in whether automation would be trusted and desired. With increasing autonomy, the requirements to being able to monitor and control the systems become more important. Challenges for the intelligent interface community include how the balance between user control and autonomy can be achieved in a flexible way without overwhelming the user with requests, and without risking undesired system actions.

Further, questions of ownership and stakeholders implicated with such an autonomous system arose during the study. Who owns the system and the data it generates and stores? Who has access to the data and the recommendations? Who is responsible if the system takes an undesired action? The user should be able to answer all these questions by accessing information through the UI, or by being notified by the system.

The insight still holds that, perhaps above all, intelligent systems need to be *intelligible* and *accountable* to be perceived as useful and trustworthy [3], particularly if the aim is that the system is adopted for use in everyday life.

CONCLUSIONS

This paper presented a system and evaluation of personalized energy-related recommendations based on household usage profiling. Based on user profiles, AgentSwitch provides comparisons of the user's current energy tariffs to the tariffs available on the market, and provides advice on how much the user can save by shifting detected deferrable loads (e.g., washing machine or tumble dryer) to off-peak times. We described the system architecture that drives the web service, including energy usage profiling based on time series of electricity consumption monitored in users' homes, deferrable load detection, and usage of up-to-date national energy tariff information to compute the recommendations.

The evaluation based on task-driven walkthroughs with 10 users with three months worth of monitored consumption data showed that AgentSwitch found cheaper tariffs for most of them (9/10). Despite potential annual savings of between £35-£390 interviews revealed a host of barriers to actually switching tariffs. As a result, we discussed interface issues that can be applied more broadly to overcome barriers to following recommendations. Moreover, anticipated regulatory as well as technological changes are needed, especially to create an environment in which load shifting can be encouraged, for example by devising persuasive systems not only to convey monetary incentives, but also to convey environmental benefits more effectively. Lastly, our evaluation supports the potential for semi-autonomous systems and we discuss some considerations relevant to intelligent UI designers, such as the need to balance user control and autonomy.

ACKNOWLEDGEMENTS

This work is supported by EPSRC grant EP/I011587/1.

REFERENCES

1. Baker, O.F., Khalil, I., and Kotsis, G. Agents for energy efficiency in ubiquitous environments. *Proc. iiWAS '09*, ACM Press (2009), 674-677.
2. Banerjee, N., Rollins, S., and Moran, K. Automating energy management in green homes. *Proc. SIGCOMM HomeNets '11*, ACM Press (2011), 19-24.
3. Bellotti, V. and Edwards, K. Intelligibility and accountability: human considerations in context-aware systems. *Human-Comp. Interact.* 16, 2 (2001), 193–212.
4. Braun, V. and Clark, V. Using thematic analysis in psychology. *Qual. Res. in Psych.* 3, (2006), 77–102.
5. Brynjarsdottir, H., Håkansson, M., Pierce, J., Baumer, E., DiSalvo, C., and Sengers, P. Sustainably unpersuaded: how persuasion narrows our vision of sustainability. *Proc. CHI '12*, ACM Press (2012), 947-956.
6. Bunt, A., Lount, M., and Lauzon, C. Are explanations always important?: a study of deployed, low-cost intelligent interactive systems. *Proc. IUI '12*, ACM Press (2012), 169-178.
7. Darby, S. Making sense of energy advice. *Proc. of ECEEE 2003*, (2003), 1217–1226.
8. MacKay, D.J.C. Sustainable energy — without the hot air. UIT Cambridge, Ltd, Cambridge, 2009.
9. Department of Energy and Climate Change (DECC) and the Office of Gas and Electricity Markets (OfGEM). *Smart Metering Implementation Programme.* 2011.
10. Diaconis, P. Bayesian numerical analysis. In S.G.J. Berger, ed., *Statistical Decision. Theory and Related Topics IV*. 1988, 163–175.
11. Dillahunt, T., Mankoff, J., Paulos, E., and Fussell, S. It's not all about "green": energy use in low-income communities. *Proc. Ubicomp '09*, Springer (2009), 255-264.
12. Frankcom, N. Household energy bills unaffordable in less than three years. 2012. http://bit.ly/LSE175. Accessed 09/01/2013.
13. Froehlich, J. and Findlater, L. The design of eco-feedback technology. *Proc. CHI '10*, ACM Press (2010), 1999–2008.
14. He, H.A., Greenberg, S., and Huang, E.M. One size does not fit all: applying the transtheoretical model to energy feedback technology design. *Proc. CHI '10*, ACM Press (2010), 927-936.
15. Hledick, R. How green is the smart grid? *Electricity* 22, 3 (2009), 29-41.
16. Ji, T., Tuo-Yu, P., Zhen-Min, Z., and Kai, L. A personalized recommendation model based on the user-state awareness. *Proc. 1st IEEE Symposium on Web Society*, IEEE (2009), 10–13.
17. Kjeldskov, J., Skov, M.B., Paay, J., and Pathmanathan, R. Using mobile phones to support sustainability: a field study of residential electricity consumption. *Proc. CHI '12*. ACM Press (2012), 2347-2356.
18. LeMay, M., Haas, J.J., and Grunter, C.A. Collaborative recommender systems for building automation. *Proc. 42nd Hawaii International Conference on System Sciences*, IEEE (2009), 1–10.
19. Lima, J.C.D., Rocha, C.C., Augustin, I., and Dantas, M´.A.R. A Context-aware recommendation system to behavioral based authentication in mobile and pervasive environments. *Proc. 9th International Conference on Embedded and Ubiquitous Computing*, IEEE (2011), 312–319.
20. Moreau, L. and Missier, P. PROV-DM: The PROV data model. 2012. http://www.w3.org/TR/prov-dm/ Accessed 09/01/2013.
21. O'Donovan, J. and Smyth, B. Trust in recommender systems. *Proc. IUI '05*, ACM Press (2005), 167-174.
22. Parnell, R. and Larsen, O.P. Informing the development of domestic energy efficiency initiatives. *Env. and Behavior* 37, 6 (2005) 787-807.
23. Parson, O., Ghosh, S., Weal, M., and Rogers, A. Non-intrusive load monitoring using prior models of general appliance types. *Proc. of the 26th AAAI Conference on Artificial Intelligence*, AAAI (2012), 356-362.
24. Pierce, J. and Paulos, E. Beyond energy monitors: interaction, energy, and emerging energy systems. *Proc. CHI '12*, ACM Press (2012), 665-674.
25. Pu, P., Chen, L., and Hu, R. A user-centric evaluation framework for recommender systems. *Proc. RecSys '11*, ACM Press (2011), 157-164.
26. Ramchurn, S.D., Vytelingum, P., Rogers, A., and Jennings, N.R. Agent-based homeostatic control for green energy in the smart grid. *ACM Trans. Intell. Syst. Technol.* 2, 4 Article 35 (2011).
27. Ramchurn, S.D., Osborne, M.A., Parson, O., Maleki, S., Rahwan, T., Huynh, T.D., Reece, S., Alam, M., Fischer, J.E., Hines, G., Costanza, E., Moreau, L., Rodden, T., and Roberts, S. AgentSwitch: smart energy tariff selection using agent technology. *Proc. AAMAS '13*, IFAAMAS (2013).
28. Rial, A. and Danezis, G. Privacy-preserving smart metering. *Proc. WPES '11*, ACM Press (2011), 49-60.
29. Scott, J., Brush, A.J.B., Krumm, J., Meyers, B., Hazas, M., Hodges, S. and Villar, N. PreHeat: controlling

home heating using occupancy prediction. *Proc. UbiComp '11,* Springer (2011), 281-290.

30. Strengers, Y.A.A. Designing eco-feedback systems for everyday life. *Proc. CHI '11*, ACM Press (2011), 2135-2144.

31. US Department of Energy. Benefits of demand response in electricity markets and recommendations for achieving them. 2006.

32. US Department of Energy. The smart grid: an introduction. 2008.

SIDNIE: Scaffolded Interviews Developed by Nurses in Education

Lauren Cairco Dukes, Toni Bloodworth Pence, Larry F. Hodges
Clemson University School of Computing
McAdams Hall, Clemson, SC 29634
{LCairco, tbloodw,LFH}@clemson.edu

Nancy Meehan, Arlene Johnson
Clemson University School of Nursing
Edwards Hall, Clemson, SC 29634
{nmeehan, aejohns}@clemson.edu

ABSTRACT
One of the most common clinical education methods for teaching patient interaction skills to nursing students is role-playing established scenarios with their classmates. Unfortunately, this is far from simulating real world experiences that they will soon face, and does not provide the immediate, impartial feedback necessary for interviewing skills development. We present a system for Scaffolded Interviews Developed by Nurses In Education (SIDNIE) that supports baccalaureate nursing education by providing multiple guided interview practice sessions with virtual characters. Our scenario depicts a mother who has brought in her five year old child to the clinic. In this paper we describe our system and report on a preliminary usability evaluation conducted with nursing students.

Author Keywords
Virtual characters; virtual patient; pediatric nursing; virtual environment; scaffolded learning; interview simulation

ACM Classification Keywords
H.5.m. Information interfaces and presentation (e.g., HCI): Miscellaneous.

General Terms
Human Factors; Design; Measurement.

INTRODUCTION

Nursing students have limited opportunities for interaction with real patients, especially with pediatric patients, and do not often receive immediate and impartial feedback on their performance during their patient interaction. In order to provide alternative educational opportunities, we have created a system for Scaffolded Interviews Developed by Nurses In Education (SIDNIE), which allows nursing students to interact with virtual characters acting as patients to practice their interviewing skills, while receiving guidance and feedback from a virtual nurse educator.

Experiential learning through simulation may help students develop the skills necessary for clinical practice and help develop the self-efficacy and critical thinking skills they need to provide the safest care possible. Also, this system has the potential to provide consistent experiences for all students with feedback and repetitive practice.

There is currently a shortage of registered nurses and nurse educators, resulting in the need for new educational pedagogies for clinical nurse education [23]. The need for registered nurses could increase as much as 500,000 by 2025. In 2007 and 2008, 84 percent of nursing schools were actively recruiting nursing faculty [23]. A shortage in nursing faculty often results in larger class numbers. Our system provides a tool to aid nursing faculty in providing scored practice opportunities for student nurses. Since children are a vulnerable population, nurses must develop appropriate pediatric skills necessary to provide safe care to infants, children, and teens. Because nursing students have limited access to pediatric patients and may not have the opportunity to practice with children, we focus on a mother and child scenario.

RELATED WORK

Simulation Learning and Patient Safety
The Institute of Medicine has recommended the use of simulation training as a method to improve health care delivery [25], and patient safety has been identified as one of the six competencies necessary to improve health care education [18]. Simulation training is an effective strategy to help promote safe clinical practices [17] and impacts the development of self-efficacy and judgment skills for nurses, that are essential to provide the safest and most effective care possible [15]. Simulation learning that mimics real world scenarios is beneficial to nursing students and will provide standardized experiences in which students can practice problem solving techniques and clinical decision making abilities [15] Five advantages to using simulation in nursing education have been identified: 1) providing opportunity for interactive learning without risk to patients, 2) boosting students' self confidence and reducing anxiety in the practice setting, 3) allowing nursing students to practice clinical decision making, and critical thinking in a controlled environment, 4) allowing skills and procedures to be repeated until proficiency is reached, and 5) providing

immediate feedback [13]. We designed SIDNIE specifically to provide repetitive practice as well as the benefits of immediate feedback.

Simulation Learning

One of the current simulation exercises in the School of Nursing involves students acting out written scenarios, where one student acts as the patient while the other acts as the nurse. SIDNIE can replace the student patient with a virtual patient, which is an artificially intelligent human representation that behaves similarly to a human patient under the same circumstance. Researchers have used virtual patients to teach communications skills to medical students, and students have rated the virtual patient experience as being as effective as a standardized patient (a paid actor) [15]. Medical students have also used virtual patients to help practice patient interviewing skills with a high level of immersion. Results indicate that using life-size virtual characters with speech recognition is useful in their education [20]. Adult virtual patients are fairly common, but virtual pediatric patients are rare. The use of virtual pediatric patients was first addressed in [13], where they were used for training and assessment for medical students. The scenario in this system included a mother and daughter, but the technology for creating virtual human behaviors had not focused on children's behaviors, therefore the realism needed for this project was not available [13]. Even with the lack of realism, the results of their study were positive in that many of the participants stated that they gained valuable experience.

Communicating with Children and Parents

In addition to the challenges presented in displaying appropriate animations for children, the dynamics related to the nurse-family-child relationship are extensive due to the many factors that enter into this relationship, including ethnicity, age, culture, and illness. During an assessment, the nurse must obtain information (verbal and nonverbal) from the parent(s) and child, and observe any interactions between them [15]. Studies by pediatric experts have shown that the nurse-family-child relationship is heavily dependent upon effective communication, which is a skill that is developed through interaction with different kinds of pediatric patients and families [10]. Student nurses must be aware of the interactions that may negatively or positively affect their communication skills, therefore affecting the relationship. This study also showed that a positive nurse-family-child relationship will promote the health of the child [10].

Scaffolding in Learning

Since SIDNIE is designed for nursing student education, we want to provide an efficient pathway for students to be able to achieve some level of competence in interviewing techniques before they reach the clinical setting. We previously developed a prototype system to support freeform interviewing with a pediatric patient using speech recognition. However, during a usability study, we found that even experienced nurses had difficulty using the system, since there was no guidance for which questions our system could answer, and because of problems with visual and behavioral fidelity. Additionally, to give a user feedback on his or her performance required the attention of a nurse, since there was no automated scoring system. To better support learning and reduce difficulty, we decided to build a scaffolded system for interview practice.

Instructional scaffolding is a teaching and learning strategy that provides temporary support to a learner while he or she achieves competency in a task that he or she would not be able to accomplish unaided [24]. Traditionally, scaffolding occurs in an apprentice-learner context, with a subject expert aiding a less experienced learner; however, any method of support provided during learning is considered a form of scaffolding [16]. Holton and Clarke have classified scaffolding techniques based on agency (who provides the scaffolding) and domain (whether the scaffolding helps teach a concept, or helps teach a heuristic method) [16]. There are three possible scaffolding agencies: expert, when a domain expert aids a learner; reciprocal, when peers working together aid each other through their individual strengths; and self, when an individual can apply his or her related knowledge to a new problem. Conceptual scaffolding provides problem-specific aid, while heuristic scaffolding provides principles that are useful for solving generalized problems. Any agency can provide either of the domains. Since the final goal of scaffolding is learner independence, self-scaffolding is especially desirable [16].

Educators have successfully applied scaffolding to many domains, including mathematics [16], medicine [19], and science [22]. Several researchers have applied expert scaffolding to pharmacy students learning to conduct patient interviews. Planas et al. developed a scaffolded communications skills development system that students used as a part of their course on clinical communications [21]. This system provided scaffolding through several means. Students worked in groups, providing reciprocal scaffolding, and received feedback from faculty members and standardized patients, providing expert scaffolding. Students also were required to evaluate their own performance, encouraging self-scaffolding. As the course progressed, support in the form of peer and instructor guidance lessened and students became more competent. Comparing the assessments of a standardized patient interview before the course and one after the course, students performed significantly better ($p < 0.01$) as rated by faculty, peers, standardized patients, and students themselves [21]. Stupans et al. developed several tools for scaffolding patient counseling skills, including rubrics for student evaluation, a flexible protocol for counseling sessions, tools to aid in self-critique and peer-critique of interviews, roleplaying, and use of expert scaffolding, especially early in the experiential learning process. Although they have not yet tested its effect on performance, students generally responded positively to the idea of scaffolded opportunities for learning [26].

Crossing into the electronic domain, Simmersion has developed several systems designed to teach interaction for specific scenarios, providing aid through a "virtual coach" who gives feedback as users ask questions [6]. Simmersion systems show a videotaped human who acts as the interview partner in a large portion of the screen. The user selects a question from a list of questions to ask the interview partner, then the partner responds through a videotaped clip. A virtual coach provides nonverbal feedback on the question selection through motions such as applauding or shaking her head, and provides text feedback if clicked. One example product is a system that gives people with autism practice in social conversation. With eleven learning objectives, a complex conversational model determines how the interview partner responds to user questions. The system keeps a points-based score for user choices and allows the user to review the interview script. A user study on this system showed that the users enjoyed their interaction with the system but would have appreciated a system with more conversational choices, and that the mean scores improved from the first use of the system to the last use of the system [27]. The Simmersion systems provide expert, conceptual scaffolding, since the virtual agent gives choice-by-choice feedback specific to the current conversation. Due to the complexity of the learning objectives and the videotaped interactions, these systems are difficult to extend. Additionally, there is no leveled scaffolding—the same feedback is provided to the user by the virtual coach regardless of the user's experience level.

Extending the success of these systems and the apprenticeship model already present in nursing education, we designed our system to provide leveled heuristic scaffolding through expert agency while supporting maximum extensibility. Our virtual agent serves as the expert scaffolder, teaching heuristic knowledge by providing information on criteria that pediatric patient interviews should meet and broad categories that an interview should cover. The virtual agent provides scaffolding by giving instruction on the criteria and categories, and by giving feedback on user selections. We encourage progressive learner independence by providing several levels of scaffolding, ranging from heavy guidance to minimal feedback. Additionally, we preserve extensibility through our database-driven design, criteria-based scoring, and virtual patients, whose actions and speech can be easily modified.

KEY CONTRIBUTIONS

There are no reports in the literature of applying scaffolded learning and standardized feedback to training in interview skills for any e-learning scenario, much less in the pediatric nursing domain. There are existing e-learning systems for teaching communication skills that offer question-by-question feedback or overall scenario scoring. However, no system found in the literature offers scaffolded support for learners by progressively decreasing guidance through the interview task, or standardized scoring based on specific criteria. Our work is novel in that it offers a framework for scaffolding and feedback for any interaction task, given a set of criteria and scored question-answer pairs. It is also a contribution to the nursing community, since the current training techniques of peer role play and standardized patient (actor) interviews are typically unscored and students receive feedback based only on a peer or instructor's personal perception of the interaction.

SYSTEM DESCRIPTION

SIDNIE is designed to teach nursing students pediatric patient interview techniques by providing interview practice with guidance and feedback from a virtual agent named Sidnie. Sidnie guides the user through several scaffolded practice opportunities and provides feedback on user choices. The user conducts an interview with the virtual patients by selecting questions from a preset list of questions developed by experienced nurses, and the virtual patients respond appropriately. The user can also view interview playbacks and score them as if they were an instructor, encouraging knowledge application to new situations. The application runs on a standard desktop computer and a single monitor, and the user interacts with the system using the mouse.

Scenario Development

We worked with experienced nursing faculty to develop a patient-nurse interaction scenario for a five year old child with an earache. The nurses generated a set of possible questions and scored each question according to two criteria important for pediatric interviews: age appropriate, and unbiased. Age appropriate in this context primarily means that questions addressed to the child used language children would understand, and that necessarily complex questions were addressed to the parent. For example, "Hello Sarah, I am the RN who will be your nurse" is not age appropriate, since a child would not know that RN stands for "Registered Nurse." Unbiased questions do not make implicit assumptions or lead the patient to respond in a particular way. For example, "Sarah, your tummy hasn't been hurting, has it?" leads the child to respond negatively, and is therefore biased. Additionally, the nurses categorized the questions into broad categories and subcategories, and provided us with the subset of categories that are essential for a nurse to cover in every patient interview. The subset of categories and subcategories that are essential are: Introduction/Introducing Yourself, Introduction/Confirming Patient Identity, Chief Complaint, History of Present Illness, Related Systems, and Past Medical History. This detailed structure enables us to provide feedback to users on their question selections and interview thoroughness. This meets our goal of providing heuristic scaffolding, since these criteria and categories can be applied to any pediatric patient interview.

Sidnie

A male nurse named Sidnie serves as our virtual nurse educator during the interview simulation. Sidnie's role is to

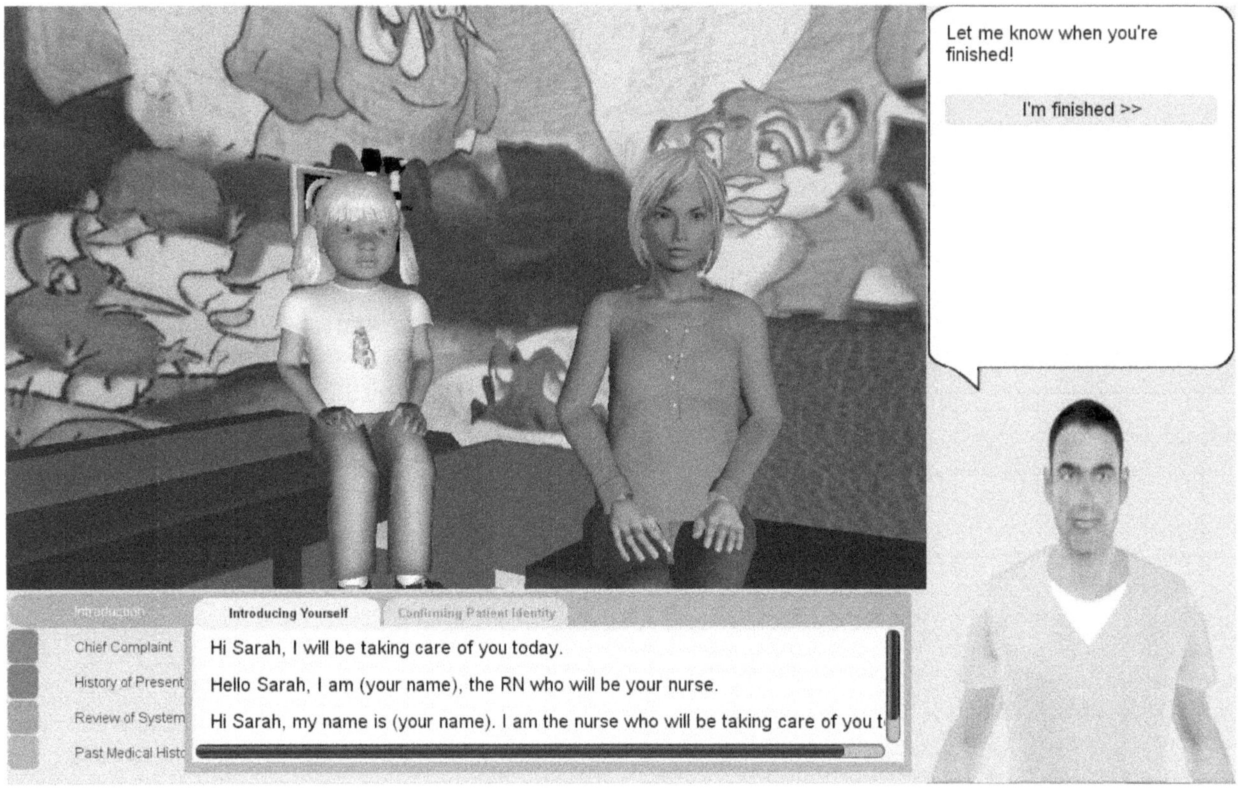

Figure 1. SIDNIE permits a user to interview the virtual patients by selecting question categories and subcategories using a tabbed interface at the bottom of the screen. The user clicks a question, then the virtual patients respond with speech and animations.

provide instruction on how to use the other interaction modules, to give feedback to the user on his or her performance, and to demonstrate patient interviews. Sidnie is represented by a static image of a male nurse in the lower right hand corner of the screen. We chose not to animate Sidnie or support additional interaction with him because we felt that an additional animated character would distract from the patients' behaviors and animations. Sidnie has a quote bubble above his head that is used to display instructions or give feedback.

Tutorial

When each session begins, Sidnie introduces himself through text and guides the user through a tutorial that outlines how to use the level using screenshots with accompanying text. The user must click "Next" to proceed through each slide until the tutorial is finished. Sidnie can give additional text or image instructions according to what is present in the database.

Electronic Health Record

After the tutorial, our system displays a simple electronic health record (EHR) for the patient. The EHR features information on the patient's current statistics including a photo of the patient, the patient's birthday, weight, temperature, immunization record, medications, allergies, parents' names and contact information, and reason for the visit. The user can access this information using buttons to select categories of information. Once the user has reviewed the medical record, he or she clicks a button to proceed with the scenario.

Pediatric Patient Interview

During the scenario, the majority of the screen displays the virtual patients in their environment. For our current simulation, a mother and her five year old daughter sit in a pediatric patient room. In an idle state, the virtual characters sit quietly. When responding to questions, the patients perform appropriate speech and animations. Depending on the chosen scaffolding level, the user may either conduct a patient interview with guidance or may observe an interview and score it for the chosen criteria.

Conducting an Interview

Our database stores a set of questions that the user may ask, and the corresponding character responses. For ease of use, we display the questions according to their categories and subcategories in the question selection interface. The question selection interface is displayed at the bottom of the screen when the user is permitted to conduct an interview with patients. On the left side of the screen, colorful tabs permit the user to select top level categories, which are dynamically loaded in from the database. Users may select subcategories using a set of tabs along the top of the list of questions. Under the tabs, we display the list of questions belonging to the selected category and subcategory. We randomize the order the questions are displayed with each run of the application so that repetitive use is still slightly

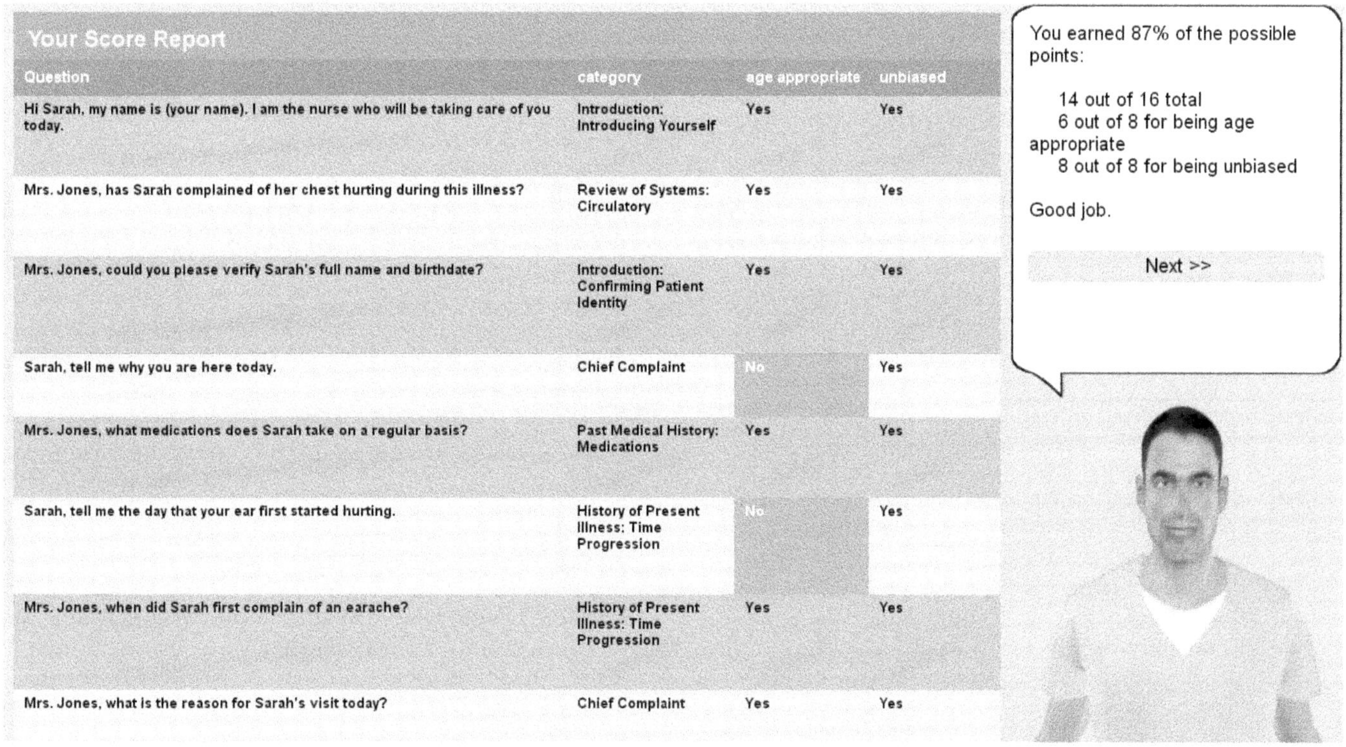

Figure 2. Sidnie gives feedback in chart and percentage form after a scaffolding level is completed.

varied. To select a question, the user simply clicks on the displayed question. The question is highlighted, then the characters respond appropriately with speech and/or animation. After the characters respond, the user may proceed to select questions until the session is complete.

Grading an Interview

Sidnie may also prompt the user to grade another interviewer's questions to encourage the user to apply his or her knowledge to a new problem. In this module, the application retrieves a prerecorded sequence of questions from the database. Sidnie "reads" a stored question using text to speech, then the virtual patient and/or parent responds with the corresponding answer stored in the database. After the characterss finish responding, in his quote bubble, Sidnie prompts the user to grade the question on the stored criteria, and to categorize the question into the correct category & subcategory. We provide a checkbox for each criteria, where the user should check the checkbox if it meets the criteria, and then a scroll down list, where the user must select a category before proceeding. After submitting the score, the interview playback proceeds.

Feedback Mechanisms

To promote user learning, we provide two types of feedback for the user depending on the selected scaffolding level. Immediate feedback provides selection-by-selection scoring so that the user can correct his or her mistakes immediately during the interview, and is used in the lower scaffolding levels. Summative feedback is provided at the end of each scaffolding level and provides the user with an overall score and overview of his or her performance for the entire scenario.

Immediate Feedback

When the user is conducting an interview, Sidnie may give immediate feedback on user question selection in his quote bubble. When the user selects a question, we query the database to see whether the question meets the stored criteria. We use the query results to generate a string that Sidnie may immediately display in his quote bubble to indicate how the user performed. For example, for a question the user selected that meets both criteria, Sidnie may say, "Good job! The question you asked was unbiased and age-appropriate."

When the user is scoring an interview, Sidnie also may provide immediate feedback on the submitted score. When the user submits a score, we query the database to find the actual question's scoring and category, then compare them to the user selected characteristics and build a string to provide feedback. For example, the correct category was chosen but both criteria were scored incorrectly, Sidnie may say, "You selected the appropriate category for this question: 'Introduction: Confirming Patient Identity.' You scored the question incorrectly as: unbiased when it was not unbiased, not age appropriate when it was age appropriate."

Summative Feedback

At the end of each session, the user may receive summative feedback in chart form as well as an overall percentile score for his or her performance. Each row in the chart represents a question the user asked, along with its scoring data.

If the user conducted the patient interview, we highlight the cells for the scored criteria based on whether the selected questions met the criteria. Pink cells show the user that the question did not meet the criteria, while green cells show that the question met the criteria. Additionally, we display a pink row with the category name for each essential category that the user neglected. If the user scored a patient interview, we highlight the cells based on whether they scored the question correctly. Pink cells show the user that they made a mistake in scoring or categorizing the question.

In the summative feedback screen, Sidnie displays percentage and proportion scores in his quote bubble. If the user conducted an interview, we calculate the percentage score and proportion score by counting how many questions met the criteria and how many of the essential categories the user covered. We generate speech for Sidnie based on those scores. For example, for a user who asked seven questions, and covered each essential category, but did not meet the scoring criteria for every question, Sidnie may say, "You scored 12 out of 20 points, for a score of 60%. You scored 6 out of 6 points for category coverage, 5 out of 7 points for being unbiased, and 1 out of 7 points for being age appropriate." We calculate scores similarly for users who score an interview, except we score them for choosing the correct category and for correctly grading the question for the criteria instead of choosing questions that met criteria and covered essential categories.

SCAFFOLDING LEVELS

Our goal in this system is to provide leveled scaffolding so that an inexperienced student may progressively gain enough confidence, knowledge, and simulated experience to ease the transition into actual patient interviews. Currently we have implemented four scaffolding levels for our simulation designed to progressively remove scaffolding until the student can perform an interview without aid.

We based our scaffolding levels on scaffolding used for in-person pharmacology interviews[21,26]; however, our approach is innovateive in that we use one set of criteria to score each question, so that students learn overall concepts to be applied for each question in addition to the steps needed for a complete interview.

Level 1: Baseline Measurement

To enable measurement of user progress, we first require the user to conduct a patient interview using our system without any training or guidance. During the tutorial phase, Sidnie explains how to select a question using our system. The user reviews the medical record and proceeds with the interview, selecting as many questions as he or she desires. Sidnie does not give immediate feedback on the question choices. When the user is finished with the interview, the session concludes without any summative feedback.

Level 2: Guided Interview with Immediate Feedback

The second level begins the scaffolded learning by guiding the user through a short pediatric patient interview. During the tutorial phase, Sidnie explains how to select a question using our system, and then describes the criteria that the questions should meet and the categories that an interview should cover. The user initially reviews the medical record then continues to the guided interview. The system preselects the first essential question category in the question selection interface and disables the user from changing the category. Then Sidnie instructs the user to select a question. When the user selects a question, the patients respond, then Sidnie gives immediate feedback on whether the question met the criteria. If the question did not meet each of the criteria, Sidnie informs the user of which criteria were not met and instructs the user to try again. The user must continue to select questions until he or she chooses a question that meets both criteria. Then, the system advances to the next essential category. The process continues until each essential category is covered, then shows summative feedback to the user.

Level 3: Grading an Interview

The third level requires the user to score a prerecorded interview by watching and listening to each question and response, then identifying the category. The tutorial phase explains the interview playback process and the grader interface. The user then views Sarah's electronic medical record and proceeds to the interview. As described in the previous section on grading an interview, the user grades the interview question by question, and Sidnie gives immediate feedback on his or her grading, but does not require the user to correctly grade the question before moving to the next question. Once the user finishes scoring the interview, he or she receives summative feedback on the scoring.

Level 4: Evaluation

Finally, the fourth level evaluates the user's learning by providing unguided interaction similar to Level 1. The tutorial phase again explains the system and the scoring criteria, and then the user proceeds through the interview by selecting as many questions in as many categories as they wish. The user clicks a button when he or she is finished. Lastly, they receive summative feedback on their interview based on their category coverage and whether their questions met the criteria.

IMPLEMENTATION DETAILS

Our system is implemented primarily in Unity 3D [8] as a set of related modules implemented in Boo or C#. We created the virtual environment using Blender [1] and imported it into Unity. We rigged and animated the characters using Poser Pro [5] and Blender [1]. Using Unity's plugin interface, we built a C++ plugin as an interface to SAPI 5.3 [4]. We used IVONA voices [2] for our virtual characters: Sarah's voice is Ivy, Mrs. Jones' voice is Kendra, and Sidnie's voice is Joey. In addition to the animations triggered by responding to user questions, our characters exhibit baseline animations such as breathing and blinking.

Although our virtual characters and environment are static at this point, the remainder of our program is database-driven, providing flexibility to change scenarios, scoring criteria, instructions, and required categories. We store our scenario data in a SQLite 3 database [7] and access it through Unity's plugin interface. Additionally, each question selection and scoring action is timestamped and recorded in the database, keyed on the user ID and the scaffolding level for easy data processing.

Character Response Queueing

When a user clicks on a question, we retrieve the answer the characters should give from the database. We store the answer as a sequence of animations and text to speech, with each record in the response representing one animation or line of speech. Each action is accompanied by an identifier that associates it with one of the virtual characters, and a delay that denotes when in time the action should occur. Within our Unity application, we keep a queue of these actions with their delays. While the queue still contains items, we use a coroutine to keep track of elapsed time and check whether it is time to perform an action. When it is time to perform an action, we call the appropriate function and remove the action from the queue.

Animating a character is a simple Unity function call to trigger a preset animation. When a character's response requires speech, the process is more complex. Because timings in the database may be inexact, and creating many SAPI instances causes performance problems, we also keep a text-to-speech queue that holds any text to speech to be rendered. When a new question is selected, we count the number of speech items contained in the response, then send that number ahead to the plugin so that it can indicate to Unity that it is busy until there are no more items to be spoken. Using a coroutine, while there is speech in the queue, our application checks to determine whether the text-to-speech engine is currently rendering speech. When the engine is not busy, it sends the next item in the queue, then waits for it to be non-busy again. To keep the count of items to speak up to date, within the plugin, we handle the SAPI event for finished speech and use it to decrement the counter.

We send the string to SAPI via the C++ plugin, along with parameters to select an appropriate voice based on the character's age and gender. This increases our system's extensibility since it would cause the most appropriate voices to be selected on a system that does not have our chosen voices installed. Since Unity's default behavior is to call a plugin as a part of its own thread, and SAPI voice loading events are blocking function calls, within our plugin we launch a thread to render the text to speech so that the Unity application may continue to render the virtual characters with appropriate animations and lipsyncing. Within the launched thread, the plugin loads the appropriate SAPI voice and renders the string through text-to-speech. Inside the plugin we store the current viseme for each character (mouth shape) by handling SAPI viseme events as the text to speech is rendered. In the Unity application's update function, we query the plugin to gather each character's current mouth shape. If the mouth shape has changed since the previous update, we trigger an animation to change the character's mouth shape to match the speech SAPI is rendering, using a modification of the Metamorph script[3] to apply shapekey morphs to our characters' faces.

In order to encourage the user to be attentive to the characters' responses, we disable the question selection interface while the character is performing animation or speaking. We do this by checking to determine whether the response queue is empty and whether the text to speech plugin has more speech to render. While the queue is nonempty or text to speech has more lines to render, we overlay the question selection interface with a translucent screen and place text over the interface and in Sidnie's text bubble to indicate that the user should wait for the characters to finish their response. After the character has finished her response, the question selection interface is enabled and Sidnie provides appropriate instructions for the scaffolding level.

EXPERIMENTAL PROCEDURE

We conducted an experiment to gather initial impressions on SIDNIE's usability and to measure learning outcomes for a student completing all three scaffolding levels. Each of the scaffolding levels used the same scenario: a mother with her five year old daughter, who has an earache.

Participants completed a demographics questionnaire and read the informed consent form the morning before the experiment. When the participants came to the experiment site, we greeted them then gathered their demographic questionnaires, which included questions about previous computer usage, experience in healthcare, and exposure to virtual environments. The participant then signed the informed consent. We seated the participant at a desktop computer and began the SIDNIE system on scaffolding level 1. We asked the participant to view the beginning tutorial screens, which instructed them on how to use the system but included no information on the required question categories or the scoring criteria, then to conduct an interview with the patients to the best of their ability, and to let us know when they had finished.

After the participant completed the initial interview, we began the SIDNIE system on level 2. We told the participants that SIDNIE would guide them through their interview this time, and that they would receive feedback on their choices. The participants then proceeded through the guided interview and notified the experimenter upon completion. The participant continued through levels 2 and 3 similarly, with the experimenter briefly commenting on each level then starting the application.

After completing every level, the participant filled out the System Usability Scale (SUS) [12] and was given the

	Age appropriate		Unbiased		Category Coverage	
	Mean	SD	Mean	SD	Mean	SD
Level 1	75.12	12.04	70.65	10.76	91.67	19.34
Level 2	94.22	10.14	93.46	11.18	n/a	
Level 3	82.14	8.75	80.10	13.19	n/a	
Level 4	93.52	9.72	90.26	8.39	100.0	0.00

Table 1. Percentage means and standard deviation for each scaffolding level.

opportunity to provide any written feedback. Finally, the participant completed an interview with the experimenter, where we asked questions about his or her opinion of the system.

Our primary hypothesis was that participant performance in terms of essential category coverage and choosing questions that met the criteria of age appropriateness and unbiasedness would increase between the level one baseline measurement and the level four evaluation measurement. We also expected participant performance to increase between each scaffolding level, and expected participants to report our system to be usable.

RESULTS

Fifteen undergraduate students seeking their Bachelor of Science in Nursing (BSN) at Clemson University participated in our experiment as an optional extra credit assignment for their Nursing Care of Children class. All of the participants already have received a bachelors degree in another field. Fourteen of the fifteen students are a part of the accelerated second degree program, while the remaining participant is a traditional BSN student.

Twelve of the participants were female, and three of the participants were male. Participants' ages ranged from 23 to 48 (mean=30.13, sd=7.28). Participants reported a high level of computer use. Participants reported some level of healthcare experience, experience with children, and experience in a healthcare setting, and somewhat lower levels of experience with children in healthcare, virtual human exposure, and virtual reality exposure. See Table 1 for detailed demographic information. When asked about their previous experience with virtual reality, virtual humans, or avatars, participants cited their experience in the nursing simulation lab, which has physical dummies that exhibit instructor-controlled symptoms. Most of the students also participated in an experiment in the previous semester that required them to take vital signs for a virtual human in a virtual hospital displayed on a desktop computer and record the results in an electronic health record.

Technical difficulties caused five sessions to terminate prematurely. We gave these participants the option to try the session again, or to continue on with the next level. Three participants chose to redo the session, while two participants continued onto the next level. We were able to recover sufficient data for all but one participant, who chose not to complete level three. We excluded her data from the quantitative analysis but kept her usability data. We recovered the three participants' data who made a second attempt at level completion by splicing together their data from the two session attempts by keeping all choices made in the first attempt before the program crashed and discarding all choices in the second attempt up until they reached the same point in the level as they were in the first session. For the final participant who chose not to retry a level, we considered her data in terms of proportions only, to give a fair basis for comparison to others who completed the level.

Our primary interest in this evaluation was to determine whether user scores improved between the level one baseline measurement and the level four evaluation measurement. Levels one and four were identical except for the instructions during the tutorial phase and the summative feedback at the end of the interview in level four. We calculated the percentage of questions the user asked that were age appropriate, the percentage of questions the user asked that were unbiased, and the percentage of the essential categories that the user covered. Using a two-tailed t-test for paired samples, we found significant differences in each of the scores for the criteria, indicating that participants' performance improved as a result of the use of our system ($p < 0.01$ for each criteria). We did not find a significant difference in the percentage of categories covered. See Table 1 for detailed statistics.

Progress through Scaffolding

To gauge which of our scaffolded levels were effective for learning, we analyzed whether participants' scores improved over each level. Levels two and three are significantly different from levels one and four, so it is somewhat difficult to make a direct comparison in user performance. We chose to compare the levels based on the two criteria: age appropriateness, and bias. Comparing category coverage was not possible since level two forced all essential categories to be covered, and level three played back a predetermined interview that covered all essential categories. We calculated the criteria percentages for levels one, two, and four for each of these criteria by finding the proportion of questions the user asked that met the criteria. For level three, since users were scoring an interview instead of conducting an interview, we calculated the proportion of questions correctly scored in regards to that criteria.

Using a two-tailed t-test for paired samples, we found significant differences in scores between each of the consecutive scaffolding levels (every $p < 0.01$), however, the mean scores were not always increasing, as we would have expected. The scores for level three were significantly lower than the scores for level two and level four (see Table 1). For nonconsecutive levels, there was no significant difference between levels two and four, but a significant difference in both criteria between levels one and three

	Mean	SD
Healthcare experience	3.80	1.37
Experience with children	4.40	1.96
Experience in a healthcare setting	3.60	1.77
Experience with children in healthcare	2.80	1.78
Computer use	6.47	0.74
Virtual human exposure	2.87	1.51
Virtual reality exposure	2.20	1.26

Table 2. Demographic information for the study participants (1= no experience, 7= very experienced)

(both p's < 0.03), with higher scores in level three.

Usability and Qualitative Feedback

Overall, participants seemed to find the system easy to use. Our system received an average SUS score of 80.33% (sd=12.20%). The highest scoring prompts were, "I didn't need to learn a lot of things before I could get going with this system" and "I didn't think there was too much inconsistency in the system", both with means of 5.6 out of 6 and the lowest standard deviation of any question as well (sd =0.63). The lowest scoring prompt was "I felt very confident using the system" with a mean score of 3.93 out of 6 (sd=1.75). See Table 2 for other detailed results.

When asked, every participant said that they thought they and their peers would use our system if it were made available to them. Comparing this technique of interview practice to other techniques (such as roleplay, standardized patients, or reading case studies), all participants felt they would have performed the same or worse using another practice technique. Reasons cited for improved performance using our system included less performance anxiety, being able to select from provided choices instead of coming up with questions on their own, being able to get immediate feedback, and being able to take our system more seriously than roleplay with their peers.

Three of the fifteen participants said that the child's symptoms were not realistic for a five year old with an earache. Two participants were not sure since they did not have much experience with children. The remaining ten participants said the child's symptoms were realistic, citing examples such as the data in the electronic medical record, the child pulling her ear, not responding to questions that weren't age appropriate, and responding nonverbally. Participants suggested that the patients should have appropriate facial expressions, and that Sarah could be more whiny, fidgety, or irritable. Three participants thought that the mother's voice sounded "mean", but one participant commented that a disagreeable parent is realistic in a clinical setting.

When asked what they liked about the system, nine of fifteen participants mentioned some aspect of the program that related to the scaffolding, including guidance and feedback, time to think about choices, and being able to try multiple questions in an interview with no risk of offending a patient. The most common aspects that participants disliked were the mother's voice and the scoring interface.

DISCUSSION

Our primary hypothesis was confirmed—participants' performance did improve from the baseline to the evaluation. However, the scores did not monotonically increase over each scaffolding level as we expected, and determining which scaffolding levels are effective for learning is difficult. There was a significant difference in performance between levels one and two, where the only training received was the tutorial preceding level two, and the immediate feedback for each question selected in level two. At level two, it seems that the scores hit a "ceiling", with participants scoring upwards of 93% for each criteria. In fact, nine out of the fifteen participants showed perfect scores in the second level. These scores do not leave much room for improvement in the similar task for level four, and in fact, we did not find significant differences in the performance between level two and level four.

The "ceiling effect" in the scores for levels one, two, and four may be explained by considering literature in the learning domain such as the Revised Bloom's Taxonomy [14], [9]. Our goal is to encourage the highest levels of learning, which in the new taxonomy are titled "creating" and "evaluating". In the first and fourth scaffolding levels, we aimed to permit users to "create" an interview scenario with limited choices. However, because there were only a few choices in each category and subcategory, and a participant was potentially exposed to each of those questions and their corresponding responses and scores multiple times, by the time the user reached the fourth level, the task became a low-level learning exercise of "remembering" or "understanding", or at best, "applying" the meaning of the criteria and categories to select appropriate questions.

In retrospect, given our limited question base, a more appropriate baseline and evaluation may have been to require the user to score an interview before and after some training. The scoring task reaches the "evaluating" level of the learning taxonomy, and the lower percentage scores in the third level of scaffolding can possibly be attributed to the higher level of learning required.

The lower scores for the third level are also likely the result of usability problems. Several participants were confused by the scoring interface. Since "unbiased" is a negative word and was paired with a checkbox, several participants asked questions like, "Do I check this box if it is biased, or unbiased?" In future iterations of the design, we will change to a radio button interface where the user can select "Yes" or "No" to clarify the scoring. Additionally, several users mentioned that they did not realize until far into the session that they could scroll down to select categories besides

	Mean	SD
I think that I would like to use this system frequently	4.2	0.94
The system was not unnecessarily complex	5.13	1.25
I thought the system was easy to use	4.13	1.85
I don't think I would need the support of a technical person to be able to use this system	5.13	0.92
I found the various functions in the system were well integrated	4.4	1.18
I didn't think there was too much inconsistency in the system	5.6	0.63
I would imagine that most people would learn to use this system very quickly	4.67	1.59
I didn't find the system very cumbersome to use	5.4	0.83
I felt very confident using the system	3.93	1.75
I didn't need to learn a lot of things before I could get going with this system	5.6	0.63

Table 3. Results of the System Usability Scale (SUS). Scores range from 0 (strongly disagree) to 6 (strongly agree). In this table we have modified the original questionnaire and scores so that higher scores are always better.

those in immediate view. Unity3D's default scrollbars are dissimilar to standard scroll controls and do not feature up and down arrows, so we will modify their appearance to match more traditional interfaces, or we will change the scrollable view to a drop-down box. Lastly, although our system currently supports a question belonging to only one category, several students felt that some of the questions could have fit in multiple categories. In the future, we will consider allowing questions to be part of multiple categories.

Although there is always room for improvement, our SUS scores as well as the feedback from our debriefing interview shows that our system has good usability, confirming our final hypothesis. The lowest scoring SUS question was about user confidence. Although we did not gather data on specific sources of anxiety, since each participant reported that they and their peers would use the system if it were offered to them, and that they would expect similar or worse performance using another interview technique, the low score for this question may reflect a user's lack of confidence in their ability to conduct pediatric interviews instead of their confidence in actually using the system.

FUTURE WORK

In addition to correcting usability problems, there are two primary areas we plan to extend our project. First, we will extend our project to provide a broader range of interview opportunities along several dimensions. For the existing scenario, we intend to add variety and attempt to reduce learning effects by adding more questions and answers within each category to the database, then showing randomly selected subsets of the questions each session. We will also add more scoring criteria to increase complexity. Additionally, we will develop more scenarios including different medical conditions as well as patients from various socioeconomic, ethnic, religious, and health backgrounds. During the debriefing interview, several students mentioned their interest in practicing interviews with people who were outside of the perceived norm, since those patients may require extra care during interaction.

Second, we would like to extend support for learning. From the scaffolded learning perspective, our current system covers several levels of the Revised Bloom's Taxonomy[9]. We promote "remembering" and "understanding" by requiring users to recall question categories and criteria in each scaffolding level, and enable "applying" that knowledge by requiring the user to select questions for their interviews. We also support "evaluating" by letting users score prerecorded interviews. However, for future work, we would like to provide scaffolding to cover the remaining levels of "analyzing" and "creating". We are currently working with natural language processing techniques to enable freeform patient interviews by matching typed or spoken user input to questions present in our database, enabling the user to truly "create" an interview while maintaining automatic scoring and feedback. We may also be able to support "analysis" by requiring users to describe or interpret why questions meet or fail to meet the given criteria. We may also consider incorporating the knowledge dimension of the Revised Bloom's Taxonomy into our scaffolding system by promoting factual, conceptual, procedural, and meta-cognitive knowledge to support holistic learning.

ACKNOWLEDGEMENTS

This research was supported, in part, by the NSF Graduate Research Fellowship Program (fellow numbers 2009080400 and 2011095211), an Interdisciplinary Research Innovations Grant from the College of Health Education and Human Development at Clemson University, and a grant from the Agency for Healthcare, Research, and Quality (RO3#HS020233-01). We would also like to thank Jeffrey Bertrand for the many hours he spent sharing his expertise in character animation.

REFERENCES

1. Blender. 2012, 1/19/2012. http://www.blender.org/
2. Anonymous. IVONA Text-to-Speech Voices | TTS Voices | Text To Voice 2012, 6/29/2012. http://www.ivona.com/en/
3. Anonymous. MetaMorph for Unity | Rezzable 2012, 6/29/2012 http://rezzable.com/blogs/foolish-frost/presenting-metamorph-toolkit-blender-and-unity
4. Anonymous. Microsoft Speech API (SAPI) 5.3 2012, 6/29/2012. http://msdn.microsoft.com/en-us/library/ms723627(v=vs.85).aspx
5. Anonymous Poser 3D Animation & Character Creation Software - Official Website 2012, 6/29/2012. http://poser.smithmicro.com/
6. Anonymous. SIMmersion.com - SIMmersion LLC, your training systems solution. 2012, 7/5/2012. http://www.simmersion.com/
7. Anonymous. SQLite Home Page 2012, 6/29/2012 ().
8. Anonymous. UNITY: Game Development Tool 2012, 1/19/2012. http://www.sqlite.org/
9. Anderson, L. W., Krathwohl, D. R., Airasian, P. W., Cruikshank, K. A., Mayer, R. E., Pintrich, P., Raths, J. and Wittrock, M. A taxonomy for learning, teaching, and assessing: A revision of Bloom's taxonomy of educational objectives. (2000).
10. Ball, J. W., Bindler, R. C. and COWEN, K. J. Child health nursing. (2006).
11. Bloodworth, T., Cairco, L., McClendon, J., Hodges, L. F., Babu, S., Meehan, N. K., Johnson, A. and Ulinski, A. C. Initial Evaluation of a Virtual Pediatric Patient System. Carolinas Women in Computing, (2012).
12. Brooke, J. SUS-A quick and dirty usability scale. Usability evaluation in industry, 189(1996), 194.
13. Durham, C. F. and Alden, K. R. Enhancing patient safety in nursing education through patient simulation. Patient safety and quality: An evidence-based handbook for nurses, 6, 3 (2008), 221-250.
14. Forehand, M. Bloom's taxonomy. Emerging perspectives on learning, teaching, and technology, (2005).
15. Hockenberry, M. J. and Wilson, D. Wong's nursing care of infants and children. Recherche, 67(2006), 02.
16. Holton, D. and Clarke, D. Scaffolding and metacognition. International Journal of Mathematical Education in Science and Technology, 37, 2 (2006), 127-143.
17. Hubal, R. C., Deterding, R. R., Frank, G. A., Schwetzke, H. F. and Kizakevich, P. Lessons learned in modeling virtual pediatric patients. Stud. Health Technol. Inform., (2003), 127-130.
18. Johnsen, K., Dickerson, R., Raij, A., Lok, B., Jackson, J., Shin, M., Hernandez, J., Stevens, A. and Lind, D. S. Experiences in using immersive virtual characters to educate medical communication skills. In Anonymous *Virtual Reality, 2005. Proceedings. VR 2005. IEEE.* . IEEE, 2005, 179-186.
19. Lua, J., LAJOIE, S. P. and WISEMAN, J. Scaffolding Collaboration in Simulated Medical Emergencies. In Anonymous *International Conference on Computers in Education.* (). Hong Kong: Asia-Pacific Society for Computers in Education., 2009, 285-292.
20. McKeon, L. M., Norris, T., Cardell, B. and Britt, T. Developing patient-centered care competencies among prelicensure nursing students using simulation. J. Nurs. Educ., 48, 12 (2009), 711-715.
21. Planas, L. G. and Nelson, L. E. A systems approach to scaffold communication skills development. Am. J. Pharm. Educ., 72, 2 (2008).
22. Quintana, C. and Fishman, B. Supporting science learning and teaching with software-based scaffolding. American Educational Research Association (AERA), (2006).
23. Rothgeb, M. K. Creating a nursing simulation laboratory: A literature review. J. Nurs. Educ., 47, 11 (2008), 489.
24. Sawyer, R. K. *The Cambridge handbook of the learning sciences.* Cambridge Univ Pr, , 2006.
25. Stevens, A., Hernandez, J., Johnsen, K., Dickerson, R., Raij, A., Harrison, C., DiPietro, M., Allen, B., Ferdig, R. and Foti, S. The use of virtual patients to teach medical students history taking and communication skills. Am. J. Surg., 191, 6 (2006), 806-811.
26. Stupans, I., Owen, S., Ryan, G., Woulfe, J. and McKauge, L. Scaffolding patient counselling skills in Australian University Pharmacy programs. Asia-Pacific Journal of Cooperative Education, 11, 2 (2011), 29-37.
27. Trepagnier, C. Y., Olsen, D. E., Boteler, L. and Bell, C. A. Virtual conversation partner for adults with autism. Cyberpsychology, Behavior, and Social Networking, 14, 1-2 (2011), 21-27.

Helping Users with Information Disclosure Decisions: Potential for Adaptation

Bart P. Knijnenburg
Donald Bren School of
Information and Computer Sciences
University of California, Irvine, USA
bart.k@uci.edu

Alfred Kobsa
Donald Bren School of
Information and Computer Sciences
University of California, Irvine, USA
kobsa@uci.edu

ABSTRACT
Personalization relies on personal data about each individual user. Users are quite often reluctant though to disclose information about themselves and to be "tracked" by a system. We investigated whether different types of rationales (justifications) for disclosure that have been suggested in the privacy literature would increase users' willingness to divulge demographic and contextual information about themselves, and would raise their satisfaction with the system. We also looked at the effect of the order of requests, owing to findings from the literature. Our experiment with a mockup of a mobile app recommender shows that there is no single strategy that is optimal for everyone. Heuristics can be defined though that select for each user the most effective justification to raise disclosure or satisfaction, taking the user's gender, disclosure tendency, and the type of solicited personal information into account. We discuss the implications of these findings for research aimed at personalizing privacy strategies to each individual user.

Author Keywords
Recommender systems; information disclosure; user experience; satisfaction; user characteristics; adaptive interfaces; privacy; trust

ACM Classification Keywords
H.1.2 [**Models and Principles**]: User/Machine Systems, H.5.2 [**Information Interfaces and Presentation**]: User Interfaces–*evaluation/methodology, theory and methods*, K.4.1 [**Computers and Society**]: Public Policy Issues–*privacy*

General Terms
Design, Experimentation, Human Factors, Measurement

INTRODUCTION
User modeling and personalization typically rely on implicitly gathered or explicitly requested personal information about the user [1]. Privacy research has however shown that quite a few people do not feel comfortable disclosing diverse personal information [2,3]. A typical remedy in this conflict is to give users control over what information they disclose [4], since this would allow them to trade off the potential personalization benefits of disclosure with the ensuing privacy risks [5,25]. However, users often have a hard time making this trade-off, since they lack knowledge about its positive and negative consequences [6,7]. This paper explores strategies to help users with their disclosure decisions in such a way that the amount of disclosure increases without decreased user satisfaction. We demonstrate that there is a potential for adaptation in this endeavor: the optimal strategy depends on the characteristics of the user and the optimization goal of the system (increasing the disclosure of two types of requested information, and/or raising users' satisfaction). Our work thus stands in the tradition of tailoring privacy to users' needs [8]. We discuss how the potential for adaptation that became manifest in our work can be translated into real-world systems that adapt their information request strategy to the user, in order to improve information disclosure while at the same time respecting users' privacy and satisfaction.

RELATED WORK

Strategies for Helping Users with Disclosure Decisions
Recent studies show that users can be assisted in their disclosure decisions by means of *justifications*. For instance, by informing users about the disclosure decisions of other users [9], or more specifically their friends [10], they become slightly more likely to conform to the perceived social norm in their own disclosure decisions. Others suggest justifications that inform users about the reason for requesting certain information [11] or the benefit of disclosing the information [8,12].

Another way to influence users' disclosure decisions is by changing the *order* of the disclosure requests. Acquisti et al. [13] showed that the average level of disclosure was higher when requests were made in decreasing order of intrusiveness. This was especially true for the more intrusive requests.

Potential for Adaptation
In [21, 27], we compared the effect of four different types of justifications against a system without such justifications. To our surprise, the system *without* justifications resulted in the most disclosure and highest satisfaction. Upon further analysis of these surprising results, we noticed that the

optimal justification depended on the characteristics of the user, type of information requested, and the goal of the system. In this paper we present this analysis, but we first outline existing work that corroborates our general findings.

User characteristics

Privacy concerns vary extensively across the population. One of the most cited results in privacy research is that people can be divided into three broad categories: privacy fundamentalists, pragmatists, and unconcerned [14]. Moreover, females and older people tend to have higher privacy concerns [15], especially when it comes to their location [16]. Due to these personal differences in privacy concerns, optimal strategies to assist disclosure decisions may not be universal, but may rather depend on the characteristics of each individual user.

Type of information requested

Users have different attitudes towards disclosing different types of information. Specifically, information that the user provides explicitly (demographic data) seems to raise less concern than information that the system extracts from user behavior on the quiet (context data). Although the latter is more convenient, it is also less controllable and may be incorrectly interpreted [17,18]. Due to these differences, the optimal strategy may be different for these two types of information.

Optimization goal of the system

Most studies on information disclosure have a behavioral goal: they try to increase the amount of users' disclosure. If these strategies are effective, one could argue that this is because they reduce privacy fears and/or increase trust in the company's privacy practices [12]. However, the increased disclosure may be unrelated to rational decision processes [13]. In fact, the same strategies that increase disclosure could inadvertently increase users' privacy fears and decrease their trust. While increased disclosure may eventually lead to higher personalization benefits, these unintended effects could at the same time lower user satisfaction. It therefore seems crucial to strive for both goals simultaneously.

ONLINE EXPERIMENT

Experimental Setup

Our experiment tests the hypothesis that the optimal strategy to help users with their disclosure decisions depends on the characteristics of the user, the type of information requested, and the optimization goal of the system. It considers a mockup of a mobile app recommender, which uses demographic data (e.g. age, hobbies, income) and context data (e.g. app usage, calendar, location) to provide users with recommendations for new applications for their phones [19]. The experiment only concerns the part of the system that collects personal information (i.e., no recommendations are given). The mockup does not run on a phone, but in an Internet browser. In order to make the experiment more realistic, users were told that their data would in fact be disclosed to the developer, a company named "Appy"[1]. We reinforced this belief by ostensibly transferring users to the "Appy" website (with its own URL and branding) for the disclosure part of the experiment (see Figure 1).

Participants

441 participants were recruited via Amazon Turk, a recruitment source that has become very popular for conducting user studies [20]. We only allowed participants from the United States and asked a number of reverse-coded and comprehension-testing questions to ascertain validity. An additional 52 participants were recruited via Craigslist, and we found no significant differences between the two groups. All 493 participants (223 males, 266 females, 4 did not disclose) were adult smartphone users, with a median age range of 25-30.

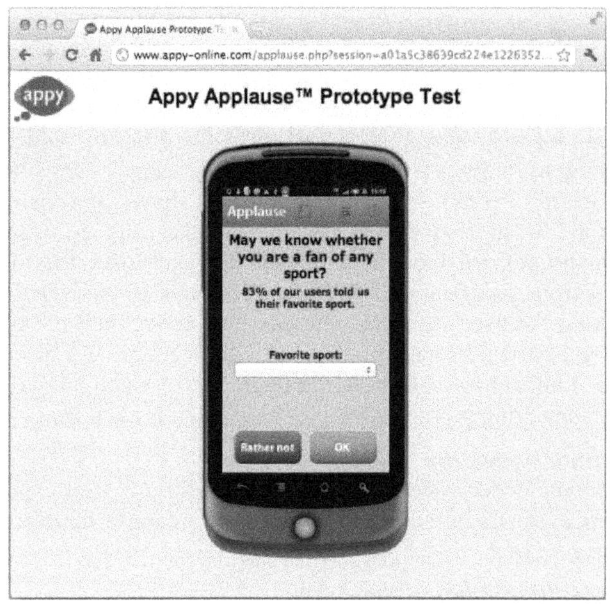

Figure 1: The website of "Appy", on which participants perform the disclosure part of the experiment.

Procedure

Participants were first given a short introduction to the mobile app recommender, and were specifically informed that they would be helping the Appy company to test the information disclosure part of the system. They were then randomly assigned to one of the experimental conditions (see below) and transferred to the Appy website. There, the system would make 31 disclosure requests, for 12 pieces of context data and 19 pieces of demographic data. In the context data requests, users were asked to indicate whether or not they would disclose the respective data (with 'yes' and 'no' as answers). In the case of demographics requests, they were asked to provide the actual information or decline

[1] This name was perceived as familiar and trustworthy in a pre-test that compared seven different company names and logos.

its disclosure[2]. We logged users' disclosure decisions in our database. After 31 decisions, participants were transferred back to the experimenters' website, where they answered questions about their subjective valuations.

Conditions: Type of Justification and Request Order

Four different justifications (see Table 1) are tested against the baseline of no justification, resulting in a total of five conditions. The 'useful for you' and 'useful for others' justifications explain the benefits of disclosure (cf. [12]) in two different ways. The 'number of others' justification appeals to the social norm (cf. [9,10]). The 'explanation' justification gives the reason for requesting the information (cf. [11]). The percentages that are shown in some of the justifications are randomly generated in the mockup, which makes the justifications more realistic. The reason presented in the explanation also varies enough per item to avoid excessive monotony.

Since our app recommender requests both demographic data and context data, we also manipulated the order in which these types of data are requested: demographic data first or context data first.

Justification	Message to user
None	[no justification message]
Useful for you	"The recommendations will be about [XX]% better for you when you tell us/allow us to use…"
Number of others	"[XX]% of our users told us/allowed us to use…"
Useful for others	"[XX]% of our users received better re–commendations when they told us/let us…
Explanation	"We can recommend apps that are [reason for request]"

Table 1: The justification messages evaluated in our study. Figure 1 shows how these messages are presented to the user.

User Characteristics: Gender and Disclosure Tendency

Two user characteristics are considered that may influence the relative impact of our strategies: gender and disclosure tendency[3]. Disclosure tendency is measured by splitting the users into two groups: one with a low disclosure tendency (up to 22 disclosed items), which comprises 33.3% of the participants, and one with high disclosure tendency (23-31 disclosed items). Several researchers found that people's actual disclosure behavior is only weakly related to their stated concerns [22,23,24], which is why we opt to split users based on their actual behaviors. The results of our analyses are robust under different splits: a 25-75% split provided very similar results, and also a three-way split failed to provide additional insights.

Gender and disclosure tendency each split the participants into two groups. To gauge the differences between these groups, we measured several other user characteristics in the post-experimental questionnaires, subjected them to a Confirmatory Factor Analysis, and regressed them on disclosure tendency and gender:

- Stated privacy concerns (3 items, adapted from [17]; e.g. "I am concerned about threats to my personal privacy today")
- Data collection concerns (5 items, adapted from [17]; e.g. "I'm concerned that online companies are collecting too much personal information about me")
- Control concerns (2 items, adapted from [18]; e.g. "Control of personal information lies at the heart of online privacy")
- Mobile internet usage (2 items, e.g. "I regularly use my phone to browse the Internet")
- Tech-savviness (3 items, e.g. "People ask me to fix their computer")

Participants with a low disclosure tendency have higher stated privacy concerns (β = 0.379, p = .001) and data collection concerns (β = 0.696, $p < .001$), are less phone-savvy (β = -0.388, $p < .001$) and less tech-savvy (β = -0.222, p = .035). Moreover, females are less tech-savvy (β = -0.766, $p < .001$). Finally, the percentage of people with a low disclosure tendency is not significantly different between males (32.7%) and females (33.1%).

Dependent Variables

We consider three different goals in our system: increasing the disclosure of context data, increasing the disclosure of demographic data, and increasing the users' subjective experience of the system. The first two goals are tested in a single analysis in which disclosure is regressed on the conditions and moderators; the type of data (demographic vs. context data) is included as an additional moderator.

Several subjective valuations of the disclosure process are measured with questionnaires, which are submitted to a Confirmatory Factor Analysis (CFA)[4] and regressed on the conditions and moderators:

- Perceived disclosure help (3 items, e.g. "The system helped me to make a tradeoff between privacy and usefulness")
- Perceived privacy threat (3 items, e.g. "The system has too much information about me")

[2] The fact that the (real) demographics data disclosure was actually *higher* than the (make believe) context disclosure suggests that participants answered both demographics and context requests as if they were real.

[3] A third analyzed characteristic, age, turned out to be non-significant in the analyses.

[4] A CFA tests the internal consistency of a set of indicators, and combines them into a single, normally distributed scale.

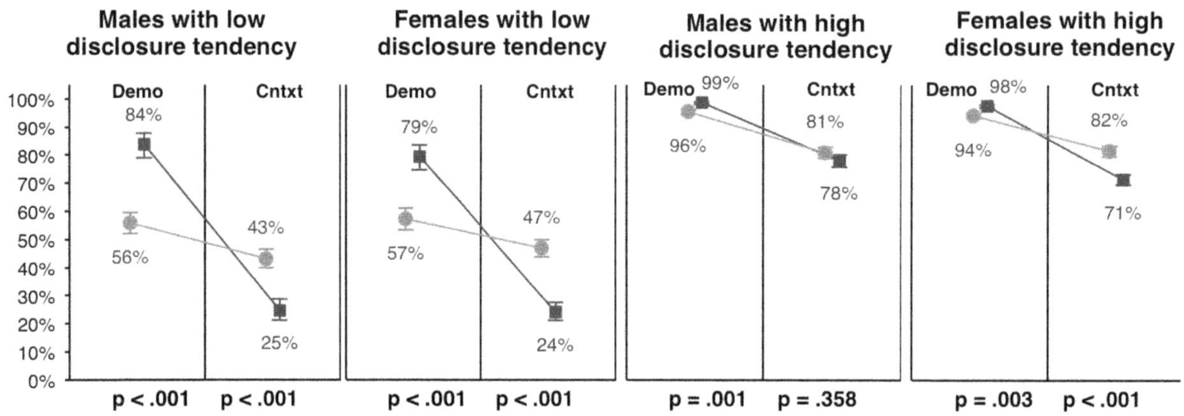

Figure 2: The effect of request order on disclosure per user group (disregarding justification type). Error bars are ±1 standard error.

- Trust in company privacy practices (3 items, adapted from [18]; e.g. "I believe this company is honest when it comes to using the information I provide")
- Satisfaction (6 items, from [22]; e.g. "Overall, I'm satisfied with the system")

RESULTS

Disclosure Behavior

The effect of our strategies[5] on subjects' disclosure decisions is analyzed using General Estimating Equations (GEE) with a log link function[6]. The dependent variable is the decision of participant x to disclose item y (yes/no). Because the 31 decisions of each participant are correlated, we impose a compound symmetric covariance structure.

The independent variables are the "strategies": the justification types (tested against no justification), the order of the disclosure requests (demographics first vs. context first), as well as their interaction. The interactions of the strategies with the user characteristics (gender and disclosure tendency) are also included. Finally, in order to make a distinction between the two goals of increasing context data disclosure and increasing demographics disclosure, the interactions of all aforementioned variables with the type of data (context data vs. demographics) are tested as well. The highest-order effect tested is thus: justification type × order × gender × disclosure tendency × type of data.

Disregarding justification type, the request order has a significant effect in almost all groups, and the main trend is that the disclosure of a certain type of data is higher if that data type is requested first (i.e. demographics disclosure is higher when demographics are requested first, and likewise for context data, $F(1,481) = 65.62$, $p < .001$). This effect is stronger for participants with a low disclosure tendency than for those with a high disclosure tendency (interaction: $F(1,481) = 43.68$, $p < .001$), but there is no difference between males and females. The mean disclosure rate for each request order and the p-value of the difference within each user group are displayed in Figure 2.

The request order differences can be explained in two ways: a growing concern with the accumulated information collected by the system, or boredom/fatigue resulting from answering 31 requests. If the latter were the case, the order effect should be most pronounced for demographics, because in our study disclosure is more laborious for demographics than for context data (selecting the answer from a dropdown menu vs. clicking a 'yes'/'no' button). However, the effect of order is stronger for context data than for demographics. The order effect is thus most likely *not* due to boredom or fatigue.

Figure 3 displays the combined effect of justification type and request order (i.e. the effect of the strategy) for the four user groups (males/females with low/high disclosure tendency). An ANOVA test of the five-way interaction of justification type × order × gender × disclosure tendency × type of data showed that the best strategy differs by gender, disclosure tendency and data type ($F(4,449) = 2.95$, $p = .020$). Aside from this five-way effect, there are significant lower-level interactions of strategy and disclosure tendency ($F(4,449) = 4.25$, $p = .002$) and strategy and data type ($F(4,449) = 2.87$, $p = .023$).

Within each user group, we compare the best strategy for each data type (marked with an arrow in Figure 3) against all other strategies. Strategies that perform significantly worse[7] than the best strategy are labeled with a p-value.

---

[5] We define "strategy" as the combination of a certain type of justification and a certain request order. We thus test 5×2 = 10 strategies.

[6] Our outcomes are correlated (each participant is represented by 31 data points) and non-normal (the data consists of 0's and 1's). GEE models are linear regression models that can robustly handle correlated, non-normal data.

[7] To reduce the risk of incorrectly claiming that a certain strategy performs equally well as the best strategy (Type I error), we take p < .10 as our cut-off value.

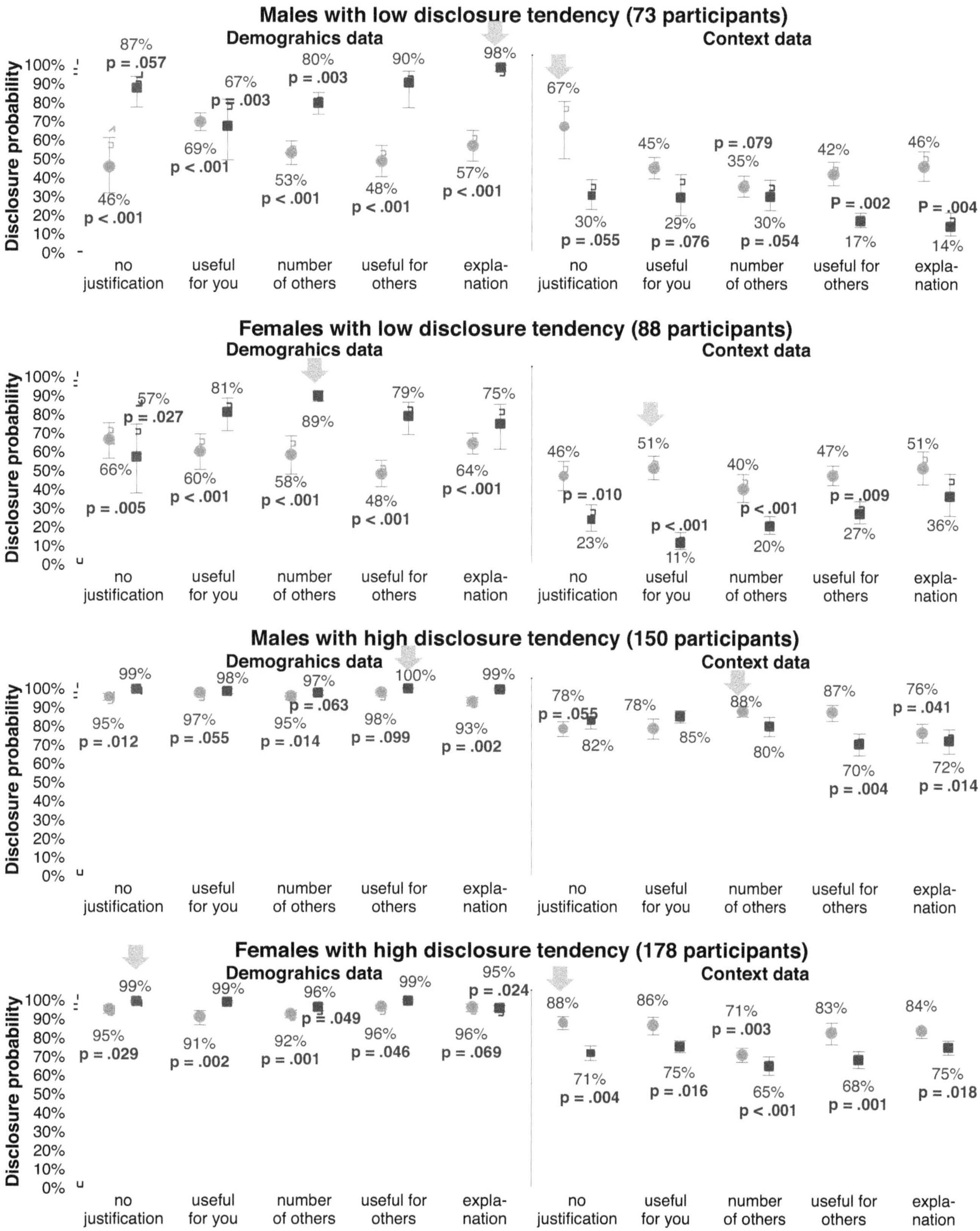

Figure 3: The effects of justification type and request order on disclosure (for each type of data, gender, and disclosure tendency). Error bars are ±1 standard error. The best strategy is labeled with an arrow; strategies with a p-value perform significantly worse.

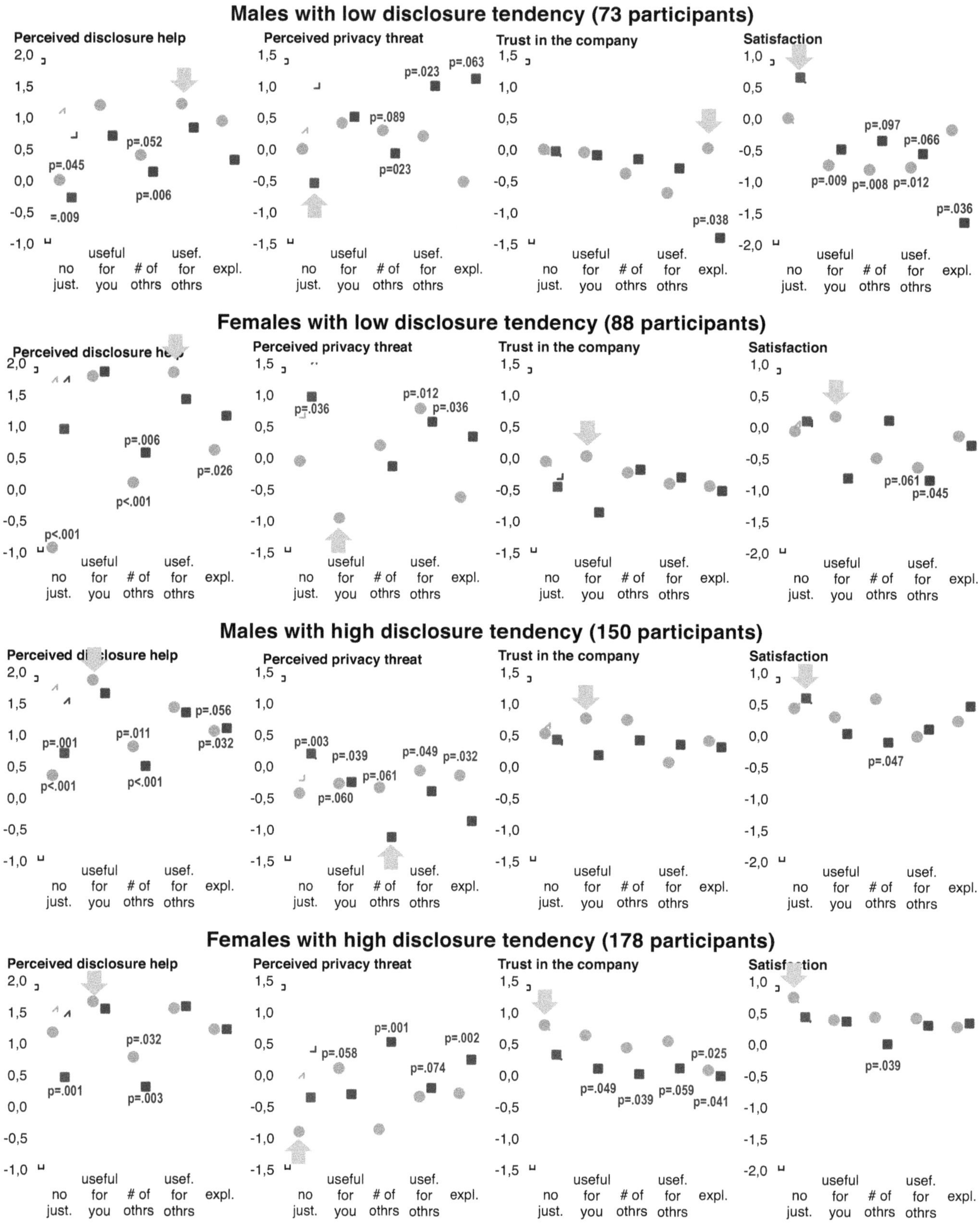

Figure 4: The estimated effects of justification type and request order on user satisfaction for each gender and disclosure tendency. Since the outcomes are scale-free factor scores, the y-axis is scaled in sample standard deviations (i.e. 95% of the participants fall within a 4.0-range), and the value for [male, low disclosure tendency, context first, no justification] is set to zero.

Subjective Valuations

We analyze the effect of the strategies on subjective valuations by submitting the questionnaire items to a Confirmatory Factor Analysis and by regressing resulting satisfaction factors on the strategies and user characteristics. The dependent variables in these analyses are: perceived disclosure help, perceived privacy threat, trust in company privacy practices, and overall satisfaction. The independent variables are the strategies (5 justification types × 2 orders), and the interactions of the strategies with gender and disclosure tendency. In effect, each dependent variable is regressed on justification type × order × gender × disclosure tendency.

Figure 4 displays the estimated effects of justification type and request order on the subjective valuations for each gender and disclosure tendency. Disregarding justification type, the request order has a significant effect on perceived disclosure help for males with a low disclosure tendency ($\beta = -0.533$, $p = .023$), where requesting context data first generally leads to a higher level of perceived disclosure help. The request order also has a significant effect on perceived privacy threat ($\beta = 0.425$, $p = .024$) and trust in the company ($\beta = -0.340$, $p = .043$) for females with a high disclosure tendency, where requesting context data first leads to less threat and more trust.

Figure 4 compares for each group the best strategy (marked with an arrow) against all other strategies. Strategies that perform significantly worse than the best strategy are labeled with a p-value.

HEURISTICS FOR SELECTING THE BEST STRATEGY

The results show that the best strategy depends on users' disclosure tendency and gender. It also depends on the goal of the system: some strategies increase disclosure of one type of data but not the other, and some increase disclosure but at the same time reduce users' satisfaction. We therefore suggest that the strategy should be adapted to the optimization goal of the system and the characteristics of the user. Table 4 outlines heuristics for selecting the best strategy for each type of user, given a certain system goal. Below we reflect on these suggested heuristics.

Best Strategy to Achieve High Demographics Disclosure

To get high demographics disclosure, one should ask for demographics first. Users with high disclosure tendency do not require a justification. Users with low disclosure tendency require a justification, the best one being 'number of others' for females and 'explanation' for males.

Best Strategy to Achieve High Context Data Disclosure

To get high context data disclosure, one should ask for context data first. No justification is required, but males with high disclosure tendency disclose more with the 'number of others' or 'useful for others' justification.

Best Strategy to Achieve High Total Disclosure

Since it is best to ask demographics first to increase demographics disclosure, and context first to increase context disclosure, increasing total disclosure requires a compromise. The best way to attain this compromise is to first choose a preferred request order, and then to select a

User type	Context first	Demographics first
Males with low disclosure tendency	The 'useful for you' justification gives the highest demographics disclosure.	Providing no justification gives the highest context disclosure.
Females with low disclosure tendency	Providing no justification gives the highest demographics disclosure.	The 'explanation' justification keeps context disclosure on par.
Males with high disclosure tendency	The 'useful for others' justification keeps demographics disclosure almost on par.	The 'useful for you' justification keeps context disclosure on par.
Females with high disclosure tendency	Providing no justification gives a high demographics disclosure.	The 'useful for you' justification gives the highest context disclosure.

Table 2: Best strategies to achieve high overall disclosures.

User type	Best strategy
Males with low disclosure tendency	Demographics first with 'useful for you'.
Males with high disclosure tendency	The 'useful for you' justification in any order.
Females with low disclosure tendency	Context first with 'useful for you'.
Females with high disclosure tendency	Context first with no justification, but 'useful for you' is second best.

Table 3: Best strategies to achieve high user satisfaction.

justification message that minimizes the disclosure decrease in the data that is requested last. The best message for this purpose depends on user characteristics (see Table 2).

Best Strategy to Achieve High User Satisfaction

To get high subjective valuations, the 'useful for you' justification generally works well, but see Table 3 for a more detailed appraisal.

Best Strategy Overall

When both the disclosure rates and satisfaction are to be optimized, one has to strike a compromise. This is possible with the following strategies: For users with low disclosure tendency, request demographics first, and use no justification for males and the 'explanation' justification for females. For users with high disclosure tendency, request demographics first with the 'useful for you' message for males, and request context first with no justification for females.

Best strategies for MALES with LOW disclosure tendency	
Goal	*Best strategy*
High demographics disclosure	Demographics first, 'explanation' justification.
High context data disclosure	Context first, no justification.
High overall disclosure	Context first, 'useful for you' justification.
High satisfaction	Context first, 'useful for others' justification or demographics first, 'useful for you' justification.
All of the above	Demographics first, no justification.
Best strategies for FEMALES with LOW disclosure tendency	
Goal	*Best strategy*
High demographics disclosure	Demographics first, 'number of others' justification.
High context data disclosure	Context first, 'useful for you' justification.
High overall disclosure	Demographics first, 'explanation' justification.
High satisfaction	Context first, 'useful for you' justification.
All of the above	Demographics first, 'explanation' justification.
Best strategies for MALES with HIGH disclosure tendency	
Goal	*Best strategy*
High demographics disclosure	Demographics first with any justification except 'number of others'.
High context data disclosure	Context first, 'number of others' or 'useful for others' justification.
High overall disclosure	Demographics first with no justification or the 'useful for you' justification, or context first with 'useful for others' justification.
High satisfaction	Demographics first, 'useful for others' or 'explanation' justification.
All of the above	Demographics first, 'useful for you' justification.
Best strategies for FEMALES with HIGH disclosure tendency	
Goal	*Best strategy*
High demographics disclosure	Demographics first with no justification, the 'useful for you' justification, or the 'useful for others' justification.
High context data disclosure	Context first with no justification.
High overall disclosure	Context first with no justification.
High satisfaction	Context first with no justification.
All of the above	Context first with no justification.

Table 4: Heuristics to find the best strategy, based on user characteristics (gender, disclosure tendency) and optimization goals.

Implementing the Strategies

To follow the heuristics, a system would have to discover the users' characteristics before or during the interaction. Gender can just be the first item to request. In fact, gender disclosure was the highest of all items in our study (94.9%), and hence we expect that asking for it first will not raise any concerns. To correctly determine the users' disclosure tendency, the system would have to first ask a number of potentially invasive questions, which is not desirable. Alternatively, one could ask about (or otherwise determine) the users' stated privacy concerns, mobile Internet usage and/or tech-savvyness, since these characteristics are related to users' disclosure tendency (see the section on user characteristics, and also [15,16]).

CONCLUSION AND FUTURE WORK

Information disclosure by users is an indispensible prerequisite for personalized systems, and strategies that increase disclosure may improve the accuracy of personalization. Our study shows that there is no single best justification strategy for all users to raise disclosure. Yet, heuristics can be developed to select an optimal strategy given the user characteristics, the type of information requested, and the optimization goal.

In terms of complexity, the heuristics presented in this paper fall between simple HCI design guidelines and more complex user models often used in adaptive systems. Although they can be realistically implemented, we do not have an intuitive rationale behind the specific heuristics we found. Future work should aspire a more fundamental understanding of the context-dependence of privacy behaviors (e.g. [26]).

In our current research, a user is only exposed to one of five types of justifications (including "none") for all information requests, and only to one of two request orders. A simple improvement would be to use different justifications for demographics and context requests. Although we have not tested this option, Figure 2 suggests that some improvements in disclosure can be attained in this way (for males with high disclosure tendencies, for instance, one could request demographics first with the 'useful for you' justification, and then request context data with the 'useful for others' justification). A fully adaptive system could go much further though: it could select the optimal justification for each specific requested item, and order the requests dynamically to ensure the highest possible disclosure (without reducing satisfaction, of course). Our results suggest that such a fully adaptive system is viable, but one should note that a lot of data is needed to optimize its performance. Although this is not feasible in an academic research setting, a commercial system will likely provide enough data to implement this adaptive approach.

Participants in our study tested the information disclosure part of a mobile app recommender system. It will still need to be verified whether different types of systems may result in different user behaviors, and whether moving from a mockup study to real-world systems bears any differences. Moreover, different types of justifications, such as privacy protection reassurances (which play more on the risk side of the risk-benefit trade-off) may work better than the justifications tested in our study (e.g. [8]). Despite these limitations, we feel confident that a careful consideration of user characteristics and optimization goals can significantly improve strategies for helping users with information disclosure decisions.

ACKNOWLEDGEMENTS

This work has been supported through NSF grants IIS-0308277, IIS-0808783 and CNS-0831526, and by the Samsung R&D Research Center.

REFERENCES

1. Kobsa, A. Tailoring Privacy to Uses' Needs. In: Bauer, M., Gmytrasiewicz, P.J., and Vassileva, J. (eds.) *UM 2001. LNAI, vol. 2109*, pp. 303--313. Springer, Heidelberg (2001). DOI: 10.1007/3-540-44566-8_52
2. Kobsa, A. Privacy-Enhanced Web Personalization. In: Brusilovsky, P., Kobsa, A., and Nejdl, W. (eds.) *The Adaptive Web: Methods and Strategies of Web Personalization*. pp. 628--670. Springer, Heidelberg (2007). DOI: 10.1007/978-3-540-72079-9_21
3. Assad, M., Carmichael, D., Kay, J., Kummerfeld, B. Giving Users Control Over Location Privacy. In: *Workshop on Ubicomp Privacy*. (2007).
4. Teltzrow, M., Kobsa, A. Impacts of User Privacy Preferences on Personalized Systems: a Comparative Study. In: Karat, C.-M., Blom, J., and Karat, J. (eds.) *Designing Personalized User Experiences for eCommerce*. pp. 315--332. Kluwer, Dordrecht (2004). DOI: 10.1007/1-4020-2148-8_17
5. Culnan, M.J. and Armstrong, P.K. Information Privacy Concerns, Procedural Fairness, and Impersonal Trust: An Empirical Investigation. *Organization Science*. 10(1), 104--115 (1999). DOI: 10.1287/orsc.10.1.104
6. Chellappa, R.K., Sin, R.G. Personalization Versus Privacy: An Empirical Examination of the Online Consumer's Dilemma. *Information Technology and Management*. 6, 181--202 (2005). DOI: 10.1007/s10799-005-5879-y
7. Brodie, C., Karat, C.-M., Karat, J. Creating an E-Commerce Environment Where Consumers are Willing to Share Personal Information. In: Karat, C.-M., Blom, J.O., and Karat, J. (eds.) *Designing Personalized User Experience for eCommerce*. pp. 185--206. Kluwer, Dordrecht (2004). DOI: 10.1007/1-4020-2148-8_11
8. Kobsa, A., Teltzrow, M. Contextualized Communication of Privacy Practices and Personalization Benefits: Impacts on Users' Data Sharing Behavior. In: Martin, D. and Serjantov, A. (eds.) *PET 2005*. 329--343.

Springer, Heidelberg (2005). DOI: 10.1007/11423409_21

9. Besmer, A., Watson, J., Lipford, H.R. The Impact of Social Navigation on Privacy Policy Configuration. In: *6th Symposium on Usable Privacy and Security*. ACM Press, New York (2010). DOI: 10.1145/1837110.1837120
10. Patil, S., Page, X., Kobsa, A. With a Little Help from My Friends. In: *ACM 2011 Conference on Computer Supported Cooperative Work*. pp. 391--394. ACM Press, New York (2011). DOI: 10.1145/1958824.1958885
11. Consolvo, S., Smith, I., Matthews, T., LaMarca, A., Tabert, J. and Powledge, P. Location disclosure to social relations: why, when, & what people want to share. In: *ACM SIGCHI Conference on Human Factors in Computing Systems*, pp. 81–90. ACM Press, New York (2005). DOI: 10.1145/1054972.1054985
12. Wang, W., Benbasat, I. Recommendation Agents for Electronic Commerce: Effects of Explanation Facilities on Trusting Beliefs. *Journal of Management Information Systems*, 23, 217--246 (2007). DOI: 10.2753/MIS0742-1222230410
13. Acquisti, A., John, L.K., Loewenstein, G. The Impact of Relative Standards on the Propensity to Disclose. *Journal of Marketing Research*. (2011). DOI: 10.1509/jmr.09.0215
14. Privacy and American Business: Consumer Privacy Attitudes: A Major Shift Since 2000 and Why. *Privacy and American Business Newsletter*, 10, (2003).
15. Cho, H., Rivera-Sánchez, M., Lim, S.S. A Multinational Study on Online Privacy: Global Concerns and Local Responses. *New Media & Society*, 11, 395--416 (2009). DOI: 10.1177/1461444808101618
16. Li, N., Chen, G. Sharing Location in Online Social Networks. *IEEE Network*, 24, 20--25 (2010). DOI: 10.1109/MNET.2010.5578914
17. Smith, H.J., Milberg, S.J., Burke, S.J. Information Privacy: Measuring Individuals' Concerns About Organizational Practices. *MIS Quarterly*, 20, 167--196 (1996).
18. Malhotra, N.K., Kim, S.S., Agarwal, J. Internet Users' Information Privacy Concerns (IUIPC): The Construct, the Scale, and a Causal Model. *Information Systems Research*, 15, 336--355 (2004). DOI: 10.1287/isre.1040.0032
19. Davidsson, C., Moritz, S. Utilizing Implicit Feedback and Context to Recommend Mobile Applications from First Use. *IUI 2011 Workshop on Context-awareness in Retrieval and Recommendation*. pp. 19--22. ACM, New York (2011). DOI: 10.1145/1961634.1961639
20. Kittur, A., Chi, E.H., Suh, B. Crowdsourcing user studies with Mechanical Turk. *Proceedings of the twenty-sixth annual SIGCHI conference on Human factors in computing systems*. pp. 453--456. ACM press, New York (2008). DOI: 10.1145/1357054.1357127
21. Knijnenburg, B.P., Kobsa, A., Saldamli, G. Privacy in Mobile Personalized Systems: The Effect of Disclosure Justifications. In: *SOUPS Workshop on Usable Privacy & Security in Mobile Devices*. (2012). URL: http://cups.cs.cmu.ecu/soups/2012/u-prism/soups12-mobile-final1.pdf
22. Knijnenburg, B.P., Willemsen, M.C., Gantner, Z., Soncu, H., Newell, C.: Explaining the user experience of recommender systems. *User Modeling and User-Adapted Interaction*. 22, (2012). DOI: 10.1007/s11257-011-9118-4
23. Spiekermann, S., Grossklags, J.: E-privacy in 2nd Generation E-Commerce: Privacy Preferences versus actual Behavior. In: *3rd ACM Conference on Electronic Commerce*. pp. 38--47. ACM Press, New York (2001). DOI: 10.1145/501158.501163
24. Tsai, J.Y., Egelman, S., Cranor, L.F., Acquisti, A.: The Effect of Online Privacy Information on Purchasing Behavior: An Experimental Study. *Information Systems Research*. 21, (2010). DOI: 10.1287/isre.1090.0260
25. Laufer, R.S., Wolfe, M.: Privacy as a Concept and a Social Issue: A Multidimensional Developmental Theory. *Journal of Social Issues*. 33(3), 22--42 (1977). DOI: 10.1111/j.1540-4560.1977.tb01880.x
26. Knijnenburg, B.P., Kobsa, A., Jin, H.: Dimensionality of Information Disclosure Behavior. *Submitted to the International Journal of Human-Computer Studies, special issue on Privacy Methodologies in HCI*. http://bit.ly/privdim
27. Knijnenburg, B.P., Kobsa, A.: Making Decisions about Privacy: Information Disclosure in Context-Aware Recommender Systems. *Accepted to the ACM Transactions on Interactive Intelligent Systems, special issue on Human Decision Making and Recommender Systems*. Available as ISR tech report: http://www.isr.uci.edu/tech_reports/UCI-ISR-12-1.pdf

Vibrobelt: Tactile Navigation Support for Cyclists

Haska Steltenpohl
Intelligent Systems Lab Amsterdam
University of Amsterdam
The Netherlands
haskasteltenpohl@gmail.com

Anders Bouwer
Intelligent Systems Lab Amsterdam
University of Amsterdam
The Netherlands
andersbouwer@uva.nl

ABSTRACT
Tactile displays can be used without demanding the attention from the human visual system, which makes them attractive for use in wayfinding contexts, where visual attention should be directed at traffic and other information in the environment. To investigate the potential of tactile navigation for cyclists, we have designed and implemented Vibrobelt. This belt, worn around the waist, gives waypoint, distance and endpoint information using directional tactile cues. We evaluated Vibrobelt by comparing it to a visual navigation application. Twenty participants were asked to cycle two routes, each route with a different application. We measured the spatial knowledge acquisition and analyzed the visual focus of the participants. We found that Vibrobelt was successful at guiding all participants to their destinations via an unfamiliar route. Participants using Vibrobelt showed a lower error rate for recognizing images from the route than users of the visual system. Users of the visual system were generally navigating faster, and were better at recalling the route, showing a higher contextual route understanding. The endpoint distance encoding was not always correctly interpreted. Future research will improve Vibrobelt by making a clearer distinction between waypoint and endpoint information, and will test users in more complex navigational situations.

Author Keywords
Tactile Display; Vibrobelt; Bicycle Traffic Safety; Navigation Support

ACM Classification Keywords
H.5.2 User Interfaces: Haptic I/O

INTRODUCTION
Navigation devices have become increasingly popular since their introduction in the eighties. Unfortunately, with the growing market penetration of these navigation devices we see a rise in related traffic accidents. According to a recent report from the American National Highway Traffic Safety Administration (NHTSA) [1], 17% of reported car crashes are caused by some sort of driver distraction. Navigation systems are among the devices that cause these distractions.

As a result of these findings NHTSA issued a set of guidelines restricting the use of equipment in cars.

Similar to car drivers, cyclists are also distracted when using navigation systems. They are more vulnerable in traffic and lack orientational support such as mirrors. For bicycle rides, the context also plays an important role. For example, a holiday bike ride on an unknown island requires information about the locations of points of interests [2]; a bike ride on a track for exercise by a blind person requires detailed directional information to steer along the track [3]; navigating on a bicycle from point A to point B through an urban environment, which is the focus of this paper, requires information about directions and distance to follow a route, and special attention to safety.

Besides the problem of drawing visual attention away from the environment, another problem with visual navigation systems is understanding the information on the screen and mapping it to the environment. Even pedestrians, who travel at a low speed, encounter problems while navigating with mobile maps, such as misunderstanding their position and orientation, missing turns, and taking wrong turns [4]. Visual navigation systems often employ features for zooming, rotation, and other changes to the visualization, which may be useful for finding out directions and distance information, but are difficult to control while riding a bicycle, with both hands at the handlebars.

Most modern navigation devices currently support spoken directional feedback (e.g., Andoid, IPhone, TomTom). This helps users to focus their visual attention on the traffic around them but potentially withholds the user from important auditory traffic information.

We propose to communicate directional information using the sense of touch. A belt, worn around the waist of the user, can give vibrotactile feedback in the direction of the next waypoint. Different patterns signify the distance of the user towards the next waypoint. We presume that using tactile feedback instead of visual will allow users to keep their attention to the road, resulting in safer traffic situations.

A limitation of using a belt to communicate directional information when compared with visual navigation information systems is the lack of context information. When we use visual navigation systems we can see our location on the map. We can also see additional information such as street names, points of interest (POI), distance information and the route we want to take. This study aims to investigate the trade-offs between the tactile and visual modality for navigation on a bicycle.

In this paper we discuss previous work on tactile navigation, the design and implementation of Vibrobelt and the results of an evaluation study with cyclists in an urban area. After discussing the results we present our conclusions and recommendations for future work.

RELATED WORK

Nokia maps use vibrotactile feedback to attract the attention of users when they have to change their course to stay on a predefined route. The user is then required to look at the screen for directional information. Using a belt that fits around the waist makes users feel the direction of the vibrations and therefore makes it very suitable for directional information.

The idea of using a vibrotactile belt for navigation is not new. Tsukada and Yasumura [5] developed and tested a tactile belt with eight vibrotactiles worn on the user's waist. They developed five applications for using the device, one of which was a navigation application. Using this application, called "FeelNavi", participants received endpoint and distance information. A continuous vibration pattern communicated the direction of the endpoint. When the participant got closer to this point, the pulse intervals of the vibrations and the vibrations themselves became shorter. They found that users were able to understand the directions but failed to recognize vibrations shorter than 500 milliseconds.

Pielot et al. performed multiple studies in which pedestrians received navigation information using a similar tactile display as Tsukada and Yasumura. They tried to improve directional information by interpolating vibration strength between six vibrotactiles on a waist belt but found no improvement when communicating waypoint information [6]. They also effectively used a tactile display to make video game players aware of their team members' locations [7]. In one experiment participants received navigation information beyond the upcoming waypoint in the route [8]. In an effort to increase the spatial knowledge acquisition they communicated the coming waypoint and the one after that in alternating order, using differences in rhythm and intensity. They found no significant difference in the spatial knowledge acquisition between their Tactile Wayfinder and a Tom Tom system. They also found that users experienced less near-accidents but took more wrong turns using the Tactile Wayfinder.

Soldiers trying to find their way trough an unfamiliar area benefit highly from a system that allows them to keep their eyes on their environment. Duistermaat [9] compared a waist belt with eight vibrotactiles to a regular GPS based visual navigation system and the Land Warrior System (LWS). This last system was a head mounted display that assists soldiers in their information needs on the battlefield. A continuous vibration pattern communicated the direction of the endpoint. They found that all soldiers preferred the tactile system over the visual GPS system. In most cases the tactile system was rated as high as or higher than the LWS system.

Robinson et al. [10] argue that users (and especially tourists) are not always looking for the fastest route. They would like to enjoy the route and have some freedom in choosing a certain route. In order to give users this freedom they developed a system that communicates route endpoint information rather than waypoint information. Using a mobile phone that increasingly vibrates when it is pointed towards the endpoint of the route they found that all participants were able to find the endpoint of the route.

Poppinga et al.'s Tacticycle [2] helps tourists reach their destination using tactile feedback in the bicycle handlebars. They divided "100% vibration" between the right and left handlebars. A balance of 25% left and 75% right would direct the user in a 45 degree angle to the right. Participants were also able to see a PDA screen with their location and destination, but without any map information. Although participants showed a low accuracy in recognizing the vibrotactile signals, they found that users were easily able to find their destinations. Their system presents tactile cueing directions to POIs "as the crow flies", but no specific turn-by-turn signals. In a later version, they also included a visual map showing the user's location and nearby POIs [11]. Kern et al. [12] and Hwang and Ryu [13] describe tactile displays in car steering wheels, which were tested successfully in office settings. A limitation of these approaches is that handlebars or car steering wheels are only felt at places where the user touches them, whereas a belt can vibrate in multiple directions around the body, which can provide a more direct spatial mapping.

Solely relying on tactile feedback for effective navigation withholds the user from contextual information usually shown in visual navigation systems, such as distance information. Van Veen et al. investigated five different coding schemes for distance encoding to the next waypoint and recorded the average speed [14]. The coding schemes included two forms of three-phase models, two monotonic models, and a control condition in which no distance encoding was used. The two three-phase models gave the user feedback at three different distances when approaching a waypoint, using different rhythms. In the monotonic condition participants received continuous feedback about the distance and direction towards the next waypoint. They found no significant difference in the distance encoding schemes for users navigating in an open field. Similar results were found by Straub et al. using blind participants [15]. They performed a series of experiments: one with fixed frequency and intensity, one with varying frequency and intensity, and one with varying frequency and patterns. The latter showed the best results of the experiments but they found no significant difference in the mean travel time when compared to navigation without distance encoding. Asif et al. [16] experimented with three styles of distance encoding for car navigation using a tactile belt: only rhythm, rhythm and intensity, and rhythm and duration They gave the user continuous distance feedback in four stages; very far (200-150 meters away), far (100-80 meters away), near (50-30 meters away) and turn-now, which was given at 10 meters from the waypoint. They found the best results using rhythm and duration for distance encoding.

HYPOTHESIS

A driving question for this research is whether we can improve navigation on bicycles using tactile feedback. Improving navigation has been operationalized as less navigation errors and less distractions by the navigation application. We use the same definition of navigation errors as used by Pielot and Boll [8]. Navigation errors are wrong turns, near-accidents and disorientation. We also want to know how users experience this system and how we can improve it. Although tactile displays have proven to be effective for navigation we also want to investigate the shortcomings of this type of navigation. In order to improve tactile displays we need to investigate which information is missing.

We constructed three hypotheses to test our application:

Hypothesis one: When people use the tactile navigation application, they will be better at recognizing images taken on the route when compared to people using the visual navigation application.

Hypothesis two: When people use the visual navigation application, they will have a better overview of the route and therefore take less wrong turns than users from the tactile application.

Hypothesis three: When people use the visual navigation application they will be better at recalling the route when asked to draw a line covering the route when compared to the tactile navigation application.

With the first hypothesis we aim to prove that users are distracted from the surrounding traffic when using the visual application. Pielot et al. [8] found that pedestrians using a tactile navigation device take more wrong turns. Hypothesis two aims to determine if cyclists show the same results. Using a tactile display withholds the user from more extensive navigational information, such as points of interest and contextual route information. Hypothesis three aims to shed more light on this issue.

SYSTEM DESIGN

We have constructed two applications: a tactile navigation application (Vibrobelt) and a visual navigation application.

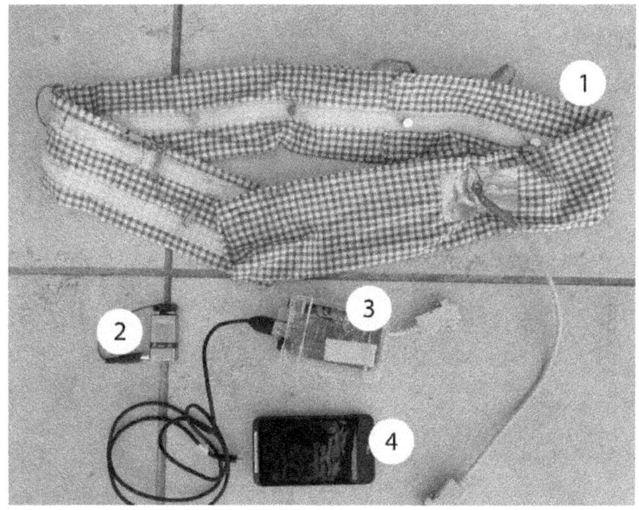

Figure 1. Hardware setup Vibrobelt

Vibrobelt gives the user tactile waypoint information and aims to give the user a sense of context awareness by adding endpoint-distance and -direction information.

The system gives the user turn-by-turn feedback by making the belt vibrate in the direction of the next part of the route. At the same time we have the belt vibrate in the direction of the endpoint of the route. The endpoint information is continued throughout the route and is only interrupted to give waypoint information at the right moment. In addition, a visual map application was developed as a baseline to compare with Vibrobelt.

Vibrobelt

Vibrobelt consists of a hardware and a software part.

Hardware

The hardware parts of Vibrobelt are displayed in Figure 1: a custom made belt with eight vibrotactiles (1) and a power source (2), an Arduino Mega ADK (3), and an Android phone (4).

The Android device used for this project was the HTC Desire HD. The Desire HD was chosen for the precision of the GPS chip and the operating system (Android 3.4.5).

Arduino is an open source prototyping board that can be programmed to drive our vibrotactiles. The Arduino is connected to the HTC Desire via a usb cable and connected to the vibrotactiles using custom wiring.

The belt was made from textile and velcro. The eight vibrotactiles in the belt were of the round Pico Vibe 10mm Vibration Motor type. They were chosen for their small size, their ability to operate on 3V and they can be made to vibrate at 250 Hz, as recommended by Boff et al. [17].

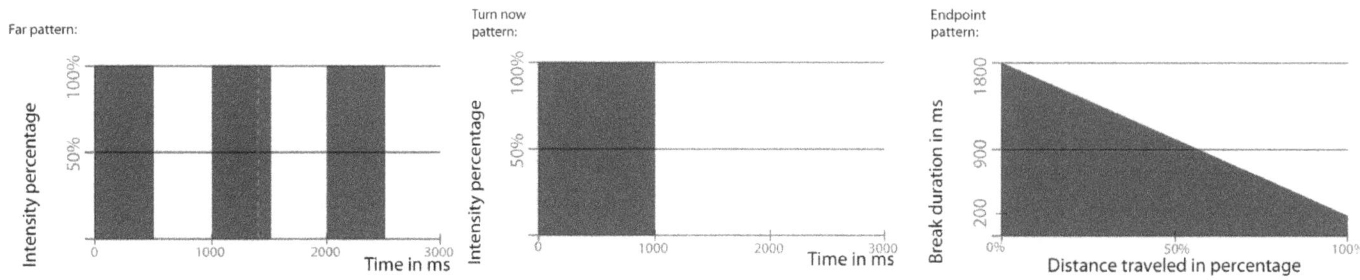

Figure 2. The patterns used for vibrobelt. Left: the "far" pattern (50 meters from target). Middle: the "turn now" pattern (10 meters from target). Right: the "endpoint" pattern.

Software

The Vibrobelt software consists of two applications, one for the Arduino and one for Android. The two applications communicate by sending a Byte array over the usb cable.

The Android application contains the rest of the programming logic, which makes use of the compass, GPS and internet capabilities. The GPS updates trigger the application to check the user's location against the known locations along the route. The route is collected by requesting a KML file from the Google API. When the user misses one of the waypoints, a new route is requested.

In our application we distinguish between starting point, waypoints and endpoint. The starting point is the first location of the route, waypoints are locations on the route where we want to give the user new information about the direction they should take, and endpoint is the end location of the route. When the user starts the application and we get an update from the GPS that has an accuracy of 10 meters or better, the application gives the user feedback about his/her initial bearing. This is the bearing to get to the first waypoint of the route. We use a two-phase rhythm and duration distance encoding design following the results of Asif et al. [16]. If a user is in a range of 50 meters from a waypoint that has not been visited, the application triggers the "far" pattern. This pattern (sent to the arduino) turns the vibrotactile on for 500 milliseconds and off for 500 milliseconds. This cycle repeats two times after the first cycle (see Figure 2 left). If the user is in a range of 10 meters from that same point we trigger the "turn now" pattern (Figure 2 middle). This pattern turns the vibrotactile on for one second. The target of the vibration is calculated using the user's orientation and the direction from the next waypoint to the one after that.

The waypoint information is triggered by the location of the user and is only active when the user approaches such a location on the route. Similar to Robinson et al. [10], we wanted to provide the user with contextual information about the route. We decided to add an additional pattern that makes the user feel in which direction the endpoint of the route is. This pattern continues to be active throughout the whole route and conveys information about the endpoint of the route by making the belt vibrate in the direction of the endpoint. By reducing the breaks between each vibration when the user comes closer to the endpoint, the user can feel its relative position in between start- and endpoint (see Figure 2 right). The length of the vibration stays at a constant 200 milliseconds and the breaks between vibrations varies between 1800 milliseconds in the beginning of the route to 200 milliseconds when the user reaches his or her endpoint.

Visual Map

We created a visual based map as a baseline comparison application for Vibrobelt. The Visual map consists of an Android device running a software application developed especially for this purpose.

Hardware

The hardware used for this application was the same HTC Desire HD as used in the Vibrobelt application. This ensured the same quality of GPS signals as used for Vibrobelt.

Software

A blue line covering the route that users have to take is shown on the map together with a visual representation of all the streets in the area (Google Maps). The user is able to zoom in on the map using two fingers and moving them away from each other. The opposite is achieved by bringing the fingers closer together. A small blue/white circle shows the location of the user and the location uncertainty is shown with a see-trough blue circle surrounding the blue white dot. When we receive a location update from the GPS, the map is centered on the newly acquired location.

METHODOLOGY

To test our hypotheses, an evaluation study was carried out, comparing Vibrobelt to the visual navigation application. In this section we describe the participants, the routes, the procedure and how we analyzed the data.

Participants

Twenty participants volunteered to take part in our study, sixteen male and four female. The average age of the participants was 26 (SD = 8.31) and 15 of them owned a smartphone for an average of 3.1 year (SD = 2.49). They all received higher education (BSc or higher degree). One of the participants had a problem with his vision. He indicated having albinism that has reduced his vision capabilities to seeing only 15% of what normal people can see.

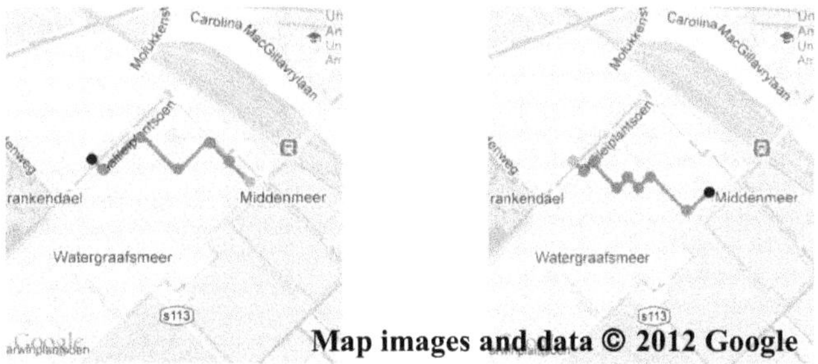

Figure 3. The two routes used for testing our applications, left is the first route and right the second. The green dot signifies the beginning of the route, the black dot the end. The dots in between signify the waypoints. Map images are from GoogleMaps © 2012 Google.

The participants rated their navigation skills and map reading skills above average (Median (Mdn) = 6.00, Interquartile Range (IQR) = 4.75-6.00 and Mdn = 6.00, IQR = 4.75-6.00, respectively) when asked to rate it on a 7 point likert scale. The participants were familiar with using route planners (more than once a week, on average), but they were unfamiliar with the area (Mdn = 1.5, IQR = 1.00-3.75).

Routes

We selected two routes that each participant was asked to follow (see Figure 3). The first route had four waypoints and five locations where vibrotactile feedback was given and measured 950 meters. On the straight part of the route between the start and the first waypoint the participant received additional information telling him/her to go straight. This was done to ensure the participant he or she was still on the right path. The second route had seven waypoints and measured 900 meters. Both of the routes were in the same quiet residential area in the east of Amsterdam.

Procedure

To test Vibrobelt we asked the twenty participants to cycle two routes in an urban environment, one time with Vibrobelt and one time with the visual map. We used a combination of a between subjects and a within subjects experimental design. Each consecutive participant performed the first route with a different application. If the last participant started the first route with the visual map, the next one started the first route with Vibrobelt. Our quantitative data comes from the between subjects design part comparing the results from these two groups. The qualitative results come from asking the participants for their opinion about both applications using a within subjects design.

The participants were asked to meet the researcher at a location close to the testing environment. After filling in the consent and demographics forms we fit the participant with Vibrobelt. Since each person has a different waist size, we activated each vibrotactile to see if we needed to adjust its location. When the participant was satisfied with the locations of the vibrotactiles we performed a test to check if the participant was able to correctly recognize the locations of the vibrations. In this test we turned on all vibrotactiles one to three times in pseudo-random order. Figure 4 shows how the vibrotactiles are divided around the waist.

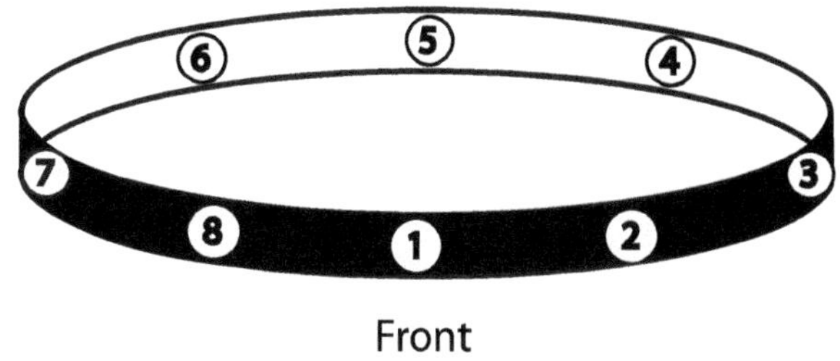

Figure 4. The locations of the vibrotactiles on the belt with numbering.

Figure 5. A participant on the bike to start route one.

The next test was the cycling test. In the Vibrobelt condition, the belt was connected to a box on the steering wheel of the bike containing all the hardware. In the Visual map condition we placed the Android device on the box using a see-through plastic cover. Participants were able to see and operate the application through the plastic cover. In both conditions (Visual map and Vibrobelt) we placed a camera on the steering wheel filming the participant's face. The participant was also asked to wear a helmet with a camera on top. The video material of both cameras was used to determine in which direction the participant was looking (see Figure 5). In this image we see the belt connected to the Arduino in the box on the steering wheel. The Arduino in turn is connected to the Android in the same box. The camera on the steering wheel was pointed at

Statement	Visual		Tactile	
	Mdn	IQR	Mdn	IQR
The application was easy to use.	6	5 – 7	6	5 – 6
The application is user friendly.	6	5 – 6.75	5	5 – 6
It was clear to me how close I was to the next waypoint.	5	3.25 – 6	5	3.25 – 6
I would like to use this system again.	6	5 – 6	6	5 – 7
It was clear to me in which direction the endpoint of the route was.	5.5	3.25 – 6.75	6	5 – 6
It was clear to me in which direction the next waypoint was.	6	5 – 7	6	5 – 6
I felt distracted by the application.	5.5	3 – 6	3.5	2 – 5
It was clear to me what my distance was to the endpoint of the route.	4	2 – 5.75	2	1 – 3.75

Table 1. Median and interquartile range comparison between Visual and Tactile condition for usability questions.

the face of the participant, the camera on the helmet registered what the participant is looking at while cycling. All the participants used the same bike as shown in Figure 5 for both routes.

After performing each route the participant was asked to draw a line covering the route they took on a black and white map of the testing area. With this test we aim to learn more about the spatial knowledge acquisition of the participant. The participant was also asked if he or she recognized a series of six images taken from the environment. Three of these images were on the desired route.

The last part of the procedure was the user experience questionnaire. In this questionnaire we tried to determine if the user found the applications user friendly, if they felt distracted by the application and if they were able to feel the vibrations correctly.

Analysis

The video data was synchronized and analyzed. We paid attention to navigation errors such as wrong turns, being disoriented (standing still for more than three seconds) and near-accidents (having to break to avoid collision or making others do the same). We also timed the number of seconds that users were looking at the screen.

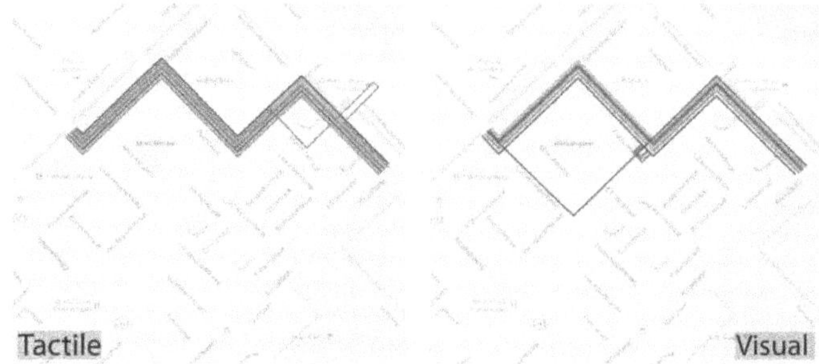

Figure 6. The traveled routes by participants from route one, left with the tactile application and right with the visual application.

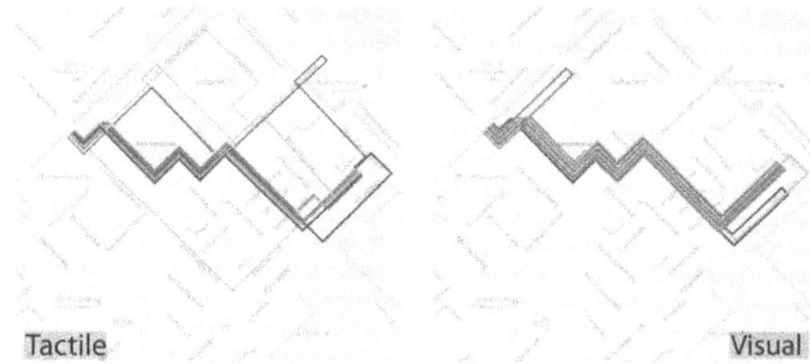

Figure 7. The traveled routes by participants from route two, left with the tactile application and right with the visual application.

The route drawing was either right or wrong; we logged a "1" if the participant was able to draw the route correctly and a "0" if it was wrong. The locations where the images were taken were matched with the route the participant took. This way we knew which image was correctly recognized and which was wrong.

Before we performed our tests on the data we tested it for normal distribution. If a question was normally distributed we could proceed with a t-test, if no normality was found we tested the data with a Mann-Whitney U test.

RESULTS

In this chapter we discuss the results from our research. We had to deal with a heterogeneous data set. We had quantitative data such as recognizing images from the route, time taken for the route, demographics etc. but also qualitative data resulting from questions about good and bad points of the system and other usability questions. On top of that we also have information from the researcher himself who followed every participant on his/her route.

Quantitative Data

The results from the belt check test showed that participants made on average 1.25 mistakes in fifteen trials (92 percent correct), with slightly higher error rates for the activations corresponding to vibrotactiles seven and three (15 and 13 percent errors, respectively). When an error was made the participant was never more than one motor away from the right answer, however.

The data to test H1 has a normal distribution and can therefore be analyzed using an independent samples t- test. We found no significant difference between people using the tactile or the visual application for either routes when asked to recognize the images. The data does however indicate a slight advantage for the tactile application. When users were asked to recognize images from route one, people using the visual application made on average 0.3 more mistakes ($p = 0.43$) than users using the tactile application (Visual: $M = 1.00$, $SD = 0.67$ vs. Tactile: $M = 0.70$, $SD = 0.95$). The difference was even higher ($p = 0.45$) when users cycled route two (Visual: $M = 1.40$, $SD = 1.08$ vs. Tactile: $M = 1.00$, $SD = 1.25$).

Regarding our second hypothesis, participants took slightly less ($p = 0.58$) wrong turns using the tactile application with route one (Visual: $M = 0.40$, $SD = 0.52$ vs. Tactile: $M = 0.30$, $SD = 0.68$) and more ($p = 0.28$) in the second route (Visual: $M = 0.40$, $SD = 0.70$ vs. Tactile: $M = 0.80$, $SD = 0.79$). However, the means of the two groups did not significantly differ (using a Mann-Whitney U test, since the data was not normally distributed).

With respect to the third hypothesis, users who cycled the second route and used the visual navigation application ($M = 0.90$, $SD = 0.32$) were on average better at recalling the route than users using the tactile application ($M = 0.50$, $SD = 0.53$), but we could not show a significant difference (t-test, $p = 0.06$). We also found no significant difference ($p = 0.63$) between the means for the first route (Visual: $M = 0.70$, $SD = 0.48$ vs. Tactile: $M = 0.80$, $SD = 0.42$).

It took participants on average 298.7 seconds to cycle route one (Visual condition: $M = 280.00$, $SD = 79.00$; Tactile condition: $M = 317.40$, $SD = 71.99$) and 309.10 seconds for route two (Visual condition: $M = 287.30$, $SD = 113.94$; Tactile condition: $M = 330.90$, $SD = 134.22$). Although participants spent an average 28.17% of their time looking at the screen in the visual condition, they were faster than participants using the tactile application. We recorded two near-accidents when using the visual navigation application and zero in the tactile condition. Both instances occurred when the participant was looking at the screen and came close to colliding with another cyclist.

Qualitative Data

Although half of the participants made navigation errors, all of them were able to reach their endpoint. They found both applications relatively easy to use and user friendly (See Table 1).

Visual

Most of the participants (12/20) found the tactile application less distracting than the visual application. Having to look at the screen was one of the most common (11/20) complaints about the visual navigation system. They also mentioned (7/20) that the reflection of the screen made it difficult to see the information. Others (2/20) found it difficult to operate the device while cycling and therefore very distracting. When participants were unable to see the screen due to the intensity of the sun they often found some shade and stood still while orientating. Positive points about the visual navigation system were the route overview (10/20), participants often browsed trough the route using the application to get a general idea about the waypoints. Participants (2/20) also mentioned feeling comfortable using a familiar navigation system.

Tactile

The tactile navigation application was appreciated for its intuitive usage (3/20). Participants felt they got the right information at the right time (3/20) allowing them to concentrate on the surrounding traffic. It was also mentioned (3/20) to be fun and exciting to use this new form of navigation. Negative points participants noted were about the strength of the vibrations (10/20) and the ability to differentiate between waypoint and endpoint information (6/20). They were also missing the overview of the route (4/20) which they had when using the visual system. One participant suggested the application would work better without the endpoint feedback while another felt it gave him not just the ability to feel the endpoint of the route but also assured that the application was still active and working.

Although the endpoint feedback was highly appreciated for its directional purpose ($Mdn = 6$, $IQR = 5\text{-}6$), it did not seem to help users get an idea about their distance to the endpoint of the route. Participants averagely rated their endpoint distance knowledge acquisition as 2 (Mdn) on a 7 point likert scale ($IQR = 1\text{-}3.75$).

Participants were slightly insecure when using the tactile belt in the beginning. They cycled slower and seemed unsure if the belt would give them the right information. After the first few waypoints they showed more confidence taking the turns indicated by the belt. Route one did not appear to be difficult for the participants and almost resulted in a perfect score but the second route showed more navigation errors. Three participants who had trouble feeling the vibrations took wrong turns in the beginning of the second route. These three participants went right either too early or too late (see Figure 7). The remaining seven in this group seemed to have no trouble following the cues from Vibrobelt until they came to the last waypoint where three participants made a wrong turn. They turned left either before or after the desired waypoint; this error was quickly corrected by following the newly calculated route or following the vibrations of the endpoint feedback. Three other participants were unable to feel all the vibrations, which resulted in slightly different routes towards the desired endpoint. While going in the wrong direction, one of these participants was asked if she still felt the vibrations. She answered that she felt it vibrating in her back.

Visual vs Tactile

When asked to indicate their preference comparing both applications on a seven point Likert scale (one being absolute preference for the tactile and seven for the visual application) they answered with a Median 4 (IQR = 2.25-5). Three participants indicated to have an absolute preference for the tactile system, one of which was the visually impaired participant. It took this last person 199 seconds longer than average to cycle the first route with the visual condition while he was 7 seconds quicker than average with the tactile condition in the second route.

DISCUSSION

The belt check test resulted in high error rates for the 6th and 12th time a vibrotactile was activated. These activations correspond to motor numbers 3 and 7, on the left and right side of the waist. The other activations of motor 3 or 7 did not result in higher error rates. It would be interesting to investigate if the order of motor activations has an influence on the recognition of the vibration location.

Users spent on average 28% of their time looking at the screen when using the visual navigation system. Having to look at the screen was therefore not surprisingly one of the most heard complaints about the visual application. We found two near-accidents when participants used the visual application. Pielot and Boll also found the visual condition to lead to significantly more dangerous situations in a similar study with pedestrians [8]. We specifically chose a quiet residential neighborhood for our tests so the chance of an accident would be as low as possible and encountered therefore no accidents during our tests. Cycling in a more dynamic environment could produce clearer results but would be unethical to ask from our participants. Using a virtual cycle tour setup as used in Poppinga et al. [2] could explore more dangerous traffic situations.

Participants were better at recalling the route when using the visual application. This might be due to the fact that they were able to see the route on the screen. Users cycling the first route were unaware they had to recognize images and recall the route in advance. It is therefore likely that users paid more attention to the surroundings and the route while cycling the second route. The fact that we only found a high significance value for the second route seems to support this rationale. We could therefore say that users are better at recalling the route when using a visual navigation system and they know they have to memorize the route. When they are unaware of the test, participants did not show a significantly increased contextual route understanding.

The visual condition resulted in faster route completion. When participants used Vibrobelt they seemed to have difficulties trusting the application to give them the right information. This made them cycle slower than participants using the visual application, anticipating new feedback at every road crossing. This result stands in contrast to Pielot and Boll who found participants using the tactile application to be slightly faster [8]. Most participants showed more confidence taking turns after the first few waypoints. A longitudinal study could determine if users can grow accustomed to using a tactile navigation device such as Vibrobelt.

Confusing the waypoint and endpoint information caused disorientation for some participants. The 50 meter waypoint feedback made a vibrotactile vibrate in the direction of the coming waypoint, turning it on and off three times for three seconds in total (see section Software). This pattern got less distinguishable from the endpoint feedback near the end of the route. As the participant approached the endpoint of the route, it became more frequent, making it more similar to the 50 meter waypoint feedback. Although none of the patterns were communicated simultaneously, some participants found this very confusing, making them stop cycling to reorientate. Future versions of Vibrobelt should support a clearer distinction between the two patterns. This could be done by using a predefined pattern to signify the user to expect waypoint information or turning the endpoint feedback off altogether. Users should be able to adjust these features in a settings menu to meet their personal preferences.

It is unclear if adding the endpoint information in Vibrobelt helped participants find their way. Participants were better aware of the endpoint direction than using the visual application but gave a low score to their distance knowledge acquisition. We used rhythm and duration to encode distance as recommended by Straub et al. [15] and Asif et al. [16]. Future research could compare a version with and without endpoint feedback. A better familiarity with the workings of the system might show more appreciation for the endpoint feedback. This feedback does not only provide users with contextual information but also allows users to take more initiative while cycling [10]. When people take an alternative route, or when map information is outdated, knowing the endpoint direction and distance could enable users to make better informed navigational decisions.

Because we used endpoint feedback and dynamic route calculation, all the participants were able to reach their destination using Vibrobelt without ever having seen the destination or the route towards it. Our system could therefore be very helpful for tourists discovering a new city or visually impaired people such as one of our participants. Tourists are often seen looking at a map, trying to discover the correct route. With a system such as this they could free their attention from reading maps and look at the interesting sceneries around them. Visually impaired people would highly benefit from a system that does not require them to look at a screen. We were able to test our system with a person with low visibility and the results looked promising. While the average participant had slower routes when using the tactile condition he was more than 2.5

minutes faster using Vibrobelt and made no navigation mistakes.

Regarding the vibrations, we used 3 volts round 10mm pico vibration motors. Some users complained that the vibrations these motors produced were difficult to feel. In some cases it resulted in participants missing their waypoint. We asked participants to fit the belt as tightly (but still comfortable) as possible to maximize the effect of the vibration sensation. In three cases the participant told the researcher that extending their waist by taking in air improved his or her sensitivity to the vibrations. Although all participants were able to sense the vibrations, user satisfaction and performance could be improved by using more powerful vibration motors.

CONCLUSION

To investigate the potential of tactile navigation for cyclists, we have designed and implemented Vibrobelt. This belt, worn around the waist, gives waypoint, distance and endpoint information using directional tactile cues. Our experiment focused on discovering the tradeoffs between visualand tactile navigation. Twenty participants cycled two routes, one with Vibrobelt and one with the visual navigation application. We tested the participants on contextual route understanding and route image recognition. At the end of the experiment the participants were asked for their opinions regarding the two applications.

The results showed that all participants were able to reach a destination unknown to them using the tactile instructions of Vibrobelt. The two-stage waypoint feedback instructions of Vibrobelt enabled participants to anticipate the waypoint and prepare to make a turn. The endpoint distance encoding was not always correctly interpreted. It rather confused participants when the patterns got more frequent near the end, making it similar to waypoint information. A future version of Vibrobelt needs to make a clearer distinction between waypoint and endpoint information.

Using the tactile application resulted in more wrong turns but less near-accidents which is similar to findings by Pielot and Boll [8]. Since participants used 28% of their cycling time looking at the screen in the visual condition it is not surprising that users felt distracted by the visual navigation application. A contrasting result however concerns the route completion times. Using Vibrobelt seemed to make participants hesitant at crossings, trying to assess if there was new navigation information. This resulted in slower routes when compared to the visual navigation application. Because participants showed more confidence after the first few waypoints we think a study in which participants are able to use the system for a longer amount of time may show greater benefits of using Vibrobelt.

Although the Vibrobelt design allowed the participants to distinguish eight different directions with an accuracy of 92 percent, as shown by the belt check test, the routes in the cycling experiment included only 90 degree turns. A future study will also investigate how users react to more heterogeneous routes including more complex turns.

Although the current experiment did not lead to statistically significant results, several findings point in the direction of potential advantages of the Vibrobelt system over visual maps. These include lower error rates, on average, for recognizing pictures taken along the route, higher participant ratings of clarity of the direction of the endpoint of the route, and lower participant ratings of feeling distracted by the tactile application, compared to the visual map application.

A study with more participants could determine if these potential advantages of vibrotactile feedback over visual maps can indeed be confirmed. Despite the drawbacks (confusion between waypoint and endpoint information, longer route completion times), the findings that all participants could find their destinations using only the vibrotactile feedback, and their enthusiasm for using it, shows that the Vibrobelt system may be a viable alternative for using visual map applications, in particular for navigation on bicycles.

ACKNOWLEDGEMENTS

This work is supported by the European Union as part of the Eurostars Program, project SmartINSIDE (E! 5262). We would also like to thank all participants for taking part in our study.

REFERENCES

1. National Highway Traffic Safety Administration, Visual-Manual NHTSA Driver Distraction Guidelines for In-Vehicle Electronic Devices, Notice of proposed Federal guidelines, 77 FR 11199, pp. 11199-11250 (2012). https://federalregister.gov/a/2012-4017 (Accessed August 11, 2012).
2. B. Poppinga, M. Pielot, and S. Boll, "Tacticycle: a tactile display for supporting tourists on a bicycle trip", in Proc. of MobileHCI'09, ACM Press (2009), pp. 1–4.
3. S. Levine, "Blicycle: A Bicycle for the Blind, Principles and Practice of Assistive Technology", Unpublished student project report, MIT (2011). http://web.mit.edu/sjlevine/www/projects/Blicycle/sjlevine_FinalReport.pdf (Accessed Dec 1, 2012).
4. A. Bouwer, F. Nack, and A. E. Ali, "Lost in navigation: Evaluating a mobile map app for a fair", in Proc. of ICMI'12, ACM Press (2012), pp. 22–26.
5. K. Tsukada and M. Yasumura, "Activebelt: Belt-type wearable tactile display for directional navigation", in Proc. of UbiComp 2004, Springer (2004), pp. 384–399.
6. M. Pielot, N. Henze, W. Heuten, and S. Boll, "Evaluation of continuous direction encoding with tactile belts", in Proc. of HAID 2008, Springer (2008), pp. 1–10.

7. M. Pielot, O. Krull, and S. Boll, "Where is my team: supporting situation awareness with tactile displays", in Proc. of CHI 2010, ACM Press (2010), pp. 1705–1714.
8. M. Pielot and S. Boll, "Tactile Wayfinder: comparison of tactile waypoint navigation with commercial pedestrian navigation systems", in Proc. of Pervasive 2010, Springer (2010), pp. 76–93.
9. M. Duistermaat, "Tactile land navigation in night operations", Tech. report, TNO Defence, Security and Safety, Dec. (2005).
10. S. Robinson, M. Jones, P. Eslambolchilar, R. Murray-Smith, and M. Lindborg, "I did it my way: moving away from the tyranny of turn-by-turn pedestrian navigation," in Proc. of MobileHCI'10, ACM Press (2010), pp. 341–344.
11. M. Pielot, B. Poppinga, W. Heuten, and S. Boll, "Tacticycle: Supporting exploratory bicycle trips", in Proc. of MobileHCI'12, ACM Press (2012), pp. 21–24.
12. D. Kern, P. Marshall, E. Hornecker, Y. Rogers, and A. Schmidt, "Enhancing navigation information with tactile output embedded into the steering wheel", In Proc. of Pervasive 2009, Springer (2009), pp. 42–58.
13. S. Hwang and J. Ryu, "The haptic steering wheel: Vibrotactile based navigation for the driving environment", in Proc. of IEEE Int. Conf. on PERCOM Workshops (2010), pp. 660-665.
14. H. Van Veen, M. Spape, and J. B. F. V. Erp, "Waypoint navigation on land: different ways of coding distance to the next waypoint", in Proc. of EuroHaptics (2004), pp. 160–165.
15. M. Straub, A. Riener, and A. Ferscha, "Distance encoding in vibro-tactile guidance cues", in Proc. of MobiQuitous 2009, IEEE (2009), pp. 2–3.
16. A. Asif, W. Heuten, and S. Boll, "Exploring Distance Encodings with a Tactile Display to Convey Turn by Turn Information in Automobiles", in Proc. of NordiCHI 2010, ACM Press (2010), pp. 32–41.
17. K. R. Boff and J. E. Lincoln, User's guide: Engineering data compendium: human perception and performance. Harry G. Armstrong Aerospace Medical Research Laboratory (1988).

Haptic Interface for Non-Visual Steering

Burkay Sucu and Eelke Folmer
Department of Computer Science and Engineering
University of Nevada, Reno
{bsucu,efolmer}@cse.unr.edu

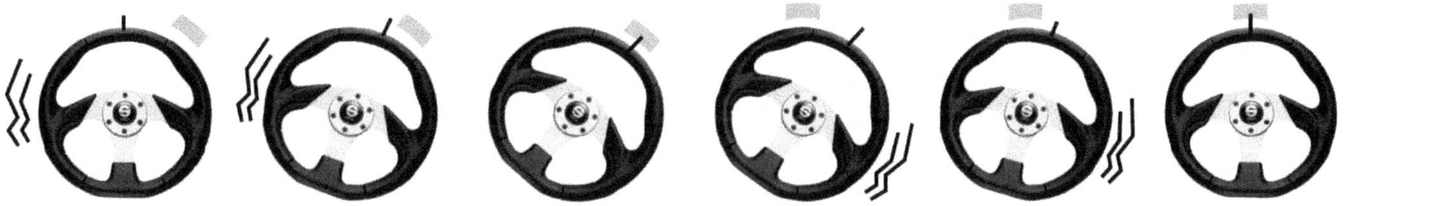

Figure 1. Steering cues are provided through a vibrotactor integrated in the left and right of the steering wheel. Drivers steer away from a cue felt in either hand, in order to find a dead-band window that indicates the target orientation of the wheel, which changes as the car drives through the curve.

ABSTRACT
Glare significantly diminishes visual perception, and is a significant cause of traffic accidents. Existing haptic automotive interfaces typically indicate when and in which direction to steer, but they don't convey how much to steer, as a driver typically determines this using visual feedback. We present a novel haptic interface that relies on an intelligent vehicle position system to indicate when, in which direction and how far to steer, as to facilitate steering without any visual feedback. Our interface may improve driving safety when a driver is temporarily blinded, for example, due to glare or fog. Three user studies were performed, the first study tries to understand driving using visual feedback, the second study evaluates two different haptic encoding mechanisms with no visual feedback present, and a third study evaluates the supplemental effect of haptic feedback when used in conjunction with visual feedback. Studies show this interface to allow for blind steering through small curves and that it can improve a driver's lane keeping ability when combined with visual feedback.

Author Keywords
Haptic Interfaces, Steering, Automotive UI, Safety.

ACM Classification Keywords
H.5.2 HCI: Haptic I/O

INTRODUCTION
Glare, caused by sunlight or headlights is a significant cause of vehicle accidents, as visibility is a basic requirement for safe driving [12]. Especially in winter, due to a lower elevation of the sun and the presence of snow and ice, there is a significant increase in traffic accidents due to glare. Depending on the type of exposure, it may take an eye between 1 and 7 seconds to adjust to glare [26, 30, 5]. As a person ages, the ability to focus and recover from glare continues to diminish [25] and as a result nearly 40% of drivers involved in accidents due to glare are older than 45 years [12]. Though glare can occur in various contexts, one of the more dangerous situations is when a driver is steering through a curve, as there is a greater risk of getting blinded due to the significant change in direction. Unlike driving on a straight road, steering through a curve requires continuous adjustment of the steering wheel, therefore a temporary blindness could have major consequences.

In recent years there has been increasing interest in improving automotive safety using haptic interfaces. For example, lane keeping [15] or lane changing [22] systems are commercially available where haptic cues warn the driver of impeding danger. Other systems [19, 7, 21] aim to reduce overloaded modalities, where haptic feedback conveys high level navigation instructions. Haptic feedback has some desirable properties over other modalities in that it is private and doesn't distract any passengers. Haptic feedback provided through the steering wheel allows for robust and efficient communication of rich tactile information [20], as the driver is always holding it. For steering, existing systems (see related work) have only explored the use of haptic feedback to indicate when to steer and in which direction, but not how far to steer, as the user typically evaluates this by looking at the curvature of the road. If a driver is temporarily blinded through glare, the information provided using haptic feedback in these systems is not sufficient for steering a vehicle through a curve.

We present a haptic steering interface, that relies on an intelligent vehicle positioning system and a map of the road, to indicate when and in which direction to steer, but also how much to steer. This allows for steering without visual feedback in contexts, i.e., steering through a curve at high speed, where getting blinded is most lethal.

BACKGROUND AND RELATED WORK

Within the HCI community a steering task is typically associated with using a pointing device for steering a mouse cursor within the confines of a 2D tunnel, for example, navigating hierarchical menus. The human performance of steering is modeled by the Steering law [6]. Studies show that different modalities of error feedback affect the accuracy of steering but not movement time, with tactile feedback improving accuracy more than visual or audio feedback [28].

The problem addressed in this paper involves performing a steering task, with the difference that instead of a pointing device, a steering wheel is used that can turn left or right to control the direction in which a vehicle is moving. Another difference is that most steering tasks, such as navigating cascading menus, assume an overhead view, whereas driving a vehicle uses a first person view. Bateman [9] has explored how different types of views affect driving performance in a simulator and found driving using a first person view to yield significantly better performance than using an overhead view.

Haptic feedback is already available in certain car systems, for example, Ford's *Lane Keeping System* [15], or *Lane Change Assist* systems used by Audi, Volkswagen, BMW, Porsche, and Mazda [22]. These systems make use of state of art technology to check if the car stays on the lane or not, and warn the driver using haptic cues if the car crosses the lane line before the driver uses the signals or if changing lanes is not safe due to a car present in the blind spot. These systems build on nearly a decade of research in automotive user interfaces, which we will summarize here, specifically focusing on steering.

Enriquez [14] was one of the first to implement a tactile display in a vehicle context. Different types of warnings, e.g., errors on various gauges, are conveyed through pulsations of varying frequencies on the drivers hands by embedding inflatable pads in the steering wheel. User studies show a significant decrease in response time and demonstrate the feasibility of using frequency to convey different warnings.

Van Erp et al [29] implement a tactile display by embedding eight vibrotactors in the driver's seat. Turning left or right is indicated by activating the vibrotactors under the driver's corresponding leg. The distance to a turn is conveyed using pulse length modulation. User studies show a significant increase in driving performance over using visual feedback alone with a decrease in cognitive load.

Griffiths and Gillespie [16] developed a driving simulator where the steering wheel is both held by the driver and motorized for automatic control. The motion of the steering wheel is a response to the sum of forces acting from the human grasp, from the automatic control motor, and from the steering linkage. Feeling the actions of the wheel, the driver can either comply with it or override it by applying more force. User studies show significant increase in the user's lane keeping ability while decreasing the visual demand and reaction time.

As part of the blind driver challenge [10] an autonomous vehicle developed for DARPA's Urban Challenge [13] was modified to allow a user who is blind to drive it [18]. Audio provided using a headset is used for steering, e.g., sonification using frequency indicates the direction and magnitude of a turn. A modified massage chair provides haptic feedback to indicate speeding up or slowing down using a series of vibrotactors. No user studies were conducted.

Kern et al. [20] present a steering wheel with six integrated vibrotactors to convey navigation information to the driver. Spatial cues on the wheel indicate to turn left or right. User studies evaluated the effectiveness of supplemental directional information in different modalities (audio/tactile) and found that haptic feedback impedes driving performance, with no significant effect for the other modalities. They further explored using dynamic patterns for conveying the steering direction, by sequentially activating vibrotactors in the direction the wheel needs to be turned. Qualitative results are reported, i.e., users preferred audio over the haptic interface.

The "haptic steering wheel" [19] embeds 32 linear vibrotactors in a steering wheel, which allows for communicating information regardless of where the drivers hold their hands and further allows for displaying tactile illusions, such as sensory saltation. Spatial and temporal patterns (clockwise/counterclock wise activation) are used to indicate whether to steer left or right, as well as to convey various types of alerts. Three different spatial encodings, three different stimulus times and three different tactile illusions are evaluated. User studies evaluate the user's ability to successfully recognize these patterns and perform corresponding actions, but not the effect on driving. The highest recognition rate is achieved for 450ms stimulus time, an overlapping spatial encoding and the sensory saltation tactile illusion.

Asif and Boll [7] propose a vibrotactile belt that conveys navigation information using eight vibrotactors. Drivers wear this belt while driving and the location of a turn is indicated by the location of the active vibrotactor and distance through different temporal patterns. User studies show increase in navigation performance but no change in cognitive workload.

Kim et al. present a haptic steering wheel with 20 vibrotactors [21]. Turning directions are indicated using clockwise or counterclockwise activation of vibrotactors. User studies evaluate multimodal feedback for younger and elderly drivers and found significant improvement in performance for haptic feedback provision.

Most of these systems provide high-level navigation instructions, e.g., turn left or right, where the required steering task (how much to steer) is performed by the driver based on visual input. Only a single system [18] allows for non-visual steering as it facilitates blind people to drive a vehicle. This system relies on an autonomous vehicle capable of determining its position on the road using GPS and a map of the environment with drivable roads. How much to steer is indicated using audio provided using a headset. Because many states ban the use of headsets that cover both ears while driving [1] and audio provided using a speaker can be annoying for passengers to hear, we explore solutions using haptic feedback to convey steering information.

DESIGN OF A HAPTIC STEERING INTERFACE

Where most studies with haptic driving assistance have evaluated the ability of haptic feedback to reduce the driver's cognitive load -when provided in conjunction with visual feedback- we are specifically interested in performing a steering task using haptic feedback alone. In existing systems, haptic cues only indicate when to steer and in which direction, but not by how much as the driver typically determines that using visual feedback, e.g., by looking at the curvature of the road. In particular contexts, for example, when the driver is temporarily blinded by glare or their view is limited by fog, knowing how much to steer is essential information for keeping the car in the lane.

A steering task can be considered to be some form of a choice response task, i.e., providing a particular input based on a certain stimulus. Various studies with subjects performing choice response tasks have shown that a stimulus represented in multiple modalities simultaneously can be detected at lower thresholds, faster, and more accurately than when information is provided separately in each modality [23, 17]. Based on these studies, one can argue that a haptic driving assistance system that also indicates how far to steer when used in conjunction with visual feedback, could allow a driver to more closely follow the median of the lane than using visual feedback alone.

Before designing a haptic interface that indicates how far to steer, we conducted a study with the goal to better understand how humans perform a steering task using visual feedback.

Study 1: Understanding Driving

Steering is required in various driving contexts, for example, parking, stopping at an intersection and turning into another lane. However, in these situations the vehicle is moving at a low speed and –when blinded– the driver can simply stop the vehicle without jeopardizing the safety of other drivers. Steering at higher speeds typically happens when changing lanes or taking an exit, in which case the driver only has to steer for a very brief period (less than a few seconds). Steering for longer periods at a constant speed only occurs when there is a curvature in the road, with the most extreme case when a driver has to take a 270° loop ramp when driving over a cloverleaf highway interchange. Haptic feedback would be the most useful in this context as drivers have a greater risk of getting blinded due to the significant change in direction and a greater risk of an accident due to having to steer for a prolonged period. For this study, we therefore analyze driving behavior when driving on a curved road.

Participants

We recruited eight computer science students (2 female, average age 27.3, SD=3.5) to participate in a user study. All subjects were right handed and none reported any non-correctable impairments in perception or motor control. Subjects had an average of 5.5 years (SD=3.8) driving experience.

Instrumentation

An open source driving simulator created in Microsoft XNA [3] was modified to suit our study. We designed four different

Figure 2. Screenshot of simulator we modified to analyze driving behavior using visual feedback.

Figure 3. Four different roads with curve angles: $180°, 135°, 90°, 45°$

roads where each road starts and ends with a 50 meter straight section connected by a circular curve with a radius of 50 meters. Using standard design dimensions recommended by the federal highway administration, we designed a two-lane road with a lane width of 3.6m [4] and used an average car width of 1.85m. We used four different angles for curving roads: $45°, 90°, 135°$ and $180°$ (see Figure 3). The radius of the right curves' lane median is 48.2 m and radius of left curves' lane median is 51.8m. Subjects drive each of these roads in both directions to understand how the radius affects steering performance. For a curve radius of 50m the department of transportation recommends a speed between 40 and 48km/h [2] but since our simulator doesn't take into account friction, we set the speed of the car in the simulator to 50km/h. These values were chosen as to have approximately between 3 and 12 seconds of steering input required from the driver, which is long enough for the vehicle to leave the lane, when the driver is temporarily blinded. Figure 2 shows a screenshot of the simulator used.

For input, we used a simulator grade racing wheel, the Logitech G27 Racing Wheel, with an 28 cm diameter (see Figure 5) that was attached to a desk. Every 100ms, we log the position of the car and the steering wheel, which ranges from -1,000 (left) to 1,000 (right) for a 180° turn of the wheel, with 0 being the neutral position.

Procedure

Participants were seated in front of the steering wheel facing the screen. Participants were instructed that they only needed to steer the vehicle to maintain its position in the lane

Table 1. Prelim. study results: average deviation (stdev) in meters

CURVATURE	LEFT	RIGHT
45°	.490 (.167)	.422 (.243)
90°	.563 (.282)	.621 (.218)
135°	.621 (.278)	.584 (.294)
180°	.557 (.281)	.557 (.223)
All	.558 (.054)	.546 (.087)
	.552 (.277)	

while the vehicle drove through the curve. Participants were allowed to try a few roads for practice as to minimize any learning effects and when they felt comfortable enough, the experiment would start. Participants would drive each of our four roads in both directions three times in random order for a total of 24 trials. The vehicle automatically starts driving at the beginning of each track and upon completion of the track, is teleported to the beginning of the next track.

Results

For every single trial, we calculate the standard deviation of the vehicle from the median of the lane. Since keeping the wheel at the neutral position is enough to keep the vehicle on the lane's median for the straight sections, these are excluded from our calculation as they decrease standard deviation significantly and don't involve any steering. Table 1 lists the results for each type of curve. A repeated measures ANOVA with a Greenhouse-Geisser correction found no statistically significant difference between left and right curves and between different curvatures ($\boldsymbol{F}_{1.83,12.78} = 1.51, p = .26$). The average deviation from the lane's median for all curves is .552 m (SD=.277).

Figure 4 lists the average values for all subjects for the steering wheel position for all right curves. The graphs for different curvatures are the same because the radius is the same and only differ in the amount of time that the wheel needs to be held in a maximum position (T_{right}=~225). The graphs for left curves are similar with a maximum value of T_{left}=~-200. Our study confirms there is a linear relationship between the radius (r) of the curve and the maximum value of the steering wheel (T). Each graph in Figure 4 can be approximated with a function $t(\phi)$, which depends on the position (ϕ) of the vehicle on the curve and the curve's radius (r), curvature θ; and the velocity (v) of the vehicle and which yields the target position T' of the steering wheel.

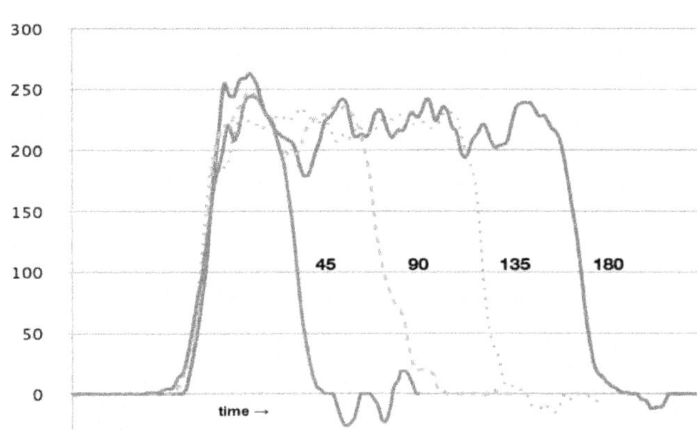

Figure 4. Average steering wheel values for the right turns

Haptic Steering Interface

Existing haptic driving assistance solutions [19, 20, 21] are often overly complex in terms of haptic technology used, for example, arrays of vibrotactors are required as to allow for providing sophisticated tactile illusionary tactile effects. Such solutions may be expensive to implement and more prone to breaking due to the large amount of hardware involved. It can be argued whether rich tactile effects, such as sensory saltation [19] are superfluous in conveying the information that is required for steering. The design of our haptic interface is therefore largely motivated by identifying the smallest amount of haptic feedback required for steering.

The information that needs to be conveyed using haptic feedback is the target position T' of the steering wheel as the vehicle follows the curve. Haptic feedback can be provided using various technologies including, force feedback, skin stretch or thermal feedback. Most commonly, haptic feedback is provided through vibrotactile feedback, for example, mobile devices typically feature a single rotary mass motor that provides on/off vibrotactile feedback with a fixed frequency. However, their latency limits the use of sophisticated drive signals [24]. For our steering interface we use vibrotactors due to their low cost and their compact size. We designed a physical interface where vibrotactors are integrated into the steering wheel, which is motivated by the following reasons: haptic feedback provided through a belt [7] or seat [29, 18] may be impeded by the driver's clothes, receptors in a driver's hips and back are also not sensitive enough to distinguish complex stimuli [19], hands are most sensitive due to an abundance of tactile receptors in the fingertips [8], and getting feedback from the steering wheel itself may be more intuitive as it may allow the driver to control the wheel using an associated physical mapping [20].

Because a driver needs to steer either to the left or right, we integrate a vibrotactor in the left and the right side of the wheel. Our interface is inspired by how rumble strips or Bott's dots work, which provides tactile feedback to a driver when they drift from their lane. When the current position of the steering wheel is to the left of the target position T' the left vibrotactor will vibrate and if it is to the right the right vibrotactor will vibrate. The next subsection details what haptic cues can be provided. Upon feeling a cue on a side the driver needs to steer away from the cue, e.g., a left cue requires the driver to turn the wheel to the right, until haptic feedback stops. Figure 1 illustrates how our technique works for steering through a curve. T' is achieved when no haptic feedback is felt, which makes sense as prolonged exposure to vibrotactile feedback may temporarily decrease the haptic sensitivity of the driver's hands, which is undesirable. Study 1 showed that the wheel is at most turned 40° so this mapping avoids confusion on how to interpret the haptic cues. This interface is similar to the interface used by Hong et al [18], that uses sonification to indicate steering information. As it is difficult to precisely hold the wheel in the target position T', drivers will keep oscillating between steering left and right. Oscillation can be minimized by implementing a dead-band window of size w around the target position T' in which no vibrotactile feedback is felt. For w a tradeoff must be made between oscillation and reduced accuracy in being able to follow $t(\phi)$, with a risk of the vehicle possibly leaving the lane.

Haptic Encoding Scheme: Our haptic steering interface is minimal in terms of number of vibrotactors required but also with regard to the haptic encoding scheme used, as we use a simple on/off cue with feedback being provided at a frequency (275Hz) that the human skin is most sensitive to. A problem with this design is that the driver can only find the target orientation by steering, with a risk of steering too slowly leading to understeering or when steering to fast; missing the window and oversteering. This problem may be solved by using vibrotactors that allow for frequency modulation and use frequency to indicate how far to steer. The vibrotactors' perceivable range of frequencies can be linearly mapped to the interval $[w/2, T_{max}]$ since we know in advance what the maximum steering error can be, for a given curvature using available map information.

Frequency modulation is better for conveying steering magnitude than using pulse delay, since T' is indicated using no vibrotactile feedback, which would be difficult to sense when pulse delay is increased as the driver gets closer to T'. A reverse encoding scheme (pulse increase) would require a transition from 0 pulse delay to no feedback, which drivers may perceive as confusing. A related study with virtual object manipulation also finds better performance for amplitude than pulse delay modulation [27]. Tactons [11] could be defined to indicate magnitude, but this requires drivers to memorize their meaning and requires discretization of magnitude, where frequency modulation is more intuitive and allows for a linear mapping.

STUDY 2: EVALUATING HAPTIC ENCODING SCHEMES

The second user study focuses on evaluating the effectiveness of both proposed haptic steering encoding schemes, e.g., no magnitude (NM) versus frequency magnitude (FM).

Participants

We recruited 12 computer science students (4 female, average age 28.6, SD=5.9) to participate in a user study. All subjects were right handed and none reported any non-correctable impairments in perception or motor control. Subjects had on average 7.1 years (SD=6.2) of driving experience.

Instrumentation

We used the same simulator as in the first study and we use it as a proxy for an intelligent vehicle positioning system with map information, as this suffices for evaluating the effectiveness of each haptic encoding scheme. For haptic feedback provision we used a commercially available wireless motion-sensing controller (Sony Playstation Move), which has an integrated vibrotactor that allows for frequency modulation with a perceivable range of 91 to 275Hz. Two controllers were used, where each was attached to the left or right front of the steering wheel using tape (see Figure 5). By having the drivers place their hands over the controllers, we maximize the surface area of the hand that touches each controller and achieve maximum sensitivity to vibrotactile feedback. The controller lights did not convey any information. A value for the dead-zone width (w) was determined experimentally using preliminary trials, where a value of $w = 50$ would minimize oscillations with an acceptable deviation from the lane's median. Because there is a small delay before each vibrotactor is activated, haptic cues are provided 380ms ahead of when the user must steer in order to accommodate this. For indicating steering magnitude using frequency, we linearly map the perceivable range of the vibrotactor $[91, 275Hz]$ to $[25, T_{max}]$, with a higher frequency indicating a larger steering error. For this study, we adjust T' as described by $t(\phi)$ but not T_{max} depending on the position of the car with regards to the median of the lane, e.g., there is no auto correction. Preliminary experiences with using autocorrection found to yield significant oscillations, which typically lead to the car leaving the road. Instead we keep T_{max} at the values found in our first study, and our study thus focuses on how well each haptic encoding scheme allows a driver to approximate $t(\phi)$.

Figure 5. Vibrotactors attached to the left and the right side of the steering wheel, with drivers placing their hands on top of them.

Procedure

Participants were randomly assigned into two six-people groups (A,B) where group A played the simulator using no magnitude (NM) and group B using frequency magnitude (FM). A between-subjects study design is justified to avoid interference effects, e.g., when participants have mastered one haptic encoding scheme it may confuse their ability to learn and use another. We used the same procedure as for the first study, except subjects were unable to see a display. Because simulating a temporary blindness with varying durations at various points in the curve could lead to significantly different results, and would require a large number of studies to be performed, we limit our study to steering without any visual feedback. This provides us with a worst-case performance in the case a driver is completely blinded, but this allows for an accurate comparison between both haptic encoding mechanisms. Participants were instructed on how to interpret the haptic cues provided for each encoding scheme and were allowed to try a few roads for practice, to minimize any learning effects. When subjects felt comfortable enough, the experiment would start. Participants would drive each of our eight roads three times in random order. The vehicle would automatically start driving and at the end of the straight section teleport to the next road.

Table 2. Study 2 results: average deviation (stdev) in meters

CURVATURE	NO MAGNITUDE	FREQUENCY MAGNITUDE
45°	1.457 (1.100)	2.073 (.950)
90°	2.778 (1.296)	4.036 (1.862)
135°	3.433 (1.777)	6.719 (2.879)
180°	2.972 (1.720)	8.007 (2.623)
All	2.660 (.847)	5.209 (2.667)

Results

Because our first study did not detect any significant differences between left and right turns, data for both turns was combined for each curvature. Straight sections were excluded from calculating the lane deviation as little deviation was observed and it doesn't involve steering. For each set of data, a Grubb's test was performed to detect significant outliers. Three data points for FM were removed from the collected data for the 180° curves. Table 2 lists the results. We found an average error of 2.660m for NM and 5.209 m for FM. A one-way MANOVA found a statistically significant difference between haptic encoding mechanisms ($\boldsymbol{F}_{4,7} = 5.226$, $p < .05$, Wilk's $\lambda = .251$, partial $\varepsilon^2 = .749$). Pairwise comparisons using a Bonferroni correction revealed a statistically significant difference in lane deviation between both encoding schemes for 180° curves ($p < .05$) but no statistically significant differences between the other curve angles.

STUDY 3: EVALUATE MULTIMODAL EFFECT

The second study shows significantly better performance for NM encoding. As multimodal feedback increases performance over using unimodal feedback [23, 17], a third study investigates the effect of NM encoding on steering performance when used in conjunction with visual feedback.

Participants

We recruited 8 computer science students (2 female, average age 27.9, SD=4.4) to match the number of subjects in our initial study. 5 participants had previously participated in the second user study using NM encoding but none of the other subjects had participated in the second study. All subjects were right handed and none reported any non-correctable impairments in perception or motor control. Subjects had an average of 6.2 years (SD=6.0) of driving experience.

Instrumentation & Procedure

We used the same setup and procedure as in the second study with the difference that subjects would use a display. To minimize interference effects, the 3 subjects who had not participated in the second study, received a significant amount of time to familiarize themselves with the haptic feedback provision and drove a number of roads without visual feedback.

Results

Table 3 lists the results of study 3 combined with the results of study 1. We found an average error of .552 m for visual and .221 m for visual and haptic feedback. A one-way MANOVA found a statistically significant difference between types of feedback ($\boldsymbol{F}_{4,11} = 3.710$, $p < .05$, Wilk's $\lambda = .426$, partial $\varepsilon^2 = .574$). Pairwise comparisons using a Bonferroni correction revealed a statistically significant difference ($p < .05$) between visual and visual+haptic feedback for all angles.

Table 3. Study 1&3 results: average deviation (stdev) in meters

CURVATURE	VISUAL	VISUAL+HAPTIC
45°	.456 (.184)	.207 (.089)
90°	.592 (.216)	.232 (.102)
135°	.603 (.239)	.215 (.100)
180°	.557 (.215)	.231 (.088)
All	.552 (.067)	.221 (.012)

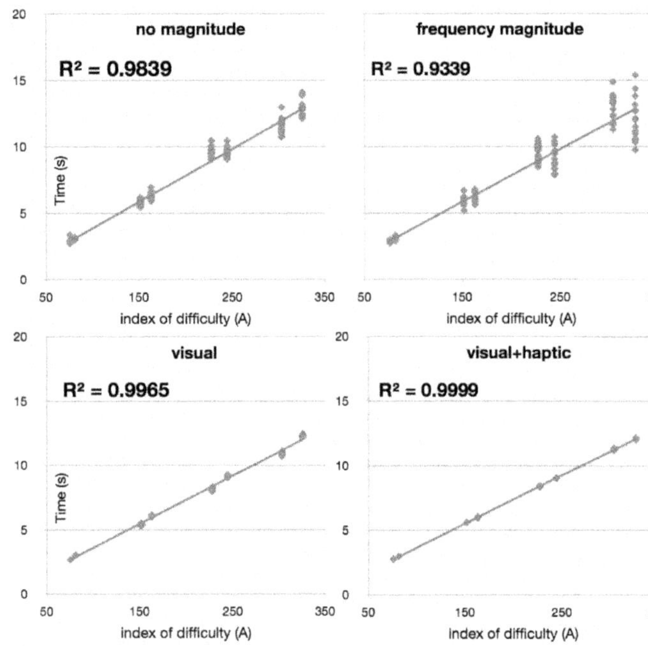

Figure 6. Correlation between steering time and index of difficulty for no magnitude, frequency magnitude, visual and haptic+visual feedback.

Modeling human movement. Using data collected from all studies, we analyze steering time (ST) as a function of index of difficulty (ID) of the steering law [6], e.g,

$$ST = a + b * \int_C \frac{d(s)}{W(s)} \quad (1)$$

Where ST is the average time to navigate through the path, C is the path parameterized by s, $W(s)$ is the width of the path at s, and a and b are experimentally fitted constants. Because the speed of the vehicle in the simulator and the width of the road are constants in our study this function is simplified to:

$$ST = a + b * A \quad (2)$$

with the index of difficulty only including the length of the path (A) [31]. Analyzing driving time versus curve length (excluding the straight parts) yields the following values for R^2; no magnitude (.9839), frequency magnitude (.9339), visual (.9965) and visual & haptic (.9999). Regression plots for each type of feedback can be found in Figure 6. Using the Fisher r-to-z transformation a statistically significant difference was found between no magnitude and frequency magnitude ($\boldsymbol{Z} = -6.044, N = 144, p < .05$) and visual and visual & haptic feedback ($\boldsymbol{Z} = -16.503, N = 192, p < .05$).

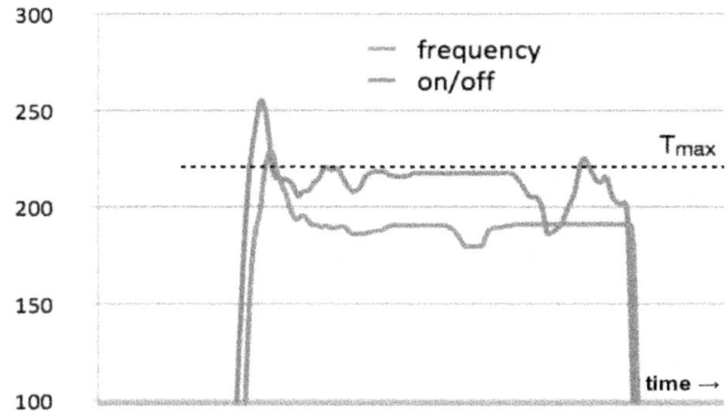

Figure 7. Average steering wheel values for the 180° turn

DISCUSSION AND FUTURE WORK

The results from our second study show that conveying how far to steer using frequency has a detrimental effect on steering performance as compared to using NM encoding. We anticipated that FM would reduce oversteering as it allows drivers to sense how far to steer, but it actually leads to understeering. An analysis of average steering wheel values for all drivers for all curvatures reveals (see Figure 7 for 180° turn) that using FM, drivers generally respond slower. When the controller vibrates with a lower frequency, drivers would only turn the steering wheel slightly, with the result of T' hovering around the edge of the window, generally leading to understeering and a significantly larger deviation from the lane's median. Using NM, drivers do oversteer but this is corrected much faster and allows T' to remain much closer to T_{max} than using FM. It seems using a higher frequency alerts drivers more quickly than when using a lower frequency. Possibly a combination of both mechanisms, e.g., a high frequency "wake up" followed by FM encoding may increase performance.

The second study yields an average median lane deviation of 2.660 m (SD=.847) for NM and 5.209 m (2.667) for FM for all curves. Blind steering can only be safely achieved for curves of 45° as NM has an average deviation of 1.457 (SD=1.100), which is small enough for a car to stay in their lane on a two lane road. To contextualize these results, we evaluated a driver's ability to steer only using haptic feedback, which is the most extreme case in which a driver is blinded completely for the whole duration of driving through the curve. Typically, glare from headlights takes an eye between 1-3 seconds to recover [5], but recovering from sunlight (flash blindness) may take longer. In these specific contexts, as the driver is only temporarily blinded and some residual visual feedback may be available, we anticipate a better performance for our interface than when no visual feedback is available. As simulating a temporary blindness is subject to many variables, we are confident study 2 and 3 accurately identify an upper and lower bound on the performance of our interface.

Our third study confirms that multimodal feedback yields significantly better performance than unimodal feedback [23, 17]. This result could be slightly misleading, as using visual feedback only, a few subjects were observed to deviate slightly from the lane's median towards the apex of the curve as this is faster. This was only observed for right turns and not for the left turns, as this would include veering into the other lane. These differences were not statistically significant. Using haptic feedback, drivers are forced to more closely follow the lane's median, which improves safety.

A practical consideration of using our interface could be that it may not be very comfortable for drivers to be continuously exposed to haptic feedback, especially when multiple consecutive curves are involved as this could numb the driver's hands and reduce the sensitivity to haptic feedback temporarily. Alternatively, an intelligent vehicle system could turn the haptic interface on automatically when it senses a greater chance of getting blinded, e.g., with a low sun, with icy roads, or at night due to headlights.

A number of problems need to be addressed before our interface can be implemented in a real vehicle. Our system relies on an intelligent vehicle positioning system for determining the car's position and curvature of the road. A driving simulator was used as a proxy in our study, but using a real vehicle positioning system may pose some significant constraints on our approach, e.g., GPS may be used to determine the car's position but most existing systems use camera's to track markings on the road. Though road curvature is typically known ahead of time using map information, the car's exact position may only be known hundreds of milliseconds in advance, which may limit being able to provide haptic cues slightly ahead of time to accommodate their startup delay.

Providing haptic feedback through a steering wheel is efficient as drivers always hold it [20], but drivers may not always hold it with their hands in the recommended position [19]. A possible solution would be to use multiple vibrotactors and sense the position of the hands [19] but an easier solution would be to use a butterfly steering wheel, i.e., a wheel that can only be held in one particular way. Our system can be integrated in existing lane keeping systems [15, 22] such as to create a single system for improving driving safety.

Future work will focus on investigating the following issues. Our interface doesn't implement auto correction, as preliminary studies using this found it to lead to significant oscillations. Similar findings were experienced by Hong [18] using audio. Problems with oscillation are challenging to solve, but a possible solution could be to dynamically adjust the window along the curve, e.g., window size could increase when the user steers from 0 to T_{max} and then decrease while the user holds T' at T_{max}, which could improve accuracy and decrease oscillations. Depending on the type of localization system used there may be some constraints on implementing auto correction. Our interface currently only includes steering, but maintaining and adjusting speed are just as important for driving a vehicle. We plan to investigate low-cost tactile solutions for conveying desired driving speed. On/off encoding without visual feedback has an average lane deviation of 2.660 m, which is not large enough to stay in a single lane, but could be large enough to drive a car on a racetrack, which are generally much wider. We further plan to investigate the usefulness of our interface with regard to the blind driver challenge [10] by conducting user studies with blind users.

CONCLUSION

Temporary blindness, caused by glare or fog while driving can lead to serious traffic accidents. We present a novel haptic interface that improves over existing haptic steering systems by not only conveying when and in which direction to steer, but also how much, which facilitates steering with limited or no visual feedback. Steering cues are provided through a vibrotactor integrated in the left and right side of the steering wheel, similar to how rumble strips work. Drivers steer away from a cue felt in either hand in order to find a dead-band window that indicates the target orientation of the wheel, which is adjusted as the car drives through the curve. User studies evaluate two different haptic encoding mechanisms and assess the effect of haptic feedback on steering performance when used in conjunction with visual feedback. Results show that our steering interface allows for blind steering through small (45°) curves and that it improves a driver's lane keeping ability when used in conjunction with visual feedback.

REFERENCES

1. Department of motor vehicle vc section 27400 wearing of headsets or earplugs, `http://www.dmv.ca.gov/pubs/vctop/d12/vc27400.htm`, access date: 10-10-2012.
2. Department of transportation, roadway design manual, `http://www.state.nj.us/transportation/eng/documents/RDM/sec4.shtm`, access date: 8-8-2012.
3. Driving simulator in XNA, `http://www.codeproject.com/Articles/29323/Driving-Simulation-in-XNA`, access date: 4-6-2012.
4. Federal highway administration, recommended lane width. `http://safety.fhwa.dot.gov/geometric/pubs/mitigationstrategies/chapter3/3_lanewidth.htm`, access date: 9-12-2012.
5. Lighting research center, recovery time of visual acuity after exposure to a glare source, `http://www.lrc.rpi.edu/resources/newsroom/pdf/2004/readaptation.pdf`, access date: 10-17-2012.
6. Accot, J., and Zhai, S. Beyond fitts' law: models for trajectory-based hci tasks. In *Proc of CHI '97*, ACM (1997), 295–302.
7. Asif, A., and Boll, S. Where to turn my car?: comparison of a tactile display and a conventional car navigation system under high load condition. In *Proc. of AutomotiveUI '10*, ACM (2010), 64–71.
8. Bach-y Rita, P., and W Kercel, S. Sensory substitution and the human-machine interface. *Trends in Cognitive Sciences* 7:12, (2003), 541–546.
9. Bateman, S., Doucette, A., Xiao, R., Gutwin, C., Mandryk, R. L., and Cockburn, A. Effects of view, input device, and track width on video game driving. In *Proc of GI '11* (2011), 207–214.
10. The blind driver challenge, `http://www.blinddriverchallenge.org/`, access date: 12-1-2011.
11. Brewster, S., and Brown, L. M. Tactons: structured tactile messages for non-visual information display. In *Proc. of AUIC '04*, Australian Computer Society. (2004), 15–23.
12. Choi, E.-H., and Singh, S. Statistical assessment of the glare issue – human and natural elements. In *Proc. of the Federal Committee on Statistical Methodology Workshop* (2005).
13. Darpa urban challenge, `http://archive.darpa.mil/grandchallenge/`, access date: 10-10-2011.
14. Enriquez, M., Afonin, O., Yager, B., and Maclean, K. A pneumatic tactile alerting system for the driving environment. In *Proc.of PUI '01*, ACM (2001), 1–7.
15. Ford lane keeping system, `http://media.ford.com/article_display.cfm?article_id=35776`, access date: 5-6-2012.
16. Griffiths, P., and Gillespie, R. Shared control between human and machine: haptic display of automation during manual control of vehicle heading. In *Proc. of HAPTICS '04* (2004), 358 – 366.
17. Hershenson, M. Reaction time as a measure of intersensory facilitation. *Journal of Experimental Psychology*, Vol 63 (1962), 289–293.
18. Hong, D., Kimmel, S., Boehling, R., Camoriano, N., Cardwell, W., Jannaman, G., Purcell, A., Ross, D., and Russel, E. Development of a semi-autonomous vehicle operable by the visually-impaired. In *Proc of MFI'08*, IEEE Computer Society (2008), 539 –544.
19. Hwang, S., and hee Ryu, J. The haptic steering wheel: Vibro-tactile based navigation for the driving environment. In *Proc. of PERCOM'10*, IEEE Computer Soc. (2010), 660 –665.
20. Kern, D., Marshall, P., Hornecker, E., Rogers, Y., and Schmidt, A. Enhancing navigation information with tactile output embedded into the steering wheel. In *Pervasive Computing'09*, Springer Berlin / Heidelberg, (2009), 42–58.
21. Kim, S., Hong, J.-H., Li, K., Forlizzi, J., and Dey, A. Route guidance modality for elder driver navigation. In *Pervasive Computing'12*, Springer Berlin / Heidelberg, (2012), 179–196.
22. Smartmicro's lane change assist system. `http://www.smartmicro.de/index.php?option=com_content&view=article&id=59&Itemid=67`, access date 7-4-2012.
23. Miller, J. Divided attention: evidence for coactivation with redundant signals. *Cogn Psychol 14*, 2 (1982), 247–279.
24. Morelli, T., and Folmer, E. Twuist: A discrete tactile-proprioceptive display for eye and ear free output on mobile devices. In *Proc. of Haptics Symposium '12*, IEEE Computer Society (2012), 443–450.
25. Sanford, L. Why lighting is important for the aging eye, `http://www.lighthouse.org/eye-health/the-basics-of-the-eye/the-aging-eye/lighting/`. In *Lighthouse International's Aging & Vision newsletter*. 1999.
26. Schieber, F. Age and glare recovery time for low-contrast stimuli. *Proc. of the Human Factors and Ergonomics Society Annual Meeting 38*, 9 (1994), 496–499.
27. Stepp, C. E., and Matsuoka, Y. Vibrotactile sensory substitution for object manipulation: amplitude versus pulse train frequency modulation. *IEEE Trans Neural Syst Rehabil Eng 20*, 1 (2012), 31–37.
28. Sun, M., Ren, X., and Cao, X. Effects of multimodal error feedback on human performance in steering tasks. *Information Processing Society of Japan 51*,12 (2010), 284–292.
29. van Erp, J. B., and van Veen, H. A. Vibro-tactile information presentation in automobiles. In *Proc. of Eurohaptics'01* University of Birmingham (2001), 99–104.
30. Xiong, K., Xiang, Z., and Ge, J. Evaluation of the human eye glare after strong exposure. In *Proc. of BMEI '08*, IEEE Computer Society (2008), 660–663.
31. Zhai, S., and Woltjer, R. Human movement performance in relation to path constraint - the law of steering in locomotion. In *Proc. of VR '03*, IEEE Computer Society (2003), 149–156.

Non-Visual Skimming On Touch-Screen Devices

Faisal Ahmed† **Andrii Soviak** **Yevgen Borodin** **I.V. Ramakrishnan**
†NetApp Inc., Wichita, KS
Stony Brook University, Computer Science Department, Stony Brook, NY 11790-4400
†ffahmed@gmail.com, {asoviak, borodin, ram}@cs.stonybrook.edu

ABSTRACT
While reading on touch-screens, sighted users can quickly pan through content, skim it, and pick out bits and pieces of information before deciding to read it more carefully. In contrast, blind users have to rely on the screen reader to narrate the content to them. To go through the text quickly, blind users employ gestures that direct the screen reader to skip to the next line or the next paragraph. However, the serial audio interface of the screen reader makes it difficult for blind users to get a sense of what is important before listening to, at least, a part of the content. This makes ad hoc skimming with gestures slow and ineffective. We address this problem in this paper; specifically we propose a non-visual skimming interface that enables blind users to control the amount of content with simple pinch-in and pinch-out gestures. This interface simulates the skimming experience enjoyed by sighted people, and enables blind users to listen to the gist of content, while controlling the speed of information intake. We report on a user study demonstrating that the proposed interface significantly outperforms ad hoc skimming techniques employed by blind users. Our results suggest that the proposed approach holds promise in empowering blind users to access digitized information much faster.

Author Keywords
Skimming; Blind; Speed Reading; Screen Reader; Summarization; Accessibility; Touch Interface.

ACM Classification Keywords
H.5.2 [Information Interfaces and Presentation]: User Interfaces -*Input devices and strategies (e.g., mouse, touchscreen)*; H.5.4 [Information Interfaces and Presentation]: Hypertext/Hypermedia -*navigation*.

General Terms
Human Factors; Algorithms; Design; Experimentation.

INTRODUCTION
Touch-screen devices are quickly becoming ubiquitous. A reason for their popularity is that they provide an easy and intuitive way to accomplish a variety of tasks by interacting directly with the content. For instance, while reading, it feels natural to flip pages in iBooks or flick to scroll rapidly through PDF documents.

Blind users are also embracing small-factor touch screens because they are both portable and provide direct access to the two-dimensional layout of the content. However, there is a big difference between how blind and sighted users interact with touch interfaces. Blind users employ screen readers which narrate the content of the screen using text-to-speech and allow users to navigate through the content. For example, VoiceOver screen reader on iOS devices uses swipe left/right to go to previous/next item, the two-finger "rotor" to switch between types of content such as headings, links, etc. One can also drag the finger over the surface and listen to the content under the finger.

Because of the low bandwidth of a serial audio interface and the fact that one has to hear the information before deciding if it is relevant, blind people spend considerably more time identifying the information they need [3].

Skimming is a speed-reading technique that allows sighted readers to get a general idea of the content and sift through information very quickly, without reading the entire content and, most importantly, without sacrificing basic understanding of the content.

Sighted people can skim through text quickly, picking out the important points and getting the gist of the content. Unfortunately, little has been done to develop an effective method for automated skimming, so that blind people could process information faster than they currently can. For example, having found the beginning of an article in a web page, screen-reader users cannot just scan through the article. In fact, increasing the speech rate and jumping between items are the *only* strategies employed by screen-reader users to skim through text on desktop computers [1].

In [2], we had proposed a non-visual skimming technique for screen reading with keyboard interfaces that employs an extractive summarization algorithm to choose the most salient words and phrases in sentences. The users can then seamlessly switch between reading the full text and skimming the compressed version. The results of experiments with screen-reader users showed that the proposed non-visual skimming was effective for reading. However, this approach was tested with keyboard interfaces only and did not allow users to vary the compression ratio. In this paper, we build on that prior work and propose an approach that enables non-visual skimming on touch-screen devices. The proposed skimming interface enables blind users to control the information flow and vary their reading speed by using pinch-in and pinch-out gestures which change the size of the narrated content.

In the remainder of this paper, we present the related work on summarization, as well as on the use of touch interfaces by blind people; we explain why the existing interfaces cannot be used to enable effective non-visual skimming on touch screens; we outline our algorithm that enables variable-size summarization and describe the proposed non-visual skimming interface driven by this algorithm; finally, we present the results of the user study with 15 blind subjects, confirming the effectiveness of our approach.

BACKGROUND

We review here the most relevant work on generating text summaries/abstracts of different size. A comprehensive review of summarization approaches appears in [2]. Telegraphic text reduction, a variable-size audio scanning service for blind people, was introduced in [6], where eight different levels of text reduction, based on different parts of speech, verb groups and syntactic relations, were introduced. The following extraction rules were used for the reduction: 1) only the proper names and no subclasses, 2) only subjects, object nouns, no sub-clauses, 3) only subjects, head verbs, object nouns, no sub-clauses, etc. This approach has several shortcomings. Firstly, it selects only individual words, rather than phrases that provide more meaning by preserving the relationship between words [1]. Secondly, this kind of summarization cannot produce a predefined amount of content (e.g., 20% or 50%) because the distribution of words between different parts of speech can vary widely within and between texts. Thirdly, the approach assumes that one part of speech is always more important/meaningful than another part of speech. But what is important depends on the context. Lastly, there was no user study done with blind users. The summarization approach proposed in our paper does not suffer from any of the above-listed limitations.

The JAWS screen-reader has a naïve implementation of "skimming" [10] that allows users to read the first line or the first sentence of each paragraph. This still does not offer a truly functional tool for skimming, and does not follow the same skimming protocol used by sighted folks.

Summate [7] provides variable-length summaries based on sentence position in a document. It selects the first sentence of each paragraph based on the parsed DOM tree of a web page. The summary can have at most four sentences: 1) the first sentence of the document; 2) the first sentence of the last paragraph; 3) a sentence from the upper (75%) quartile; 4) a sentence from lower (25%) quartile. This approach is ad hoc and suffers the same drawbacks as that in JAWS.

Several Firefox plug-ins [4] for summarizing text have been reported notably GreatSummary [14], Pluribo-Instant-Summaries [13], and SummaryFox [8]. GreatSummary, specifically designed for reviewing web articles, lets the user manipulate the number of sentences in the summary (1-100). Pluribo-Instant-Summaries is a special-purpose summarizer of product reviews at Amazon.com. In the Mac-based SummaryFox [8] users highlight the text to be summarized and use a slider to vary the summary size. Summaries produced by these plug-in summarizers do not retain any correspondence between the summary and the original content. Consequently blind users cannot preserve their reading position while switching between reading the summary and the original text.

In [12] a statistical keyword extraction technique is described to summarize text without using a corpus. This method is based on the extraction of frequent words and the words that co-occur with frequent words. The main drawback of this algorithm is that it relies on the entire document to compute word frequencies. What this means is that the quality of the summary is dependent on the size of the text. Furthermore the summary may not cover the entire text. In our previous work, we demonstrated that users do not trust summaries with poor coverage [1]

In this paper, we present an extractive text summarization algorithm that: (i) generates variable-size summaries of arbitrary length; (ii) summarizes each sentence separately to provide good coverage of the text; (iii) extracts phrases to retain meaningful connections between the words. This algorithm forms the basis of the non-visual skimming approach presented in the ensuing sections of this paper.

GENERATION OF VARIABLE-SIZE SUMMARIES

Basis of the Approach

Our approach to variable-rate skimming is rooted in our previous work on accessible skimming [2]. We overview it now in order to provide context to the variable rate accessible skimming algorithm proposed in this paper.

Accessible Skimming Overview: It works as follows: Firstly, every sentence is parsed to extract grammatical relations amongst its words. Secondly, a lexical tree based on these relations is constructed, where each node of the tree represents a word in the sentence. Thirdly, for every word in this tree, its grammatical (e.g., part of speech) as well as structural features (e.g., in-degree/out-degree) are extracted. These features are given to a trained classifier to determine whether or not to include the word in the skimming summary. Finally a subtree consisting of the selected words is constructed. This subtree represents the skimming summary that users interact with via an interface.

To capture the relationships between words in a sentence, we used the Stanford Parser [11], which is a probabilistic natural language parser that can analyze the grammatical and syntactical structure of sentences and extract relations - "typed dependency relations" per [11]. A subset of typed dependency relations extracted by the parser from the sentence *"Chewing gum can improve memory, say UK psychologists."* is given below:

Adjectival modifier (gum-2 → chewing-1);
Nominal subject (improve-4 → gum-2);
Auxiliary (improve-4 → can-3)
Noun compound modifier (psychologists-8 → uk-7)
Direct object (say-6 → psychologists-8)

In the 1st relation *Adjectival modifier* is the relation type, *gum-2* and *chewing-1* are the ($word_i$-$position_i$ → $word_j$-$position_j$) pairs with $position_i$ and $position_j$ denoting the position of $word_i$ and $word_j$ respectively in the sentence.

Using the grammatical relations generated by Stanford Parser a sentence tree is constructed, where the nodes are the words and the edges are the relations between word pairs. For the example above each word-position will be represented by a node in the tree. An edge corresponds to a typed dependency relation. The relation *Adjectival modifier (gum-2 → chewing-1)* will be represented by an edge from the node representing *gum-2* to the node representing *chewing-1*. The incoming type of relation associated with the node representing *chewing-1* is *Adjectival modifier*. The *root node* in the tree is the one with no in-degree, which means it is not dependent on any other node

Word features – derived from this graph – such as the number of outgoing edges of a node, its level in the tree, number of (its) descendants, the incoming relation type, and the part-of-speech tag of the word are used for training a SVM classifier. The training data set consisted of over 600 summarized sentences spanning assorted articles. Features of the words included in these summaries were used to train the SVM. Details of the training appear in [2].

Given a word in a sentence the trained classifier will determine if the word is to be included in the summary. It associates a confidence score (between 0 and 1) with the (binary) classification outcome.

Algorithm for Variable-size Summary Generation

Now note that we can set a threshold and include only those words with a confidence score above the threshold in the summary. Thus we can utilize the availability of the confidence score to generate summaries of different sizes.

An important aspect of variable size summary, in so far as skimming is concerned, is that the larger summaries should include smaller summaries. Formally, suppose $S_n(\sigma)$ denotes a summary of a sentence σ such that it includes at least n words from σ. Then the summary sequence $< S_1(\sigma), S_2(\sigma), .., S_n(\sigma) >$ is a *subsuming* sequence whenever $S_1(\sigma) \subseteq S_2(\sigma) \subseteq \cdots \subseteq S_n(\sigma)$. We are interested in subsuming sequences because they enable retention of "continuity" of content to some degree when skimming at variable speeds. Sentence summary sequences produced by our algorithm are subsuming.

Putting it all together

To enable variable-size summarization, we put a threshold on the confidence scores output by the classifier, i.e., any word with a confidence score lower than the specific threshold, is not included in the summary. Words can be ranked by their scores. The ranks provide a "sense" of their importance enabling linear control over the summary size.

The classifier outputs the words to be included in the sentence summary. They are sorted w.r.t. the confidence scores. The sorted words are arranged in a sequence such that the word positions in the sequence is consistent w.r.t. their positions in the original sentence. Table 1 below illustrates the process of ranking:

Original Sentence:	*"Amy is a busy student"*
Words with confidence score (SVM)	*(Amy, 1.0) (is, 0.6) (a, 0.5) (busy, 0.8) (student, 0.7)*
Sort by Confidence Score	*(Amy, 1.0) (busy, 0.75) (student, 0.5) (is, 0.25) (a, 0.0)*
Reorder by original position	*(Amy, 1.0) (is, 0.25) (a, 0.0) (busy, 0.75) (student, 0.5)*

Table 1. Annotating words: illustrative example

To control the size of the summary, we use a threshold parameter. Using it we can control the summary size in terms of percentage of the original text. The parameter ranges from 0.0 to 1.0. For example, if it is set to 0.5, then all the words whose confidence score is greater or equal to 0.5 will be included to the sentence summary. This means that the summary will contain around the 50% of the original sentence. We always include the root word.

Summary	Threshold
Afterwards, they often spray their skin with a protective coating of dust.	0.0 (original)
Afterwards, they spray their skin a protective coating dust.	0.2
Afterwards, they spray skin protective coating dust.	0.4
they spray skin coating dust.	0.6
spray skin coating.	0.8
spray.	1.0

Table 2. Variable size summaries for different threshold

This will let us preserve the mapping between the original sentence and its summary. As a result, the user can switch between original content and its summary seamlessly, preserving the reading position. Table 2 shows an example of a sentence and its associated summaries of variable length.

Algorithm *VariableSummary* below captures the informal description above in algorithmic form. It takes a sentence and a confidence-score threshold as parameters and generates a summary of a certain size.

Algorithm: *VariableSummary*:

Set of Typed Dependency Relations $\{(W_{g1}, W_{d1}), (W_{g2}, W_{d2}),.., (W_{gn}, W_{dn})\}$ between words in a sentence, $1 \leq i \leq n$.

SN: Set of <confidence score, word node> tuples: $\{(CS_1, N_1), (CS_2, N_2),..,(CS_n, N_n)\}$.

T: SentenceTree

Input: S: sentence to be skimmed; CT: Confidence Score Threshold
Output: M: summary as list of words

```
1. SN←{ }//set of<confid. score, word node> tuples
2. M←[ ]//initialize list of summary words
3. R←TypedDependencies(S)//from parser
4. T←ConstructTree(R)//from dependencies
5. For each node N in T
6. Do O←#ofOutgoingEdges(N)
7. L←LevelInTree(N)
8. C←#ofDescendants(N)
9. I ← IncomingRelationType(N)
10.   P ← POSTags(N)
11.   F ← <O, L, C, I, P>//feature vector
12.   confd_score←getConfdScore(F)
13.   SN.add(confidence_score, N)
14.   M ← WordsAboveThreshold(S, CT)
15.   Return M
```

Following initialization, in line 3 we find all the typed dependency relations in the sentence. These relations are used to construct the sentence tree in line 4. For each word associated with a node in the tree its features are extracted in lines 6,7,8,9 and 10. In line 12 the trained classifier is called with these features. And it outputs a confidence score for the word's inclusion in the summary. This is added to SN in line 14. In line 13 *WordsAboveThreshold* (shown below) is called to construct the summarized sentence.

Algorithm: *WordsAboveThreshold*

Input: SN: set of <confidence score, word node> tuples;

CT: Confidence ScoreThreshold

Output: M: summary as list of words

```
1. M←[ ]//initialize list of summary words
2. FN←{ }//initialize final set of nodes
3. SortedSN←{ }//init list of<score, node> tuples
4. SortedSN←Sort SN by confid. score
5. For each tuple <S, N> in SortedSN
6. Do If S >= CT
7. Then FN.add(N)
8. M←OrderNodesGetWords(FN)//reorder
9. Return M
```

In line 4 the set SN is sorted based on the confidence scores of the nodes in the set. Lines 5-7 add only those words whose confidence score is above the threshold CT. In line 8 the sorted words are arranged in a sequence such that the word positions in the sequence is consistent w.r.t. their positions in the original sentence.

Note that selecting words above the threshold and reordering them to form a consistent sequence results in making variable length summaries subsuming.

DESIGNING TOUCH BASED SKIMMING INTERFACE

VoiceOver Screen Reader for iOS

A lot of research has been done in the area of touch-screen interfaces. However, there are few commercial products that make touch screen interfaces accessible to people with visual impairments. Among those few products, VoiceOver [15] for iOS is the screen reader of choice because of its general usability and simplicity of use.

VoiceOver supports single-finger navigation gestures such as left and right swipes for going to previous and next element. The two-finger "rotor" gesture enables the selection of the type of content, e.g., link, heading, etc. "Two finger swipe down" instructs VoiceOver to read continuously from the current reading position. This is convenient for listening to the entire content without having to interact with the device. A two-finger tap stops reading. Pinch-in/out unselects/selects the text while editing.

While the above gestures do not take into account finger coordinate(s), VoiceOver also makes it possible for users to interact with content directly. A single-finger tap-and-hold makes VoiceOver read out the content under the finger; if the user drags the finger, VoiceOver will start reading the new content that is touched by the finger.

Our Interface

Due to the lack of public API access to VoiceOver screen-reader, we chose to implement our skimming interface on the Android [5] open-source mobile platform. This platform is widely supported by different manufacturers of mobile phones, tablets and even TVs. Android also provided us with a powerful development API to manage the User Interface and backend hardware. Finally, Android provides flexible and intuitive application model, which bridges/ supports all Android devices. As a result, once we develop an application for Android platform, it can be deployed to a wide range of devices (tablets, smart-phones, etc.). To be able to compare with the state-of-the-art touch-enabled screen reader, we implemented a screen-reading interface replicating the main gestures of VoiceOver. We did not implement the "rotor" gesture because we focused on accessing simple text so there was no need to switch to navigating different types of content. Furthermore, we used pinch-in and out gestures, in a different way than VoiceOver uses. All supported gestures supported in our prototype are illustrated in Figure 1. These include: left/right single-finger swipe to reads the previous/next sentence; two-finger down swipe to read continuously from the current position; two-finger tap pauses and resumes the narration (VoiceOver only pauses); single-finger tap-hold-

and-drag, reads the sentence directly under the finger (VoiceOver reads a paragraph), pinch-in/out gestures change the compression ratio (change the size of content).

The pinch-in/out gestures are typically used for zooming-out/in respectively on touch-screen devices. By analogy, we used these gestures to increase and decrease the skimming speed respectively; this assignment (and not the other way around) was found to be the most logical by several participants of pilot user studies. On pinch-in/-out, the underlying algorithm changes the compression level of the text summary and, thus, decreases or increases the amount of narrated content. While using the pinch-in/out gestures the user will hear audio feedback – short sounds of different pitch depending on the level of compression.

For the convenience of sighted users, we also included a slider that appears at the top of the screen to indicate the compression level of the summary (Figure 1). The left most end of the slider corresponds to the lowest compression level (0%), which means that the entire content will be read. The right end of the slider corresponds to the highest compression level (100%), at least one word per sentence will be read in this mode. The positions in between correspond to 20%, 40%, and 60% compression. While our initial prototype enabled continuous control of the compression ratio, the blind pilot subjects found that controlling the compression ratio was considerably more usable if there were just a few discrete positions.

In summary, the interface we designed supports most of the typical navigation gestures used by the highly acclaimed touch-based iOS screen-reader VoiceOver [15]. In addition, in order to give the user the control over the skimming speed, we used the pinch-in/out gesture. We next report on the evaluation of our skimming interface in real world scenarios by people with vision impairments.

USER STUDY

Experimental Setup

To evaluate the proposed skimming interface, we conducted a user study with 15 participants. Six of them were male and nine were female. The age of the participants was evenly distributed from 25 to 62. All participants were comfortable with screen-readers and have been using JAWS as their primary desktop screen reader. Many participants have been using or have been previously exposed to VoiceOver. In order to compare the touch-screen and the keyboard-based interfaces, we implemented a keyboard based skimming interface described in [2].

We used a Samsung Galaxy Tablet 10.1 as device to run a user study. In addition, we used IVONA Text To Speech engine(TTS) [9] with voice *"Amy"* and 180 words per minute speech rate. We have selected this speech rate based on the interviews and user studies described in [1].

In the experiment, we measured the time needed to complete tasks. Statistical significance tests (e.g., two-tailed paired t-test and analysis of variance) were used to compare the effects of the interfaces on the dependent variables.

In a within-subjects experiment that had a 5 by 5 cell design, we asked each subject to skim/read through 5 different 5-paragraph articles using a touch-based skimming interface (without skimming, with single-speed skimming (50% compression ratio), with variable-speed skimming) and keyboard interface (without skimming, with single-speed skimming). The tasks were counterbalanced across subjects to avoid bias. In each task, subjects had to find an answer to a question in the article. They were instructed not to use the keyword search feature because the questions we asked could not be answered by searching for keywords.

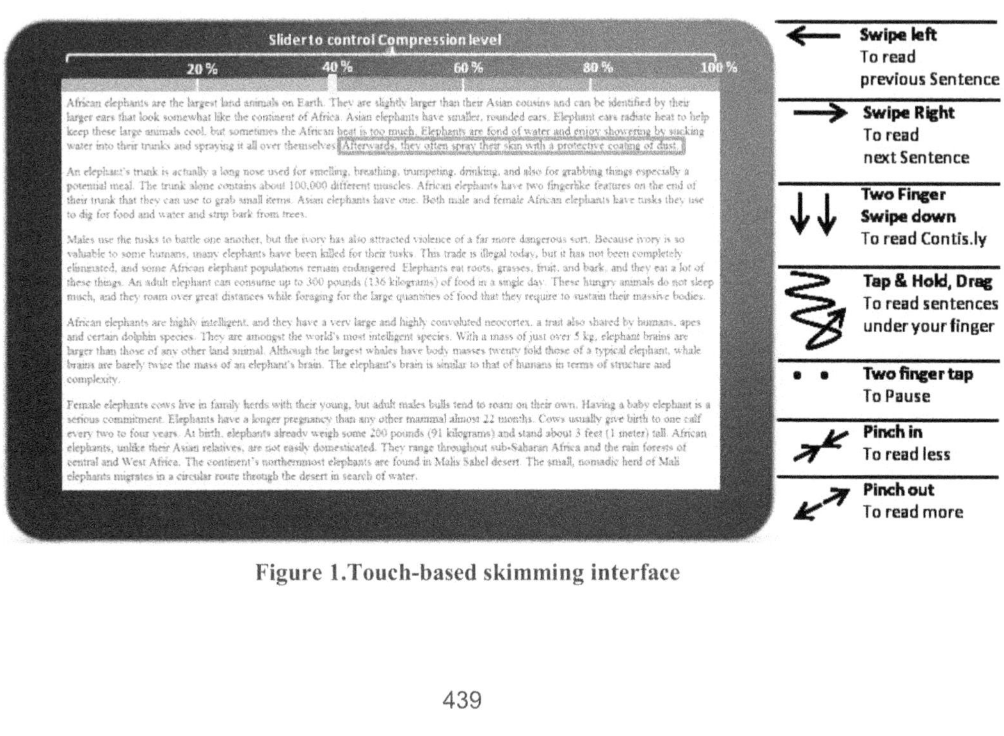

Figure 1.Touch-based skimming interface

The answer to the question was contained in the last (5th) paragraph of each article to increase the time required to find the answer. Having the answer in the beginning of the articles would have caused the users to find the answers equally fast with and without skimming, defeating the purpose of the experiment. Varying the location of the answer would have increased the variation of the completion times across articles. In addition, in order to avoid the learning bias, in between all real tasks, we introduced dummy tasks where the answers appeared randomly in different paragraphs. In order to evaluate task completion, we recorded: 1) the time users spend to navigate to the sentence containing the answer and 2) the time users spend to give the answer verbally. We let subjects practice with a sample tasks before doing the real task, until they were comfortable with the new interface.

Each task took around 10 minutes. At the end of each task we asked subjects to evaluate the complexity of this task on a 5-point Likert scale (1=Very Easy to 5=Very Hard). In addition, we administered post completion questionnaires.

Hypotheses and Results

We next present here results of our user study. In what follows, the Hi's are the hypotheses tested in the study.

H1: Finding information using touch-based interface with variable-speed skimming is faster than ad-hoc navigation.

Result: While recording time for task completion, we considered two measures. First, the time the user takes to navigate to the sentence containing the answer and the TTS reads out the answer. Second, the time it takes the user to read the answer, comprehend it, and give the answer verbally. In Figure 2 we referred to these measures as "time for TTS" and "time for subject". While searching for information, subjects took an average of 128.07 seconds (St. Dev. = 29.60) to get the answer using variable-speed skimming and 296.86 seconds (St. Dev. = 56.21) using ad-hoc touch based navigation (Figure 2). There was a significant difference in the speed of navigation (t=14.47, df=14, p<0.0001). The time it took the subjects to actually answer the questions was an average of 130.93 seconds (St. Dev. 29.14 seconds) and 300.60 seconds (St. Dev. = 56.84 seconds) for skimming and reading respectively. The one-tailed paired t-test (t=14.22, df=14, p<0.0001) found this difference to be statistically significant. Thus, we accept H1. We did a normality test on individual data series to validate our assumption of normal distribution of the data. The Shapiro-Wilk test statistics were (W=0.80, p=0.1182) and (W=0.91, p=0.1171) respectively with a significance level of 1%, confirming the data was normally distributed. An F test did not reveal a significant difference in the variances of these two groups (F(15,14) = 3.6, p=0.011).

Discussion: Subjects were able to navigate to the answer location 2.3 times faster using touch-based interface with skimming compared to touch-based interface without skimming. In answering questions, subjects were 2.2 times faster while using skimming compared to no skimming. These results indicate that touch-based skimming interface can be efficient for skimming long documents.

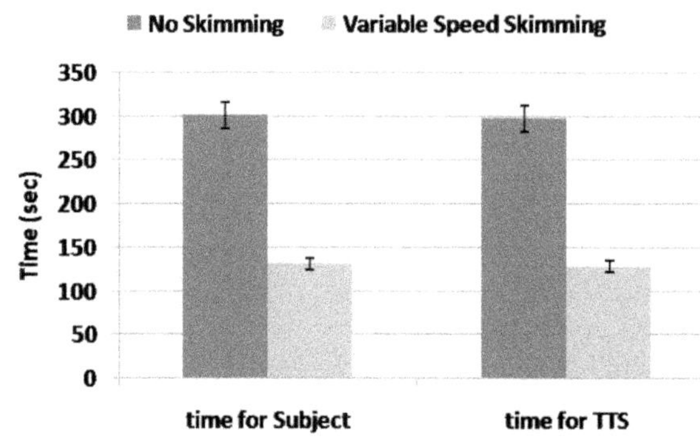

Figure 2.Average time to reach and understand the answer to a question with variable speed skimming vs. no skimming on a touch interface (St. Dev.)

H2: Variable sizes skimming on touch based interface was easier than ad hoc touch-based navigation.

Result: We found that, on average, people rated the difficulty of the tasks using variable-speed skimming as 1.60 (St. Dev. = 0.63) and the difficulty of tasks without skimming as 3.10 (St. Dev. = 0.79). Using the one-tailed paired t-test, we found skimming appeared to be significantly easier than ad hoc navigation (t=8.88, df=14, p<0.0001), rejecting the null hypothesis. The Shapiro-Wilk test statistics were (W=0.76, p=0.0112) and (W=0.82, p=0.0161) respectively with a significance level of 1%, confirming that the data was normally distributed. An F test did not reveal a significant difference in the variances of the two groups (F(15, 14) = 1.59, p=0.19). The medians of these two groups were 2 and 3, respectively. A Wilcoxon Signed-rank test showed that there was a significant effect of Group (W = 120, Z = 3.39, p = 0.0003).

Discussion: This was an unexpected finding, especially considering the fact that the subjects had little experience with skimming. In our preliminary experiments, users rated listening to the text with the lowest compression level (full text) as the easiest ones for comprehension. However, they rated the touch interface with variable-size skimming to be relatively easier than the regular touch-based interface

H3: Finding information with touch-based skimming is faster than keyboard-based fixed-speed skimming.

Result: The average time spent on arriving at the answer using touch-based skimming was 148.06 seconds (St. Dev. = 29.60), whereas with keyboard-based skimming it was 174.93 seconds (St. Dev. = 46.22). According to one-tailed paired t-test, the difference in speed was statistically significant (t=3.11, df=14, p=0.0038). For answering questions, the subject needed an of average 150.33 seconds (St. Dev. = 29.14) for touch-based skimming interface and 176.93 seconds (St. Dev. = 45.77) for keyboard-based skimming. A one-tailed paired t-test showed the difference of the speed was statistically significant (t=3.087, df=14, p=0.0040) (Figure 3). Thus, we accept **H3**.

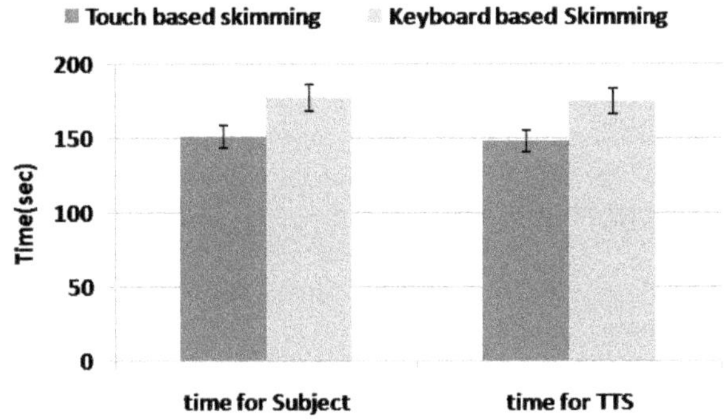

Figure 3. Average time to reach and understand the answer to a question with touch-based skimming vs. keyboard-based skimming (St. Dev.)

The Shapiro-Wilk test statistics were (W=0.80, p=0.1026) and (W=0.86, p=0.1022) respectively with the significance level of 1%, confirming the data was normally distributed. An F test did not reveal a significant difference in the variances of the two groups (F(15, 14) = 0.40, p=0.05).

Discussion: Subjects could also use dragging gesture which got them to the answer faster than if they had to skip through the summary using shortcuts.

H4: Finding information using touch-based skimming interface is easier than keyboard-based skimming.

Result: We found that, on average, people rated the difficulty of the tasks with touch-based skimming as 1.96 (St. Dev. = 0.85) and the difficulty of tasks with keyboard-based skimming as 2.46 (St. Dev. = 0.83). Using the one-tailed paired t-test, touch-based skimming was found to be significantly easier compared to keyboard-based skimming (t=3.094, df=14, p=0.0040), rejecting the null hypothesis. The Shapiro-Wilk test statistic were (W=0.80, p=0.0126) and (W=0.84, p=0.0146) respectively, significance level of 1%, confirming that the data was normally distributed. An F test did not reveal a significant difference in the variances of the two groups (F(15, 14) = 1.05, p=0.46). The medians of these two groups were both 2. A Wilcoxon Signed-rank test showed that there was a significant effect of Group (W = -43, Z = -2.17, p = 0.015).

Discussion: Subjects were more comfortable using touch-based skimming interface because it was intuitive and, unlike keyboard-based skimming, they did not have to remember the position of keys for numerous shortcuts.

H5: Keyboard based skimming is faster than ad-hoc keyboard based navigation.

Result: Subjects took an average of 174.53 seconds (St. Dev. = 46.21) to reach the answer using keyboard based skimming and 288.27 seconds (St. Dev. = 89.81) using ad-hoc searching. One tailed paired t-test (t=6.541, df=14, p<0.0001) showed significant difference in speed. To find the answer to the question, users needed an average of 176.93 seconds (St. Dev. 45.77 seconds) and 298.8 seconds (St. Dev. = 89.21 seconds) for skimming and ad hoc navigation respectively. One tailed paired t-test (t=8.201, df=14, p<0.0001) showed that the speed difference was statistically significant. The Shapiro-Wilk test statistic were (W=0.89, p=0.0169) and (W=0.85, p=0.0155) respectively with a significance level of 1%, confirming that the data was normally distributed. An F test did not reveal a significant difference in the variances of the two groups (F(15, 14) = 3.71, p=0.01).

Discussion: Subjects were able to find the answer almost twice as fast using skimming, compared to using regular screen-reader navigation shortcuts. This result demonstrates that skimming can save screen-reader users a substantial amount of time depending on the size of the text.

Post Completion Questionnaires

At the end of the experiments, we read several statements, pertaining to variable-speed skimming to the subjects and asked them to rate the statements on a 5-point Likert scale (1=Strongly Disagree to 5=Strongly Agree);Table 3 summarizes their ratings. The ratings in the questionnaires show that the majority of the subjects agreed that touch-based skimming was faster than mere touch-based navigation or keyboard-based skimming. They also expressed interest in using this technology in the future.

General Statements	Avg. (St. Dev.)
I wish I could look through articles faster than I can with a screen reader	4.60 (0.63)
I experience difficulties in fast navigation in an article with regular touch interface	4.13(0.74)
Touch based skimming made reading articles faster than regular touch navigation	4.67(0.48)
Touch based skimming is easier than keyboard based skimming	4.13(1.12)
I want to use the touch based skimming feature in the future	4.67(0.48)

Table 3. Post completion questionnaire for touch-based skimming (1=Strongly Disagree to 5=Strongly Agree)

TESTIMONIALS

Herein we provide verbatim quotes of our subjects commenting on the skimming interface:

"This is my first experience with touch. Once you are familiar with the touch interface, it's pretty easy. With the touch interface, I got the impression that I can move faster than with the keyboard based interface. I think, with 1-2 weeks of practice I can get used to the touch interface."

"For keyword search, skimming is the second option to look for info. For getting an overview of text, skimming is

the first option. I think it's faster, and touch can be equally good as keyboard."

it picks up keywords and main points…I prefer touch more than keyboard based because you don't have to remember the key locations. It's easier to remember gestures…I loved the way various-speed skimming is implemented. It gives me control on how much information I need…I don't think much practice is necessary"

"I like the touch-based interface much more compared to keyboard-based interface. I wish I never had to use the keyboard other than for typing. On the other hand, touch interface is intuitive (flipping page, pinch out, pinch in). Touch based skimming is really cool."

"Usually I don't like compressed article, but even with compression it's better because I have independent control of the speed….. It's useful. Skimming is faster is some situation, but reading this way is not very much fun. It's not for serious reading or study. But it's definitely useful to get a quick idea, when you are in short of time. … I like touch more than keyboard, because it's easier. I do not have to learn the command keys and shortcuts."

"My brain was synthesizing the bits and pieces of the article and forming up complete picture of the story. …..I like the touch commands. …..It's faster more efficient. Touch commands are very intuitive and easier to remember. I had to put less effort to get used to them. I did not have to search for key locations or remember the shortcuts like the way I do in keyboard-based interface."

"Skimming is good, simple. Swiping is intuitive. I did not know touch is faster than keyboard. If I can practice it, I will make the keyboard an alternative device."

"I want to use touch interface…..Touch interface helps me stay focused. By the time I find the answer using keyboard, I fall asleep, I become bored and lost. Skimming is something that gets me to the point, and using touch-based skimming made it even more efficient."

"Skimming is much faster, concise compared to the way I typically read. Touch-based interface is more convenient, quicker than key-based. In key-based approach I have to remember all the shortcuts and finds out key locations"

"I use a lot of software, so I have to remember all the shortcuts they have, when I use them. But because in touch device you don't need to remember any shortcuts, it's just general intuition… It makes reading a lot faster. I feel like I don't have to sit and get bored with info that I am not interested in…..I am more willing to use skimming with touch, I have already learned a lot of keyboard shortcuts. I don't want to remember new ones"

We did not get any negative comments about skimming. One subject made this interesting comment: *"Skimming feature made the reading a lot faster. But I love keyboard more than touch based skimming because I have dexterousness problem".*

CONCLUSION AND FUTURE WORK

In this paper we proposed a gesture-based non-visual skimming interface for touch-screen devices. We described a variable-size summarization algorithm powering the skimming interface. We also reported on a user study. Results of the study demonstrate the promise and potential of the approach. By enabling non-visual skimming on touch interfaces we have "pushed the envelope" in computer accessibility, taking blind users a step closer to experiencing the benefits of speed reading.

There are a number of enhancements that can be done to improve the skimming interface and the underlying summarization algorithm. For example, we can increase the corpus for training the classifier used for summarization. Hybrid approaches combining different summarization techniques can be used, e.g., a common English writing pattern is to put the topic sentence first in a paragraph and the summary sentence – last. Therefore, we could pick more words from the first and last sentences.

While we have explored skimming on general text interfaces, it can be further extended to work on general web content, which may require developing different summarization algorithms for different types of content.

ACKNOWLEDGMENTS

Research reported in this paper was supported by NSF Awards IIS-1218570, IIS-0808678, and CNS-0751083. We thank Dr. Terri Hedgpeth and the Arizona State University Disability Support Center for helping us conduct the study.

REFERENCES

[1] Ahmed, F., Y. Borodin, Y. Puzis, and I.V. Ramakrishnan, *Why Read if You Can Skim: Towards Enabling Faster Screen Reading*, in *International Cross-Disciplinary Conference on Web Accessibility*. 2012.

[2] Ahmed, F., Y. Borodin, A. Soviak, M.A. Islam, I.V. Ramakrishnan, and T. Hedgpeth, *Accessible Skimming: Faster Screen Reading of Web Pages*, in *to be appeared in UIST*. 2012, ACM: Cambridge, Massachusetts, USA.

[3] Borodin, Y., J.P. Bigham, G. Dausch, and I.V. Ramakrishnan, *More than meets the eye: a survey of screen-reader browsing strategies*, in *Proceedings of the 2010 International Cross Disciplinary Conference on Web Accessibility (W4A)*. 2010, ACM: Raleigh, North Carolina. p. 1-10.

[4] Firefox. *Firefox Addon*. Available from: https://addons.mozilla.org/en-US/firefox/.

[5] Google. *Android*. Available from: http://www.android.com/developers/.

[6] Grefenstette, G., *Producing Intelligent Telegraphic Text Reduction to Provide an Audio Scanning Service for the blind*, in *Workshop on Intelligent Text*

Summarization. 1998, American Association for Artificial Intelligence Spring Symposium Series: Menlo Park, California. p. 111-117.

[7] Harper, S. and N. Patel, *Gist summaries for visually impaired surfers*, in *Proceedings of the 7th International ACM SIGACCESS Conference on Computers and Accessibility*. 2005, ACM: Baltimore, MD, USA.

[8] hihayash. *SummaryFox* 2009; Available from: https://addons.mozilla.org/en-US/firefox/addon/summaryfox-47140/?src=search.

[9] IVONA. *IVONA multi-lingual speech synthesis system*. 2005; Available: http://www.ivona.com/.

[10] JAWS_Skimming. *Skim Reading*. 2011; Available: http://www.freedomscientific.com/Training/Surfs-up/Skim_Reading.htm.

[11] Marneffe, M.-C.d., B. MacCartney, and C.D. Manning, *Generating Typed Dependency Parses from Phrase Structure Parses.*, in *LREC* 2006.

[12] Matsuo, Y. and M. Ishizuka, *Keyword Extraction From a Single Document Using Word Co-occurrence Statistical Information.* International Journal on Artificial Intelligence Tools, 2004. **13**(1): p. 157-169.

[13] Pluribo. *Pluribo: Instant Summaries*. 2008; Available: addons.mozilla.org/en-US/firefox/addon/pluribo-instant-summaries/?src=search.

[14] Team, G. *GreatSummary* 2008; Available from: https://addons.mozilla.org/en-US/firefox/addon/greatsummary/?src=ss.

[15] VoiceOver, *Screen reader from Apple*. 2010. http://www.apple.com/accessibility/voiceover.

Multi-Tap Sliders: Advancing Touch Interaction for Parameter Adjustment

Sashikanth Damaraju
Department of CSE
Texas A&M University
College Station
sashi@cse.tamu.edu

Jinsil Hwaryoung Seo
Department of Visualization
Texas A&M University
College Station
hwaryoung@tamu.edu

Tracy Hammond
Department of CSE
Texas A&M University,
College Station
hammond@cse.tamu.edu

Andruid Kerne
Interface Ecology Lab
Texas A&M University
College Station
andruid@ecologylab.net

ABSTRACT
Research in multi-touch interaction has typically been focused on direct spatial manipulation; techniques have been create to result in the most intuitive mapping between the movement of the hand and the resultant change in the virtual object. However, as we attempt to design for more complex operations, the expectation of spatial manipulation becomes infeasible.

We introduce Multi-tap Sliders for operation in what we call abstract parametric spaces that do not have an obvious literal spatial representation, such as exposure, brightness, contrast and saturation for image editing. This new widget design promotes multi-touch interaction for prolonged use in scenarios that require adjustment of multiple parameters as part of an operation. The multi-tap sliders encourage the user to keep her visual focus on the target, instead of the requiring to look back at the interface.

Our research emphasizes ergonomics, clear visual design, and fluid transition between the selection of parameters and their subsequent adjustment for a given operation. We demonstrate a new technique for quickly selecting and adjusting multiple numerical parameters. A preliminary user study points out improvements over the traditional sliders.

Author Keywords
multi-touch; parametric spaces; exploratory interfaces;

ACM Classification Keywords
H.5.2. User Interfaces: Ergonomics, Graphical User Interfaces (GUI), and Interaction Styles.

INTRODUCTION
This research promotes the use of multi-touch as a modality for supporting creative design tools. We describe a motivation from an analysis on what the operation requires. A new interaction technique is presented that merges the operations of selection and adjustment of numerical parameters.

Historically, *command line interfaces* (CLIs) constituted the first modality of human computer interaction. The user had to memorize commands acceptable to the computer. Commands were designed with ease of repetition by expert users as a priority. Shortened textual notations of described actions was the norm: *ls* for list, and *rm* for removing files. As computing resources improved, displays allowed the visual representation of complex content on the screen.

Graphical user interfaces (GUIs) adopted the paradigm of Windows, Icons, Menu, and Pointer (WIMP) for presenting and interacting with content. The *menu* emphasized recognition of operations from a visible set of menu items, over the recall of how to invoke a command from a vast number of options, as was the case in CLIs.

In 1983, Shneiderman [30] introduced the term *direct manipulation* to mean interaction with elements of the GUI using a pointer. The pointer, controlled by the physical movement of a mouse by the human, operated on visual targets such as buttons or menu items.

However, with multi-touch, the human can now interact with a computer by directly placing her hands on the visual. The pointer is no longer a required part of the interaction between the human and the computer.

This research investigates the design space of multi-touch interaction beyond direct spatial manipulation. Inspired by the use of multiple fingers of a single hand for quick command selection in keyboard shortcuts, we demonstrate how numerical parameters can be quickly selected and adjusted.

The summarized contributions of this paper are:

- Motivating the new design space of parameter adjustment.
- Demonstrating a new technique for merging selection and adjustment of a small sets of parameters with touch interfaces.
- Initial studies showing drawbacks and benefits of using touch for relative parameter adjustment.

MOTIVATION

Engaging in visual design tasks often requires users to adjust multiple parameters for an associated action. These are typically presented to the user as a set of sliders. Parameter adjustment requires the user to shift visual focus away from the target to acquire the thumb of the slider. Design often requires iterations of the following sequence of subtasks: parameter selection, adjustment, and observing the effect on the target. The duration of each iteration is further extended when the user needs to switch between different parameters. This leads to to-and-fro visual saccading between an interactive component and the target object, even if the interface is located close to the target.

Jacob [17] presents a dual classification of how humans perceive combinations of attributes: *integral* or *separable*. Attributes such as the x and y points of a location are perceived as an integral whole. Manipulation of location includes both the parameters. However, the tuple of attributes size and saturation are not perceived together, but are separable. We attempt to bring the user an experience that allows the integration of the multiple parameters of an operation as close at hand as possible.

These distractions of repeated saccading during tasks with high cognitive loads, such as visual design, lead to break downs in the user experience. This context is similar to that of visual analytics, wherein the visual is not a design, but a visualization of large sets of data. The problems describe above apply to interactions that require problem-solving and analysis of data. Our research attempts to develop new forms of interaction for manipulation in such multi-dimensional abstract parameter spaces that do not have an obvious 2D or 3D spatial representation.

Photo Editing

Creative fields such as post-processing of a photograph taken by a digital camera is a delicate balancing act. The photographers take great care in making minute adjustment of a large number of parameters available to them. Figure 1 shows a set of four parameters that manipulate the tone curve. The values of each of such parameters are used to perform a complex set of mathematical calculations to alter the pixel color values.

Even though photographers may not fully comprehend the details of the implementation, they understand the resultant visual change. As their expertise with the software grows, their knowledge of the relationship between the several groups of parameters increases. However, this does not imply

Figure 1. The Multi-tap slider seen overlayed in context with Adobe Photoshop Lightroom 3®.

that given a photograph, an expert photographer can uniquely identify the desired parameter values without interaction.

There is no correct answer. The user interface exposes a set of knobs that feed into complicated algorithms that ultimately change pixels. Details are abstracted away from the user to simplify the experience, while delivering as much power from the algorithms as possible. Providing more knobs would overwhelm the user, where as providing fewer might take away control. The software attempts to find a balance between the two.

The operation demands play. There is a constant exploration of what the photograph could look like with different values. Each parameter is constrained to a fixed range. However, even with just four parameters, under the menu Tone Curve, the possible combinations are in the millions. The operation is purely subjective. The experience and design sense of the photographer can aid in identifying a satisfactory combination of the parameter values. This selection is the primary purpose of the interaction. Devoting more visual and cognitive faculties of the brain, will aid the user in making a qualitatively improved product.

INTERACTION DESIGN

We use this defined motivation and context to establish the goals for our design.

- Promote integrated selection and manipulation of parameters. A group of parameters are considered *integrated* for an operation, the interaction should emphasize this integrality.
- Optimize visual cognition: Use the tactility of touch to leverage selection, instead of requiring targeting a slider thumb.
- Ergonomics: Long term use, relaxed hand posture. Minimizing muscle movement during use.
- Supporting expert users for complex tasks: Utilizing manual dexterity as a learned skill.

This research utilizes indirect interaction via a visual. The visual described is an intermediary between the target of the interaction (a photograph) and the human hand, providing

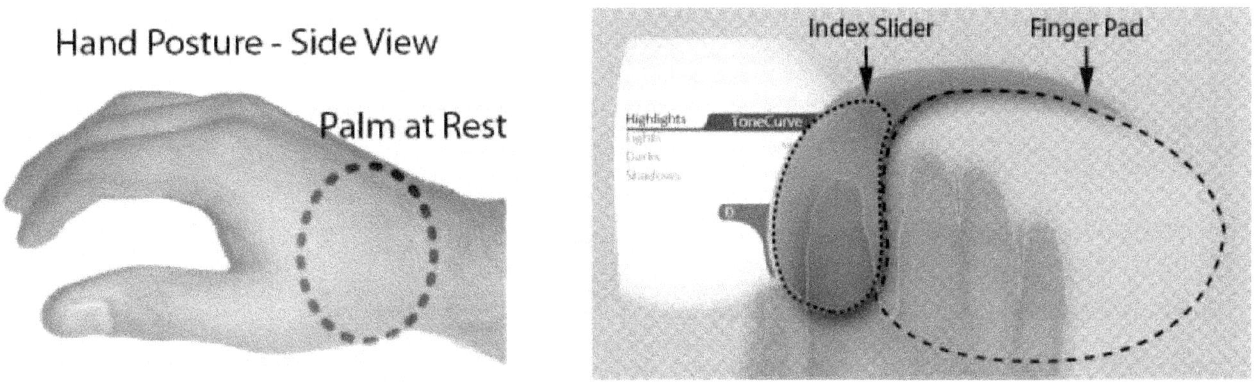

Figure 2. On the left is the relaxed hand posture that is used during operation. The functional components of the Multi-tap Slider are emphasized on the right: the *index slider* for adjustment, and the *finger pad* for selection.

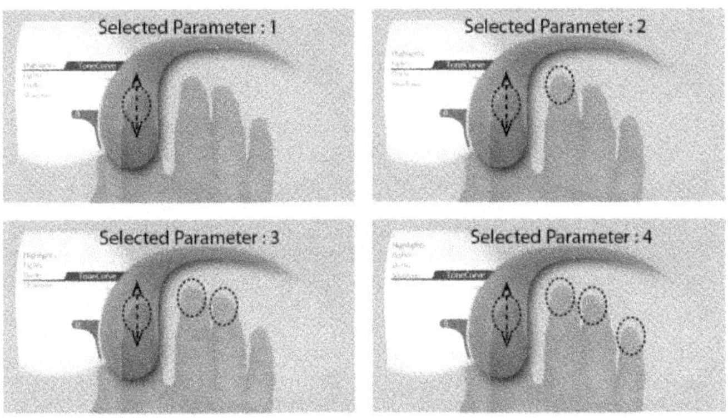

Figure 3. Illustration of parameter selection. The dashed ellipses indicate fingers making contact with the screen. The index finger performs the adjustment through forward and backward movements. When a parameter is selected, the index finger can be raised, re-positioned and lowered as needed. On the left, the selected parameter is underlined.

feedback on two states, that of the interaction, and that of the system. This interface has been designed for use with the wrist being rested on the screen, and the hand in a relaxed posture, as it were clutching a mouse. For increased comfort, the angle of the touch screen is raised to 30°, like an architects drafting table.

The Multi-tap Slider consists of two functional subcomponents: the *index pad*, which behaves as a relative slider for the selected parameter, and a *finger pad* that determines the currently selected parameter based on the number of fingers making contact with it. Figure 2 shows an annotated view of the Multi-tap Slider.

This design operates in two modes, the parameter *adjustment* mode and the parameter *set selection* mode. Each set of parameters is considered as a unique operation that requires frequent repetitions of selection and adjustment of the contained parameters.

Adjustment Mode

We use contact of fingers with the screen (specifically the finger pad) as a quasi-mode selection. The ring, middle and little fingers only perform the function of modifiers. The degrees of freedom of these fingers are limited, only the index finger is used for all adjustment.

For selection, fingers are raised and lowered onto the screen. With no fingers on the finger pad, the first parameter (Highlights) is selected, one finger on the finger pad selects the second parameter (Lights), two selects the third (Darks) and three fingers on the finger pad selects the third parameter (Shadows).

To adjust values, the index finger performs a forwards-backwards movement. This is similar to the operation of a scroll wheel on a mouse. Upward and downward movements can be precisely performed with little or no training. The resulting interaction with this widget requires limited muscle movement.

The user receives immediate tactile feedback as to which parameter is currently selected. The visual optimizes the utility of screen space that is usually occluded by the hand. The large target areas for the index pad and the finger pad allows the user to use the slider without visually focusing on the presented interface, even though their hand occludes most of the visual. Visual feedback of the current state of the interface is provided with a representation of the mapping between number of fingers and the parameter. The slider visualizes the maximum and minimum permissible values, while showing the current value of the parameter.

Resting the wrist on the screen increases the comfort of operation, and increases the precision of the interaction with individual fingers. Without this rest, the weight of the hand is supported by the arm, and the single finger in contact with the screen. Prolonged use on a multi-touch screen without adequate wrist support is likely to build up fatigue in the arm.

Set Selection Mode

Although the sliders can operate on a small set of four parameters, we broaden the scope by providing an upper level menu. This is accessible by performing a double tap with the index finger over the *index slider*. Figure 4 shows the presentation of the upper level menu. By moving the index finger along the index slider, the selection can be changed in the same way the parameter is adjusted. Performing a single

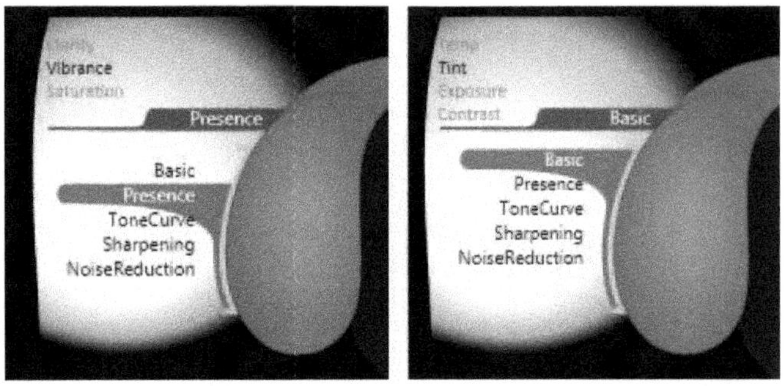

Figure 4. On performing a double tap of the index slider, the set selection mode is presented. Shown here are two selected sets, with the parameters within displayed on the top left of each. A single tap selects the parameter set.

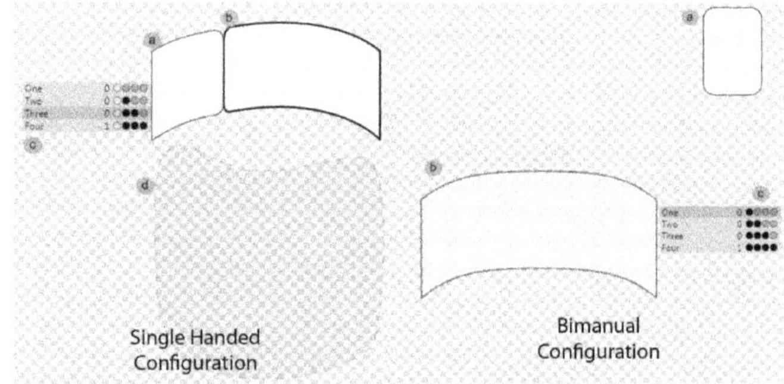

Figure 5. Previous iteration of the Multi-tap slider for a comparative study. The two configurations considered are the for one and two handed use of the Multi-touch SliderPad showing a) the index pad for parameter adjustment, b) the finger pad for parameter selection c) visual feedback of selected parameter and current values and d) for the single handed configuration, a region for palm support

tap will select the set, and the Multi-tap Slider will go back into the parameter adjustment mode.

We provide visual feedback for different states of interaction, as it allows the user to uniquely identify erroneous interaction (as described in [33]). The index slider has a blue glow when it is being operated on. The entire slider can be translated and scaled using the top portion (the gray above the finger pad in Figure 2). A blue glow along the entire shape represents that the translation is being performed. The selection of parameters is also visualized by change in text color and position. As shown in Figure 2, the currently selected parameter black, with other parameter names in gray.

COMPARATIVE USER STUDY

With an earlier prototype of this design (then called the SliderPad), we performed a comparative user study. The differences between the presented version and the study are: 1) No menus in the first prototype, and 2) The visual was modified with improved aesthetics. This is not of concern to the results, as they only performed tasks with a single set of four parameters. These changes are purely cosmetic and have no impact on the applicability of the results.

Figure 5 shows the two configurations of the Multi-touch SliderPad, single handed and bimanual.

We conducted a within-subjects experiment to investigate whether finger count can be used as a parameter selection mechanism, compared to the traditional interfaces of sliders. The task is to select and adjust a parameter to a target value. We designed the experiment with three conditions, the single handed and bimanual configurations of Multi-touch SliderPad and the traditional slider interface. We noted that the two Multi-touch SliderPad conditions and the relative sliders require a relative adjustment of values, whereas the traditional slider interface requires an absolute adjustment of values. To measure the differences in relative and absolute adjustments, we added a fourth condition of relative sliders. The relative sliders (shown in right of Figure 6) are four rectangles of fixed size, placed vertically, and adjacent to each other. The user selects a parameter by placing their finger on one of these rectangles, and could adjust the corresponding target parameter.

Task and Procedure

The task presented the user with four parameters, visualized as bars in the center of the screen, with the height of each bar mapped to the corresponding parameter value. The target parameter is visualized with a mark at the target value. The sliders in all conditions are towards the user on the bottom of the screen. The user selects the appropriate parameter and adjusts it until the target rectangle's height matches the mark on screen. The parameters have a range from zero to one, and the task is considered complete when the parameter value matches the target with .01 accuracy.

We measured two dependent variables, one being the time to select a parameter for adjustment, and the other the time to reach the target value. Time to adjust the parameter begins when the previous parameter reaches the target value, and ends when the correct parameter is adjusted. The completion time begins on adjustment of the parameter, and ends when the user lifts off their finger at the correct target value. The two Multi-touch SliderPad conditions and the relative sliders adjust the parameter based on the acceleration of the finger over the interface, allowing for more precise adjustments to use finger rolls and coarser adjustments to use flicks of the finger.

We had a total of 13 participants, 1 female and 12 male, all right handed. Each of them performed 24 trials with each of the 4 conditions resulting in a total of 13 participants $\times$ 24 trials $\times$ 4 conditions = 1,248 total trials. The order of conditions was counter-balanced across participants. Each of the conditions used a fixed set of parameter values presented in random order. Participants were given a short demonstration before each condition, and had a few minutes of practice trials to accustom themselves to the interface.

Results

Participants reported that they had no problems learning the two Multi-touch SliderPad conditions. After initial practice, multiple subjects reported that they were more comfortable than the relative sliders and traditional sliders. A repeated-measures analysis of variance (ANOVA) run showed a significant effect on technique for parameter

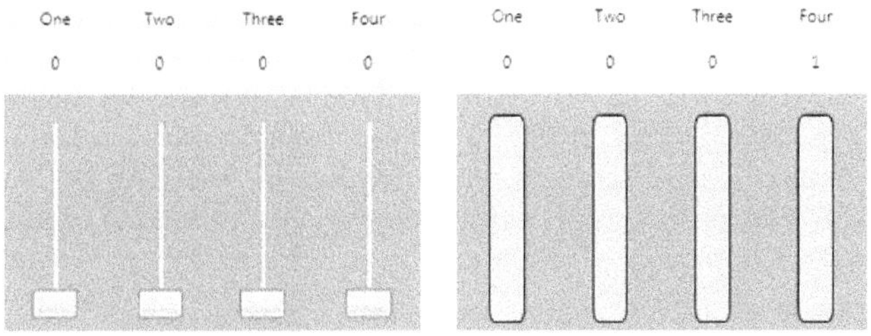

Figure 6. Control conditions with the traditional sliders on the left and the relative sliders on the right

selection time ($F_{3,30} = 3.8$, $p < 0.02$). Participants were faster at switching between parameters for the three conditions using relative parameter adjustment (Multi-touch SliderPad Single Handed = 1.43s, Bimanual = 1.54s, Relative Sliders = 1.28s) than the traditional sliders (1.85s), with no significant difference between the first three. This shows that acquiring the slider thumb affects the parameter selection time. An ANOVA on the completion time shows no significant difference between the conditions ($F_{3,36} = 2.7, p = 0.054$) with a Fischer's Least Significance Difference of 0.72 seconds. This result shows that after a short practice, participants are faster at switching parameters with the SliderPad than the traditional sliders.

However, the SliderPad conditions were not faster than relative sliders. We observed that the presented target has a strong visual correspondence with the sliders in both the relative and traditional conditions. This gave relative sliders a visual advantage over the SliderPad conditions, as the selection of parameters is aided by the presented target. This will not be the case while working on design tasks because there is no fixed target spatially configured like the sliders.

The comparable results for the single handed and bimanual conditions are interesting. On the one hand, the bimanual condition can be seen as a kind of kinematic chain in which the parameter selection by the non-dominant hand is framing the precise value adjustment by the dominant hand. At the same time, the mapping individual fingers to parameters in the multi-touch condition results in a form of direct embodiment. More situated research will be required to discover if there are context in which the kinematic chain or the direct multi-touch embodiment is more valuable.

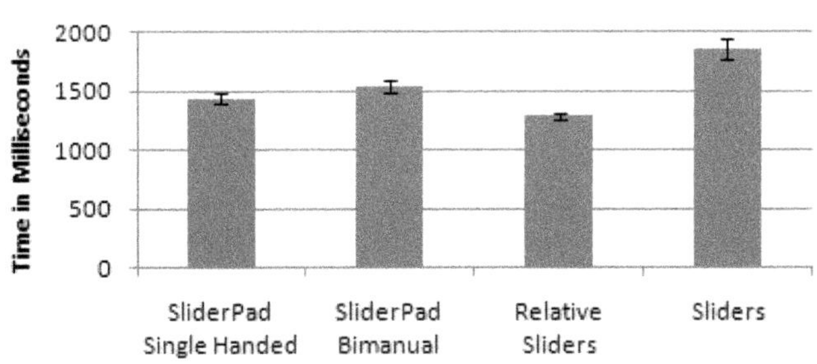

Figure 7. Time to select between parameters for each of the conditions. Bars indicate standard error.

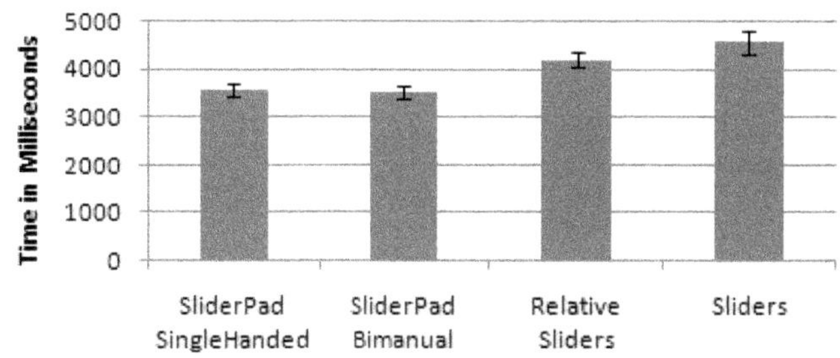

Figure 8. Time to complete the parameter adjustment for each of the conditions. Bars indicate standard error.

For our user study, we did not specify exactly how participants should place their hand and perform the task: where exactly their hand should be placed, whether their wrist or arms should be rested. They used it as they found comfortable.

While operating the relative sliders, we observed that participants rarely rested their palms on the table, as targeting different sliders required repositioning of the hand. We observed participants were quickly fatigued and tended to rest between tasks. This was not a problem with the single handed and bimanual Multi-touch SliderPad conditions, as the palm can rest on the screen without moving throughout the operation.

RELATED WORK

Our research draws from several related fields in touch interaction. Recent interest in the field has increased considerably due ubiquity of input devices, and the low cost for entry to do-it-yourself multi-touch screens. To frame our research, we consider below the breadth of research in touch interaction.

Legacy interfaces

Initial touch research focuses on overcoming the initial obstacle of precise selection. Early research by Schneiderman et al [29] raise the issue and present *take-off* as a promising technique, wherein a cursor is presented to the user with an fixed offset to their finger. Zoom-pointing [6] is developed using graphical scaling of the target area, increasing the motor control space available to the user. Albisson and Zhai [2] develop multiple techniques to improve the precision of the finger on a screen, using 2D levers, an interface that allows precise manipulation of the cursor position.

In the interest of supporting general purpose use of computer using the touch modality, researchers developed techniques to emulate the mouse, and its buttons. The fluid DTMouse [11] describes a mapping using multiple fingers to emulate mouse move while avoiding occlusion (mouse cursor is moved at the mid point of two fingers) and mouse drag (a third finger toggles drag mode). Benko et al, [7] introduce a menu for a bimanual operation that facilitates magnification, controlling speed of cursor movement (indirect manipulation of the cursor) and snapping the cursor to items. Matejka et al [24] develop a new design (SDMouse) for multi-finger chorded mouse emulation.

Direct Spatial Manipulation

Following the paradigm of direct manipulation, research on multi-touch interaction emphasizes focus on altering the spatial attributes of elements. Traditionally, the term direct manipulation was used for graphical buttons that could be clicked to perform a command. With touch, manipulation is more direct.

We use the term *direct spatial manipulation* to specifically identify techniques that alter spatial appearance of a visual. Direct spatial manipulation makes the selection of commands of rotation, translation and scaling *implicit*. These commands are selected through the use of *mappings*, a relationship between the movement of the human hand across the surface to a command or operation executed on an item on screen. The result of these manipulations is the adjustment of visual parameters of items, namely their X, Y location, their angle of orientation, and their scale.

Research has developed interaction techniques for translation of virtual items [36], using two fingers for rotation for 2D[18, 19] and 3D[15, 28]. Additional attributes of pressure for layering of multiple elements on a touch screen [10]. When multiple simultaneous activities are performed with a single movement, there is an inevitable loss of accuracy. Martinet et. al.,[23] raise issues of coordination, and find that simple techniques of differentiating actions with number of fingers helps specify intent.

Gestural Interaction

Research in human-computer interaction deals with the unambiguous understanding and processing of human intent. A goal of *natural user interface* [1, 34] is to the human to express their intent comfortably, using actions we commonly use in the world. The mappings to non-spatial operations are not self evident. Sensing technologies additionally can sense different parts of the hand that make contact with the screen, such as palms, or the side of the hand.

Wu et al [?], use the DiamondTouch table to explore possible mappings of the hand for activities beyond the literal. Their implementation, a photo browser application, enables annotation, wiping (erasing), cut/copy-pasting, and the expansion and collapse of piles.

Advances in hardware has allowed recognition of more qualities of touch, such as detecting the palm, side of the hand and close fist. ShadowGuides [12] introduces a new feedforward visualization that is aimed at teaching such gestures. Using play to alter the perceived cost of learning, Gesture Play [8] describes a physical simulation with springs, dials, and props to teach specific gestures to the user.

Changes to spatial attributes are a great fit for direct spatial manipulation techniques. The mappings from body movements to changes in the visual are clear and explicit. The resulting experience can be considered natural to the user.

However, the question of what mappings are obvious is not easy to answer. Although mappings can be made, there isn't a clear objective design process that allows for the development of gestural mappings to an arbitrary set of commands. What may be considered natural or intuitive for one person, may not be for another. The context of the mappings may have a similar effect, the gesture may be more natural when mapped to a different operation in a different context. This leads to an ambiguity in selecting the most obvious gesture. This subjective variance in human opinions makes designing a vocabulary of gestures for complex actions a difficult problem.

Considering that most commands lack a literal obvious real-world counterpart, their association to a hand movement is an important interaction design topic. One process of development of this mapping is described by Wobbrock, Morris and Wilson [26, 35]. They use a *participatory design* approach to elicit a gesture vocabulary from the users, without first imposing a rigid set of pre-defined gestures. We find that this approach has a demonstrable benefit to designing gesture sets, especially if the participants in the process match the intended demographic for the resultant product.

Multi-touch Menus

The cognitive overhead of memorizing a large set gestures increases. Taking a clue that signified the paradigm shift from CLIs to GUIs, this overhead can be reduced by encouraging recognition over recall: visualize possible commands in a clear and consistent manner to the human.

We call this form of command selection *explicit*. The user must be able to *navigate* to a commands from within a menu, making available commands *visible*. Traditional menus are functional, and can be operated by touch interfaces. The need new fluid multi-touch techniques for command selection is evident.

The introduction of a visualization of the menu in some form at the finger contact. We describe two categories of menus, 1) stroke-based marking menus, that may or may not have a visual representation of operations at all times, and 2) visual menus that emphasize a consistent visual representation during their operation.

Lepinski, Grossman and Fitzmaurice [21] translate work on marking menus[20] from the domain of stylus / pen based interaction to multi-touch. While regular marking menus use directional strokes for each menu level, they explore the use of hand chords for the top level menu selection. A chord is identified by a detecting which combination of fingers make contact with the screen. These techniques are aimed at facilitating a smooth learning curve for a novice user to become an expert.

However, from personal experience, attempting to quickly alter between the chords repeatedly is physically difficult, and induces undue stress in the hand. Their evaluation neglects to raise these experiential issues that are extremely relevant to their techniques adoption in the real-world.

Bailly et al [3, 4] extend the marking menus to bimanual interaction. Instead of using hand chords, they use only the number of fingers to encode the selection of the first level. The use of the second hand allows for a larger selection. For selection at the next menu level, they use two techniques, directional strokes and simple multi-finger tapping. The motivation behind this set of techniques is that with some training, a human can remember spatially, and kinaesthetically (with muscle memory) the mappings between a hand movement and a command. However, the also implement the finger count method for at-a-distance interaction.

Considering the pace of adoption of the multi-touch modality in research, it is surprising that, to our knowledge, there have only been a handful of publications that develop novel techniques for presenting visual menus to the user.

Stacked Half Pie menus [16] use a single touch to navigate a hierarchy, visualized as a semi-circle. A goal of the design is to reduce the distance that the hand must traverse to access items of the menu. Banovic et al.,[5] present a menu activated by the thumb, the menu can be accessed using the little, ring, middle or index fingers. Attribute gates [31] allow the user to set multiple attributes of an element (given a discrete set of options for each) using a single stroke with co-location tabletop collaboration as the context. In his dissertation, Malik [22] describes an exploration of single-handed multi-finger interaction. He introduces the use of natural movement of the thumb as it spans an arc to select from a discrete set of items, and also manipulate a slider over a continuous range of values.

Parameter Adjustment

Techniques for the selection and subsequent adjustment of numerical parameters have been designed for other interaction modalities. Pook et al introduce *control menus* [27] for the mouse or stylus. A radial pie menu presents available options, on moving a threshold distance away from the center selects an action, and subsequent movement of the cursor or mouse performs adjustment of that menu. In the same year Guimbretière et al., present *flow menus* [14] that allow chaining of operations by re-entering the center of the menu. A single fluid stroke of the stylus can perform several operations. Results from a laboratory study by Guimbretière et al. showed that techniques which merge selection of the command with adjustment of the parameter outperformed the other techniques [13].

FaST Sliders [25] again use marking menus for selection of parameters, but have an improved adjustment stage. The cursor is 'captured', and adjustments do not require dragging of the cursor. A mouse-click completes the adjustment. The in-context slider [32] is a mouse based technique that can be raised and adjusted without a click. Hovering over a circular affordance raises a single slider, whose value can be set with a single click.

These techniques emphasize the fluid selection and adjustment of a *single* parameter with a mouse or stylus. The parameters may be nested in a hierarchical menu. To operate on several parameters within a certain menu would require additional steps. Damaraju and Kerne[9] describe a multi-touch technique for adjusting a small set parameters without navigating a menu. They present findings on a user study to manipulate parameters of color (hue, saturation and value) using single handed multi-finger mappings. Their technique shows an improvement over a base line of traditional menu. The multi-touch technique uses number of fingers and simple finger disambiguation to allow quick repeated selection and adjustment of one of the three parameters.

DISCUSSION

Within the current state of the art in multi-touch research, we frame this research as introducing a new design space. From our results, we find that improving ergonomics and designing for expert use. Our user study shows that traditional sliders can be outperformed by a simple rectangular relative slider. The advantage of not grabbing the thumb of the slider improves selection time. However, we show that our design for parameter selection could improve over this relative slider. The index finger is consistently used for adjustment regardless of which parameter is selected.

FUTURE WORK

To understand the impact of this technique for subjective tasks, it is important to perform evaluations in context. We are working with a Digital Photography course, being taught at an undergraduate level, to conduct studies over multiple sessions to evaluate the long term affects on the ergonomics and comfort. We acknowledge that the novelty of the interaction requires a certain amount of learning, it is unclear as to exactly how long it would take. From our user studies, we found that from a 5-10 minute training phase, users were able to outperform the baseline of traditional sliders.

From preliminary pilot studies, we found that more features could complement the interaction without increasing complexity. One such feature that would immediately impact the utility over the keyboard/mouse combination is using the thumb for the Undo operation. A simple tap to undo and a swipe to re-do from the thumb will allow simple, quick adjustments. The Multi-tap Slider has been initially designed for manipulation of numerical values, however, discrete item selection can also be easily performed.

Although the technique is designed for non-spatial parameters, it could be integrated with spatial tools. For example a simple brush tool in Adobe Photoshop has associated parameters such as size, brush head, opacity, flow. These parameters could be adjusted with the hand, while the use of a single finger could use the brush itself. Alternatively, the non-dominant hand could operate the tool parameters while the dominant hand uses a stylus for operation. Other contexts such as music and video production, digital painting have similar integration of parameters that will benefit from using the Multi-tap Slider.

REFERENCES

1. Abowd, G. D., and Mynatt, E. D. Charting past, present, and future research in ubiquitous computing. *ACM Transactions on Computer-Human Interaction 7*, 1 (Mar. 2000), 29–58.
2. Albinsson, P.-A., and Zhai, S. High precision touch screen interaction. In *Proceedings of the conference on Human factors in computing systems - CHI '03*, ACM Press (New York, New York, USA, Apr. 2003), 105.

3. Bailly, G., Lecolinet, E., and Guiard, Y. Finger-count & radial-stroke shortcuts: 2 techniques for augmenting linear menus on multi-touch surfaces. In *Proceedings of the 28th international conference on Human factors in computing systems*, CHI '10, ACM (New York, NY, USA, 2010), 591–594.
4. Bailly, G., Müller, J., and Lecolinet, E. Design and evaluation of finger-count interaction: Combining multitouch gestures and menus. *International Journal of Human-Computer Studies 70*, 10 (Oct. 2012), 673–689.
5. Banovic, N., Li, F. C. Y., Dearman, D., Yatani, K., and Truong, K. N. Design of unimanual multi-finger pie menu interaction. In *Proceedings of the ACM International Conference on Interactive Tabletops and Surfaces - ITS '11*, ACM Press (New York, New York, USA, Nov. 2011), 120.
6. Bederson, B. B., and Hollan, J. D. Pad++. In *Proceedings of the 7th annual ACM symposium on User interface software and technology - UIST '94*, ACM Press (New York, New York, USA, Nov. 1994), 17–26.
7. Benko, H., Wilson, A. D., and Baudisch, P. Precise selection techniques for multi-touch screens. In *Proceedings of the SIGCHI conference on Human Factors in computing systems*, CHI '06, ACM (New York, NY, USA, 2006), 1263–1272.
8. Bragdon, A., Uguray, A., Wigdor, D., Anagnostopoulos, S., Zeleznik, R., and Feman, R. Gesture play. In *ACM International Conference on Interactive Tabletops and Surfaces - ITS '10*, ACM Press (New York, New York, USA, Nov. 2010), 39.
9. Damaraju, S., and Kerne, A. Comparing multi-touch interaction techniques for manipulation of an abstract parameter space. In *Proceedings of the 13th international conference on multimodal interfaces - ICMI '11*, ACM Press (New York, New York, USA, Nov. 2011), 221.
10. Davidson, P. L., and Han, J. Y. Extending 2D object arrangement with pressure-sensitive layering cues. In *Proceedings of the 21st annual ACM symposium on User interface software and technology*, UIST '08, ACM (New York, NY, USA, 2008), 87–90.
11. Esenther, A., and Ryall, K. Fluid DTMouse: better mouse support for touch-based interactions. In *Proceedings of the working conference on Advanced visual interfaces*, AVI '06, ACM (New York, NY, USA, May 2006), 112–115.
12. Freeman, D., Benko, H., Morris, M. R., and Wigdor, D. ShadowGuides: visualizations for in-situ learning of multi-touch and whole-hand gestures. In *Proceedings of the ACM International Conference on Interactive Tabletops and Surfaces - ITS '09*, ITS '09, ACM Press (New York, New York, USA, Nov. 2009), 165–172.
13. Guimbretière, F., Martin, A., Winograd, T., and Ere, O. I. S. G. Benefits of Merging Command Selection and Direct Manipulation. *ACM Transactions on Computer-Human Interaction 12*, 3 (Sept. 2005), 460–476.
14. Guimbretiére, F., and Winograd, T. FlowMenu: combining command, text, and data entry. In *Proceedings of the 13th annual ACM symposium on User interface software and technology*, UIST '00, ACM (New York, NY, USA, 2000), 213–216.
15. Hancock, M., Carpendale, S., and Cockburn, A. Shallow-depth 3d interaction. In *Proceedings of the SIGCHI conference on Human factors in computing systems - CHI '07*, ACM Press (New York, New York, USA, Apr. 2007), 1147.
16. Hesselmann, T., Flöring, S., and Schmitt, M. Stacked Half-Pie menus: navigating nested menus on interactive tabletops. In *Proceedings of the ACM International Conference on Interactive Tabletops and Surfaces*, ITS '09, ACM (New York, NY, USA, 2009), 173–180.
17. Jacob, R. J. K., Sibert, L. E., McFarlane, D. C., and Mullen Jr., M. P. Integrality and separability of input devices. *ACM Trans. Comput.-Hum. Interact. 1*, 1 (Mar. 1994), 3–26.
18. Kruger, R., Carpendale, S., Scott, S. D., and Greenberg, S. Roles of Orientation in Tabletop Collaboration: Comprehension, Coordination and Communication. *Computer Supported Cooperative Work (CSCW) 13*, 5-6 (Dec. 2004), 501–537.
19. Kruger, R., Carpendale, S., Scott, S. D., and Tang, A. Fluid integration of rotation and translation. In *Proceedings of the SIGCHI conference on Human factors in computing systems - CHI '05*, ACM Press (New York, New York, USA, Apr. 2005), 601.
20. Kurtenbach, G., and Buxton, W. The limits of expert performance using hierarchic marking menus. In *Proceedings of the INTERACT '93 and CHI '93 conference on Human factors in computing systems*, CHI '93, ACM (New York, NY, USA, 1993), 482–487.
21. Lepinski, G. J., Grossman, T., and Fitzmaurice, G. The design and evaluation of multitouch marking menus. In *Proceedings of the 28th international conference on Human factors in computing systems*, CHI '10, ACM (New York, NY, USA, 2010), 2233–2242.
22. Malik, S. *An exploration of multi-finger interaction on multi-touch surfaces*. PhD thesis, Toronto, Ont., Canada, Canada, 2007.
23. Martinet, A., Casiez, G., and Grisoni, L. The effect of DOF separation in 3D manipulation tasks with multi-touch displays. In *Proceedings of the 17th ACM Symposium on Virtual Reality Software and Technology - VRST '10*, ACM Press (New York, New York, USA, Nov. 2010), 111.
24. Matejka, J., Grossman, T., Lo, J., and Fitzmaurice, G. The design and evaluation of multi-finger mouse emulation techniques. In *Proceedings of the 27th international conference on Human factors in computing systems*, CHI '09, ACM (New York, NY, USA, 2009), 1073–1082.
25. Mcguffin, M., Burtnyk, N., Kurtenbach, G., and Street, K. FaST Sliders: Integrating marking menus and the adjustment of continuous values. Graphics Interface (2002). 35–42.
26. Morris, M. R., Wobbrock, J. O., and Wilson, A. D. Understanding users' preferences for surface gestures. In *Proceedings of Graphics Interface 2010*, GI '10, Canadian Information Processing Society (Toronto, Ont., Canada, Canada, 2010), 261–268.
27. Pook, S., Lecolinet, E., Vaysseix, G., and Barillot, E. Control menus. In *CHI '00 extended abstracts on Human factors in computing systems - CHI '00*, ACM Press (New York, New York, USA, Apr. 2000), 263.
28. Reisman, J. L., Davidson, P. L., and Han, J. Y. A screen-space formulation for 2D and 3D direct manipulation. In *Proceedings of the 22nd annual ACM symposium on User interface software and technology*, UIST '09, ACM (New York, NY, USA, 2009), 69–78.
29. Sears, A., and Shneiderman, B. High precision touchscreens: design strategies and comparisons with a mouse. *International Journal of Man-Machine Studies 34*, 4 (Apr. 1991), 593–613.
30. Shneiderman, B. Direct Manipulation: A Step Beyond Programming Languages. *Computer 16*, 8 (Aug. 1983), 57–69.
31. Sulaiman, A. N., and Olivier, P. Attribute gates. In *Proceedings of the 21st annual ACM symposium on User interface software and technology*, UIST '08, ACM (New York, NY, USA, 2008), 57–66.
32. Webb, A., and Kerne, A. The in-context slider: a fluid interface component for visualization and adjustment of values while authoring. In *Proceedings of the working conference on Advanced visual interfaces*, AVI '08, ACM (New York, NY, USA, 2008), 91–99.
33. Wigdor, D., Williams, S., Cronin, M., Levy, R., White, K., Mazeev, M., and Benko, H. Ripples: utilizing per-contact visualizations to improve user interaction with touch displays. In *Proceedings of the 22nd annual ACM symposium on User interface software and technology*, UIST '09, ACM (New York, NY, USA, 2009), 3–12.
34. Wigdor, D., and Wixon, D. *Brave NUI World: Designing Natural User Interfaces for Touch and Gesture*. Morgan Kaufmann, 2011.
35. Wobbrock, J. O., Morris, M. R., and Wilson, A. D. User-defined gestures for surface computing. In *Proceedings of the 27th international conference on Human factors in computing systems*, CHI '09, ACM (New York, NY, USA, 2009), 1083–1092.
36. Wu, M., and Balakrishnan, R. Multi-finger and whole hand gestural interaction techniques for multi-user tabletop displays. In *Proceedings of the 16th annual ACM symposium on User interface software and technology*, UIST '03, ACM (New York, NY, USA, 2003), 193–202.

Author Index

www.ingramcontent.com/pod-product-compliance
Ingram Content Group UK Ltd.
Pitfield, Milton Keynes, MK11 3LW, UK
UKHW051413290926
15471UKWH00009B/1579